Encyclopedia of
SOCIAL
THEORY

Encyclopedia of
SOCIAL
THEORY

VOLUME II

EDITOR

GEORGE RITZER

University of Maryland, College Park

A SAGE Reference Publication

SAGE Publications
Thousand Oaks ▪ London ▪ New Delhi

For information:

Sage Publications, Inc.
2455 Teller Road
Thousand Oaks, California 91320
E-mail: order@sagepub.com

Sage Publications Ltd.
1 Oliver's Yard
55 City Road
London EC1Y 1SP
United Kingdom

Sage Publications India Pvt. Ltd.
B-42, Panchsheel Enclave
Post Box 4109
New Delhi 110 017 India

Printed in the United States of America

Library of Congress Cataloging-in-Publication Data

Encyclopedia of social theory / George Ritzer, editor.
    p. cm.
Sage reference.
Includes bibliographical references and index.
ISBN 0-7619-2611-9 (cloth : acid-free paper)
   1. Sociology—Philosophy—Encyclopedias. I. Ritzer, George.
HM425.E47 2004
301´.01—dc22

                                      2004003251

This book is printed on acid-free paper.

04   05   06   07   10   9   8   7   6   5   4   3   2   1

Acquisitions Editor:	Jerry Westby
Production Editor:	Denise Santoyo
Copy Editors:	Carla Freeman
	Barbara Coster
	Linda Gray
Typesetter:	C&M Digitals (P) Ltd.
Indexer:	Kathy Paparchontis
Cover Designer:	Michelle Lee Kenny

List of Entries

Reader's Guide

TOPICS AND CONCEPTS IN SOCIAL THEORY

Affect Control Theory
AGIL
Alienation
Anomie
Authority

Body
Bureaucracy

Capital
Capitalism
Celebrity
Citizenship
Civil Society
Civility
Civilizing Processes
Collective Conscience
Collective Memory
Commitment
Compulsory Heterosexuality
Consumer Culture
Crime
Cultural Capital
Culture and Civilization

Deconstruction
Democracy
Deviance
Dialectic
Discourse
Disneyization
Distributive Justice
Dramaturgy

Emergence
Emotion Work
Enchantment/Disenchantment
Essentialism

Exchange Coalitions
Exchange Networks
Exploitation

Family Wage
Feminism
Feminist Epistemology
Feminist Ethics
Film
Fordism and Post-Fordism
Frame Analysis

Gender
Genealogy
Generalized Exchange
Globalization
Governmentality
Graph Theoretic Measures of Power
Green Movements

Habitus
Herrschaft (Rule)
Hollywood Film
Holocaust
Hyperreality

Ideal Type
Identity
Imperialism
Impression Management
Individualism
Industrial Society
Internet and Cyberculture
Intimacy

Lesbian Continuum
Levels of Social Structure
Lifeworld
Logocentrism

THEORISTS

Veblen, Thorstein
Virilio, Paul

Wallerstein, Immanuel
Weber, Marianne
Weber, Max
White, Harrison
Willer, David
Wright, Erik Olin
Wuthnow, Robert

Žižek, Slavoj
Znaniecki, Florian Witold

SCHOOLS AND THEORETICAL APPROACHES

Actor Network Theory
Annales School

Behaviorism

Cognitive Sociology
Collège de Sociologie and Acéphale
Complexity Theory
Conflict Theory
Conversation Analysis
Cosmopolitan Sociology
Critical Pedagogy
Cultural Marxism and British Cultural Studies
Cultural Studies and the New Populism

Ecofeminism
Ecological Theory
Elementary Theory
Ethnomethodology
Evolutionary Theory

Feminism
Feminist Cultural Studies
Figurational Sociology
Frankfurt School

Game Theory
General Systems Theory
German Idealism

Hermeneutics
Historical and Comparative Theory
Historical Materialism
Historicism

Institutional Theory

Labeling Theory
Learning Theory
Liberal Feminism

Marxism
Media Critique

Neo-Kantianism
Network Exchange Theory
Network Theory

Phenomenology
Philosophical Anthropology
Political Economy
Positivism
Post-Marxism
Postmodernism
Postsocial
Poststructuralism
Pragmatism
Psychoanalysis and Social Theory

Queer Theory

Radical Feminism
Rational Choice
Rhetorical Turn in Social Theory
Role Theory

Scottish Enlightenment
Semiology
Situationists
Social Constructionism
Social Darwinism
Social Exchange Theory
Social Studies of Science
Sociologies of Everyday Life
Standpoint Theory
Structural Functionalism
Structuralism
Structuralist Marxism
Structuration
Symbolic Interaction

World-Systems Theory

CULTURAL THEORY

Althusser, Louis

Bellah, Robert
Benjamin, Walter
Bourdieu, Pierre
Butler, Judith

MARXIST AND NEO-MARXIST THEORY

FEMINIST THEORY

FRENCH SOCIAL THEORY

GERMAN SOCIAL THEORY

BRITISH SOCIAL THEORY

MACROSOCIOLOGICAL THEORIES

NATIONALISM

Social theory has approached nationalism most as a political ideology structuring relations of power and conflict. It has focused on nationalism's relationship to ethnic violence and war, on the production of beliefs that one's own country is the best, and on the invocation of national unity to override internal differences. It has seen nationalism first through bellicose international relations and second through projects by which elites attempt to mobilize mass support. This has been an influential view both among scholars of nationalism (such as Michael Hechter) and among general social theorists (such as Jürgen Habermas) who have tended to see nationalism largely as a problem to be overcome.

A second strain of social theory, associated with modernization theory and anticipated by both Weber and Durkheim, has seen nation building as a crucial component of developing an effective modern society, one capable of political stability and economic development. Nationalism, as the ideology associated with such nation building, is thus important to a phase on the process of becoming modern and also a normal reflection of industrialization and state formation. Ernst Gellner, Charles Tilly, and Michael Mann are key representatives. But however normal to a developmental phase nationalism may be, all see it as also deeply implicated in power relations and conflicts and prone to problematic manipulation by state elites.

These first two lines of theory both emphasize politics and the state and treat nationalism mainly as a feature of the modern era. A third strain of social theory recognizes the role of nationalism in politics and conflict but stresses also its more positive contributions to the production of culture, the preservation of historical memory, and the formation of group solidarity. Many of the most influential theorists in this group also place much greater stress on the sources of

nationalism in ancient ethnicities that provide the basis for identities prior to any specific political mobilization. Anthony Smith is the foremost representative of this view. A related point is that nationalism ought not to be approached only through its most extreme manifestations, but also grasped in its more banal forms—in a variety of ceremonial events, for example, and the organization of athletic competitions. These contribute not only to specific group loyalties but to the reproduction of the general view that the world is organized in terms of nations and national identities.

Here the study of nationalism as a topic of social theory intersects with the more reflexive question of how nationalism has shaped a crucial unit of analysis in social theory, that of society. While "sociality" may be universal to human life, the idea of discrete, bounded, and integrally unitary "societies" is more historically specific. It appears in strong form as one of the characteristic, even definitive, features of the modern era.

This reflects political features—as, for example, both state control over borders and intensification of state administration internally help to produce the idea of bounded and unified societies, and as arguments for political legitimacy increasingly claim ascent from the people rather than descent from God or inherited office. It also reflects cultural features, although many of these are not ancient inheritances but modern inventions or reforms, such as linguistic standardization, common educational systems, museums as vehicles of representation, and the introduction of national media. In one of the most influential recent studies of nationalism, Benedict Anderson (1991) has described it as productive of "imagined communities." By this he means that nations are produced centrally by cultural practices that encourage members to situate their own identities and self-understandings within a nation. Reading the same news, for example, not only provides people with common information, and common images of "us" and "them" but helps to reproduce a collective narrative in which the manifold different events and activities reported fit together like narrative threads in a novel and interweaves them all with the life of the reader. Practices and institutions of state administration are central to this production of nations as categories of understanding—imagining—but they are not exhaustive of it, and those who wield state power do not entirely control it.

To simplify the field, then, we can see four main themes in theories of nationalism (which may be combined in different ways by different authors): (1) nationalism as a source or form of conflict, (2) nationalism as a source of political integration, (3) nationalism as a reform and appropriation of ethnic inheritance, (4) nationalism as a new cultural creation. These themes are deployed in debates over "civic" versus "ethnic" nationalism and over the "modernity" or "primordiality" of nations. But before we turn to debates within the field, we should consider further the underlying problem of nationalism as a source and a shaper of the notion of society itself.

NATIONALISM AND THE PRODUCTION OF "SOCIETIES"

Human beings have always lived in groups. The nature of these groups has, however, varied considerably. They range from families and small bands through clans and other larger kin organizations to villages, kingdoms, and empires; they include religions and cultures, occupational groups and castes, nations, and more recently, even global society to the extent that it knits all humanity into a single group. In most of these cases, the self-understanding of members is crucial to the existence of the group—a kingdom, a religion, or a caste is both an "objective" collection of people and pattern of social organization and a "subjective" way in which people understand how they belong together and should interact. This is clearly true of the idea of nation. Without the subjective component of self-understanding, nations could not exist. Moreover, once the idea of nation exists, it can be used to organize not just self-understanding but categorizations of others.

The most basic meaning of nationalism is the use of this way of categorizing human populations, both as a way of looking at the world as a whole and as a way of establishing group identity from within. In addition, nationalism usually refers not just to using the category of nation to conceptualize social groups but also to holding that national identities and groups are of basic importance (and often that loyalty to one's own nation should be a commanding value). Nationalism is thus simultaneously a way of constructing groups and a normative claim. The two sides come together in ideas about who properly belongs together in a society and in arguments that members have moral obligations to the nation as a whole—perhaps even to kill on its behalf or die for it in a war.

Nationalism, then, is the use of the category "nation" to organize perceptions of basic human identities, grouping people together with fellow nationals and distinguishing them from members of other nations. It is influential as a way of helping to produce solidarity within national categories, as a way of determining how specific groups should be treated (for example, in terms of voting rights or visas and passports), and as a way of seeing the world as a whole. We see this representation in the different-colored territories on globes and maps, and in the organization of the United Nations. At the same time, clearly the boundaries of nations are both less fixed and more permeable than nationalists commonly recognize.

Central to nationalist discourse is the idea that there should be a match between a nation and a sovereign state; indeed, the nation (usually understood as prepolitical and always already there in historical terms) constitutes the ground of the legitimacy of the state. Kedourie (1993) has argued, for example, that nationalism was invented in Europe at the beginning of the nineteenth century. In his view, it "pretends to supply a criterion for the determination of the unit of population proper to enjoy a government exclusively its own, for the legitimate exercise of power in the state, and for the right organization of a society of states" (p. 1). The core elements of the doctrine are simple: Humanity is naturally divided into nations; nations are known by certain empirically identifiable characteristics; and the only legitimate type of government is national self-government.

Gellner (1983) likewise avers that nationalism is "a political principle, which holds that the political and the national unit should be congruent" (p. 5). Yet nationalism is not merely a "political principle." It depends also on reproduction through banal practices such as Olympic competitions (Billig 1995) and imaginative construction, for example, in museums, censuses, and habits of reading (Anderson 1991). And, of course, whether or not ethnicity explains nationalism, it facilitates national integration and identification.

A variety of claims are made about what constitutes "proper" nations. For example, they are held ideally to have common and distinct territories, common and distinct national cultures (including especially languages), and sovereign states of their own. It is very difficult to define nations in terms of these claims, however, since there are exceptions to almost all of them. To take language as an example, there are both nations whose members speak multiple languages (Switzerland), and languages spoken by members of different nations (English). Likewise, nationalist ideologies may hold that all members share distinctive common descent, constituting in effect a large kin group, but this is not definitive of nations in general. Nations are organized at a scale and with an internal diversity of membership that transcends kinship. No definition of *nation* (or of its correlative terms such as *nationalism* and *nationality*) has ever gained general acceptance.

In this sense, nationalism is a "discursive formation." It is a way of speaking that shapes our consciousness but also is problematic enough that it keeps generating more issues and questions. As a discursive formation, nationalism is implicated in the widespread if problematic treatment of societies as bounded, integral, wholes with distinctive identities, cultures, and institutions. Charles Tilly, Rogers Brubaker, and most important, Pierre Bourdieu have all called for a relational approach, by contrast to ideas about clear collective identities. Their critiques have hardly ended the problematic usage, partly because it is so deeply embedded in the way we speak and think. This is not an unmotivated error by social scientists; it is a participation, perhaps unwitting, in the nationalist rhetoric that pervades public life and contemporary culture.

ETHNIC AND CIVIC NATIONALISM

The category of nation has ancient roots. Both the term and two of its distinctive modern meanings were in play in the Roman Empire. For the Romans, the term referred to descent groups (usually understood to have common language and culture as well). But the Romans commonly used such ethnic categorizations to designate those who were not Roman citizens. National origins, in this sense, were what differentiated those conquered by or at war with Romans from those fully incorporated into the Roman state, not what Romans claimed as the source of their own unity. But in the very distinction, we see two sides of the discourse of nations ever since: first, an attribution of common ethnicity (culture and/or biological descent) and an idea of common membership of a state (citizenship, and more generally respect for laws and standards of behavior, which can be adopted, not only inherited).

These two sides to the idea of nation shape an enduring debate over the extent to which a legitimate people should or must be ethnically defined, or can or should be civically constituted and what the implications of each might be. Ethnic nationalist claims, based on race, kinship, language, or common culture, have been widespread throughout the modern era. They sometimes extend beyond the construction of identity to the reproduction of enmity, demands that members place the nation ahead of other loyalties, and attempts to purge territories of those defined as foreign. As a result, ethnic nationalism is often associated with ethnic violence and projects of ethnic cleansing or genocide. However, ethnic solidarity is also seen by many as basic to national identity as such and thus to the notion of the nation-state. While this notion is as much contested as defended, it remains influential.

In such usage, ethnic nationalism is commonly opposed to civic nationalism. The latter is understood as the loyalty of individual citizens to a state based purely on political identity. Habermas (1998) has theorized this as "constitutional patriotism," stressing the extent to which political loyalty is to a set of institutional arrangements rather than a prepolitical culture or other extrapolitical solidarity. Ethnic nationalism, in such usage, refers precisely to rooting political identity and obligation in the existence of a prepolitical collective unit—the nation—which achieves political subjectivity by virtue of the state. The legitimacy of the state, in turn, is judged by reference to the interests of the nation.

The contrast of ethnic to civic nationalism is heavily influenced by that of Germany to France. The contrast has been enduring and has resulted in different understandings of citizenship. France has been much more willing, for example, to use legal mechanisms to grant immigrants French citizenship, while Germany—equally open to immigration in numerical terms—has generally refused its immigrants German citizenship unless they are already ethnic Germans (Brubaker 1992). Other countries vary on the same dimension (and in Europe, the European Union is developing a mainly civic, assimilationist legal framework), but it is important to recognize that the difference is one of proportion and ideological emphasis. As Smith (1986) has remarked that all nations are shaped by both territorial and ethnic approaches to identity, and all represent an uneasy confluence of "civic" and "genealogical" or ethnic models of sociocultural organization. Not all scholars accept the distinction or hold it to be sharp; those who do use it often attribute ethnic nationalism to countries that are "late modernizers" (see p. 149).

Central to the idea of civic nationalism is the possibility for citizens to adopt national identity by choice. This is most commonly discussed in terms of the assimilation of individual immigrants into nation-states; civic nations can in principle be open to anyone who agrees to follow their laws. Citizenship in the state is seen as primary rather than prior membership in a descent group or cultural tradition. The distinction is fuzzy, however, as a rhetoric of civic nationalism and citizenship can mask underlying commitments to particularistic cultural or racial definitions of what counts as a "proper" or good citizen. Thus (in a recently prominent example) even law-abiding Muslims may not seem sufficiently French to many, and conversely the French state may pass laws ostensibly enforcing neutrality on religion but in fact expressing particular ethnocultural mores. It is particularly difficult to frame rationales for limits on immigration in civic nationalist terms without falling back on ethnic nationalism.

At the same time, the civic nationalist tradition contains another thread. This is the notion that the nation itself is made, is a product of collective action. This is symbolized by revolutions and the founding of new states (which may include more or less successful efforts to call forth national solidarities). The idea of choice here is not simply that of individual membership but of collective determination of the form and content of the nation itself—the effort to take control of culture as a historical project rather than merely receiving it as inheritance. When the revolutionary French National Assembly reformed the calendar and systems of measurement, thus, it was engaged not merely in administration of the state but in an effort to make a certain sort of nation—one with a more modern, rational culture. And, of course, the tension between attempting to make a new culture and preserve the old has been played out in the educational system ever since.

While much nationalist ideology has claimed definitive ethnic roots, social scientists are divided on the question, and most prominent twentieth-century analysts of nationalism have sought to challenge the explanation of nationalism by ethnicity. Kohn (1944) stresses the crucial role of modern politics, especially the idea of sovereignty. Hobsbawm (1990) treats nationalism as a kind of second-order political movement based on a false consciousness that ethnicity helps to produce but cannot explain because the deeper roots lie in political economy, not culture. The dominant approach in contemporary scholarship approaches nationalism largely as an ideological reflection of state formation (Mann 1993; Tilly 1990). Gellner (1983) emphasizes industrialization and also stresses the number of cases of failed or absent nationalisms: ethnic groups which mounted either little or no attempt to become nations in the modern sense. This suggests that even if ethnicity plays a role, it cannot be a sufficient explanation (although one imagines the nineteenth-century German romantics would simply reply that there are strong, historic nations and weak ones destined to fade from the historic stage). Hayes (1931) argues for seeing nationalism as a sort of religion. Hechter (2000) analyzes it in terms of strategic individual action aimed at maximizing mostly economic and political benefits. Kedourie (1993) approaches nationalism as an ideology and attempts to debunk nationalism by showing the untenability of the German romantic cultural-ethnic claims. Indeed, in their different ways, all these thinkers have sought to debunk the common claims nationalists themselves make to long-established ethnic identities.

Against this backdrop, Smith (1986) acknowledges that nations cannot be seen as primordial or natural but nonetheless argues that they are rooted in relatively ancient histories. Smith argues that the origins of modern nationalism lie in the successful bureaucratization of aristocratic ethnie (ethnic community), which were able to transform themselves into genuine nations only in the West. In the West, territorial centralization and consolidation went hand in hand with a growing cultural standardization. Nations, Smith thus suggests, are long-term processes, continually reenacted and reconstructed; they require ethnic cores, homelands, heroes and golden ages if they are to survive. "Modern nations and nationalism have only extended and deepened the meanings and scope of older ethnic concepts and structures" (p. 216). Nationalism brings some degree of universalization, but even modern "civic" nations do not fully transcend ethnicity or ethnic sentiments. Consider the fact that France is the primary example of civic nationalism, and yet imagine France without French culture: language, cheeses, styles of social theory, and all.

The ethnic similarities and bonds that contribute to the formation of nations may indeed be important and long standing, but in themselves they do not fully constitute either particular nations or the modern idea of nation. While some critics of ethnic explanations of nationalism emphasize the influence of state formation or other "master variables," a number assert that nations are created by nationalism—by this particular form of discourse, political rhetoric, or ideology—not merely passively present and awaiting the contingent address of nationalists (Anderson 1991; Chatterjee 1986; Gellner 1983; Kedourie 1993).

An emphasis on preexisting ethnicity—even where this is rightly identified—is unable to shed much light on why so many modern movements, policies, ideologies, and conflicts are constituted within the discourse of nationalism. Indeed, as Gellner (1983:8–18, 61) has suggested, the very self-recognition of ethnicities or cultures as defining identities is distinctively modern. Walker Connor (1994) uses a similar point to distinguish ethnic groups as "potential nations" from real nations: "While an ethnic group may, therefore, be other-defined, the nation must be self-defined" (p. 103).

Explanations of nationalism, thus, need to address the contemporary conditions that make it effective in people's lives, their attempts to orient themselves in the world, and their actions. Such conditions are, of course, subject to change, and nationalist constructions are apt to change with them. Thus, Indian nationalists from the nineteenth century through Nehru were able to make a meaningful (although hardly seamless or uncontested) unity of the welter of subcontinental identities as part of their struggle against the British. The departure of the British from India changed the meaning of Congress nationalism, however, as this became the program of an Indian state, not of those outside official politics who resisted an alien regime. Among other effects of this, a rhetorical space was opened up for "communal" and other sectional claims that were less readily brought forward in the colonial period (Chatterjee 1994). Similarly, the proliferation of nationalisms in Eastern Europe attendant on the collapse of communist rule involved a "reframing" of older national identities and nationalist projects; the nationalisms of the 1990s were neither altogether new nor simply resumptions of those that predated communism (Brubaker 1996). The opposition between primordiality and "mere invention" leaves open a very wide range of historicities within which national and other traditions can exert real force. As Renan ([1871]1990) famously stressed, nationalist histories are matters of forgetting as well as remembering, including forgotten the "deeds of violence which took place at the origin of all political formations" (p. 11).

Nationalism is partly a matter of narrative construction, the production (and reproduction and revision) of narratives locating the nation's place in history. As Anderson (1991) puts it, nations move through historical time as persons move through biographical time; each may figure in stories like characters in a novel. This is one reason why the continuity of ethnic identities alone does not adequately explain nationalism: The narrative constructions in which it is cast change and potentially transform the meaning of whatever ethnic commonalties may exist. Ironically, the writing of linear historical narratives of national development and claims to primordial national identity often proceed hand in hand. Indeed, the writing of national historical narratives is so embedded in the discourse of nationalism that it almost always depends rhetorically on the presumption of some kind of preexisting national identity in order to give the story a beginning. A claim to primordial national identity is, in fact, a version of nationalist historical narrative.

MODERNITY VERSUS PRIMORDIALITY

A long-running debate in the literature on nationalism pits arguments that it is an extension of ancient ethnicity (Smith 1986) against those who argue that it is essentially modern (Gellner 1983; Greenfeld 1992; Hobsbawm 1990). Majority scholarly opinion tends toward the latter view, although explanations differ. "Modernists" variously see nationalism rooted in industrialization (Gellner 1983), state formation (Mann 1993; Tilly 1990), the rise of new communications media and genres of collective imagination (Anderson 1991; Deutsch 1966), and the development of new rhetorics for collective identity and capacities for collective action (Calhoun 1997). While many favor specific factors as primary explanations, most recognize that several causes are interrelated.

Many nationalists but few scholars see nationalism as ubiquitous in history and simply the "normal" way of organizing large-scale collective identity. Most social scientists point, rather, to the variety of political and cultural forms common before the modern era—empires and great religions, for example—and the transformations wrought by the rise of a new kind of intensive state administration, cultural integration, popular political participation, and international relations. Many of these social scientists argue that nations and nationalism in their modern sense are both new. In particular, they would argue that ethnicity as a way of organizing collective identity underwent at the least a substantial reorganization when it began to be deployed as part of ethnonationalist rhetoric in the modern era. Others, however, including notably Anthony Smith and John Armstrong,

argue that there is more continuity in the ethnic core of nations, although they too would agree that modernity transformed—if it did not outright create—nationalism.

The attraction of a claimed ethnic foundation to nations lies largely in the implication that nationhood is in some sense primordial and natural. Nationalists typically claim that their nations are simply given and immutable rather than constructions of recent historical action or tendentious contemporary claims. Much early scholarly writing on nations and nationalism shared in this view and sought to discover which were the "true" ethnic foundations of nationhood. It is no doubt ideologically effective to claim that a nation has existed since time immemorial or that its traditions have been passed down intact from heroic founders. In no case, however, does historical or social science research support such a claim. All nations are historically created.

Noting this, one line of research emphasizes the manipulation of popular sentiments by the more or less cynical production of national culture by intellectuals and state-building elites. Hobsbawm and Ranger (1983), for example, have collected numerous examples of the ways in which apparently definitive cultural markers of national identity can in fact be traced to specific acts of creation embedded in political (or sometimes marketing) projects rather than reflecting preexisting ethnicity. The Scots tartan kilt is a famous example, dating not from the mists of primordial Highland history but from eighteenth-century resistance to Anglicization (Trevor-Roper 1983) and early nineteenth-century romantic celebrations of a no-longer-troubling ethnic Scottishness. Likewise, nineteenth-century Serbian and Croatian intellectuals strove to divide their common Serbo-Croatian language into two distinct vernaculars with separate literary traditions. But as this example makes clear, it is not obvious that because the "traditions" of nationalism are "invented," they are somehow less real or valid. Anderson (1996) finds the same fault with Gellner: "Gellner is so anxious to show that nationalism masquerades under false pretences that he assimilates 'invention' to 'fabrication' and 'falsity,' rather than to 'imagining' and 'creation'" (p. 6).

Hobsbawm and Ranger (1983) imply that long-standing, "primordial" tradition would somehow count as legitimate, while by contrast various nationalist traditions are of recent and perhaps manipulative creation. Many ideologues do claim origins at the dawn of history, but few scholars have doubted that cultural traditions are constantly renewed. What so-called primordialists have argued is that certain identities and traditions—especially those of ethnicity—are experienced as primordial. Sociologically, thus, what matters is less the antiquity of the contents of tradition than the efficacy of the process by which certain beliefs and understandings are constituted as unquestioned, immediate knowledge. This has more to do with current bases for the reproduction of culture than with history as such. Ethnicity or cultural traditions are bases for nationalism because they effectively constitute historical memory, because they inculcate it as "prejudice," not because the historical origins they claim are accurate (prejudice means not just prior to judgment, but constituting the condition of judgment.). Moreover, all traditions are "invented" (or at least in a more diffuse sense, created); none are truly primordial. This was acknowledged, although rather weakly, even by some of the functionalists who emphasized the notion of primordiality and the "givenness" of cultural identities and traditions (see especially Geertz 1963). All such traditions also are potentially contested and subject to continual reshaping, whether explicit or hidden. Some claims about nationality may fail to persuade because they are too manifestly manipulated by creators or because the myth being proffered does not speak to the circumstances and practical commitments of the people in question.

Notions of nations as acting subjects are distinctively modern, part of a new way of constructing collective identity. This said, there is no scholarly agreement about when nationalism began. Greenfeld (1992) dates it from the English Civil War, Anderson (1991) from Latin American independence movements, Alter (1989) from the French Revolution, and Breuilly (1993) and Kedourie (1993) both from German romanticism and reaction to the French Revolution. Calhoun (1997) suggests that rather than trying to identify a single point of origin, scholars should see nationalism as drawing together several different threads of historical change. As a discursive formation, it took on increasingly clear form through the early modern period and was fully in play by the Napoleonic era.

CONCLUSION

The idea of nation became a more fundamental building block of social life during the early modern period, especially the eighteenth and nineteenth centuries. While it is fruitless to search for a precise origin point for modern nationalism, it is possible to identify some of the social changes and conditions that helped to make it important.

First, nationalism reflected a growing scale of social organization, larger than cities (which had previously been primary units of belonging and common culture for elites), villages, or kin groups. This was made possible partly by improved communication that enabled larger populations to interact with greater density—a matter simultaneously of roads, the spread of literacy, and wars that brought large populations together in common military organization and movements (Deutsch 1966). It was also facilitated by increased integration of trade among different regions within contiguous territories and by the mobilization of new kinds of military and state power.

Second, nationalism constituted a new ideology about primary identities. In this it competed not only with localism

and family but with religion (Anderson 1991; Hayes 1931). In fact, nationalism was often furthered by religious movements and wars—notably in the wake of the reformation—and national self-understandings were frequently religiously inflected (as in the Catholicism of Poland or the Protestantism of England). But nationalism involved a kind of secular faith and a primary loyalty to the nation that was and is distinct from any religion that may intertwine with it.

Third, nationalism grew hand in hand with modern states and was basic to a new way of claiming political legitimacy. States furthered social integration among their subjects by building roads, mobilizing militaries, sponsoring education, and standardizing languages (Breuilly 1993). But they also were shaped by a cultural change that introduced a new, stronger idea of "the people" who were both governed by and served by a state. Indeed, the idea of the state as providing necessary services for the "commonwealth" was basic, and with it came the notion that the legitimacy of the state depended on its serving its people effectively, being recognized by them, or both. This placed a new stress on the question of who the people might be. The notions that they were those who happened to have been born into the domain of a monarch or who conquered in war were clearly inadequate. The idea of nation came to the forefront. It represented the "people" of a country as an internally unified group with common interests and the capacity to act.

The last point is crucial. The idea of nation not only laid claim to history or common identity. It purported to describe (or construct) a collective actor: "we the people," as articulated in the U.S. Constitution or the French people who collectively stormed the Bastille and joined in the levée en masse.

The constitution of nations—not only in dramatic revolutionary acts of founding but in the formation of common culture and political identities—is one of the pivotal features of the modern era. It is part of the organization of political participation and loyalty, of culture and identity, of the way history is taught and the way wars are fought. It not only shapes practical political identity and ideology, it also shapes the very idea of society in which much social theory is rooted.

— Craig Calhoun

See also Citizenship; Collective Memory; Historical and Comparative Theory; State; Tilly, Charles

FURTHER READINGS AND REFERENCES

Alter, Peter. 1989. *Nationalism.* London: Edward Arnold.

Anderson, Benedict. 1991. *Imagined Communities.* Rev. ed. London: Verso.

———. 1996, "Introduction." In *Mapping the Nation,* edited by Gopal Balakrishnan. London: Verso.

Billig, Michael. 1995. *Banal Nationalism.* London: Sage.

Breuilly, John. 1993. *Nationalism and the State.* Rev. ed. Chicago, IL: University of Chicago Press.

Brubaker, Rogers. 1992. *Citizenship and Nationhood in France and Germany.* Cambridge, UK: Cambridge University Press.

———. 1996. *Nationalism Reframed: Nationhood and the National Question in the New Europe.* Cambridge, UK: Cambridge University Press.

Calhoun, Craig. 1997. *Nationalism.* Milton Keynes, UK: Open University Press.

Chatterjee, Partha. 1986. *Nationalist Thought and the Colonial World: A Derivative Discourse?* Atlantic Highlands, NJ: Zed.

———. 1994. *The Nation and Its Fragments: Studies in Colonial and Post-Colonial Histories.* Princeton, NJ: Princeton University Press.

Connor, Walker. 1994. *Ethnonationalism.* Princeton, NJ: Princeton University Press.

Deutsch, Karl W. 1966. *Nationalism and Social Communication: An Inquiry into the Foundations of Nationality,* 2d ed. Cambridge: MIT Press.

Geertz, Clifford. 1963. *Old Societies and New States.* New York: Free Press.

Gellner, Ernest. 1983. *Nations and Nationalism.* Oxford, UK: Blackwell.

Greenfeld, Leah. 1992. *Nationalism: Five Paths to Modernity.* Cambridge, MA: Harvard University Press.

Habermas, Jürgen. 1998. *The Inclusion of the Other: Studies in Political Theory,* edited by Ciaran Cronin and Pablo De Greif. Cambridge: MIT Press.

Hayes, Carlton J. H. 1931. *The Historical Evolution of Modern Nationalism.* New York: R. R. Smith.

Hechter, Michael. 2000. *Containing Nationalism.* New York: Oxford University Press.

Hobsbawm, Eric. 1990. *Nations and Nationalism Since 1780: Programme, Myth, Reality.* Cambridge, UK: Cambridge University Press.

Hobsbawm, Eric and Terence Ranger. 1983. *The Invention of Tradition.* Cambridge, UK: Cambridge University Press.

Kedourie, Elie. 1993. *Nationalism.* 4th ed. Oxford, UK: Blackwell.

Kohn, Hans. 1944. *The Age of Nationalism.* New York: Harper & Row.

Mann, Michael. 1993. *Sources of Social Power.* Vol. 2. Cambridge, UK: Cambridge University Press.

Renan, Ernst. [1871] 1990. "What Is a Nation?" Pp. 8–22 in *Nation and Narration,* edited by Homi Bhabha. London: Routledge.

Smith, Anthony. 1986. *The Ethnic Origins of Nations.* Oxford, UK: Blackwell.

Tilly, Charles. 1990. *Coercion, Capital and European States, AD 990–1990.* Cambridge, UK: Blackwell.

Trevor-Roper, Hugh. 1983. "The Invention of Tradition: The Highland Tradition of Scotland." Pp. 15–42 in *The Invention of Tradition,* edited by E. Hobsbawm and T. Ranger. Cambridge, UK: Cambridge University Press.

NEGOTIATED ORDER

Negotiated order is a theoretical perspective developed primarily by Anselm Strauss (1917–1996), who argued that virtually all social order is negotiated order. To accomplish tasks in social settings, people chiefly negotiate with each other. Through ongoing processes of negotiation, social actors alternately create, maintain, transform, and are constrained by, social structures. The negotiated-order perspective provides a means to understand the processes involved in both structural change and stability and to identify the social structures and conditions that shape those processes. It also permits researchers to address one of the central concerns in sociology—the link between individuals and society—by specifying how social actors respond to and changed social structure, whether they act on their own behalf or as organizational representatives.

The negotiated-order perspective enables researchers to examine patterned negotiations between social actors embedded in organizations and between organizations, occupations, professions, industries, markets, social worlds, or nations. Negotiations occur whenever acting units encounter ambiguity or uncertainty, when they define organizational routines differently, when they differ in their approach to problems, or when they create exceptions or loopholes for previously established rules and policies. When social actors settle on new practices, those patterns become part of the stable structure or "organizational background" that guides future negotiations. The perspective thus encourages researchers to incorporate historical data in their analyses by investigating how structural conditions arose in the past and observing how those conditions influence present negotiations.

Strauss (1978) offered this description of negotiated order at the organizational level:

> The negotiated order on any given day could be conceived of as the sum total of the organization's rules and policies, along with whatever agreements, understandings, pacts, contracts, and other working arrangements currently [operate]. These include agreements at every level of the organization, of every clique and coalition, and include covert as well as overt agreements. (pp. 5–6)

With roots in the symbolic interactionist tradition, Strauss and his colleagues conceived of negotiated order as a critical response to structural-functionalist characterizations of social structure as immutable and as exerting a one-way influence on social behavior. They wanted to document and analyze social change by placing negotiation in the forefront without sacrificing respect for social structure.

While the perspective claims that practically all social orders are negotiated orders, this does not make structure a fictional concept, nor does it make stability impossible, despite some critics' charges that negotiated order overemphasizes indeterminacy. Proponents argue that not all aspects of society can be negotiated at any given time, but they also contend that stability in organizational life cannot be taken at face value—people must work together continuously to achieve and then maintain it. Moreover, they charge that because social conditions change through a negotiated process, any current arrangement that participants treat as inviolate may be the product of past negotiations. Simply examining a professional organized sport and comparing its rules and structure with the original game will demonstrate how today's stability was achieved through yesterday's negotiation and exchange.

The negotiated-order perspective provides a conceptual framework for studying *mesostructure* (see Maines 1982), a term that represents the intermediate social realm where individual action and social structure meet and where social orders are developed and invested with meaning. Negotiations occur within a *negotiation context,* which is defined as a set of structural conditions that surround and directly affect the content, process, and consequences of negotiations. Past negotiations may shape future courses of action, modify structural conditions, or undergo a process of *sedimentation,* whereby they join the set of standard operating procedures and become part of the social structure. Enveloping the negotiation context is a *structural context,* which consists of larger social patterns and interlocking demographic, economic, and political conditions. A structural context may influence multiple negotiation contexts for a given organization or for interconnected organizations. For example, if one looks at the corrupt practice of insider trading in the stock market, the structural context would include the regulatory policies of the U.S. Securities and Exchange Commission established via sedimentation from previous negotiation processes; policies and patterns of trade developed in publicly held firms; organizational and market conditions that inspire marketable information; the divisions of labor and workers' relationships that operate in law, banking, and brokerage firms; the web of investor relations in the marketplace; and the political climate surrounding the organizations and individuals involved in trade.

In this perspective, negotiation concerns interpersonal, not intrapersonal, interactions. Negotiation may be defined narrowly, as in brokering agreements, mediating, and bargaining, or loosely, as in compromising, making concessions, and colluding. Alternatives to negotiation may occur as well, such as manipulation or persuasion, sometimes even to the exclusion of negotiation. This invites a reasonable theoretical and methodological complaint about the negotiated-order perspective: Just what is, and what isn't, negotiation? When laying the groundwork for the perspective, Strauss gently criticized contemporary theorists for either omitting negotiation altogether as an important consideration or for focusing so narrowly on certain kinds of negotiations that they excluded significant transactions between social actors or acting units.

Although Strauss and his colleagues deliberately created a broad definition of negotiation to accommodate diverse social and organizational interactions, negotiated-order researchers differ in whether they define negotiation generically or specifically. Consequently, they may publish contradictory or inconsistent findings depending on how they operationalize the concept of negotiation. For example, while one researcher may define the absence of face-to-face communication between coworkers of different ranks and occupations as an example of a lack of negotiation, another researcher might assume that their cooperative working arrangements resulted from previous negotiations or "silent bargains" that became routine and taken-for-granted. Through previous negotiations, coworkers may base their actions on what they think others want, or how they imagine others will respond, such as to retaliate. Researchers may also disagree on whether one must observe active negotiations firsthand or accept respondents' or other researchers' reports that negotiations occur.

Although the definition of negotiation may be unclear, using the perspective enables researchers to carefully and closely analyze the conditions that modify negotiations in the surrounding negotiation context. Factors that matter in analyzing how, when, where, and why negotiations take place in a social setting can be grouped by the characteristics of participants, negotiations, issues, and alternatives.

Regarding the characteristics of negotiation participants, researchers need to identify which social actors get to negotiate, their experience with negotiation, what loyalties they maintain to different groups or identities, what cultural backgrounds they come from, what they stand to lose or gain from negotiation, and what degree of power, authority, and autonomy they possess in relation to other participants. To further understand negotiators, researchers may examine how social actors develop their negotiation skills and how they perceive their surroundings. Just how negotiators interpret the social setting, other participants, and situational constraints such as organizational rules and policies will influence the negotiation context. When different participants do not share assumptions about who has more power, what is open to negotiation, or just what they need to negotiate, their differing perceptions complicate the negotiation process.

Characteristics of negotiations themselves also inform the negotiation context. Negotiations may exhibit particular patterns in timing and composition, such as whether they occur singly, repeatedly, in combination with others, and so forth. They may also differ in their visibility to members of the social setting, even to negotiation participants, if one or more sides have hidden agendas. Negotiations may consist of particular kinds of subprocesses, such as renegotiation after a party violates an agreement or a new issue appears, or trade-offs, concessions, and payoffs to keep negotiations open and ongoing.

Characteristics of the issues involved in negotiations compose another aspect of the negotiation context. Issues may differ on the basis of their meaning, complexity, priority, and legitimacy to participants, all of which may contribute to the process of negotiation. For example, if an issue matters more to one party than to another, it may add to that party's urgency to negotiate at the same time that it weakens their bargaining position with the other party, who may try to stall the process in order to magnify their relative power. Or when organizational members negotiate with each other and represent different occupations, divergent organizational goals, or different cultural backgrounds, they may disagree on the significance of particular issues, especially if they favor some participants over others. Even the organization's legitimacy in the eyes of the public may become a dominant issue around which participants negotiate. Issues may be interconnected—the death penalty, for example—such that participants cannot negotiate on one concern without addressing others.

The last set of factors that may bear on the negotiation context—and on each of the other factors discussed previously—concerns the availability of alternatives to negotiation. Alternatives may consist of persuasion, manipulation, appealing to the rules or to a higher authority, or coercion. These options seem to relate closely to the distribution of power between participants in the social setting or between negotiating organizations. The alternatives may also shape how, and if, any negotiation occurs. Researchers of political processes may be particularly interested in analyzing under what conditions negotiation assumes a higher priority than alternatives like coercion, oppression, or rebellion.

Factors in the structural context—which encompass multiple negotiation contexts—can also be organized and studied along similar lines as those in the negotiation context when examining negotiations between complex organizations. When organizations of various size, power, composition, experience, ideological commitments, and goals negotiate with each other at the same time that they negotiate internally, structural conditions that influence their negotiations multiply quickly. Proponents of the negotiated-order perspective argue that when researchers fail to analyze those interlocking processes of negotiation, they ultimately fall short of understanding the product: social order.

Although the studies that adopt the negotiated-order perspective vary in scale from interpersonal to interorganizational negotiations and cover a wide variety of substantive areas, most applications of the perspective contribute to a few main areas of sociological interest. On the basis of the publication record to date, researchers have employed the negotiated-order perspective most often in the areas of work, occupations, and professions; simple and complex organizations, including the shared theoretical ground between negotiated order and organizational theory; and in social worlds/arenas theory, which joins the negotiated-order perspective with the study of collective action, social movements, and organizations.

The emphases on occupations, professions, and organizations originated with research published in 1963 by Strauss and his colleagues Leonard Schatzman, Danuta Ehrlich, Rue Bucher, and Melvin Sabshin, who studied the interactions of personnel and patients at two psychiatric hospitals. Through their observations, Strauss and his colleagues recognized hospitals as "professionalized locales" in which members of professional and nonprofessional groups hold different ideologies, aims, and statuses but nevertheless manage to work together as a whole. The authors drew attention to the multiple and repeated transactions between hospital participants that helped shape their collective understanding of rules and policies as "structure." This approach by Strauss and his colleagues displayed a strong departure from contemporaneous studies of formal organization that downplayed internal changes and interactions.

Although many researchers have continued to examine negotiated order in hospital settings, in alternative health organizations, among workers in health-related occupations, or between different health-related organizations, far more studies have examined organizations and occupations outside the health care field. Research settings have included families, communities, schools, prisons, factories, restaurants, accounting firms, universities, and government agencies. Other researchers have focused their attention on the machinations of particular industries and markets, such as liquor and automobiles; social institutions, such as politics, law, and marriage and family; or complex social relationships, such as the division of labor and criminal activity.

Some applications of negotiated order follow a more microsociological bent, examining situated negotiation between social actors in the process of accomplishing specific work-related tasks. Researchers have analyzed transcripts of interactions between coworkers or between clients and service providers to capture unfolding processes of negotiation. Some of these studies blur the boundary between the concept of negotiated order and Goffman's concept of "interaction order," which addresses face-to-face interaction, often guided by actors' shared assumptions about how to act in given situations.

Collectively, these different applications of negotiated order demonstrate the strengths of the perspective in working with multiple levels of analysis and substantive areas. Despite the demonstrated utility of negotiated order—the perspective offers a powerful and practical link between micro- and macrosociology and provides a clear framework for studying the connections between individual action and social structure—researchers have not developed it further in a cumulative sense. The perspective's influence remains limited, even in interactionist and organizational sociology, where it seems most useful.

Within the symbolic interactionist perspective, more researchers have adopted a social constructionist (or reality constructionist) than a negotiated-order approach. Although the negotiated-order perspective shares the assumption that social structures arise through a process of social construction, and social constructionists agree that reality may be negotiated, the emphasis on negotiation skirts an interactionist concern with the reproduction of inequality and the consequences of an unequal distribution of power for social actors. Inequality itself may be understood simultaneously as a negotiated order, a coerced order, and a manipulated order—all possibilities that Strauss argued could operate alongside each other—but few researchers have answered the call to investigate how they may overlap in society.

In organizational sociology, applications of other theoretical perspectives far outnumber negotiated order and have effectively excluded the negotiated-order perspective. Three theoretical approaches bear mention regarding the common ground they share with negotiated order: social network theory, organizational ecology, and institutional theory. Social network theory offers powerful models for examining the strategic positioning of social actors or organizations in a network structure and enables researchers to attend to social structural constraints and exchanges between network participants. Organizational ecology, like the negotiated-order perspective, examines the structural and environmental contexts in which organizations operate and offers the opportunity to observe patterns in interorganizational cooperation and competition. Institutional theory emphasizes the importance of social structure, process, and historical change and enables researchers to study how organizations impinge on each other. What these perspectives primarily offer, beyond their theoretical and methodological sophistication, is the flexibility to consider exchanges other than negotiation, no matter how that concept is defined. However, they lack the interactionist sensibility of negotiated order; they do not exhibit a strong concern for how social actors collectively maintain, conform to, and change social structure.

The strongest development of the negotiated-order perspective appears in Strauss's social worlds/arenas theory. *Social worlds* comprise groups that share particular concerns or activities and mobilize their resources to act collectively, but not necessarily cooperatively (sciences, industries, religions, media, etc.). Multiple social worlds may be joined by their participation in an *arena* of concern (HIV research, environmental issues, legal actions, wars, etc.). Several former students and colleagues of Anselm Strauss (Adele E. Clarke, Joan Fujimura, and Susan Leigh

Star) have melded social worlds/arenas research with social studies of science and, more generally, with science and technology studies. By honoring a Strauss dictum to "study the unstudied," they focus on a central concern of the negotiated-order perspective—to understand how social change occurs and to accurately track how social actors and groups accomplish it—in a variety of scientific and technological contexts.

Adele E. Clarke (1998) has studied the origins and transformations of twentieth-century reproductive science by examining the involvements of actors representing different worlds such as scientists from diverse academic disciplines; research sponsors; consumers; markets; and contraceptive manufacturers, advocates, and opponents. She and her colleagues have also called attention to elements of scientific infrastructure that intersect social worlds, studying the growth and development of research materials and tools on which scientists and students depend (Clarke and Fujimura 1992) and that, like scientific knowledge itself, arise through a collective process of conflict, negotiation, and exchange.

Taking an ecological approach to work, knowledge, and organizations, Susan Leigh Star has explored how the nature and character of seemingly mundane infrastructure (computer networks, electronic codes, information standards, power supplies, legal codes, etc.), can influence the structural conditions in both negotiated order and social worlds/arena research. Along with James R. Griesemer (Star and Griesemer 1989), she introduced the analytic concept of *boundary objects,* which can be understood as social objects that connect multiple social worlds and facilitate collective action. Boundary objects have a common structure that permits translation between social worlds, yet in each particular social world, members adapt and modify them to suit their local needs.

Joan H. Fujimura (1992) has advanced a conceptual companion to boundary objects, *standardized packages,* which are more structured and concrete in that they combine theory and a set of methodological practices that do not vary from one social world to another. For example, Fujimura applied the concept of standardized packages to analyze how recombinant DNA technologies from molecular biology, combined with oncogene theory, came to dominate cancer research. She demonstrated that standardized packages contribute to negotiated order when they act as interfaces for social worlds and form an infrastructure that changes and constrains the practices, skills, and knowledge in each social world. Thus, science itself—facts, theories, and methodologies—is profitably understood as a collection of negotiated orders.

— Martha Copp

See also Institutional Theory; Network Theory; Social Constructionism; Social Studies of Science; Social Worlds; Strauss, Anselm; Symbolic Interaction

FURTHER READINGS AND REFERENCES

Clarke, Adele E. 1998. *Disciplining Reproduction: Modernity, Life Sciences, and "the Problems of Sex."* Berkeley, CA: University of California Press.

Clarke, Adele E. and Joan H. Fujimura, eds. 1992. *The Right Tools for the Job: At Work in Twentieth-Century Life Sciences.* Princeton, NJ: Princeton University Press.

Fine, Gary Alan. 1984. "Negotiated Orders and Organizational Cultures." *Annual Review of Sociology* 10:239–62.

Fujimura, Joan H. 1992. "Crafting Science: Standardized Packages, Boundary Objects, and 'Translation.'" Pp. 168–211 in *Science as Practice and Culture,* edited by Andrew Pickering. Chicago, IL: University of Chicago Press.

Maines, David R. 1982. "In Search of Mesostructure: Studies in the Negotiated Order." *Urban Life* 11:267–79.

Star, Susan Leigh and James R. Griesemer. 1989. "Institutional Ecology, 'Translations' and Boundary Objects: Amateurs and Professionals in Berkeley's Museum of Vertebrate Zoology, 1907–39." *Social Studies of Science* 19:387–420.

Strauss, Anselm. 1978. *Negotiations: Varieties, Contexts, Processes, and Social Order.* San Francisco, CA: Jossey-Bass.

Strauss, Anselm, Leonard Schatzman, Danuta Ehrlich, Rue Bucher, and Melvin Sabshin. 1963. "The Hospital and Its Negotiated Order." Pp. 147–69 in *The Hospital in Modern Society,* edited by Eliot Freidson. New York: Free Press.

NEO-KANTIANISM

At the end of the nineteenth century, various philosophers critical of Hegel's metaphysics, Nietzsche's vitalism, and Marx's materialism, proposed to return to Kant's epistemology, focusing on the problematic relationship between knowledge and reality, concepts and experience. This so-called neo-Kantianism was also prompted by the emerging social sciences, psychology and sociology in the first place, and their search for a logic and methodology that could match those of the natural sciences. Neo-Kantianism was an influential stream of thought and research until 1933 when the rise of Nazism put an end to it. After World War II, it was surpassed by French and German existentialism, Anglo-Saxon analytical philosophy, and phenomenology.

Neo-Kantianism is a label for often vastly different currents of thought and research, but usually two main schools are distinguished: the Marburg School and the South-West German, or Baden School. Wilhelm Windelband (1846–1916) is generally viewed as the founder of the latter. He commanded a comprehensive knowledge of the history of philosophy and was a fierce opponent of speculative, metaphysical systems of philosophical thought. He searched above all for a logic of the sciences

(*Wissenschaftslehre*) that would avoid the pitfall of scientism or positivism, which models such a logic after the natural sciences. In his view, the world of historical values and meanings (i.e., the world of the *Geist*) needed method of scientific scrutiny that differs from the way nature ought to be investigated. In other words, there is not an essential difference between *Geisteswissenschaft* and *Naturwissenschaft* (i.e., between humanity and science) but, rather, a logical and methodological difference. In *Geisteswissenschaft,* history in the first place, there is a focus on what is unique, different, and individual. It is a predominantly descriptive, *idiographic* approach of reality. In *Naturwissenschaft,* the focus is rather on what is general, repetitive, and lawlike. This is a *nomothetic* approach to reality. Windelband's successor, Heinrich Rickert (1863–1936), elaborated this idea in the much broader context of a philosophy of values. To avoid the introduction of psychology into the logic and methodology of social sciences, as was recurrently done by his contemporaries, Rickert proposed to replace the word *Geisteswissenschaft* by the concept of *Kulturwissenschaft. Geist* after all, is easily associated with "psyche" or "soul," while *Kultur* refers to the immaterial reality of values and meanings. The basic idea of his rather complex logic is that the natural-scientific approach, characterized by the search for general laws of development, will run up against its limits the moment one has to deal with values and meanings, which, after all, function within specific, historically unique, and individual contexts. His *opus magnum, The Limits of Concept Formation in Natural Sciences: A Logical Introduction to the Historical Sciences* (1896–1902), is an attempt to design a methodology for the historical discipline and the related "cultural sciences." In Rickert's view, social sciences such as psychology and sociology can legitimately be executed in a natural-scientific manner and thus search for general laws of psychic and social developments, but the moment they also want to focus on values and meanings—that is, on culture—they will have to work with individualizing, historical methods. This idea had a decisive influence on the logic and methodology of Max Weber, who always tried to combine a generalizing, "natural scientific" approach (see his *Economy and Society*) with an individualizing, historical method (see his essays on the economic ethics of the world religions).

The main philosopher of the Marburg School was Ernst Cassirer (1874–1945). His knowledge was that of a Renaissance man, since he was an expert in mathematics, physics, religion, magic, esoteric philosophies, linguistics, and the history of philosophy. It drives him far beyond the philosophy of Kant, whose critique of reason he broadened into a critique of culture. He also extended Kant's epistemology into a historical and comparative analysis of the evolutionary development of human knowledge. Language (speech), religion, myth, magic, art, and science are analyzed and compared as various specimens of knowledge. Despite vast differences, they share a similar function, since they are expressions of man's ability to gain knowledge of reality by means of *symbolic forms.* That is, human beings do not just experience reality but supply their experiences with meaning and apply words, names, and concepts to them, which are accompanied by various acts and actions. These words, names, and concepts—coined by speech, myths, magical formulas, religious doctrines, and scientific theories—are symbolic forms whose function it is not only to constitute human knowledge but, in a sense, also to construct reality. Cassirer developed this basic idea in the three volumes of his *opus magnum, Philosophy of Symbolic Forms* (1923–1929).

Rickert's philosophy of values and logic of the natural and cultural sciences was rather abstract, rationalistic, and radically opposed to the vitalism of Nietzsche, Bergson, Dilthey, and others. His fame declined rapidly after World War I, when students were no longer eager to delve into detailed epistemological debates. It was, rather, Rickert's student and family friend Martin Heidegger who satisfied their thirst for an existentialist approach to their surrounding world. Ludwig Wittgenstein's scathing attacks on traditional philosophical thought and Karl Popper's critique of historicism contributed also to the fact that Rickert is almost completely forgotten today. However, as to social theory, his influence on Max Weber's methodology of the social sciences should not be underestimated. Moreover, present postmodernist vitalism still meets in Rickert's philosophy of values a formidable opponent who should not be dismissed too easily. Cassirer's neo-Kantian legacy, on the other hand, has remained influential throughout the decades after World War II. As to social theory, his philosophy of symbolic forms will remind many sociologists of George Herbert Mead's "social behaviorism," or "symbolic interactionism." In view of the "linguistic turn" of philosophy, which has always been important for the social sciences as well, Cassirer's approach to language (speech) still deserves attention far beyond the boundaries of philosophy.

— Anton C. Zijderveld

See also Blumer, Herbert; Cassirer, Ernst; Dilthey, Wilhelm; Mead, George Herbert; Phenomenology; Symbolic Interaction; Weber, Max

FURTHER READINGS AND REFERENCES

Cassirer, Ernst. [1923-1999] 1997. *Philosophie der symbolischen Formen* [Philosophy of Symbolic Forms]. Vol. 1: *Die Sprache* [Language/Speech]; Vol. 2: *Das mythische Denken* [Mythological Thought]; Vol. 3: *Phänomenologie der Erkenntnis* [Phenomenology of Knowledge]. Darmstadt, Germany: Primus Verlag.

Oakes, Guy. 1987. "Weber and the Southwest German School: The Genesis of the Concept of the Historical Individual."

Pp. 434–46 in *Max Weber and His Contemporaries,* edited by Wolfgang J. Mommsen and Jürgen Osterhammel. London: Unwin Hyman.

Ollig, Hans-Ludwig, ed. 1982. *Neukantianismus. Texte der Marburger und Südwestdeutschen Schule, ihrer Vorläufer und Kritiker* [Neo-Kantianism. Texts of the Marburg and South-West German Schools, Their Predecessors and Critics]. Stuttgart, Germany: Reclam.

Rickert, Heinrich. [1926] 1986. *Kulturwissenschaft und Naturwissenschaft* [Cultural Science and Natural Science]. Stuttgart, Germany: Reclam.

———. 1986. *The Limits of Concept Formation in Natural Sciences: A Logical Introduction to the Historical Sciences,* edited by Guy Oakes. London. Cambridge University Press.

NETWORK EXCHANGE THEORY

An important aspect of social life is the way valued resources are allocated and exchanged among people and groups. Network Exchange Theory (NET) investigates phenomena of this type. It was formulated as a way to understand and predict how a network's shape affects the power of some members to accumulate resources at the expense of others. NET is constructed as a *formal* theory in that all its most important terms are clearly defined, all its central claims are expressed in the form of explicit axioms, and it employs a system of logic that permits anyone—or even a computer program—to derive its predictions.

To date, most of the research inspired by NET has been in the form of careful experimental tests conducted under controlled laboratory conditions. Nevertheless, the scope of the theory is sufficiently broad that it can be used to help interpret a wide range of natural social phenomena. For example, one may study decision-making power in adolescents' friendship networks as it is affected by each member's location in the network and by his or her desire to avoid being excluded. At the group level, the study of organizational power may be informed by considering the structure of relationships between firms competing within the same industry.

BACKGROUND

The intellectual roots of NET can be traced to the classical sociological theories of Karl Marx and Max Weber. Two more recent sources provided the direct inspiration, however: David Willer's "elementary theory" (ET) and Richard Emerson's "power-dependence theory" (PDT). Although offering different basic assumptions and, at times, mutually contradictory predictions, ET and PDT address issues of structural power using a "bottom-up" approach—that is, from a foundation composed of explicit assumptions concerning how individuals make choices in social contexts. Both theories tackle the question of how a social *actor* (person or group) interacting with others to obtain valued *resources* realizes advantages or disadvantages due to the pattern or *structure of relationships* with other actors. Thus, in its own way, each theory focuses on how power—or powerlessness—can arise based on one's social position rather than on one's personal qualities.

Emerson applied his PDT to simple social structures; however, his collaborators at the University of Washington also played a crucial role in extending PDT into the realm of exchange networks. In an influential article published in 1983, Karen Cook, Richard Emerson, Mary Gillmore, and Toshio Yamagishi used PDT to help interpret the ways that actors affect one another directly and indirectly in exchange network contexts. The basic PDT argument is that the power of Actor A over Actor B is greater to the extent that B has low dependence on resources that A controls and that alternative sources for B are readily available. The authors were especially interested in the implications for power and dependence when multiple A–B relationships overlapped, such as in a network of the form shown in Figure 1. If exchange processes in each relationship are permitted to unfold independently, then A has no special advantage by virtue of its central location. However, the moment that events in one "branch" of this little structure affect exchanges in the other branch, it becomes more than just a pair of overlapping A–B exchange relationships: It is an integrated *exchange system*. Researchers at the University of Washington were especially interested in what transpires under a "1-exchange rule"—that is, in cases where both Bs want to obtain resources through negotiations with A, while A may negotiate and exchange with either B *but not with both* in a given period of time. PDT could then predict that A has power over the Bs and that A will achieve higher profit than either of the Bs every time an exchange occurs.

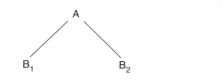

Figure 1. A "Branch" Approach

Before 1983, PDT lacked an explicit and general model for analyzing exchange networks. Ideally, such a formulation would permit one to evaluate networks of any shape and size, allowing investigators systematically to derive predictions for relative power and exchange profits. Along with their PDT-based interpretations of several specific exchange networks, the University of Washington group

published the first experimentally tested mathematical model for predicting the relative power levels of different positions in exchange networks.

In contrast to the PDT approach that inspired it, the *vulnerability model* for exchange network analysis was considerably more explicit, objective, and testable. The model was so named because it equated a given position's power with the vulnerability of resource flows to the position's removal from the network: The more disruptive a position's hypothetical removal, the greater its predicted power to garner resources through exchange with others. The vulnerability model demonstrated an ability to predict the ordering of exchange profits in laboratory experiments using the 1-exchange rule—cases where traditional centrality-based measures for social networks failed. In retrospect, the model also proved to be seminal as indicated by the wave of competing theories that arose over the ensuing years.

NET was among the earliest theories to contest the vulnerability model, emerging as an outgrowth of ET several years after the appearance of the vulnerability model. At the time the vulnerability model was published, ET offered a typology of social relationships (including exchange, conflict, and coercion) and general principles governing social transactions, along with some tools for predicting the relative power associated with positions in small exchange networks.

Just as PDT provided the intellectual backdrop for the vulnerability model, ET played a similar role with respect to the newly developed NET. Viewing network exchange processes through the lens of ET suggested a simple approach: All else being equal, actors are assumed to have more power when they are in positions with numerous ties to other positions, but less power to the extent that they are connected to positions that are high in power. The task was to devise a set of rules—a mathematical model—essentially to automate the process of taking into account characteristics of positions' network environments to determine their relative advantages and disadvantages for accumulating resources from exchanges. The result, described next, was the first experimentally tested alternative to the vulnerability model.

FIRST VERSION OF NET

The first version of NET was published in 1988 by Barry Markovsky, David Willer, and Travis Patton. It was designed specifically to correct limitations that its authors discovered in the vulnerability model. This included rectifying logically impossible vulnerability predictions, providing *scope conditions* to clarify and delimit the applicability of the theory, and extending the theory to some new phenomena, such as networks that break apart and networks that have distinct substructures.

NET has several components, but at its heart is a mathematical model called the *graph-theoretic power index*

(GPI). Graph theory is a branch of mathematics concerned with the logical and numerical properties of *graphs,* which, in the context of this theory, consist of sets of points or *nodes* linked by sets of lines or *edges.* For NET's purposes, graph theory suggested ways to calculate power in social exchanges by treating networks as graphs, positions as nodes, and potential exchange relations as edges.

To illustrate the GPI, consider the star network in Figure 2. A GPI value must be calculated for all positions in the network to determine each position's power relative to those around it. As noted earlier, a key aspect of structural power is the number of direct links or "1-paths" to other positions. C_1, C_2, and C_3 each has one such connection, whereas each B has two and A has three. Continuing the process, the GPI tallies the number of nonoverlapping 2-paths stemming from each position. For example, there are two 2-paths stemming from B_1, including B_1—A—B_2 and B_1—A—B_3. Because these paths from B_1 overlap at A, only one of them is added to the tally of 2-paths. The situation is the same for B_2 and for B_3, each of which also has one nonoverlapping 2-path. A has three separate 2-paths, and each C has one. Continuing this analysis, A does not have any 3-paths; however, each B has one nonoverlapping 3-path, as does each C. Finally, each C has one 4-path.

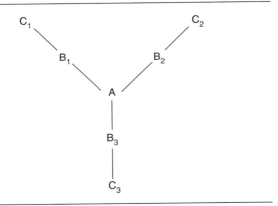

Figure 2.　A "Star" Network

All the path counts are summarized in Table 1. The GPI is obtained by summing these values, where odd-length beneficial paths are counted as positive and even-length detrimental paths are counted as negative. As indicated in the table, the power in this network resides in the B positions. This occurs because the four actors in the C and A positions seek to exchange with only three Bs. The *structure* favors the Bs: None of them is necessarily excluded from exchange, but one of the other four has to be excluded. This means that the Cs and A must compete among themselves by making increasingly attractive offers to the Bs, much to their own detriment.

Table 1　　Path Analysis for the Star Network

Position	1-paths (+)	2-paths (−)	3-paths (+)	4-paths (−)	GPI
A	3	3			0
B	2	1	1		2
C	1	1	1	1	0

The T network in Figure 3 has some interesting properties that helped establish a direct test of GPI against vulnerability. The two theories make different predictions for the relative power of positions in the T. The axioms of NET specify conditions under which one is to apply a repeated or *iterated* procedure to identify breaks in the network—that is, exchange relations that go unused because one or both of its members benefit more by not exchanging in the relationship. The result is that some networks are predicted to split apart into smaller networks. In the T network, the first iteration of GPI produces the values shown in the upper portion of Table 2. The theory claims that C will seek exchanges with D because of its lower GPI, but not so with B because of its higher GPI. Therefore, the network breaks, and the GPI is recalculated separately for the A_1–B–A_2 line and the C–D dyad. Now, as shown in the bottom portion of Table 2, B has power over the As, and C and D exchange with each other at equal power. Vulnerability predicted equal and high power for B, C, and D and was silent in regard to the breakup of the network. Experimental tests confirmed NET's predictions.

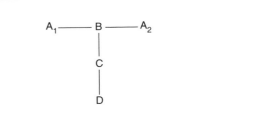

Figure 3.　A "T" Network

Thus far, all the discussion of vulnerability and NET's GPI has assumed a 1-exchange rule governing exchanges. An additional feature of NET's first version was the generalization of this rule so as to permit any given number of exchanges. The theory predicted—and experiments found—that such rule changes could radically alter a network's distribution of power and resources, and could produce new complexities, such as overlapping, analytically distinct subnetworks within a larger network.

Table 2   Path Analysis for the T Network

Position	1-paths (+)	2-paths (−)	3-paths (+)	GPI
		1st iteration		
A	1	1	1	1
B	3	1		2
C	2	1		1
D	1	1	1	1
		2nd iteration (no B–C tie)		
A	1	1		0
B	2			2
C	1			1
D	1			1

LATER VERSIONS

NET has developed along a number of fronts since its first appearance in 1988. For example, two different approaches were developed to predict the effects of structural power by modeling the negotiation behavior of actors responding only to their local network environments. One of these, the X-Net computer simulation, allows the user to explore virtually a limitless combination of network structures, exchange rules, and decision strategies, many of which would be difficult or impossible to study in laboratory experiments or in natural settings. X-Net simulations were instrumental in the discovery of a *weak power* phenomenon, which later was verified experimentally. In contrast to situations like those in Figures 1–3 where the structurally favored positions can accrue virtually all available resources, some networks manifest a weaker and more subtle basis for power. For example, X-Net simulations found slight but consistent power advantages for the A positions in the B_1–A_1–A_2–B_2 line network. Later these simulation results were verified experimentally and accommodated by a refinement of NET's axioms. Weak power turns out to be very important because, among other reasons, profit distributions in weak power structures are more prone than strong power structures (such as the branch) to being altered by the strategic actions of individual actors.

The other actor-level approach used to predict exchange network phenomena is the *resistance* model for dyadic bargaining developed by Douglas Heckathorn and David Willer in the early 1980s. Willer and his colleagues have adapted this mathematical model for the analysis of a variety of exchange network phenomena. An actor's resistance to a given exchange offer is represented as the ratio of two differences: the best conceivable outcome minus the actual offer, and the actual offer minus the worst possible (or "confrontation") outcome. A compromise and an exchange between two actors are assumed to occur at the mutual offer for which resistance is equal for both actors. In network settings, some actors must conduct multiple negotiations simultaneously. Therefore, the values that are plugged into the resistance model are selected in a manner that takes into account any contingencies introduced by virtue of the added relations. For instance, in the branch (Figure 1), A's expected conflict outcome when negotiating with B_1 would be the profit A would anticipate receiving from B_2 should negotiations with B_1 reach a stalemate.

The theory has also expanded to accommodate different kinds of network connections. In general, *exclusive* connections exist when a position needs or wants fewer exchanges than it has connections to others. An example is a new car buyer with multiple dealers vying for her business. *Inclusive* connections exist when a position needs or wants a combination of exchanges with others before it may obtain resources. For instance, a manufacturer must exchange money for a combination of raw materials needed to assemble its product for subsequent distribution. Finally, in *null* connections, negotiations and exchanges are independent across relations. NET has developed several techniques for dealing with these different types of connections and with more complex situations involving combinations of different types within the same network.

NET continues to spawn a variety of new theoretical lines designed to solve more specialized problems and to increase the theory's precision. There are now models for decomposing and analyzing more complex and subtle networks, and others for predicting the long-run probabilities of exchange occurring in any two linked positions. One of NET's refinements takes into account actors' misperceptions of their structural power. Another variant allows members of a network to manipulate the structure itself. There is even a computer program that automates the systematic comparison of predictions from two or more theories to potentially an unlimited number of different network configurations, informing the user of test cases that differentiate the theories.

RECENT WORK

Power and status are related but distinct social processes, both of which depend on social relations for their existence and both of which have an impact on the actors in those relations. Since the late 1990s, NET researchers have been building and testing theoretical bridges that help to understand interactions between power and status. For example, power based on structural advantages in exchange networks can be used to gain social status, along with the honor, esteem, and capacity to influence others that is accorded to the status-advantaged. Conversely, status affects power. Research has shown that goods possessed by those of higher status are viewed by others as having higher value than the same goods possessed by lower-status actors. The result is that in social exchange settings, greater power accrues to those with higher status.

One other research area bears mention. Some experiments and simulations conducted in conjunction with NET have suggested possible links to *complexity theory*—an emerging multidisciplinary field that deals with systems containing large numbers of interacting elements that respond to feedback from dynamic environments. Complex systems are characterized by spontaneous and surprising *macrophenomena* that emerge from *microprocesses* without the benefit of any "top-down" guidance or plan, and some networks do in fact exhibit odd exchange patterns not predicted by current theory. As the scope of NET continues to expand and to address more complicated structures and exchange conditions, the likelihood seems high that NET will continue to develop its bridge to complexity theory.

COMPETING THEORIES AND CRITICAL TESTS

As is the case with any scientific theory, NET always will be a work in progress. The developers of NET have encouraged and welcomed competing formulations, both among themselves and from other theoretical traditions. When NET theorists suggest new or alternative axioms to one another, their collective analysis helps to improve the theory by filtering out weaknesses such as untenable assumptions or ambiguous terms. When new competing theories appear outside the NET program, they also help to stimulate improvements by suggesting new phenomena to address, new empirical tests to conduct, and new ways to solve intellectual puzzles.

With the publication of the first version of NET in 1988, there soon followed a number of alternatives from different researchers working through a variety of theoretical perspectives. Those perspectives included game theory, expected value theory, power-dependence theory, identity theory, and rational choice theory. Predictions from these theories are very similar or identical for most networks. However, owing to their different fundamental assumptions, it is always possible to identify specific test cases in which a given theory's predictions depart from those of one or more of the other theories. NET researchers have identified such cases and subjected their theory to critical testing against the alternative predictions. In all such tests, NET has performed no worse than any alternative theory and has shown superior accuracy in the great majority of specific comparisons with those alternatives.

— Barry Markovsky

See also Elementary Theory; Exchange Coalitions; Emerson, Richard; Exchange Networks; Graph Theoretic Measures of Power; Markovsky, Barry; Power-Dependence Relations; Rational Choice; Social Exchange Theory; Status Relations; Theory Construction; Willer, David

FURTHER READINGS AND REFERENCES

Cook, Karen S., Richard M. Emerson, Mary R. Gillmore, and Toshio Yamagishi. 1983. "The Distribution of Power in Exchange Networks: Theory and Experimental Results." *American Journal of Sociology* 89:275–305.

Markovsky, Barry, David Willer, and Travis Patton. 1988. "Power Relations in Exchange Networks." *American Sociological Review* 53:220–36.

Willer, David, ed. 1992. *Social Networks* (special issue on locating power in exchange networks) 14(3–4):187–344.

———, ed. 1999. *Network Exchange Theory*. Westport, CT: Praeger.

NETWORK THEORY

Network theory is based on the idea that human behavior can be most fully accounted for by an understanding of the structure of social relations within which actors are situated. Network theorists assume that these structures have a more profound impact on behavior than do norms, values, or other subjective states. Network theory is distinct from network analysis, which is a set of techniques that apply network theoretical ideas. This essay will focus on the former, although it will include references to the latter.

THE ROOTS OF NETWORK THEORY

Network theory is a branch of structural sociology. In structural sociology, human action is viewed as a function of the constraints and opportunities provided by forces that exist outside the individual. The roots of structural sociology go back to the works of Karl Marx, Émile Durkheim, and Georg Simmel, but the approach emerged in contemporary sociology in reaction to the dominance of the earlier normative approach. The structural critique of the normative approach is examined in this section, followed by a discussion showing how network theory constitutes a unique version of structural sociology.

Normative Sociology in the Mid-Twentieth Century

Sociology in the West, especially in the United States, was dominated between the 1930s and the early 1970s by a perspective variously termed the *normative, order,* or *functionalist* approach. In this view, societies were seen as largely stable entities held together by shared values (generalized beliefs) and norms (expectations of behavior). The primary proponent of this approach, which drew on one version of Durkheimian theory, was Talcott Parsons. The shared values and norms at the root of this approach were viewed as learned through socialization, primarily from family, school, and the larger culture. For norms to operate effectively, it was necessary that they be internalized—that is, taken for granted. Without the existence of internalized norms, the only way to maintain social order was by an intensive system of monitoring. Such a system was ultimately unworkable, however, since without internalized norms there were no assurances that the monitors themselves would behave appropriately.

Given the importance of shared norms and values, the empirical research that emerged from this model focused heavily on the attitudes of individuals, which were assumed to reflect the values that they held. This led to the proliferation of survey research, which dominated much sociology in the West in the period after World War II. Sociology, which had begun as the study of social structure, increasingly focused on distributions of individual characteristics and attitudes.

A primary difficulty with the normative model was that it was extremely difficult to verify the existence of internalized norms. First, a number of studies indicated that attitudes and behavior were often not highly correlated. Second, even when actors behaved in accordance with accepted norms, it was rarely possible to know whether the behavior resulted from the internalization of the norms or from a fear of sanctions. When someone refrains from stealing something, for example, is it because he or she has internalized the norm that stealing is wrong or because he or she fears the possibility of being caught?

One possible way to address these problems would be to conduct interviews with respondents in an attempt to uncover the motives behind their behavior. This approach assumes that motives are knowable or reasonably decipherable, however; yet actors' awareness of their motives, which often exist at several different levels of consciousness, is frequently unclear. It also assumes that certain motives will produce a consequent set of behaviors, without taking into account the potential obstacles to such behavior. Simply because a majority of voters favor a certain policy, for example, does not ensure that they will either organize politically to pursue the policy or that even if they do organize, they will successfully achieve their goals. To assume a connection between collective beliefs and political outcomes thus requires a leap of logic that may have little empirical foundation. It may be more fruitful to examine the opportunities and constraints that facilitate or impede such outcomes.

Structural Sociology

The empirical and logical problems with the normative approach led sociologists during the 1970s to turn toward more structural explanations of behavior. Structural sociology is based on the idea that social structures have a more pronounced effect on human behavior than do cultural norms or other subjective phenomena. This approach has its roots in Marx's statement, in *A Contribution to the Critique of Political Economy* that "it is not the consciousness of [people] that determines their existence, but, on the contrary, their social existence determines their consciousness" (p. 43) as well as in Simmel's concern with the formal properties of social life. The structural critique of normative sociology had a significant impact on a range of substantive areas. In the study of social movements, for example, models focusing on the subjective feelings of frustration as the source of movement activity were replaced by those that emphasized the resources available to actors. In the study of development, models focusing on the cultures of underdeveloped nations as explanations for their poverty were replaced by those that emphasized the resistance these nations faced from developed countries. Models of cross-group interaction that focused on personal preferences were replaced by those that emphasized the size distributions of the various groups. In each of these cases, the primary determinant of behavior and outcomes was sought in forces beyond the individual. For example, in explaining social interaction Peter Blau, in *Inequality and Heterogeneity* (1977), suggested that when one group contained 90 percent of the population and a second group only 10 percent, members of the minority would be considerably more likely to interact with those of a different group than would members of the majority, irrespective of personal preferences, simply on the basis of the greater number of nongroup members in the population. In accounting for why strike activity increased during periods of wage growth, Edward Shorter and Charles Tilly, in *Strikes in France, 1830–1968* (1974), argued that the cause was not the rising expectations created by improved conditions but, rather, that wage increases tended to occur during periods of labor shortages, when worker leverage was highest.

Although to many sociologists the structural accounts of behavior provided a more fruitful set of theoretical explanations than did the more subjective orientation of the normative model, these accounts shared a problem of their own: They continued to treat human actors in primarily attributional terms. Blau's focus, for example, was on distributions of variables such as class, income, gender, or race. Actors were viewed primarily in categorical terms, such as capitalist or worker, male or female. This focus, although useful, concealed the fact that actors operate within social structures, or regularized patterns of interaction, that exert a significant influence on their behavior. The focus on attributes often obscured the fact that the categories and boundaries by which sociologists traditionally classified social groups are rarely fixed or clear. Social relations crosscut and transcend individual attributes. Members of socially defined racial or gender groups vary considerably in the nature of their social relations. Even those with comparable levels of education and income may have widely varying opportunities depending on the nature of their social ties. The focus on social relations, as distinct from aggregated categories of actors, required an alternative theoretical approach.

NETWORK THEORY

As noted earlier, network theory is closely linked with the methodological approach known as network analysis. Network analysis has its roots in the sociometry of psychiatrist J. L. Moreno, who, in the 1930s, pioneered the idea of drawing graphs that represented social ties among actors. In the 1950s and 1960s, British anthropologists John Barnes, Elizabeth Bott, and J. Clyde Mitchell used the term *social networks* to describe webs of interactions among villagers. Network analysis became the study of the effects of patterns of social relations on human behavior. The classical theoretical roots of this approach go back to Durkheim and Simmel. In *The Division of Labor in Society,* Durkheim (1893) argued that the basis of social order in complex societies could be found in the interdependence among actors, which was both cause and consequence of the increased intensity of interaction. Simmel argued that the number of actors in a group affected the nature of the social relations in the group by altering patterns of interaction. In one of his best-known discussions, Simmel (1950) showed that a two-person situation, the dyad, contains only one social relation but the addition of one person into the interaction not only triples the number of relations, thus significantly complicating the group process, but also alters the relation between the original two actors. The addition of each new actor causes the number of possible relations in a group to increase geometrically. This explains in part why it becomes so difficult to maintain cohesion as the size of a group increases.

The theoretical basis of the study of social networks in contemporary sociology is generally attributed to Harrison White, who relied heavily on the anthropologist S. F. Nadel. White's basic principle was that the structure of relations between actors determines the content of those relations. This can be seen by comparing two simple three-person groups. In Group 1, Actors A, B, and C each can communicate with one another. In Group 2, Actors A and B can each communicate with C, but not directly with one another. In network theory, the relations in Group 1 will be egalitarian in character because no single actor has an advantage over any of the others in terms of communication paths. The relations in Group 2 will be asymmetric in nature, however, because C controls the path of access between A and B, giving C an advantage over both actors. The content of the A-C relation in Group 2 is thus very different from that of the A-C relation in Group 1. The difference is accounted for by the different structures of the two groups.

White's theoretical project went well beyond the general point about structure determining content. One of White's primary goals was to reconceptualize the sociological concept of the role in relational terms. In normative sociology, roles were viewed as positions occupied by social actors that had associated sets of culturally prescribed behaviors. "Boss," "teacher," and "mother" were examples of social roles, each of which possessed a set of scripts, or norms. White argued that although roles were indeed characterized by specific scripts, these norms did not define the role. Rather, roles actually represented similar positions in a structure of social relations. In Group 2 from the previous example, Actors A and B play the same role because they are in identical structural positions in the network.

White originally operationalized the concept of a role in terms of what Francois Lorrain and he (1971) called "structural equivalence," defined as a situation in which actors share identical relations with all other actors in the system. Actors A and B are structurally equivalent in Group 2 because both have a relationship with Actor C. In a larger group, two actors are viewed as structurally equivalent to the extent that they have relations (such as friendship ties) and nonrelations to the same other actors. One problem with using structural equivalence to capture the concept of a role is that it requires actors to be tied to exactly the same alters (other actors in the situation). Imagine a third group, identical in structure to Group 2 except that we have three new Actors, D, E, and F, where D and E are each tied to F but not to one another. Actor F in this group is in the same structural position as actor C in Group 2, but Actors F and C are not structurally equivalent because they are not tied to the same alters. In an early critique of White's formulation, Christopher Winship (1988) suggested the need to use a less restrictive conception of equivalence to capture the idea of a social role. Winship, and scholars such as Stephen Borgatti and Martin Everett (1989), devised new definitions of equivalence that identified Actors F and C as playing the same role.

In addition to the emphasis on the structure of the network, network theorists have also distinguished the ties by which actors are connected. In a seminal formulation, Mark Granovetter (1973) argued that the stronger the relation between two actors, the more likely that both were tied to the same alters. Two close friends are more likely to have the same other friends than are two casual acquaintances, for example. This meant that actors who were strongly tied were more likely to be in the same communication paths. Actors are therefore more likely to receive new and unique information from their casual, or weak, ties than from their strong ties. Granovetter used this formulation to argue that the rapid spread of rumors and other information is most likely to occur through weak rather than strong ties.

Granovetter's distinction between strong and weak ties was important because it turned attention to the processes by which information diffused in social groups. This, along with White's concept of structural equivalence, helped spawn a protracted debate over the nature of social influence. We examine this debate in the following section.

Cohesion Versus Equivalence

One of the central questions with which network theory has dealt is the spread of ideas and behaviors. In traditional network theory, information is seen as diffusing through direct communication paths. In a classic study of the adoption of a new drug, tetracycline, by physicians in four Illinois communities, James Coleman, Elihu Katz, and Herbert Menzel (*Medical Innovation* 1966) found that the adoption process flowed through social network ties between physicians. A given physician was likely to adopt the drug when one with whom he regularly communicated had himself previously adopted it. This finding, and numerous ones like it, suggested that cohesive relations between actors was the source of the diffusion of practices.

In a subsequent formulation, however, Ronald Burt (1987) argued that in addition to being influenced by those with whom one has cohesive ties, social actors are likely to be influenced by their competitive relations with those who occupy similar social positions. Structurally equivalent actors, as we have seen, share relations with the same alters. In this sense, they are substitutable—that is, they are redundant from the point of view of the alters with whom they are tied. The alters gain no more information from relating to both actors than they do from relating with only one of them. Members of industries that purchase steel may benefit from the existence of multiple steel producers, but they need not buy from both simultaneously and, in fact, can use their leverage to divide the steelmakers. This suggests that structurally equivalent actors are likely to be competitive with one another. If this is the case, if one actor adopts a behavior, its structurally equivalent peers are likely to follow suit. In this formulation, behavior diffuses among structurally equivalent actors rather than through cohesive ones. It is possible that structurally equivalent actors adopt the same behaviors because they share cohesive relations with the same alters and are being directly influenced by them in the same ways. Which of these alternative interpretations is more accurate has not been resolved. Considerable evidence exists to suggest that diffusion of behavior proceeds via both processes.

NETWORK THEORIES OF ACTION

Much of the early work in social network theory operated with a broadly rational choice theory of action, in which human action was viewed as a response to interests rather than emotions or sentiment. The reason for this is not surprising. The structural critique of normative sociology emphasized the difficulty of relying on internalized norms as a source of behavior. Structural sociologists preferred to focus on the fear of sanctions rather than on the internalization of norms as the reason for behaving in a normatively prescribed fashion. In most early network studies, the rational choice assumptions were implicit. They were made explicit by Burt, in his 1982 treatise, *Toward a Structural Theory of Action,* and by Granovetter in his 1985 article, "Economic Action and Social Structure: The Problem of Embeddedness."

Burt proposed a model in which social structure has both direct and indirect effects on action, the latter through its effects on actor interests. He distinguished three types of action: atomistic, normative, and structural. Atomistic action is the form posited by neoclassical economists, in which actor preferences are assumed to be exogenous and fixed, and action can be understood entirely as a function of these individual preferences. Normative action is roughly the form described above, in which action is motivated by values and beliefs. Structural action is driven by interests that are endogenously formed on the basis of actors' positions in social structures. Actors that are structurally equivalent, in Burt's view, will have similar interests and will therefore behave similarly. Burt views the concept of structural action as capturing the best features of both the normative and atomistic models: the normative model's focus on the social context within which action occurs, and the atomistic model's deductive rigor. A conception of interest-directed action within social structural constraints is Burt's solution to the problems posed by both traditional approaches. To gain this analytic leverage, Burt relies on an interest-driven conception of action consistent with rational choice principles, in which actors weigh the costs and benefits of various actions and proceed accordingly.

Granovetter's (1985) discussion in "Economic Action and Social Structure" parallels Burt's. Granovetter criticizes economists for using an "undersocialized" conception of action (a notion similar to Burt's concept of atomistic action) and criticizes many sociologists for using an "oversocialized" conception (a notion similar to Burt's concept of normative action). Consistent with other network formulations, Granovetter argues that behavior is best understood in terms of the social relations within which actors operate. In market transactions, opportunistic behavior is most likely to occur between strangers and one-time business partners, whereas more cooperative behavior is most likely to occur between those who have ongoing transactions and who, as a result, have developed feelings of trust. Despite Granovetter's view of trust as a largely affective phenomenon, he remains reluctant to dispense with the assumption of rationality. "While the assumption of rational action must always be problematic, it is a good working hypothesis that should not be easily abandoned. What looks to the analyst like nonrational behavior may be quite sensible when situational constraints . . . are fully appreciated" (p. 506). For many network theorists, then, actors can be treated as rational, while operating within social structural constraints.

A more recent network approach developed by Harrison White includes an alternative theory of action. In *Identity and Control* (1992), White argues that actors must be treated as constellations of identities, each of which seeks a predictable and tractable environment for itself. Social structures are characterized by a differentiated set of roles, and actors succeed by seeking unique niches for themselves within these structures. In part, White's model parallels that of Burt, for whom joint occupancy of a position is viewed as a disadvantage because the structurally equivalent actors are potential substitutes for one another. In addition to seeking a unique niche, however, White's actors also seek to create ambiguity for those with whom they are socially tied, while maintaining predictability for themselves. One means by which actors create ambiguity among their alters is to maintain a central position between clusters of otherwise disconnected groups. In this situation, those directly tied to ego (an actor) are disconnected from one another, but these alters are themselves embedded in dense networks. The lack of connection among the alters allows ego to control the flow of information, keeping the alters in a perpetual state of confusion.

This formulation is consistent with Burt's concept of "structural holes" (*Structural Holes* 1992). A structural hole is a position in which a single actor has ties to disconnected alters, who themselves are densely connected. As in White's model, an occupant of a structural hole experiences an advantage because each of its ties provides unique information, whereas many of its alters' ties provide redundant information. To the extent that actors can occupy relatively unique positions while their alters occupy "crowded" positions, they will experience benefits, or, as in White's model, gain control over their environments. Burt has shown that members of industries that are highly concentrated and whose trading partners are highly competitive enjoy relatively high profit margins. He has also shown that corporate managers who occupy sparse personal networks experience more rapid promotions than those who occupy dense personal networks.

The strategy of controlling the flow of information and maintaining a state of confusion among one's alters has been termed "robust action" by Padgett and Ansell (1993). In a study of the rise of Cosimo de' Medici in Renaissance Florence, Padgett and Ansell attribute Cosimo's success to his ability to avoid making his intentions known, as well as his skill at keeping his options open (what they call "flexible opportunism") and creating ambiguity for others. "Contrary to Machiavelli's portrait in *The Prince* of effective leaders as decisive and goal oriented, eyewitness accounts describe Cosimo de' Medici as an indecipherable sphinx" (p. 1262), Padgett and Ansell write.

One could argue that this conception of action is compatible with a rational choice model. There is no reason that actors could not act rationally to render their opponents' goals manifest while simultaneously creating confusion about their own goals. Where robust action deviates from a rational choice model of action is in its eschewing of the importance of goals. As Padgett and Ansell (1993) note, "Crucial for maintaining discretion is *not* to pursue any specific goals" (p. 1264, emphasis in the original). Rational actor models normally begin with such an assumption. Still, as Padgett and Ansell show, it was that he occupied a structural hole in the networks among Florentine elite families that allowed Cosimo to be successful in this strategy.

CRITICISMS OF NETWORK THEORY

Given its origins in a critique of well-known approaches within sociology, it is not surprising that network theory has itself been subjected to a number of criticisms. The two most prominently identified difficulties with the theory have revolved around its alleged failure to consider the importance of culture and its allegedly underdeveloped conception of human agency. Both concerns speak to a more general issue about how we account for the origins of social networks.

Networks and Culture

By focusing on the opportunities and constraints created by social structures, structural and network sociologists gained considerable analytical and predictive power. At the same time, network theorists have tended to ignore or minimize the role of subjective factors in human behavior. This has created difficulties for many applications of network theory. Some of these problems involve measurement, such as the question of how researchers identify the content of the ties that constitute the social networks they study. Equally important have been the meanings that actors attribute to various events, which, according to critics, network theorists often take for granted.

One example, raised by Emirbayer and Goodwin (1994) in their critique of network theory, comes from Doug McAdam's study of participation in the Freedom Summer project, a program during the civil rights movement in which activists from around the United States spent a summer in Mississippi helping to register African American voters. In attempting to explain why some applicants who were accepted for the program ultimately participated while others did not, McAdam (1986) shows that because virtually all applicants strongly supported the civil rights movement on normative grounds, ideology cannot account for participation. Rather, the primary determinants of participation were whether an applicant was a member of multiple movement organizations and whether he or she had friends who were also participating. In criticizing McAdam's argument, Emirbayer and Goodwin (1994) assert that without the strong normative commitment to the movement's ideals in the first place, the networks that later affected individual participation would not have been established. Normative commitments may therefore be causally prior to the formation of social networks. Emirbayer and Goodwin raise a similar criticism of Padgett and Ansell's (1993) study of Cosimo de' Medici. A major basis for the Medicis' accession to power was the relabeling of the earlier ruling family groups, who had previously been characterized as "public citizens of the state," as "oligarchs," which occurred after they attempted to politically repress the previously neutral "new men." Emirbayer and Goodwin argue that it was only because of the powerful meanings associated with terms such as public citizens and oligarchs that the significance of this relabeling can be understood.

Certainly, taking into account the processes by which norms and meanings were established might have lent further richness to the McAdam (1986) and Padgett and Ansell (1993) studies. Whether either would have provided additional explanatory power is less clear. To demonstrate this, it would be necessary for critics to show that taking these norms and meanings into account might have actually reduced or nullified the predictive power of the social structural factors identified in both studies. Simply pointing out that exogenous factors have prior causes is by itself an inadequate basis for critique.

In response to critiques such as those by Emirbayer and Goodwin, network theorists have begun to pay more attention to the role of both culture and subjectivity in human action. Culture for network theorists is a set of practices and meanings constructed within structures of social relations. A meaning system emerges, in this view, through either direct social interaction, as in the cohesion model, or shared positions in a social structure, as in the structural equivalence model. These formulations have been successful in accounting for social attitudes (Erickson 1988). They have been less successful in accounting for shared meanings that are not associated with either direct or indirect network ties. How can one account for the fact that social workers in a wide number of locales will share certain political views, for example, despite operating in very different social networks? One approach to handling this issue is to use the concept of role equivalence. Role-equivalent actors are those, such as Actors F and C in the earlier example, that share the same type of position even in otherwise unconnected social structures. At this writing, there is not nearly as much evidence of homogeneity among role-equivalent actors as there is for cohesive and structurally equivalent ones. The idea that shared meanings across networks are associated with shared network roles remains a promising means of accounting for the construction of meaning. Network theorists have been unable to account for the

origins of the meanings themselves, but simply treating these meanings as exogenous, as cultural sociologists have tended to do, also fails to account for their origin.

Networks and Attributes

An alternative cultural critique of network theory has been raised by Brint (1992). Brint argues that even if attributes have been socially constructed in networks, the meanings associated with them often take on lives of their own. Race, for example, could be viewed in network terms as a set of categories that were socially constructed as a means of exploitation or exclusion. Once race becomes recognized as a category, however, it may have an independent effect on behavior. Those who share characteristics of disadvantaged racial categories may be denied access to existing networks that would be permitted to members of privileged racial categories. In this sense, the formation of or changes in networks can be viewed as endogenous to previously existing attributional factors.

Brint's critique raises important issues that network theory has not fully addressed. The network argument that categories must be seen as social constructions themselves is a powerful alternative to approaches that treat these variables as if they were immutable traits. It is also true, as network theorists note, that there are enormous variations in outcomes within these categories that network analyses are well suited to capture. A study by Petersen, Saporta, and Seidel (2000), for example, showed that the discriminatory behavior by a firm against minorities and women could be explained by network ties. Minorities and women who had network connections with members of the firm faced no disadvantages based on their racial or gender status. The disadvantages faced by minorities and women were due primarily to their disadvantaged network positions. Petersen et al. are unable to account for why minorities and women experience disadvantaged network positions in the first place, and in that sense Brint is correct that these categories may have independent effects. The solution to this problem appears to be a synthesis, in which network ties and categorical factors are viewed as interacting. This will be a fruitful approach as long as researchers are able to analytically distinguish the roles of both factors in explaining social phenomena.

Networks and Agency

Network researchers have focused primarily on the effects of social structures on various outcomes. Action has therefore most often been viewed as a consequence of structure. Contrary to some critics, however, network theorists have paid considerable attention to the issue of agency. In Burt's earlier work, discussed above, structure was viewed as affecting both interests and action, but the model included a feedback loop in which action then operated back on the structure. In his more recent work, Burt (1992) has argued that structural holes can be actively created by actors, by strategically selecting nonredundant ties. Burt's earlier model was criticized because it still gave analytical precedence to the structure (see Ira J. Cohen, *Structuration Theory,* 1989), and both models are open to the criticism that Burt does not develop an explicit analytical framework for the role of agency. White (1992), in *Identity and Control,* makes an explicit attempt to build human agency into his framework through a focus on narratives. Identity, White's key concept, involves "any source of action . . . to which observers can attribute meaning" (p. 6). The search for control, an attempt to make one's environment predictable, is the primary engine of his model. As does Burt, White views the narratives through which identity is constituted as embedded in social structures, and as with Burt, White has been criticized for this. Whereas White argues that culture cannot be separated from social networks but is inextricably linked with them, Emirbayer and Goodwin (1994) argue that culture must be treated as having its own internal logic and structure, one that constrains action by placing limits on possible courses of action. Ultimately, however, Emirbayer and Goodwin argue that any empirical event must be viewed as structured "*simultaneously* by the dynamics of societal as well as cultural structures" (p. 1443, emphasis in the original). One's position in this debate may hinge on whether it is possible to gain superior analytical leverage from viewing one phenomenon as endogenous to another, even as one understands that in theory, both are operating simultaneously. The limits that culture places on possible courses of action ultimately have their origins in the social communities that defined those courses.

CONCLUSION

The study of social networks has been viewed more as a series of techniques than as a theory in its own right. Those who have practiced the approach have adopted a wide range of theoretical models, from rational choice theory to social constructionist approaches. In recent years, more attention has been given to the theoretical principles behind the network approach, both by practitioners and critics. The debates described here provide evidence that these theoretical principles remain contested. There is no shortage of issues that require attention, but the analysis of social networks has become far more than a set of methodological tools.

— Mark S. Mizruchi

See also Actor Network Theory; Exchange Networks; Levels of Social Structure; Network Exchange Theory; Social Capital; Social Exchange Theory; Strength of Weak Ties; White, Harrison

FURTHER READINGS AND REFERENCES

Borgatti, Stephen P. and Martin G. Everett. 1989. "The Class of All Regular Equivalences: Algebraic Structure and Computation." *Social Networks* 11:65–88.

Brint, Stephen. 1992. "Hidden Meanings: Cultural Content and Context in Harrison White's Structural Sociology." *Sociological Theory* 10:194–208.

Burt, Ronald S. 1987. "Social Contagion and Innovation: Cohesion versus Structural Equivalence." *American Journal of Sociology* 92:1287–1335.

Emirbayer, Mustafa and Jeff Goodwin. 1994. "Network Analysis, Culture, and the Problem of Agency." *American Journal of Sociology* 99:1411–54.

Erickson, Bonnie H. 1988. "The Relational Basis of Attitudes." Pp. 99–121 in *Social Structures: A Network Approach,* edited by Barry Wellman and S. D. Berkowitz. New York: Cambridge University Press.

Granovetter, Mark S. 1973. "The Strength of Weak Ties." *American Journal of Sociology* 78:1360–80.

———. 1985. "Economic Action and Social Structure: The Problem of Embeddedness." *American Journal of Sociology* 91(3):481–510.

Lorrain, Francois and Harrison C. White. 1971. "Structural Equivalence of Individuals in Social Networks." *Journal of Mathematical Sociology* 1:49–80.

Marx, K. 1959. "Excerpt from *A Contribution to the Critique of Political Economy.*" In *Marx and Engels: Basic Writings on Politics and Philosophy*, edited by Lewis S. Feuer. Garden City, NY: Doubleday.

McAdam, Doug. 1986. "Recruitment to High-Risk Activism: The Case of Freedom Summer." *American Journal of Sociology* 92:64–90.

Padgett, John F. and Christopher K. Ansell. 1993. "Robust Action and the Rise of the Medici, 1400–1434." *American Journal of Sociology* 98:1259–1319.

Petersen, Trond, Ishak Saporta, and Marc-David Seidel. 2000. "Offering a Job: Meritocracy and Social Networks." *American Journal of Sociology* 106:763–816.

Simmel, Georg. 1950. "The Isolated Individual and the Dyad." Pp. 118–44 in *The Sociology of Georg Simmel,* edited by Kurt Wolff. New York: Free Press.

Winship, Christopher. 1988. "Thoughts About Roles and Relations: An Old Document Revisited." *Social Networks* 10:209–31.

OUTSIDER-WITHIN

The concept of the outsider-within has been developed most fully by Patricia Hill Collins. Two of Collins's works, *Fighting Words: Black Women and the Search for Justice* (1998) and *Black Feminist Thought: Knowledge, Consciousness, and the Politics of Empowerment* (1990), are considered by many to be classics of feminist theory. In these works, Collins explores the unique social location of black women as a historically situated group, and explores the power relations inherent in the construction of knowledge that help influence a notion of critical theory. This is part of one of the broader themes found in both texts—that knowledge is inextricably connected to power. Collins analyzes social theory in this context and notes that "[f]ar from being neutral, the very meaning and use of the term social theory represents a contested terrain" (1998:ix).

Attending a predominately white school, and being black herself, Collins came to understand what it was like to be on the "inside" and yet still remain an outsider. Although her concept of an outsider-within has grown and changed over time, the core of the idea has always remained the same. Originally, the term was used to describe the location of individuals who find themselves in the border space between groups; that is, who no longer have clear membership in any one group. Collins disliked this usage, however, as she felt it reduced the concept to an identity construct that too closely resembled the "marginal man" found in early sociology. In more recent years, Collins has used this term to "describe social locations or border spaces occupied by groups of unequal power" (1998:5). These locations contain a number of contradictions for the individuals who occupy them. They appear to be members of the more powerful group because they have the necessary qualifications for and surface level rights of member standing. However, this does not necessarily mean that they have all of the *real* rights and privileges afforded to formal members. Collins uses African Americans in the United States as exemplars of this situation; they have citizenship rights but they are often treated as second-class citizens.

In addition to the definition cited previously, Collins's concept of the outsider-within also states that "[u]nder conditions of social injustice, the outsider-within location describes a particular knowledge/power relationship, one of gaining knowledge about or of a dominant group without gaining the full power accorded to members of that group" (1998:6). In *Fighting Words,* Collins points out that it is the multiplicity of oppressions that help distinguish the knowledge developed from an outsider-within location from the knowledge of both elite locations and oppositional locations. She uses the term "hidden transcripts" from the work of James Scott to describe the type of information that is granted only to members inside of a group (1998:7).

Collins's search for justice begins with a group-based approach. Although she recognizes the importance of individuals, she views justice as something that can only be achieved on a group level. This is not to say that Collins wishes to make broad generalizations about groups of people. Quite the contrary, she advocates focusing on the unique social location of individuals based on the intersection of their various social positions (class, gender, race, sexual orientation, etc.). However, she argues that without a sense of a collectivity, a critical social theory that expresses the realities confronting a particular group cannot exist.

Collins is interested in the ways in which the standpoint of many minorities (black women are her particular concern) have been excluded from most social theory. Part of her interest in developing the concept of the outsider-within came from her desire to create a body of knowledge that was specific to black women and their unique social location in order to insert an identity into the stream of theoretical consciousness that had long been missing. She believes that social theory is both knowledge and lived institutional practices that attempt to answer the questions and concerns facing groups based in specific political, social, and historical situations. Thus, it does not derive from the ivory tower of the intellectuals but rather from actual groups of people in specific institutional settings. They are the ones who legitimate such theory and whose concerns should be reflected in such theory. This ideology demonstrates Collins's concern with placing outsider groups at the core of her analysis.

Collins also hopes that the idea of an outsider-within will carry a political message. By making black women visible, Collins hopes to create "issues where absence has long been the norm" (1998:105). Her final line in *Fighting Words* is perhaps the best summary of Collins's view on social theory and justice: "If critical social theory manages to move people toward justice, then it has made a very important difference" (1998:251).

— Michael Ryan

See also Collins, Patricia Hill; Standpoint Theory

FURTHER READINGS AND REFERENCES

Collins, Patricia Hill. 1990. *Black Feminist Thought: Knowledge, Consciousness, and the Politics of Empowerment.* London: Unwin Hyman.

———. 1998. *Fighting Words: Black Women & the Search for Justice.* Minneapolis, MN: University of Minnesota Press.

P

PARADIGM

A paradigm is a fundamental image of the subject matter within a science. It serves to define what should be studied, what questions should be asked, how they should be asked, and what rules should be followed in interpreting the answers obtained. The paradigm is the broadest unit of consensus within a science and serves to differentiate one scientific community (*or subcommunity*) from another. It subsumes, defines, and interrelates the exemplars, theories, and methods and instruments that exist within it.

The most famous use of the paradigm concept is that of Thomas Kuhn. As influential as the concept, and the theory of scientific revolutions in which it is embedded, were, there is great ambiguity in the way Kuhn used the concept. One critic found 21 *different* definitions in his original work. This very ambiguity may have helped to make the concept influential since it could be interpreted and used in many different ways.

The definition offered above is consistent with at least one of Kuhn's definitions, his sense of a paradigm as what he called a "disciplinary matrix." Some take issue with this definition, claiming that the idea of a disciplinary matrix was an early conceptualization and that later Kuhn defined paradigms *as* exemplars, that is, as concrete solutions to scientific problems and puzzles. They have in mind definitive laboratory experiments that serve as models for scientists who work in a given tradition.

The later Kuhn did seem to want to restrict the paradigm concept to concrete solutions to puzzles, but this idea works best when applied to the hard sciences where breakthroughs in the lab do serve as models for others. However, few social sciences have much in the way of laboratory research. Exemplars, at least used in this way, will not help us get a better sense of the structure of the social sciences and the ways in which they change. Indeed, the theory of scientific

revolutions, of which the paradigm is a central component, has little applicability to the social science where few, if any, "revolutions," at least in the Kuhnian sense, occur. Social sciences may change dramatically and suddenly but it is rarely the result of dramatic new laboratory developments.

For Kuhn, the dominance of a paradigm allows for "normal science" as the paradigm is fleshed out (but not questioned in any fundamental way). Change occurs as normal science leads to findings that cannot be explained by the dominant paradigm. As these anomalies mount, a crisis phase is reached and the science moves toward a situation where a new paradigm can arise that will better explain both what the old paradigm did as well as most, if not all, of the anomalies. Once the new paradigm is in a position of preeminence, the stage is set for the process to recur.

If, as is the case with the social sciences, there is no dominant paradigm, but multiple paradigms, then the process described by Kuhn is called into question. Anomalies require the existence of an agreed-upon paradigm, and without one it is hard to see how anomalous findings will come about, let alone create a crisis. Rather, the crisis for the social sciences is the coexistence of multiple paradigms in basic disagreement.

In the mid-1970s, when the paradigm concept was at the height of its influence, sociology was characterized by three basic paradigms—the "social facts," "social definition," and "social behavior" paradigms. These differed fundamentally in their image of the subject matter of sociology, with the social facts paradigm focusing on large-scale social structures and institutions, the social definition paradigm on the way people construct their social worlds and act and interact on the basis of those constructions, and the social behavior paradigm on behavior that is less dependent on social constructions. Given these differences in image of the subject matter, adherents of each paradigm have different exemplars, here defined as orientations and bodies of work that serve as icons and models for practitioners within each paradigm. To the social factist it is the work of Émile Durkheim (who created the term "social fact"), to the social definitionist it is that of Max Weber on social action, and to the social behaviorist it is the work of the preeminent psychological behaviorist, B. F. Skinner. Based on these differences in image of the subject matter and exemplar, those within each paradigm tend to develop and use different methods and theories that fit best with that image of what is to be studied and with the basic orientation of the exemplar. Thus, sociology tended to be characterized by three distinct paradigms, each with its own set of images, exemplars, theories, and methods. These paradigms tended to be deeply at odds with one another, questioning each other's focus and most basic assumptions. This prevented researchers from doing the normal science that is a prerequisite to the development of a paradigm, to the uncovering of anomalies, and to scientific revolutions.

Fields change, and sociology's paradigmatic status is quite different today. The fortunes of extant paradigms wax and wane and new ones come to the fore. In the case of sociology, it has become harder to identify the leading paradigms, with the result that the field looks more chaotic than it did several decades ago. Yet, there are disadvantages to the hegemony of a limited number of paradigms (debilitating conflict over basic assumptions) and advantages to a more chaotic science (scientists are less restricted by paradigmatic allegiances). Thus, we must not simply assume that the decline in paradigm hegemony, and the increase in chaos, is counterproductive, especially for a field like sociology already characterized by multiple paradigms.

The paradigm concept, and the theory of scientific revolutions of which it is part, remains an important touchstone for anyone interested in a better understanding of the structure of scientific fields, including, and perhaps especially, the social sciences.

— George Ritzer

See also Behaviorism; Ritzer, George; Social Constructionism; Social Facts

FURTHER READINGS AND REFERENCES

Eckberg, Douglas E. and Lester Hill. 1979. "The Paradigm Concept and Sociology: A Critical Review." *American Sociological Review* 44: 925–37.

Hoyningen-Huene, Paul. 1993. *Reconstructing Scientific Revolutions: Thomas S. Kuhn's Philosophy of Science.* Chicago, IL: University of Chicago Press.

Kuhn, Thomas. 1970. *The Structure of Scientific Revolutions.* 2d ed. Chicago, IL: University of Chicago Press.

Ritzer, George. 1980. *Sociology: A Multiple Paradigm Science.* rev. ed. Boston, MA: Allyn & Bacon.

———. 2001. "From Exclusion to Inclusion to Chaos (?) in Sociological Theory." Pp. 145–53 in *Explorations in Social Theory: From Metatheorizing to Rationalization* by George Ritzer. London: Sage.

PARETO, VILFREDO

Vilfredo Pareto (1848–1923) is best known for his views that the rationalizations people use for their behavior change, while their reasons or motivations do not; that the successful use of power justifies itself; and that elites rule sometimes by the use of force and sometimes by cunning.

Few theorists have elicited more intense reactions than Pareto. One writer calls him "the adversary of humanitarian democracy" (Zeitlin 1994:192). Another describes him as "a humanist who fought ceaselessly for democracy [and] for freedom of any sort" (Lopreato in Pareto [1916]1980:xx). Why such differing interpretations? The answer lies in Pareto's changing responses to the times in which he lived and others' fragmentary knowledge of his work.

Vilfredo Pareto was born in Paris to an Italian political-exile father and a French mother. When Vilfredo was a small boy, the family moved back to Italy, where he became imbued with humanitarian/democratic ideals.

The powerhunger of Europe's leaders, culminating in World War I, was paralleled by Pareto's increasing cynicism about political life. The cynical portions of his work became known in the West before his earlier works, and his writings about fascism, especially that of Mussolini in Italy, were misunderstood as sympathetic with the brutal totalitarianism that developed in Italy after Pareto's death.

Not only did events in Europe affect Pareto's view of society and politics, but so did his personal life. In 1882, he ran for office in Florence, and was defeated by a government-supported candidate. This defeat he attributed to the corrupt practices of Italy's ruling elite. Soon thereafter, his friend Maffeo Pantaleoni was forced to resign his teaching post because he had criticized a customs duty on wine. Pareto considered himself partly to blame because he had quoted Pantaleoni's incriminating article in print.

In 1893, Pareto was appointed to the chair of political economy at Lausanne, where he taught for 20 years. In 1901, he inherited a substantial fortune and moved to a villa at Celigny. Later that year, his wife ran off with a servant—a deeply disturbing experience for Pareto. After that, he came to be known in intellectual circles as "the hermit of Celigny," although he continued to entertain his friends, including both Pantaleoni and theorist Robert Michels.

PARETO'S CENTRAL THEORIES

Pareto was greatly influenced by the work of another Italian, Niccolo Machiavelli. In *The Prince* (1532), Machiavelli had set for himself the problem of discovering "the best means available to princes for holding their power" (Pareto [1916]1980:254). Although Machiavelli argues that princes *should* stay in power, the methods he described included deceit and force, as well as the use of argument. Pareto thought that Machiavelli's insights helped to explain history and society.

Residues and Derivations

The core and most controversial portion of Pareto's work was his general theory of residues and derivations. Put simply, residues are the reasons or motives for behavior, while derivations are the excuses (justifications, rationalizations) we give for our actions.

By residues Pareto meant the bases of human action. He used the term interchangeably with instinct, need, motive, and especially with sentiment (Pareto [1916]1980:xxxi). Of these "springs of human action," six are most important: (1) the instinct for combinations (change), (2) persistence of aggregates (nonchange), (3) self-expression or activity—the need to do something, to express ourselves, (4) sociality or sociability, (5) integrity or integration with one's social setting, and (6) sex residues (Pareto [1916]1980:120–22).

Although all these had a place in Pareto's theory, the first two—change and nonchange—were central. Just as human beings exhibit an intermingling of the residues for new combinations and persistence, so societies are characterized by both change and nonchange, with some dominated by one or the other. In the course of human history, the residues never change, since they are the bases for all human action.

While the mix of residues differs, the residues themselves never change; they are the essential underlying motives and sentiments. What change, according to Pareto, are the derivations—the intellectual systems of justification with which individuals camouflage their motives in order to appear rational. Derivations are the reasons we give for behaving as we do, or for wanting someone else to behave in a certain way. One's explanation is almost always a rationalization, argued Pareto, seldom expressing the real reason for basis for behavior. "Man, although impelled to act by non-logical motives, likes to tie his actions to certain principles; he therefore invents these *a posteriori* in order to justify his actions" (Pareto [1901]1968:27).

Examples of derivations can be seen in the persuasive mechanisms people use to get others to behave in certain ways. One is an appeal to human authority: "Because I said so" or "Because I am your mother." Another is metaphysical, appealing to external authority: "Because God will punish you if you don't." Pareto noted that people often state their aims in such terms, while the practical purpose is their own, or their society's, welfare and prosperity. Finally, people offer verbal proofs: "Vote for me because I favor democracy and will work for the people." Here reliance is on catchphrases such as "democracy" and "work for the people," with the hope that no one will ask what is actually meant.

The relationship between residues and derivations involves the problem of logic and illogic. Logic, according to Pareto, is derived from success. If we act in a way that brings about the outcome we desire, we have acted logically. Logic is not based on confessing or even recognizing our real motives; it is based on doing/saying whatever gets us what we want. A by-product of this view, drawing upon Machiavelli, is Pareto's political cynicism. An effective derivation is logical; believing one's own message while failing in one's aim is illogical. Politically, then, cynical or hypocritical political leaders who do not believe their own message are more logical. This is because the ability to change their viewpoint to suit an audience is more likely to bring success. True believers act illogically, because they are incapable of altering what they say to fit the situation. Thus, hypocrisy may be necessary to be successful in politics—and success, for Pareto, is logical. Pareto believed that the majority of politicians are nonlogical, because they believe what they say (especially if they repeat it enough times).

The Circulation of Elites

According to Pareto, "[S]ociety is always governed by a small number of men, by an elite, even when it seems to have a completely democratic organization" (Pareto [1906] 1971:312). Both democracy and mass revolution were inconceivable to Pareto. "Almost all revolutions have been the work, not of the common people, but of the aristocracy" (1906:92). However, sometimes the poorer classes "derive some advantage, as a by-product, from the struggle between elites" ([1906]1971:301).

Pareto suggested that elites may use force or cunning to achieve their aims, but a new elite ordinarily takes control by force. Then, as their authority is legitimated or legalized, they are followed by perpetuators or administrators, shrewd but cowardly individuals who are easily overthrown by new violence, either from abroad or from within. These administrators are "timid but often honest souls who believe in the efficacy of the law against force of arms. They are constantly declining in vigor" and, as Karl Marx would say, are busy digging their own graves (Pareto [1916]1980:342, 384).

These mechanisms result in the circulation of elites, as "lions" are followed by "foxes"—that is, as leadership by force is followed by leadership by cunning. *Circulation* does not imply historical change or progress, but going around and around.

Why do elites continue to circulate? The weakening of those in power is not so much a result of their becoming lazy and unconcerned as it is a result of their inherent conservatism. Their support for, or conservation of, a system that is becoming increasingly anachronistic leaves them open to overthrow by a forceful new elite with (supposedly) new ideas.

Usually the lions and foxes simply take turns feeding on the sheep—the masses. As Pareto put it: "The world has always belonged to the strong. . . . Men only respect those who make themselves respected. Whoever becomes a lamb will find a wolf to eat them" (Bucolo 1980:125). If the masses threaten to cause trouble for the elite in power, Machiavelli had said, they will be either cajoled or exterminated (Machiavelli 1532). Pareto's version was that the masses would be absorbed or eliminated—bought off or wiped out.

In short, Pareto's theory of political elites was that they use derivations to seek and hold power, circulate between lions and foxes, and keep the masses under control by absorption or elimination.

The Nature of Society, Humans, and Change

Pareto's ideology changed gradually during his life. He began as a cautious liberal. But his position altered from the liberal notion of tinkering with the world to make it better, to the belief that nothing could be done to improve the world. It is clear that, during the last 25 years of his life, he became increasingly conservative—though he would call himself a nonideological realist—about society and power.

Over time, then, Pareto became cynical about human nature. He did not say that humans are evil, but rather that in seeking power they camouflage their motives to seem more altruistic than they are. Pareto did not see society as good or evil but as a mixture of primarily self-seeking actors and actions. He saw history and change as resulting from the combination of unchanging residues and the circulation of elites. He would doubtless argue that the combination of his view of cynicism, hypocrisy, and nonchange made him not a conservative but a realist.

As for gender, Pareto believed that patriarchy was the natural and universal social form among civilized peoples. Pareto had little time for the equality claims of feminists. Like some present-day commentators, Pareto believed that feminists were hysterical women "in want of a mate," who persecuted "women who have lovers simply because they have been unable to find men of their own" (Pareto [1916]1935, vol. 2:696). He also contended that feminism could only arise when a society is wealthy.

Pareto viewed women as naturally fickle and promiscuous. He was scathing about the reformist assumption that capitalism was the primary cause of prostitution. Whatever the economic context, Pareto insisted that there would be women willing to sell themselves: "The woman of the petty bourgeoisie sells herself to get a stylish hat, the society woman sells herself to get a string of pearls—but they both sell themselves" (Pareto [1916]1935, vol. 3:1318). Pareto's misogynistic views, as already noted, had some basis in his personal experience.

Pareto's Economic Theories

Though Pareto's views of society and elites were his primary foci, he also sought to understand economics. Although few economists have adopted it, Pareto used the term *ophelimity* to mean the pleasure that a certain quantity of a thing affords an individual. According to Pareto, differences in ophelimity are due to differences in taste, coupled with the obstacles encountered in gratifying one's tastes. Markets and prices do not by themselves determine economic behavior, but depend on "the opposition of tastes and obstacles" ([1906]1971:152). The more intense and widespread the taste for an item, and the more obstacles to obtaining it, the higher its value and its price.

Another important part of Pareto's economic theory is capital, of which he listed three kinds. *Land capital* is immovable property that can be mined or developed. *Mobile* capital includes machines, transport means, household goods, and money. *Human capital* is "the cost of production of a human being . . . what is strictly necessary to keep him alive and train him" (Pareto [1906]1971:300). The concept of human capital has been expanded in economics, but Pareto was one of the earliest writers to recognize its importance. These three forms of capital are used in the free market system to increase one's bargaining position relative to others.

Although individual economic behavior was of some interest to Pareto, he was more concerned with economic systems, their upswings and downswings. According to his analysis, upswings result when entrepreneurs expand production by transferring savings into development, often using credit. Investors likewise extend themselves to have a part in a productive boom. Downswings occur when markets become glutted and/or stagnate (because tastes are satisfied with few obstacles for the individual) and the producers and investors reduce and retrench (Pareto [1906]1971:321–83).

According to Pareto, "[I]t is customary to assume that man will be guided in his choice exclusively by consideration of his own advantage, of his self-interest" (Pareto [1906]1971:105. This premise for human behavior was later expanded into exchange theories, which argue that humans seek the most profit at the least cost.

PARETO IN THE COMMUNITY OF SCHOLARS

Pareto's relation to other theorists begins with Gaetano Mosca, who published *The Ruling Class* (1884) 20 years before Pareto's *Manual of Political Economy* appeared. When Pareto's book appeared, it was apparent to many, but especially to Mosca, that Pareto's discussion of elites paralleled Mosca's. In fact, he accused Pareto of having "copied shamelessly." Pareto's response was to eliminate the few references to Mosca in a subsequent printing of his book.

Pareto's criticism of Karl Marx began, as did that of most non-Marxists, with a rejection of the inevitable final revolution. Whereas Marx had seen the "history of all hitherto existing societies" as class conflict, Pareto wrote that "the history of man is the history of the continuous replacement of certain elites: as one ascends, another declines (Pareto [1901]1968:36).

Pareto's criticisms often had a sarcastic, cutting edge to them. He was critical of those like Émile Durkheim, who thought a new morality could be built on scientific principles and understanding. People do not and never will operate thus, Pareto wrote, but will excuse and rationalize their behaviors. He criticized not just revolutionaries or radicals, such as Marxists, but later in life he also criticized liberal humanitarians who thought society could be made better by tinkering with it. Pareto was also critical of evolutionary thinking that assumed progress and improvement. Society, he said, never changes much, and when it does make progress, as toward freedom, it is an indirect result of elites' striving for personal goals.

All in all, Pareto appeared to gain satisfaction from criticizing the work of his colleagues as based upon their derivations. He wrote to his friend Pantaleoni: "Not because of any merit of my own, but because of the circumstances in which I found myself, I have no prejudices of any kind . . . which hinder others to do scholarly work in this field. I am not tied to any party, any religion, or any sect; therefore, I entertain no preconceived ideas about phenomena" (Pareto in de Rosa 1962). He was understandably unpopular among those committed to an ideology or cause, and among scholars in general.

In summary, Pareto's insights included, first, his "contribution" to the fascist concept of order and control. Following Machiavelli, he argued that power is inevitable, is its own justification, is based on the best use of derivations, and is usually cynical when employed correctly and successfully. Second, He pointed out the illogic in human behavior, distinguishing motives, or residues, from the reasons people give and often believe. The central issue raised by Pareto's theory is whether society is primarily the result of an ideological overlay of rationalizations. Third, Pareto argued that elites merely circulate between lions and foxes while feeding on the sheep or masses.

Pareto saw himself as the only real theorist, the rest being ideologues. His critics would say he was not a theorist at all, because he explained nothing regarding the course of human history. Given that the residues never change, he was dealing with constants, with only superficial derivations changing as people think up new rationalizations.

— Bert N. Adams

See also Durkheim, Émile; Marx, Karl; Political Economy

FURTHER READINGS AND REFERENCES

Bucolo, Placido. 1980. *The Other Pareto*. New York: St. Martin's.

de Rosa, Gabriele. 1962. *Carteggi Paretiani, 1892–1923*. (Pareto's Letters). Rome, Italy: Roma.

Machiavelli, Niccolo. [1532] 1979. *The Prince*. Middlesex, UK: Penguin.

Mosca, Gaetano. [1884] 1939. *The Ruling Class*. New York: McGraw-Hill.

Pareto, Vilfredo. [1901] 1968. *The Rise and Fall of the Elites*. Totowa, NJ: Bedminster.

———. [1906] 1971. *Manual of Political Economy*. New York: Augustus Kelley.

———. [1916] 1935. *The Mind and Society*. 4 vols. Edited by Arthur Livingstone. London: Jonathan Cape.

———. [1916] 1980. *Trattato di Sociologia Generale* [The Mind and Society]. Edited and abridged by Giulio Farina. Minneapolis, MN: University of Minnesota Press.

Zeitlin, Irving. 1994. *Ideology and the Development of Sociological Theory*. 5th ed. Englewood Cliffs, NJ: Prentice Hall.

PARK, ROBERT

A journalist and sociologist, Robert Park (1864–1944) was one of the charismatic figures around whom the Chicago School of urban sociology coalesced in the 1920s and 1930s. Influenced by Georg Simmel's conception of sociology as the study of patterns in human behavior that result from the "formal" properties of social interaction, Park added a dash of Herbert Spencer's social Darwinism and envisioned society as an ecological order where individuals cooperate and compete in the struggle for survival. Before joining the Chicago department at the age of 50, Park worked as a newspaper reporter in Minneapolis, Detroit, New York, and Chicago and later as a public relations consultant for Booker T. Washington and the Tuskegee Institute. These settings helped forge his substantive interests: in cities, the press, and in the lives of members of racial and ethnic minority groups. He is best remembered today for his PhD dissertation, *The Crowd and the Public* (1904), an early attempt at formulating a theory of social movements; for three essays—"The City" (1915), "The Urban Community as a Spatial Pattern and a Moral Order" (1926), and "The City as a Social Laboratory" (1929)—which laid out the research agenda of the Chicago School; for his theory that immigration initiates a "race relations cycle" beginning with contact and competition between a majority and minority group, proceeding through a conflict and then accommodation stage, and ending with the minority group's eventual assimilation; and for giving intellectual succor to students like Nels Anderson, Horace Cayton, Frederic Thrasher, and Lewis Wirth, whose ethnographic investigations of Chicago became classics in their own right.

LIFE AND CAREER

Park was born in Pennsylvania but spent his formative years in the town of Red Wing, Minnesota, the fourth child of Hiram and Theodosia Park, a grocer and school-teacher, respectively. Park was not a studious child; he passed his days in play, characteristically crossing ethnic divides to befriend children from Red Wing's Swedish and Norwegian immigrant communities. Despite his poor academic showing, Park went on to the University of Minnesota and then transferred after a year to the University of Michigan, where he received a degree in philosophy in 1887, coming under the influence of John Dewey, who was at that point more a Hegelian than a pragmatist.

Park had been a reporter for the student newspaper at Michigan. Upon graduation he entered the newspaper business, working briefly for a short-lived paper affiliated with Dewey and then for various big-city commercial presses. In 1894, he married Clara Cahill, an artist and writer, and in 1898 the couple moved to Cambridge, Massachusetts, where Park took an MA in philosophy from Harvard, studying with William James. Park took to heart James's critiques of dogmatic philosophies that have no practical bearing on human affairs, and was impressed by James's willingness to fold into philosophy the real-world experiences that people from all walks of life had shared with him. (For a reading of Park that places more emphasis than I do here on his pragmatist roots, see Joas 1993.)

Led in this way from philosophy to social science, Park became intent on studying social psychology and making it the basis for a doctoral dissertation on the press. He moved with his family to Germany, which remained, even at the turn of the century, a mecca for those wishing to learn how to approach the human sciences empirically. Simmel's courses in sociology at the University of Berlin held tremendous interest for Park, and left a permanent imprint on his thinking, but he wrote his dissertation under the direction of Wilhelm Windelband, a neo-Kantian philosopher and historian of science. On returning to the United States, however, Park found himself despairing of spending more time in ivory towers, and declined an offer from Albion Small, the chair of sociology at the University of Chicago, to teach there on a temporary basis. Instead, he

took a job as press secretary for the Congo Reform Association, whose goal was to publicize the brutality of Belgian colonial rule. This was an odd job for Park to have taken, for, despite his desire to return to the "real world," his days as a reporter had left him with serious misgivings about the motivations and consequences of social reform activity. His tenure at the association was predictably brief. In 1905, he was hired away by Washington. Traveling frequently between Tuskegee, Alabama, and his family's home in Massachusetts, and often accompanying Washington on fact-finding expeditions and publicity tours, Park became intimately acquainted with the problems faced by African Americans in the post-Reconstruction South, and cowrote with (or ghost authored for) the busy Washington numerous articles, tracts, and books.

In 1913, however, the opportunity again arose to join the Chicago department, which had begun to gain a reputation as a leading American center for sociological research. Perhaps sensing that this would be his last chance at academic respectability, Park took the job. He quickly developed intellectual friendships with W. I. Thomas, who, like Park, had drunk deeply from the well of American pragmatism, and with Ernest Burgess, with whom Park would coauthor the immensely popular *An Introduction to the Science of Sociology* (1921), a sourcebook of readings from which an entire generation of sociologists learned the field. Park was productive at Chicago, especially for someone who had started his academic career so late. During his more than 20 years there, he wrote five books (depending on how you count), more than 50 articles, and supervised scores of doctoral dissertations, the introductions to which he was often called upon to write after they were published. His interests ranged widely and helped set the agenda for his extensive travels, both in the United States and abroad—travels that reinforced his desire to understand patterns in ethnic and racial interaction. He retired from Chicago in 1934 and took a position at Fisk University in Atlanta, a historically black college where one of Park's former students, Charles Johnson, taught. Park continued working on various sociological projects, including an autobiography that was never completed, until his death in 1944.

MAJOR THEORETICAL THEMES

Although not always remembered as a contributor to sociological theory, Park in fact made important theoretical advances at both the presuppositional and substantive levels—advances that were obscured by the unsystematic and essayistic style of his writing. At the presuppositional level, Park was hardly alone among sociologists of his day in incorporating evolutionary themes into his thinking. What made his approach distinctive, however, was the insistence that social-ecological environments are characterized by processes of both cooperation *and* competition.

Park recognized two primary forms of cooperation: on one hand, urbanization and an advanced division of labor create situations of economic interdependence in modern societies; on the other hand, institutions—ranging from the family to the press—help integrate actors into a common moral and symbolic order. As for social competition, Park saw it centering on struggles for "dominance," which may occur at different levels: the individual competes with others for employment in the limited number of satisfying vocations, neighborhoods vie to become centers of social power in cities, established institutions jockey with not yet established ones for legitimacy, and so on. According to Park, cooperative and competitive social processes often unfold in recurring patterns of "succession." Park's most famous example of succession was drawn from research on population patterns in Chicago, where immigrants regularly moved from city centers outward as they established more secure footholds in their new country.

Methodological precepts followed from these presuppositions. Park's interest in studying social processes relating to "symbiosis"—or the interaction of different entities in a social ecosystem—as they play out over time ruled out in advance any static approach. Instead, Park sought to re-create "natural histories" of the individuals, groups, and institutions he wrote about, that is, accounts in which their present condition can be explained as a function of their complex social-ecological trajectories. Park believed that recovering such trajectories requires a multimethodological way of proceeding in which a wide range of factual material is used to understand actors from the viewpoints from which they themselves perceived their situations at crucial junctures. (This insistence, which owed a great debt to George Herbert Mead, a longtime acquaintance of Park and later colleague of his at Chicago, was then programmatized by Park's student, Herbert Blumer, and became one of the bases for symbolic interactionism.) In light of these concerns, Park saw in-depth life history interviews, participant observation in unfamiliar social worlds, probing and imaginative reportage, and—given the concern with spatiality inherent in the notion of social ecology—the making of social maps, as the most fruitful methods of social research. It was these he employed in his own empirical investigations—of the immigrant press, for example, or in his classic essay on "The Natural History of the Newspaper" (1923). Drummed into the heads of his graduate students, these methods became synonymous with Chicago sociology.

At the level of substantive theory, Park's most significant contributions were to extend Simmel's work on urbanism and to turn his process-oriented eye toward racial and ethnic relations. In both of these domains, his earlier interest in social psychology loomed large. The anonymity and intensity of urban life, he argued, combined with the fact that in cities, relationships of dependence often center on monetary exchange, has a profoundly detraditionalizing effect, breaking up informal patterns of social control, especially among newly arrived immigrants subject to the potentially conflicting demands of assimilation versus ethno-political loyalty. In Park's view, this meant that the city environment is inherently an unstable equilibrium. The downside of this, as he saw it, is that cities thereby become prone to crime and vice, to social crises, and to the irrationality of the mob. But the upside—and for Park this was more than adequate compensation—is that cities are also red-hot centers of social and cultural ferment and experimentation, places where new institutions, ideas, and artistic forms are likely to arise, both out of need (given endemic crises demanding resolution) and because a conscience freed from the strictures of traditional morality is a conscience primed for creativity. Cities thus represented, for Park, the leading edge of modernization and social change, and he directed his students to pay special attention to them.

Park's theory of a race relations cycle in immigration, for its part, has been out of fashion for some time, on the grounds that it posits assimilation to the norms and values of the host society as desirable and inevitable, whereas the accumulated empirical evidence suggests that immigrant groups, in the second generation and beyond, often retain key features of their ethnic heritage and modify the culture of their host countries as much as they are modified by it. These charges are not without merit. Park did regard assimilation as both thoroughgoing and desirable. For example, in his 1914 paper "Racial Assimilation in Secondary Groups with Particular Reference to the Negro," Park asserted that "[t]he immigrant readily takes over the language, manners, the social ritual, and outward forms of his adopted country"—a process he coded as good because, as he saw it, the women and men who were thus "emancipat[ed]" from their traditional practices would thereby gain the "room and freedom for the expansion and development of . . . [their] individual aptitudes" (1914:607). He did not, however, view the race relations cycle as an iron law—indeed, he explicitly noted that the assimilation process may become blocked for those groups whose members bear "a distinctive racial hallmark" (1914:611), or for a variety of institutional reasons discussed in *The Immigrant Press and Its Control* (1922), a book written on the heels of the first Red Scare. His reputation among contemporary scholars of immigration may also be bolstered slightly by pointing out that with the exception of Karl Marx, Park was virtually alone among classical and postclassical theorists in stressing the complex relationship between immigration and colonialism, recognizing this to be the proper context for understanding the race relations cycle in the United States and Europe.

— Neil Gross

See also Ecological Theory; Mead, George Herbert; Simmel, Georg; Symbolic Interaction; Urbanization

FURTHER READINGS AND REFERENCES

Joas, Hans. 1993. *Pragmatism and Social Theory*. Chicago, IL: University of Chicago Press.

Matthews, Fred H. 1977. *Quest for an American Sociology: Robert E. Park and the Chicago School*. Montreal and London: McGill-Queen's University Press.

Park, Robert E. [1904] 1972. *The Crowd and the Public, and Other Essays*. Translated by Charlotte Elsner. Chicago, IL: University of Chicago Press.

———. 1914. "Racial Assimilation in Secondary Groups with Particular Reference to the Negro." *American Journal of Sociology* 19:606–23.

———. 1915. "The City: Suggestions for the Investigation of Human Behavior in the City Environment." *American Journal of Sociology* 20:577–612.

———. 1922. *The Immigrant Press and Its Control*. New York: Harper.

———. 1923. "The Natural History of the Newspaper." *American Journal of Sociology* 29:273–89.

———. 1926. "The Urban Community as a Spatial Pattern and a Moral Order." In *The Urban Community,* edited by Ernest W. Burgess. Chicago, IL: University of Chicago Press.

———. 1929. "The City as a Social Laboratory." In *Chicago: An Experiment in Social Science Research,* edited by T. V. Smith and Leonard D. White. Chicago, IL: University of Chicago Press.

Park, Robert E. and Ernest W. Burgess. 1921. *An Introduction to the Science of Sociology*. Chicago, IL: University of Chicago Press.

Raushenbush, Winifred. 1979. *Robert E. Park: Biography of a Sociologist*. Durham, NC: Duke University Press.

PARSONS, TALCOTT

The contribution of Talcott Parsons (1902–1979) to sociology can be differentiated into three theoretical elements: (1) a theory of order, (2) a theory of society as a production process, and (3) a theory of societal evolution.

THE THEORY OF ORDER

Parsons's theory of order starts with his analysis of Hobbes's problem of order in his seminal work, *The Structure of Social Action* ([1937]1968). Hobbes's question was how social order in the sense of mutually expectable behavior and expectations of two or more actors in a situation is possible under the condition that each actor is free in choosing goals and means to attain his or her goals. Hobbes's prediction for such a situation was the war of all against all (state of nature). According to Hobbes, recognizing this dilemma and striving for survival should suffice to lead everybody to the conclusion of concluding a contract with each other to build a central authority with a monopoly of power, which is in charge of establishing and enforcing rules defining rights and obligations so that social order will be guaranteed. In order to exclude destabilization, the subjects of the authority have no right to resistance, and the founding of the authority in the belief in God's will should help to avoid any questioning of it.

Parsons's criticism of Hobbes's solution says that it leads to the utilitarian dilemma. If there is no precontractual bond between the individuals, there is no reason why they should step out of the situation to see and enact a solution to their problem from the external position of an observer. Within their situation, there is no mutual trust on which to rely in order to conclude a contract that would deprive them of their own sanctioning power. Thus, there are only two extreme solutions to the problem: a very unstable coincidence of interests, which provides for accidental order, or external constraint that produces compulsory order. Both are types of what Parsons calls factual order. Neither type is stable in itself. Accidental order possibly endures for moments of time only, while compulsory order provokes counterforce and is always in danger of resulting in a spiral of force and counterforce. Thus, according to Parsons, a purely positivistic theory of action, which conceives of action as being merely guided by freely chosen goals and means to attain these goals under given external conditions, is unable to provide a satisfying answer to the question of how social order is possible.

It is at this point that Parsons introduces his "normative" solution to the problem of order. He distinguishes normative order from purely factual order in the sense that it relies on precontractual commonly shared values and norms. There must be minimal bonds between people in order to share a minimal set of values and norms. Under this condition, they learn to subordinate their I-perspective to a we-perspective and to reconcile individual interests within a common frame of reference. In order to do so, they need to share a feeling of mutual belongingness, which is furthered by external demarcation and minimal internal homogeneity of the society. For Parsons, it goes without saying that such preconditions of commonly shared norms cannot come about by the convergence of individual interests or by external constraint. They follow their own logic of production, namely, external demarcation and internal homogenization; the differentiation between a sacred core of unchangeable values and norms and a profane periphery of changeable technical rules in Durkheim's sense; the recurrent reinforcement and re-creation of the validity of values and norms in commonly shared rituals; inclusion of members in such rituals; the identification of members with the social unit (group, organization, society); socialization of new members through identification with representatives of the social unit; legitimation of more specific norms and practices by reference to more general values and norms. We have to account for these prerequisites as regards the existence of commonly shared values and norms if we want to understand and explain a concretely existing social order.

For Parsons, the "normative" solution to the problem of order, however, does not mean that any concrete social order is only the result of norm constitution outside the effects of interests and power. To do so would result in the counterposition to positivism, which is idealism according to nineteenth-century German philosophy. Idealism tries to understand human action and social order as an "emanation" of ideas and pure reason and leads to the dilemma of having to choose between the two extreme poles of a purely ideal order coming about through the realization of reason, or a purely traditionalist conformistic order existing in a closed community without any change. A concrete order is, as a rule, neither purely factual nor purely normative in character, but rather the result of the interpenetration of normative and conditional factors. This is the way in which Parsons resolves the contradiction between positivism and idealism in his "voluntaristic" theory of action. This means that the outlined processes of norm constitution penetrate the satisfaction of interests and the application of power and vice versa.

An example might explain how this kind of order building has to be conceived of. According to Max Weber, the marriage of ascetic Protestantism and modern capitalism has resolved the contradiction between the traditional religious ethics of brotherhood and the unbrotherly world of business, market competition, and market exchange between strangers through the establishment of what can be called *business ethics,* which is located in the zone of interpenetration (overlap) of ethics and business. It is both ethics and business, namely, the ethics of business, and has to be distinguished from the pure ethics of brotherhood and the pure satisfaction of business interests. The new business ethics is put into law in trade, corporation, competition, and contract law. According to Weber, the new thing about business ethics, trade, corporation, competition, and contract law is that they break down the differentiation between in-group and out-group morality. Formerly, the ethics of brotherhood prevailed within the community, whereas outside the community there was unbrotherliness, force, deceit, and mistrust. With the establishment of business ethics and economic law, the interaction within communities and between members of different communities became guided by identical norms. Market and business penetrate the community, turning members of a closed community into self-responsible individuals; the formation of a wider and more abstract community of a common faith and of economic law penetrates the market to turn insecurity, mistrust, deceit, and force into ethically and legally regulated, predictable, and trustful business activity. The new economic order is both the result of expanding markets and expanding ethical and legal regulation. This is exactly what we can call the interpenetration of normative and

conditional factors in the production of a concrete social order in terms of Parsons's voluntaristic theory of action.

The question as to whether Parsons completely discarded his voluntaristic theory of action, when he turned to functionalism and systems theory, resulting in the publication of *The Social System* in 1951, has been frequently debated. At least, the parallel publication of *Toward a General Theory of Action* in 1951 (Parsons and Shils 1951) gives clear evidence that there was no intention to do so. Also, Parsons's final collection of essays, *Action Theory and the Human Condition,* published in 1978, refers to action theory in its title. It is, however, also clear that action theory was complemented by analytical functionalism and systems theory and that theoretical problems were now expressed in terms of the new theoretical language. Nevertheless, what can be maintained is the continuing importance of the problem of order and of its solution in terms of Parsons's voluntaristic theory of action. In *The Social System,* Parsons introduces three systems in order to analyze human action and its order: the social system composed of interactions, the personality system composed of need dispositions, and the cultural system composed of symbols with meaning (language, values, norms, expressive symbols, cognitions). The problem of order now occurs in three different forms: as double contingency of actions within social systems, as motivational problem in the relationship between social and personality systems, and as legitimation in the relationship between social and cultural systems.

THE THEORY OF SOCIETY AS AN ONGOING PRODUCTION PROCESS

In the further development of his systems theory, Parsons introduced a fourth action subsystem, which was originally called behavioral organism and was then renamed behavioral system following the advice of Victor and Charles Lidz. The four subsystems make up the complete action system. Each one of them fulfills a specific function within the four-function paradigm (AGIL scheme) introduced in the *Working Papers in the Theory of Action* (Parsons, Bales, and Shils 1953), which became later on systematized by way of crossing two dichotomies: instrumental versus consummatory and internal versus external orientation of action: Adaptation (A), Goal-attainment (G), Integration (I), Latent pattern maintenance (L).

Providing for adaptation, the behavioral system is the organizational unit of learning in the broadest sense, from simple conditioning up to reflective abstraction. The interpenetration of the behavioral system with the personality system ensures a change of the personality through learning and direction of learning by personal goal setting, its interpenetration with the social system provides for collective learning and for the social organization of learning, its interpenetration with the cultural system induces cultural change on one hand, and the cultural framing of learning processes on the other hand.

Parsons elaborated his model of the action system in two directions. In *Economy and Society,* Parsons and Smelser (1956) subdivided the social system into the four functional subsystems, which were eventually named the economic system (A), the political system (G), the societal community (I), and the fiduciary system (L). In his late work collected in *Action Theory and the Human Condition* (1978), Parsons embedded the action system into the system of the human condition: physicochemical system (A), organic system (G), action system (I), and telic system (L). The production, reproduction, renewal, and transformation of order is now a problem of the balanced fulfillment of the specific functions by the subsystems and of their balanced interpenetration. The latter is outlined in a theoretical model of the double interchange of factors and products between the functional subsystems, which is carried out by generalized media of interchange (or communication): (A) money, (G) power, (I) influence, (L) value commitments for the social system; (A) intelligence, (G) performance capacity, (I) affect, (L) definition of the situation for the action system; (A) empirical ordering, (G) health, (I) meaning, (L) transcendental ordering for the human condition.

Here, we enter the domain of Parsons's theory of society as an ongoing production process, which includes value creation, ups and downs, and inflationary-deflationary spirals. We might explain this model with the example of the political system as the societal subsystem, which is specialized in the production and implementation of collectively binding decisions in order to accomplish societal goals. To fulfill this societal function, it needs to generate power, because power is exactly that means, which allows the enforcement of collectively binding decisions, though a plurality of alternative decisions is always articulated and desired by groups and individuals who intend to oppose. According to Max Weber's ([1922]1976:28) definition, power is the chance to enforce one's will against resistance. The ultimate means needed to enforce collectively binding decisions is the establishment of a monopoly of physical force by the state, which authorized representatives of the state can apply in case of resistance.

What is crucial and what represents the voluntaristic solution of the problem of order in the production model is the fact that the generation of political power is not self-sufficient, but needs extra-political resources in order to be stabilized and enhanced. And these extra-political resources must be produced through procedures following their own logic. Financial resources have to be produced according to economic laws and cannot be produced politically, as the failure of the socialist regime of the Soviet Union has demonstrated (mobilization of money). Support has to be produced by processes of inclusion and participation in decision making (mobilization of influence). Legitimacy has to be produced by processes of consensus-formation in public discourse (mobilization of value commitments). Parsons represents this political production process in a model of the double interchange of factors and products carried out on the basis of specialized media of interchange.

What is furthermore crucial is the involvement of generalized media of interchange (communication) in the societal (political) production process. The specific features of the media help to advance this process far beyond the limits of what would be an economic barter business, or direct political application of force, or particularistic solidarity, or traditional consensus of a shared lifeworld. The media are generalizations of more concretely effective means of motivating action.

The media are of a symbolic nature. Money symbolizes purchasable goods and services, power signifies enforceable collectively binding decisions, influence means cooperation that can be mobilized, value-commitments design the consent available. They are generated and applied according to institutionalized norms: money/economic law, political power/constitution, influence/order of competencies, value-commitments/rules of public discourse (Parsons 1969a, 1969b, 1969c).

The media allow for credit lending and a corresponding process of value creation. The voters invest their votes in political parties as in banks, which, in their turn, invest the votes they received in governmental programs. The return for the party-bank is enhanced support as a result of successful programs, for the voters it is farther-reaching, collectively binding decisions that they could not achieve on their own account. In this political process of value-creation, zero-sum conditions of power are overcome. The power of one group of voters does not rule out the power of other groups of voters, because the range of collectively binding decisions is continually extended so that a growing spectrum of desired decisions is being served. There are measures of functioning of the production process, which is effectiveness as value principle and compliance as coordination standard for political power.

The dynamic nature of the production process implies waves of ups and downs and inflationary-deflationary spirals. An inflation of political power occurs when there is an overinvestment of support so that desires for political decisions run beyond the limits of production. The return for votes is diminishing in this case. The result is declining trust in political investments, which might lead to the growing recall of investments like the running recall of investments in banks. Investments are shifted to secure units, over which one has direct control (one's own group). This implies deflation with diminishing power available for party-banks, which, therefore, cannot invest in farther-reaching programs. The effect is a shrinking capability of political production. Parsons gives an interpretation of

McCarthyism in the United States in the 1950s, which applies the model of an inflationary-deflationary spiral. The end of World War II had increased the external and internal power of the United States government enormously. The investment of voters in supporting the government was insecure in its return, because it could not be predicted what the government would do with its increased power. Senator McCarthy made use of this insecurity and turned it into a basic mistrust in incumbents of authority positions of any kind that they would deviate from true American values and support communism. As a result, it was intended to establish close control on incumbents of authority positions so that the scope of decision making beyond immediate return was shrinking. The inflation of power turned into a deflationary spiral, which, however, came to a halt, when the constricting effects of McCarthy's position were realized and increasingly opposed to across party lines.

In an article on an empirical survey on voting behavior, published by Berelson, Lazarsfeld, and McPhee (1954), Parsons explains what he conceives as a balanced production of leadership responsibility and political decisions in the interchange between the political system and the societal community in the American society. There is a double interchange of factors producing specific enforcement power and products providing for general leadership power. Interest demands are articulated by groups in the societal community and transmitted to the political system through influence; political decisions are transmitted from the political system to the societal community through political power. Support from groups in the societal community is turned into power in the political system via elections; leadership responsibility is taken by the government on this basis and turned into influence to convince people and groups in the societal community of the preference for certain political programs.

According to Parsons, the political production process has to keep balance between three sets of opposing requirements: (1) stability versus flexibility, (2) consensus versus conflict, and (3) conservation and progression. In his analysis of the empirical voting study, he gives the following explanation on how this balance is achieved in the American political system.

Stability versus flexibility. The consequences of political decisions are far too complex so that not even experts would be able to predict their outcome. Thus, there would be chaos if voters tried to vote on the basis of rational grounds. This is prevented by the fact that a majority of voters decide on "nonrational" grounds simply in line with group alliances within their milieus. Their traditionalism is the guarantor of predictability and stability in the system. The resulting danger of rigidity is counteracted by the voting of people, who are not firmly included in a one-dimensional milieu but are socially less included or experience cross-cutting loyalty demands from different group memberships. They change their party preference more often than the average voter from one election to the other or during the campaign for an election. In the "normal" case of inclusion, they will shift toward the majority, which is emerging during a campaign. In the "pathological" case of alienation, they withdraw from voting or support radical movements opposing the system in general.

Consensus versus conflict. The polarization between the conservative Republicans and the liberal Democrats is embedded in a consensus on the rules of the game, in commonly shared values of the constitution, in mutual trust to let the winner of an election lead the nation for the next term and in cross-cutting memberships.

Conservation versus progression. The Republicans represent the principle of conservation, which implies less inclination to change the given parameters of society (especially the economy) through political intervention, whereas the Democrats stand for the wish to change society in the direction of the basic constitutional values, especially to provide for more inclusion of marginalized people and justice through political intervention. Progress on the basis of enduring structures is particularly possible, since changes carried out by the legislation of one government are mostly not revoked by the next government, even if its members had opposed it severely in the legislation process.

THE THEORY OF SOCIETAL EVOLUTION

Approaching Parsons's theory of the evolution of societies, we might start with his representation of the voluntaristic model of the interpenetration of normative and conditional factors in his functional systems theory in terms of the cybernetic hierarchy of conditions and control, where energy is high and information is low at the bottom, but energy is low and information high on top in the order of the systems, from the adaptation system at the bottom via the goal-attainment system and the integration system up to the latent pattern maintenance system on top.

According to our example of the interpenetration of ethics and business, we could say that the expansion of markets via the creation of the European single market conditions disturbance in the political system (G) of the member states of the European Union by making their regulation of the economy ineffective and causing corresponding political alienation in the electorate; it also breaks up the solidarity structure (I) of the member states and produces a rift between the winners and losers of this modernization process; and it creates legitimation deficits (L), because the established notion of justice as approaching equal living conditions for the whole national community through redistribution is challenged by increasing pressure from the market in the direction of a greater spread of income. The disturbance caused by the expansion of markets in the political systems, societal communities, and fiduciary systems of cultural communication in the nation-states calls for restructuring activities from the top down to the regulation of the economy in the new multilevel system of European Union, nation-states, regions, and local communities by way of building a multilevel polity (G), transnational solidarity, and reinclusion of marginalized groups (I) and consensus on a new idea of justice, which would go in the direction of a more individualized conceptualization in the sense of providing for equal opportunity and fairness (L).

We might also apply Parsons's scheme of pattern variables to describe this transformation. It decomposes Tönnies's dichotomy of community and society and Durkheim's dichotomy of mechanical and organic solidarity to allow for a greater variety of compositions of the elements.

We could say that the organization of the national welfare state preserved elements of community and mechanical solidarity, whereas the evolution of the European multilevel system makes a step forward toward an extended society and organic solidarity. However, this does not completely rule out the maintenance of elements of community and mechanical solidarity in the new system, particularly within the smaller units of family, but also local communities, regions, and even nation-states. The establishment of some basic mechanical solidarity of commonly shared feelings of belongingness is also possible on the European level and helps to stabilize the multilevel system.

Applying his AGIL scheme to societal evolution, Parsons (1966, 1971) outlines four basic dimensions of this process: (A) adaptive upgrading, (G) structural differentiation, (I) inclusion, and (L) value generalization. In our example of European integration, the European single market provides for adaptive upgrading because of the economy's enhanced performance. It necessitates structural differentiation of institutions in the multilevel system; it also requires complementation through the inclusion of groups in the periphery excluded thus far, and of newly marginalized groups in the center, that is, the resolution of conflicts between winners and losers of modernization. Finally, there is a need for value generalization in the sense that notions of justice as partaking collectively in produced wealth are being replaced by a notion of justice as equal opportunity and fairness.

In his book *Societies* (1966), Parsons presents an outline of evolution according to the four basic dimensions by looking at the advancements of archaic societies (Egypt and Mesopotamia) compared to primitive societies, and of the historical empires (China, India, and the Roman Empire) compared to archaic societies, and he also highlights the advancements produced by the "seedbed societies" of Israel and Greece that were taken up later on in the emergence of modern Western societies.

In *The System of Modern Societies* (1971), he describes the major advancements achieved by the Reformation, the Enlightenment, and the crystallization of the system in Northwestern Europe, and concludes with an account of the special achievements of American society and a look at countermovements against modernization. He also dares the prediction that the Soviet system cannot be regarded as a stable type of modern society.

In an article on "Evolutionary Universals in Society" (1967), he provides a brief description of institutional inventions, which can be called evolutionary universals in the sense that they further evolution. First prerequisites are religion, language, kinship systems, and technology. Evolutionary universals are social stratification, cultural legitimation, bureaucratic organization, money and the market complex, generalized universalistic norms, and democratic association.

According to his analysis in *The System of Modern Societies* (1971), three major revolutions have brought about major breakthroughs in modernity: the industrial revolution (A), the democratic revolution (G), and the educational revolution (I, L). The process involves consecutive steps in the establishment of civil, political, and social rights, according to Marshall's analysis of the development of citizenship in the United Kingdom. Though the development in Britain was not replicated everywhere in the same way, it is nevertheless of a paradigmatic nature, because it presents a model of what Parsons calls a modern societal community, which establishes a solidarity of citizenship beyond any primordial group membership. In Parsons's eyes, it is the peculiar achievement of the United States to develop such a pluralistic, yet integrated, societal community even further. In an analysis of ethnicity, however, he sees this achievement in danger of regression due to the return to primary ethnic solidarity as a reaction to the insecurity of status enhanced by rapid social change. This is what has become the controversy on multiculturalism and group rights versus pluralism and individual rights (Parsons 1977).

Evolutionary advancement is not guaranteed. There is always the danger of retrogression. Parsons's major example of this is Nazi Germany. According to his explanation, the modernization of science, technology, economy, and administration was not complemented by a concomitant modernization of social structure, political organization, and culture. There were strong tensions between modern technical rationality and traditionalistic social structure and culture, which caused a longing for the return to the securities of *Gemeinschaft* that was successfully promoted by the Nazi movement.

CONCLUDING REMARKS

Talcott Parsons's contributions to sociological theory can be subdivided into the three elements of a theory of order, a theory of society as a production process, and a theory of societal evolution. It is still worthy of application, refinement, renewal, and extension. It is fair to say that its potential still calls for efforts of realization.

— Richard Münch

See also AGIL; General Systems Theory; Luhmann, Niklas; Smelser, Neil; Social Action; Social Structure; Structural Functionalism

FURTHER READINGS AND REFERENCES

Berelson, B. R., P. F. Lazarsfeld, and W. N. McPhee. 1954. *Voting*. Chicago, IL: University of Chicago Press.

Haas, Ernst B. 1958. *The Uniting of Europe*. Stanford, CA: Stanford University Press.

———. 1975. *The Obsolescence of Regional Integration Theory*. Berkeley, CA: University of California Press.

Marx, Karl. 1969. *Zur Kritik der politischen Ökonomie*. MEW, Bd. 13. Berlin, Germany: Dietz.

Münch, Richard. 1988. *Theorie des Handelns*. Frankfurt, Germany: Suhrkamp.

———. 1995. *Dynamik der Kommunikationsgesellschaft*. Frankfurt, Germany: Suhrkamp.

Parsons, Talcott. [1937] 1968. *The Structure of Social Action*. New York: Free Press.

———. 1951. *The Social System*. Glencoe, IL: Free Press.

———. 1964. *Social Structure and Personality*. New York: Free Press.

———. 1966. *Societies: Evolutionary and Comparative Perspectives*. Englewood Cliffs, NJ: Prentice-Hall.

———. 1967. "Evolutionary Universals in Society." Pp. 490–520 in *Sociological Theory and Modern Society* by T. Parsons. New York: Free Press.

———. 1969a. "On the Concept of Influence." Pp. 405–38 in *Politics and Social Structure* by T. Parsons. New York: Free Press.

———. 1969b. "On the Concept of Political Power." Pp. 352–404 in *Politics and Social Structure* by T. Parsons. New York: Free Press.

———. 1969c. "On the Concept of Value Commitments." Pp. 439–72 in *Politics and Social Structure* by T. Parsons. New York: Free Press.

———. 1969d. "Voting and the Equilibrium of the American Political System." Pp. 204–40 in *Politics and Social Structure* by T. Parsons. New York: Free Press.

———. 1971. *The System of Modern Societies*. Englewood Cliffs, NJ: Prentice-Hall.

———. 1977. "Some Theoretical Considerations on the Nature and Trends of Change of Ethnicity." Pp. 383–404 in *Social Systems and the Evolution of Action Theory* by T. Parsons. New York: Free Press.

———. 1978. *Action Theory and the Human Condition*. New York: Free Press.

Parsons, Talcott, R. F. Bales, and E. A. Shils. 1953. *Working Papers in the Theory of Action*. Glencoe, IL: Free Press.

Parsons, Talcott and G. M. Platt. 1973. *The American University*. Cambridge, MA: Harvard University Press.

Parsons, Talcott and E. A. Shils, eds. 1951. *Toward a General Theory of Action*. Cambridge, MA: Harvard University Press.

Parsons, Talcott and Neil J. Smelser. 1956. *Economy and Society*. New York: Free Press.

Weber, Max. [1922] 1976. *Wirtschaft und Gesellschaft* [Economy and Society]. Tübingen, Germany: Mohr Siebeck.

PATRIARCHY

Patriarchy is the seemingly ubiquitous system of sex-based oppression that is incorporated throughout society. It refers to the power differential between men and women in society that allows men to dominate and control women. It is not the unanticipated consequence of capitalism or some other social arrangement but rather a purposeful system held in place by those who are reaping the benefits of its unjust systematic abuse of women.

Several types of feminism have grappled with the issue of patriarchy. Psychoanalytic feminists believe that all men everywhere are responsible for enforcing patriarchy in their daily lives and that women do little to challenge them. This branch of feminism offers two reasons for the dilemma. First, they posit that men strive to maintain the system because they fear death. Women do not have such an intense fear of death because they are more closely linked to the process of reproduction and life-giving. This causes men to try to control the reproductive abilities of women and women themselves to try to create objects that will immortalize them (monuments, belief systems, nuclear bombs, etc.) and to distance themselves as far as possible from signs of their own mortality (sexuality, disease, birth, etc.).

The second explanation for patriarchy put forth by psychoanalytic feminists is related to the experiences of early childhood personality formation. They assume that people are forever attempting to balance (but never quite can) their own quest for individualism with the need to belong to something larger than themselves. They also assume that the earliest, and most crucial, stages of emotional development occur primarily with the mother figure (whether the biological mother or not is irrelevant). At these early stages, especially prior to the formation of linguistic skills, infants are dependent upon the mother for happiness as well as frustrated and angered by her punishment or lack of cooperation in satisfying desires. Infants have ambivalent feelings toward the father figure since he is only an occasional being with whom they have interaction and on whom they rarely depend to satisfy some need. This causes males to grow up and use women for emotional fulfillment and to also seek to manipulate them for their own satisfaction.

Women grow up with ambivalent feelings about themselves as women and seek to reenact the role of mother with their male counterparts. Hence, psychoanalytic feminism explains patriarchy as rooted in the anxious energy exerted by men out of fear of their own death as well as their ambivalent feelings toward their mothers. Women are not inclined to oppose the system because they lack a similar emotional energy to resist.

Radical feminism is another branch of feminist thought that seeks to explain patriarchy. They hold the belief that women everywhere should be valued positively and that women everywhere are violently oppressed by the system of patriarchy. They see patriarchy as the most oppressive system of domination in society, even more so than racism, heterosexism, or class. They believe that patriarchy manifests itself violently throughout society, whether it is through the physical infliction of harm or more ideological violence such as the idealized and nearly unattainable image of the perfect female body, ideas about women's sexuality, practices related to motherhood and pregnancy, or in the devaluing of household labor. Overt physical violence, however, is the most important of these forms to radical feminists. They believe that rape, prostitution, hysterectomies, and other forms of physical violence against women are at the core of patriarchal oppressive practices. Men maintain this system because of the advantages it brings to them. They are able to use women to pass on their genes, do their household labor, and serve as signifiers of their own social status. Radical feminists suggest two strategies for resisting patriarchy. The first is to band together in a "sisterhood" and oppose domination wherever and whenever it is present. The second is to retreat into all-female communities. This latter alternative represents the particularly vibrant strand of radical lesbian feminists.

Cultural feminists are primarily concerned with the ways in which women are different from men. Unlike psychoanalytic feminists, they are not concerned with where these differences came from, and unlike radical feminists, they are not necessarily concerned with arguing that women are always the victims of violence. What they do argue is that women have a different way of being and that this way, one which is generally seen as more moral and caring than that of men, might be a better base for society. They view patriarchy as the current system of male domination and argue that women's greater capacity for nurturance and caring would serve as a better model for social organization.

Liberal feminists, unlike cultural feminists, claim that women can claim an equality with men because of their shared capacity for morality. They do not claim that one is better than the other but rather that the two are equal. This equality, however, is not expressed under the tyrannical system of patriarchy that seeks to dominate women through falsely constructed ideas about what is "natural." Liberal feminists seek to use the state and an appeal to the public's sense of moral reason to undo the system of sex inequality inherently pervasive under patriarchy.

Socialist feminism also seeks to deal with patriarchy, particularly as it relates to the capitalist system. Growing out of the writings of Marx and Engels, socialist feminists seek to unite feminist concerns with Marxian class analysis. This relationship has been termed an "uneasy marriage" (Hartmann 1981), as it is often the case that women's concerns are merely added to the issues of class domination rather than being presented as an independent, though interrelated, issue. Socialist feminists argue that it was with the advent of property relations that women first came to be exploited as men began seeing women as objects to be owned and controlled. Using historical materialism as a base, capitalist patriarchy is thus defined as the union of oppressions under the capitalist system and the system of patriarchy.

Capitalism and patriarchy are seen as mutually reinforcing systems of domination. For example, women being kept in the private sphere ensures that there is always a reserve army of labor, a necessity for keeping labor costs low. It also allows for the reproduction of the worker at no cost to the system, as women's work at home is unpaid. Patriarchy clearly benefits from this same separation of public and private spheres, as it keeps women from earning their own incomes and hence maintains their dependence on men. Patriarchy also permits women to be sexually harassed on the job and in other public places, which acts as a deterrent to their seeking jobs in the public sphere and hence keeps them in the homes where they can be most easily exploited. This form of sex oppression reinforces both patriarchal and capitalist ideologies. The generally lower wages of women for equal work, if they are able to make it into the workplace at all, is another means of maintaining the status quo of male domination.

While all of these arguments are valuable insights into the concept of patriarchy, most of them (with the exception of radical feminism) assume heterosexuality. This assumed heterosexuality is a weak spot for many of these theories, as they fail to adequately deal with the arrangements found in same-sex relationships. An analysis into the workings of gay male and lesbian relationships and the ways in which patriarchy enacts itself in those situations would help enhance the quality and strength of the argument against patriarchy. This is not to say that such an endeavor has not been undertaken already. Indeed, many have been interested in this issue since the early days of the Stonewall Revolution and before, but the place of same-sex relationships is undoubtedly one of the key areas for further development for those wishing to combat patriarchal oppression.

— Michael Ryan

See also Feminism; Liberal Feminism; Radical Feminism

FURTHER READINGS AND REFERENCES

Chodorow, Nancy. 1990. *Feminism and Psychoanalytic Theory.* New Haven, CT: Yale University Press.

Friedan, Betty. 1963. *The Feminine Mystique.* New York: Dell.

Hartmann, Heidi. 1981. "The Unhappy Marriage of Marxism and Feminism: Towards a More Progressive Union." In *Women and Revolution,* edited by Lydia Sargent. Boston, MA: South End.

Hartsock, Nancy. 1983. *Money, Sex and Power: Towards a Feminist Historical Materialism.* New York: Longman.

———. 1998. *The Feminist Standpoint Revisited & Other Essays.* Boulder, CO: Westview.

Lengermann, Patricia Madoo and Jill Niebrugge-Brantley. 2000. "Contemporary Feminist Theory." Pp. 307–55 in *Modern Sociological Theory,* edited by George Ritzer. Boston, MA: McGraw-Hill.

Rich, Adrienne. 1980. "Compulsory Heterosexual and Lesbian Experience." Pp. 62–91 in *Women, Sex, and Sexuality,* edited by C. R. Stimson and E. S. Person. Chicago, IL: University of Chicago Press.

Tong, Rosemarie Putnam. 1998. *Feminist Thought: A More Comprehensive Introduction.* 2d ed. Boulder, CO: Westview.

PHENOMENOLOGY

In the course of their everyday activities, people do not doubt the validity of the world that surrounds them. But from the philosophical point of view, this validity, which is quasi "automatically" given to us, presents a problem. How does our consciousness gain the reality of the world that we take for granted in our "natural attitude"? Phenomenology, as developed by Edmund Husserl, is a philosophical school of thought that intends to clarify this problem by describing how the constitution of reality in the acts of our consciousness occurs. Thus, phenomenology aims at basic processes bestowing meaning on the human world, and its results are significant for those crucial questions of social theory asking how actors construct and interpret their reality and how they define situations to give orientation to their actions. Accordingly, in the field of social theory, phenomenological thought is fundamental for the interpretative approaches in the theory of action, for the sociology of knowledge, culture, language, and—in general—for constitutive theories of society.

PHENOMENOLOGY AS A RIGOROUS SCIENCE AND AS THE SCIENCE OF THE LIFEWORLD

The concept of phenomenology was primarily developed by the philosopher Edmund Husserl in the first decades of the twentieth century He was born in 1859 in a German Jewish family in Prostejov, Moravia, which was a part of the Austro-Hungarian empire and which is currently a part of the Czech Republic. He studied mathematics and philosophy at Leipzig, Berlin, and Vienna and taught philosophy at the Universities of Halle, Göttingen, and Freiburg, where he died in 1938. The genesis of his work can be divided into three periods: (1) investigation of the philosophical presuppositions of logical thought, (2) investigations into the meaning of establishing acts of consciousness, and (3) the theory of lifeworld.

Husserl begins with a critical assessment of the contemporary currents of philosophical thought. At that time, the philosophical thought concerning the starting points that form our knowledge were divided into approaches stressing methodological (neo-Kantianism) or logical (Frege, Vienna Circle) operations, on one hand, and the originality of lived experience (philosophy of life—Dilthey, Bergson), on the other. Husserl's conception cuts across the boundaries separating those positions. His programmatic aim was to make the "characteristic correlation between ideal objects (*ideale Gegenstände*) of the purely logical sphere and subjectively lived experience as constitutive action (*bildendes Tun*) a topic of research" (Biemel 1959). This aim, which sounds purely philosophical, had an enormous impact on the state of discussion at that time, since it helped to bridge the gap between the logical systematic approach to epistemological problems and its opposite, the analysis of consciousness as a stream of lived experience where intuitive introspection is the preferred method. Husserl, who had started out as a mathematician, emphasized the self-evident necessity of pure logic for any science. At the same time, however, he demonstrated that logic itself required a philosophical foundation in order to illuminate the context of meaning in which logical thought takes place. He conceived consciousness as a stream of acts that always are "intentional," that is, that always are correlated with a reality that they are able to grasp. Thinking means for him primarily "thinking of something," so that the "empty" formal mode of thought represented by pure logic needs to be seen as a secondary derivation from those primary acts. Husserl is interested in the structure of acts of consciousness that, as intentional experience (*intentionales Erleben*), always represents a unity of content and form of experience and hence is the basis of the human approach to reality in its every mode (Husserl 1975–1984 2:9, 401). This does not mean that he would neglect the significance of logic for the sciences and scientific procedures. But if it is to claim to be a rigorous science providing a foundation of all individual sciences, philosophy must achieve both: It must employ pure logic and at the same time be able to clarify its basis in the stream of intentional consciousness itself.

In the second period of his work, Husserl (1976) develops a specific method for this enterprise called the "phenomenological reduction" (*epoché*). He is concerned with investigating experiences as meaning establishing acts of consciousness and looks for a method to make them evident. He suggests putting the self-evident validity of the experiences "into brackets" and reflecting on the acts of consciousness that constitute that taken-for-granted self-evidence itself. Husserl contends that to reveal those acts would mean to disclose the processes in our consciousness that endow our experience with meaning, that is, which do construct all the "facts" given in our mind. By the means of the *epoché,* an experience is viewed as a phenomenon as it is happening and as it is constituted in the acts of consciousness that makes this phenomenon what it is for us. The phenomenological procedure is intended to reveal the self-givenness of experiences, that is to say, to let them appear as they really are. That is what Husserl means by his famous appeal, "Return to the things themselves" (Husserl 1975–1984 2:1, 6). Hence, Husserl not only demonstrated that logic and lived experience do not contradict one another, but also showed that they are closely intertwined and that we can get direct evidence about it when we use phenomenology as a deep reflective philosophical method. Thus, Husserl's phenomenological analysis of the constitutive acts of our consciousness appeared to indicate the way to the clarification of all scientific knowledge and, in addition, opened up an area of research that apparently contained the conditions for the constitution of all human knowledge. He believed that it must be possible by means of the phenomenological reduction to reveal the self-givenness of basic structures and processes of meaning establishment, which constitutes the condition of possibility of the validity of the world and must hence be regarded as an a priori of this validity. He was convinced that a consistently conducted phenomenological analysis would not only reveal the meaning-establishing acts of our consciousness but can also reach a level of abstraction on which its results would gain a transcendental validity.

Thus, he suggested conceiving the phenomenological reduction as a three-step procedure. The first step would transform our specific experience into a "phenomenon" showing the acts necessary to constitute the experience as an "empirical" content of mind (for example, a table). In the second step, we would vary all possible forms of that experience and its constitutive acts to find out the typical structures that cannot be ignored if the experience (of a table) should keep its identity instead of changing into an experience of something else (a chair). So while imagining all possible forms of tables, we also become aware of typical features that are invariant for our object of imagination and that distinguishes it from all other possible objects. Husserl calls these typical structures "eidetic structures," and the procedure for how to reveal them is called the "eidetic variation."

Starting from those typical eidetic structures of consciousness, we can now reflect on the necessary conditions of consciousness to create meaningful and valid experiences that have to be given before any experiencing can start, that

is "a priori." With this step, we reach the level of a transcendental consciousness belonging to transcendental ego, which refers to the general structure representing the precondition of knowledge. In this way, Husserl (1965) supposed that he had completed the transition to philosophy as a universal, rigorous, and radical science and that he could shed light on both the foundation of knowledge in the prescientific "natural attitude" of humans and the scientific constitution of knowledge. He was convinced that phenomenological analysis meets the requirements of the sciences of nature with regard to the foundation of a theory of science by clarifying the basis of meaning of the validity of pure logic. At the same time, it would also provide a philosophical foundation of the cultural sciences showing the basic structure of meaning constitution in the "natural attitude" that underlies any constitution of knowledge, any attempt to interpret and understand the world.

But which fundamental features of the meaning constitution do appear through the prism of the phenomenological reduction? While the results of phenomenological analysis discussed above represent the structural features of consciousness and belong to the field of phenomenological research called the "static phenomenology," Husserl (1950) also developed a "genetic" phenomenological approach within "constitutive phenomenology" that stresses the temporal, processing character of consciousness and its activity. He distinguished between "active" and "passive" genesis as two types of meaning constitution. In the active constitution, we combine our experiences and create our cultural reality in its various shapes. The acts of the passive constitution are those on which our active thought is based and which are to be seen as its universal preconditions. In both cases, Husserl concentrates again on the general, that is, transcendental level of meaningful constitution of reality. Here he disclosed the temporality proper to the stream of consciousness (1966) that allows for the synthesis of separate perceptions into complex objects of thought as well as for their duration and identity in mental processes (due to this temporality—for example—we do not perceive a series of separate tones but a continuous melody that can be recognized again). As temporal objects, the "facts" and operations of our mind are always transitive and therefore changeable constructions. Secondly, there is a basic form of our lived experience based on the temporality of consciousness that Husserl (1976) calls the "noetic-noematical" structure of experience. He holds that all experience always consists of two inseparable parts: its intentional content (noema) and the specific attitude of consciousness we adopt in the moment of perception (noesis); for example, the experience of an apple becomes different if we perceive it with the feeling of hunger or in an aesthetic attitude. That means again that the contents of our consciousness are not mere "fact" but always interpreted constructions whose meaning depends on temporal configuration of their constitution.

The reflexivity and thus the cultural and historical plasticity of our consciousness is mainly based on its temporality and noetic-noematical structure. But there are not only mental acts that bestow meaning on objects of lived experience. One of the substantial sources constituting the meaning of reality for the subject is its body. From the embodied experience of reality emerges the conception of our life space in which our body represents the central point of a coordinates' system that situates ourselves in the world and leads our actions. It is also embodiment that provides a prerequisite for the reflexivity of consciousness. The experience of reflexivity results here from experiencing my own movement, on one hand, as it is experienced inwardly in kinesthesia and, on the other hand, as a movement of something that happens in the outside world. I can observe myself in one way or another; I am not clearly bound to an experience in a fixed way, but rather can take up one position or another toward it. I can exist in several conditions simultaneously, and live in more than one possibility. Husserl is, of course, aware of the fact that the conditions forming the validity of meaningful experiences cannot be described adequately as the achievement of a solitary subject. To the universal features of consciousness, creating the validity of meaningful experiences in the active genesis that phenomenological reduction can reveal, it also belongs that there are different others in the world whose meaningful acts are to be understood. One of the substantial features of the meaningful constitution of human reality consists therefore in its intersubjectivity.

The search for a solution to the problem of intersubjectivity, that is, how sociocultural knowledge is shared and the understanding of others is possible, led Husserl to his concept of lifeworld to which the final period of his work is devoted (1954). He defined the lifeworld as "a realm of original evidence" representing a transcendental structure of knowledge that is generated intersubjectively in the "natural attitude" (pp. 126–35). The concept of lifeworld, again, aims in a radicalized manner at the questions that Husserl tried to solve before. The "natural attitude" is seen here as the original mode of the human approach to the reality preceding science or philosophy and thus forming the basis of meaning for all human knowledge. It is the meaning structure of this attitude that results in a typology of the lifeworld that Husserl investigates by means of phenomenological reduction, and it is also this structure on which scientific knowledge is based. The philosophical foundation of sciences can therefore only take place by the means of radical reflection on evidence from the lifeworld.

Hence, phenomenology in this last period of Husserl's work must be understood as a science of lifeworld. But this reformulation of the task of phenomenology entails a radicalisation of Husserl's concept of the foundation of science. He contends that in their formalised and abstract form, modern sciences have become estranged from their lifeworldly

task, that is, from contributing to an understanding of the world, and have the opposite effect, that of obscuring a satisfactory worldview by repressing their lifeworldly origins (1954–1995). In order to integrate the sciences into the framework of their original humanistic purpose, we have to disclose their roots in the structure of lifeworld again. The aim of phenomenological philosophy in this sense is not to create a new system of knowledge to be implemented into society but rather to provide methods based on the *epoché* that would disclose the structure of the intersubjective, sociocultural lifeworld, that is, which would reveal the general patterns according to which people do make sense of their world. Thus, the phenomenological theory of lifeworld in Husserl's sense aims at three tasks: (1) clarification of the conditions of the intersubjective constitution of knowledge in the "natural attitude," (2) foundation of science on the basis of these conditions, and (3) a criticism of the alienated shape of sciences that results from the modernisation of society.

THE IMPACT OF PHENOMENOLOGY ON PHILOSOPHY AND SOCIAL AND CULTURAL SCIENCES

Due to its aims, phenomenology was widely perceived in the cultural and social sciences as a research programme requiring a new basic orientation in many disciplines and opening new perspectives as well as new fields of investigation. Husserl's thoughts influenced psychology and psychiatry (Ludwig Binswanger, Karl Bühler, Karl Jaspers), mathematics (Oskar Becker), linguistics (Roman Jacobson), anthropology (Frederik J. J. Buytendijk), jurisprudence (Gerhard Husserl), and sociology (Alfred Schütz). The impact of Husserl's approach was, of course crucial for the development of philosophy itself. Generations of his followers formed an influential international "Phenomenological movement" (Spiegelberg 1965), which spread phenomenological thought to Eastern Europe (Roman Ingarden in Poland, Jan Patocka in Czechoslovakia, Gustav Spet in Russia), Japan (Kitaro Nishida), and the United States (Dorion Cairns, Aron Gurwitsch). The reception of his works influenced numerous philosophers who shaped the thought of the twentieth century: the "fundamental ontology" of Martin Heidegger, the philosophy of embodiment of Maurice Merleau-Ponty, the existentialism of Jean-Paul Sartre, Ortega y Gasset's philosophy, as well as the hermeneutics of Hans-Georg Gadamer. Especially in France, Husserl's and Heidegger's approaches inspired a series of influential thinkers, such as Jean-Francois Lyotard, Paul Ricoeur, Emmanuel Levinas, Jacques Lacan, and Jacques Derrida, and offered a framework in which poststructuralist and postmodern thinking was developed. Currently, phenomenological philosophy finds creative continuation in France (Marc Richir, Michel Henry), in Germany (Bernhard

Waldenfels, Klaus Held, Elisabeth Ströker, Thomas Seebohm), in Spain (Javier San Martín, Maria Luz Pintos), in the United States (Lester Embree, Joseph J. Kockelmans, Don Ihde, John Drummond, Anna-Teresa Tymieniecka, Robert Sokolowski), in Argentina (Roberto Walton), and in Japan (Wataru Hiromatsu, Hiroshi Ichikawa, and Tani Toru).

The phenomenological approach has also provided a substantial impulse for the development of social theory. One of the most encompassing attempts to synthesise phenomenological thinking with the results of human sciences occurred in the field of "philosophical anthropology" represented by Max Scheler and Helmuth Plessner in the first decades of the twentieth century in Germany. Scheler traces the constitution of meaningful human reality to cognitive as well as the organic conditions of mankind and posited sociality as the creative process mediating between those two poles of the human existence. As a consequence of this, he conceived all forms of human knowledge as a social construction and formulated an extended concept of the sociology of knowledge. He is the first scholar who coined this term. Plessner radicalised Scheler's concept and tried to describe the "natural artificiality" of humans as a result of their natural history.

The critical intention of the lifeworld concept, which described the alienating tendencies of modernity, provided an opportunity for engagement with Marxian thought. Marx's early critique of capitalism as a restrictive social system preventing humankind from unfolding its natural conditions corresponds with the Husserlian criticism of modernity. This congruency gave birth to a "phenomenological Marxism" in the 1960s and in the 1970s (in the work of Enzo Paci, Lucien Goldmann, Pier-Aldo Rovatti, Paul Piccone, and Tran Duc Thao). This tendency was intensified by the reformulation of phenomenology in the work of Martin Heidegger (1977). Heidegger changed the basic question of Husserlian phenomenology, which asked how the world becomes valid for us, into an ontological question asking about the conditions of the being of humankind and its reality itself. He defined the mode of everyday existence as a necessary but alienated one and distinguished it from a proper existential mode that can be only gained if individuals could change their praxis and deconstruct the everyday surface of their existence. It was Herbert Marcuse, one of the leading personalities of the Frankfort school and a disciple of both Husserl and Heidegger, who synthesised the Husserlian and Heideggerian impulses with Marxian concepts and developed a radical critique of capitalism as a one-dimensional society based on alienating mass culture, science, politics, and economy. His theory strongly influenced the student protest movement in Germany and France in the 1960s and the 1970s.

Husserl's efforts to disclose the meaningful structure of the lifeworld as well as the processes of its constitution paralleled the search for interpretative approaches in the sociology initiated by Max Weber's and Georg Simmel's cultural conception of society as a context of meaningful action. If sociology is to describe society as something meaningful that always is interpreted and understood by its members, then Husserl points the way by drawing attention to the fact that the basis of constitution of meaning is to be found in the everyday practical reality of the lifeworld, that is, in the process of establishing intersubjectively valid meaning by the actors themselves in their everyday life. This mutual interest of the sociological and philosophical perspectives contains the original basis for the intrinsic affinity of phenomenology and interpretative sociology from which "phenomenological sociology," based on the work of Alfred Schütz, was to emerge. Schütz's primary intention was to give a philosophical and methodological foundation to Max Weber's concept of interpretative sociology. For this purpose, he developed a "phenomenology of mundane sociality" (Schütz 1932). He adopts the Husserlian idea of a lifeworld as a basic meaning structure of reality constituted by subjects in their "natural attitude," but he adds to the consideration of the meaning constitution in the acts of consciousness also the analysis of the meaning constitution in the everyday action and its practices themselves. Lifeworld in the sense of a meaningful social reality is then seen as a result of processes of interaction and communication. In the field of methodology, Schütz applied Husserl's idea of founding sciences on the meaning structure of the lifeworld and formulated the "postulate of adequacy," urging scientific concepts in sociology to respect the features of everyday knowledge of actors. Called "phenomenological sociology" (Psathas 1973) or "sociology of everyday life," the Schützian approach has gained paradigmatic relevance in the interpretative social sciences as well as in the theory of action since the second half of the twentieth century. In the United States, where a theoretical alternative to the Parsonian system theory was sought, the Schützian concept served as a starting point for new approaches in sociological theory focussing on the constitution of social reality in everyday practices of actions. Due to the reception of Schütz's theory since the 1960s, the attention of sociology was drawn to inquiries into everyday interaction and communication as well as to the insight that society has to be considered as a construction produced in these processes. Sociologists influenced by Schütz started to examine the practices of everyday action, communication, and interpretation from which social reality emerges. Harold Garfinkel's ethnomethodology, aimed at the formal properties of everyday practices, led to a series of case studies covering a wide range of everyday life in society and its institutions. Examinations of everyday communication in continuation of this research were provided by Emmanuel A. Schegloff and Harvey Sacks, whose conversation analysis became a widespread method in qualitative sociological research. Aron Cicourel's cognitive sociology reveals the constructed character of data in social institutions as well as in science and thus initiated a series of studies in the sociology of organisation and the sociology of science. Also, Erving Goffman's investigations into the logic of everyday interaction draws inspiration from phenomenological theory. The social construction of reality was conceived by Peter L. Berger and Thomas Luckmann (1966) as a general process by which cultural worlds emerge. Their work gave new impulse to both the sociology of knowledge and the sociology of culture (reconceived now in terms of mundane phenomenology). In this context, the Schützian impact can be seen in the sociology of language and in the sociology of religion (Berger, Luckmann). The spread and the empirical application of the Schützian approach enforced the search for qualitative research methods. In addition to ethnomethodology and conversation analysis, this search led to a refinement in the techniques of narrative interviews and in biographical research. At the present time, phenomenologically oriented approaches in social theory as well as in social research are at work in the United States (George Psathas, Egon Bittner, Edward Rose), in Japan (Kazuhisa Hishihara, Hisashi Nasu, Mototaka Mori, Yoshikuni Yatani), in England (Christian Heath), in France (Daniel Cefai), in Switzerland (Thomas Eberle), and in Germany (Thomas Luckmann, Hansfried Kellner, Richard Grathoff, Ilja Srubar, and Walter L. Bühl), where the phenomenological approach developed into a variety of theoretical contributions to methods and research fields. The ongoing research in the sociology of knowledge, culture, communication, and language (Thomas Luckmann, Roland Hitzler, Hubert Knoblauch, Angela Keppler, Bruno Hildenbrand, Jörg Bergmann, Ilja Srubar) was paralleled by methodological reflection and has led to new concepts of social hermeneutics (Hans-Georg Soeffner), social ethnography (Anne Honer) and social geography (Benno Werlen).

Once established in the 1970s, the phenomenological paradigm influenced the mainstream of sociological theorizing. *Lifeworld* in the sense of a basic level of social reality provided by humans in their "natural" intercourse became one of the central terms in social theory and was widely accepted as a concept allowing for an approach to the culture strata of social reality (Clifford Geertz, Zygmunt Bauman). The Husserlian opposition of lifeworld and formalised science often transformed in this perspective to an opposition between social reality formed in informal spontaneous interactions and social systems structured by powers of political and economic institutions. Along these lines, Jürgen Habermas contrasts the lifeworld as a basic stratum of social reality where spontaneous communication takes place to the "system" understood as societal structures where alienating pressures of domination and economics prevail. In a similar manner, Anthony Giddens distinguishes in his theory of social structuration between social and systemic integration and suggests conceiving the processes of social integration as everyday practices in the sense of the phenomenological paradigm. Pierre Bourdieu's work, which—similar to Anthony Giddens's—seeks to overcome the gap between the microlevel theories of action and the macrolevel of systemic approaches, also draws important impulses from phenomenological sociology. His concept of "*le sens pratique*" leading to everyday actions as well as his idea of "habitus," as embodied patterns of social structure forming the individual preferences to collective lifestyles, emerge from the phenomenological ideas of the lifewordly "natural attitude" and of embodiment as a basic feature of a meaningful human approach to reality. The phenomenological conception of meaning constitution reformulated in the sense of an autopoiesis (self-creation) of social and psychic systems also influenced the development of the contemporary system theory in sociology (Niklas Luhmann). Luhmann's "radical constructivism" conceives the psychic, as well as the social systems, as meaning-processing structures. Husserl's description of meaning constitution in the activity of consciousness represents for Luhmann a paradigm of the systemic self-generation of reality that is proper to the psychic systems, while parallel self-creating processes based on communication are fundamental to social systems. Thus, the evolution of societies is only explainable as a coevolution of both the conscious and the communicative self-creation of reality. Even if many of the authors mentioned above transcend the field of "phenomenological sociology," the results of the phenomenological paradigm are deeply embedded in contemporary sociology.

— Ilja Srubar

See also Bauman, Zygmunt; Bourdieu, Pierre; Frankfurt School; Garfinkel, Harold; Giddens, Anthony; Goffman, Erving, Habermas, Jürgen; Luhmann, Niklas; Scheler, Max; Schütz, Alfred

FURTHER READINGS AND REFERENCES

Bell, David. 1990. *Husserl.* London: Routledge.

Berger, Peter L. and Thomas Luckmann. 1966. *The Social Construction of Reality.* New York: Doubleday.

Biemel, Walter. 1959. "Die entscheidenden Phasen der Entfaltung von Husserls Philosophie." *Zeitschrift für philosophische Forschung* 13:187–214.

Bühl, Walter L. 2002. *Phänomenologische Soziologie.* Konstanz, Germany: Universitätsverlag.

Embree, Lester et al., eds. 1997. *Encyclopedia of Phenomenology.* Dordrecht, Netherlands: Kluwer.

Heidegger, Martin. [1911] 1965. *Phänomenologie als strenge Wissesnchaft.* Frankfurt, Germany: M. Klostermann.

———. [1913] 1976. *Ideen zu einer reinen Phänomenologie und phänomenologischen Philosophie, Erstes Buch, Huserliana 3/l.*

The Hague, Netherlands: Nijhoff. Translated as *Ideas Pertaining to a Pure Phenomenology and to a Phenomenological Philosophy*. First Book (The Hague, Netherlands: Nijhoff, 1982).

———. [1927] 1977. *Sein und Zeit*. Frankfurt, Germany: M Kostermann.

———. [1928] 1966. *Zur Phänomenologie des inneren Zeitbewußtseins, Husserliana 10*. The Hague, Netherlands: Nijhoff. Translated as *On the Phenomenology of the Consciousness of Internal Time* (Dordrecht, Netherlands: Kluwer, 1991).

———. [1931] 1950. *Cartesianische Meditationen und Pariser Vorträge, Husserliana 1*. The Hague, Netherlands: Nijhoff. Translated as *Cartesian Meditations* (The Hague, Netherlands: Nijhoff. 1960).

———. [1936] 1954. *Die Krisis der europäischen Wissenschaften und die transzendentale Phänomenologie, Husserliana 6*: The Hague, Netherlands: Nijhoff. Translated as *The Crisis of European Sciences and the Transcendental Phenomenology* (Evanston, IL: Northwestern University Press 1970).

———. 1962. *Being and Time*. New York: Harper & Row.

Husserl, Edmund. [1900–1901] 1975–1984. *Logische Untersuchungen*. 2 vols. The Hague, Netherlands: Nijhoff. Translated as *Logical Investigations* (London: Routledge & Kegan Paul, 1970).

Psathas, George, ed. 1973. *Phenomenological Sociology, Issues and Applications*. New York: John Wiley.

Schütz, Alfred. 1932. *Der sinnhafte Aufbau der sozialen Welt*. Vienna, Austria: Springer. Translated as *The Phenomenology of the Social World* (Evanston, IL: Northwestern University Press, 1967).

Spiegelberg, Herbert. 1965. *The Phenomenological Movement*. The Hague, Netherlands: Nijhoff.

PHILOSOPHICAL ANTHROPOLOGY

In contrast to empirical, biological, as well as cultural and social anthropology, the aim of philosophical anthropology is to take up and tie together the results of such empirical research to come to fundamental and comprehensive statements on the peculiar nature and form of the existence of humans. Important contributions to philosophical anthropology have been made by Johann Gottfried Herder and in particular by Immanuel Kant (*Anthropologie in pragmatischer Hinsicht abgefasst* 1798) and Ludwig Feuerbach, who for his part adopted pivotal themes from French Enlightenment thinkers (Helvetius, d'Holbach, D'Alembert, Voltaire). Ludwig Feuerbach's criticism and inversion of theology became decisive for the Marxian perspective, especially Marxist anthropology.

In Feuerbach and Marx and later in the work of Friedrich Nietzsche, anthropology is regarded not as a part of philosophy but as the only possible "primary philosophy." As such, philosophical anthropology takes the part of the traditional ontology (in terms of an onto-theology) or metaphysics: "The new philosophy makes man . . . the *only, universal* and *most prominent* subject of philosophy—the anthropology thus . . . an universal science" (Feuerbach *Werke*:3:319). In this a tendency is expressed that has become a characteristic principle for modern philosophy as a whole, namely, in Martin Heidegger's (1963) words, to conduct reasoning "starting from man and towards man" (p. 86).

This far-reaching intention loses its predominance in the philosophical anthropology of the twentieth century. Here, above all, the works of Max Scheler (*Die Stellung des Menschen im Kosmos* [Man's Place in Nature]), Helmut Plessner (*Die Stufen des Organischen und der Mensch* [Man and the Stages of the Organic]) and Arnold Gehlen (*Der Mensch. Seine Natur und seine Stellung in der Welt* [Man: His Nature and His Place in the World]) have to be mentioned. Their influence on sociological theorizing all in all was not as strong as could have been expected for material reasons. For the most part, this may be explained by the fact that these works were not translated into English or only with great delay. However, especially phenomenological sociology was inspired substantially by the thinking of Helmut Plessner, while the anthropology of Arnold Gehlen and the theory of institutions founded on Gehlen's work became seminal for one of the most influential works of twentieth-century sociological theory, Peter L. Berger's and Thomas Luckmann's *The Social Construction of Reality*. Furthermore, this anthropology supplied decisive philosophical presuppositions for Niklas Luhmann's "functional structural" theory of social systems, especially with its assumption of an essential openness to the world (*Weltoffenheit*) and of homo sapiens as a "deficient being" (*Maengelwesen*).

The pivotal axiom of philosophical anthropology was already formulated by Herder, when he spoke of man as the "nondetermined" animal. This living being can only exist if it behaves toward itself and toward the reality surrounding it and if it defines and interprets itself and its world. In this sense, Gehlen says, "By nature man is a cultural being." Similarly, Ernst Cassirer has defined man by extending the traditional designation of man as animal rationale and by describing him as "animal symbolicum" (meaning, a symbol-using animal).

The destination, even constraint, to culture is, according to the concurring insight of philosophical anthropology, not to be added to the naturalness of humanity; rather, it is intended if not demanded by this naturalness (defined by eccentricity, reduction of instinct, abundance of impetus, brain of great volume, upright walk). In this respect, philosophical anthropology contradicts a dualism of body and soul, as it has, deriving from Descartes, dominated modern philosophy for a long time. Likewise, philosophical anthropology opposes old and new variants of an anthropological reductionism, where humans are explained either exclusively by their animality (as recently in certain directions of sociobiology or molecular biology) or is understood in the way of machines which they themselves have created. The latter also arose very early (cf. Jean d'Alembert's "l'homme machine") and refers nowadays above all to research on artificial intelligence and the development of intelligent machines (robots) inspired by it.

The criticism of philosophical anthropology is directed against a view according to which one could reach in this way at last a substantial, definite, and absorptive definition of humanity. Seen from its perspective, it is a question of a possible but by no means exclusive and concluding kind of self-interpretation of humanity that has its own reasons and merits but also its specific preconditions, limits, and problematic implications.

Philosophical anthropology stands in a peculiar relation of affinity and rivalry with the philosophy of existence, which, too, following its predecessor Søren Kierkegaard, emerged in the first half of the twentieth century (Karl Jaspers, Martin Heidegger, Jean-Paul Sartre). Because the philosophy of existence does not treat humanity on the whole and in general but the particular existing human being, it issues a challenge for sociology. This challenge has rarely been picked up in sociology so far, most of all by the mediation of recent French social theories (Michel Foucault, Jacques Derrida, etc.), who themselves are frequently assigned to a "historical anthropology."

— Johannes Weiss

See also Body; Cassirer, Ernst; Culture and Civilization; Derrida, Jacques; Foucault, Michel; Luhmann, Niklas; Marx, Karl; Sartre, Jean-Paul; Scheler, Max

FURTHER READINGS AND REFERENCES

Bidney, David. 1966. *"Ernst Cassirers Stellung in der Geschichte der philosophischen Anthropologie."* Pp. 335–403 in *Ernst Cassirer,* edited by Paul A. Schilpp. Stuttgart, Germany: Kohlhammer. Originally published in *The Philosophy of Ernst Cassirer,* edited by P. A. Schilpp (Evanston, IL: Library of Living Philosophers, 1949).

Cassirer, Ernst. 1944. *An Essay on Man: An Introduction to a Philosophy of Human Culture.* New Haven, CT: Yale University Press.

Feuerbach, Ludwig. 1975. *Werke in sechs Bänden.* Vol. 3. Frankfurt, Germany: Suhrkamp.

Gehlen, Arnold. [1962] 1988. *Man: His Nature and His Place in the World.* 7th ed. New York: Columbia University Press. Originally published as *Der Mensch. Seine Natur und seine Stellung in der Welt.* 7th ed. (Frankfurt, Germany: Klostermann, 1940).

Heidegger, Martin. 1963. *Holzwege.* Frankfurt, Germany: V. Klostermann.

Kant, Immanuel. [1798] 1964. "Anthropologie in pragmatischer Hinsicht abgefasst." Pp. 399–690 in *Werke* 12. Frankfurt, Germany: Suhrkamp.

Plessner, Helmut. [1928] 1965. *Die Stufen des Organischen und der Mensch* [Man and the States of the Organic]. 2d ed. Berlin, Germany: de Gruyter.

Scheler, Max. 1961. *Man's Place in Nature.* New York: Noonday Press. Originally published as *Die Stellung des Menschen im Kosmos* (Muenchen, Germany: Nymphenburger Verlagsbuchhandlung, 1928).

POLITICAL ECONOMY

Until about 1880, the term *political economy* encompassed the area of social thought subsequently known as economics, and a great deal besides. More recently, it has acquired a range of different meanings. With the rise to dominance of neoclassical economics in the twentieth century, it was used increasingly in reference to nonneoclassical economics, and particularly to Marxian theory. Heterodox economists have largely concurred, describing their own work as political economy in order to distinguish it from the mainstream. However, in recent decades, orthodoxy itself has come to embrace what it regards as legitimate political economies that seek to explain institutions, including those of politics, along with government policies, in terms of rational choice theory. This entry concentrates on Marxian political economy, which is still the predominant reference of the term. It begins with the classical predecessors of Marx and ends with an outline of the development of political economies within neoclassical theory.

Classical political economy emerged toward the end of the seventeenth century and flourished in the eighteenth century with the work of the Physiocrats in France and their Scottish contemporaries, above all Adam Smith, whose *Wealth of Nations* (1776) was a major landmark. It reached its peak in the early nineteenth century with Ricardo's great *Principles of Political Economy and Taxation* (1817). These classical writers concentrated their attention on the production and distribution of the means of subsistence. They explained the evolution of modern economies in terms of the fundamental conflict between the different social classes in a predominantly agricultural society where the producers enjoyed a bare minimum standard of living and the surplus product was shared between landlords and capitalist farmers. The size of the surplus, relative to total output, set a maximum limit on the rate of growth; actual growth depended on the relative shares of thrifty capitalists and prodigal landlords. In most versions of classical political economy, the rate of profit on capital was expected to fall, and with it the rate of economic growth; Ricardo and many of his contemporaries anticipated an eventual stationary state, where growth would simply peter out. This classical vision of political economy, formalized and extended to deal with industrial production and much else, was rehabilitated after 1960 by theorists influenced by the Cambridge-Italian economist Piero Sraffa (Kurz and Salvadori 1995).

Marx saw himself as the heir of classical political economy. He argued that, beginning in the 1820s, honest scientific investigation had increasingly given way to apologetics, as economists' emphasis shifted from questions of production, distribution, and accumulation toward the much less important issues of individual consumption decisions and market relationships. For this reason, he paid little attention to post-Ricardian economic thought, but no doubt, he would have condemned the neoclassical economics that rose to dominance after 1880 as evidence of continuing intellectual decay. "Vulgar economy," for Marx, was both ideologically driven and superficial in nature. Classical political economy, in contrast, had represented an honest and profound attempt to understand the operation of the capitalist mode of production, penetrating beneath the surface world of mere appearances to expose the underlying reality.

Marx defined the subject matter of the political economy of capitalism as the production, distribution, consumption, and exchange of commodities, which are useful products of human labour destined for sale on markets rather than for direct use. Moreover, in Marxian political economy, production is privileged in its explanatory status over the other categories. This is true not only for the explanation of distribution, consumption, and exchange, but also for the nature of the state and forms of social consciousness. Here there is a continuation and significant refinement of Adam Smith's "four stages theory of history" and a sharp difference with neoclassical economics, which privileges consumption and exchange and has until very recently ignored most other matters of concern to political economy.

HISTORICAL MATERIALISM

According to the principle of historical materialism, the relations that define the economic system, and the institutions of politics and the law, as well as the dominant forms of social consciousness, are all ultimately determined by the requirements of the productive forces, which consist of means of production and human labour power. The productive relations are relations of power, and usually also of ownership, over the productive forces. Three propositions are central to historical materialism. The development thesis states that human creative intelligence, reacting to scarcity, makes the productive forces develop over time. The primacy thesis asserts that it is the level of development reached by the productive forces that explains the nature of the productive relations, which in turn account for the nature of the superstructure (noneconomic institutions such as the legal

system and the state). Most important for the dynamic of history, the fettering thesis states that, when the productive relations become a shackle on the development of the productive forces, they will change in order to break the fetters.

Marx distinguished several modes of production, characterised by the different ways in which surplus labour was performed and the resulting surplus product was appropriated. In primitive communism, there was little or no surplus and no class stratification. In classical antiquity, the critical social relation was that between slaves and slave-owners, while under the feudal mode of production, surplus labour was extracted through the serf's obligation to work, without remuneration, for several days each week on the lord's land. In none of these early modes of production were market relations of overriding importance; the production of commodities was not central to the way in which they operated. In classical antiquity and feudalism, the exploitation of the producers was directly observable. Capitalism, by contrast, is defined by the dominance of commodity production and above all by the fact that human labour power has itself become a commodity. This gives rise to the appearance that every hour of work is paid for, concealing the underlying reality of surplus labour, which is now produced in the form of surplus value (see below).

The theory of historical materialism maintains that the classical, feudal, and capitalist modes of production followed each other in chronological sequence, each serving at first to develop the forces of production but eventually becoming a fetter upon them. Capitalism would in its turn give way to socialism/communism, which, Marx believed, constituted the final stage in the unfettering of human productive potential, with the eventual abolition of the market and the direct regulation of production by society in accordance with genuine human needs. This claim has proved extremely contentious, however, and the remainder of this entry is devoted to the political economy of capitalism, which has been the core of all Marxian theory.

There are two additional areas of controversy. The first is Marx's assertion that there was a unique *Asiatic mode of production,* which he invoked to explain the allegedly unchanging nature of Indian and Chinese society for many centuries prior to the impact of European colonisation. The second is the suggestion that classless, *simple,* or *petty commodity production* constituted a further mode of production, either during the transition from feudalism to capitalism in Western Europe or (a much more ambitious claim, associated more closely with Friedrich Engels than with Marx) in many parts of the world for millennia prior to the emergence of capitalism.

CAPITALISM

Most of the central features of the capitalist mode of production were identified by Marx and Engels as early as

1848 in the *Communist Manifesto,* and their analysis has formed the basis for all subsequent developments in Marxian political economy. These core features are: exploitation; alienation and fetishism; compulsion to accumulate; concentration and centralisation of capital; constant revolutionising of the means of production; global expansion; social and economic polarisation; intensification of class conflict; increasingly severe economic crises, accompanied by the growth of a reserve army of unemployed workers; development of socialist relations within capitalism; and the eventual replacement of capitalism by socialism/communism through proletarian revolution.

The defining characteristic of capitalism is the relationship between wage labourers and capitalists: capital is defined as a social relation, not as a sum of value or a collection of machines and buildings. In this relationship, workers are not only exploited, that is, forced to perform surplus labour or required to work for longer than would be necessary to produce the means of subsistence that they need to keep them alive and able to work, but they are also alienated, in the sense that the products of their labour have escaped their control and have instead become external forces that increasingly dominate their own producers. Marx sometimes referred to alienation as human self-estrangement, meaning by this that although people exist in a social world of their own collective making, they relate to it only as strangers. They do not control their own lives but instead are, predominantly, the puppets of structural forces. Alienation is an objective social condition. Its reflection in human consciousness takes the form of commodity fetishism, a distorted view of the economic world in which historically contingent social relations are seen as the natural properties of things. "Vulgar economy," with its exaggerated emphasis upon consumption and its marginal productivity theory of income distribution, is one influential example of this fetishism of commodities.

All premodern legal, political, religious, and cultural constraints on competition are progressively eliminated as capitalism develops and the pressure on individual capitalists intensifies. Machine production drives out the earlier technology of manufacturing (literally, making things by hand), so that the economic advantages of large-scale production are increasingly evident and the processes of concentration and centralisation of capital accelerate. Individual units of capital become larger, and the number of capitalists able to survive in any branch of industry diminishes. Peasants, petty traders, and small handicraft producers disappear as the polarisation of society between large capitalists and propertyless wage labourers becomes more and more extreme. Increasingly, this occurs on a global scale, as capitalists pursue a world market for their commodities.

Hours of work increase, as do the intensity of labour and the workers' experience of alienation. Real wages may fall, remain constant, or even rise somewhat, but relative to profits they continually decline, and the insecurity of proletarian existence grows. This is the material basis for increasingly acute class conflict, which is accentuated by the socialising effects of the factory system. Working-class radicalism is further provoked by periodic economic crises, which throw many of them out of work and demonstrate that capitalism has itself now become a fetter on the development of the productive forces. Its own technology and social organisation point unerringly toward the socialist/communist future that will be realised, sooner rather than later, through proletarian revolution.

This vision of the capitalist mode of production has guided all subsequent work in Marxian political economy, although there has inevitably been dissent on many specific issues. Marx and (especially) Engels were forced to reassess their expectations concerning the increasing severity of economic crises and the pauperisation and homogenisation of the working class, and also to consider the possibility (for example, in Russia) that peasants rather than proletarians might be the first to create a socialist future. From the 1890s, revisionists like Eduard Bernstein argued that peaceful, piecemeal reform of the capitalist system would not only benefit the workers but also permit a gradual and nonviolent transition to democratic socialism. They were opposed by more orthodox Marxists, some of the most important of whom, including Karl Kautsky and Rudolf Hilferding, later came to accept much of the revisionist position. In the 1920s, Hilferding finally identified a new stage of development, which he termed "organised capitalism," in which the most objectionable features of competitive capitalism had been superseded by the growth of monopoly, increased trade union power, and government regulation of the market in the interests of the working class.

Against them, the revolutionaries, such as Vladimir Ilych Lenin and Rosa Luxemburg, maintained that capitalism had reached the new and much more dangerous stage of imperialism, in which the means of violence monopolised by the state were used by capitalists to suppress the working class at home and to extend their reach across the globe. In Stalinist orthodoxy, these ideas were crystallised in the conception of state monopoly capitalism as the last, decadent, and by far the most vicious stage of the capitalist mode of production. Echoes of both the reformist and the revolutionary positions can be found in the post-1945 literature on the stages of capitalist development, including Paul Baran's and Paul Sweezy's analysis of monopoly capital, Ernest Mandel's notion of late capitalism, and the work of the French regulation school.

VALUE AND EXPLOITATION

Marx attempted to formalise his vision of capitalism into a systematic model of accumulation and crisis. For this he needed a theory of value so that the fundamental relationships could be expressed in a clear and coherent manner. The *qualitative* dimension of Marx's value theory expresses the profound but frequently neglected truth that a social division of labour underpins each individual act of market exchange. People relate to each other not merely through buying and selling in the marketplace but also, and more fundamentally, by cooperating in a social process of production. Since the physical properties of commodities differ, the only quality that they have in common is that they are products of human labour, and this defines their value. The *quantitative* dimension of Marx's theory of value is concerned with the magnitude of value. This, he argued, depends on the amount of labour embodied in a commodity, although this need not and in fact normally will not equal the price at which the commodity is actually sold.

Marx distinguished dead from living labour, where dead labour is contained in the produced means of production (machinery and raw materials) that are used in the course of production. Only part of the workers' living labour is paid for; their unpaid or surplus labour is what produces surplus value (s), which is in turn the source of profit, interest, and rent. Capital has two components. The first is constant capital (c), the value of which is merely transferred from the means of production to the final product without increasing in quantity. The second is variable capital (v), embodied in the wage-goods consumed by the workers, which expands its value during production because of the performance of surplus labour. Thus the value of any particular commodity has three components, c, v, and s, and the same is true of the total product of society as a whole.

Some of the difficulties with this quantitative labour theory of value were acknowledged by Marx himself, in particular the problems associated with the payment of rent, the distinction between productive and unproductive activities, the application of the law of value to the market for labour power, and the continuing diversity of the working class in terms of its skills and capabilities. Even more troublesome was the so-called transformation problem. Competition in the market for labour power would tend to equalize the rate of exploitation ($e = s/v$) in all industries, but there was no reason to suppose that the ratio of constant to variable capital (which Marx termed the organic composition of capital, $k = c/v$) would also be equalized. This would lead to differences in the rate of profit (r) between industries, since $r = s/(c + v) = (s/v)/(c/v) + (v/v) = e/k + 1$. In a competitive capitalist economy, however, such differences are inconsistent with the free mobility of capital. Marx's solution was to distinguish the labour value of a commodity from the price of production at which it was actually sold and also to distinguish the profits accruing to individual capitalists from the surplus value produced by their workers. In industries with an above-average organic composition of capital, price of production would exceed value, and profits would be greater than surplus value; the reverse would be true if the organic composition was below the average. In aggregate, though, the sum of values would equal the sum of prices, and more important, the sum of profits would equal the sum of surplus value. Marx concluded that value determined price and surplus value determined profit, even though competition inevitably transformed the first of these categories into the second.

There are well-known objections to Marx's solution to the transformation problem, and many subsequent writers have attempted to improve on it. The reformulation of Ricardian economics by Piero Sraffa pointed the way to a more satisfactory solution to the transformation problem than Marx was able to provide but also suggested the irrelevance of the entire discussion, since a theory of value founded on the objective conditions of production rather than on the subjective preferences of individuals does not require that any reference be made to labour values, and the existence of exploitation can be established independently of the notion of surplus value. These claims remain profoundly controversial.

ACCUMULATION AND CRISIS

In Volume 2 of *Capital*, Marx used his value categories to set out a formal model of capital accumulation and to explain why the process of accumulation necessarily involved cyclical crises. He distinguished two sectors, one producing capital goods and the other consumer goods; sometimes he drew a further distinction between wage-goods and luxuries. His models of simple reproduction (zero growth) and expanded reproduction (positive growth) reveal that the rate of accumulation depends on the proportion of surplus value that capitalists decide or are compelled to devote to accumulation, and also on the rate of profit. Marx's objective here was not to demonstrate that smooth growth was likely but precisely the opposite: to show why it is not likely to occur.

Specific numerical relations between the sectors are necessary (but not sufficient) for smooth growth to occur; disproportionality will lead to crises, perhaps in the form of underconsumption, which occurs when the incomes of the working class are too small to allow wage-goods to be purchased at prices that realise the surplus value (profit) contained in them. Interpreted as a contradiction of the capitalist mode of production, underconsumption was probably the majority view among the Marxian political economists of the Second and Third Internationals. It survived after 1945 through the work of Josef Steindl and of Paul Baran and Paul Sweezy.

An alternative (and inconsistent) account, also found in Marx, is in terms of cyclical movements in the rate of exploitation due to fluctuations in the size of the reserve army of the unemployed. In boom conditions, when unemployment falls, real wages tend to rise and the pace of work slackens. This reduces both the rate of exploitation and the rate of profit, causing capitalists to cut back on accumulation, thereby provoking a realization crisis of a different nature from that produced by underconsumption. In 1967, Richard Goodwin formalised Marx's insights into a mathematical model of the business cycle that represents one of the earliest examples of chaotic dynamics in political economy. Less formal arguments were often used by Marxists to explain the profit squeeze crisis of the later 1960s/early 1970s.

In Volume 3 of *Capital,* Marx developed a model of the falling rate of profit that was inspired by that of Ricardo but was also very different. Ricardo had relied on the Malthusian population principle, together with diminishing returns in agriculture, to generate a falling rate of profit. Marx emphasized rising productivity, reflected in a tendency for the organic composition of capital to increase more rapidly than the rate of exploitation. His analysis was neglected by later generations of Marxian political economists, with a few notable exceptions such as Henryk Grossmann, but it was revived in the 1970s and given an essentialist twist, in which the falling rate of profit was seen as an inescapable necessity in any advanced capitalist economy. Powerful objections were raised to this, and to Marx's less dogmatic prognosis, by critics like Natalie Moszkowska, Joan Robinson, Ronald Meek, and Nobuo Okishio.

If the rate of profit does tend to fall, either because of a rising organic composition or a declining rate of exploitation or persistent underconsumption, this will eventually result in a falling rate of accumulation, which would vindicate the fettering thesis that is central to historical materialism. But this again remains very contentious.

NEOCLASSICAL POLITICAL ECONOMY

Marx ignored neoclassical economics, and Marxists subsequently have continued the neglect, believing it to be superficial and ideological. For their part, neoclassicals have reciprocated in kind, claiming that it is they who are genuinely scientific and regarding Marxism as an (unappealing) political project riddled with analytic errors and empirical inaccuracies. Moreover, there has been a marked difference in focus, with neoclassicals traditionally ignoring the problems at the heart of Marxian political economy and concentrating instead on the equilibria achievable by optimising consumers and producers operating in well-developed markets. Typically, neoclassicals have paid no attention to how actual markets have emerged and changed, or with what class structures and political forms they have been associated, and neoclassicals have also tended to believe markets are capable of fully reconciling diverse interests and coordinating action. However, in the latter half of the twentieth century, and particularly since the 1970s,

neoclassical economics has evolved various forms of political economy. Three strands are now evident.

First, the approach associated with Gary Becker and James Buchanan centres on the belief that rational choice in the context of scarcity is the most important quality in all human action. Hence, the concepts and theorems of traditional neoclassicism are not limited to economic analysis narrowly understood, but constitute a science of society, including politics. All social processes are considered analogues of the market, and the basic results of established neoclassical theory are generalised beyond the contexts of their original formulation.

Second, beginning with Kenneth Arrow and Mancur Olson, there has been a broader appreciation of the importance of public and collective goods, along with the significance of nonmarket provisioning institutions. Arrow's *Social Choice and Individual Values* (1951) used neoclassical reasoning to argue inter alia that genuine liberal democracy was incapable of consistent decision making unless preferences took restricted forms. The relevance for political economy is obvious, and a massive amount of research has since been devoted to elaborating, extending, and amending Arrow's results. The influence of Mancur Olson's *Logic of Collective Action* (1965) has, if anything, been even more substantial, discussing as it does the circumstances in which atomised and rational individuals can cooperate in collective action to achieve common interests, and when they are most likely to fail to do so. Olson himself used his theory very innovatively, analysing, among many other problems, the emergence of the state, the development of democracy, and the collapse of communism.

Third, two concepts—transactions costs and asymmetric information—previously on the margins of neoclassical economics have been elevated into the core by Oliver Williamson and Joseph Stiglitz. This has brought major changes to conclusions about the types of integration achievable through markets and the efficiency of various nonmarket processes. Transactions costs, as distinct from production costs, are those associated with mechanisms of coordination, such as hierarchical command, markets, and networks, as well as coercion and violence, and they can be appealed to as important determinants of the different and changing mixtures of these institutions evident in all societies throughout history. The closely related idea of asymmetric information refers to circumstances in which different people interested in transacting with each other have different information about what is to be exchanged, and this can be used to account for the different institutional forms in a way similar to that provided by a direct appeal to differential transactions costs.

As a consequence of these developments, neoclassical economics has generated political economies in which economic phenomena are held to be significant determinants of the political arrangements characterising different societies.

They have also affected Marxism, with the emergence in the 1970s of a "rational choice Marxism" that attempted to marry the rational choice perspective of neoclassical economics with the problems typically treated by Marxism. Nonetheless, it remains the case that the bulk of Marxists, and also the majority of neoclassicals, would repudiate the union.

— Michael C. Howard and John E. King

See also Alienation; Capitalism; Historical Materialism; Imperialism; Marx, Karl; Marxism; Means of Production; Socialism

REFERENCES AND FURTHER READINGS

Brewer, A. 1984. *A Guide to Marx's Capital.* Cambridge, UK: Cambridge University Press.

Cohen, Gerald A. 1978. *Karl Marx's Theory of History: A Defense.* Princeton, NJ: Princeton University Press.

Dobb, Maurice H. 1973. *Theories of Value and Distribution since Adam Smith.* Cambridge, UK: Cambridge University Press.

Eggertson, Thráinn. 1990. *Economic Behaviour and Institutions.* Cambridge, UK: Cambridge University Press.

Howard, Michael C. and John E. King. 1985. *The Political Economy of Marx.* 2d ed. Harlow, UK: Longman.

———. 1989. *A History of Marxian Economics.* Vol. 1, *1883–1929.* London: Macmillan.

———. 1992. *A History of Marxian Economics.* Vol. 2, *1929–1990.* London: Macmillan.

Kurz, Heinz D. and Neri Salvadori. 1995. *Theory of Production.* Cambridge, UK: Cambridge University Press.

POPULAR MUSIC

Popular music describes music intended for consumption by a mass public, containing imagery and voicing feelings, needs, and desires of ordinary people, mostly about interpersonal love or loss. It also comments on, or protests, aspects of personal existence or public policy (or its lack). Most commonly, the term refers to music as a cultural commodity, created by professional musicians, recorded by and marketed by media corporations, to be sold to the mass public. Originally, the term denoted an authentic expressive creation by nonprofessional musicians, now sometimes called folk music (or related categories of country or blues or ethnic music), opposed to studio, professional, high, classical, or art music. Rarely in the twentieth and twenty-first centuries does popular music occur in an unmediated form. All popular music is influenced by earlier models. As early as the sixteenth century, sheet music for sale existed in the form of "broadside" cheap printed songs on single sheets of paper, designed to be sung by anyone, some selling as many as 2.5 million copies.

Before the twentieth century, a supposed "traditional culture" served as background for a musical culture in which authentic traditional music was transmitted via oral means, without writing or mechanical/electronic recording. In the regional folk, country, and blues traditions in the United States, such oral transmissions occurred in the nineteenth and early twentieth centuries, but since the spread of recordings for home use and advent of radio in the 1920s, most "popular" music has reflected their influences. Instead of gathering to hear songs played or sung by family members, learned via oral transmission (or from printed sheet music), people listened to radio broadcasts of singers, such as Bing Crosby, or the Grand Ol' Opry. The latter radio program began on radio station WSM, Nashville, Tennessee, in 1925, representing an idealized, nostalgic public notion of a southern and rural American regional culture, itself in the process of erosion and change.

Erosion of U.S. regional musical culture was a complex process. Phonograph records in the South, from the beginning of recording, sold to markets wanting to hear their own kinds of music. As early as 1923, U.S. record companies sent talent scouts to comb the South for local musicians, who were recorded and sold to black and white populations in those areas and marketed to other areas of the country. The complex process of mediation of allegedly natural or authentic or folk forms of popular music is illustrated by the primitive black bluesman Howlin Wolf (Chester Burnett), born in the Mississippi Delta region in 1910, becoming known during the 1940s in Memphis for his distinctive falsetto moan, once thought to have been acquired via the oral transmission process in his original home, the Delta. Yet Wolf said he developed his style through emulating the blue yodel on records of *white* singer Jimmy Rodgers, known as the singing brakeman, who dominated the popular music industry in the years 1927 to his death in 1933, virtually creating a national style of popular country music, recorded in northeastern studios by RCA Victor and sold across the nation on Victor 78 RPM records. Rodgers was the first major country music performer to use unidentified sidemen in the studio, including jazz great Louis Armstrong, establishing the common pattern in popular music of "the star" and anonymous accompaniment. Rodgers's career illustrates the complex process of mediation of "natural" and "folk" forms of popular music, providing an example of ethnic cross-influence and interaction, all based on a process of oral and aural transmission, combining personal appearances in local settings with the individualized listening via phonograph records and radio (and, later, from the 1940s on, via television) that continue into the twenty-first century on HBO and MTV.

Popular music in the present era is a part of a complex cultural process: its products highly mediated cultural commodities, yet not imposed on an unsuspecting public by what T.W. Adorno once called "the culture industries." Popular music, no matter how commodified, has, like other cultural commodities, always been directed by its creators and distributors at the preferences of particular demographic sectors of the larger population. Its market, like the market for popular film, is complex and difficult to predict. While records cost much less than movies, more than 60 percent of commercial recordings are heard by nobody— never bought or played on the air; only a small percentage of the rest cover their cost of production. Only 1 percent to 2 percent of releases generate major sales and significant revenue for companies. Most songs played on radio are heard by a small percentage of listeners. Once heard, a still smaller percentage of recordings are actually bought. Only then, as mass popular musical commodities, are they available for use in personal efforts at self-definition or identity creation, and—perhaps unconsciously, among smaller numbers—as part of a quest for free space and affective emotional alternatives. Popular music is also used in creating community, responding to and critiquing the stresses and anxieties of social transformation, in nostalgic reflecting back on the erosion and loss of earlier ways of life, or—in a minority of cases—as a form of cultural resistance.

Popular music, as one part of a process of making and use of popular culture, reveals tensions and conflict over things preferred and those to be transformed. This process encompasses relations, on the surface, appearing purely personal, but reflecting deeper social transformations and conflicts over broader conceptions of society. Given the $40 *billion* business it has become, popular music must contain, within its commodified creations for sale, currents and tensions within the larger culture and society. Through individual styles of diverse performers, a diversity of images and feelings permit audiences to utilize it in ways both containing and fulfilling their desires. Through fantasy and substitute imagery, it strategically satisfies via "symbolic containment structures" of popular songs or integrated collections of songs (once called albums) now on a single compact disc (CD) or retrospective, multidisc collections.

Popular music is an interactional form of expressive activity—an ongoing struggle between artist and corporation, and corporation and consumer. Within the limits defined by "product" judged by its purveyors as potentially profitable, the listener/consumer may create a world of meaning by manipulating and using the imagery in the music heard. Artist creativity in the twenty-first century is mediated through larger, ever fewer global corporations marketing recordings, and through radio and television disc and video playlists, and concert ticket sales, increasingly sold through integrated radio/concert ticket companies. Audience needs are similarly mediated, yet a degree of reciprocity exists; how much is a matter of dispute among scholars. Frith (1981), in *Sound Effects,* noted that realist approaches assume that media operate with transparency,

communicating the meaning of artists but suggesting that ownership affects what the audience hears. Constructivist approaches stress the way media corporations construct reality for the audience, stressing that the ideological meaning of popular music lies in the way it is commercially produced, in its commodity form. Such oppositions recall the position of Adorno versus Walter Benjamin's (1973) notion in "The Work of Art in the Age of Mechanical Reproduction" that the ideological meaning of popular artifacts (popular music, in this case) is decided in the process of consumption—meaning that popular music becomes what people make of it. Adorno saw media corporations imposing meaning on passive listeners.

Such elitist versus creative subject approaches reveal divergent tendencies in the analysis of the meanings of popular music, evident in the explosive energies of the varieties of rock music in the 1960s through the 1980s and in emergent hip-hop/rap subcultures in the 1990s and into the twenty-first century. Popular music has a fundamentally paradoxical and contradictory character as both creative expression and commodity. It has potentials for liberation and domination, providing opportunities for creativity and resistance, yet its meanings are "squeezed out" between conflicting pressures: on one hand, of publishers and manufacturers, each following the obsolescence principle, constantly promoting new artists and crazes; on the other, youth (and succeeding generations) seeking a medium to express their experience in the contemporary world, to resist the dominant culture, to define their own unique identities. In popular music, this contradiction exists in a particularly intensified form. Popular musical artists must—to make any money—take account of it, some adopting tried commercial formulas, others insisting on being pure artists and cultural revolutionaries whose productions are not diluted by commercial pressures, nor corrupted, bought off, or bought out. This distinctive paradox of popular music reached its nadir (or peak) in 1970, when Columbia Records widely advertised their recordings with the slogan, "The Revolution is on Columbia Records."

— Ray Pratt

See also Benjamin, Walter; Cultural Marxism and British Cultural Studies; Media Critique

FURTHER READINGS AND REFERENCES

Benjamin, Walter. 1973. "The Work of Art in the Age of Mechanical Reproduction." Pp. 217–52 in *Illuminations.* Translated by Harry Zohn. Glasgow, Scotland: Fontana/Collins.

Garofalo, Reebee. 2001. *Rockin Out: Popular Music in the U.S.A.* 2d ed. New York: Prentice-Hall.

Kellner, Douglas. 1995. *Media Culture: Cultural Studies, Identity and Politics between the Modern and the Postmodern.* New York: Routledge.

Pratt, Ray. 1990. *Rhythm and Resistance: Political Uses of American Popular Music.* New York: Praeger.

PORNOGRAPHY AND CULTURAL STUDIES

Pornography is a hotly debated area in academic feminist circles, with the pro-pornography feminists arguing that the pornographic text is polysemic with emancipatory value to develop transgressive desire (see Strossen 1995). The anti-pornography feminists, on the other hand, argue that pornography causes harm to women in both the production and consumption of pornographic material (see Dworkin 1981). To suggest that there was disagreement among the writers is to minimize the enormous differences between the various camps as to the definition, nature, effects, and legal status of pornography. Some of the central points of contention concern the nature of human agency, social structure, and cultural production. Those feminists who have adopted an anti-pornography position posit a social structure, which conditions, limits, and determines human agency. While not adopting a wholly social determinist position, anti-pornography feminists see women's lives as patterned and structured by macrosystems of domination that work to provide the pornography industry with a steady flow of bodies that can be used as raw material in the production of pornography. The anti-pornography feminists thus call for an analysis of pornography production that foregrounds systems of inequality where a ruling class has the power to own and control the means of material and cultural production.

The main focus of this discussion is to highlight the ways in which the debates within media studies can be applied to the study of pornography. Critical media studies scholars such as Kellner (2003) have for some time argued that cultural studies in the United States has lost its political edge by focusing primarily on the text rather than on the social and economic contexts of media production. The original project of cultural studies, developed at the University of Birmingham in England, was to create an area of study that would foreground the political economy of communication in order to develop a theory of dominance in industrial capitalist societies that would lead to social change. According to critical media scholars in this country, the political potential of cultural studies has been replaced with an apolitical approach that ignores wider questions of power and social change.

Political questions about the nature of cultural production are at the forefront of the academic study of the political economy of communication. These theorists, like the anti-pornography feminists, see the society as marked by inequality, oppression, and domination, where domination is seen as those practices used by the ruling class to control the conditions of production. Built into the analysis is a social activist agenda that calls for a transformation in both the material and the ideological levels of human experience, and while classical Marxism has privileged the former, contemporary Marxist critics have called for an analysis that links the material conditions of a society to its systems and processes of signification and representation.

In his article on the future of media studies, McChesney (2000) criticizes media studies for abandoning the central questions that a political economy of media raises. The result, he argues, is that much of communication research ignores the structural factors that influence the production of media content. This same criticism can be leveled against the pro-pornography scholarship in that the focus of analysis is the text rather than the context of pornography production. This is not to argue that a close reading of the text and the study of audience pleasures have little to offer the study of pornography, but that the privileging of these two areas of research fails to examine the political process involved in the production, distribution, and consumption of media texts (McChesney, 2000). Moreover, it is not enough to say that much of the contemporary research on pornography is uninterested in questions of political economy, but rather, that it actually trivializes this line of inquiry. In those few academic books that do look at how pornography is produced, there is a tendency to limit the discussion to either a first-person account by a "sex-worker" (usually Nina Hartley) or to focus on woman-owned or woman-produced pornography. While this type of research does shed light on the workings of the various sectors of the industry, it cannot stand in for a critical macrolevel approach that explores how capitalism, patriarchy, racism, and first-world economic domination provides the economic and cultural space for international, mass-scale pornography production. To focus only on those women who have the resources to produce and distribute pornography is as limited as looking at worker-controlled cooperatives to explore how labor is organized under capitalism.

The anti-pornography feminists are one of the few groups to take seriously how the production of pornography is tied to larger systems of inequality. These feminists explore the nature of pornography production using theories and methods developed within a critical paradigm that explores how pornography production produces and reproduces the unequal systems of relations that define women as a subordinate class. The picture that is beginning to emerge from this research is one of international trafficking in women that suggests that poor women (particularly of color) may well be the ones whose location in the nexus of class, gender, and race relations allow for the continuation of an industry that some first-world members of the intellectual and financial elite see as beneficial to women. In terms of production, from the limited research, it would seem that the making of pornography is anything but positive for the actual women whose bodies are used as the raw material in pornography. Women who have worked within the industry often speak of a system of sexual slavery that preys on poor women, abused women, and young women running away from sexually abusive households. Evelina Giobbe (1995), director of education and public policy at Whisper, works with women who have been used in the making of pornography, and argues that most of the women come from backgrounds of poverty, abuse, and parental deprivation, and were forced into the pornography industry as teenagers.

To foreground the lives of the women who are used in pornography presents a very different view of the pornography industry. Without a scholarly analysis of the political economy of pornography, the pro-pornography position is truncated, depoliticized, and ultimately serves the interests of those in power.

One of the major underlying projects of critical media studies is to provide an intellectual and theoretical framework for both individual empowerment and social and political change (Kellner 2003). This radical potential of critical media studies makes it particularly compatible with a feminist analysis that seeks also, through consciousness raising, theoretical debates, political organizing, and educational practices, to transform the material and ideological relations of patriarchy. Because critical media studies take as a founding principle the ways in which theory and politics are connected to the control of knowledge, they call for the linking of theory with activism. In this way, a feminist analysis of pornography that is located in critical media studies needs to include a strategy for change that will ultimately deny the pornographers access to women by changing those conditions that force women to "choose" pornography as the only means of "employment."

The debate thus needs to shift to a new level where we take seriously the systems of inequality that define the nature of the production of pornography. This calls for new research methods and strategies that critical media scholars use to explore how media is produced within a global capitalist framework. This will not only provide a more sophisticated understanding of pornography but will also encourage critical media theory to include discussions of gender and race since much of this scholarship foregrounds class as *the* system of inequality. It is abundantly clear that we can no longer understand how class inequality functions without a theoretical and empirical analysis of how class, gender, and race work together to produce multiple social and material locations for individuals and groups. Critical cultural studies are well situated to take on this task and to become an example of how academics can ask questions and provide answers that engage with the reality of the world, the world where the majority of the population is exploited, dehumanized, and rendered worthless for the sake of increased profits for multinational industries such as pornography.

— Gail Dines

See also Cultural Marxism and British Cultural Studies; Feminist Cultural Studies; Radical Feminism

FURTHER READINGS AND REFERENCES

Dworkin, Andrea. 1981. *Pornography: Men Possessing Women.* New York: Perigee.
Giobbe, Evilina. 1995. "Surviving Commercial Sexual Exploitation." Pp. 314–18 in *Gender, Race and Class in Media: A Text-Reader,* edited by Gail Dines and Jean Humez. Thousand Oaks, CA: Sage.
Kellner, Doug. 2003. "Cultural Studies, Multiculturalism and Media Culture." Pp. 9–20 in *Gender, Race and Class in Media: A Text-Reader,* 2d ed., edited by Gail Dines and Jean Humez. Thousand Oaks, CA: Sage.
McChesney. Robert. 2000. "The Political Economy of Communications and the Future of the Field." *Media, Culture and Society* 22:109–16.
Russell, Diana. 1998. *Dangerous Relationships: Pornography, Misogyny, and Rape.* Thousand Oaks, CA: Sage.
Strossen, Nadine. 1995. *Defending Pornography: Free Speech, Sex, and the Fight for Women's Rights.* New York: Scribner.

POSITIVISM

Positivism, in its most general sense, is a doctrine that maintains that the study of the human or social world should be organised according to the same principles as the study of the physical or natural world. In simple terms, positivism maintains that the social sciences should be modelled on the natural sciences. This broad definition encompasses numerous variants, depending first on what are taken to be the characteristic features of the natural sciences and second on which of these features are to be applied in the social sciences. Accordingly, a very wide range of social theories have been designated positivist, even though they show little similarity in terms of notions of data, mode of analysis, or explanatory objective.

Historically, the popularity of positivism has waxed and waned as enthusiasm for science has fluctuated, most notably from the optimism 150 years ago that science provided the basis for the progressive understanding and control of the natural and social worlds to the current pessimism about science's part in the despoliation of the natural environment and degradation of the human condition. Particularly influential on positivism's rise and fall has been the varying strength of the counter doctrine, which maintains that the social world—the actions and interactions of human beings—cannot be studied according to scientific principles. This counter doctrine too has taken a variety of forms, depending on what properties of individual people or social collectivities are considered to be beyond scientific analysis.

THE EARLY ROOTS

Positivism has its origin in the eighteenth-century French Enlightenment, the doctrine being a key component of what is now known as the modernist project, which was founded on the belief that human endeavours—especially the rational pursuit of empirical scientific inquiries—would generate knowledge that could be deployed for human betterment. The term *positivism* was coined by Auguste Comte to describe the ideas, largely drawn from earlier thinkers, that he set out in a series of lectures and which were later published in the six-volume *Cours de philosophie positive* (1830–1842). From his conspectus of the sciences, Comte believed he had established a law of three stages through which knowledge in all disciplines necessarily progresses. In the first, theological stage, people explain by appeal to divine agents. In the second, metaphysical stage, explanations are proposed in terms of abstract forces and powers. In the third and final, scientific or positive stage, explanations eschew appeal to mysterious abstractions and are instead cast in terms of invariable natural laws relating observable phenomena and events, with Newton's laws of motion being the paradigmatic case. Different disciplines pass through the three stages at different rates, and therefore fall into a natural hierarchy, with the highest and most complex taking the longest to arrive at the positive stage. The queen of the sciences, argued Comte, is sociology, for its laws guide the application of the lower sciences for the benefit of humanity. The *Cours* is, in effect, a sustained argument that a natural science of society, comprising a set of laws tested against experience, is both possible and necessary for progress. Societal disorder can be overcome, Comte proposed, once the laws of society have been scientifically established so that people can accommodate to them. In this way, order and progress can be jointly pursued.

There are three core themes in Comte's positivism: first, the notion that historical progress is built on advances in scientific knowledge; second, an empiricist theory of knowledge (or epistemology) according to which all sound or positive knowledge is based ultimately on observation (as opposed to divine decree or human reason alone); and third, a unity of science thesis, according to which all disciplines, natural and social, can be integrated into a unified system of natural laws.

In the later part of the nineteenth century, the evolutionary social theory of Herbert Spencer became popular, forming part of the social Darwinist movement that extended ideas from evolutionary biology to the social sciences. Although explicitly dissenting from some of Comte's philosophy, Spencer is commonly identified as having bolstered the positivist spirit of the age and as having been a significant forerunner of twentieth-century positivism. He was committed to the central tenet of positivism, the unification of the natural and social sciences, in his case under the principle of natural evolution. He believed that all causes have multiple effects, with the result that all domains—the natural, biological, and human—become increasingly differentiated. Historical progress is a result of competition between individuals with different characteristics; the struggle of each differentiated individual against the others powers the internal dynamic of the natural and social worlds, just as Charles Darwin (1809–1892) had accounted for the dynamic of the biological world in *On the Origin of the Species* published in 1859. This theory of progress differs sharply from Comte's—in which increasing harmony is achieved by subjugating individuals to the scientific laws of society. In opposition to this collectivist approach, Spencer's is an individualistic theory, in accord with the laissez-faire ethos of his day. He argued against intervening in the natural historical competitive evolutionary process in the attempt to address inequalities. However, as the destructive social effects of unregulated competition were highlighted by the poverty surveys conducted by social reformers in the early twentieth century, laissez-faire doctrines lost support and interest in Spencer's sociology had all but disappeared by the 1930s.

Meanwhile, Comte's ideas had become institutionalised in French universities at the beginning of the twentieth century through Émile Durkheim's sociology, which adopted the central themes of the unity of the sciences, an empiricist epistemology and the application of knowledge for the progressive benefit of humankind. To these, Durkheim added a further strand—statistics, or the collection and analysis of quantitative descriptions of social facts. While Durkheim's own analyses were relatively unsophisticated, statistics became embedded in academic social sciences over the first half of the twentieth century. Particularly influential in this development were the heads of the newly established university social studies departments in the United States who sought to demonstrate that their emerging disciplines were scientific by encouraging the dispassionate and rigorous application of statistical methods to precisely measured social facts. Many also believed that numerical data was objective and therefore statistical analysis value-free. The view that science can be unified through the impartial collection and statistical manipulation of quantitative data in all disciplines, natural and social, has become a common way of characterising what has been called professional practice positivism. It is a view that has been constantly challenged on both technical and epistemological grounds.

LOGICAL POSITIVISM

There was a remarkable resurgence of interest in positivist philosophy in the 1920s and 1930s, centring on a group of philosophers, scientists, and mathematicians who became known as the Vienna Circle. They were committed to two of the core themes of the earlier positivism: the unification of the sciences and empiricism. Again, the initial impetus was to ensure that all disciplines would become scientific, and the group's efforts were directed at utilising recent advances in logic to analyse how legitimate scientific knowledge could be demarcated from unscientific ideas. However, although keen that only genuine scientific knowledge be used to guide action, they did not attempt to formulate general theories of progress because they did not believe it possible to argue from what is—which is what science tells us—to what ought to be. In other words, they believed that science is morally neutral; advances in science could be of benefit but were not necessarily so. To emphasise this difference from earlier positivism, the Circle gave their work the name logical positivism. Philosophy, including logic, was to concern itself solely with clarifying the abstract form of science, rather than with its substance. Positive philosophy was, therefore, to be separated from social philosophy, including arguments about what social arrangements are desirable and what constitutes progress.

Logical positivists were able to incorporate logic into science because, although logical truths are a priori—meaning that they are known to be true without appeal to experience—they are analytic, in the sense that they are not about experience. In this way, the logical positivists could retain their commitment to empiricism: Science is composed of empirical statements about the natural and social worlds, of course, but also logical propositions (including mathematical expressions) about the relations between empirical statements. The inclusion in science of logical propositions does not jeopardise empiricism—the requirement that knowledge be grounded in experience—since this applies only to knowledge of facts and not to the analytic propositions of logic that do not purport to describe the world.

The logical positivists' approach can be illustrated by Carl G. Hempel's analysis of scientific explanation: Formally an explanation consists of a statement describing an event (the explanandum) that is explained by deducing it from a set of other statements (the explanans), including a covering law and a set of initial conditions. For example, to recast part of Durkheim's explanation of suicide rates, the high rate of suicide experienced in a particular province is explained by deducing it from the initial condition that the province is experiencing rapid economic development together with the covering laws (1) that sudden economic success is accompanied by high levels of anomie (this latter being Durkheim's term for the situation in which the norms that guided behaviour in more straightened times no longer

apply) and (2) that anomie encourages suicide. This Hempelian deductive-nomological schema is the basis for unifying the sciences since it offers a formal model for explanations in all disciplines.

Because laws form a crucial role in scientific explanations, the logical positivists devoted considerable effort to elucidating the nature of laws. There were two related problems to solve. First, in order to guarantee that the explanandum is deducible from the explanans, the law included in the latter must be an unrestricted universal statement, of the form that all As, without exception, are also Bs. Second, in order to distinguish universal laws from mere accidental generalisations, the former must incorporate a relation between antecedent and consequent that is stronger than mere covariation. Both these are versions of the problem of induction, which is particularly acute for empiricists. First, no matter how extensive our observations of As that are Bs, this cannot conclusively establish that all As are Bs, only that those hitherto examined are. Second, whenever something extra, beyond covariation, is proposed as characteristic of laws but not accidental generalisations, it is mostly something that is beyond immediate observation, which violates the commitment to empiricism. This is the case, for example, when the distinguishing feature of laws is said to be that they express causal connections.

Although the logical positivists pursued several inventive approaches to these problems, a widely adopted way of avoiding them was most fully developed by Karl Popper, who communicated with the logical positivists but distanced himself from their philosophy. He proposed that universal laws have a provisional character, being accepted as true only until proved false. Science proceeds by trial and error—by the hypothetico-deductive method, which involves conjecturing a hypothetical universal law, deducing from it an expected observation and then investigating empirically whether or not this expectation is fulfilled. If it is, we continue to subscribe to the law, whereas if it is not, the putative law is rejected as false. In this way, laws are corroborated by our experience but never verified, that is, never demonstrated to be true for all time. Science progresses by the gradual elimination of falsified conjectures. What is crucial for the sciences—social and natural—is that their conjectured explanatory laws are falsifiable, that is, can be subject to empirical test. Conjectures that are not falsifiable are to be expunged from science. The sciences are to be unified around a body of falsifiable but not yet falsified laws.

The importance for social theory of logical positivism and Popper's philosophy was that for a period in the middle of the twentieth century, they became the received view about the nature of science. It became widely believed that the deductive-nomological schema was not merely a theory about scientific explanation but instead a description of natural scientists' objectives. In a similar fashion, Popper's hypothetico-deductive procedure was treated not as a theory of scientific progress but as a description of natural scientists' practical inquiries. As a result, the unity of science thesis was stated in terms of requiring social theorists to use hypothetico-deductive methods to corroborate general laws and cast their explanations in the deductive-nomological form. To this end, in many substantive areas, quantitative inquiries using statistical techniques were undertaken in order to establish the strengths of relationships between variables and the likelihood that relationships found in samples existed in the populations from which the samples were drawn. In effect, statistical analyses were directed to separating laws from accidental generalisations (or spurious correlations) and to corroborating laws.

POSTPOSITIVISM

The positivist hegemony in the social sciences had always been precarious and at no time has it been free of challenges from rival doctrines. The tenuous dominance achieved in the mid-twentieth century disintegrated under increasing pressure from several directions over the following years. A sustained attack came in the 1950s, when the Frankfurt school of critical theorists articulated a Hegelian-Marxist critique, arguing that natural and social scientific knowledge, like all products of human activity, serves sectional interests rather than being value-free. In positivism's case, the interest is in technical control, which is as invidious as class oppression, and which can be overcome only by a radical transformation of society to overcome inequalities.

A second source of pressure on mid-twentieth-century positivism was the rejection of empiricism for failing to account adequately for the part played by theory in science. Realist philosophers argued that this was better captured by an epistemology that allowed a place for modelling the underlying structures and their powers, beyond the reach of immediate experience, that are causally responsible for the observable outcomes of their operation. The paradigmatic case is the structure of atoms being causally responsible for the observed behaviour of gases, liquids, and solids. One advantage of the realist conception of science is that it provides a solution to the persistent problem within empiricism— noted above—of satisfactorily distinguishing causal laws from accidental generalisations. Although first invoked as a philosophy of the natural sciences, realism was extended to social sciences as a way of retaining the unity of science while at the same time rejecting other strands of positivism, in particular its empiricism. Realist social scientists argued that underlying structures, for example of the sort identified by Marx, are generative mechanisms that have a determinate effect on social relations.

But the unity of science thesis in both its positivist and realist guises came under extensive criticism, especially

from social theorists interested in the meaningfulness of social practices, who took the view that it is actors' culturally specific conceptions of their own and others' activities that guide their actions and interactions, rather than these being either law-governed or generated by underlying causal structures. To make sense of social practices, the social theorist's task is to obtain an understanding of the locally embedded meanings in terms intelligible to the actors involved. The unity of science is rejected: Because the social world, unlike the natural world, is pervaded by meanings, there is a radical division between the social and the natural sciences, with the former concerned to elucidate the situated meanings of actions and not to seek laws. Empirical studies focus on the interactions between people in particular milieux, using ethnographic fieldwork techniques, to understand, for example, the processing of sudden deaths by the police and coroners' courts that produces suicide rates. This interpretivist perspective draws on several sources. One is the earlier hermeneutic tradition, which had influenced Max Weber at the beginning of the twentieth century. It stressed that the method of *verstehen,* or interpretive understanding, is central to the study of human activities because it provides access to the meanings of those activities shared by the people engaged in them. The interpretivist perspective drew further support from ordinary language philosophy, which flowered in the mid-century in opposition to positivist philosophy and which focused on the customary uses of languages within particular linguistic communities. This approach was extended to the social sciences by Peter Winch, who argued that rather than applying the methods of the natural sciences, they should be concerned to grasp the rules that guide social practices, enabling the meanings those practices have to the actors involved to be understood. The interpretivist perspective was also inspired by symbolic interactionism that had its origin in the Chicago school community studies of the 1920s and 1930s. These used participant observation, life histories, and depth interviews to discover how, in their everyday interactions, people constructed, negotiated, and modified the meanings they gave to their activities.

By the end of the twentieth century, the various strands of the interpretivist approach were commonly seen as contributing to social constructionism. which, in its most radical guise, proposes that all human activities are contingent practices whose sense is constructed in the to and fro of social intercourse. This applies to our representations of the natural and social world too: The natural and social sciences are products of their historical and social environment, and they could have been quite different in different circumstances. This marks a loss of faith in the modernist project: No longer does it seem that any philosophy of science can be legitimated by appeal to a universal standard, that science can be successfully separated from ideology, or that scientific knowledge can provide the basis for progress. Postmodernism therefore presents positivism with a potent challenge.

— Peter Halfpenny

See also Comte, Auguste; Durkheim, Émile; Hermeneutics; Positivismusstreit; Postmodernism; Social Constructionism; Social Darwinism; Spencer, Herbert; Symbolic Interaction; Verstehen; Weber, Max

FURTHER READINGS AND REFERENCES

Halfpenny, Peter. 2001. "Positivism in the Twentieth Century." Pp. 371–85 in *Handbook of Social Theory,* edited by G. Ritzer and B. Smart. London: Sage.

Halfpenny, Peter and Peter McMylor, eds. 1994. *Positivist Sociology and Its Critics.* 3 vols. Aldershot, UK: E. Elgar.

POSITIVISMUSSTREIT (THE POSITIVIST DISPUTE)

The term *Positivismusstreit* was coined by Theodor Adorno to characterize a dispute that started formally at a meeting of the German Sociological Association in Tübingen in 1961 and that shook the sociological community in Germany from the 1960s to the early 1970s including the revolts around 1968. In addition to Adorno, this dispute included the most prestigious social thinkers such as Hans Albert, Ralf Dahrendorf, Jürgen Habermas, Harald Pilot, Karl R. Popper, and later Niklas Luhmann. In effect, the dispute is ongoing, and may possibly never end, as it is a fundamental dispute about the paradigms within social thought. In effect, it continues a dispute that started at the beginning of the twentieth century and was known as the Methodenstreit (dispute over methodology), and in which the most prestigious German social scientists of that time were engaged, like Max Weber and Gustav Schmoller.

Actually Adorno's term is misleading because the main protagonists on the other side did not understand themselves as positivists. For example, Karl R. Popper, probably the most well known among the participants, was never a member of the Vienna Circle, which launched the debate in the 1920s and 1930s. They gave their approach the name of logical positivism and may therefore be called neopositivists. They had developed rather distinctive arguments in comparison to the original school of positivism. Hans Albert agrees with this typification in regard to himself, though he designates his own methodology as Kritischer Rationalismus (Critical Rationalism). But certainly neither Ralf Dahrendorf nor Niklas Luhmann can be subsumed under this heading. As a result, Hans-Joachim Dahms (1994) summarizes the dispute as a multifront one: the

Frankfurt school against logical positivism, American pragmatism and critical rationalism. The debate was continued namely by Jürgen Habermas and Niklas Luhmann—then the younger generation—in a book under the title *Theorie der Gesellschaft oder Sozialtechnologie* (Theory of Society or Social Technology) in 1971.

What is so important about this dispute? Is it only a German ideological dispute? It is interesting to see that some of the most influential social theorists took part in the ongoing dispute. This includes work by Anthony Giddens (1974, 1978) and three volumes by Peter Halfpenny and Peter McMylor (1994). This dispute is described in all dictionaries and encyclopedias, and in Germany it is even included in encyclopedias intended for the lay public. However, in the English-language encyclopedias and dictionaries it shows up only within an article on "positivism" as such.

In part we may explain the resurgence of the debate on positivism in postwar Germany by attending to the difficult situation there. Different schools, both inside and outside of Germany, were fighting for hegemony after National Socialism. Remigrants like Theodor W. Adorno and Max Horkheimer, but also René König, and emigrants like Karl R. Popper fought against those such as Helmut Schelsky who had survived the war with a chair in occupied Strasbourg. In 1949, while still in exile, René König wrote a book with the title *Soziologie heute* (Sociology Today). Several years later, in 1959, Helmut Schelsky responded to this book by providing his definition of German sociology. The conflict was also about the role and character of the German Sociological Association and who should preside over it. It is necessary to understand this struggle for influence in order to understand the dispute over positivism in Germany. This also makes it understandable why Adorno chose—consciously or unconsciously—a misleading title.

A second dimension, which is relevant to understanding the dispute, is the political situation in Germany in the 1960s. A widespread social revolt from Berkeley through to Paris and Frankfurt to Berlin made it such that sociology became a sort of central intellectual tool to understand exploitation and social conflicts and contribute to the possibility of emancipation. In opposition to the call for social change, "critical rationalism" became a sort of fundamental credo for a large number of politicians, who wanted to organize society like a company. The former German chancellor Helmut Schmidt was a protagonist of this kind of politics and governance. In addition, even today German sociology is much more grounded in philosophy than the Anglo-Saxon sociology ever was. So it does not seem to be a hazard that the Frankfurt school is classified in the United States under the label social philosophy and not sociology.

The main arguments made by the representatives of the Frankfurt school are as follows: (1) a Critical Theory of Society has to understand the totality of society as a life context, which is always approached through an a priori concept of reality, because social phenomena cannot be isolated from the societal totality; therefore (2) sociological theory construction has to start from a prescientific experience of society, and the relation between theory and experience cannot be reduced to a controlled and reproducible ex-post check of hypotheses; (3) social theory has to describe "historical laws of movement" (*historische Bewegungsgesetze*); and (4) social theory has as its very reason to contribute to the emancipation of society and the acting individual.

The protagonists of critical rationalism counterargue that (1) the notion "societal totality" is an empty concept as long as it is not clear how the social phenomena can be structured and checked through hypothesis testing. An a priori understanding may be a false theory, which again has to be checked and criticized; (2) experience is at best a critical instance but nothing that can be a basis of cognition; (3) it is impossible to predict the development of history, as this depends on our knowledge, and it is logically impossible to forecast the future of knowledge (cf. Popper's critique of "historicism"); (4) to change the whole society is an impossible exercise in holistic planning and has for that reason to be refuted; and finally (5) the ideal of *Wertfreiheit* (value freedom) does not mean the negligence of interests and values in the research process but the recognition of "objective truth" as the leading value (Klima 1995:506–507).

Since the 1970s and 1980s, both positivism and the Frankfurt school increasingly came under attack from different sides: from philosophy (Ludwig J. J. Wittgenstein, Paul Feyerabend), from French postmodernists (Jean Baudrillard, Michel Foucault, Jacques Lacan, François Lyotard), and from feminists (Sandra Harding; for more details see Halfpenny and McMylor 1994).

What remains of the positivist dispute today? There is no doubt that today's mainstream social sciences are still dominated by different variants of neopositivism, especially in the Anglo-Saxon world. Their utilitarian, pragmatic orientation, the dominance of the natural sciences—which in English reserve only for themselves the title of science; the other disciplines are just arts and/or humanities—make it difficult to realize a critical theory of society. Not that this is a new situation. Even in Germany, where philosophical approaches to sociology are more common, the Frankfurt school has always been in the minority because of their anti- and postpositivist approaches.

Nevertheless, both positions have a similar aim: to contribute to the goals of the Enlightenment—though with different means and paradigms. Since the 1970s, Claus Offe has tried to overcome the fundamental differences between these two schools of thought through a compromise. However, it is only very recently that this seems like a possibility due to Bent Flyvbjerg's rediscovery of the Aristotelian principle of *phronesis*, that is, the search for a "good society." *Phronesis* is placed between *episteme*, the basis for the arts and humanities, and *techne*, the basis for natural sciences and technologies. *Phronesis* has its own logic and methodology, which overcomes the now outdated dichotomy, and by this it also aims to overcome the problems central to the positivist dispute.

— György Széll

See also Frankfurt School; Luhmann, Niklas; Marxism; Paradigm; Positivism; Postmodernism

FURTHER READINGS AND REFERENCES

Adorno, Theodor, Hans Albert, Ralf Dahrendorf, Jürgen Habermas, Harald Pilot, and Karl R. Popper. 1976. *The Positivist Dispute in German Sociology.* London: Heinemann.

Dahms, Hans-Joachim. 1994. *Positivismusstreit: Die Auseinandersetzungen der Frankfurter Schule mit dem logischen Positivismus, dem amerikanischen Pragmatismus und dem kritischen Rationalismus.* Translated as *The Positivist Dispute: The Heated Discussion of the Frankfurt School against Logical Positivism, American Pragmatism and Critical Rationalism* (Frankfurt, Germany: Suhrkamp).

Flyvbjerg, Bent. 2001. *Making Social Science Matter: Why Social Inquiry Fails and How It Can Succeed Again.* Cambridge, UK: Cambridge University Press.

Frisby, David. 1976. *The Positivist Dispute in German Sociology.* London: Heinemann.

Giddens, Anthony, ed. 1974. *Positivism and Sociology.* London: Heinemann.

———. 1978. "Positivism and Its Critics." In *A History of Sociological Analysis,* edited by Tom Bottomore and Robert Nisbet. New York: Basic Books.

Habermas, Jürgen and Niklas Luhmann, eds. 1971. *Theorie der Gesellschaft oder Sozialtechnologie* [Theory of Society or Social Technology]. Frankfurt, Germany: Suhrkamp.

Halfpenny, Peter and Peter McMylor, eds. 1994. *Positivist Sociology and Its Critics.* 3 vols. Aldershot, UK: Edgar Elgar.

Klima, Rolf. 1995. *Positivismusstreit* 3d enl. ed. (The Positivist Dispute)." Pp. 505–507 in *Lexikon zur Soziologie* [Dictionary of Sociology], edited by Werner Fuchs-Henritz, Rüdiger Lautmann, Otthein Rammstedt, and Hanns Wienold. Opladen, Germany: Westdeutscher Verlag.

König, René, 1949. *Soziologie heute* [Sociology Today]. Zurich, Switzerland: Regio-Verl.

Meja, Volker and Nico Stehr, eds. 1987. *Modern GermanSsociology.* New York: Columbia University Press.

Schelsky, Helmut, 1959. *Ortsbestimmung der deutschen Soziologie.* Düsseldorf, Germany: Diederichs.

POSTCOLONIALISM

There is no agreed-upon definition of postcolonialism, as it is a highly complex and contested arena of thought and practice. Postcolonial discourse constitutes a transdisciplinary arena of critical discourse that is most generally associated with developing theories and activisms related to globalization and the politics of representation (race, class, gender/sexuality, ethnicity, nationalisms, religion) as well as to economic, political, social, and psychic dimensions of colonization, neocolonialism, recolonization, and postcolonial conditions. Furthermore, it includes the advancement of liberatory and resistant politics that support decolonization and engages subaltern experience, which involves the perspectives of dominated, marginalized, oppressed, and subordinated peoples.

Many scholars argue that the development of postcolonial culture must be understood within the historical and imperialist context of the European colonialism of the so-called third world or, as many postcolonial theorists describe it, the "tricontinental" (i.e., the southern continents of Latin America, Africa, and Asia), that began over 500 years ago. This violent history of colonization involved massive appropriation of land and territories, slavery, institutionalized racism, enforced migration, murder, torture, genocide, obliteration of cultures, and the imposition of Eurocentric, ideological sociopolitical, economic, and cultural values of the colonizers. This process escalated during the imperialist expansion of the eighteenth, nineteenth, and early twentieth centuries. And although political, cultural, and economic reforms characterized many of the former colonies, which gained independence after the Second World War, one of the most deleterious effects of the multileveled process of colonization has been the development and implementation of a global supercapitalist economic system that is primarily controlled by the West and ultimately mediates all global relations.

Given this context, it is hardly surprising that much of colonial and postcolonial critique emerges before, during, and after the numerous struggles for liberation and decolonization in the twentieth century and employs a critical Marxian perspective, which translates from and transforms classical Western Marxist analysis. Hence, much postcolonialist critique involves the advancement of Marxian analysis that is developed from the perspective and position of the colonized and is situated within the complexities of relations that define the postcolonial experiences and realities. There is a strong focus on the kinds of cultural politics associated with the ideas and practice of cultural revolutions within primarily the tricontinents, which espoused resistance and devised strategies to combat ideological forces of colonialism and neocolonialism. Thus, one of its distinctions from orthodox, European Marxism is identified, by many postcolonial scholars, as "combining critique of objective material conditions with detailed analysis of their subjective effects" (Young 2001:5).

However, some critics argue that an overemphasis on the subjective dimensions of colonization and decolonization in postcolonial discourse is given primacy over the material and concrete conditions, such as class. Yet it is this concern with the dialectics of the relations between the "self" and "other" and the "subjective with the objective" that distinguishes anticolonialist writings and postcolonial critique from more one-dimensional theories of oppression. Indeed, a central feature of anticolonial and postcolonial thought is the recognition that colonization is a sophisticated and multileveled ideological process, which operates both externally and internally. In reality, colonization is not restricted to physical deprivation, legal inequality, economic exploitation, and classist, racist, and sexist unofficial or official assumptions.

In fact, there is a psychopathological dimension of colonization that was described by Frantz Fanon (1967) as "psychic alienation." Fanon, a psychoanalyst and revolutionary anticolonial scholar from Martinique, worked in colonial Algeria and later joined the Front de Liberation National. He employed the Hegelian "master/slave dialectic" that depicts the contradictory relationship between the dominator and dominated, in which the master needs to be recognized by the slave as the master and hence convince the slave of her or his inherent inferiority and "otherness"—to depict the relationship between colonizer and colonized. It is in this sense that the colonized become their own oppressor, in that they exert the colonizers' imaginary suppositions of inferiority upon their own self-esteem. In this sense, it involves the objectification and dehumanization of the colonized.

Moreover, Fanon and, later, Paulo Freire (1972), argued that the colonizer, through the use of "tokens," or the aid of "collaborators," what postcolonial scholar Homi Bhaba (1994) describes as "mimic men" or women, ensures that the colonized remain in a "false" or "imaginary" consciousness. They not only reinforce the master's ideological values but often occupy a place of honor and power within the colonizers' regime. Hence, it is only through critical consciousness, what Brazilian educator and anticolonial pedagogue Paulo Freire called *conscientizacao*, that psychic and material decolonization can begin to take place. Therefore, anticolonial and postcolonial scholars are especially concerned with both the theoretical and practical dimensions of dialectics as an empowering process of decolonization in which the "colonized Self" can be liberated from the "tyrannical Other" and hence achieve liberation as well as "authentic individuality." It is important to note, as Edward Said (in Eagleton, Jameson, and Said 1990) reminds us, that this transformation of social consciousness must transcend and go beyond national consciousness, which often retains or develops colonized dimensions.

The topic of imperialisms' effects on both colonization and anticolonial resistance is a significant dimension of postcolonial analyses and critique of the kinds of master narratives that mediate sociopolitical, economic, and cultural relations, as well as help construct and transform the politics of representation. Much of this postcolonial work is associated with arenas of literary criticism and, to a lesser extent, deconstruction theory with its emphasis on nonessentialism and the arbitrary, rather than the fixed, nature of language. Many postcolonial critics are deconstructing normalized assumptions about the nature of language and texts by critiquing the cultural imperialism that underlies this discourse as well as resisting and reappropriating imperial literature and ideological frameworks. Hence, they criticize the kinds of master narratives that characterize dominant white, Christian, Western, patriarchal, heterosexual thought and discourse (sometimes described as "the canon") that are produced and reinforced by both the dominant and the collaborator.

Moreover, anticolonialist and postcolonial critics are especially concerned with the provocation, authentification, and celebration of the "voice" of the "Other." Such narratives capture the multiplicities of differences and diversities of the subaltern, who have been silenced for too long under colonialist and neocolonialist constraints and practices. These discourses resituate colonized people within the location of the center, rather than the margins of the local and global world. Such postcolonial works have been especially evident within feminist domains, in particular in the criticisms and writings of women of color, who, in part, challenge the notion of the essentialization of women as a universal category. Indeed, critical feminists like Jacqui Alexander and Chandra Mohanty (1997) and bell hooks (1994) point out that the identities of marginalized women and/or othered peoples are constructed by the dominant ideology. Much of this kind of postcolonial critique has been expressed in terms of "a third space" or "borderland" epistemologies or standpoints that recognize and highlight the experiences and practices of sexism, racism, classicism, and homophobia within the context of cultural, historical, geographic, national, political, economic, and social differences at both local and global levels. Hence, the dialectics of divergent and shared experiences frames the resistant and global coalition politics of many postcolonial critics. Postcolonial research and activist work seek thus to resist and transform the legacies and realities of colonial, neocolonial, and postcolonial conditions.

— Rhonda Hammer

See also Cultural Marxism and British Cultural Studies; Feminism; Political Economy

FURTHER READINGS AND REFERENCES

Alexander, M. Jacqui and Chandra Talpade Mohanty, eds. 1997. *Feminist Genealogies, Colonial Legacies, Democratic Futures.* New York: Routledge.

Eagleton, Terry, Frederic Jameson, and Edward Said. 1990. *Nationalism, Colonialism and Literature.* Minneapolis, MN: University of Minnesota Press.

Fanon, Frantz. 1967. *Black Skins, White Masks.* New York: Grove.

Bhaba, Homi. 1994. *The Location of Culture.* London: Routledge.

hooks, bell. 1994. *Teaching to Transgress: Education as the Practice of Freedom.* New York: Routledge.

Freire, Paulo. 1972. *Pedagogy of the Oppressed.* New York: Herder & Herder.

Williams, Patrick and Laura Chrisman, eds. *Colonial Discourse and Post-Colonial Theory: A Reader.* New York: Columbia University Press.

Young, Robert J. C. 2001. *Postcolonialism: An Historical Introduction.* Oxford, UK: Blackwell.

POST-MARXISM

If Marxism is what comes after Marx, post-Marxism is what comes after Marxism as a theory and practice in its organised and relatively disciplined form characteristic of the twentieth century. Post-Marxism can be seen as an ex post facto category referring to developments in and after Marxism with the 1980s crisis of Marxism, the collapse of Eurocommunism, and the collapse of the Soviet empire. Post-Marxism is highly varied and contradictory in nature; it corresponds with the postmodern sense that anything goes, in theory, that any theory goes with any other theory. At the same time, post-Marxism can be more Marxist than the Marxists. The idea of post-Marxism has a complicated semantic relationship with the idea of the postmodern. Just as postmodern theory can place the emphasis on either of the two terms against the other—some postmoderns have a stronger sense of being post, or after, others of remaining in reviving modernity or modernism—so with post-Marxism. Some views in this field are more vehemently post, or after Marx or Marxism; others revive Marx or Marxism as a universal theory of the modern.

The historical semantics involved are also suggestive. In the first place, the idea of post-Marx is either truistic or ironic: We are, of course, after Marx; even the Marxists are after Marx. The "post" refers to the sense that something significant has changed since Marx; yet post-Marxism also seems often to involve a Marxist orthodoxy of a kind less frequently encountered since the 1930s or 1960s. The idea of post-Marxism therefore logically follows that of the postmodern, but with these further refractions, that Marxism (or Marx's theory) is thought to be the fundamental critique of modernity. If Marx is the great modern or modernist, and we are now after modernism, then we are also after Marx, so we must all be post-Marxist. More specifically, if, as in the Soviet experience, Marx and Marxism are identified with a particular, failed, alternative path to modernity, then for the peoples of the old Soviet empire we are definitionally post-Marxist, because postcommunist. In addition, the idea of post-Marxism can be aligned with the earlier sociological notion of postindustrialism and the more recent category of poststructuralism, where pluralism claimed to replace the alleged monism of structure.

So where does the post-Marxist move begin, theoretically? One obvious point indicating the shift beyond Marxism is in the work of Michel Foucault, or at least its reception, in the Foucault effect. One aspect of the Foucault effect is the opening up of orthodox Marxism to methodological pluralism. Even if Foucault's power ontology is ultimately misleading, Foucault practically pluralises power. Beyond the economic sphere or the point of production, there are other institutions based on different aspects of power, on the model of Bentham's Panopticon rather than the image of the factory in Marx's *Capital*. Foucault's effect for orthodox Marxists in the 1970s and after is a belated echo of the Weber effect on nascent critical theory in the1920s, where rationalisation or bureaucratisation is a world historic problem alongside commodification, alienation, or capitalism. It is impossible, however, to imagine the Foucault effect or the extraordinary hegemony of his influence without contemplating the incredible influence of French Marxism in this period. Foucault happened, for the Anglo Left, because he followed Louis Althusser. If Foucault was German, his influence would have been negligible. While Foucault's reception in the United States was mediated differently, in terms of the history of systems of thought and especially with reference to law, discourse, and sexuality, in Great Britain and Australia, Foucault was presented as what came next for Marxists after the crisis of Marxism.

Althusser is the crucial connection here, as his Marxism managed to combine the most orthodox of Leninist and then Maoist claims with an importation of thinkers completely unholy for communism, from Freud and Lacan to Spinoza and Montesquieu. The apparently random nature of this mix, compared, say, to the more coherent integration of different themes in the work of Henri Lefebvre, itself prefigures what is now often called post-Marxism—on the one hand, a stubborn orthodoxy, on the other, a rough use of whatever theory passes by. This is the beginning of a trend that results in post-Marxism, exemplified in the work of Slavoj Žižek, where Lacan meets Hitchcock and Marx is coupled with Lenin. There was an alternative prospect in the 1970s connected with the project of Nicos Poulantzas, where the challenge in principle at least was to integrate the Weberian insights of Foucault and the realization of the centrality of democracy into a more originally orthodox Marxist framework. Instead, the work of Foucault was too often accommodated into Marxism for its occasional radical insights to prevail. Foucault met Marx and Althusser on at least one ground: the unshiftability of structure.

An alternative path of development for post-Marxism could be plotted out through the work of Jean Baudrillard. Baudrillard's (1975) first great work to become available in the English language was *The Mirror of Production,* a kind of Marxian critique of Marx. Here the alternative French legacies of Surrealism and Situationism seemed to be far more potentially generative than the weary clichés of orthodox Marxism. Baudrillard's trajectory through anthropology into culture and culture studies signals another kind of post-Marxist route, increasingly influential with the rise of cultural studies itself. For if the world seemed to consist of surfaces and random issues, then theory, and Marxism, should also be so. Post-Marxism, in this way, has more impact on cultural studies than on sociology; alternatively, its presence can be observed in geography, where Marx has just arrived, and radical political economy, where he has been revived.

An alternative path again can be connected to the work of another lapsed Marxist, Jean-François Lyotard. Lyotard's (1984) *Postmodern Condition* claimed to criticise grand narratives in general, but in Paris there was one narrative grander than all others, Marxism itself. The argument for the plurality of voices coincided with the rise of identity politics. The alternative to the stern orthodoxy of Marxism was a playful academic politics, with as many voices as the Tower of Babel. The connection with the postmodern here was undeniable. Marxism was modernism par excellence.

The presence of post-Marxism in sociology is more limited. This reflects the mixed reception of the postmodern in sociology, as well as territory disputes with cultural studies. The work of Zygmunt Bauman is one obvious candidate for the description of postmodern and post-Marxist sociology: Postmodern, because his work takes the postmodern seriously, at least at the level of a sociological phenomenon to be explained; post-Marxist, because his intellectual formation was Marxist up until his exile from Poland in 1969, and remains so afterward, in the broad sense that Marx's questions and key concerns—capitalism, consumption, reification—remain frames for his own work. Bauman's own critical categories can be applied here, stretched from his own working distinction between a postmodern sociology and a sociology of postmodernity. The first, postmodern sociology, enters and embraces the postmodern labyrinth. The second, a sociology of postmodernity, takes on the phenomena of the postmodern from the perspective of a critical sociology. By extension, there will also be a post-Marxist sociology, a sociology where the horizons of post-Marxism frame the task of sociology, and a sociology of post-Marxism, whose project would be not only to enter but also to interpret and then exit from post-Marxism.

If we view some of the fields of the post-Marxist regionally, some of its differences emerge. Eastern and Central Europe is a primary field for post-Marxist activity. Bauman's work is a central example of a project that is more closely defined as post-Marxist than postmodern, with the distinction that the emphasis in post-Marxism is on the Marxist in the context of a broad sympathy for classical sociology, critical theory, and continental philosophy. The work of the so-called Budapest school is another central project. Agnes Heller and Ferenc Feher both responded early to the European sense of being postmodern or post-histoire. Heller's trajectory, like Bauman's in its lineage though distinct in its detail, is also best described as post-Marxist rather than postmodern. The connection with the Weberian Marxism of Lukács means that, in Heller's case, the significance of Foucault is less marked. The work of Foucault can, however, be seen to have a significant impact on Bauman's (1982) work in exile, in *Memories of Class,* as a complement to Marx's factory-based critique. In France, Lefebvre pioneered the post-Marxist road by creatively building on Marxian themes with other materials from Surrealism to Nietzsche. One of his leading books here was called *Beyond Marxism* (1970), which might also in post-Marxist spirit be rendered as "With Marx, Against Marx." The influence of Althusser was never so high in Paris as beyond, via the work of its English importers. Other thinkers living in France who pioneered post-Marxism include Cornelius Castoriadis, who long before Baudrillard took the attitude that if you could be a Marxist or a revolutionary, then the only path was the revolutionary one; in order to be a Marxist in spirit, you had to be a post-Marxist, after Marx.

In Italy, where for the ultra-Left Gramsci was part of the problem of sclerotic communism, the most prominent post-Marxist is Antonio Negri, though here the anomalous nature of the term is apparent in full light: Negri is also the most orthodox of automatic Marxists, following the tradition where it is capital and capitalism itself that is the most revolutionary force on the planet, and will revolutionize the planet. The phenomenal success of Hardt and Negri's (2000) *Empire* needs to be seen in this context. Negri's work emerges out of the context of the Italian ultra Left of the 1960s and 1970s. The key word of this movement was its claim to workers' autonomy; often known as the *autonomista*, they advocated workerism, a kind of revolutionary syndicalism after Marx. The emphasis on workers' autonomy or voluntarism went together with an automatic Marxism, where capitalism was viewed as necessarily containing and heading toward socialism. The result, in a book like *Empire,* is a kind of magical Marxism. Where others earlier viewed capitalism as doing socialism's work, globalization here is viewed as a kind of socialization from within. Capital and empire here are autopoetic machines of power. Capital ravishes the planet but prepares the way for socialism in so doing. Proletarian struggles nevertheless persist in constituting the motor of capitalist development. The primary task, however, is not getting into but getting out of modernity. Information technology, which involves immaterial labour, in this way of thinking offers potential for a kind of spontaneous and elementary communism. The

contradiction in the argument is familiar: On the one hand, capitalism revolutionizes itself; on the other, socialism is the result of the conscious action of the new workers. The post-Marxist contradiction is the old Marxian contradiction revisited. These arguments seem to appeal to the remaining American radicals who want to insist both on the necessity of socialism and the centrality of intellectual militancy.

In the United Kingdom, Gramsci has been one of the connectors to post-Marxism. The most influential text here is that by Ernesto Laclau and Chantal Mouffe (1985), *Hegemony and Socialist Strategy,* itself an exemplary text in the sense that it juxtaposes the orthodox wisdom of Marx's 1859 Preface with Lacan and Wittgenstein. If anything goes, why not? The conduct of social theory becomes an eclectic mix, with the distinction for post-Marxism that the mix involves this combination of Marxian axioms and cultural theses from afar. Here, in *Hegemony and Socialist Strategy* at least, the emphasis is post-Marxist in equal proportions. A more synthetic approach is that taken by Stuart Hall, whose work in this sense places the emphasis on the Marxist rather than the post. Yet the very idea of "a Marxism without guarantees" places Hall firmly in the revisionist, or extensionist stream, for what was orthodox Marxism if not a theory of necessary guarantees? In the United Kingdom, one striking spinoff of post-Marxism was the adoption of the "New Times" motif by the Left magazine *Marxism Today* prior to its collapse into New Labour. Here the politics of post-Marxism took an alternative route to the new vanguard indicated earlier by bolshevism. As in the case of the modernization of the Australian Labor Party before it, Marxist intellectuals left the Communist Party and joined forces with the new revisionism of Blair. Gramsci's New Prince was no longer the Communist Party but the new Labour Party. A distinct trajectory followed Althusser out through Foucault into political theory (Barry Hindess) or via a return to the British radical thought of Cole and Laski toward the project of associative democracy (Paul Hirst).

In the United States, the influence of Althusser was more narrow, and that of Foucault more broad than in the United Kingdom or Australia. The broad appeal of Marxism into the 1930s shifted elsewhere, into pragmatism. Marxism showed considerable influence in the 1960s revival of critical theory via phenomenology, as in the journal *Telos.* America had its maverick Trotskyists, including the Hegelian Marxists who made up the Johnson-Forrest Tendency of the Socialist Workers Party, whose most eminent intellectual leaders were C. L. R. James and Raya Dunayevskaya. Dunayevskaya was emphatically Marxist, finding all kinds of new secrets in the less popular texts of Marx. James made a greater impact as an incipient postcolonial than as a post-Marxist, though he had also followed the earlier Marxian clue that socialism was the invading society within capitalism, the theme followed through by Hardt and Negri in *Empire.* Today, the followers of post-Marxism are scattered around places like western Massachusetts and North Carolina. A leading journal here is *Rethinking Marx,* sometimes abbreviated as *Remarx.* A leading book is *The End of Capitalism as We Knew It* (1996) by Catherine Gibson-Graham. The most influential Marxist intellectual writing on culture today, Fredric Jameson, is equally a candidate for the prize of post-Marxism, though his trajectory is more consistently aligned to the melancholic element of critical theory than to French Marxism. Perhaps the most exemplary case of post-Marxism in the mixed sense is Žižek. Žižek's mix of bolshevism and psychoanalysis is wilfully provocative and iconoclastic. Combining a strong sense of humour, sparkling prose, and vernacular example from film and television, Žižek manages nevertheless to remain a bolshevik comic in a decisively postbolshevik world. In his essay in *Revolution at the Gates* (2002), as in Hardt and Negri's *Empire,* Lenin is reconstructed as a nice guy who stumbled into bolshevism, but whose practice remains exemplary. Žižek postmodernizes Marxism by putting Lenin into cyberspace. Where Lenin in 1917 called for socialism = electrification and Soviets, Žižek calls for socialism as free access to the Internet and Soviets.

The irony of post-Marxism abounds. As with the postmodern, Marxists cannot be after themselves. The awkwardness of the category reflects the long and ambivalent relationship between Marxism and intellectual revisionism. An ever-changing world needs a changing theory. Marxism has to be open to revision; this is what compelled Western Marxists like Lukács and Korsch to insist that Marxism was a method, not a set of axioms, and which led Gramsci not to talk about Marxism but to do it by applying it to the local, Italian situation. In terms of social theory, the controversy over post-Marxism or revision indicates the fundamental nature of the Marxist claim to universal or total knowledge. Through its twentieth-century history as a social theory, Marxists have sought out supplements to strengthen Marx's work or to make it comprehensive—or to cover its lack—Darwin, Hegel, Freud. In sociology they have added Weber, in philosophy analytic or rational choice categories; for Althusser, Freud and structuralism, for Žižek, Lacan. Viewed from a distance, this theoretical will-to-synthesise in order to strengthen Marxism looks like an attempt to save Marxist theory against the world. In the long run, post-Marxism will surely be known as Marxism. An alternative approach, more often adopted by Marxist historians like Eric Hobsbawm or Bernard Smith, is to wear Marxism as a light cloak, to seek to apply it historically and comparatively. A more generalised cultural approach would be to acknowledge that Marxism emerged from European modernity and allow it to return there, to cease to be Marxist, truly to be after Marx.

— Peter Beilharz

See also Marxism; Revolution; Structuralist Marxism

FURTHER READINGS AND REFERENCES

Beilharz, P. 1994. *Postmodern Socialism.* Melbourne, Australia: Melbourne University Press.

Hardt, M. and A. Negri. 2000. *Empire.* Cambridge, MA: Harvard University Press.

Laclau, E. and C. Mouffe. 1985. *Hegemony and Socialist Strategy.* London: Verso.

Lefebre, Henri. 1970. *Beyond Marx.* Paris: PUF.

Sim, S. 2000. *Post-Marxism: An Intellectual History.* London: Routledge.

———, ed. 1998. *Post-Marxism: A Reader.* Edinburgh, Scotland: Edinburgh University Press.

Wright, S. 2002. *Storming Heaven: Class Composition and Struggle in Italian Autonomist Marxism.* London: Pluto.

Žižek, S. 2002. *Revolution at the Gates.* London: Verso.

POSTMODERNISM

The current historical moment goes by a variety of names, including postmodern, postnational, global, transnational, postindustrial, late capitalist, and the society of the spectacle. The ingredients of postmodernism and the postmodern self are given in three key cultural identities, those derived from the performances that define gender, social class, race and ethnicity. The patriarchal, and all too often racist, contemporary cultures of the world ideologically code the self and its meanings in terms of the meanings brought to these three cultural identities. The postmodern self has become a sign of itself, a double dramaturgical reflection anchored in media representations, on one side, and everyday life, on the other. All too often this self is reduced to its essential markers, which carry the traces of these three terms.

The postmodern terrain is defined almost exclusively in visual terms, including the display, the icon, the representations of the real seen through the camera's eyes, captured on videotape, and given in the moving picture. The search for the meaning of the postmodern moment is a study in looking. It can be no other way. This is a televisual, cinematic age.

Classical sociological ways of representing and writing about society require radical transformation. If sociology and the other human disciplines are to remain in touch with the worlds of lived experience in this new century, then new ways of inscribing and reading the social must be found (Lemert 1997; Lyon 1999).

DEFINING AND WRITING THE POSTMODERN

The postmodern as postmodernism is four things at the same time. First, it describes a sequence of historical moments from World War II to the present. These moments include the Vietnam War, the two Gulf Wars, the worldwide economic recessions of the 1970s and 1980s, the rise to power of conservative or neoliberal political regimes in Europe and America, the failure of the Left to mount an effective attack against these regimes, the collapse in the international labor movement, the emergence of a new, conservative politics of health and morality centering on sexuality and the family, totalitarian regimes in Europe, Asia, Latin America, and South Africa, the breakdown of the Cold War and the emergence of glasnost, and increased worldwide racism.

Second, the postmodern references the multinational forms of late capitalism that have introduced new cultural logics and new forms of communication and representation into the world economic and cultural systems. Third, it describes a movement in the visual arts, architecture, cinema, popular music, and social theory that goes against the grain of classic realist and modernist formations. Fourth, it references a form of theorizing and writing about the social that is antifoundational, postpositivist, interpretive, and critical.

Postmodern theorizing is preoccupied with the visual society, its representations, cultural logics, and the new types of personal troubles (AIDS, homelessness, drug addiction, family and public violence) and public problems that define the current age. At the most abstract level, the cultural logics of late capitalism define the postmodern moment (Jameson 1991).

But postmodernism is more than a series of economic formations. The postmodern society is a cinematic, dramaturgical production. Film and television have transformed American, and perhaps all other societies touched by the camera, into video, visual cultures. Representations of the real have become stand-ins for actual, lived experience. Three implications follow from the dramaturgical view of contemporary life.

First, reality is a staged, social production. Second, the real is now judged against its staged, cinematic-video counterpart. Third, the metaphor of the dramaturgical society or "life as theater" has now become interactional reality. The theatrical aspects of the dramaturgical metaphor have not "only creeped into everyday life" (Goffman 1959:254), they have taken it over. Art not only mirrors life, it structures and reproduces it. The postmodern society is a dramaturgical society.

Accordingly, the postmodern scene is a series of cultural formations that impinge upon, shape, and define contemporary human group life. These formations are anchored in a series of institutional sites, including the mass media, the economy and the polity, the academy, and popular culture itself. In these sites, interacting individuals come in contact with postmodernism, which, like the air we breathe, is everywhere around us: in the omnipresent camera whenever lives and money exchange hands, in the sprawling urban shopping malls, in the evening televised news, in soap operas and situation comedies, in the doctor's office and the police station, at the computer terminal.

The cultural formations of postmodernism do not have a direct, unmediated effect on the worlds of lived experience. The meanings of postmodernism are mediated and filtered through existing systems of interpretation. These meanings may be incorporated into a group's ongoing flow of experience and become part of their collective vocabulary and memory (i.e., the New York postmodern art scene during the 1970s and 1980s). Here the postmodern supports and strengthens a group's scheme of life. On the other hand, the multiple, conflicting cultural meanings of postmodernism may be judged to have no relevance to what the members of a group do, and hence be rejected (i.e., the rejection of postmodernism by mainstream American sociologists). Still other groups may incorporate portions of the postmodern and reject its other features (i.e., the cultural conservatives who value nostalgia). In this case, the postmodern will have a disjunctive effect, settling into one part of a group's way of life, without incorporation into its overall interpretive scheme. For still other groups, postmodernism may disrupt a way of life and even undermine it, as when postmodernists in the academy challenge the traditional literary canons of Western civilization and propose radical new reading lists that express the positions of racial, ethnic, and gender minorities.

In writing about this historical moment, the sociologist understands that there is no privileged position of absolute spectator, for how can the postmodern self write about itself when the very postmodern stuff it is made of conditions what it says, sees, feels, and hears? Of course, any hint of objectivity predicated on the privileged position of the absolute spectator must be relinquished. As an observer of the postmodern scene, I must recognize that I am grafted into every action and situation I write about. My point of contact with the contemporary postmodern world is the origin of my insights into this world.

THE TERM *POSTMODERN*

The term *postmodern* is a paradoxical oxymoron with a short history. How can something be post, or after the modern, when the modern represents the present, or recent moment (Hassan 1985:121). What comes after the present but another present, or period in history, which is a continuation of the present? It is a paradoxical oxymoron because it comes at the end of a series of other "post-isms," most important, poststructuralism, that amorphous theoretical formation that has theorized language, meaning, and textuality after the semiotic-structural revolution inspired by Saussure (1959). In a sense, postmodernism should have come first, for it describes the very conditions of experience these earlier isms responded to. Predictably, as postmodernism emerges as a distinct theoretical formation, it comes under attack from the very perspectives it seeks to surround and make sense of.

Users of the word are attempting to describe fields of political, cultural, aesthetic, scientific, and moral experiences that are distinctly different from those that were taken for granted in an earlier historical, commonly called modern or Enlightenment, phase of world history. It is not possible to give a precise date to the beginning of the postmodern period, as Virginia Woolf did for modernism, which she said began "in or about December, 1910" (Hassan 1985:122), although we may with, Hassan (p. 122), "woefully imagine that postmodernism began 'in or about September, 1939.'"

For present purposes, postmodernism will be defined as the cultural logic of late capitalism (see Jameson 1991). I intend the following meanings with this phrase. First, I reference the self-reflective working through of a multitude of contradictory meanings and understandings concerning human experience and its aesthetic, sociological, media, and textual representations in the current historical moment. This is commonly called intertextuality. Second, I ask, after Mills (1959), "[W]hat varieties of men, women [and children] now prevail in this . . . period" (p. 7), what personal troubles and public issues define this epoch, and how are these troubles and lived experiences represented in the cultural texts that cultural experts like sociologists, anthropologists, journalists, politicians, philosophers, and artists write?

Third, by cultural logic, I designate the logics of use, utility, exchange, and status or prestige value (Baudrillard 1981:66), which surround the production, distribution, and consumption of cultural commodities in the present moment, including human experience. That is, how are cultural objects transformed into instruments, commodities, symbols, and signs that circulate in fields of productive and conspicuous consumption (Baudrillard 1981:125–26)? A political economy of signs, unique to late capitalism, now mediates the worlds of cultural objects and lived experience. A double ideology of prestige and work ethic invades the signs that surround the objects that are consumed in this culture (Baudrillard 1981:32–3). This ideology is stitched into the linguistic fabrics of everyday life. More deeply, this ideology is now communicated via the print and electronic media in a way that transcends pure production and consumption. The new cold universe of the TV screen becomes a site where, as one skips from channel to channel, multiple texts split and fracture the self and its images. A near obscene, ecstasy of communication, which has eliminated all boundaries between the public and private self, is experienced. The viewer quietly sits with a channel switcher in hand, moving from one world to another, controlling a universe of experiences emanating from the cold screen that just sits and stares (gazes) back.

Fourth, by late capitalism is meant contemporary multinational, state-sponsored capitalist activities that cross-cut political regimes and national boundaries. Late capitalism corresponds to Baudrillard's (1983:25–6, 83) fourth historical order, the hyperreal, or the fourth order of the simulacrum (the previous three historical orders being pre-Renaissance, Renaissance, and the Industrial Age, and the previous regimes of representation being the orders of: sign = reality (pre-Renaissance), the counterfeit (Renaissance), and the simulation (Industrial Revolution).

This extended definition views postmodernism as a worldview, or unique set of structured experiences, shaped by late capitalism and given expression in new artistic, representational, and theoretical practices. Postmodernism may not be what we want it to be, but it is, as Jameson (1991:56) and Lemert (1997:xiii) argue, a condition that is no longer an option.

— Norman K. Denzin

See also Baudrillard, Jean; Deleuze, Gilles; Fordism and Post-Fordism; Jameson, Frederic; Modernity; Postmodernist Feminism; Simulation; Virilio, Paul

FURTHER READINGS AND REFERENCES

Baudrillard, Jean. 1981. *For a Critique of the Political Economy of the Sign.* St. Louis, MO: Telos.

———. 1983. *Simulations.* New York: Semiotext.

Goffman, Erving. 1959. *The Presentation of Self in Everyday Life.* New York: Doubleday.

Hassan, Uhab. 1985. "The Culture of Postmodernism." *Theory, Culture and Society* 2:119–32.

Jameson, Fredric. 1991. *Postmodernism, or the Cultural Logic of Late Capitalism.* Durham, NC: Duke University Press.

Lemert, Charles. 1997. *Postmodernism Is Not What You Think.* Malden, MA: Blackwell.

Lyon, David. 1999. *Postmodernity.* 2d ed. Minneapolis, MN: University of Minnesota Press.

Mills, C. Wright. 1959. *The Sociological Imagination.* New York: Oxford University Press.

Saussure, F. de. 1959. *Course in General Linguistics.* New York: Philosophical Library.

POSTMODERNIST FEMINISM

Like ecofeminism, postmodernist feminism is an amalgam of two distinct perspectives. This strand of feminist theory combines postmodernist with feminist standpoints, albeit in diverse shapes. The result is extremely powerful expressions of resistance to or rejection of Enlightenment notions, especially universalism, human nature, and sociopolitical progress. Postmodernist feminists join other postmodernists in rejecting or at least radically chastening these notions, and they bring to postmodernism women-centered concerns that go so far as to problematize the very notion "woman."

By rendering the identity and the concept of woman problematic, postmodernist feminists illustrate some of the key theoretical underpinnings of postmodernism. To wit, postmodernist feminists argue that no universal identity or reality undergirds "woman." From their perspective, theorizing as if this category represents some universal status results in theorizing away the multitude of differences gathered together and erased under this conceptual aegis. For postmodernist feminists, then, there is no female "nature" any more than there is a single, unitary human nature throughout human history and across human societies. Furthermore, postmodernist feminism rejects or substantially refashions the tales of progress for girls and women implied in modernist narratives of progress for humankind. Aware of all those girls and women around the globe whose lives have worsened as "progress" supposedly marched on, these feminist theorists resist the erasure of differences that sustains misbegotten dreams and perpetuates biased theorizing.

Postmodernist theorizing among feminists exhibits the same propensities toward ambiguity, irony, and paradox found elsewhere in the world of postmodernism. These feminist theorists also exhibit a parallel feel for how localized and embedded knowledge inevitably is. Thus, they criticize the exaggerated claims of other scholars, particularly around issues of objectivity as well as generalizability.

Three postmodernist feminist theorists whose ideas have wielded widespread influence are Judith Butler, Donna Haraway, and Laurel Richardson. Some of Butler's (1990) most important work theorizes about the cultural "intelligibility" of only some few identities, so that other identities get rendered as nothing more than deviations reflective of what is perverse, maladapted, or abnormal. Butler treats identity as a performative phenomenon heavily regulated within institutionalized regimes that construct some enactments as "real"—that is, intelligible—versions of a given identity and other enactments as something *other than* versions of that identity. For example, "womanhood" is recognizable only within socially regulated boundaries. Some versions hardly get seen at all. Some women's behavior, then, gets recognized as little more than self-centeredness, man hating, opinionated stridency, or bitchiness rather than versions of womanliness. Butler (1992:15–16) argues that "part of the project of postmodernism . . . is to call into question the ways in which such 'examples' and 'paradigms' serve to subordinate and erase that which they seek to explain." More generally, Butler (1992:15–16) treats identity as something normative, regulatory, and exclusionary.

For Haraway (1993:257, 258), feminist postmodernism or postmodernist feminism revolves around "politics and epistemologies of location, positioning, and situating" as well as around a rejection of universalism. Her feminism greatly favors what is partial and limited as the key to claims that are rational and meaningful. Haraway (1990:190–91) considers irony more than a rhetorical tool. For her, it is also a political strategy that revolves around serving as a "valid witness" who is modest as well as allied with diverse other witnesses. Best known perhaps for her contributions to feminist science studies as well as feminist epistemology more generally, Haraway has greatly affected how feminist theorists think about issues of knowledge construction, including scientific methodology and scientific writing.

Richardson's (1997:55) "feminist-postmodernist practice" rests on seeing that feminist theorists themselves have built up a number of crucial quasi-narratives emanating from the goals of social change and cultural transformation. Richardson casts her critical consciousness on these as well as other narratives. In large measure, her work revolves around questions about representation, including issues of voice, ethics, and genre as well as issues of hierarchy and power. Perhaps more than any other English-language social theorist, Richardson has interrogated writing practices not only for their biases and erasures but also for their transformative promise.

Richardson's interrogation has included bold experiments with diverse genres in her own theoretical work. Her creative, critical explorations of literary and other genres for writing social theory put Richardson in the company of other feminist theorists insistent on bursting representational limits. For example, two feminist social theorists—Katherine Gibson and Julie Graham—have published their collaborative work using the pseudonym "J. K. Gibson-Graham" and then proceeded to use a lot of first-person *singular* voice. (Gibson-Graham 1996) Ultimately, what Richardson and these other postmodernist feminists are theorizing is how narrative conventions constrain what can be said, who is authorized to say it, and who can expect to read it in meaningful, effective ways. Not surprisingly, many feminist theorists are critical of or ambivalent toward postmodernism. Often uncomfortable with and sometimes confused about postmodernists' stances toward modernist values such as equality, some feminist theorists advocate skepticism toward postmodernist approaches. Gibson-Graham (1996:236) argues, for example, that postmodernism may have burst a lot of epistemological limits but has at the same time "shackled" politics. Still, Gibson-Graham's (p. 241) stance sufficiently illuminates possibilities such as politicizing the very project of "discursive destabilization" that informs much postmodernist work.

— Mary F. Rogers

See also Butler, Judith; Feminism; Feminist Epistemology; Postmodernism

FURTHER READINGS AND REFERENCES

Butler, Judith. 1990. *Gender Trouble: Feminism and the Subversion of Identity.* New York: Routledge.

———. 1992. "Contingent Foundations: Feminism and the Question of 'Postmodernism.'" In *Feminists Theorize the Political,* edited by Judith Butler and Joan W. Scott. New York: Routledge.

Gibson-Graham, J. K. (1996) "Reflections on Postmodern Feminist Social Research," In *Bodyspace: Destabilizing Geographies of Gender and Sexuality,* edited by Nancy Duncan. London: Routledge.

Haraway, Donna. 1990. "A Manifesto for Cyborgs: Science, Technology, and Socialist Feminism in the 1980s." In *Feminism/Postmodernism,* edited by Linda J. Nicholson. New York: Routledge.

———. 1993. "Situated Knowledges: The Science Question in Feminism and the Privilege of Partial Perspective." In *Feminism and Science,* edited by Evelyn Fox Keller and Helen E. Longino. Oxford, UK, and New York: Oxford University Press.

Richardson, Laurel. 1997. *Fields of Play: Constructing an Academic Life.* New Brunswick, NJ: Rutgers University Press.

POSTSOCIAL

Postsocial analysis attempts to develop an understanding of current changes of social forms and of sociality in general. Broadly speaking, what postsocial theory aspires to is the analysis and discussion of an environment in which the social principles and structures we have known hitherto are emptying out and other elements and relationships are taking their place. While it may be correct that human beings are by nature social animals, forms of sociality are nonetheless changing, and the change may be pronounced in periods of cumulative historical transitions. The term *postsocial* shines an analytic light on contemporary transitions that challenge core concepts of human interaction and solidarity and that point beyond a period of high social formation to one of more limited sociality and alternative forms of binding self and other. Postsocial developments are sustained by changes in the structure of the self; these changes are captured by models that break with Meadian and Freudian ideas proposed during a period of high sociality and that emphasize the autoaffective side of the self and its nonsocial engagements. The notion *postsocial* refers to the massive expansion of object worlds in the social world and to the rise of work and leisure environments that promote and demand relations with objects. A postsocial environment is one where objects displace human beings as relationship partners and embedding environments, or where they increasingly mediate human relationships, making the latter dependent upon the former. Postsociality also implies a shift in the collective imagination from social and political preoccupations to other topics. We no longer seek salvation in society but elsewhere—in the biological sciences, in financial futures, in information knowledge. What some of these areas promise can be captured by the idea of life rather than by that of society and by the notion of enhancement rather than that of salvation.

SOCIALITY AS A HISTORICAL PHENOMENON: EXPANSIONS AND RETRACTIONS

The current retraction of social principles and structures is not the first in recent history. One of the great legacies of classical social thought is the idea that the development of modern society involved the collapse of community and the loss of social tradition. Yet what followed was not an asocial or nonsocial environment but a period of high social formation—a period when the welfare state was established, societies became societies of (complex) organizations and structures, and social thinking took off in ways that stimulated institutional changes.

The first region of expansion of social principles during the course of the nineteenth century and throughout the early decades of the twentieth was that of social policies, and this was linked to the rise of the nation-state. Social policies as we know them today derive from what Wittrock and Wagner (1996) call the "nationalization of social responsibility" (p. 98ff.)—the formulation of social rights alongside individual rights and the positing of the state as the "natural container" and provider of labor regulations, pension and welfare provisions, unemployment insurance, and public education. A second region of expansion, connected to the first, was that of social thinking and social imagination. A corollary of the institutionalization of social policies were new concepts of the forces that determine human destiny: They were now more likely to be thought of as impersonal, social forces. Rather than assuming the automatic adaptation of individuals to changing environmental conditions, these ideas focused on the prevailing imbalances and their social causes: the social causes of occupational accidents would be an example (Rabinbach 1996). Sociology played an important role in bringing about the shift in mentality through which individuals came to be seen as the bearers of the individual costs of collective structures. When Mills (1959) argued for a "sociological imagination," he tried to capture in one concept the phenomenon of societal processes that individuals do not recognize but that affect and change their lives. A third area of expansion of social principles and structures was that of social organization. The rise of the nation-state implied the rise of bureaucratic institutions. The growth of industrial production brought with it the emergence of the factory and the modern corporation. The advent of universal health care became embodied in the clinic, and modern science in the research university and laboratory. Industrial, nation-state societies are unthinkable without complex modern organizations. Complex organizations are localized social arrangements serving to manage work and services in collective frameworks by social structural means. A fourth area of expansion was that of social structure. The class differentiation of modern society is itself an outgrowth of the Industrial Revolution and its political consequences as well as of processes of social and political measurement and categorization.

It is central to our experience today, however, that these expansions of social principles and of socially constituted environments have come to a halt. In many European countries and in the United States, the welfare state, with all its manifestations of social policy and collective insurance against individual disaster, is in the process of being "overhauled"; some would say "dismantled." Thatcherism in Britain and "neo-liberalism" in general could be viewed as a partially successful attempt to contest some of the social rights acquired in the previous half century (Urry 2000:165). Social explanations and social thinking run up against, among other things, biological and economic accounts of human behavior against which they have to prove their worth. The mobilization of a social imagination was an attempt to identify the collective basis for individuals' predicaments and dispositions to react. This collective basis is now more likely to be found in the similarity of the genetic makeup of socially unrelated members of the population. Social structures and social relations also seem to be losing some of their hold. The individual of industrialized society had already been portrayed as a "homeless mind"—an uprooted, confused, and inchoate self, whose predicaments contributed to the expansion of social principles discussed before (Berger, Berger, and Kellner 1974). But well into the twentieth century, this self appeared to be sustained by traditional family relations. What analysts see disintegrating today are these "primordial social relations" (Lasch 1978). When complex organizations are dissolved into networks, some of the layered structural depth of the hierarchically organized social systems that organizations used to represent gets lost on the way. The global architecture of financial markets, for example, is enabled and supported by complex technological rather than social organizational systems. The expansion of societies to global forms does not imply further expansions of social complexity. The installation of a "world-society" would seem to be feasible with the help of individuals and electronically mediated interaction structures, and perhaps becomes plausible only in relation to such structures. The concept of society itself, geared as it is to the nation-state and to horizontal concepts of social structure, loses much of its plausibility in an era of globalization.

Postsocial transitions of this kind imply that social forms as we knew them have become flattened, narrowed, and thinned out; they imply that the social is retracting, in all of the senses just described. What sociologists have posited, accordingly, is a further boost to individualization (e.g., Beck 1992). This interpretation is not wrong in pinpointing subject-centered rather than collective structures as being on the rise in contemporary cultures. But it is nonetheless one-sided in looking at current transitions only from the perspective of a loss of human relationships and received forms of the social. What postsocial theory offers in the stead of the scenario of simple "desocialization" is the analysis of alternative forms of binding self and other, changes in the structure of the self that accommodates these forms, and forms of social imagination that subordinate sociality to new promises and concerns.

SOCIAL AND POSTSOCIAL SELVES: FROM THE INNER CENSOR TO STRUCTURES OF WANTING

The core model of the "social" self of the period of high sociality is the idea of the self as composed of an ego and an internalized "other" that represents society and functions as an inner censor. In Mead, the inner censor is called the "generalized other"; it is closely coupled to the intrasubjective conformist past of the self and the self as an object, which Mead calls the "me." At the opposite end of this side of the self lies the "I," the spontaneous, unpredictable, disobeying self. The "I" has the power to construct reality cognitively, and by redefining situations, can break away from the "me" and the norms of society. The "me" and the "generalized other" can be likened to Peirce's "you"; Peirce held the "you" to be a critical self that represented society and to which all thought was addressed. These notions are also roughly similar to Freud's "super-ego," the rule-carrier that functions as a regulative principle in an internal dynamic of morality and deviance. In Mead's theory, the self first originates from such a dynamic. It arises from role taking, from taking the perspective of the other first interpersonally, when engaged with a close caretaker, and then also intrapersonally.

This "I-you-me" system of the social self and its most sophisticated version (Wiley 1994:34ff., 44ff.) can be contrasted with a second model that understands the self not as a relation between the individual and society but as a structure of wantings in relation to continually renewed lacks. This notion of the self can be derived from Lacan, among others (Wiley 1994:33). Like Freud, Lacan is concerned with what "drives" the subject, but he derives this wanting not as Freud did from an instinctual impulse whose ultimate goal is a reduction in bodily tension but rather from the mirror stage of a young child's development. In this phase, the child becomes impressed with the wholeness of his or her image in the mirror and with the appearance of definite boundaries and control—while realizing that she or he is none of these things in actual experience. Wanting or desire is born in envy of the perfection of the image in the mirror (or of the mirroring response of the parents); the lack is permanent, since there will always be a distance between the subjective experience of a lack in our existence and the image in the mirror, or the apparent wholeness of others (Alford 1991:36ff.).

The two conceptions may seem similar in that both emphasize the discrepancy between the "I" and a model, but they are in fact quite different. From the idea of the self as composed of an inner censor results an ego subjected to feelings of guilt, experiencing rebellion, and attempting to "live up to" social expectations. In contrast, the self as a permanently reiterated lack gives rise to the desire, also permanent, to eliminate the lack. The former model would seem to result in actions that are perpetually curtailed as an ego attempts to adapt them to internalized norms; it will also result in deviant actions that transgress boundaries of which the actor is well aware. The second model yields actions spurred on by the unfulfillability of lacks, or by new wants opening up simultaneously with the (partial) fulfillment of old ones. In the first model, the actors' free fall from society is continually broken as they catch themselves (or are caught by others) in compliance with social rules and traditions, and return to their ontological security. In the second case, no society of this sort is in place any longer to provide ontological security. The "you" is the idealized self in the mirror or the perfect other. The actor would seem to be freed from guilt complexes; but he or she is like a vagrant perpetually searching, stringing together objects of satisfaction and dismantling the structure again as he or she moves on to other goals.

This search system is autoaffective and self-sustaining, indeed self-energizing; as a structure of wanting, the self is extended through continually renewed and discovered lacks that renew its motivation and affectivity. The Meadian "I-you-me" system neglects the autoaffective side of the self, which is not its self-love but its willingness to become engaged in circuits that renew wanting. What we need to retain from the Lacanian "mirror" stage is the idea of a self that is susceptible to such autoaffective pursuits. We need not find the mirror stage itself plausible as a description of what actually happens to the infant when it first recognizes itself in a mirror. In contemporary society, the mirror is exteriorized in a media, image, and knowledge culture; it is no longer either a physical mirror or the caretakers' activity of "back-projecting," their activity of "reflecting," like a mirror, the child's being in relation to parental idealizations and expectations. Instead, the mirror response is articulated by the media and professional image industries that project images and stage "wholeness." The mirror is also present in the "cathedrals of consumption" Ritzer (1999:8ff.) analyzes

in the shopping malls and other places that offer enchanted displays of possible selves.

In a media, image, and knowledge culture that continually reactivates a lack-wanting dynamic, the reflexive (mirror image) self may describe contemporary selves better than the "I-you-me" system and may in fact be in the process of displacing and reshaping it. In this sense, a media, image, and knowledge culture is also a postsocial culture that stimulates and sustains postsocial selves. The seeming fit of the lack-wanting model with contemporary life may also result from the problems of primordial social relations, which no longer offer the kind of normative guidance and tight structures of control that are needed to give rise to an inner censor and a dynamic of guilt and rebellion, compliance, and transgression. The liberalization of partnership and family life that Lasch (1978) and Beck (1992), among others, describe, the detraditionalization of education and the individualization of choice, all conspire to prevent a strong "I-you-me" dynamic founded on the internalization of a censor. Mead, Freud, and others who contributed to the "I-you-me" model were not only proposing abstract theories of the self. Their conceptions were also rooted in existence, in particular patterns of attachment and socialization that are no longer dominant in contemporary society.

BINDING WORK AND THE BINDING OF SELF AND OTHER

If a media and image culture plays into postsocial trends, so does a knowledge culture. The self that is caught in a lack-wanting dynamic can easily be tied to the "wanting" objects of knowledge-oriented environments. This extends questions of postsocial development to contexts of work and brings up the issue of nonhuman objects.

A knowledge society is characterized by professional work that can hardly be seen as corresponding to the Marxian notion of alienated labor. Industrial ("instrumental," "alienated") labor has been characterized in terms of its machinelike functionality where the action of the worker becomes an intrinsic part of a machine process, its lack of uniqueness or general reproducibility by anyone with comparable training, its measurability, the divisibility of the work into components that seem freely exchangeable, and the separation of means from ends such that the work is abstract and divorced from the product (Berger et al. 1974:24, 39). The logic of the production process may also dictate the management of social relations and cause the identity of others at the workplace as well as one's own identity to become divided and anonymized. But in today's Western societies, under 20 percent of the workforce are employed in the production sector. An increasing percentage of employees work in knowledge-based industries and services that include the image industries and science and education. These industries and services are marked by a complexification of the work process rather than by job simplification and rationalization: sophisticated instruments replace simple machines, performance criteria relate not so much to speed, quantity, and large volume than to quality, innovation, and personalized service, there are fewer specific rules and room and demand for human agency, and an emphasis on information seeking and the upgrading of knowledge (Hage and Powers 1992:50ff.). The objects of this work are not only the goal and output of activities but things to which workers relate; they make relational demands and offer relational opportunities to those who deal with them. As objects of innovation and inquiry, they are characteristically open, question-generating, and complex. They are processes and projections rather than definitive things (Rheinberger 1992). Work with them reveals them by increasing rather than reducing the questions they raise. In this sense, they are the polar opposite of tools like hammers and drills. These tools and instruments are like closed boxes. Objects of knowledge-based work, on the other hand, are more reminiscent of open drawers filled with folders extending indefinitely into the depth of a dark closet. Since objects of knowledge are always in the process of being materially defined, they continually acquire new properties and change the ones they have. But this also means that these objects cannot quite ever be fully attained, that they are, if you wish, never quite themselves. What we encounter in the work process are stand-ins for a more basic lack of object.

The open, unfolding character of such objects uniquely matches the "structures of wanting" by which the postsocial self was characterized: Objects provide for the continuation of a chain of wantings through the signs they give off of what they still lack, and subjects (experts) provide for the possibility of the continuation of these objects by attempting to define and articulate them. This basic mutuality binds self and object. Object relations of this sort imply a level of reciprocity, perspective-taking, and at times solidarity (exemplified in Knorr Cetina 1997) between human subjects and nonhuman objects. Intimate object relationships of this sort may also be realized in industrial work, but they would seem to be far more of a structural requirement—and a source of innovation—of knowledge-based work. It is difficult to imagine a successful scientist or a high-tech specialist who is not intimately involved with his or her object of work. These involvements illustrate object relations as forms of binding self and other. As the respective work environments expand and encroach upon home life, object-relations may substitute for and mediate human relations. Objects may also be the risk winners in the context of the increased relationship risks in human relationships. Empirical studies suggest that for many in these industries, work is by no means a negative experience, but rather the place where they feel emotionally more at home than in their actual home life (Hochschild 1997).

Object relations have expanded into the domain of consumption, an area that takes us back to the working of the media and image industries but that can also be considered in the light of the objects involved. Objects that are acquired to be used also make relational demands, offer binding sites for desires, and display similar qualities to those in knowledge-based work environments. Many consumer objects have a dual structure in that these objects can simultaneously be ready-to-hand usable things and, absent objects of inquiry, developed further by technological research (cars, computers), artistic design (fashion, commercials), or analysis (finance). This duality repeats itself when a device like a computer is on the one hand "ready" to be used but also retains an interior indefiniteness of being—a potential for further discovery and exploration involving a relational engagement of the subject with the object. In addition, a subject that develops an intrinsic relationship with a consumer object like a car, a computer, or a fashionable outfit will be lured into further pursuits by the referential nexus of objects and their continuous transmutation into more attractive successor versions. Thus, consumption illustrates the sense in which objects not only attract a person's desire but allow wanting to continue, by giving it its serial, chainlike structure.

Object relations tend to involve more than a formal correspondence between a self as a chain of wanting and the transmutational character of postindustrial objects. They are enriched by a semiotic dimension (an object signaling what it still lacks and a subject interpreting these signals), role-taking (subjects putting themselves in the position of the object), crossover (objects occupying a subject's mind), and flow experience (the subject becoming a "flow" of concentrated object experience). All these dimensions together account for the lure of object relations. The different relational components are marked by an interspecies reciprocity of a subject doing one thing and an object "reciprocating" with another. Postsocial binding is a form of liminal sociality, when compared with human binding.

THE CULTURE OF LIFE AND THE RISE OF A LIFE-CENTERED IMAGINATION

Object relations as construed above point away from a human-centered picture of society and back to nature and the material world. On the subject's side, they point not only to a temporalized self—pursuing wants in object worlds—but also to the possibility that this self is closer to material objects and to "nature" than the enlightenment concept of humans, that has been foundational for sociology, suggested. As assumptions about rationality give way to research into human cognition, homo sapiens loses IQ and gains emotions and visceral definition (Elster 1998). He or she also gains openness and "transmutability"—through technological, biological, genetic, and surgical as well as psychological enhancements and alterations. Just as the notion of an object in a knowledge and media era no longer fits in with received concepts of objects as fixed material things, so the notion of a subject no longer fits in with received notions of humans as defined by reason, intentions, and agency and perhaps inner conflicts, as the main characteristics of interest to the social sciences. The postsocial subject is also a posthumanist subject. Yet it is part of a "culture of life," by which is meant a culture capacitated by and centered on material, technological, and informational processes.

The expansion of a social imagination had involved, since the Enlightenment, hopes for the perfectibility of human society in terms of equality, peace, justice, and social welfare, with the high point being Marxist visions of a socialist revolution. These ideas have not disappeared with the retraction of social principles and the collapse of Marxism. But the promise and hope and the excess imagination that went into visions of social salvation have been extended to other areas where they find progressive inspiration. What has become thinkable today is the perfectibility of life—through life enhancement on the individual level, but also through the biopolitics of populations, through the protection and reflexive manipulation of nature, through the idea of intergenerational (rather than distributional) justice. The notion of life can serve as a metaphor and anchoring concept that illustrates a cultural turn to nature and how it replaces the culture of the social. "Life" bridges divisions between the natural, the human, and the information sciences and stands for an open-ended series of phenomenological, biological, economic, and other significations and processes. In the social sciences, "life" thinking is illustrated by those areas that have turned the individual and its search for Ego and "I"-related pleasures and affirmations into topics of investigation. But from a broader perspective, many areas focusing upon the subject can be seen to play into life-centered thinking—and in the social sciences today, the phantasized unit is more the subject than society. Theories of identity and identity politics and of the self and subjectivity provide examples of such trends, as do ideas embodied in the vast numbers of self-help books derived from psychology that counsel individuals about how to enhance their lives. Hope and promise in reference to individual life also come from finance, where excess imagination—supported by the profession of financial analysts—is invested in financial scenarios as ways of enriching the self and the life course. What feeds into this situation are institutional changes in pension schemes that have moved from solidarity-based principles, where income from the working population is redistributed to retirees, to personal investment schemes where one plans and pays for one's retirement benefits over the course of a lifetime. One massive source of life-centered thinking is the life sciences themselves. They produce a stream of research that inspires imaginative elaborations of the human individual as enriched by genetic, biological, and technological supplements and upgrades. These ideas relate to the enhancement of life through preimplantation genetic diagnosis and screening, germ-line engineering (genetic changes that can be passed down to an individual's offspring), psychotropic drugs that improve emotions and self-esteem, biotechnological means of enhancing the life span, and human cloning. The ideas suggest the perfectibility of individual life, but they also strongly implicate unrelated populations, those sharing particular genes, exposures, or histories of adaptation to environmental conditions, and benefiting in the aggregate from genetic measures and drugs. On a more conceptual and theoretical level, a return to human nature-based theories of rights and justice can be associated with life-centered ideas (Fukuyama 2002), as can Heidegger's temporal notions of human existence as "being towards death" and vitalist concepts (Lash 2003) that can be linked to Bergson and Tarde. The lack-wanting temporalized self and its processual, transmuting objects captures dimensions of this vitality. A theoretical notion used in several fields is that of flow. Though authors define flow differently, with concepts ranging from flow as a state of consciousness and experience to that of information as flow, the notion captures the dynamic dimensions and temporal structuring that "life" suggests.

LIMINAL SOCIALITY

For neo-Marxist thinkers, post-Fordist knowledge-based systems appropriate workers' lives rather than their labor, with work encroaching upon and difficult to distinguish from free time and coinciding with the individual's lifetime. The life-enhancement literature, bioethical controversies about the rights to genetically and technologically enrich lives and gene lines, and the literature depicting individuals lured into object pursuits and searching for optimal experience would suggest individuals and populations deeply involved in the appropriation of their lives and those of their offspring. Conflicts over the "appropriation of life" (Lash 2003) rather than over the appropriation of surplus value—between economic agents, individuals, *and* the state and nonhuman objects (such as viruses)—may well be what defines postsocial environments. But the divides may not run along traditional lines; for example, many of the individuals mentioned pursue their wants in structural cooperation and collusion with (rather than in structural opposition to) their corporate environments—with the knowledge firms and services in which they work, or with the media, image, and aesthetic industries that collect individual pursuits in sports, fashion, and design into marketable lifestyles. In knowledge areas, the new constellation is one of knowledge workers empowered by object relations and finding additional embeddedness in epistemic communities that collect around object worlds. In areas of self-testing "edgework" (extreme sports, high-speed trading, etc.), individuals also appear to gain empowerment from their engagements and show a similar tendency to aggregate in object-focused groups. Human relations may take second place vis-à-vis these engagements. The welfare state, with its goals of social solidarity and redistribution, also operates in terms of a logic orthogonal to a culture of life. It is geared to horizontal social structural divisions rather than to intra- and intergenerational life, skeptical vis-à-vis some of the newly feasible life advantages, and dedicated to the provision of services that often seem deficient in the light of projected and phantasized technological possibilities and the powers of collective human, nonhuman, and hybrid agents.

Postsocial systems include sociality, but in reconfigured, specialized, more mediated, and limited ways, as liminal forms of sociality. Postsocial relations are human ties triangulated with object relations and forming only with respect to these relations. A postsocial system may be one where information structures have replaced previous forms of social coordination, as when sophisticated hardware and software systems substitute for social networks and enable expanded, accelerated, and intensified global financial markets. Postsocial is what one might call a level of intersubjectivity that is no longer based on face-to-face interaction and may in fact not involve interaction at all but rather "communities of time" formed by the joint observation of common, electronically transmitted content. Postsocial systems may arise around the sort of relatedness enabled by the Internet, for which the characteristics that have traditionally defined human relationships (feelings of obligation and trust, etc.) are not constitutive or even relevant. Postsocial forms are not rich in sociality in the old sense, but they may be rich in other ways, and the challenge is to analyze and theorize these constellations.

— Karin Knorr Cetina

See also Actor Network Theory; Consumer Culture; Freud, Sigmund; Identity; Individualism; Latour, Bruno; Mead, George Herbert; Self and Self-Concept; Social Studies of Science

FURTHER READINGS AND REFERENCES

Alford, C. Fred. 1991. *The Self in Social Theory: A Psychoanalytic Account of its Construction in Plato, Hobbes, Locke, Rawls, and Rousseau.* New Haven, CT: Yale University Press.

Beck, Ulrich. 1992. *Risk Society: Towards a New Modernity.* London: Sage.

Berger, Peter L., Brigitte Berger, and Hansfried Kellner. 1974. *The Homeless Mind: Modernization and Consciousness.* New York: Vintage.

Elster, Jon. 1998. "Emotions and Economic Theory." *Journal of Economic Literature* 36:47–74.

Fukuyama, Francis. 2002. *Our Posthuman Future: Consequences of the Biotechnology Revolution.* New York: Farrar, Straus & Giroux.

Hage, Jerald and Charles H. Powers. 1992. *Post-Industrial Lives: Roles and Relationships in the 21st Century.* Newbury Park, CA: Sage.

Hochschild, Arlie R. 1997. *The Time Bind: When Work Becomes Home and Home Becomes Work.* New York: Metropolitan Books.

Knorr Cetina, Karin. 1997. "Sociality with Objects. Social Relations in Postsocial Knowledge Societies." *Theory, Culture and Society* 14:1–30.

Lasch, Christopher. 1978. *The Culture of Narcissism: American Life in an Age of Diminishing Expectations.* New York: Norton.

Lash, Scott. 2003. "Empire and Vitalism." Presented at the annual meeting of the Eastern Sociological Society, Philadelphia, PA.

Mills, C. Wright. 1959. *The Sociological Imagination.* New York: Oxford University Press.

Rabinbach, Anson. 1996. "Social Knowledge, Social Risk, and the Politics of Industrial Accidents in Germany and France." Pp. 48–89 in *States, Social Knowledge, and the Origins of Modern Social Policies,* edited by D. Rueschemeyer and T. Skocpol. Princeton, NJ: Princeton University Press.

Rheinberger, Hans-Jörg. 1992. "Experiment, Difference, and Writing: I. Tracing Protein Synthesis." *Studies in History and Philosophy of Science* 23:305–31.

Ritzer, George. 1999. *Enchanting a Disenchanted World: Revolutionizing the Means of Consumption.* Thousand Oaks, CA: Pine Forge.

Urry, John. 2000. *Sociology beyond Societies: Mobilities for the Twenty-First Century.* London: Routledge.

Wiley, Norbert. 1994. *The Semiotic Self.* Chicago, IL: University of Chicago Press.

Wittrock, Björn and Peter Wagner. 1996. "Social Science and the Building of the Early Welfare State: Toward a Comparison of Statist and Non-Statist Western Societies." Pp. 90–116 in *States, Social Knowledge, and the Origins of Modern Social Policies,* edited by D. Rueschemeyer and T. Skocpol. Princeton, NJ: Princeton University Press.

POSTSTRUCTURALISM

Poststructuralism is a loosely connected set of reflections on and extensions and critiques of structuralism that emerged mostly in France in the mid-1960s. Poststructuralism does not advocate a wholesale rejection of the premises and arguments of structuralism; rather, poststructuralist thought is best viewed as a sequel to the structuralist works of Ferdinand de Saussure and Claude

Lévi-Strauss. It is most often associated with the work of thinkers such as Roland Barthes, Hélène Cixous, Gilles Deleuze, Jacques Derrida, Michel Foucault, Luce Irigaray, Julia Kristeva, and Richard Rorty, although few of these theorists apply the term to their work. Poststructuralism is known primarily for its critiques of humanism, essentialism, and foundationalism; its rejection of the search for absolute meanings and lawlike generalizations; its decentering of the subject and the death of the author; and its skeptical attitude toward the so-called project of modernity.

Structuralism, as exemplified in the linguistics of Ferdinand de Saussure, the anthropology of Claude Lévi-Strauss, and the early literary theory of Roland Barthes, sought to create a theoretical apparatus that would become a foundation for rigorous analysis and research in all of the human and social sciences. Structuralism propounds four basic tenets. First, it rejects the argument that all meanings, practices, and actions can be understood in terms of and are propelled by subjective consciousness. Second, structuralism holds that meanings, practices, and actions can be explained only by studying the relations among elements in structures or systems. Third, structuralism views the binary opposition as the key to understanding structural relationships among elements (e.g., signifier/signified, raw/cooked, male/female). Finally, structuralists tend to be concerned mainly with synchronic analysis, that is, studying the relations among elements of a structure at a moment in time. Poststructuralists generally agree with the first tenet, but for various reasons to be explored in what follows, reject the others. For present purposes, the work of Jacques Derrida and Michel Foucault best illustrates the poststructuralist critique of structuralism.

Derrida's most trenchant critique of structuralism takes issue with the second and third tenets of structuralist thought. Derrida argues that the structuralist view of language as a stable system that can be studied only by reference to the relations among its elements relies on a number of untenable assumptions. The most problematic of these assumptions is what Derrida calls logocentrism, which is, moreover, a problematic assumption of most of Western thought. Logocentrism is a term that describes the tendency of Western thinkers to privilege one term in a binary opposition over the other term, thus creating a hierarchy that organizes thought (e.g., speech over writing, male over female, reason over superstition). This hierarchy then appears to be a stable and natural one that has its roots in a stable system of language and its elements. Derrida aims to upset these hierarchical relationships by showing that binary oppositions are rarely exhaustive and mutually exclusive, and are often contradictory, rendering the binary useless for any descriptive or epistemological purposes. In addition, the two terms of a binary opposition define themselves against each other (which he calls supplementarity), and any hierarchy is therefore merely arbitrary. Derrida's

project can be described as the deconstruction of logocentrism, which involves breaking down the ways in which logocentrism operates in order to dismantle its hegemony in Western society. In short, Derrida takes aim at the assumed stability of language and the ways in which structuralists construct binary oppositions.

Foucault's early work on the archaeology of knowledge, particularly *The Order of Things* (1966), proceeds in structuralist fashion and actually praises structuralism for providing the human sciences with a theoretical framework for analysis that discards the centrality of meaning and action based on subjective consciousness and its representations. The "death of man," according to Foucault, opens up opportunities for social science to think about phenomena of life, language, and labor without encountering the many philosophical pitfalls of subjectivity. Foucault's archaeology of knowledge also demonstrates the early influence of structuralism in his work insofar as it represents a search for the rules that govern what can be said in any particular discourse at a given historical moment.

While Foucault's *The Order of Things* and other archaeological works employ structuralist methods and underscore the ingenuity of structuralist thinking, they also provide many reflections on the shortcomings of structuralist thought. The most important critique of structuralism, for present purposes, concerns its inability to explain how systems and structures change over time. Foucault considered himself a historian of systems of thought, and, as a historian, he was interested in how systems and structures change (change over time is diachronic), while structuralism limits itself to studying the relations among elements of structures in synchronic fashion, that is, at one moment in time.

In order to ask and answer questions about historical change, then, Foucault began to develop a method of inquiry that became known as the genealogy of power, which is exemplified in his book *Discipline and Punish* (1979). Adopting a genealogical method provides a way to approach historical problematizations of knowledge and governing. A genealogical method, according to Foucault, studies events, but not the events of traditional political history or the history of great men; rather, genealogy may take the formation and articulation of a problem (e.g., how a society deals with those who have violated its laws) as its event. Genealogy focuses on problems, moreover, in order to study the heterogeneous lines of descent that form assemblages of practices, the multitude of problematizing discourses that such practices generate, and the regimes of truth that these practices and problematizing discourses instantiate. In addition, Foucault characterized the genealogy of power as a "history of the present." This does not, however, imply that the present is a necessary outcome of past historical events. Instead, it tries to make use of history to understand the present and to demonstrate the contingency of what has transpired historically. The genealogy of power is therefore often viewed as a form of social criticism.

Foucault's genealogy of power contends that power and knowledge are inextricably linked. This is known as the power/knowledge nexus. Critical to Foucault's genealogy is the contention that power is a source of dynamism that is productive (i.e., not simply repressive) and dispersed throughout society into many local centers. Through this lens of power, Foucault traces the ways in which early modern European states responded to such problems of governing as criminality, the practices of punishment and social control that emerged as ways of dealing with criminality, and the bodies of knowledge (e.g., penology, criminology, and other social sciences) that emerged alongside these practices. Foucault adds that, while power is pervasive, it always meets some form of resistance. While Foucault's genealogy of power does not indict bodies of knowledge that emerge from practices of power as false or invalid (some of them may even state universally objective truths), it does challenge scholars and practitioners to consider alternative practices and discourses in order to counter the established regimes of truth and practice.

James M. Murphy

See also Deconstruction; Deleuze, Gilles; Derrida, Jacques; Foucault, Michel; Irigaray, Luce; Kristeva, Julia; Lévi-Strauss, Claude; Logocentrism; Postmodernism; Rorty, Richard; Saussure, Ferdinand de; Structuralism

FURTHER READINGS AND REFERENCES

Culler, Jonathan. 1982. *On Deconstruction: Theory and Criticism after Structuralism.* Ithaca, NY: Cornell University Press.

Derrida, Jacques. 1974. *Of Grammatology.* Baltimore, MD: Johns Hopkins University Press.

———. 1981. *Dissemination.* London: Athlone.

Foucault, Michel. 1966. *The Order of Things: An Archaeology of the Human Sciences.* New York: Vintage.

———. 1979. *Discipline and Punish: The Birth of the Prison.* New York: Vintage.

Sarup, Madan. 1993. *An Introductory Guide to Post-structuralism and Postmodernism.* Athens, GA: University of Georgia Press.

POWER

In its broadest sense, *power* refers to the capacity to produce effects on the world, to bring about changes in it. The entity or agent possessing this capacity may be natural, organic, or human. Thus, we speak of the power of windstorms, electric grids, and animals, including human beings. Both Thomas Hobbes's definition of power as "man's present means to any future apparent good" and Bertrand Russell's as "the production of intended effects" refer solely to humans and are therefore relevant to the social sciences, Russell's on the assumption that humans alone are capable of full intentionality, that is, of conscious purposive action. Hobbes identified power with the possession of "means" to achieve desired ends (or "goods"), whether they are employed to that effect or not, but like Russell he restricted power, at least implicitly, to intended action. Russell's definition by contrast specifies only the actual exercise of power rather than regarding power as a *capacity* or *potential* when not exercised. These limits are overcome by defining human power broadly as any capacity for action that produces effects or outcomes and then proceeding to enumerate the diverse forms it may take. Such a definition recognizes the possession, or latent existence, of power when it is not actually being exercised, nor does it exclude the unintended effects of an action. These may on occasion be more consequential than those intended, although since most human conduct involves intended action, unintended effects are often one of its by-products.

Power as the production of effects by some persons on others clearly includes social interaction with at least a minimal mutuality or reciprocity of influence, which indeed *defines* social interaction. "Power" and "influence" are here synonymous. Asymmetrical power "over" other people exists when an actor regularly produces more and greater effects on others than the reverse, although so long as there is some reciprocal response by the subordinate party, it is a *social* rather than a physical relation affecting only a person's body, as in bodily obstruction or confinement or violence and the infliction of pain. Such regular *social* power relations are clearly a primary concern of the social sciences.

Power may be exercised over few or many persons; its scope, the spheres of life and range of actions of the power subject it governs, may be narrow or comprehensive; it may be limited or intensive in its effects, that is, relatively unrestricted in the kinds of effects it produces from life-and-death concerns to minor adjustments of behavior. Power described as "absolute" is highly comprehensive and intensive but is likely to be low in extensiveness, even limited to a single person, as in the power of a master over a slave (Aristotle's original example of unrestricted power), a parent over an infant or small child, or a jailer over a prison inmate, although such dyadic power relations are usually regulated by law and custom. The extremely comprehensive, intensive, and extensive power exercised in the twentieth century by several states with large populations, notably Nazi Germany and Soviet Russia, came to be described as "totalitarian" and was regarded as identifying a new and altogether unprecedented kind of political regime dependent on recently invented technologies of surveillance and communication able to penetrate and intervene in the private lives of its subjects. The enforcement of ritual affirmations of such regimes (as in "Heil Hitler" salutes) by all citizens had the effect of cowing potential dissidents into silence and the appearance of passive acquiescence.

The phrase *naked power* is often used to mean the imposition or threat of sanctions, that is, of some penalty or deprivation for noncompliance with an order. In popular usage the term *power* often misleadingly carries at least a faint suggestion of coercion that is lacking in the case of such cognates as *influence* or *authority*. The broader definition advanced here eliminates that restrictive implication. Compliance with an order or directive achieved through the offering in exchange of rewards rather than the imposition of penalties, in short the inducement of obedience by "positive" rather than "negative" sanctions, is also a form of power, although once "rewards" have become habitual, like wages or salaries for regular work, their threatened or actual withdrawal is apt to be experienced as economic coercion. A person's compliance with another's directive out of a felt sense of obligation to obey is clearly a separate and distinct form of power, often called "legitimate authority," or even "authority" *tout simple,* and contrasted with coercion and positive inducement. The obligation to obey is a corollary of the power holder's right, often enough obligation, to direct or command. Even *persuasion,* which implicitly appears to presuppose in form the equality of the interacting parties, becomes a power relation when one party possesses much greater persuasive abilities than another. The collective power of mass persuasion possessed by modern communications media—newspapers, cinema, radio and television, even billboards in public places, et al.—is undeniable in modern society. *Manipulation,* defined as the concealment of the power holder's intention from the power subject, is also a form of power, one that may involve acting on the environment to induce a desired response without necessarily engaging in face-to-face social interaction at all.

The right or obligation to command and the corollary obligation to obey are vested in positions or roles that are part of the structure of social institutions. They typically form a hierarchy, or in military parlance, a chain of command. The emergence of managerial or directive roles, exercising power when different activities performed by many separate people need to be coordinated to achieve a desired goal, is inevitable. Sheer assembled but undifferentiated aggregates of people forming crowds, mobs, mass demonstrations, and audiences have certainly played crucial parts in history, notably in revolutions, but their survival in contrast to that of major institutions is inherently contingent and transitory. Markets, strikes of labor, and elections are institutionalized procedures enabling dispersed aggregates of people to exercise collective power despite the very limited power of any single individual member.

Western thinkers since at least Plato's attribution to Thrasymachus of "justice is the interest of the stronger" in *The Republic,* including Machiavelli, Hobbes, and the early twentieth-century Italian thinkers labeled the neo-Machiavellians, have insisted on the primacy of coercive force in all politics. Marx and Weber have sometimes been too one-sidedly assigned to this tradition, although their views of power were more complex. Yet even Machiavelli, the most famous or at least notorious of these figures, regarded love as well as fear as necessary to secure the power of princes, though he thought fear more essential. Max Weber's definition of power as the ability to enforce one's will even in the face of conflict or resistance, which certainly indicates coercion, has probably been the most widely accepted definition among sociologists and has often been assimilated to the cynical realist canon, although his "even" implies that command—obedience relations need not be based on force or threatened force. Moreover, Weber is also famous for having identified three forms of the "legitimation" of power: traditional, rational-legal, and charismatic, which have been widely adopted and elaborated by later social scientists. Tradition appeals to custom rooted in the practices of "eternal yesterday"; rational-legal authority is based on the need to coordinate specialized roles in large organizations or on imputed expertise or greater knowledge in the case of the professions ("doctor's orders"); charismatic authority is belief in a particular individual's prophetic mission or destiny. Weber's definition of the state as that agency possessing "a monopoly of the legitimate use of force" in society explicitly combines coercion and legitimacy. The definition suggests diverse motives for obeying political power, a "fear-love" mix in Machiavellian terms, distributed among a plurality of different subjects yet also conceivably coexisting in the breasts of single individuals. Totalitarian regimes have been described as ruling through "terror and propaganda," which clearly connotes a combination of threats of force and appeals to legitimacy.

Highly differentiated and complex modern societies include many different power-wielding roles distributed among its institutions. Whether the holders of power constitute a coherent group or power elite promoting either their own distinctive values and interests or those of a larger group forming a ruling class are essentially contested issues rooted in ideological conflicts unlikely ever to be definitively resolved to everyone's satisfaction. When power is broadly defined simply as the *power to* satisfy wants, inequality in the distribution of material wealth and social prestige or status is obviously a phenomenon of power, as Weber recognized, although its individual beneficiaries need not exercise direct power over anyone else. The Marxist conception of class domination takes this for granted while assuming that many or most subjects possess *false consciousness,* a term that acknowledges, if invidiously, the legitimacy of power in their eyes. Marxism asserts the primacy of economic power in regarding the state as the mere executive organ of an economic ruling class. The autonomy of political power is thereby denied or minimized, although it has been stressed by thinkers from Machiavelli to Weber, who have by no means denied the frequent interdependence of economic and political power. Autonomous political power is maximized by autocratic rulers, from the absolute monarchs of the past to modern dictators who have often been military leaders directly controlling armed forces. Constitutional democracies with regular elections based on universal suffrage allow the many component groups in complex urbanized societies to influence and shape political decisions.

Power is often grouped with material wealth and prestige or status as a universal object of striving. Aspirants to power are said to be driven by a "will to power," a "power lust" or "power drive" just as deeply rooted in human nature as economic self-interest and the wish for approval from others. While there undoubtedly are such persons, it is doubtful that commanding and forbidding are widely desired in and of themselves because of the intrinsic satisfactions they afford rather than for their instrumental value in serving widely varied aims and purposes. Defined as *power to,* as any means to any desired end, power is certainly universally desired, if rarely for its own sake as a direct source of pleasure. Power is not therefore a psychological desideratum on the same plane as material wealth and prestige or status, although it may be sought as a means of attaining wealth or status and as a source of status and social honor in its own right. In institutionalized social roles, the exercise of power over others is a normative requirement of the role itself, although the fact that it involves personal judgments not reducible to sheer routine decision making makes it prone to abuse by being diverted to serve the power holder's own personal interests or that of unauthorized others. Nor is there an "instinct" of submission motivating the obedience of subordinates correlative to the alleged will to power, the two motives either separating two distinct psychological classes of individuals or coexisting in the psyches of single persons.

Its susceptibility to abuse and in its extreme forms to tyranny accounts for power often being described as a necessary evil. Yet it might just as plausibly be labeled a necessary good, for the many achievements of advanced modern societies that benefit humanity could not exist in the absence of marked institutionalized inequalities of power by no means limited to the sovereignty of states.

— Dennis H. Wrong

See also Foucault, Michel; Hegemony; State; Surveillance and Society; Weber, Max

FURTHER READINGS AND REFERENCES

Aron, Raymond. 1960. "Macht, Power, Puissance: prose democratique ou poesie demoniacque?" *Archives Europeenes de Sociologie* 1:27–51.

Bierstedt, Robert. 1974. *Power and Progress: Essays on Sociological Theory.* New York: McGraw-Hill.

Giddens, Anthony. 1984. *The Constitution of Society.* Cambridge, UK: Polity.

Jouvenal, Bertrand de. 1958. "Authority: The Efficient Imperative." Pp. 159–69 in *Authority,* Nomos 1, edited by Carl J. Friedrich. Cambridge, MA: Harvard University Press.

Lukes, Steven. 1974. *Power: A Radical View.* London: Macmillan.

Poggi, Gianfranco. 2001. *Forms of Power.* Oxford, UK: Blackwell.

Russell, Bertrand. 1938. *Power: A New Social Analysis.* London: George Allen & Unwin.

Wrong, Dennis H. 1995. *Power: Its Forms, Bases, and Uses.* New Brunswick, NJ: Transaction.

POWER-DEPENDENCE RELATIONS

Power-dependence relations refers to exchange relations between actors, emphasizing the dynamics of power in those relations. The term comes from a seminal 1962 article by Richard Emerson that introduced the relationship between power and dependence in exchange relations as a key element of the perspective in sociology known as exchange theory, and the cornerstone of most approaches to the study of exchange in networks. The analysis of power and dependence in exchange relations is applicable to any realm of social interaction in which entities exchange. Consequently, it has been used and developed in a number of areas of sociology. This includes relations between parents and between parents and children in studies of the family; relations between employees and between bosses and employees within formal organizations; relations between formal organizations; relations between managed care organizations, physicians, and patients; and relations between political actors.

The relationship between power and dependence in an exchange relation may be stated as a simple power-dependence principle: *In an exchange relation between two actors, the actor who is least dependent has the most power.* An actor is an entity, typically a person or organization, that has likes it acts to obtain and dislikes it acts to avoid. An exchange relation is a tie between two actors in which each does something to benefit the other and that exists for that reason. *Power* is a term many scholars have defined and used differently. However, in the statement of the power-dependence principle, power means power *over* the exchange partner, or the ability to affect the partner's behavior. *Dependence* refers to the degree to which a particular exchange partner has control over the supply to its partner of its partner's likes and dislikes. Another version of the power-dependence principle is the principle of least interest: *In a relationship between two actors, the actor with the least interest in the relationship has the most power.*

The explanation for the power-dependence principle is not difficult. Let us assume that the more an actor wants something, the more cost the actor will be willing to bear to get it. Then the more Actor B wants what Actor A provides, the more cost B will be willing to bear to get it; and the more superior A is as a source of what B wants, the more B will be willing to bear the cost of doing what A wants. In other words, the more dependent B is on A, the more power A has over B. In his 1962 article, Emerson points out the two roots of dependence: the importance to A of what B can provide and the availability to A of alternative sources for what B provides. Dependence is greater the more what B provides is valued and the less alternative sources are available.

Emerson next took the important and influential step of extending study of power-dependence relations to study of networks of such relations. In these exchange networks, the network structure is the source of variation in the dependence of exchange partners. According to the power-dependence principle, this in turn causes variation in power. For example, consider a simple three-person exchange network: A linked to B linked to C (diagrammatically, A—B—C), in which A and C are alternative sources of the same good for B. Alternatively, the exchange in question could be spending time together, for example, on a date. In this network, B has two sources of its desired good, while its two partners have only one source each, B. This makes B less dependent on them than they are on B and hence gives B more power. Stemming from the theoretical and empirical work of Emerson and his colleague Karen Cook, the study of exchange networks has been an active and productive area of research for several decades.

In early work on power-dependence relations, several ancillary issues arose. With subsequent emphasis on exchange networks and structural sources of dependence and power, some of these early issues have had little attention, although they have not been settled. One such issue concerns what happens to power when it is used. If using power entails satisfying the exchange partner's dependence, then using power may diminish it. However, under some circumstances, that may not be the case. This issue clearly is important for understanding power in exchange relations over the long term and needs further investigation.

Another such issue concerns value: What do actors value, how much, and why? What makes goods and resources mutually substitutable to an actor, and to what extent? How does that affect dependence and thus power? Emerson discussed some of these questions in his 1972 chapters and was working on them further at the time of his premature death. Since value—likes and dislikes—is an important root of dependence, understanding value is crucial for understanding power-dependence relations. Nevertheless, work and progress in this area has been relatively scanty.

Finally, coercion is one issue that has seen extensive work and development, primarily by Linda Molm and her students and associates. Exchange may involve coercion, in that what one or both parties offer and give the other may be not some good or reward but instead relief from punishment. The coercive exchange relation is indeed a power-dependence relation, but what creates the dependence is current punishment or a credible threat, perhaps involving prior occurrence of punishment. The dynamics of power-dependence relations involving coercion and of exchange networks incorporating such relations can be quite different from the dynamics of those involving only goods.

— Joseph M. Whitmeyer

See also Emerson, Richard; Exchange Networks; Game Theory; Molm, Linda; Power; Rational Choice; Social Exchange Theory

FURTHER READINGS AND REFERENCES

Cook, Karen S., Richard M. Emerson, Mary R. Gillmore, and Toshio Yamagishi. 1983. "The Distribution of Power in Exchange Networks: Theory and Experimental Results." *American Journal of Sociology* 89:275–305.

Emerson, Richard M. 1962. "Power-Dependence Relations." *American Sociological Review* 27:31–41.

———. 1964. "Power-Dependence Relations: Two Experiments." *Sociometry* 27:282–98.

———. 1972. "Exchange Theory, Part I: A Psychological Basis for Social Exchange" and "Exchange Theory, Part II: Exchange Relations and Network Structures." Pp. 38–87 in *Sociological Theories in Progress,* vol. 2, edited by J. Berger, M. Zelditch Jr., and B. Anderson. Boston, MA: Houghton Mifflin.

Molm, Linda D. 1997. *Coercive Power in Social Exchange.* Cambridge, UK: Cambridge University Press.

PRAGMATISM

Pragmatism is the distinctive contribution of American thought to philosophy. It is a movement that attracted much attention in the early part of the twentieth century, went into decline, and reemerged in the last part of the century. Part of the difficulty in defining pragmatism is that misconceptions of what pragmatism means have abounded since its beginning, and continue in today's "neopragmatism."

Pragmatism is a method of philosophy begun by Charles Sanders Peirce (1839–1914), popularized by William James (1842–1910), and associated with two other major early representatives, John Dewey (1859–1952) and George Herbert Mead (1863–1931). Pragmatism was defined in 1878 by Peirce ([1878]1992) as follows: "Consider what effects that might conceivably have practical bearings, we conceive the object of our conception to have. Then, our conception of these effects is the whole of our conception of the object" (p. 132).

William James's book *Pragmatism* ([1907]1977) gathered together lectures he had been giving on the subject since 1898 and launched a much broader interest in pragmatism and also controversy concerning what the philosophy means. Most early critics took James as the representative of pragmatism, yet Peirce claimed that James misunderstood his definition in holding the meaning of a concept to be the actual conduct it produces rather than the conceivable conduct. Early European critics such as Georg Simmel, Émile Durkheim, and Max Horkheimer took pragmatism to be an example of an American mentality that reduced truth to mere expediency, to what James unfortunately once expressed as "the cash value of an act." There has also been a tendency to confuse the philosophy with the everyday meaning of the word *pragmatic* as expedient, yet Peirce, citing Kant, was careful to distinguish *pragmatic* from *practical.*

PRAGMATIC OR PRACTICAL?

James was interested in the experiencing individual, for whom practical events marked the test of ideas. As he put it in *Pragmatism:* "The whole function of philosophy ought to be to find out what definite difference it will make to you and me, at definite instants of our life, if this world-formula or that world-formula be the true one" ([1907] 1977:379). Philosophy is taken by James to be a means for practical life, whereas for Peirce, pragmatism was a method for attaining clarity of ideas within a normative conception of logic, that is, within the norms of continuing, self-correcting inquiry directed toward truth. Logical meaning, for Peirce, is not found in "definite instants of our life" but in the context of the community of self-correcting inquiry. And truth is that opinion the community would reach, given sufficient inquiry, and which is known fallibly by individuals.

The earliest roots of pragmatism are to be found in the remarkable series of papers from around 1868, published when Peirce was 29 years old. In "Some Consequences of Four Incapacities," and its four denials of Cartesianism, he destroyed the Cartesian foundations of modern philosophy. Against Descartes's attempt to base science on the indubitable foundations of immediate knowledge, Peirce argued that we have no powers of *introspection* or of *intuition,*

using these terms in their technical logical sense as meaning direct, unmediated, dyadic knowledge. Cognitions are instead determined by previous cognitions, and all cognitions are inferences or mediate signs that, in turn, address interpreting signs. The possibility of scientific truth does not derive from indubitable foundations but by the self-correcting process of interpretation. Peirce, who rejected foundationalism, proposed a regulative ideal of an unlimited community of inquirers, capable of inquiry into the indefinite future as a basis for fallible, objective knowledge. It is within this context of a general community of interpretation that the "conceivable consequences" of pragmatic meaning are to be found.

Peirce's pragmatism must be understood within his conceptions of semiotic (doctrine of signs) and of inquiry, as must his separation of it from practical life. Peirce differed from the other pragmatists in keeping theory separate from practice, not out of elitism, but because in this master scientist's view, the scientific method is not vital enough to run society or one's individual life. In his view, practical decisions often need to be based on beliefs and gut feelings, which produce the "definite difference" of James, whereas theoretical life can only be based on fallible *opinions,* always subject to correction within the unlimited community of inquiry. Pragmatic meaning is found, as he put it elsewhere, not in a particular experiment but in *experimental phenomena,* not in "any particular event that did happen to somebody in the dead past, but what *surely will* happen to everybody in the living future who shall fulfill certain conditions" (1931–1938, vol. 5, para. 425).

The term *conceivable* marks the difference between Peirce's and James's pragmatic maxims. In reducing Peirce's "conceivable consequences" to consequences, James seemed not to understand why conceivable consequences are not exhausted by actual instances, and why "pragmatic," in the philosophical sense, is very different from "practical," in the everyday sense.

What works today, in a practical sense, may not work tomorrow, and may not work tomorrow because conceivable consequences not yet actualized today came to fruition, and may yet come to further fruition. "Ye may know them by their fruits," is pragmatic, when one considers those fruits as conceivable consequences, capable of further fruition, that is, as general.

The pragmatic meaning of a stop sign is that it will determine consequences in general and not simply the individual autos that stop. It is also the autos that would stop, that is, the conceivable consequences. For these reasons, Peirce attempted to distinguish his own original version of pragmatism from the one James popularized and that others, such as F. C. S. Schiller and Giovanni Papini, drew their own versions from. So he renamed his original version *pragmaticism,* a term, he added, "ugly enough to be safe from kidnappers."

PRAGMATISM AS GENERAL OUTLOOK

Peirce and James first met as students at Harvard University, yet neither held PhDs. Peirce had a master's degree in chemistry and James received an MD. John Dewey received one of the first PhDs in philosophy in the United States from Johns Hopkins University in 1884, where he studied briefly with Peirce. Dewey met Mead, who received a PhD from Harvard, when they taught briefly at the University of Michigan, and a few years later, after being named chairman of philosophy, psychology, and pedagogy at the University of Chicago, brought Mead there. Late in his life, penniless, Peirce added a middle name of "Santiago"—St. James—in thanks to a fund James put together on his behalf.

One sees a broad range of topics in the writings of these four "classic" pragmatists, in contrast to the growing demands for technical "specialization" that marked the course of academic philosophy. But when these early pragmatists are invoked, it is usually not only for their particular doctrines of pragmatism but rather their larger philosophical outlooks in general that are included as "pragmatist thought" and that do share some similarities. So the term *pragmatism* is often used to describe the broader philosophical movement, including Peirce's doctrine of signs, Dewey's philosophy of "instrumentalism," and Mead's developmental model of the self.

Pragmatism in general was an attempt to undercut the Cartesian-Kantian problem of starting with a subject and an object and then figuring out how to put them together. It denied that knowledge was reducible either to a knowing subject or to an immediate sensation of an object, thus rejecting rationalism and the sensationalism of British empiricism. Pragmatism denied the myth of a private and asocially constituted subject or object by locating meaning in the vital tissue of the generalized community. It began instead with triadic mediated sign-acts, from which could be prescinded a "subject" and an "object." Objectivity is thus thoroughly social and mediate, rather than individual and immediate.

Though James may have been short on philosophical rigor, his writings brimmed with ideas and vigor. In *Pragmatism,* for example, he set out in the opening chapter his distinction between *tough-minded* and *tender-minded* outlooks. In his *Principles of Psychology* (1890), he coined the term *stream of consciousness,* and he developed the idea of "The Moral Equivalent of War" in 1910 in an essay of that title, a mobilization for a kind of peace corps.

In his later work, James developed his philosophy in *The Will to Believe* (1897), in which truth again is viewed from the experiencing individual, and in *A Pluralistic Universe* (1909), where he emphasized multiple perspectives over a "monistic" theory of truth. Against what he saw as a "block universe" in idealism, James argued for a pluralistic and open-ended universe that would allow for the qualitative uniqueness of experience.

All four pragmatists carved out phenomenological aspects of their theories. Peirce literally founded a phenomenology around the same time as Edmund Husserl, though he settled on the term *phaneroscopy* to avoid confusing it with Hegel's *Phenomenology of Spirit.* James began with the phenomenon of religious experience rather than belief or authority in his study of *The Varieties of Religious Experience* (1902). Qualitative immediacy is an element of communicative conduct in Dewey's and Mead's theories of aesthetic experience, of the problematic situation, of Mead's discussions of the place of emergence and novelty, and of his work *The Philosophy of the Present* (1932), of Peirce and Dewey's discussions of the first stage of inquiry—Peirce's "abductive inference" and Dewey's "problem finding"—and of Peirce, James, and Mead's discussions of the "I" as an element of the "I" "me" internal dialogue that constitutes thought.

James and Dewey, the chief public spokespersons for pragmatism, were also powerful manifestations of the modernist impulse in the early twentieth century. Their ardent optimism, pluralism, and situationalism showed new ways to reconceive mind as vitally continuous with nature, experience, and conduct. Dewey was the most widely known public philosopher in America in the first half of the twentieth century, and social reform was a central preoccupation of his public philosophy. He had become associated with Jane Addams and Ellen Gates Starr and their social settlement Hull House in the 1890s, which they founded in Chicago shortly before Dewey arrived there. Mead shared Dewey's interests in social reform and the possibilities for reconstructing democratic life in America. Though his work was hardly known outside academic circles, Mead became a mainstay in sociology, even as Dewey's reputation went with pragmatism into eclipse in mid-century philosophy. Through his student Herbert Blumer, philosopher and social psychologist Mead became a representative of "Chicago sociology" and what Blumer termed "symbolic interactionism."

It should be noted that all four pragmatists were active as psychologists: Peirce and James were active in experimental psychology, and Dewey and Mead were interested in developmental psychology, and specifically in the "genetic epistemology" movement in America in the 1890s and on. Dewey published a key functional psychology article in 1896, "The Reflex Arc in Psychology." There he argued that the stimulus-response arc model needed to be reconceived functionally as a "circuit, a continual reconstitution," rather than an arc, in which both stimulus and response occur within a mediating organic coordination rather than as only externally related. This kind of argument reappears in his later turn to the context of the situation and in his late view of meaning as transaction.

Mead is perhaps most known to sociologists for his developmental theory of the self, which involves a progressive internalization of the other, beginning in a "conversation of gestures," through a level of "play" involving specific others, and culminating in a "generalized other," an inner representation of community who is "me" in that internal dialogue of "I" and "me" that comprises the self of self-consciousness. In Mead's view, it is the internalized "attitudes" and values of the community, and not only a specific role model, that mark the fully developed human self.

The human ability to engage in gestural conversations retains its preconscious animal sensing and emotional communicative origins while yet embedded in the inner representation of social life that is the generalized other. Mead termed this representation "the significant symbol," which is a gesture, sign, or word simultaneously addressed to the self and another individual.

Communicative mind is a semiotic process for Mead and the other pragmatists, involving neural processes, though not reducible to them. Mind is viewed not as internal to the brain but as in transaction with its environment. Mind, as the communicative organ of the self, involves the further interpretations and pragmatic consequences it engenders.

ECLIPSE AND REEMERGENCE

Part of the confusion over pragmatism has to do with the peculiar history of thought in the twentieth century as philosophy became institutionalized in American universities and as scientific modernism swept away American philosophy. Though he was Mead's former student and editor of the publication of Mead's lectures, *Mind, Self, and Society* (1934), Charles Morris believed that logical positivism and its claim to dyadic knowledge based in "thing-sentences" (or semantic reference) provided philosophical foundations more scientific than pragmatism. The open-ended Chicago pragmatism of Dewey and Mead, centering on the human being within a live social environment—a human capable of criticism, cultivation, emergence, and continued growth in the community of interpretation—was replaced in the 1930s at the University of Chicago by the closed positivist dream of the completion of philosophy personified by Morris and Viennese refugee Rudolph Carnap, and later by the even more stringent technicalism of analytic philosophy that in turn replaced positivism.

In his 1938 monograph *Foundations of a Theory of Signs,* Morris systematically reduced Peirce's triadic view of signs to a dyadic-based positivism without acknowledgment of Peirce or of Peirce's logical arguments for signs as triadic inferences (as Dewey pointed out in an essay written when he was in his late 80s), although Morris did acknowledge Peirce a couple of decades later. A number of Morris's inverted Peircean semiotic terms, such as "pragmatics," have become institutionalized, despite their reversal of Peirce's definitions. To use Peirce's term *pragmatism,* and then claim originality for the term *pragmatics* as a specifically semiotical term, without describing the relation of Peirce's pragmatism to semiotic, or how Morris's view radically departed from the source terms he uses—claiming that it is about "the relations of signs to their users," as though the users are not also signs—amounts to the further "kidnapping" of the meaning of pragmatism.

Philosophical pragmatism resurfaced as a significant part of intellectual life in the last decades of the twentieth century. What had been a body of thought reduced largely to the influence of Mead in academic social science, and passing references to James, Dewey, and Peirce, reemerged with significance for semiotics, philosophy, literary criticism, and other disciplines. There are ongoing collected works projects for all four pragmatists.

James's and Dewey's situationally based philosophies now seemed to provide a vital alternative to the narrowly positivist/language analysis world in which academic philosophy had become enclosed in the Anglo-American context. Strangely enough, Mead's fortunes rose in the 1940s and 1950s in sociology just as his work and that of the other pragmatists were being eclipsed in philosophy. Symbolic interactionism had functioned in mid-century to keep the Meadian stream of pragmatic thought flowing, though it lost sight of the other pragmatists. Now Mead has begun to be taken seriously by philosophers again.

NEOPRAGMATISM

Jürgen Habermas and Richard Rorty are two widely discussed thinkers closely associated with the renewal of interest in pragmatism. Both are heavily influenced by the "linguistic turn"—by the dominant postwar Anglo-American "language analysis" (out of which Rorty in particular derives)—and both are contributors to attempts to link Anglo-American and continental philosophies.

Influenced both by his colleague Karl-Otto Apel's inquiry into Peirce and the tendency of critical theorists, such as Max Horkheimer, to view pragmatism as positivism, Habermas depicted the pragmatisms of Charles Peirce and John Dewey in his early work *Knowledge and Human Interests* (1971), as having critical potential, yet as ultimately ingredients in the development of modern positivism. He viewed pragmatism from a Kantian and Weberian standpoint as a doctrine of inferential inquiry legitimized by transcendental structures of instrumental action.

Habermas missed Peirce's crucial rejection of Kant's transcendental philosophy: To put it tersely in Kantian terms, science is not the "synthesis" of the immediate, as Kant thought, but rather the "analysis" of the mediate, of signs. Habermas also imposed a Weberian concept of strategic, "instrumental action" that was alien to Peirce's community of interpretation framework and that of the other pragmatists as well, including Dewey's "instrumentalism."

Nevertheless, the explosion of interest in Habermas, in connection with Apel's inquiries, also sparked interest in pragmatism both in Europe and America. Apel, who translated Peirce into German, helped to show how Peirce's rejection of foundationalism had, in effect, transformed Kant's transcendental subject into a "transcendental" unlimited community of inquirers as the limit of knowledge. Apel's reintroduction of the term *transcendental*, in its technical sense, to Peirce's philosophy is problematic, since Peirce believed that the pragmatic maxim denied Kant's concept of incognizable things-in-themselves and thereby the concept of transcendental underpinnings.

Habermas's appreciation of pragmatism grew since those early works, and he attempted to develop a "theory of communicative action," based on a concept of "linguistically generated intersubjectivity" influenced in part by Mead. Although Habermas sought to come to terms with the body of pragmatism as a whole, his theory of communicative action remains grounded in Kantian dichotomies at variance with the pragmatic tradition.

Rorty claims to be a pragmatist influenced by Dewey, as well as such seemingly distant sources as Martin Heidegger and Ludwig Wittgenstein. The pragmatic vision Rorty extols is that of philosophy as conversation instead of a quest for truth or wisdom. In his book *Consequences of Pragmatism* (1982), Rorty depicted pragmatism as a doctrine rooted in a conception of inquiry, but inquiry as unconstrained conventional conversation.

Rorty's pragmatist bears an uncanny resemblance to the language game approach of later Wittgenstein and his rejection of his early "picture theory of knowledge." The pragmatists also rejected such foundationalism, beginning with Peirce's bold anti-Cartesian articles of the late 1860s and culminating with Dewey and Bentley's *Knowing and the Known* in 1949, but they did so by articulating a fallibilist, experiential model of inquiry that showed, in contrast to Rorty's statement, how the "nature of objects" and the evolutionary biosocial genius of the human mind tempered or constrained inquiry toward truth and "self-knowledge."

Despite Rorty's claim of being a pragmatist, a number of his leading ideas are at odds with pragmatism. Peirce, James, Dewey, and Mead were all genuinely interested in exploring the place of biology in human conduct, yet Rorty denies the influence of biology. Peirce, Dewey, and Mead developed theories of meaning that involved more than conventional signification, yet Rorty views signs as purely conventional. The four earlier pragmatists all viewed experience as an element of conduct, yet Rorty (1989) limits conduct to conventional or contingent meaning, claiming that people are solely products of socialization—"There is nothing to people except what has been socialized into them." (p. 177). Unlike Dewey, Rorty denies continuity between the self and its community.

Finally, pragmatism is at heart a philosophy of purport, yet Rorty's postmodern outlook denies authentic purposiveness, viewing meaning as sets of conventions. Meaning is simply what one happens to believe, subject to arbitrary "redescriptions," and the pragmatic criterion of consequences is undone.

Despite shortcomings in contemporary neopragmatism, the ongoing reengagement with the earlier pragmatists shows that significant consequences for social theory are still being discovered.

— Eugene Halton

See also Habermas, Jürgen; Mead, George Herbert; Rorty, Richard; Self and Self-Concept; Symbolic Interaction

FURTHER READINGS AND REFERENCES

Dewey, John. 1960. *Dewey on Experience, Nature, and Freedom.* Edited by Richard J. Bernstein. Indianapolis, IN: Bobbs-Merrill.

Habermas, Jürgen. 1987. *The Theory of Communicative Action.* 2 vols. Translated by Thomas McCarthy. Boston, MA: Beacon.

Halton, Eugene. 1995. *Bereft of Reason: On the Decline of Social Thought and Prospects for its Renewal.* Chicago, IL: University of Chicago Press.

James, William. 1977. *The Writings of William James: A Comprehensive Edition.* Edited by John J. McDermott. Chicago, IL: University of Chicago Press.

Joas, Hans. 1985. *G. H. Mead: A Contemporary Re-examination of His Thought.* Translated by Raymond Meyer. Cambridge, MA: MIT Press.

Mead, George Herbert. [1922] 1981. "A Behavioristic Account of the Significant Symbol." In *Mead: Selected Writings,* edited by A. J. Reck. Chicago, IL: University of Chicago Press.

Peirce, Charles Sanders. [1878] 1992. "How to Make Our Ideas Clear." In *The Essential Peirce: Selected Philosophical Writings,* vol. 1, *1867–1893,* edited by Nathan Houser and Christian Kloesel. Bloomington, IN: Indiana University Press.

———. 1931–1938. *The Collected Papers of Charles Sanders Peirce.* 6 vols. Edited by Charles Hartshorne and Paul Weiss. Cambridge, MA: Harvard University Press.

Rorty, Richard. 1989. *Contingency, Irony, and Solidarity.* New York: Cambridge University Press.

Shalin, Dmitri, ed. 1992. "Habermas, Pragmatism, and Critical Theory." Special issue of *Symbolic Interaction* 15:3.

PROCEDURAL JUSTICE

Any interaction among people involves procedures or processes through which the people involved coordinate their actions. Procedural justice is the study of people's subjective evaluations of the justice of those procedures—whether they are fair or unfair, ethical or unethical, and otherwise accord with people's standards of fair processes for interaction and decision making. Procedural justice is usually distinguished from subjective assessments of the fairness of outcomes (distributive justice) and the degree to which people feel that they are gaining or losing resources in the group (outcome favorability).

The procedures found in groups, organizations, and societies have several key elements. First, there are those aspects of interaction linked to problem solving or decision making—that is, to managing group tasks. Second, there are the broader interpersonal dynamics of people's interactions with others—that is, the socioemotional aspects of procedure. Both aspects of procedures can be distinguished conceptually from the outcomes of group interaction and decision making, although in practice the procedures of a group and the outcomes it arrives at are typically found to be related.

Group procedures can potentially be evaluated objectively by considering the quality or content of interactions within a group, or they can be evaluated subjectively by asking people to report about their judgments about particular procedures. The distinction involved is that objective evaluations are linked to what actually occurs within the group, while subjective evaluations examine people's judgments and evaluations. Objective and subjective procedural assessments are typically studied separately, although procedures can be evaluated against both objective and subjective criterion at the same time.

Irrespective of whether they are making objective or subjective evaluations, people can potentially evaluate procedures along many dimensions, dimensions such as their speed, their accuracy, their degree of bias, and so on. Within social psychology, a large literature has developed that focuses on evaluations of procedural justice. This literature focuses on one key dimension of procedures—their justice or fairness. In the procedural justice literature, people are typically asked to evaluate a procedure along a general continuum of fairness-unfairness.

Procedural justice studies can focus on the objective features of procedures that are associated with their subjective fairness. Thibaut and Walker's (1975) classic work on procedural justice, for example, is concerned with the fairness of two forms of trial procedures—the adversarial and the inquisitorial. Their work codes features such as the actual impact of bias on decisions to determine which procedures have objective features, like neutrality, that the researchers associate with fairness. This leads to evaluations of the objective quality of different procedures, when judged against performance criterion identified by the researchers.

In contrast, the subjective study of procedural justice explores people's evaluations of the fairness of procedures. It is concerned with what people judge to be a fair process or procedure (Lind and Tyler 1988; Tyler 2000; Tyler et al. 1997). Such subjective evaluations may or may not be linked to particular objective characteristics of procedures. While both aspects of procedural justice have been studied by psychologists, most of the recent work on procedural justice has focused on subjective evaluations of fairness.

WHY IS PROCEDURAL JUSTICE IMPORTANT?

Subjective procedural justice judgments have been the focus of a great deal of research attention by psychologists because they have been found to be a key antecedent of many types of cooperative behavior in groups, organizations, and societies. The viability of groups depends upon the cooperation of the people within them. Furthermore, people are found to vary widely in their degree of cooperation. This makes the question of what motivates cooperation a key one for groups, organizations, and societies. Two literatures focus on the issue of cooperation and explore the motivations underlying cooperation: the literature on regulation and that on performance.

The literature on regulation is concerned with bringing people's behavior into line with group rules and the decisions of group authorities. Because social life requires people to follow social guidelines, the effective exercise of authority must involve the ability to motivate rule-following behavior. While important, regulation is not the only form of cooperation that groups need. The second literature focuses on performance—the ability to motivate people to engage in positive actions that help to promote the group's goals. For example, in addition to not stealing from their workplace, employees also need to do their jobs well. Cooperation of both types can be studied in the context of cooperation with particular decisions, or as a general level of everyday cooperation with the group.

Regulation

One reason that people might cooperate is that they receive desirable rewards for cooperating and/or fear sanctioning from the group for not cooperating. Such instrumental motivations are found to be effective in motivating cooperation in a wide variety of social settings, and shape both reactions to particular decisions and everyday behavior in groups. Studies suggest, however, that instrumental mechanisms have only a weak influence on behavior. In addition, they do not promote voluntary cooperation. People cooperate when they feel that their behavior is linked to whether they will be rewarded and sanctioned, but not when their behavior is not being observed or when authorities lack the ability to effectively dispense rewards and sanctions.

An alternative reason that people might cooperate is that they are motivated by their sense of justice to accept what they feel is fair, even if it is not what they want. The basic problem of social regulation is that everyone cannot have everything they want at the same time. Hence, people must sometimes defer to others and receive less than they desire. People's views about what is just or fair are a social mechanism through which interaction among people and groups is enabled because they provide guidelines for appropriate forms of cooperation with others. Social justice provides a set of shared values that minimizes social conflicts and contributes to the continuation of productive interactions among people.

The question is whether justice is effective in resolving conflicts and disagreements when people cannot have everything they want. Underlying the potential contribution of justice to the resolution of social conflicts is a view of human nature that suggests that people will defer their personal needs and interests when they feel that doing so is just. In other words, the belief that justice has the power to influence people's feelings and actions. Norms of social justice effectively resolve coordination problems when people accept them and defer to decisions that give the people involved less than they want, as well as being motivated to contribute to groups and relationships in which they experience justice. To the degree that people defer because allocation decisions are fair, justice is an important factor in creating and maintaining social harmony.

Research on procedural justice suggests that social justice can act as a mechanism for resolving social conflicts. The results of procedural justice research are optimistic about the ability of social authorities to bridge differences in interests and values and find differences that the parties to a dispute will accept. Furthermore, the findings of procedural justice research suggest how authorities should act to pursue such procedural justice strategies.

Thibaut and Walker (1975) presented the first systematic set of experiments designed to show the impact of procedural justice. Their studies demonstrate that people's assessments of the fairness of third-party decision-making procedures shape their satisfaction with their outcomes. This finding has been widely confirmed in subsequent laboratory studies of procedural justice (Lind and Tyler 1988). The original hope of Thibaut and Walker was that the willingness of all the parties to a dispute to accept decisions that they view as fairly arrived at would provide a mechanism through which social conflicts could be resolved.

Subsequent laboratory and field studies have supported the finding that when third-party decisions are fairly made, people are more willing to voluntarily accept them. What is striking is that the procedural justice effects are widely found in studies of real disputes, in real settings, involving actual disputants. Procedural justice judgments are found to have an especially important role in shaping adherence to agreements over time. For example, the procedural fairness of initial mediation sessions is the primary determinant of

whether people were adhering to mediation agreements six months later.

Similarly, procedural justice is central to gaining deference to social rules over time. For example, Paternoster and his colleagues (1997) interviewed men who had dealt with police officers called to their homes because they were abusing their wives (i.e., due to domestic violence). They explored which aspects of police behavior during the initial call predicted subsequent compliance with the law against domestic violence among the men interviewed. It was found that those men who felt fairly treated during the initial encounter with the police adhered to the law in the future. Interestingly, procedural justice judgments during this initial encounter with the police were more powerful predictors of subsequent law-abiding behavior than were factors such as whether the police arrested the men during the initial contact, fined them, and/or took them into the police station.

Beyond the acceptance of decisions, procedural justice also shapes people's values concerning the legitimacy of the authorities and institutions with which they are dealing, and through such feelings, their willingness to defer to those authorities and institutions. Studies of the legitimacy of authority suggest that people decide how much to defer to authorities and to their decisions primarily by assessing the fairness of their decision-making procedures. Hence, using fair decision-making procedures is the key to developing, maintaining, and enhancing the legitimacy of rules and authorities and gaining voluntary deference to social rules.

Performance

The importance of procedural justice is not confined to the arena of regulation, and more recent research on procedural justice has moved beyond an early focus on regulation to a broader focus on a variety of types of cooperative behavior. The findings of this work demonstrate that when people experience procedural fairness, they are also found to be more cooperative and to work harder on behalf of groups (Tyler and Blader 2000). Groups generally benefit when those within them engage in voluntary cooperative actions that help the group, and research suggests that people voluntarily cooperate with groups when they judge that group decisions are being made fairly. Fair decision-making procedures encourage voluntary cooperation with groups because they lead to supportive attitudes, that is, identification with and loyalty and commitment toward groups.

MODELS OF SOCIAL COORDINATION

These findings are hopeful and optimistic. They demonstrate that providing people with procedural justice can be an important and viable mechanism for gaining deference to decisions made by authorities. This effect occurs across a variety of settings, including both hierarchical and non-hierarchical situations, in political, legal, managerial, interpersonal, familial, and educational settings and when important issues of outcomes and treatment are involved. Hence, conflict resolution efforts can gain viability through the use of fair decision-making procedures.

Procedural justice is especially important because it is central to creating and maintaining internal values that support voluntary cooperative behavior on the part of the members of groups. The importance of developing and maintaining such values is increasingly being recognized, as social scientists recognize the limits of strategies of conflict resolution that are based upon seeking to shape the rewards and punishments received by the parties to a dispute. Because social science thinking has been dominated by rational choice models of the person, command and control, deterrence, or social control strategies have dominated discussions about social regulation during the past several decades. These models focus upon the individual as a calculative actor, thinking, feeling, and behaving in terms of potential rewards and costs in the individual's immediate environment.

Increasingly, social scientists have recognized the limits of instrumental approaches to managing conflict. In political and legal settings, authorities have recognized that both regulation (Tyler 1990) and the encouragement of voluntary civic behavior (Green and Shapiro 1994) are difficult when authorities can only rely upon their ability to reward and/or punish citizens. Similarly, organizational theorists are recognizing the difficulties of managing employees using command and control strategies (Pfeffer 1994).

The alternative to command and control approaches are approaches that focus upon the development and maintenance of internal values. If people have internal values that lead them to voluntarily defer to authorities and act to help the group, then authorities need to seek to compel such behavior through promises of reward or threats of punishment. In other words, the recognition of the importance of creating a "civic culture" or an "organizational culture" that supports the development and maintenance of internal values among group members is increasing as the limits of command and control approaches to managing conflict become increasingly clear. To manage effectively, authorities need the consent and cooperation of those being governed. Procedural justice is central to both developing and maintaining (1) judgments that authorities are legitimate and (2) feelings of commitment and identification with groups, organizations, and societies.

CRITERIA OF PROCEDURAL FAIRNESS

To utilize these findings, it is important to consider what people mean by a fair procedure. What characteristics lead to procedural fairness? Studies typically find seven, eight, or even more elements that contribute to assessments of their fairness. However, four elements of procedures are the primary factors that contribute to judgments about their fairness: opportunities for participation, a neutral forum, trustworthy authorities, and treatment with dignity and respect.

People feel more fairly treated if they are allowed to participate in the resolution of their problems or conflicts. The positive effects of participation have been widely found, beginning in the work of Thibaut and Walker (1975). Furthermore, people value participation even when they think that their participation is not shaping outcomes. People are primarily interested in sharing in the discussion over the case, not in controlling decisions about how to handle it. Instead, people often look to authorities to make decisions about which legal or managerial principles govern resolution of their dispute. In other words, they expect authorities to make final decisions about how to act based upon what they have said.

People are also influenced by judgments about neutrality—the honesty, impartiality, and objectivity of the authorities with whom they deal. They believe that authorities should not allow their personal values and biases to enter into their decisions, which should be made based upon rules and facts. Basically, people seek a level playing field in which no one is unfairly disadvantaged. If they believe that the authorities are following impartial rules and making factual, objective decisions, they think procedures are fairer.

Another factor shaping people's views about the fairness of a procedure is their assessment of the motives of the third-party authority responsible for resolving the case. People recognize that third parties typically have considerable discretion to implement formal procedures in varying ways, and they are concerned about the motivation underlying the decisions made by the authority with whom they are dealing. They judge whether that person is benevolent and caring, is concerned about their situation and their concerns and needs, considers their arguments, tries to do what is right for them, and tries to be fair.

Studies suggest that people also value having respect shown for their rights and for their status within society. They are very concerned that, in the process of dealing with authorities, their dignity as people and as members of the society is recognized and acknowledged. Since it is essentially unrelated to the outcomes they receive, the importance that people place upon this affirmation of their status is especially relevant to conflict resolution. More than any other issue, treatment with dignity and respect is something that authorities can give to everyone with whom they deal.

— Tom R. Tyler

See also Civil Society; Distributive Justice

FURTHER READINGS AND REFERENCES

Green, Donald P. and Ian Shapiro. 1994. *Pathologies of Rational Choice Theory.* New Haven, CT: Yale University Press

Lind, E. A. and T. R. Tyler. 1988. *The Social Psychology of Procedural Justice.* New York: Plenum.

Paternoster, R., R. Brame, R. Bachman, and L. W. Sherman. 1997. "Do Fair Procedures Matter? The Effect of Procedural Justice on Spouse Assault. *Law and Society Review* 31:163–204.

Pfeffer, J. 1994. *Competitive Advantage through People.* Cambridge, MA: Harvard University Press.

Thibaut, J. and L. Walker. 1975. *Procedural Justice.* Hillsdale, NJ: Lawrence Erlbaum.

Tyler, T. R. 1990. *Why People Obey the Law.* New Haven, CT: Yale University Press.

———. 2000. "Social Justice: Outcome and Procedure." *International Journal of Psychology* 35:117–25.

Tyler, T. R. and S. Blader. 2000. *Cooperation in Groups.* Philadelphia, PA: Psychology Press.

Tyler, T. R., R. Boeckmann, H. J. Smith, and Y. J. Huo. 1997. *Social Justice in a Diverse Society.* Denver, CO: Westview.

Tyler, T. R. and Y. J. Huo. 2002. *Trust in the Law.* New York: Russell Sage.

Tyler, T. R. and H. J. Smith. 1997. "Social Justice and Social Movements. Pp. 595–629 in *Handbook of Social Psychology,* 4th ed., vol. 2, edited by D. Gilbert, S. Fiske, and G. Lindzey. New York: Addison-Wesley.

PROFESSIONS

Professions are occupations that claim control over specific tasks through the mastery of abstract knowledge. Most theoretical development in the professions has focused on defining professional work, explaining the rise and dominance of professional groups, developing models of professional organization, and discussing systems of professions and knowledge claims.

Control over abstract knowledge confers legitimacy on professional groups, and this legitimacy usually translates into social prestige, power, and rewards for professionals. A key to understanding professions is the knowledge claims that professional groups make. These are rhetorical and institutional claims that professionals have exclusive control over specific tasks because the professional has mastered the abstract knowledge necessary to understand when, where, how, and under what conditions specific tasks will be performed.

In addition to knowledge claims, professions usually claim control over a specific task domain. A task domain is a set of specific behaviors and activities that can be linked, directly or indirectly, to the abstract knowledge claims of the profession. The combination of abstract and esoteric knowledge and monopoly or near monopoly over a task domain means that professionals usually have considerable autonomy over their work tasks. Whether this autonomy over the execution of tasks translates into the ability to determine the terms and conditions of work is one of the major long-term research problems addressed by students of the professions.

In the ideal-typical profession, control over a specific task domain and the abstract nature of knowledge claims place clients in dependent positions relative to professionals. In exchange for autonomy and control, professions are expected to require their incumbents to act in the best interests of their clients and the broader culture. These expectations often are embodied in codes of ethics that require professionals to act in the best interests of their clients or in accordance with abstract ideals (respect for the law, justice, fiduciary responsibility, etc.).

Professional work usually addresses some culturally important value (legal rights, health, scientific progress, safety, etc.). The fact that clients usually approach professionals at times when these values seem most salient to them increases the dependency of clients on professional practitioners.

Most professions are organized into professional associations that protect the interests of professionals by regulating the terms and conditions of work and developing codes of conduct that regulate behavior. Professional associations also regulate the qualifications necessary to enter the profession, and many professions have competency tests (bar exams and medical board exams being the two most prominent examples) that determine when would-be practitioners are ready to assume professional roles.

TRAIT THEORIES AND DEFINITIONS OF PROFESSIONS

Most early attempts to define professions developed sets of traits or characteristics that separate professions from other occupations. These treatments are referred to as trait theories of professions. While differing in their specific emphasis, there has been a common focus on eight broadly conceived characteristics that distinguish professions: (1) knowledge based on theory and substantively complex techniques, (2) mastery of knowledge that requires a long period of university-based training that socializes trainees into the culture and symbols of the profession, (3) tasks that speak to relevant and key social values that are inherently valuable to societies, (4) practitioners that are oriented toward clients' welfare and service to the profession, (5) task performance characterized by a high degree of autonomy, (6) practitioners that exhibit long-term commitments to their work, (7) practitioners who enjoy a well-developed sense of community, and (8) a well-developed code of ethics that guides practitioner behavior and defines the profession's core values. Occupations are evaluated based on their conformity to this, or some other, list of traits. Trait theories of professions were popular in the 1950s and 1960s and were identified with structural functionalist desires for precise definitions of professional activities.

Trait explanations do not explain the development of professions very well, nor do they outline a detailed process of change in the professions. Instead, they provide a set of institutional markers whose appearance or disappearance would signal change in the status and relative power of specific occupational groups. They provide a set of places or practices to observe when studying potential changes in professional life.

Since the 1970s, students of the professions have grown dissatisfied with trait theories of professions. There has been relatively little agreement about which traits are critical and which are superfluous for professional development. Most trait theories were silent regarding the manipulative actions taken by professions and professionals themselves to enhance their own power and prestige. Some observers have questioned whether the ability or inability to conform to a list of professional traits is influenced by forces outside of the functional importance of the knowledge professions allegedly control. Others questioned whether codes of ethnics were actually adhered to or whether such codes are ploys to avoid scrutiny and control by outside observers.

THEORIES EXPLAINING THE RISE AND DOMINANCE OF PROFESSIONS

Recent theoretical development in the study of the professions often focuses on the rise and dominance of professions as institutions. Professions as macrolevel institutions represent distinct and identifiable structures of knowledge, expertise, work, and labor markets with distinct norms, practices, ideologies, and organizational forms. These theories explain the rise and dominance of professions by focusing on the knowledge systems or power relationships that shape these institutions.

Liberal/technocratic theories explain the rise of professions as a by-product of distinct role demands created by postindustrial capitalism. These theories claim that increasing technological complexity leads to the creation of highly specialized roles and a search for qualified people to fill them. The process of filling and enacting these roles produces a technocratic professional elite that applies their knowledge to a broad spectrum of problems. Modernity in this context is characterized by the susceptibility of ever-wider sets of problems to technocratic solutions.

While much liberal/technocratic writing sounds decidedly functionalist, some theorists offer other interpretations within the liberal/technocratic framework. Some authors speak with great concern about the creation of a globalized,

highly technocratic economy that produces alarming levels of social inequality and social dislocation. These writers point to social and community dislocation, residential segregation, and the concentration of the poor and unemployed in forgotten sections of the inner city as some of the consequences of a technologically sophisticated economy that demands a highly educated workforce. Globally, nations compete for scarce pools of highly educated labor, producing a brain drain from the less developed world to the developed world that is linked to rising residential, cultural, and social segregation in urban areas. Some writers even speak of the creation of a "global overclass" of economically prosperous, highly educated scientists, technicians, and financiers who share a common, segregated, elite subculture.

Other, less apocalyptic issues addressed by liberal/technocratic models include whether there are changing social and cultural links between professionals and other highly educated workers. The purpose of these inquiries is to investigate whether professionals and experts are starting to occupy distinctive positions in the social structure of advanced capitalism. Most of these investigations discuss the existence of a *new class* of economically prosperous, postmaterialist, socially liberal citizens with distinctive worldviews and political orientations. These orientations do not easily fit into traditional conservative or liberal political ideologies. The empirical evidence for the existence of this new class is considerable, though writers and commentators disagree about the social and political implications.

Criticisms of early versions of liberal/technocratic theories focused on the benign roles assigned to technology and economic development as a creator of professional roles. These theories were criticized for the (seemingly) unconscious development of role demands to which professionals were the natural and inevitable solution. Scholarship in the sociology of work since the 1970s has questioned whether many aspects of the contemporary division of labor are natural or inevitable, nor is there an easy one-to-one relationship between specific technologies and specific methods for organizing work tasks. More recent scholarship on the new class is not prone to this criticism. Most writers examining the political and social distinctiveness (or lack thereof) of professionals and expert workers are agnostic concerning the existence of professional roles, and focus on the consequences of occupying these roles for other dimensions of social life. Some writers in this latter group examine whether professional roles are under attack and whether defense of professional "life space" constitutes a basis for distinctive political organizations.

POWER THEORIES OF THE PROFESSIONS

Power theories of professions focus on the prerogatives and status accruing to professionals. Within this group there is considerable variation in basic themes and implications.

All power theories begin with the observation that professionals possess considerable power and social status. However, power theories are skeptical that professional status and prerogatives flow from the mere possession of expert knowledge. Instead, rewards flow from attempts by professionals from the exercise of social control or the extraction of economic and social benefits from consumers. However, power theories vary in their evaluation of who benefits from the monopolization of professional knowledge and whether professional knowledge constitutes a distinctive, superior way to understand the increasingly technical problems of late modernity.

Some power theories locate professional power within the organization of professional associations. Professional associations attempt to exert control over the supply and production of new professionals as well as control over the locations and conditions of professional work. Professional associations often exert control by enforcing stringent educational requirements that bear only a marginal relationship to the performance of professional roles. Attempts to create licensed monopolies also are used to regulate the supply of professionals, driving up prices and limiting practice to accepted, established methods. These theories assume that professional groups extract financial and social benefits from their knowledge for the benefit of professionals themselves.

A variant of this first group of theories claims that the organization of professional work exerts a different social closure function. In addition to restricting the supply of professionals in order to keep demand and fees high, this variant of power theories claims that educational and licensing requirements are part of a larger agenda to limit professional practice to high-status groups: whites, men, and (in an earlier age) Protestants. This group of theories views the rewards that accrue to the professions as a by-product of high-status occupants. These variants of power theories are used to explain gender and racial inequality within subfields of the professions in addition to examining the relatively privileged position of professionals themselves.

Another variant of this first group of theories explains inequality among subspecialties within the professions themselves. These theories point to increasingly skewed distributions of rewards in the direction of glamorous and visible subspecialties and away from routine, frontline work that is more indicative of the "service ideal" that most professions ascribe. The high status of medical specialties that engage in drastic interventions against life-threatening disease relative to the low status of preventative care, health promotion, and public health is cited as evidence of this trend, as are the wide differences in rewards between public interest and constitutional law relative to corporate legal practice.

Marxist variants of power theories would locate the source of the status, rewards, and prerogatives of professions outside of professional associations. Instead, they point to structures of professional incentives that are tilted toward specialties that serve the rich and powerful. The funding of professional research and financial rewards in the form of fees encourage professionals to take up subspecialties with paying, relatively affluent customers. In their minds, this explains the skewed distribution of professional activity away from the provision of basic services that benefit most members of society toward activities that protect or enhance the safety, health, or convenience of elites.

Still other variants of power theories question whether professional knowledge is distinctive or valuable. These variants of power theory have a decidedly postmodern cast to them, and question the very existence of professional knowledge as a tool of power and domination. These variants of power theory go beyond the question of whether the organization of professional service delivery is distorting the distribution of professional and societal rewards. Instead, these theories cast a critical eye on the knowledge claims of professionals and claim that professional dominance of specific task domains privileges scientific and technical knowledge at the expense of intuitive, practical, grounded practice. The effect of the expansion of professional expertise to ever-expanding areas of life is the political and social disenfranchisement of nonprivileged, nonprofessional groups.

While the historical trend in theorizing the professions is to explain the growth in professional power and prerogatives, there is distinctive theorizing within the power tradition that claims that those prerogatives and powers are being eroded. This group of scholars asks whether the control and prerogatives of professional work have shifted from professionals themselves and toward dominating, superordinant organizations that do not represent the interests of professionals. These scholars suggest that professional prerogatives have been under attack by an increasingly skeptical public and by other occupational groups who seek to control service costs. This variant of power theory claims that an increasingly educated, reflexive, knowledge-consuming, and organized set of consumers and third-party payers are seeking to reorganize professional services to streamline service delivery and lower its cost. Almost all of these reorganization attempts seek to limit professional discretion and autonomy, and connections often are made to the deskilling and proletarianization of skilled craft workers in earlier historical periods.

Power theories focus our attention on the activities of professionals themselves and the economically powerful and influential interests and benefactors that finance much leading-edge professional activity. These theories tend to ignore the actions or desires of average consumers, or assume that these tastes are easily manipulated. Furthermore, power theories often make it sound as if professional manipulation of the symbolic environment around them is easy and their success assured. The more recent development of scholarship explaining attacks on and the reorganization of professional work (both from modernist and postmodernist perspectives) serves as a useful counterpoint to the focus on professional dominance.

MODELS OF PROFESSIONAL ORGANIZATIONS

Theories that focus on the organizational settings where professional work takes place have developed several ideal-typical terms to describe professional work organizations. The classic mode of professional practice is summarized under the head of the autonomous professional organization. Autonomous professional organizations are dominated by professionals who maintain authority and control over the terms and conditions of work and evaluate themselves as a group. The traditional, freestanding law firm or group medical practice is a classic example of an autonomous professional organization. In these organizational types, partners or senior professionals hire other professionals and work in a freestanding, collegial setting where peer group decision making is the norm, status differences between professionals are minimized, and all nonprofessional employees are subordinate to those with recognized professional status.

Heteronymous professional organizations are work settings where considerable control is exercised over professional work. Managed care organizations and other health care plans that review and attempt to control the behavior of professionals and house attorneys practicing law within large corporations are examples of heteronymous work organizations. Some commentators have speculated that heteronymous work organizations for professionals are increasing in dominance, given some of the trends observed by students of the declining power of professional groups. Finally, conjoint organizations involve professionals and administrators operating in separate domains of expertise and sharing the benefits that derive from collaboration. There are relatively few examples of such organizations in the literature, though university relationships between faculty and administrators and relationships between administrators and researchers in research institutes and think-tanks come the closest to this organizational form.

SYSTEMS OF PROFESSIONS AND KNOWLEDGE CLAIMS

Most recent theorizing and research on the professions has focused on systems of professions and knowledge claims. This newer tradition does not focus on a specific profession but instead focuses on entire groups of professions making competing claims to the same task domain, or on the entire system of professional claims within a specific culture or society.

This perspective focuses on the ability to claim jurisdiction over specific task domains in competition with other occupational groups. Here the emphasis is not on the rationales or explanations given to consumers or the relationship between professionals and the interests of dominant elites. Instead, this perspective focuses on boundary disputes over task domains (doctors and nurses, traditional medicine and holistic approaches to healing, lawyers and accountants, accountants and managers, etc.). These competitions (and their outcomes) eventually determine the relative prestige of professional groups. Very prestigious occupations almost never have their task domains challenged and do not have trouble winning challenges when they do occur. But far more numerous are occupations where professional prerogatives and task domains are continually challenged (e.g., teachers, nurses, pharmacists, and psychologists). By watching and studying these competitions, researchers can study how task domains are controlled and how challenges to the conventional organization of professional work transpires.

A variant of this focus on the system of professions can be found in the theory of countervailing powers. Here, the dynamics of change in the status of professions is linked to a given profession's location in a field of institutional and cultural actors. A profession may gain dominance by subjugating the needs of other groups that, over time, will mobilize their own resources and connections to counter this dominance.

— Kevin T. Leicht

See also Bell, Daniel; Durkheim, Émile; Fordism and Post-Fordism; Social Studies of Science

FURTHER READINGS AND REFERENCES

Abbott, Andrew. 1988. *The System of Professions: Essays on the Expert Division of Labor.* Chicago, IL: University of Chicago Press.

Brint, Steven. 1994. *In an Age of Experts: The Changing Role of Professionals in Politics and Public Life.* Princeton, NJ: Princeton University Press.

Friedson, Elliot. 1994. *Professionalism Reborn: Theory, Prophesy and Policy.* Chicago, IL: University of Chicago Press.

Illich, Ivan. 1982. *Medical Nemesis: The Expropriation of Health.* New York: Pantheon.

Larsen, M. S. 1977. *The Rise of Professionalism: A Sociological Analysis.* Berkeley, CA: University of California Press.

Leicht, Kevin T. and Mary L. Fennell. 2001. *Professional Work: A Sociological Approach.* Oxford, UK: Blackwell.

Scott, W. R. 1982. "Managing Professional Work: Three Models of Control of Healthcare Organizations." *Health Services Research* 17:213–40.

Wilensky, H. L. 1964. "The Professionalization of Everyone?" *American Journal of Sociology* 70:137–58.

PSYCHOANALYSIS AND SOCIAL THEORY

FREUD AND SOCIAL THEORY

Since its origins, psychoanalysis has been inextricably linked with the history of twentieth-century social theory. Sigmund Freud, the founder of psychoanalysis, responded to unprecedented events in his own political culture, particularly World War I, the resurgence in Austria of anti-Semitism, and the rise of Nazism, fascism, and other mass movements, and applied his developing science to a theory of society. Psychoanalysis is predicated on a fully elaborated set of postulates concerning human nature, a metapsychology that describes the inner world of a human being as governed by both rational and nonrational impulses. In various writings beginning in the 1920s, Freud sought to explain the ways in which the psychological makeup of the individual, rather than helping to realize it, limited the achievement of reason in the social world.

The theorist of the unconscious described the special problem faced by "civilization" that required for its survival the thwarting of human instinct. Developing in particular a theory of the death drive, or Thanatos, Freud explored its expression in individuals, its necessary repression by social systems, and the pathology that can derive from it, to explain the mass politics with which he was confronted. Here Freud appears to be a more modern Thomas Hobbes, suggesting that social institutions are required to limit, restrict, and restrain these fundamentally antisocial inclinations of individuals. Consistent with Freud's elaboration of an individual's intrapsychic conflict that requires repression of pleasure on behalf of a reality principle, he posits that the social order too insists upon repression of instinct, and as such, society, from the family to the state, inserts itself as the agency of individual domination.

Unlike Hobbes, who posits an identity of interest between the needs of the individual (i.e., to prevent premature death through the war of one against all) and the interests of the sovereign (i.e., in place to preserve the Leviathan), Freud identifies an inherent conflict between the needs or requirements of social institutions and their capacity to distort or pervert individual possibility. Here, more like Nietzsche than Hobbes, Freud insists that society, rather than establishing the conditions for human self-realization, can impede them. While civilization ensures greater happiness for the species, because without it disease, war, and earlier death would be more common, society nonetheless interferes with a person's pleasure principle, creating a social being at war with authority and, as that authority becomes internalized, at war with itself.

This is the Freudian conundrum: Individuals are dependent upon a social world that makes possible instinctual gratification. Nonetheless, they find themselves in a struggle against social power that requires of them excessive restriction both of libidinal or erotic and aggressive impulses. The result is the internalization of external authority in the form of moral conscience, generating often an overly repressive form of self-discipline and restraint. Because of these contending sentiments and imperatives, the lived experience of individuals is defined by the production of ambivalence and dominated by the experience of guilt. Love and hate coexist, directed at times at oneself, at others, and at the social world that enables those feelings. While the victory of a reality principle over pleasure alone is the aim, the result often is pathology. The individual drive to satisfaction with socially imposed restrictions on gratification defines the dialectical relationship that, for Freud, is a permanent feature of the world in which we live and is always fraught with the possibility for failure. While much of Freud's career was devoted to exploring the ways in which psychological illness was a product of an individual's inability to successfully navigate the waters of pleasure and restraint with which he or she was confronted, Freud's later writings increasingly turned to the inextricable connection between the death drive of individuals and the forces of social order and constraint that colluded in the simultaneous production of excessive repression and pathology.

Freud, in the end, remains agnostic as to whether the emancipatory potential of the individual might ever be achieved despite the requirements of a collectivity that requires a surplus of repression. Writing in *Civilization and Its Discontents* ([1930]1975), Freud states, "A good part of the struggles of mankind centre around the single task of finding an expedient accommodation—one, that is, that will bring happiness—between the claim of the individual and the cultural claims of the group; and one of the problems that touches the fate of humanity is whether such an accommodation can be reached by means of some particular form of civilization or whether this conflict is irreconcilable" (p. 96). And while Freud, writing in the interwar years, assumes an understandably despairing tone about our capacity to construct collective institutions that balance group needs with personal self-expressiveness, psychoanalysis firmly established its centrality to understanding the relationship between individual and society and, more pointedly, laid the theoretical terms for a twentieth-century preoccupation with the tension between social constraint and human potentiality.

CRITICAL THEORY

Freud's anthropological claims about the human being were first taken up outside psychoanalysis by members of the Institute for Social Research, later known as the Frankfurt School of Critical Theory. In the late 1920s and early 1930s, a generation of scholars—Max

Horkheimer, Leo Loewenthal, Erich Fromm, and Theodore Adorno—interested in breaking out of an instrumental utilitarianism then characteristic of Marxist thought sought to marry the psychology of Freud to the economics and philosophy of Marx. Because of their interest in applying psychoanalysis to social theory, the early members of the school were successful in having an Institute of Psychoanalysis established in Frankfurt in 1929, and created the first formal relationship of its kind between a Freudian training center and a university. The result, for a time, was a vigorous exchange between psychoanalytic practitioners, visiting psychoanalysts, and members of the Institute of Social Research, establishing a model of interaction between clinicians and intellectuals rarely paralleled anywhere since. Throughout the century and currently, those who identify with the Frankfurt School and its intellectual and political legacy, including Herbert Marcuse, Jürgen Habermas, Jessica Benjamin, and Axel Honneth, have been the most insistent interlocutors of psychoanalysis, continuing to critically engage the field for its social and political implications.

Ironically, while Freud in the early 1930s became interested in specifying the contours of the death drive and its collaboration with societal forces demanding excessive restraint, these first-generation Frankfurt school theorists, in a bold effort to wrap anticapitalist, antistatist and antifascist politics around a psychology of human emancipation, were drawn to psychoanalytic ideas that offered a vision of the postcapitalist individual, when alienation—including psychological estrangement—might be overcome. Thus, Freud was criticized for his new emphasis on Thanatos with the critical theorists rejecting this shade of antihumanism in his thought. The presence of the death drive implied that the forces of domination might be justified in demanding its repression. Horkheimer insisted rather that Thanatos was a historically specific expression of impulses existing in modern capitalist society, now carried forth by individuals. While quarrelling with Freud in this regard, he nonetheless embraced fully Freud's insistence on the nonidentity between society and psychology, the irreducibility of the social to the psychological and vice versa. Freud's most fundamental contribution, he argued, lay in his demonstration of a stratum of human existence—the unconscious—that was out of reach of the totalizing effects of society. The Freudian unconscious became a theoretical bulwark against a sense of total defeat as the forces of society, through the 1930s and 1940s, seemed to overwhelm any indications of human capacity for resistance. The extent to which individual unconscious stands as a line of last defense against a totalizing system of societal domination remains a central node of contemporary theoretical controversy involving psychoanalytic thinkers, those that identify with the critical theory school, as well as contemporary postmodern and poststructural theorists.

As a result of Nazism, the Frankfurt school was forced to relocate; most of its members moved to New York, renaming the school as the International Institute for Social Research and housed at Columbia University. Other members, while still affiliated, emigrated farther west to California. In America, Adorno, Horkheimer, and Marcuse continued to demonstrate the centrality of Freud to their thinking. Adorno, for example, influenced by the psychoanalytic writings of Fromm and Wilhelm Reich, who were attempting to explain mass support for fascism, turned his attention in the 1940s to a study of anti-Semitism that later expanded to an explanation of psychological authoritarianism. Linking up with empirical researchers at Berkeley, Adorno (1950) published *The Authoritarian Personality,* where he argued that authoritarianism is a consequence of a publicly expressed ethnocentric ideology overlaid on a conflicted personality structure created by punitive child-rearing practices and inconsistent parental affection. And in a kind of companion piece, Adorno (1951) published "Freudian Theory and the Pattern of Fascist Propaganda." He argued here that mass movements, in addition to being understood from the bottom up, or from the perspective of individuals' pathology helping to foster authoritarianism, require an appreciation of the ways in which propaganda skillfully fosters from the top down primitive identifications with the leader and with the group. As political events of the 1940s and 1950s unfolded, the nonidentity principle, while not explicitly abandoned, was being seriously undermined: Was there any aspect of the individual unconscious invulnerable to external manipulation? Adorno and others were finding it more difficult to understand the unconscious as anything more than a function of political and social repression. Adorno was to call both the culture industry and fascist propaganda "psychoanalysis in reverse," and their capacity to subdue the individual through primitive psychological mechanisms extraordinarily impressive.

But with the publication of *The Authoritarian Personality,* a psychoanalytically informed critical theory became wedded for a time to American empirical social science, and the critical theoretical issues raised by the findings were subsumed to the question of the validity and reliability of its quantitative findings and statistical measures. The controversy over the volume was effectively drained of any political meaning; almost instantly, it was subject to considerable scrutiny, with strong criticisms directed especially at its empirical findings. The result was a setback for the institutionalization of a critical psychoanalytic theory within American social science. The institute reopened in Germany in 1949, and Horkheimer and Adorno returned to Frankfurt.

In contrast to Horkheimer and Adorno, who sought to discover in Freud support for an increasingly pessimistic formulation of the possibilities of social transformation, Herbert Marcuse offered a utopian reconciliation between Freud and Marx. Marcuse, who remained in America, published in 1955 *Eros and Civilization: A Philosophical Inquiry into Freud.* He argues that the erotic instinct, Eros, has produced the material and technical preconditions necessary to end scarcity in society. But advanced industrial society, characterized by people's mastery over the natural world, also resulted in their estrangement from nature. For Marcuse, the death instinct expresses this form of alienation, a negation of what he terms the Nirvana principle, that is, the oceanic feeling of oneness with the world. Like other critical theorists' historicized treatments of Thanatos, Marcuse identifies the death instinct as the source of people's unhappiness. Yet in contradistinction, he identifies the death drive as a human being's quest to reunite with inorganic nature, and insists that by re-eroticizing a person's relation both to other people and to nature it is possible to overcome alienated labor. Invoking a less pessimistic reading of Freud, Marcuse conceptualizes the possibility of a convergence between the pleasure and Nirvana principle. The sexual tyranny of the genitals, Marcuse proclaims, is the expression of a historically specific form of estrangement. Polymorphous perversity, in contrast—the eroticization of all of life itself—constitutes a possibility now, for the first time. The shift from production to consumption in modern capitalism, Marcuse argues, promotes the conditions by which the repressive needs of an industrializing society has given way to a more liberated consumer society. The individual personality has become freed—never before possible in human history—of the requirement of excessive repression. *Eros and Civilization,* while profoundly utopian, was also inherently political: Overcome the performance principle imposed by advanced industrial civilization, Marcuse proclaims, and a fulfilling, playful, and eroticized life will emerge.

Norman O. Brown (1959), writing *Life against Death: The Psychoanalytic Meaning of History* shortly after *Eros and Civilization,* struck a complementary chord. An American scholar who was not a member of the Frankfurt school, Brown nonetheless similarly politicizes Freud by suggesting that human sociability possesses a regressive, backward-looking, death-driven character because of human beings' unwillingness to acknowledge the reality of mortality. By uncovering the powerful role of the death instinct, Brown argues, Freud now enables a conception of a healthy human being: The human neurosis is now, for the first time, made conscious and, therefore, eradicable. Together, for a time, with Marcuse and Brown its commanding officers, a new American school of psychoanalytically informed political criticism appeared to be emerging.

But psychoanalysis as political critique gave way to a kind of mystical celebration of the erotic and communal. Marcuse's and Brown's subsequent writings became read as celebrations for an eroticized collectivity, utopian visions capable of being realized through the strength of communalism. Contributing to an apolitical celebration of the sensuous,

Marcuse's (1964) *One-Dimensional Man* and Brown's (1966) *Love's Body* in the 1960s were treated as complementary pieces (despite Marcuse's own efforts to differentiate between them), with each assuming a cultlike status to a countercultural and communitarian politics that was more cultural than political. The identification in public thinking between Freud and claims for nonrepressive sexuality is reminiscent of Freud's reception in turn-of-the-century Vienna: psychoanalysis as synonymous with free love. Psychoanalysis as political critique was eclipsed. Its fate in America was now tied to that of the counterculturalism of the 1960s.

In 1971, Jürgen Habermas, a third-generation critical theorist writing in Germany, published *Knowledge and Human Interests.* He describes psychoanalysis as an exemplar of "undistorted communication," in which the presuppositions of both parties to a communicative exchange are subject to reflexive examination. Reflecting perhaps a more hopeful climate in Western Europe, Habermas identifies a rationalistic and emancipatory core to the practice of psychoanalysis— "the only tangible example of a science incorporating methodical self-reflection"—and employs it as a normative model for social communication. While criticized for minimizing the significance of the asymmetries of power between analyst and analysand, Habermas nonetheless, on behalf of emancipatory possibility, describes in the relationship between analyst and analysand a model of communicative action demonstrably achievable, capable of challenging systemic structures of power and domination. Habermas's turn toward communication signaled a broader theoretical reorientation to language that extended beyond critical theory, which included the ideas of the psychoanalyst Jacques Lacan, who described the unconscious as structured like a language. But while Lacan became a central figure in postmodern and poststructural social theory, Habermas stood firm against the deconstructive turn, imagining instead nondistorted communication as a vehicle to transform subjective irrationalities held privately by individuals into an objectively grounded and reflexive radical democracy. By describing a concrete possibility for emancipatory practice, Habermas remains true to his critical theory origins, resisting wholesale abandonment of an emancipatory social project. Indeed, throughout the last several decades, he has been among the most prominent stalwarts against abandoning a commitment toward the realization of reason and promoting Enlightenment ideals in social life.

At the same time, Habermas also makes clear the limits of his interest in aligning his emancipatory interest to psychoanalysis, a discipline that similarly harbors utopian aspirations. He writes pointedly against the psychoanalytic theorizing of Cornelius Castoriadis, a French analyst contemporary with Habermas. Castoriadis (1997) asserts the "monadic core of the subject," that is, an unconscious untouched by the social world, and identifies the psychoanalytic project of "making the unconscious conscious" with an emancipatory "project of autonomy." Habermas distances himself from psychoanalysis by insisting on the primacy of the intersubjective—not the subjective—and the sufficiency of knowing the subject through the language being spoken between social members. He disclaims any interest in the Freudian unconscious. There is an irony, as Joel Whitebook (1997) notes, that in a postmodern political environment hostile to claims about reason's potential for human emancipation, Habermas rejects the substantive claims of a discipline that shares with him a similar belief in the possibilities of reason. Yet Habermas remains consistent with his earlier writings, insisting that psychoanalysis is of interest only for its epistemological stance toward self-discovery and its claims that genuine communication is possible as countervailing possibility despite existing structures of asymmetric power and authority.

More recently, the writings of Jessica Benjamin (1995) and Axel Honneth (1996), in contrast, reveal a substantive involvement with psychoanalytic ideas, ones intended to specify the specific contours of emancipatory possibility in the modern world. Reviving the substantive engagement with psychoanalysis in the early years of critical theory, they each reestablish the link between a progressive social theory and a depth-psychological understanding of the human being. Moving beyond the monistic theorizing of Freud (and Castoriadis, as well), both draw heavily upon the writings of D. W. Winnicott, an English psychoanalyst, writing in the 1950s and 1960s. Winnicott describes the developmental process of the individual as one moving from absolute dependency, at the time of birth, toward independence. This process is not foreordained but is an achievement requiring a *good-enough environment* that enables the individual to develop "the capacity to be alone." Winnicott captures the link between healthy individual development and a providing social world, internalized in the person, characterized by a community of loving and caring others.

The struggle for recognition—being known and knowing others through love, respect, and self-esteem—describes for Honneth and Benjamin an imperative that defines the human project in a social world. Recognition as a concept draws upon both Hegel and post-Freudian psychoanalytic thought, and its achievement can become derailed as a result of interpersonal failures (the focus especially for Benjamin) linked to inadequacies in the social environment. At the same time, recognition also establishes normative criteria upon which contemporary societies and the social relations they engender are understood as deficient. The grounds for transformative political action are defined by the struggle to produce the conditions that enable recognition.

AMERICAN STRUCTURAL FUNCTIONALISM AND SOCIAL SCIENCE

Among American theorists of the twentieth century, Talcott Parsons, more than any other, has been interested in integrating Freudian thought within a fully elaborated social theory. Parsons identifies as the central sociological question the problem of social order—the Hobbesian problem—or how potentially egoistic and conflictual aspects of human nature are inhibited so as not to destroy stable social relationships. In synthesizing the writings of Weber, Durkheim, Pareto, and other European theorists, Parsons identifies various structural arrangements that function in order to generate order, including the deployment of legal and political authority and the institutionalization of patterns of lawful economic competition. But he argues, in addition, that social order possesses a crucial affective component, a primary attachment of individuals to goals and rules of social action that link them both to the particular social relations of families and to more generalized normative models of rule-governed behavior. Parsons utilizes psychoanalysis both for a "theory of action," in which individual motivation is understood as intrinsically necessary to social structure, and a theory of how, through the process of socialization, social actors internalize cultural symbols and values. Within social theory, Parsons argues, a remarkable convergence occurs between Durkheim, who, beginning from the social whole, theorizes about the ways in which individuals internalize collective norms and values, and Freud, who, starting from the individual personality and the acquisition of the superego, theorizes about the internalization of collective norms and values in the individual. For Parsons, seeking a grand, synthetic theory of society, the fundamental differences between Durkheim, who denies individual monism, and Freud, who built a science based upon it, are of far less interest than the ways in which the former turned to the problem of individual internalization and the latter moved toward a theory of object-relations to each produce a rendering of the articulation of the social whole through its individual participants.

Writing about psychoanalysis and theory mostly in the 1950s and early 1960s, Parsons offered a complex theory of the interchange between personality and social structure that was far less critical and pessimistic than those writing in the tradition of critical theory. While documenting the sources within the individual personality for social strain, Parsonian theory nonetheless emphasizes the complementarity between individual and society, social institutions as mediating agencies, and the mutually reinforcing forces that produce and reproduce social order. The result is a theory of social structure and function whose analytical focus is to describe the forces that naturally move a society and individuals toward equilibrium and stasis rather than those that account for conflicting interests between individual and society.

Various students of Parsons have built upon his work to further develop a psychoanalytically informed social science. Philip Slater (1963), for example, in an article that appeared in the *American Sociological Review,* argues that while social systems depend upon libidinal diffusion, social anxiety encourages regressive impulses that threaten the social collectivity. Here he offers his response to Freud's concern with the power of Thanatos in social life. Particular institutions, Slater claims, like the incest taboo, marriage, and socialization necessarily counteract those threatening impulses and attempt to preserve libidinal attachments to the broader collectivity. And Neil Smelser, Parsons's research assistant for his most explicitly psychoanalytic book, *Family, Socialization and Interaction Processes* (1955), undertook a full clinical training in psychoanalysis. During the course of Smelser's own career as a sociologist at the University of California, Berkeley, he has considered psychoanalysis and its relation to sociology both in terms of the epistemological and methodological obstacles to inter-disciplinarity and the rethinking of defense mechanisms in light of an elaborated understanding of the social contexts in which they operate. His engagement with these themes culminated in *The Social Edges of Psychoanalysis* (1998), a collection of his psychoanalytic-sociological essays. In 1997, Smelser delivered as a presidential address to the American Sociological Association, "The Rational and the Ambivalent in the Social Sciences." Not since 1939 on the occasion of Freud's death when the *American Journal of Sociology* devoted an entire issue to Freud and sociology has psychoanalysis been as prominently represented in the field.

These metathemes of civilization, Thanatos, and guilt have not been the only ones in which social theory has engaged psychoanalysis. Since the 1913 publication of *Totem and Taboo*, where Freud declares the birth of culture as a result of the killing of the primal father, anthropologists have been in dialogue with psychoanalysis, at a more microlevel, concerning culture, its meaning, and the relation between cultural forms and its carriers. The dialogue, at times, has paralleled that of metatheory, especially as it has focused on issues, for example, of the universality of the Oedipal complex and other bioevolutionary and instinctual universals underlying culture. But less controversial for psychological anthropology are the Freudian-inspired ideas of the pervasiveness in all cultures of sexuality, aggressivity, attachment, and loss, and the interest in understanding their cross-cultural variation. Significant debates are ongoing about the interrelation between individual personality and cultural forms. Do socialization practices reflect the disciplining of individuals to conform to specific cultural or social forms? Or does the reality of instinctual needs driven by the individual—even the child—require a more complex understanding of the dynamic relation between personality and culture? How might one better understand the interpenetration of conflictual intrapsychic patterns alongside the presence of a multivalent culture? These themes have been explicitly explored in, for example, Jean Briggs's (1998) *Inuit Morality Play: The Emotional Education of a Three Year Old*. A Durkheimian-inspired understanding

that social and cultural organization precedes the individual and creates and shapes the individual's worldview and orientation to social action, in short, vies with a Weberian nominalist effort to characterize individuals ideal-typically. As Gannath Obeyeskere (1990) in *The Work of Culture* observes in support of this latter rendering, anthropology is an enterprise that, in order to explain cultural forms and their transformations over time, requires holding an idea of the interpenetration between a personal symbol—based on the personal life and experience of individuals—and the cultural symbol that helps to shape for individuals their experiences of social reality. Here, external reality and individual perception are not easily parsed, an insight profoundly indebted to Freudian psychoanalysis and one that requires the anthropological quest to generalize ideal-typically about the "native's point of view."

POSTSTRUCTURALISM, POSTMODERNISM, AND FEMINISM

The publication in 1974 of Juliet Mitchell's *Psychoanalysis and Feminism: A Radical Reassessment of Freudian Psychoanalysis* marked the resurgence of psychoanalysis as political critique, and psychoanalytic ideas now remain as an integral component in contemporary feminist criticism. Indeed, through feminist discourse, psychoanalysis persists as a key contributor to contemporary social theory. *Psychoanalysis and Feminism* signaled to those interested in feminism, by a writer whose credentials were already well established as a feminist, that psychoanalysis could not be ignored in a social analysis of the sources of sexual oppression. The broadly based receptivity of contemporary psychoanalytic writings, as in the works of Nancy Chodorow, Jessica Benjamin, Jacqueline Rose, Helene Cixous, Luce Irigaray, Julia Kristeva, and Judith Butler, were enhanced by Mitchell's assertion of the significance of psychoanalytic thought in feminist social analysis.

Mitchell reinterpreted Parsons's model of unconscious identifications and gender roles as fruitful difference and complementarity to be, rather, a description of socially enforced deficit and inequality. She is a British socialist influenced by Lacan and the French Marxist Althusser, who argued that Freud, despite clear evidence of his own misogyny, nonetheless provided the theoretical basis to understand how masculinity, femininity, heterosexuality, and gender become deeply inscribed in the individual psyche. Psychoanalysis demonstrates the cultural basis of patriarchy, not its naturalness; it also explains, Mitchell argues, the reasons for its deep resistance to change. At the same time, the psychological basis for sexual domination provides a theory for its radical undoing, though mindful of the power of the idea in reproducing gendered inequality.

Yet the widespread invocation of psychoanalysis on behalf of a feminist social analysis implied no unanimity in terms of its application: It has rather helped to define the terms of the debate. On the one side, engaging directly with Mitchell's work are feminists, largely in Europe, who understand sexual domination as a function of language and discourse and as hinging on the perception and acceptance of unequal genital difference: the phallus and its lack. Building upon Foucault, Althusser, and Lacan, the prism of explanation for domination is the historical development of gender dualism in which man is viewed as self-determining and autonomous and woman as Other. Language itself encodes definitions of gendered identity; as Lacan argues, entry to the symbolic realm is subordination to a structure of distinctions that position individuals almost irretrievably in a cognitive prison in which only certain thoughts and desires are thinkable. Psychodynamically, the Oedipal father is decisive in reinscribing sexual difference and establishing phallic primacy from one generation to the next. The works of Irigaray, Cixous, and others are reactions against the formulation of women as lack, but they nonetheless provide an alternative linguistic rendering to account for gendered difference. Still interested in the Oedipal triangle and the failure of mothers to resist the passing on of male domination, these authors assert nonetheless the possibility for "women's language" and "writing the body" that valorizes feminine experience and the female body.

North American feminists provide an alternative theory to explain gender domination, though one no less inspired by psychoanalysis. But unlike the Lacanian and neo-Lacanians described, these writers rely on Freudian and post-Freudian insights on the pre-Oedipal object relations ties, especially between child and mother—"the first bond," to help explain gendered inequality. Nancy Chodorow (1978), in *The Reproduction of Mothering*, describes the intense identification that occurs, in isolated middle-class mother-dominated child-rearing families, between mothers and daughters, creating in girls a more fluid and relational sense of selfhood, as compared to boys, and establishing in girls the capacities and desires for mothering. Boys tend to more sharply individuate themselves against their mothers, simultaneously becoming more autonomous and emotionally constrained. Jessica Benjamin (1995) in *The Bonds of Love, Psychoanalysis, Feminism and the Problem of Domination* similarly focuses on the pre-Oedipal experience, emphasizing the writings of Winnicott rather than Freud's, to explore the psychological persistence of gendered inequality in a social environment that, in all other respects, celebrates formal equality. Domination, she argues, is a complex social process deeply intertwined in family life, sexual relations, and other social institutions, and has it roots in the earliest patterns of relatedness between mothers, fathers, and boys and girls. Dorothy Dinnerstein and Carol Gilligan too share in this perspective in which pre-Oedipal gender relations are identified as crucial dimensions of social inequality.

CONCLUSION

The relation between psychoanalysis and contemporary social theory remains a vexed one. In one respect, postmodernism and poststructuralism reject a conception of a generalized human nature, the idea of an immutable psychic structure, a sense of the "knowability" of an individual, as well as a concept of the singularity of the self. But while in certain ways Freudian psychoanalysis has been an easy foil by which to articulate a more relativistic, contextually based, skeptical, and multivalent understanding of the person and his or her relation to the social world, it has not withered in the face of its detractors. In fact, it has demonstrated over the last century a rather remarkable resilience, revealing a dynamic capacity to address similar challenges within its own discursive frame. Thus, an emphasis on a one-person psychology has given way to elaborated conceptions of intersubjectivity, drive, or instinct theory to object-relatedness, the primacy of the Oedipal triangle in defining the parameters of the adult personality to pre-Oedipal dyadic patterns. To current epistemological challenges about historical objectivity and certainty, it has offered its own reformulations, inspired by Freud himself but also employing post-Freudian analysts, about memory and the reconstruction of the past. In sum, as a result of its own adaptability to new understandings and sets of concerns, psychoanalysis has proven to be an inestimable resource for present-day social theory. Indeed, as contemporary theory increasingly turns toward issues of selfhood, identity, intimacy, and sexuality in the postmodern condition—questions that directly engage the relation of the individual to the social world—it is now no longer conceivable to consider social theory without psychoanalysis as a dimension of it. Beyond that, psychoanalysis helps frame the question that has organized theoretical argument throughout the twentieth century and into the twenty-first: Is the individual unconscious a deposit of the cultural and social world that surrounds it, or does it possess imaginary possibility, relatively immune to social determinations, that is capable of transforming the social world on behalf of the human being? This is the question Freud originally posed, and in various respecifications, it continues today to structure theoretical controversy.

— Jeffrey Prager

See also Benjamin, Jessica; Castoriadis, Cornelius; Chodorow, Nancy; Deleuze, Gilles; Frankfurt School; Freud, Sigmund; Gilligan, Carol; Habermas, Jürgen; Irigaray, Luce; Kristeva, Julia; Lacan, Jacques; Parsons, Talcott; Smelser, Neil; Žižek, Slavoj

FURTHER READINGS AND REFERENCES

Benjamin, J. 1995. *Like Subjects, Love Objects: Essays on Recognition and Sexual Difference.* New Haven, CT: Yale University Press.

Castoriadis, C. 1997. *World in Fragments.* Stanford, CA: Stanford University Press.

Chodorow, N. 1999. *The Power of Feelings: Personal Meaning in Psychoanalysis, Gender and Culture.* New Haven, CT: Yale University Press.

Elliott, A. 1999. *Social Theory & Psychoanalysis in Transition: Self and Society from Freud to Kristeva.* 2d ed. New York: Free Association Books.

Freud, S. [1913] 1975. *Totem and Taboo,* Standard edition, 12. London: Hogarth.

———. [1930] 1975. *Civilization and Its Discontents.* Standard edition, 21. London: Hogarth.

Honneth, A. 1996. *The Struggle for Recognition: The Moral Grammar of Social Conflicts.* Cambridge, MA: MIT Press.

Obeyesekere, G. 1990. *The Work of Culture: Symbolic Transformation in Psychoanalysis and Anthropology,* Chicago, IL: University of Chicago Press.

Prager, J. 1998. *Presenting the Past: Psychoanalysis and the Sociology of Misremembering.* Cambridge, MA: Harvard University Press.

Slater, P. 1963. "On Social Regression." *American Sociological Review* 28:339–64.

Smelser, N. 1998. *The Social Edges of Psychoanalysis.* Berkeley, CA: University of California Press.

Whitebook, J. 1997. "Intersubjectivity and the Monadic Core of the Psyche: Habermas and Castoriadis on the Unconscious." In *Habermas and the Unfinished Project of Modernity,* edited by M. Passerin D'entreves and S. Benhabib. Cambridge, MA: MIT Press.

PUBLIC SPHERE

The public sphere describes a space of reasoned debate about politics and the state. The public sphere is the arena of political participation in which ideas, alternatives, opinions, and other forms of discourse take shape. We can recall the ideas of John Stuart Mill in *On Liberty* to think of the public sphere as the space in which persons come to join a contest over true, partially true, and wrong ideas about how the state and politics should address the major issues of the day. Along with debate, the public sphere also encompasses the arena of political action, by both individuals and groups. In modern democracy, the public sphere is, in particular, the arena of social movement activity, as collective action seeks to bring issues to the fore that have hitherto been excluded from, or at least marginalized in, the important political debates of the day. As a space of collective action, the public sphere encompasses both narrative and textual discourse (which includes speech, journalism, letters, articles, broadsheets, songs, popular theater, etc.) and performative actions that communicate about politics

(which includes all the forms of contentious demonstration or protest that remain civil, even if civil disobedience, and peaceful).

The contemporary theory of the public sphere is rooted in the work of the Frankfurt School and critical theory. Jürgen Habermas's 1962 dissertation, *The Structural Transformation of the Public Sphere: An Inquiry into a Category of Bourgeois Society,* provided a clear history of the development of public debate about politics in various European settings in the eighteenth and nineteenth centuries. Great Britain was the case in which the public sphere developed earliest and most fully, and Habermas traces the emergence of debate in salons, letter writing, and other venues. He identifies the public sphere as a space opened up by private citizens who took control of political debate from the state. Habermas identifies a free public sphere open to the participation of all comers as a prerequisite of democracy; indeed democracy is staked on the equality of entry and participation in the public sphere. Yet, by the 1950s, Habermas concluded that the mechanisms of communication in the public sphere were increasingly controlled by a few, small corporate concerns. The advent of big media threatened (in the late 1950s) a privatization of the public sphere, privileging the concerns of big media and corporate power. Public debate and with it liberal democracy, Habermas concluded, were under grave threat.

Habermas's work was well ahead of its time. These are the debates that emerged in the Anglo-American world only after the 1970s. Habermas's dissertation was not translated into English until 1989, and discussion of the public sphere in the Anglo-American world remained somewhat muted until then. Meanwhile, Habermas continued to develop his interest in the communicative politics of public interaction; moreover, he was searching for ways to understand the potential for public politics and social transformation in the contemporary era. Through the 1970s and 1980s, he developed the theory of communicative action, as a way of understanding how public politics could proceed to empower ordinary people even in a situation where the mass media really reflected the views of a small corporate oligarchy and sought to control and constrain public debate (the opposite of the public sphere's origins in free, equal, and reasoned debate).

In 1989, Habermas's original 1962 dissertation on the public sphere was translated into English, sparking a major debate in the Anglo-American world. Social theorists and researchers of women's and other minority political communities took issue with Habermas's formulation of the open public sphere as a critical component of modern democracy. These critics noted that the public sphere that Habermas had discussed was in fact a highly exclusionary arena of politics, confined mainly to male, bourgeois, European (white), actors, leaving out of the story of the development of democracy other actors, who included the vast majority of the population in Great Britain and other Western democracies—nonpropertied or less affluent males, the working class, women, members of the African and other diasporas, youth, homosexuals, and other marginalized groups. Yet these critics by and large remained open to the notion that public spheres were important to the development of democracy, and Habermas responded in the 1990s by formulating what he called a "discourse-centered" theory of democracy that embraced the pluralist notion of dominant and popular public spheres that, along with the action of social movements, pushed democracy along even while the bourgeois public sphere had been, according to his earlier analysis, largely co-opted by private, market forces in the mass media.

Other researchers began to develop empirical analyses of the kinds of historical and documentary evidence that supported a thesis claiming that the public sphere was a crucial feature of modern democracy. By the late 1990s, the public sphere literature had broadened to include not only the dominant public sphere controlled by privately owned mass media but also the actions of social movements and other collective actors that created popular and oppositional public spheres that described the actions of "counterpublics" striving for inclusion in public politics. Understandings of the public sphere by this point now included not only media studies but also social movement studies, feminist theory, African American and Afro-diaspora politics, queer theory, and studies of popular movements and collective action in general.

These developments in public sphere studies were matched in the real world of politics by the "Third Wave" democratizations in Southern Europe, Latin America, and across the developing world. The Third Wave began in the mid-1970s in Southern Europe, exploded in the 1980s across Latin America, and in the 1980s and 1990s came to affect countries across the developing world. Latin American analysts, in particular, have been keenly aware of how movements to develop public politics were key forces that helped to destabilize military regimes and hasten their exit from power. At this time, we see the reemergence of civil society in writings on democratization and transitions from authoritarian rule, which is matched by the emphasis on voluntary organization and civil society in both the analysis of and political discourse of neoliberalism, the political philosophy and program that emerged from the Thatcher and Reagan administrations in Great Britain and the United States, respectively. In development programs supported by the World Bank in the developing countries, for example, we see an emphasis on the participation of persons affected by development through civil society and social movement organizations in a way that explicitly acknowledges the role of public politics in the implementation and success of policies.

— John Guidry

See also Civil Society; Democracy; Frankfurt School; Habermas, Jürgen; Social Movement Theory

FURTHER READINGS AND REFERENCES

Avritzer, Leonardo. 2002. *Democracy and the Public Space in Latin America.* Princeton, NJ: Princeton University Press.

Calhoun, Craig, ed. 1992. *Habermas and the Public Sphere.* Cambridge, MA: MIT Press.

Dawson, Michael. 1994. "A Black Counterpublic? Economic Earthquakes, Racial Agenda(s), and Black Politics." *Public Culture* 7:195–223.

Habermas, Jürgen. [1962] 1989. *The Structural Transformation of the Public Sphere: An Inquiry into a Category of Bourgeois Society.* Translated by T. Burger with F. Lawrence. Cambridge, MA: MIT Press. Originally published as *Strukturwandel der Öffentlichkeit: Untersuchung zu einer Kategorie der bügerlichen Gesellschaft.*

———. 1992. "Further Reflections on the Public Sphere." Pp. 421–61 in *Habermas and the Public Sphere,* edited by Craig Calhoun. Cambridge, MA: MIT Press.

———. 1996. *Between Facts and Norms: Contributions to a Discourse Theory of Law and Democracy.* Translated by William Rehg. Cambridge, MA: MIT Press.

Zaret, David. 2000. *Origins of Democratic Culture.* Princeton, NJ: Princeton University Press.

QUEER THEORY

Queer theory has its roots in poststructuralism and literary deconstructionism. Hence, the works of Foucault, Derrida, and Lacan are seen as largely influential. Queer theory is tied to the rise in multicultural theory in sociology. Both of these in turn owe much to the rise of postmodern social theory in helping to give voice where none had previously been present.

The rise of poststructuralism played an especially important role in setting the stage for queer theory. Counterintuitively, one reason for this is that poststructuralism leaves a lot of unanswered questions. In fact, poststructuralists delight in their belief that there is no single answer to any question. While this may be frustrating to many, it is also a source of joy and freedom for many others. It promotes the tearing apart of existing social theories by subjecting them to harsh critical analysis and ultimately stimulates many to be revised, re-envisioned, and improved, thereby leading to a strengthening of such theories. Poststructuralism also has the positive side effect of promoting the idea that all social phenomena can, and should, be deconstructed. This idea is similar to the mainstream sociological goal of debunking social myths and shows how poststructuralism can provide many valuable insights for those who have been oppressed, ignored, or silenced by social theory.

One of the key contributors to poststructuralism, as well as one of the most influential founders of queer theory, is Michel Foucault. Specifically, two of Foucault's main ideas—"archaeology of knowledge" (1966) and "genealogy of power" (1969)—have had the greatest influence. The archaeology of knowledge represents a search for the universal rules that govern what can be said in a particular discourse at a given historical moment. Foucault's goal is not to develop a traditional understanding of these documents but rather to describe them, analyze them, and organize them. He does not believe that one can, or even should, pinpoint origins. The focus should be on analyzing what actually is, not where it came from. This idea has been readily adopted by queer theorists as they also frequently proceed with a goal of understanding, not defining.

A genealogy of power for Foucault represents his concern with what he saw as the inextricable linkage between knowledge and power. Genealogy as a method of intellectual history is very distinct in that it does not seek to describe things based on the lawlike ways they unfold or even on their arrival at a given historical goal. Instead it outlines their trajectories, which are seen as open-ended, thereby allowing for a multiplicity of pathways. Thus, everything is relational and contingent. Genealogy also implies an inherent criticism toward the way things are perceived to be "naturally" (i.e., men and women, heterosexuals and homosexuals, etc.). This idea has become a cornerstone of relational politics and queer theory alike as they seek to disrupt notions of essence and "natural" identity.

The genealogy of power also demonstrates an interest in how people regulate themselves and other members of society through the production and control of knowledge. Although Foucault is interested in the ways in which the power derived from knowledge is used to dominate society by members of the ruling class, he does not see those elites as consciously exerting their rule. Instead, he is more interested in the structure between knowledge and power than with the actors and their positions within that structure.

It was not until the groundbreaking work of Michel Foucault ([1978]1980) that the topic of sexuality, and homosexuality in particular, was given much attention in academic environments. The founding fathers of sociology had paid little, if any, attention to such issues. There was, however, some interest in topics related to sexuality and homosexuality prior to Foucault, although much of it took place outside the discipline of sociology. Alfred Kinsey and

Sigmund Freud, for example, both explored various tenets of sexuality and disrupted many of the traditional ways of thinking about the issues related to the topic. It was not until the work of Foucault, however, and especially in the late 1980s, that an independent area of queer theory first began to take hold in the academy.

The onset of the public attention given to the AIDS epidemic, combined with liberalizing attitudes toward homosexuality, fostered an environment in which lesbian and gay studies were finally able to take hold in academic settings. It was during this time (roughly the mid to late 1980s) that many in academia sought to stake out the boundaries of what it meant to be gay or lesbian and wanted to advance causes that related specifically to these identities. This parallels the rise of interest in identity politics that was also occurring at this time. However, a transition similar to the one that turned interest from identity politics to relational politics also occurred in lesbian and gay studies leading to the emergence of a field of queer theory.

The term "queer theory" was specifically chosen by those in the field over "lesbian and gay studies" because of the fixed identity and exclusivity the latter term seemed to imply. One of the goals of those interested in the topics that would become queer theory was to displace many of the commonly held notions about lesbian and gay people and to, in fact, destabilize those categories of identity. Hence, an area known as lesbian and gay studies would seem contradictory and confining. Such a limited term would also seem to exclude many who have found refuge in queer theory, such as transsexuals, transvestites, sadists, fetishists, and others whose sexuality has been labeled deviant.

The use of the word *queer* carried a negative connotation for many decades. Since the Stonewall Revolution of 1969, however, a number of gay and lesbian advocacy groups have made gallant strides in reclaiming the word and transforming it into a neutral, if not positive, term. It has since come to represent not that which is different in an inherently negative way but, rather, that which is different in a unique, liberating way. Groups such as ACT UP (AIDS Coalition to Unleash Power), which rallied in support of bringing increased attention to the AIDS epidemic, were particularly influential in this battle.

Although it is hard to define any particular identifying characteristics of queer theory (in fact, most queer theorists would abhor such an attempt), Arlene Stein and Ken Plummer (1996) have noted several "hallmarks" of queer theory. First, there is a conceptualization of sexuality in a way that views sexual power located in different aspects of social life. This power is given form discursively and is enforced and reinforced through the policing of boundaries and polarizing binary divides. Second, there is an attempt to displace categories of sex, gender, and sexuality. A lot of work has been done in queer theory to call into question the uneasy concept of identity in general and,

more specifically, how we claim to know identity. Third, many in the field reject civil rights strategies "in favor of a politics of carnival, transgression, and parody which leads to deconstruction, decentering, revisionist readings, and an anti-assimilationist politics" (p. 134). Fourth, there is no opposition to doing work in areas not normally thought of as related to sexuality, and there is a desire to reinterpret texts through "queer readings," which are viewed as heterosexualized or not sexualized at all.

The emergence of queer theory led to an understanding of the identity of the homosexual that is both comparable to and contrastable with the identity of the heterosexual. It also allowed for the homosexual to be taken as a subject in and of itself. Queer theory is often seen as a standpoint theory, one that is particular to the viewpoint of sexuality, and most usually homosexuality. It seeks to insert the social location and viewpoint of homosexuals and others labeled as sexual deviants into the mainstream of social theory.

Queer theory is more complex than this, however, and Steven Seidman (1994) would argue that what sets queer theory apart is its rejection of any single unifying identity. Instead, individuals are seen as composed of multiple identities that are all unstable and always shifting. In this way, Seidman believes that queer theory is moving away from a theory of the homosexual and in the direction of a more general social theory, especially a more general postmodern social theory.

Diana Fuss (1989, 1991) is another theorist who is pushing to move queer theory beyond simply a heterosexual/homosexual dichotomy. Fuss believes that the "interior" of an identity is primarily constituted by reference to its "exterior," or that which it is not. Hence, she argues that heterosexuality and homosexuality are each given meaning only by virtue of their relationship to the other; they are what they are because of what they are not. Fuss believes that asserting an identity as queer only helps to validate the existing dichotomy and its consequent oppression. She contends that a more relational approach should be taken to issues of sexuality.

Jennifer Terry (1995) argues that the category of homosexual has always been thought of as something that lies distinctly separated from and most generally opposed to the category of heterosexual. Terry also speaks to how the body is an important factor in maintaining this distinction. Homosexuals have been maintained at a safe distance from heterosexuals first through an implication of biological differences, then with Kinsey through statistical differences (although Kinsey's distinctions brought up the unsettling problem of the possibility of anyone being capable of being a homosexual), and finally back full circle to many modern-day arguments that homosexuality is indeed biologically determined. "It would appear that a century-old tendency toward binary thinking that separates a friendly 'us' from a dangerous 'them' makes great use of the body as a site wherein difference is imagined to materialize" (p. 163).

Scientists and laypeople alike have been interested in how to determine if one is gay or straight since the term *homosexual* first appeared in Germany around 1869 (Terry 1995:131). It seemed immediately necessary to make clear who was and, more important, who was not a homosexual. As noted above, scientists originally, and once again in recent years, turned to the physical body for signs of determining sexual orientation. Although they are no longer searching for signs of degeneracy (at least not as often as before), they are still using the body as a means of making definite determinations of sexual orientation (through things such as the search for the gay gene or assertions that gay men have larger fingers, etc.). Terry argues that the body is still considered an important source of information for trying to determine the sexuality of individuals and that this information is then used to categorize and, often, oppress them.

The nonscientific community has more commonly relied on another means of determining sexual identity—namely, gender. In fact, Seidman (2002) argues that gender is the principle means for determining sexual identity in contemporary American society. In addition, Butler (1990) sees the equation of sex equals gender equals sexuality as the dominant paradigm in most of America, and she seeks to unsettle this cultural fallacy. She makes the sex/gender/sexuality connection in the examples of employment and sexual harassment by saying,

> Gay people, for instance, may be discriminated against in positions of employment because they fail to "appear" in accordance with accepted gender norms. And the sexual harassment of gay people may well take place not in the service of shoring up gender hierarchy, but in promoting gender normativity. (p. xiii)

Whatever methods are used to identify homosexual individuals, the goal is almost always the same—to keep the dividing line between heterosexuality and homosexuality clear and present.

Eve Kosofsky Sedgwick is one of the pioneering queer theorists who has helped conceptualize this dividing line between straight and gay. In her book *The Epistemology of the Closet*, Sedgwick (1990) explores the concept of the closet, which she believes is "the defining structure for gay oppression in this century" (p. 48). The closet is paired against "coming out" as two concepts that have come to respectively represent the secrecy and revelation of almost any "identity" that is seen as politically charged. In particular, these ideas seek to crystallize the identity of the homosexual. The term homosexual itself has been resistant to efforts of deconstructionists, not because it is particularly significant to those who are categorized under its label but because it is considered invaluable to those who wish to categorize themselves outside that label.

Another innovative idea derived from Sedgwick's piece is that one can never truly be out of the closet. No matter how many times people reveal themselves and their "true identity" (a concept she clearly does not agree with in the first place), they will still most likely find themselves in situations in the future in which it will be necessary to do so again. Hence, the process of coming out is a never-ending one. Another important question posed by Sedgwick is coming out to where? After people come out of the closet, where does this leave them?

Similar to Foucault's interest in the genealogy of power, the relevance of coming out also constitutes a knowledge-power relationship for Sedgwick. The ideas are based on secrecy and outings. It creates possibilities for others to gain power by using knowledge of one's sexuality against him or her. It can also lead to other forms of power found in knowledge that are not reducible to other understandings of a knowledge-power relationship.

Another of the most influential queer theorists, and also one of the most influential feminist theorists and social theorists more generally, is Judith Butler. For Butler (1997), sexuality is simply a performance based on repetition. Compulsory heterosexuality, through its constant repetition and enactment (even many times by those who are not heterosexual), has come to lay claim to titles of what it means to be "natural" or "normal." In this way, homosexuality is seen as a copy, albeit a far inferior copy, of heterosexuality. However, since Butler views all sexuality as a repetitive performance, there can be no original template and hence no inferior version. She argues against the idea that the performance of sexuality is in any way an expression of "a psychic reality that precedes it" (p. 309).

Sexuality, then, is considered a form of drag. Individuals do not always consciously "perform" their sexuality, but there is a performance going on nonetheless. This idea led Butler to offer something of a solution to the crisis of compulsory heterosexuality. She posits the idea of a "repetitive disruption," which would be one way that sexuality could work against identity. In this way, although no true stable identity would come to light, there would be the hope "of letting that which cannot fully appear in any performance persist in its disruptive promise" (p. 313).

For Butler (1993), as for many other queer theorists, the use of the term queer, because it can be so broadly defined and so easily co-opted by a wide spectrum of "identities," more often implies an anti-identity, or even a nonidentity, than a stable, discernable group of people. Butler believes that it is this sense of a nonidentity that helps make the use of the term queer so effective because it calls into question our sense of what constitutes an identity at all. In this way, the term queer and the broader concept of a queer theory are both ideas that have no predictable direction because they are in a constant state of formation and reformation.

Overall, queer theory has sought to do what many other newly emergent disciplines have sought to do—disrupt the accepted hierarchies of privilege and dispel myths related to identity. In fact, queer theory has sought to dispel the notion of identity in its totality. It is difficult to predict exactly where queer theory will be led in the future, but it seems apparent that it has already made a number of inroads into the established world of academia and that it has provided insights considered invaluable to academics and laypeople alike.

— Michael Ryan

See also Butler, Judith; Compulsory Heterosexuality; Foucault, Michel; Gender; Lesbian Continuum; Sexuality and the Subject; Standpoint Theory

FURTHER READINGS AND REFERENCES

Butler, Judith. 1990. *Gender Trouble: Feminism and the Subversion of Identity.* New York: Routledge.

———. 1993. *Bodies That Matter: On the Discursive Limits of "Sex"* New York: Routledge.

———. 1997. "Imitation and Gender Insubordination." Pp. 300–16 in *The Second Wave: A Reader in Feminist Theory*, edited by Linda Nicholson New York: Routledge.

Foucault, Michel. 1966. *The Order of Things: An Archaeology of the Human Sciences.* New York: Vintage.

———. 1969. *The Archaeology of Knowledge and the Discourse on Language.* New York: Harper Colophon.

———. [1978] 1980. *The History of Sexuality.* Vol. 1, *An Introduction.* New York: Vintage.

Fuss, Diana. 1989. *Essentially Speaking.* New York: Routledge.

———. 1991. *Inside/Outside: Lesbian Theories, Gay Theories.* New York: Routledge.

Sedgwick, Eve Kosofsky. 1990. *Epistemology of the Closet.* Berkeley: University of California Press.

Seidman, Steven. 1994. "Symposium: Queer Theory/Sociology: A Dialogue." *Sociological Theory* 12:166–77.

———. 2002. *Beyond the Closet: The Transformation of Gay and Lesbian Life.* New York: Routledge.

Stein, Arlene and Ken Plummer. 1996. "'I Can't Even Think Straight': 'Queer' Theory and the Missing Sexual Revolution in Sociology." Pp. 129–44 in *Queer Theory/Sociology,* edited by Steven Seidman Cambridge, MA: Blackwell.

Terry, Jennifer. 1995. "Anxious Slippages Between 'Us' and 'Them.'" Pp. 129–67 in *Deviant Bodies,* edited by Jennifer Terry and Jacqueline Urla. Bloomington, IN: Indiana University Press.

R

RADICAL FEMINISM

This strand of feminist ideas and practices has as its hallmarks a disdain for, if not rejection of, hierarchy and a commitment to cultural as well as political transformation. Seeking more than the reformist measures associated with liberal feminism, radical feminism can be seen as revolutionary or at least aiming at wholesale rather than piecemeal social change. During the nineteenth and early twentieth centuries, such feminist luminaries as Lucretia Mott, Sojourner Truth, Matilda Joslyn Cage, Angelina and Sarah Grimke, Ida Wells-Barnett, and Charlotte Perkins Gilman forged strong grounds for radical feminist theory. Their work was pivotal in, though not typical of, the *first wave* of feminism during that time period, which began receding from public attention as Western women's right to vote gained constitutional stature.

During the 1960s, radical feminism found renewed, powerful expression in Western societies. In the hands of theorists such as Eve Figes, Shulamith Firestone, and Kate Millet, radical feminism took a shape that both linked it with and distinguished it from New Left politics. During the 1970s and early 1980s, this *second wave* of feminist expression produced pathbreaking works such as Sheila Rowbotham's *Women, Resistance, and Revolution* (1972), Ti-Grace Atkinson's *Amazon Odyssey* (1974), Adrienne Rich's *Of Woman Born: Motherhood as Experience and Institution* (1976), Susan Griffin's *Pornography and Silence* (1981), and Kathleen Barry's *Female Sexual Slavery* (1984). Figures such as Gayle Rubin and Mary Daly emerged as still other influential purveyors of a feminist vocabulary built up around the notions of oppression, exploitation, patriarchy, domination, and resistance. Unlike their liberal feminist counterparts, these radical theorists emphasized transgressive and subversive tactics for overhauling social structure. They built their frameworks around the understanding that *the personal is political*—that is, that power pervades human association and shapes the structures wherein some groups, such as men, dominate and oppress other groups, such as women. From their perspective, the personal and interpersonal levels demand critique and transformation just as thoroughly as large-scale organizations and the institutional order do.

One of the best-known radical feminists who emerged during this period is Angela Y. Davis. Her political activism brought her notoriety in many circles. The publication of *Women, Race & Class* (1981) gained her attention in academic circles. Davis's book includes an incisive survey of the class and racial biases that had infiltrated first-wave feminism. Alongside her historically grounded critique Davis offers a parallel critique of her contemporary radical feminists. In the antirape movement spearheaded by radical feminists, for example, Davis finds considerable racism centering on stereotypes of African American men as rapists. Working mostly from a Marxian perspective, Davis links women's and other groups' political struggles and treats them all as necessitating the defeat of monopoly capitalism. From her perspective, femininity is above all an ideology of inferiority produced primarily by industrialization, which displaced women's productive labor in and around the household. Eradicating that ideology, then, means eradicating the conditions of its genesis and development.

More than 15 years later Davis published *Blues Legacies and Black Feminism* (1998), which focuses on how working-class African American women's feminism found powerful expression in their contributions to blues music. Centering on the works of Bessie Smith, Gertrude "Ma" Rainey, and Billie Holiday, this study provides rich empirical grounds illustrative of Davis's earlier contentions about the linkages among race, class, and gender in capitalist economies. At the same time, it offers historical insights into African American women's contributions to feminism that amount to a cultural and political legacy that bears further investigation.

Although Davis herself introduced few, if any, new terms into the feminist vocabulary, one colorful contribution of radical feminist theorists has been their distinctive vocabulary, which includes a variety of neologisms. Daly can scarcely be outdone on this front. With *Gyn/Ecology: The Metaethics of Radical Feminism* (1978) she introduced a variety of hard-hitting terms such as *anti-androcrat* and *Amazon Voyager* unlikely to win respect in mainstream contexts, including academe where she herself labored as a feminist theologian. Robin Morgan (1982:8, 106) introduced the notion of "sexual fundamentalism," which involves suppressing sexuality or denying its joyful character, and emphasized how women have gotten saddled with religion in lieu of philosophy and morality in lieu of ethics as well as other male-serving displacements that further feminine inferiorization. Ann Ferguson added to the vocabulary of male dominance and oppression the notion of "gyandry," aimed at valorizing distinctively female resources. Much in the spirit of radical feminism, Ferguson (1991:211) argued that the "gynandrous" ideal is preferable to the "androgynous" one because femininity itself has to be appreciated in order to promote an "autonomous yet caring" personhood that transcends the limits of androgyny within patriarchal systems. In all this work, although more explicitly in some, women's desires and sexuality and pleasure get priority alongside women's other rights and needs.

Widely portrayed as man hating and male bashing, radical feminists deny the efficacy of gaining women's rights and equality by relying primarily or even heavily on the law and public policy. The world of everyday life thus commands a lot of their theoretical and practical attention. As radical feminist Andrea Dworkin (2002) puts it, "The worst immorality is in living a trivial life because one is afraid to face any other kind of life" (p. 202). What Annie Rogers (1974) has called *ordinary courage* thus lies at the core of what radical feminism presupposes not only in theory but also in practice.

— Mary F. Rogers

See also Davis, Angela; Feminism; Liberal Feminism; Postmodernist Feminism

FURTHER READINGS AND REFERENCES

Dworkin, Andrea. 2002. *Heartbreak: The Political Memoir of a Feminist Militant.* New York: Basic Books.

Ferguson, Ann. 1991. *Sexual Democracy: Women, Oppression, and Revolution.* Boulder, CO: Westview.

Morgan, Robin. 1982. *The Anatomy of Freedom: Feminism, Physics, and Global Politics.* Garden City, NY: Anchor Press/Doubleday.

Rogers, Annie G. 1993. "Voice, Play, and a Practice of Ordinary Courage in Girls' and Women's Lives." *Harvard Educational Review* 63(3):265–92.

RATIONAL CHOICE

Rational choice's emergence within sociology began with the pioneering work of James Coleman in the 1960s. Drawing on the "purposive action framework" (see *The Mathematics of Collective Action,* 1973), he proposed an analysis of collective action that was eventually extended into analyses of social norms, marriage markets, status systems, and educational attainment (*Foundations of Social Theory,* 1990). His work established the theme that continued to define rational choice sociology, a focus on explaining macro-social phenomena in ways grounded in micro-social choices of social actors. As thus conceived, rational choice has two essential features. The first is a view of social action as purposive; thus behavior is oriented by a system of values, aims, or goals. The second is a commitment to some form of methodological individualism wherein social structures and institutions are viewed as the products of social action.

Coleman's approach to rational choice sociology drew directly on neoclassical economic theory. He viewed a wide range of phenomena in market terms. For example, a marriage system can be viewed as a market for mates in which those with highly valued attributes have the greatest value in the marriage market. Similarly, a status system can be viewed as a market for access to individuals with highly valued attributes. High-status people gravitate toward one another, thereby defining the upper reaches of the stratification system, and lower-status people have no choice but to settle for one another and thereby define the lower levels. This emphasis on market models carried over to Coleman's proposals for institutional design. The problem he addressed was the diminishing portion of the gross domestic product going to homes with children resulting from the increasing proportion of single-parent households. He proposed resolving this problem by creating a micromarket in child care services, in which families would earn governmental payments based on to their ability to raise effectively functioning children. The intended effect was to strengthen the incentives for families to invest in their children while also providing them with the resources to do so. Therefore, one form of market failure—a failure of the marriage market to provide adequately for the needs of children—was to be resolved through creating a secondary market. This approach resembles the economic approach to institutional design. For example, the failure of the mortgage market that contributed to the Great Depression of the 1930s led to the creation of a governmentally administered secondary mortgage market.

During this early phase, contributions to rational choice grew quietly, with contributions from a growing number of scholars. These include Anthony Oberschall's (1973) analyses of social movements, Heckathorn's (1983) analyses of bargaining and networks of collective action, Pamela Oliver's (1980) work on the organizational processes underlying collective action, Karl-Dieter Opp's (1982) analyses of norms and social movements, and Lindenberg's studies of sharing groups (1982). While sharing Coleman's focus on explaining macro-social phenomena in ways grounded in micro-social choices of social actors, these works were grounded, not in microeconomic theory but, rather, either in various forms of social psychology, which had long been dominated by rational choice perspectives, or in game theory.

A second phase in rational choice's emergence within sociology began in the mid-1980s with the publication of two programmatic statements that called for its expansion (Coleman 1986; Hechter 1983). These statements emphasized the continuity between rational choice and traditional approaches to theorizing. For example, Coleman approvingly described Weber's explanation of bureaucratic, traditional, and charismatic forms of organization in terms of a microfoundation of purposive action. Weber was thereby embraced as the first rational choice sociologist. These programmatic statements were also critical of traditional approaches to theorizing in sociology and emphasized the unique contribution that rational choice could offer by providing a more nuanced means for analyzing the link between macro- and micro-social levels.

The essential theme in these statements, although not expressed in precisely these terms, was that the lessons from the collapse of structural functionalism had not been learned. For the widely condemned view of social actors as oversocialized had been replaced by a functionally equivalent "structural embeddedness paradigm" that viewed actors as mere puppets of the culture or structure in which they were embedded. The problem with this approach is that it precludes upward causation, from the micro- to the macro-social levels. In contrast, the distinctive contribution of rational choice is to provide a framework within which the role of agency can be fully appreciated through analyzing the reciprocal process by which actors both transform the contexts within which they act and are, in turn, shaped by those structures.

The chapters in Hechter's (1983) book demonstrated the viability of this approach to a broad range of areas of macrosociology and social science theory in other disciplines. These include Mary Brinton's analysis of the Japanese family, Douglass North's analysis of institutional change, and Hechter's analysis of highly solidary groups such as charismatically organized religious sects using an expanded form of power-dependence theory. During this period, the growth of rational choice sociology was reflected in institutional developments such as the founding of the journal *Rationality and Society* in 1989 and the formation of a rational choice section in the American Sociological Association in 1994.

This period was also characterized by a vigorous debate between proponents (e.g., see Coleman and Fararo 1992) and critics (e.g., see England and Kilbourne 1990), a debate that also occurred within political science (see Friedman, *The Rational Choice Controversy*, 1995; Green and Shapiro, *Pathologies of Rational Choice Theory*, 1994) where the adoption of rational choice perspectives had occurred earlier. The harshest critiques came from postmodernists and some feminists who equated rational choice with what they saw as pernicious values. For example, Seidman (1991) portrayed a hypothetical rational choice scholar who was confronted by the criticism that the theory "devalues expressive, relational, feminine, and democratic values," as responding with the following statement: "As a utilitarian individualist who believes that male elites should rule the key social institutions, the social and moral implications of this discourse are fully consistent with [my] values" (p. 189). Thus Seidman depicts the rational choice scholar as a self-proclaimed elitist, sexist, and enemy of democracy.

Owing to this debate, four traditional critiques of rational choice came increasingly to be recognized as misconceptions. First, rational choice is not wedded to a grim view of actors as ruthless opportunists. Indeed, much sociological rational choice analysis focuses on altruistic and other nonegoistic behaviors (Hechter, *Principles of Group Solidarity*, 1987; Mansbridge, *Beyond Self-Interest*, 1990). Second, rational choice is not wedded to any particular political position. Rational choice scholars range from free-market conservatives (James Buchanan) through political moderates (James Coleman) to Marxists (Jon Elster [1990] and John Roemer). Third, rational choice theory does not require that actions have only intended consequences; indeed, primary emphasis has been placed on analyzing social dilemmas, such as the prisoner's dilemma, in which individually rational actions combine to produce a collective loss. Finally, rational choice is not an alien import, but as emphasized by Coleman and others (Swedberg, *Max Weber and the Idea of Economic Sociology*, 1998), it has deep roots within sociology, in particular the methodological individualism of Weber.

A third phase in rational choice's emergence within sociology began in the mid 1990s when it became apparent that the hopes of some, and the fears of others, were disappointed. Rational choice did not sweep the discipline. Instead, it took its place as one among many alternative approaches in general sociological theory. Significantly, this development occurred at a time when the decline of general sociological theory was continuing, because for decades the principal focus of intellectual action within the discipline had been shifting to substantive fields such as inequality, organizations, and political sociology. It is within these more intellectually active fields that rational choice has continued to expand. It has also become increasingly interdisciplinary, drawing on and contributing to the works of scholars from economics, political science, anthropology, law, and philosophy. This expansion has also been accompanied by a shift in the microfoundation of rational choice theory toward less reliance on microeconomics and social psychology and greater reliance on varying forms of game theory.

This expansion continued in the area in which rational choice first became prominent, social movements and collective action. Marwell and Oliver (*The Critical Mass in Collective Action*, 1993) had argued that contrary to conventional wisdom (see Olson, *The Logic of Collective Action*, 1965), increases in both group size and heterogeneity promotes collective action. This occurred, they argued, because the larger and more diverse a group, the greater would be the number of individuals with an especially strong interest in promoting collective action. This group would then serve as a "critical mass," which would trigger the emergence of collective action. This analysis considered only a single way in which collective action could be organized, voluntary cooperation in which each individual chooses independently whether to contribute to the collective endeavor. They therefore ignored selective incentives.

In contrast, Heckathorn (2002) showed that depending on the circumstances, heterogeneity can either promote collective action or it can cause the group to fragment into mutually antagonistic factions. The latter can occur when what is for some a collective good is for others a collective bad or when costs of contribution vary. Such cases are common in real-world collective action problems. For example, when environmentalists promote regulation to protect what they see as valuable and fragile ecosystems, the affected industries often complain about loss of jobs. The analysis further showed that polarization is especially likely when collective action is organized through selective incentives. For selective incentives compel even those who lack any interest in the collective good to contribute and thereby provide those individuals with an incentive to mobilize in opposition. This was an issue Marwell and Oliver did not consider, because they considered only voluntary contributions. However, public policies reflect recognition of the potentially divisive nature of selective incentives. Politicians are frequently reluctant to support use of public funds for controversial programs. For example, in New York, state-sanctioned needle exchanges do not receive public funds. They operate through private donations. This ensures that individuals who oppose these exchanges will not be taxed to support a program they do not agree with and thereby weakens their incentive to mobilize in opposition to the exchanges. This example illustrates the cumulative nature of theoretic development made possible by the theoretic coherence and constancy of the rational choice paradigm. For a detailed discussion and analysis of this cumulative development in collective action theories see Marwell and Oliver (2002).

Rational choice analysis also expanded to other core areas, including stratification. Roger Gould (2002) began by observing that analyses of stratification fall within two rival camps. Some view stratification as deriving from a system of domination, in which those occupying positions of power use it to maintain their privileges. Others view stratification in more meritocratic terms, as reflecting differing endowments of socially valued attributes. Gould constructed a model broad enough to encompass both models yet specific enough to provide testable hypotheses regarding when one or the other model, or a blend of the two, could be expected to apply. This was achieved by conceptualizing stratification as arising from two distinct processes. First, consistent with the assumption of bounded rationality, judging the attributes of others always involves uncertainty. Therefore, the judgments of others provide useful information through a relational signaling process. However, he showed that operation of this mechanism alone would trigger a positive feedback process that would produce implausibly high levels of stratification in which those with initial status advantages would gain ever-higher status. He then introduced a second opposing mechanism wherein offering recognition that is unreciprocated entails a risk of being placed in a socially inferior position. The resulting multimechanism model was tested and found considerable empirical support using several social network-based data sets. Gould's analysis shows how rational choice theory can provide the basis for theoretic integration of opposing models drawn from mainstream sociology into a consistent and coherent integrative model.

Rational choice theories of emotions have also been proposed. In complementary analyses, Robert Frank (*Passions Within Reason*, 1988) and Jack Hirshleifer (1993) argue that negative emotions such as anger serve to ensure the credibility of threats, while positive emotions such as love and affection serve to ensure the credibility of promises to cooperate. More generally, emotions resolve the "commitment" problem that arises when actors could benefit by entering binding commitments that they also would be tempted to violate. Frank and Hirshleifer's analyses draw on evolutionary game models of the sort popularized by Robert Axelrod's (1984) *Evolution of Cooperation*. They provide a game theoretically grounded account of both the conditions under which emotions are elicited and the form of emotions that arise in each setting, establishing in this way the link between emotions and rational action. Emotions serve somewhat like the bindings that prevented Ulysses from rushing toward the Sirens. Emotions block actions that are rational within a narrow time frame but irrational when more distant consequences are considered. In this way emotions confer survival advantages. This view contrasts sharply with the stereotypical view of emotions as producers of impulsive and irrational behavior. In the Frank and Hirshleifer models, emotions allow us to act in ways compatible with our long-term interests, rescuing us from short-term maximizing that would be to our long-term detriment.

The Frank and Hirshleifer models provide complementary accounts of the role of emotions. Hirshleifer focuses on fundamental processes, such as the distinction between "affections," somewhat stable patterns of benevolence or malevolence such as love or hate, and "passions," transient orientations such as anger and gratitude that are triggered by specific acts. In contrast, Frank focuses on the structural implications of his account of emotions. He shows that when emotions are incorporated into economic models, a variety of new phenomena become explicable. These range from charitable giving and trust to the market failures that have led to government regulation of workplace safety, working hours, minimum wages, and savings for retirement.

Economic sociology has emerged as major area within sociology and also for applications of rational choice. This development results, in part, from the collapse of the Soviet Union in 1989 and associated events in East Asia that expanded the scope of economic sociology by eliminating all but a handful of noncapitalist economies. More important, it initiated a vast natural experiment on market transition. Many classic works in economic sociology, including Weber's *The Protestant Ethic and the Spirit of Capitalism* and Polanyi's *The Great Transformation,* examined the emergence of capitalism in Western societies. However, after 1989, market transition could be studied using contemporary intellectual and analytic tools. The result has been a growing body of rational choice-based work on market transition (Nee and Matthews 1996) that has substantially enriched the empirical literature in economic sociology. Important themes in the market transition literature include the displacement of political capital as the organizing principle of production by economic, human, and social capital, and debates about whether the transition process will produce market systems that converge or remain distinct.

Rational choice-based economic sociology has, in a sense, reversed what had originally been seen as the relationship between rational choice and economic theory. Whereas the earliest work in sociological rational choice relied on microeconomic theory as a foundation, in contrast, economic sociology focuses on what is left out of market models, including the webs of norms and the hierarchies in which markets are embedded and upon which they rely to establish and secure systems of property rights and define norms of economic conduct. Therefore, the analyses of markets on which economics has specialized is supplemented by analyses of hierarchies and norms, institutional forms about which sociologists have much to contribute intellectually.

Other areas in which rational choice sociology is expanding include gangs (Jankowski, *Islands in the Street: Gangs*

and American Urban Society, 1991), medical sociology (Heckathorn 2002), sociology of education (Morgan 1998), organizations (Miller, *Managerial Dilemmas,* 1992), socialization (Yamaguchi 1998), preference change (Hechter et al., 1993; Lindenberg and Frey 1993), institutional analysis (Brinton and Nee 1998), the sociology of religion (Stark 1999), the family (Brinton 1993), trust (Cook, *Trust in Society,* 2001; Gautschi, *Trust and Exchange,* 2002), narrative analysis (Anthony et al. 1994; Kiser 1996; also see Bates et al., *Analytic Narratives,* 1998), immigration and assimilation (Alba and Nee, *Remaking the American Mainstream,* 2003), and historical analysis (Brustein, *The Logic of Evil,* 1996; Hopcroft, *Regions, Institutions, and Agrarian Change in European History,* 1999). Consequently, whereas rational choice as a part of general sociological theory has remained durable, its contributions are increasingly being made in the substantive areas in which the discipline has long been most intellectually dynamic.

As rational choice extends into the discipline's substantive areas, a clear theoretic core remains that renders the approach distinctive and provides the basis for communication among scholars working in disparate areas. This derives from the requirement that the criteria governing the choices of social actors be made *explicit*. It might seem that making an assumption explicit would be a minor matter. However, it has important implications, for it imposes a common structure on rational choice models. Each must specify a core set of theoretic terms, including (1) the set of actors who function as players in the system; (2) the alternatives available to each actor; (3) the set of outcomes that are feasible in the system, given each actor's alternatives; (4) the preferences of each actor over the set of feasible outcomes; and (5) the expectations of actors regarding system parameters. Rational choice models can also vary along many dimensions. They may be expressed mathematically or discursively; they can correspond to one-shot games in which an actor makes only a single choice or to processual models in which each actor's choices affect the conditions under which the actor and others will make subsequent choices; they may assume materially based instrumental preferences or include preferences for social approval, altruism, or justice; they may assume that information is complete (i.e., knowing the structure of the game, including others' preferences), perfect (i.e., also knowing others strategies), or incomplete and reflect either risk (i.e., knowing the probability of occurrence for each uncertain event) or uncertainty (i.e., not knowing these probabilities); they may include individual actors, corporate actors, or a combination of both types of actors. Despite such variations, because of the common structure of rational choice theories, they share a common theoretic vocabulary. This common vocabulary permits rational choice to function as the interlingua of the social sciences and ensures that theoretic developments in one substantive area will have implications in other substantive areas, both within sociology and across social science disciplines.

— Douglas D. Heckathorn

See also Coleman James; Commitment; Game Theory; Social Dilemma

FURTHER READINGS AND REFERENCES

Anthony, Denise L., Douglas D. Heckathorn, and Steven M. Maser. 1994. "Rational Rhetoric in Politics: The Debate over Ratifying the U.S. Constitution." *Rationality and Society* 6(4):489–518.

Buchanan, James M. 1975. *The Limits of Liberty*. Chicago: University of Chicago Press.

Brinton, Mary C. 1993. *Women and the Economic Miracle: Gender and Work in Postwar Japan*. Berkeley: University of California Press.

Brinton, Mary C. and Victor Nee, eds. 1998. *The New Institutionalism in Sociology*. New York: Russell Sage.

Coleman, James S. 1986. "Social Theory, Social Research, and a Theory of Action." *American Journal of Sociology* 91:1309–35.

———. 1993. "The Rational Reconstruction of Society." *American Sociological Review* 58:1–15.

Coleman, James S., and Thomas J. Fararo, eds. 1992. *Rational Choice Theory: Advocacy and Critique*. Newbury Park, CA: Sage.

Elster, Jon. 1990. "Marxism, functionalism, and game theory." Pp. 87–117 in *Structures of Capital: The Social Organization of the Economy*, edited by S. Zukin and P. DiMaggio. Cambridge, UK: Cambridge University Press.

England, Paula and Barbara Stanek Kilbourne. 1990. "Feminist Critiques of the Separative Model of Self: Implications for Rational Choice Theory." *Rationality and Society* 2(2):156–71.

Gould, Roger V. 2002. "The Origin of Status Hierarchies: A Formal Theory and Empirical Test. " *American Journal of Sociology* 107:1143–78.

Heckathorn, Douglas D. 1983. "Extensions to Power-Dependence Theory: The Concept of Resistance." *Social Forces* 61(4): 1206–31.

———. 2002. "Development of a Theory of Collective Action: From the Emergence of Norms to AIDS Prevention and the Analysis of Social Structure." Pp. 79–108 in *New Directions in Sociological Theory: Growth of Contemporary Theories*, edited by J. Berger and M. Zelditch. Lanham, MD: Rowman & Littlefield.

Hechter, Michael, ed. 1983. *Microfoundations of Macrosociology*. Philadelphia: Temple University Press.

Hechter, Michael, Lynn Nadel, and Richard E. Michod, eds. 1993. *The Origin of Values*. New York: Aldine de Gruyter.

Hirshleifer, Jack. 1993. "The Affections and the Passions: Their Economic Logic." *Rationality and Society* 5:185–202.

Kiser, Edgar. 1996. "The Revival of Narrative in Historical Sociology: What Rational Choice Theory Can Contribute." *Politics and Society* 24:249–71.

Lindenberg, Seigwart. 1982. "Sharing Groups: Theory and Suggested Applications." *Journal of Mathematical Sociology* 9:33–62.

Lindenberg, Seigwart and Bruno S. Frey. 1993. "Alternatives, Frames, and Relative Prices: A Broader View of Rational Choice Theory." *Acta Sociologica* 36:191–209.

Macy, Michael W. 1990. "Learning Theory and the Logic of Critical Mass." *American Sociological Review* 55:809–26.

Marwell, Gerald and Pamela Oliver. 2002. "Recent Developments in Critical Mass Theory." Pp. 172–193 in *New Directions in Sociological Theory: Growth of Contemporary Theories*, edited by M. Zelditch and J. Berger. Lanham, MD: Rowman & Littlefield.

Morgan, Stephen L. 1998. "Adolescent Educational Expectations: Rationalized, Fantasized, or Both?" *Rationality and Society* 10:131–62.

Nee, Victor. 1996. "The Emergence of a Market Society: Changing Mechanisms of Stratification in China." *American Journal of Sociology* 101:908—49.

Nee, Victor and Paul Ingram. 1998. "Embeddedness and Beyond: Institutions, Exchange, and Social Structure." Pp. 19–45 in *The New Institutionalism in Sociology*, edited by M. C. Brinton and V. Nee New York: Russell Sage.

Nee, Victor and Rebecca Matthews. 1996. "Market Transition and Societal Transformation in Reforming State Socialism." *Annual Review of Sociology* 22 (1996):401–36

Oberschall, Anthony. 1973. *Social Conflict and Social Movements*. Englewood Cliffs, NJ: Prentice Hall.

Oliver, Pamela. 1980. "Rewards and Punishments as Selective Incentives for Collective Action." *American Journal of Sociology* 85:1356–75.

Opp, Karl-Dieter. 1982. "The Evolutionary Emergence of Norms." *British Journal of Social Psychology* 21:139–49.

Seidman, Steven. 1991. "Postmodern Anxiety: The Politics of Epistemology." *Sociological Theory* 9:180–90.

Stark, Rodney. 1999. "A Theory of Revelations." *Journal for the Scientific Study of Religion*, 38:287–308.

Yamaguchi, Kazuo. 1998. "Rational-Choice Theories of Anticipatory Socialization and Anticipatory Non-Socialization." Rationality and Society 10:163–199.

RATIONALIZATION

The concept of rationalization as it is used in social science and social theory refers in general to complex processes in which beliefs and actions become more coherent, consistent, systematic, and goal oriented. It is often used to describe and account for large-scale social and historical processes, such as the increasing secularization of society or the transformation from a traditional autarchic agrarian economy to a modern market-oriented industrial economy. Rationalization in these instances may involve the elimination of magic and superstition from religious belief systems in favor of the methodical systematization of rational beliefs and ethical norms. Or it may entail the shift from wasteful and hidebound labor practices to more efficient, calculable, and technologically adept modes of production. Rationalization can thus be both a social and a mental or intellectual process. In either case it involves organizing belief and action so as to maximize the probability of achieving a defined end: attaining a rational belief system and methodical way of life or attaining an economic system oriented toward improving the standard of living and increasing the production of wealth.

The concept of rationalization can also be used to describe and account for the internal logic of significant changes in belief systems, ideational forms, and action orientations. In this respect, what becomes most important is the increasing logical consistency and systematic coherence within a set of beliefs or a pattern of action. To gauge consistency, it is often useful to distinguish between formal and substantive rationalization of belief systems or moral and legal principles. In general, formal rationalization has to do with the logical consistency of rules or procedures and their application, while substantive rationalization is a matter of providing logical clarity to the content of a norm and its meaning. In addition, it is useful to recognize that when applied to action orientations, rationalization can be especially pronounced when a pattern of action is consistently goal oriented, purposeful, or instrumental, thus requiring a precise matching of means with ends and a calculation of intended and unintended consequences.

When employing the concept of rationalization, whether in its historical-developmental or logical sense, one should note that it is not identical to or synonymous with the notion of rationality. That is, a rationalization process or logic may be rational from one point of view but entirely irrational from another contrasting standpoint. This contradiction is particularly apparent when the different points of view are economic or political on one hand and ethical or aesthetic on the other. For example, technical rationalization leading to more efficient productivity may be rational if the economic goal is solely to increase wealth but entirely irrational if the ethical goal is exclusively the conservation and protection of endangered environmental goods. Or the formal requirement of "equal treatment" regardless of class, race, ethnicity, or gender may clash with the substantive aim of correcting a particular social injustice based on one of these differentiating ascriptive characteristics. The modern world is replete with these kinds of opposed standpoints and contradictions.

In social theory, the leading ideas about rationalization were introduced in their most striking form in the thought of Max Weber (1864–1920). In his early work on agrarian economies, Weber was concerned with transitions from less developed to more highly developed economies. Building on an older language of economic types and developmental stages, he began to speak of a rationalization process characterized by structural differentiation in social organization, functional specialization in the division of labor, technological innovations, and a tendency toward secularization of culture. He saw that rationalization in these senses could occur internal to a specific sphere of activity in a given society, such as the economy of the large estates, the *Gutswirtschaft,* of eastern Germany, where economic, social, and political transformation was triggered in large part by technological innovations and the competitive pressures of grain production for an international market. In this instance, rationalized capitalism based on wage labor, oriented to the calculation of profit, and chained to the logic of competitive markets tended to undermine and supplant the older and traditionalist patriarchal systems of social and economic organization.

Weber considered the traditional forms of production and exchange doomed over the long term, as did a number of other political economists, including Karl Marx and Friedrich Engels. Like Marx and Engels, he thought the forces of capitalist production would eventually penetrate into the farthest reaches of the globe and affect every culture and civilization. The question was not whether it would occur, but how, when, where, and in what sequence. In the case of his own Germany, Weber recognized that politically powerful groups, such as the owners of the large estates in the eastern provinces, the Junkers, could attempt to resist and redirect such development. He believed, however, that such efforts would tend to increase rather than resolve economic and social tensions, and thus impede successful development. In an effort to counter resistance and educate skeptical contemporaries, as a young scholar Weber even devoted considerable attention to explaining the operation of the stock market as an efficient institutionalized mechanism for dealing fairly in an international competitive environment with commodity prices and capital accumulation. Later during World War I, much of his political writing about Germany sought to analyze the legacy of resistance to economic change and the prospects for recasting the national constitutional order and its basis in the socioeconomic system.

Starting with these ideas about rationalization in the economic sphere, particularly as reflected in the development of capitalist modes of production in the West, Weber began to elaborate this grand theme in a number of ways. When discussing the categories of social action in *Economy and Society* (Weber 1968), for example, he postulated four possible action orientations: instrumental, or goal oriented; value oriented; traditional; and affective. His discussion of charisma and charismatic authority attached to the last orientation, while the first (*Zweckrationalität* was his important term) gave him a powerful tool for understanding a particular type of rationalization that appeared to become increasingly dominant in the modern world and seemed opposed to the personal gifts associated with charisma. These notions were elaborated further and from a somewhat different historical point of view, addressed to the origins of particular forms of rationality, in *The Protestant Ethic and the Spirit of Capitalism* (Weber 1958a) and his later essays in the sociology of religion.

In these latter texts, much of Weber's most engaged thinking converges in one central location, the essay translated by Hans Gerth and C. Wright Mills as "Religious Rejections of the World and Their Directions" (Weber 1946), or more literally "Intermediate Reflections" ("Zwischenbetrachtung"). Noting that the world of human affairs can be conceptualized as consisting of different life orders or spheres of value—principally the ethical, economic, political, aesthetic, erotic, and intellectual—Weber suggested that each of these orders could be subject to the forces of rationalization, although in different ways, at different rates, and in different directions. (Paradoxically, each could also be reinterpreted and exploited *in opposition to* perceived threats of rationalization.) There was what he called an internal and lawlike autonomy, a logic to these orders that could be seen in increasing coherence and consistency in relation to postulated goals or ends. Economic examples, such as the introduction of wages and double-entry bookkeeping to calculate profit and loss more precisely, provide perhaps the most obvious instances of the application of instrumental, purposive, or goal-oriented rationality to a particular order. But this type of internal logic can take hold also even in religious ethics, with the development of a systematic and rational theology to deal consistently with problems of morality and belief, including in all the great world religions solutions to the challenge of theodicy. So it is also with the aesthetic and erotic spheres, the political order, and of course science itself, the sphere of knowledge and intellectual mastery of the world.

Weber wrote with great insight and imagination about a number of these orders himself. His theory of the origins of modern capitalism, tracing the "elective affinity" between an ascetic religious ethic emphasizing mastery of the self and the world (the Protestant ethic) and the spirit of capitalist enterprise is the most famous instance of rationalization associated with his contributions to social science. In this case, Weber explored the controversial connection between rationalization in the ethical realm and rationalization in the economic sphere and based on his investigations postulated *historical association* between the two, although not a causal connection. Historically, he found a social carrier of the new rationalist ethos in the voluntaristic Protestant sects, where a notion of vocation or calling encouraged mastery of the material world. For Weber, this concatenation

of circumstances accounted for the specific sites and eras in which modern capitalism emerged in world civilization. Although the sources for its emergence had long since disappeared, capitalism's legacy was for Weber the most powerful and fateful force in the modern world.

In addition, Weber's well-known theory of bureaucracy and the development of the modern administrative state was cast in terms of a historic and consequential rationalization of the political order, particularly in the West, where principles of rulership, authority, legitimacy, rule of law, and citizenship became institutionalized in particular political and legal arrangements. In Weber's view, expressed most concisely in one of his last speeches and essays, "Politics as a Vocation," the leading characteristics of bureaucratization in the modern state—specialization of tasks and jurisdictions, specialized training of salaried employees in a lifetime career, procedural rules for decision making, hierarchy of command, emphasis on achievement norms and impartial application of rules, and the tendency to monopolize information in recorded files—represented one of the most powerful instances of rationalization in the modern age. While sharply critical of this trend and concerned about its consequences for individual liberty, he saw it as an inevitable and irreversible outgrowth of the demands placed on the modern state to provide security and defense, social welfare and health, the means of communication, access to education, and a seemingly endless array of other public goods and services. He also understood that bureaucratization would be extended everywhere, into the modern business enterprise, the corporation, political parties, labor unions, hospitals and clinics, schools and universities, the workplace—indeed any kind of human association, whether voluntary or compulsory, that required organization in order to be effective. Like the forces of rational capitalism, bureaucracy seemed to Weber an inevitable consequence of the pervasive rationalization of the modern world, the extension everywhere of instrumentally oriented systems of action.

One of Weber's most unusual contributions was his exploration of the aesthetic value sphere, particularly the Western musical aesthetic. This untitled work was left incomplete and published posthumously. Indeed, Weber planned to write more extensively on art, architecture, and literature in an effort to investigate the rationalization of the contents of culture. This larger intention was never realized, however, aside from scattered remarks on the rationalization of style in art and architecture and in a monograph on music. In the comparative study of music, he elaborated a view of occidental harmonic rationalization proceeding with the solution to the symmetrical division of the octave with tempered intonation, a corresponding system for compositional notation, polyphonic harmonies, and the evolving technology of particular instruments. He also pointed out that elements of tonality and instrumentation had been affected by political and religious considerations, not solely by aesthetic principles. In modern occidental music, the forces of rationalization were particularly transparent, he thought: evident in the continuing exploration of atonality, dissonance, new instruments, electronic technologies, and even the incorporation of contrasting tonal systems.

Last, with regard to science, intellectual inquiry and the pursuit of knowledge, Weber added one capstone to his life work on rationalization, summed up in the notion of disenchantment, or more literally, demagification (*Entzauberung*). In one of his last essays, the revised 1917 speech "Science as a Vocation" and in the 1920 introduction to the *Collected Essays on the Sociology of Religion* (the *Religionssoziologie*), Weber developed the view that a long-term historical process of intellectualization had been at work in Western civilization in which magical and mysterious forces had been progressively mastered by calculation and technical means. This trend is of course exemplified by the revolution in science and technology, dating especially from the seventeenth century. In fact, rationalization today has come to mean most fundamentally the production and application of scientific and technical knowledge, invading virtually every sphere of life. It is as if no cultural enclaves and protected zones can truly avoid the march of scientific rationalism. Thus, as Weber recognized, disenchantment must also be understood as an existential condition capable of provoking cultural and political expressions of regret, loss, nostalgia, resistance, and efforts at reenchantment. Although choosing to cast his lot with science and the pursuit of knowledge, Weber recognized in the countercultural movements of his own time the kind of deep discontent that could be produced by the disenchantment of the world. In the twenty-first century, these discontents are as pronounced as they ever were in Weber's era, and they will undoubtedly remain so.

The significant rationalization themes developed in Weber's writings have been taken up subsequently in a number of different ways. One line of thought, developed early in the work of Norbert Elias and later in some of the writings of Michel Foucault and Pierre Bourdieu, has investigated the evolution of civilization, the civilizing process, and the rationalization of manners, morals, cultural lifestyles, norms of civility, and modes of discipline. Much of this work has been motivated by a desire to understand the ways in which socialization occurs and the social forms emerge that make up what we call civilization. By tracing the reciprocal interaction between socioeconomic and political forces on one hand and individual conduct on the other, one is able to unmask the sources of control and their justifications, whether through the long sweep of history or in discrete contemporary contexts. These analyses of civilization always raise questions about rationalization processes and are often highly critical of its consequences for the modern human condition.

Another important critical direction has been charted by those representatives of the Frankfurt School of social theory,

such as Walter Benjamin, Theodor Adorno, and Max Horkheimer, who developed a form of cultural criticism with Marxist roots. For example, in his celebrated essay from the 1930s, "The Work of Art in the Age of Mechanical Reproduction," Benjamin (1969) explored the ways in which technical innovations and new media, such as film and photography, had begun to rationalize the production and commodification of art and our sense of what art is, how it functions, and what the artist as producer's relationship is to the consumers of art. Like Benjamin, Adorno and Horkheimer also perceived a radical break, a rupture in cultural practices. In *Dialectic of Enlightenment* (Horkheimer and Adorno 1987), they extended this perception to an analysis of the capacity for rational technique to turn against itself, for rationalization to become irrational and form an encompassing totality. Theirs was an argument that both revealed the ruthless domination of technique in a homogenized "culture industry" and exposed the self-destructive dynamic of scientific progress. Instead of liberating creative powers, disenchantment had in this bleak view become repressive and totalizing. It would take a new movement of the dialectic to point toward avenues of escape from the impasse, as Herbert Marcuse and others argued politically in the 1960s.

Within the critical theory tradition of the Frankfurt School, undoubtedly the most systematic and comprehensive theoretical treatment of rationalization has come from the prolific social theorist, Jürgen Habermas. Much of his thinking on the subject is stated in his two-volume work *The Theory of Communicative Action* (Habermas 1984). Building on Weber's notion of instrumental or purposive rationality, he sets out to show that this form of rationalization has been extended into every domain, colonizing the human lifeworld and affecting cognitive, ethical, and aesthetic modes of communication. What Weber called life orders or value spheres, Habermas conceives as rationalization complexes, of which three are primary: science, morality, and art. Each is aligned with different interests—cognitive-instrumental, moral-practical, and aesthetic-expressive—and each is responsive to different claims for validity: propositional truth, normative rightness, and subjective truthfulness. Like Weber, he acknowledges the potency of instrumental rationality among the different competing forms of rationality, and he realizes that rationalization can proceed in quite different ways within each complex. But in contrast to Weber, he develops the notion that immanent within these rationalization processes is the possibility for the emergence of a transformative emancipatory project.

In this regard the most original aspect of Habermas's treatment of rationalization is his invention and argument for the rationality of what he calls communicative action and the critical reasoning that he constructs on a basic distinction between labor and interaction. In his terminology, labor embodies strategic calculations and instrumental rationality, and it is oriented toward success, power, and control over nature. It is what Weber has in mind when he writes about instrumental rationality and its expression in bureaucratic organizations. Interaction, on the other hand, embodies communicative rationality and is oriented to the realization of the rational potential of communication. For Habermas, the latter potential can be made visible in a theory of communicative competence that establishes the possibility of intersubjectivity and uncoerced and undistorted communication. To achieve this possibility obviously requires a public process of expressing opinion and forming consensus, and it is thus a possibility realizable only with democratic norms.

Habermas insists that our understanding of rationalization must be broadened to include communicative action and communicative competence. In his view, only with this expanded understanding will it be possible to envisage a rational and just society in which instrumental rationality is controlled and directed by human reason. The challenge for his position, notwithstanding its rigor and depth of argumentation, remains one of showing that in the face of rationalization in its instrumental sense, as adumbrated with such persistence by Weber, there can be a just social order that meets the test of rationality in its most comprehensive communicative sense.

At the beginning of the twenty-first century, the scientific and public discussions of rationalization take numerous different forms and are dispersed variously in economic and cultural sociology, art history and criticism, organization studies and theory, studies of development and modernization, investigations of the state, discussions of the environment and sustainability, and the most recent attempts to deal with the global economy. There is continuing interest in applications to particular spheres of modern life—the economy, the polity, the cultural sphere—that are very much in the spirit of Weber. There is renewed interest in understanding efforts at reenchantment of the world in new social movements. Needless to say, the long-standing critical discussion of capitalist development that began in the nineteenth century will continue in the spirited exchanges over globalization and its discontents. However they are depicted, the many faces of rationalization will be with us far into the future.

— Lawrence A. Scaff

See also Bureaucracy; Culture and Civilization; Globalization; Habermas, Jürgen; Industrial Society; Modernity; Weber, Max

FURTHER READINGS AND REFERENCES

Benjamin, Walter. 1969. "The Work of Art in the Age of Mechanical Reproduction." Pp. 217–51 in *Illuminations,* edited by H. Arendt. Translated by H. Zohn. New York: Schocken.

Braun, Christoph. 1992. *Max Weber's "Musiksoziologie."* Laaber, Germany: Laaber-Verlag.

Collins, Randall. 1986. *Weberian Sociological Theory.* Cambridge, UK: Cambridge University Press.

Elias, Norbert. 1982. *The Civilizing Process.* 2 vols. Translated by E. Jephcott. New York: Pantheon.

Habermas, Jürgen. 1984. *The Theory of Communicative Action.* 2 vols. Translated by T. McCarthy. Boston, MA: Beacon.

Horkheimer, Max and T. W. Adorno. 1987. *Dialectic of Enlightenment.* Translated by J. Cumming. New York: Continuum.

Scaff, Lawrence A. 1989. *Fleeing the Iron Cage: Culture, Politics, and Modernity in the Thought of Max Weber.* Berkeley: University of California Press.

Schluchter, Wolfgang. 1989. *Rationalism, Religion, and Domination: A Weberian Perspective.* Translated by N. Solomon. Berkeley: University of California Press.

Sica, Alan. 1988. *Weber, Irrationality, and Social Order.* Berkeley: University of California Press.

Swedberg, Richard. 1998. *Max Weber and the Idea of Economic Sociology.* Princeton, NJ: Princeton University Press.

Turner, Stephen, ed. 2000. *The Cambridge Companion to Weber.* Cambridge, UK: Cambridge University Press.

Weber, Max. 1946. "Religious Rejections of the World and Their Directions." Pp. 323–58 in *From Max Weber: Essays in Sociology.* Translated and edited by H. Gerth and C. W. Mills. New York: Oxford University Press.

———. 1958a. *The Protestant Ethic and the Spirit of Capitalism.* Translated by T. Parsons. New York: Scribner's.

———. 1958b. *The Rational and Social Foundations of Music.* Translated and edited by D. Martindale et al. Carbondale, IL: Southern Illinois University Press.

———. 1968. *Economy and Society,* edited by G. Roth and C. Wittich. New York: Bedminster.

REFORM

In Western societies, political reform comprises attempts to expand the reach of politics. Social and economic progress is said to depend on the repoliticization (reform) of productive and distributive outcomes, which, since the Enlightenment, have been subject mainly to individual, entrepreneurial, and market-driven decision-making criteria. Consequently, reform is an assertion of the efficacy of collective, deliberative, and democratic efforts to ameliorate, transform, or disrupt the processes and the tendencies implied by an unregulated capitalist "mode of accumulation." The possibilities of reform presuppose that political development and political capacities are not as "structurally" constrained by economic conditions as radicals and political pessimists have feared. Reform, therefore, elevates political will, Machiavellianism, and sedulous institution building to an importance admitted by neither its liberal nor radical opponents. Its claim is that political arrangements can be constructed to reassert some of the political autonomy lost in the social experiments of economic-liberal rationalism.

The many rationales for political reform produced by social science, particularly antiliberal political economy, all imply that the scope for politics increases as economic development releases us from the realm of necessity. Wealth and democracy are seen as mutually reinforcing. Unregulated capitalist economies are seen as flawed by their chronic propensity to underuse important resources (most significantly, labour) and thereby to produce lower standards of living than are technically possible. In other words, reformists assume there are nonvolitional conditions tending to enhance the impact of distinctively political (and collectively mandated) decisions and correspondingly to diminish the province of unregulated (or privately initiated) activity, while facilitating economic prosperity. This presumption seems warranted, since the proportion of total income appropriated and spent by governments has increased from about 10 percent to about 40 percent over the past century. More significant than the empirical reality is the question why.

Arguments for an expanded role for political activism predate capitalist modernism and the classical era. Systematic and principled state support for industry development characterized the mercantilist era and the city-states of the fifteenth century when synergies flowing from advances in science, knowledge, and technological advance were first recognized. "Renaissance" or neomercantilist economic doctrines today continue to insist that free-trade ideologies emerged not as the justification or blueprint for development but as a way of frustrating the leading industrialized countries' challengers. (Britain, whose early productive supremacy was based on the strength of its navy and its access to cheap raw materials from abroad, was particularly anxious to keep continental economies undeveloped.) In the nineteenth century, Friedrich List in Germany popularized the idea of industry protection (learned from the Americans under Alexander Hamilton) and initiated an antiliberal strand of developmental doctrine that claimed that free trade would impoverish those nations at lower levels of affluence that engaged with it. Commensurately, much contemporary "reformism" has taken the form of attempts to construct state institutions to foster national development in a still-developing economic environment where affluence is nonetheless not guaranteed by its capitalist qualities alone.

A generation later, the mature political economy of Karl Marx's *Capital* unwittingly contributed to reformists' efforts by demonstrating that the underlying social relations of capitalism (private property relations, market mechanisms of allocation, profitability criteria, commodity production, the commodification of labour, and undemocratic control of production) would not always remain the best underwriters of wealth creation. Political interventions of various sorts could be expected to emerge as antiliberal forces sought to impose their preferences on what would otherwise be autonomous processes of capital accumulation or as business itself sought state assistance (for example, to regularize conflicts or markets or intersectoral problems). Conventionally, only the first of these forms of interventions have been referred to as "reform." Perhaps surprisingly, Marxism has usually been loath to champion the reforms its analysis has prefigured.

By the 1890s, the rationales for reform had begun to diversify considerably, with sociology, anthropology, Christian social thought, and institutionalism all suggesting that interferences with the market processes of development and adjustment were not aberrant but inevitable. From this time, the discursive dimensions of arguments for and against reform began to assume an intellectually significant role. Liberals struggled, for the most part successfully, to create a climate wherein market outcomes would be seen as natural while societal preferences (for equality or security or democratic engagement or civic amenity or even just faster rates of development than autonomous market mechanisms would normally allow) were deemed illegitimate. Their opponents, sometimes nascent leftists, sometimes conservative antiliberals, became marginalized in their endeavours to insist that tradition and prejudice and rigidity and national peculiarity and collective proclivity and other forms of antirationalism could not be so easily dismissed as expendable and antiprogressive. Émile Durkheim, for example, argued that economic activity was always underwritten, even constituted, by noneconomic conditions such as the general spiritual and cultural well-being of the populace. This implied that institutions (not necessarily state institutions) to monitor morality or professional integrity or social integration were justified and might be economically beneficial, even if they imposed constraints on private behaviour and private organizations. Reform efforts would then be oriented both to proposing functionally important social controls on certain types of activity and to building institutions able to devise and implement policy that could try to achieve explicitly deliberated outcomes.

Controls on private entrepreneurial activity had been advocated by what is now known as the "social economy" tradition in economic analysis, largely associated with papal encyclicals in the nineteenth and early twentieth centuries. The churches confirmed the sanctity of private property, inheritance, and subsidiarity, but they nonetheless insisted that winners should accept obligations to losers and that trade unions (and attempts to secure industrial or workplace democracy) were legitimate organizational responses to the undemocratic nature of the capitalist division of labour. Their hostility to the commodification of labour has been notable and influential. Such themes also permeate institutional political economy with Thorstein Veblen, for instance, arguing that work and labour should not be seen as a "disutility," the burdensome price to pay for income.

Rather, effort and inventiveness were necessary for humanity, with most people developing an "instinct for workmanship," the collective willingness to be productive and competent. Consequently public processes would be needed to ensure that work was as well remunerated, safe, meaningful, democratic, and socially oriented as possible. Such aspirations and accomplishments are frequently seen by liberals as inflexibilities.

Max Weber, too, insisted that even though rationalistic processes were hallmarks of the Enlightenment's dismantling of arbitrary decision making, people were entitled, through political processes, to discard "formally rational" (rule-based) outcomes if they were adjudged to be substantively irrational. Reform then would involve reestablishing public competences able to secure outcomes that would not otherwise occur. These are increasingly referred to as state capacity. Weber developed a form of enquiry initially associated with List in the 1840s and the German "Historical School" from then until the 1890s that opened up one of the great methodological fissures in the history of social science and that marks the divergent approaches to reform still. On one hand, economic rationalism, shared by liberals and Marxists alike, bases analysis and prescription on the belief that knowledge of abstract processes (such as the logic of the market or the logic of accumulation) define the structure and development and consequences of actual economies. On the other hand, antirationalists have always maintained that more empirical methods—based, for example, on observation of historical legacies, existing institutions, and political preferences—need to be fostered, without presuming that social impediments to markets are unwarranted.

Joseph Schumpeter's and Karl Polanyi's writings in the first half of the twentieth century extended these ideas, thereby also broadening the sociological underpinnings of the reform project—for example, by defending the appropriateness of large (as opposed to competitive) organization in the public and private spheres. "Bigness" was seen as an effect of economies of scale (efficiencies) in both production and service provision. Meanwhile, the licence of welfare state development, a means of effecting income security, was defended in the name of the "self-protection of society" and the resulting decommodified provision helped to sever the link between individual success and living standards. Together the changes implied by this rethinking of the connections between economy and society (denying causal primacy to the former) set the scene for the post-1945 emergence of the concept and reality of the "mixed economy."

Keynesian economic management is probably the most well-known reformist intervention into the capitalist economy. However, insofar as national macroeconomic management necessitated a public commitment to countercyclical policy and the "socialization of investment" (both intended to ameliorate recession), it was not honoured. Keynesianism's real test came not during the 1945 to 1974 long boom, when near full employment in the rich countries was guaranteed by spontaneous and demographic conditions, but in the subsequent recession, after 1974, when (global) structural change caused the return of mass unemployment and the institutional underdevelopment of the previous decades allowed no prophylactic. John Maynard Keynes's expectations from the 1930s, that civilized nations would never again permit unmediated economic forces to wreak havoc, was proven overly optimistic. From the experience of "bastard Keynesianism" in the 1950s and 1960s and from the subsequent anti-Keynesian era, we must conclude that reforms do not necessarily stick, that "path dependency" is weaker than often imagined, and that the "default position" in global economic policy making is usually a liberal one.

The struggle for reform is an aspect of the perennial conflict between social democratic extenders and conservative defenders of state activism, on one hand, and liberal opponents and Marxist sceptics of deliberative and interventionist policy making, on the other.

Reform in both theory and practice is underanalyzed and underdeveloped largely because of the intellectual influence throughout most of the twentieth century of Marxian approaches to political economy that emphasized the self-determining character of capital accumulation and the implied impotence of a distinctive or autonomous realm of democratic politics. Nonetheless, a reformist strand of Marxism can be construed, in accordance with Marx's mature political economy. From this viewpoint, capital accumulation, investment, growth, and development depend on political (and social) infrastructure that can be provided only collectively—that is, according to a political rather than an economic logic. This argument differs from that which postulates a "role" for the "capitalist state" as primarily to secure the economic conditions for a (class-biased) accumulation process. Consequently, politicization of economic activity, organized by left political parties or trade unions or public bureaucracies or corporatist arrangements composed by elements of each, may be both genuinely democratic and sufficiently compatible with macroeconomic success to withstand the political obstacles it is likely to encounter. Indeed, the contradictions embedded in a "normally" functioning capitalist economy may become dysfunctional enough to allow conscious political action (including state building) to reverse the usual power imbalance between controllers of capital and the democratic impulse. Reform, then, is the attempt to ensure that the undemocratic nature of private economic life is transformed—against the objections of liberals who insist the transformation is undesirable and the dogmatic Marxists who maintain it's impossible.

Thanks to its a priori hostility toward crucial aspects of modern democratic development—the "capitalist state" is something more intractable than a state or political realm in capitalist society—large parts of the Marxist tradition have remained sceptical of the possibilities of political reform, asserting that the structural logic of the economy renders an independent, majoritarian democratic polity unlikely. In this respect, Marxist orthodoxy has neglected one of the central observations of Marx's political economy—namely, that crisis tendencies are usually not determinant but are confronted by "countertendencies," which may be spontaneous, as Polanyi implied, or deliberated, as "reformists" suppose. In either case, reformist political possibilities depend on the potential of the countertendencies to economic crisis to frustrate the market logic. Marxists have usually been dismissive of state efforts to "manage" the economy (particularly during recession or structural change), state attempts to ensure or to hasten accumulation (normally under the rubric of industry policy), state policies that "decommodify" the provision of services or infrastructure, state development of public enterprise (with distinctive political responsibilities), and state sponsorship of nonmarket auspices for economic development. While Marx doubted that governments would typically choose, or be able, to enact such interventions, they have in fact characterized modern economic development in all the countries of advanced capitalism. Yet their emergence does not violate the analysis of capitalist development he provided.

The tradition of social democratic reform, then, particularly when its orientation has been analytical and progressive rather than opportunistic and electoral, has seen both political possibilities and political responsibilities in the exploitation of structural changes such as the century-long trend toward big government in capitalist societies. It is this that has allowed a concomitant extension of social provision outside the market (for example, through taxation-financed health and education and income replacement expenditures). More arguably, the encroachment of national or macrolevel or long-term criteria onto decision making that, in conventional liberal democratic polities, would remain unconsolidated in the private sector, is both a means to and an outcome of political reform. By broadening the range of collective input into economic decision making (particularly with respect to structural change that otherwise occurs in capricious or unwanted ways), increased government spending facilitates a significant decommodification of social provision. It has allowed a considerable measure of democratization, constructed a platform from which those political movements or social forces opposed to liberalism can mount successful campaigns for further democratization, and transformed the relations between economic conditions and their sociopolitical environment in such a way that outcomes are improved. An underlying presumption in social democratic strategies to transform the auspices under which economic decisions are made is that both private interests and collective outcomes

are advanced by state interventions that successfully maximize the rate of capital accumulation or achieve full employment or eliminate recession or usurp the labour market or replace market calculation by deliberated arrangements.

Reform proposals aim either to shift the balance between market determination and politicized determination of economic outcomes or to prevent erosion of the "social embeddedness" of the economy. These are the concerns of political economy and economic sociology. From each tradition, state building or institution building is advocated. The most acknowledged instances of public institutions are those required to subject investment, income distribution, the "labour market," corporate governance, and civic amenity to democratic process. The reformist purpose behind these five institution-building responsibilities in modern polities is, respectively, to control the boom-bust cycles of capitalism, to avert the possibilities of inflationary conflicts over wages and profits, to politicize the remuneration and deployment of labour, to increase community participation in what are really society's productive organizations, and to generalize the societal decencies that law and public authority can ensure. In these cases, the imagined "new political institutions" would most likely be corporatist; that is, decision making would be by functionally important institutions, usually intermediated with or in collusion with other functionally important institutions (commonly, peak organizations of labour and capital, interacting on a routine basis with state institutions). Much of the contemporary effort to create such unorthodox networks and arrangements has been categorized as constituting "social capital," implying that, like physical and financial capital, the nonmaterial bases of economic progress are ineliminable but also deliberative and with a stream of future benefits that can be bequeathed to future generations.

Contemporary contributions to reformist theory have come not from the social democratic left but from notionally conservative neo-Weberian or statist critics of liberalization and globalization. The theory of state capacity, with its overtones of List, draws from observations that domestic political processes have been influential in helping "late industrializers" catch up and can be expected always to play a role in industrial upgrading. Industry policy and closely regulated relationships between financial and productive sectors within capitalist economies are typical means for the enhancement of the "infrastructural power" of the state. State capacity therefore implies that global or market determinants of economic change do not necessarily account for ultimate outcomes; political institutions can be definitive. Of course, as with other instances of policy reform, such public capacities may not withstand the resistances they are subjected to both from within and outside the polity. Political achievements are always contingent, provisional, and readily dismantled.

So a final caution: Over recent decades, the term *reform,* particularly in the context of microeconomic reform, competition policy reform, and labour market reform, has been applied to attempts by governments to reverse the reforms of the past. Advisedly though, such politically inspired policy efforts are more accurately seen as part of the normal oscillation between interventionist and noninterventionist proclivities of social movements, public institutions, and policy elites. Like politics generally, reformist politics is best characterized as humanity's recurrent attempt to control its destiny, not the equally recurrent attempt to ensure that the state smoothes the path only for what would have happened anyway.

— Geoff Dow

See also Capitalism; Institutional Theory; Political Economy; Social Capital; Social Market Economy

FURTHER READINGS AND REFERENCES

Higgins, Winton and Nixon Apple. 1983. "How Limited Is Reformism?" *Theory and Society* 12(5):603–60.

Hodgson, Geoffrey M. 2001. *How Economics Forgot History: The Problem of Historical Specificity in Social Science.* London: Routledge.

Jessop, Bob. 2002. *The Future of the Capitalist State.* Cambridge, UK: Polity Press.

Robinson, Joan. 1973. "What Has Become of the Keynesian Revolution?" Pp. 1–11 in *After Keynes,* edited by Joan Robinson. Oxford, UK: Basil Blackwell.

Weiss, Linda. 2003. "Introduction: Bringing Domestic Institutions Back In." Pp. 1–33 in *States in the Global Economy: Bringing Domestic Institutions Back In,* edited by Linda Weiss. Cambridge, UK: Cambridge University Press.

REIFICATION

The concept of reification is closely associated with the thinking of Karl Marx (especially his idea of "fetishism of commodities") and Marxian theory, especially the work of György Lukács. However, it has long since come to be accepted and used by a wide range of social theorists because of its utility in thinking about the modern social world.

Reification is based on the idea that people create their social worlds, especially larger social structures and institutions. However, over time, people come to lose sight of this fact, or are led to lose sight of it by those who control the larger structures and institutions. Instead, these structures and institutions come to be seen by people as "things" (hence, "thingification" is often used as synonymous with reification) that exist independently of the actors who created them. In other words, they are seen as having a life of their own. Instead of being in control of these larger entities, people see themselves as being controlled by them. Even when people perceive these structures and institutions as malfunctioning, and even oppressive, they feel that there is little that they can do about them and the problems they create.

In the end, this becomes more than merely a matter of peoples' perceptions. Because they think and act as if they are in the thrall of these larger entities, they eventually come to be controlled by them. These entities, especially those who control them, come to see themselves as, and eventually come to be, independent and capable of acting on people without their consent or knowledge. Instead of actively creating and controlling large structures and institutions, people come to be created (through socialization) and controlled (through social control mechanisms) by them.

Reification is closely related to Marxian thinking on class, especially false consciousness. That is, agents, especially as a collectivity, with class consciousness would never lose control over, let alone be controlled by, large social entities. However, because they lack such class consciousness, people fall prey to the process of reification. Instead of class consciousness, people have false consciousness, especially in this case the false belief that they are controlled by larger structures and institutions rather than being in control of them.

The solution, at least in Marxian theory, lies in praxis, in this case the retaking of control over these reified phenomena, the destruction of them, or both. This, in turn, requires the development of class consciousness. "True" class consciousness would emerge in tandem with the praxis oriented to gaining control over reified structures. Once they are under the control of people who have class consciousness, it would be impossible, at least from the point of view of Marxian theory, for reified structures and institutions to reemerge.

Given its roots in Marxian theory, the economy is the central arena of the process of reification, and the market is the prime example of it. The market is nothing more than the sum total of the actions of agents who participate in it. Thus, the labor market and the stock market are nothing more than the sum total of the actions of buyers and sellers of labor power or stocks. However, in capitalist society we have become accustomed to thinking of these markets as "things," as structures that have dynamics of their own. They are seen as not only acting independently but in determining what people do. That is, in the case of the labor market, people accept unemployment, low-paying work, or alienating jobs because of the operation of the market. Similarly, stocks are seen as going up or down because of the "market"—the market did this or that—and not because of the actions taken by people who *are* the market.

While it has its roots in Marxian thinking on economics and economic structures, it is easy to see how the idea of reification can be extended to all social structures and institutions in all types of societies, not just capitalist societies. Thus, one could have thought of structures and institutions in the former Soviet Union as being reified. While the Soviet Union is long gone, it remains possible and useful to think of social structures and institutions in the twenty-first century, in modern and even postmodern society, as being reified.

— George Ritzer

See also Frankfurt School; Lukács, György; Marx, Karl

FURTHER READINGS AND REFERENCES

Lukács, Georg. [1923] 1971. *History and Class Consciousness: Studies in Marxist Dialectics.* Translated by R. Livingstone. Cambridge: MIT Press.

Marx, K. [1867] 1977. "Chapter 1: The Commodity." Pp. 125–77 in *Capital: A Critique of Political Economy.* Vol. 1. New York: Vintage.

RELATIONAL COHESION

Relational cohesion is a testable theory that explains how a network of social exchange produces more cohesion and commitment in some relations than in others. Cohesion and commitment develop in particular relations because exchanging valued outcomes with others produces emotions—that is, individuals feel good or feel bad as a result. If the exchange is successful, they feel good (e.g., pleased, satisfied, enthused, excited); if it is unsuccessful, they feel bad (e.g., sad, depressed, dissatisfied). The theory of relational cohesion specifies the conditions under which individuals associate these emotions with their relationship or group affiliation. Positive emotions from exchange thereby strengthen relations, whereas negative emotions weaken relations. The theory was formulated and tested by Edward J. Lawler and his colleagues, Jeongkoo Yoon and Shane Thye. It has important implications for when and why people stay in relations that produce fewer rewards than available elsewhere, why they invest more time and effort in some relations than others, and why norms and trust are stronger in some relations.

Relational cohesion has a structural basis. Following Richard Emerson, the structure involves a network with three or more actors; power dependence is a key dimension of this structure. The original idea for relational cohesion theory can be traced to Emerson's structural definition of cohesion as the degree of mutual dependence between a pair of actors in a network. Relational cohesion theory expands this structural definition by adding relative dependence (degree of equality or inequality). Structural cohesion is greater if individuals are mutually dependent and equally dependent on each other.

Relational cohesion is defined as the degree that actors perceive their relation as a distinct object apart from self and other. This definition of relational cohesion implies that actors consciously or unconsciously perceive their relationship to one another as real. The social constructionist theory of Peter Berger and Thomas Luckmann terms this the *objectification* of a social unit. Similarly, the social identity theory of Henri Tajfel would portray this as *psychological group formation.* If the relation is real to actors, it operates as a *third force* in the social situation, and individuals orient their behavior in part to their relation, not just to each other or to the task they are doing. This means they will conform to the norms of that relation, trust each other more, and develop a commitment to their relationship. Commitment is defined as behavior that reflects an individual's attachment to a social unit (relation, group, organization); it is the outcome or result predicted by the theory of relational cohesion.

In relational cohesion theory, individual emotions or feelings mediate the effects of structure (network, power dependence) on relational cohesion and commitment behavior. Four key points of the theory are as follows: First, social structures tend to produce varying rates or frequencies of exchange among a set of actors. Actors choose relations that they expect to provide them the greatest benefit, and the network structure determines the incentives for particular relations to form. Choosing exchange partners in a network is fundamentally a rational choice process. Repeated exchange by the same individuals forms an exchange relation. Second, success at exchange has positive emotional effects. When people exchange items of value with another, it gives them an *emotional buzz.* If they fail at efforts to exchange, then they experience an *emotional down.* Third, positive emotions or feelings make the relation itself more salient and an object of attachment for actors. Repeated exchange produces repeated positive feelings that, in turn, underlie the sense of a cohesive, unifying relation. The emotions enhance cohesion in the exchange relation formed. Fourth, the theory of relational cohesion, as elaborated by a subsequent affect theory of exchange, predicts that emotions generate relational cohesion to the degree that individuals have a sense of shared responsibility for the success at exchange—for example, if actors believe it is hard to differentiate their individual contributions to the joint effort. Under such conditions, individual feelings from exchange are more closely associated with relational or group affiliations, and feelings about these affiliations are affected, accordingly. The mechanisms linking network properties to commitment, therefore, involve an *exchange to emotion to cohesion* process. This is the heart of the theory of relational cohesion.

Relational cohesion affects an individual's commitment to a relation or group. Three forms of commitment behavior have been explicitly studied: (1) staying in the relation despite equal or better alternatives, (2) providing benefits or giving gifts to another without strings attached, and (3) engaging in risky behavior that opens one to malfeasance or exploitation by the other. Research on relational cohesion confirms that more frequent exchange produces more positive emotions, more positive emotions produce a more cohesive relation, and greater cohesion generates more commitment behaviors of these types. There is strong and consistent empirical support for the theory of relational cohesion.

Generalizing further, relational cohesion theory suggests that people experience positive or negative emotions or feelings when they interact with others to accomplish joint tasks. If the emotions are positive and experienced repeatedly, they attribute these emotions in part to their relationship or common group membership, especially if they perceive a joint task and shared responsibility. The commitment to their relation, therefore, has an emotional or affective basis. These effects are strongest when the social structure creates equal and high mutual dependence between the actors. They also are strongest when social exchange has a productive form in which two or more actors are collaborating on a joint effort and weakest when the social exchange has a generalized form in which actors give benefits to different persons than they receive benefits from. Negotiated and reciprocal forms of exchange produce degrees of cohesion and commitment that fall between productive and generalized forms.

— Edward J. Lawler

See also Commitment; Rational Choice; Social Exchange Theory; Trust

FURTHER READING AND REFERENCES

Lawler, Edward J. 2001. "An Affect Theory of Social Exchange." *American Journal of Sociology* 107:321–52.

Lawler, Edward J. and Jeongkoo Yoon. 1996. "Commitment in Exchange Relations: Test of a Theory of Relational Cohesion." *American Sociological Review* 61:89–108.

————. 1998. "Network Structure and Emotion in Exchange Relations." *American Sociological Review* 63: 871–94.

Lawler, Edward J. and Shane R. Thye. 1999. "Bringing Emotions into Social Exchange Theory." *Annual Review of Sociology* 25:217–44.

Lawler, Edward J., Shane R. Thye, and Jeongkoo Yoon. 2000. "Emotion and Group Cohesion in Productive Exchange." *American Journal of Sociology* 106(3):616–57.

RELIGION

Sociology of religion experienced renewed vigor in the last quarter of the twentieth century, paralleling a coincident resurgence of traditional religion in much, although not all, of the world. For several decades in the middle of the century, years bracketed by the emergence of Talcott Parsons as a social theorist in the 1930s and the campaign of Jimmy Carter for U.S. president in the 1970s, Western social theorists broadly assumed that traditional religion was fated either to retreat into insignificance or to merge into the universalistic value system of modern society. Such assumptions became untenable in view of the growing public confidence of evangelicalism and corresponding malaise of liberal Protestantism in the United States and the rise of militant Islam in the Middle East. Soon, theorists' attention was drawn to the worldwide rise of Islamism and Pentecostalism, Evangelicalism's close cousin, and "fundamentalist" variants of all faiths. Some assertively "progressive," yet recognizably religious forces, such as the civil rights and sanctuary movements in the United States, also gained notice. Religion as conventionally defined—beliefs and practices centered on communal devotion to a god or some other representation of sacredness—was back on theorists' agenda. This article will briefly discuss the theoretical issue of defining "religion," will then unpack at length the elaborate but frequently unsatisfactory debate over "secularization," and will conclude with theorists' attempts to understand the role of religion as one among many persistent societal and cultural complexes in contemporary society.

DEFINING RELIGION

Durkheim's classic definition, paraphrased above, is always the starting point for sociologists, especially his recognition that religion involves at least two dimensions, a cognitive or propositional one and a ritual or behavioral one. He deferred to commonsense social constructions to the extent of accepting Buddhism as a religion, despite the absence of theism in its classic formulations. Thus, for Durkheim, not theism but "the sacred" must be the defining characteristic of the phenomenon. He also insisted that religion pertained to a moral community: a "private religion" would be a contradiction in terms. Durkheim's influence was not least in setting off extensive discussion on what came to be called "substantive" versus "functional" definitions of religion, the former corresponding to Durkheim's "sacred"—what religion *is*—and the latter to his "community"—what religion *does*. In the middle of the century, the possibility that the future might belong to one or another of the warring political ideologies of the time gave theorists reason to assess the potential of movements such as fascism or communism as functional successors to the religions of the past. By the end of the century, however, those possibilities seemed increasingly remote, and conceptual attention reverted to the substantive question of what it is that defines religion. The desideratum was a definition that would encompass not only the conventionally recognized world religions (i.e., Christianity, Islam, Buddhism, Hinduism, Judaism, etc.) but also newer, smaller, more indigenous and more subaltern religions such as Scientology, Wicca, Voodoo, and Shamanism. As with Durkheim, at issue was whether attributes such as gods (or goddesses), the supernatural, and the sacred could sufficiently capture this diversity without privileging one or another variant. Just as "god" may be a limiting concept confined to the Abrahamic faiths, so also "the sacred" may carry its own theological baggage. Recently, Rodney Stark, in *One True God* (2001), has proposed not a new definition but a proposition that only religions with a personal, monotheistic god have power to shape history. In this view, some religions, especially the Abrahamic faiths, are more powerful than others, especially Buddhism. Many of those who oppose Stark's formulation of rational choice theory (see below) would agree at least that there is something distinctive about religion by definition that should not be lost in the urge to generalize about all human activity. The result of these two discussions (i.e., the one in regard to Durkheim's definition of religion, the other in regard to the critique of rational choice theory) is that for the purposes of social theory, religion remains what it is conventionally taken to mean.

DEBATING SECULARIZATION VERSUS PERSISTENT RELIGION

The religious resurgence that began to be noticed in the 1970s did not settle the issue of the ultimate fate of religion in the modern world. For one thing, at the same time that religion seemed to have renewed vigor in the United States and much of the third world, its apparent decline became all the more precipitous in most of Europe. Those predicting religion's imminent demise have not retreated in the face of those who are convinced of religion's staying power, and it is easy to gain the (nonetheless superficial) impression that contemporary sociology of religion boils down to a debate over something called secularization theory. This lengthy section will examine three aspects of this contentious literature: (1) efforts to clarify debate by specifying the meaning of the concept of secularization, (2) efforts to explain the persistence of religion through the alternative theory of rational choice, and (3) efforts to specify paradigms of religious systems as contexts for the play of dynamics such as secularization and religious "markets."

Conceptualizing Secularization. Theorists of secularization have rightly protested that they do not and need not insist that religion will ultimately disappear. They are no more responsible for Marx's vision that religion will be abolished along with its basic cause, class oppression, than the discipline of sociology is for Durkheim's intemperate assertion that society is the true object of worship. Stemming from the theories of both Durkheim and Weber, secularization is properly understood as the process of religion's diminishing social significance, and it can be understood and measured in several ways.

Historically, the first meaning of the concept was the separation of church and state, according to which one of the first and most thoroughly secularized nations was none other than the United States, at least at the federal level. Yet if the sociological concept were so delimited, there would be no debate, and secularization would be a definitional truth. The debatable empirical claim, shared by some theorists of secularization and some religious authorities, is that separation of church and state must ultimately lead to the diminution of religion. More broadly, secularization is taken by sociologist Frank Lechner to mean the increasing *differentiation* of religion from other spheres of society, not only the polity but also education, the economy, the professions, and civil society generally, which are rendered autonomous from religion in the process of secularization. Much work has been done in this vein to document secularization of the American system of higher education from its initially religious roots.

Eventually, in this perspective, religion will pertain only to the household. Furthermore, as the authority of patriarchal household heads erodes, religion will be embraced only by individuals, for whom in turn, because of the differentiation of religion from other social spheres, religion will ultimately have no other than the psychological function of being a source of solace and personal exploration. This is secularization as *privatization,* which, by Durkheim's definition, means the evisceration of religion at its core.

Other theorists, such as Peter Berger (1969), tended to approach the matter social psychologically, where secularization is identified with decreasing assent to religious doctrines, or, more simply, increasing unbelief. Insofar as religious belief systems are inherently precarious—based as they admittedly are on evidence of things hoped for but not seen—they are made plausible only through socially elaborate mechanisms by which the faithful are enmeshed in networks and practices of cobelievers and insulated from unbelievers and those who adhere to different faiths. As a society becomes more pluralistic through exploration and migration and its culture more rational through scientific and scholarly development, and as mass media spread awareness of all these novelties, religion loses its *plausibility structures.* Widespread defection is the expected result.

Structural differentiation and societal pluralism being two components of modernity, it is therefore proposed at the grandest level of analysis that modernity is inimical to religion, or, more precisely, predictive of secularization. One response to the *prima facie* contradiction to this proposition posed by the case of societies, like the United States, characterized by both modernity and high levels of self-reported religious belief and practice, is to separate out these two aspects of secularization. Thus, some theorists maintain that secularization applies, through differentiation, at the level of public institutions and public discourse but, plausibility theory to the contrary notwithstanding, not at the level of personal belief. In this manner, jurist Stephen Carter claims that a public "culture of disbelief" coexists in the United States with a pattern of private piety. Accordingly, one definition of secularization is diminished scope for religious authority instead of diminished religious belief.

The strengths of the secularization perspective are precisely its attention to conceptualization. Its typical weaknesses are the vagueness of its propositions (e.g., modernity is conducive to secularism) and its frequent failure to specify a baseline of comparison to modern conditions (e.g., merely assuming that the past was a time of greater religiosity than the present). If it is proposed that modernity is inimical to religion, when did "modernity" begin and when are its alleged effects supposed to set in? Too often a study is said to evince support of secularization theory when it demonstrates that one or another aspect of religion in a modern society is weaker than, by some unspecified standard, it supposedly used to be or still, if religion were powerful, ought to be. Exponents of secularization have responded to such criticisms by specifying the causal force not as a global social property such as modernity but as a property that varies across discrete units (e.g., rates of religious pluralism in U.S. counties). They have also sought to marshal time series data on religious social indicators (e.g., religious attendance over time).

Theories of Rational Choice. Some of the recent improvements in the secularization perspective have come in response to a competing perspective, rational choice theory (RCT) applied to religion. Indeed, some methodological techniques employed by secularization theorists were pioneered by exponents of RCT. Thus, it is a mistake to see RCT as only an alternative to secularization and the manifest conflict between them as zero sum. RCT has a different agenda. Whereas secularization theorists struggle to find ways to speak of the diminished role of religion in contemporary society that they observe or fully expect to observe, exponents of RCT use their approach to explain upward *and* downward variations in religious phenomena in the same society as well as variable levels of religious activity across different societies.

RCT emerged in the 1980s from two sources, neoclassical economics and U.S. religious history. Economist Laurence Iannaccone offered an elaborate formal explanation of why it makes sense for sectarians to take on what might seem to be gratuitous burdens. Sociologists Roger Finke and Rodney Stark used 100-year-old U.S. census data from religious denominations to refute the proposition, derived from secularization theory, that religious pluralism depresses religious participation. (Some years later, sociologist Daniel Olson demonstrated both errors in Finke and Stark's specific findings and the futility of the general pluralism-by-participation research program based on ecological-level denominational data. That program is fatally flawed by multicollinearity: In effect, the data sources did not allow the independent and dependent variables to be specified in a sufficiently mutually exclusive manner. Meanwhile, however, a large literature had emerged both in support of and critical of the proposition that pluralism promotes religious vitality.) By the mid-1990s, two of RCT's most influential statements had appeared, Finke and Stark's explanation of religious mobilization in the nineteenth-century United States as a function of the competition of sects in a *religious market* and Iannaccone's claim that religiously conservative groups grow because of, not despite, their *strictness*.

In common with the secularization perspective, RCT has its micro, or social psychological, and macro, or structural, sides, which in RCT are called *demand-side* and *supply-side* perspectives. Stark has led the way in proposing that religious demand, pertaining to the human condition, is more or less constant across time and space. (Stark's proposition of constant demand is consistent with the assumption of classical economics that wants are given.) It follows that variation in religious involvement (e.g., church attendance) provides no evidence of variation in religious interest. Instead, religious pluralism promotes religious involvement by offering outlets for different kinds of (not levels of) religious tastes. Downswings in religious involvement are similarly attributed to the effects of religious monopolization. Finke explained the widespread post-1960s decline in Catholic religious vocations as a consequence not of lack of faith on the part of would-be recruits but of church-imposed diminution of the specially honored status of clergy and religious. Implicit in RCT from the beginning of its development, and occasionally made explicit, is the idea that no special psychology distinguishes religious people. Far from being vulnerable to erosion once all the facts are known, as secularization theorists presuppose, religious involvement makes rational sense.

The supply-side perspective focuses on the ways that religious leaders, ranging from entrepreneurs to large bureaucratic firms, respond to the incentives made available to them as rational actors by a less or more regulated religious market. When support is guaranteed by the state, or when there is no competition, religious suppliers will have no incentive to reach out to extant or potential clients. The result, in state church or monopolistic regimes, is a low level of religious activity across the society. But when state support is unavailable or cut off by disestablishment, and barriers to entry are lowered, there is ample incentive for aggressive religious firms to mobilize the population on a voluntary basis. As seen in the flurry of religious activity in the early republican period of U.S. history (the half-century after the revolution), the result of disestablishment may be a flourishing religious system. Recently, supply-side thinking has been applied by political scientist Anthony Gill to the situation of the Catholic Church in various Latin American countries, where the bishops who adopt the Church's "preferential option for the poor" are said to do so because they face competition from Protestant rivals for the allegiance of the poor.

The strengths of RCT are its attention to the formulation of testable propositions, its attention to variation in religious activity, and its stimulus for the theoretically informed use of survey and census data. In Robert Merton's sense, RCT is truly a sociological theory, and there can be no doubt that its arrival on the scene has contributed to the health of the research field. Its weaknesses are the frequent looseness of its empirical operationalizations; the implausibility, to some, the unattractiveness of its presuppositions; and its lack of attention to scope conditions. Critics have questioned whether, for example, the churches Iannaccone and his followers would call "strict" are properly so called. (This critique, in turn, has spawned studies to define what additional properties of such churches, including their possible "distinctiveness," may be conducive to their growth.) Many have called into question the assumption that individuals make religious choices in the same way that they make economic choices, and some have complained that the influential assumption that they do so itself tends to erode what would otherwise be their disinterested devotion to their faiths. RCT, it is said, contributes to the individualization and instrumentalization of social life that is already too rampant in the postmodern world.

Paradigms or Conceptual Maps of Religious Systems. Doubts about the unspecified scope conditions of RCT have led some scholars to propose that inquiry is needed into the attributes of religious systems that make RCT's religious market viable. Following received sociological wisdom that a market is an institution and that an "unregulated market" is therefore a contradiction in terms, they have asked how the kind of open religious market that surely does characterize the United States comes about. Perhaps the religious market is a specifically American phenomenon. But theorists have equally questioned whether secularization theory can make sense in societies that have historically lacked a monopolistic state church. Noticing that most proponents of secularization theory are Europeans, they suspect that secularization is just European religious history writ large.

In such manner, Stephen Warner (1993) proposed that most of RCT is an aspect of a *new paradigm* that is emerging specifically for the understanding of U.S. religion, and Grace Davie (2002) has proposed that secularization theory applies only to Europe as an "exceptional case" in a world of varied *conceptual maps* for religion. (In the past two decades, Peter Berger, author in the 1960s of some of the most influential statements of secularization theory, has himself come to think that the theory is limited to the case of Western Europe.)

Learning from religious historians that religious activity in the United States flourished in the wake of postrevolutionary disestablishment, Warner recognized that pluralism and vitality in U.S. religion was not so much the product of a newly opened market as a precondition of it. Colonists with conflicting, often assertive, religious identities had previously settled in different regions of the nation-to-be. Thus, the religious establishments that some of them passed into law were already plural prior to disestablishment, and the majoritarian electoral system the new nation quickly evolved made no provision for political representation of minorities. Cultural pluralism was greatly augmented by immigration from more and more European, then East Asian and Middle Eastern countries. Even "involuntary migrants" from Africa, and later Latin America, eventually found social space for cultural expression in religious institutions of their own devising. Thus, the U.S. paradigm is not that of a primitive, unregulated religious market. It is that of a society with high levels of religious interest and high levels of diversity that find expression through and reinforce a developed, open religious market.

For her part, Davie finds a continuing pattern of "believing without belonging" in Britain, a society in which, true to the secularization perspective, the church has lost much of the significance it once had, but an "unchurched" society more than a truly secular one. Britain may well be one of many "post-Christian" societies in Europe, but these societies are decidedly post-*Christian*, with more or less suspicion of new or non-Christian religious movements, little inclination to disestablish the church, persisting involvement in religious rites of passage, and moderately high levels of religious belief. While Europeans do little to support their churches, they regard them positively as significant "public utilities," letting someone else, quite often the state, do the work of maintaining them. In that sense, these Europeans adhere to what Davie calls *vicarious religion.* Exceptional cases within Europe—the continuing high levels of both religious activity and belief in Ireland, Poland, and Greece—are due to the harnessing of religion to national feeling in these countries (in contrast one might say, to the historic divorce of religion and nationalism in France, Italy, and Turkey).

Regardless of its complexity, the European conceptual map should not automatically be applied elsewhere. The basic historical condition behind it—the Constantinian paradigm of a state church commanding the allegiance of the entire population in a given territory—is itself distinctly European, a legacy of the Roman Empire. Those parts of Latin America where a colonized and superficially evangelized population was once presided over by a monopoly church and are now being mobilized by Pentecostal movements—Brazil and Guatemala come to mind—may perhaps be understood as in transition between the European and the American paradigms, but religious systems elsewhere in the world—Africa, East Asia, South Asia, and the Middle East—require their own conceptual maps. India, to take just one case of a country with extraordinarily high levels of both religious activity and religious diversity, cannot be understood in terms of either secularization or religious market theory. An Indian paradigm is overdue.

RELIGION AS AN ORGANIZATIONAL AND CULTURAL COMPLEX

Relieved, temporarily at least, of the burden of defending or dismissing religion's role as a persisting feature of modern society, social scientists are free to explain structural and cultural aspects of religion using general social theory, as well as to contribute to the development of theory using religion as a case study. Within the field of sociology, Paul DiMaggio has argued that sociologists of religion have much to learn from organizational theory, and Christian Smith that social movement theory has much to learn from students of religion. The fact that U.S. religious institutions are major employers with highly varied rules of recruitment and career trajectories and often meticulous record-keeping systems makes the sociology of the clergy a fertile nongovernmental subfield within the sociology of occupations and professions. The 300,000 local religious assemblies ("congregations") in the United States are now a prime research field for students of voluntary associations, including theorists of social capital. That congregations tend to be homogeneous makes them a convenient site for the application of the theory of homophily to race and ethnic differentiation. One source of the successful effort in the 1990s to organize a section of the American Sociological Association devoted to sociology of religion was indeed the conviction that the social scientific study of religion should not be relegated to an intellectual ghetto, where the ambitions of religion to chart the future would be either nurtured or discouraged. Religion is here to stay for the long time being, part of the world that social theorists are obliged to understand.

In a noted exercise in organizational sociology, Mark Chaves draws on the theoretical school known as the *new institutionalism* to understand why it is that some American denominations grant full formal leadership credentials to qualified women (they "ordain women"), while others do not. Chaves shows that the practical issue of supply and demand for clergy labor has little correlation with whether women's contributions are welcomed. Instead, regardless of whether the decision to open or close ordination to women is formally based in scriptural authority or the sacramental role of clergy, it functions symbolically as a signal to maintain the legitimacy of the institution in the eyes of allied churches whose goodwill is needed. In this instance, social theory explains how churches behave the way other complex organizations are thought to do.

But religious institutions can be theorized as having their own structural dynamics. While secularization theorists point to recent declines in mainline Protestantism as vindication of their expectations, political scientist Robert Putnam, in *Bowling Alone* (2000), considers the possibility that the relative strength of conservative Protestant churches may be an exception to the post-1960s decline of nearly every other form of voluntary association in the United States, a general pattern he calls "bowling alone." Religion is different. Sociologist Nancy Ammerman studies ways that religious institutions, most of which specialize in the production of what Putnam calls *bonding social capital,* internal solidarity, also reach outside themselves to produce *bridging social capital* to the benefit of the society.

The "cultural turn" in social theory has involved religion as well as other cultural complexes. One of the most influential recent studies of culture is *Habits of the Heart,* whose authors conducted depth interviews on topics such as occupation, civic participation, and family, as well as religion, to learn not so much how Americans think about these aspects of their lives but how they talk about them. Arguing that the languages American use to speak of their social involvements derive from different streams in American culture, the authors tried to show that, across the board, instrumental and expressive languages (where things are viewed as "rewarding" or "feeling good") increasingly trump republican and Biblical languages (where talk is about one's "duty" and "God's will"). Theorists have discerned such linguistic devolution even in evangelical Protestant sermons (or teachings, as they are often called), where the urge to be relevant in the interest of attracting participants may dilute truly religious language. Nonetheless, because of religious pluralism (and social stratification), countercultural discourses flourish. According to sociologist Mary Pattillo-McCoy, the black church, filled with expressions of collective obligation and God's power, serves as a template for secular social activism in the African American community.

Combining structural and cultural perspectives, sociologist Michael P. Young, in his account of the rise of the antislavery and temperance movements in the antebellum

United States, offers amendments to the *contentious politics* and *life politics* perspectives in the study of social movements. These two influential movements emerged, Young shows, in interaction not with the state, which was in a period of weakness in the 1830s, but with Protestant religious institutions. Informed by the cultural schemas of both elite northern churches and populist sects, adherents of these movements intended to bring about not only structural but also personal change. Studies of American religious cultures by priest-sociologist Andrew Greeley, among others, have pointed to the contribution of distinctively Catholic themes of "communalism" and "incarnational theology" to liberal politics. In these instances, the study of religion contributes to the understanding of the role of culture in shaping society.

Various of the studies mentioned in this section might be invoked to bolster one or another of the major perspectives discussed earlier (secularization, rational choice, and new paradigm). Yet such is not their primary significance for religion and social theory, a nexus that is now emancipated from the never-ending, frequently ideological and even theological, problematic of the fate of religion in modern society.

— R. Stephen Warner

See also Durkheim, Émile; Modernity; Rational Choice; Rationalization; Secularization; Social Capital; Weber, Max

FURTHER READINGS AND REFERENCES

Berger, Peter L. 1969. *The Sacred Canopy: Elements of a Sociological Theory of Religion.* Garden City, NY: Doubleday.

Casanova, José. 1994. *Public Religions in the Modern World.* Chicago: University of Chicago Press.

Davie, Grace. 2002. *Europe: The Exceptional Case: Parameters of Faith in the Modern World.* London: Darton, Longman & Todd.

Demerath, N. J., Peter Dobkin Hall, Terry Schmitt, and Rhys H. Williams, eds. 1998. *Sacred Companies: Organizational Aspects of Religion and Religious Aspects of Organizations.* New York: Oxford University Press.

Luckmann, Thomas. 1967. *The Invisible Religion: The Problem of Religion in Modern Society.* New York: Macmillan.

Stark, Rodney, and Roger Finke. 2000. *Acts of Faith: Explaining the Human Side of Religion.* Berkeley: University of California Press.

Tschannen, Olivier. 1991. "The Secularization Paradigm: A Systematization." *Journal for the Scientific Study of Religion* 30:395–415.

Warner, R. Stephen. 1993. "Work in Progress Toward a New Paradigm for the Sociological Study of Religion in the United States." *American Journal of Sociology* 98:1044–93.

RELIGION IN FRENCH SOCIAL THEORY

The problem of religion and society has been central to French social thought from the time of the seventeenth-century religious philosopher Blaise Pascal. It becomes particularly prominent during the period after the French Revolution in the work of figures such as Auguste Comte and Joseph de Maistre. In the twentieth century, religion, magic, myth, and related topics became central concerns for figures such as Émile Durkheim, Marcel Mauss, Henri Hubert, and their school as well as other French or Francophone authors such as Arnold van Gennep, Lucien Lévy-Bruhl, and Henri Bergson. A variety of other more recent writers, including Georges Bataille, Claude Lévi-Strauss, and Lucien Goldmann have renewed this interest in differing ways.

Important sociological insights concerning the role of religious experience in social existence are already found in Pascal's *Pensées* (written during the years before his death in 1662). There, he discusses topics such as the Christian roots of the idea of the dualism of human nature, the role of popular social diversions as a defense against existential reflection about ultimate religious concerns, the tensions between religious belief and social status claims, and the relationship between religion and scientific thought. He also presents an early version of what has come to be known as the "rational choice" perspective on religion in his theory of the necessity of a wager in favor of belief in God and eternal life. Pascal's emphasis on the reasons of the heart as the root of religious sensibility found a later echo in Rousseau and other French thinkers. In general, his theological discussions of the aforementioned issues posed challenges for later thinkers such as Émile Durkheim, who were interested in providing sociological answers to questions such as the dualism of human nature.

French Enlightenment thinkers generally attacked religion in the name of the powers of a human reason rooted in nature. However, religion and related moral issues remained on the theoretical agendas of many thinkers of this period. Voltaire investigated the history of customs and morals in a manner compatible with current historical sociology. Montesquieu presaged Max Weber's later work by noting the interesting congruence of religion, democracy, and industrial development in England. Rousseau supplemented the purely secular rationality of the Enlightenment with the idea of a new cult, which he called "civil religion" and which would bind the citizen to the state by more than the powers of either self-interest or pure reason.

The turmoil in French politics, society, and culture during the half century after the revolution of 1789 led to an even wider quest for new principles of order, including a critique of the Enlightenment and a quest for new religious and moral ideals. The result was a proliferation of utopian and counterutopian proposals from the left as well as the right of the political spectrum. Those writers once described by Frank Manuel as the "prophets of Paris" (e.g., Saint-Simon, Comte, Fourier, Cabet, and others), combined new ideals with versions of established religious ideas and organization drawn from a newly renovated Christianity. The result was a startling array of utopian amalgams, including Saint-Simon's "new Christianity," Fourier's designs for utopian communities called "phalanxes," and Auguste Comte's positivism and religion of humanity.

Saint-Simon sought to create a "new Christianity" better suited to the needs of a society of scientific, industrial, and technical specialists. His former secretary, Auguste Comte, became an independent theorist and proposed a sweeping theory of three stages of historical development. This theory argued that human thought evolved from theological to metaphysical to positive thought. In the process, he detailed the internal progress of the theological stage, from primitive fetishism to polytheism and, finally, to a mature monotheism. In his early philosophic synthesis, the *Cours de Philosophie Positive* (1830–1846), Comte emphasized the need to transcend religious and metaphysical thinking in favor of a more positive (i.e., scientific) approach to knowledge and social reform. However, his later work embodies a new religious standpoint, emphasizing the reform of society through the ideal of altruism, the worship of the Great Being, and the creation of a new Religion of Humanity, in which mankind would celebrate the accomplishments of its best and brightest by means of a calendar of yearly rites. This Church of Humanity combined elements of the older Roman Catholic veneration of saints with modern humanistic ideals and provides a theoretical rationale for more recent efforts to elevate notable public figures to quasi-religious standing (e.g., birthdays of Abraham Lincoln, Martin Luther King, and others).

By contrast, critics of revolution and utopia, such as Joseph de Maistre, drew on religious traditions to struggle against what they viewed as the inevitable excesses emerging from an exclusive reliance on human reason. The ideas of Maistre and the later Comte were similar in some respects, partly because of Comte's influence on Maistre, but also because of their shared attachment to Roman Catholicism as the archetype of a church organization and a model for the creation of sociomoral integration. For Maistre, only a traditional religious organization could root a society with sufficient strength and depth to avoid what he saw as the destructive potential of revolutionary change. In his view, political constitutions derived not from human reason, but from divine authority. Maistre found this authority and support for social stability especially in the Papacy and the Roman Catholic Church.

Other French thinkers also saw a positive role for religion in society. Alexis de Tocqueville, in his two-volume work, *Democracy in America* (1835, 1840), analyzed the role of religion in American society and distinguished between the role of Protestantism and Catholicism in modern society. In his view, religion could, under given historical conditions, function to support modern democracy rather than be a bulwark of reaction. He thought Protestantism was compatible with the development of modernity. Since most Americans were Protestants, there existed a common religious and cultural inheritance in churches and sects that promoted moral discipline and social order. Protestant congregationalism also served as a workshop for democratic participation, and the multiplicity of Protestant sects helped advance not only the separation of church and state, but also the social organization of Americans by serving as the prototype of all voluntary associations. By contrast, Tocqueville found none of these conditions in the old regime in France, where church, state, and aristocracy combined to thwart the growth of the democratic spirit.

In the later nineteenth century, the examination of religion's role in society shifted to the study of earlier historical periods and to primitive societies. For example, Numa Denis Fustel de Coulanges, in his influential work on *The Ancient City* (1864), compared the history of religion, social institutions, and political organization in Greece and Rome. His treatment of the changing relationships between religion and social and political organization as well as his use of the comparative method made the book an important reference point for later French sociologists and historians such as Émile Durkheim and Marc Bloch. Fustel's history was written in a republican spirit and emphasized the dangers to individual freedom posed by increasingly centralized political organization. Fustel generally saw the changes in religious belief and practice as the driving force behind political change. In his view, the earliest religion of the Greeks and Romans was a familial cult, or cult of male ancestors. This cult provided the basis for social and legal authority, succession to property, and stability of the family space. With each subsequent stage in the development of society, there necessarily occurred a change in religious practice. The formation of the *polis* involved the creation of gods of the city, while the formation of larger empires was paralleled not only by the cult of the divinity of the emperor, but also the rise of new religions such as Christianity and a variety of mystery cults which would, in the future, satisfy the growing need for a more personal and individual religiosity. In general, Fustel saw the increasing growth of the political circle from family to *polis* to empire as involving a concomitant decrease in individual freedom. Only with Christianity is a new religious and political principle introduced.

The major breakthrough in the study of religion in French social theory came in the twentieth century with the work of Émile Durkheim and the school of sociology that emerged around the journal *L'Année Sociologique*. This group included not only Durkheim but also Marcel Mauss, Henri Hubert, Celestin Bouglé, Robert Hertz, and several others. The sociology of religion was one of their main interests. They studied the main categories of religious beliefs and rites such as the sacred, sacrifice, magic, sin and expiation, prayer and oral rites, and others. They emphasized the social roots of religion but also the influence of religion on social institutions, thought, and conduct. Mauss and Hubert wrote together on *Sacrifice* (1899) and on the *General Theory of Magic* (1904), while Mauss separately investigated topics such as prayer, or oral rites. Bouglé examined the religious ideas that supported the hierarchical caste system of India and strongly influenced the theories of later investigators of India such as Louis Dumont. A younger member of the school, Robert Hertz, published a highly influential investigation on the preeminence of the right hand, or religious polarity, as well as a study of the collective representation of death He was also interested in folklore. His study of sin and expiation in religions was left unfinished when he died in fighting at the front in World War I. Only the introduction was published posthumously by Mauss. Maurice Halbwachs, who focused on the study of collective memory, authored a study of the legendary topography of the Gospels in the holy land. In general, the work of the Durkheim school was part of a broader contemporaneous Francophone analysis of religion that included the work of the Belgian anthropologist, Arnold van Gennep, whose analysis of "liminality" in his book on *The Rites of Passage* (1909) became a major influence on the work of later figures such as Victor Turner.

Durkheim's own mature theory of religion was developed in his book, *The Elementary Forms of Religious Life* (1912). There, he defined religion as a system of beliefs and practices concerning the sacred, ones that united those who followed them into a moral community called a church. In the process of examining the social origins and functions of the principle rites and beliefs of primitive religion, he also claimed to discover the social roots of the fundamental categories of human understanding (i.e., time, space, causality, etc.). Durkheim's influential study combined a substantive definition of religion, in terms of the opposition between the sacred and the profane, with a functionalist view of its social effects in causing social integration. Durkheim also distinguished between religion and magic by emphasizing that religion forms church and is an inherently collective phenomenon, while magic involves a clientele attached to the rites of an individual practitioner.

Henri Bergson was a Nobel Prize–Winning French philosopher whose book *The Two Sources of Morality and Religion* (1932) both criticized Durkheim's purely sociological conception of religion and offered an alternate view rooted in Bergson's vitalistic philosophy. Bergson argued that there were two forms of religion, the static and the dynamic. The former established religious myth and ritual as institutions necessary for the coherent organization of society. However, dynamic religion, which Bergson viewed as the vital source of religious sentiment and new religious ideas, emerged from the inner flow of individual consciousness. It was more directly related to mystical experiences and an openness to love of fellow human beings as well as to God.

Claude Lévi-Strauss combined Mauss's ideas with perspectives drawn from comparative linguistics, Freud, and other sources to create a new and influential theory of structuralism. Although he applied his new framework initially to the study of kinship structures, he increasingly focused his attention on the comparative study of mythology, a field that was also being developed in France by other investigators such as George Dumezeil. At the same time, Mircea Eliade, who was Romanian by birth and upbringing, but wrote extensively in French, advanced a broadly comparative historical phenomenology of religion that attempted to identify, through a method of generalizing comparison, the fundamental forms of the sacred manifested in all societies. Similarly, Georges Bataille provided another view of religion that emphasized the relationships between violence and the sacred. While the social theory of religion has not figured as prominently in recent French thought, exceptions can be found in Lucien Goldmann's *The Hidden God* (1959), a study of Pascal's thought from the standpoint of a genetic structuralism that draws inspiration simultaneously from Marxism and Piaget, and in the later investigations of Foucault into sexuality, the self, and religious thought.

— Donald A. Nielsen

See also Bataille, Georges; Durkheim, Émile; Lévi-Strauss, Claude; Maistre, Joseph de; Religion

FURTHER READINGS AND REFERENCES

Bergson, Henri. 1935. *Two Sources of Morality and Religion*. Translated by R. Ashley Audra and Cloudesley Brereton, with the assistance of W. Horsfall Carter. New York: Henry Holt.

Durkheim, Émile. 1995. *The Elementary Forms of Religious Life*. Translated by Karen Fields. New York: Free Press.

Nielsen, Donald A. 1999. *Three Faces of God: Society, Religion and the Categories of Totality in the Philosophy of Émile Durkheim*. Albany, NY: State University of New York Press.

Wernick, Andrew. 2001. *Auguste Comte and the Religion of Humanity*. New York: Cambridge University Press.

REVOLUTION

Revolution: in modern times, the fact or idea of violent, abrupt, or radical change. In the philosophical discourse of modernity, the idea of revolution is associated with sociology's view that contemporary institutions and culture are the result of the three great revolutions—the French, American, and Industrial. The idea of revolution has a long premodern history, where its meaning is connected less to rupture or break and more to the sense of circular or cyclical meaning or movement. From the Greeks to the Renaissance, revolution is more like its physical or mechanical counterpart, indicating the complete turn of a wheel or a full cycle of the seasons. Here, revolution alternates with restoration, indicating a cyclical conception of time. Modernity inaugurates a new conception of revolution as rupture, absolute innovation, which rests on a linear or stadial, progressivist or evolutionary conception of time.

The sensibility of sociology is that more actually changed in the period since the Great Revolutions than across the longer time span of the many centuries before. The French Revolution, in the sociological imagination, saw the application or pursuit of Enlightenment or humanist principles, where the self emerged as a project, and the prospect of geographical and, especially, social mobility meant that individuals and society could in principle be made in their own image. Hard lines of estate or status were replaced with class structures, which could in principle be transversed. The third estate, or the people, could pit their collective will against the state, kings, and clerics. Socialism, democracy, and the prospect of social engineering became practical values. Liberty, fraternity, and equality would be established as social goals, and their achievement would be viewed as within human reach.

The connotations of the American Revolution were less connected to this sense of rupture with the tradition of aristocracy or feudalism and more celebrative of the idea of establishing a new republic in the New World, where the initial founding project of the 13 colonies of New England would come together as the United States and democracy and liberalism would flourish. The founding of the American colonies and the American Revolution was imagined as a clean break into the field of pure modernity, a view that in different ways influenced modern social theory from Locke through Tocqueville to Weber. As historians from Marx observed, however, those who set out to make the world anew often reached back to old or ancient symbols to do so. They set out actively to make the future in the image of the past. This sensibility, which is connected to the more recent idea articulated by Eric Hobsbawm of the invention of tradition, helps explain the presence of Greek and Roman motifs and design in great experiments such as the construction of Washington D.C. These connections between past and future indicate that even the new, ruptural sense of revolution associated with modernity was never itself complete but still drew on these older cyclical senses of revolution as repetition.

If in retrospect these senses of social and political revolution associated with the French and American events

exaggerate the ruptural sense of change, the image of the Industrial Revolution retains its power as an indicator of degree of extraordinary change over the period of a century from, say, 1800 to 1900. While the idea of the Industrial Revolution as an overnight change has long been dismissed, the extent of the change and its consequences are beyond question. By the end of the twentieth century, the idea of industrial revolution was often subsumed to that of technological revolution, a revolution in permanence, suggesting either revolution upon revolution in the modern manner or ongoing cyclical revolution in the traditional sense, or some combination of both. Together with the sense of a revolution in culture, not least as afforded by the informational revolution, we live today in the West with a sense that nothing can or ought to stay the same. Revolution in this sense has been normalized, or at least we have come to think of the idea as second nature. Perhaps revolution has simply lost its meaning in everyday use, in response to the heightened sense that change is the only thing now that stays the same.

If the Industrial Revolution opened the way to the sense of permanent technological revolution, then the French and American Revolutions opened a phase where political revolution, democracy and dictatorship became normalized or predictable features of modern politics. Later in the nineteenth century, magazines ran columns with titles such as "The Week's Revolutions." Political instability was the immediate face of modern times. The key connecting idea was that of socialism. While the French Revolution was often cast as the great bourgeois revolution, the arrival of socialist doctrine into the nineteenth century resulted in the frequent identification of socialism and revolution. The French Revolution was often viewed not only as a bourgeois revolution but as the first breath of socialist revolution. The Bolsheviks conducted the Russian Revolution in the shadow of the French Revolution as the metanarrative legitimating their project. The spirit of Jacobinism became a major frame of reference for both the Bolsheviks and their opponents—Lenin cast, for example, as Robespierre, the Great Terror as the precedent for Red Terror. Both the democratic and the socialist project were grounded in the French Revolution. Socialist demands could be directed against tradition, crossing over with the democratic movement as in Chartism in England or against the new and iniquitous results of the Industrial Revolution, as in machine breaking or Luddism. The emergence of Political Economy saw the appearance of the discourse of value. Who produced this new industrial wealth, and who claimed it?—so that the rights of labour became part of political discussion. One powerful argument, which fed into Marxism, indicated that labour should retain or cover the right to the whole of its product.

Prior to the emergence of mass parliamentary democracy later in the nineteenth century, the appeals of revolution were obvious. If the powerful could not be expected voluntarily to relinquish their privileges, the poor would have to take them for themselves. Significant revolutions occurred across Europe in 1848, in 1871 with the Paris Commune, 1905 and 1917 in Russia. The Russian Revolution generated its own controversies. Was October the beginning of a process of world revolution, or a specific and containable event? Trotsky and others had argued for the idea of Permanent Revolution in 1905, and Trotsky returned to this theme in 1930, staking his claim against Stalin's slogan of socialism in one country. In Trotsky's thinking socialist revolution could not be brooked. Revolutions would be telescoped. Revolution must be permanent in two senses; if it commenced as bourgeois, it would result in socialist revolution, and if it commenced in one country it must spread to the next, until the whole planet was socialist.

The more prominent revolutions of the interwar period were Nazi or fascist, in Italy and especially in Germany. The idea that fascism was a popular revolutionary movement took some time to make an impact on the consciousness of Marxists, who imagined hitherto that the Left had some kind of monopoly on revolutionary credentials, which made fascism counterrevolutionary by definition. The period after the Great War saw revolutions or insurrections break out across Europe, although the great remaining symbolic events of revolution took place in 1949 in China and 1959 in Cuba. The Soviet Union enacted revolution from above, at the point of the bayonet, through Eastern Europe after 1945. The citizens of Eastern and Central Europe asserted their own revolutionary demands for autonomy in East Germany in 1953, Hungary and Poland in 1956, Czechoslovakia and beyond in 1968, all to be defeated by Soviet tanks. The May events in Paris 1968 and elsewhere in Europe are often thought of as revolutionary. The great period of coerced labour and chaotic politics in China went under the name of the Great Proletarian Cultural Revolution, for here the question arose how revolutionaries could renew their power and legitimacy as revolutionaries once the initial carnival of the revolution was over. The Chinese students made something like their own revolution in Tienanmien Square in 1991. The greatest revolution of our own time was the so-called Velvet Revolution following Gorbachev's reforms from 1989 to 1991, with the reunification of Germany and the collapse of the old Soviet Empire. If the idea of technological or cultural revolution has become normalized, the idea of political revolution has since evaporated, recycled as nostalgia for Bolshevism as a fashion item.

The connection of revolution to Marxism remains strong and significant, however, not least because of Marx's ambivalence about capitalism. Reform or revolution? Capitalism, for Marx, needed to be revolutionized, socialized, but it was also at the same time itself the most revolutionary force in history. This was one theoretical source of the great revisionist controversy of the German Social Democrats, resting in this unresolved contradiction in the work of Marx himself. Was capitalism itself revolutionary, would socialism arrive automatically by itself from within the womb of capitalism, or did the revolutionary party have to make it? Marx's failure to resolve this issue gave pretext to the Bolsheviks, who returned to the idea of the conspiratorial or Jacobin party in order to keep history moving. Marx's own work portrayed socialism as a qualitatively new society and yet as one whose economic dynamics were capitalist, for they represented the growth capacity of the ever-expanding productive forces that would break through the old, capitalist relations of private ownership of property. Yet as generations of scholars and activists have pointed out, all revolutions made in the name of Marxism have occurred not in the homelands of capitalist Europe or America, but in lands where the peasantry rather than the proletariat was numerically dominant.

With the Bolshevik seizure of power in 1917 Marxism not only became a state ideology but became an ideology of economic modernization, for Marx had insisted that socialism could not be based on the universalization of poverty, and the Bolsheviks agreed. Where Kautsky and the other Social Democrats followed Marx in waiting, the Bolsheviks set out to force history, to generate the communist version of primitive industrial accumulation, forcing peasants into the proletariat or against the wall. The contradiction of Marx's legacy allowed both Bolsheviks and Social Democrats to claim that they were his faithful followers. If Marx had fueled the giganticism of Kautsky, where socialist industry would be even bigger than capitalism, he also called out Lenin's *State and Revolution,* where the idea of utopia jostled with the administrative image of socialism as the post office writ large. The early Marx imagined revolution as a purgative process, from whence humanity liberated would start again, perhaps in the image of the small working community like a guild, perhaps in that classical utopian space where time would stand still, stasis prevail.

The early Marx connected the idea of revolution necessarily to its bearer, the revolutionary proletariat. The revolution would not occur because the proletariat would be convinced that it was a good idea; it was, rather, inscribed into its very existence, as the last class, the class after aristocracy and bourgeoisie, after whom there would be no more classes and, by implication, no future revolutions; after the rupture of proletarian revolution, the real history of humanity would begin. For this reason, however, Marx had no need of a theory of organisation. The party was the mass, the class. There was no party outside the revolutionary proletariat, whose vocation it was to be revolutionary. Thus, Marx wrote, in the statutes of the First International (International Workingmen's Association), that socialism could only be the results of the efforts of the workers themselves. Leaders could not substitute themselves or their desires for the masses. The infamous idea of proletarian dictatorship, to be identified by the Bolsheviks with their own reign, in Marx stood for an interregnum, a transitional interval opening the door from socialism to the higher state of communism. Marx's embrace of political economy indicates a shift in his thinking about revolution, for henceforth the argument does not start with claims as to the revolutionary subject or bearer but, rather, with assertions as to capitalism's revolutionary dynamic and self-destructive capacities. Revolution shifts in the early Marx, from the political sphere or superstructure to political economy or structure in the later Marx.

In the 1859 *Contribution to the Critique of Political Economy,* revolution results from the contradiction between the ever-expanding dynamic of productive forces and capitalist social relations, which constrain production. Then, alternatively, in *Capital,* the tendency for profit rate to fall leads to the self-destruction of capitalism and the emergence of the collective labourer as its new master, which inaugurates the social regime of the associated producers. Alternatively again, in the *Grundrisse,* it is technology in the specific form of automation that enables labour to step aside from production except as its minder so that freedom emerges beyond labour rather than through it. Here, the proletariat is the beneficiary of the further path of capitalist industrial development, now in its socialist form, rather than the central and necessary actor whose political revolution calls the new order out.

In the early work, Marx has the proletariat initiate socialism as an act of conscious will. This is the spirit that later informs Western Marxism, and especially the work of Gramsci. By the *Communist Manifesto* of 1848, the opening tension in Marx's theory of revolution is already apparent. The *Manifesto* opens with the strong claim that it is class struggle rather than economic development that dominates history. Yet Marx's project is also to link the future of the proletariat and socialist revolution to historical necessity, this connection offering Marx's theory the scientific edge over alternative left-wing utopias based on nothing but desire. The *Manifesto* offers the theorem of class polarization between proletarian and bourgeois forces, viewed practically as opposed military camps. Yet within pages, Marx is singing his hymn for the extraordinary achievements of capitalism, the extraordinary force that knows no limits, that is itself redeemably revolutionary, even if its power overwhelms its bearers, making of the bourgeoisie nothing more than the sorcerer's apprentice. This is the prompt for a different, non-Marxian approach like that of Joseph Schumpeter in *Capitalism, Socialism and Democracy,* where capitalist dynamism is viewed as the major force of creative destruction in modernity. This is clearly one implication of Marx's hymn in the *Communist Manifesto* that it is capitalism rather than socialism that is really revolutionary.

Thus, the embracing of the image of Marx on parts of Wall Street into the 1990s, where Marx is hailed not as the fomenter of socialism but as the great advocate of capitalism as revolution. More recently, this trend has opened the way for critics such as Luc Boltanski and Jeremy Rifkin's argument that there is a new kind of capitalism, which takes some of the old romantic or bohemian impulse into the spirit of capitalism. On all accounts, socialism here is a lost cause, except in the sense that socialism was viewed by some, such as Kautsky in his middle period, as the icing on the cake of capitalist development. Plainly capitalism even in its revolutionary impetus fails historically to generate socialism from within, although this view has recently been revived by post-Marxists. The victorious view of capitalism, like the old-fashioned view of Marx, however, indicates its own limits even as it draws attention to modernity as capitalism. This is a view of modernity that reduces the field to capitalism or economy; it works against the legacy of complexity introduced into the analysis of capitalism as modernity by Max Weber, and developed by later critical theory, Habermas and Heller, or differently in Luhmann. Capitalism here is granted great complexity and even protean capacities itself, but state bureaucracy and rationalisation here are all subsumed to capitalism as complex in itself. The logic of this view appeals, as globalization reinforces the sense that capitalism is the only form of economic organization available to us after 1989.

The counterargument, that capitalism is only ever part of modernity, continues to inform not only the methodological pluralism of critical theory but also the tradition of comparative historical sociology, where the key contributions on the theme of revolution include works such as Barrington Moore's *Social Origins of Dictatorship and Democracy* and Theda Skocpol's *States and Social Revolutions.* The alternative legacy, suggested by Hannah Arendt's *On Revolution,* saw revolution as an Atlantic project connected with the pursuit of freedom, where the American example was more pure than the French, with its distraction into the politics of social provision. If capitalism has really taken over the idea of revolution, then the only freedom left to us will be capitalist freedom.

— Peter Beilharz

See also Capitalism; Marxism; Reform; Socialism

FURTHER READINGS AND REFERENCES

Arendt, H. 1963. *On Revolution,* New York: Viking.

Boltanski, L. 2002. "The Left after 1968 and the Longing for Total Revolution." *Thesis Eleven: Critical Theory and Historical Sociology* 69:1–20.

Draper, H. 1977–1986. *Karl Marx's Theory of Revolution.* 4 vols. New York: Monthly Review.

Furet, F. 2000. *The Passing of an Illusion.* Cambridge, MA: Harvard University Press.

Kimmel, M. 1990. *Revolution.* Oxford, UK. Polity.

Moore, B. 1966. *The Social Origins of Dictatorship and Democracy.* London: Allen Lane.

Skocpol, T. 1979. *States and Social Revolutions.* Cambridge, UK: Cambridge University Press.

Wagner, P. 1999. "The Resistance That Modernity Constantly Provokes: Europe, America and Social Theory." *Thesis Eleven: Critical Theory and Historical Sociology* 58:35–58.

THE RHETORICAL TURN IN SOCIAL THEORY

During the past two decades, the "linguistic" or "rhetorical" turn has emerged as an important intellectual movement in the human and social sciences. It has become a commonplace that society can be viewed as a text and that social and cultural reality, and the sciences themselves, are linguistic constructions. In this view, reality and truth are formed through practices of representation and interpretation by speakers and their publics. This view can be located in the contexts of sociolinguistics, sociology of knowledge, poststructuralism, feminist theory, critical rhetoric of inquiry, and social studies of science, as well as several other intellectual traditions. All these tendencies of thought reject the simple bifurcations of reason and persuasion, discovery and invention, or of thought and its expressions. Instead, knowledge, and human experience itself, are viewed as poetically and politically constituted, "made" by human communicative action that develops historically and is institutionalized politically.

In this view, realistic representations become true descriptions not by correspondence to noumenal objects, but by conformity to orthodox practices of writing and reading. These practices are largely guided by root metaphors that define the basic character of a world and all that it might contain. Indeed, insofar as a representation is regarded as objectively true, it is viewed that way because its metaphors and methods of construction have become so familiar that they operate transparently. Absolutist conceptions of truth are made plausible only by those modes of metaphoric representation that have "made it" socially and thence deny their necessary partiality.

Thus, for those who follow the rhetorical turn, distinctions between fact and fiction are softened because both are seen as the products of, and sources for, communicative action; both are viewed as representations of reality that also represent various groups, interests, ideologies, and historical impositions. By untangling the relationship between objectivistic, metaphoric, and political practices, rhetorical (that is, poetic and political) analysis helps us gain insight into the ways in which the true has been fashioned and could be refashioned anew.

In the presence of such a relativization of formerly privileged discourses of truth, many people feel nostalgia for a lost foundation for lawlike knowledge or ethical absolutes. That is, even after metaphoric or deconstructive criticism has done its work, we still are faced with the challenge of establishing cognitive authority and inventing affirmative values as central elements of any rational moral polity. The research program of the linguistic turn, therefore, includes the critical assessment of the deconstructivist, rhetorical effort to date, a clearer understanding of its dialectical relationship to intelligibility within historical communities of discourse, and an analysis of how academic discourses both reflect and influence their larger political contexts of production. In other words, rhetorically oriented social thinkers need to analyze the methods by which people encode and create what is taken as real, normal, and to be accepted without question and even without awareness. In this sense, the "new rhetoric" goes beyond classical rhetorical theory in three ways. It makes the ontological claims that representation and communication help to make that which is represented and communicated. It extends the scope of rhetoric to all representation, not merely political or public address. And it is critical in showing how anything stated could be otherwise represented.

Such a research program has the potential to radicalize the methods, objects, and very conceptions of the academic enterprise. In particular, the rhetorical transvaluation of epistemology wrenches us away from our most treasured beliefs about the constitution of science, knowledge, and even reason itself. It does so by leading us to question the traditional foundations of knowledge and scientific inquiry; then it invites us to adopt a linguistically reflexive posture as we are subsequently faced with redefining, metatheoretically, what theory and research are and should be.

In the modernist and especially positivist periods, our understanding of how science and knowledge were constituted relied on an assumed polarity and hierarchy between truth and its media of expression. Foundationalist epistemology and modern scientific method insisted that objective truth existed independently of any symbols that might be used to convey it. In this bifurcation, reason was authoritatively superior to its own external systems of expression. Since the Enlightenment, science has thrived on the self-endorsing assumption that the "metaphoric" by definition is separate from the true, ontologically and epistemologically. By contrast, rhetorical approach subverts the authority of modernist philosophy of science by radically conflating the traditionally bifurcated hierarchies of truth and expression, *doxa* and *episteme,* rationality and language, appearance and reality, and meaning and metaphor. It does so by focusing on the *how* rather than the *what* of knowledge, its poetic and political enablements rather than its logical and empirical entailments.

Through such shifts of focus, the rhetorical turn relocates knowledge in the act of symbolic construction, and knowledge is no longer regarded as that which symbols subserviently convey. Humans *enact* truth not by legislating it scientifically, but by performing it discursively, in science, in politics, and in everyday life. Our knowledge of truth is not based on some extralinguistic rationality, because rationality itself is demystified and reconstituted as a historical construction and deployment guided by root metaphors that themselves have no ultimate referent or foundation.

Accordingly, the image of knowledge and research is shifted from explanation and verification to a conversation of scholars (rhetors and dialecticians) who seek to guide and persuade themselves and each other through discourses soaked with metaphors. This picture of the scholarly enterprise suggests that critique of theory and method must be permanently immanent precisely because theories and methods themselves cannot be universalized, since their intelligibility and elaboration is possible only within some basic metaphor. This view requires us to acknowledge our own linguistic constitution—ourselves as subjects and our fields as disciplinary objects—and then to maintain and apply the consciousness and the practice of linguistically reflective awareness.

What is the relationship, then, between this metaphoric perspective and the *telos* of nonideological, emancipatory discourse? That is, can rhetorically sensitive social theory also contribute to a more reflexive, more enlightened polity? An adequate paradigm for democratic civic communication must join efficiency in managing complex systems with self-understanding and significance in the lifeworld. That is, it must enable us to govern our polities in a rational manner to ensure collective survival, while providing us with meaning and dignity in our existential experience of ourselves. Hence, such a discourse must be adequate not only on the level of science and technique but also on the level of ethics and politics. After we have deconstructed traditional humanism and traditional science in terms of their metaphoric encodements, we still confront these challenges. But with what intellectual resources and with what disciplinary strategies? What additional problems are we likely to confront? How might they be usefully framed and resolved?

The view of scientific and social realities as rhetorical constructions helps us to address such questions. First, it allows us to abandon the views both of social structures as objective entities acting on individuals, and of subjective agents inventing their worlds out of conscious intentions. Instead, both structure and consciousness are seen as practical, historical accomplishments, brought about through everyday communicative action, the result of rhetorical and dialectical struggles over the nature and meaning of reality.

In this discursive view, language is not a natural fact of daily life or a mere epiphenomenon of forces and relations of production. Instead, language expresses and enables a social "covenant." As de Saussure (1965) put it, this covenant is

the social side of language, [which operates] outside the individual, who can never create or modify it by himself; it exists only by virtue of a sort of contract signed by the members of the community. The community is necessary . . . ; by himself the individual cannot fix a single value. Each time I say [a] word I renew its substance. (pp. 14, 113, 109)

In such a manner, absolutist dichotomies of structure and agency or of base and superstructure may be dissolved in the metaphor of society as textual enactment. The structure (language) is both a constraint and a resource for performance (speech). The semiotic moment of this approach deals effectively with structure; its hermeneutic moment addresses meaning and action. Both these dimensions—syntactics and grammatics, on one hand, and semantics and pragmatics on the other—are contained and logically consisted within the image of social reality and knowledge as metaphoric.

The discursive approach also abandons the distorting notion of disciplines as well as of positivist and hermeneutic dichotomies within these disciplines. Instead, it enables us to slice modes of argumentation differently and to understand the construction of theories as itself the deployment of various rhetorical strategies. Such an approach highlights the presuppositions and metalogics of all forms of knowledge and thus brings values back to the fore.

Indeed, in abandoning the antirhetorical rhetoric of positivism, the rhetorical turn recovers the ancient function of social thought as a moral and political practice. In this view, in constructing theories, we should attend not only to logical propositions and empirical contents but also to linguistic methods and existential functions. We then see the metaphoric dimension of all knowledges as an integral part of their truth or falsity to social life. When seen metaphorically, such truth is also an implicit call to action. Its existential *telos* is self-understanding, critique, and emancipation. Positivists have sought to silence this existential dimension of knowledge by treating it as an object external to society that makes no personal moral claim on us. But different knowledges also convey different existential truths. And unlike propositional truth, existential truth is not merely to be cross-examined. Instead, when it speaks, we ourselves become the "object," for it is we who are addressed.

— Richard Harvey Brown

See also Dilthey, Wilhelm; Discourse; Hermeneutics; Postsocial; Postmodernism; Saussure, Ferdinand de; Social Constructionism; Social Studies of Science

FURTHER READINGS AND REFERENCES

Aristotle. 1991. *On Rhetoric: A Theory of Civic Discourse.* Translated by George A. Kennedy. Oxford, UK: Oxford University Press.

Brown, Richard Harvey. 1989. *Social Science as Civic Discourse: Essays on the Invention, Legitimation, and Uses of Social Theory.* Chicago, IL: University of Chicago Press.

Burke, Kenneth. 1969. *A Rhetoric of Motives.* Berkeley: University of California Press.

de Saussure, Ferdinand. 1965. *Cours de Linguistique Generale.* Paris: Presses Universitaires de France.

Farrell, Thomas. 1993. *Norms of Rhetorical Culture.* New Haven, CT: Yale University Press.

Jasinski, James. 2001. *Sourcebook on Rhetoric: Key Concepts in Contemporary Rhetorical Studies.* Thousand Oaks, CA: Sage.

Perelman, Chaim and Lucy Olbrechts-Tyteca. 1971. *The New Rhetoric: A Treatise on Argumentation.* Notre Dame, IN: Notre Dame University Press.

RIEFF, PHILIP

An American social theorist and analyst of culture, Philip Rieff (b. 1922) is best known for two acclaimed books on Freud and his influence on twentieth-century culture, *Freud: The Mind of the Moralist* (1959) and *The Triumph of the Therapeutic: Uses of Faith after Freud* (1966), and as the editor of the 10-volume edition, *The Collected Papers of Sigmund Freud* (1963). Educated at the University of Chicago and for many years a member of the sociology faculty at the University of Pennsylvania (1961–1993), Rieff is a wide-ranging theorist who has focused on developing a concept of culture that draws heavily from the humanities and religious sources. Within the discipline of sociology, Rieff is most deeply indebted to the works of Max Weber and Charles Horton Cooley. Broadly speaking, Rieff has explored the implications of the rise of psychology for Western culture and the decline of cultures of faith. More specifically, Rieff can fairly lay claim to having originated the concept of "therapeutic culture" and tracing its emergence in Western societies. In his later writings, Rieff has attempted to advance a moral theory of culture that is notable for its uncompromising critique of therapeutic culture and that is closely linked to his efforts to clarify a concept of the sacred.

Rieff's early work, which culminated with the publication of *Freud: The Mind of the Moralist,* argued that Freud, more than any other modern intellectual figure, charted the spiritual course of the twentieth century for America and Europe because he was "the first completely irreligious moralist . . . without even a moralizing message" ([1959] 1979:xi). As a secular guide to the conduct of life, Freud exemplified the strange new ideal of "psychological man" who has nothing left to affirm except the self. Offering neither religious nor political salvation, Freud counseled that individuals should strive for no ethical heights but, rather, settle for training in an "ethic of honesty" that teaches a certain detachment from communal ideals and tolerance toward the irresolvable complexities of the self. According to Rieff, the Freudian ethic demanded lucid insight rather than sincere action, self-awareness rather than heroic commitment, to escape the dialectic of hope and despair, illusion and disillusion, to which human beings are prone. Rieff points out that in practice, however, Freud's cautious, stoic ethic became popularized into therapeutic doctrines of liberation from normative constraints—sexual, political, and otherwise—which Freud never intended.

In *The Triumph of the Therapeutic,* Rieff proceeded to clarify how "the analytic attitude" of Freud was corrupted and abandoned by seminal cultural figures directly influenced by Freud, such as C. G. Jung, Wilhelm Reich, and D. H. Lawrence, who were the predecessors of a full-blown therapeutic culture, which Rieff saw emerge in the 1960s. Although Rieff wrote largely in defense of Freud's analytic attitude against those who advocated some variety of therapeutic liberation, the ironic and irenic style of *The Triumph of the Therapeutic* sometimes leaves readers in doubt as to where the author stands. In subsequent writings, Rieff leaves little doubt that he rejects not only the triumphant therapeutic culture but also Freud's analytic attitude, which he holds at least partially responsible for the therapeutic revolution.

Fellow Teachers (1973) and other central works of the 1970s, such as "The Impossible Culture: Wilde as a Modern Prophet" ([1970] 1982–83) and the 1978 epilogue to the third edition of *Freud: The Mind of the Moralist,* exhibit much more explicit condemnations of therapeutic culture and (especially in the latter work) even Freud himself. But they also build on earlier attempts to formulate a theory of culture in terms of controlling and releasing motifs, which is pivotal to Rieff's theoretical project.

In the works of the 1970s, Rieff regularly begins to identify the primary controlling forms of all high cultures as "interdicts," the secondary releasing forms as "remissions," and outright violations of interdicts as "transgressions." Every viable culture is thereby conceived of as achieving an intricate balance of dominant, implicitly understood "shalt nots" and subordinate remissions, an ingenious symbolic system of limitations and permissions, that make individuals intelligible and trustworthy to one another. "In point of psychiatric and historical fact, it is *no,* rather than *yes,* upon which all culture and inner development of character, depend" (*The Feeling Intellect,* p. 284). Consequently, it is when the *yeses* expand, growing increasingly subversive and eventually transgressive, overwhelming the interdictory *no's,* that a culture may be said to be in crisis. According to Rieff, we are living through such a period of crisis today that is particularly acute because not only is there no new system of interdicts on the cultural horizon but our therapeutic culture rejects interdictory forms as a matter of principle.

Much of Rieff's *oeuvre* from the 1970s, 1980s, and 1990s remains unpublished, including his magnum opus *Sacred Order and Social Order*. But from the work, which has been published and various public lectures, it is clear that beginning in the 1970s, Rieff launched a sustained intellectual effort to develop a cross-cultural theory of the sacred. Central to this effort has been his attempt to counter the compelling psychological theories of Freud and his predecessor Nietzsche with his own analytic arsenal of concepts. By appropriating, in particular, pivotal Freudian concepts such as "repression," "negation," and "sense of guilt," Rieff has attempted to turn the brilliant psychological reductionism of the predecessors of therapeutic culture against its inadvertent founders. Beyond this, Rieff has given powerful hints of a comprehensive theory of sacred order.

At present, Rieff's influence on social theory and the discipline of sociology is restricted to a relatively small group of scholars who are familiar with his work, within sociology probably most significantly represented by James Davison Hunter and his students. Outside the discipline, Rieff's influence has been more widespread, as evidenced in works by figures such as historian Christopher Lasch (*The Culture of Narcissism*), philosopher Alasdair MacIntyre (*After Virtue*), and others who explore the relations between morality and society. Indeed, Rieff could easily be characterized as what is now commonly termed a "public intellectual." But as an intellectual, Rieff has consistently adopted a stance of opposition toward the very model of the public intellectual in the twentieth century, which was inspired by *les philosophes* and arose from the Dreyfus Affair, because of the intellectual's close affiliation with the "remissive" world of public celebrity and political power. In its dual opposition to narrow academic specialization and intellectual celebrity, Rieff's work stands out as an unusual effort to employ social theory in defense of the interdictory forms that he sees as inseparable from all high cultures.

— Alan Woolfolk

See also Culture and Civilization; Freud, Sigmund; Psychoanalysis and Social Theory

FURTHER READINGS AND REFERENCES

Lasch, Christopher. 1995. "Philip Rieff and the Religion of Culture." Pp. 213–29 in *The Revolt of the Elites and the Betrayal of Democracy*. New York: Norton.

Rieff, Philip. [1959, 1961] 1979. *Freud: The Mind of the Moralist*. Chicago, IL: University of Chicago Press.

———. [1970] 1982-83. "The Impossible Culture: Wilde as a Modern Prophet." *Salmagundi* 58–59:406–26. Expanded version of introduction to *The Soul of Man Under Socialism and Other Essays* (New York: Harper & Row, 1970).

———. [1972, 1973] 1985. *Fellow Teachers: Of Culture and Its Second Death*. Chicago, IL: University of Chicago Press.

———. [1966] 1987. *The Triumph of the Therapeutic: Uses of Faith after Freud*. Chicago, IL: University of Chicago Press.

———. 1990. *The Feeling Intellect: Selected Writings*. Edited and with an Introduction by Jonathan B. Imber. Chicago, IL: University of Chicago Press.

RISK SOCIETY

What do events as different as Chernobyl, global warming, mad cow disease, the debate about the human genome, the Asian financial crisis, and the September 11, 2001, terrorist attacks have in common? They signify different dimensions and dynamics of (global) risk society.

Premodern dangers were attributed to nature, gods, and demons. Risk is a modern concept. It presumes decision making and inherently contains the concept of control. As soon as we speak in terms of "risk," we are talking about calculating the incalculable, colonizing the future. In this sense, calculating risks is part of the master narrative of (first) modernity. In Europe, this victorious march culminates in the development and organisation of the welfare state, which bases its legitimacy on its capacity to protect its citizens against dangers of all sorts. But what happens in risk society is that we enter a world of *uncontrollable risk*. "Uncontrollable risk" is a contradiction in terms. And yet it is the only apt description for the second-order, *un*natural, human-made, manufactured uncertainties and hazards beyond boundaries we are confronted with in (second) reflexive modernity.

Risk society does not arise from the fact that everyday life has generally become more dangerous. It is not a matter of the *increase*, but rather of the *de-bounding* of uncontrollable risks. This de-bounding is three-dimensional: spatial, temporal, and social. In the spatial dimension, we see ourselves confronted with risks that do not take nation-state boundaries, or any other boundaries for that matter, into account: climate change, air pollution, and the ozone hole affect everyone (if not all in the same way). Similarly, in the temporal dimension, the long latency period of dangers—such as, for example, in the elimination of nuclear waste or the consequences of genetically manipulated food—escapes the prevailing procedures used when dealing with industrial dangers. Finally, in the social dimension, the incorporation of both jeopardizing potentials and the related liability question lead to a problem—namely, that it is difficult to determine, in a legally relevant manner, who "causes" environmental pollution or a financial crisis and who is responsible; these are mainly due to the combined effects of the actions of many individuals ("organized irresponsibility"). This then also means that the boundaries of private insurability dissolve, since it is based on the fundamental potential for compensation of damages and on the possibility of estimating their probability by means of quantitative risk calculation. So the hidden central issue in risk society is *how to feign control over the incontrollable*—in politics, law, science, technology, economy, and everyday life (Adam, Beck, and van Loon 2000; Allan 2003; Beck 1999; Giddens 1994; Latour 2003).

We can differentiate between at least three different axes of conflict in risk society. The first axis is that of *ecological* conflicts, which are by their very essence global. The second is *global financial* crises, which, during the first stage of modernity, can be individualised and nationalised. Financial risks threaten or devalue personal property (capital, jobs) so they are more individualized than ecological risks; if there is a collective definition, it tends to be a national one. And the third, which suddenly broke upon us on September 11, 2001, is the threat of global terror networks, which empower governments and states. Terrorism raises the question of who defines the identity of a "transnational terrorist." Neither judges nor international courts do, but the governments of powerful states do. They empower themselves by defining who is their enemy. Terrorist enemy images are de-territorialized, de-nationalized, and flexible state constructions that legitimate global interventions by military powers.

When we say these risks are global, this should not be equated with a homogenisation of the world—that is, that all regions and cultures are now equally affected by a uniform set of nonquantifiable, uncontrollable risks in the areas of ecology, economy, and power. On the contrary, global risks are per se unequally distributed. They unfold in different ways in every concrete formation, mediated by different historical backgrounds and cultural and political patterns. In the so-called periphery, global risk society appears *not* as an *endogenous* process, which can be fought by means of autonomous national decision making but rather as an *exogenous* process propelled by decisions made in other countries, especially in the so-called centre. People feel like the helpless hostages of this process insofar as corrections are virtually impossible at the national level. One area in which the difference is especially marked is in the experience of global financial crises, whereby entire regions on the periphery can be plunged into depressions that citizens of the centre do not even register as crises. Moreover, ecological and terrorist network threats also flourish with particular virulence under the weak states that define the periphery.

There is a dialectical relation between the unequal experience of being victimized by global risks and the transborder nature of the problems. But it is the transnational aspect, which makes cooperation indispensable to their solution, that truly gives them their global nature. The collapse of global financial markets or climatic change affects regions quite differently. But that doesn't change the principle that everyone is affected, and everyone can

potentially be affected in a much worse manner. Thus, in a way, these problems endow each country with a common global interest, which means that the globalized public reflection ("mass media") of global risk conflicts produces the basis of a global community of fate. Furthermore, it is also intellectually obvious that global problems have only global solutions and demand global cooperation. But between the potential of global cooperation and its realization lie a host of risk conflicts. And yet these conflicts still serve an *integrative* and enlightenment function, because they make it increasingly clear that global solutions must be found and that these cannot be found through war but only through negotiation and contract.

A further distinction can be made, however, between ecological and financial threats on one hand and the threat of global terrorist networks on the other. Ecological and financial conflicts fit the model of modernity's self-endangerment. They both clearly result from the accumulation and distribution of "bads" that were tied up with the production of goods. They result from society's central decisions but as unintentional side effects of those decisions. Terrorist activity, on the other hand, is intentionally bad. It aims to produce the effects that the other crises produce unintentionally. Thus, the principle of *intention* replaces the principle of *accident*. Active trust becomes active mistrust. The context of individual risk is replaced by the context of systemic risks. Private insurance is (partly) replaced by state insurance. The power of definition of experts has been replaced by that of states and intelligence agencies, and the pluralization of expert rationalities has turned into the simplification of enemy images. It is the very flexible hybrid character of the "transnational terrorist enemy" representation that ultimately reinforces the hegemony of already powerful states.

Having outlined their differences, it should be no surprise that the three kinds of global risk—ecological, financial, and terrorist threat—also interact. And terrorism again is the focal point. On one hand, the dangers from terrorism increase exponentially with technical progress. Advances in financial and communication technology are what made global terrorism possible in the first place. And the same innovations that have individualized financial risks have also *individualized war.*

But the most horrifying connection is that all the risk conflicts stored away as potential could now be intentionally unleashed. Every advance from gene technology to nanotechnology opens a "Pandora's box" that could be used as a terrorist's tool kit. Thus, the terrorist threat has made everyone into a disaster movie scriptwriter, now condemned to imagine the effects of a homemade atomic bomb assembled with the help of gene technology or nanotechnology and so on. But this is a one-sided view. It ignores the new terrain. In an age where trust and faith in God, class, nation, and government have declined considerably, humanity's common fear has proved the last resource for making new bonds.

— Ulrich Beck

See also Beck, Ulrich; Cosmopolitan Sociology; Globalization

FURTHER READINGS AND REFERENCES

Adam, B., U. Beck, and J. van Loon. 2000. *The Risk Society and Beyond.* London: Sage.

Allan, S. 2003. *Media, Risk and Science.* Buckingham, UK, and Philadelphia, PA: Open University Press.

Beck, U. 1999. *World Risk Society.* Cambridge, UK: Polity.

Giddens, A. 1994. *Beyond Left and Right.* Cambridge, UK: Polity.

Latour, B. 2003. "Is Re-modernization Occurring—And If So, How to Prove It?" *Theory, Culture & Society* 20(2):35–48.

RITZER, GEORGE

George Ritzer (b. 1940) is Distinguished University Professor of Sociology at the University of Maryland. His most important work has been in sociological theory, especially metatheory, and the application and development of theory in the sociology of consumption. Outside sociology, George Ritzer is best known for his term, *McDonaldization.* He has other and perhaps stronger claims to significance in sociology, but this article will begin with McDonaldization, because it is one of the few recent ideas that have originated in sociology and connected with a general intellectual public.

As Ritzer recognized, McDonald's has become a key symbol that connects the process of socialization through mundane activities (our childhood experiences of dining out) to global capitalist developments (the golden arches as one of the most prominent signs of American imperialism). However, Ritzer argues that the *process* of McDonaldization is of greater importance than the actual McDonald's. As described in *The McDonaldization of Society,* this process means a focus on efficiency, calculability, predictability, and control, but it is accompanied by the seemingly inevitable irrationality of rationality. McDonald's is the epitome of this, but McDonaldization is a process that is increasingly evident in a wide range of settings (e.g., the McDonaldization of education, the church, the health system, criminal justice, and so on).

The idea of McDonaldization is an elaboration of Max Weber's theory of rationalization. For Weber, the bureaucracy was the embodiment of the increasing formal rationality of the modern world, but Ritzer argues that the bureaucracy's vanguard role has been taken over by the fast-food restaurant. Like the bureaucracy before it, the fast-food restaurant both exemplifies this rationalization in its organizational form and, at the same time, constitutes one of the main vectors for its further dissemination. The bureaucracy allowed formal rationality to dominate our political and economic life. The fast-food restaurant opens up the realm of mundane activities and personal taste.

McDonaldization provides a key point from which to understand Ritzer's evolution as a theorist. Before McDonaldization, Ritzer was mainly concerned with delineating the existence of multiple paradigms in sociology and encouraging their integration. McDonaldization is, in part, an outgrowth of this work, since it integrates Weber's theory of rationalization with Marx's theory of capitalism, as well as neo-Marxist work on control. However, despite its deep roots in classical sociology, there is something new in Ritzer's concept. The rationalization of consumer organizations is different from the rationalization of administrative and production organizations. Therefore, McDonaldization can be seen not only as an outgrowth of Ritzer's early work but also as the beginning of his more recent interest in consumption.

Ritzer's early work in sociological theory concerned metatheory—that is, the systematic study of the underlying structure of sociological theories. *Sociology: A Multiple Paradigm Science* was an assessment of Thomas Kuhn's idea of paradigms and an application of this concept to sociology. Ritzer argued that sociology is divided into three fundamental paradigms. The social facts paradigm focuses on large social structures and external social constraints such as norms and values. The social definition paradigm focuses on the way in which actors define their social situation. The social behavior paradigm focuses on the social causes and effects of the unthinking behavior of individuals. This examination of paradigms allowed Ritzer to look at fundamental commonalities between seemingly disparate theories, as well as identify theorists who "bridged" these paradigms.

This led to Ritzer's proposal for an integrated paradigm for sociology. He maintained that the three paradigms could be seen as dealing with the major "levels" of social reality, which Ritzer delineated through the juxtaposition of the macroscopic-microscopic and objective-subjective continua. His integrated paradigm, designed to complement extant paradigms, deals with the interrelationships among *all* these levels. This work, completed by the early 1980s, anticipated the rise in interest in micro-macro and agency-structure integration in late twentieth-century social theory.

In *Metatheorizing in Sociology,* Ritzer established three distinct uses of metatheory: to attain a deeper understanding of sociological theory; as a prelude to theory development; and as a source of new metatheories. He also introduced a fourfold typology for a deeper understanding of sociological theories using the dimensions of internal-external and intellectual-social influences. We can use this tool to understand Ritzer's theories. He had no strong allegiance to any theoretical approach (internal-intellectual) because he got his Ph.D. at Cornell University in industrial and labor relations and therefore was not socialized in any particular sociological school (internal-social). His professional career began at the same time as Kuhn's book was having an impact on philosophy and science studies (external-intellectual) and as the dominant sociological school, structural functionalism, was unraveling (external-social). This provided Ritzer with a relatively unique standpoint from which to understand and compare sociological theories. This metatheoretical approach can also be seen in the eclecticism that characterizes his textbooks on sociological theory.

Ritzer's more recent work involves theorizing about consumer culture. Both *Expressing America* and *The McDonaldization Thesis* can be seen as attempts to bring more theoretical resources to the understanding of consumer culture. In *Expressing,* Ritzer draws on C. W. Mills and Georg Simmel to understand the effects of credit cards on society. In *The McDonaldization Thesis* he draws on Karl Mannheim to further understand McDonaldization. However, it is in his book *Enchanting a Disenchanted World* that Ritzer outlines the challenge that consumer culture presents to social theory.

McDonaldization had originally been intended as a fairly straightforward application of Weber's theory of rationalization to current problems. One of the most important tenets of Weber's theory is that rationalization leads to an increasing disenchantment of our view of the world. The world is demystified, less magical, a more predictable and calculable place. For Weber, this has certain psychological and moral disadvantages, but it does not really interfere with the workings of the rationalized systems themselves. Ritzer shows that for consumer culture, disenchantment becomes a central problem for the system. Continued consumption requires enchantment and belief in the promise of magic. Disenchanted production and administrative systems can run quite well; disenchanted consumption systems cannot. Ritzer examines the ways in which disenchanted consumption systems attempt to reenchant their practices.

This recognition of the centrality of consumption in modern society led Ritzer to cofound the *Journal of Consumer Culture* with Don Slater and to propose in his latest book, *The Globalization of Nothing,* a daring new theory that the spread of consumer culture is accompanied by the dominance of a social form that is centrally conceived and controlled while being relatively devoid of substantive content. He creates a new term, "grobalization," to complement the popular idea of glocalization in globalization theory and focuses on the growing proliferation of nothing in consumer culture throughout much of the world. Building on Marc Augé's concept of nonplaces (e.g., a shopping mall), he develops the ideas of nonthings (e.g.,

Gucci bags), nonpeople (e.g., Disney "cast members"), and nonservices (those of ATMs), and he argues that all are being increasingly grobalized.

— Douglas J. Goodman

See also Augé, Marc; Consumer Culture; Globalization; Mannheim, Karl; McDonaldization; Metatheory; Mills, C. Wright; Rationalization; Simmel, Georg; Weber, Max

FURTHER READINGS AND REFERENCES

Ritzer, George. 1980. *Sociology: A Multiple Paradigm Science.* Boston, MA: Allyn & Bacon.
———. 1981. *Toward an Integrated Sociological Paradigm: The Search for an Exemplar and an Image of the Subject Matter.* Boston, MA: Allyn & Bacon.
———. 1991. *Metatheorizing in Sociology.* Lexington, MA: Lexington Books.
———. 1995. *Expressing America: A Critique of the Global Credit Card Society.* Thousand Oaks, CA: Pine Forge.
———. 1998. *The McDonaldization Thesis: Explorations and Extensions.* London & Thousand Oaks, CA: Sage.
———. 1999. *Enchanting a Disenchanted World: Revolutionizing the Means of Consumption.* Thousand Oaks, CA: Pine Forge.
———. 2004. *The Globalization of Nothing.* Thousand Oaks, CA: Pine Forge.
———. [1993] 2004. *The McDonaldization of Society: Revised New Century Edition.* Thousand Oaks, CA: Pine Forge.

ROLE THEORY

The term *role theory* refers to an expansive and variegated body of analyses examining the linkages between social organization, culture, and the performances that humans give while engaged in interaction. Contemporary role theory within sociology is the progeny of two dominant theoretical traditions in social psychology—structural role theory and symbolic interactionism. Recent theorizing within postmodern, feminist, and critical-dramaturgical perspectives in role theory have integrated the insights of both traditions, creating a hybrid emphasizing the political, economic, and cultural as well as performative aspects of social roles. Building on the early insights of anthropologist Ralph Linton, structural role theory provided a conventional definition of *role* as the duties and obligations associated with a single position or "status" and defined the way in which one carried out his or her role, a "role performance." For Linton, interaction was governed by the role expectations of actors' respective statuses. The fundamental proposition of the structural role theory is that shared expectations serve as a cultural script or blueprint that ensures conformity because it is either obtrusive in the social context, has been internalized by actors before they enter into it, or both. A decidedly sociological variant of structural role theory was provided by Talcott Parsons in his theory of "informational control." Parsons theorized roles as the crucial social mechanism that positioned individuals in social structure but, more important, inculcated culture as individuals were socialized into them.

One of the most reliable sociological findings is that people's attitudes and behaviors vary according to the social position they occupy in the social structure. Contemporary research in the *social structure and personality* paradigm within sociological social psychology has provided evidence of the linkage between social class, parental values, and the psychological attributes of children. The questions historically addressed within social science—How is society organized? How is social order possible? How is prediction of behavior possible? How and why people are constrained?—are answered by structural role theory, which emphasizes that "status" or structural position is the fundamental, constituent element of social organization determining the allocation of social roles. Exploring the linkage between adult work experiences and childhood development, Mortimer, Lorence, and Kumka (1986) write: "Social class . . . determines the conditions of occupational life to which the individual is exposed. Men who have self-directed work activities value self-direction in themselves as well as in their children" (p. 188). Structural role theorists argue that social organization and interactional regularity are possible because of cultural consensus regarding role expectations. While this feature of social life may lead to people feeling constrained in the way that they enact various roles, habituated behavior also produces an "economy of effort." Hence, the prediction of behavior becomes possible for social scientists as the actors in everyday life "construct predictability."

Structural role theory, then, views individuals largely as conformists. A central criticism leveled at the theory is that it does not adequately explain deviance in terms other than psychologistic ones. Other problems also remain. Biddle (1986) observed that not all roles may be associated with identified social positions. In friendship groups, status structures may be precariously absent or minimal and roles may be shared. Moreover, norms may or may not be shared within an entire social system, and thus they may or may not lead to conformity or sanctioning. Symbolic interactionists have traditionally eschewed asking questions concerning the stability of personality characteristics, criticizing early structural role theory for, as Dennis Wrong argued, providing an "overly socialized" conception of human behavior. Instead, symbolic interactionists have focused on the ways in which roles are molded and adapted in the course of a performance—that is, interaction. Following the work of

sociologists such as Herbert Blumer and Ralph Turner, psychologists Paul Secord and Carl Backman have emphasized a less deterministic view of human action. These scholars conceive of interaction as an interpretive process in which meanings evolve and change over the course of interaction. Roles are viewed as emerging out of the interactional process. Interpersonal negotiation leads to shared role definitions, which, in turn, lead to stable, individual behavior. As a symbolic interactionist role theory, this approach focuses on the roles of individual actors and the way in which roles evolve through social interaction. Roles are thought to "reflect norms, attitudes, contextual demands, negotiation, and the evolving definition of the situation as understood by the actors" (Biddle 1986:71). Role-taking and role-making processes are central to understanding this approach.

ROLE TAKING AND ROLE MAKING

Responding meaningfully to our interaction partners requires us to "take the role of the other"—that is, to anticipate communicative as well as nonverbal action on the part of others. Social philosopher George Herbert Mead viewed roles as strategies for coping that evolve as individuals interact with other persons. Mead emphasized the need for a "reciprocity of perspectives," or understanding the perspective of others ("role taking"), if lines of interaction are to be effectively aligned with others. Relying on the insights of Mead and phenomenologist Alfred Schütz, sociologists Peter Berger and Thomas Luckmann theorized that role taking proceeds on the basis of typifications—that is, definitions about the "type," character, or nature of the person we encounter. Knowing the status of a person, we immediately attempt to take the role or perspective of that person. If we know that we will be at a dinner gathering with a medical doctor, a social worker, and a pianist, we come to that gathering with certain role expectations of these individuals, given the positions they occupy. We might think of possible topics of conversation that would be appropriate to discuss with these individuals. We are perhaps most aware of role-taking processes when we fail at interaction and commit a social blunder.

While role playing presupposes the ability of people to take the role of the other, *role making* entails constructing, changing, adapting, and modifying a role in the course of a role performance. Formal rules may govern and limit the kind and degree of innovation in a performance, but outside of highly bureaucratized institutions such as the military, hospitals, convents, or monasteries, where performances may be marked by rigid enforcement, most roles allow for some degree of improvisation and creativity.

In Turner's approach, interaction is always a tentative process, as the individual tests the conception the other has of her role. Turner critiqued structural role theory as emphasizing only one way in which role-taking and role-playing processes may occur—through conformity, expectation, and approval. For Turner (1962), role processes are interactive. However, problems exist for this theory, as well, to the degree that it neglects the constraining effects of the role framework provided by groups. Indeed, as Biddle (1986) notes, little attention is given to actors' expectations for other persons or to the structural constraints placed on expectations and roles.

THE LANGUAGE OF ROLE

In their discussion of the nature and history of role theory, Thomas and Biddle (1966) examine role metaphors—"the use and extension of which have greatly increased the articulateness of the role language" (p. 13). A clear example is the dramaturgical metaphor. Analyzing social interaction as if it were a theatrical performance, sociologist Erving Goffman's approach relies heavily on the concept of role. Indeed, the dramaturgical model of human behavior has inspired metaphorical concepts such as role enactment, role playing, role taking, altercasting, front, presentation of self, mask, and persona. In his analysis of fantasy games involving the construction of fictitious roles, Gary Alan Fine (1983) used Goffman's concept of "keying" in demonstrating how fantasy role gamers transform the "everyday" quality of their surroundings into theater as they move their game pieces around the board. The term "upkeying" is appropriated by Fine to describe the fanciful flight from the frame of everyday reality and entry into the role of a make-believe character that gamers socially construct as they play such games as *Dungeons and Dragons.* "Down-keying," in the context of fantasy role-playing games, denotes the process of social psychologically exiting the game frame and returning to the conventional frame of everyday reality.

But to what degree do people personally identify with their roles? In what ways do roles become salient for people as they define their own identity and see, think, talk, and act in the social world? When the roles that people perform are ones that completely saturate the way they think, see themselves, and interact with others, they are engaged in *role engulfment.* Role engulfment was readily observed among the fantasy game players studied by Fine (1983). Gamers playing *Dungeons and Dragons* spent much time constructing fictitious characters through role playing, embracing the role so strongly that they would use the identity outside of the game context when penning letters. Moreover, according to some of the players' parents, fantasy gamers "had become so thoroughly engrossed that they had difficulty retreating back into everyday life and conventional morality." Groups concerned that the game promoted "mind control" argued that students should not be allowed to play the game (Martin and Fine 1991:112).

If role engulfment defines a state in which a role is all encompassing, it is also true that people may disassociate themselves from the roles that they play. *Role distance* refers to the inner separation that people feel from the role they are playing as they disinvest themselves in its performance. As performers engage in role distance, they may directly or inadvertently indicate that they are not to be identified with the role they are playing. As Peter Berger (1963) commented, every strongly coercive situation will produce "the playing of a role tongue-in-cheek, without really meaning it. . . . this kind of duplicity is the only way by which human dignity can be maintained" (p. 135).

In her field research on women prison guards working in all-male prisons, Lyn Zimmer (1987) found that women resisted some elements of the guard role as it was traditionally performed by men. While most aspects of their role performance were indistinguishable from their male counterparts, female guards relied on skills at relational work and eschewed coercive strategies, such as rescinding privileges, commonly used by male guards. By making small concessions, women humanized the guard role, transforming some of their contact with prisoners into times when they could provide counseling, help prisoners write letters, or help inmates search for jobs as they anticipated parole. While female guards received lower performance reviews and less staff support for failing to enact a more masculine script in the guard role, this adaptation garnered higher degrees of compliance from the prisoners.

As Zimmer's study reveals, the degree to which people resist the requirements of their role is quite variable and depends, in part, on their assessment of the "objective" features of the context over which they may have no control. Female guards resisted and transformed the guard role until it was transparent that they would receive little or no assistance from their male counterparts even in dangerous situations. As role players resist the unpleasant aspects of their role, that resistance may take a variety of forms. Where the consequences of resistance may be acutely felt, resistance may only be internal, in the form of distancing oneself from the role. Secondary adjustments may be used as performers begin to sense that the opportunity for role making is small and that they are "stuck" in the role. Where more autonomy in role playing is realized, actors may engage in role making, transforming features of the role in ways that are more humanizing. The shift, in recent years, from structural role theory to more interactionist understandings of role dynamics allows for more complete and dynamic conceptions of this crucial sociological concept.

ROLE THEORY: AREAS OF STUDY

Gender Roles. In gender analyses of both family and work settings, emphasis is commonly placed on role specialization, role conflict, and socialization. In recent years, feminist research has focused on the effects of changing occupational roles as women have challenged male-dominated structures in the division of household labor as well as in the workforce. Arlie Hochschild, in her book *The Second Shift* (1989), demonstrated that while in the role of homemaker, the workload of working women was exacerbated as husbands refused to create a more equitable distribution of household chores by altering their own roles. More recently, Scott Coltrane (1998) found that while household work regarding children is shared more or less equally by women and men, some chores continue to be allocated according to very traditional gender roles: Women still do most of the clothes care, while men do lawn care.

Ethnic Roles. Research on race and ethnicity has focused on children's socialization into a "race role." Joan Ferrante (2000), for example, observing the play of Palestinian children noted that the most popular part to play in the children's game is that of Israeli soldier, because the role is one on which power and status in everyday life is conferred. Focusing on the dramaturgical repertoire required of young black men, Brent Staples noted that white racism forces young black men to play accommodating roles. At night, to avoid being hassled by police or confronted by frightened, hostile white pedestrians like subway shooter Bernard Goetz, young black men use several strategies: They increase the physical distance between themselves and white pedestrians they may be following; they allow lobbies of buildings to clear rather than be caught alone with a white person; and, they allow sufficient physical space on train and subway platforms. *In toto,* the weight of the culture is on black men to develop and use interactional strategies that alleviate white fear of the stereotypical role they are presumed to play—one that is dangerous, criminal, and suspect.

Class Roles. Another process elucidated by role theory is social class. Children are socialized into social class and learn the class role. Robert Granfield's (1991) study of working-class students at Harvard Law School uncovered two distinct options that working-class students may exercise in playing the student role. Students may engage in "covering"—that is, trying to fit in without revealing their working-class roots. Yet this strategy may be plagued with "disidentifiers." Students may not be able to afford the clothes that don the same labels as their classmates, their diction may be deficient when speaking, or their social graces may be suspect as they attend mixers with faculty, parents, and other students. By contrast, working-class students may, instead, play the role of "working-class hero" demonstrating that, whatever upward social mobility they may experience, ideologically, they embraced their working-class roots. Wearing flannel shirts, talking about labor issues, and demonstrating that their aspirations include fighting for workers' causes are included in the repertoire of the working-class law student.

THE POSTMODERN SHIFT

In recent years, the work of sociologists and psychologists has increasingly emphasized the concept of identity rather than role. Postmodern theories, in particular, have shifted the theoretical focus from roles to identity, emphasizing the fractious and segmented nature of both the performance demands governing the self and the cultural narratives used in constructing and understanding it (see especially the work of psychologist Kenneth Gergen as well as the work of sociologists Jaber Gubrium and James Holstein). Changes in the structure of society reflect (and partially account for) this theoretical shift. Ralph Turner's (1962) masterful analysis observed that, in premodern and modern societies, the self is expressed in and through a given role performance; it is affirmed as people live up to the institutional expectations for their role. Yet the levels of mass production and consumerism achieved under industrial capitalism increased the possibility as well as the cultural expectations for greater consumption and personal expression through it. According to Turner—and more recently, postmodern theories of the self—greater levels of consumption are accompanied by a cultural shift in the locus of self from institutionally based roles to its expression in impulse. New cultural movements such as the self-help movement provide increasing attention on the self, creating narratives and vocabularies that glorify it in a culture of narcissism. The focus on the expression of the self as identity, as a cultural and social object, and on the signifiers that accompany it now characterizes much of the contemporary theoretical work being done in the area of role theory.

— Daniel D. Martin and Janelle L. Wilson

See also Dramaturgy; Gender; Identity; Mead, George Herbert; Parsons, Talcott

FURTHER READINGS AND REFERENCES

Berger, Peter L. 1963. *Invitation to Sociology.* Garden City, NY: Anchor.

Biddle, Bruce J. 1986. "Recent Developments in Role Theory." *Annual Review of Sociology* 12:67–92.

———. 2000. "Role Theory." Pp. 2415–20 in *Encyclopedia of Sociology.* 2d ed. Vol. 4, edited by Edgar F. Borgatta and Rhonda J. V. Montgomery. New York: Macmillan Reference.

Coltrane, Scott. 1998. *Gender and Families.* Thousand Oaks, CA: Pine Forge.

Ferrante, Joan. 2000. *Sociology: A Global Perspective.* Belmont, CA: Wadsworth.

Fine, Gary Alan. 1983. *Shared Fantasy: Role-Playing Games as Social Worlds.* Chicago, IL: University of Chicago Press.

Goffman, Erving. 1961. *Encounters: Two Studies in the Sociology of Interaction.* Indianapolis, IN: Bobbs-Merrill.

Granfield, Robert. 1991. "Making It By Faking It: Working-Class Students in an Elite Academic Environment." *Journal of Contemporary Ethnology* 20:331–51.

Martin, Daniel and Gary Alan Fine. 1991. "Satanic Cults, Satanic Play: Is Dungeons & Dragons a Breeding Ground for the Devil?" Pp. 107–26 in *The Satanism Scare,* edited by James T. Richardson, Joel Best, and David Bromley. Chicago IL: Aldine de Gruyter.

Mortimer, Jeylan T., Jon Lorence, and Donald S. Kumka. 1986. *Work, Family and Personality: Transition to Adulthood.* Norwood, NJ: Ablex.

Secord, Paul F. and Carl W. Backman. 1964. *Social Psychology.* New York: McGraw-Hill.

Staples, Brent. 1992. "Black Men and Public Space." Pp. 29–32 in *Life Studies,* edited by David Cavitch. Boston, MA: Bedford Books.

Thomas, Edwin J. and Bruce J. Biddle. 1966. "The Nature and History of Role Theory." Pp. 3–19 in *Role Theory: Concepts and Research,* edited by Edwin Thomas and Bruce Biddle. New York: John Wiley.

Turner, Ralph H. 1962. "Role Taking: Process versus Conformity." Pp. 20–40 in *Human Behavior and Social Processes,* edited by Arnold M. Rose. Boston, MA: Houghton Mifflin.

Zimmer, Lyn. 1987. "How Women Shape the Prison Guard Role." *Gender & Society* 1:415–31.

RORTY, RICHARD

Rorty, Richard (b. 1931), American pragmatist and self-described bourgeois, liberal ironist, established himself as philosophy's "anti-philosopher" in his 1979 book *Philosophy and the Mirror of Nature.* In this work, Rorty critiques the epistemological and metaphysical foundations of modern philosophy and, in particular, rejects the belief of knowledge as representation. According to Rorty, we should be critical of epistemology because it is the equivalent of foundationalism and suspicious of metaphysics because it amounts to essentialism. There is no universal truth for Rorty, and we should be weary of any discipline, especially philosophy, that attempts to provide a theory of knowledge to ground science, art, politics, or morality. Thus, Rorty's pragmatism is informed by an antirepresentationalism, antifoundationalism, and anti-essentialism, which is captured in all his work from the *Philosophy and the Mirror of Nature* (1979), through his *Philosophical Papers,* volumes one (1991), two (1991), and three (1998), to *Contingency, Irony, and Solidarity* (1989).

Rorty is not alone in his rejection of knowledge as representation, and in *Philosophy and the Mirror of Nature,* he discusses who he feels are the three most important philosophers—Ludwig Wittgenstein, Martin Heidegger, and James Dewey—that also realized that the mind was not merely a mirror of nature. Wittgenstein, Heidegger, and Dewey recognized that language is contingent. Thus, the vocabulary employed by philosophers during the Enlightenment is specific to their own time and place, and we therefore need to invent a new vocabulary to describe our own historical experiences. This is another critical theme that informs much of Rorty's writings as he hopes that hermeneutics, especially conversation, will provide the space for social justification and, possibly, agreement. In particular, Rorty is indebted to Wittgenstein for understanding language as a tool, not a mirror; to Heidegger for the historicist notion that there is no knowing subject that is the source of truth; and especially to Dewey for conceiving of knowledge as social practice. Rorty describes Wittgenstein, Heidegger, and Dewey as "edifying" philosophers who engaged in "abnormal discourse" and were "reactive" and "destructive" rather than "systematic." Their philosophies offer parodies instead of arguments and aim at "continuing a conversation rather than discovering a truth." This is critical, for Rorty himself provides what could be characterized as an edifying philosophy, which hopes to disrupt the reader into questioning his or her taken-for-granted attitudes and through this practice of questioning become new human beings.

Rorty perhaps best articulates what he means by pragmatism in an essay from *Consequences of Pragmatism* (1982) titled "Pragmatism, Relativism, and Irrationalism." Rorty describes three characteristics of pragmatism, including its anti-essentialist understanding of truth, language, and knowledge; its rejection of the distinction between morality and science; and its belief in contingency. This last point, according to Rorty, is the most important because it means that no constraints exist in our attempts to understand the social world and ourselves except those we encounter with our conversational partners. However, conversational constraints, Rorty informs us, cannot be anticipated. Therefore, we are never precisely certain when we have reached the truth, or even if in conversation we have come closer to the truth. Instead, we have to accept the contingent nature of conversation as having no beginning and no end and that success in conversation means continuing to converse. Although Rorty's notion of conversation sounds similar to Jürgen Habermas's ideal speech situation, Rorty reminds us that Habermas qualifies his conversation as one that is "undistorted." According to Rorty, Habermas treads into a transcendental realm by delineating principles of what constitutes undistorted conversation. For Rorty, these principles will not do because as a pragmatist he believes only those engaged in conversation have the capacity to agree on what *undistorted* means according to their own criteria. Rorty admits that this understanding of conversation is ethnocentric but believes that we can attempt to justify our beliefs only to those who already share them.

Rorty, true to spirit of the early American pragmatists, is optimistic about the prospects for human solidarity and the possibility of what he calls a liberal utopia. However, as he discusses in *Contingency, Irony, and Solidarity* (1989), the only way to achieve this utopia is to relinquish the modern quest of uniting the public and the private. For Rorty, there exists an irreconcilable tension between an individual's public struggle for social justice and private project of self-creation. Therefore, to live in a just and free society, we need to allow individuals to realize their aesthetic projects of self-creation in the private realm as long as these individual efforts do not cause harm to others. This is the goal of what Rorty calls the "liberal ironist." Liberals are those individuals who believe that inflicting harm or cruelty on others is the most base thing we can do, while ironists are those who understand the contingency of their beliefs and desires. Liberal ironists, according to Rorty, realize that human solidarity is a goal to be achieved through imagination, not inquiry, because it is only through imagination that we can feel the pain of others. Rorty hopes that if we increase our sensitivity to the pain of others, then it will be more difficult for us to marginalize them and we will, indeed, begin to see them as fellow sufferers.

— Wendy A. Wiedenhoft

See also Democracy; Habermas, Jürgen; Pragmatism; Taylor, Charles

FURTHER READINGS AND REFERENCES

Rorty, Richard. 1991. *Objectivity, Relativism, and Truth: Philosophical Papers.* Vol. 1. Cambridge, UK: Cambridge University Press.

———. 1991. *Essays on Heidegger and Others: Philosophical Papers.* Vol. 2. Cambridge, UK: Cambridge University Press.

———. 1998. *Truth and Progress: Philosophical Papers.* Vol. 3. Cambridge, UK: Cambridge University Press.

———. 1998. *Achieving Our Country: Leftist Thought in Twentieth-Century America.* Cambridge, MA: Harvard University Press.

ROUSSEAU, JEAN-JACQUES

Jean-Jacques Rousseau (1712–1778) was born of parents of modest means in 1712 in Geneva, a city that he quit as an adolescent but to which he would occasionally return, both physically and spiritually. He led a rather picaresque early life, working variously as a servant, private tutor, music copyist, and ambassador's secretary, eventually making his way to Paris, where he consorted with the *philosophes*. In 1749, while walking to Vincennes, he had an "illumination" that was to result in the *Discourse on the Arts and Sciences* and subsequent notoriety. A steady stream of writings extended his fame across Europe, although the controversial nature of these writings meant that he was often on the move, a tendency exacerbated by increasing signs of paranoia as he advanced in age. He died in 1778 in his final refuge in Ermenonville. At the height of the French Revolution, his remains were transferred to the Panthéon, only to be removed and scattered with the Bourbon Restoration.

Jean-Jacques Rousseau is an enigma. He has been variously described as a figure of the Enlightenment and as its critic, as an individualist and a collectivist, a democrat and a totalitarian, the founding figure of the modern cult of the inner life, and the posthumous "author" of the French Revolution. Such very different judgments stem in part from the diversity of his writings, which can be grouped into the following categories: historical anthropology (*Discourse on the Origin of Inequality, Essay on the Origin of Languages*), political theory (*The Social Contract, Discourse on Political Economy*) and political practice (*The Government of Poland, Constitutional Project for Corsica*), education (*Emile*), the arts (*Discourse on the Arts and Sciences, Letter to M. Alembert on the Theatre*), fiction (*Julie or La Nouvelle Hélöise*), autobiography, introspection, and self-justification (*The Confessions, Reveries of the Solitary Walker, Rousseau Judge of Jean-Jacques*), not to mention his writings on botany and music (or his musical and operatic compositions). But such very different judgments also stem from the fact that the same works have been subjected to the most contradictory interpretations. Rousseau's writings are infinitely rich and complex, subject to considerable internal tensions.

If one adopts the perspective of a specifically social theory, one might begin by noting that the widespread use of the term *social* in the nineteenth century owed much to the fame of *The Social Contract*. This work, however, is decidedly more a work of political than social theory. The society of the social contract is an exclusively political society: For it is formed by a political act, held together by a political will, and ordered relative to political ends. Moreover, the members of this society must present themselves exclusively as citizens, not as social actors. And yet Rousseau radicalizes the premises of contract theory to the point where the political constitution of society begins to implode. It is at this point of implosion that Rousseau can be read, retrospectively, as a social theorist.

The social contract forms, and is formed by, the general will, which in turn establishes the general laws that constitute the collective order and constitute it as a just order. This contract is established both between individuals (as a decision to live together under the same laws) and within each individual (as a decision to live according to the law). With the contract, all citizens agree to alienate their entire "natural" liberty to the collective body, and they acquire in return, through their participation in that body, a properly social or, better, political liberty. This latter liberty implies not just a principle of collective self-determination as given by the general will, but a principle of individual self-determination: For once one has left the presocial state and become self-conscious, one will want to be free to determine one's own law (as well as the general law). The two laws, individual and collective, coincide in principle. Otherwise individuals would not agree to the terms of the contract, even as there could be no individual law without the "social" state formed by the contract. The fact that the general will is to be truly general, deriving from and applying to everyone equally, determines its three principal characteristics: its inalienability, indivisibility, and infallibility. It is inalienable in that it cannot be transferred to a less general will, as in the case of its representation. It is indivisible, insofar as it cannot be general if divided against itself. And it is infallible in that its generality guarantees its rightness (the empirical will of all, should it fail to present the general interest, would not be truly general if everyone knew what that interest was). These claims must be understood as having an axiomatic nature, as belonging to the social contract's definitional logic. As the contract and the will formed by the contract are, by reason of their generality, entirely abstract, it is not immediately clear what their relation is to empirical reality and its particulars.

This definitional logic implies at least two radical innovations relative to the tradition of contract theory exemplified by Hobbes and Locke. First, it pushes contract theory in a radically democratic direction. Being inalienable, the sovereign general will belongs to everyone at all times, not just at its origins. (Although one must be careful to understand in what sense Rousseau's contract is democratic. The general will refers to political society, not to government; the former establishes the general laws, while the latter, composed exclusively of the executive and judicial functions, is limited to particular decrees. Political society, then, is necessarily and directly democratic, but government—understood as a delegation of power and not as a representation of the sovereign will—can be monarchic, aristocratic, or democratic.) Second, the distinction between nature and culture is radicalized so as to emphasize the mutability of the human condition. In the state of nature protohumans are without language, morality, self-consciousness, or consistent relations with others, while their desires are restricted to needs that can be satisfied without toil. Consequently, even though nature's impulse can never be entirely extinguished, social existence entails a radical historicity. Note that even as the social contract marks the transition from the state of nature, its preconditions (e.g., language, morality, and reason) can emerge only after the transition's completion. Moreover, in *The Discourse on Inequality*, Rousseau claims that the self-sufficient, harmonious character of the state of nature could only have been disrupted by a catastrophic accident that introduces traits—notably the egoism of *amour propre* and the division of property—that undermine the contract's ethical content. All this only renders the question of the social contract's status relative to empirical reality all the more problematic.

Rousseau is quite aware that the definitional axioms of the social contract cannot but appear as absurd paradoxes. He constantly speaks of the obstacles to the contract's realization, and sometimes he speaks of them as insuperable. What then is the status of the social contract? Some have interpreted it as a utopia, the most perfect society, the end product of the species' perfectibility, where all the tensions between the individual and collective, nature and culture, reason and passion, virtue and happiness, have been overcome. Others have seen the society of the contract less as a utopia than as a second-best solution to civilization's discontents, an alienated response to an alienated world. Thus, they note that, while the general will seeks to limit *amour propre,* social inequalities, and private property, it cannot eliminate them. Still others would understand the social contract as an ideal form in Plato's sense, one that necessarily underlies all collective life, but whose empirical manifestation is always, to one degree or another, corrupt. All the interpretations pose a disjunction between the ideal collectivity constituted by the contract and all real collectivities. It is relative to this disjunction or, more precisely, to the subsequent instability, that one can speak of the implosion of the idea of society's specifically political constitution. And it is in relation to this implosion, which here takes on a heightened, almost self-conscious character, that one can speak of the social dimension in Rousseau's thought. This dimension allows of several possible approaches.

The first would be to read Rousseau's social theory, as drawn largely from his historical anthropology, against the political theory of the contract, treating the former as pointing to the obstacles to the latter's realization. Here, the social dimension of his thought would consist of his critique of the division of labor, private property, the power differentials in the political and judicial structures, and the growth of the egoistic passions. These themes could be woven into a narrative of humanity's fall from a state of natural grace and the betrayal of the social state's promise. In short, Rousseau as a social theorist would be identical to Rousseau as a critic of bourgeois society.

A second strategy would draw attention to what might be called the social supplement necessary to realize the political "solution." Rousseau often appears to claim that it is extremely difficult, even impossible, to realize the social contract politically—that is, by the development of a consensus based on reason. Whether because of ignorance or immorality, little is to be expected from really existing public opinion. The people require "guidance," and this guidance will be all the more effective if it employs methods that "trick" the general will's claim to encompass the participation of all in full consciousness. One can point to the figure of the legislator as a sort of extra-political *deus ex machina,* who breaks through the circle of civilizational alienation while adapting contractual principles to local circumstances. And one can describe all the infrapolitical instruments that the legislator employs to inscribe the contract's clauses in the citizens' hearts, if not their minds. The social dimension of Rousseau's theory, then, would speak to his discussion of identity formation, civil religion, the patriotic rites and ceremonies of emulation, and more generally, all the half-submerged institutional and civilizational mechanisms that seem to underpin every conscious, volitional consensus. Such a discussion would open onto larger ethical questions concerning a pedagogy of freedom where, unbeknownst to oneself, one is made to be free. The *Émile* provides particularly rich resources in this regard.

A third and final approach would read the social theory into the tensions, if not the seeming impossibility of a purely political "solution." If the social contract appears in the form of an exchange, it can never be upheld solely on the basis of a purely rational calculation. As a moral relation, the social bond is underwritten by the sentiment of virtue. And virtue is the expression of both the individual's absolute moral autonomy and his or her desire to submit to (as well as the duty to uphold) the general law of the community. This double character of virtue follows from the definitional axiomatics of the social contract. And yet if the definition appears clear, Rousseau's work vents the very real tensions that such a doubled sentiment implies. Sometimes virtue appears in the purely individual terms of an authenticity of feelings rooted in an inner nature (the phylogenetic equivalent of the ontogenetic state of nature). But the love of self (*amour de soi*) and sense of pity characteristic of the natural state barely imply a relation with others, let alone a moral or ethical relation. In other words, virtue here appears fundamentally asocial. At other times, virtue appears in the most austere terms of social heteronomy, demanding the sacrifice of one's desires, happiness, and even children in the name of patriotism. One suspects that, given these two virtues, the conflict between individual and community cannot but exist even in the best of societies. And this conflict between the individual and collectivity is repeated within the individual who is torn between his or her asocial nature, social passions, and political obligations. It is as though, once individuals become aware of themselves in relation to others, they develop the social passions of an *amour propre* (as borne by imaginary fears, dreams of omnipotence, and desires for domination) that resist the demands of both inner conscience and external duty. Social theory here, then, would insinuate itself between the natural individual and the political whole, and speak to the impossibility of living entirely comfortably within either.

Not only have the *Émile* and *The Nouvelle Héloïse* been seen as illustrating the tensions between nature and culture, conscience and public opinion, individual desire and communal imperatives with exceptional psychological acuity, both books have been variously interpreted as providing, relative to these conflicts, a genuine resolution, a "magical" resolution, and the (unconscious or conscious) demonstration of the impossibility of any resolution. But however one interprets these works, what is certain is that in Rousseau's personal life, these conflicts were never resolved. Instead, within the darkness of a developing paranoia, he retreated from a seemingly hostile world into a solitude from which he could proclaim an inner goodness that only a virtuous posterity would recognize.

— Brian C. J. Singer

See also Bonald, Louis de; Citizenship; Democracy; Individualism; Maistre, Joseph de; Montesquieu, Charles Louis de Secondat; Power; Revolution; State; Utopia

FURTHER READINGS AND REFERENCES

Althusser, Louis. 1972. "Rousseau: The Social Contract (The Discrepancies)." Pp. 111–60 in *Politics and History: Montesquieu, Rousseau, Marx.* Translated by Ben Brewster. London: NLB.

Derathé, Robert. 1950. *Jean-Jacques Rousseau et la science politique de son temps* [Jean-Jacques Rousseau and the Political Science of His Time]. Paris: Presses Universitaires de France.

Durkheim, Émile. 1960. "Rousseau's Social Contract." Pp. 65–138 in *Montesquieu and Rousseau: Forerunners of Sociology.* Ann Arbor, MI: University of Michigan Press.

Horowitz, Asher. 1987. *Rousseau, Nature and History.* Toronto, Canada: University of Toronto Press.

Starobinski, Jean. 1988. *Jean-Jacques Rousseau: Transparency and Obstruction.* Translated by Arthur Goldhammer. Chicago, IL: University of Chicago Press.

Swenson, James. 2000. *On Jean-Jacques Rousseau: Considered as One of the First Authors of the Revolution.* Stanford, CA: Stanford University Press.

RUBIN, GAYLE

Gayle Rubin (b. 1949) has been writing articles that have energized gender studies and feminist theory since the 1960s. Her research is pivotal to studies in queer theory, and her essays continue to be republished, translated, cited, and referenced. While studying at the University of Michigan in the late 1960s, she constructed a major in women's studies by taking advantage of the open-ended honors program. The thesis she worked on for this major later became the often cited essay, "The Traffic in Women:

Notes on the 'Political Economy' of Sex." She earned her PhD in anthropology and continues to teach and write. She is also a longtime activist in gay and lesbian politics.

Rubin's (1975) essay, *Traffic,* examines Levi-Strauss' kinship models and shows how women have been constructed as commodities to be traded and owned by husbands, brothers, and fathers. She extensively analyzes what Adrienne Rich describes with the concept "compulsory heterosexuality." In arguing that "kinship systems do not merely exchange women. They exchange sexual access, genealogical statuses, lineage names and ancestors, rights and people—men, women, and children—in concrete systems of social relationships" (Rubin 1975:177), she makes concrete the economic and political oppressions that women face historically and currently on a daily basis. Furthermore, *Traffic* examines the way that Freudian and Lacanian binary theoretical models support the political institutions and power structures that are born from these oppressive kinship relations. Her purpose here, as well as in much of her work, is to deconstruct how these power inequities and underlying assumptions continue to shape and codify the way we build our social and, thus, sexual selves.

"Thinking Sex: Notes for a Radical Theory of the Politics of Sexuality" (1984) continues to examine how sexuality and sexual identity is constructed. In contrast to her previous work, this essay is more focused on how deviance and difference is constructed and legally maintained. Here, she roots sexual oppression in historical contexts and, in the tradition of Michel Foucault, shows how medical and legal institutions construct and maintain sexual difference for political ends. In particular, this essay is useful for its discussion of the concept of sexual essentialism. Sexual essentialism is the idea that our sexual selves and our experience of sexual difference are innate and biologically determined. Sexual essentialism tends to demonize those who reject the hegemonic model of acceptable sexual practices. Finally, it maps out a sex hierarchy, or what Rubin (1984) refers to as the "charmed circle" and "the outer limits." In this hierarchy, acceptable sexual practices are those that are "heterosexual, married, monogamous, procreative, non-commercial, in pairs, in a relationship, same generation, in private, no pornography, bodies only, vanilla" (p. 13).

Rubin is an advocate for the sexual others who are marginalized and criminalized in our current heterosexist culture. Furthermore, Rubin examines how feminist theory and gay and lesbian activists themselves have contributed to this marginalization in their attack on sadomasochism, pornography, sex professionals, pedophiles, and transsexuals and transgendered persons. Her essay "Of Catamites and Kings" (1992) takes up the oppressive practices that exist within feminism and lesbian feminism when those who self-identify as butch/femme are attacked. Here, she brings voice and agency to those who typically are vilified and in doing so traces the history by which these voices have been silenced. She illustrates how "playing with" dominant categories of sexual identities can actually disrupt the very premises that these identities rely on for their continued legitimation. More generally, she shows that the ongoing attacks from both the dominant culture and the feminist and lesbian communities maintain the oppressive forces that work to constrain all persons.

Rubin has also worked within these communities for voice and change. She is one of the founders of Samois, the first sadomasochist feminist lesbian organization, which published *Coming to Power: Writings and Graphics on Lesbian S/M* (1981). This anthology is particularly pertinent for its combination of activists' and academics' writings on sexuality and power. In this collection, Rubin's essay "The Leather Menace: Comments on Politics and S/M" continues to examine the ways that certain sexual practices are legitimately maintained and prioritized while others are designated as deviant and dangerous. She shows how this practice contributes to larger oppressive practices and that privilege and power are contained in concepts of sexual freedom of speech and the possibilities of consent. In this work, she calls for a politics of sexuality and otherness that allows for sexual diversity. She argues that sexual diversity, as well as all forms of diversity, is crucial to the continuing fight against totalizing tendencies that strain toward homogeneity.

— Marga Ryersbach

See also Feminism; Lévi-Strauss, Claude; Postmodernism; Radical Feminism

FURTHER READINGS AND REFERENCES

Rich, Adrienne. 1986. "Compulsory Heterosexuality and Lesbian Existence (1980)." Pp. 23–75 in *Blood, Bread, and Poetry: Selected Prose, 1979–1985.* New York: Norton.

Rubin, Gayle. 1975. "The Traffic in Women: Notes on the 'Political Economy' of Sex." Pp. 157–210 in *Toward an Anthropology of Women,* edited by Rayna R. Reiter. New York: Monthly Review.

———. 1981. "The Leather Menace: Comments on Politics and S/M." Pp. 194–229 in *Coming to Power: Writings and Graphics on Lesbian S/M,* edited by Samois. 3d ed. Rev. and updated. Boston, MA: Alyson.

———. 1984. "Thinking Sex: Notes for a Radical Theory of the Politics of Sexuality." Pp. 267–319 in *Pleasure and Danger: Exploring Female Sexuality,* edited by Carole S. Vance. Boston: Routledge. Reprinted in *The Lesbian and Gay Studies Reader,* edited by Henry Abelove, Michele Aina Barale, and David M. Halperin (New York: Routledge, 1993).

———. 1992. "Of Catamites and Kings: Reflections on Butch, Gender, and Boundaries." Pp. 466–42 in *The Persistent Desire: A Femme-Butch Reader,* edited by Joan Nestle. Boston, MA: Alyson.

RUDDICK, SARA

Sara Ruddick (b. 1935), an American philosopher and feminist theorist, is best known for theorizing maternal practice, maternal thinking, and feminist maternal peace politics. She wrote the influential article "Maternal Thinking" (1980), where she argues that maternal practice, like the practice of any discipline, has the capacity to produce distinct forms of thought. She developed this idea further in *Maternal Thinking: Toward a Politics of Peace* (1995), arguing that maternal thought is a resource for a feminist politics of peace. In these and other works, Ruddick treats mothers as thinking persons and maternal thought as potentially valuable to community, national, and global relations. In so doing, she debunks traditions in Western thought that elevate abstract reason over anything defined as particularistic, emotional, bodily, or feminine. Educated in the 1950s and 1960s at Vassar, Radcliffe, and Harvard, Ruddick taught philosophy and feminist theory for many years at Eugene Lang College at the New School University in New York City.

Challenges to Western thought's sexist bifurcations pervade Ruddick's first two books, both coedited collections on the place of chosen work in women's lives: *Working It Out: 23 Women Writers, Artists, Scientists, and Scholars Talk about Their Lives and Work* (1977), and *Between Women: Biographers, Novelists, Critics, Teachers, and Artists Write about Their Work on Women* (1984). In autobiographical essays in these books, Ruddick describes her educational and academic experiences as sometimes exhilarating but as alienating her from anything womanly and eventually rendering her unable to write. Her compelling experiences as a mother, the deep pleasure she took in Virginia Woolf's writing, and the support of a feminist community helped her to integrate love and work and to embrace intellectual writing. This integration is apparent throughout her work.

In *Maternal Thinking* and more recent work, including articles on fatherhood, Ruddick articulates the gendered character of mothering and of caring work in general. She resists biological determinism, insisting that men are as capable as women of caring for children and developing maternal thought. Nonetheless, she rejects gender-neutral terms such as *parenting*. While she recognizes the risks of acknowledging sexual difference, she argues that denying the gendered character of care work holds more serious dangers. Ruddick also theorizes giving birth as at once different from and connected to mothering. She proposes that the experience of pregnancy and birth may give rise to *natal reflection*, characterized by active waiting, chosen pain, and a distinct conception of self and other.

Since *Maternal Thinking*, Ruddick has been concerned with the complexities of an ethics of care. In "Care as Labor and Relationship" (1998), she argues that care must be theorized not only as work, which was her focus in *Maternal Thinking* and which tends to overemphasize its burdens, but also as relationship, which emphasizes the wide range of emotions that caregivers and care recipients feel. The complexities of an ethics of care, and its relationship to an ethics of justice, also show up in Ruddick's articles on adolescent motherhood and assault and domination in families. She tackles these issues again in *Mother Troubles* (1999), which addresses the scapegoating of "bad" mothers and mothers' responsibility for the harm they sometimes inflict on children.

Ruddick's recent writing on peace politics also demonstrates the complexities inherent in theorizing urgent social problems. In " 'Woman of Peace' " (1998), she suggests that contemporary global relations compel peace feminists to consider whether violence is sometimes necessary. She acknowledges that feminists disagree because of their radically different locations and vulnerabilities in relation to threats of violence. She articulates rather than resolves conflicts within peace feminism, conflicts created by tensions among identities that have inspired peace feminists in the past (mourning mother, outsider, peacemaker). Most recently, Ruddick (2003) has formulated the particular evil embodied in the September 11, 2001, attacks, connecting it to and distinguishing it from other historical and contemporary forms of terror.

— Susan E. Chase

See also Feminist Epistemology; Feminist Ethics; Maternal Thinking

FURTHER READINGS AND REFERENCES

Hanigsberg, Julia E. and Sara Ruddick. 1999. *Mother Troubles: Rethinking Contemporary Maternal Dilemmas.* Boston, MA: Beacon.

Ruddick, Sara. 1980. "Maternal Thinking." *Feminist Studies* 6:342–67.

———. 1995. *Maternal Thinking: Toward a Politics of Peace,* 2nd ed. Boston, MA: Beacon.

———. 1998. "Care as Labor and Relationship." Pp. 3–25 in *Norms and Values: Essays on the Work of Virginia Held,* edited by J. G. Haber and M. S. Halfon. Lanham, MD: Rowman & Littlefield.

———. 1998. "'Woman of Peace': A Feminist Construction." Pp. 213–26 in *The Women and War Reader,* edited by L. A. Lorentzen and J. Turpin. New York: New York University Press.

———. 2003. "The Moral Horror of the September Attacks." *Hypatia* 11:212–22.

S

SACRED AND PROFANE

The sociological concepts of the sacred and the profane have their main roots in the theories of Émile Durkheim. The source of modern religion was one of the most important questions for Durkheim. However, a modern world that was highly secularized and characterized by competing ideologies made this a very difficult issue with which to deal. To overcome these difficulties, Durkheim studied primitive societies and the sources of religion within them. Given his core methodological orientation that only one social fact can cause another social fact, Durkheim reached the conclusion that primitive religion (and hence modern religion) was created by society itself. Society (through individuals) is able to create religion by differentiating between what is considered sacred, those things set apart from everyday life and deemed forbidden, and what is considered profane, or basically everything not so defined (the mundane, utilitarian). Those things that are profane, however, can be transformed into that which is sacred if they come to be viewed with an attitude of respect, reverence, mystery, and a general awe—in other words, if they come to be associated with the same attitudes as those linked to that which is sacred.

According to Durkheim, the differentiation between the sacred and the profane is the basis for the development of religion. Other conditions—beliefs, religious rites, and a church—are also necessary; however, the true essence of religion is found in what society deems sacred. Therefore, an extension of this argument would imply that what is sacred (the church, religious symbols, and even God) and what is society are one and the same. This view contributed to Durkheim's opposition to any form of social revolution and to his efforts to promote social reforms that would improve the functioning of society.

Durkheim believed that religion and God come from some superior moral power but that could not be a supernatural power. Rather, it is society that is the superior power at the base of these phenomena. Society is a power greater than we are that transcends us and makes demands on us. One of the ways that society exercises power over us is through its representations, and God and religion are such representations. Thus, to Durkheim, God is nothing more than society transfigured and expressed symbolically.

— Michael Ryan

See also Bataille, Georges; Collège de Sociologie and Acéphale; Durkheim, Émile; Religion; Religion in French Social Theory; Social Facts

FURTHER READINGS AND REFERENCES

Durkheim, Émile. [1912] 1965. *The Elementary Forms of Religious Life.* New York: Dutton.

SAINT-SIMON, CLAUDE-HENRI DE

Among the social theorists exerting influence since the early nineteenth century, Claude-Henri Comte de Saint-Simon (1760–1825) remains prominent. He was the first to forecast our modern industrial societies. He provided guidance and insight for both the social sciences and the practice of politics and economics. He therefore became not only a "founding father of sociology" and an early advocate of socialism, but he also enriched technocratic thinking and "managerial philosophies." He also advocated European unification.

As a French officer, Saint-Simon fought in the American independence war: a "crucial experience" for him. After returning to France, he also appreciated the great revolution, even though he was imprisoned for several months. Speculations made him a rich man, but he soon became impoverished due to wasteful spending and sponsorship. He enlarged his knowledge as an autodidact and lived in numerous social settings, including proletarian neighbourhoods. In 1815, he worked as librarian at the Paris "Arsenal" collections. Later, he lived as a publicist, supported by private sponsors, and finally rallied a close group of pupils.

Saint-Simon's numerous papers—composed between 1802 and 1825—form a confusing conglomerate. They mostly lacked the formal scientific standard, but they provided new findings and insights.

Saint-Simon was a son of the Enlightenment and the revolution, opponent of the antiquated "Ancien Régime," a progress optimist, and a friend of the working class. His works centered on the following central ideas. First, Saint-Simon advocated a *unity of the sciences*. He argued that all sciences should emanate and operate from the deductions of history and observation. Especially the new social sciences ("Science Politique") must apply scientific procedures. This is vital for the future of mankind and peace.

Second, in his understanding of social development and progress, Saint-Simon contributed his own model to the theories that schematize the social history of humanity. His developmental scheme—which Auguste Comte largely adopted—distinguishes three stages: (1) a "theological" stage that includes fetishism, polytheism, and monotheism; (2) a "negative" stage that includes metaphysics, religious criticism, and the elimination of obsolete social models and ideas; and (3) a final "positive" stage in which the senses are controlled through scientific knowledge. Furthermore, he argued that in social history, "organic" periods alternate with periods of "crises" that prepare the movement to higher stages. The crises are based on the tremendous inadequacy of previous social systems and often result in revolutions.

A third important idea contributed by Saint-Simon is that social analysis requires a clear distinction between the elements of productive work and parasitic factors. It is important to apply the related findings to social strata, classes, and occupational functions. Saint-Simon used the image of drones and bees. The distinction was effectively expressed in his utopian masterpiece, the so-called Parable (*L'Organisateur*, 1819), wherein he compares the loss of thousands of excellent performers in all sectors with the one of needless dignitaries and idle parasites. The first case would present a disaster for prosperity; the second would be irrelevant.

Saint-Simon identified productive work with industrial work: An industrial man works to produce goods or to provide the society with means for the satisfaction of needs and wants. This definition of industry includes all kinds of mental or physical productive work, regardless of the sector, the sciences as well as literature and arts included.

Fourth, even though Saint-Simon offered utopian visions of society, his was not an egalitarian utopianism. In arguing that "Not everyone can be in the lead" (*L'Industrie*, 1817),

he suggested that some people in a society occupy elite positions. This applies not only to social development but also within the individual social structures. The importance lies in the special significance of particular social functions. In certain societies, the leading role of warriors and priests was just as ordinary and important as the top functions of economic leaders, scientists, and engineers in modern societies. Those performances and activities required by a society shall be rewarded with both material remunerations and social appreciation. With regard to political governments ("a necessary evil to fight the worst threat: anarchy"), Saint-Simon had various utopian visions.

Finally, for Saint-Simon a modern industrial society is a kind of an *extensive fabricating organization*, to which everybody has to contribute. He argued that it was necessary to acquire the support of the "poorest class with the highest number of members," especially the emerging working class proletariat. The entire society has need of solidarity that can be ensured only by general and effective moral conceptions. In this regard, Saint-Simon focuses on a renewed Christianity. His last, unfinished writing "Nouveau Christianisme" (1825) was a contribution to this end.

Saint-Simon's conceptions were mainly disseminated by his pupils. Auguste Comte, who assisted the master from 1817 to 1824, extensively worked out the main ideas of his teacher and gave them a scientifically readable structure. He had first idolized Saint-Simon, then—after the breach in 1824—totally ignored him. But questions of priority are secondary; Comte retains his own rank.

The school, editorial community, and bizarre sect of the so-called Saint-Simonians (the most famous sect leaders included Saint-Amand Bazard and Barthélemi-Prosper Enfantin) had the same significance for the distribution of Saint-Simon's ideas. These ideas contributed to the articulation of an early socialism. Saint-Simon had never disliked private property, as long as it remained productive. However, in the eighteenth and nineteenth centuries, private property—and therewith the hereditary right to private property—was considered a problem, which some Saint-Simonians wanted to abolish. These Saint-Simonians also discussed women's rights and the problems of civil marriage. The writings and magazines of the Saint-Simonians (most notably the *Globe*) impressed Europe, but in this, Saint-Simon's name was sometimes misused to advocate extreme social postulates and pseudoreligious sect activities. The so-called doctrine of Saint-Simon, which the above circle disseminated, is often mistaken for his own works.

Outside of France, Saint-Simon's influence can mainly be seen in Germany and England. Marx and Engels referred to Saint-Simon, especially with regard to the terms *class* and *class conflict*, which they radicalized. John Stuart Mill also refers to him, and Herbert Spencer's work reflects some of his ideas. Practically, Saint-Simon's ideas have affected fields as diverse as railroad construction, banking (credit business), and corporate philosophies.

— Richard Martinus Emge

See also Comte, Auguste; Industrial Society; Socialism

REFERENCES AND FURTHER READING

Emge, Richard Martinus. 1987. *Saint-Simon.* Munich, Germany: Oldenbourg.

Manuel, Frank E. 1963. *The New World of Henri Saint-Simon.* 2d ed. Notre Dame, IN: University of Notre Dame Press.

Saint-Simon, Claude Henri de. 1966. *Œuvres* [Collected Works]. Paris: Anthropos.

Taylor, K., ed. 1975. *Henri Saint-Simon (1760–1825): Selected Writings.* New York: Holmes & Meier.

SARTRE, JEAN-PAUL

Jean-Paul Sartre (1905–1980) was a French existentialist; a Marxist philosopher, dramatist, and novelist; and a major political figure on the French Left during the 1950s and 1960s. His chief works of relevance for social theory include *L'ego et la Transcendance* (The Ego and Transcendence, 1937), *l'Être et le Néant* (*Being and Nothingness*, 1943), "l'Existentialisme est un humanisme" ("Existentialism and Humanism," 1946), and *Critique de la Raison Dialectique* (Critique of Dialectical Reason—Vol. 1, 1960; Vol. 2, 1985). He was also the founder-editor of the journal *Temps Modernes.* His most important philosophical influences were French Hegelianism and the phenomenology of Husserl and Heidegger.

Sartre's existentialism, which he developed over the first part of his life, achieved a wide popularity, especially through his novels (*La Nausée* [Nausea], 1938), and *l'Age de la Raison* (The Age of Reason, 1945), and plays (*les Mouches* [The Flies], 1943; *Huis Clos* [No Exit], 1944). It was underpinned, at the same time, by a complex philosophy that he continually developed. Very different philosophers can be lumped together under the label "existentialist," and about the only thing they have in common is summed up in the slogan "existence precedes essence," the direct opposite of Descartes' "I think, therefore I am." We cannot assume anything about the nature of human beings; there is no a priori essence or human nature from which we can derive an understanding of human thought and action.

Sartre's early work is concerned with developing an ontology, a philosophy of Being. What is Being? And what sort of Being exists in the world? In keeping with Heidegger's (1962) *Being and Time.* Being—a subjectless verb—is to be distinguished from beings, or particular entities, and is to be studied through the rigorous inspection of human consciousness. Sartre developed a critique, however, of Husserl and his pupil, Heidegger, that led him to posit a radical freedom and a radical individualism. For Husserl, consciousness *constituted* its object, just as, for modern social constructionists, language or discourse constitutes its objects. Sartre argued that if this was the case, then consciousness could only ever be conscious of itself. Yet consciousness is always consciousness *of* something, a relation to something else. This something else must transcend the individual ego. He argued that consciousness was a "Nothingness," a hole in the solidity of Being. Consciousness (the "for-itself") is only a relationship to Being (the "in-itself"); most important, Being cannot determine consciousness—there is nothing between the two, no channel through which Being can seep into consciousness, no causal mechanism by means of which it can determine actions and thoughts. Consciousness itself is negation. If I look around my study and think that I would like to change it in some way, I am negating what is there and positing something different in a free act that is not determined by anything operating on my consciousness. This ability to negate is my freedom. There is a sense in which my freedom is an unbearable burden and I seek to lose it in my relationship with Being. My consciousness and freedom are always in relation to a situation. I have no choice but to choose a relation to the situation in which I find myself. I am condemned to be free. Even if I am hung upside down and left to die, I must adopt a relationship to the situation of my death. This choice is not something I think about or decide on; it does not happen at a cognitive level, but at a prereflective level. Consciousness is split. The prereflective is seen by Sartre as a flight toward Being, a solidity that can never be achieved, and the relationship between the reflective and prereflective is like that between two mirrors, constantly reflecting each other. Consciousness has no content; there is no unconscious, and it relates to everything, including the ego, the self, and language, as external objects.

There is, however, another form of Being in Sartre's ontology. In addition to Being-for-itself and Being-in-itself, there is Being-for-others. For myself, my future is always open; I am able to make choices. In the eyes of others, I am a physical object. What for me are possibilities in my life are for them probabilities; I experience my body as something that I live and that can be an object for me but that is not me. Others see my body as me, and in this exterior reduction of me to my body is the source of shame through which I experience the Other. We have three fundamental reactions to the Other, each of which fails. The first is love: I want to be a privileged object for the Other, and I must seduce the other but he or she must give love freely; this is one contradiction. If I win the other's love, then he or she becomes a privileged object for me, and I am thrown back onto my own subjectivity, which I was trying to escape. This is a second contradiction, and the two together lead to a breakdown in love. My second possible attitude to the Other is indifference. I refuse to recognise his or Being-for-itself as a transcendent power, although I am haunted by it and by my fear of it. Sartre sees sexual desire as an attempt to capture the consciousness of the other and subdue it, but immediately after the sex act, I become aware again of the Other's transcendence. Finally, I am left with hatred; I can destroy the other, but I cannot destroy the fact that he or she has existed and seen me as an object and that he or she has seen my shame. Thus, all relationships fail; we cannot avoid experiencing ourselves as shameful objects for other people: In the words of a character in *Huis Clos* (No Exit), "Hell is other people."

Sartre's concept of radical freedom also implies an ethics of responsibility. If choice is inescapable, one must take responsibility for one's prereflective choices. This is perhaps best understood through its opposite—"bad faith." Bad faith involves the denial of choice, in the sense of denying to myself that I am doing something—allowing myself to be seduced, choosing to be a bad lover, denying my responsibility for my relationship to Being and the Being of the Other.

In addition to his philosophical contributions, Sartre's work also has relevance for social theory. This is at first sight paradoxical, since his existentialism was deeply opposed to social ontologising, particularly of the kind associated with classical French sociology. (In *The Watchdogs,* Sartre's friend Paul Nizan gives a good picture of the "New Sorbonne," dominated by the moralistic spirit of Durkheim and neo-Kantianism, against which radical students in the 1920s were rebelling.) Yet Sartre's relation to social theory is not just that of a challenging critic. His thought adds a dimension, by identifying a level of experience that we cannot see from the outside. The social theorist—at least, of the kind that strives for scientific objectivity—is always the Other, turning the people who are studied into objects, perhaps shameful objects. Not only may such theory be unable to grasp the immediate experience of those we study, it may not even recognise that our objects have such immediate experiences.

Especially important, however, for social theory is the line of thinking that begins with Sartre's early discussion of the "situation" and the "project," ideas that were to be developed in his later work into a sophisticated theory of action and social action. At first, as elaborated in *Being and Nothingness,* these notions were used to describe the exercise of our individual freedom. I am born into the world, and I find myself in a situation that I have not chosen; I have to choose what I do about this—I cannot not choose—I have to negate this situation and posit something else, choosing from what the situation offers me. I cannot choose *ex nihilo;* sometimes, the situation offers me very limited choices but I nonetheless have to choose. But after and as a result of the Second World War, Sartre became more concerned with real situations in which people had to make real choices rather than with the ontological foundations of choice. This shift in focus is reflected in the two volumes of *The Critique of Dialectical Reason.*

Sartre was a prolific writer, and it is impossible to deal with the details of his development in a short article. The most important influences that led to his development of an elaborate social philosophy and theory were political. From 1940 to 1941, he was imprisoned in a German prisoner of war camp, escaped, and then attempted to set up a resistance group when he returned to Paris. After the war, he tried with others to set up a left-wing political party (*Rassemblement Démocratique Révolutionnaire*), which would provide an alternative to the Communist Party and the American-backed Right. In the 1950s, he became involved in the movement against the repressive, anti-independentist, French policy in Algeria. Over this time, he became a prominent public figure, a role in France often occupied by philosophers. He also broke with Albert Camus, another prominent French existentialist, over the question of political engagement. He was clearly on the radical Left and found himself sometimes very close to the Communist Party, not because of any Stalinist sympathies but because of his detestation for what he saw as the political and moral bankruptcy of the anticommunists. For the rest of his life, he maintained this radical allegiance. He campaigned against the Vietnam War, joined the student revolt in 1968, and then remained active in the far Left. When he died, tens of thousands of people attended his funeral.

Sartre's later philosophy, which attempted to combine Marxism with an existentialist standpoint, was addressed, however, not only to the question of freedom and political choice in the face of capitalist alienation. Like most other socialist intellectuals in Western Europe he was concerned to understand the failures of communism in Eastern Europe as well as the apparent emptiness and rigidity of intellectual life in the communist movement. He kept his concern with the way we might individually and collectively understand and transcend our situation, but he felt he had to come to grips with collective life and social institutions in a way that his earlier philosophy did not allow. This led him to develop a typology of forms of social being, their implications for human freedom, and what was involved in the passage from one to the other. At one end of the scale was the *series,* an inessential group like a bus queue in which each individual was only externally connected to the others. Then came the *group-in-fusion,* in which individuals were transitorily combined for the achievement of some common task, like a hunting party. Next came the *pledge group,* in which each was subordinated to the "we" it constituted and participated in the group subordination of other individuals. At the end of the sequence was the *collective* or true community, in which the condition of the freedom of each was the freedom of all. The problem of freedom in a social context was defined in terms of the dialectic between individual freedom and the *practico-inert,* constituted, as in Marx's account of capital as dead labour weighing on the living, by the institutional sedimentation of past praxis and its constricting effects on present praxis.

As he moves from his earlier to his later work, Sartre struggles to move from the ontological to the ontic, from Being in general, to concrete-historical circumstances, attempting in various ways to overcome the original dualism. His early philosophy was criticised precisely for this dualism, particularly by his political and philosophical (as well as personal) colleague Simone de Beauvoir, who was later to develop a subtle phenomenology of personal and interpersonal perception focused on women as "the other sex." In *Being and Nothingness* Sartre talked briefly about a "We-subject" and "Us-object," but these terms were not sustainable given the ideas that had preceded. When he returned to the problem in the two volumes of *The Critique,* it was clear that he recognised the weight of the earlier criticisms.

His intellectual and political conflicts with the French Communist Party, one of the most Stalinist in Europe, led to a philosophical attempt to provide a philosophical foundation for Marxism not as a body of rigid truths, but as a flexible form of thinking about the world, able to produce new knowledge and understanding and able to act as a practical guide in a politics of collective self-transcendence. His attempts were still in the framework of his original ontology, the in-Itself and the for-Itself, but one modification (in the second volume) was that he talked of them enveloping each other—each providing the limit or boundary for the other. The for-Itself was no longer the complete negation and transcendence of the in-Itself, but neither was the latter a determinant of the former. Even if the world does not force my action, I have tot take notice. Sartre called this position "ontological realism."

However, most of his later work was concerned with History, with a capital "H." It was a philosophy of history, an attempt to understand how history is possible, how it is intelligible as a movement from past to future; in other words, it is concerned with the relative rather than the absolute of ontology. He was also concerned with dialectical thought, sometimes reified as "the" dialectic but taken by Sartre as the basis of open and creative thinking about the world. Dialectical thinking moves to and fro consistently between the part and the whole. It is the process through which all understanding takes place, and the notion of totality is at the centre. To understand the sentence I have just written, I must move from word to the whole sentence and back again. Understanding history involves the same movement, from event to whole. Here, we move back to the original concern with ontology, but Sartre's later argument re-thinks being in the light of "the dialectic," taken to be at once a human product, the form of human thinking, and the structure of human praxis. Generally, in the *Critique of Dialectical Reason* (Vol. 2), praxis replaces the for-Itself. Praxis is best understood as human action in its widest sense, the way in which the for-Itself lives its activities and its situation as a whole. Praxis plays the same role as, but has a wider compass than, labour in the philosophy of the early Marx. Praxis is "totalising." When I act on my situation, I implicitly draw together all its aspects. Even if I only act on one part of it, the whole is changed because the parts are related to each other through the whole.

Sartre's postwar dominance of the French intellectual scene was challenged by structuralists like Lévi-Strauss in the late 1950s and early 1960s and by poststructuralists in the late 60s. Althusser attacked Sartre's rendering of Marxism as a humanism; Derrida criticised his humanist interpretation of the early Heidegger. Sartre has been out of fashion since then, and although recent translations may revive interest, his later work has been little examined.

— Ian Craib and Andrew Wernick

See also Althusser, Louis; Beauvoir, Simone de; Derrida, Jacques; Durkheim, Émile; Lévi-Strauss, Claude

FURTHER READINGS AND REFERENCES

Derrida, J. 1982. "The Ends of Man." Pp. 111–36 in *Margins of Philosophy.* Translated by Alan Bass. Chicago, IL: University of Chicago Press.

Howells, Christina, ed. 1991. *The Cambridge Companion to Sartre.* New York: Cambridge University Press.

Nizan, Paul. 1973. *The Watchdogs.* New York: Monthly Review Press.

Sartre, Jean-Paul. 1957. *Transcendence and the Ego.* New York: Noonday.

———. 1977. *Existentialism and Humanism.* Brooklyn, NY: Haskell House.

———. 1989. *No Exit and Three Other Plays.* New York: Vintage.

———. 1993. *Being and Nothingness.* New York: Washington Square Press.

———. 2001. *Critique of Dialectical Reason,* Vol. 1, *Theory of Practical Ensembles.* New York: Verso.

SAUSSURE, FERDINAND DE

Ferdinand de Saussure was born in Switzerland in 1857. Saussure's scientific precocity was evident at an early age. In either 1872 or 1874, at the age of 15 or 17, he wrote a piece titled "Essai pour Reduire les Mots du Grec, du Latin & de l'Allemand a un Petiti Nombre de Racines" [Essay for Reducing the Words of Greek, Latin, & German to a small

Number of Roots] (see Saussure 1978). From 1876 to 1880, he studied at the University of Lepizig, where he was taught and influenced by leading exponents of the neogrammarian school, such as Curtius, Ostoff, and Brugmann. In 1879, at the age of 21, Saussure published his monograph, the *Mémoire* (see below) while he was a student at the University of Leipzig. During the period 1881 to 1882, Saussure completed his doctoral thesis in the Faculty of Philosophy at the University of Leipzig. His thesis was titled "De l'Emploi du Génitif Absolu en Sanscrite" [On the Use of the Absolute Genitive in Sanskrit]. In 1880, Saussure left Leipzig for Paris, where he taught at the *Ecole des Hautes Etudes* and was involved in the activities of the *Société de Linguistique de Paris*. He remained in Paris until 1891. In that year, he returned to Geneva to take up his appointment as chair professor in general linguistics at the University of Geneva. Saussure remained in Geneva until his death in 1913.

THE RECEPTION OF SAUSSURE IN THE LIGHT OF THE 1916 EDITION OF THE *COURS DE LINGUISTIQUE GÉNÉRALE* (*CLG*)

The reception of Saussure's work has been largely based on the posthumously published edition of the *Cours de Linguistique Générale* (1916) [hereafter *CLG*] that was edited and published by Charles Bally and Albert Sechehaye in collaboration with Albert Riedlinger. Significantly, Riedlinger was the only one of these three individuals who actually attended and made notes on the lectures on general linguistics that Saussure gave between 1907 and 1909 at the University of Geneva. The significance of this fact lies in the way in which so many of the interpretations and assumptions about Saussure's thinking have been based on a text that, thanks to the editorial hands of Bally and Sechehaye, has substantially played down, altered, or omitted important aspects of the lectures, and their organization, that Saussure gave to his students at the University of Geneva. Readers may refer to the reviews of *CLG* by Jules Ronjat (1916), André Oltramare (1916), and J. Wackernagel (1922) for a sense of the early reception of the 1916 edition.

Moreover, a substantial body of previously unpublished notes and manuscripts by Saussure on diverse areas of research that occupied him at various stages throughout his career, as well as new editions of the *CLG*, based on the notes of the students who attended the lectures, have helped to shed light on a much richer, more complex, more diverse, and more dynamic thinker than the posthumous version of the *CLG* that was bequeathed to posterity by Bally and Sechehaye in 1916.

In the following sections, Saussure's work will be examined in terms of a number of different thematic areas that representing the major areas in the development of his thinking about language, seen as a semiological system of signs.

THE MÉMOIRE SUR LE SYSTÈME PRIMITIF DES VOYELLES DANS LES LANGUES INDOEUROPÉENNES

Saussure's *Mémoire sur le Système Primitif des Voyelles dans les Langues Indoeuropéennes* [Memory on the Primitive System of the Vowels in the Indo-European Languages] (1879) is the only monograph that Saussure published during his lifetime. In some respects, it is a further development of his 1877 article "Essai D'une Distinction des Différentes *a* Indoeuropéens" [Essay Concerning a Distinction of the Different Indo-European *a*]. In that article, Saussure assigned the *e* vowel to both Indo-European and to the prehistorical phase of Sanskrit on the basis of a number of negative observations concerning the correspondences between the vowels *a* and *o* in the Western European languages and the vowels *i* and *u* in Indo-Iranian (see "'Sistema' e 'fonema' nel primo Saussure" [System and Phoneme in the Early Saussure], Vincenzi 1976:232).

Saussure wrote his *Mémoire* during the period 1877 to 1878 at the age of 20 to 21, while he was studying at the University of Leipzig. The use of the term *system* closely follows the use of this term in the theoretical tradition established by the work of Curtius, Schleicher, and Brugmann on the Indo-European vowel system (Vincenzi 1976). In citing these scholars in the opening pages of the *Mémoire*, Saussure uses the term system in the sense of a "schema" or "framework" for the purposes of comparing the relations between the Indo-European languages, including the various stages of their evolution.

Saussure was concerned with trying to establish the early vowel system by using a pan-synchronic approach to languages as a basis for comparison. He analyzed both phonetic and morphological data, in particular the *ablaut*, to establish the primitive vowel system of the Indo-European languages. He was not concerned with questions regarding the historical origins of the phonemes *o* and *e* or with determining whether Sanskrit was the oldest among the sister languages.

Saussure's *Mémoire* was innovatory in the way in which he sought *morphophonemic* evidence of changes in the *ablaut*. In other words, he sought to reveal the relationships between the phonetic *and* morphological levels rather than isolating the phonetic value, as his predecessors in comparative linguistics had done. Saussure's approach therefore focused on the ways in which sounds function and have values *qua* linguistic units in relation to other levels of linguistic organization (Saussure 1972:326–27). Kruszewski ([1880] forthcoming), in his review of both Brugmann's article "Nasalis Sonans in der Indo-Germanischen Grundsprache" [A Syllable Forming Nasal in the Indo-Germanic Protolanguage] (1876) and Saussure's *Mémoire*, was perhaps the first to properly grasp and appreciate the significance of Saussure's insights.

In adopting this approach, Saussure began the task of defining languages as systems based on differential and relational terms rather than on the basis of the material properties of their phonetic substance. The *Mémoire* is significant for the break that it represents with the atomistic and substance-based approaches of nineteenth-century comparative linguistics at the same time that it is a work thoroughly steeped in the practices of historical and comparative linguistics, especially the neogrammarian school whose leading exponents included Curtius, Ostoff, Brugmann, and Paul.

There is no suggestion in the *Mémoire* that Saussure was consciously developing a radical new approach to the study of language as semiological system. Rather, Saussure's insistence on looking beyond the material characteristics of linguistic sounds to examine intrinsic levels of their properly linguistic (morphophonemic) organization on the basis of the position of each element in a system of interrelated terms is itself a departure from the analytical criteria that were generally practiced at the time by his contemporaries. With hindsight, we can say that this approach represents an important early stage in the development of Saussure's semiological theory of language.

A FURTHER NOTE ON THE PHONEME IN SAUSSURE'S THEORETICAL THINKING: IMPLICATIONS FOR THE DEFINITION OF THE LINGUISTIC SIGN

Saussure's thinking about the phoneme was very probably influenced by Baudouin de Courtenay's (1895) distinction between sounds and functional linguistic units (see De Mauro's comments in Saussure 1972:306, note 6; Koerner *Ferdinand de Saussure: Origin and Development of His Linguistic Thought in Western Studies of Language,* 1973: 135, 142) as well as the neogrammarian, Eduard Sievers (*Grundzüge der Phonetik* [Principles of Phonetics] 1876; see Koerner 1973:125–29). Saussure's use of the term *phoneme* is different from the modern sense, which is more directly traceable to the phonological studies of Prague School linguists such as Trubetzkoy (*Principles of Phonology* [1939]1971). In Saussure's (1879) *Mémoire,* a phoneme is a *material* unit of sound; it refers to the material characteristics of the signifier. In the first course in general linguistics, Saussure succinctly defines the phoneme as follows: "Le phoneme = son/acte phonatoire [the phoneme = sound/act of phonation]" (1993, p. 29). The phoneme, in this view, is a unit of sound as seen from the point of view of its articulatory dynamics (*l'acte phonatoire*). It refers to the concrete level of material segments into which speech sounds can be analyzed rather than to the more abstract level of the functional differentiations that constitute a given language system and which are, in any case, always abstracted from concrete speech sounds in *parole* (specific instances of language as speech).

In the section on phonology in the third course in general linguistics, Saussure (1993) makes a distinction between "les sons de la parole" [the sounds of speech] (p. 262) and the "impressions acoustiques" [acoustic impressions] that belong to *la langue* [the language system] (p. 262). The term "impression acoustique" is subsequently changed to "image acoustique" [acoustic image] in the later section of the third course titled "Nature du Signe Linguistique" [Nature of the Linguistic Sign] (285). Here, Saussure says, "L'image acoustique n'est pas le son materiel, c'est l'empreinte psychique du son" [The acoustic image is not the material sound, it is the psychic imprint of the sound] (285). It is the "image acoustique," which is related to the "concept" by an associative link in the creation of the linguistic sign. The more abstract and psychic definition of the "image acoustique" that Saussure makes here, as distinct from the material character of the phoneme in his definition, may be seen as a more likely precursor of the categorical theory of the phoneme that was later developed in the structuralist phonology of the Prague School (see also Komatsu's "Introduction" in Saussure 1993:3).

In any case, the importance of Saussure's innovative approach in the *Mémoire* lies in his understanding that the phonetic and morphological levels of linguistic organization are distinct and that phonetic distinctions function to specify meaningful distinctions on the morphological level.

THE HARVARD MANUSCRIPTS: NOTES TOWARD A TREATISE ON *PHONÉTIQUE*

Jakobson ("Saussure's Unpublished Reflexions on Phonemes" [1969]) first drew attention to the existence in the Houghton Library of Harvard University of a large body of manuscripts known as the Harvard Manuscripts. The manuscripts are catalogued in the Houghton Library of Harvard University as bMS Fr 266 (1)–(9). These manuscripts consist of some 638 sheets and 995 pages of material. In addition to the Saussurean manuscripts catalogued by Godel (see *Les Sources Manuscrites du Cours de Linguistique Générale de F. de Saussure* [1957]; "Inventaire des Manuscrits de F. de Saussure Remis à la Bibliothèque Publique et Universitaire de Genève" [1960]) and stored in the *Bibliotheque Publique et Universitaire* in Geneva, the Harvard Manuscripts constitute an important resource in the study of Saussure's thinking.

The Harvard Manuscripts mainly date from Saussure's earlier years, including the 10-year period of his stay in Paris prior to his return to Geneva in 1891. Marchese argues, on the basis of the authors cited by Saussure, that the most likely period for the writing of the greater part of these manuscripts was between 1881 and 1885 ("Introduction," in Saussure 1995:xiv). The manuscripts that have been catalogued as bMS Fr 266 (8), consisting of 177 pages of unpublished material, bear the handwritten title *Phonétique* [Phonetics] and are generally believed to be notes and reflections for a treatise on phonetics that Saussure never completed (Jakobson 1969; Saussure 1995:xi).

A critical edition of the complete manuscripts catalogued as bMS Fr 266 (8) has been published by Maria Pia Marchese (Saussure 1995). Selected excerpts with interpretative commentary from the entire collection have been published by Parret ("Les Manuscrits Saussuriens de Harvard" [The Harvard Saussure Manuscripts] 1993). Both Jakobson and Marchese concur that one of the prime motivations for the material Saussure wrote with a view to publishing a treatise on phonetics was to respond to Osthoff's (1881) criticisms of Saussure's *Mémoire*.

The importance of the Harvard Manuscripts lies, in part, in the light they shed on the further development of Saussure's theoretical thinking on Indo-European and articulatory phonetics since the publication of his *Mémoire*. The major themes of the Harvard Manuscripts may be summarized as follows: (1) the study of the functional roles of the Indo-European phonemes in relation to the opposition between consonants and sonants, (2) the syllabic basis of articulation, (3) the concept of the phoneme as "unité phonétique" [phonetic unit], (4) the form and substance of speech sounds, (5) the combining of phonemes in *parole;* (6) the role of the voice and of the ear, (7) the physiological and physical dimensions of speech sounds, (8) intention and will as agencies that modulate speech sounds in *parole,* and (9) the diverse temporal spheres of *parole*.

In the other manuscripts in this collection, Saussure's notes cover many diverse topics. These include (1) the Armenian *kh* final, (2) the Sanskrit genitive, (3) the absolute genitive, (4) Vedic literature, (5) a discussion of a book by Paul Oltramare (*Histoire des Idées Théosophiques dans l'Inde, Vol. 1, La Théosophie Brahmanique* [*History of Theosophical Ideas in India,* Vol. I, *Brahman Theosophy*] 1907) on ancient Indian theosophy, (6) the Indo-European *a,* (7) the Vedic and Hindu mythology, (8) ancient Greek linguistics, and (9) a draft of Saussure's doctoral thesis (see also Parret "Réflexions Saussuriennes sur le Temps et le Moi' [Saussurean reflections on time and the me], 1995).

The publication by Marchese in 1995 of a critical edition of the complete manuscript bMS Fr 266 (8), entitled *Phonétique,* provides Saussure scholars with an important opportunity to better comprehend and assess the evolution of Saussure's semiological theory of speech sounds both in relation to his previous thinking on Indo-European vocalism in his *Mémoire,* as well as in relation to the later treatment of the phoneme in the *Cours*. In the *Mémoire,* Saussure first developed his systemic conception of phonemes as functional terms whose values derive from their place in an overall system. In manuscript bMS Fr 266 (8), Saussure defines his semiological phonetics as follows:

semiological phonetics:

it is concerned with sounds and the succession of sounds existing in each idiom in so far as they have a value for an idea (acoustico-psychological cycle). (Saussure 1995:120)

As the discussion of the "image acoustique" in the previous section showed, the play of oppositions between acoustic images (previously "acoustic impressions") in *la langue,* rather than the material sounds uttered in acts of *parole,* constitutes a system of values and, when associated with what Saussure variously refers to as ideas or concepts, forms the signs of the language system. Both acoustic images and ideas have values in *langue*. On this basis, Saussure proposes a semiological phonetics, as defined in the above quotation, whereby acoustic impressions or images function to distinguish one idea from another at the same time that they enable the ear to distinguish one material sound from another in virtue of the principles of classification intrinsic to *la langue* (see Saussure 1993:263; see also section 7).

SAUSSURE'S ANALYSIS OF AND THEORETICAL REFLECTIONS ON THE GERMANIC LEGENDS

Saussure's extensive notes on the Germanic legends are preserved and catalogued in the *Bibliothèque Publique et Universitaire* in Geneva with the following numbers: ms. fr 3952.4 122v-122r; ms. fr. 3958.1–8; ms. fr. 3959.1–9; ms. fr. 3959.10; and ms. fr. 3959.11. A critical edition of Saussure's notes, with editorial commentary, has been prepared by Marinetti and Meli (Saussure 1986). The editorial work of Marinetti and Meli constitutes a significant step in the recovery of previously unpublished material by Saussure and in a form that renders this important body of research, undertaken by Saussure during the period roughly from late 1903 to 1910 and possibly even until his death in 1913, accessible to Saussure scholars.

In the first instance, Saussure's interest is empirical: His basic hypothesis is that the legends are based on and traceable to historical events (see Prosdocimi, "Sul Saussure delle Leggende Germaniche" [On the Saussure of the Germanic Legends] [1983]; see also Meli 'Per una Lettura Degl'inediti di F. de Saussure sulle Leggende Germaniche' [For a Reading of Saussure's Unpublished Works on the Germanic Legends] in Saussure 1986:451–502, 457). Saussure uses a technique that he calls "approximation" to establish connections between original historical events and the legends that have their genesis, as Prosdocimi points out, in "an historical research that Saussure intends to carry out on Geneva and its surroundings" (Saussere 1986:42–43). Saussure uses the analytical technique of "coincidences" to establish relations of identity between the events, characters, and so on described in the legends and the historical events that form the original basis of the legends (see, for example, fragment 3858.7.34v-35r, in Saussure 1986:141; see also Saussure 1986:388). On this basis, Saussure proposes transformational processes of "transposition" and "substitution" whereby particular historical elements are integrated into the legends on the basis of larger-scale social processes. Other processes described by Saussure include the "displacement" of, for example, places and the phenomenon of *oubli* [forgetting] attributable to the individual tellers of particular versions of a given legend.

According to Meli, the theoretical observations made by Saussure on his analysis of the legends are "sporadic and marginal reflections," which "regard the theory and not the method" (Saussure 1986:459). Meli (Saussure 1986) cites a contradiction in Saussure's notes regarding the transposition of names and the transposition of biographical details to back up his point. However, it is difficult to see how Saussure's admittedly infrequent theoretical observations in his notes on the Germanic legends are not in some way intrinsically related to the very many rich and dense analytical observations that he makes about his corpus.

First, Saussure's analyses of the processes of transposition, substitution, and displacement are quintessentially intertextual processes, even though Saussure never uses the term *intertextuality*. These processes are not simply empirical questions that regard a particular analytical method for establishing the coincidences between historical material and mythical material. Histories—spoken and written—of historical events are themselves texts, as are stories about and mythical transformations of these events. The inherently intertextual character of these processes has important consequences for the second point, as discussed below.

Second, Saussure's analytical technique, in actual fact, raises important theoretical questions concerning the ways in which semiological processes across different timescales both influence and amplify the ways in which actors and events in real historical events in the distant past themselves have semiological significance in other times and places. This fact entails the intersection of very diverse timescales such that it becomes difficult to neatly distinguish one timescale from another. In other words, Saussure's analysis shows how the historical and the mythical timescales interpenetrate, thereby showing that the very notion of history, at least in the Western European tradition, implies a complex diversity of semiological scales in a given sociocultural system. This much is evident in the following reflection that Saussure makes on the notion of the symbol with reference to an author's epic account of a battle between two armies that gets transformed over time into a duel between two chieftains:

The duel between chieftain A and chieftain B (inevitably) becomes symbolic since this particular combat represents the overall result of the battle, perhaps the conquest of vast tracts of land, and a political and geographical upheaval, but a *symbolic intention* did not exist during this time at any moment. The reduction of the battle to a duel is a natural fact of semiological transmission, produced by a temporal duration between tales. (Saussure 1986:129–30 [italics in original])

Saussure's discussion of the role of the symbol in the legends shows that these cannot simply be reduced to historical events that once took place in some distant time and place. Nor is the resulting mythical transformation of this event reducible to the objective scientific study of ancient systems of belief. Instead, the processes of symbolization that Saussure refers to show how myth is a more abstract system of meanings for which objective historical events constitute the raw material. The symbolic transformations of this raw material—themselves processes of "semiological transmission"—are abstract symbolic resources that provide answers concerning the meanings and values of concrete human experiences on other timescales and in other situations far removed from the original historical event on its timescale. That, surely, is a key aspect of the significance of myth. Saussure's theoretical interpellations, far from being "marginal," would appear to have grasped very well the significance of this for a semiological theory of textual processes and their transformations over time.

Without having recourse to notions such as "Saussure, precursor of Propp" in the development of narratological theory, as suggested by Avalle (*Ontology of the Sign in Saussure* 1986), it seems not unreasonable to claim that both the method adopted by Saussure and the theoretical observations that he makes concerning the results obtained by this method demonstrate his emerging awareness of the semiological character of the Germanic legends *qua* texts that belong to a complex intertextual system on multiple timescales. The objects of his analysis are thus revealed to be complex systems of interacting signs and their respective functions. Moreover, words and whole texts can be used as symbols whose implications cannot be fixed in the word or symbol itself. Rather, the implications of the symbol are emergent properties that become apparent only over time in the context of a particular sociocultural community with its collective history and memory. Saussure (1986) draws attention to this emergent, time-bound property of symbols as follows: "The identity of a symbol can never be fixed from the moment that it is a symbol, that is to say, directed to the social mass that fixes its value at each instant" (p. 30). Speaking of the identity of symbols, Saussure also observes:

Each of the characters [*personnages*] is a symbol of which one can see vary—exactly as in the case of the rune—a) the name, b) its position vis-à-vis others, c) the characteristics, d) the function, the actions. If a *name* is transposed, it may follow that some of the actions are transposed, and, reciprocally, or that the entire plot changes because of an accident of this kind. (p. 31; emphasis in original)

THE COURSES IN GENERAL LINGUISTICS AND THE DERIVATION OF *LA LANGUE* AS THE OBJECT OF STUDY FOR A SEMIOLOGICAL SCIENCE OF SIGNS IN SOCIAL LIFE

Saussure gave his three courses in general linguistics at the University of Geneva from 1907 to 1911. In 1916, Saussure's colleagues, Charles Bally and Albert Sechehaye, published their edition of *CLG*. This edition was to remain overridingly influential for some decades after its publication in spite of the many lacunae and editorial liberties that they took with the students' notes of Saussure's lectures, which Sechehaye collated for the preparation of the 1916 edition. Both the publication of Godel's *Sources Manuscrites* (1957) and Engler's *Édition Critique* (Saussure 1967–1968) reveal the many discrepancies between the editorial legacy of Bally and Sechehaye's 1916 text and the students' notes. The third course (1911) is the basis of the 1916 edition of *CLG* published by Bally and Sechehaye, although Saussure's ordering and organization of his material, as presented in his lectures, was significantly altered by the editors of the 1916 edition.

The changes introduced by Bally and Sechehaye were due to the editors' decision above all to present a general theory of *la langue,* whereas Part 1 of Saussure's third course began with a series of reflections on the geographical diversity of *les langues* and the causes of this diversity. Only in the second part of this course did Saussure present his general theory of *la langue.* Sechehaye's *Collation* of the students' notes as the basis for the 1916 edition clearly reflects the editors' intention to reorganize Saussure's third course along lines that clearly conformed to the requirements of the editors rather than to accurate transmission of what Saussure's students had annotated.

Harris (*Saussure and His Interpreters,* 2001:19–20) points out that the decision of the editors of the 1916 edition to drastically scale down Saussure's survey of the history and description of the Indo-European languages has important consequences both for the latter-day perception of the importance that Saussure assigned to the body of knowledge accumulated throughout the nineteenth century by the comparative philologists and for the definition of "general linguistics" that Saussure and his students took for granted. While the proportion assigned to the survey of comparative philology varies over the three courses, there can be no doubt, Harris (2001:21–22) argues, that Saussure appeals to an already established body of facts about the Indo-European languages as the starting point for his

development of a general linguistics on semiological grounds as an academic discipline.

Indeed, Saussure (1993) begins the first course on a cautious note by declaring, in effect, that that it would be premature to begin with an "interior" definition of linguistics as "la science du language ou des langues" [the science of language or of language systems] (p. 11). It should be clear that Saussure's notion of general linguistics does not start out by claiming that language is distinct from other domains of knowledge or that the linguistic description should necessarily be pitched at such a high level of generality so as to cover all languages or that certain linguistic facts (e.g., grammatical mood) are universally valid for all languages. Rather, the epithet "general" appeals in the first instance to an accepted body of facts about the Indo-European languages to which the linguist can appeal and around which a certain scientific consensus has gathered.

Instead, Saussure (1993) announces that the first course will begin by defining linguistics from the outside (*de l'extérieur*) (p. 11). Saussure then provides a brief survey of linguistics in relation to ethnology, philology, logic, and sociology before then embarking on a discussion of the errors of linguistic analysis in relation to the confusion between "corruption" and linguistic change and the distortions that written documents have brought about in the study of "le signe parlé" [the spoken sign] (p. 15).

Harris (2001:28–30) also points out that Saussure's distinction between *langue* and *parole,* rather than having its basis in an independent reflection on "les faits de langage" [the facts of language], can be traced to Saussure's discussion in the first course of the processes of analogical change (see also Thibault, *Re-Reading Saussure,* 1997:92–93, 104–105).

According to Saussure (1993), analogical change is, above all, a grammatical process. On the emergence of the form *je trouve* [I find], he makes the following observations:

Everything is grammatical in the phenomenon of analogy, but in the grammatical operation two aspects must be distinguished: the comprehension of the relationship between the forms that are compared (generating, inspiring forms) and secondly the product that they suggest, the form which is engendered, inspired, which is the *x* in the proportion: *nous poussons*: *je pousse = nous trouvons → je trouve,* ↔ (*je treuve*). (pp. 90–91)

The newly engendered form—*je trouve,* in Saussure's example—is created on analogy with already existing forms in the language system. Moreover, the new form, as Saussure (1993) remarks, "avant d'être produite est d'abord voulue pour répondre à une idée précise que j'ai dans l'esprit: le première personne du singulier" [before being produced is first of all wanted in order to respond to a precise idea that I have in my mind: the first person singular]

(p. 90). The new form is, in other words, coupled with an idea that one has in mind, that of the French "first person singular." This observation further shows that there is no fixed relationship between forms and ideas in Saussure's theory. A particular idea such as first person singular—in actual fact, a term or value in the French language system—can be decoupled from its usual coupling to a particular (grammatical) form—*je treuve*—and recoupled to a new form on analogy with already existing forms which can be said to "generate" or to "inspire" the new form.

Analogy is shown to be a powerful semiological resource for the creation of new signs through the generation of new couplings of ideas and forms. It is therefore a source of variation and of new meanings in a given language system. Saussure's discussion also shows that grammatical units such as *je trouve* are themselves signs composed of the coupling of an idea with a grammatical form. Therefore, the definition of the linguistic sign is not confined to couplings of acoustic images (signifiers) and concepts (signifieds) but also includes relationships between grammatical forms and meanings.

Saussure (1993) clarifies and renders more apparent the opposition between the two spheres—*langue* and *parole*—by opposing them within the individual (p. 91).

Each individual is in possession of an individual *langue,* which is located in the "sphere intérieure de l'individu" [interior sphere of the individual] (Saussure 1993:92). By the same token, *la langue qua* object of linguistic analysis can be derived from the sum of the individual language systems in this interior sphere of each individual speaker (p. 92). *La langue* in this second sense can be seen as being distributed across the individuals who use a given language. Each individual's *langue* is also social because it has gotten into the individual's interior (the brain) in the first place through the mediating effects of usage in the "sphère extérieure de la parole" [exterior sphere of speech].

Harris (2001:15–16) reports a puzzle that worried Riedlinger concerning Saussure's distinction between a social *parole* and an individual *langue,* as presented in Saussure's first course (Saussure 1993:92). Saussure's formulation here appears to contradict the notion of an individual *parole* and a *social* langue. Saussure (1993:91) had previously pointed out in the same discussion that *le langage,* from which the opposition between *langue* and *parole* is derived, is itself social. *Parole* is the exterior means whereby individuals participate in social discourse; in this sense it is social. Each individual has also interiorized a version of *la langue* in his or her brain. In this sense, *langue* is individual. However, Saussure is careful to point out that this individual *langue* only gets inside the individual in the first place through the social activity of the individual's participation in acts of *parole*. In this sense, *la langue* is also social because it is analytically derived from the sum of the many individual *langues* as the distributed product of these

in a given society at the same time that it is seen as being located in individuals through the mediating effects of social usage in the sphere of *parole*. While it is true that Saussure extended and further modified his distinction in the third course in his description of "le circuit de la parole" [the speech circuit] (pp. 277–80), the distinctions he makes in the first course between *langue* and *parole*, *individual* and *social*, and *interior* and *exterior* suggest a much more complex and dynamic epistemology of language than one based on static oppositions between the two terms in each of these pairs.

On the evidence of Saussure's discussion of the processes of analogical change in the first course, Saussure, Harris (2001:29–30) argues, derives the distinction between *langue* and *parole*. As Saussure (1993) goes on to say in the section of the first course, titled "Le classement intérieure" [Interior classification], which follows the section discussed above, *la langue* constitutes a principle of order and classification whereby forms are associated with ideas (pp. 92–93). The alternative would be, Saussure says, "un chaos dans chaque tête" [a chaos in each head] (p. 92). Saussure speaks of two types of association at work in *la langue:* (1) between form and idea and (2) the association of form with form (p. 93).

Without exploring this further here, we begin to see how the establishment of *la langue* as the object of study of his semiological science of signs has its basis in a consideration of the ways in which innovations in *parole* are "une force transformatrice de la langue" [a transformative force in the language system] (Saussure 1993:89). One could say that "a momentary forgetting" of the old form by a given language user in a particular act of *parole* on its here-now timescale provides the basis for more far-reaching transformations in *la langue* on its far greater evolutionary timescale (p. 89).

In parallel fashion, we saw in the previous section on the Germanic legends that an epic author's recount of a battle between two armies in Saussure's example may, in successive retellings over time, become a duel between two chiefs and so on, without presupposing a specific "symbolic intention" on the part of the teller. Thus, transformative processes of "transposition," "substitution," "displacement," and "oubli" [forgetting] of the original historical material can lead to changes both in specific legends as well as in entire intertextual systems of legends.

This process of "semiological transmission," Saussure pointed out, depends on the duration of time between tales in the process of transforming the historical event into a legend, as part of a system whose symbolic values can vary just as the processes of analogical change can lead to variation in the relations of association between forms and idea and between forms and forms, and therefore to the entire system of values, on the evolutionary timescale of the language system.

This suggests that Saussure's research on the Germanic legends and his development of a semiological theory of *la langue* are informed by the same social-semiological concerns at least insofar as both are concerned with the emergence of values and changes in these values through the agencies of both time and what Saussure calls "la masse sociale" [the social mass].

— Paul J. Thibault

See also Derrida, Jacques; Lacan, Jacques; Logocentrism; Poststructuralism; Semiology; Structuralism

FURTHER READINGS AND REFERENCES

Avalle, D'Arco Silvio. [1973] 1986. *L'Ontologia del Segno in Saussure*. 2d ed., revised and expanded edition. Turin, Italy: Editore G. Giappichelli.

Kruszewski, Mikolaj Habdank. [1880] Forthcoming. "Novejsie Otkrytija v Oblasti Ario-Evropejskogo Vokalisma" (The Latest Discoveries in the Area of Indo-European Vocalism). Translated by Gregory M. Eramian. In *Saussure: Critical Assessments*, edited by Paul J. Thibault. London & New York: Routledge. (Originally published in *Russkij Filologičeskij Vestnik*. [*Russian Philological Herald*] 4:33–45.)

Saussure, Ferdinand de. 1879. *Mémoire sur le Système Primitif des Voyelles dans les Langues Indoeuropéennes* (Memory on the Primitive System of the Vowels in the Indo-European Languages) Leipzig, Germany: Teubner.

———.1881. "De l'Emploi du Génitif Absolu en Sanscrite" (On the Use of the Absolute Genitive in Sanskrit). Doctoral thesis, Faculty of Philosophy, University of Leipzig. (Reprinted in Saussure 1922.)

———.1922. *Recueil des Publications Scientifiques de Ferdinand de Saussure* (Collected Scientific Publications of Ferdinand de Saussure), edited by Charles Bally and M. Léopold Gautier. Geneva, Switzerland: Éditions Sonor.

———. 1967–1968. *Cours de Linguistique Générale* (Course in General Linguistics), edited by Rudolf Engler. Critical edition in 3 Vols. Wiesbaden, Germany: Otto Harrassowitz.

———. 1916. *Cours de Linguistique Générale* (Course in General Linguistics), edited by Charles Bally and Albert Sechehaye. Lausanne & Paris: Payot.

———. [1916] 1971. *Cours de Linguistique Générale* (Course in General Linguistics), edited by Charles Bally and Albert Sechehaye. 3d ed. Paris: Payot.

———. 1972. *Corso di Linguistica Generale* (Course in General Linguistics), edited by Tullio de Mauro. Critical edition in Italian. Bari & Rome: LaTerza.

———. 1978. "Essai pour Reduire les Mots du Grec, du Latin & de l'Allemand à un Petit Nombre de Racines" (Essay for Reducing the Words of Greek, Latin, & German to a Small Number of Roots), edited by B. Davis. *Cahiers Ferdinand de Saussure* 32:73–101.

———. 1986. *Le Leggende Germaniche: Scritti Scelti e Annotati* (The Germanic Legends: Selected and Annotated Writings), edited by Anna Marinetti and Marcello Meli. Padua, Italy: Libreria Editrice Zielo–Este.

———. 1993. *Cours de Linguistique Générale: Premier et Troisième Cours D'après les Notes de Reidlinger et Constantin* (Course in General Linguistics: First and Third Course Based on the notes of Reidlinger and Constantin), edited by Eisuke Komatsu. Collection Recherches Université Gaskushuin n° 24. Tokyo, Japan: Université Gakushuin.

———. 1995. *Phonétique: Il Manoscritto di Harvard* (Phonetics: The Harvard Manuscript), edited by Maria Pia Marchese. *Houghton Library bMS Fr 266 (8)*.Quaderni del Dipartimento di Linguistica, Università degli Studi di Firenze–Studi 3. Florence, Italy: Unipress.

Vincenzi, Giuseppe Carlo. 1976. "'Sistema' e 'fonema' nel primo Saussure" [System and phoneme in the early Saussure]. *Studi Italiani di Linguistica Teorica ed Applicata* (Italian Studies of Theoretical and Applied Linguistics) 1–2:229–51.

SCHELER, MAX

Max Scheler (1874–1928) was a German philosopher and social theorist, who significantly contributed to the anthropological and phenomenological turn in German philosophy at the beginning of the last century. Scheler studied philosophy and sociology under Dilthey, Simmel, and Eucken in Munich, Berlin, and Jena. Influenced also by the work of Brentano, Husserl, Heidegger, and Nietzsche, Scheler taught at Jena, Munich, Göttingen, Cologne, and Frankfurt/M. While his actual contribution to the laying of new foundations of contemporary European philosophy is often underestimated in the light of his influential contemporaries Husserl and Heidegger, it was Scheler who most vividly pursued an application of the new philosophical framework beyond the confines of narrow philosophical debate. He applied phenomenological thinking to subjects and topics as varied as values, capitalism, sympathy, elites, world age, Christianity, and Buddhism, as well as pacifism and feminism, to name just a few. Especially during the First World War, Scheler engaged in the political debate, not just in writing. His rather patriotic position during that time leaves room for interpretation. However, some years later, Scheler was one of the few scholars who warned of the dangers of the Nazi movement, which once in power suppressed his work. Despite a spread of interests and his rather nonsystematic and aphoristic style of writing, all Scheler's thoughts radiate toward a central issue: What defines human personality, and what is the position of human existence within this world? In pursuit of an answer, Scheler developed a distinctly nontranscendental and contextual understanding of human nature and existence. Much of his persistent enthusiasm for this issue has to be seen against the background of a continuous engagement with Catholic religion. His most influential works are *Formalism in Ethics and Non-Formal Ethics of Values* (1916), his attempt to outline an applied phenomenology; *Man's Place in Nature* (1928), in which he sets out his philosophical anthropology; and *The Forms of Knowledge and Society* (1925). Scheler is the philosopher of "love" and "sympathy" who stresses the role of the emotional as constituting for the human milieu. But at the same time, he maintains the importance of "world-openness" as the uniquely human potential to reach outside a given environment. With his emphasis on the emotional, Scheler distinctly moves away from a pre-Kantian and Kantian understanding of human nature as defined by reason and intellect, while with his emphasis on milieu, he attempts to understand humans not as beings above nature but as intrinsically embedded in this world via certain historical and cultural environs. In developing his ideas concerning the human milieu, Scheler also made a significant contribution to the sociology of knowledge through reemphasizing the role of situated practical knowledge(s) as opposed to universal scientific knowledge. Scheler managed only to sketch out his ideas of a phenomenolgically based philosophical anthropology, as his life, marked by intellectual as well as emotional restlessness, came to a premature end at the age of 54. His work has influenced thinkers such as Cassirer, Heidegger, Berdyaev, Gehlen, and Mannheim. Outside Germany, he had lasting influence in the Spanish-speaking world, mainly through the mediation of the work of Ortega y Gasset.

Scheler's thinking focuses around a nonformal understanding of values as a way to understand human personality and society. According to Scheler, human action and behavior is guided by an "ordered rank of values," which is given by the "intuitive evidence of preference" and not accessible through logical deduction. As such, the "ordo amoris," as Scheler famously called this frame of value preferences, has a priori character in two directions. First, value evidence is given beyond any contingent experience. For example, we continue to cherish the idea of friendship despite having been let down by a friend. Second, acts based on love and sympathy are immediate responses to the world that cannot be referred back to intellectual decision making. For example, a child might spontaneously interrupt game play to give his or her mother a kiss. The "emotional a priori" offered by Scheler thus differs distinctly from Kant's "formal a priori" in that it is not rooted in the universal law of human mind or reason but instead is immediately given before any acts of rationality. Moreover, while the rank of values as such remains stable, the actual patterns of intuitive preference and putting after of values in practical life change with historic development and across different social and cultural environments. This again stands in stark contrast to Kant's a priori, which relies on universal knowledge deriving from universal logical necessity. What we find in Scheler's argument is thus an implicit criticism of Kantian metaphysic as Eurocentric despite its universal claim.

While Scheler's argument concerning the role of values for human existence is carried by a philosophical drive, many of his insights are of sociological significance. So he argues that the "macrocosm" of ranked values is mirrored and reflected in the "microcosm" of those frames of reference that guide social units and individuals in daily life. Thus, the "milieu" in which we conduct our everyday lives is structured by a constant "ethos" or "disposition" through which we relate to our surroundings, effectively providing the "alphabet" of the lifeworld. As such, "milieu" in Scheler's sense implies a stable configuration of meaning and action that we carry around with us and that effectively takes in more *and at the same time* less than the immediate environment. It takes in more, insofar as it relates to distant and absent things and happenings, and less insofar as it filters out elements in our immediate surroundings that are of no practical relevance to us. In its knowledge structure, the milieu is described by Scheler as a "relative natural view of the world." It is *natural* in that it provides structures of meaning that are given without question and incapable of justification. It is *relative* insofar as the contents of these frames of reference differ for coexisting milieus as well as across historical epochs. Moreover, human milieus, according to Scheler, are not fixated and static but have to be actively maintained under changing external conditions. Scheler further outlines this crucial distinction between human milieu and animal environment in his anthropological writings. Here, he stresses that as a "person" possessing "spirit" beyond "instinct" and "practical intelligence," we are able to transcend our milieu, even if only momentarily. This human capacity of "self-transcendence" manifests itself, for example, in the capabilities of humor and irony. This is what Scheler refers to as "world-openness," describing the tendency of human beings to reach outside any given environment.

—Jörg Dürrschmidt

See also Mannheim, Karl; Phenomenology; Philosophical Anthropology; Schütz, Alfred

FURTHER READINGS AND REFERENCES

Frings, Manfred. 1965. *Max Scheler: A Concise Introduction into the World of a Great Thinker.* Pittsburgh: Duquesne University Press.

Scheler, Max. 1961. *Man's Place in Nature.* Translated and introduction by Hans Meyerhoff. New York: Noonday.

———. 1973. *Formalism in Ethics and Non-Formal Ethics of Values: A New Attempt Toward a Foundation of an Ethical*

Personalism. Translated by Manfred S. Frings and Roger L. Funk. Evanston, IL: Northwestern University Press.

————. 1980. *Problems of a Sociology of Knowledge.* Translated by Manfred Frings. Edited and introduction by Kenneth W. Stikkers. London: Routledge & Kegan Paul.

SCHÜTZ, ALFRED

Austrian-born phenomenologist and social theorist Alfred Schütz made charting the structures of the lifeworld his life's work. In the course of this endeavor, he added a host of terms to the vocabulary of social science, including "typification," "in-order-to and because-motives," "course-of-action and personal ideal types," "multiple realities," "finite provinces of meaning," and "the social distribution of knowledge." Following his death in 1959, his devoted students published his collected papers, unfinished manuscripts, and an intellectual biography; arranged to have his first book translated into English (Schütz 1967); and integrated his concepts into a new theoretical perspective called social constructionism (Berger and Luckmann 1966). A number of scholars in Europe and America continue to undertake phenomenological research in the Schützian style. A group of economists explores Schütz's relationship to the Austrian school of economics while applying his analyses of temporality and the ideal type to the reform of the neoclassical paradigm. Many contemporary social theorists incorporate Schützian concepts into their own distinctive systems of thought.

Born into an affluent Viennese family in 1899, Schütz—he would drop the umlaut after immigrating to New York City in 1939—received a rigorous classical education at the Esterhazy Gymnasium, where he distinguished himself as a pianist and student of European musical history and literature. After service in the First World War, he abandoned his hopes for a career in music for one in international law and finance. Completing his degree on an accelerated schedule, he served as executive secretary for the Austrian Bankers Association in Vienna for seven years before joining a private bank as an attorney in 1929. Schütz remained in banking until 1956, by which time he had been teaching at the émigré-staffed New School for Social Research for 12 years.

Schütz's three major intellectual mentors were French philosopher Henri Bergson, sociologist Max Weber, and Edmund Husserl, the founder of phenomenology. Weber had taught one semester at the University of Vienna in 1918, just before Schütz matriculated there, and greatly impressed the economics faculty, particularly Ludwig von Mises. After Schütz completed his degree in 1922, Mises invited him to join his private seminar, where the issues of objectivity,

historicism, apriorism, *Verstehen* (understanding), holism, and methodological individualism were debated by a host of brilliant figures, many of whom became lifelong friends of Schütz's. During the 10 years that he participated in the seminar, Schütz tried to reconcile the inconsistencies in Weber's use of the term "subjective meaning" and to show how the methods of *Verstehen* and the ideal type can yield objective knowledge in the disciplines that take human action as their foundation. He first tried, unsuccessfully, to use Bergson's analyses of "duration" and memory as the bridge from subjective to objective meaning, then found in Husserl's analysis of internal time-consciousness the starting point he needed. After reading parts of it in the seminar, Schütz published *Die Sinnhafte Aufbau der socialen Welt: Eine Einleitung in die verstehende Soziologie (The Meaningful Construction of the Social World: An Introduction to Interpretive Sociology)* in 1932.

The discovery of duration, internal time-consciousness, or the stream of consciousness (as William James called it) was central to Schütz's account of subjective meaning. Subjective meaning arises through the retrospective unification of segments of a perennial, heterogeneous flux of sensations, perceptions, and reactions into experiences of this or that "type." Only through disciplined reflection can one disentangle the layers of anticipation and interpretation involved in the typification of the simplest experience and reconstruct the stages through which a given phenomenon is constituted in its typicality. In Husserl's formulation, meaning arises through a "monothetic glance" over the "polythetic" flux that preceded it. The crucial fact is the temporal one: Meaning always arises *retrospectively.* Even one's prospective intentions are linguistically formulated in the future perfect tense—as actions one *will have executed* in the anticipated way.

This discovery allowed Schütz's to clarify Weber's methodological concepts. According to Weber, the social scientist-observer understands the subjective meaning that an actor attaches to his or her action when he or she realizes that the actor intends to accomplish a certain end by the observed efforts. On the contrary, Schütz argued, the alleged subjective meaning is only a hypothetical formulation of the actor's in-order-to motive. The lived experience of another is inaccessible to the social scientist, for he or she can apprehend neither the polythetic stages nor the monothetic glance that unified the intention subjectively. Moreover, the social scientist brings to observation analytical and methodological imperatives alien to the actor's own meaning constitution. History, sociology, law, and economics can adopt the subjective point of view only in the formal sense of using analytical models that refer back to the shared typifications that actors use to make sense of their own experience.

By eliminating the residual romantic-emphatic elements in Weber's methodology, Schütz felt he had resolved the long-standing conflict between the "individualizing" and "generalizing" cultural sciences—they employ personal and course-of-action ideal types of different levels of concreteness—and, in the process, validated Husserl's conception of phenomenology as a science of the foundations of the sciences. The book's publication led to an invitation to meet Husserl in person and to a lifelong affiliation with the phenomenological movement. But the book was poorly understood by Weber scholars and had little effect on the methodological debates of the day, save for a few students of Mises who realized that ideal types provided a better account of the basic concepts and laws of economics than did "intellectual intuition."

Alfred Schütz was the kind of thinker who returned repeatedly to a core set of intellectual problems. The transcendental turn in phenomenology, which Husserl pursued from 1913 to 1935, was one. Schütz's misgivings about this project were vindicated in 1938 when Husserl turned back to the lifeworld, the world of commonsense realities. Pragmatism was another. Schütz's most sustained exploration of pragmatism can be found in the unfinished manuscript, *Reflections on the Problem of Relevance* (1970). A series of papers on the methodology of the social sciences—the most famous being "Common-Sense and Scientific Interpretation of Human Action"—fleshed out and updated the lessons of his first book. Another series of papers on "The Stranger," "The Well-Informed Citizen," and "The Homecomer" recalled his early enthusiasm for Georg Simmel's studies of social types. The last series, along with "Making Music Together," represent Schütz's most important contributions to interpretive sociology.

As individually profound and influential as these essays were, they distracted Schütz from the task he first envisioned in 1932—to trace the multidimensional, multistoried meaning-structures of the lifeworld back to the constitutive operations of mundane subjectivity. He further advanced this project in the essays "On Multiple Realities" and "Symbol, Reality and Society," but was unable to complete it. As his health began to fail in 1957, he outlined a final work that could do no more than summarize his progress to date. Thomas Luckmann faithfully and lovingly executed his teacher's plan in *The Structures of the Life-World.*

The Structures of the Life-World represents Schütz's foremost contribution to intellectual history. Following Husserl's "law of oriented constitution," Schütz analyzed the commonsense realities of everyday life into layers of meaning extending outward from a primordial "null point"—a mundane ego representing pragmatic subjectivity as such. The resulting stratifications of the lifeworld—temporal, spatial, social, and signative—incorporate all of Schütz's familiar concepts so that the reader can clearly see the unity of his life's work.

One of the most original and beloved figures of twentieth-century social theory, Alfred Schütz will long be remembered as the inspiring mentor of the social constructionist perspective. His intellectual achievements were rarely appreciated on their own terms, however, for reasons he well understood: The requirements of theory construction in the social sciences preclude systematic inquiry into the cascading syntheses that make analysis and inference possible. Even as Schütz's writings were becoming widely available in the 1960s and 1970s, the rival paradigms of structuralism and poststructuralism ceased to look to human subjectivity for the origin of meaning, but to systems of contrasting signs and discursive practices.

— Christopher Prendergast

See also Ideal Type; Lifeworld; Phenomenology; Social Constructionism

FURTHER READINGS AND REFERENCES

Berger, Peter L. and Thomas Luckmann. 1966. *The Social Construction of Reality: A Treatise in the Sociology of Knowledge.* New York: Doubleday.

Embree, Lester, ed. 1999. *Schutzian Social Science.* Dordrecht, Netherlands: Kluwer.

Schütz, Alfred. 1962. *Collected Papers I: The Problem of Social Reality.* The Hague, Netherlands: Martinus Nijhoff.

———. 1967. *The Phenomenology of the Social World.* Translated by G. Walsh and F. Lehnert. Evanston, IL: Northwestern University Press.

Schütz, Alfred and Thomas Luckmann. 1973. *The Structures of the Life-World.* Translated by R. M. Zaner and H. T. Engelhardt Jr. Evanston, IL: Northwestern University Press.

Wagner, Helmut R. 1983. *Alfred Schutz: An Intellectual Biography.* Chicago: University of Chicago Press.

THE SCOTTISH ENLIGHTENMENT

The Scottish Enlightenment refers to a historical event in northern Britain between approximately 1740 and 1790 that found expression in a significant body of literature embedded in changing political and economic conditions; novel institutional developments such as clubs, societies and academies; and a concurrent efflorescence of associational relations and public communication comparable to what characterised the Enlightenment elsewhere in Europe. The intellectual achievement of eighteenth-century Scotland was so considerable that it not only impressed contemporaries such as Benjamin Franklin, Thomas Jefferson, and Immanuel Kant but is today still regarded as having been responsible for the remarkable distinction that Scotland attained among the countries that participated in the Enlightenment.

The vast intellectual literature containing the basic ideas of the Scottish Enlightenment was produced by different generations of authors over a 50-year period but found its most characteristic focus roughly in the third quarter of the century during which a whole series of famous titles were published by David Hume (1711–1776), William Robertson (1721–1793), Adam Smith (1723–1790), Adam Ferguson (1723–1816), John Millar (1735–1801), and others. While this literature as a whole represented virtually the full range of modern knowledge, from experimental natural science and medicine through philosophy to what Hume referred to as "the moral subjects" or "the science of man" and later after Condorcet came to be called "the social sciences," it is interesting to note here that it is particularly the latter branch of this literature that has retained its relevance and significance. At times, it indeed seemed as though the larger part of this social theoretic literature had fallen into oblivion, yet a certain line of continuity can be observed, and somewhat unexpectedly, the second half of the twentieth century has inaugurated a veritable renaissance in Scottish Enlightenment studies.

FRAMEWORKS OF INTERPRETATION

The contemporary interest in the social theory of the Scottish Enlightenment is by no means due, as some suggest, solely to the resurgence since the late 1970s of the New Right in the guise of neoconservatism and neoliberal economics and politics. It is indeed indisputable that some authors approach the Scottish intellectual heritage from within this interpretative framework, yet there is ample evidence that other factors also have been relevant.

From a social scientific point of view, it is obvious that the demise of positivism and the growing postempiricist emphasis on the history and sociology of science have played their part in generating a heightened concern with the Scottish Enlightenment. Since the 1960s, these developments were followed by an increasing impatience with textbook disciplinary histories and a renewed desire to clarify the foundations of the social sciences. This epistemological and methodological shift in emphasis has thus sharpened the sensitivity of historically minded social scientists toward theoretical options, approaches, or traditions that are lesser known or have become marginalized, suppressed, excluded, or even eclipsed.

Perhaps the most important force behind the increased interest in the Scottish Enlightenment, however, is the recent momentous transformation of historical consciousness. Against its background, an alternative political-ideological framework of interpretation has arisen that, far from a narrow neoliberalism, somehow brings together the liberal focus on rights and the republican stress on participation with the discursive or deliberative concern with the mediation of potentially contrary values and interests under fragile conditions of existence.

THE FORMATION OF NORMS AND THE CONSTITUTION OF NORMATIVE ORDERS

The difference between these two contrary frameworks for the interpretation of the Scottish Enlightenment is indicative of something of theoretical importance. It concerns the question of the formation of norms and the constitution of normative orders or regimes that lies at the heart of the contribution of the Scottish authors.

According to neoliberalism, which sees its own free-market capitalist position as the culmination point of the Scottish understanding, patterns of behaviour are spontaneously generated as by-products or unintended consequences of other activities and related contingent factors that then, to the extent that they benefit a significant number, become stabilised through the self-regulative maintenance of relations between the component parts. The economist Friedrich von Hayek defended precisely this view of the Scottish Enlightenment and, on that basis, concluded that since markets emerge spontaneously, they should indefinitely be left to regulate themselves recursively, regardless of the consequences. Inspired by Hayek, Louis Schneider sought to offer a functionalist interpretation of the sociology of the Scottish authors, while Ronald Hamowy insisted that the core of the Scottish contribution to sociology is represented by their view of spontaneous order.

This functionalist perspective indeed finds a foothold in Adam Smith's political economy in which he traced the emergence of the modern capitalist economic system, as well as more generally in the Scottish emphasis on benefit or utility over authority. Extrapolating Hume's analysis of local trade relations into the idea of a national economy by focusing on the intelligible form of the system, Smith ([1776]1976) for instance showed in *An Inquiry into the Nature and Causes of the Wealth of Nations* how supply and demand, or production and consumption, represent an autonomous and self-regulating mechanism at the core of the modern system of commerce which gives rise to the market price—a "system of natural liberty" that establishes and maintains itself "of its own accord" (IV.ix.51).

Contrary to the neoliberal interpretation, however, Smith ([1776]1976) went considerably further than this systemic logic of self-regulation. Over and above an autonomous economic system, Smith considered also the possibility of economic and social crisis and the concomitant need for intervention in the self-regulative mechanism of the economy in order to secure the "natural price" (I.vii.7) in the sense of the socially and ethically minimum wage consistent with a developed economy. In this case, he invoked the collective normative standard of what he called "common humanity" (I.viii.24) rather than simply insisting on individual benefit or utility. Under certain circumstances, then, the systemic logic of self-regulation calls for interruption by the social logic of self-organisation. In this latter respect,

Adam Ferguson and John Millar went far beyond Smith and thus, by implication, drew a line between economics and sociology.

FROM "COMMERCIAL SOCIETY" TO "CIVIL SOCIETY"

Although Smith ([1776]1976) effectively refused to conceive of "commercial society" (I.vi., I.vii., IV.i) strictly in systems theoretical terms, his focus nevertheless remained fixed on the economic system and its environment. The limits of his position were defined by the fact that he was fundamentally tied to John Locke's (1632–1704) economic or "mercantile" (Smith [1776]1976:IV.i.3) model of society and, hence, belonged to the Lockean tradition in the conceptualisation of society or the "L-stream," as Charles Taylor called it. Ferguson and Millar differed from Smith in that they took the social route much more emphatically. In fact, many regard them as the first authors to have recognised social reality as such and to have dealt with it in its own right. That this sociological concern with the historically variable "state of society" had been prefigured by Hume, who exhibited an interest in the "moral subjects" since his first book *A Treatise of Human Nature* ([1739–1740] 1964) and continued to ask moral philosophical questions about society, by no means detracts from the achievement of these authors.

While ascribing a socially significant self-reflective capacity to the individual under such titles as "sympathy" and "impartial spectator" (Smith [1759]1982:I.i.1, I.i.5.8), Smith consistently kept to the English individualist tradition that, at least since Thomas Hobbes (1588–1679), saw the individual as self-loving, egoistic and self-interested. Ferguson and Millar, by contrast, not only followed their Scottish predecessors such as Francis Hutcheson who took a social turn beyond the Earl of Shaftesbury but also adopted more specifically the view of their French example, Montesquieu, that human beings are social by nature. To this they added one of their most characteristic insights: that human beings are capable of both learning and the development of their latent capacities within the social structures into which they were incorporated. Although being vehemently against the Hobbesian "selfish system," Ferguson and Millar nevertheless did not allow this opposition to mislead them into accepting a collectivism that reduces or obliterates the individual, as for instance Auguste Comte would do in the nineteenth century. For them, the individual as active agent and bearer of rights retained importance, but they incorporated it into a genuinely sociological concept of society.

Rather than equating social reality or society simply with Smith's "commercial society," Ferguson and Millar drew in addition also on Montesquieu's sociopolitical model put forward in 1748 in *The Spirit of the Laws* with its characteristic emphasis on politically mediated cultural and social differences, inequalities, conflicts, and power balances. To conceive sociologically of society as "civil society," as Ferguson ([1767]1966) famously called it, they thus creatively combined the "L-stream" and the "M-stream." For Ferguson and Millar, therefore, modern society was by no means exclusively a prepolitical economic complex that regulated itself recursively, but more fully a dynamic set of social relations, characterised by cultural, social, and power difference and inequalities leading to tensions, contradictions, ambiguities, and conflicts that those involved were required to organise themselves. A logic of self-regulation carried by an autonomous system was embedded in and complemented by a logic of self-organisation for which the rights-bearing, active members of society took responsibility. Ferguson and Millar's understanding of both history and of the study of society reflects their twofold Lockean-Montesquieuian conception of civil society.

THEORETICAL HISTORY OF THE "NATURAL HISTORY" OF CIVIL SOCIETY

The most striking feature of the social theory of the Scottish Enlightenment is its historical orientation. Ferguson's *An Essay on the History of Civil Society* ([1767] 1966) gives paradigmatic expression to this Scottish sensibility and program, but it receives even more explicit elaboration in the writings of Millar, from his *The Origin of the Distinction of Ranks* ([1771]1806) to his *An Historical View of the English Government* ([1787]1803). Not only did they regard society as having its own history, what they called its "natural history," but they also put forward their own characteristic type of social scientific study of that history, what they called "theoretical history."

Proceeding from certain assumptions about the nature of human beings, both Ferguson and Millar regarded society as acquiring structural and institutional features through a process of historical development that unfolds and accumulates largely of its own accord. Due to lack of imagination, inadequate anticipation of the future, unconscious adaptation to circumstances, individual actions having incalculable social ramifications, and involuntary production of unintended outcomes and consequences, society has a "natural history" (Millar [1771]1806:11) that runs its course with a minimum of purposiveness and without a script. Government, parliamentary procedure, civil laws, and institutions in general, all arose in this manner in the historical process, mediated by "custom," conflicting "projects and schemes," and the given "circumstances" (Ferguson [1767] 1966:122–23). Millar agreed fully with Ferguson's ([1767] 1966) observation that societies "stumble upon establishments, which are indeed the result of human action, but not the execution of any human design" (p. 122). In spite of such imputation of low rationality to history and high complexity to society, however, both Ferguson and Millar nevertheless emphasised the importance of public opinion, active participation in public life, and deliberate action in politics—with Millar, for instance, supporting the American War of Independence and the French Revolution. Whereas this twofold emphasis led Schneider to the discovery of an unresolved tension in the Scottish contribution, Habermas more acutely appreciated that the sociology of the Scottish Enlightenment had both a conservative and a critical side. In fact, this duality was a characteristic feature of their theoretical history. While assuming the achievements of the natural history of society, both Ferguson and Millar insisted on the possibility of, and need for, the critique of modern society, including existing institutions and authorities. Their critical focus was trained in particular on the division of labour and its negative social consequences, as in the case of Ferguson, and on ecclesiastical institutions and private and public abuses of power made possible by the class structure, as in the case of Millar. A clear distinction has to be drawn, therefore, between the Scottish authors' understanding of the natural history of society, on one hand, and their view of how to study that history and for what purpose, on the other.

The Scots' characteristic concern was a type of social scientific investigation for which they did not yet have an appropriate name. Millar had a clear idea of what was intended when he referred to himself as a "philosophical historian" (cited in Lehmann 1960:135). What he had in mind was in the first instance a social theorist who seeks to discover a pattern in, and thus to account for, the facts made available by the historian. In addition, he was convinced that this theoretical activity should be discharged in a critical and public way so as to provide the educator, the politician, and the public with some basis for the determination of the desired direction of development. In want of a fitting name, Dugald Stewart (1854) therefore proposed to call it provisionally "Theoretical or Conjectural History" (p. 34).

The social science of the Scottish Enlightenment presupposed the indigenous British traditions of empirical science, as represented by Bacon, Newton, and Hume, and of moral philosophy and civil jurisprudence, as put forward by Cumberland, Shaftesbury, Carmichael, Hutcheson, Berkeley, and Hume. The most conspicuous influence on their "theoretical history," however, was Montesquieu, the most widely read French Enlightenment thinker, whom they regarded as the Bacon of their own science. Montesquieu himself can be regarded as an early theoretical historian—or sociologist, as Raymond Aron suggests—in the sense of an author who explicitly sought to make history theoretically intelligible. Ferguson freely admitted that not only his point of view but much of his information also depended directly on the Frenchman. And Millar identified the latter unambiguously as the fountainhead of the

program of the Scottish Enlightenment, which Smith, Ferguson, and he himself were pursuing:

> Upon this subject he [Smith] followed the plan that seems to be suggested by Montesquieu; endeavouring to trace the gradual progress of jurisprudence, both public and private, from the rudest to the most refined ages, and to point out the effects of those arts which contribute to subsistence, and to the accumulation of property, in producing correspondent improvements or alterations in law and government. (Stewart 1854:12)

This passage outlining the Scottish program of social theory could be taken as paradigmatic reference point of a range of more or less prominent conflicting twentieth-century interpretations of its direction and value.

MODERNITY

It is generally accepted that the Scottish Enlightenment is one of a number of events that marked the historical moment when modern society emerged, which implies that there is an intrinsic relation between social theory and modernity. Given this connection, the different commentators' interpretations of the social theory of the Scottish Enlightenment obviously correlate with their respective periodizations and theories of modernity.

The most widely accepted interpretation in the history of social theory, generally speaking, links modernity with what Eric Hobsbawm called the "dual revolution"—that is, the political dispensation inaugurated by the French Revolution and the rise of industrial capitalism in the wake of the Industrial Revolution. Since the Scottish Enlightenment had occurred largely prior to the culmination of the great transition in the dual revolution, however, the defining moment in Scottish history, the Union of Parliaments of 1707, became the reference point for contrary interpretations.

Starting from the deep unpopularity of the Union in Scotland itself and drawing on classical republicanism, many authors have interpreted the Scottish Enlightenment as a defence of the independent, virtuous Scottish citizen against the modern Whig order resting on the pillars of patronage, office, and credit that was imposed from London. In opposition to this perspective drawn from political theory in the sense of classical republicanism stressing "virtue," others have sought instead to present Scottish social theory from an economic angle stressing "wealth" instead. From this point of view, it was either part of the attempt to overcome the barbarous and parochial nature of Scottish life by associating with the socioeconomic order introduced by the Whig oligarchy or an ideological articulation and justification of the commercial capitalism of the British bourgeoisie. As against these alternatives, a third interpretative paradigm has been put forward according to which the continental tradition of civil jurisprudence or modernized natural law was central to Scottish social theory in a way that distinguished it sharply from English thought. Instead of virtue or wealth, the predominant semantics in this case was shaped by law and included not only words such as *rights, liberty*, and *constitution* but also *politeness* and *taste*, which give the distinction between the rude and the polished a completely different sense than in the case of the earlier commercial-liberal interpretation. Rather than either a political or an economic theory of the emergence of modernity, Eriksson put forward a cultural-intellectual theory, but instead of law, his focus is on science. To make sense of the social theory of the Scottish Enlightenment, therefore, he traces modernity back to the line of development leading from Galileo through Bacon and Descartes to Newton. According to this scientistic interpretation, the latter's theory of gravity led Smith, followed by Ferguson and Millar, to transpose "subsistence" into the core conceptual category of social theory.

From a contemporary perspective, it is apparent that the preceding political, economic, cultural-jurisprudential, and cultural-scientific interpretations each indeed strikes on a plausible dimension of the social theory of the Scottish Enlightenment, yet represents a one-sided reading because it rests on a single-factor theory of modernity. To do justice to the multidimensional nature of the work of the Scottish authors, by contrast, it has become clear that it is necessary to see early modernity in its integrity. The different dimensions must be seen in their dialectical interrelation. An increasingly accepted way of doing this is to see the Scottish Enlightenment as having formed part of and having been an outgrowth of the Europe-wide practical discourse of the time about how the survival of society could be secured and social solidarity created through rights in the face of the domination, violence, and disorder emanating from a range of forces. Among the latter were the dissolution of the religious worldview and fragmentation of its institutional underpinnings and communal basis, the process of state formation, the differentiation of civil society from the state, the emergence of capitalism, and the development of technology and science. Taking into account the interplay of these dynamic forces, particularly the contradiction of capitalism and democracy within civil society, both Ferguson and Millar regarded society as becoming visible in the tensions, ambiguities, contradictions, and conflicts that emerge from the struggle against dominating and depleting forces, on one hand, and for the realization of freedom and inclusion, on the other. For them, society was the "scene in which the parties contend for power, privilege and equality" (Ferguson [1767]1966:135), yet one in which a more equitable and just arrangement and a more complete existence could be achieved through law, the distribution of rights, constitutionalism, and, hence, active participation, public spiritedness, and public opinion

(Ferguson [1767]1966:136, 154–67, 190–91, 261–72; Millar [1771]1806:230–42).

CONTEMPORARY RELEVANCE

A standard feature of scholarship on the Scottish Enlightenment, which is also present in the majority of the above interpretations, is the assumption that a stage theory of the progress of society from a savage or rude to a civil or polished state forms a core component of the social theory of Smith, Ferguson, and Millar. Although it has under the influence of Ronald Meek come to be called the "four stages theory," this does not apply to Ferguson, who identified only three stages, and applies only with difficulty to Millar, who worked with a flexible three- to four-stage concept. As is apparent today, however, the major problem with twentieth-century interpreters is that they read Scottish social theory from a nineteenth-century liberal, socialist, and evolutionary point of view, thus imputing to it not merely an inappropriately strong concept of progress but indeed the untenable assumptions of the philosophy of history. The prerevolutionary Enlightenment, including the stage theorists, did not yet dispose over a concept of universal history and progress transposed into a temporal utopia projected into the future but, rather, assumed a dualistic and cyclical viewpoint and entertained nearly as much cultural pessimism as optimism. The Scottish authors, particularly the leading social theorists Ferguson and Millar, therefore combined a deep-seated sense of the possibility of decline and decay of societies with the conviction that the pursuit of public good and happiness was nevertheless worthwhile. Considering society in a historically grounded and politically informed way, they were sensitive to the unavoidability of contingency, openness, and uncertainty. Far from progress being a foregone conclusion, it was a question of how society dealt with both ineliminable internal class and status differences and external political, economic, and other exigencies.

It is precisely in the particular historical consciousness of authors such as Ferguson and Millar that the contemporary relevance of the social theory of the Scottish Enlightenment is to be found. Beyond the historical consciousness of universality of the past two centuries with its emphasis on unmitigated notions of development, progress, evolution, and the realization of universality, our newfound late twentieth- and early twenty-first-century consciousness of generality or globality, marked as it is by its stress on the simultaneity and connectedness of different forms of life under fragile conditions of existence, reproduces, albeit in its own particular form, the consciousness of generality characteristic of the late eighteenth-century Scottish authors. Their awareness of the vicissitudes and fragility of society and our forced acknowledgement of, for instance, the ecology crisis, the hollowing out of the nation-state, the privatisation of violence, and the vulnerability of the world financial system at the end of high modernity, are bringing us together in such a way that we are compelled to recognise today that we need to be much more modest and, hence, sensitive to differences, contradictions, and ambiguities under conditions of an open history, contingency, and uncertainty than our predecessors had been during the past 200 years.

— Piet Strydom

See also Alienation; Capitalism; Civil Society; Social Class; Conflict Theory; Democracy; Modernity; Montesquieu, Charles Louis de Secondat; Political Economy

FURTHER READINGS AND REFERENCES

Eriksson, Björn. 1993. "The First Formulation of Sociology: A Discursive Innovation of the 18th Century." *European Journal of Sociology* 34:251–76.

Ferguson, Adam. [1767] 1966. *An Essay on the History of Civil Society.* Edinburgh, Scotland: Edinburgh University Press.

Habermas, Jürgen. 1969. "Kritische und konservative Aufgaben der Soziologie" [Critical and Conservative Tasks of Sociology]. Pp. 215–30 in *Theorie und Praxis* [Theory and Practice]. Neuwied, Germany: Luchterhand.

Hume, David. [1739–1740] 1964. *A Treatise of Human Nature.* Vols. I-II. London/New York: Dent/Dutton.

Lehmann, William C. 1930. *Adam Ferguson and the Beginning of Modern Sociology.* New York: Columbia University Press.

———. 1960. *John Millar of Glasgow, 1735–1801: His Life and Thought and His Contribution to Sociological Analysis.* London: Cambridge University Press.

Meek, Ronald L. 1971. "Smith, Turgot, and the 'Four Stages' Theory." *History of Political Economy* 3:9–27.

Millar, John. [1787] 1803. *An Historical View of the English Government: From the Settlement of the Saxons in Britain to the Revolution in 1688; to which are Subjoined Some Dissertations Connected with the History of Government from the Revolution to the Present Time.* Vols. I-IV. London: Mawman.

———. [1771] 1806. *The Origin of the Distinction of Ranks: Or, an Inquiry into the Circumstances Which Give Rise to Influence and Authority, in the Different Members of Society.* Edinburgh, Scotland: Blackwood.

Schneider, Louis, ed. 1967. *The Scottish Moralists: On Human Nature and Society.* Chicago: University of Chicago Press.

Smith, Adam. [1776] 1976. *An Inquiry into the Nature and Causes of the Wealth of Nations.* Vols. I-II. Oxford, UK: Clarendon.

———. [1759] 1982. *The Theory of Moral Sentiments.* Indianapolis: Liberty Fund.

Stewart, Dugald. 1854. *The Collected Works of Dugald Stewart.* Vol. X. Edinburgh, Scotland: Constable.

Strydom, Piet. 2000. *Discourse and Knowledge: The Making of Enlightenment Sociology.* Liverpool, UK: Liverpool University Press.

Swingewood, Alan. 1991. *A Short History of Sociological Thought.* Houndsmills, UK: Macmillan.

SECULARIZATION

The word *secularization* comes from the Latin *sæculum,* which could be taken to mean an age (or era) but also, at least by the fourth and fifth centuries, "the world," probably as an extension of the idea of a "spirit of an age." By this date, too, the word had already developed an ambiguous meaning. It could be used to mean something like unending time (the phrases "world without end" or "forever and ever" that still often appear at the end of formal Christian prayers are translations of the Latin *in sæcula sæculorum*), or the world "out there" (monastic priests, who were "enclosed" and under a formal "rule of life," were distinguished from "secular" clergy, meaning the parish clergy who served the people "out in the world"), but it was also used to mean a life or lifestyle that is at odds with God (thus, people would enter monastic life to flee "the world"). Later the term would come to be used to distinguish between civil and ecclesiastical law, lands, and possessions. In the nineteenth century, the term was adopted by the British freethinker G. J. Holyoake, who founded the Secular Society as a group committed to a just world order and moral program of individual action that would address human problems without the use of supernatural explanations. Hence, the term had an increasingly negative use by the time it was adapted into social science: Secularization conceptualized and gave "scientific" status to the advance of secularism.

The term *secularization* was introduced by Max Weber, but ever so lightly, in his Protestant Ethic essays and was adapted by his sometime associate Ernst Troeltsch. To the extent that one may reference a single integrating focus in a body of work as extensive as Max Weber's corpus, it must be said to be that of *rationalität,* or *the processes of the rationalization of action,* the specific form of *social change* that enabled the "modern world" to come into being. Weber was interested in how it was that methods of rational calculation had come to dominate virtually the entirety of modern life. He referred to this as the "spirit of capitalism." His studies convinced him that, from the sixteenth century forward, a process had been occurring in Western civilization as a result of which one after another sphere of life had become subject to the belief that explanations for events could be found within worldly experience and the application of human reason.

The consequence of this worldview was that explanations referring to forces outside this world were constantly being laid aside. The flip side of rationalization

Weber termed *Entzauberung*—a word usually translated as *disenchantment,* although perhaps more accurately rendered de-magi-fication or de-mystery-ization. Disenchantment did not simply mean that people did not believe in the old mysteries of religion but, rather, that the concept of mystery or "the mysterious" was itself devalued. Mystery was seen not as something to be entered into but something to be conquered by human reason, ingenuity, and the products of technology. Weber gave the name secularization to this double-sided rationalization-disenchantment process in religion. Secularization was both the process and the result of the process; however, it is also the case that the term occurs only rarely in Weber's writing.

It is not clear that Weber himself considered secularization to be a specific domain of the sociology of religion. In his essay "Science as a Vocation," *intellectualization* is used as a virtual synonym; hence, it could be argued that secularization ought to be more properly considered an aspect of the sociology of knowledge—to deal with questions of *epistemology,* the ways people "know" or the conditions on which we receive "knowledge" of "the ways the world works." Weber's claim is that appeals to divine authority have lost credibility relative to the past as providing sure knowledge for social action and that practical economic considerations (contrasted to a heavenly bank account) have come to play an increasing role in measuring the worth of knowledge. At most, "the religious point of view" will be treated as one among many competing claims to authority. Priests, ministers, rabbis, and mullahs are less sought after for solving world problems than economists, physicists, and political scientists, while psychologists, social workers, and medical doctors are the societally recognized experts at the individual or microsocial level. Mark Chaves, for example, explicates secularization along these lines in referring to it as a "declining scope of religious authority."

SECULARIZATION IN AMERICA

Secularization did not become a significant concept in American sociology until the late 1950s. An important figure in this development was the popular essayist Will Herberg, whose work had circulation beyond the academy and was at the same time not tightly bound by the canons of scholarship that characterized academic sociology. In spite of a cautionary article by Larry Shiner as early as 1967 about the muddled meanings that had come to be attached to the term—hence his suggestion that "we drop the word entirely"—by the early 1970s, secularization was the reigning dogma in the field for understanding the contemporary religion-and-society nexus.

Twenty years would pass between Shiner's expression of reservations about secularization "theory" and the next major assault on the thesis. In between, Bryan Wilson, Peter Berger, Thomas Luckmann, and Karel Dobbelaere would become the principal proponents of the concept. Not insignificantly, Wilson, Luckmann, and Dobbelaere are Europeans, and Berger is a European emigré to the United States. All were products of a European Christian intellectual heritage and educational system that, we might now say, romanticized the religious past of their nations. Among them, only Berger has now fully recanted his earlier position, perhaps a sign of a fuller Americanization. Even now, the most aggressive proponent of the concept is the British sociologist Steve Bruce.

In his 1986 presidential address to the Southern Sociological Society, Jeffrey Hadden presented a clear, comprehensive, and trenchant analysis of the weakness of secularization theory—both in its genesis and its predicted outcomes. The core of his argument is that in and from its genesis secularization constituted a "*doctrine* more than a theory" based on "presuppositions that . . . represent a taken-for-granted *ideology*" of social scientists "rather than a systematic set of interrelated propositions"; over time in social scientific circles (which continued to widen in their influence), "*the idea of secularization became sacralized,*" that is, a belief system accepted "on faith" (Hadden 1987:588). Even more than a statement about the present, the ideology of secularization relies on beliefs about the past.

The second thrust of Hadden's attack is a fourfold challenge: (1) Secularization theory is internally weak in its logical structure—basically Shiner's 1967 critique. (2) Such secularization *theory* as does exist is unsupported by data after more than 20 years of research. (3) New religious movements (NRMs) have appeared and persisted in the most supposedly secularized societies. And finally, (4) religion has emerged as a vital force in the world political order. These four points are the heart of the contemporary critique of the secularization concept.

In the boldest terms, as Shiner (1967) points out, however, secularization theory's claims mean the "decline of religion"—that is, religion's "previously accepted symbols, doctrines and institutions lose their prestige and influence. The culmination of secularization would be a religionless society" (p. 209). Rodney Stark, perhaps the preeminent contemporary critic of secularization theory, also fully accepts this definition as paradigmatic of secularization theory, and it is this one with which he takes issue.

Two important observations arise here: The first is that *secularization,* secularity, or the secular *is always relative to* some definition of *religion* or the religious. As Edward Bailey (1998) writes, the meaning of secular "keeps changing yet remains consistent. It always means, simply, the opposite of 'religious'—whatever that means" (p. 18). This not only suggests that the "definition of religion question" is not an arcane philosophical debate, but it also shows how premises can influence evidence and outcomes, hence why it is important to examine premises carefully. The second observation is that the "truth" of secularization claims depends on *historical* evidence. If we say, "people are less religious now than they were a hundred years ago," we have not only invoked some presumed definition of religion, but we have also said that we know how religious people were 100 years ago.

THE MEANING OF CHANGE

All the propositions advanced by secularization theorists share a common presupposition—namely, that there has been an enormously significant *change* in the ways in which society and religion have interacted in the past from the ways they do now.

At the purely descriptive level, secularization may be said to refer to the process of the separation of state and church in Europe, which was much more complex than it was in the United States. Olivier Tschannen (1991:397) has provided a graph that summarizes the "exemplary infrastructure" or "primitive cognitive apparatus" that may be derived from the efforts of various secularization theorists. Application of his map shows that the one element they have in common is that of institutional *differentiation.* According to Ralf Dahrendorf, for example, the entire European social system was characterized by a state of *superimposition* wherein one institutional system overlay another and each had a hand in the other. Church, state, education, health and welfare, the law, and the like were so intertwined that sundering them caused a significant shock to all sectors of the system, from which religion was not immune. The United States, by contrast, was characterized by relative pluralism from its earliest years. Church and state were constitutionally separated, and free-market, *laissez-faire* economics circumscribed the role of the state as far as other institutional sectors of the social system were concerned. Nevertheless, even in the United States a view has grown that "religion" is in decline.

There is no question that in most of the Western world there has been at least sufficient separation of church and state, the primary locus of differentiation, that people are capable of living their lives apart from direct "interference" on the part of religion and that people may choose among various religions without suffering civil disabilities. If this is all that is meant by secularization, then there is no debate over "the secularization thesis." But if this is all that secularization meant, there would also have been far less excitement about the topic. It would not have been so much something to investigate as simply something to state as a factual condition (or as not existing in other parts of the world). Indeed, on this basis, one could develop a fairly simple classification system of those societies that had or had not been legally "secularized" in much the same way that we can determine whether or not a business has been incorporated or is a partnership or a sole proprietorship.

There is no doubt that the separation of church and state has consequences for religious organizations and for the lives of individual citizens. At the organizational level, for example, a previously established religion may lose tax support; on the other hand, other religious organizations gain free access to the religious "market"—that is, other religions get to operate on an equal basis. Whether or not this means the decline of religion, therefore, becomes an empirical question. Individuals no longer may be required to pay taxes to support religion, and they may also be required to conform to certain state norms. These may open or close religious options and freedoms, as people can choose to support or reject religious alternatives.

The principal thrust in secularization theory has, however, been stronger than simply church-state issues or the scope of religious authority. It has been a claim that, in the face of scientific rationality, religion's influence on all aspects of life—from personal habits to social institutions—is in dramatic decline. Regardless of the sociostructural level of the argument, the underlying assumption is that "people" are becoming "less religious." Many social theorists doubted that modernity could combine religious traditions with the overpowering impersonal features of our time: scientific research, humanistic education, high-technology multinational capitalism, bureaucratic organizational life, and so on. Reacting on the basis of a functional definition of religion, religion appeared to these theorists denuded of almost all the functions it had previously appeared to perform. In this view, religion harked back to some prior level of human evolution and was now uselessly appended to the modern cultural repertoire. People today are awed by human achievements, not divine forces; societies of the future would be constructed around these, not antiquity's notion of the "sacred."

The underlying religious myth of secularization theory, as Stark notes, is that in "the past" people were significantly more religious than they are today. That is, that in the past there was a solidary Age of Faith in which "the world was filled with the sacred." According to this myth, the Age of Faith gave way to the Age of Reason. Europeans and Euro-Americans often point to the medieval era as the site of the Age of Faith. Yet there is a growing consensus among historians that both the Catholic Middle Ages and the Protestant Age of Reformation are creations of nineteenth-century Europe, when the new mass media and the schooling of the entire population made the Christianization of everyone a reality. In short, the Age of Faith myth reflects an educational process that did not begin to occur until about 200 years ago. What happened in that process was that precisely as a serious attempt was made to "Christianize" the entire population, a counterattempt at resistance also emerged. The "Age of Faith," if it ever existed, did so for at most a few decades of the nineteenth century.

PLURALISM

What can we say of secularization now? We can say that over time our epistemologies have changed, that our ideas of "the ways the world works" have changed, and that these have entailed corresponding shifts of emphasis in global explanatory structures or bases on which we attribute credibility or truth. When we consider the relatively short history of the scientific worldview, it is not surprising that its epistemology has not fully jelled; furthermore, the phenomenon of globalization creates a contestation among religious epistemologies themselves that, although it has analogs in the past, is unprecedented in its scope today.

The theory of secularization as a self-limiting process as proposed by Stark and Bainbridge, however, can help us to understand some of the important social dynamics that lie behind religious developments in our own day. In many respects, secularization theory was an attempt to account for how *pluralism* was reshaping the religious map—both geographically and cognitively; that is, there is a world religious ferment of contesting epistemologies going on without limit around the globe. Contemporary pluralism means that far more religious worldviews are in immediate competition with each other than has ever been the case in the past. Whereas the United States could once settle on a shared "Judeo-Christian" ethic, its religious map now must accommodate Muslims and Buddhists in increasing numbers.

Furthermore, the nature of pluralism is multiplicative. Each "new" religion (or newly imported religion) spawns more new religions, and as some secularization theorists rightly noted, ever-increasing pluralism does undermine the element of absolute certainty that has been claimed by at least some religions, although new religions will simultaneously continue to arise making precisely this claim. That is, the more one becomes aware of more and more religions competing in a marketplace-like setting, the harder it becomes to assert that any one religion contains all truth and that others must be all wrong. While it is certainly possible to make "better" and "worse" type comparisons, all-or-nothing rigidity simply does not hold up.

Religious (or, more broadly, ideological) pluralism clearly creates a marketplace of ideas wherein absolute claims for ultimacy are always at some degree of risk. This gives rise to a model of religious competition or marketplace, and in a double sense. Not only is there competition among religions themselves, but there is also the freedom on the part of buyers (people) to pick and choose among the ideological wares different religions proffer. This has been referred to as "religion à la carte" and the result as *bricolage*. The outcome of increased competition is clearly a shifting of market shares. However, Finke and Stark have shown that the reality of increasing religious competition in American cities was not a decrease in religious mobilization but an increase. Stark has also shown that this increase

extended to rural areas but that these changes were often unreported because newer, "marginal" churches were not counted in religious censuses. European religious activity follows this pattern least well, perhaps because the state-church tradition there has created a mind-set to which any and all religion is simply a less desirable "good" than it is elsewhere, due to its having been taken for granted for so long, hence so closely identified with a taken-for-granted culture. With certain notable exceptions, European religious participation has been historically low; yet curiously, for example, European immigrants to the United States generally acted quickly to re-create the church of their homeland, and along with their immediate descendants were *much more* religious (or at least organizationally active) than was the custom in their countries of origin.

That people are more likely to want their religion à la carte does not necessarily mean that they are "less religious." The metaphor is helpful: People who order meals à la carte often actually spend more than they would have if they bought a *prix fixe* meal. What choosing à la carte does mean is that people do not simply take whatever is dished out to them. However, it should not be assumed that as a result they will eat irresponsibly—three desserts and no veggies. People may just as often use the *carte* to choose wisely, passing over rich sauces and heavy starches. Certainly it is true, as Chaves has noted, that the authority of religious officers is reduced in this process; on the other hand, it must be remembered that religious officers are nothing but layfolk who have become supercharged by a religious message. The quality of motivation that leads to becoming a religious officer may change, but in fact this may again result in more rather than less: Consider the surplus of (male and female, married and single, straight and gay) priests in the Episcopal church, compared with the shortage of (celibate) priests in the Roman Catholic church where hierarchical clerical authority is still maximized. Episcopal church membership has shrunk while its number of clergy has grown, whereas Roman Catholic membership has grown while its number of clergy has shrunk.

With respect to the secularization thesis, then, two aspects of pluralism must be taken into consideration. On one hand, there is a substantial body of evidence that pluralism of belief—including disbelief—has been an option throughout history that is simply intensified by globalization. On the other hand, pluralism forces us to make a distinction between secularization and what might be called "de-Christianization": That is, new religious movements may emerge or other world traditions may gain dominance over Christianity in the West. Leaving Christianity for another religion is not secularization. *Religious change* of course has occurred, and this will have consequences for the societies in which it takes place.

The underlying assumption of secularization theory that pluralism thus challenges is the idea that "religion" is something fixed. Instead, sociologists need to recognize the tentativeness and fragility of religious structures of meaning. Religious concepts easily lend themselves to reification. As ideational systems, religions are always in interaction with material culture, social structure, other cultural systems, and individual personalities. The theological bias of secularization theory within the sociology of religion (especially via Troeltsch and Herberg) has underwritten conceptions of "religion" as essentially fixed rather than essentially variable. *Sociologically,* however, there is far more reason to conceive religion as variable—indeed, whereas among social institutions religion deals uniquely with a nonempirical, "uncontrollable" referent, religion is *infinitely* variable in a way that other action orientations are not. Theological, rather than sociological, presuppositions and prejudices warrant the notion of religious fixity; thus, sociological theories of religion need to be attentive to change as *inherent* in religion, just as change is in other institutional spheres and cultural dimensions, precisely because religion is a sociocultural institution.

— William H. Swatos Jr.

See also Dahrendorf, Ralf; Parsons, Talcott; Religion; Weber, Max

FURTHER READINGS AND REFERENCES

Bailey, Edward. 1998. "'Implicit Religion': What Might That Be?" *Implicit Religion* 1:9–22.

Chaves, Mark A. 1994. "Secularization as Declining Religious Authority." *Social Forces* 72:749–74.

Dobbelaere, Karel. 1981. *Secularization: A Multidimensional Concept.* London: Sage.

Finke, Roger and Rodney Stark. 1992. *The Churching of America, 1776–1990: Winners and Losers in Our Religious Economy.* New Brunswick, NJ: Rutgers University Press.

Hadden, Jeffrey K. 1987. "Toward Desacralizing Secularization Theory." *Social Forces* 65:587–611.

Shiner, Larry. 1967. "The Concept of Secularization in Empirical Research." *Journal for the Scientific Study of Religion* 6: 207–20.

Stark, Rodney and William Sims Bainbridge. 1985. *The Future of Religion: Secularization, Revival, and Cult Formation.* Berkeley: University of California Press.

Swatos, William H. Jr. and Daniel V. A. Olson. 2000. *The Secularization Debate.* Lanham, MD: Rowman & Littlefield.

Tschannen, Olivier. 1991. "The Secularization Paradigm: A Systematization." *Journal for the Scientific Study of Religion* 30:396–415.

Weber, Max. 1946. *From Max Weber,* edited by C. Wright Mills and H. H. Gerth. New York: Oxford University Press.

———. [1922] 1978. *Economy and Society.* Reprint. Berkeley: University of California Press.

———. [1904–1906] 1998. *The Protestant Ethic and the Spirit of Capitalism.* Reprint. Los Angeles: Roxbury.

SELF AND SELF-CONCEPT

At the end of the nineteenth century, the Harvard psychologist William James laid down a cornerstone of modern self theory. In his 1890 *Principles of Psychology,* James distinguished between the *self as knower* (the I) and the *self as object known* (the Me, or self-concept). This formulation offered a language for talking about matters that had been obscured by reifications such as psyche, mind, soul, spirit, and ego. Following James, the self could be seen as both a process—acts of perception and knowing—and the outcome of that process—knowledge about the knower. James's distinction remains basic to self theory today.

The origins of self theory lie in human prehistory. As our hominid ancestors sought to explain the world around them, they likewise struggled to explain themselves. The world of dreams, images, thoughts, and feelings was perhaps no less troubling a mystery than the outer world of animals, plants, weather, and landscape. Where did these inner forces come from, and how did they relate to the outer world? What made one person different from another? To wrestle with these questions was to begin to theorize about the self.

Reflecting on the capacities, dispositions, and inner processes that make us human may thus be as old as consciousness. By the time such reflections began to be recorded, people surely had been thinking about human nature for ages. When Socrates (470–399 BCE) urged "know thyself," he presumed an intellectual framework within which disciplined introspection made sense. The Socratic admonition leaves open, however, the question of precisely what it is we should seek to know. And that is the question that has occupied subsequent social theorists.

To try to identify a history of thought regarding the self raises, first, the question of whether there exists a body of thought that constitutes a coherent tradition of theorizing about the self. By modern standards of scholarship, the answer is no, at least prior to the nineteenth century. Before then, one can find a great deal of philosophical and theological discourse about the inner processes—or, more often, "essences"—that constitute human nature. Absent is conceptual consensus or continuity. Psyche, soul, spirit, mind, proprium, and ego may all be answers to roughly the same question, but the answers, cast in such disparate terms, refuse to add up.

A major shift in thinking began to appear in the eighteenth century. Before this, Leibniz, Descartes, and other rationalist philosophers of the sixteenth- and seventeenth-century Renaissance period embraced a neoclassical view of the human being. In this view, the mind—that which made us self-aware and uniquely human—is an indisputably natural, indeed axiomatic, feature of individuals. This was expressed in Descartes's famous dictum: *I think, therefore I am.* By the end of the nineteenth century, however, this dictum was supplanted by one that has remained foundational ever since: *I am social, therefore I can think.*

This shift had vast implications for theorizing about the self as a social phenomenon and a matter for empirical study. The eighteenth-century Scottish moral philosophers, notably David Hume and Adam Smith, drew attention to how social life engendered the moral habits and sentiments that make us human. Hume and Smith (and later Marx, Weber, and Durkheim) saw how capitalist industrialization was altering social relationships, giving rise to new categories and groups, creating new moral strains, and in these ways, generating new patterns of thought. In light of such changes, it was no longer tenable to see the human mind as insulated from social life. The inner processes that make us human were coming to be seen as inexorably linked to the organization of social life.

James's contribution opened the way to deeper understandings of these connections between self and society. In James's view, the self as object known—what he called the *Me*—becomes more complex as society becomes more complex. The more different ways it is possible to exist in a given society—materially, socially, and spiritually—the more different ways we can know ourselves. The complexity of the Me is also enhanced by the multiple relationships that can exist between individuals and groups. As James (1890) put it in a key passage,

> Properly speaking, a man has as many social selves as there are individuals who recognize him and carry an image of him in their mind. To wound any one of these his images is to wound him. But as the individuals who carry the images fall naturally into classes, we may practically say that he has as many different social selves as there are distinct *groups* of persons about whose opinion he cares. (p. 294)

This passage foreshadows Charles Horton Cooley's notion of the *looking-glass self,* which refers to self-conceptions that derive from imagining how others judge us. The emphasis on feelings attached to self-images also foreshadows Erving Goffman's discussion of the self as a virtual reality created in interaction. Further implied is a central idea of reference group theory: Behavior is aimed at pleasing the audiences that most powerfully affect our self-conceptions.

Following in the pragmatist tradition, John Dewey and George H. Mead built on James's ideas concerning the social nature of the self. Dewey emphasized the "I" as a conditioned subjectivity: a configuration of habits shaped by our relationships with others and by our choices in response to the moral dilemmas inherent in social life. Dewey's contribution was thus to highlight the self as both a social product and an agent of its own making. Mead drew

on James, Dewey, and Cooley, powerfully and creatively extending their ideas (see Mead [1934] *Mind, Self, and Society*). Mead's profound contributions lay in theorizing about the development of the self, the role of language in this process, and the relationship between mind and self.

Although Mead adopted James's "I" and "Me" terminology and sometimes referred to these as alternating phases of the self, Mead uniquely conceived of the self as an internalization of the social process of communication. According to Mead, this process entails the use of significant symbols, which are those that evoke, by virtue of learned convention, a similar response in the user and the perceiver. Using such symbols requires taking the perspective of the other—that is, sympathetically imagining the other's response to the symbol (be it gestural, oral, or textual). Taking the perspective of the other implies, in turn, the ability to look back on oneself as an object. To do this—to act and then, in the next moment, perceive the meaning of that act from the standpoint of an other—is, for Mead, what it means for an individual to have a self.

In Mead's view, the self is not inborn but emergent. This occurs as the child learns to use language (rather than impulsive cries and gestures) to evoke responses in others. To use language in this way requires perspective taking, which in turn enables perception of oneself as actor/object. As the child masters the use of language to evoke precise responses in others, the child also learns to carry on the process imaginarily. The unfolding of this internal conversation—in which one's acts, the reactions of others, and one's reactions to those reactions are represented in consciousness—is the process that constitutes the self. Further development occurs as the individual gains facility with language and the ability to take the perspectives of diverse others. Adult development is achieved when individuals are able to take the perspective of a community, or what Mead called the *generalized other.*

Mead's view also distinguishes self from mind. Rather than use the static term *mind,* Mead preferred to speak of *minded behavior,* by which he meant behavior that was not merely impulsive but was mediated by internal representations—imagery—of external objects and completed acts. Mead argued that the highly complex human nervous system enables the internal representation and imaginary manipulation of complex external states. This use of imagery and cognitive manipulation occurs "in the field of mind," wherein also arises the process of self as described above. A prominent feature in the field of mind is the Me—the person as a social object—which is taken into account, along with other persons and objects, in forming minded behavior, or what contemporary symbolic interactionists call a "line of action."

James and Mead are the giants of classic social theorizing about the self. They conceived the self as distinct from and not reducible to psyche, spirit, mind, or ego. Both theorists also linked the self—as process and object—to social life. The distinction between self as knower and self as object known also has been enormously important for later work on the self. It would be fair to say that twentieth-century social-psychological study of the self is not merely indebted to James and Mead, but barely imaginable without them.

CONTEMPORARY THEMES

Beginning early in the twentieth century, the self has been one of the most heavily studied topics in social psychology. Review articles began to appear in the early 1900s (e.g., Mary Calkins [1919]). Yet most of the theoretical and empirical work on the self throughout the century can be seen as moving along paths cut by classical self theorists. Four themes, or focal concerns, thus continue to dominate self theory: (1) the nature of the self as knower; (2) the content, causes, and consequences of self-conceptions; (3) the interactive construction of virtual selves through expressive and interpretive behavior; and (4) the etiology of the self.

Until the 1980s, little effort was made to further theorize the self as knower. It was as if this aspect of the self, the *I* of James's formulation, simply had to be assumed rather than explained. The cognitive revolution in psychology changed this. Under the influence of ideas associated with computer science, the brain was now seen as a kind of organic computer, and mind as "software" that ran on this organic platform. Some social psychologists, mostly in psychology, took this computer metaphor seriously and used it to reconceive the self as knower.

In this view, the self as knower is theorized as a *schema*. A schema is not static but rather, as Greenwald and Pratkanis (1984) define it, "an active, self-monitoring knowledge structure" (p. 142). A knowledge structure that can assimilate information, manipulate that information using a stable set of algorithms, and then modify itself as a result, is, in essence, a highly sophisticated computer program. Theorists who take this approach treat the self as a program for which the original code is not directly accessible. The empirical task, then, is to observe how the program functions—that is, how the self as knower processes information—and thereby infer its hidden operating logic.

Perhaps because it seemed more empirically accessible, far more attention has been paid to the self as object known, or what is now called the *self-concept*. Theorists have thus sought to specify, first, the content of the self-concept—that is, the kinds of knowledge we have about ourselves. We know ourselves, for example, in terms of public and private roles, categorical and group identities, and a set of character traits. Study of the content of the self-concept has also examined the organization of this knowledge. Some theorists have suggested, for example, that the self-concept is a theory we have about ourselves—a theory consisting of axioms, first-order propositions, and a host of logical implications.

Also recognized as key parts of the self-concept are *self-evaluations* and *self-esteem*. Although the self, like any object, can be evaluated in many ways, it has been suggested that the two main dimensions of self-evaluation, in Western societies, are competence (also referred to as self-efficacy) and morality (also referred to as self-worth). Self-esteem is then often defined as the affective response to these evaluations. Theorists have also posited two kinds of self-esteem: (1) "global," referring to chronic, generalized feelings of positive or negative self-regard, and (2) "situational," referring to more transitory feelings about the self that are influenced by events in a particular context.

Among all the concepts associated with self theory, self-esteem has gained the greatest currency in popular culture (see Hewitt 1998). Folk psychologists and moral entrepreneurs often invoke self-esteem as the cause of all manner of behaviors, good and bad. Crime, teenage pregnancy, unemployment, and failure in school have been alleged to result from low self-esteem. The obvious solution is then held to be *raising* self-esteem. Research has consistently found, however, that self-esteem is of only slight predictive value, relative to situational variables, when trying to explain social behavior.

The self-concept is universally seen as social in origin. Roles and identities derive from one's place in a social order; the meanings of identities are socially constructed and situationally variable; terms for character traits, as well as criteria for applying them, are aspects of culture; standards for self-evaluation are likewise socially learned. This view suggests that the self-concept is not only a product of social life but that its shape and content mirror the culture and social organization in which an individual develops. There is also agreement that the self-concept is formed by, and remains subject to the influence of, feedback from others (reflected appraisals); the ways we measure ourselves against others (social comparisons); and our observations of what we do and make happen (self-perceptions).

Three self-concept motives have been posited to explain how the self-concept shapes behavior. The tendency to behave in ways that affirm central identities is attributed to a *self-consistency* or *self-verification motive*. The tendency to behave in ways that generate positive reflected appraisals (from important audiences), favorable social comparisons, and perceptions of morality and competence is attributed to a *self-esteem motive*. And the tendency to behave in ways that produce observable and valued effects on the world is attributed to a *self-efficacy motive*. Theorists have thus sought to understand the self-concept not only as a social product but also as a social force.

A different approach to the self is found in theoretical work associated with the dramaturgical and semiotic perspectives. In the dramaturgical view, associated with Erving Goffman, the self is a "dramatic [or rhetorical] effect," that is, an attribution of character that is interactively constructed through expressive and interpretive behavior. The only self that matters, in other words, is the one attributed to us based on our acts of signification, because this is the self to which others respond. Other than presuming a concern for protecting the feelings attached to cherished self-images, the dramaturgical perspective has little to say about cognition or self-conceptions. The semiotic perspective similarly focuses on expressive behavior, analyzing the signifying acts (sometimes called *identity work*) through which virtual selves are created in interaction.

A related approach that also treats the self as a linguistic construction points to what Kenneth Gergen calls "narratives of the self." In this view, similar to the dramaturgical, the self is an impression, a virtual reality, created in our minds and the minds of others. This impression, however, is created not only through situated expressive behavior and reactions to that behavior but through lifelong storytelling about ourselves. Who we are is thus seen as a result of how we selectively weave the purported facts of biography into stories about ourselves. Studies of the narrative construction of the self have examined cultural templates for biographical storytelling and the interactive creation of self-narratives in therapeutic groups.

In the 1980s, there emerged a strain of self theory influenced by postmodernist social theory more generally (see Elliott 2001). The core argument was that as social life had become more fast-paced, fluid, fragmented, and soaked in media images, the self had changed correspondingly. According to postmodernist self theory, the idea of a solid, stable self as the basis of personhood is passé. "The postmodern self," as Gecas and Burke (1995) described it in a critical review of the literature, is "decentered, relational, contingent, illusory, and lacking any core or essence" (p. 57). Some theorists went so far as to argue that the self had disappeared. Critics of the postmodernist view granted that changes in society could produce changes in self-conceptions and experiences of personhood but preferred to treat any such changes as matters for empirical study rather than accepting the self's demise by theoretical fiat.

At the start of the new century, studies of the self and self-concept continue to move along the paths outlined above. Researchers remain concerned with how culture and social structure shape the self and with how the self in turn shapes thought and behavior. Narrative approaches to studying self and identity seem to be gaining ground relative to older approaches based on experiments and surveys. At the other end of the spectrum, an emerging neurobiological perspective aims to theorize the relationship between the organization of neural networks in the brain and the emergence of self-consciousness. Each path carries on the ageless human project of understanding the self as knower and as object never fully known.

— Michael Schwalbe

See also Cooley, Charles Horton; Dramaturgy; Goffman, Erving; Identity; Mead, George Herbert; Postmodernism; Pragmatism; Symbolic Interaction

FURTHER READINGS AND REFERENCES

Baumeister, Roy, ed. 1999. *The Self in Social Psychology.* Ann Arbor, MI: Edwards Brothers.

Calkins, Mary Whiton. 1919. "The Self in Recent Psychology." *Psychological Bulletin* 16:111–18.

Elliott, Anthony. 2001. *Concepts of the Self.* Oxford, UK: Blackwell.

Gecas, Viktor and Peter Burke. 1995. "Self and Identity." Pp. 41–67 in *Sociological Perspectives on Social Psychology,* edited by K. S. Cook, G. A. Fine, and J. S. House. Boston: Allyn & Bacon.

Gergen, Kenneth. 1991. *The Saturated Self: Dilemmas of Identity in Contemporary Life.* New York: Basic Books.

Greenwald, Anthony G. and Anthony R. Pratkanis. 1984. "The Self." Pp. 129–78 in *Handbook of Social Cognition,* edited by R. S. Wyer and T. K. Srull. Hillsdale, NJ: Lawrence Erlbaum.

Hewitt, John P. 1998. *The Myth of Self-Esteem.* New York: St. Martin's.

James, William. 1890 [1918]. *The Principles of Psychology, vol 1.* New York: Henry Holt.

Rosenberg, Morris and Howard B. Kaplan, eds. 1982. *Social Psychology of the Self-Concept.* Arlington Heights, IL: Harlan Davidson.

SEMIOLOGY

Semiology has its modern origins in the linguistic theory of Ferdinand de Saussure, especially in the various versions of his *Cours de Linguistique Générale* [*Course in General Linguistics*] ([1916] 1971). Some of the basic principles expounded by Saussure are also discussed by classical writers such as Plato and Aristotle, although neither of these thinkers explicitly set out to develop a science of semiology as such. In the present discussion, the term *semiology* will refer to those developments that stem from Saussure in the early twentieth century and that have contributed to the further development of Saussure's thinking. The term semiology is to be distinguished from the term *semiotics*. The latter term, at least in its modern usage, is traceable to the work of the American philosopher Charles Sanders Peirce and will not be discussed here. Increasingly, the term semiotics, irrespective of the Peircean lineage, has become the more widely used term.

In Saussure's conception, semiology is the study of systems of signs. According to the notes compiled by Riedlinger and Constantin of Saussure's third *Cours de Linguistique Générale* (Saussure 1993), semiology is defined as "studies of signs and their life in human societies"

(p. 282), Saussure's inauguration of this new science depends on establishing an object of study—the language system, or *la langue*—in order that the language system may take its place among "the human facts" [*les faits humains*] (p. 282). For reasons that the various texts of the *Cours* do not make explicit, Saussure subsumes the study of the language system and of other sign systems (e.g., writing, maritime signals, sign language) under psychology, more particularly social psychology. It is interesting to compare Saussure's classification with the observations made by Claparède (1916) in his review of the *Cours de Linguistique Générale* Claparède, who was professor of Psychology at the University of Geneva, states: "Whereas Saussure recognizes that 'all is psychology in the language system,' he distinguishes, however, linguistics from psychology in an absolute manner" (p. 94). According to Saussure (1993), "The set of socially ratified associations [between acoustic images and ideas] that constitute the language system have their seat in the brain; it is a set of realities similar to other psychic realities" (p. 282). In this sense, an essentially social phenomenon—the language system—may be said to have a psychological reality for the individual by virtue of the associations between acoustic images and ideas that each individual stores in his or her brain. A further reason for locating semiology as a branch of (social) psychology may have to do with Saussure's concern to find an academic home for the newly launched semiological study of signs.

The most essential fact about the language system *qua* semiological system is that it is a system of signs. Saussure does not offer any systematic analysis of the other sign systems that he mentions as candidates for inclusion in his newly inaugurated science of semiology. He does, however, enter into a discussion of systems of writing in relation to the ways in which, according to Saussure, writing has impeded the development of the study of the *la langue*. Nevertheless, Saussure does not develop a corresponding semiology of writing (*écriture*), based on the visual-spatial character of written signs (see Harris 2001; Thibault 1996a, 1996b). For Saussure (1993), semiology is, above all, the study of "systems of arbitrary signs, of which the language system is the principal example" (p. 288). In Saussure's famous definition, "The linguistic sign rests on an association made by the mind between two very different things, but which are both psychic and within the subject: an acoustic image is associated with a concept" (p. 285). Rather than designating a material object (tree, horse), which is outside the subject, or a material sound that one hears, the sign is an association of the two terms—acoustic image and concept—linked by the same psychic association within the individual. This fact is demonstrated, Saussure points out, by the ways in which we can both "pronounce (and hear) an interior discourse" without moving the lips. Inner language [*langage intérieur*] (Saussure 1993:287) occurs because a socially ratified language system makes possible this relationship of association between the two immaterial terms that make up the linguistic sign in the minds of the individuals who speak a given language, either in silent inner speech or in externalised speech with others.

Saussure's semiological theory of sign systems is founded on two critically important concepts. The first of these is the *arbitrary* character of the linguistic sign. The second is the concept of *value*. These two concepts will now be discussed.

ARBITRARINESS AND THE STRATIFIED NATURE OF LINGUISTIC SIGNS

The linguistic sign is arbitrary in the following way: "The concept *sœur* [sister] for example is not linked in any interior way (relationship) with the sequence of sounds s + ö + r that forms the corresponding acoustic image" (Saussure 1993:287). Signs of writing, Saussure says, also have this same arbitrary character (p. 288). More generally, Saussure points out that the future science of semiology will have to see "if it must be concerned with arbitrary signs or others" (p. 288). In any case, the primary domain of semiology, in Saussure's view, will be "systems of arbitrary signs, of which the language system is the principal example" (p. 288). Saussure further clarifies the arbitrary nature of the relationship between acoustic image and concept as follows: "as having nothing in it [the word] which particularly ties it to its concept" (p. 288). That is, there is no necessary or naturalistic relationship between a particular word and the concept that it signifies. It is important to bear in mind here that, for Saussure, the relationship between acoustic image and concept is an *internal* one between two aspects of one overall linguistic form.

Subsequent theorizing in some influential branches of linguistics often yielded different readings of Saussure's formulation. Many linguists have made a distinction between form and meaning. The relationship between these two levels is then said to be arbitrary in the sense that it is not motivated by any natural link between them on the assumption that the two levels of form and meaning are constitutively separable. The relationship between the linguistic levels of phonology and lexicogrammar is said to be arbitrary in this sense. This line of argumentation follows from theorizing about language in which meaning is separated from and seen as not systematically related to linguistic form. According to another variant of this thinking, the relationship between form and meaning is arbitrary in the sense that there is no naturalistic or necessary correspondence or resemblance between linguistic form and the real-world object or event that the form designates. There is, in this view, no naturalistic resemblance between, say, the word *butterfly* and the real-world insects that we see flying about gardens, parks, fields, and forests.

It is arguable that neither of these definitions of arbitrariness exactly captures the meaning it has in the texts deriving from Saussure's courses in Geneva. First, Saussure did not make a distinction between "form" and "meaning" in the way that later formal linguists did. Rather, both dimensions of the linguistic sign in his definition—that is, acoustic image (signifier) and concept (signified)—are aspects of linguistic form in the language system from which they derive. Secondly, Saussure's definition of the sign is not about the external relation between a given sign and the real-world object that it names. Rather, Saussure is at pains to stress that it is about the internal relationship of association between the two different dimensions of the sign's organization, as described above. It was on this basis that Saussure (1993) rejected the view of the sign as a nomenclature for naming objects in the external world (pp. 285–86).

This second reading of arbitrariness as referring to an external relationship between sign and object essentially states a banality and is, for this reason, of no great interest to linguistic theory. Linguists seek to understand the ways in which different levels of linguistic organization are systematically and functionally motivated in relation to each other. Different levels of linguistic organization such as phonology, morphology, lexicogrammar, and semantics are very often functionally and, therefore, semiologically motivated in relation to each other. Motivation in this sense follows from the fact that language and other sign systems are, as we shall see below, systems for making meanings in the contexts with which semiological (linguistic, etc.) forms are integrated and that, in part, they create in use.

To be sure, Saussure's claim that there is no naturalistic or necessary relationship between speech sounds and meaning is substantially correct. However, concrete speech sounds are not the same as phonological organization, although they are related. Phonology is an abstract level of linguistic organization that integrates with grammar and functions to make meaningful distinctions in grammar, among the other things that phonology does. There is a *functionally motivated*, rather than arbitrary, relationship between these two levels.

Rather than simply treat phonemes, say, as the constituent parts, or the building blocks, of morphemes, we can say that the level of phonology realizes the level of grammar. For example, in English, syllables (a phonological [articulatory] unit) frequently, although not always, correlate with morpheme and word boundaries on the lexicogrammatical level. One such example in English is syllable closure by the consonant / ʤ / in words such as *bridge* / brɪʤ /, *bridgehead* / briDhed /, cabbage / kæbɪʤ /, caged / keɪʤd /, *hedgehog* / heʤhɒg /, *ranger* / reɪnʤəʳ /, *ridge* / rɪʤ /, and *ridged* / rɪʤd /. Typically, a syllable closed by / ʤ / indicates the *end* of a morpheme or a word, as shown:

brɪʤ	rɪʤ	d	heʤ	hɒg
SYLLABLE	SYLLABLE	SYLLABLE	SYLLABLE	SYLLABLE
morph-finality	morph-finality		morph-finality	

Here is a second example of the functional relationship between phonology and lexicogrammar. In tone languages such as Mandarin Chinese (Pǔtōnghuà), a tonal feature from the phonological system integrates with an entire grammatical unit by extending over its entire length so as to determine its meaning. For example,

bā (level) = eight
bá (rising) = pull out, uproot
bǎ (falling-rising) = to handle, to grip
bà (falling) = dad

The Chinese examples also show us that the tonal feature is not a discrete particle. Instead, it spreads or extends over the entire grammatical unit and cannot be restricted to any single part of the overall unit.

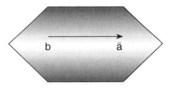

Figure 1   Prosodic Extension of the Tonal Feature [LEVEL] over an Entire Syllable Comprising a Consonant and Vowel to Indicate the Meaning [EIGHT] of the Grammatical Unit that Is Realized by the Phonological One

In Figure 1, the horizontal [gray shading] in the diagram represents both the extended nature of the tone over the entire duration of the two phonemes in the syllable as well as the feature [LEVEL] of this particular tone. The arrow indicates that the prosodic extension of the tonal feature has directionality in time.

In the English examples above, we see how the correlation of the syllable closure by a consonant with a morpheme or word indicates a specific lexicogrammatical domain. In the Chinese examples, the phonological feature—the tone—extends over the duration of an entire lexicogrammatical domain and, in combination with the given lexicogrammatical domain, specifies the meaning of that domain—the given lexeme—in the above examples.

Phonological units are not simply empty formal means for the construction of units on other levels. Instead, they make their own distinctive contribution, on their own level, to the meaning of the units that they help to constitute on other levels. The functionally motivated (nonarbitrary) relationship between units and relations on different levels works in two directions. That is, functions (meanings) and the formal means of their expression are mutually determining. Thus, the grammatical relation "morpheme finality" is realized by the phonological feature "syllable closure by consonant" at the same time that the latter realizes the former. There is, then, a two-way and functionally motivated relationship between the two levels.

Saussure's insistence on the arbitrary character of the linguistic sign no doubt stems, in spite of some qualifying observations, from his focus on *langue* as a relatively homogeneous and well-defined system, which is separated from actual uses of language (*parole*). It can also be related to the absence of a properly worked-out distinction between phonetics and phonology in the modern sense, as well as to the fact that grammatical relations above the level of the word are scarcely considered at all in his Geneva lectures. All these distinctions were to await future developments in twentieth-century linguistics.

In the functionalist perspectives inspired by semiological principles, all levels of linguistic organisation contribute to and function in meaningful ways both on their own level of organization and in relation to other levels of organization, including the discourse context. In a functionalist perspective of this kind, linguistic forms serve the purposes of language users in discourse. Language is not an end in itself, as in formal accounts, but is integrated with the semiotic activities—both internal and external—of language. The forms of a language have evolved in ways that enable integration of this kind to occur. Formal theories of language are essentially nonsemiological. They both separate an abstract language system from the contexts in which language is used and further claim that syntax is autonomous with respect to semantics.

Rather than simply treat phonemes, say, as the smaller-scale constituents—the building blocks—of the next biggest level (i.e., morphemes) as formal linguists do, we can say that phonemes function in the larger-scale contexts—morphemes, words—to which they are integrated to differentiate meaningful distinctions on that level. Thus, the phonological differentiation between the phonemes / p / and / b / in the pair / pɪt :: bɪt / differentiates the meanings of these two words. Likewise, the graphological distinction between the written letter shapes [i] and [y] differentiates the meaning of the two written words *bite* and *byte* even though the two words have the same phonological representation—phonetically / baɪt /—for speakers of English. This does not, of course, mean that in the spoken language, they are the same word.

In some respects, Saussure's definition of the linguistic sign more closely corresponds to the protolinguistic signs that infants create in the early stages of their prelinguistic development. A protolinguistic sign consists of an elementary signifier and a signified. There is no grammar between these two levels. Protolinguistic signs are integrated to their contexts in ways that are situation dependent: Their meaning depends on their relation to the here-now situation in which they are articulated. Protolinguistic signs cannot be deconstructed into different meaningful components—for example, ordering of elements, articulatory shape (vowels and consonants), prosodic contour, different mood and modality choices, different experiential contents, and so on—which can be independently varied and recombined in other ways in other signs. In protolanguage, there is a fixed correlation between a simple signifier and a simple signified.

Now, Saussure is clearly not talking about infant protolanguage as such. The point is that his theory of the sign correctly captures the way in which signs embody different layers of organization, but he does not show that each of the two levels of signifier and signified in the linguistic sign is itself internally stratified.

Thus, Saussure's signifier (acoustic image) is internally stratified into phonetics and phonology. Phonology is a purely abstract level of linguistic form in which sounds are organized into a language-specific system. Phonetics refers to the articulatory and acoustic properties of speech sounds from the points of view of their production and perception by the human body. The relationship between the sounds we actually produce and perceive tends to stand in a functionally motivated relationship to the more abstract system of phonological categories. The phonological system selects which features of the many degrees of topological freedom—the dynamical continuously varying features—of actual speech sounds will be criterial for distinguishing one sound from another or for assigning two or more perhaps very different articulations to the same abstract phonological category. It therefore selects which patterns from among the many possible patterns on the articulatory level will be significant on its level at the same time that it constrains the degrees of freedom of the lower level so that few patterns get selected. There is no direct correspondence between the actual sounds uttered and heard and the phonological categories to which they are assigned. Instead, their assignment to this or that category depends on the ways in which a given combination of articulatory features is integrated to its larger-scale linguistic context.

A similar point can be made with respect to the visual shapes that we arrange in particular visual-spatial configurations on treated surfaces of various kinds in writing. Saussure did not develop a semiological theory of writing comparable to his semiological theory of the spoken language system (see Harris 2001). However, the written signifiers in alphabetic languages such as English or Italian can be stratified into two levels of organization on analogous, although not identical, lines, as follows. First, a highly limited set of written shapes, including their upper- and lowercase variants (26 of each in the English alphabet), along with various punctuation signs, and so on, can be traced or copied onto a surface by somatic or extra-somatic means. Second, this limited inventory of visual forms—the letters of the alphabet—can be combined into larger visual-spatial configurations on different scalar levels of organization, such as letter clusters, orthographic words, phrases, sentences, paragraphs, and so on.

In other words, an abstract graphology systematizes the visual-spatial organization of letters into letter clusters, orthographic words, and so on, to allow these visual-spatial configurations to be integrated with the level of lexicogrammar in functionally motivated ways specific to a given language. Clearly, both written English and written Italian use many of the same visual shapes (letters) in their respective alphabets. However, the principles of their combination into larger-scale units, such as letter clusters, words, and so on, depend on more abstract principles of organization that can be explained in terms of the different principles that operate on the *graphological* level of organization of the two written language systems and how this, in turn, is integrated into the lexicogrammar of the two languages. This graphological level refers to purely visual-spatial principles of organization and must be distinguished from the (different) principles of organization that pertain to the sounds of the spoken language.

Likewise, the signified (concept) is stratified into the two levels of lexicogrammar and semantics. The relationship between the semantics and the grammar is also functionally motivated. Consider the following clause: *On October 1, 1949, Chairman Mao Zedong proclaimed the founding of the People's Republic of China at a grand inauguration ceremony held in Tiananmen Square, Beijing.* This clause consists of the following sequence of grammatical items: prepositional phrase + nominal group + verb + nominal group + prepositional phrase in the clause. Each item in the sequence also expresses a semantic function. This sequence realizes the following configuration of semantic functions: [Circumstance: Time]^[Participant: Sayer]^[Process: Verbal]^[Participant: Verbiage]^[Circumstance: Location]. The relationship between the sequence of grammatical items and the semantic configuration this realizes is functionally motivated: The grammar of the clause organizes the event as a configuration of two circumstances, a process, and the participants involved in that process. It does so in ways that correspond to our sense that our experience of the world can be analysed and interpreted in terms of component parts and how they play a role in the larger wholes to which they belong. Thus, the clause in question construes the given situation as a verbal action in which one of the participants performs and in so doing brings into being the other participant—that is, that which is said (semantically, the functional role of Verbiage). Moreover, this situation is further analysed in terms of both time and location circumstances specifying when it took place and where.

Saussure instates *langue* as a social fact, yet he does not show how a language is constrained by the ways in which it is used by human beings in a wide range of different kinds of social contexts. Instead, the emphasis is on the relatively homogeneous character of *langue* as a system of reciprocally defining differences. For Saussure, the system of differences is indifferent to the constraints emanating from particular forms of social organization and their associated meaning-making practices. *Langue* is described in a note to the diagram illustrating the separation of *langue* from *parole* in relation to *langage* in the Riedlinger-Constantin notes to the third *Course* as follows: "Social code, organizing language [*langage*] and forming the tool necessary for the exercise of the language faculty" (Saussure 1993:280). Saussure's insistence on the intrinsically social and semiological character of *langue* notwithstanding, it is not difficult to see how his characterization of *langue* as an object which is "definable and separable from the totality of language acts" and which can be studied separately from the "other elements of *langage*" (p. 281) has also led to the formalist and essentially nonsemiological project in much of twentieth-century linguistics. In that project, language has been seen as a stable and autonomous system of purely formal constraints, usually formalised as rules for explaining constraints on formal patterns.

SAUSSURE'S SEMIOLOGICAL THEORY OF VALUE AND THE RELATIONAL CHARACTER OF SIGNS

Semiology, in Saussure's (1993) definition, is a science concerned with values that are "arbitrarily fixable" (p. 326) in contrast with those values that have their roots in things. Moreover, *langue* is a system that must be considered as a totality (p. 329). These two aspects of Saussure's conception of linguistic value must be seen together if we are to understand the importance of his notion of linguistic value. Saussure defines value as follows: "The language system represents a system in which all the terms appear to be linked by relations. . . . The value of a word will only result from the coexistence of different terms. The value is the counterpart of coexisting terms" (pp. 358–59).

The value of a given term in the language system is defined in terms of its differential relationships with the other terms with which it contrasts in that system. The language system is a system of differences in this sense. The differences that pertain to a given language system may be said to be the semiologically salient differences recognized and used by the members of a given social group. The meaning of a given sign is a function of its position in relation to the other signs in the same system. The sign has neither meaning nor value in itself.

When Saussure (1993) points out that "the purely conceptual mass of our ideas, the mass separated from the language system represents a sort of unformed cloud" (p. 362), he is showing how a typological system of categorical differences—that is, the terms and their respective values—in a language system can emerge from and, in turn, give meaning to the continuously varying, topological domain or substrate of what he calls "ideas" (see Thibault 1997:164–73). The semiological principle of value thus has the potential to contextualize the phenomena of human experience in and through the system of semiotically salient differences that characterize a particular language system. Saussure's semiological theory of value shows the relational character of signs, although he did not build on this radically important insight to develop a semiological theory that is both relational *and* fully contextual.

The system of differences so postulated is, as Saussure recognized, an abstraction from actual uses of language in *parole*. It is the system of the *possible* kinds of meanings that language users can make in the various types of social contexts and social relationships in which language is used. This system of possible kinds of meanings can then be connected to the various ways in which meanings are actually made, in which types of contexts, and by which social participants. In such a theory, it would be possible to specify how signs contrast with each other in ways that depend on the wider contexts in which they function in the making and negotiating of meanings in human life. This is a step that Saussure did not actually take, although it is one that a social-semiological theory of language would need to make to account for the "life of signs in human societies."

The differential basis of the semiological notion of value can be illustrated with reference to the system of Mood in English grammar, as set out in Figure 2.

The system of MOOD in English is a grammatical system based on an initial "choice" between either *indicative* or *imperative*. The horizontal (right to left) dimension entails a move in delicacy (specificity) such that the selection of a given less delicate feature (e.g., indicative) becomes the point of entry for the selection of a still more delicate (more specific) feature (e.g., *declarative* and then *exclamative*). The selection of the feature or term indicative entails a choice between the terms indicative or *interrogative*. When the term indicative is selected, then either declarative or interrogative must be selected. If the subsystem declarative is then entered, a choice is made between either *affirm* or *exclaim*. Thus, the network orders the terms in this subsystem of English grammar as a set of increasingly delicate features that contrast with and therefore mutually define each other in terms of their respective values. This set of contrasts does not specify the meanings that particular uses of the mood options have, although it does exercise its own constraints on the kinds of meanings that can be made when selections from the MOOD system are used in particular contexts. The meanings can be determined only by the ways in which they are used in particular contexts.

The same general principle can be illustrated with reference to the system of contrasting terms or features that constitute the system I shall call [EYEBROW MOVEMENT], itself a subsystem of the larger system of [FACIAL EXPRESSION]. Figure 3 shows that the choice of the [EYEBROW MOVEMENT] system entails the simultaneous selection of choices from the three subsystems of "distance apart," "movement," and "duration."

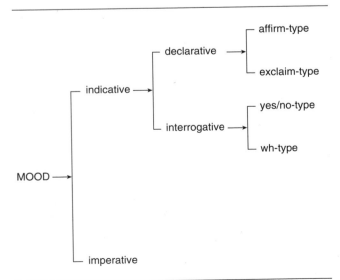

Figure 2   Basic Mood Options in English, Seen as a Network of Contrasting Terms

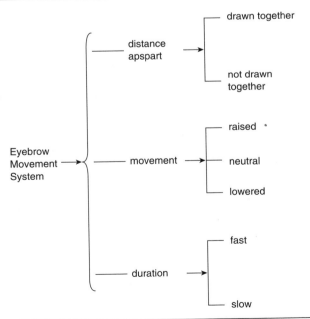

Figure 3   Eyebrow Movement System, Showing Contrasting Features in Relation to Three Simultaneously Accessed Subsystems

The [EYEBROW MOVEMENT] system can, therefore, be characterized as a clustering of the three closely related subsystems mentioned above. Thus, the subsystem distance apart shows a systematic contrast between eyebrows "drawn together" and eyebrows "not drawn together." These contrasting features are potentially meaningful each in their own right, as well as in combination with selections of features from other subsystems in the [EYEBROW MOVEMENT] system, the [FACIAL EXPRESSION] system as a whole, or with selections from other semiological systems such as language. For example, an interrogative clause selected from the English mood system may be combined with "raised eyebrows," which is a selection from the "movement" subsystem, to produce a more complex syntagmatic structure, the meaning of which is something like [ASK QUESTION/EXPRESSS DOUBT/SEEK ATTENTION, etc.]. The two selections from the two different semiological systems co-contextualize each other as parts in a more complex, multimodal syntagm.

The distinctions I have made here between terms like declarative mood and interrogative mood in language and eyebrows raised and eyebrows not raised in the eyebrow movement system are formal resources that have a range of possible meanings. The network notation that I have adopted here is a means of formalising the ways in which these terms and their respective values derive from their place in a system of contrasting terms. The basic logic is the same in the two cases. The forms are the means in and through which meanings are made. There is no suggestion that the forms have fixed, already preexisting meanings. The semiological principle of value allows for the fact that forms and meanings may be uncoupled to create new couplings of forms and meanings in different contexts. This possibility is intrinsic to Saussure's relational theory of semiological value. Obviously, the eyebrow system is considerably more restricted in its possibilities for meaning making than is the vastly more complex system of a given language. Yet, even here we can see this principle at work. For example, raised eyebrows may be coupled to the meanings question, seek attention, express doubt in different contexts, and in combination with other signs from the larger facial expression system, or from other semiological systems such as language.

DISCOURSE, CONTEXT, AND THE MODERN SCIENCE OF SIGNS BASED ON SEMIOLOGICAL PRINCIPLES

The modern "science of signs" that has its roots in Saussure's semiology is based on text and discourse rather than on single signs. Moreover, language is no longer the sole or even necessarily the primary object of study. Increasingly, the functionalist principles outlined above have been extended to the study of the kinds of semiological partnerships that occur in discourse between language and other sign systems. Language—spoken and written—is always integrated with other sign systems—gesture, facial expressions, visual images, sound, spatial relations, body movement—and never occurs on its own. Texts or discourses, in relation to their contexts, are seen as complex systems of systems of interrelated signs that serve many different simultaneous and overlapping functions. Moreover, texts and discourses are not static entities. Rather, they are dynamical meaning-making processes in and through which social agents make meanings in contextually relevant and constrained ways. They do so by integrating the material signifiers in the here-now of bodily activity to other processes, activities, happenings, and so on, on other space-time scales, beyond the here-now scale of the text *qua* material artifact, or signifier.

Rather than simple couplings of atomistic signifiers to their signifieds, texts are seen as semiotic-material artifacts for mediating and integrating the local, smaller timescales of real-time meaning-making activity to more global, larger timescales in some social-semiological system. In ways that Saussure's relational conception of the sign foreshadowed, yet did not fully develop, signs are *made*, not given in advance, through these processes of contextual integration across different scalar levels of semiological and material organization.

— Paul J. Thibault

See also Deconstruction; Discourse; Poststructuralism; Saussure, Ferdinand de; Structuralism

FURTHER READINGS AND REFERENCES

Claparède, Ed. 1916. Review of the *Cours de Linguistique Générale* (C. Bally and A. Sechehaye, eds, Lausanne & Paris: Payot, 1916). *Archives de Psychologie* 61:93–95.

Harris, Roy. 2001. *Rethinking Writing*. London & New York: Continuum.

Saussure, Ferdinand de. [1916] 1971. *Cours de Linguistique Générale* [Course in General Linguistics], edited by Charles Bally and Albert Sechehaye. 3d ed. Paris: Payot.

———. 1993. *Cours de Linguistique Générale: Premier et Troisième Cours D'après les Notes de Reidlinger et Constantin* [Course in General Linguistics: First and Third Course Based on the Notes of Reidlinger and Constantin], edited by Eisuke Komatsu. Collection Recherches Université Gaskushuin No. 24. Tokyo, Japan: Université Gakushuin.

Thibault, Paul J. 1996a. "The Problematic of *Écriture*." Lecture 2 in the course Saussure and Beyond. University of Toronto, Cyber Semiotics Institute. Retrieved February 27, 2004 (http://www.chass.utoronto.ca/epc/srb/cyber/thi2.html).

———. 1996b. "Speech and Writing: Two Distinct Systems of Signs." Lecture 1 in the course Saussure and Beyond. University of Toronto, Cyber Semiotics Institute. Retrieved February 27, 2004 (http://www.chass.utoronto.ca/epc/srb /cyber/thi1.html).

———. 1997. *Re-reading Saussure. The Dynamics of Signs in Social Life*. London & New York: Routledge.

SEXUALITY AND THE SUBJECT

The study of sexuality is a vital area of contemporary social theory. During the course of the twentieth century, in Western society, thinking on sexuality shifted from a conception of sex as a biological, essential, and fixed aspect of human "nature" to theorizations of sexuality as a social construct, shaped and regulated through cultural discourses and other social formations.

In large part, this shift was a direct result of feminist challenges to a binary understanding of gender that traditionally rested on fixed, mutually opposed categories of "male" and "female." A number of feminist scholars pointed to the lack of clear-cut biological differences between the two sexes; and increasingly, gender was theorized to be an ideological enterprise rather than a natural fact. The French feminist Simone de Beauvoir (1908–1986) catalyzed these debates when she famously wrote, "One is not born a woman, but rather becomes one." Her argument for the social construction of gender was taken up by feminists seeking to attack the gendered power differences that were at the heart of women's oppression. Yet these theoretical breakthroughs led to a quandary: If the category is eradicated, how then can women unite for political action against oppressions based on that category? The problem is one of a politics of identity. Debates within the feminist movement continue to hinge on whether women share certain "essential" characteristics or whether "woman" is a socially constructed category.

Radically questioning these essentialized categorizations of gender has had powerful implications for the related notion of *sexuality.* The ways in which medical and legal definitions of gender impinge on sexuality offer an understanding of sexuality, too, as shifting and ideologically driven rather than natural or essential. As a result of such theorization, the idea of sexuality has changed from a binary conception of hetero- versus homosexual to the more pluralistic notion of *sexualities* that are not biologically determined. In this area, as well, debates rage over whether sexuality is genetically based, whether it is a matter of individual agency, or whether it is ideologically directed. These theoretical discussions have powerful implications for our understanding of identity or subjectivity, because gender and sexuality are constitutive elements in the formulation of the self.

In these debates over essentialism and social constructionism, there has been a growing recognition of the mechanisms of ideology through which gender and sexuality are given meaning in society. The field of feminist cultural studies focuses on the analysis of representations of gender and sexuality and their interactions with social processes and human behaviors. As part of such analyses, the related functions of race, ethnicity, nationality, class, age, and other

social vectors have been noted. The social struggles and movements of the mid-twentieth century were especially significant in revealing the multiple imbrications of anti-hegemonic identity politics. Thus, feminist analysis, which in its early manifestations was centrally concerned with gender and power, now seeks to account for the variety of factors that work together to construct hierarchies of power and privilege in society. Gay and lesbian theorists and critical race theorists have also engaged in multiperspectival approaches to understanding power and oppression and how cultural discourses and texts reproduce hierarchies of class, gender, race, and sexuality.

On all these fronts, sexuality offers a powerful lens through which the mechanisms of society can be investigated. The ways in which sexuality is tied to subjectivity or individual identity can shed light on social configurations and processes; there is a dialectic at work between the sexualized self and its social environment that raises important issues of gender, race, class, and power.

THE EMERGENCE OF SEXUALITY

The term *sexuality* itself is barely a century old; and just as the term entered social discourse, sexuality began to be linked with individual personalities and behaviors. Since classical times, sexual practices had been recognized and categorized, but only in the late 1800s did sexuality become linked with personhood or subjectivity. Terms like *homosexual, transvestite,* and *sadist* entered the parlance then; prior to that time, sex was a medical and biological function. Medical scientists had catalogued and named various sexual practices and "perversions," which were seen as biological or genetic attributes. The science of *sexology* was thus born. Much attention was paid during the course of the nineteenth century to crafting legal and medical definitions and explanations for sexual practices. It was only later that sexuality began to be understood as being psychologically significant.

Toward the middle of the nineteenth century, sexologists began to consider sexuality in terms of "abnormality" or "perversion"; these concepts alluded to sexual practices that had been deemed socially and morally unacceptable and that were characterized as illnesses attributed to hidden psychological drives as well as genetic or anatomical defects. Richard von Krafft-Ebing's (1814–1902) encyclopedic book, *Psychopathia Sexualis* (1886), was a highly influential catalog of sexual mental disease: Early editions of this book presented sexual perversions as curable deviancies, but later ones shifted to arguments that sexual deviance was involuntary and irremediable. The debates around sexuality in this period tended to center on homosexuality, its causes and correctives; these sexological discussions offered definitions of masculinity and femininity in socially prescriptive formulations that had legal and cultural implications. The writings of the sexologists wavered among various positions on sexuality, often deeming it at once an unchangeable instinct and a condition that could be cured through therapeutic intervention. The work of the British sexologist Havelock Ellis (1859–1939) is notable in that it addressed sexuality as normal, healthy, and complex. His seven-volume opus, *Studies in the Psychology of Sex* (published between 1897 and 1928), are his best-known work and were a precursor to Albert Kinsey's later investigations; the work did much to depathologize many sexual practices, although it was uneven in many ways. Ellis also advanced the notion that sexual deviations were socially constructed, although he characterized white male heterosexuality as normative.

On the whole, however, the work of the sexologists was centered on taxonomies and classifications of sexual behaviors. These systems of classification brought into circulation the terms *homosexual, heterosexual,* and *bisexual* and then confined the understanding of sexuality to the homo/hetero binarism that later (particularly feminist and gay/lesbian) scholars repudiated. In addition, these taxonomies tended to privilege heterosexual, monogamous relations as the norm against which all other sexual activities were characterized as deviant. Even later versions of such sexology, carried out by Albert Kinsey in the 1940s and 1950s, and William Masters and Virginia Johnson in the 1960s, strayed little from these early positions, defining sexuality as biological and physical, susceptible to external influences and capable of being changed by medical intervention.

PSYCHOANALYSIS, SEX, AND THE SUBJECT

Coming on the heels of the taxonomic sexology that developed in the 1800s, the invention of psychoanalysis near the turn of the twentieth century was instrumental in radically repositioning sexuality in relation to individual identity or subjectivity, and developments from psychoanalysis most substantively challenged the sexological and essentialized conceptions of sex. Later critiques of psychoanalysis and the rise of social constructionism led to the analysis of social forces through which subjects are constituted. The emergence of feminist scholarship, queer theory, postmodernism, and deconstructionism broached central questions regarding the linkages between sexuality, subjectivity, and cultural, ideological, and discursive formations. Some of these questions are as follows: How are subjects *sexed* or made sexual? Are gender and sexuality synonymous? What is the relationship of gender identity to subjectivity? What is the relationship of sexual identity to subjectivity? To what extent is sexual identity socially determined? And conversely, to what extent do sexual identities and practices shape society?

The psychoanalytic theory of Sigmund Freud (1856–1939) offered the first insights into the nexus between sexuality and subjectivity. Generally speaking, Freud's conceptualization of the human psyche in terms of the unconscious destabilized Enlightenment notions of a rational, autonomous subject. This *Cartesian* subject (so called because it was most closely associated with the writings of French philosopher René Descartes, 1596–1650) had formed the basis of centuries of philosophy on the human condition: its basic premise (that *reason,* or the human capacity to understand one's own existence, defined the self) had given rise to formal theories of society such as liberalism, idealism, and humanism; modern conceptions of democracy stemmed from the Enlightenment notion of a centered being whose capacities of reason, consciousness, and action impelled him or her toward the pursuit of knowledge, happiness, and freedom. This being, or *subject,* was also an *agent*—that is, an individual with the power to act independently. The power of self-governing action came from an innate essence, a capacity for rational autonomy that separated humankind from beasts.

Freud's conception of the subject presented a radical challenge to the very core of those ideas. Freud explicated the human psyche in terms of the conscious and the unconscious. In his writings, these concepts are variously labeled conscious, unconscious, and subconscious—or later, id, ego, and superego. The latter terms do not directly correspond to the former but, rather, represent a more developed theorization of the human personality, in which the id refers to unconscious drives and impulses, while the ego and superego operate between the subject's external and internal worlds, negotiating the borders of the conscious and unconscious. The *consciousness* that defined and animated the Cartesian subject was in Freud's view only the superficial functioning of a self motivated by unconscious desires and drives. In Freud's conception, the conscious is not aware of the workings of the unconscious; rather, it operates in constant and incognizant interplay with it. The ego or the *conscious* channels energies that Freud termed *libidinous:* These are pleasure-seeking drives, primarily sexual, that play out in the ego's relationships with external and internal objects and functions.

These concepts are crucial to understanding Freud's theories of sexuality and the subject, as well as the various revisions thereof that followed from scholarly critiques of his ideas. To Freud, libidinal energies shape the contours of the self; the ego develops in relation to the subject's relations with itself and others. Freud's early writings on sexual development centered on the repression of various libidinous desires.

To Freud, sexuality was a primary force underlying human behavior and psychology. His early theories of sexual development were predicated on a progressive attention to various erotogenic zones of the body. These theories were premised on notions of infantile sexuality and erotic desires felt by a child for its parents, which were repressed by society. The various sexual repressions experienced at each stage of development, and their attendant anxieties, guided the development of the human psyche, in Freud's formulation. The ways in which these sexual desires were expressed or repressed were posited by Freud to explain subsequent behaviors and pathologies. Freud later offered theories of society grounded in parallel notions of the repression of sexual/libidinal urges.

Thus, for Freud, sexuality shaped the contours of the unconscious and was the primary factor in understanding human development. While his theories have been the target of substantial criticism and challenge, in large part because of the apparent misogyny underlying his problematization of female sexuality, his work has also contributed a great deal to contemporary understandings of sexuality. Yet it should be noted that his work centered on the analysis of male sexuality and identity development, and when he dealt with girls and women, his ideas were undertheorized and largely devaluative. While some feminist scholars have brought to light these aspects of Freud's analyses, others have made some attempts to recuperate Freudian theory in relation to female sexuality, arguing that he was describing rather than endorsing the conditions of patriarchy.

Freud's theories were notably advanced by the French psychologist Jacques Lacan (1901–1981), whose rethinking of Freudian concepts are key to contemporary formulations of sex and subjectivity. Lacan posited the emergence of the subject to be tied to what he termed "the mirror stage"—the moment at which an infant recognizes himself or herself in a reflection. According to Lacanian psychology, this moment of recognition serves to unify an identity that previously was fragmented; this unification is corporeal as well as psychic. In the mirror stage, the infant's subjectivity is formed into a cohesive whole. The body is thus irrevocably bound up with the psyche; the recognition of the physical contours of the body leads to a recognition of the self.

But Lacan also wrote that the integrity of the self and the body can only be sustained in terms of the social discourse that sexually differentiates bodies into *male* and *female* and then organizes them within a gendered system of power. This social discourse is played out through language. Lacan refers to this discursive system as the "symbolic order." The symbolic is organized in terms of social structures, such as the taboo on incest, that regulate all human relationships. The symbolic is a patriarchial system that exercises authority through the "phallus," Lacan's term for hegemonic masculine power. In Lacan's view, language shapes sexuality and subjectivity together, and sexuality binds subjects to culture. Thus, the Lacanian view of sexuality and the subject offered a bridge between psychoanalysis and social theory.

Freudian and Lacanian theories of sex and the subject are the point of entry for the considerations of sexuality and society that followed throughout the twentieth century and into the twenty-first. As Juliet Mitchell (1974) expresses it, "Psychoanalysis gives us the concepts with which we can comprehend how ideology functions; closely connected with this, it further offers an analysis of the place and meaning of sexuality and of gender differences within society" (p. xx). Both masculinist and heterosexist at their core, Freud's and Lacan's ideas provide a baseline to which later theorizations refer.

Feminist scholars, in particular, have developed notions of sexuality and the subject beyond psychoanalysis, working to connect the interiorized processes of sexuality posited by psychoanalytic theory with the sociological structures that intersect and act on them. For feminist writers, there is an action agenda at the heart of such investigations: The emancipatory goals of social change and the dissolution of gender inequity are tied to feminist projects. Feminisms share this orientation with other theoretical strands such as Marxism, critical race theories, ethnic studies, and gay and lesbian studies. Sexuality and the subject have been addressed from all of these perspectives, and these critiques have troubled and complicated our understandings of the role of desire in contemporary social formations.

On one hand, some feminist psychoanalysts criticize psychoanalytic theory for its inability to provide a model for social change, but others support it for its insights into how femininity is inculcated by patriarchal society. A key aspect of such reflections on psychoanalytical constructions of sex and the subject is the shift toward understanding sexuality as a sociocultural construction as well as in terms of individual internal traumas; the struggle to link the two approaches is a hallmark of more recent considerations of sexuality.

SEXUALITY AND DISCOURSE

Perhaps the most significant break with psychoanalytic schools of thought on sexuality came from the French philosopher Michel Foucault (1926–1984), whose three volumes on the history of Western sexuality postulate that discourses on sexuality and their importance in shaping knowledge are functions of power. From the perspective of gay politics, Foucault argues that desire has been produced through various historicized discourses; the ways in which sexuality is articulated socially in a sense determines how it manifests itself. These multiple articulations serve to constrain and delimit sexuality, as well as to enable new forms of sexuality to emerge; thus, the sexual body is the site on which hierarchies of power are played out. Sex, then, is neither *natural* nor *repressed* by society; rather, what Foucault calls the *machinery* of sex tells us much about the social order.

Contemporary theorists of sex and sexuality build on Foucault and psychoanalytical theorists to invent new understandings of sexuality in society. Judith Butler's engagement with the sexed body and its relationship to gender is a reformulation of Freud, Lacan, and feminist theorists such as Luce Irigaray and Julia Kristeva. Like Foucault, Butler sees sexuality as well as bodies themselves as discursive effects; bodies and their sexuality, she writes, cannot be dissociated from the regulatory norms that provide their context and determine their meanings. Her most crucial point is that identity, or subjectivity, is achieved as an effect of assuming a sexual location and that this assumption of a sexual identity is performative in that it repeats the behaviors governed by discourse. Yet this idea does not prohibit resistance to such socially determined constraints; in assuming a sexual identity, another is discarded, and that discarded or *abject* identity offers the seeds of resistance and change.

Susan Bordo, too, tracks Foucault in her examinations of femininity and masculinity in Western culture. Bordo sees discourse as vital in shaping the body and its functioning. She argues that the discursive meanings and significations of the body have serious, and often dangerous, material impacts. The cultural emphasis on the heterosexual desirability of the slender body and its privileged position in popular representation, for example, can be a contributing factor to the incidence of eating disorders in Western societies and to the maintenance and reproduction of existing power relations.

Gay and lesbian scholars contemplate sexuality and subjectivity in similarly complex ways. In these writings, the argument that social conditions and discourse shape sexual identification is countered by the notion that sexuality is an inherent and instinctual *orientation*. The sociopolitical implications of various theorizations of sex and subjectivity are clear in these works. Homophobia, social stigma, and political action are tied to how sexual identity can be understood. Representation is, again, a key factor in the privileging of heterosexuality and the marginalization of alternative sexualities, although increasing challenges from gay, lesbian, bisexual, and other activists mark cultural texts as contested terrain in which existing social struggles are reproduced and conflicting political discourses are reflected.

The issue of race further complicates the question of sexuality in society. Again, building on Foucault, critical race theorists recognize that discourses of sexuality reify power hierarchies. The early sexologists privileged white male heterosexuality as the moral ideal, characterizing the sexuality of women, Jews, and people of color as wanton and degraded. Sociocultural discourses of sex have since then conflated deviance with physical signs of difference, especially race. Cultural tropes of racial Otherness, such as exoticization, hypersexualization, and pathologization, again reinscribe power differentials in society. Within racial minority groups, aberrance from the heterosexual norm is also problematic.

In part, the sexual behaviors ascribed to various racial, class, and gender categories of people are circulated via cultural representation. The idea that all cultural representations are political is a major theme of the cultural theories of the last few decades. In particular, feminist and other oppositional social activists have attacked the stereotypes and biased images of their groups. These critiques of sexism, racism, homophobia, and other biases made it clear that images and representations are never innocent of political effect: Positive, negative, or ambiguous depictions of social groups can counter or reinforce social oppression. Early interventions in the politics of representation concentrated primarily on *images of* particular social groups, decrying negative images and affirming more progressive ones. The limitations of such approaches quickly became apparent, and by the 1970s, more sophisticated analyses began emerging of how texts position audiences, of how narratives, scenes, and images can be ideological instruments. In the 1980s, the turn toward audiences offered more complex notions of meaning making, recognizing audiences as active creators of meaning from texts rather than passive victims of manipulation. Thus, a dialectical relationship between audience and text was posited, with implications for subjectivity: Engagement with cultural texts was theorized to shape ideas of selfhood. Reading culture began to be seen as a political event. Representations were interpreted not just as replications of the real but as constructions of complex technical, narrative, and ideological apparatuses. The politics of representation focused on both the ideological encoding of textual messages and their decoding by audiences.

In this vein, feminist cultural studies have investigated sexual texts and audiences as corollaries of power, yet within the field there are widely ranging perspectives on representation, sexuality, and subjectivity. Radical feminist views on sexuality take the position that women are objectified and dehumanized in mainstream mass cultural representations of sex and that these representations not only place women in danger of sexual violence but influence both men and women to accept or even condone such violence. Such texts have also been criticized for their reinforcement of the hetero/homosexual binarism, their racism, and their preclusion of more progressive formulations of sex. But other voices defend mainstream representations of sexuality, either as a free-speech issue or by situating women and sexual minorities as active and knowledgeable consumers and producers of these texts.

Feminist activism and the gay and lesbian social movements of the late twentieth century are in part sociosexual configurations that have opened up alternative sexologies, one's that challenge the orthodoxy of the sexual tradition. The intellectual and political discourses that have arisen from these movements are redefining sexuality and subjectivity in an ongoing sense. Thus, sexuality can be understood as a historicized term that emerged in a moment when medical science and taxonomy were on the rise and continue to be central to the understanding of human social life. Sexuality is also a significant component of media culture that cultural studies attempts to critically engage.

It is possible that the concept of *sexuality* itself may fade with future social shifts. But at this point in time, it remains a key axis of identification and organization in contemporary societies.

— Meenakshi Gigi Durham

See also Beauvoir, Simone de; Butler, Judith; Feminism; Foucault, Michel; Freud, Sigmund; Lacan, Jacques; Psychoanalysis and Social Theory; Queer Theory

FURTHER READINGS AND REFERENCES

de Beauvoir, Simone. 1952. *The Second Sex.* New York: Knopf.
Butler, Judith P. 1999. *Gender Trouble: Feminism and the Subversion of Identity.* New York: Routledge.
Duggan, Lisa and Nan D. Hunter. 1995. *Sex Wars: Sexual Dissent and Political Culture.* New York & London: Routledge.
Freud, Sigmund. 1962. *Three Essays on the Theory of Sexuality.* New York: Basic Books.
Foucault, Michel. 1978. *The History of Sexuality: An Introduction.* New York: Vintage.
Gilman, Sander. 1985. *Difference and Pathology.* Ithaca, NY: Cornell University Press.
Lacan, Jacques. 1977. *Ecrits: A Selection.* Translated by Alan Sheridan. New York: Norton.
McKinnon, Catherine. 1993. *Only Words.* Cambridge, MA: Harvard University Press.
Mitchell, Juliet. 1974. *Psychoanalysis and Feminism.* New York: Vintage.
Weeks, Jeffrey. 1986. *Sexuality.* London: Tavistock.

SIMMEL, GEORG

WORK AND BIOGRAPHY

Georg Simmel (1858–1918) was a philosopher, although sociologists consider him a founder of the humanist branch of sociology and recognize his contributions to an interpretive approach to the study of society. Contemporary theorists are deeply indebted to him as is amply documented by the frequent references to his work in recent publications. His theoretical method is rooted in his philosophy of life. From that he develops four epistemological approaches: pragmatism, constructivism, interactionism, and evolutionism. These serve as the context for Simmel's heuristic tools: (1) dealing with perspectives as realities, (2) seeing mental constructs as bridges across the gap between the subjective and the objective, (3) the dialectic of form and content, and (4) the tension between center and periphery. Simmel applies his unique method of study to various topics, including a famous analysis of "the stranger," a book-length investigation of money, the theoretical topic of historical materialism, and culture as it appears in music and in religion.

From 1858 until 1914, his home was Berlin. He spent the last four years of his life, however, which coincided with World War I, as a full professor at the University of Strasbourg. He died there of liver cancer on September 26, 1918 (not on September 28, as several sources report). Simmel was of Jewish origin and belonged to a Protestant church. He grew up the youngest of seven children and received a sizable inheritance after the death of his father. This allowed him to pursue his natural inclinations toward intellectual autonomy.

Simmel earned his doctorate degree from the University of Berlin, which enjoyed considerable international reputation then. Among those intellectuals who came from abroad to study there were George Herbert Mead and Robert Ezra Park. In Berlin, as well as elsewhere in Austria, Germany, and other parts of Europe, it had been—and still is—the tradition not to promote a scholar from within his or her department to the rank of full professor. This old custom, by which intellectual inbreeding was to be minimized, excluded Simmel from eligibility for a professorship at the university where he had been a student, a PhD candidate, and a *Privatdozent*. That is one of the reasons why Max Weber tried to get him a professorship at Heidelberg, which failed, most likely due to anti-Semitic prejudices.

PHILOSOPHY OF LIFE

After Simmel was diagnosed with liver cancer, knowing that his days were numbered, he completed his philosophy of life and presented it in his *Lebensanschauung: Vier metaphysische Kapitel (Life-anschauung: Four Metaphysical Chapters)* in 1918. Simmel's sociology is consistently based on this philosophy. He appears to pick up and modify statements by Plato, Spinoza, and Kant. These greats help Simmel to find his own position, which he then compares with the work of Goethe, Marx, Schopenhauer, Nietzsche, and others: To Simmel, reality is too vast and complex for the human mind to grasp. The only chance humans have is to create tools for selecting, describing, and placing in context segments of reality that correspond to their interests and emotions. The construction of ideal types as recommended by Max Weber is for Simmel essentially all we ever do: Scholarship is—whether admitted or not—the creation of heuristic tools. This insight and the message that reality is socially constructed have their origin in Simmel's epistemology.

Simmel incorporates Marx's concept of alienation into his philosophy of life. Mental activity can be defined as producing something that is self-significant and self-regulating ("*eigenbedeutsam und eigengesetzlich*" [Simmel 1918:25]) and, accordingly, has the potential of becoming alien to its origin. Life then cannot be seen in any way other than as the subject continually grasping for the unfamiliar and bringing forth from itself that which becomes alien. While Marx considers that a deplorable defect of capitalist society, Simmel sees in it the inevitable mark of the human condition in general. Like in a parent-child relation, the mental product can be seen as emancipated rather than alienated. It is not a runaway extension of the subject who made it but, instead, may legitimately stand by itself. This is what Simmel calls "*Mehr-als-Leben-Sein*" ("to be more than life" [Simmel 1918:25]).

Simmel cannot be counted among philosophical idealists. Their view, according to which the world is what one sees, is not acceptable to him because it makes all that transcends life an illusion. Instead, Simmel wants to accept what is out there as objective reality in its own right, facing us *prima facie* as alien and yet as created by a life we can identify with. This method leads him to a dualism that "not only does not contradict the unity of life but rather is the way in which unity exists" (Simmel 1918:25). Thus, Simmel's philosophy of life is founded on a human type of existence which *finds* itself in *transcending* itself and which bestows form (or *gestalt*) on its individuality that will enable the person continually to reach across its boundaries (Simmel 1918:27).

EPISTEMOLOGICAL APPROACHES AND HEURISTIC TOOLS

Pragmatism

The search for reliable insight can only be successful if the subject who strives for knowledge is active. What is demanded is autonomous and potentially creative conduct. Building on Kant, Simmel creates the epistemology of an active human being, an approach that William James was to name pragmatism. Because in the process of acting, the interests of the subject flow into the process of gaining knowledge, Simmel sees as the central concern of Kant's system not *thinking* but the *will*. What matters to Simmel is this: A given body of knowledge must be assumed to guide and command action, even if its validity cannot be tested, let alone proven. No matter how far removed that knowledge may be from objective reality, it will produce action, and nobody can deny that then the results will be real. Since sociology is (also) the study of human conduct, the pragmatist approach as suggested by Simmel makes it plausible to assign types of knowledge a status of potential reality not according to what has preceded it but, rather, according to what action may potentially result from it.

Constructivism

From Simmel's point of view, ideas are on one hand simply conceptual products that are postulated. They are created *ad hoc* as tools of thought, like Max Weber's ideal types. On the other hand, they also serve the purpose of "understanding the existence of a truth" (Simmel 1910:106), a truth that therefore must exist, whether grasped by humans or not. Thus, Simmel's epistemology is caught up in the conflict of accepting the realm of ideas as only the product of human creation on one hand yet on the other hand anticipating that ideas will provide access to an objective truth. It is therefore incorrect to call Simmel a relativist. He did not see before his eyes a multiplicity of possible ultimate values but, rather, many presentations of the one. What must be constructed then is not the truth, but tools needed to access it. The "You" we encounter in everyday life is Simmel's most persuasive example: It is both a true person whom in his or her uniqueness nobody will ever fully grasp *and* a social construction that is necessary to enable interaction. The same applies to the "I": Individuals to not *really* know themselves beyond construction! In interpersonal dialogue then, the criticism "you do not know me, you only form an image of me" is in Simmel's view a rebellion against the inevitable.

Interactionism

If the heuristic aspect of reality is a *social* construction, it is constructed in interaction. The forms and processes of interaction are to be studied as sources of reality. The most widely known application is Simmel's concept of the stranger (*der Fremde,* see below). He is the alien who represents another reality in our own midst. Simmel defines the stranger in terms of "a particular form of interaction" (Simmel 1908:685). Elements of closeness and distance are both present. The interaction between native and stranger represents a rather exceptional and particularly interesting quality of an encounter.

Evolutionism

Throughout Simmel's writings, there are frequent indications that he pursues the notion of social and cultural evolution. Given the other three components of his method, that does *not* mean that to him there is an ultimate reality that evolves. All Simmel assumes is a dynamic aspect of the sphere of human constructs: society and culture. A convincing substantive area of scholarly work to which Simmel's evolutionism can be applied is his research on religion (Simmel 1997). Any answer to the question of whether there is a sacred absolute in the beyond and what it may be like, lies clearly outside the competence of empirical scholarship. The sociologist of religion can neither confirm nor deny any statement for or against the reality of any god or deities. But the bodies of religious knowledge, the holy scriptures, the theological teachings and similar creations of faithful humans can be studied as heuristic tools that have been constructed for the purpose of relating to the beyond in a more or less satisfactory fashion (while leaving entirely open the possibility that there may be nothing in the beyond). Simmel assumes that in the history of humankind there is an evolution of the way in which humans go about creating and using such tools.

Four Heuristic Tools

Simmel and G. H. Mead (Mead 1927) agreed to give reality status to perspectives. To Simmel, the central perspectives are art, religion, and scholarship. The totality of the world can be seen and experienced from each of these, and it is absurd to find them competing with each other. Simmel calls the reality in which humans create art, religion, or scholarship the *third realm* because it mediates between the other two: the subject and the object. Again, the study of religion is a good illustration (Simmel 1997). Simmel's first heuristic tool, viewing religion not as an ensemble of things but as a specific *perspective,* and the second tool, according to which religion is a reality of its own, capable of *bridging the rift* between the subjective and the objective, are connected by him with yet a third heuristic device: the *dialectic of form and content.*

Simmel uses *historical materialism* as an example of this relation between form and content (Simmel 1977; see below). He interprets this Marxian philosophy as deriving the *content* of historical life from the *forms* of the economy. Examples of *content* are law, philosophy, and religion; these are determined by the *form* in which humans organize their food supply. Simmel criticizes historical materialism by pointing out that one sector of human life is exaggerated to the point of appearing as its sole content. This view, however, is unfit to grasp historical change: According to Simmel, history advances through the process in which form and content are transmuted into one another. The continuity of history would not be possible unless the same content (e.g., government) were to appear in different forms (e.g., aristocracy, dictatorship, democracy) or unless the same form (e.g., autocratic leadership) were to shape various contents (e.g., family, state, church).

A fourth heuristic tool is Simmel's description of the relationship between *center* and *periphery.* Simmel writes that human beings are free to the extent that the center of an individual determines his or her periphery. What is unique and utterly personal would fill the center; that which many people have in common can be only peripheral to the individual. Simmel observes that Christian churches have tended to emphasize that which all or many believers have in common rather than encouraging each individual to let its unique talents bring fruit.

APPLICATIONS OF HIS METHOD

The Stranger

Simmel's reflections on being a stranger are based on the concept of two separate populations. Originally, each population inhabits its own living space. The individual newcomer is regarded as an alien insofar as he or she is seen as a representative of the other group. Confrontation with the whole of the other group would be considered threatening, but contact with an individual representative is interesting, perhaps instructive—in any case, out of the ordinary. The stranger is not "the wanderer who comes today and goes tomorrow; he is the one who comes today and stays tomorrow—the potential wanderer, as it were" (Simmel 1908:685).

The advent of the stranger shatters native society's illusion of being universal. Self-satisfied society witnesses how the stranger who has joined it unexpectedly cannot be forced to acquiesce to its order. In the presence of the stranger, a supposedly universal orientation is revealed as locally restricted and provincial. Thus, the stranger has both a destructive and constructive effect, as a representative of alternative patterns of thought and an initiator of social change. He or she destroys for many what Karl Mannheim called life's instruments of concealment and illusion. The stranger is initially and principally an individual who is not integrated into the host society, and very often one who does not wish for such integration. In many historical instances, he or she will compensate for the burden this places on him or her with a strong belief in predestination or divine election.

Money

The *Philosophy of Money* (1907) is primarily a reflection on highly complex forms of interaction. The social principle of culture by which interactions between subjects invest objects with values acquires a concrete form in money. People shape sensory impressions into objects, and this allows them to experience reality. People's distance or detachment from objects means that, in their wish to overcome this distance, they experience the value of an object. In exchanging objects, they assess the expectations of the individuals involved of overcoming the distance and compare values. They thereby become aware of the value relations of the goods exchanged. These relations then become separated from the goods whose comparison they originated from and appear as an independent factor: They are given the form of money: Money thus becomes the expression of the "interdependence of people, their relativity, by which the satisfaction of one person's wishes is always dependent on another person" (Simmel 1907:134).

Money is the most general form of social relationship. The conscious mind, occupied with the social construction of reality, invests money with such a well-defined sense of independent existence that we forget in the course of everyday life that the origin and effect of money is an expression of the interdependence of people. Where interpersonal relationships are not social, where individuals are not interactive and do not enter into exchanges with one another but instead treat each other as objects, money becomes meaningless. In Simmel's opinion, the same applies to law. Law is nothing but an empty abstraction until it becomes the form of a living relationship. People can treat each other rightfully or do each other wrong only if they are interacting with one another. "In reality, law is merely a relationship between people and is executed only in the interests, objectives or power play" (Simmel 1907:95).

Simmel considers the money economy with ambivalence. On one hand, it facilitates an ever-increasing degree of substantialization and, at the same time, greater internalization. Money (as relationship) becomes the "guardian of the innermost depths" (Simmel 1907:532). But whether it allows the person concerned to become more refined, unique, and differentiated or, conversely, makes him or her into a tyrant over other people—precisely because of the easiness with which it is obtained—has nothing to do with money but with people. Here, too, the money economy appears in its formal relationship to socialist conditions. Both forms of relationship—that of money and of socialism— are expected to bring the same blessing: "deliverance from the individual struggle for existence" (Simmel 1907:532). They can be substituted one for the other: Whoever has money does not need socialism.

Historical Materialism

"Historical Materialism," a Misnomer

Simmel first contends that the followers of historical materialism have not labeled it correctly. The name is misleading because it raises incorrect ideas about the character of this theory. What the idea seems to offer is a unitary psychological interpretation of historical occurrences. The theory has nothing to do with metaphysical materialism but, rather, is compatible with every monistic or dualistic opinion about the essence of physical processes. Therefore, materialism could only mean here that history, in the final analysis, depends on inorganic energies. However, this contradicts the generic content of the theory, according to which history is "psychologically motivated" (Simmel 1977:185). The unfortunate defect of being falsely named does not take away Simmel's admiration for its heuristic potential. It is the grandeur of the theory that it wants to make visible the driving force behind the oppositions and changes of history, a force that, by its elementary simplicity, is qualified to portray unity in the total, immense bustling of historical life. It is nothing but "a psychological hypothesis" (Simmel 1977:186). A psychological hypothesis, however, cannot sensibly be called "historical materialism."

Obscuring the Process of Formation

Simmel acknowledges historical materialism as a system of heuristic tools, and he concedes, in the terminology of Max Weber, its ability to construct useful ideal types. But Marxian theory is firmly tied to the claim of presenting a true picture of reality. It is to Simmel therefore just another form of historical *realism,* and as such contradicts Simmel's constructionist premises. According to Simmel, there is hardly another approach that shows with such clarity the process by which the gradual mental formation of the data is carried out. A picture of reality emerges like a portrait that is created one-sidedly—polemically one could say, as a caricature of reality. Therefore, the claim presented in the name of historical materialism is not acceptable methodologically. In its context, the preeminence of the economic realm is stated, not to create a heuristic instrument for gaining knowledge but, rather, because the reality of economics is seen as the factual foundation of all other occurrences. Here, the point is reached beyond which Simmel cannot accept historical materialism.

Music

Simmel quotes Darwin's statement that "'musical utterances represent one of the foundations for the development of language'" (Simmel 1882:261). Simmel's opposition to this thesis is disarmingly simple: "Were that the case, then it would not be understandable why man ever should have progressed to speech, since he was able after all to express everything in tones" (Simmel 1882:263). This more amusing than convincing line of reasoning is then augmented with a reference to the "speechless song" that would have to exist if Darwin's thesis were correct, but that Simmel can find nowhere with the exception of yodeling. If the speechless song "would be that much more natural than language, would it not have survived at least at the lowest level of culture, such that he (man) somehow, sometime breaks out in that 'speechless yodel'?" (Simmel 1882:263). Since Simmel finds, despite wide-ranging research in the materials of cultural history and of ethnology, everywhere (except for the yodeling in parts of Bavaria and Switzerland) the combination of text and song, not song without language, he is convinced that music did not precede language in evolution but, rather, that language came first. One may or may not find the content of this question interesting. Essentially, this is the method of the early Simmel:

1. He sees culture in the tradition of the theory of progeny as having developed in evolutionary steps, and he speaks in this connection also about "early man" and

language as that bridge that "leads the animal to the human being" (Simmel 1882:265). He picks up the impulses originally emanating from Darwin and applies them to philosophy; from the start, he orients the method of his own work accordingly.

2. Generating objective culture in the process of formation is another topic in Simmel's article on music. The model along which he thinks through this problem is that of interaction or, in the language of Dilthey and Simmel, the *Wechselwirkung* between the lead singer and a group of listeners who are emotionally touched by the song. Members of the group react to the presentation of the individual singer by spontaneously singing along: This is still pure subjectivity; the song of the first singer as such is entirely irrelevant. What carries an effect here is the emotion that is thereby stirred up, which could just as well have been produced by almost any other causal source. Ever so gradually, when objectivity has gained a little more headway and when at the same time the sense for melodic tunes has found its track, one will, aroused by a song, sing along (Simmel 1882:286). The transformation of subjective experience into objective culture is seen by Simmel as an evolutionary process. Both concerns—the process of formation and evolutionism—are connected without contradiction.

3. A third perspective that can be drawn on to demonstrate the continuity in Simmel's method is that of the dynamics of exchange between sensory experience and mental formation in the life of the subject. In an alternating exchange over time between them, these two ways of gaining knowledge continue to grow side by side. In a circular course, which Simmel says begins with sensory perception, pure thinking develops out of experiences, and this again feeds into new experiences. This ring-shaped movement always leads the subject through the empirical world. Vital-emotional feelings are being shaped into forms and these in turn create and reinforce emotional moods. For Simmel, the social aspect of the process of formation is placed alongside the process of objectification in accordance with his epistemological position. The former he illustrates with the example of a lead singer and the group of listeners who are spontaneously aroused to sing along, the latter with the exchange between subjective emotional mood and the song as an objective form of art. These basic threads of his theory of the process of formation are linked with the evolutionist approach.

Religion

Simmel writes in a letter to Martin Buber on April 10, 1916,

> Dear Doctor! Thank you cordially for sending me your book. . . . Also I have some reservations with regard to the way you describe the religiosity of the Jews,

however beautiful and deep it may be. It seems to me that what you describe is the essence of religiosity always and everywhere. (Buber 1972:426–27)

Simmel prepares scholarship for a global perspective on religion. Like society, religion is possible because the content of the conscious mind is not merely a reflection on something untouched by such reflection but itself contributes to the shaping of reality. If religion is compared to society, they are not different in principle; religion is a specific social formation. The initiative to create religious experiences by means of the formative process does not emanate from an outer-worldly sphere but from the shared experience of social life. Religion is reality because it is not disprovable; the religious person tends to experience things in such a way that they cannot be any different from what his religiousness allows them to be.

Simmel compares the creative act of love, which enables love itself to generate a new form, and the creative act of the religious person, which is necessary for the content of faith to become factual (Simmel 1997:163). Of course, faith is linked to concrete phenomena that are open to varying interpretations. Yet religious feelings and faith are never a necessary conclusion to be drawn from the facts, as seeking to prove the existence of God. The adoption of faith is always a free choice; in fact, the question of whether a person is able to adopt such faith is a question of his or her own experiences and feelings.

SIMMEL'S LEGACY

Reliable translations and interpretations of Simmel's works into English have been published by Donald N. Levine (1977), Guy Oakes (Simmel 1977), and others. Tamotsu Shibutani (1955) and Anselm Strauss (1959) helped correct the notion that Simmel's method was formal sociology or useful only in microsociological research. In *The Social Construction of Reality,* Berger and Luckmann (1966) refer to Simmel in six different places, but the most impressive application and continuation of Simmel's work has been presented in Erving Goffman's *Frame Analysis* (1974). Simmel's *form* becomes Goffman's *frame.* In addition, Neil J. Smelser (1995) sums up Simmel's achievements in his Georg Simmel Lectures, and the methodological impetus that the field owes to Simmel lives on in the theoretical reflections on individualization and globalization by authors like Anthony Giddens and Ulrich Beck. Simmel will continue to be one of the most important authors for all humanities. This is true because hardly anyone else foresaw the enormous changes in culture, politics, and social conditions in general that would occur in the course of the twentieth century. It is also true because he discovered a new way of thinking, one that made this premonition of dramatic change possible.

What makes the work of Simmel enlightening as well as frustrating is his attitude toward reality. In opposition to those who declare dreaming as dangerous in school and college teaching and who would rely on hard facts only, Simmel points out that it would be a dangerous dream precisely to assume that anyone can reproduce reality without manipulating it in the process. His point of view, of course, hinges entirely on the evaluation of our faculty of perception. If we believe that sooner or later humans will have registered and clearly presented everything that is worth knowing because that, after all, is the goal of scholarship, then we must reject Simmel as an unwelcome source of doubt. If, however, one assumes that reality is so all encompassing and complex that individuals will always need to introduce their own interests in selecting data, then we can learn from him.

Simmel's work has been controversial from the start. In the tradition of Spinoza, he confronted the dogmatism of some philosophers with fresh insights into human nature that were subsequently accepted by Max Scheler and others. Simmel preferred to see sociology in the companionship of philosophy, history, social psychology, and other humanities. This meant of course that to him sociology is *not* a distant relative to physics, biology, or physiology. As a philosopher of ethics (*Moralwissenschaft*), he proposed a dynamic approach to human behavior and was conscious of the relevance of human emotions. Thus, he antagonized those who view human behavior as subject to eternal or never-changing codes of conduct. He is a precursor to Max Weber and Erving Goffman, and he influenced many other scholars. He also created a version of pragmatism that is similar to the one Charles S. Peirce, William James, and John Dewey developed later.

Simmel's critics suggest that the diversity of his subject matter is confusing. Thus, many claim that sociologically he did not know what he was doing. They point out that Simmel simply drifted from one area of interest to the next. This implies the absence of any systematic order in his scholarly activities. However, if we see Simmel as a scholar who spent his entire life searching for a method that would fit the study of culture and society, we can dispel this negative impression. The diversity of Simmel's topics is the way he *tested his epistemology*. Once he succeeded in devising the proper method for social inquiry, it proved fruitful in his investigations on the stranger, the adventurer (Wanderer 1995), the poor (Draghici 2001), art, love, and religion. Decades before Berger and Luckmann (1966), the message that reality is socially constructed is clearly evident in Simmel's writings.

— Horst Jürgen Helle

See also Frame Analysis; Goffman, Erving; Intimacy; Pragmatism; Scheler, Max; Social Constructionism; Weber, Max

FURTHER READINGS AND REFERENCES

Berger, Peter L. and Thomas Luckmann. 1966. *The Social Construction of Reality: A Treatise in the Sociology of Knowledge.* Garden City, NY: Doubleday.

Buber, Martin. 1972. *Briefwechsel aus sieben Jahrzehnten* [Correspondence from Seven Decades], vol. 1, *1897–1918,* edited by Grete Schaeder. Heidelberg, Germany: Verlag Lambert Schneider.

Draghici, Simona. 2001. *The Pauper/Georg Simmel.* Washington, DC: Plutarch.

Goffman, Erving. 1974. *Frame Analysis: An Essay on the Organization of Experience.* Cambridge, MA: Harvard University Press.

Helle, von Horst J. 2001. *Georg Simmel: Introduction to His Theory and Method.* München & Wien, Germany: R. Oldenbourg Verlag.

Levine, Donald N. 1977. "Simmel at a Distance: On the History and the Systematics of the Sociology of the Stranger." *Sociological Focus* 10:15–29.

Mead, George Herbert. 1927. "The Objective Reality of Perspectives." Pp. 100–13 in *Proceedings of the Sixth International Congress of Philosophy*, edited by E. S. Brightman. New York: Longmans, Green.

Shibutani, Tamotsu 1955. "Reference Groups as Perspectives." *American Journal of Sociology* 60:562–69.

Simmel, Georg. 1882. "Psychologische und Ethnologische Studien über Musik" [Studies in Psychology and Cultural Anthropology on Music]. *Zeitschrift für Völkerpsychologie und Srachwissenschaft* 13:261–305.

———. 1907. *Philosophie des Geldes* [Philosophy of Money]. 2d ed. Leipzig, Germany: Duncker & Humblot.

———. 1908. *Soziologie: Untersuchungen über die Formen der Vergesellschaftung* [Sociology: Inquiries into the Forms of Socialization]. Leipzig, Germany: Duncker & Humblot.

———. 1910. *Hauptprobleme der Philosophie* [Main Problems of Philosophy]. Leipzig, Germany: G. J. Göschen.

———. 1918. *Lebensanschauung: Vier metaphysische Kapitel* [Life-anschauung: Four Metaphysical Chapters]. München & Leipzig, Germany: Duncker & Humblot.

———. 1977. *The Problems of the Phosophy of History: An Epistemological Essay.* Translated and edited, with an introduction by Guy Oakes. New York: Free Press.

———. 1997. *Essays on Religion.* New Haven, CT, & London: Yale University Press.

Smelser, Neil J. 1995. *Problematics of Sociology: The Georg Simmel Lectures.* Berkeley: University of California Press.

Strauss, Anselm. 1959. *Mirrors and Masks. The Search for Identity.* Glencoe, IL: Free Press.

Wanderer, Jules J. 1995. "Adventure in a Theme Park." Pp. 171–88 in *Georg Simmel between Modernity and Postmodernity,* edited by Dörr-Backes and L. Nieder. Würzburg, Germany: Königshausen & Neumann.

SIMULATION

Simulation refers to a theory proposing the absolute loss of reality in contemporary society. Often associated with postmodernism, the theory's major protagonist, Jean Baudrillard, moved from an attempt to update Marxism to a refusal of all political doctrines on the grounds of the fundamentally illusory nature of society and meaning. Reacting against the structuralist school, Baudrillard proposed that what is perceived as the social is really an effect of the self-replication of a code. The term *code* derives from structural linguistics, where it denotes the unit of discourse; from genetics; and from information science. Amalgamating these concepts with a residual Marxism and with the media theory of Marshall MacLuhan, Baudrillard proposed that the equivalence of commodities in exchange implied the equivalence of signs in communication. Just as commodities had been freed from use-value in consumerism, so signs had been freed of the necessity of reference to reality. In historical stages, signification had moved from masking reality to masking its absence and, finally, to circulating without reference to reality at all. Both value and meaning proliferate without distinction, de-realizing the world and devaluing all values. The economics of production have been superseded by those of equivalence in which, since all differences are suppressed, all specificity and therefore all reality also disappear. In a nod to Guy Debord, Baudrillard suggests that the era of the spectacle is over, superseded by that of the hyperreal.

The concept of hyperreality has had the broadest use of the terms developed in simulation theory. In Plato's *Republic,* the term *simulacrum* (or its Greek equivalent *eidolon*) was used to define an extreme degree of removal from the foundations of reality: The ideal table was imitated by the real carpenter, but the painter who made an image of the result was no longer in touch with the ideal, and his work was therefore not a representation (like the carpenter's) but a simulacrum. In Baudrillard, the use-value of commodities, what distinguishes them as real, has disappeared first under exchange value but now under sign-value, so that the original use is so remote as to have vanished. Since the definition of the real is that which can be represented, but since all representation is serial in form, the real has become indistinguishable from its representations, distinguishable if at all only by its startling resemblance to itself. The real that is already an imitation and a representation, and one now lacking an original, becomes subject to a spiral of self-realizing code, producing ever more extravagant and ever less grounded figurations and hallucinations.

One of Baudrillard's examples is public opinion: on one hand, an artefact of the questions asked, on the other the sole proof of the existence of a public that otherwise has no presence in the social world. The opinion poll thus achieves a greater degree of reality than the public whose opinion it supposedly expresses. At the same time, there can be no question of an ideological analysis of opinion polls, since there is by definition no reality behind them that would give the lie to the ideological. Like the perfect recording of music that has only ever existed as a technological mediation, the media and social technologies of simulation abolish the distance between audience and performer, observer and observed, even ruler and ruled, on which meaning and political action are premised. As a result, global politics enters the age of the stalemated Cold War.

Warfare appears as the source of simulation in the work of urbanist Paul Virilio. The twentieth-century development of strategies of camouflage, disinformation, propaganda, and surveillance has entered ("endo-colonised") modern societies. Characteristic of militarization is the acceleration of daily life, an acceleration that, for Virilio, results in the loss of dimensionality. On one hand, distance technologies like rockets, radar, telephony, and television reduce space to the vanishingly small. At the same time, the time left by nuclear weaponry or Internet news services for a political decision-making process is now negligible and, consequently, responses must be automated. The result is a near-static population surrounded by a frenetically rapid communications and transport infrastructure. From TV set via commuter automobile to office computer, contemporary citizens are functionally immobilized, while windscreens and windows merely reduplicate the moving landscapes of TV. German media historian Friedrich Kittler advances the militarization thesis in case studies, including an analysis of the encryption protecting large areas of consumer computer hard drives from the consumers. User-friendly interfaces actively dissuade and eventually refuse permission to users wishing to reach these protected zones, resulting in a relationship in which most computers run their consumers rather than vice versa. In Kittler's work, the mechanization of media technologies parallels and induces the divorce of signification from reference, and of discourse from dialogue, again resulting in the simulation of society and the loss of its reality. In a more politically informed manner, Dutch media theorist Geert Lovink argues that there is no point in seeking the power "behind" media, since the media themselves not only have power, but because apathetic slumping in front of a screen is now a job requirement, they are power.

When, in 1991, Baudrillard published a series of articles arguing that the Gulf War had not taken place, the concept of simulation became public property. At the heart of the argument were a series of axioms. Most obviously, this was a media war and therefore a war of disinformation. Moreover, it was a war waged without political objective, merely as a warning not to start a "real" war. Finally, the restoration of Saddam Hussein to power proved to Baudrillard that no one wanted to believe the war had happened and that the dead were merely props designed to prove that something had happened when in fact it had not. Baudrillard's tactic here was to exaggerate the rhetoric of clean, surgical, minimal war to the point at which the very existence of combat disappears under the weight of its representations.

In terms developed by the Slovenian psychoanalyst Slavoj Žižek, the problem is that reality ceases to be available to consciousness when consciousness is instead entranced by the concept of reality. Like the French philosopher Gilles Deleuze, Žižek counters Baudrillard's nihilism with the argument that the concept of origin, of a reality that exceeds and denies human knowledge, is itself simulacral, but where Deleuze finds here a Nietzschean rationale for foundational, ontological repetition, Žižek sees a more Hegelian dialectic in which the acceleration of unreality may lead to the reemergence of reality in a new guise.

A rather different interpretation appears in the work of Italian semiotician (and celebrated novelist) Umberto Eco, for whom hyperreality refers to the imitation of imitations; for example, the fake Michaelangelos decorating North American graveyards. Eco offers a critical theory of simulation in arguing that, while simulation may govern the lexicon of signification, it does not govern the encyclopedic structures of common sense, which is why it is possible to raise a critique and to discern the excesses of imitations without originals. While this recourse to common sense is vulnerable to both Baudrillard's and Virilio's beliefs that without individuality and therefore community, there can be no common sense, Eco's argument is that the central role of signification is to communicate, not to represent. In this milder form, hyperreality and simulation are portrayed as symptoms of a collapsing of reality and representation in a period when the powers of media become as real as the events they depict, while increasingly, political statements, wars, protests, and even crimes are stage managed to be circulated as media events. In this variant, it is not so much that reality has disappeared but, rather, that the nature of reality and of social relations with it have changed as signification and communication become both more prevalent and more commercialised and commodified. More extreme statements of simulation theory concerning the death of the social and the end of history can then be seen as themselves simulacra, in which, however, lies an analytic tool of some power, the democratization and universalization of systematic doubt.

— Sean Cubitt

See also Baudrillard, Jean; Debord, Guy; Hyperreality; Media Critique; Post-Marxism; Semiology; Virilio, Paul; Žižek, Slavoj

FURTHER READINGS AND REFERENCES

Baudrillard, Jean. 1994. *Simulacra and Simulation.* Translated by Sheila Faria Glaser. Ann Arbor: University of Michigan Press.

———. 1996. *The Perfect Crime.* Translated by Chris Turner. London: Verso.

Eco, Umberto. 1986. *Faith in Fakes: Travels in Hyperreality.* Translated by William Weaver. London: Minerva.

Kittler, Friedrich A. 1997. *Literature, Media, Information Systems: Essays.* Edited and with an introduction by John Johnston. Amsterdam, Netherlands: G+B Arts International.

Virilio, Paul and Sylvère Lotringer. 2002. *Crepuscular Dawn.* Translated by Mike Taormina. New York: Semiotext(e).

SIMULATIONS

In the context of theoretical inquiry, simulations are tools by which theorists examine the consequences of assumptions. In that respect, it is equivalent to logical analysis, which seeks to derive additional propositions from a set of assumptions. Logical analysis, if possible, is always preferable: Consequences asserted as a result of the outcomes of simulations are open to the criticisms that (1) a slightly different instantiation of the assumptions would have produced different results, (2) the outcomes produced are critically dependent on the initial conditions assumed in the model, and (3) the generalizations proposed hold only for the particular space of parameter values examined. Simulations as theoretical tools are quite distinct from simulation put to other purposes such as training or entertainment (e.g., flight simulators).

As a theoretical tool, simulations are typically used for two reasons. First, a proposed model contains probabilistic elements or nonlinear relations among a large set of variables and the overwhelming complexity of possible outcomes makes it impractical or impossible to derive closed-form solutions of key properties. This use of simulations in these circumstances has a long history in social science; for instance, Rapoport in the 1950s used a deck of cards to simulate a link-tracing process on a biased net, a network composed of ties constructed from random and biased forces (1953). The second use of simulations is somewhat more recent, although it has a precursor in Schelling's famous model of segregation (1969). In this arena, agent-based modeling, the nature of the modeling exercise requires that simulations be used to analyze the model's consequences— the aim is to derive complexity at the aggregate level from the interaction of agents following relatively simple rules at the microlevel. Such complexity is "emergent" relative to the lower-level rules of interaction and agent-state change and thus, in principle, not predictable from these rules. Therefore, simulations must be used to detect such emergent regularities. In such a model, there are typically many agents, and often, probabilistic considerations figure in the determination of who interacts with whom and in the determination of the changes of agent-state change. Logical analysis of such a system is not feasible. The only way to explore consequences is through simulations. Both uses of simulations have been greatly aided by the development of very fast computation easily available on desktop workstations.

A simulations study can be divided into three phases: model setup, model implementation and execution, and inductive analysis of model output. In the model setup phase, decisions must be made about how variables are interconnected or how agents may interact and what rules govern their changes of state. In the implementation and execution phase, the system of agents or variables must be encoded in a computer program and various executions of this program conducted. The output of these executions must then be analyzed for patterns or regularities that can be reasonably attributed to the underlying assumptions about the connections among variables or the behavior constraints on agents encoded in the program. Care must be exercised to avoid the attribution of substantive meaning to regularities that are artifacts of the program implementation. In the best of all possible worlds, the simulation study is convincing because (1) the assumptions about behavior or variable connection are clear and intuitively reasonable or based clearly on existing theory, (2) the program implementation is transparent, (3) a full range of initial conditions and values of basic parameters is explored, and (4) clear regularities emerge and variation in these regularities can be interpretively explained in terms of the model's original assumptions.

Simulations have been called a third way of doing science (Axelrod 1997) because research using simulations has features of both deduction and induction. As does deduction, simulations require that research start with an explicit set of assumptions but no theorems are proved; rather, the output of systematic executions of the algorithmic implementation of these assumptions are then inductively analyzed for patterns and regularities. Unlike induction, however, the data analyzed are not generated by empirical measurements. This third way of doing social science, termed "generative social science" by Epstein and Axtell (1996), relies on the more recent type of simulations, agent-based modeling. Such models have a number of common features. Attention focuses on systems consisting of multiple agents and the emergence of system regularities from local interactions among agents. Agents have internal states and behavioral rules, and the rules may be fixed or changeable through experience and interaction. Agents are boundedly rational; they have only limited information-processing and computational capacity. Agents interact in an environment that provides resources for their actions. Typically, agents and the rules they use thrive or die based on their success in obtaining resources. Agent-based models are the paramount tools for "generative social science," social science in which the key research imperative is to explore what microspecifications of agents and their interaction protocols are sufficient to generate macro-phenomenon of interest. The macrophenomena explored cover a wide range: the polarization of attitudes, the articulation of political structures, global performance of organizations, cooperation in social dilemmas by strangers, retirement behavior and social networks, historical change in primitive societies, and labor markets, to name but a few.

— John Skvoretz

See also Actor Network Theory; Agency-Structure Integration; Cognitive Sociology; Complexity Theory; Network Theory; Statics and Dynamics

FURTHER READINGS AND REFERENCES

Axelrod, R. 1997. "Advancing the Art of Simulation in the Social Sciences." Pp. 21–40 in *Simulating Social Phenomena*, edited by R. Conte, R. Hegselmann, and P. Terna. Berlin, Germany: Springer-Verlag.

Epstein, J. and R. Axtell. 1996. *Growing Artificial Societies: Social Science from the Bottom Up.* Cambridge, PA: MIT Press.

Rapoport, A. 1953. "Spread of Information through a Population with Socio-structural Bias: III. Suggested Experimental Procedures." *Bulletin of Mathematical Biophysics* 16:75–81.

Schelling, T. C. 1969. *Models of Segregation.* Memorandum RM-6014-RC. Santa Monica, CA: RAND.

SITUATIONISTS

Situationists are members of the Situationist International (SI) (1957–1972), a European avant-garde art movement whose embrace of radical politics gave them a significant role in the student uprisings of the late 1960s. Initially, a breakaway group of the Lettrist International, the SI sought to create "situations," moments of radical disruption in which the possibilities of a different society more attuned to "real" desires, might be envisaged or temporarily realised. Members of the group included Dutch architect Constant Nieuenhuys, a cofounder of the Amsterdam Provos and the painter Asger Jorn; Italian painter Pinot Gallizio; in the United Kingdom, Donald Nicholson-Smith, the poet Alexander Trocchi and art historian T. J. Clark; and in France, utopian architect Ivan Chtcheglov (Gilles Ivain), Michèle Bernstein, Raoul Vaneigem, and Guy Debord. Also associated with the movement (but after its official demise) were "punk" activists, including Sex Pistols manager Malcolm MacLaren, fashion designer Vivienne Westwood, and graphic designer Jamie Reid.

Among techniques developed to explore the possibility of creating new situations were the theory of "unitary urbanism," which sought to unearth complementary and transforming moments of city life, the *dérive,* a narrative walk or simultaneous walks through the urban environment (sometimes connected by walkie-talkie) designed to stimulate an awareness of the utopian potential available in the built environment, especially its more forgotten corners, and "psychogeography," at once a practice, similar to the *dérive,* aimed at defining the emotional tenor of specific areas and an architectural intervention in urban development aimed at creating previously unheard of new environmental emotions. The ludic influence of Johan Huizinga's theories of play in *Homo Ludens* and the critical urban studies of Lewis Mumford is visible in many of these activities. In all of them, the contrast is drawn between the abstract space of representation, including sociological representation, and the gritty reality of city streets. Abstraction is seen as the intellectual equivalent of the homogenisation of space brought about by the ascent of the commodity to the status of spectacle, pure sign. Similarly, the situationists were concerned to distinguish their *dérive* from the random wanderings of the surrealists, criticising both the class-specific aristocracy of an irresponsible enjoyment and the surrealist concept of chance as a last bastion of freedom. Rather, they recognised the role of planning in urban geography and sought tactics for changing the ways in which the planned and administered environment might be inhabited.

In the late 1950s and early 1960s, the group's interest in practical experiment gave way to a more theoretical and intensely negative assessment of consumer capitalism, a theme captured in the phrase "the colonisation of everyday life" borrowed from Henri Lefebvre, for a time an associate of the SI. The last remaining element of the art practice was *détournement,* the practice of reorienting advertisements, political slogans, and media catchphrases for revolutionary or simply ironic purposes. Much of their art in this period is therefore also sociologically critical of the circumstances of both the art and the society in which they found themselves. Such was Gallizio's semiautomated industrial painting, sold by the metre, as ironic comment on the commodification of painting and of the self-expression that it was understood to communicate. In a related gesture, Debord's film *Hurlements en faveur de Sade* (*Howlings in Favor of de Sade,* 1952) contains a 24-minute passage of darkness and silence intended to destroy the possibility not only of vision but of the spectacularisation of the self, otherwise unavoidable in the society of the spectacle. This sequence might also be taken to illustrate the situationist thesis that the spectacle makes visible the simultaneous presence and absence of the world that is typical of the world of the commodity in general and of the spectacle of the commodity in consumerism in particular. In this way, Debord's film is a *détournement* of the cinema apparatus. In a postsituationist example, Debord photographed reporters following him after he was implicated

in a society murder, thus denying journalism its claim to truth through anonymity.

From its vanguard beginnings, the SI devoted itself to a root-and-branch critique of the art world that rapidly expanded to embrace the conditions of society as a whole. By the mid-1960s, the group was devoted to a wholesale critique of the Communist and Socialist parties, not simply as betrayers of the working class but as fellow travelers of the society of the spectacle, the integration of representational politics with the consumption of commodities reduced to signs. For many of the group, the analysis of an alienated and fragmented society was material for a hedonistic practice of anarchist pleasure seeking, developed in the case of Raoul Vaneigem into a political platform directed specifically at students and widely disseminated in France during May 1968. For others, the route led toward anarchism and to armed struggle—for example, Mustapha Khayati, who left the SI to join the PLO. Like the surrealists, the situationists embraced the criminal underworld, invoking a *détournement* of the language of social organization into a lexicon of gangs, rackets, and protection.

While the more hyperbolic and sloganeering work published in the name of the SI was devoted to internal strife, to quarrels with rival factions, and to interventions in long-forgotten local campaigns, much of it offered intelligent critique. Science is pilloried for its autonomy from daily life and for the hypocrisy of its claim to serve humanity in a period of vastly expensive projects like the space race. The fragmentation of knowledge into isolated disciplines incapable of a total critique of a total and totalitarian society was a pale imitation of that autonomy. Praising the Paris Commune and the revolutionary anarchism of Barcelona in the Spanish Civil War as models for the self-organization of workers' struggles, the SI advocated the power of riot as both festival and revolution. Professionalized trades unions were accused of a Stalinist triumph of dictatorship by bureaucracy, and the claim was made that the Cold War hid the deep similarities in workers' oppression on either side of the Iron Curtain. The conscious domination of history by the people who make it was to be the core revolutionary project, since without the conquest of history, the proletariat was doomed only to inherit the tawdry wealth of the spectacular commodity—as was the case under reformist governments like the British Labour Party of the mid-1960s. In an influential pamphlet of November 1966 addressed to "The Poverty of Student Life," students were accused of complicity in their own bureaucratization, in the fragmentation of knowledge, and in submission to the disciplines of power. Against these were raised, especially by Vaneigem, the possibility of living according only to one's desires.

In the major works of the SI, Debord's *La Société du spectacle* (*The Society of the Spectacle*) and Vaneigem's

Traité de savoir-vivre à l'usage des jeunes générations, both of 1967, the central preoccupation is with the degradation of everyday life. For Vaneigem, whether cloaked in religion or the false glamour of spectacular consumer goods, the poverty of daily life was based in humiliation and reification, shame for desiring otherwise than permitted, and the objectification of humanity. This objectification leads directly to isolation, while the society of the spectacle provides only an illusion of community and nationhood. Social organization is then only the distribution of constraints, including the production of isolation and alienation, and as such is deeply contradictory, leading either toward despair, apathy, and at least a moral and intellectual suicide or toward the erruption of a spontaneous revolutiuonary revulsion with the cheapness of the world on offer.

The situationists developed a high art of invective, as often as not employed against one another during the series of expulsions and splits that characterised the history of the movement. Such splits were rationalized as the necessary radicalism of a revolutionary theory that rejected as spectacular ideology any attempt to represent the working class. A revolutionary organisation was held to require absolute separation from the "world of separation" characteristic of the division of art from politics and both from life. Such radical negation required in turn a readiness to negate itself, a task to which the Situationist International turned in 1972.

— Sean Cubitt

See also Alienation; Debord, Guy; Lefebvre, Henri; Marxism; Media Critique; Revolution

FURTHER READINGS AND REFERENCES

Knabb, Ken, ed., trans. 1981. *Situationist International Anthology.* Rev. ed. Berkeley, CA: Bureau of Public Secrets.

McDonough, Tom, ed. 2002. *Guy Debord and the Situationist International: Texts and Documents.* Cambridge, MA: MIT Press.

Plant, Sadie. 1992. *The Most Radical Gesture: The Situationist International in a Postmodern Age.* London: Routledge.

Sussman, Elizabeth, ed. 1989. *On the Passage of a Few People Through a Rather Brief Moment in Time: The Situationist International, 1957–1972.* Cambridge, MA: MIT Press.

Vaneigem, Raoul. [1979] 1983. *The Book of Pleasures.* Translated by John Fullerton. London: Pending Press.

SMELSER, NEIL

Future historians will write about Neil Smelser (b. 1930) as an iconic figure in twentieth-century sociology's second half. Smelser has had an extraordinarily active career, not only as scholar but as teacher and organizational leader. His impressive and varied performances as organizational leader are perhaps less well known, but they speak equally clearly of scholarly power exercised in a more political manner. His roles have included adviser to a string of University of California chancellors and presidents; referee of the nation's most significant scientific training and funding programs, from NSF (National Science Foundation) to the departments of leading universities; organizer of the *Handbook of Sociology* and the *International Encyclopedia of the Social and Behavioral Sciences;* and director of the Center for Advanced Study in the Behavioral Sciences.

In many respects, both Neil Smelser and the social sciences matured together in the last half of the last century. Smelser expanded his areas of research to include sociology, psychology, economics, and history, at the same time that newly synthetic cross-disciplinary programs, area studies, and applied programs appeared. Through his work with commissions and foundations and as a spokesperson for the social sciences, he sought a greater public role for sociology, and helped to foster the gradual infiltration of their findings and methods into other disciplines, practical settings, and popular culture. Smelser's early interest in comparative international studies anticipated their expansion, an increase in international collaboration, and greater awareness of globalization issues. His move from optimism about positivist approaches and functionalism in the 1950s, to a more guarded optimism and plurivocality today has paralleled broader doubts within the academy and greater tolerance for other ways of knowing.

There is one fundamental respect, however, in which Smelser has broken with dominant trends. The last one-third of the twentieth century was marked by increasing fragmentation and seemingly endless specialization. It was an age of centrifugal conceptual forces and centripetal methodological rigor. These post-1960s intellectual developments have unfolded against a background of ideological jeremiads, the continuous reference to social crisis, and alternations between elegies and eulogies to revolutionary social change. Through all this, Smelser has continued to uphold generality and synthesis as worthy scientific goals. He has maintained his intellectual commitment to uniting divergent disciplinary perspectives and even expanded significantly his own disciplinary reach. He has become ever more dedicated to bridging various conceptual and methodological divides. He has also maintained a quiet and impressive serenity about the continuing possibility for progressive social reform and democratic political change.

Neil Smelser's active life as theorist and researcher has spanned more than 50 years. In 1962, at the age of 32, he became editor of the *American Sociological Review,* the most influential editorial position in the discipline. Almost 35 years later, in 1996, he was elected president of the American Sociological Association, in recognition not only of his lifetime achievement but of the influence, both scientific and organizational, that he continued to wield over those decades.

Smelser began his public life as a *Wunderkind*. Having barely settled into Oxford as a Rhodes Scholar in 1952, he was tapped by Talcott Parsons, his Harvard mentor, to advise him about preparing for the Marshall lectures at Cambridge. Parsons wanted to demonstrate that his newly developed AGIL theory could handle economics. (AGIL refers to the four "pattern variables" in Parsons's theory of social action. In particular, they refer to: A = adaptation; G = goal attainment; I = integration; L = pattern maintenance, later changed to Latency.) Yet he had stopped reading in that discipline before Keynes' *General Theory*. Smelser was *au courrant* with the Keynesian revolution and AGIL besides.

During their collaboration, it was actually Smelser, not Parsons, who suggested the scheme of double interchanges that allowed AGIL to be applied to social systems. This brilliant conceptual innovation formed the core of their jointly written book, *Economy and Society* (1956), which accomplished what its subtitle promised: an integration of economic and social theory. Along with Smelser's later work, especially *The Sociology of Economic Life* (1963), *Economy and Society* laid the foundations for the new field of economic sociology that has become so central to the discipline today. Only three years later, Smelser published the extraordinarily innovative and deeply researched book *Social Change in the Industrial Revolution: An Application of Theory to the British Cotton Industry* (1959), and only three years after that he brought out the equally pathbreaking *Theory of Collective Behavior* (1962).

While Smelser gained great distinction for this rush of early work, he also aroused great controversy. It was high noon for the functionalist paradigm. Smelser was its crown prince and its clear leader in waiting. His work was not only systematic, original, and erudite but intellectually provocative and aggressive. It brimmed with great ambition and utter self-confidence, and it seemed to suggest that, with the emergence of action theory, the solution to sociology's struggles had arrived. Revealingly, the second chapter of *Social Change in the Industrial Revolution* was titled "Some Empty Boxes," and the chapter that followed was titled, "Filling the Boxes." In *Theory of Collective Behavior,* Smelser began with the pronouncement that "even though many thinkers in this field attempt to be objective," they had not succeeded. Because of their failure, "the language of the field . . . shrouds its very subject in indeterminacy" (p. 1). The aim of his study, he proclaimed, would be to "reduce this residue of indeterminacy" by "assembling a number of categories" so that "a kind of 'map' or 'flow chart'" could be constructed of the "paths along which social action moves" (p. 1). While strongly assertive, his goal appropriately was to *reduce,* not eliminate, the residue of indeterminacy.

The youthful Neil Smelser did, in fact, succeed in filling his boxes, forever broadening our view of the industrial revolution as a multidimensional social process—political, economic, familial, cultural, scientific, and very much contingent, all at the same time. He also managed to create an utterly new and fascinating conceptual social map, one that simultaneously separated and intertwined the different dimensions of collective behavior, social structure, and social movements in a value-added manner never before achieved. What he could not do, however, was ensure the continuing sovereignty of functionalist theory. In the history of social science, much more than conceptual precision and explanatory power is involved. Every powerful approach tends to overreach and is partial and to a degree situationally conditioned.

Thirty years after his unabashed and triumphal entrance on the sociological scene, Neil Smelser penned a "concluding note" to his penetrating essay on "The Psychoanalytic Mode of Inquiry" (in *The Social Edges of Psychoanalysis*, 1998). He warned his readers to be careful of their imperialist urge. Was he not looking back with rueful reflection on the grand ambitions and urgent polemics of those early years?

Whenever a truly novel and revolutionary method of generating new knowledge about the human condition is generated—and the psychoanalytic method was one of those—there emerges, as a concomitant tendency, something of an imperialist urge: to turn this method to the understanding of everything in the world—its institutions, its peoples, its history, and its cultures. This happened to the Marxian approach (there is a Marxist explanation of everything), to the sociological approach generally (there is a sociology of everything), and to the psychoanalytic approach (there is a psychoanalytic interpretation of everything) (Smelser 1998a:246).

In the halcyon days of the Parsonian revolution, there had always been a functionalist approach to everything—although few, if any, could rival the power and insight generated by the approaches developed by Smelser himself.

By the late 1960s, the functionalist approach had stalled. Attacked as ideologically conservative, accused of every imaginable scientific inadequacy, functionalism eventually lost its position of dominance. Yet Smelser's postfunctionalist career has also been an extraordinary one. He did not blame the enemies of functionalism for his tradition's weakening. Instead, he targeted the nature of Parsonian thinking itself. He engaged in implicit self-criticism. This required courage and maturity.

Smelser accused foundational functionalism of hubris, of overreaching conceptually, and underreaching empirically. He dressed it down for being one-sided and polemical. After making those observations on the imperialism of every "truly novel and revolutionary method" noted above, Smelser's later reflections continue with the suggestion that "it is always legitimate to ask about the relative *explanatory* power of the method in settings and circumstances in which it was not invented." Only on the basis of such further reflection will it be possible to be objective about "what are the emergent strengths *and weaknesses* of the method" (Smelser 1998a:246, italics added).

It was just such a commitment to the task of explanation, over and above the allegiance to any particular theory, that allowed Smelser not just to stay afloat but to flourish after the functionalist ship sank. When Parsons published his first collection of articles, in 1949, he called them *Essays in Sociological Theory.* When, two decades later, Smelser published his own, he called them *Essays in Sociological Explanation* (1968). His ambitions were tied to the scientific goals of discipline, not to any particular approach.

In 1997, in his presidential address to the ASA, Smelser developed what has already become the most influential essay of his later career. In "The Rational and the Ambivalent in the Social Sciences," (in *The Social Edges of Psychoanalysis*, 1998), he developed an argument that exposed one-sided intellectual polemics as a simplistic defense against the ambivalence that marks human life. "Because ambivalence is such a *powerful, persistent, unresolvable, volatile, generalizable,* and *anxiety-provoking* feature of the human condition," Smelser suggested, "people defend against experiencing it in many ways." For intellectual life, the "most pernicious" of these defenses is splitting, which involves "transferring the positive side of the ambivalence into an unqualified love of one person or object, and the negative side into an unqualified hatred of another" (1998:176–77, original italics). Smelser went on to directly apply this critical observation to sociology itself. Admonishing his colleagues that "in our search for application of the idea of ambivalence, we would do well to look in our own sociological backyard," he observed that "there is almost no facet of our existence as sociologists about which we do not show ambivalence and its derivative, dividing into groups or quasi-groups of advocacy and counteradvocacy" (p. 184).

In his third major historical-cum-theoretical monograph, *Social Paralysis and Social Change: British Working-Class Education in the Nineteenth Century* (1991), Smelser demonstrated how this advice generalized from the path that he had now chosen for himself. Rather than declaring all preceding theoretical boxes empty and announcing that he would now proceed to fill them in, his new approach made carefully circumscribed criticisms. It proposed a theoretical model based on reconciliation and synthesis. After reviewing Whiggish, functionalist, Marxist, and status group approaches to the history of British working-class education, Smelser suggests that each must be "criticized as incomplete, limited, incapable of answering certain problems, and perhaps even incompatible with the others." The alternative, he writes, is "to develop a perspective that is

synthetic," that "incorporates insights from approaches known to have usefulness" (Smelser 1991:16–18).

From his first, vivid entry into the field of intellectual combat, Neil Smelser exhibited one of the most lucid and coherent minds that ever set sociological pen to paper. As his career continued to develop, he revealed another distinctive capacity: He became one of the most incorporative and inclusive of thinkers as well. In fact, we would suggest, it has been Smelser's penchant for combining opposites—the acceptance of sociological ambivalence without fear or favor—that has perhaps most distinctively marked his intellectual career.

He is one of the most abstract of theorists, yet he became an acknowledged "area specialist" in British history.

He is a grand theorist, but he employed grand theory exclusively to develop explanations at the middle range.

He is a functionalist, but he devoted his theoretical and empirical attention almost entirely to conflict.

He is a liberal advocate of institutional flexibility, but he has written primarily about social paralysis and the blockages to social change (see Smelser 1974). He is a psychoanalyst who has highlighted the role of affect, but his major contributions have attacked psychologistic theorizing and explained how to fold the emotional into more sociological levels of explanation (e.g., Smelser 1998a, 2002; Smelser and Wallerstein 1998).

He is a trained economist, but he has strenuously avoided economism, and he is a persistent student of economic life who has demonstrated how it is thoroughly imbedded in noneconomic institutions (e.g., 1968). He is a systems theorist who devoted his final historical monograph to exploring the unbending primordiality of class.

He is a close student of social values (e.g., Smelser 1998a) who rejects any possibility of purely cultural explanations.

He is a theorist of social structure who eschews any form of structural determinism (1968, 1997:28–48).

He was a protégé of Talcott Parsons whom Parsons's sworn enemy, George Homans, publicly singled out for distinct praise.

By avoiding the defense against ambivalence, Smelser demonstrated a remarkable ability to take the sword from the hands of those who would destroy him. He showed how Marx and Engels could be viewed as conflict-oriented functionalist theorists (see "Introduction" to *Karl Marx and on Society and Social Change*, 1973). He made the gendered division of family labor an independent variable in social change (see *Social Change in the Industrial Revolution,* 1959), decades before many feminist theorists made arguments along these same lines. He borrowed from Tocqueville the idea of intranscient "estates" (Smelser 1974) to explain that functional positions in the educational division of labor could be understood as status groups seeking the protection of their own power. He used the idea of "truce situations," an idea that John Rex (1961) had introduced as the antithesis to functionalist consensus theory, to explain why the social differentiation, at the heart of functionalist change theory, developed in a back and forth, stuttering motion rather than in a smooth and unfolding way. He explained (Smelser 1998b) how the differentiation between instrumental and expressive activities actually had been continued, not overturned, by the feminist revolution, and how this often corrosive process of social and cultural rationalization could explain the emergence of the new kinds of child-caring institutions and the increasingly difficult and negotiated character of socialization from childhood to adulthood.

Behind these specific and intellectual innovations, two overarching metathemes have animated Neil Smelser's contributions to sociology. First, there is the insistence that social reality must be parsed into relatively autonomous analytic levels that, in empirical terms, are concretely interconnected. As he wrote (1997) in his intriguing, and continuously instructive Berlin lectures, *Problematics of Sociology,* "Even though the micro, meso, macro, and global levels can be identified, it must be remembered that in any kind of social organization we can observe an interpenetration of these analytic levels" (p. 29). There is every "reason to believe," he insisted, that all "levels of reality are analytically as important" as every other. Smelser's empirical and theoretical work consistently displays the deepest agnosticism about assigning causal apriority. His plurivocality is epistemological and insistent. He absolutely refuses to be absolute. He does not privilege any particular sector or level. Here lies the source of Smelser's famous theft from economic price theory (see the *Theory of Collective Behavior,* 1962:18–20)—the notion that causality must be conceived as a "value-added" process. This apparently simple yet, in reality, quite subtle idea represents a seminal contribution to sociological thought. Social structure, beliefs, and emotions are all important, as is every level inside them. These ideas are reflected in the title for a book honoring Neil Smelser, whose authors—all former students—comprise some of the leading figures on contemporary sociology (Alexander, Marx, and Williams 2004). Second, there is a deep sense that social structure can never, under any circumstances, be separated from the analysis of social process, from the study of social movement, from the flux and flummox of social change. Every book that Smelser has written, every article on social structure, every study of beliefs, and every discussion of emotions—has been a study in the constructive and destructive crystallization of structures.

This double preoccupation with plurality and process, in the context of accepting ambivalence and ambiguity, led Smelser in his historical monograph on working-class education to a wonderfully sociological rendering of the British notion of "muddling through."

Like all such stereotypes, this one demands skepticism and a nonliteral reading. Nevertheless, it can be argued that if any sequence of social change manifested the principle of muddling through, the one I have suited in this volume is a good candidate. . . . Almost every proposal, whether ultimately successful or not, was accompanied by a series of disclaimers. These were that past good work in the area would not be dishonored; ongoing efforts would not be disturbed; what was being added would be no more than a helpful supplement to cover certain gaps; and the claims, rights, and sensibilities of interested parties would not be offended. . . . The aim was to squeeze limited increments of social change by and through them without disturbing them. *[But] the results were often much more than proponents claimed in their modesty. And in the long run, the policy . . . revolutionized the educational system.* The road to that end was marked, however, by a great deal of muddling through. (1991:370, italics added)

Smelser writes here about the ultimate effects of what initially were intended as modest proposals for reform. He might also be speaking about the cumulative effects of the flow of theoretical proposals he has generated in the latter part of his long scientific career. They, too, were accompanied by disclaimers and by the concern not to dishonor past good work. They, too, were launched in a manner designed not to overly disturb ongoing sociological efforts of other kinds, presented as helpful supplements rather than unfriendly displacements. Indeed, Smelser did succeed in his effort not to offend the rights and sensibilities of other sociological parties. All the same, he challenged their claims, and in the long run, his work has had, if not revolutionary, then certainly fundamental intellectual effects. Over the course of 50 years in the sociological trenches, he has muddled through in a remarkable and inspirational way.

That inspiration has been of great importance to the many students Smelser has instructed as a teacher, mentor, and role model. Intellectual legacies lie not only in the substantive contributions of a scholar but also in the work of students touched by their teacher. Having chaired more than 50 PhD committees, served on numerous others, worked with myriad colleagues on joint projects and instructed so many others through his writing, Neil Smelser stands out here. He demonstrated how the division between teaching and research was often too sharply drawn. For the inspired instructor, teaching was a way of exploring new ideas and exercising intellectual curiosity.

Teaching was also a way to communicate the love of ideas and appreciation of the rich intellectual heritage we are bequeathed. In his inspired teaching, Smelser effectively communicated reverence for those giants of social and psychological thought who sought to understand the vast changes in culture, social organization, and personality associated with the development of the modern world. Yet his respect was tempered with critical analysis and the insight that every way of seeing was also a way of not seeing. He honored our intellectual past without being stifled by it.

— Jeffrey C. Alexander and Gary T. Marx

See also AGIL; Historical and Comparative Theory; Parsons, Talcott; Psychoanalysis and Social Theory; Structural Functionalism

FURTHER READINGS AND REFERENCES

Alexander, Jeffrey C., Gary T. Marx, and Christine Williams. 2004. *Self, Social Structure and Beliefs: Essays in Honor of Neil Smelser.* Berkeley: University of California Press.

Homans, George C. 1964. "Bringing Men Back In." *American Sociological Review* 29(6):809–18.

Parsons, Talcott and Neil J. Smelser. 1956. *Economy and Society: A Study of the Integration of Economic and Social Theory.* New York: Free Press.

Rex, John. 1961. *Key Problems of Sociological Theory.* London: Routledge & Kegan Paul.

Smelser, Neil. 1968. *Essays in Sociological Explanation.* Englewood Cliffs, NJ: Prentice-Hall.

———. 1974. "Growth, Structural Change, and Conflict in California Public Higher Education, 1950–1970." Pp. 9–142 in *Public Higher Education in California*, edited by Neil Smelser and Gabriel Almond. Berkeley & Los Angeles: University of California Press.

———. 1991. *Social Paralysis and Social Change: British Working Class Education in the Nineteenth Century.* Berkeley & Los Angeles: University of California Press.

———. 1997. *Problematics of Sociology: The Georg Simmel Lectures, 1995.* Berkeley & Los Angeles: University of California Press.

———. 1998a. *The Social Edges of Psychoanalysis.* Berkeley & Los Angeles: University of California Press.

———. 1998b. "Vicissitudes of Work and Love in Anglo-American Society." Pp. 93–107 in *The Social Edges of Psychoanalysis.* Berkeley & Los Angeles: University of California Press.

———. 2004. "Psychological Trauma and Cultural Trauma." Pp. 31–59 in *Cultural Trauma and Collective Identity*, edited by Jeffrey C. Alexander, Ron Eyerman, Bernhard Giesen, Neil J. Smelser, and Piotr Sztompka. Berkeley & Los Angeles: University of California Press.

Smelser, Neil J. and Dean Gerstein, eds. 1986. *Behavioral and Social Science: Fifty Years of Discovery.* Washington DC: National Academy Press.

Smelser, Neil J. and Robert S. Wallerstein. 1998. "Psychoanalysis and Sociology: Articulations and Applications." Pp. 3–35 in *The Social Edges of Psychoanalysis,* edited by Neil J. Smelser. Berkeley & Los Angeles: University of California Press.

SMITH, DOROTHY

Dorothy E. Smith (b. 1926) a Canadian sociologist, is one of the most prominent feminist theorists of the twentieth century. Educated at the University of London School of Economics (BSc), the University of British Columbia (LLD), and the University of California at Berkeley (PhD), she was one of the founders of an influential theoretical framework called feminist standpoint epistemology. Smith asserts that certain standpoints can provide a more reliable vantage point from which to assess how power is woven into institutions that contour women's daily activities. Smith's approach situates women's experiences within the local institutional practices that organize their lives. By using this "everyday world" perspective, researchers remain sensitive to women's experiences while also exploring how varying institutional practices such as welfare policy and higher education differentially organize their lives.

Smith's theoretical approach draws on a variety of traditions, including phenomenology and ethnomethodology as well as Marx's historical materialism and poststructuralism. She was on the faculty of the University of Essex, the University of British Columbia, and the Ontario Institute for Studies in Education (OISE). She also served as head of OISE's Centre for Women's Studies in Education. She was recipient of the Jessie Bernard Award for Feminist Sociology from the American Sociological Association, the Kerstin Hesselgren Professorship in Sweden, and the Lansdowne Professorship at the University of Victoria. She was also awarded the Degré Prize Lecturership at the University of Waterloo and the John Porter Lecturership of the Canadian Sociology and Anthropology Association. Her doctoral thesis, completed in 1963, was titled *Power and the Front-Line: Social Controls in a State Mental Hospital.*

In her highly acclaimed book *The Everyday World as Problematic: A Feminist Sociology,* Smith (1987) argues for a sociology that will reveal the everyday practices of people that abstractions typically developed by sociologists both "express and conceal" (p. 213). Theorizing from her own experience as a single mother of two young children, Smith developed the concept of "bifurcated consciousness" to capture the tensions women in particular experience when they enter the textually organized world of academia that is independent of the everyday world of preschool schedules, visits to doctors, and trips to the parks. As a mode of consciousness, the practice of sociology, requires distancing from the everyday world of child care and meal preparation, among other particularities. Smith argues that these different modes of consciousness are gendered and that women are constructed as the "Other" in the academic world. As a result of consciousness-raising strategies developed by the feminist movement of the late 1960s and early 1970s, women collectively articulated new issues and concerns that called into question the presumed genderless organization of the knowledge production enterprise.

Smith first published her critique of the dominant methods of sociology in a 1974 article titled "The Ideological Practice of Sociology." As a corrective to the abstractions developed by sociologists, Smith created a methodological approach to social research called "institutional ethnography" that is designed to explore links between everyday life experiences and broad-based social structural processes. Smith's methodological goal is to examine the social relations that shape everyday life experiences, revealing how local experiences are organized by relations of ruling. Smith (1987) defines *relations of ruling* as a term "that brings into view the intersection of the institutions organizing and regulating society with their gender subtext and their basis in a gender division of labor" (p. 2). The term *ruling* is used to identify organizational practices of government, law, financial management, professional associations, and other institutions that shape everyday life. Smith argues that bureaucratic procedures and textual forms that rationalize the organizational practices create a screen of neutrality that masks the gender, racial, and class subtexts of institutional activities and discourse.

Smith (1999) resists providing content to the standpoint of social actors. For Smith, a standpoint functions like an arrow on maps in malls. Standpoints are sites in and through which to explore the relationships between diverse local sites. Smith's map-making strategy helps an investigator map the activities that coordinate and reproduce oppressive systems. This strategy also provides a useful tool for activist research. It helps capture less formal activities and institutional processes that intersect in particular social or institutional locations. This knowledge can be used as a resource for social change efforts, providing an assessment of how power operates in local practices of ruling or *ruling relations* where activist interventions might be most successful.

In *The Conceptual Practices of Power: A Feminist Sociology of Knowledge,* Smith (1990a) furthers her analysis of "women's experience as a radical critique of sociology" and takes issue with what she terms "the ideological practice of sociology." *The Conceptual Practices of Power* concentrates on the ways relations of ruling are organized through texts and the ideological properties of textual accounts of factual accounts. As two examples of these practices,

Smith demonstrates how statistics on mental illness and constructions of what counts as suicide are inseparable from the professional and bureaucratic practices that give rise to these phenomena. In the first example, she calls attention to the patriarchal relations that inform the production of statistical evidence. She argues that what counts as mental illness is constructed along with the categories used to organize patients' problems into objects of psychiatry. In the second example, Smith draws on Marx's notion of "social relation" to produce a materialist analysis of the social processes that organize factual accounts and define them as "suicide." Implicated in these processes is the increasing bureaucratic and professional push to standardize organizational forms to produce coherence between the clinical encounter, the production of an account of the encounter, and the development of a specific psychiatric syndrome.

In *Texts, Facts, and Femininity: Exploring the Relations of Ruling* (1990b), Smith extends her conceptualization of relations of ruling and the social organization of subjectivity. She discusses her epistemological link to Marx's method of historical materialism and argues that "social forms of consciousness also exist only in actual practices and in the concerting of those practices as an ongoing process" (p. 7). She offers a powerful analysis of femininity as a textually mediated discourse. Smith explains that individuals in diverse locations who do not know each other are coordinated by the same texts and, consequently, new social relations are created.

Despite her interest in discourse and the power of texts to mediate social relations, Smith is critical of postmodernism and differentiates her materialist feminist approach from Foucault's theory of discourse. While Smith (1993) finds value in Foucault's analysis of discourse, she criticizes his emphasis on discourse to the exclusion of nondiscursive processes. As she explains, "There are indeed matters to be spoken and spoken of that discourse does not yet encompass" (pp. 183–84). In contrast to Foucault's "conception of discourse as a conversation mediated by texts," Smith (1999) argues for the incorporation of how people use texts and how texts coordinate an individual's activities with another's or others' activities (p. 158).

In *Writing the Social: Critique, Theory, and Investigations,* Smith (1999) further explicates her critique of postmodernism. For Smith, it is essential that analysis makes "reference to what is beyond discourse" (p. 127). Smith offers a social theory that envisions subjects of investigation who can experience aspects of life outside discourse. Smith's institutional ethnographic approach provides the methodological framework to explore the material consequences of local discourses and institutional practices for social, cultural, political, and economic processes that shape social actors' everyday lives.

— Nancy A. Naples

See also Ethnomethodology; Feminism; Feminism Epistomology; Foucault, Michel; Historical Materialism; Phenomenology; Postmodernism; Poststructuralism

FURTHER READINGS AND REFERENCES

Campbell, Marie L. and Ann Manicom, eds. 1995. *Knowledge, Experience, and Ruling Relations: Studies in the Social Organization of Knowledge.* Toronto, Canada: University of Toronto Press.

Smith, Dorothy E. 1971. "The Ideological Practice of Sociology." *Catalyst* 8:39–54.

———. 1987. *The Everyday World as Problematic: A Feminist Sociology.* Toronto, Canada: University of Toronto Press.

———. 1990a. *Conceptual Practices of Power: A Feminist Sociology of Knowledge.* Boston: Northeastern University Press.

———. 1990b. *Texts, Facts, and Femininity: Exploring the Relations of Ruling.* New York: Routledge.

———. 1993. "High Noon in Textland: A Critique of Clough." *Sociological Quarterley* 34(1):183–92.

———. 1999. *Writing the Social: Critique, Theory, and Investigations.* Toronto, Canada: University of Toronto Press.

SOCIAL ACTION

Social action occurs when thought processes intervene between a stimulus, an actor, and their subsequent response. In other words, it is a process whereby an individual attaches a subjective meaning to his or her action. This is different from reactive behavior in that a simple reaction involves a response to a stimulus with no intervening thought. The concept of social action is of particular importance to sociology because many aspects of the field are built on the principle of understanding the subjective meanings that actors attach to actions and how they come to understand the actions of others (and themselves).

The sociology of Max Weber rested on his concept of social action. He stated that the goal of sociological analysis was "the interpretation of action in terms of its subjective meaning" (Weber [1921]1968:8). This did not, however, lead him to support the psychological study of the mind but, rather, to pursue a sociological study of mental processes. He was not as concerned with the roots of action in consciousness as much as he was interested in the ways in which social structures affected individual action.

The focus of Weber's interest in social action was on the individual. He acknowledged that there were occasions when the collective had to be treated as an individual, but only as "the resultants and modes of organization of the particular acts of individual persons, since these alone can be treated as agents in a course of subjectively understandable

action" (Weber [1921]1968:13). Therefore, in contrast to what the name might imply, social action is in nearly all instances performed by the individual actor and not the social collective.

Weber outlined four basic ideal types of action. The most important to him were the two basic types of rational action because these are the ones most likely to be understood by sociologists. The first of these, means-ends rationality is based on a set of expectations of other actors and their assumed responses to environmental stimuli and other human actors. These expectations are the "means" by which the actor calculates his or her own actions in order to obtain his or her desired "ends." An example of this type of action would be extending one's hand to a new acquaintance with the expectation that that person will shake your hand and the goal of a successful social exchange. The second type of rational action, value rationality, is based on the belief that some actions must be undertaken for their own sake regardless of whether or not they will be successful. The confession of sins to a Catholic priest in hopes of saving one's soul is an example of this type of action.

The other two types of action for Weber have a seemingly more irrational basis. Affectual action is the result of the emotional state of the actor. An example of this would be throwing expensive dinner plates across the room in a fit of rage or acting in socially unprescribed ways in the name of love. Traditional action is rooted in the individual's routine systems of behavior. This would include things such as showering at night versus in the morning, having tea at a certain time every day, or celebrating one's birthday with a cake and candles.

Although Weber outlined four specific types of social action, he made it clear that nearly every instance involved some combination of these four ideal types. For example, celebrating one's birthday with candles and a cake is not only traditional action but could be interpreted as value action as well.

Weber's concept of social action led to a more general action theory. Although it has declined in popularity since the 1930s and 1940s, a number of notable theorists at that time, including Robert MacIver (1931), Florian Znaniecki (1934), and especially Talcott Parsons (1937), all engaged in action theory. It was mostly the work of Parsons, however, that brought action theory to the spotlight.

Parsons did not intend his action theory to explain all parts of social reality. Instead, he recognized that such a theory was limited primarily to the most basic forms of social life. In turn, the most basic component of his action theory is the unit act. The unit act, for Parsons, has four characteristics: (1) an actor must be present, (2) the act must have a goal to which it is oriented, (3) the situation in which the act occurs must be different from the ends that it aims to accomplish (which is not the same as saying the means must be different from the ends; Parsons saw the means as only one aspect of the situation—the parts over which the actor has control; the other subdivision of a situation is conditions, or those parts over which the actor has no control), and (4) norms and values exist for an actor that orient his or her choice of means to the desired end.

The last element of the unit act is of critical importance in helping to distinguish action from a behavioral response. The contemplation of a choice implies that the actor is engaging in voluntarism, a well-known concept developed by Parsons. Voluntarism does not mean total freedom to do as one wishes but, rather, the ability to choose from among the range or options available, given the conditions or the restraints of the situation.

In Parsons's later works, he almost entirely abandons his idea of the unit act in lieu of a focus on systems, which he sees as composed of and emerging from unit acts. In other words, he moved in a more macro direction and sought to explain those aspects of social reality that he did not feel could be explained by the individual unit act. Nevertheless, he was influential in bringing Weber's ideas of social action to the United States and to further developing them into the field of action theory.

— Michael Ryan

See also Parsons, Talcott; Weber, Max

REFERENCES

MacIver, Robert. 1931. *Society: Its Structure and Changes.* New York: Ray Long and Richard R. Smith.

Parsons, Talcott. 1937. *The Structure of Social Action.* New York: Free Press.

Weber, Max. [1921] 1968. *Economy and Society.* 3 vols. Totowa, NJ: Bedminster.

Znaniecki, Florian. 1934. *Method of Sociology.* New York: Farrar & Rinehart.

SOCIAL CAPITAL

The term *social capital* refers either to the capacity of an individual to obtain valued material or symbolic goods by virtue of his or her social relationships and group memberships or to the capacity of a plurality of persons to enjoy the benefits of collective action by virtue of their own social participation, trust in institutions, or commitment to established ways of doing things. The former capacity has been called "relational social capital" and the latter "institutional social capital" (Krishna 2000). The common element underlying both types of social capital is social embeddedness. Individual and collective action alike are enabled and constrained by the resources that actors can leverage within and between levels of social structure.

Like the complementary concept of "human capital" (the knowledge, skill, and understanding acquired by persons through training and experience), the concept of social capital stems from an analogy to physical and financial capital. Capital in general refers to finite assets available for purposive deployment in the satisfaction of future wants (rather than present consumption). Capital assets accumulate as stocks. Put to productive use, they generate flows of benefits for the asset holder and his or her exchange partners. Capital assets are said to be "fungible" (interchangeable), "transferable" (conveyable from one place or situation to another), and "alienable" (transferable in ownership). Since social capital is only slightly fungible, mildly transferable, and inalienable, some economists—for example, Kenneth Arrow—reject the analogy to capital theory. However stretched the analogy may be, the concept of social capital captures something that most sociologists consider an elemental truth—that the resources embedded in social structures facilitate individual and collective action, and generate flows of benefits for persons, groups, and communities.

No one knows who first used the term social capital in the ways defined above. Robert D. Putnam nominates L. Judson Hanifan on the basis of the Progressive educator's 1916 essay on community centers. "The individual is helpless socially, if left to himself," Hanifan (1916) observed of the rural poor in West Virginia. "If he comes into contact with his neighbors, and they with other neighbors, there will be an accumulation of social capital, which may immediately satisfy his social needs and which may bear a social potentiality sufficient to the substantial improvement of living conditions in the whole community" (p. 130). The core elements of the concept are clearly present in this quotation: agential capacitation through relationship formation, interdependent asset cumulation, and "social potentiality," the facilitation of collective ends.

Two contemporary social theorists who developed the concept's theoretical potential are Pierre Bourdieu and James S. Coleman. Bourdieu arrived at the concept independently, while Coleman built on economist and policy analyst Glenn Loury's use of the term to designate all the family, class, and neighborhood characteristics that affect actors' investments in human capital. Bourdieu and Wacquant (1992) define social capital as the actual or potential resources at play in the "field of the social"—that is, in the sphere of "mutual acquaintance and recognition" (p. 1991). For Bourdieu, modern society is an ensemble of relatively autonomous fields—for example, the religious field, the linguistic field, the economic field, each with its own strategic logic and specific form of capital—religious capital, linguistic capital, economic capital, and so on. Of these, the most important, the one that exerts the greatest force on the other fields, is the economic. Having limited social capital to the sphere of direct social relations,

Bourdieu devoted his prodigious research efforts to the study of other forms of capital, particularly cultural capital.

Coleman (1988) derived the concept of social capital from the premises of rational choice theory. Starting out from the spare premises of utility-maximizing, resource-bearing actors, each controlling assets of differential value to others, Coleman erected an impressive theoretical edifice extending to interdependent corporate groups ("corporate society"). These premises required him to see social capital as an unintended, emergent phenomenon chiefly found in social structures characterized by "closure." The effective monitoring and sanctioning of behavior that closure provides builds interpersonal trust, generates the authority required for collective action, and allows actors to pool their resources for new projects and endeavors.

Two other theorists of social capital working within the rational choice framework are Nan Lin and Ronald S. Burt. Both emphasize actors' self-conscious investments in social structural arrangements that yield high flows of benefits for themselves and others. Lin's research centers on the ways that social capital facilitates status attainment. In *Social Capital* (2001), he crafted a set of 12 postulates and propositions to integrate the literature in this area. Burt concentrates on the network configurations that confer structural autonomy on strategically located nodes, allowing the occupants of such positions to broker information and control the flow of resources. Burt (2002) theoretically derived four mechanisms (contagion, prominence, closure, and brokerage) that differentially affect the social capitals of actors situated at different nodes. Seamlessly integrating the concept of social capital into his theory of structural holes, Burt advances the proposition that high social capital accrues to positions that span structural holes (defined as weak ties between social networks or subnetworks).

In contrast to the above uses of the term, which concentrate on the empowerment of persons' strategic or instrumental action, political scientist Robert D. Putnam steered social capital research in a decidedly institutional, even communitarian direction. In *Making Democracy Work* (1993), he and his coworkers examined the effectiveness of 20 new regional governments established in Italy in 1970. Some of these new governments failed miserably, while others established successful participatory programs and spurred economic development. After controlling for political ideology, tax revenues, and other conditions, Putnam determined that the best predictor of governmental performance was a strong local tradition of civic engagement, which he measured by a host of social capital indicators, such as membership in voluntary associations and voter participation in elections. In *Bowling Alone* (2000), Putnam applied the same analysis to American communities and states. He found that, overall, social capital had declined significantly since 1960. States and localities that maintained relatively higher levels of social capital, however, were more likely to experience safer and more productive neighborhoods, better student test scores, lower levels of tax evasion, and higher levels of intergroup tolerance.

As in Putnam's work, empirical studies employing the concept of social capital typically involve dependent variables of performance or outcome, indicators of social capital at the relational or institutional level (or both), and various controls. Persons advantaged by higher social capital find better jobs more easily, organize more effective protests, and influence public opinion more decisively. The mechanisms of relational social capital include (1) access to information, organizations, or public officials; (2) the promulgation of effective norms; (3) the cashing in of outstanding interpersonal obligations ("credit slips"); and (4) being in a position to understand conflicting interests or perceptions and thus to broker solutions acceptable to different parties.

In communities where higher levels of trust, cooperation, and participation prevail, common outcome variables include institutional effectiveness and smoother adaptations to changing macroeconomic conditions. The mechanisms of institutional social capital include (1) vertical linkages between levels of social structure; (2) horizontal linkages ("bridges") between local social networks; and (3) the support of outside agencies in devising positive-sum solutions to collective action problems.

During the 1990s, social capital explanations blossomed in the fields of developmental economics, community development, criminology, social welfare, and poverty amelioration. Many of these fields saw the failures of both market-centered and government-centered programs to solve pressing social problems. For many policy-oriented researchers, social capital represents a liberating perspective.

As important as the concept of social capital appears to be for both theoretical and applied sociology, it has no shortage of critics. Many economists reject the analogy to capital theory and doubt whether social capital rises to a factor of production. Methodologists worry that too many diverse mechanisms underlay the concept's effects, that too many diverse indicators measure it, and that its effects are distributed over too many levels of social organization. They consider the concept "fuzzy" (analytically imprecise). Some theorists reject in principle the distinction between social capital and cultural capital. They insist on a joint conceptual construction or on the epistemological priority of cultural capital. Theorists inclined toward rational choice or network explanations lament the concept's extension into the macro realms of institutional social capital. Critical theorists consider the multiplying analogies to capital to be symptomatic of the social sciences' intellectual subordination to bourgeois ideology.

Social theorists long understood that the resources embedded in social structures empower actors (whether persons or collectivities) to conceive and achieve their projects. In social capital, they found a concept that focuses like a laser on precisely that idea.

— Christopher Prendergast

See also Cultural Capital

FURTHER READINGS AND REFERENCES

Bourdieu, Pierre and Loïc J. D. Wacquant. 1992. *An Invitation to Reflexive Sociology.* Chicago: University of Chicago Press.

Burt, Ronald S. 2002. "The Social Capital of Structural Holes." Pp. 148–90 in *The New Economic Sociology: Developments in an Emerging Field,* edited by M. F. Guillén, R. Collins, P. England, and M. Meyer. New York: Russell Sage.

Coleman, James S. 1988. "Social Capital in the Creation of Human Capital." *American Journal of Sociology* 94:S95–S120.

Hanifan, Lyda Judson. 1916. "The Rural School Community Center." *Annals of the American Academy of Political and Social Science* 67:130–38.

Krishna, Anirudh. 2000. "Creating and Harnessing Social Capital." Pp. 71–93 in *Social Capital: A Multifaceted Perspective,* edited by P. Dasgupta and I. Serageldin. Washington, DC: World Bank.

Lin, Nan. 2001. *Social Capital: A Theory of Social Structure and Action.* Cambridge, UK: Cambridge University Press.

Putnam, Robert D. 2000. *Bowling Alone: The Collapse and Revival of American Community.* New York: Simon & Schuster.

Putnam, Robert D, with Roberto Leonardi and Raffaella Y. Nanetti. 1993. *Making Democracy Work: Civic Traditions in Modern Italy.* Princeton, NJ: Princeton University Press.

SOCIAL CLASS

Few concepts are more contested in sociological theory than the concept of "class." In contemporary sociology, there are scholars who assert that class is ceasing to be useful (Pahl 1989) or even more stridently proclaim the death of class. Yet at the same time, there are also sociologists who write books with titles such as *Bringing Class Back In* (McNall, Levine, and Fantasia 1991), *Reworking Class* (Hall 1997), *Repositioning Class* (Marshall 1997), and *Class Counts* (Wright 1997). In some theoretical traditions in sociology, most notably Marxism, class figures at the very core of the theoretical structure; in others, especially the tradition identified with Durkheim, only pale shadows of class appear.

In what follows, there is first an examination, in broad strokes, the different ways in which the word *class* is used in sociological theory. This is followed by a more fine-grained exploration of the differences in the concept of class in the two most important traditions of class analysis, the Weberian and the Marxist.

VARIETIES OF CLASS CONCEPTS

Many discussions of the concept of class confuse the terminological problem of how the *word* class is used within social theory with theoretical disputes about the proper definition and elaboration of the *concept* of class. While all uses of the word class in social theory invoke in one way or another the problem of understanding systems of economic inequality, different uses of the word are imbedded in very different theoretical agendas involving different kinds of questions and thus different sorts of concepts. One way of sorting out these alternative meanings is to examine what might be termed the anchoring questions within different agendas of class analysis. These are the questions that define the theoretical work the concept of class attempts to do. Five such anchoring questions in which the word *class* figures centrally in the answers are particularly important.

1. *Class as subjective location.* First, the word class sometimes figures in the answer to the question: "How do people, individually and collectively, *locate themselves and others* within a social structure of inequality?" Class is one of the possible answers to this question. In this case, the concept would be defined something like this: "Classes are social categories sharing subjectively salient attributes used by people to rank those categories within a system of economic stratification." With this definition of class, the actual content of these evaluative attributes will vary considerably across time and place. In some contexts, class-as-subjective-classification revolves around lifestyles, in others around occupations, and in still others around income levels. Sometimes the economic content of the subjective classification system is quite direct, as in income levels; in other contexts, it is more indirect, as in expressions such as "the respectable classes," the "dangerous classes." The number of classes also varies contextually depending on how the actors in a social situation themselves define class distinctions. Class is not defined by a set of objective properties of a person's social situation but by the shared subjective understandings of people about rankings within social inequality (e.g., Warner [1949]1960). Class, in this sense of the word, is contrasted to other forms of salient evaluation—religion, ethnicity, gender, occupation, and so on—that may have economic dimensions but that are not centrally defined in economic terms.

2. *Class as objective position within distributions.* Second, class is often central to the question, "How are people *objectively located* in distributions of material inequality." In this case, class is defined in terms of material

standards of living, usually indexed by income or, possibly, wealth. Class, in this agenda, is a *gradational* concept; the standard image is of rungs on a ladder, and the names for locations are accordingly such things as upper class, upper middle class, middle class, lower middle class, lower class, underclass. This is the concept of class that figures most prominently in popular discourse, at least in countries like the United States without a strong working-class political tradition. When American politicians call for "middle-class tax cuts" what they characteristically mean is tax cuts for people in the middle of the income distribution. Subjective aspects of the location of people within systems of stratification may still be important in sociological investigations using this concept of class, but the word class itself is being used to capture objective properties of economic inequality, not simply the subjective classifications. Class, in this context, is contrasted with other ways that people are objectively located within social structures—for example, by their citizenship status, their power, or their subjection to institutionalized forms of ascriptive discrimination.

3. *Class as the relational explanation of economic life chance.* Third, class may be offered as part of the answer to the question, "What *explains* inequalities in economically defined life chances and material standards of living of individuals and families?" This is a more complex and demanding question than the first two, for here the issue is not simply descriptively locating people within some kind of system of stratification—either subjectively or objectively—but identifying certain causal mechanisms that help determine salient features of that system. When class is used to explain inequality, typically, the concept is not defined primarily by subjectively salient attributes of a social location but, rather, by *the relationship of people to income-generating resources* or assets of various sorts. Class thus becomes a *relational* rather than simply *gradational* concept. This concept of class is characteristic of both the Weberian and Marxist traditions of social theory. Class, in this usage, is contrasted to the many other determinants of a person's life chances—for example, geographical location, forms of discrimination anchored in ascriptive characteristics like race or gender, or genetic endowments. Location, discrimination, and genetic endowments may, of course, still figure in the analysis of class—they may, for example, play an important role in explaining why different sorts of people end up in different classes—but the definition of class as such centers on how people are linked to those income-generating assets.

4. *Class as a dimension of historical variation in systems of inequality.* Fourth, class figures in answers to the question, "How should we characterize and explain the variations across history in the social organization of inequalities?" This question implies the need for a macrolevel concept rather than simply a microlevel concept capturing the causal processes of individual lives, and it requires a concept that allows for macrolevel variations across time and place. This question is also important in both the Marxist and Weberian traditions, but as we will see later, here the two traditions have quite different answers. Within the Marxist tradition, the most salient aspect of historical variation in inequality is the ways in which economic systems vary in the manner in which an economic surplus is produced and appropriated, and classes are therefore defined with respect to the mechanisms of surplus extraction. For Weber, in contrast, the central problem of historical variation is the degree of rationalization (in this context, the extent to which inequalities are organized in such a way that the actors within those inequalities can act in precise, calculable ways) of different dimensions of inequality. This underwrites a conceptual space in which, on one hand, class and status are contrasted as distinct forms of inequality and, on the other hand, class is contrasted with nonrationalized ways through which individual life chances are shaped.

5. *Class as a foundation of economic oppression and exploitation.* Finally, class plays a central role in answering the question, "What sorts of transformations are needed to eliminate economic oppression and exploitation within capitalist societies?" This is the most contentious question, for it implies not simply an explanatory agenda about the mechanisms that generate economic inequalities but a normative judgment about those inequalities—they are forms of oppression and exploitation—and a normative vision of the transformation of those inequalities. This is the distinctively Marxist question, and it suggests a concept of class laden with normative content. It supports a concept of class that is not simply defined in terms of the social relations to economic resources but that also figures centrally in a political project of emancipatory social change.

Different theoretical approaches to class analysis build their concepts of class to help answer different clusters of these questions. Figure 1 indicates the array of central questions linked to different approaches to class analysis. Weber's work revolves around the third and fourth questions, with the fourth question concerning forms of historical variation in social organization of inequalities providing the anchor for his understanding of class. The narrower question about explaining individual life chances gets its specific meaning from its relationship to this broader historical question. Michael Mann's work on class, especially in his multivolume study of *The Sources of Social Power* (1993) is, like Weber's, also centered on the fourth question. John Goldthorpe's (1980) class analysis centers firmly on the third question. While his work is often characterized as having a Weberian inflection, his categories are elaborated strictly in terms of the requirements of describing and explaining economic life chances, not long-term historical variations in systems of inequality. For Pierre Bourdieu, class analysis is anchored in a more open-ended version of the third question. Where he differs from Weber and other Weber-inspired class analysts is in expanding the idea of life chances to include a variety of noneconomic aspects of opportunity (e.g., cultural opportunities of various sorts) and expanding the kinds of resources relevant to explaining those life chances from narrowly economic resources to a range of cultural and social resources (called "cultural capital" and "social capital"). "Class" for Bourdieu (1984), therefore, is a much more expansive concept, covering all inequalities in opportunities (life chances) that can be attributed to socially determined inequalities of resources of whatever sort. Finally, class analysis in the Marxist tradition is anchored in the fifth question concerning the challenge to systems of economic oppression and exploitation. The questions about historical variation and individual life chances

are also important, but they are posed within the parameters of the problem of emancipatory transformations.

The rest of this essay examines in some detail how these questions are played out in the Weberian and Marxist traditions, the two most important traditions of class analysis in sociological theory. The concepts of class in these two theoretical traditions share much in common: They both reject simple gradational definitions of class; they are both anchored in the social relations that link people to economic resources of various sorts; they both see these social relations as affecting the material interests of actors; and, accordingly, they see class relations as the potential basis for solidarities and conflict. Yet they also differ in certain fundamental ways. The core of the difference is captured by the favorite buzzwords of each theoretical tradition: *life chances* for Weberians, and *exploitation* for Marxists. This difference, in turn, reflects

	Anchoring questions				
	1. subjective location	2. distributional location	3. life chances	4. historical variation	5. emancipation
Karl Marx	*	*	**	**	***
Max Weber	*	*	**	***	
Michael Mann	*	*	*	***	
John Goldthorpe	*	*	***		
Pierre Bourdieu	*	*	***		
popular usage	*	***	*		
Lloyd Warner	***	*	*		

*** primary anchoring question for concept of class
** secondary anchoring question
* additional questions engaged with concept of class, but not central to the definition

The questions:

1. "How do people, individually and collectively, *locate themselves and others* within a social structure of inequality?"

2. "How are people *objectively located* in distributions of material inequality?"

3. "What *explains* inequalities in economically defined life chances and material standards of living?"

4. "How should we characterize and explain the variations across history in the social organization of inequalities?"

5. "What sorts of transformations are needed to eliminate economic oppression and exploitation within capitalist societies?"

Figure 1   Anchoring Questions in Different Traditions of Class Analysis

the location of class analysis within their broader theoretical agendas.

THE WEBERIAN CONCEPT: CLASS AS MARKET-DETERMINED LIFE CHANCES

What has become the Weber-inspired tradition of class analysis is largely based on Weber's few explicit, but fragmentary, conceptual analyses of class. In *Economy and Society* ([1924]1978), Weber writes:

We may speak of a "class" when (1) a number of people have in common a specific causal component of their life chances, insofar as (2) this component is represented exclusively by economic interests in the possession of goods and opportunities for income, and (3) is represented under the conditions of the commodity or labor markets. This is "class situation."

It is the most elemental economic fact that the way in which the disposition over material property is distributed among a plurality of people, meeting competitively in the market for the purpose of exchange, in itself creates specific life chances. . . .

But always this is the generic connotation of the concept of class: that the kind of chance in the *market* is the decisive moment which presents a common condition for the individual's fate. Class situation is, in this sense, ultimately market situation. (pp. 927–28)

In short, the kind and quantity of resources you own affects your opportunities for income in market exchanges. "Opportunity" is a description of the feasible set individuals face, the trade-offs they encounter in deciding what to do. Owning means of production (the capitalist class) gives a person different alternatives from owning skills and credentials (the "middle" class), and both are different from simply owning unskilled labor power (the working class). Furthermore, in a market economy, access to market-derived income affects the broader array of life experiences and opportunities for oneself and one's children. The study of the life chances of children based on parent's market capacity is thus an integral part of the Weberian agenda of class analysis.

This definition of class in terms of market-determined life chances is clearly linked to the third question posed above: "What *explains* inequalities in economically defined life chances and material standards of living?" Weber's answer is, In capitalist societies, the material resources one brings to market exchanges explain such inequalities in life chances. But even more deeply, Weber's conceptualization of class is anchored in the fourth question, the question of how to characterize and explain historical variation in the social organization of inequality. Two issues are especially salient here: first, the historical variation in the articulation

of class and status and, second, the broad historical problem in understanding the rationalization of social processes.

Class is part of a broader multidimensional schema of stratification in Weber in which the most central contrast is between "class" and "status" (as well as "party"). Status groups are defined within the sphere of communal interaction (or what Weber calls the "social order") and always imply some level of identity in the sense of some recognized estimation of *honor,* either positive or negative. A status group cannot exist without its members being in some way conscious of being members of the group.

This conceptual contrast between class and status for Weber is not primarily a question of the *motives* of actors: It is not that status groups are derived from purely symbolic motives and class categories are derived from material interests. Although people care about status categories in part because of their importance for symbolic ideal interests, class positions also entail such symbolic interests, and both status and class are implicated in the pursuit of material interests. Rather than motives, the central contrast between class and status is the nature of the mechanisms through which class and status shape inequalities of the material and symbolic conditions of people's lives. Class affects material well-being directly through the kinds of economic assets people bring to market exchanges. Status affects material well-being indirectly, through the ways that categories of social honor underwrite various coercive mechanisms that are in accord with the degree of monopolization of ideal and material goods or opportunities to obtain them.

The contrast between class and status provides one of the axes of Weber's analysis of historical variation in systems of inequality. One of the central reasons that capitalist societies are societies within which class becomes the predominant basis of stratification is precisely because capitalism fosters continual technical and economic transformation.

Weber's concept of class is also closely linked to his theoretical preoccupation with the problem of historical variation in the process of rationalization of social life. The problem of class for Weber is primarily situated within one particular form of rationalization: the *objective instrumental* rationalization of social order. In all societies, the ways people gain access to and use material resources is governed by rules that are objectively embodied in the institutional settings within which they live. When the rules allocate resources to people on the basis of ascriptive characteristics and when the use of those material resources is governed by tradition rather than by the result of a calculative weighing of alternatives, then economic interactions take place under *non*rationalized conditions. When those rules enable people to make precise calculations about alternative uses of those resources and discipline people to use those resources in more rather than less efficient ways on the basis of those calculations, those rules can be described as "rationalized." This occurs, in Weber's analysis, when market relations have the most pervasive influence on economic interactions (i.e., in fully developed capitalism). His definition of classes in terms of the economic opportunities people face *in the market,* then, is simultaneously a definition of classes in terms of rationalized economic interactions. Class, in these terms, assumes its central sociological meaning to Weber as a description of the way people are related to the material conditions of life under conditions in which their economic interactions are regulated in a maximally rationalized manner. Weber is, fundamentally, less interested in the problem of the material deprivations and advantages of different categories of people as such, or in the collective struggles that might spring from those advantages and disadvantages, than he is in the underlying normative order and cognitive practices—instrumental rationality—embodied in the social interactions that generates these life chances. "Class," in these terms, is part of the answer to a broad question about historical variations in the degree and forms of rationalization of social life in general, and the social organization of inequality in particular.

THE MARXIST CONCEPT: CLASS AS EXPLOITATION

The pivotal question that anchors the Marxist conceptualization of class is the question of human emancipation: "What sorts of transformations are needed to eliminate economic oppression and exploitation within capitalist societies?" The starting point for Marxist class analysis is a stark observation: The world in which we live involves a juxtaposition of extraordinary prosperity and enhanced potentials for human creativity and fulfillment along with continuing human misery and thwarted lives. The central task of the theory is to demonstrate first, that poverty in the midst of plenty is not somehow an inevitable consequence of the laws of nature but, rather, the result of the specific design of our social institutions and, second, that these institutions can be transformed in such a way as to eliminate such socially unnecessary suffering. The concept of class, then, in the first instance is meant to help answer this normatively laden question.

The specific strategy in the Marxist tradition for answering the normative question leads directly to the question about historical variation. The normative question asks what needs transforming for human emancipation to occur. The theory of history in Marx—generally called "historical materialism"—lays out an account of the historical dynamics that make such transformations possible and, in the more deterministic version of the theory, inevitable. Again, the concept of class figures centrally in this theory of historical development.

The most distinctive feature of the concept of class elaborated within Marxism to contribute to the answer of these two questions is the idea of *exploitation.* Marx shares with Weber the central idea that classes should be defined in terms of the social relations that link people to the central resources that are economically relevant to production. And like Weber, Marx sees these relations as having a systematic impact on the material well-being of people; both "exploitation" and "life chances" identify inequalities in material well-being generated by inequalities in access to resources of various sorts. Thus, both concepts point to conflicts of interest over the *distribution* of the assets themselves. What exploitation adds to this is a claim that conflicts of interest between classes are generated not simply by what people *have* but also by what people *do with what they have.* The concept of exploitation, therefore, points our attention to conflicts within *production,* not simply conflicts in the *market.*

Exploitation is a complex and challenging concept. In classical Marxism, this concept was elaborated in terms of a specific conceptual framework for understanding capitalist economies, the "labor theory of value." In terms of sociological theory and research, however, the labor theory of value has never figured very prominently, even among sociologists working in the Marxist tradition. And in any case, the concept of exploitation and its relevance for class analysis does not depend on the labor theory of value.

The concept of exploitation designates a particular form of interdependence of the material interests of people—namely, a situation that satisfies three criteria:

1. *The inverse interdependent welfare principle:* The material welfare of exploiters causally depends on the material deprivations of the exploited.
2. *The exclusion principle:* This inverse interdependence of welfares of exploiters and exploited depends on the exclusion of the exploited from access to certain productive resources.
3. *The appropriation principle:* Exclusion generates material advantage to exploiters because it enables them to appropriate the labor effort of the exploited.

Exploitation is thus a diagnosis of the process through which the inequalities in incomes are generated by inequalities in rights and powers over productive resources: The inequalities occur, in part at least, through the ways in which exploiters, by virtue of their exclusionary rights and powers over resources, are able to appropriate surplus generated by the effort of the exploited. If the first two of these principles are present, but not the third, economic oppression may exist, but not exploitation. The crucial difference is that in *non*exploitative economic oppression, the privileged social category does not itself *need* the excluded category. While their welfare does depend on exclusion, there

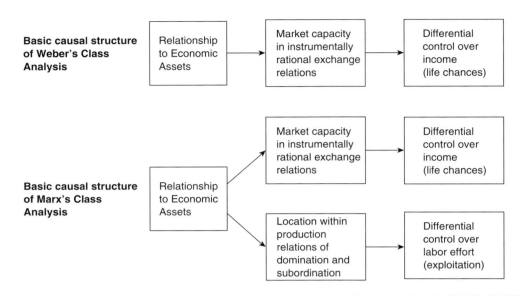

Figure 2   Core Elements in Weber's and Marx's Class Analysis

Source: Adapted and simplified from Wright (1997:34).

is no ongoing interdependence of their activities. In the case of exploitation, the exploiters actively need the exploited: Exploiters depend on the effort of the exploited for their own welfare.

This conceptualization of exploitation underwrites an essentially polarized conception of class relations in which, in capitalist societies, the two fundamental classes are capitalists and workers. Capitalists, by virtue of their ownership and control of the means of production, are able to appropriate the laboring effort of workers embodied in the surplus produced through the use of those means of production. The Marxist tradition of class analysis, however, also contains a variety of strategies for elaborating more concrete class concepts that allow for much more complex maps of class structures in which managers, professionals, and the self-employed are structurally differentiated from capitalists and workers. For example, Wright (1985, 1997) argues that managers in capitalist firms constitute a type of "contradictory location within class relations" in the sense of having the relational properties of both capitalists and workers.

The exploitation-centered concept of class provides a framework for linking the microlevel question about explaining individual material conditions and interests with the macrolevel question about historical variation and the normative question about emancipatory transformation. What needs changing in capitalism is a system of property relations that confers power on capitalists and enables them to exploit and oppress others. This social organization of class relations is not an expression of a natural law but is one form in a systematic pattern of historical variation. And

the life experiences and interests of individuals living within these relations generate patterns of conflict that have the potential of pushing these historical variations in ways that accomplish the emancipatory transformation.

THE TWO TRADITIONS COMPARED

The contrast between Marxist and Weberian frameworks of class analysis is illustrated in Figure 2. Both Marxist and Weberian class analysis differ sharply from simple gradational accounts of class in which class is itself directly identified within inequalities in income since both begin with the problem of the social relations that determine the access of people to economic resources. In a sense, therefore, Marxist and Weberian definitions of class in capitalist society share much the same *operational* criteria for class structure within capitalist societies. Where they differ is in the theoretical elaboration and specification of the implications of this common set of criteria: The Marxist model sees two causal paths being systematically generated by these relations—one operating through market exchanges and the other through the process of production itself—the Weberian model traces only one causal path, and the Marxist model elaborates the mechanisms of these causal paths in terms of exploitation as well as bargaining capacity within exchange; the Weberian model only deals with the latter of these. In a sense, then, the Weberian strategy of class analysis is contained within the Marxist model.

While the Marxist concept of class may be particularly suited to the distinctively Marxist question about potential emancipatory transformations, is it still sociologically useful if one rejects that question? There are a number of reasons why elaborating the concept of class in terms of exploitation has theoretical payoffs beyond the specific normative agenda of Marxist class analysis itself:

1. *Linking exchange and production.* The Marxist logic of class analysis affirms the intimate link between the way in which social relations are organized within exchange and within production. This is a substantive, not definitional, point: The social relations that organize the rights and powers of individuals with respect to productive resources systematically shapes their location both within exchange relations and within the process of production itself.

2. *Conflict.* One of the standard claims about Marxist class analysis is that it foregrounds conflict within class relations. Indeed, a conventional way of describing Marxism in sociological textbooks is to see it as a variety of "conflict theory." This characterization, however, is not quite precise enough, for conflict is certainly a prominent feature of Weberian views of class as well. The distinctive feature of the Marxist account of class relations in these terms is not simply that it gives prominence to class conflict but that it understands conflict as generated by *inherent properties* of those relations rather than simply contingent factors.

3. *Power.* At the very core of the Marxist construction of class analysis is not simply the claim that class relations generate deeply antagonistic interests but that they also give people in subordinate class locations forms of power with which to struggle for their interests. Since exploitation rests on the extraction of labor effort and since people always retain some measure of control over their own effort, they always confront their exploiters with capacities to resist exploitation. This is a crucial form of power reflected in the complex counterstrategies exploiting classes are forced to adopt through the elaboration of instruments of supervision, surveillance, monitoring, and sanctioning.

4. *Coercion and consent.* Marxist class analysis contains the rudiments of what might be termed an *endogenous* theory of the formation of consent. The argument is basically this: The extraction of labor effort in systems of exploitation is costly for exploiting classes because of the inherent capacity of people to resist their own exploitation. Purely coercively backed systems of exploitation will often tend to be suboptimal since under many conditions it is too easy for workers to withhold diligent performance of labor effort. Exploiting classes will therefore have a tendency to seek ways of reducing those costs. One of the ways of reducing the overhead costs of extracting labor effort is to do things that elicit the active consent of the exploited. These range from the development of internal labor markets that strengthen the identification and loyalty of workers to the firms in which they work to the support for ideological positions that proclaim the practical and moral desirability of capitalist institutions. Such consent-producing practices, however, also have costs attached to them, and thus systems of exploitation can be seen as always involving trade-offs between coercion and consent as mechanisms for extracting labor effort.

5. *Historical/comparative analysis.* As originally conceived, Marxist class analysis was an integral part of a sweeping theory of the epochal structure and historical trajectory of social change. But even if one rejects historical materialism, the Marxist exploitation-centered strategy of class analysis still provides a rich menu of concepts for historical and comparative analysis. Different kinds of class relations are defined by the specific mechanisms through which exploitation is accomplished, and these differences in turn imply different problems faced by exploiting classes for the reproduction of their class advantage and different opportunities for exploited classes to resist. Variations in these mechanisms and in the specific ways in which they are combined in concrete societies provide an analytically powerful road map for comparative research. Weber's class concept also figures in an account of historical variation, and one of its strengths is the way in which his conceptual menu draws attention to the interplay of class and status and to historical variations in the forms of rationality governing life chances. These are not issues brought into focus by the Marxist concept of class. On the other hand, the Weberian concept, by marginalizing the problem of exploitation, fails to bring to center stage the historical variability in forms of conflict linked to the central mechanisms of extraction and control over the social surplus.

— Erik Olin Wright

See also Bourdieu, Pierre; Capitalism; Conflict Theory; Dahrendorf, Ralf; Marx, Karl; Political Economy; Status Relations; Stratification; Weber, Max; Wright, Erik Olin

FURTHER READINGS AND REFERENCES

Bourdieu, P. 1984. *Distinction: A Social Critique of the Judgement of Taste.* Translated by Richard Nice. Cambridge, MA: Harvard University Press.

———. 1987. "What Makes a Social Class?" *Berkeley Journal of Sociology* 22:1–18.

Gerth, H. and C. W. Mills. 1958. *From Max Weber.* New York: Oxford University Press.

Goldthorpe, John H. 1980. *Social Mobility and Class Structure in Modern Britain.* Oxford, UK: Clarendon.

Holton, R. J. and B. S. Turner. 1989. "Has Class Analysis a Future? Max Weber and the Challenge of Liberalism to *Gemeinschaftlich* Accounts of Class." Pp. 160–96 in *Max Weber on Economics and Society,* edited by R. J. Holton and B. S. Turner. London: Routledge & Kegan Paul.

Levine, Donald Nathan. 1985. *The Flight from Ambiguity: Essays in Social and Cultural Theory.* Chicago: University of Chicago Press.

Mann, Michael. 1993. *The Sources of Social Power.* Cambridge, UK, & New York: Cambridge University Press.

Marshall, G. 1997. *Repositioning Class: Social Inequality in Industrial Societies.* London: Sage.

McNall, S. G., R. F. Levine, and R. Fantasia, eds. 1991. *Bringing Class Back In: Contemporary and Historical Perspectives.* Boulder, CO: Westview.

Pahl, R. E. 1989. "Is the Emperor Naked? Some Comments on the Adequacy of Sociological Theory in Urban and Regional Research." *International Journal of Urban and Regional Research* 13:127–29.

Pakulski, J. and M. Waters. 1996. *The Death of Class.* London: Sage.

Warner, W. L. [1949] 1960. *Social Class in America.* New York: Harper & Row.

Weber, Max. [1924] 1978. *Economy and Society,* edited by Guenther Roth and Claus Wittich. Berkeley: University of California Press.

Wright, E. O. 1979. *Class Structure and Income Determination.* New York: Academic Press.

———. 1985. *Classes.* London: Verso.

———. 1997. *Class Counts: Comparative Studies in Class Analysis.* Cambridge, UK: Cambridge University Press.

———. 2002. "The Shadow of Exploitation in Weber's Class Analysis." *American Sociological Review* 67:832–53.

SOCIAL CONSTRUCTIONISM

The argument that *social constructionism* proposes, with more or less insistence, about objects of social and cultural inquiry is in some sense the "other" to essentialisms of all sorts. To wit: Things—including even nature—are not simply given, revealed, fully determined, and as such, unalterable. Rather, things are made, and made up, in and through diverse social and cultural processes, practices, and actions. Much of the force of social constructionist argument is in this irony—its proposal that some assumedly taken-for-granted phenomenon not only could be otherwise but that its "local" form has a history that can be written to show a collection of interests, actions, and flows of power that have created and that sustain it. It seeks typically to show how some arguably social or cultural thing came about, how it is maintained, and, often by implication, how it might be changed. Social constructionist argument offers critique as a resource against all analyses that say, in effect, "This simply is the way things are and/or always have been." This emphasis on critique becomes particularly pronounced

in work where the line between constructionism and *deconstruction* blurs.

BERGER AND LUCKMANN'S SOCIOLOGY

In *The Social Construction of Reality: A Treatise in the Sociology of Knowledge,* Peter Berger and Thomas Luckmann (1966) build their argument on "classic roots" of Western sociology: the work of Marx, Durkheim, Weber, Schütz, and Mead. But classic roots for some are minor literatures for others, and Berger and Luckmann intended their book as a corrective to what they saw as an overemphasis on "purely structural" argument in the then-popular versions of structural-functionalism in U.S. sociology. They "correct" by forefronting acting and interacting human(ist) beings as the primary agents in the constitution, maintenance, and change of the social.

Berger and Luckmann (1966) contend that "reality is socially constructed and that the sociology of knowledge must analyze the process in which this occurs" (p. 1). They treat this project as one equally relevant to academic philosophy and to everyday life, but their constructionism is distinct from philosophical argument and analysis. Rather than asking ontological and epistemological questions such as "What is real?" and "How is one to know?," Berger and Luckmann shift attention to more specifically pragmatic considerations appropriate to an empirical, by which they mean "scientific," sociology. Central among these are the following: What does a collection of people located at a particular time and in a particular place take to be "real," and how is this construction to be understood as something they do? How are their conceptions linked to relevant social and historical contexts? How are differences in social realities/constructions/worlds across different collections of people understood as implicating those varying contexts? The very existence of difference in such social realities and contexts, they argue, underwrites the need for studying the *social processes* through which such difference has come about and by which it is maintained as well as changed. They assert that the sociology of knowledge "must concern itself with whatever passes for 'knowledge' in a society, regardless of the ultimate validity or invalidity (by whatever criteria) of such 'knowledge'" (p. 3).

Berger and Luckmann (1966) credit Marx with the clearest statement of the social construction of reality argument in that "man's consciousness is determined by his social being," specifically through the human activity of laboring together and the social relationships that emerge and are inextricable from that labor. For them, Marx's famous concepts of substructure and superstructure are seen most accurately "as, respectively, human activity and the world produced by that activity" (p. 6).

Berger and Luckmann (1966) propose their theory as a major redefinition of the sociology of knowledge, making it and the study of the social construction of reality central to sociological theory. They cite what they call two "marching orders" for modern sociology as at the heart of their argument: Durkheim's advice to "consider social facts as things" and Weber's statement that "both for sociology . . . and for history, the object of cognition is the subjective meaning-complex of action" (p. 18). These "orders" might be restated in their version of social constructionism as follows: Treat socially constructed realities as things, as objective; and see the meaning and action in social life that are these realities as mutually constitutive and contingent. That is, the objects that emerge in and through situated, meaningful social action can come to have precisely the "obdurate" quality that Durkheim used to describe "social facts." These then become habituated and typified in individuals' understandings of themselves, others, and their worlds and are used as resources to create, sustain, and change those objects. "Society is a human product. Society is an objective reality. Man [sic] is a social product" (p. 61). This, they say, is the essence of the social construction of reality.

Also central to Berger and Luckmann's social constructionism are the *phenomenology* of Alfred Schütz and the *symbolic interactionism* of George Herbert Mead. From Schütz, the authors take a stated focus on the natural attitude of *everyday life* and the knowledge therein and attention to how these are taken up, reiterated, and changed in and through the routine interactions and taken-for-granted understandings of the people whose lives are lived in a given locale. For Schütz, this concept of the everyday was an analytical resource with which to focus attention on how the social is continually accomplished by human beings pursuing practical but mundane projects. From Mead comes a sense of the absolute importance of human *social interaction* as symbolic interaction, suffused with and by shared meanings in language that feed back into and shape the ongoing lines of joint and always open action as well as the selves at the center of that action.

Berger and Luckmann (1966) underline the importance of processes of historically situated legitimation in carrying forward and sustaining all such social realities, realities that illustrate what they call institutionalization. *Language* and knowledge are the coordinating and integrating symbolic resources that bring a coherence to the diverse lines of situated human interaction. While the paramount or everyday realities thus constructed are mostly taken for granted by those who produce and are produced by them, "every symbolic universe is incipiently problematic" and routinely requires conscious "maintenance work" by embodied individuals who make it up (pp. 106, 116). From the analyst's view, then, as Berger and Luckmann note, "Says who?" is a critical question: "What remains sociologically essential is the recognition that all symbolic universes and all legitimations are human products; their existence has its base in

the lives of concrete individuals, and has no empirical status apart from these lives" (p. 128).

FOUCAULT'S POSTSTRUCTURALISM

The name and work of Michel Foucault are often linked to social constructionism. While, like Berger and Luckmann, Foucault wrote in conversation with a legacy of Western European, *humanist* thinkers, unlike them Foucault mostly wrote against that legacy—at least as it typically is read in the origin stories of U.S. sociology—and toward what he hoped would be a new way of thinking about human beings in social and historical terms. The proto-heroic humanist subject at the heart of Berger and Luckmann's story—and most other sociological stories—has a much less glorious role to play in the social construction work proposed here.

Drawing on their own intellectual and personal relationships with Foucault, philosopher Hubert Dreyfus and anthropologist Paul Rabinow offer a careful reading of Foucault's difference from the dominant traditions of Western European thought in the social and human sciences. They argue that Foucault was neither a *structuralist* nor an advocate of *hermeneutics*—what they call the two "poles" of the human sciences—but that he sought to develop a "new method" that would preserve "the distancing effect of structuralism, and an interpretive dimension which develops the hermeneutic insight that the investigator is always situated and must understand the meaning of his cultural practices from within them" (Dreyfus and Rabinow 1983:xii). Deeply influenced by Marx but not Marxist or Hegelian, Foucault's new method would eschew the dialectic as explanatory device in favor of a view of history as discontinuous, marked by epistemic breaks rather than linear development. More Nietzschean than Husserlian, Foucault would dismiss the search for deep meaning and truth behind social formations and practices ("texts") characteristic of hermeneutics, seeing the history of Western thought as revealing nothing to give a deep interpretation of (Dreyfus and Rabinow 1983:xxiii–xxv, 123–24, 180–83). Relying on methods that he called archeology and *genealogy,* Foucault sought—especially in his later books—not to provide a new theory of anything but, rather, to encourage a critical understanding of, "a history of," as he put it, "the present." Indeed, the human sciences themselves, and the objects and subjects that populate and define them, became prime targets for this critical and ostensibly new kind of analysis.

If Berger and Luckmann bring forward the importance of the acting and interacting individual in the context of the everyday to better understand how social realities are constructed, Foucault might be seen to diminish considerably what he called the "anthropological" theme that individual people are the prime sources of movement and force—especially through the operation of rational choice and intentionality—in society and in history. Although he later moved away from claims that the person is fully an effect of discourse, he retained through his last books on the care of the self the view that while not fully determined by prescribed cultural and institutional practices, the space of the resisting and "creative" subject should not be framed in terms of the humanist fantasies of "freedom" or "free will." Indeed, Foucault's skepticism about the optimistic stories in the legacy of humanism sets off his contributions from those carried forward by Berger and Luckmann and others who wrote more from within that tradition (and that also is apparent in the pragmatism of Richard Rorty).

In some of Foucault's most widely read books, we might say that the sources of the social construction about which Foucault writes are differentially distributed across particular *discursive practices,* their objects and subjects, and the individual, acting human beings who both take them up/are taken up by them and who give them life/are given life by them in real time and place. The distinction implied here between the body or bodies acting in time and space, on one hand, and the nature of the objects and subjects given life thereby, on the other hand, is, arguably, one of Foucault's most enduring contributions. In the focus on disciplinary practices, Foucault may be said to show us, in fine-grained empirical detail, the social and cultural machines through which docile and useful bodies and subjects were/are made into objects in service of "society." In his analysis of sexual subjects, he shows us how, through expert knowledge and discourse, culture and society create a "deep inside" essence—sexuality and the desire for sex—as the condition for the discovery of true, "healthy," and useful knowledge about each and every one of us. Here, especially, we see that which was thought to be prior and fundamental proposed, rather, as product and resource for the operation of power and "social good."

In these images of social construction, the individual still acts and interacts, but the choices are circumscribed in advance to serve and reinforce the structures that define the everyday. Although he professed very little interest in a study of the everyday realities so produced or in the meanings they had for those who enacted them—topics of central interest to Berger and Luckmann and "interpretive" philosophies and theories they wrote—Foucault was far from resigned to despair about the possibilities for change and *resistance* in the face of such structures. Most particularly, he did not see the human being in society as fully determined by the subjectivities that serve to embody that being. Perhaps particularly in his distinct but not always fully elaborated conception of *power* as always dynamic and relational, not as a commodity-like thing that some have and others do not, can we see the sense in which Foucault granted the acting individual within a constraining/enabling *subjectivity* or "self" a notable importance in society and history. For Foucault, one is "in" power as long as one is "in play" in relational dynamics with others in social and cultural sites that hierarchically allocate prerogatives, responsibilities, and duties. While there is constraint both from the subjectivities through and in which one takes up/is given an identity in such settings and from the prerogatives and responsibilities that define and link these entities together, the fact that the individual, as human individual, has the capacity to act and thus to act otherwise and in some degree of resistance to those constraints is critical to Foucault's vision. Even in social arrangements that appear to offer one party no power—for example, a woman in an abusive heterosexual relationship—Foucault's concept of power would encourage us to see how her "local" subjectivity could provide resources for possibly effecting change. While he emphasized social construction as operating beyond, around, in, and through the individual—as social and cultural processes and practices—Foucault allocated to the acting individual the possibility for both doing and thinking otherwise, something to which he himself aspired.

Beyond the notion of resistance, in his books on the care of the self, Foucault focuses attention on what he calls a "genealogy of ethics" based on careful study of life in ancient Greece. The problem of ethics there, which for Foucault is the problem of how to develop, how to craft, one's relationship with one's self, is not about resistance and power but, rather, about the ways one might put together a life. That framing does not imply, of course, an absence of social and cultural constraint, but it does bring forward the acting individual, using and adapting, applying, social and cultural codes to the mundane details of life, the space, of course, in which a life is made and made up in countless reiterations.

SUBSEQUENT LINES OF WORK

Constructing Social Problems

Against the commonsense and often social scientific wisdom that social problems exist as obviously undesirable conditions threatening social and cultural stability, health, and happiness, Malcolm Spector and John I. Kitsuse ([1977]2001), in their *Constructing Social Problems,* propose a definition of social problems and a kind of empirical analysis that draws on many of the themes in Berger and Luckmann's work and that have come to exemplify a certain kind of social constructionist theory. Both lines of work might be read in part as humanist responses to the then dominance of structural and functional analysis of social systems apparent in U.S. sociology and the corresponding de-emphasis on situated, ongoing, social interaction. Parallel work in psychology, often referred to as "constructivist," marks similar reactions against a dominant positivism there (see Burr 1995).

Social problems, Spector and Kitsuse ([1977]2001) wrote, are "the activities of individuals or groups making assertions of grievances and claims with respect to some putative conditions" (p. 75). The inquiry should focus on what they called *claims-making and responding activities* by specific persons at and in particular times and places and about things they do not/do like and hope/hope not to change. Here, the analyst is not concerned with evaluating or examining the validity or truth of the claims made about the things in question, which of course has been the conventional sociological assignment. "Even the existence of the condition itself is irrelevant and outside of our analysis. We are not concerned whether or not the imputed condition exists" (p. 76). It is, rather, the viability or "life" of such claims and responses that interest Spector and Kitsuse.

Social problems—and, by extension, all of what can be called "moral work" or "morality" understood as the making of evaluations and judgments—are thus seen as accomplishments that exist in and through claims-making, responding, and related activities. Although this gives prime place to actual language in use and the strategies those who press such claims or respond to them might adopt, Spector and Kitsuse's view also incorporates activities that participants pursue that seem to the analyst to be clearly premised on member definitions of the objects, arrangements, and theories that they imply. Attention thus is given not only to language and *discourse* but to the individual and joint activities that appear to be premised on these member understandings and interpretations.

Spector and Kitsuse's constructionism contains an explicitly *reflexive* flavor. Sociologists themselves are seen as among the primary champions of various definitions of social problems—in both the public and professional arenas in which they can be found—and these definitions easily become topic for the theory and strategy of analysis this constructionism encourages. Indeed, professional and official claims-makers of all sorts have been among the most commonly studied participants in constructing social problems in the large body of research and writing this work has stimulated. Much of the early empirical research using this perspective—studies by Stephen Pfohl on child abuse, by Peter Conrad on hyperactivity, by Joseph Schneider on alcoholism, and by Conrad and Schneider on the medicalization of deviance—focused on such professional and medical claims-makers and their interactions with various lay populations (see Conrad and Schneider 1992).

Sexuality: Identity and Body Constructed

Foucault's writing on the disciplining of the body and the shaping and embrace of subjectivity has had an enormous effect on subsequent research and theory on various aspects of sexuality across the human sciences. Among the clearest of these lines of influence are those found in the argument that *sexual identity* is socially constructed and that "the body"—and the *sexual body* in particular—and sexuality are "inscribed," "performed," and thus, too, constructed. This work offers examples of the two different ways in which social constructionism seems to be read: as at the more or less rational and intentional direction of an individual self or subject, on one hand, and as the operation of constraining but not fully determinative social, cultural, and historical processes that more or less shape/constitute subjects and their activities, on the other.

Before Foucault—and in U.S. sociology—an early and notable example of the former kind of social constructionist argument dealing with what might be called "gender identity" is Harold Garfinkel's famous case study of Agnes. Arguably paradigmatic of ethnomethodological analysis, Garfinkel drew on detailed interviews with and observations of a male-to-female transsexual to reveal the mundane practices or "methods" that Agnes had to learn and then use in order to be, to exist in the world as, a taken-for-granted, "bona fide" female and woman in society. Garfinkel shows how Agnes worked to achieve this mundane ontology and, in doing so, makes clear just how much all normalized gender identity is an accomplishment produced by and through an ongoing set of intentional practices that are the seen but unnoticed stuff of social and cultural reality. Garfinkel's ethnomethodology and subsequent work in *conversation analysis* helped us see the material real as an achievement in which human beings in local settings put society and culture together using the mundane practices that every society/culture makes available to them. (A parallel kind of analysis that is not particularly about sexual identity and is not seen as ethnomethodological but is, arguably, constructionist in a similar sense, is found in Erving Goffman's work on the presentation of self.)

Against this kind of constructionism, elements of which also can easily be found in writing on the social construction of sexual identity linked to gay and lesbian identity and social movement politics, some feminist scholars have taken up from Foucault and from poststructuralism more generally an analysis of how sexuality and sexualized bodies are inscribed and performed in and through social and cultural regulatory practices that simultaneously produce the very subjects or subjectivities through and in which human beings are said to "have *agency*." Indeed, the very possibility of "agency"—not to mention "rational choice"—is seen here as a cultural and social resource with various but circumscribed possibilities that are always politically charged. The writings of Judith Butler and Elisabeth Grosz, in their emphasis on performativity, materiality, the psyche, and the volatility of bodies have been among the most influential here. In this work, we can see a critique of the version of constructionism that highlights the intentional, choosing, and rational subject. While not erasing the significance of a moving, acting human individual, this work resituates the notion of human agency within a complex of forces that can be said to "construct" the social and cultural objects under study. Poststructural influence in scholarship on gay and lesbian sexuality has produced congenial analyses, sometimes referred to as queer theory, that aim to deconstruct sexual identity as itself a social construction that regulates and serves that which it seems to critique. In all these latter works, the emergence, force, and consequences of categories of knowledge and their related practices, never simply "used" or "directed" by the familiar humanist subject, are at the center of attention.

Posthuman Actant Networks in Technoscience Studies

A third line of work that can be seen as social constructionist in yet another sense has grown up in the interdisciplinary field of technoscience studies, particularly as found in the work of Bruno Latour and Donna Haraway. Here we come almost full circle from Berger and Luckmann's claim that social constructionism takes knowledge and its categories, their creation, history, complexity, and movement as its central topic of analysis. But this circle is not quite closed. Although Berger and Luckmann claimed that "whatever passes for 'knowledge' in society" should be subjected to constructionist analysis, they were not quite willing to subject their own kind of work—science—to a thoroughgoing or "radical" constructionism. The work referenced here does precisely that.

Pushing the decentered humanist subject even farther afield, this work might be characterized as a *posthuman* or postpersonal constructionism in which the human player does not disappear but, rather, becomes one of a diverse collection of "*actants*" linked together in a network that itself can be seen to construct facts and technoscientific knowledge. In no case is this network directed by the humans who participate in it, although they retain a special importance linked to their particular capacities as users of language and meaning and as those who can ask often difficult moral and ethical questions.

Grounded in early ethnographies of scientists at work at the bench, Latour, Steve Woolgar, and others contributed to what Latour calls an *actor-network analysis* of science. Eschewing much standard sociological explanation, Latour has seen the production of scientific knowledge and the actual work of science as collective accomplishments of a network of actants, only some of whom are human or even alive. Latour saw that scientists rely heavily on the action of the ever-expanding collection of writing machines ("inscription devices"), observations, and laboratory-sited events, and objects that ostensibly stand in for "nature" and on whose behalf the scientists hope to speak as they defend their claims to skeptical colleagues. Successful scientific knowledge becomes that which the scientist and other actant collaborators can defend against all attempts to undermine it as "subjective" or merely a human speaking for herself or himself alone.

Haraway has contributed importantly to this view of technoscience, although she writes as a socialist-feminist sympathetic to poststructuralism and who longs for what she calls a "successor science" that is networked, collaborative, partial, strongly objective, and that seriously seeks to make a better world, with less suffering and more "happiness," for all living beings. Writing explicitly against sexism, racism, and patriarchy, Haraway offers a constructionism that is considerably more open, messy, and unpredictable than versions that locate the rational human actor—historically almost always a white male European or North American—at the center of its story or that give "discourse" a determinative force. From her famous "cyborg manifesto" to later critical analyses of technoscience, Haraway urges an understanding and vision by human actants in this process—among other "material-semiotic objects"—that not only make explicit their own dependencies but that also speak their own implication in the shaping of and responsibilities for the local worlds being built. Haraway wants scientists to ask if the worlds they help to construct are worth living for, for whom this might be more or less the case, and what all life in these worlds is likely to be, being able to admit that while they know, they do not know for sure. Others have pursued work that reiterates and extends various themes of contingency, distributed cognition, and complexity in the networks that can be said to construct and embody technoscientific knowledge.

— Joseph W. Schneider

See also Butler, Judith; Conversation Analysis; Discourse; Essentialism; Ethnomethodology; Foucault, Michel; Postmodernist Feminism; Sexuality and the Subject; Social Studies of Science; Sociologies of Everyday Life; Symbolic Interaction

FURTHER READINGS AND REFERENCES

Berger, Peter L. and Thomas Luckmann. 1966. *The Social Construction of Reality: A Treatise in the Sociology of Knowledge.* New York: Doubleday.

Burr, Vivien. 1995. *An Introduction to Social Constructionism.* London: Routledge.

Conrad, Peter and Joseph W. Schneider. 1992. *Deviance and Medicalization: From Badness to Sickness.* Philadelphia: Temple University Press.

Dreyfus, Hubert and Paul Rabinow. 1983. *Michel Foucault: Beyond Structuralism and Hermeneutics.* Berkeley: University of California Press.

Garfinkel, Harold. 1967. *Studies in Ethnomethodology.* Englewood Cliffs, NJ: Prentice-Hall.

Haraway, Donna. 1997. *Modest_Witness@Second_Millennium. FemaleMan©_Meets_Oncomouse™: Feminism and Technoscience.* New York: Routledge.

Holstein, James A. and Gale Miller, eds. 1993. *Reconsidering Social Constructionism: Debates in Social Problems Theory.* Hawthorne, NY: de Gruyter.

Latour, Bruno. 1999. *Pandora's Hope: Essays on the Reality of Science Studies.* Cambridge, MA: Harvard University Press.

Price, Janet and Margaret Shildrick. 1999. *Feminist Theory and the Body.* New York: Routledge.

Seidman, Steven. 1996. *Queer Theory/Sociology.* Cambridge, MA: Blackwell.

Spector, Malcolm and John I. Kitsuse. [1977] 2001. *Constructing Social Problems.* New Brunswick, NJ: Transaction.

Taylor, Mark C. 2001. *The Moment of Complexity: Emerging Network Culture.* Chicago: University of Chicago Press.

SOCIAL DARWINISM

Social Darwinism is the application of the theory of natural selection to human society. Alfred Wallace, the theory's codiscoverer, once asked Charles Darwin whether he would follow up his *Origin of Species* with a book on human beings. Darwin replied:

> You ask whether I shall discuss "man." I think I shall avoid the whole subject, as so surrounded with prejudices, though I fully admit it is the highest and most interesting problem for the naturalist. (Cited in Hawkins 1997:20)

Darwin was understandably cautious. But others have felt less constrained, with the result that massive theoretical and political issues have arisen.

Most living creatures, Darwin and Wallace argued, produce many more offspring than are needed to reproduce their numbers. Such multiplication, if left unhindered, meant that "the earth would soon be covered by the progeny of a single pair." However, the numbers of each species remained much the same from one generation to the next. What was taking place?

A struggle for survival and reproduction must be occurring, one between individuals and the rest of nature. No two individuals are alike, each possessing variations that confer advantages and disadvantages in the struggle. Those individuals with particular advantages will be those that develop and reproduce future generations. All this, Darwin and Wallace believed, occurs in the context of inevitable resource shortages. As Malthus had argued in the late eighteenth century, populations grow at a geometric rate while food supplies grow arithmetically. The environment was therefore active in eliminating those individuals without the characteristics necessary to survive and reproduce.

Turning now to *social* Darwinism, human characteristics can also be seen as resulting from struggle to survive. Herbert Spencer, for example, looked forward to a society in which individuals are free to realize their full potential. A long evolutionary process would take place, leading to a race in which people found fulfilment in aesthetic and spiritual matters rather than in the materialism of Spencer's own day. Those individuals not adapting and developing in this way would slowly die out. Note, however, a divergence between Spencer's views and those of Darwin. Spencer had no Malthusian fear of overpopulation, believing that humans have the capacity to adapt to environmental and social change. There are also differences between social Darwinists. Spencer believed that state intervention would delay the improvement of the human species, while William Sumner, the influential Yale Social Darwinist, increasingly saw a need for social reform.

The transfer of evolutionary ideas to human beings is an intellectual and political minefield. There are five themes here; the politics of knowledge, the question of "struggle," the notion of "progress," the assumption of direction, and an "end" to which evolution is developing.

As regards knowledge, the theory of natural selection can easily be seen as a product of its era and knowledge recruited to distinctive political ends. "The struggle for survival," for example, can be seen as a transposal of the social struggle (all too apparent in Darwin's Britain) to the non-human world. Similarly, the "successful" variations are no less than the human success stories of middle-class Victorian society again transposed to the natural world. Similarly, Malthus's theory of necessary resource shortages is by no means the objective and scientific theory as he claimed. Wallace, though clearly influenced by Malthus, was also sympathetic to Owen's socialism. Such a politics argues that "resource shortages" are not inevitable. They are a product of social and property relations.

Similarly, forms of social evolutionism were well established before Darwin's *Origin*. Herbert Spencer coined the phrase "the survival of the fittest" some 10 years before the publication of *The Origin*. As applied to humanity, he meant the struggle between *races* to survive, the demise of the weakest leaving the strongest to "keep up the average fitness to the conditions of life." Here again was an apparently objective science being used to enhance an overtly political programme. Social Darwinism is sometimes seen as a "neutral instrument," albeit one capable of being recruited to by a range of political positions. Such adoption by a range of causes is a matter of historical fact. But to describe the theory as "neutral" or "objective" is probably being overdeferential to this "science."

These issues remain important today. "Neo-Darwinism" in the form of sociobiology also claimed to be an objective form of knowledge. (This time the organism, including the human organism, is seen as a carrier of and reproducer of "selfish genes" into future generations [Dawkins 1989].) But this perspective, too, can be seen as a product of its day, the "selfish gene" being no less than the selfish person of neoliberalism transferred back to the natural world. But all this said, the theory of natural selection as developed by Darwin and Wallace remains largely intact. It was a social construction (what theory is not?), but many biologists would argue that it still describes real causal mechanisms affecting both the natural and the human worlds.

The "struggle for survival" is a problematic second theme. So, too, is the linked question of "human nature." Darwin was again cautious over these matters; recognising in *The Descent of Man* that the struggle to reproduce can take a number of forms, including various forms of cooperation. Yet social Darwinism is often equated with liberalism, with attempts to prosper, and with an idea of human nature that focuses on the individual at the expense of his or her social and environmental context. Such an interpretation led to early support for social Darwinism from influential classes in North America. But alternative understandings were made in other societies. Prince Kropotkin, the Russian anarchist, argued strongly in his 1902 book *Mutual Aid* that the fundamental feature of all nature, including human nature, was mutualism and cooperation. The lesson of Darwin here was that this propensity needed active support in capitalist societies devoted to individualistic competition. Mutualistic and solidaristic interpretations of Darwin were also more common in other societies, including France.

We should also note different understandings of both the struggle to survive and of human nature in our own day. *The Bell Curve,* published in 1994 by Herrnstein and Murray, represents a contemporary form of Social Darwinism. They argue that intelligence is the prime means by which human beings succeed in modern knowledge-based societies. Some groups, particularly black people, are seen as possessing inherently low levels of intelligence. White people are better endowed and Asians have, it is argued, higher intelligence levels than both these groups. Social stratification and social success are again, therefore, seen as largely the result of individuals' assumed internal characteristics. Society, according to this position, is itself "natural." Here is another example of a science (in this case a science measuring "intelligence") that is easily recruited to a particular kind of politics. And it is a "science" that is itself highly contested by many social and natural scientists. They would especially question oversimple notions of "intelligence" and would argue that intellectual capacities are best seen as developing during a person's early lifetime.

Closely linked to the "science" of intelligence is the fact Social Darwinism has often been linked with eugenics. This is the attempted speeding up of human evolution, the selection of the "best" humans and the neglect or even killing of the supposedly "inferior." These concerns have recently resurfaced with the rise of biotechnology and cloning. Embryos deemed to be "unfit" can be modified or even destroyed. Such "unnatural selection" must be of major concern, but it is important to stay focused on the more subtle, often unintended, effects of the social and "natural" environment on people's well-being.

"Progress" is a third theme. Sumner, like Spencer, argued strongly for a sense of "progress" emerging from the struggle to survive. If human beings were allowed to realise their capacities, societies' high levels of "civilisation" would eventually be achieved. As is often still assumed, science was seen as the main means by which such progress was to be achieved. The most "intelligent" people are taken to be those best able to advance science and hence society at large. Progress, according to this perspective, therefore had distinct normative connotations. It has close links with the philosophical and sociological ideas of Georg Hegel and Auguste Comte. Progress, entailing increased scientific knowledge (including knowledge of the self) is equated both with increased civilisation and the creation of freed, emancipated selves.

Darwin was aware of the difficulties here but did not always resolve them. He claimed the "science" of natural selection to be value free. Yet much of his language describing evolutionary change implicitly adopted a notion of progress. Note, for example, the following from *The Origin:*

The inhabitants of each successive period in the world's history have beaten their predecessors in the race for life and are higher in the scale of nature; and this may account for that vague yet ill-defined sentiment, felt by many palaeontologists, that organisation on the whole has progressed. (1859:345)

Darwin also espoused aspects of Lamarckian thinking, especially in *The Descent of Man.* According to this view, acquired characteristics could be inherited by later generations. As people continued fighting for survival, and so long as governments and philanthropists did not interfere, the most favourable characteristics would emerge and be passed to later generations. Progress was again the most likely outcome.

The progress question closely links to the fourth theme, that of directionality. Spencer and much of early sociology adopted a strong notion of direction. For Spencer and writers such as Emile Durkheim, the direction of social change is away from homogeneity toward structured heterogeneity. Directionality is also a feature of much historical materialism. For Karl Marx and Friedrich Engels, European history is divided into four distinct eras; tribal, classical, feudal, and capitalist. Communism would be the final, most "progressive," outcome. Note in Marx and Engels the significance of class struggle with each society being an embryonic version of the following social form. Note also the implication in much social theory that all societies inevitably follow the same direction. Such understandings borrowed more or less explicitly from evolutionary thought. The transition from the simple to the complex was raised to a point of cosmic significance by Spencer, an understanding that applied to the human, biological, and physical worlds. Contemporary sociologists such as Niklaus Luhmann also maintain that society is increasingly characterised by autonomous "subsystems," with the result that modernity is increasingly "unsteerable." Analogies are still made between biological and social evolution. But paradoxically, and most unfortunately, these make little contribution to the increasingly urgent task of understanding how human societies are rooted in their ecological environments.

Finally, note the related theme of teleology. Marx and Engels argued that one of Darwinism's main gains was "the death of teleology"—an end to any notion that an organism or society is the result of any predetermined end. In important ways, this was achieved, with Darwinism delivering an apparently fatal blow to Christian accounts of origins. Nevertheless, there remain traces of teleology. Darwin's notion of a multiplicity of "species, genera and families of organic beings" all having "common parents" has distinct biblical overtones. Indeed, evolutionary theory is arguably another science offering itself as a God-surrogate and demanding constant uncritical adulation. Such a view can, however, be used to marginalise the real scientific insights made by Darwin, Wallace, and others.

Future work linking evolutionary and social thought must consider humans and other species as an evolved species with distinct powers. But these potentials must be seen as realised or constrained by different social and political contexts. Critical realism, as developed by Roy Bhaskar and others, is a useful way forward. It recognises the reality of causal mechanisms operating in the natural worlds (natural selection being an example) while insisting on these theories being critically assessed and taking account of how such mechanisms combine with social relations and processes to produce the societies we actually observe and experience.

— Peter Dickens

See also Evolutionary Theory; Spencer, Herbert

FURTHER READINGS AND REFERENCES

Darwin, Charles. 1859. *The Origin of Species by Natural Selection.* London: Murray.

———. 1901. *The Descent of Man and Selection in Relation to Sex.* London: Murray.

Dawkins, Richard. 1989. *The Selfish Gene.* Harmondsworth, UK: Penguin

Dickens, Peter. 2000. *Social Darwinism.* Buckingham, UK: Open University Press.

———. 2003. *Society and Nature: Evolution, Industry, Community, Risk.* Oxford, UK: Polity Press.

Hawkins, Mike. 1997. *Social Darwinism in European and American Thought.* Cambridge, UK: Cambridge University Press.

Hofstadter, Richard. 1959. *Social Darwinism in American Thought.* New York: Braziller.

SOCIAL DILEMMA

A social dilemma is formally defined as an incentive structure in which a deficient outcome is collectively achieved when each individual (in a group of two or more people) makes choices in accordance with a dominating strategy. A strategy is dominating if the *personal* consequences of behaving according to it are superior to the consequences of behaving according to all other strategies, regardless of the behavior of others in the group. The outcome is considered to be "deficient" when that outcome is preferred less than other outcomes by all members of the group. The commons dilemma, a social trap, the public goods problem, and the free-riding problem are all used to refer to a social dilemma. Real-world examples of social dilemmas range from an arms race between superpowers, the overharvesting of regenerating natural resources, protective trade policies, traffic jams, the use of modern amenities that create global warming, and so on. In these examples, the choice that follows the dominating strategy—often called the choice of "defection," or "free-riding" in some contexts—is the one that brings forth the most desirable outcome *for the individual.* Using the example of the arms race, the individual consequence for choosing to increase military power is military advantage. Using the example of overharvesting resources, the individual consequence for choosing to overharvest is the immediate profit reaped from ooverharvesting. However, if each person follows the dominating strategy and makes the choice of defection, the *collective outcome* is less desirable an outcome than if the individuals had followed another strategy and made an alternative, cooperative choice. For example, everyone benefits more if both superpowers disarm than if both expand their military power. Furthermore, everyone benefits more if the fishermen refrain from overharvesting than if they overharvest, and so on.

The current use of the term *social dilemma* summarized above is relatively new. However, the study of social dilemmas began much earlier, in the 1950s. Robyn Dawes used the term when he reviewed experimental work that had previously been described as "*n*-person prisoner's dilemmas." Social dilemmas were originally conceptualized as a group version (or *n*-person version) of the prisoner's dilemma, which usually involves only two people. The name "prisoner's dilemma" (PD) comes from a story of two individuals suspected of a crime. Two suspects who have been arrested for a serious crime are being interrogated by a district attorney. The district attorney does not have enough evidence to convict either of the suspects of the crime. Therefore, the district attorney needs a confession from at least one of the suspects. He offers a deal to each "prisoner" independently. If one of the prisoners confesses and the other prisoner does not confess, the one who confesses gets acquitted and the one who does not confess gets the maximum penalty. If both prisoners confess, both are charged with the serious crime but both will receive a lenient penalty. If neither prisoner confesses, each prisoner is charged with a minor offense (not the serious crime) and receives a minor penalty. Both prisoners face a choice between confessing and not confessing. The dominating strategy is confessing, since individually, each prisoner is better off by confessing than by not confessing no matter what the other does. For example, Prisoner A is better off when he confesses (lenient penalty for the serious crime) than when he does not confess (the maximum penalty for the serious crime), if Prisoner B confesses. If Prisoner B does not confess, A is again better off by confessing (no penalty) than by not confessing (penalty for a minor crime). However, when each takes this dominating choice of confessing, each receives a lenient penalty for the serious crime, whereas each prisoner could have avoided that penalty by not confessing.

Social dilemmas and prisoner's dilemmas have attracted the attention of researchers in various fields of the social sciences. Early empirical works, however, have been conducted mostly by a group of social psychologists called experimental game researchers. Early experimental studies of social dilemmas examined games set up in a laboratory that served as a miniature model of real-life problems such as the problems mentioned earlier. Recently, thinking of experimental games as miniature models of real social problems has been replaced by more theoretically driven approaches. Below, major factors studied in the early experimental gaming tradition are briefly summarized. Next, an overview of the theoretical issues concerning *cooperation* in social dilemmas is provided.

FACTORS AFFECTING BEHAVIOR IN SOCIAL DILEMMAS

Experimental game researchers produced an impressive list of factors that affect the cooperation-defection choice in experimental games. The list includes both individual-level factors as well as structural factors.

Individual-Level Factors

Gender. Contrary to the naive view that women are more cooperative than men, experiments on social dilemmas produced mixed results. In some studies, women are more cooperative, and in other studies, no gender difference in cooperation emerged. Yet in another set of studies, men are found to be more cooperative than women. The naive belief that females are more cooperative than males may be attributed to the fact that the nature of the tasks females face in society makes their "cooperation" more visible than the tasks males face in society.

Social Value Orientation. The individual-level factor that has been most extensively studied is what is referred to as "social value orientation" or "social motivation." Social value orientation is defined as an attitude toward self and an interdependent other. An individual's social value orientation is represented by a combination of positive and negative attitudes toward self and other. Put differently, an individual's social value orientation can be conceptualized as the degree to which an individual is concerned with his or her own welfare and with another person's welfare. Three major types of social value orientation have been studied. *Individualists* are concerned with their own welfare and have little or no concern with the welfare of the other. *Cooperators* are concerned with the welfare of both self and the other. *Competitors* are those who prefer positive "relative gain" even at the expense of their own welfare. Theoretically, other types of social value orientation can exist. However, studies of social dilemmas have repeatedly shown that these three types are the dominant modes of social value orientation. Facing social dilemmas, cooperators tend to behave in a cooperative manner, whereas individualists and competitors tend to behave in a noncooperative manner.

Trust and Expectations. One of the most consistent findings in experimental studies of social dilemmas is that there *is* an effect of the expectations of other people's behavior on the player's own behavior. That is, players who expect that other players are cooperative tend to cooperate themselves, and those players who expect that other players are not cooperative tend not to cooperate themselves. This finding is worthy of attention since individuals profit more from noncooperative behavior than from cooperative behavior *no matter what other individuals do* (see the definition of social dilemmas mentioned above). Thus, from a rational theoretic perspective, individuals who face a social dilemma situation should be indifferent to others' behavior. Despite this rational-choice theoretic prescription, an overwhelming majority of subjects do pay attention to other people's behavior and adjust their own behavior to the observed or expected behaviors of others.

Dean Pruitt and Melvin Kimmel propose the goal/expectation theory of cooperation to explain the effect of expectation on an individual's behavior. According to this theory, individuals who experience undesirable consequences of mutual defection come to prefer mutual cooperation to mutual defection but hesitate to cooperate unless they expect that others will not take advantage of their willingness to cooperate. They are "cautious cooperators" who are willing to cooperate if others do as well but are careful not to be victimized by free riders. Unconditional cooperation, that is, cooperation even when other people are not cooperating, is rarely observed in social dilemma experiments. Some students who study the effect of an individual's social value orientation suggest that the difference in social value orientations reflects the individual's general trust in other individuals. For "cautious cooperators" who believe that others are also willing to cooperate, initiating cooperation is more desirable than unilateral defection that will eventually destroy the possibility of achieving mutual cooperation. On the other hand, for those who believe that others are not willing to reciprocate, mutual cooperation is an impossible dream. Individual differences in general trust, or trust in other people in general, is thus suggested to affect individuals' proclivity to cooperate in social dilemmas. This suggestion has been consistently confirmed by a large number of studies.

Culture. Scholars expect that cooperation in social dilemmas is easier to achieve in a collectivist society than in an individualist society, since people in a collectivist society value the welfare of the group over their individual welfare. This prediction has received a mixed but generally negative support empirically. Toshio Yamagishi argues that within-group cooperation in a collectivist society is institutionally grounded, and thus people in a collectivist society cooperate at a high level in the everyday practice that takes place within institutional arrangements. On the other hand, when experimental participants face an artificially created social dilemma situation in a laboratory stripped of the institutional context surrounding everyday social dilemmas, people in collectivist cultures tend to be less trustful of others and thus less cooperative than those in individualist cultures.

Other Factors. Other individual difference factors such as group identity, information, morality, and prior experience have also been studied.

Structural Features

The ways in which structural features of the social dilemma affect an individual's cooperative behavior have been extensively studied.

One-Shot Versus Repeated Play. Achieving mutual cooperation is easier in repeated games than in one-shot games. In a one-shot game in which two players interact only once and never play the same game again, players have no means to influence their partner's behavior. When the same game is repeatedly played between the same two partners, however, one player can affect his or her partner's choice by adopting a certain strategy such as the tit-for-tat strategy. The tit-for-tat strategy is one in which a player cooperates when and only when his partner cooperated on the previous round. This strategy, despite its simplicity, has proven very effective in inducing the partner to take cooperative actions. In repeated games in which players' behavior involves "noise," another strategy called Pavlov is found to be more effective. The Pavlov strategy is one in which a player maintains the same behavior as long as the outcome is satisfactory and switches the behavior when the outcome is not satisfactory.

Incentives. The incentives that characterize a social dilemma have two components: (1) temptation for defection—how much more an individual gains by not cooperating—and (2) gain of cooperation—how much more each individual gains when all individuals cooperate compared with when none cooperates. Both are known to affect an individual's behavior in a social dilemma. Cooperative behavior decreases as the size of temptation for defection increases, and cooperative behavior increases as does the gain of cooperation. Furthermore, the former effect (of the size of temptation) is stronger than the latter effect (of the size of the gain of cooperation).

Size of Incentives. Despite the fact that defection is the dominating strategy in social dilemmas, the prediction of no cooperation (or complete defection) is seldom supported by experimental research. A sizable proportion of subjects, between 30 and 60 percent, cooperate even in one-shot games. The lack of support for the rational choice theoretic prediction of no cooperation is sometimes attributed to the weak incentives used in the experiments. Several experimental studies examined the effect of incentive size on cooperation. Some studies, comparing imaginary incentives and monetary incentives, find a higher level of cooperation when real money is at stake than when imaginary money or points are at stake. Other studies find the opposite. The size of the monetary reward is found to have no effect on the average level of cooperation. Experimental economists examined the effect of monetary size on game players' choices using the ultimatum game. They found that choice behavior is not affected very much even when the monetary stake was increased to an amount equal to a few months of the average cost of living in Indonesia and in Moscow.

Communication. The positive effect of communication and face-to-face interaction on cooperation in social dilemmas has been well documented. Similarly, cooperation level is found to be higher when subjects' choices are known to others than when their choices are anonymous.

Group Size. When there are more partners, it is difficult to detect who is cooperating and who is defecting. Furthermore, the effectiveness of one's action is distributed across many partners so that one's action does not have a strong impact on specific others. Finally, strategic actions may have negative "externalities." If a player decides to defect in a reciprocal manner in order to punish a defector, other cooperators might interpret his or her strategic action as exploitive, and might try to punish him or her by defecting themselves. This may produce a conflict spiral often observed in the repeated social dilemma experiments. While the largest difference lies between dyads and three-person groups, group size generally has a negative effect on cooperation.

Sanctions. The most straightforward means to enhance cooperation in social dilemmas is administrating selective incentives or sanctions. Experimental studies of sanctioning behavior in social dilemmas consistently demonstrate the positive effect of sanctioning on cooperation. The use of sanctioning as a means to enhance cooperation in social dilemmas, however, faces the second-order dilemma concerning the administration of sanctions. Logically, a higher level of sanctioning—the sanctioning of those who do not participate in the administration of sanctioning—is required to solve the problem of sanctioning. The sanctioning of nonsanctioners is required to maintain the "second-order sanctioning." Such a situation can create an infinite regress of ever higher-order sanctioning activities.

Other Factors. Other structural factors that have been extensively studied in social dilemmas include the territorialization or privatization of a common resource, leadership, resource variability, power distribution, type of behavior (contribution to a public good versus restraining from overuse), and the binary choice of cooperation and defection versus a varied level of cooperation.

THEORETICAL APPROACHES TO EXPLAINING COOPERATION IN SOCIAL DILEMMAS

As mentioned above, the cooperation rate is usually higher in repeated games than in one-shot games. And yet, many participants in social dilemma experiments do cooperate even in one-shot games that are anonymously played with strangers. There are currently two broad approaches to explain cooperation in such games. One is the social value orientation approach, according to which some people are endowed with a value that honors cooperation even when no gain is expected. This explanation of cooperation in one-shot games, however, immediately raises another question as to why some people have such a value and others do not. The second approach to explain cooperation in these games may be broadly called the evolutionary approach. This

approach seeks a "hidden" adaptive advantage in behaving cooperatively or reciprocally. Most studies from this perspective focus on advantages associated with some form of conditional cooperation or reciprocal cooperation.

Reciprocity. As mentioned earlier, most of the participants in one-shot games care about other people's behavior and behave in a reciprocal manner to the expected behavior of others. A correlation between the player's own behavior and his or her expectation about other players' behavior is one of the strongest findings in the social dilemma experiments. This correlation may be caused by a projection of the player's own behavior onto others. However, experiments of one-shot, sequential PD games, in which the first player makes a decision and then the second player who is aware of the first player's decision makes a decision, consistently demonstrates that people do behave in a reciprocal manner even in one-shot games. The social value orientation cannot explain such reciprocal cooperation, since those who have internalized the welfare of others should cooperate regardless of their partner's choices. Yamagishi and his colleagues argue that reciprocity is a "default" decision heuristic that is triggered when people face an interdependent situation. They further argue that having such a default response is adaptive since it helps individuals establish mutually cooperative relations at a relatively minor cost incurred by forgoing free-riding opportunities.

Strong Reciprocity. Some researchers think that humans behave not only reciprocally but also *strongly reciprocally.* Strong reciprocity translates into an inclination to punish defectors even in one-shot games. This approach seeks the adaptive advantage not in reciprocal behavior *per se* but in the reciprocity-punishment complex. This approach logically suffers from the problem of the infinite regress of higher-order sanctions mentioned previously. Most researchers who adopt this approach, however, claim that the cost of higher-order sanctioning is smaller than that of the first-order sanctioning (i.e., the cost sanctioning nonsanctioners is smaller than sanctioning defectors), and thus it is easier to solve the higher-order dilemma than the dilemma of cooperation and defection.

Selective Play and Ostracism. Another approach to explaining cooperation in social dilemmas is exit and ostracism. Students of social dilemmas have traditionally dealt with isolated relationships, and the wider context in which relationships are embedded has not been seriously examined. In the traditional research paradigm, players are locked in a particular relationship and do not have the option to leave it and join another relationship. Moreover, players do not have the option of kicking out undesirable members from their group. This traditional research paradigm is called the "forced play" paradigm because players are "forced" to interact with a particular set of partners. We sometimes face interdependent situations of this kind. An example is the U.S.–U.S.S.R. relationship during the Cold War. However, most personal as well as formal relationships entail at least some room for mobility. Although the exit option was included in some early studies of social dilemmas, it was not until the late 1980s that social dilemma researchers (although small in number) began systematic research efforts to explore the theoretical implications of the option to leave the relationship and choose a new partner. The resulting research paradigm may be called the "selective play" paradigm. Theoretical and empirical research using some form of the selective play paradigm, including the option for ostracism, generally indicate that cooperation in social dilemmas is easier to maintain when people who face a social dilemma can leave the group or when they can ostracize uncooperative members.

Signal Detection and Mimicry. The option to ostracize or to avoid interacting with uncooperative players requires that people have an ability to detect noncooperators. Evolutionary psychologist Leda Cosmides argues that humans are evolutionarily endowed with a cognitive module specialized for watching for and detecting noncooperators. However, cheater detection ability faces an arms race with the ability to mimic on the part of the defector. A game theoretic account of the arms race between signal detection ability and mimicry predicts that mimicry loses when and only when it is too costly to do so. Some of the evolutionary-based abilities found in animals to detect signals of cooperators may be replaced among humans by institutional arrangements to provide accreditation and references. Reputation is one mechanism that supports selective play and ostracism as solutions to the social dilemma problem.

— Toshio Yamagishi

See also Evolutionary Theory; Generalized Exchange; Rational Choice; Social Exchange Theory; Trust

FURTHER READINGS AND REFERENCES

Axelrod, Robert. 1984. *The Evolution of Cooperation.* New York: Basic Books.

Dawes, Robyn M. 1980. "Social Dilemmas." *Annual Review of Psychology* 31:169–93.

Fehr, Ernst and Simon Gächter. 2000. "Fairness and Retaliation: The Economics of Reciprocity." *Journal of Economic Perspective* 14:159–81.

Hayashi, Nohoko and Toshio Yamagishi. 1998. "Selective Play: Choosing Partners in an Uncertain World." *Personality and Social Psychology Review* 2: 276–89.

Kiyonari, Toko, Shigehito Tanida, and Toshio Yamagishi. 2000. "Social Exchange and Reciprocity: Confusion or a Heuristic." *Evolution and Human Behavior* 21:411–27.

Kollock, Peter. 1998. "Social Dilemmas." *Annual Review of Sociology* 24:183–214.

Olson, Mancur. 1965. *The Logic of Collective Action.* Cambridge, MA: Harvard University Press.

Pruitt, Dean G. and Melvin J. Kimmel. 1977. "Twenty Years of Experimental Gaming: Critique, Synthesis, and Suggestions for the Future." *Annual Review of Psychology* 28:363–92.

Wilke, Henk A. M., Dave M. Messick, and Christel G. Rutte, eds. 1986. *Experimental Social Dilemmas.* Frankfurt, Germany: Verlag Peter Lang.

SOCIAL EXCHANGE THEORY

Social exchange theory is one of the major theoretical perspectives in sociology. It takes its place alongside social systems theory, symbolic interactionism, structural-functionalism, and conflict theory. Three of the major exchange theorists are George C. Homans, Peter Blau, and Richard M. Emerson. This general perspective has roots in a number of disciplines in the social sciences, including the fields of psychology, sociology, anthropology, and micro-economics. Some of the early theoretical influences came from pragmatism, utilitarianism, behaviorism, and functionalism. Other sources of influence include the major works of several social psychologists and cultural anthropologists. From psychology, the work of John Thibaut and Harold Kelley, notably their prize-winning book *The Social Psychology of Groups* (1959, 1986), is closest to the analysis developed by exchange theorists in sociology, especially Homans and later Emerson. The other major influence on theories of social exchange that derived from psychology was behaviorism. It had a strong impact on the development of Homans's theory of social behavior as exchange and the early work of Richard Emerson and later the work of Linda Molm. In cultural anthropology, the works of Claude Levi-Strauss, Bronislaw Malinowski, and Marcel Mauss were especially influential.

The first formal treatment of social behavior as exchange in sociology appeared in George Homans's article published in 1958 in the *American Sociological Review*. This was also a major topic in his presidential address on "bringing men back in" at the American Sociological Association meetings. He was reacting to the growing dominance of Parsonianism and the focus on large-scale social systems in sociological theory. Homans argued that theory should focus on the subinstitutional level of analysis, specifying the determinants of "elementary" social behavior that formed the bedrock of groups and organizations. For him, this meant a primary emphasis on the actions of individuals in direct interaction with one another in contrast to the study of institutions and institutional behavior driven by social prescriptions or normative elements in society, the focus of Parsons. Homans believed that the subinstitutional elementary forms of social behavior could "crack the institutional crust," forcing changes in the institutionalized ways of doing things. Rebellion, revolution, and even more modest forms of social change often take this form. They provide the impetus for social change.

Homans' most sustained work on social exchange is his book *Social Behavior: Its Elementary Forms,* published in 1961 and revised in 1974. In this book, he lays out his propositions of elementary social behavior. These propositions are based to a large extent on the work of his Harvard colleague, B. F. Skinner and his ideas about reinforcement processes as determinants of behavior and behavioral change. Skinner defined social exchange as the exchange of activity, tangible or intangible, and more or less rewarding or costly, between at least two persons (Homans 1961:13). Influenced by deductive theorizing and logical positivism, Homans believed that many important aspects of social behavior could be derived from five simple behavioral propositions. He embraced reductionism, arguing that the behavior of collectivities could be reduced to principles of elementary behavior. For Homans, nothing emerged in social groups that could not be explained by propositions about individuals, together with the given conditions under which they were interacting.

Homans's primary focus was the social behavior that emerged as a result of mutual reinforcement of two parties involved in a dyadic exchange. His theoretical consideration of distributive justice, balance, power, status, authority, leadership, and solidarity is based on an analysis of direct exchange. Two main criticisms of Homans's work were that it was too reductionistic (i.e., it took the principles of psychology as the basis for sociological phenomena) and that it underplayed the significance of the institutional level of analysis and the social processes and structures that emerge from social interaction. These criticisms were addressed in the subsequent work of Peter Blau and Richard Emerson.

Blau (1964, 1986), in his well-known book, *Exchange and Power in Social Life,* developed a much more extensive treatment of the links between microlevel social behavior and the groups, organizations, and institutions it constitutes. For Blau, relationships between the elements of the structure create emergent processes that evolve from the interaction of the parts but that are not reducible to properties of these individual elements. Thus, a major difference between the perspectives of Homans and Blau is the latter's recognition of "emergent" processes at more complex levels of social organization. Blau framed his micro-exchange theory in terms of rewards and costs as did Homans, but he took a more utilitarian approach. Social exchange, for Blau (1964), "refers to voluntary actions of individuals that are motivated by the returns they are expected to bring and typically do in fact bring from others"

(p. 91). Blau defined exchange behavior as behavior explicitly oriented to the ends that can be achieved through interaction with others (Blau 1986:5). The microlevel exchange theory in Blau's work represents one of the first attempts to apply utilitarianism derived from microeconomics to social behavior. Later efforts include those of Gary Becker, a Nobel Prize–winning economist.

Blau focused primarily on the reciprocal exchange of extrinsic benefits and the forms of association and emergent social structures created by this kind of social interaction. In social exchange more than in economic exchange, the exact nature of the obligations to return the favor or resources of value is often not specified in advance. There is a general expectation of some future return, but it is frequently based on reciprocity norms rather than explicit negotiation. Subsequently, this form of social exchange has been identified as reciprocal or "non-negotiated" exchange in contrast to negotiated exchange in which there are explicit, often binding terms of trade.

Principles of social attraction were used by Blau to specify the conditions under which behavior leads to the initial formation of exchange relations. Social exchange processes give rise to differentiation in social status and power based on the dependence of some actors on others for the provision of valued goods and services. Much of the remaining focus of his book is on the structure of social exchange and emergent social processes at the group and organizational level. His explicit attempt to build a theory of social structure on the basis of a microlevel theory of exchange was influential in Emerson's work, although they used different theoretical strategies. Blau's discussion of dependence as a determinant of power drew on Emerson's (1962) early work on power. In addition to his effort to build a macrosocial theory of structure on the basis of a microsocial theory of behavior, Blau identified generic social processes and mechanisms that he viewed as operative at various levels of social organization. These included cooperation, collective action, legitimacy, opposition, and conflict. His work set the stage for a number of subsequent developments in exchange theory.

Homans and Blau popularized exchange theorizing in the late 1960s and early 1970s, but sustained empirical research on the topic did not begin until the mid-1970s largely as a result of the influence of Emerson's (1972) more formal theoretical work, based on his earlier treatment of power-dependence relations. Emerson built a conception of social exchange around his fundamental insights concerning power in social relations. He, like Blau, made power and inequality central to his treatment of exchange processes. And, like Blau, he viewed his theory of social exchange as the initial step toward building a general theory of social structure. The structures of primary interest were the networks formed as a result of the connections among a set of actors engaged in social exchange with one another. Two of Emerson's distinct contributions to exchange theory in sociology are his fundamental insight into the relational nature of power and his extension of exchange theory to analyze the social networks created by exchange relations. Subsequent work by Markovsky, Willer, Skvoretz, Lawler, Molm, Bonacich, Friedkin, and others built on these developments.

For Emerson, the relationship between power and social structure was the central theoretical problem in social exchange theory. From his earliest work in social exchange, Emerson (1962) defined power in relational terms as a function of the dependence of one actor on another. The *power* of actor A over actor B in the Ax:By exchange relation (where x and y represent resources of value) increases as a function of the value of y to A and decreases proportional to the degree of availability of y to A from alternative sources (other than B). These two factors (resource value and availability) determine the level of B's dependence on A and thus A's power over B. That is, *the power of A over B is a direct function of B's dependence on A in the A:B exchange relation.* The more dependent B is on A, the more power A has over B. Embedding this relationship in a network of exchange opportunities creates the basis for a structural theory of power in exchange networks.

This relational conception of power has two central features that helped to generate a large body of research on social exchange networks. First, power is treated explicitly as relational, not simply the property of a given actor. Second, power is potential power and is derived from the resource connections among actors that may or may not be used. Exchange relations are *connected* to the extent that exchange in one relation affects or is affected by the nature of the exchange in another relation. The connection according to Emerson can either be positive or negative. A *negative* connection means that exchange in one relation reduces the amount or frequency of exchange in another exchange relation involving one of the same parties (e.g., the A-B and B-C exchange relations are negatively connected at B if exchange in the A-B relation reduces the frequency or amount of exchange in the B-C relation). A connection is *positive* if the amount or frequency of exchange in one relation increases the amount or frequency of exchange in an exchange relation involving at least one of the parties to both exchanges (e.g., the A-B relation is positively connected to the B-C relation if exchange in the A-B relation increases the frequency or amount of exchange in the B-C relation). These are modal cases, however; exchange in two relations may also be "mixed" involving both positive and negative exchange connections relating to different aspects (or dimensions) of exchange. Exchange in more complicated networks often involves both positive and negative connections (see Cook, Emerson, Gillmore, and Yamagishi 1983).

Emerson expanded this important direction of development in exchange theory in subsequent publications formulating what is now known as exchange network theory. In his work with Cook (e.g., Cook and Emerson 1978), Emerson argued and experimentally demonstrated that power was clearly a function of relative dependence. Moreover, dependence was a feature of networks of interconnected exchange partners whose relative social power was the result of the shape of the social network and the positions they occupied. While Cook and Emerson concerned themselves with other exchange outcomes, particularly commitment formation, it was the connection between the use of power and the structure of social networks that became the central focus of social exchange theorists for over two decades.

The key assumptions of exchange theory, summarized recently by Molm and Cook (1995:210), include the following: (1) Behavior is motivated by the desire to increase gain and to avoid loss (or to increase outcomes that are positively valued and to decrease outcomes that are negatively valued), (2) exchange relations develop in structures of mutual dependence (both parties have some reason to engage in exchange to obtain resources of value or there would be no need to form an exchange relation), (3) actors engage in recurrent, mutually contingent exchanges with specific partners over time (i.e., they are not engaged in simple one-shot transactions), and (4) valued outcomes obey the economic law of diminishing marginal utility (or the psychological principle of satiation). Based on these core assumptions various predictions are made about the behavior of actors engaged in exchange and the effects of different factors on the outcomes of exchange. The power-dependence principle, in addition, allows for the formulation of predictions concerning the effects of increasing the value of the resources involved in the exchange and the availability of resources from alternate sources.

One of the most consistent findings in the experimental research on social exchange is that relative position in a network of exchange relations produces differences in the relative use of power, manifest in the unequal distribution of rewards across positions in a social network (Bienenstock and Bonacich 1993; Cook and Emerson 1978; Cook et al. 1983; Friedkin 1992; Markovsky et al. 1988; Markovsky et al. 1993; Skvoretz and Willer 1993). While several competing microtheories connecting network structure and power use have emerged over the past two decades, these competing perspectives converge on the prediction that power differentials relate to actor's network positions in exchange networks (see Skvoretz and Willer 1993:803). The theories differ, however, in the causal mechanisms at work in converting differentials in network position into actual power differences. The Graph-Theoretic Power Index approach uses elementary theory and focuses on the role of exclusion in networks (Markovsky et al. 1988; Markovsky et al. 1993; Skvoretz and Willer 1993). Core theory borrows from game theory and focuses on specifying the viable coalitions among exchange partners (Bienenstock and Bonacich 1992, 1993). Equidependence theory is based on power-dependence reasoning and specifies equilibrium points at which the dependence between partners reaches a "balance" (Cook and Yamagishi 1992). Finally, expected value theory (Friedkin 1992) is based on a probabilistic logic and looks at the expected value of exchanges weighted by their likelihood of occurrence (For a detailed discussion of the relative merits of these theories and their predictive abilities see Skvoretz and Willer 1993. For thorough discussions of each of these alternative formulations see the *Social Networks* special issue edited by Willer [1992]).

Bienenstock and Bonacich (1993) developed an approach to the analysis of exchange in networks of social relations based on game theoretic concepts such as the "core" (a solution set). Different network structures not only produce different power distributions, but also, different coalitions emerge as solutions to exchange. This argument implies that the structural arrangement of actors in relative position to one another can be an impetus for some subsets of actors to exchange more frequently than others. Bienenstock and Bonacich (1993) find that the core typically makes effective predictions about the frequency of exchanges as well as relative power differences among the actors in the network.

Cook and Yamagishi (1992) argue that social exchanges in a network proceed toward an equilibrium point at which partners depend equally on each other for valued resources. This "equidependence" principle has implications for partner selection as well as for exchange outcomes. They identify three different types of relations that can emerge from a network of potential exchange relations (which they refer to as an opportunity structure). Exchange relations are those in which exchanges routinely occur. Nonrelations are potential partnerships within the network that are never used and that if removed from the network do not affect the predicted distribution of power. Finally, latent relations are potential exchange relations, which also remain unused but which if removed affect the subsequent predicted distribution of power across positions in the network. The existence of latent relations can be important because they may be activated at any time as an alternative source of valued resources. When they are, they modify the distribution of power in the network.

Friedkin (1992) also argues that some relations involve more frequent interaction than others, depending on the structure of the alternative relations in the exchange network. The expected value of a particular exchange weighted by the probability of the occurrence of that exchange determines the payoffs for each exchange. The fact that some relations are used more than others is central to Friedkin's explanation of how power becomes differentially distributed across positions in a network.

The Graph-Theoretic Power Index (GPI), developed by Markovsky and Willer, predicts resource acquisition by actors in positions in exchange networks. It is a key element of what has come to be known as network exchange theory (Markovsky, Willer, and Patton 1988). GPI is based on the probability of particular partnerships being formed (see Markovsky et al. 1993:200–04 for a detailed explanation). Markovsky and his collaborators argue that some types of structures have more of an impetus toward the exclusion of some parties from exchange than do others. (In Emerson's terminology, networks that are negatively connected lead to more exclusion because they include alternatives that are competing sources of value.) Some network structures can be characterized as weak-power networks and others as strong-power networks. The main difference between these two types of networks is that strong-power networks include positions that can exclude particular partners without affecting their own relative power or benefit levels. One implication of this distinction is that strong-power networks will tend to have lower levels of behavioral commitment between exchange parties than will weak-power networks, because strong-power structures allow the arbitrary exclusion of some partners (Markovsky et al. 1993) facilitating power use.

Recent developments in Network Exchange Theory developed by Markovsky and Willer include efforts to study network dynamics, coalition formation, and the links of exchange processes in networks to other social processes like the emergence of status differences and the legitimation of inequality. In addition, Markovsky has recently worked on the linkages between the study of exchange networks and complexity theory, a rapidly developing field of interdisciplinary research.

Molm started with Emerson's two central propositions: Power is relational and power is a function of dependence, but her program of research took a direction that was distinct from the other positional theories of social exchange noted above. First, Molm focused on exchanges that are not negotiated but that are reciprocal acts of contingent giving (e.g., Molm, Peterson, and Takahashi 1999). In reciprocal exchange, actors do not bargain over the division of a finite pool of resources (or a fixed range of positive returns); rather, exchange is a process of "gift giving" or the simple act of the provision of a valued resource or service, and exchange relationships develop over time through repeated acts of reciprocal giving. The failure of reciprocity results in infrequent exchange. Second, power is not solely tied to the legitimate use of authority. Power may take the form of coercion or punishment. Whereas the other theories view the use of power as wielding structural influence through the threat and/or practice of exclusion from exchange (especially when there is a power-imbalance in the network), Molm considers how actors may impose punitive sanctions or negative outcomes on one another. The threat or practice of exclusion is most effective in networks in which there is a large power difference between the actors. And actors who are most dependent (least powerful) are most likely to be excluded from exchange in certain networks (e.g., networks in which there is a monopoly structure).

Molm's (*Coercive Power in Social Exchange,* 1997) work demonstrates that not all power use is structurally motivated. Punishment power is not used unwittingly in the same way in which exclusion can produce the unconscious use of reward power in negotiated exchange contexts. Power use can also have strategic motivations. Punishment power may be used much less frequently, but when it is used, it is most likely to be employed purposively to influence the future actions of an exchange partner. The less frequent use of punishment power results from the risk that the target of punishment will simply withdraw from the relationship altogether. Molm extends exchange theory by investigating alternative sources of power. Power use based on the application of punishment is distinct from power use that involves differential rewards. Molm's research also demonstrates how coercive power is constrained by the structures of dependence. The primary force in exchange relations is the dependence on rewards, which motivates both the use of punishment as well as reward power.

Since those involved in ongoing exchange relations frequently have control over both rewards and punishments (even if it is only the withholding of rewarding behaviors) Molm's research facilitates the investigation of more complex exchange situations. In addition, Molm has begun to specify the nature of the precise mechanisms that relate structural determinants of power with the actual use of power by those in various positions of power, something previous theorists had not yet accomplished. Norms of fairness or justice and attitudes toward risk play a central role in this analysis. Conceptions of fairness constrain the use of power under some conditions, especially the use of coercive power, and risk aversion makes some actors unwilling to use the structural power at their disposal for fear of loss. In more recent work, Molm, Takahashi, and Peterson (2003), analyze the relationship between different forms of social exchange (e.g., negotiated versus reciprocal exchange) as a key factor in predicting exchange outcomes. The relative importance of fairness, risk aversion, and the strategic use of power varies, depending on whether or not the exchange is negotiated directly between the parties involved or it involves reciprocal, non-negotiated exchange instead.

Lawler and his collaborators (e.g., Lawler and Yoon 1996) have recently developed a new theory of relational cohesion based on principles of social exchange. The focus of this work is to examine the conditions under which social exchange relations emerge from opportunities for exchange and lead to the emergence of positive emotions about the exchange relation. These positive emotions may subsequently lead to relational cohesion, commitment, or solidarity. Positive emotions develop based on positive evaluations of the outcomes of exchanges between actors and the frequency of their exchange. Low frequency and unfavorable (or less favorable) outcome exchanges are much less likely to lead to commitment to the relation, to positive feelings about the exchange and to feelings of cohesiveness or solidarity (i.e., what Lawler terms a "we-feeling"). This line of research returns to some of the earlier anthropological concerns about the nature of the links between exchange and solidarity in social relations. In addition, it expands the scope of exchange theory to include the emotional bases of exchange, commitment, and cohesion.

Empirical research on social exchange theory has also focused more recently on the effects of important factors such as uncertainty and risk on the nature and structure of social exchange (including the work of Molm). Facing uncertain environments actors involved in exchange are more likely to seek to form committed exchange relations (Cook and Emerson 1978; Kollock 1994; Lawler and Yoon 1996) or networks of trusted exchange partners. A significant effect of the emergence of commitment in many networks is that it reduces the extent to which actors seek exchange with alternative partners and thus serves to reduce power inequalities both within the exchange relation and within the network in which the relation is embedded (Rice 2003). Kollock's (1994) work demonstrates that uncertainty not only results in commitment formation as a means of reducing uncertainty, but also tends to be correlated with perceptions of trustworthiness of the actors involved in the exchange relations. Recent work on trust in social exchange relations treats trust as an emergent property in certain types of exchange settings.

Yamagishi, Cook, and Watabe (1998) report that trust emerges in exchange relations under conditions of high uncertainty when actors begin to form commitments to exclusive exchange relations in an attempt to avoid the possibility of exploitation by unknown actors who enter the exchange opportunity structure. Given low uncertainty, actors are much more likely to continue to "play the market" and to avoid forming commitments to specific partners in order to maximize their access to valued resources. (Uncertainty in these experiments refers to the likelihood of being exploited by a new partner in a network of exchange opportunities that changes over time.) In recent research on trust, uncertainty, and vulnerability to exploitation are often defined as two of the key elements of situations in which trust considerations are paramount (e.g., Heimer 2001). Cook, Rice, and Gerbasi (forthcoming) identify the types of economic uncertainty that lead to the formation of trust networks for exchange. Trust networks, if they become closed networks, actually may retard the transition to market economies under high economic uncertainty such as that characteristic of Eastern European countries and other countries making the transition from socialist to capitalist economies. Other implications of social exchange theory for economic relations are explored in Cook et al. (forthcoming).

New applications of social exchange theory to macrolevel social structures and processes are a fitting tribute to Blau's enduring influence on the development of exchange theory, despite his own skepticism about the links between microlevel theories of exchange and macrolevel social structures and processes.

— Karen S. Cook and Eric Rice

See also Blau, Peter; Commitment; Cook, Karen; Emerson, Richard; Exchange Networks; Homans, George; Molm, Linda; Network Exchange Theory; Power-Dependence Relations

FURTHER READINGS AND REFERENCES

Bienenstock, Elisa Jayne and Phillip Bonacich. 1993. "Game-Theory Models for Exchange Networks: Experimental Results." *Sociological Perspectives* 36:117–35.

Cook, Karen S. and Richard M. Emerson. 1978. "Power, Equity and Commitment in Exchange Networks." *American Sociological Review* 43:712–39.

Cook, Karen S., Richard M. Emerson, Mary R. Gillmore, and Toshio Yamagishi. 1983. "The Distribution of Power in Exchange Networks: Theory and Experimental Results." *American Journal of Sociology* 89:275–305.

Cook, Karen S., Eric R. W. Rice, and Alexandra Gerbasi. 2004. "The Emergence of Trust Networks under Uncertainty: The Case of Transitional Economies—Insights from Social Psychological Research." In *Problems of Post Socialist Transition: Creating Social Trust,* edited by Susan Rose-Ackerman, Bo Rothstein, and Janos Kornai. New York: Palgrave Macmillan.

Cook, Karen S. and Toshio Yamagishi. 1992. "Power in Exchange Networks: A Power-Dependence Formulation." *Social Networks* 14:245–65.

Emerson, Richard M. 1962. "Power-Dependence Relations." *American Sociological Review* 27:31–41.

———. 1972. "Exchange Theory, Part I: A " Psychological Basis for Social Exchange" and "Exchange Theory, Part II: Exchange Relations and Network Structures." Pp. 38–87 in *Sociological Theories in Progress,* Vol. 2, edited by J. Berger, M. Zelditch Jr., and B. Anderson. Boston: Houghton Mifflin.

Friedkin, Noah E. 1992. "An Expected Value Model of Social Power: Predictions for Selected Exchange Networks." *Social Networks* 14:213–29.

Heimer, Carol. 2001. "Solving the Problem of Trust." Pp. 40–88 in *Trust in Society*, edited by Karen Cook. New York: Russell Sage.

Homans, George C. 1958. "Social Behavior as Exchange." *American Journal of Sociology* 62:597–606.

Kollock, Peter. 1994. "The Emergence of Exchange Structures: An Experimental Study of Uncertainty, Commitment and Trust." *American Journal of Sociology* 100:313–45.

Lawler, Edward J. and Jeongkoo Yoon. 1996. "Commitment in Exchange Relations: Test of a Theory of Relational Cohesion." *American Sociological Review* 61:89–108.

Markovsky, Barry, John Skvoretz, David Willer, Michael J. Lovaglia, and Jeffrey Erger. 1993. "The Seeds of Weak Power: Extending Network Exchange Theory." *American Sociological Review* 1993:197–209.

Markovsky, Barry, David Willer, and Travis Patton. 1988. "Power Relations in Exchange Networks." *American Sociological Review* 53:220–36.

Molm, Linda D. and Karen S. Cook. 1995. "Social Exchange and Exchange Networks." Pp. 209–35 in *Sociological Perspectives on Social Psychology,* edited by Karen S. Cook, Gary A. Fine, and James S. House. Needham Heights, MA: Allyn & Bacon.

Molm, Linda D., Gretchen Peterson, and Nobuyuki Takahashi. 1999. "Power in Negotiated and Reciprocal Exchange." *American Sociological Review* 64:876–90.

Molm, Linda D., Nobuyuki Takahashi, and Gretchen Peterson. 2003. "Perceptions of Fairness and Forms of Exchange." *American Sociological Review* 68:1–160.

Skvoretz, John and David Willer. 1993. "Exclusion and Power: A Test of Four Theories of Power in Exchange Networks." *American Sociological Review* 58:801–18.

Willer, D. 1992. "Predicting Power in Exchange Networks: A Brief History and Introduction to the Issues." *Social Networks* 14:187–211.

Yamagishi, Toshio, Karen S. Cook, and M. Watabe. 1998. "Uncertainty, Trust and Commitment Formation in the United States and Japan." *American Journal of Sociology* 104:165–94.

SOCIAL FACTS

In his work on *The Rules of Sociological Method* ([1895] 1982), the French sociologist Durkheim defined social facts as ways of acting, thinking, and feeling that were external to individuals and exercised a constraint over them. Although the concept of social facts is closely identified with Durkheim, it is also relevant to the understanding of any type of social theory that treats society as an objective reality apart from its individual members. In general, it can be distinguished from theoretical paradigms that place a greater emphasis on social action or individual definitions of reality.

According to Durkheim, social facts are general to the whole society and have a distinctively collective character. They constitute the distinctive subject matter of sociology. They are often embodied in social institutions, such as religions, kinship structures, or legal codes. These institutions are the primary focus of sociology as a science. However, social facts can also appear as social forces of more diffuse type—for example, in the mass behavior of crowds and other forms of collective action or in the collective tendencies manifested in statistical rates of social phenomena such as suicide and crime.

Durkheim stated that the sociologist should treat such social facts as things. The sociologist must study these social facts as realities in their own right, with their own objective laws of organization, apart from the representation of these facts in the individual's consciousness. In Durkheim's view, if society does not exist as a distinct level of reality, then sociology has no subject matter. The social and the psychological are distinguished as different and independent levels of analysis. For Durkheim and his followers, this meant examining both the social substratum, or distribution of groups in space, as well as the collective representations or collective psychology shared by most members of society.

Durkheim also distinguished between the normal and the pathological within the sphere of social facts. Phenomena such as crime and suicide are normal for a society if they correspond to its type of social organization and level of development. For example, crime is normal in a society that also prizes individual innovation, and no progress would be possible without the actions of those great criminals who represent in their individual person the new cultural tendencies and provide a focus for new outlets for emerging currents of public opinion. In his book *Suicide*, Durkheim ([1897]1951) examined social suicide rates as a type of social fact. He argued that suicide rates varied regularly with differing social circumstances, and he proposed a theory of four social causes of suicide, two of which were particularly central to modern society. Egoistic suicide resulted from the lack of integration of the individual into social groups and was the most common type of suicide in modern society. Based on his examination of suicide rates, Durkheim constructed a formula that stated that the rate of egoistical suicide varies inversely with degree of integration of familial, religious, and political society. Durkheim thought that familial, religious, and political ties were generally weakened in modern society and, therefore, suicide rates were higher. He argued generally that society needed to supplement these weakened ties with new and stronger ones rooted in important emerging realities such as the occupational or professional group.

Anomic suicide resulted from failure of social norms to regulate the individual's wants, needs, and desires. It was found especially in periods of rapidly changing or fluctuating economic circumstances but could occur in other forms, wherever individuals' normal standards of conduct and expectations were suddenly disturbed. For Durkheim, both of these social causes operated independently, apart from the individual incidence of suicide, and pointed to a level of social facts that could be understood only sociologically.

Since his book's publication, Durkheim's work has been faulted for its underestimation of the interpretive aspects of the classification of actions as suicides and also for its neglect of the role of motives and intentions in the understanding of individual suicides. In a later study titled *The Causes of Suicide*, another member of the Durkheim school, Maurice Halbwachs (1930), had already placed a more equal emphasis on the psychological as well as the social dimensions of suicide and, thus, counteracted the school's inherited objectivism. Jack Douglas's (1967) work on *The Social Meanings of Suicide* reviews this tradition of research. He questions the validity of an objectivist account of suicide as a purely social phenomenon and calls for a study that does justice to the complexity of the socially embedded meanings connected with acts of suicide.

Durkheim and the members of his school investigated a wide range of other social facts, including family and kinship structures, the division of labor, religion and magic, systems of symbolic classification, and the dynamics of whole societies. Their focus on studying social facts as objective realities led them to emphasize social morphology—that is, the study of the number, distribution, and social arrangement of populations in space and over time. This approach combined the disciplines of geography, history, and demography into a synthetic sociological analysis of what they called the social substructure. Among the Durkheimians, Maurice Halbwachs wrote most extensively on social morphology, although all the members of the school, including Durkheim himself, used this perspective in their explanations of social phenomena.

The emphasis on social morphology was part of a more general methodological principle in which Durkheim argued that the causes of changes in social facts are to be sought in historically antecedent social phenomena. For example, in *The Division of Labor in Society*, Durkheim (1893) examined the transformation of whole societies from mechanical to organic solidarity. Mechanical solidarity was based on likeness among its members due to a strongly developed collective consciousness and was organized around segmental groups, primarily extended kinship structures. Organic solidarity was based on the mutual interdependence of performances in a complex division of labor. Increased division of labor and organic social solidarity also promoted greater individuation and a decreased influence of the collective consciousness. This overall transformation from one type of solidarity to another was caused by changes in social morphology, in particular, an increase in the total population volume, a greater number of persons in given territories (i.e., material density), and an enhanced degree of communication and interaction among groups (i.e., moral or dynamic density). At the same time, Durkheim identified a modern pathological form that he titled the anomic division of labor. In this type of social organization, the division of labor failed to create social solidarity because of the absence of sustained contact between segments in the division of labor. It is noteworthy that this explanation of social change operates entirely at the level of interrelated social facts.

In his study on *Seasonal Variations in Eskimo Society*, Durkheim's (1904–1905) close collaborator, Marcel Mauss, found a similar cause of change in religious ritual, law, family organization, economic life, and other aspects of Eskimo society in the seasonal variation of population concentration and dispersion and their concomitant effects on moral density. In their study of *Primitive Classification*, Durkheim and Mauss (1901–1902) argued that the central categories of thought and elementary forms of classification of objects in the world in primitive societies corresponded to the social organization of those societies and could be understood without reference to individual psychology. In a related study of "The Preeminence of the Right Hand," Robert Hertz (1909) argued that the unequal evaluation placed on the right versus the left hand was not rooted as much in biological realities as in social and especially religious definitions of the sacred versus the profane. This study subsequently generated a large literature on dual systems of classification that ultimately helped give rise to structuralist theories of culture and society.

Although the concept of "social facts" is associated with Durkheim and his school, and with the positivist tradition generally, other social theories that emphasize the constraint of objective social conditions over individuals share something in common with this view. Marxist social theory has a strong positivist or objectivist dimension in its focus on forces and social relations of production that confront individuals as objective conditions of existence. Although Marx noted that individuals make history, he added that they did so under conditions independent of their will. Social existence determines consciousness rather than the other way around. In Marx's writings, individuals appear largely as representatives or personifications of social classes or objective economic forces. When Marx does emphasize the role of actors in history, they are usually collective actors such as social classes like the bourgeoisie or the proletariat. Capitalism as an economic system dominates the experience of both worker and capitalist. The capitalist's individual motives are unimportant in understanding capitalism. They are merely representatives of the economic dynamics of the system. However, Marx sometimes strikes a more activistic chord, for example, when he speaks of the revolutionary action of the proletariat as a necessary part of the historical transformation from capitalism to communism. This ambiguity divided later Marxists (e.g., Gramsci and Althusser) over the question of the deterministic versus voluntaristic implications of Marx's work. This division was enhanced with the discovery of the writings of the young Marx, with their more humanistic emphasis on individual alienation and their Hegelian language of self-consciousness. These writings seemed to contradict the economistic and deterministic emphasis of his mature writings.

Emphasis on the objective reality of society and factual character of social existence helped generate a variety of functionalist and structuralist approaches to social theory. Although Talcott Parsons began his work with a theory of social action, he rapidly moved toward the development of a macrosociological, structural functional theory that all but eliminated the study of individual action and actors. This theory emphasized the role of common values in creating social integration and, in consequence, examined the individual largely in terms of the successful (or unsuccessful) socialization and internalization of these values. When individual action was emphasized, it was thought to take place within a culturally determined set of choices among institutionalized value orientations—what Parsons called the schema of patterned variables. For example, the choice between universalism versus particularism, or achievement versus ascription, is a culturally defined choice in which individual actors may choose their particular orientations to action but do so within a cultural system that has already valorized one or another of the competing value orientations.

In *The Social System*, Parsons (1951) also began to develop a theory of social systems that focused on the idea that any social system, including whole societies, needed to accomplish four basic functions in order to survive (i.e., adaptation to environment, goal attainment, social integrative, and cultural pattern maintenance). The analysis of the interchanges among institutions (e.g., economy, polity, household, school, law, etc.), serving these four functions became a major focus of theory building and was applied by Parsons to a variety of concrete problems. For example, in *Economy and Society*, Parsons and Neil Smelser (1956) provided a detailed analysis of the economy as a social system and charted its internal interchanges as well as its relations with other noneconomic systems. In *Family, Socialization and Interaction Process*, Parsons and several collaborators (1955) also examined the social system of the family, in particular, the distribution of instrumental and integrative roles among men and women. His followers developed this perspective in varying directions, including most notably Kingsley Davis and Wilbert Moore, in their attempt to demonstrate the functional necessity of social stratification in society and the aforementioned Smelser who extended this approach to social change in the industrial revolution and to the study of collective behavior. All these studies focus on the objective analysis of social and cultural systems without significant reference to individual agency as a constituting factor.

Robert K. Merton's functionalist theory also emphasized the study of objective social structures and their consequences. Merton focused on the distinction between the manifest (i.e., intended and foreseen) and latent (i.e., unintended and unforeseen) functions of social structural arrangements. In his influential essay "Social Structure and Anomie," published originally in 1938 in the *American Sociological Review*, Merton traced the ways in which an anomic American social structure inordinately emphasized the goal of success and downplayed the role of legitimate means to that goal or limited access to their achievement by the lower classes. As a result, this particular social structure promoted a variety of role adaptations, including criminaloid innovation, ritualist withdrawl of effort, full-scale retreat from social engagement, and rebellion against established values and norms. Merton and his students generally adopted a more flexible functionalist method than Parsons. This allowed them to discuss a variety of internal dynamics of "middle-range" social phenomena (e.g., conflict, bureaucracy, reference groups) that escaped the more wholistic and systematic functionalism of Parsons. However, the Mertonian brand of functionalism remained devoted to an image of society as an objective social phenomenon susceptible to analysis without substantial reference to the motivation of individual actors.

Later twentieth-century French social thought produced a particularly large number of variations on Durkheim's sociological objectivism, including the structuralism of the anthropologist Claude Lévi-Strauss, the historical investigations of the *Annales* school, especially the work of Braudel and his followers, the work of Michel Foucault, and the writings of Louis Althusser.

Lévi-Strauss drew heavily on linguistic models to create structural theories of kinship, myth, and culture generally. His theories eliminated individual experience and response in favor of establishing the reality of enduring, perhaps even eternal human structures. Human experience and expression in differing cultures could then be viewed as variations on these structures, but operating strictly within their confines. The second generation of *Annales* historians rejected the study of history in terms of actors and events and emphasized structures of the *longue duree,* especially the stabilizing influence of objective environmental forces, including even climate, and enduring socioeconomic and civilizational structures. This approach is best exemplified in Fernand Braudel's (1949) work on *The Mediterranean* but also in the studies of Immanuel Le Roy Ladurie, whose examinations of the economic and social impact of climatic fluctuations has entertained the possibility of a "history without people." Michel Foucault's studies also attempt to establish a history without the individual subject. His studies of madness, changing forms of knowledge, the clinic, and the prison trace fundamental shifts or epistemological breaks in the discourses about these topics without necessarily searching for causal sequences or viewing the changes as emerging from the actions of individuals. Instead, actors instantiate the words and deeds made possible by the reigning discourses. These various approaches to society, culture, and history reach perhaps their fullest development in Louis Althusser's structuralist Marxism. Althusser rejected the early humanist in favor of the later scientific Marx. He created a structural theory of society that entirely eliminates any effects of human agency in favor of the self-evolving character of internally dynamic socioeconomic and political structures.

The objective, scientific study of social facts is generally opposed by social theorists who emphasize human agency and social interaction. For example, Max Weber's social action theory; the symbolic interactionism of George Herbert Mead, Herbert Blumer, and their followers; phenomenological sociologists such as Alfred Schütz; and several related perspectives can be opposed to theories that emphasize the objective reality of social facts. Weber's work rests on an assumption of "methodological individualism," which insists that all objective social processes—for example, relations of power and authority—can in principle be reduced to the actions of individuals. Mead, Blumer, and their followers view society as a process rather than an object and see human beings as creators of systems of meaning through the use of symbols in social interaction. For both Weber and the symbolic interactionists, these symbolic systems need to be interpreted by the actors involved as well as by the sociological investigator—in the latter case, through a hermeneutic retrieval of meanings. Schütz's approach suggests that we begin with the taken-for-granted knowledge and conceptions of everyday life of actors and build our scientific concepts about social processes from that starting point. In general, when the objective structures of society are emphasized by interpretive sociologists, they are thought to be a moment in a larger necessary process of objective creation and subsequent reappropriation of meanings and institutions.

There have been many efforts to combine the objective study of social facts inherited from the Durkheimian, Marxian, structuralist, functionalist, and related traditions with an equal focus on the subjective experience and response of actors. The work of Peter Berger and Thomas Luckmann, Anthony Giddens, and Pierre Bourdieu are particularly worth mentioning. In *The Social Construction of Reality*, Berger and Luckmann (1966) traced the social processes of objectivation, institutionalization, socialization, and internalization through which culture and society are first created as an objective and even alien reality but then reappropriated and reinterpreted in new ways by individuals. Bourdieu's (1972) book, *Outlines of a Theory of Practice*, emphasized the concepts of habitus, practices, and reproduction. He views social and cultural structures as inherently embodied in actors without seeing any opposition between social facts and actors' experiences. Actors reproduce structures through their practices while at the same time making these structures real and removing their purely objective status as externalities. In general, sociologists today increasingly emphasize the equal significance of what Giddens (1984), in his book *The Constitution of Society*, calls "structure" and "agency." In his view, social structures provide the symbolic and institutional resources required for human agency to actually exist, yet actors working within these structures also simultaneously renew and transform them through their very action.

Although these and other efforts at synthesis have produced fruitful results, it is not clear that they have fully resolved the basic dilemma involved in the creation of a systematic social theory that must do justice to both the objective realities of historical economy, society, and culture and the equally compelling reality of individual experience and response. This is a dilemma perhaps inherent in sociology as a social science.

— Donald A. Nielsen

See also Durkheim, Émile; Historical Materialism; Marxism; Parsons, Talcott; Positivism; Structuralist Marxism; Structuration

FURTHER READINGS AND REFERENCES

Althusser, Louis. 1970. *For Marx.* Translated by Ben Brewster. New York: Vintage.

Durkheim, Émile. [1897] 1951. *Suicide: A Sociological Study.* Translated by John Spaulding and George Simpson. New York: Free Press.

———. [1895] 1982. *The Rules of Sociological Method.* Translated by W. D. Halls. New York: Free Press.

Giddens, Anthony. 1979. *Central Problems in Social Theory.* Berkeley: University of California Press.

Gilbert, Margaret. 1992. *On Social Facts.* Princeton, NJ: Princeton University Press.

Nielsen, Donald A. 1999. *Three Faces of God: Society, Religion and the Categories of Totality in the Philosophy of Emile Durkheim.* Albany: State University of New York Press.

Ritzer, George. 1980. *Sociology: A Multiple Paradigm Science.* Boston: Allyn & Bacon.

SOCIAL INTERACTION

Social interaction is the process through which two or more social actors reciprocally influence one another's actions. Although it may involve corporate actors of varying size, from pairs of individuals acting in concert to complex organizations, it commonly refers to processes of mutual influence among individuals. Individuals always influence one another's action in some form when in one another's immediate physical presence but may also do so through varied media of communication when spatially and temporally separated. However, until recently, the study of social interaction or what is commonly called *microsociology* has focused primarily on its face-to-face varieties.

Social interaction is the critical link between the individual and society. It is the medium through which culture and society directly influence individuals and through which individuals collectively produce and reproduce culture and social arrangements. However, social theories vary greatly in the relative emphasis they place on social interaction. Many suggest that patterns of social interaction directly reflect participants' psychological characteristics, internalized cultural values and social norms, or the influence of larger social entities and structures. Although these theories generally recognize that processes of social interaction constitute and uphold social arrangements and systems, they imply that the processes and outcomes of social interaction are largely predictable from anterior or other external factors. In contrast, other social theories argue that social interaction cannot be deduced from anterior or external factors and requires direct investigation.

Erving Goffman was the strongest advocate for treating social interaction as a subject in its own right. Goffman repeatedly argued that the orderliness of social interaction could not be reduced to the psychology of participants. Whatever is in individuals' minds, according to Goffman, they must make their behavior understandable to others. That requires an orientation to expressive conventions and consideration of the meanings one is likely to convey to others through either upholding or violating those conventions. For Goffman, social interaction involved not a meeting of minds but moves in an orderly game of collective definition.

Goffman also argued that what are commonly called social structures, such as diffuse social statuses or organizational positions, influence patterns of social interaction only indirectly. He maintained that social interaction consists of processes and structures specific to it. According to Goffman, there is only a "loose coupling" between interactional practices and encompassing social structures. The introduction of social structural factors into social interaction requires their translation and transformation into interactional terms. Hence, patterns of interaction cannot be directly deduced from social structural factors without consideration of the rules of their transformation into interaction specific processes and structures.

Goffman's own analyses of social interaction focused on the dramatic character of its definitional dynamics and its ritual order or structure. Goffman argued that social actors reach a working consensus about the definition of the situation that governs their interaction by mobilizing a variety of expressive resources, such as their appearance, voices and bodies, physical objects, and the fixed equipment of the setting. They thereby enact characters, stage scenes, and play through social narratives using techniques similar to those used by theatrical actors. Goffman also argued that an implicit but complex code of ritual conventions governed the interactional dramas of everyday social life. According to Goffman, much expressive conduct is ritual in both the ethological sense of being stylized and virtually automatic and, borrowing from Émile Durkheim, in the religious sense of expressing respect and regard for objects of ultimate value. Goffman argued that interactants ritually express respect and regard for each other's self or "face," as if it were sacred. He demonstrated how social actors do so by avoiding intrusion on one another's various self-territories, such as personal space and private information, and by celebrating their past or anticipated relations with one another.

Goffman's analyses of social interaction provide a compelling answer to one of the central questions of social theory: What is the basis of social order? Individuals who hope to influence one another must make their actions understandable to one another. To do so, they must subject their conduct to the constraints of mutually understood expressive conventions, such as the grammatical rules of spoken language or the ritual prescriptions and proscriptions of interpersonal conduct. Failure to do so results in misunderstanding or not being understood at all. Hence, engagement in effective social interaction and enlistment of others in one's own endeavors necessarily involves an implicit commitment to an expressive order that is the foundation of all social order.

To demonstrate the anchorage of social order in interaction rituals, Goffman concentrated much of his attention on interaction in public places. The individuals who populate such places, at least in contemporary urban settings, often have widely varied personal and social characteristics and little, if any, knowledge of and, hence, grounds for trusting one another. Yet as Goffman illustrated time and again, their public encounters are commonly orderly, routine, and unremarkable. Such routine and orderly public interaction demonstrates that individuals, despite their many differences and lack of familiarity with one another, are mutually oriented to similar expressive conventions and committed to upholding what Goffman came to call "the interaction order."

According to Goffman, "the interaction order" is not a product of blind conformity to informal norms of public interaction. He recognized that public actors routinely violate the ritual conventions of social interaction both inadvertently and for a variety of practical reasons. Yet he showed that violations are commonly followed by apologies and explanations or what he called "remedial work." The seeming offender thereby acknowledges the potential offense and demonstrates his or her understanding of and commitment to the ritual conventions of interaction, despite the apparent evidence to the contrary. In addition, Goffman demonstrated that the ritual expectations governing interaction serve as enabling conventions that render both conformity to and violations of them mutually meaningful. For example, the implicitly understood prohibition against staring at strangers makes stares from strangers menacing, flirtatious, or otherwise meaningful. The ritual prescriptions and proscriptions of interaction are not invariant norms but constitute a common idiom of expression that social actors strategically use for a variety of expressive purposes.

Those whom Goffman inspired have primarily focused their attention on strategic uses of the ritual idiom of interaction in public places. Following Goffman's advice to study the varied ways individuals treat and are treated by others and then deducing what is implied by them through that treatment, many have concentrated on how patterns of interaction both express and reproduce cultural conceptions of different categories of people and relations among them. For example, they have shown how adults commonly deny children the same expressions of respect and regard in public places that they grant one another. Adults thereby imply that children are less than full-fledged persons, and the young commonly respond to that treatment in ways that confirm adults' unflattering conceptions of them. Others have documented the varied ways that men publicly harass women by violating their self-territories and right to be let alone. Men thereby expressively assert their dominance over public places and situationally disadvantage women who must tolerate men's uninvited overtures, evaluative remarks and gazes, and attempts to extract personal information. Still others have shown how whites tend to respond to African Americans, especially younger males, with obvious suspicion and fear in public places, often provoking hostile and intimating responses. The result is a kind of interactional choreography of the tension and misunderstanding that embodies the state of race relations in contemporary American society, both expressing and reproducing those strained relations.

Other students of social interaction have examined how individuals infuse usually impersonal and anonymous public encounters with sociality and intimacy. For one, Lyn Lofland has detailed how public encounters are not limited to fleeting relations, as when one stranger asks another for directions or the time, or routinized ones, such as those between taxi drivers and their fares or the panhandler and potential donor. What has been called quasi-primary relations of transitory sociality are also common in public places when strangers recognize that they share a common interest, a common social identity, a common focus of attention, or territory. For example, unacquainted dog owners often stop for a friendly chat about their canine companions, gay men may mutually recognize their special "kinship," unacquainted onlookers sometimes exchange critical commentary on street art and performances, and seatmates on buses and users of laundromats may engage in conversation for the duration of their time together. Longer-lasting intimate-secondary relations are also common among those who routinely encounter one another in public places. The regular customers and staff of diners, bars, and coffee shops; regular riders of bus or subway routes; and regular shoppers and retail clerks may begin to exchange personal information and, over time, a degree of intimacy, however circumscribed. In any case, this diversity of relations in public arguably provides residents of urban settings at least some of their sense of belonging, place, and community.

Those who followed Goffman's lead into the study of public interaction have also demonstrated, in a variety of ways, that the social glue of what Durkheim called collective ideas and sentiments is anchored in ritual patterns of interaction. In both public and less accessible places, individuals dramatically enact presumed differences among people and reproduce collective conceptions of stages of life, gender, race, and other social distinctions. They honor one another's privacy but seek out and celebrate sociability with others. Each encounter that goes beyond the fleeting and routine creates what Durkheim called collective effervescence, fellow feeling, and collective identification.

The interactional production and reproduction of collective identity is most apparent among those who establish relations of continuing interaction. Using the example of little league baseball players, Gary Alan Fine has shown how members of interacting groups create distinguishing styles of appearance, their own argot or specialized language, inside jokes, and collective myths that constitute a distinctive group culture that Fine terms "idioculture." Those distinctive cultural practices expressively mark the group's boundary, distinguish those who are "us" from "them," and encourage a sense of personal identification with the group. This and other examples illustrate that social interaction is the source of cultural creation and change and of social solidarity, whether among small groups of friends or larger communities.

The apparent connection between social interaction and solidarity has led some students of interaction to consider how built environments encourage or discourage casual contacts. Most have concentrated their attention on how suburbanization, the policies that promote it, and the consequent demise of corner stores, neighborhood bars, and other urban gathering places have diminished opportunities for unexpected encounters and casual interaction among residents. Although largely speculative, they argue that the diminishment of those opportunities also diminishes residents' sense of community identification and solidarity.

Inspired in part by Goffman but more significantly by *ethnomethodology,* conversation analysts have conducted more detailed studies of social interaction than other followers of Goffman's lead. Conversation analysts extend the ethnomethodological concern with the taken-for-granted but methodical procedures of everyday social life to the study of conversational interaction. They maintain that an adequate understanding of the methodical procedures of conversational interaction requires studious attention to its empirical detail. They argue that those details are often lost in and concealed by the glosses and summaries of observational field notes and insist on the necessity of audio and/or video recording and detailed transcription of social interactions. Conversation analytic transcripts include interactional details such as phonetic representations of pronunciation and notations of simultaneous talk, inhalations and exhalations, and length of silences, often in fractions of seconds.

Conversation analysts have identified a number of processes and structures of conversational interaction based on these empirical materials. They include the procedures of opening and closing conversations, of introducing and developing topics, and of turn allocation in conversation. The study of turn taking in conversation has been particularly revealing. It demonstrates that speakers commonly demonstrate some understanding or appreciation of the prior turn or turns of talk in their current turn. That allows the previous speaker or speakers to assess how well she or he has been understood and to attempt clarification of any misunderstanding in subsequent turns of talk. The turn-taking structure of conversational interaction thereby serves as a general mechanism for the continual achievement and maintenance of mutual understanding, providing, in the words of one conversation analyst, the very architecture of intersubjectivity.

Conversation analysts have also studied what they call the preference format of conversational interaction, using the expression "preference" in a precise and peculiar sense. They use that expression to refer not to conversationalists' motivations or to statistical regularities but to the way responses to certain kinds of turns at talk are delivered. Preferred responses are delivered in a straightforward manner and without delay while dispreferred responses are delayed, qualified, and/or explicitly explained or justified. Conversation analysts' investigation of such "preference formats" tends to confirm Goffman's observations about the ritual and cooperative character of social interaction. For example, acceptance of invitations, offers, and requests is the preferred response, while refusal is dispreferred. The delay, qualification, explanation, and/or justification of a refusal are mechanisms of avoiding insult and conflict. Hence, conversational interaction exhibits a systematic bias in favor of cooperation, social solidarity, and order.

Conversation analysts initially limited their attention to the organization of mundane, everyday conversations but have more recently investigated the distinctive features of conversational interaction in particular institutional settings. These studies suggest that the ways conversational organization in such settings diverge from that of mundane conversation serve "to talk" those very institutional contexts of interaction into being. For example, in mundane conversations, any conversationalists can select himself or herself as the next speaker when the current speaker approaches the end of her or his turn at talk, but participants in classroom discussions usually honor the teacher's right to allocate turns at talk by waiting to speak until recognized by the teacher. It is in large part that restrictive organization of turn taking that distinguishes classroom discussion from the casual conversations that commonly occur in classrooms before and after classes and that makes it possible for students easily to disrupt classroom discussions by speaking "out of turn."

— Spencer E. Cahill

See also Conversation Analysis; Dramaturgy; Ethnomethodology; Goffman, Erving; Symbolic Interaction

FURTHER READINGS AND REFERENCES

Anderson, Elijah. 1990. *Street Wise: Race, Class and Change in an Urban Community.* Chicago: University of Chicago Press.

Cahill, Spencer and Lyn Lofland, eds. 1994. *The Community of the Streets: Research in Community Sociology,* Supplement 1. Greenwich, CT: JAI.

Fine, Gary Alan. 1979. "Small Groups and Culture Creation: The Idioculture of Little League Baseball Teams." *American Sociological Review* 44:733–45.

Gardner, Carol Brooks. 1995. *Passing By: Gender and Public Harassment.* Berkeley: University of California Press.

Goffman, Erving. 1967. *Interaction Ritual.* New York: Random House.

———. 1971. *Relations in Public.* New York: Harper and Row.

———. 1983. "The Interaction Order." *American Sociological Review* 48:1–17.

Heritage, John. 1984. "Conversation Analysis." Pp. 233–92 in *Garfinkel and Ethnomethodology,* by John Heritage. Cambridge, UK: Polity.

Lofland, Lyn. 1998. *The Public Realm: Exploring the City's Quintessential Social Territory.* New York: Aldine de Gruyter.

SOCIAL MARKET ECONOMY (*SOZIALE MARKTWIRTSCHAFT*)

The term "social market economy" was coined at the end of the 1940s by Alfred Müller-Armack, a German economist and social theorist of the so-called Freiburg School of Law and Economics, a neoliberal branch, often referred to as "ordoliberals." Walter Eucken is known as the founder of "ordoliberalism," and Wilhelm Röpke, Alexander Rüstow, and Karl Böhm have been other prominent representatives of this group. The idea of a social market economy became a leading political and economic ideologem for the rebuilding of the German society after World War II, closely attached to the myth of the German *Wirtschaftswunder* and the name of Ludwig Erhard. Reviewing general social debates as well as studying the relevant scientific discussions, it is not easy to distinguish the definition of the social market economy from "welfare society" and

various concepts concerning "social state regulations" (*Sozialstaatlichkeit*). There is consensus, however, that social market economy combines principles of competitive democracy—that is, a free market economy—with the idea of an active state regarding standards of social equilibration and responsibility. According to Alfred Müller-Armack, systemic mechanisms (i.e., the "automatism" of the market system) enforce "guidelines" by "meaningful" regulations reflecting general social and human values. The goal of such regulations is to find a "new balance between the divergent interests of social security and economic freedom" (Müller-Armack 1966:236).

Eucken and his followers argued for supplementing the private law society with an institutional guarantee of open markets to ensure that market competition can display its central function as "the most ingenious instrument to emasculate power" (Böhm 1961:22). In its German reality after 1948, social market economy is based on three main areas of societal governance and political regulations. First, it covers rules of guaranteeing qualitative competition; second, it embraces arrangements regarding social security, health care, and so on; third, it is backed by the institutionalization of the so-called labor-capital compromise (industrial conflict).

Thus, social market economy has to be grasped as a societal project to bridge the systematically built-in contradictions between the dynamics of liberal market economy, on one hand, and the institutionalization of standards regarding social values on the level of societal community, on the other. A broader understanding of the idea of social market economy focuses not only on macrolevel national economic policies but also on ethics and on issues of a specific social philosophy concerning the role of the state, the regulative functions of the intermediate organizations and institutions, and the "positioning" of—respectively, the "embedding" of—individuality.

THE HISTORICAL CONTEXT OF THE EMERGENCE OF THE SOCIAL MARKET ECONOMY

The project of a social market economy arose against the background of the developments and historical experiences of Germany between the late 1890s and the first half of the twentieth century. One can observe philanthropic and state legal reactions to the new social challenges of industrial capitalism, urbanization, and proletarization in all European societies during the nineteenth century—starting with special legislation in England even before 1850. Germany was a "latecomer" to industrialization and, as a relatively newly established nation-state, developed an intense and elaborated social debate over these issues. In contrast to other European countries, the so-called *Soziale Frage*—"how to integrate the working class into a bourgeois society?"—became a core element of the German nation. Against the background of a controversial debate under the regime of Fürst Bismarck, the "Deutsches Reich" introduced the most advanced social state regulations of the time concerning health care, unemployment pay, and social welfare, on the one hand (*Sozialgesetzgebung* [social legislation] 1883–1889). On the other hand, it initiated suppression of the social protest by the police and launched tough laws against socialist movements in the country (*Sozialistengesetze* [socialist laws]

(1878). Bismarck's welfare state led to a configuration of corporatist interest intermediation as a central element of coordinated capitalism.

Nation building and the political debate during the so-called Weimar Period were very much profiled by the *Soziale Frage* and the industrial conflict issue. The fate of the Weimar Republic was linked to two controversies: First, there was an emphasis on the building of a modern, more or less Western-oriented civil society versus strong and aggressive feudal and militaristic traditions. Second, there were the efforts toward a societal institutionalization and regulation of the capital-versus-labor conflict. The programmatic and political actions of the Weimar Parties referred mainly to these two areas of society building. Class abatement was seen as a main task of welfare-state action beyond inquest particularism. Interestingly, the conservative revolt ending the Weimar Period targeted the party pluralism as well as the "irresponsible" social costs of the welfare system. One of the intellectual starting points of early ordoliberal thinking in the 1930s has been the experience of a specific "failure of the state" (*Staatsversagen*) and the "corporatism" of the Weimar Republic facing the needs of a modern market economy.

From the very beginning, the specific German approach toward regulating industrial class society via an active state had an emphasis not only on social integration and social pacification but on economic performance, too. Because Germany had no colonies and an inferior position regarding natural resources, social pacification, vocational training, and the "production" of a state-loyal and skilled labor force became essentials of the German way toward industrial modernity.

THE FOUNDATION OF THE FEDERAL REPUBLIC OF GERMANY

Social policy discussion and societal decision making regarding labor organization and economic development did not start in a historical situation of "tabula rasa" after 1945 but was built on a tradition of substantial "social state regulations" and a broad theoretical debate regarding welfare issues and class abatement well before the end of the 1920s. As profound as the ideological changes and political regulations of the Nazi Regime may have been, main elements of the power structure and its institutional framework

still worked or were quickly restored at the end of World War II. The pre-Nazi union movement quickly regained power on the factory level, and Germany had a relatively developed institutional setting regulating labor politics and labor law (e.g., labor courts) as well as chambers of commerce and industry. Returning emigrants and a young generation of intellectuals started enthusiastic debates on the future structure of the German society. Among the leading intellectuals there was no doubt that some sort of "socialist" governance system should be implemented to resist "fascism," on one hand, and to avoid the social misfits and imbalances of "crude capitalism," on the other. Even the Christian Democratic Union (CDU), which was prominent for its "free-market" position later, favored socialist elements for the socioeconomic order of the new Germany (*Aalener Programm*, which proclaimed steel industry, coal, and mining as state-owned economic assets). It is necessary to recall that the concept of *Soziale Marktwirtschaft* entered the debate not by way of left-wingers but through moderate conservative discussants as a program to curb socialist and interventionist aspirations.

Doubtless, the emphatic energy was centered on the idea of the market—the free market controlled by a strong state but *not* managed or manipulated by an interventionist state. Literature shows an almost theologian association, as Philip Manow (2002) stresses:

> Ordoliberalism thus transferred the idea of "Staatskirchentum" to the economic sphere: The economy was supposed to function freely, according to its own "liturgy" of a free competition and efficient resource allocation, but the state was supposed to oversea and protect this free and undistorted functionate against all undue interference. The authoritarian leanings of ordoliberal thought thus drew heavily upon the protestant concertion of the proper role of the state. (p. 13)

However, intellectual modeling of socialist ideas for (re)building societies after 1945 has not been only a German topic. Everywhere in Europe more or less socialist models for the reconstruction of economy and society were on the agenda. This is true for Great Britain, France, and also for Italy. Despite the attraction of the prosperous material culture in the United States, the example of American capitalism did not get much credit among European social theorists immediately after World War II. The rise of the Cold War, however, laid ground not only for political anti-communism but also for rigid opposition against socialist ideas in general. The debate on society building got caught at the beginning of open confrontation between the two political blocks. The events in Greece and Yugoslavia and especially the Korean War influenced and restricted substantially the intellectual dispute and political reasoning throughout Europe and, due to the peculiar border situation, in West Germany in particular. Against this background, the idea and the concept of social market economy clearly bridged "free market economy ideology" and the European—and especially German—tradition of social policy. Alfred Müller-Armack formulated the idea, and Ludwig Erhard became its symbol of realization.

The main structural elements characterizing the realization of the social market economy concept are the following:

• The organization of efficient regulations on competition, fighting, and limiting distortions and deterioriation of market procedures through monopolization and trusts and the like. However, the basic idea was not to call for the state as economic actor but to call for an active state in terms of ensuring "contextual direction."

• The implementation of an elaborated social security system and of various welfare society standards guaranteeing a relatively high level of minimum income for all, including health care, unemployment and sickness payments, and other procedures of "social state" qualities (*Sozialstaatlichkeit*); favoring especially in these areas the active—regulating and caring—state. These welfare-institutions turned out to be "real" identifying qualities for social market economy through the 1960s and 1970s.

• The institutionalization of the industrial conflict and especially the stabilization of independent unions not only as an economic bargaining power but as an element of the political structure of society. Of particular importance are regulations concerning codetermination of workers and workers' interest organizations on enterprise and branch levels (*Mitbestimmungsgesetze* [laws of codetermination] 1951/52, 1972). The institutionalization of industrial conflict did not fit the original ordoliberal doctrines pushed by Eucken, Rüstow, and others, but surely it became essential historically, to the working concept of social market economy in Germany from the 1950s on.

During the 1950s, the more puristic ordoliberal concepts fused with welfare state achievements. The cartel law, the central bank law, and the pension reform were enacted in 1957; principles of liberal economic order and elements of a corporatist welfare state were implemented simultaneously. The social market economy model is strongly related to what has been discussed by Ralf Dahrendorf and others as the career of the social democratic consensus scenario in postwar industrial societies in Europe.

Screening the situation of social policies and labor strategies after World War II, we find variations of this social democratic consensus. Of particular relevance for theoretical and political debate has been the Swedish model (a model that has its roots in the late 1920s), but the French model of "planification" has provoked special interest, too. The different phases of social disputes and, especially, industrial conflicts in postwar Italy fueled ambitious

modeling and provoked intellectual curiosity as well as tough controversies. Great Britain—apparently the "hero" of the Anglo-Saxon heritage of liberalism and free-market economy—had a rather interesting postwar history of state-regulated welfare economy. As different modes of regulating industrial conflicts and economy in general were implemented in all industrial societies during the twentieth century, the workers' codetermination of regulations became a special "qualifying" element of the German system of industrial conflict management. The introduction of the social market economy transformed the "negative integration" of the working class (Güenther Roth) into some degree of positive conflictual partnership.

SOCIAL MARKET ECONOMY AS THE GERMAN SUCCESS STORY

The success of the German social market economy lies in its continuous generation of competitive production and productivity by way of effective workers' involvement (*Leistungsbereitschaft* [readiness to perform]) and a widely shared culture of rationalization, on one hand, and in its "catalyser" function in producing stable relationships between the different-interest parties in economic conflict, on the other. The social effectiveness of the social market economy system and its obvious economic efficiency, ideologically backed by a relatively high legitimacy of an "active state," were the foundations of what was seen from outside as the "German model," especially during the 1960s and 1970s. Low strike losses, high-quality production, the influx of millions of the skilled refugees from Eastern Germany, and the import of hundreds of thousands unskilled workers ("guest workers") from Italy, Spain, the Balkan countries, and Turkey made possible the so-called German *Wirtschaftswunder* during the first two decades after World War II, which realized high growth rates and impressive productivity gains (the gross domestic product doubled during the 1950s and labor productivity rose on an annual average of 5.7 percent). This "miracle" did hide systemic tensions and contradictions. Growing world markets, increasing competitiveness of German products, low defense expenses—these and other factors contributed to the peculiar configuration of the German economic and social success story. Strike figures, productivity, economic growth, and terms-of-trade figures show that in almost all relevant data sets, Germany took a favorable position in the statistics.

Only in the late 1960s did a short recession interrupt a continuous positive economic development. This short economic crisis showed the integrative function of the German system of industrial conflict regulation. Even though wildcat strikes gave evidence that even the German consensus model was based on antagonistic structures, the conflict histories in France and in Italy demonstrated to the

European public that the German model of social integration and economic progress had considerable advantages regarding the overall "benchmarking" between the early industrialized nations in an increasingly competitive world market.

This success story received admiration from outsiders and sometimes was looked on with envy and mistrust from European neighbors—but overall, it was welcomed as a historical development that stabilized German society politically and guaranteed its strong Western ties. There is no doubt that a socially and economically unstable and therefore unreliable German Federal Republic would have been a difficult burden for the European unification process and the East-West confrontation.

Germany could build its new economy under the military shield of the United States and NATO and with considerably fewer defense expenditures and input into military research and development than other countries. Therefore—like Japan—the German economy could concentrate on consumer and investment products with a strong export orientation. It might be disputed therefore as to what degree the social market economy system alone guaranteed progress and prosperity in Germany during the postwar decades or to what degree the externally "sponsored" economic growth-dynamics stabilized the model of the social market economy. Obviously there has been a positive interaction (*Wechselwirkung*).

The German path of economic and social development continued through the mid-1970s and was then redesigned due to qualitatively new challenges and uncertainties related to new technologies, globalization, new economic power structures, and the world financial markets. During the late 1970s and the 1980s, the German mode of capitalism lost its reputation, as the German economy increasingly showed the same problems as other Western Nations.

At the end of the twentieth century, the classic model of industrial society as conceptualized by economists, historians, and the first generation of sociologists in the late nineteenth century, was called into question. What is currently on the agenda of the political and social science discourse is first the future of the so-called Taylor-Ford regulation model, which has essentially characterized the process of industrialization for the last 60 years or so; second, the future of European variations of social welfare societies, which were established in the postwar period; and third, the impact of globalization—the emergence of the "global age" (Martin Albrow).

SOCIOECONOMIC CHANGES AND CRITICAL ARGUMENTS SINCE THE 1970s

Along with the trend toward "globalization" and "internationalization," economies increasingly experience strong pressures regarding mobility of capital investment, flexibility of labor use, and decentralization of production,

research, and development activities in order to reduce costs. The key formulas are lean management, just-in-time-production, global sourcing, global marketing, and global production. National institutions lose some of their earlier regulative importance. Globalization has more impact on activist states like Germany as the state loses its capacity to direct economic activity within its borders and is on the defense against Anglo-Saxon-style capitalism.

Moreover, "internal" factors like demographic developments and changes of the social structure (composition of workforce regarding gender, education, age, etc.). as well as new sociocultural standards of consumption and leisure, generate new framing conditions for modeling the built-in tensions and contradictions for policies focusing on economic efficiency and social effectivity.

Relatively early, critical analysts have spotted weak points of the German model regarding economic efficiency and market competition: highly legalized and regulated work relations, rigid unions that back inflexibility of work input and block industrial change, the increasingly unbearable social costs, and the welfare costs endangering prosperity in the long run, creating a "negative progressive circle" of economic data dynamics. The positive aspects of the German social market economy fade against its negative aspects. During the 1980s, the world economic scenario and developments at the national level reduced the attractivity of the German model considerably: More and more, export-oriented German producers were faced with strong competition on many important markets—for example, on the important U.S. market—from Asian competitors, especially from Japanese industry. The classical "super-aditum" of German industrial production on the world market—the label "Quality Made in Germany"—lost its particular profit value. Especially the machine tool, textile, and chemical industries could no longer rely on "Made in Germany." Even the auto industry—traditionally the most important product symbolizing German engineering—had to face fierce competition from Japanese competitors. With its highly regulated labor market, relatively strong legalizations regarding many products (especially biotechnics and the like), and its high labor costs, Germany lost its former strong position as an attractive economic place for foreign investments, too.

Negative effects of formerly positive enterprise cultures and consensus policies at the firm level, such as recruitement of long-term, high-quality workers, trust in local economic networks, and so on, showed up more and more as elements of inflexibility and as problems for innovation and structural change. The very qualities of the German success story (Hans-Joachim Braczyk et al.) became the foundations of the German economic difficulties in the 1980s: trust relations, long-term regional cooperation, and the tradition of conflictual cooperation in industrial relations. Demographic developments challenged modern social welfare systems in most European countries—and also in Japan—but hit the German situation harder, as the legalized demands regarding social transfer payment became more and more costly.

The fall of the Iron Curtain after 1990 and the integration of former East Germany (GDR) into the West German societal model proved to be a crucial test area regarding the German model. The enlargement of the institutional and normative system of West Germany's social state principle (*Sozialstaatlichkeit*) combined with the integration of a very problematic, inefficient economic structure has been a "fantastic" economic macro-experiment. The integration of the GDR resulted in a massive de-industrialization and destruction of economic resources, on one hand, and in the production of huge costs for the welfare society institutions, on the other. In effect, this pushed the German model to its limits. The size of the German economy and its still-strong industrial core as well as the good name of "DM" (Deutschmark) helped resist to some degree the very serious economic challenges. However, since the beginning of the 1990s, the German economy has been in a critical condition, displaying over 4 million unemployed, reduced profit margins in many branches, and the slowdown of investments in new technologies and new products. The situation has not improved much since then. Three indicators expose the critical condition of Germany's economy at the end of the twentieth century:

1. The German economy is still very much oriented toward heavy industry, manufacturing, and machine tool and vehicle engineering, and it remains relatively underdeveloped in industries associated with the postindustrial economy, such as biotechnology, knowledge service, and so on. These facts are seen as an important weakness by some observers. In Germany, more than one-third of the working population is still engaged in the so-called industrial sector, compared with only about one-quarter in the United States. Despite some problems of statistical equivalencies, there is no doubt that the German economy with its strong position in automobile production and machine tool industry is still more industry oriented and less service oriented than other modern economies.

2. Flexibility of labor is progressing only very slowly in Germany, in contrast to the United States and Japan and also, for example, the Netherlands. Institutional and cultural support for traditional work patterns such as the "normal working day" and long-term work contracts is still strong. Labor costs are also at the highest level compared with other nations, while the comparative advantage of a high-quality labor force diminishes with the expansion of lean production methods. Overall, the German labor market is rather resistant to the introduction of new types of low-income work with flexible time arrangements and new income configurations to reintegrate the long-term unemployed.

3. The positive interaction of free-market conditions with state interventionists' welfare policies obviously has turned into a negative spiral. Against this background, there has been an ongoing debate over the last few years about the *Standort Deutschland* (Germany's position as an attractive location for investment) versus the *Modell Deutschland* (the German model). Recent government rhetoric and a wide range of economic literature and, in particular, strategic arguments made by entrepreneurs has been aimed at remodeling the German model. The workers' interest organizations have definitely lost power. The model of the social market economy was put on trial as there was a broad consensus between experts and leading social politicians that facing first the Japanese success story and second—from the 1990s on—the new American success story, German socioeconomic doctrines had passed their best times.

SOCIAL MARKET ECONOMY, EUROPE, AND GLOBALIZATION: REFORM OF DISSOLUTION

Economic data in the 1980s and especially in the 1990s clearly show the diminishing attraction of the German model. In terms of growth dynamics and employment, Germany has fallen behind most of its European and global competitors—and some experts labeled Germany as "the sick man of Europe," pointing to a 0.7 percent growth rate in 2001 and 2.7 percent of GDP fiscal deficit in 2002.

Nevertheless it should be noted that in social science debates and in popular discussions neither the Japanese success story nor the new Anglo-Saxon success story led to a complete dismissal of the idea and the model of social market economy in Germany. The controversial debate among experts and politicians regarding Rhinish capitalism versus Anglo-Saxon capitalism involved considerable polemics at the beginning. Through the 1990s, it developed more and more into a sophisticated discussion reflecting various options of systemic aspects of different socioeconomic developments and regulations (Friedrich Buttler). The evidences of systemic problems of "classical" welfare policies were put on the agenda as well as the not less systemic problems resulting from neoliberalism.

The historical defeat of the "real socialism" and the difficulties of softly adapting European social welfare achievements to the new challenges of global economy and the impact of new technologies, on one hand, and undeniable deficiencies and social risks of "pure" capitalism, on the other, force current debates into new perspectives. Key words are *deregulation* versus *reregulation, shareholderism* versus *stakeholder values,* and *globalization* versus *regionalization.* Surely there is need for new answers to old problems and for answers to new problems: the ecological question, nonintended consequences of global economic processes and strategies, the troubles with the "new economy" at the end of the twentieth and the beginning of the twenty-first century, particular economic risks related to financial "bubble" phenomena, and a new quality of international terrorism after September 11, 2001.

On the level of social theory, new emphasis is put on "communitarianism" (Rawls, Walzer et al.) and on the role of the state as a regulator in global economic relations as well as on the increasing impact of nongovernmental organizations (NGOs) on the international level and the role of international organizations (World Bank and World Trade Organization), as well as the ILO (International Labour Office) in Geneva. The fabulous career of the notion of "governance" and its normative disciple "good governance" in relevant socioeconomic literature stands for a new interest in grasping the tensions between free market economy principles and the institutionalization of social justice and social equilibration related to basic social and human values. As the idea of and the demand for a "world government" still remains highly poetic, discussions on the further institutionalization of international and transnational rules and standards regarding labor force use and nature resource management have progressed. After a short period of unquestioned dominance of the Anglo-Saxon model of socioeconomic deregulation, the current debate is much more cautious and ambivalent about this, and there is "curiosity" in modeling a new economic efficiency that includes *social* effectivity. Reflecting the economic and worldwide turbulences at the beginning of the twenty-first century, it does not seem risky to predict that the debate about social market economy will gain new ground in the coming years. Eventually, social scientists will excavate the original concepts "designed" by Walter Euken, Alexander Rüstow, Alfred Müller-Armack, and others.

Struggling with serious problems, the German economy has faced during the last 10 to 15 years, there should be the historical chance for further developing a social market economy that works. The recent economic history of the Netherlands, Denmark, and other countries impressively demonstrates that European welfare societies have laid down rather solid grounds for reshaping themselves without betraying the basic social philosophical and political ideas and ideals that led to their creation after the catastrophes of the economic crisis in the 1930s. There is evidence that the German social market economy will undergo important changes during the coming years—reform of the health care system, new labor arrangements like the Volkswagen 5000 × 5000 model, and strategies for flexibility of income and work time regulations.

Many experts' judgment is clear: The German state that now spends almost 50 percent of the national income (and most of this for social transfers and social security) cannot and will not survive macro-economic challenges ahead. Surely, resistance of vested interests, the reluctance of the incumbent politicians, and the "imago" of the caring state in Bismarckian tradition will be tough. However, the recently fashionable formula "new social market economy" will have to be materialized sooner or later. And there are a lot of issues waiting for disagreement: strengthening consumers' purchase power versus favoring firms' investment activities, lowering business taxes versus public expenses, and so on.

FINAL REMARKS: SOCIAL MARKET ECONOMY, GLOBALIZATION, EUROPEAN UNIFICATION

The German project of a social market economy is one of the models representing the tradition of European capitalism and welfare society development after the Second World War. Notwithstanding internationalization of economic activities, new labor market realities due to immigration and demography, and new modes of economic organization on national, European, and international (and even transnational) level—the issue of the state's role in developing and/or stabilizing political and cultural identity will not vanish from the social sciences catalogue of controversies. The debate on adequate alignment of a state interventionism versus free-market dynamics referring to institutions and generalized ideas regarding well-being and standards of communal life will stay on the agenda of society building in Europe and elsewhere. For sure, in the near future, the notion of social market economy will not be identified as a doctrine but more or less as a "project" directed toward the balance of different societal interests—more precisely, as *one* project among others mirroring the multiplicity of developing capitalisms (Soskice et al.). Against the background of globalization and international competition, social market economy will face alternatives regarding the conduct of civil society—and as the ideas and political concepts of social market economy will "process" in future, social market economy will be opposed by more individualist, Anglo-Saxon-type, free-market-oriented conceptions of the civil society. Certainly, the most important "advancement" of the German social market economy model is to be expected with its integration into the emerging European political, economic, and social order. In many respects, the German "status" of social market economy will give way to overriding European strategies and policies. Thus, nowadays the debate on social market economy becomes part of the broader intellectual and political discussion concerning the basic construction principles of the "European House"—that is, the building of a "European home state" as laid down in the Presidency Conclusion of the Lisbon European Council in March 2000, under the headline: "Modernizing the European Social Model by Investing in People and Building an Active Welfare State."

— Gert Schmidt

See also Weber, Max

FURTHER READINGS AND REFERENCES

Abelshauser, Werner. 1997. "Erhard oder Bismarck? Die Richtungsentscheidung der deutschen Sozialpolitik am Beispiel der Reform der Sozialversicherung in den Fünziger Jahren" [Erhard or Bismarck? Strategical Options of German Social Policy: The Debate on the Social Security System in Germany in the 50s]. *Geschichte und Gesellschaft* 22:376–92.

Aust, Andreas, Sigrid Leitner, and Stephan Lessenich, eds. 2000. "Sozialmodell Europa: Kontouren eines Phänomens" [The Social Model of Europe: Outline of a Phenomenon]. *Jahrbuch für Europa- und Nordamerikastudien*. No. 4. Opladen, Germany: Leske and Budrich.

Böhm, Franz. 1961. "Demokratie und ökonomische Macht" [Democracy and Economic Power]. Pp. 1-23 in *Institut fuer Auslaendisches und Internationales Wirtschaftsrecht* [Institute for Foreign and International Economic Law], edited by Kartelle und Monopole im modernen Recht [Cartels in Modern Law]. Karlsruhe, Germany: Mueller.

Braczyk, Hans-Joachim and Gerd Schienstock, eds. 1996. *Kurswechsel in der Industrie. Lean Production in Baden-Württemberg* [Change of Direction in Industry. Lean Production in Baden-Württemberg/Germany]. Stuttgart, Germany: Kohlhammer.

Buttler, Friedrich, ed. 1995. *International Frameworks and Labor Market Performance. Comparative Views on the US and German Economies.* London: Routledge.

Dahrendorf, Ralf. 1979. *Life Chance: Aproaches to Social and Political Theory.* Chicago: University of Chicago Press.

———. 1988. *The Modern Social Conflict: An Essay on the Politics of Liberty.* New York: Weidenfeld & Nicolson.

Hall, Peter A. and David Soskice, eds. 2001. *Varieties of Capitalism: The Institutional Foundations of Comparative Advantage.* Oxford, UK: Oxford University Press.

Lisbon European Council. 2000, March 23–24. "Modernizing the European Social Model by Investing in People and Building an Active Welfare State." Presidential Conclusions. Lisbon, Portugal. (http://www.ces.fas.harvard.edu/working_papers/ Manow.pdf) Manow, Philip. 2002. *Modell Deutschland as an Interdenominational Compromise.* Max Planck Institute for the Study of Societies—Program for the Study of Germany and Europe, Working Paper No. 00.3. Cologne, Germany. Müller-Armack, Alfred. 1966. *Wirtschaftsordnung und Wirtschaftspolitik* [Economic Order and Economic Policy]. Freiburg, Germany: Krombach.

Roth, Guenther. 1963. *The Social Democrats in Imperial Germany: A Study in Working-Class Isolation and National Integration.* Totowa, NJ: Bedminster.

Schmidt, Gert with Karen Williams. 2002. "German Management Facing Globalization: The 'German Model' on Trial." Pp. 281–93 in *Challenges for European Management in a Global Context: Experiences from Britain and Germany,* edited by Mike Geppert, Dirk Matten, and Karen Williams. Houndsmills, UK: Palgrave Macmillan.

SOCIAL MOVEMENT THEORY

Social movement theory attempts to explain the origins, growth, decline, and outcomes of social movements. Current theory builds on several different approaches: European *new social movement* theory and North American *collective behavior, resource mobilization,* and *political process* theories. The field has expanded enormously and made important theoretical advances in the past 30 years. Current theory is at a stage of synthesizing ideas from different approaches, tackling neglected problems, defining scope conditions, and devising new research agendas. Although much social movement theory has been developed through studies of movements in Western countries, research is increasingly conducted in other parts of the world, and theories are beginning to incorporate this work as well as to deal with the globalization of social movements. Key areas of social movement theorizing include movement organization, political opportunities and processes, culture, and social psychology.

ORGANIZATION IN SOCIAL MOVEMENTS

Resource mobilization theory brought organization to the forefront of social movement theorizing. Although earlier collective behavior theories recognized organization as a factor in the rise of social movements, they tended to explain movement mobilization by focusing on determinants such as discontent and the emergence of generalized beliefs. Early resource mobilization work identified the "social movement organization" (SMO) as a key entity within movements. More recently, movement analysts have examined a broad range of "mobilizing structures" in social movements, including movement organizations, social networks, preexisting organizations, and alternative institutions. Scholars have analyzed and debated the ways in which preexisting organizations affect movement emergence and maintenance, the effects of different types of SMO structures on strategy and outcomes, interorganizational cooperation and competition, and the changing organizational composition of movements.

Resource mobilization theorists have viewed organization as critical to both the emergence and maintenance of movements. A variety of preexisting organizational forms, such as social networks and established institutions, are involved in the process of mobilization. Preexisting organizations connect new recruits to movement participants and provide leaders and frames that can be adapted for collective action. New social movement theorists such as Alberto Melucci emphasize how movements develop out of the "submerged networks" of everyday life. Through interactions in small groups, individuals experiment with new cultural forms and develop collective identities, creating the cultural bases for collective action.

To explain movement survival and change, scholars have examined the evolution of various types of organizational structures, including social movement organizations and other organizational forms within social movement communities. After the decline of a period of visible movement activity, movements are sustained through various means. In some cases, movement organizations that attract an exclusive group of participants with a shared culture or that are staffed by professionals keep a movement alive during slow periods. In other cases, a loosely knit movement community, including cultural groups and alternative institutions, sustains a movement during periods of scant political action. One of the interesting avenues of current research is an examination of the ways in which movements move into institutional and cultural domains, creating social changes and spreading movement ideology to these arenas.

Studies of organizational structures are critical to our understanding of social movement strategies and outcomes. In a seminal study, William A. Gamson (1975) demonstrated how organizational characteristics, such as bureaucratization and centralization, affect a challenging group's ability to remain mobilized and achieve movement goals. Further research has continued to specify the advantages and disadvantages of different types of organizational structures, including both the internal characteristics of movement organizations and networks among participants and groups within and across movements. In a study of efforts to unionize California farmworkers, Marshall Ganz (2000) shows how organizational structures that create connections to constituents, opportunities for meaningful and open deliberations among leaders, and leadership accountability are associated with the capacity for effective strategies. Research also suggests that linkages between national and local organizations and connections between a movement and other social movements result in more effective strategies than those employed by movements without such ties.

Studies of interorganizational dynamics have demonstrated the importance of looking at the effects of organizations and movements on one another. Sidney Tarrow's (1998) analysis of "cycles of contention" points to the importance of early movements in demonstrating political opportunities and creating models of protest for movements that come later in a protest cycle. Research suggests that the size of social movement industries and the social movement sector, consisting of all movement industries, is important; the expansion of a population of organizations creates legitimacy for protest strategies and also generates competition among organizations. The ideological composition of movement industries is also significant; radical organizations may have both positive and negative "radical flank effects" on more moderate organizations within a movement. One effect of radical organizations, as Herbert Haines

(1984) found in his analysis of radical flank effects in the civil rights movement, might be to increase funding for moderate organizations. Researchers have also analyzed the ways in which movements influence one another through shared activists and organizational, tactical, and ideological influences.

Movement organizations operate within multiorganizational fields consisting of other movement organizations as well as other types of organizations, such as established voluntary organizations. These organizations cooperate or compete with one another and influence one another's goals and tactics. Analysts have looked at the ways in which internal characteristics of movement organizations as well as overlapping memberships and other ties among organizations facilitate cooperation or encourage competition. They have also examined the ways in which mesolevel groups and organizations coordinate the actions of individual actors. Although macrolevel environmental factors are also important, organizational analyses show that the ways in which organizations are structured, and the nature of connections among groups, affect cooperation and competition within and among movements.

The characteristics of a "social movement industry," consisting of all SMOs working for the same general goals, change over time, affecting mobilization, strategies and tactics, and outcomes. The number and size of organizations in a movement expands or shrinks, and the forms of movement organizations change. For example, some movement organizations become more professionalized over time; some become influential within institutions; and some become decentralized and submerged. Research suggests that organizationally dense movements are likely to generate more protest. Movement industries that contain formalized and professionalized organizations are most likely to persist but are not necessarily more conservative in their strategies. Besides political movement organizations, social movement communities consist of a variety of organizational forms, including cultural and institutional entities. The impact of movement industries and communities on the culture and organization of other domains is a pressing concern for social movement theory.

POLITICAL OPPORTUNITIES AND PROCESSES

While resource mobilization theory focuses our concern on organizational dynamics, political process theory (which might be considered an extension of the resource mobilization approach) brings to center stage the interactions of states and social movements. *Political opportunities* are elements of the political environment that affect perceptions as to the likelihood that collective action will succeed or fail. There has been much debate over the concept of political opportunity, and scholars have proposed various factors as components of the "political opportunity structure."

One key issue is how broad the concept should be and, particularly, whether cultural factors should be included. Some scholars argue for a narrowly political use of the concept, lest it lose all meaning, and some propose distinctions between cultural and political opportunities. Tarrow's (1998) elaboration of the major elements of political opportunity, which is confined to key political variables, is widely employed. In his schema, political opportunity includes the extent of openness in the polity, shifts in political alignments, divisions among elites, the availability of influential allies, and repression or facilitation by the state (pp. 77–80).

A focus on political opportunities directs our attention to the structural obstacles and opportunities for collective action in various political systems. Critics have argued, however, that the approach neglects agency in its focus on political opportunities as structures. Movements are not only influenced by political opportunities; they also create opportunities for themselves and other social movements. Although some elements of political opportunity, such as characteristics of state institutions, are relatively stable, other dimensions, such as policy changes, are more subject to movement influence. Movement strategies are critical to political processes because collective action can produce new opportunities and because movement leaders must perceive and interpret opportunities. However, perceptions of opportunities are influenced by organizational structures, and both agency and structure are clearly important in understanding the creation and impact of political opportunities.

Another important issue for political process theory is the role of political opportunities in the emergence of social movements. Political opportunities are often viewed as encouragements to collective action; when opportunities expand generally, we are likely to see a "cycle of contention" such as the widespread protest of the 1960s. Movements that are "early risers" in a protest cycle open up opportunities for later movements by exposing the vulnerabilities of opponents (Tarrow 1998:77). Doug McAdam (1996:32–33) argues, however, that in reform movement cycles, there is not necessarily an increase in system vulnerability for "spin-off" movements. In fact, political opportunities may contract for movements that come later in a cycle as the state is preoccupied with the demands of the early movements. McAdam suggests that the diffusion of protest tactics, ideologies, and organizational forms may be more important to the emergence of spin-off movements than are political opportunities.

Theorists have also recognized that *threats* as well as opportunities mobilize movements by outraging constituents and increasing the costs of failing to act. Thus, favorable conditions for *mobilization* are different from opportunities for winning *new advantages*. Adherents flock to movements during times of threat, when they feel their contributions are most needed and when they feel emotionally upset or outraged, but they are more difficult to mobilize when there is less opposition to movement goals and conditions are more advantageous for making gains. The appearance of a *countermovement* to oppose movement goals is particularly effective in stimulating movement participation. Assessment of political opportunity and its effects is therefore complicated and involves analysis of the interactions of challengers and a variety of other actors within changing political contexts.

McAdam, Tarrow, and Tilly (2001) argue for a dynamic model of mobilization in which opportunities and threats are not objective structures but are subject to attribution by potential challengers. They contend that the political process model is overly static, failing to capture the interactions among multiple actors involved in attributing threats and opportunities, appropriating sites of mobilization, constructing meanings, and devising collective action. To develop a more dynamic approach, McAdam et al. call for identification of the mechanisms and processes underlying contentious politics. Although this approach has not yet achieved the authors' goal of revolutionizing the field, political process researchers are clearly moving toward the development of more dynamic, interactive models that identify common patterns in the workings of contentious politics. Comparative analysis of movements in different types of political and cultural contexts is critical to this research agenda.

CULTURE AND SOCIAL MOVEMENTS

Criticisms of resource mobilization and political process theorists for focusing too heavily on political organization and interactions with the state have resulted in a "cultural turn" in social movement theory. This new emphasis on culture returns to some of the themes from collective behavior theory and also incorporates ideas from new social movement theory into social movement research. Three of the major topics addressed are the cultural conditions and opportunities that encourage movements, the internal cultures of movements, and the cultural outcomes of movements. A large literature on social movement *framing* and a growing body of work on *collective identity* are central to social movement theorizing about culture.

Collective action frames are ways of presenting issues that identify injustices, attribute blame, suggest solutions, and inspire collective action. *Master frames* perform similar functions on a larger scale, making them useful to a number of different movements and organizations. Preexisting organizations and institutions are a source of cultural meanings and leaders, who adapt meanings and create collective action frames based on their experiences in such institutions. By drawing on cultural resources and developing frames that can be used to mobilize participants and win new advantages, movements then create cultural opportunities for subsequent movements. The availability of master frames, developed within both preexisting organizations and movements, helps to account for the growth of protest cycles (Snow and Benford 1992).

Master frames and other elements of culture cannot, however, simply be selected or manipulated at will. Social movement culture necessarily draws on the larger culture, which can both facilitate and constrain movement frames and strategies. Existing political discourse sets boundaries on the range of issues considered appropriate for meaningful public debate and policy action. If current political discourse does not include understandings that can be expanded or adapted as collective action frames, it is difficult for movements to create effective frames. Large-scale changes may be needed before movements can spread new discourse. Although theorists often treat cultural and structural opportunities as distinct, there are important connections between cultural and structural changes.

As in the case of political opportunities, both agency and structure are important to our understanding of cultural dimensions of movements. Large-scale cultural changes open up ideological space for social movements, but participants must actively develop and disseminate new cultural understandings. Thomas Rochon (1998) suggests that cultural change often occurs through a two-step process: New ideas and values are first developed "within a relatively small, interacting, self-conscious critical community" (p. 57) and later spread to a wider public by a mass movement. An important question for social movement theorists is how such critical communities develop in different types of cultural and political contexts. In some times and places, lack of "free space" or civil society may constrain the emergence of social movements as much as lack of political opportunity.

Once social movements arise, they not only influence public discourse, but they create their own internal cultures, which influence movement growth, survival, and strategies. In addition to generating collective action frames, movements develop values, collective identities, rituals, and discourse. Research on the women's movement has been particularly important in demonstrating the role of culture in sustaining movements and in shaping their organizational structures and strategies. During abeyance periods, feminism is found in the submerged networks of institutional and cultural venues as well as in surviving political organizations. Protest may take the form of discourse aimed at cultural and institutional as well as political targets. Shared political identity, nurtured through movement culture and the submerged networks of movement communities, is critical in keeping feminism alive.

Internal movement cultures foster the development of collective identities, which influence movement emergence, recruitment, strategies and tactics, and outcomes (see Polletta and Jasper 2001). As new social movement theorists have emphasized, large-scale socioeconomic changes such as urbanization make it possible to mobilize around new identities such as homosexuality. New identities are shaped within networks and institutions, and recruitment to movements builds on these structures and identities. Collective identities are incorporated into the frames that movement organizations devise to mobilize activists, and they influence the choice of strategies and tactics. Depending on their collective identities, activists prefer certain organizational forms and tactics. Identities may also be used strategically, with differences between activists and mainstream actors emphasized or de-emphasized depending on the political and cultural context. The deployment of movement identities through collective action frames and tactics potentially changes the broader culture by introducing new ideas, values, and lifestyle choices to the public.

In focusing on goal achievements such as the passage of legislation, early resource mobilization theory tended to neglect the cultural consequences of movements. Recently, however, theorists have attempted to assess outcomes such as changes in public discourse and the placing of issues on the public agenda as well as changes in everyday life, such as gender relations. For example, changes in consciousness brought about by the women's movement influenced the decisions of women to run for public office in the early 1970s, and the rhetorical strategies of Quebec nationalists influenced aboriginal peoples in Canada to use similar discourse. In both cases, cultural changes had political implications, demonstrating the importance of analyzing the interactions between "culture" and "politics" rather than treating the two as separate domains.

THE SOCIAL PSYCHOLOGY OF SOCIAL MOVEMENTS

Concepts such as framing and collective identity suggest the importance of social psychology in movement theory. And, indeed, a renewed interest in the social psychology of social movements accompanied the cultural turn in movement theory. Lack of attention to social psychology by early resource mobilization and political process theorists was in part a reaction to those collective behavior theories that depicted movement actors as irrational and their actions as strictly expressive rather than instrumental. In distancing themselves from such approaches, scholars emphasized continuities between collective protest and institutional action, rational choices over emotional reactions, and organization over spontaneity. They tended to neglect even those collective behavior theories that made no assumptions about the irrationality of participants in emphasizing grievances and emergent norms. By the 1980s, however, social movement theorists began to return to social psychology as theorists attempt to synthesize approaches and address neglected topics.

A number of theorists who turned to social psychology criticized rational choice theory as an inadequate conception of human motivation and group relations. By treating individuals as rational actors making separate choices, critics argue that rational choice theory fails to explain differences in participation, levels of involvement, and ongoing commitment. In response to such criticism, some theorists have worked to revise rational choice theory, moving "away from models of individual decisions toward models of group mobilization processes" (Snow and Oliver 1995:585). Others have turned to alternative social psychological concepts to address key questions regarding individual motivation and commitment.

Bert Klandermans (1997) examines the processes involved in recruiting individuals to social movements and maintaining or losing their commitment, including the generation of collective action frames, the transformation of discontent into action, and the erosion of support. In doing so, he attempts to combine resource mobilization and political process approaches with social psychological concepts, connecting different levels of analysis. Collective action framing involves both the societal level *construction* of pools of beliefs through public discourse, persuasive communication during mobilization campaigns, and consciousness-raising during episodes of collective action and the individual level *appropriation* of frames through cognitive information processing and interpersonal interactions. The mobilization of participation involves the interaction of structural and social psychological factors. Movements reach out to potential supporters through networks, demonstrations of effectiveness, and persuasive communications, while individuals make calculations about costs and benefits and the likelihood of movement success. Disengagement results from insufficient gratification and a decline of commitment on the part of individuals, which is related to both macrolevel factors, such as shifts in public opinion, and the mesolevel structures that keep individuals connected to movements.

Collective identity, consisting of "an individual's cognitive, moral, and emotional connection with a broader community, category, practice, or institution," (Polletta and Jasper 2001:285) is an important concept for understanding the participation, ongoing commitments, and departures of individuals from social movements. Individuals who share a preexisting sense of common identity with a group are likely to participate in collective action, although collective identity does not necessarily precede movement involvement; identities are also created and reinforced after recruitment through interactions within movements. Taylor and Whitter (1992) argue that collective identity is constructed within movement communities in three ways: (1) through the erection of *boundaries* differentiating challenging group members from dominant groups; (2) through the development of *consciousness* as a group with common

interest opposed to the dominant order; and (3) through *negotiation* of new ways of thinking and acting, both privately and publicly.

Individuals who continue to participate in the process of constructing collective identity are likely to remain committed to a movement, whereas those who no longer feel identified with the group are likely to withdraw. Collective identities change with shifts in movements and organizations, such as the influx of new activists (Klandermans 1997:136). Activists entering movement organizations at different times, under different political conditions, are likely to have different collective identities, and long-lived organizations typically need to negotiate conflicts among cohorts. Although some theorists have discussed collective identity primarily in terms of cognitive beliefs and interests, others have noted "the emotional satisfactions of collective identity" (Polletta and Jasper 2001:290). Many individuals participate in collective action because they find the experience emotionally rewarding and because participation allows them to act on personal values.

Until recently, the emotional aspects of collective action were neglected as social movement theorists focused on the instrumental, politically targeted actions of collective actors and shied away from any implication that social movement participants are irrational. However, new scholarship argues that rationality and emotion are not dichotomous, and that we need to recognize the role of emotion in individual decisions to participate in collective action, framing processes, collective identity, and protest tactics. Empirical research is beginning to demonstrate how emotions are central to organizational, political, and cultural processes. For example, Deborah Gould (2002) analyzes the ways in which emotions were critical to the development of ACT UP and militant AIDS activism. She shows how the negative political opportunity structure of the 1980s helped to change gay and lesbian ambivalence into anger, and how ACT UP's "emotion work" affected its interpretation of the AIDS crisis and fueled militant direct action.

CHALLENGES FOR SOCIAL MOVEMENT THEORY

Social movement theory has advanced greatly in the past 30 years, yet fundamental theoretical challenges remain. One of the key unresolved issues has to do with the very nature of the phenomena studied by social movement theorists. McAdam et al. (2001) argue that social movements should be treated as one form of "contentious politics" along with revolutions, nationalism, and strike waves. These forms of "collective political struggle" are all episodic and public interactions among claimants that involve governments as either claimants, targets, or mediators. The "public" part of this definition of contentious politics excludes "claim making that occurs entirely within well-bounded organizations, including churches and firms" (p. 5).

At the same time, McAdam et al. challenge the distinction between institutionalized and noninstitutionalized politics, arguing that the parallels and interactions between conventional and nonconventional contentious politics need to be analyzed.

Other scholars have also proposed broadening the scope of the social movement field, offering different takes on the problem. Mayer N. Zald (2000) suggests that we think of movements as including all actions shaped by ideological concerns or as "ideologically structured action." This approach would connect collective action to culture and allow theorists to explore, at the microlevel, how individuals develop and maintain commitments and, at the meso- and macrolevels, how movements penetrate institutions, political parties, and government. Although Zald focuses on extending movement analysis into political parties and government agencies, his approach is in line with research on movement activity within institutions and with efforts to locate movements within loosely shaped movement communities and the structures of everyday life. Zald shares McAdam et al.'s (2001) view of the connections between social movements and institutionalized actions, but in contrast to them, he includes nonpublic activity within bounded organizations as ideologically structured action.

David A. Snow (2002) argues that the concept of "contentious politics" advocated by McAdam et al. (2001) is too restrictive in that it excludes social movement activity that is not connected in some way to the state, such as religious movements and self-help movements. He warns that the emerging dominance of the contentious politics approach hinders consideration of alternative conceptualizations such as Zald's ideologically structured action approach. Snow proposes that we think of social movements as collective challenges to systems or structures of authority, including governmental units, but also various types of nongovernmental structures such as corporations, universities, and religious denominations. This approach directs students of social movements to examine cultural and institutional as well as political challenges, and to compare processes of change in different arenas.

The challenge of broadening the scope of social movement theory is related to central theoretical problems facing social movement scholars, including the need to connect levels of analysis and organizational, political, cultural, and social psychological processes. To adequately explain movement mobilization, strategies and tactics, and outcomes, social movement theory needs to examine the ways in which microlevel transformations and reactions are connected to mesolevel organization and macrolevel cultural and political structures. How are perceptions of political opportunities affected by organizational structures and cultural understandings? How do social psychological reactions vary across political and cultural contexts? How does movement organization affect culture and organization in other domains? These and other key questions require detailed empirical examinations of movement processes across levels of analysis.

Most important, social movement theory needs to examine these processes dynamically, showing how interactions among collective actors, their targets, and other actors change over time along with organizational, political, cultural, and social psychological developments. This poses both methodological and theoretical challenges. Case studies continue to be an important means for examining movement growth, development, and change, but other methods are also required, including comparative studies of movements in different countries. McAdam et al. (2001) argue that episodes of contentious politics in a wide variety of settings need to be compared so that underlying mechanisms and processes of change, rather than general laws, can be identified. This approach holds great promise, but critics note that the precise nature of mechanisms and processes remains unclear. Thus, social movement theorists continue to search for ways to examine the dynamic, interactive workings of social movements in different historical, political, and cultural settings.

— Suzanne Staggenborg

See also Discourse; Emotion Work; Feminism; Frame Analysis; Historical and Comparative Theory; Identity; Rational Choice; Revolution; Tilly, Charles

FURTHER READINGS AND REFERENCES

Gamson, William A. 1975. *The Strategy of Social Protest.* Homewood, IL: Dorsey.

Ganz, Marshall. 2000. "Resources and Resourcefulness: Strategic Capacity in the Unionization of California Agriculture, 1959–1966." *American Journal of Sociology* 105(4):1003–62.

Gould, Deborah B. 2002. "Life during Wartime: Emotions and the Development of ACT UP." *Mobilization* 7(2):177–200.

Haines, Herbert H. 1984. "Black Radicalization and the Funding of Civil Rights: 1957–1970." *Social Problems* 32(1):31–43.

Klandermans, Bert. 1997. *The Social Psychology of Protest.* Oxford, UK: Blackwell.

McAdam, Doug. 1996. "Conceptual Origins, Current Problems, Future Directions." Pp. 23–40 in *Comparative Perspectives on Social Movements,* edited by Doug McAdam, John D. McCarthy, and Mayer N. Zald. Cambridge, UK, & New York: Cambridge University Press.

McAdam, Doug, Sidney Tarrow, and Charles Tilly. 2001. *Dynamics of Contention.* Cambridge, UK: Cambridge University Press.

Polletta, Francesca and James M. Jasper. 2001. "Collective Identity and Social Movements." *Annual Review of Sociology* 27:283–305.

Rochon, Thomas R. 1998. *Culture Moves: Ideas, Activism, and Changing Values.* Princeton, NJ: Princeton University Press.

Snow, David A. 2002. "Social Movements as Challenges to Authority: Resistance to an Emerging Cultural Hegemony." Paper presented at the conference on "Authority in Contention" sponsored by the Collective Behavior and Social Movements section of the American Sociological Association, August 14–15, University of Notre Dame, South Bend, Indiana.

Snow, David A. and Robert D. Benford. 1992. "Master Frames and Cycles of Protest." Pp. 133–55 in *Frontiers in Social Movement Theory,* edited by Aldon D. Morris and Carol M. Mueller. New Haven, CT: Yale University Press.

Snow, David A. and Pamela E. Oliver. 1995. "Social Movements and Collective Behavior: Social Psychological Dimensions and Considerations." Pp. 571–99 in *Sociological Perspectives on Social Psychology,* edited by Karen S. Cook, Gary Alan Fine, and James S. House. Boston: Allyn & Bacon.

Tarrow, Sidney. 1998. *Power in Movement: Social Movements and Contentious Politics.* 2d ed. New York: Cambridge University Press.

Taylor, Verta and Nancy E. Whitter. 1992. "Collective Identity in Social Movement Communities: Lesbian Feminist Mobilization." Pp. 104–29 in *Frontiers in Social Movement Theory,* edited by Aldon D. Morris and Carol M. Mueller. New Haven, CT: Yale University Press.

Zald, Mayer N. 2000. "Ideologically Structured Action: An Enlarged Agenda for Social Movement Research." *Mobilization* 5(1):1–16.

SOCIAL RATIONALITY

The term *social rationality* covers a family of conceptions of goal-directed behavior that have one feature in common: they proceed from the assumption that each individual's ability to pursue goals more or less intelligently and the way goals are pursued (the mode of rationality) are strongly influenced by social conditions. This conception stands in contrast to "natural rationality" in which the individual's ability to pursue goals more or less intelligently is assumed to be naturally given and the same for all. The latter even holds for a great number of "bounded rationality" approaches in which human biases in judgment and limitations in calculatory ability are explicitly admitted. Important assumptions of the natural rationality approach include the veridicality of expectations, common knowledge (i.e., cognitive coordination) of interacting individuals, and ordered preferences as naturally given. All these assumptions are challenged by social rationality approaches.

Social rationality assumptions are quite old in sociology. For example, Simmel and Weber worked explicitly with such a conception. However, goal-directed behavior was sidelined in sociology for some time in favor or role-playing behavior, and economists used increasingly natural rationality conceptions, often as a simplifying assumption for the sake of tractability and deductive rigor. As a consequence, when sociologists began to pay more attention to goal-directed behavior again (in the 1970s), they often borrowed the conception of natural rationality from economics and game theory, which led to a predominance of natural rationality assumptions in "rational choice sociology" (with James Coleman as a major proponent). In the meantime, social rationality approaches have developed and begun to spread in sociology. There is no single dominant approach yet, but most of the approaches have learned a great deal from natural rationality approaches and from cognitive and evolutionary psychology. In that sense, they have evolved far beyond the beginnings in classical sociology.

A direct result of this difference in assumptions is that in the natural rationality approaches, social and cultural conditions can improve or diminish the joint goal pursuit (also called "collective" rationality or Pareto optimality) but not individual rationality. By contrast, for social rationality approaches, social and cultural conditions can affect positively or negatively *both* individual and collective rationality. This has important consequences for the kind of social arrangements (especially institutions) being considered and for the interdependence among these arrangements. For example, in social rationality approaches, humans are assumed to be forward looking, but they don't naturally look far into the future. The ability to consider the far future (often called "farsightedness" and "rational expectations" in natural rationality approaches) is thus assumed to depend on social arrangements that make it easy to do so by (1) standardizing events and (2) making it possible to predict classes of contingencies. A school system, for instance, and institutions that make it stable over time, allow parents to anticipate possible choices and contingencies far into their child's future. There is no "natural" farsightedness involved. Creating social arrangements for the improvement of collective rationality is often dependent on having arrangements for enhanced individual rationality in place. Institutional design for the improvement of collective rationality is an important task for sociology. However, it presupposes a high level of individual sensitivity to incentives and thus a high level of individual rationality that responds to changes in incentives. Yet contrary to the assumptions in natural rationality approaches, expectations are often not veridical, preferences are often not ordered, and there is no cognitive coordination. Thus, the social conditions under which expectations are more or less veridical, preferences are more or less ordered, and cognitions of interacting partners more or less coordinated must be investigated, and that is one of the tasks of social rationality approaches.

Social conditions can affect virtually all aspects of individual rationality, from the mode of rationality to the abilities that jointly constitute the core of rationality (such as the ability to generate expectations and learn from experience, the ability to set goals, the ability to "define" situations, and the ability to substitute and the ability to create nongiven alternatives), to the motivation in goal pursuit (such as improvement versus maximization). Especially important is the influence of goals on the criteria of goal achievement and thus on the "mode" of rationality (such as calculativeness, appropriateness, and emotional "rightness"). Social influences on goals thus become particularly important for the way people will go after goal realization. Recent developments in psychology that trace the impact of motivations (emotions and goals) on cognitions ([self-] categorization, interpretation, social perception, beliefs) are highly relevant for sociological work on social rationality, especially for tracing the social influence on rationality through the influence of social arrangements on emotions and goal salience. The same can be said about evolutionary psychology. In this sense, the traditional disciplinary lines are far less clear than, say, 20 years ago. This also holds for the borders between sociology and economics. Social rationality approaches are decidedly not radically "sociological." Contrary to the conception that rationality itself is entirely a social construction (which leaves no theory of action), social rationality approaches generally share the assumption that human beings are endowed with rationality, and that social conditions will affect it positively or negatively and will affect its mode but not "create" it. Thus, the very dispositions to give meaning to situations (e.g., through framing effects and the use of simple heuristics), to generate expectations, to set goals, and to look for (given and nongiven) alternatives, allows social rationality approaches to actually use these features in theories of action. Sociobiology and evolutionary psychology have greatly aided this view by showing how social influences in the past can find their way into "hardwiring" now and how, in turn, this hardwiring makes people wide open for ongoing social influences on rationality. On its basis, even the core elements of rationality, including its seemingly noncalculative modes, can be interpreted as being generated socially in the course of evolution *and* the daily course of interaction.

— Siegwart Lindenberg

See also Coleman, James; Rational Choice; Weber, Max

FURTHER READINGS AND REFERENCES

Diekmann, A. and S. Lindenberg. 2001. "Cooperation: Sociological Aspects." Pp. 2751–56 in *International Encyclopedia of the Social and Behavioral Sciences,* edited by N. J. Smelser and P. B. Baltes. Vol. 4. Oxford, UK: Pergamon-Elsevier.

Lindenberg, S. 2001. "Social Rationality versus Rational Egoism." Pp. 635–68 in *Handbook of Sociological Theory,* edited by J. Turner. New York: Kluwer Academic/Plenum.

Stinchcombe, A. 1986. "Reason and Rationality." *Sociological Theory* 4(2):151–66.

SOCIAL SPACE

The past few decades have seen a renewed interest in space as a concept for social theory. This "spatial turn" has occurred at a time when ever-denser flows of goods, capital, information, services, and people around the globe have led to what Karl Marx called the "annihilation of space by time" or, to put it more carefully, time-space compression. This thinking is in line with the dominant strand of sociological thinking throughout much of the twentieth century, which has seen the process of differentiation of modern society being inextricably linked to emancipation from spatial factors. In a nutshell, theorists such as Georg Simmel and Émile Durkheim assumed that space would gradually lose in significance as abstract forms of social organization (*Vergesellschaftung*), such as monetarized exchange, become more pervasive.

Yet the resurgence of theorizing on space raises the question whether modernity, late modernity, or postmodernity is indeed characterized by a decoupling of space and time. It could be hypothesized that even time-space compression may not lead to a disappearance of space but to a regrouping of space-time orders. After all, space—very much like the much more theorized concept of time—is a crucial element of *Vergesellschaftung*.

Social science concepts of space have been influenced by and built upon mainly two distinct, ideal typical understandings derived from physics—absolutist and relativist (Albert Einstein). The *absolute* understanding of space is based on a Euclidian view and posits a dualism between space and social life and bodies. According to this view, space exists as a contextual background condition, independently of social action and human perceptions. Social action thus proceeds within an unmovable and fixed space. This sort of container is not thought to be part of social action. By contrast, a *relative* understanding views space as constituted by the structure of the relative positions of the bodies and objects to each other. Accordingly, spaces do not exist independently of social relations defined by the positions of actors, social action, and social goods such as status and power. Social relations flow into the production of spaces, their formation, and their institutionalization.

ABSOLUTIST CONCEPTS OF SPACE

Three distinct concepts can be identified in the absolutist vein of thinking about space, viewing it as territory, as place, or as form.

Space as territory has figured prominently in early twentieth-century approaches to political science and sociology. Geopolitics was a specific form of geodeterminism. This idea has been largely discredited by political practice; especially the national socialist quest for "living space"

(*Lebensraum*). Nevertheless, geopolitical views raise important questions about the potentially exclusive character of social space as political space. The political theory of sovereign nation-states assumes that states can fulfill their integrative function as the final arbiter in making collectively binding decisions only because there is no second state occupying the same territory. The modern form of state organization with territorially defined, territorially fixed, and mutually exclusive state formations is based on the existence of a public sphere with central authorities exercising legitimate use of force and external sovereignty. Over the past decades, this historical configuration has been called into question by newer developments of global governance, such as international regimes and supranational organizations.

Early versions of urban sociology did not embrace territorial determinism. The classic approach of the Chicago School of Sociology posited that people adapt to their urban environment and configure group settlements or communities in what are seen as natural areas. This human ecology approach results in an ideal typical model of the city, which can be modeled as a series of concentric circles. This allowed for the development of concepts such as segregation and succession of groups. In short, the social ecology approach assumes a "synomorphy" of physical and social distance. Yet the concept of space was never explicitly developed.

Space as place can be found in time-space geography, developed by Torsten Hägerstrand and his associates, who came to be known as the Lund school of geography. In this concept, all actions are mapped as local activities. The goal is to trace the spatial expression of everyday, or even lifetime, routines and practices and to thus identify the impact of space on the average day or life course of an average person. Since time-space geography emphasizes the measurement of social activities within the daily environment of persons, it conceptualizes space as a physical environment. The "stations," at which persons carry out their activities, define the "momentary thereness" of "interrelated presences and absences." From here, it is not far to a decidedly behavioral and individualist perspective according to which movement in space involves *mental maps*. Such maps can be thought of as the result of learning and are socially impregnated. Mental maps include topographic representations of places and distance and value judgments—for example, positive and negative images. These cognitive maps imbue places with meaning.

Space as a form transfigures the concept of space into an epistemological tool. This approach is vaguely based on Immanuel Kant who held that space and time are basic "intuitions" and who argued against the view that space has its own reality. Kant held that space is a principle of order, a *conditio sine qua non,* which precedes all experience. Very similar to Kant, Georg Simmel viewed space as existing independently and prior to human cognition. Simmel also viewed space as a mere "form," akin to forms such as social groups, poverty, and conflict. He considered only the "content" of social ties to be sociologically relevant. Society originates, according to Simmel, if the isolated elements are put together into certain forms. Therefore, space is a formal condition but has no relevance as a cause for processes of *Vergesellschaftung.*

Absolute concepts of space have been useful in answering questions about the placement of persons and groups in places and territories, the impact of macrostructures on human behavior, and the mutual conditioning of action and structure. The movement of actors in space exists, but spaces are not moving; space is fixed. An absolutist understanding of space does not pose questions about the social constitution of space going beyond place and territory. Furthermore, the existence of places and territories is taken for granted. It is not considered how places and territories may also be a product of the constitution of spaces. Also, keeping space as a background condition does not suffice to explore how several spaces intersect in or occupy the same place. This is where the relativist understanding of space comes in. The relativist understanding of space has guided thinking concerned with the constitution, construction, formation, and development of social space. The relative positions of elements involved in the production of space—depending on the view, for example, positions of material objects, places, ties between individual or collective actors—offers a convenient vantage point for conceptualizing space as the duality of presence and absence, space as sites of power and resistance, space as flows, and space as glocalization.

RELATIVIST CONCEPTS OF SPACE

Relativist accounts of social space go beyond a purely physical viewpoint that would look at the placement and relationship of "bodies" in space. They also encompass "action," a sphere conventionally attributed to "time."

In his theory of structuration, Anthony Giddens picks up this thread and uses the concept of space as a device to conciliate the age-old problem of agency and structure. Giddens does not juxtapose societal structures to the actor as objective realities. Rather, he sees structures—defined as recursively reproduced social practices—to flow into the very actions, which in turn create structures. Giddens's theory places social action and structures in a spatial-temporal order. Social practices "take place" in time and space and persons construct their own places. While time-geography treats physical environment as a restricting variable only, Giddens contends that these processes may simultaneously be enabling and restricting to social actors. The place of modern societies is the nation-state. This means that Giddens transcends time-geography in emphasizing the structuration of place and space by power and representation as resources. Overall, the theory of structuration offers a connection between social integration and system integration, expressed spatially as the difference between presence and absence—*space as the duality of presence and absence*. Giddens conceptualizes the problem of social order as one of "time-space distanciation." In his analysis of globalization Giddens is interested in how processes of social integration—such as trust, intimacy, and family—change, when distant and "absent" structures influence "present" in everyday places. Yet the mechanisms mediating between the present and the absent remain hidden.

The notion of *space as power and resistance* highlights how "presence" and "absence" have mixed in new and volatile ways in processes through domination and countermovements. According to Henri Lefebvre ([1974]1991), social space is a social product. Through time-space colonization, abstract space (*l'espace abstrait*) has been imposed on the concrete space of everyday life (*l'espace vécu*). In a conceptualization reminiscent of Jurgen Habermas's "colonization of the life world," Lefebvre identifies the two master processes: commodification and bureaucratization of and through space. In terms of bureaucratization through space, the state is the master of space in subjecting social life to systematic surveillance and regulation. However, the very outcomes of master processes are always contested terrain, as there are efforts toward the production of a genuinely public and democratic space.

While the concept of time-space colonization describes the reconfiguration of space as caused by exogenous factors that destroy the lifeworlds of persons, what could be called time-space disorientation emphasizes endogenous factors, a crisis of capital accumulation, the move from modernity and postmodernity, and the ensuing crisis in representation. For the lifeworld, this means that commodities and images change radically. Everyday routines become pervaded by global relations and communication. It also involves the transformation of locality so that places are revalorized: Products and images may even profit from global differentiation (as David Harvey describes in *The Condition of Postmodernity*, 1990) Another change in locality is the spread of "nonplaces" (a term developed by Marc Augé in *Non-places: Introduction to an Anthropology of Supermodernity*, 1995), such as holiday clubs, hotel chains, and supermarkets, which are largely devoid of the characteristics of place—namely, space defined by unique history, set of relations, and identity. Instead, these nonplaces are stifling the creative lifeworld by placing uniformity and bureaucratic manners on persons. The differentiation between "place" and "nonplace" should be seen as an ideal typical distinction in the Weberian sense, not least because nonplaces are sites that, in principle, offer opportunities for social ties to be restored and resumed.

Time-space dislocation also raises the identity question "to what space/place do we belong?" Some authors place the decentered or fragmented subject in "in-between spaces" or "third spaces." On a collective level, imagination creates communities of sentiment, groups that imagine and feel things together. "Imagined communities" composed of people who were never in face-to-face contact, constituted the perquisite for the formation of nation-states. Communities of diasporic people now crossing the borders of nation-states carry the potential of moving from shared imagination to collective action (Arjun Appadurai 1996). Processes such as international migration create a new instability in the creation of subjectivities, challenging the narratives of nationally bounded communities.

Space as flows questions the boundaries of societal units such as national states. Some notions in this vein consider the nation-state as anachronistic and emphasize the unbounded space of flows. They overlook the manifold tendencies of reconfiguring political spaces. One of them is the formation of transnational spaces within and across national territories, such as global cities. Technology enables a faster exchange of goods, ideas, and services as well as making travel faster. Persons interact in simulated environments. Place disappears. At the same time, close distance as a bodily experience turns into informational distance. In a macroperspective, global cities are nodes in the space of flows. A partial decoupling of cities from their national economies and states can be observed. Nonetheless, global cities are a mélange of parts of different cities. This suggests that various spaces may intersect in one and the same place, producing a new "power-geometry" (Doreen Massey). Picking up this thread, others have seen Los Angeles as "the quintessential postmodern place," in which developments and changes occurring around the globe are reflected and duplicated in this city (Edward Soja 1989). The "landscape" of Los Angeles is represented from a series of vantage points through which Soja contemplates variations of abstract geometries.

In contrast to space as flows the concept of *space as "glocalization"* (Ronald Robertson 1995) treats space as concomitant processes of generalization and specification, of globalization and localization. The production of space can be considered a dialectical process. On one hand, globalization allows a deplacing from concrete territorial places (*space of flows*). On the other hand, global flows have to be anchored locally in specific places (*space of places*). Space is conceived as a relational process of structuring relative positions of social and symbolic ties between social actors, social resources and goods inherent in social ties, and the connection of these ties to places.

On a macrolevel, the reconfiguration of social space is visible, for example, in the political realm. In a process of "unbundling" territoriality (John G. Ruggie 1993), various types of functional regimes have come to intersect territorially defined nation-states. Such institutions include common markets, border-crossing political communities and inter- and supranational organizations. Nonterritorial functional space-as-flows and territorial nation-states as space-of-places are the grids wherein international or global society is anchored. Such ruptures render the conventional distinction between internal and external increasingly problematic because there are various tiers of making collectively binding decisions. It also calls into question the concept of state sovereignty as an expression of a single fixed viewpoint and the research strategy of "methodological nationalism," which takes for granted national states as containerlike units, defined by the congruence of a fixed state territory, an intergenerational political community, and a legitimate state authority. In its stead, multilayered systems of rule, such as the European Union, demand a multiperspectival framework.

On a mesolevel, the dialectics of flows and places go hand in hand with the possibility of transfer of resources in space. Financial capital, for example, is distinctly more mobile than social capital. It is therefore often seen as the prototype of a global good. By contrast, social capital, such as networks of solidarity and trust, are place-bound, local assets, which can be rendered mobile across space only by social ties in kinship groups, organizations, and communities that connect distinct places. Any conceptualization of space across borders would therefore depend on the type of ties and (social) goods to be exchanged. Glocalization then means, first, that the local is produced—to a large extent—on the global or transnational level. Second, the local is also important in reconfiguring place. An empirical example for this approach is "transnational social spaces." Transnational social spaces consist of combinations of ties and their contents, positions in networks and organizations, and networks of organizations that can be found in at least two internationally distinct places. The concept of transnational social spaces probes into the question by what principles geographical propinquity, which implies the embeddedness of ties in place, is supplemented or transformed by transnational flows. This raises the question about the transaction mechanisms embedded in social ties and structures, such as exchange, reciprocity, and solidarity.

SPACE AND TIME: SOCIAL RELATIONS AND CHANGE

To conclude, the social sciences have used space in manifold ways, ranging from a conceptual tool to a metatheoretical concept. The same seems to be true for its twin sibling, time. Space and time share important commonalities and distinctions. Both refer to social action and social institutions, based on relations between positions in processes. The analysis of social processes requires that both actors and their (physical) environment are treated holistically, not separately. In Norbert Elias's thinking, each change in "space" implies movement in "time" and vice versa. For example, one cannot be perfectly immobile in a

room while time is passing. One's heart is beating, cells are dying and growing—change is continuous in "time and space." In the end, space and time may be expressions of two sides of the same coin. Space relates to relations between positions within sequences of events and action, abstracting from the fact that these relations are forever changing. Time, by contrast, is taking into account that such relations are continuously changing.

— Thomas Faist

See also Capitalism; Cosmopolitan Sociology; Globalization; Internet and Cyberculture; Time

FURTHER READINGS AND REFERENCES

Appadurai, Arjun. 1996. *Modernity at Large: Cultural Dimensions of Globalization.* Minneapolis: University of Minnesota Press.

Elias, Norbert. 1990. *Über die Zeit: Arbeiten zur Wissenssoziologie II* [On Time: Studies on the Sociology of Knowledge]. Frankfurt, Germany: Suhrkamp.

Giddens, Anthony. 1986. *The Constitution of Society: An Outline of the Theory of Structuration.* Reprint. Cambridge, UK: Polity Press.

Hägerstrand, Torsten. 1984. "Presence and Absence: A Look at Conceptual Choices and Bodily Necessities." *Regional Studies* 18:373–80.

Lefebvre, Henri. [1974] 1991. *The Production of Space.* Oxford, UK: Blackwell.

Robertson, Roland. 1995. "Glocalization: Time-Space and Homogeneity-Heterogeneity." Pp. 25–44 in *Global Modernities,* edited by Roland Robertson et al. London: Sage.

Ruggie, John Gerard. 1993. "Territoriality and Beyond: Problematizing Modernity in International Relations. *International Organization* 47:139–74.

Simmel, Georg. 1903/1995. *Soziologie: Untersuchungen über die Formen der Vergesellschaftung* (Sociology: Studies on the Forms of Social Organization). Gesamtausgabe, Band 11. Edited by Ottheim Rammstedt. Frankfurt, Germany: Suhrkamp.

Soja, Edward W. 1989. *Postmodern Geographies: The Reassertion of Space in Critical Social Theory.* London: Verso.

SOCIAL STRUCTURE

The idea of social structure is closely linked to an intellectual tradition that goes back to the work of Émile Durkheim, as well as to the structural functional theory that owes such a deep debt to his work.

Famously, Durkheim distinguished between nonmaterial and material social facts. All social facts are external to and coercive over individuals (or, at least, should be treated that way). Nonmaterial social facts (e.g., norms, values, social institutions) exist in the realm of ideas, while material social facts have a real, material existence. One type of material social fact is a social structure. Thus, social structures can be defined as real material social facts that are external to and coercive over actors. For example, the state is such a social structure, as is the market in the realm of the economy.

Durkheim's work played a key role in the development of both structural functionalism and structuralism. The latter, however, is based on Durkheim's later work (e.g., *The Elementary Forms of Religious Life*) and moves off in a different direction in search of the "deep" structures that undergird social thought and social action. Thus, structural functionalism played a key role in developing the notion of social structures (and social institutions), according it a central role in social analysis.

As the name suggests, structural functionalists were interested in the "functional" analysis of social structures. That is, they were interested in analyzing the consequences of given social structures for other social structures, as well as the larger society. The American sociologists Talcott Parsons and later Robert Merton provided the most extensive elaborations of the structural functionalist theory. Parsons developed a complex theory in which he argued that social systems are regulated by four functional needs: adaptation, goal attainment, integration, and latency (often abbreviated with the acronym AGIL). To survive, a social system must be structured to ensure that these needs are adequately and efficiently met. Although, as a student of Parsons, Merton shared many of the basic assumptions of structural functionalism, he was also critical of its more extreme functionalist views. For example, in contrast to the assumption that all elements in a social structure are functional for a society, Merton claimed that certain social beliefs and practices could be dysfunctional, or even nonfunctional. In elaborating this concept of dysfunction, he drew on Durkheim's famous concept of "anomie" to argue that certain social structures can lead to deviant behaviors. Critics outside the structural functionalist paradigm argued that structural functionalists tended to ignore agents or to see them as being controlled by social structures. Thus, structural functionalism was an extreme example of the tendency of some social theories to treat actors as what Harold Garfinkel called "judgmental dopes."

Of course, it is possible, even desirable, to look at the *relationship* between social structures and actors without giving priority to the former (or the latter as did, for example, phenomenologists, symbolic interactionists, and the like). Indeed, a great deal of recent social theory can be seen as according roughly equal weight to social structures and actors. Prime examples are Anthony Giddens's structuration theory and Pierre Bourdieu's work on the relationship between habitus and field. Indeed, the whole idea of structuration (a term that is sometimes also associated with Bourdieu's approach) is that what are termed here (although not necessarily by Giddens) as social structures cannot be examined without simultaneously examining the agents who are involved in them and who are their creators.

In George Ritzer's integrated sociological paradigm, the argument is made that there is a need for a paradigm that focuses on the dialectical relationship among four "levels" of social analysis. The macro-objective level encompasses social structures (and more generally Durkheim's material social facts) and the macrosubjective encompasses social institutions (and Durkheim's nonmaterial social facts, more generally). These levels must be looked at in relationship not only to one another but also to the microlevels—micro-objective (behavior, action, and interaction) and micro-subjective (mind, self, thought, the social construction of reality). The key point from the perspective of this discussion is that social structures cannot be examined in isolation from all these "levels" of analysis.

Thus, social structure remains central to social theory, but the long-term trend has been away from treating it in isolation from the rest of social reality. Rather, today social structure is seen as one aspect of the social world that must be seen in relationship to all other aspects. It affects, but is affected by, all the others. Thus, contemporary social theory has a more balanced view of social structures and their role in the social world.

— George Ritzer

See also Durkheim, Émile; Merton, Robert; Parsons, Talcott; Ritzer, George; Social Facts; Structuration

FURTHER READINGS AND REFERENCES

Durkheim, E. [1895] 1964. *The Rules of Sociological Method.* New York: Free Press.

Merton, R. K. 1949. *Social Theory and Social Structure.* New York: Free Press.

Parsons, T. 1949. *The Structure of Social Action.* 2d ed. New York: McGraw-Hill.

Ritzer, G. 1981. *Toward an Integrated Sociological Paradigm: The Search for an Exemplar and an Image of the Subject Matter.* Boston: Allyn & Bacon.

SOCIAL STUDIES OF SCIENCE

Social studies of science, or science studies, is a transdisciplinary research field that investigates historical, political, cultural, conceptual, and practical aspects and implications of the sciences. Because modern sciences are deeply intertwined with technology, the more comprehensive name science and technology studies (STS) is often used to identify the field. Regardless of which name is used, it is widely understood that social studies of science cover a broad range of historical and contemporary developments associated with natural and social science, pure and applied mathematics, engineering, and medicine. Social studies of science draw on the literature, concepts, and methods of philosophy, history, and sociology, but such studies make up an emergent field in its own right and not a branch or subfield of any other established social science or humanities discipline. The field has dedicated journals and professional associations, and numerous universities have STS departments, programs, and research centers. Participants in the field often hold appointments in history, sociology, anthropology, philosophy, and other university departments, but their research typically has a hybrid character.

Social studies of science include a number of different theoretical orientations. Some of these are offshoots of preexisting schools of social theory. For example, during its heyday in American sociology, structural functionalism was the dominant approach to sociology of science (as represented by Robert Merton's and his students' research on institutional norms and rewards in science). Boris Hessen, J. D. Bernal, and other Marxist scholars and scientists also had leading roles in the early development of social studies of science, especially in Europe. More recently, critical theory, symbolic interactionism, ethnomethodology, semiotics, cognitive psychology, feminist cultural studies, poststructuralist literary theory, and various approaches to globalization have been represented in social studies of science and science policy. Two approaches that developed within the field in a distinctive way are the *sociology of scientific knowledge* (SSK) and *actor network theory* (ANT). These and some of the other current approaches often are labeled as *constructionist* or *constructivist* treatments of scientific knowledge.

THE STRONG PROGRAMME AND SSK

SSK developed in the early 1970s and was strongly influenced by the writings of Thomas Kuhn, Paul Feyerabend, and other influential critics of positivist and logical empiricist philosophies of science. Several members of the Edinburgh University Science Studies Unit (which was founded in the 1960s) had a leading role in a successful effort to reorient the sociology of knowledge to engage the material practices and contents of the sciences. Leading figures in the Edinburgh School (also known as the "Strong Programme" in the *sociology of knowledge*) included David Bloor, Barry Barnes, David Edge, Steven Shapin, and Donald MacKenzie, who published a series of programmatic arguments and social-historical case studies starting in the early 1970s. In 1970, Edge and Roy MacLeod cofounded the journal *Science Studies* (renamed

Social Studies of Science after a few years), which provided an outlet for the new approach and became the leading journal in the field.

The "strength" of the Strong Programme lay in its proposal to extend the sociology of knowledge to cover even the most robust mathematical procedures, physical laws, and scientific facts. Conceived in the early twentieth century, the sociology of knowledge was an empirical research program that aimed to explain the historical formation and social distribution of collective beliefs and ideologies. Instead of evaluating the truth or rationality of beliefs, sociologists of knowledge endeavored to explain the connections between particular beliefs and the characteristics of the social groups that held them. Persons promoting a doctrine typically emphasize its intrinsic truth and rationality, but a sociologist of knowledge attempts to be noncommittal about inherent truth of a belief, while examining the history, socialization practices, and collective interests in the community of believers. Karl Mannheim, an early exponent of the sociology of knowledge, endowed the perspective with broad scope to cover religious and metaphysical systems, political ideologies of all kinds, and controversial scientific theories. However, Mannheim made an exception for the most robust, generally accepted scientific and mathematical knowledge. Mannheim held that because such knowledge no longer bears the imprint of the cultural and historical conditions of its emergence, the sociology of knowledge had no basis for explaining it as a function of particular traditions and practices. He recognized that modern science and mathematics were historically and culturally "conditioned," but he argued that "existential factors" were "merely of peripheral significance" for explaining the status of such knowledge (Mannheim 1936:271). Proponents of the Strong Programme refused to accept the idea that selected facts, laws, and procedures, which are currently accepted as invariant, rational, and true, should be exempted from social and cultural explanation. To set up the possibility of such explanation, Bloor, Barnes, and other adherents to the Strong Programme recruited philosophical arguments about the conventionality of mathematical practices, the theory ladenness of observation, the tacit underpinnings of experimental method, the incommensurability of competing paradigms, and the underdetermination of theory choice by empirical evidence. Such philosophical arguments were used to suggest that the resolution of controversies and the formation of consensus in scientific communities was not due to evidence alone. Empirical study of particular cases would then be used to identify historical conditions, social interests, and collective alignments that may have had some influence on the relevant scientific communities.

The Strong Programme is often summarized by a set of four principles that were formulated by David Bloor (1976) in his influential *Knowledge and Social Imagery:* causality, impartiality, symmetry, and reflexivity. Although studies associated with the Strong Programme rarely adhered to all four principles (e.g., many SSK studies do not advance clear-cut causal explanations), and the effective meaning of each principle left much to the imagination, the *symmetry* principle was frequently cited as an emblematic feature of the "new" sociology of knowledge. As Bloor defines it, symmetry means that the same general type of explanation should be used for any belief studied, regardless of whether it is held to be true or false. This idea flies in the face of the "sociology of error"—the commonplace idea that erroneous (and also unverifiable) beliefs are to be explained by reference to social and psychological causes (mass persuasion, cultural tradition, vested interests, personal bias, compensation for low status, false consciousness, etc.) and that true beliefs are to be explained by reference to their correspondence to reality and/or their derivation from rational procedures of inquiry. Symmetry, together with the principle of *impartiality,* is a methodological heuristic and not an ontological position. It does not imply that all "knowledges" are equally valid; it simply counsels the sociologist of knowledge to put aside judgments about the validity of a doctrine or practice when seeking to explain why it is *held* to be valid by particular historical and social groups. So, for example, existential factors (socialization institutions, regional cultures, traditions, local authorities, etc.) can be cited to explain belief in evolution and natural selection as well as ascription to special creationist doctrines. To follow through with such explanations does not imply that the competing doctrines are equally good or equally true or that both deserve an equivalent place in biology textbooks. Instead, it implies only that socialization, tradition, and so forth, explain the social distribution of the particular beliefs, regardless of their ultimate truth. Proponents of SSK hold that the ultimate truth of a conviction is irrelevant to an effort to explain why particular communities happen to hold it.

SOCIAL HISTORICAL AND ETHNOGRAPHIC STUDIES

SSK includes two predominant forms of case study, one of which is social-historical in scope and the other ethnographic in design. Typically, social-historical case studies focus on specific episodes of scientific change and/or controversy. These include relatively recent controversies about gravity waves, cold fusion, and solar neutrinos, as well as more remote historical controversies about the discovery of oxygen, the germ theory of disease, or the theory of relativity. Cases include marginal or rejected science (phrenology, spontaneous generation, cold fusion, etc.) as well as established theories and empirical discoveries. Many case studies have a conceptual focus: (1) tracing historical changes in notions of experience, experiment,

matters of fact, and objectivity or (2) challenging established conceptions of experimental test or replication. *Ethnography* is a method for studying the beliefs and practices of contemporaneous groups. It is perhaps best known as an anthropological method for studying exotic "tribes" and attempting to elicit and document cultural practices and understandings characteristic of the tribes studied. The related, but lesser known, sociological approach of *participant observation* is no less significant for suggesting themes and methodological strategies for ethnographic studies to science. Participant observation is a method for studying groups, often living within the sociologist's society, whose beliefs and activities are unusual, "deviant," exotic, or in some other way interesting from the point of view of sociologists, their readers, and their students. Like an ethnographer of an exotic tribe, a participant observer attempts to describe a way of life "from within," and extensive contact with the relevant group is necessary to develop a degree of fluency, skill, and mutual trust necessary for gaining deep access to that way of life.

Another sociological orientation, *ethnomethodology,* also influenced ethnographic (as well as some of the sociohistorical) studies of science. Like ethnographers and participant observers, ethnomethodologists integrate their research methods with the discursive and embodied production of the practices being studied. The engagement with the practices studied tends to be more intimate and detailed than one typically finds in other ethnographic and participant observation approaches. Some of the earliest ethnomethodological studies by Harold Garfinkel and his students reflexively examined social science research practices for transliterating and codifying data. Years later, ethnomethodologists turned their attention to the situated practices of natural scientists, mathematicians, and computer programmers. Such studies attempt to describe the coordination of discursive and representational practices and to elucidate how such practices constitute stable ways of life. Unlike many of their colleagues in social studies of science, ethnomethodologists eschew causal explanation, cognitive modeling, social and cultural criticism, and global theorizing. They are more interested in describing how the practices they study reflexively deploy social as well as technical concepts, models, discourses, theories, and ideal types (see Lynch 1993).

ACTOR NETWORK THEORY

Several ethnographies of scientific laboratories were conducted in the late 1970s, the best known of which was Bruno Latour and Steve Woolgar's (1979) *Laboratory Life: The Social Construction of Scientific Facts,* a study at Salk Laboratory in San Diego. Their book was notable for its bold and explicit argument about the "construction" of a particular biochemical "fact" and also for its adoption of vocabularies from literary theory to describe how laboratory practices using "inscription devices" make fugitive microbiological phenomena visible, stable, transportable, and resistant to "deconstruction." Latour and several of his colleagues later developed "actor network theory" (ANT), an entire ontology of scientific and technical innovation (see Latour 1986). ANT shares with ethnomethodology an orientation to the "local" or "endogenous" production of society, but it places far stronger emphasis on the semiotic inscription, translation, transportation, and stabilization of marks, graphisms, and other literary traces and representations of scientific practices and phenomena. The key move is to connect the practices and products of science from their point of production (the laboratory or field site) through multiple, globally distributed networks of literary reproduction. Studies taking up the ANT approach attempt to "follow" chains and networks of association through which literary traces travel on their way to publication and dissemination; chains and networks that handle, translate, transform, and reproduce inscriptions, thereby constituting the global infrastructures in which science and society are coproduced in a dynamic and contingent way.

Consistent with the ANT emphasis on distributed networks of scientific production (often organized around "centers of calculation" that articulated standards and controlled expensive means of production), and also stimulated by trends in anthropology, it became popular in social studies of science to pursue multisited ethnographies, which "follow" global developments, sequences of practical transformation, and social networks related to a phenomenon of interest. So, for example, current controversies about global climate change involve a complex array of scientific researchers working in several specialties, as well as members of government and nongovernment organizations, industrial spokespersons and lobbyists, and various specialized and popular media. Although it may be desirable to seek in-depth understanding of the different—and competing—points of view of the constituent actors, to do so requires interviews and documentary research at multiple research sites. In studies of contemporary (or very recent) cases, such research tends to blend the aims and methods of social historical research with those of ethnography.

A distinctive, though disconcerting and unevenly adhered to, aspect of ANT is its radicalization of the theme of symmetry from SSK. Symmetry in SSK is the methodological principle of giving the same (social) form of explanation to (allegedly) true as well as false beliefs. ANT compounds SSK's methodological indifference to truth and falsity with an ontological indifference to the status of any given "entity" as "social" or "natural." So instead of framing technical innovation as having been "caused" in linear fashion by "social" antecedents or "conditioned" by social circumstances, ANT abandons the effort to discriminate types of cause and, instead, "explains" innovations by tracing out hybrid networks of association composed of human and nonhuman "actors" ("actants" in the jargon of semiotics). This monistic ontology can be viewed as an alternative (perhaps a mirror image) of the more prevalent scientistic monism in which social actions, cultural traditions, and individual consciousnesses are explained (speculatively) by reference to material and micromechanical principles. Instead of placing "nature" (represented, for example, by cognitive science and sociobiological models) at the center of an explanatory system, ANT deploys a vocabulary of actions, actors, and agencies, to encompass "natural" as well as "social" relations. ANT has had broad influence on STS research, but many researchers who borrow from ANT fail to animate the nonhumans and, instead, focus selectively on the machinations of the human actors held responsible for a successful or failed innovation.

CONSTRUCTIONISM

Starting with the publication of Latour and Woolgar's ethnography, social studies of science became identified with the theme of the social construction (or simply construction) of scientific facts, objective representations, and other research products. Social-historical case studies and ethnographies (some of which went into considerable length to describe specific experimental practices and scientific discourse) began to speak of the "construction" of phenomena such as physical subparticles and organic molecules. The term *social construction* was first used by Peter Berger and Thomas Luckmann (1966) in their sociological treatise, *The Social Construction of Reality,* and *constructionism* later became a buzzword for a confusing array of critical theories, disciplinary approaches, and empirical studies in many social science and humanities fields. The idea that established natural scientific "facts" were constructed went well beyond Berger and Luckmann's original effort to explain the distinctive way in which "social" phenomena develop and are organized. Berger and Luckmann took for granted that natural reality differs from constructed (social) reality; their aim was to address the question of how concerted social actions emerge and become reified. The idea that "natural" reality also is constructed seemed much more startling, and it touched off considerable interest and controversy. The term *construction* is remarkably protean, but when used in connection with a term such as *fact,* it seemed to imply that the phenomenon in question was somehow different, or even less real, than a fact. Moreover, the theme encouraged arguments and investigations that challenged the universality of scientific knowledge and scientific methods, thus raising the specter of relativism and begging questions about the grounds of constructionist claims (see Hacking 1999).

Consistent with social theoretical trends toward feminist epistemology, deconstructionism, postcolonialism, and so-called postmodernism, and encouraged by SSK and

ANT research and argumentation, studies proliferated in the 1980s and 1990s that politicized the idea that the very nature and contents of science were "socially constructed" (see Haraway 1991). The earlier argument that scientific representations (facts, laws, etc.) were not inevitable or determined by "nature" alone was compounded by explicit denunciations of particular scientific representations (of gendered bodies, racial characteristics, normal and pathological conditions, etc.) and of conceptions of scientific objectivity (as "male," exploitative of "female" nature, expressing cultural privilege and domination). Social construction—both the SSK version and the more politicized cultural studies version—became a target of a flurry of books, articles, conferences, and a massive number of Web postings in the 1990s. The *science wars* were epitomized by the publication in the cultural studies journal *Social Text* of a "hoax" article by physicist Alan Sokal, which argued for a conceptual affinity between poststructuralist literary theory and current theories in quantum gravity physics. Sokal's hoax was celebrated by many opponents of constructionism and related "relativist" trends in the humanities and social sciences, and for a short time it attracted unwanted media attention to the social studies of science field. During the science wars, debates about the "construction" of science were rarely argued with much care or philosophical sophistication, and by the end of the 1990s, the heated rhetoric began to be toned down (see Labinger and Collins 2001). The field of social studies of science continued to thrive, despite the highly charged polemics about it in the 1990s, and much (indeed most) research in the field consists in uncontroversial studies of (often controversial) developments in science, engineering, and medicine. Consistent with the tendency to question conceptual boundaries between science and nonscience and between science and technology, current research explores the complex way in which science has become embedded in, and inflected by, popular social movements, legal cases and regulations, economic institutions, and systems of governance.

— Michael Lynch

See also Actor Network Theory; Ethnomethodology; Feminism; Feminist Epistemology; Garfinkel, Harold; Latour, Bruno; Merton, Robert; Postcolonialism; Postmodernism; Social Constructionism; Symbolic Interaction

FURTHER READINGS AND REFERENCES

Hacking, Ian. 1999. *The Social Construction of What?* Cambridge, MA: Harvard University Press.

Haraway, Donna. 1991. *Simians, Cyborgs, and Women: The Reinvention of Nature.* New York: Routledge.

Jasanoff, Sheila, Gerald Markle, James Peterson, and Trevor Pinch, eds. 1994. *Handbook of Science, Technology & Society.* Beverly Hills, CA: Sage.

Labinger, Jay and Harry M. Collins, eds. 2001. *The One Culture? A Conversation about Science.* Chicago: University of Chicago Press.

Latour, Bruno. 1986. *Science in Action.* Cambridge, MA: Harvard University Press.

Lynch, Michael. 1993. *Scientific Practice & Ordinary Action: Ethnomethodology and Social Studies of Science.* New York: Cambridge University Press.

Mannheim, K. 1936. *Ideology & Utopia.* London: Routledge.

Sokal, Alan D. 1996. "Transgressing the Boundaries: Toward a Transformative Hermeneutics of Quantum Gravity." *Social Text* 46/47:217–52.

SOCIAL WORLDS

Combining notions of culture, social structure, and collective action, *social worlds* are collections of actors with shared understandings and shared institutionalized arrangements that convene, communicate, and coordinate behaviors on the basis of some shared interest. The conceptualization originally stems from work by Tamotsu Shibutani, Anselm Strauss, and Howard Becker, with roots traceable to John Dewey.

Social worlds is a symbolic interactionist concept that distinguishes social actors as they negotiate interactions with one another. Actors negotiate conflict when their perspectives are different, since they represent different social worlds within the same *arena*. When their perspectives are shared, the actors develop and maintain a social world as they communicate with one another and coordinate their behaviors in regard to the phenomenon of interest. Whether it is a baseball game, a soap opera, an advertising campaign, or a medical treatment program, a social world emerges as those with shared perspectives on the phenomenon interact with one another about that phenomenon. In contrast, as those with different perspectives experience conflict over it, different social worlds within a single arena can be identified.

As an interactionist concept, social worlds can be applied at micro-, meso-, or macro-levels of interaction. However, most research using the social worlds concept has been either at the micro-level, such as research on "serious leisure"—including studies on role-playing computer games, bridge playing, and bass tournament fishing—or at the meso-level in science and technology studies (STS). While the former body of research has tended to focus on how social worlds are developed and maintained, the latter STS research has tended to describe how conflicts between social worlds are negotiated at the organizational and institutional levels.

The social worlds analysis in STS is most attributable to Strauss, who thought of social worlds as the unit of interaction in society. The concept allows the analyst to account for any actor involved in a contested phenomenon. Actors can include those who are little more than observers—such as consumers, an electorate, or community members—who help form the context of the contest. As actors become increasingly involved in the contest and mobilize their resources, their social world becomes more important in determining the contest's outcome. In this way, social worlds analysis is able to account for the influence of social movements and a society's emergent awareness of social problems on how phenomena are defined and treated.

Indeed, researchers in STS using social worlds analysis see conflict as the generic social process they study; cooperation and collaboration typically have to be mandated and cannot be taken for granted. The model of scientists producing science and recruiting supporters of it on the basis of reason and evidence was first challenged by an interests model in the 1970s. That model has since been supplanted by a number of others, including that of social worlds analysis. Unlike other perspectives, social worlds analysis tends to include nonscientific actors in its models.

Social worlds analysis raises the issue of how social worlds are distinguished. To address this issue, Adele Clarke developed the concept of *boundary objects:* things about which there is disagreement among members of different social worlds interacting in the same arena. Debate over the meaning of those boundary objects can reveal the conflicting nature of the different perspectives delineating the social worlds. For example, religious texts, government documents, and organizational policies can all constitute boundary objects; they serve as referents for common identity and consensus at a general level but can also be interpreted specifically and quite differently at local levels. The emergent conflicts over the meaning of boundary objects can thus reveal the varied perspectives constituting the different social worlds of the parties involved. Using such concepts, social worlds analyses often uncover the conflict beneath what is supposedly harmonious. These analysts have, for example, found that seeming congruous collaborations brought together by funding opportunities for democratic and community-oriented appearances are often characterized by mistrust and misunderstandings.

While social worlds analysis focuses on the mesolevel in STS, examining strategies and tactics used in conflicts between worlds, social worlds theory, used more often at the microlevel of interaction, concentrates more on the causes and consequences of an individual's involvement in a given social world, the patterns of functioning of social worlds in general. Among the questions addressed in such research are how social worlds are developed and maintained, what kinds of systems of power and hierarchy exist within them, and how personal identity and commitment to social worlds emerge.

Personal involvement is critical to social worlds. Among the findings to have emerged from this research are categorizations of involvement. Unruh describes four types of social

world members: strangers, tourists, regulars, and insiders. Strangers participate little, tourists occasionally, and regulars routinely, but insiders perform the tasks critical to the creation and maintenance of the social world. Insiders tend to have the most time, experience, and resources invested in the social world and are the most committed to its existence.

An additional use of the phrase "social worlds" is a psychologically subjective use, referring to constellations of actors held in an individual's imagination. "Imaginary social worlds" has been a concept central to some dream research, which has found such worlds to reflect individuals' culture and social surroundings. For example, Caughey (1984) found that nearly 11 percent of his sample of subjects had media figures in their dreams. He also points out that all our social worlds (in the individually subjective sense) must be imaginary to some degree, in that we are all expected to know people in our society whom we have never met. Last, social worlds have also been used in reference to the social development of children. Scholars have described how in the course of developing identity, displaying mastery, and gaining a sense of agency, children's social worlds tend to coalesce around characteristics they hold in common, such as age, gender, ethnicity, religion, and skill.

— Loren Demerath

See also Social Studies of Science; Strauss, Anselm; Symbolic Interaction

FURTHER READINGS AND REFERENCES

Caughey, J. L. 1984. *Imaginary Social Worlds.* Lincoln: University of Nebraska Press.
Clarke, Adele. 1991. "Social Worlds/Arenas Theory as Organizational Theory." Pp. 119–58 in *Social Organization and Social Processes: Essays in Honor of Anselm Strauss,* edited by David R. Maines. New York: Aldine de Gruyter.
Fine, G. A. 1983. *Shared Fantasy: Role-playing Games as Social Worlds.* Chicago, IL: Chicago University Press.
Star, S. L. and J. R. Griesemer. 1989. "Institutional Ecology, 'Translations,' and Boundary Objects: Amateurs and Professionals in Berkeley's Museum of Vertebrate Zoology, 1907–1939." *Social Studies of Science* 19:387–420.
Strauss, A. 1993. *Continual Permutations of Action.* New York: Aldine de Gruyter.
Unruh, D. R. 1980. "The Nature of Social Worlds." *Pacific Sociological Review* 23:271–96.

SOCIALISM

Socialism is the theory and practice directed toward shared ownership and collective property holding of social goods and services. Socialism has been enormously influential in sociology and social theory, because it shares the root concern with the social. Socialism is often identified with Marxism, but this is misleading. Socialism precedes Marxism by 50 years. The word *socialism* came into use in the 1820s. It is also larger and more varied than Marxism, for its usages refer to a wider range of places than Western Europe, where classical Marxism emanates from Germany, and to a broader set of claims and practices than the idea of scientific socialism.

In its earliest usages, the term socialism was reactive, but less against the idea of capitalism than against the idea of individualism. Socialism in its earliest phases was understood less as an alternative social system to capitalism and more as an antidote to the corrosive effects of laissez-faire and its individualism. By the twentieth century, the success of the Russian Revolution saw the installation of orthodox Marxism as the most influential type of socialism, as movement and as theory. Alongside Marxism, there were always practical reforming socialisms of different kinds, best represented emblematically by Fabianism in England and progressivism in the United States. Wherever capitalism emerged, socialists responded, often in local and pragmatic terms rather than in those of Marxism as a social theory. Socialisms are thus characterised by diversity and often by internal conflict and contradiction. In some cases, as in England and Australia, socialisms could be characterised as the confluence of middle-class ideas and their intellectual bearers with working-class strategies and their bearers in union-based social involvements. There have always been middle-class and working-class socialisms, and there have always been socialist theories and movements that do not always meld. There have always been modernist and anti-modernist streams within socialism, some expressing the utopian need or desire to return to precapitalist days, others arguing to the contrary that it was necessary to have more factories but no capitalists. There have always been substantial tensions between socialist arguments for efficiency in material provision and other claims for democracy and freedom. There have often been tensions between the idea that small cooperative organization is beautiful, and the increasingly influential twentieth-century demand that the state should run society. Often these contradictions or tensions are evident within the same thinkers, as evidenced in the work of Marx or Gramsci or G. D. H. Cole, or else they emerge across the historical paths of development of their thought.

The earliest uses of the word socialism in the English language occur in England, in connection with the emerging cooperative movement. *Cooperation* is a leading example of a kind of practical, rather than theoretical, socialism. Cooperation spread across the nineteenth century in two forms, as cooperatives of consumption and production. In the first case, working people would pool their resources, buy consumer goods collectively, distribute them socially and share profits as dividends. Such practices were directed against the so-called truck system or closed economies of company towns, where wages might be paid in kind, where wage-labour relations were not formally free, and consequently where workers were even more oppressed than elsewhere, having no alternative but to buy or receive adulterated or substandard goods in lieu of wages. The history of producers' cooperatives is more complicated, as producers' co-ops are often formed in moments of crisis—for example, as an alternative to the closure of firms, where workers buy their capitalists out and introduce the strategy of self-management. Both types of cooperation are open to the Marxist criticism that they seek capitalism without capitalists. They have nevertheless been viewed as exemplary by radicals, as they demonstrate the redundancy of capitalist domination. The knowledge and skill of production belong to the workers, not their bosses. The secondary issue, that capitalists often know how to trade even if they do not know how to produce, is lost in the equation. Both types of cooperation facilitate some degree of worker self-management, a theme that resurfaces into the 1960s, where workers take over the functions of capital and seek to run firms democratically. Here, the telling criticism comes rather from the syndicalists, for whom it is bad enough that workers have to work in factories—now you expect us to run them, as well?

Cooperation remains a powerful subordinate theme in socialism, not least because it plays on the social theme in socialist argument: Shared problems warrant shared solutions. Even capital is a social product, not an individual entitlement. The dominant socialist argument in England and Australia, however, is *labourism,* a tradition that becomes more fully reconciled to the state rather than the local level as the appropriate realm of action. Labourism refers to the socialism of the organised labour movement, where the object is the defense of the interests of workers and their families, represented by unions and labour parties. Labourism is associated with the social security measures "from the cradle to the grave" of the welfare state, though welfare states were generally engineered by middle-class liberals like Keynes and Beveridge (in America, Franklin Roosevelt) rather than by labour's intellectuals. Labourism involves incremental reforms generated through "parliamentary socialism." In this, it coincides with, and is often driven on by, Fabianism. *Fabianism* is the British intellectual tradition of middle-class reform that is often associated with British sociology and social administration; by virtue of the Empire, it is also the dominant reforming ideology in Australia. Its primary educative institution was the London School of Economics, established by the Fabians in 1895. Originally an alternative life group, the Fabians became the first think tank; intellectual reformers prepared to work with any political leaders if the connection would further their ends. This was an approach identified with Sidney and Beatrice Webb (nee Potter), but pioneered by Beatrice Potter in her apprenticeship with Charles Booth's survey of poverty in London. Its middle-class roots ran in tandem with the Christian Settlement tradition of Toynbee Hall, where young men and women like Potter would do good work with the poor; the parallel American experience is that associated with Jane Addams and Hull House in Chicago. Systematic social research should lead to publicity and then to reform. In this way, health, housing, education, transport, and so on, could incrementally but systematically be reformed, and the end result of this process would be socialism. This is the kind of socialism that the Polish revolutionary Marxist Rosa Luxemburg would ridicule as socialism by the instalment plan. Not all English socialists were Fabians, however. The romantic revolutionary William Morris called for revolution, although like his Boston reformist opponent Edward Bellamy, was coy as to how precisely socialism might come about.

Other English ethical socialists such as Richard Tawney rejected revolution but insisted that while you could peel an onion layer by layer, you could less easily peel the tiger of capitalism claw by claw. Socialists like Tawney saw inequality, rather than wage-labour, as the major problem. Social service was the solution to aristocratic parasitism. Others like G. D. H. Cole, who travelled from guild socialism to Fabianism, insisted that the problem with most socialists was that, asked to identify the central issue, they would say poverty, whereas it was really slavery (here, wage-slavery) that was at fault. The *guild socialists,* as the name indicates, wanted really to go back, to the medieval guilds, or forward to some modified modern version of guildism, where the scale of social organization was small, and work depended on the transferred traditions of skill between masters and apprentices. Later British socialists like Harold Laski followed Cole in arguing that power needed best to be dispersed: pluralism, not medievalism, was the appropriate response. Other Catholic radicals such as Hilaire Belloc argued for what they called "distributism," the breaking up of modern monopoly and state concentration and the reconstruction of a rural smallholding society. Antimodernists like these saw cities as a major problem and eulogized the image of England's green and pleasant land as a lost social alternative. A different socialist or reforming current can be traced to the influence of John Stuart Mill. Later in life, Mill offered a theoretical dispensation to the socialist idea and to the fact of cooperation. The most influential liberal of the twentieth century, John Maynard Keynes, followed Mill's agnosticism regarding the perpetuity of capitalist civilization. At the very least, Keynes seemed to be arguing, capitalism itself needed civilizing (and this is, by default, the logic of most non-Marxist socialism—the advocacy of the mixed economy, where the state fills the gaps in market activity and underwrites

social development through the welfare state). This was a less muscular socialism than the Fabians had in mind, though by the mid-twentieth century, there is some merging of horizons as Fabianism becomes the defacto theory of labourism and aristocratic liberals such as Keynes and Beveridge supply the practical blueprint for a civilized capitalism.

While the English tradition developed cooperation, the French tradition pioneered utopian socialism. Comte is usually credited with coining the idea and one version of the project of sociology; Saint-Simon and then Fourier developed ideas and schemes for utopia, ranging from urban meritocracy to the permanent rural retreat. As elsewhere, socialism in France was to rest on this central conflict between antimodernism and modernization. The greatest socialist modernizer of reform was Durkheim. Through the nineteenth century, antimodern arguments were to dominate. Georges Sorel developed the argument for the myth of revolution. Paul Lafargue, Marx's son-in-law, sought to introduce Marxism into the Latin socialist tradition, but his major contribution was an antimodern tract criticizing not only capitalism but civilization in general. It was called *The Right to Be Lazy.* With the Russian Revolution and the Bolshevization of the Socialist parties, communism came to dominate the Left in a way without parallel, save, in Britain, where labourism ruled. Communism and the French Communist Party became something of a compulsory haven or benchmark for French intellectuals, from Jean-Paul Sartre to Maurice Merleau-Ponty. The most interesting of French Marxists remained those who developed out of surrealism and existentialism into urban studies, like Lefebvre, or maverick postwar Trotskyists such as Castoriadis and Lefort, who developed major alternative social and political theories. Into the 1960s, the new wave of structuralism saw Louis Althusser displace this humanist legacy. Although Marxism came to exert a greater influence here than in any other parallel experience except Italy, it remains the case that Durkheim's influence persists across the whole period from 1890.

Durkheim argued in a series of texts from *The Division of Labor in Society* to his lectures on socialism and Saint-Simon that communism was passé. Communism was a philosophy of simplicity, austerity, and stasis, reaching back to Plato. Socialism, in comparison, was modern and modernizing, especially if it was harnessed to the new science of sociology. Contrary to the romantics, the division of labour would be used to civilize society and to cultivate interdependence, not least through the encouragement of professional associations that might fulfill some of the old integrative functions of the guilds. The parallels with English guild socialism are striking, except that Durkheim was no medievalist. Like Tawney, he believed that individuals still should serve society and each other, and he viewed unions or work-based associations as the means that might mediate between society or state and individual. Contrary to Marx, labour here is viewed not as alienated but as potentially integrative; anomic social forms may occur, but as in the Fabians, social problems are viewed as open to analysis, research, and publicity, thence to legislative resolution. Unlike Lafargue and the romantic tradition, Durkheim offers a model of society as the working institution, where identity and purpose and social cohesion are all work generated. Work is the great social integrator. Socialism in the United States follows a broadly similar pattern, where the romanticism or communalism of the nineteenth century gives way to progressivism by the twentieth. Utopian or communal socialism thrived in the earlier parts of the nineteenth century in America, perhaps more than in any other case. It was in America, in the New World, that enthusiasts often set out to apply communal plans developed elsewhere, on the continent by the French, in Britain by Robert Owen or John Ruskin (Owen's model factories in Scotland remained exemplary of nonagrarian social experiments).

By the end of the nineteenth century, the closing of the American frontier and the emergence of crisis in the cities saw a hesitant shift to a modernizing socialism, best exemplified in the extraordinarily influential work of Edward Bellamy, *Looking Backward.* Bellamy clubs arose to propagate the cause of an industrial army-based utopia spread across the United States and as far afield as Australia. Bellamy's social model resembled Durkheim's, at least cosmetically, for both saw the construction of new forms of industrial solidarity as the challenge. By some of Durkheim's criteria, however, Bellamy's utopia remained uncomfortably close to communism in its premodern predilections. Bellamy aspired to complete equality, whereas Durkheim's image of society was closer to that of civilizing rather than negating capitalism. Bellamy, for his part, largely eschewed the language of socialism because of fear of red ragging; earlier, he called his utopia nationalist, later referring to it as a kind of public capitalism. The impulse of the Bellamy clubs was dispersed into the twentieth century. It informed the progressivist case that found its way into Roosevelt's New Deal, alongside the Keynes-Beveridge welfare state in the United Kingdom. Bellamy's socialism was a transitional phenomenon, responding to the Gilded Age, seeking to bridge country and city through the small-town tradition so central to American political culture. As the cities came to dominate American social and political life, so did socialist thinking become more urban and modernizing. In Detroit and Chicago and across the Midwest, a different transitional movement flourished briefly before the First World War. Generically called *syndicalism,* and with strong French and Italian precedents connected to anarchism, its leading movement was the Wobblies, or Industrial Workers of the World. Here unions or syndicates, rather than guilds, were the model of the new society. The transitional nature of the movement is indicated in the fact that many of the members were rural workers, itinerants, residuals of the old way of life rather than bearers of the new world of Fordism.

The success of the Russian Revolution again saw the emergence of American communism and Trotskyism in response. But the peculiar character of American socialism in the cities—in New York, Chicago, and Milwaukee—was its Germanic influence. Thanks to its immigrants from Central Europe, the Marxism of the German Social Democrats, which in turn influenced Poles, Russians, and Ukrainians, became the substance of American socialism over the turn of the century. As participant critics such as Daniel Bell then argued, Marxism discredited itself in America by failing to Americanize. This was the socialism of the ghetto, of the old country rather than the New World. American Marxism, on this account, was not of this world. As the subsequent paths of American Marxists such as Max Eastman and Sidney Hook show, Marxism seeks to renegotiate local tradition through American pragmatism, right through to the contemporary work of Richard Rorty, while others, such as Cornell West, were to claim not a new Marxism but a new progressivism as the American radical politics for the twenty-first century. Having been outflanked by the Bolsheviks and then crushed by the Nazis, the German Social Democrats led the way into the postwar period with a managerial version of civilized capitalism. The Keynesian consensus ruled, until its defeat into the 1970s and 1980s by neoliberalism. The social infrastructure facilitated by state intervention and cooperation remain a subordinate note in most industrial countries, with the qualified exception of the United States.

— Peter Beilharz

See also Capitalism; Marxism

FURTHER READINGS AND REFERENCES

Beilharz, P. 1992. *Labour's Utopias: Bolshevism, Fabianism, Social Democracy.* London: Routledge.
———. 1994. *Postmodern Socialism.* Melbourne, Australia: Melbourne University Press.
Cole, G. D. H. 1953–1960. *A History of Socialist Thought.* 5 vols., 7 parts. London: Macmillan.
Lipset, S. M. and G. Marks. 1999. *It Didn't Happen Here: Why Socialism Failed in the United States.* New York: Norton.
Sassoon, D. 1996. *One Hundred Years of Socialism.* London: Tauris.
Wright, A. 1986. *Socialisms.* New York: Oxford University Press.

SOCIALIZATION

Socialization is a process by which the larger societal and cultural norms and values are transmitted to the individual. Successful socialization also involves an internalization of the larger norms and values into the consciousness of the individual actor. This process usually takes place when adults teach small children "right" from "wrong." Children learn what is expected of them from the social system as well as what to expect from the social system and are simultaneously bound to the system by those expectations. Childhood socialization equips the individual with only a very general sense of how to respond to social situations, and a continued lifelong socialization process is necessary to prepare individuals with how to deal with more specific situations.

The first sociologist to truly grapple with the topic of socialization was Émile Durkheim. Durkheim held the view that human beings are riddled with innate human passions that at every moment threaten to overtake them and society at large. The only way to restrain these passions is through a collective morality, or a collective conscience. These ideas led Durkheim to an interest in how social morals are internalized through education and socialization.

Durkheim defined education and socialization as the processes through which a given group or society transmits its ways to its members. It is a means by which the actor is able to learn the necessary physical, mental, and most important to Durkheim, moral tools he or she will need to function properly in a given group or society.

Durkheim believed that moral education and socialization more generally had three important goals. First, their goal is to teach the individuals the necessary discipline they will need in order to control their passions. It is only by limiting these passions that individuals can ever achieve a sense of happiness and good moral health. Second, these processes provide individuals with a sense of autonomy. This is not a traditional sense of autonomy, however, because it does not imply free will but, rather, an understanding of why the larger social norms and values should be desired of one's own free will. Third, socialization and moral education seek to instill within the individual a strong sense of devotion to the larger society and its moral system.

Another sociologist who dealt heavily with the topic of socialization was the structural-functionalist, Talcott Parsons. Parsons believed that socialization was a means whereby the normative order was able to control the behavioral order. He assumed that actors were passive recipients of the norms, values, and morals taught to them by means of socialization and that they would largely successfully internalize these standards of the larger social system. This would ensure that even when actors were pursuing what they believed to be their own best interests, they would also, in fact, be pursuing the best interests of the social system as a whole.

There are instances, however, when individuals seem to be not in line with what is expected of them by the larger social system. These "deviants" can pose a threat to the social order, and the use of what Parsons called "social controls" might be in order. He believed that these social controls should be used sparingly, however, because a flexible social system is stronger than a rigid one. In this way, socialization in combination with social control helps keep the social system in balance.

In contrast to the view of socialization taken by Parsons, many ethnomethodologists argue that socialization is not a one-way process of internalization. For example, Speier (1970) argues that "socialization is the acquisition of interactional competencies" (p. 189). Thus, many ethnomethodologists support the view of socialization as a two-way process involving the interaction of both instructor and recipient. Robert W. Mackay has used the example of childhood socialization as an exemplar of the differences between normative sociology and ethnomethodology. He argues that whereas normative sociology sees socialization as a series of stages whereby "incomplete" children are taught by "complete" adults, ethnomethodologists see socialization as an interactive process in which children are active participants in the construction of the social order.

— Michael Ryan

See also Durkheim, Émile; Ethnomethodology; Parsons, Talcott

REFERENCES

Durkheim, Émile. 1973. *Moral Education: A Study in the Theory and Application of the Sociology of Education.* New York: Free Press.

Mackay, Robert W. 1974. "Words, Utterances and Activities." Pp. 197–215 in *Ethnomethodology: Selected Readings*, edited by R. Turner. Harmondsworth, UK: Penguin.

Parsons, Talcott. 1951. *The Social System.* Glencoe, IL: Free Press.

Speier, Matthew. 1970. "The Everyday World of the Child." Pp. 188–217 in *Understanding Everyday Life*, edited by J. Douglas. Chicago: Aldine.

SOCIOLOGIES OF EVERYDAY LIFE

Sociologies of everyday life are qualitative sociologies that examine small-group interaction and place a primacy on understanding and reporting the lives of the members of everyday life as they see it or as close as possible to it. They all share a common concern with the members' perspective about society and a qualitative methodological approach to the study of human interaction. Sociologies of everyday life encompass a variety of sociologies, most of which never refer to or associate themselves with the name *sociologies of everyday life*. The term itself comes from a book by Jack Douglas and some of his graduate students (Douglas et al. 1980).

The origins of the sociologies of everyday life are diverse. Douglas attributes its origin to the nineteenth-century Scottish moral philosophers. Perhaps more direct is the derivation from the two philosophical currents known as pragmatism and phenomenology. Pragmatism, especially in the works of George H. Mead, Charles Horton Cooley, and John Dewey, is the recognized foundation of some sociologies of everyday life. The stress on the study of small-group interaction and the symbols used by the members of society in communication are paramount features of the sociologies of everyday life, as informed by the pragmatist philosophies.

Phenomenology, similarly, focuses on the study of society based on the meaning attributed to it by its members. Stemming loosely from the philosophy of Edmund Husserl with its centrality on understanding the phenomena of the world, phenomenology was applied to sociology primarily by Alfred Schütz (1962), whose work shares fundamental social principles with the pragmatists, especially Mead, and informs some of the sociologies of everyday life. Schütz and Mead both focused on the socialization process (common stock of knowledge) of the members of society, their ability to interact (reciprocity of perspective), and the relevance of understanding the meaning they attributed to everyday life.

Other phenomenologists stressed the incarnate nature of humans, collapsing the dichotomy of self as established by René Descartes. Martin Heidegger refers to it as *dasein* (being-in-the-world). Maurice Merleau-Ponty also places emphasis on being in the world (*étre-au-monde*). Phenenologists (along with others) reject human attributes that can be grasped outside of the realm of everyday life. We (*qua* humans) are irremediably embedded in this world through the carnality of our bodies—we are our bodies. Thus, the sociologies of everyday life embed the members of society in the world of everyday life while focusing on the negotiated meaning of their interactions.

The sociologies generally considered to be "of everyday life" are the following: *symbolic interactionism, dramaturgy, labeling theory, ethnomethodology, existential sociology,* and *postmodern sociology.* They all share some common ideas, which has led to their grouping together, yet at times, they have marked differences.

The first concept shared by the sociologies of everyday life is the concern with maintaining the integrity of phenomena. Researchers must spend time with the members of the group studied to gain an understanding of how the group views and describes the social world, as well as the members' daily concerns. Researchers must not superimpose any theoretical preconception on the study but must, instead, derive their notions as they stem from the accounts of the members themselves. Thus, all the sociologies of everyday life would rely on the methods of participant observation, in-depth-interviewing, or both and on inductive reasoning to reach a better understanding and minimize distortions of the phenomena studied.

The second concept shared is with understanding the symbols used by the members of society in interacting with each other. Since symbols can vary and mean different things for different cultures or subcultures the researchers must become familiar with the group studied and their use and interpretation of symbols. The emphasis would be different for different sociologies. For instance, symbolic interactionism and labeling theory would focus on the symbols used in interaction, dramaturgy would look at the symbols used by the actors in their presentation of self, ethnomethodology would ponder why some symbols are used rather than others, existential sociology would emphasize the emotional component of symbols, and postmodern sociology would observe the interplay between everyday life and media-presented symbols.

The third concept shared concerns the methods used by the members of society to create and sustain their reality (Gubrium and Holstein 1997). The focus here is not so much on what the events are but on how the members of everyday life create and describe their lives. The sociologies of everyday life and especially ethnomethodology would reflexively study the accounts of the members of society—what stories do they tell about themselves and how do they tell them to gain certain effects?

There are marked differences among various sociologies of everyday life. Symbolic interactionism, dramaturgy, labeling theory, and ethnomethodology continue in the tradition of mainstream sociology and wish to conduct research in an objective and neutral fashion. Existential sociology and postmodern sociology reject the assumption of objectivity and instead advocate partisanship and cooperation with the group under study (often an oppressed or disadvantaged group).

Another difference is in the emphasis of rational behavior versus the role played by feeling and emotions in decision making by the members of society. Existential sociology and postmodern sociology emphasize feelings rather than rational elements in trying to understand what makes people act in certain ways.

A final difference among the various sociologies of everyday life is in the reporting procedures used to describe research studies. Most of the sociologies of everyday life continue to use the sparse language of science and traditional methods of reporting, while existential sociology (Kotarba and Johnson 2002) and postmodern sociology (Fontana 2003) experiment with new modes of reporting. Thus, rather than taking the form of conventional journal articles, postmodern modes use the short-story format or make use of performances or even poetry.

— Andrea Fontana

See also Blumer, Herbert; Cooley, Charles Horton; Dramaturgy; Ethnomethodology; Goffman, Erving; Labeling Theory;

Mead, George Herbert; Postmodernism; Sartre, Jean-Paul; Symbolic Interaction

FURTHER READINGS AND REFERENCES

Blumer, H. 1969. *Symbolic Interactionism.* Berkeley: University of California Press.

Dickens, D. R. and A. Fontana. 1994. *Postmodernism and Social Inquiry.* New York: Guilford.

Douglas, J., P. A. Adler, P. Adler, A. Fontana, C. R. Freeman, and J. Kotarba. 1980. *Introduction to the Sociologies of Everyday Life.* Boston: Allyn & Bacon.

Fontana, A. Forthcoming. "The Postmodern Turn in Interactionism." *Studies in Symbolic Interaction.*

Goffman, E. 1959. *The Presentation of Self in Everyday Life.* New York: Anchor.

Gubrium, J. and J. Holstein. 1997. *The New Language of Qualitative Methods.* New York: Oxford University Press.

Kotarba, J. and J. Johnson, eds. 2002. *Postmodern Existential Sociology.* Walnut Creek, CA: Alta Mira.

Schütz, A. 1962. *Collected Papers I: The Problem of Social Reality.* The Hague, Netherlands: Martinus Nijhoff.

SOMBART, WERNER

Werner Sombart (1863–1941) was a German economist and founding figure of sociology. While he was very well known during his lifetime, he was largely forgotten after his death. Outside Germany, Sombart is perhaps best known for his essay *Why Is There No Socialism in the United States?* first published in 1906 (Sombart 1976). To this day, political scientists, historians, and labor specialists refer to the "Sombart question" when addressing the exceptional character of the American labor movement.

Sombart came from a liberal bourgeois family. He obtained his doctoral degree under Gustav Schmoller in Berlin in 1888 with a dissertation on the Roman Campagna. At the recommendation of Schmoller, but against the opposition of the faculty, two years later he was appointed associate professor at Breslau. It was not until the end of the First World War that Sombart became full professor in Berlin, where he succeeded one of his teachers, Adolph Wagner. Before that, Max Weber tried twice, unsuccessfully, to get him appointed as his successor, first in Freiburg, later in Heidelberg. In 1904, Sombart became one of the editors of the *Archiv für Sozialwissenschaft und Sozialpolitik* (Archive of Social Science and Social Policy) along with Max Weber and Edgar Jaffé. The *Archiv* was the most influential German social science journal of the time until its closure in 1933.

His main work is *Moderner Kapitalismus* (Modern Capitalism), first published in two volumes in 1902 and reissued in a much-enlarged second edition from 1916 to 1928, albeit never translated entirely into English. While Sombart was not the first to use the term *capitalism* (Louis Blanc is considered to have coined the term in the 1850s), the title of this work puts the term capitalism in a prominent position. Marx had never used the noun but spoke of the "capitalist mode of production." The book offers in the eyes of many contemporary social scientists a classical analysis of the origins and the nature of capitalism. He also develops a kind of methodological and epistemological manifesto for a modern social science. In contrast to the "historical school" in economics from which he started (being a pupil of Gustav Schmoller), he started to aim for explanations based on ultimate causes. For Sombart, historical appearances build up to a social system that can be grasped by theory (and here he mentions explicitly the theory of Marx). However, he still considers himself a member of the historical school. Sombart did not follow the intellectual agenda of Marx's base-superstructure theorem in which productive forces are the most basic layer in society, on which relations of production are erected and are, in turn, overlaid with an ideological sphere. In Marx, the primacy is with the former two, in Sombart, with the latter—he gives definite priority to the spiritual sphere of society. Sombart thus was not a Marxist in the strict sense, but he was sympathetic to the socialist cause (Lenger 1994).

Among the recurring themes in Sombart's works are race, Judaism, Germanness, capitalism and technology, Marxism, fashion, consumption and leisure, and methodological issues. The first three are somewhat odd for a sociologist; nevertheless, they were of central importance to him. He also advocated a new program for sociology, which he called "Noo-sociology" and which attracted hardly any followers. A noological sociology is based on the premise that all society is spirit (*Geist*) and all spirit, society. Its fields of investigation are forms and cycles of civilization. Its methods, therefore, cannot be those of the natural sciences. It is committed to emergent social phenomena that must be understood and placed in restrictive sociohistorical and institutional contexts—for example, religion, the state, the church, or the economy. It is worth noting that Sombart calls the scientific approach "Western" and the noological approach, "German" sociology.

If one were to summarize Sombart's intellectual development, one could say that he radically changed his mind about two crucial issues: Marxism and Germany. He started out as an ardent fighter for the cause of the socialist movement. This earned him the recognition of Friedrich Engels. In this period, Sombart did not try to reject or transcend Marx. Instead, he attempted to complete the Marxian perspective by adding a sociopsychological and sociocultural dimension to the analysis of the genesis and the nature of capitalism.

After the turn of the century, Sombart became a fervent anti-Marxist, with some anti-Semitic overtones. His relation to Germany was marked by an equal shift of valuation: In his early writings, Sombart had many reservations about his country, but around 1910, he turned into a strident nationalist. His intellectual development can also be followed through different editions of the same book, *Sozialismus und Soziale Bewegung* (Socialism and the Social Movement), which first appeared in 1896. While the first nine editions were sympathetic to the socialist movement, the 10th edition (1924) revealed Sombart as a critic of Marx and socialism. This edition had the title *Proletarischer Sozialismus (Marxismus)*. In 1934, when the final edition of the book appeared, it was called *Deutscher Sozialismus* and supported the Nazi rulers. Princeton University Press published an English translation of this book under the title *A New Social Philosophy* in 1937.

Sombart and Weber both attempted to explain the origins of capitalism by invoking the importance of religion. While Weber saw the Protestant ethic as root cause for the emergence of capitalism, Sombart awarded this role to the Jewish religion. While Weber and Sombart largely agreed about the role of the Jews in economic history as being traders and moneylenders, they disagreed about the Jews' role in the development of capitalism and about the role of race. While Sombart was beset with issues of race, Weber was not. Most important, Sombart mixed these contested issues with ethical and moral aspects. His analysis of causes of capitalism is coupled to a discussion about an attribution of blame. Since he abhorred capitalism and free markets, he did not stop at analytical statements about the sociohistorical role of the Jews (no matter how contested such observations may be) but linked these observations to moral judgments. Likewise, his discussion about the course of civilization is interspersed with arguments about "superior" and "inferior," "mixed" and "pure" races. He states, for example, "One can be sure that the Jews have had a significant share in the genesis of capitalism. This follows from, among other things, their racial disposition" (Sombart 1902:390). Sombart emphasizes the dominance of willpower, egotism, and abstract mentality in the "Jewish race."

In another context, he identified two "worldviews" contesting each other during World War I. On one side were the nations of shopkeepers and merchants; on the other was the land of heroes, philosophers, and soldiers, prepared to sacrifice themselves for higher ideals. For Sombart, England represented the former set of worldviews, and Germany, the latter. In this instance too, he changed his views in the course of his life quite fundamentally.

In Sombart's book *Die deutsche Volkswirtschaft im Neunzehnten Jahrhundert* (The German Economy in the 19th Century, published in 1903), he points to a manifest link between the national character of the German people and the spirit of capitalism. While retaining his hostility toward capitalism, he would, however, slowly develop a "strategy" of reconciliation with "*Deutschtum*." (Germanness). The distinction between two types of capitalists—entrepreneurs and traders—became crucial. While the entrepreneur is quick in comprehension, true in judgment, and clear in thought, with a sure eye for the needful and a good memory, the trader's "intellectual and emotional world is directed to the money value of conditions and dealings, who therefore calculates everything in terms of money" (Sombart [1913]2001:39–40). Sombart was to identify this role as occupied by the "Jewish species." The peoples less inclined to capitalism were the Celts and a few of the Germanic tribes, the Goths in particular. Wherever the Celtic element predominated, capitalism made little headway.

Sombart persistently dwelled on the topic of racial categories. It cannot come as a surprise therefore that he welcomed the Nazis' rise to power, whose chief ideologue he imagined himself to be—a feeling that was not reciprocated. And he was quite naive at that, given that even in his most nazified book (Sombart 1937), he time and again mentions Marx as an intellectual authority.

It should also be noted that Sombart is held in high esteem by some Jewish scholars, who are followers of the capitalist economic order and therefore applaud his attempt to establish their beneficial role in the emergence and development of capitalism. For example, Werner Mosse (1987) concludes his book with a quote from Sombart that emphasizes the beneficial consequences of the Jews for the German economic development.

Sombart's work on culture, consumption, and luxury is still regarded as "classic." This field had been left almost exclusively to economists who treat consumer behavior in an ahistorical framework of assumptions and consider it to be basically the same for all peoples at all times.

Sombart suggested a close connection between the insatiable patterns of consumption in early modern court life and the growth of capitalist production. The demand for luxury was not so much connected to a pursuit of comfort as to social ambition and mobility, a point also made by Norbert Elias who argued that the highly complex and expensive culture of consumption within the court was not only there to distract a bored aristocracy but was a central means by which Louis XIV controlled the French aristocracy. Aristocrats became especially passionate about assembling rare objects from around the world. The display of these objects, plants, and animals prefigures Veblen's conspicuous consumption. Where Veblen would stress the point that this was wasteful consumption, Sombart sees it as a way to mark ranks where social stratification was unclear. Others have pointed out that a materialist consumer culture oriented around products and goods from all over the world was the "prerequisite for the technological revolution of industrial capitalism" (Appadurai 1986:37) not its result.

— Reiner Grundmann and Nico Stehr

See also Capitalism; Consumer Culture; Elias, Norbert; Historicism; Marx, Karl; Political Economy; Veblen, Thorstein; Verstehen

FURTHER READINGS AND REFERENCES

Appadurai, Arjun, 1986. *The Social Life of Things: Commodities in Cultural Perspective.* Cambridge, UK: Cambridge University Press.

Grundmann, Reiner and Nico Stehr. 2001. "Introduction." Pp. ixl–xii in *Werner Sombart: Economic Life in the Modern Age,* edited by N. Stehr and R. Grundmann. New Brunswick, NJ, & Oxford, UK: Transaction.

Lenger, Friedrich. 1994. *Werner Sombart 1963–1941: Eine Biographie.* München, Germany: C. H. Beck.

Mosse, Werner. 1987. *Jews in the German Economy.* Oxford, UK: Clarendon.

Sombart, Werner. 1902. *Der Moderne Kapitalismus.* Leipzig, Germany: Duncker & Humblot.

———. 1937 *A New Social Philosophy.* Translated and edited by Karl F. Geisser. [Translation of *Deutscher Sozialismus*]. Oxford, UK: Oxford University Press.

———. 1976. *Why Is There No Socialism in the United States?* London: Macmillan.

———. [1913] 2001. "The Origins of the Capitalist Spirit," Pp. 33–54 in *Werner Sombart: Economic Life in the Modern Age,* edited by N. Stehr and R. Grundmann. New Brunswick, NJ, & Oxford, UK: Transaction.

SOROKIN, PITIRIM

Pitirim Alexandrovich Sorokin was born in Russia in 1889. During the Russian revolution, he was a member of the Social Revolutionary Party. He was active in opposing both the Czarist government and the Communists, being arrested and imprisoned by both regimes. Sorokin served in the cabinet of the post-Czarist Kerensky government in 1917. After his second arrest by the Communists, his death sentence was revoked, and he was allowed to return to graduate work at the University of St. Petersburg, where he was awarded his doctorate in 1922. Later that year, he was exiled from Russia by the Communists. After coming to the United States, he taught at the University of Minnesota. In 1930, he became the first chairperson of the Sociology Department at Harvard University. Sorokin later founded the Harvard Research Center in Creative Altruism. He was elected president of the American Sociological Association in 1965. Sorokin died in 1968.

Sorokin is the most published and translated writer in the history of sociology. During his career, he wrote 37 books and more than 400 articles. His contributions to sociology are original, fundamental, and comprehensive. Sorokin's most important writings are in the areas of cultural structure and change, social differentiation, social stratification, social conflict, and the causes and effects of altruistic love. He also made major contributions in the classification and critical analysis of theories, epistemology, methodology, the analysis of social space and time, the sociology of revolution, and the sociology of crisis.

His work taken as a whole constitutes a comprehensive general system of sociology that integrates the scientific, reformist, and practical traditions of the discipline. Following this cosmopolitan character of his system of thought, Sorokin's writings range from complex and insightful scientific formulations to writings intended to inform the general public on problematic conditions and provide suggestions for their resolution.

Sorokin was the first theorist to explicitly identify culture, society, and personality as the basic frame of reference of sociology. This perspective on the subject matter of sociology pervades his work.

CULTURAL STRUCTURE AND DYNAMICS

Cultural Integration

Sorokin is best known for his theory of cultural organization and change. His work in historical sociology is a major effort in applying both quantitative and qualitative methods to cultural and social trends over a 2,500-year period, primarily in Western civilization. Collaborating scholars who were not aware of the overall purpose classified data representing a time period typically ranging from 600 B.C. to 1925 A.D. This data is tabulated by varying intervals of time ranging from 20 to 100 years. In some instances, correlation methods are also employed. Sorokin's culture types and his analysis of cultural and social change are thus based on a massive compilation and analysis of empirical data.

The meaningful aspect of culture is considered foundational. Behavior and material products objectify these ideological aspects of culture. Cultures vary in their degree of integration. A culture is integrated to the degree that its components are logically consistent, interrelated, and interdependent. The basis of integration is the predominant cultural definitions pertaining to four major premises: the nature of reality, the needs and ends to be satisfied, the extent of their satisfaction, and the methods of their satisfaction.

On the basis of contrasting definitions of these universal questions, two polar types of integrated culture can be considered—the ideational and the sensate. All existing cultures fall somewhere on the continuum between these two ideal types. In an ideational culture, the nature of reality is regarded as supersensory and superrational, organized in reference to some idea of God or the Ultimate Reality. The needs and ends are thus primarily spiritual and otherworldly, their satisfaction is maximum, and the primary method of satisfaction is modification of the self to conform to transcendental standards. In a sensate culture, the nature of reality is viewed as limited to that which is physical and material. Needs and ends are thus of this nature, and their satisfaction is to the maximum. The primary method of satisfaction is engagement with the external environment to take from it or change it in some manner to satisfy needs. A third type of integrated culture, the idealistic, later called the integral, represents a harmonious synthesis of these two polar types, with the ideational content of basic premises being foundational.

Variations in the content of these basic premises are reflected in differences in what Sorokin termed the compartments of culture. For example, in an ideational culture the system of truth and knowledge is based primarily on the truth of faith, which is considered as the revealed truth of God. In direct contrast, in a sensate culture, induction and empiricism are the sources of truth. In an idealistic culture, reason is used to combine these contrasting ontologies and epistemologies into a harmonious system of truth and knowledge. In ethics, ideational ethics consists of absolute principles derived from transcendental sources and intended to guide the lives of individuals according to ultimate values. In contrast, sensate ethics consists of relative and changeable rules made by humans to maximize human happiness. Idealistic ethics combines these contrasting types into an integrated system in which the absolute principles of ideationalism are fundamental. Basic differences between ideational and sensate cultures can be observed in other compartments of culture such as philosophy, law, and art of various types.

Cultural Change

Change is immanent, in the sense that its source is the properties and processes of the system itself. Sociocultural systems change because they are composed of individuals, ideas, and material vehicles, all of which are constantly changing. However, the range of this change is limited. This is because almost all basic sociocultural systems and processes can assume a relatively small number of distinctive forms. The principles of immanence and of limits explain the recurrence of sociocultural phenomena over time.

These principles of change are the basis of understanding the recurrence of ideational, idealistic, and sensate culture forms in Western civilization. Further understanding of this change in culture types rests on the idea that the true reality contains empirical-sensory, rational-mindful,

and superrational-supersensory aspects. When a culture approaches too close to the polar type of either ideational or sensate, it moves further from the nature of true reality and thus becomes increasingly false. Since culture provides the framework through which individuals and groups adapt to reality, if the false parts of culture are too great, both individual and social life are impoverished. Basic human needs are not met and social life becomes unnecessarily limited and problematic. Because of these conditions, increasing numbers of individuals question established definitions of reality and search for alternatives. A fundamentally opposite culture begins to emerge and eventually becomes dominant. This explains the fluctuation from ideational to sensate culture types. The explanation of change is somewhat different for the idealistic culture that combines sensate and ideational in a harmonious system. This type of culture is considered to be relatively short-lived because of the difficulty of maintaining a balance of components that are essentially opposite. Historically, it has been transitional between ideational and sensate.

SOCIAL STRUCTURE AND DYNAMICS

Sorokin's writings contain conceptual and theoretical formulations in a number of major areas in the study of social structure and dynamics. His major ideas can be organized by three general topics: social differentiation, social stratification, and social conflict.

The analysis of society is based on the assumption that meaningful interaction is the most basic sociocultural phenomenon. It has three components: two or more thinking and acting individuals; meanings, values, and norms that are exchanged and realized in interaction; and behavior and material vehicles that objectify and socialize the ideas involved in interaction. A second basic assumption is that there are three inseparable components of all sociocultural phenomena: culture, society, and personality.

Social Differentiation

There are three universal types of social relationship: familistic, contractual, and compulsory. Almost all social groups are a combination of these pure types. In the familistic type, solidarity is high, interaction is extensive, typically of long duration, and includes the important values of the interacting parties. Contractual relationships are typically limited in extensity and duration and are based on the interacting parties' mutually fulfilling obligations and gaining from the relationship. Compulsory social relations are antagonistic. In these relations, one party imposes conduct on the other party contrary to the second party's desires or benefit.

Social relationships in major institutional groupings from the eighth to the twentieth century in Europe are analyzed with this typology. Ideational culture tends toward familistic social relationships, while sensate is conducive to both contractual and compulsory relationships.

Groups are classified according to the number and nature of the meanings, norms, and values in terms of which the group is organized. Unibonded groups are organized around one set of meanings, norms, and values, multibonded groups around two or more. Some unibonded groups are organized around the meanings associated with a biosocial characteristic, such as sex or race, others around sociocultural characteristics such as occupational or political groupings. Important multibonded groups include the family, social class, and nation.

Social Stratification

The essence of social stratification is the unequal distribution of power, influence, privileges, privations, and responsibilities. Stratification involves the hierarchial arrangement of groups into upper and lower strata. Stratification is pervasive and universal, although its forms can vary considerably. All organized groups are stratified internally and in relation to other groups. In some instances, strata are formally organized and have the characteristics of organized groups. In other instances, such as that of social class, the organization is less developed.

As with groups, stratification can be unibonded or multibonded. Race, sex, and age are examples of unibonded stratification. In multibonded stratification, strata are superior or inferior on a number of criteria. Castes, orders, and classes are examples of this type of stratification. When multibonded stratification involves disparate positions, such as low state position but high wealth or vice versa, it can create pressures for change.

Social mobility is universal, although it may vary considerably in degree. It involves the movement of individuals or groups upward or downward in a system of stratification. Mobility takes place through the channels of circulation provided by major social institutions, such as the political, military, or educational. Within these channels, mobility is regulated by testing mechanisms, the criteria that determine what types of individuals may move up or be prevented from doing so.

Mobility into elite groups becomes a crucial problem in the modern era because of the concentration of power. Considerable historical data indicates frequent dualism in morality and intelligence of rulers and other elites. In general, these groups are found to be more criminal than the general population, although this criminality decreases when the power of elite groups is limited.

Social Conflict

Sorokin's theory of war and of internal disturbances is based on extensive historical research. For example, various quantitative indicators are used to study 967 wars in Greece, Rome, and Europe from 500 B.C. to 1925 A.D. A total of 1,622 internal disturbances are ranked according to magnitude by a multiple-factor index. Fluctuations over time in both types of conflict are studied.

Culture is an important factor in both kinds of conflict. The basis of international peace is compatibility of the basic values of nations that are in contact rather than similarity or difference of values in itself. The occurrence of war is greatest in periods when basic values are in transformation. Internal peace is also based on the compatibility of values of the various factions within a nation. Civil wars and other major internal disturbances are most likely to occur when there is a basic and rapid change in the values of one segment of a society.

Revolutionary change is an internal disturbance of high magnitude aimed at extensive changes in values and institutions. It is typically rapid and involves the use of force. Revolutions involve a destructive phase in which values and institutions are destroyed. During this phase, ethical polarization occurs, with the negative predominating over the positive. Thus, antisocial behavior increases, as does mental illness and mob psychology. The destructive phase is followed by a declining phase in which some values and institutions are restored and the society returns to a higher degree of stability and solidarity.

Sorokin also developed a general theory of solidarity and antagonism. Such a theory is considered important because if we knew how to increase solidarity and decrease antagonism, and were able to apply the knowledge effectively, social tragedies such as war and coercion could be reduced or eliminated. The most important factor in the relative incidence of solidarity and antagonism in both interpersonal and intergroup interaction is the character of cultural values and norms. Values and norms that stress mutual aid and sympathy will increase solidarity interaction. Conversely, values and norms that stress egoism and competition for limited resources will generate antagonistic interaction. A second factor in the relative predominance of solidarity or antagonism in interaction and intergroup relations is the concordance or discordance of values and norms of the interacting parties. Concordance increases solidarity, while discordance increases antagonism. This is particularly so if the discordant values and norms themselves encourage antagonism. These effects of culture are increased to the degree that the predominant values and norms are manifested in behavior.

PERSONALITY

There are four levels of personality. Most fundamental is the biological unconscious, which consists of various biological energies. Next are conscious biological egos, such as sex or age. The third level is the multiple conscious sociocultural egos. Each ego reflects the influence of one of the various groups to which the individual has belonged. Much of the individual's mentality is derived from these group affiliations. The fourth level is the supraconscious, or soul. It operates through intuition and is important in creativity, spirituality, and in basic conceptions of truth, beauty, and goodness.

CRITICAL SOCIOLOGY AND THE CALL FOR REFORM

On the basis of his historical and comparative research and analysis, Sorokin formulated a critique of contemporary culture and society and issued a call for reform. The focal point of his critique was the inadequacy of the declining sensate culture. Its false parts have become greater than the true; hence, it does not provide for orderly relations between groups or the meeting of basic human needs. The profound crisis engendered by the decline of sensate culture is the most important and fundamental event of the historical era that began with the twentieth century. The locus of this event is primarily Western civilization. However, its effects are worldwide due to the decreasing separation of East and West because of factors such as communication, transportation, technology, and cultural diffusion.

The loss of vitality and creativity in sensate culture is evident in all its compartments. The system of truth is characterized by skepticism, relativism, and the separation of scientific endeavor from any criteria of the good. The ethical compartment of culture emphasizes expediency, relativism, hedonism, and subjectivism. Without universal standards, the ethical system cannot provide positive motivation or control behavior. Art is focused on giving pleasure and enjoyment and is often antisocial and amoral. Sensate ideas of freedom multiply desires without instilling restraint.

This cultural system contributes to the decline of familistic relationships, the breakdown of equity in contractual relationships, and the rise of the compulsory. Great power is held by a limited number, and its use is not adequately controlled. Because of the lack of universal standards and the proliferation of wants generic to sensate culture, an anomic situation is created in which interpersonal and intergroup conflicts, including war, are frequent, often intense, and inevitable.

PRACTICAL SOCIOLOGY AND RECONSTRUCTION

Sorokin believed that an increase in altruistic love represents the best practical solution to the problems of this historical era. Altruistic love, love that is unselfish, disinterested, and sacrificial, is one of the greatest powers in the universe. Evidence is presented to show that it has numerous positive effects on individuals and on society. Love of this nature contributes to mental and physical health, longevity, and the most beneficial development of personality. At some minimal level, altruistic love is necessary for social solidarity. This love provides for the cooperation, mutual aid, and justice that make creativity and social harmony possible.

In Sorokin's view, any practical solution to the human and social problems of this era depends on the recognition that culture, society, and individual personality must all be changed. Society and culture are ultimately the creation of the actions of individuals. Therefore, reconstruction must begin with the conscious and deliberate efforts of individuals to increase their own capacity and practice of altruistic love. A planned reconstruction of culture in all its compartments and of social relations rests on this foundation.

Social science can help provide the knowledge and understanding of how love can be increased. Altruistic love has five dimensions: intensity, extensity, duration, purity, and adequacy. The relationships between these dimensions are considered. On this foundation, the techniques of altruistic transformation are described and illustrated with case study examples on both the individual and group level.

The necessary reconstruction of society and culture can be effected on the foundation of the altruistic transformation of individuals. The basic premise pertaining to the nature of reality is the foundation of cultural integration. Therefore, Sorokin believed that changing this premise to an integral one in which sensory, rational, and superrational aspects of reality are recognized is the most effective way to transform the culture. This will shift the system of values from egoism toward the impersonal, inexhaustible, and universal values of truth, beauty, and goodness. Within this cultural context, the power of elites can be effectively limited and a social order in which familistic relationships will predominate can be created. Different cultures will become more compatible with the infusing of spiritual principles and values. As a result, interpersonal and intergroup conflict can be reduced.

INTEGRALISM AND THE SOCIAL SCIENCES

The foundational idea in much of Sorokin's system of thought is integralism. It is expressed in his analysis of cultural organization and change and represents the basis of his vision of personal, social, and cultural reconstruction. Integralism is also the guiding principle in the ontology and epistemology of his system of sociology.

Sorokin considered the adoption of an integral perspective a necessary condition for vitality and creativity in the social sciences. The basic assumption of integralism is that reality contains empirical-sensory, rational-mindful, and superrational-sensory components. It thus requires a different ontology and epistemology from that of contemporary social science.

An integral system of truth would incorporate empirical, rational, and supersensory modes of cognition. The last of these sources of truth would involve intuition, including the revelation and mystical intuition of religious conceptions of sources of truth. Each method of cognition is fallible by itself. When combined into a harmonious integral system, they can cross-validate each other, thus providing a more powerful epistemology. Integralism would unite science, philosophy, and religion in the common endeavor of providing knowledge and understanding of how personal, social, and cultural reconstruction can be achieved and maintained. In this context, the practice of science would be directed toward the realization of greater altruistic love, the ethical principles of the major world religions, and the universal values of truth, beauty, and goodness.

The integralism advocated by Sorokin is a complete system of sociology incorporating the scientific, reform, and practical traditions of the discipline. It involves rigorous scientific research, an explicit commitment to reform that engages social science in public debate of desirable ends, and a scientifically based program of means to achieve personal, social, and cultural reconstruction.

— Vincent Jeffries

See also Culture and Civilization; Historical and Comparative Theory; Metatheory

FURTHER READINGS AND REFERENCES

Allen, Philip J., ed. 1963. *Pitirim A. Sorokin in Review.* Durham, NC: Duke University.

Johnston, Barry V. 1995. *Pitirim A. Sorokin: An Intellectual Biography.* Lawrence: University Press of Kansas.

Sorokin, Pitirim A. 1941. *The Crisis of Our Age.* New York: E. P. Dutton.

———. 1947. *Culture, Society, and Personality.* New York: Harper & Brothers.

———. 1954. *The Ways and Power of Love.* Boston: Beacon.

———. 1957. *Social and Cultural Dynamics.* 1-vol. ed. Boston: Beacon.

———. 1959. *Social and Cultural Mobility.* Glencoe, IL: Free Press.

———. 1966. *Sociological Theories of Today.* New York: Harper and Row.

SPENCER, HERBERT

Herbert Spencer (1820–1903) was one of the most influential thinkers of his time. To understand why, one must read Spencer as an evolutionary theorist. This is how he saw himself and how his contemporaries responded to him and his work. It is what marked his place in the history of sociology and what accounts for his influence far beyond the confines of the discipline he helped to found.

Who is Spencer? Spencer was born on April 27, 1820, at Derby, England, the only surviving child of William George Spencer and Harriet Holmes. In his autobiographical writings, Spencer offers a brief intellectual history of himself, identifying how key aspects of his life were linked to the origins and transformations of his evolutionary ideas. Not surprisingly, he begins with the nonconformist upbringing he received at the hands of the Spencer family and the family of his mother. To this upbringing and, in particular, his father, he attributes the early development of emotional and intellectual traits that were to operate throughout his life: a willingness to resist arbitrary authority no matter the source (church or state) or the cost (financial or health); the mental habits of seeking natural causes, analyzing, and synthesizing; and a love of completeness that would reach its fullest expression in a 10-volume *Synthetic Philosophy* that covered religion, philosophy of science, biology, psychology, sociology, and ethics. George Spencer was a teacher, but poor health prevented him from educating his son. Spencer thus went to a day school until 1830 when his uncle William Spencer resumed teaching at the school that he had inherited from his father. Spencer remained there as one of a select number of pupils until 1833 when he moved to Hinton to attend a school run by another uncle, Thomas Spencer, who, like his brothers, emphasized science and mathematics at the expense of the classics. This education prepared Spencer for the career as a civil engineer he began with the London and Birmingham Railway at the age of 17. Lasting off and on until 1846, this career in civil engineering provided opportunities to exercise mental habits developed in childhood and boyhood and resulted in several of the inventions that Spencer would make during his lifetime. It also rekindled a boyhood interest in collecting fossils, prompting Spencer to read Charles Lyell's *Principles of Geology* (1831–1833). During this period, his uncle Thomas encouraged him to write the series of 12 letters on the proper sphere of government that were published in *The Nonconfomist*—a newspaper established by and for the advanced dissenters. But it was not until he became the subeditor of *The Economist* in 1848 that he began the literary career that, despite major ups (e.g., the legacies from his uncles Thomas and William, endorsements of the *Synthetic Philosophy* by the chief men of science, leading men of letters and statesmen) and downs (e.g., persistent health problems, financial difficulties) was to occupy him for the rest of his life.

Spencer was a prolific writer. In addition to the *Synthetic Philosophy,* he published *Social Statics* (1855), *Education* (1861), *The Study of Sociology* (1873), *The Man versus the State* (1884), three series of *Essays* (1857, 1863, 1874),

Various Fragments (1897), *Facts and Comments* (1902), *Descriptive Sociology* (1873–1881), *An Autobiography* (1904), and "The Filiation of Ideas," a natural history of his evolutionary theory that was completed in March of 1899 and included in David Duncan's biography, *Life and Letters of Herbert Spencer* (1908). Throughout his life, Spencer was a regular contributor to the major general periodicals and specialty journals both as an author and as a reviewer. He was a member of the famous X Club, nine leading men of science who successfully challenged the cultural authority of the clergy by advocating scientific, naturalistic explanations of world. His election to the Athenaeum Club in 1867 by the committee under Rule 2 (a rule allowing the committee to select chief representatives of science, literature, and art) solidified his place in the elite intellectual circles of his day. By also publishing widely in magazines and newspapers, he established himself not just as a prominent member of the scientific community but also as a popularizer of science and, in particular, evolutionary theory.

What does it mean to say that Spencer is an evolutionary theorist? To answer this question, it is necessary to distinguish between the ways in which "evolution" and "evolutionary theory" are used in sociology and biology. Sociologists routinely use evolution and development as synonyms to denote unfolding models of change. In biology, evolution and development are universally recognized as distinct and fundamentally different processes. Development is an unfolding of preexisting potentials inherent in an organism at the time it begins life. Because this is a process of immanent change, environmental factors can only speed up, slow down, or stop the process of unfolding; they cannot create new potentials. Evolution, in contrast, depends on organism-environment interactions. There are no predetermined paths or preset goals. Environmental contingency, historical specificity, and probabilism are hallmarks of evolutionary theories.

Spencer's social theory is evolutionary in the modern biological sense of the term *evolution*. What are its central ideas and arguments? How did Spencer arrive at it? How was it received by his contemporaries? What was its subsequent fate? Answering these questions requires a historically contextualizing evaluation of Spencer that captures how his theory of organic evolution, his reconciliation of religion and science, and his philosophy of science helped shape the content, development, and reception of his evolutionary social theory.

SPENCER'S THEORY OF ORGANIC EVOLUTION

Spencer developed his theory of social evolution by participating in the nineteenth-century debates about the fact and mechanism of organic evolution. To establish the fact of evolution, the first evolutionists had to successfully challenge the special creation solution to the organic origins problem. In his biological works, Spencer used standard nineteenth-century arguments from classification, embryology, morphology, and distribution to challenge the hypothesis of special creation. By demonstrating that the hypothesis of evolution can explain facts that anti-evolutionists claimed could be explained only by special creation and facts that special creation cannot explain, these works help to establish the fact of evolution.

To explain the fact of evolution, Spencer turned to use inheritance, arguing that structures that organisms acquire during their lives through use or disuse of organs in response to environmental influences (e.g., the stronger legs [use] and weaker wings [disuse] of domestic fowl) can be passed on to their offspring. Spencer discovered the Lamarckian formulation of use inheritance in 1840 when he read Lyell's *Principles of Geology*. Most of the scientific community agreed with Lyell's conclusion that this explanation of organic evolution was unscientific—but not Spencer. In use inheritance, he found the evolutionary explanation of organic change that would remain one of the cornerstones of his theory of organic evolution. The introduction of its other cornerstone, Karl Ernst von Baer's law of individual development, in 1857 left the Lamarckian foundation of his theory unchanged. Spencer used this law of individual development to specify the course of organic change as a movement from homogeneity of structure to heterogeneity of structure through a process of successive differentiations and integrations. Explained by use inheritance, the transition from homogeneity to heterogeneity is contingent on favorable environmental conditions. A more heterogeneous structure will develop only if the environment demands more complex habits. Otherwise, there will be stasis or retrogression.

In his early biological works, Spencer used evolution and use inheritance as synonyms. Then in 1859, Charles Darwin published his alternative explanation of organic evolution, natural selection, in *On the Origin of Species*. Unlike most of his contemporaries, Spencer immediately adopted the environmental selection of random variation as a cause of evolutionary change. In *The Principles of Biology*, in his other post-1859 works, and in post-1859 editions of earlier works, Spencer followed Darwin and argued that neither use inheritance nor natural selection was a sufficient cause of organic evolution. But where Darwin argued that natural selection was the principal mechanism of organic evolution in all times and all places, Spencer concluded that natural selection was the principal cause of organic change only for inferior plants and animals and for the early evolutionary stages of superior plants and animals. In higher life forms, including humans, use inheritance is the primary mechanism of organic evolution. And where Darwin stressed that he was concerned only with organic evolution, Spencer made the concept of evolution the linchpin of a synthetic philosophy that included not just his

Principles of Biology but also his *Principles of Sociology,* his *Principles of Psychology,* and his *Principles of Ethics.* Together, these works explored the implications of Spencer's understanding of the course and mechanism of organic evolution for society, mind, and morals.

By the time Spencer began work on the synthetic philosophy in the spring of 1860, the debate about implications of evolutionary theorizing for connections among science, religion, and theology had intensified. Natural theologians had little difficulty accommodating the fact of evolution. They simply interpreted apparent design in nature (e.g., eyes, wings of birds, economy of nature) as empirical evidence for the existence of God. Evolutionary explanations of organic evolution were another matter altogether because they eliminated both design and designer from nature. Nowhere were the repercussions of doing this more evident than in the response to Darwin's theory of evolution by means of natural selection. This theory was attacked on religious and scientific grounds by some of the most influential philosophers, theologians, and scientists of the day. Spencer realized that if he hoped to convince the scientific community of the validity of his own evolutionary explanations of the natural and social worlds, he had to confront these attacks head on. The reconciliation of religion and science set out in Part I of *First Principles,* the first volume of his synthetic philosophy, and the philosophy of science that followed in Part II were intended to do just this.

SPENCER'S RECONCILIATION OF RELIGION AND SCIENCE

Spencer's reconciliation of religion and science started from the widely held view that the key to reconciling religion and science was facing the limits of each. For Spencer, the domain of religion was matters of faith and belief or what he called "The Unknowable." The domain of science, in contrast, was made up of matters of fact or knowledge. By making the domain of science coterminous with "The Knowable," Spencer could claim for science not just nature but man, mind, and morality.

Spencer deduced this view of the domains of religion and science from arguments about the nature of the human mind and how it obtains knowledge. If, as he had argued in his psychological writings, the human mind is incapable of knowing anything but phenomena that can be apprehended by the senses, and if "thinking is relationing," then all knowledge is relative, and that which is infinite, absolute, and unconditioned (i.e., God) cannot be grasped by the human mind. But because we can believe in what we cannot know, recognizing that God transcends the reach of human intelligence and the limits of knowledge in no way implies that God does not exist.

This defense of the limits of religion and science was not original to Spencer. Nor was the use of The Unknowable

and The Knowable to demarcate the domains of religion and science. Spencer took them from the Scottish philosopher Sir William Hamilton and the theologian Reverend Henry Longueville Mansel, author of the much-debated Bampton Lectures on the limits of religious thought. The originality of Spencer's reconciliation of religion and science became clear when he turned to the question, "What must we say concerning that which transcends knowledge?" (1862/1911:64). Where Hamilton and Mansel concluded that the absolute or infinite could be apprehended only negatively (i.e., from the consciousness not of what is but of what is not), Spencer countered that the same laws of thought that preclude knowledge of an infinite, absolute God affirm that there is a God. The necessity of thinking in relations makes it impossible for humans to rid themselves of the consciousness of an actuality lying behind appearance. From a scientific point of view, then, the conclusion that there is a nonrelative that passes the sphere of the intellect is unavoidable. Because this indestructible belief in the existence of a mystery absolutely beyond comprehension is the fundamental truth that religion asserts in the absence of science, this is the common ground that reconciles science and religion.

Spencer was prepared to take full credit for arriving at what he presented as the only possible reconciliation of religion and science. But as he points out in his autobiographical writings, what really mattered to him was what this reconciliation of religion and science said about his own evolutionary theory: First, his evolutionary theory could and, indeed, did contest theological explanations of the natural and social worlds. Special creation, miracles, and design (and designer) in nature are legitimate targets of evolutionary science. Second, his evolutionary theory did not and, indeed, could not contest religion "properly understood," and therefore, it could not be dismissed as irreligious, purely materialistic, or inherently atheistic. By allowing Spencer to attack theology without undermining faith, this reconciliation helped to undermine the authority of the clergy in matters of fact. Third, his evolutionary theory had no place for metaphysical principles where metaphysics is understood as the study of the absolute. Against this backdrop, Spencer could ask readers to set aside disagreements about religious and metaphysical beliefs when considering the essential part of *First Principles*—the philosophy of science set out in Part II, "The Knowable."

SPENCER'S PHILOSOPHY OF SCIENCE

The 1830s and 1840s were the most important period in the development of philosophy of science in Britain. Like his contemporaries, Spencer accepted that John F. W. Herschel, William Whewell, and John Stuart Mill had identified the kind of theory and the kind of evidence that were necessary for good science. By first combining the methodological principles they shared in his own philosophy of science and then using this philosophy of science to ground his synthetic philosophy, Spencer hoped to convince the scientific community that his evolutionary biology, sociology, psychology, and ethics conformed to this canonical standard for science.

The law of evolution and the persistence of force are the central ideas of Spencer's philosophy of science. As philosophical truths, they are defined by their relationship to scientific truths: Standing in the same relation to the highest scientific truths as these truths do to lower scientific truths, they integrate scientific knowledge by grouping laws of coexistence and sequence of phenomena into higher, more extended generalizations. For Spencer, the only thing that sets philosophy apart from science is its higher degree of generality. Philosophy is the science of the sciences.

Spencer organized his philosophy of science around the two kinds of laws that Whewell, Herschel, and Mill had argued were necessary for good science: Phenomenal laws describe empirical regularities in the succession and coexistence of phenomena (e.g., the planets move in ellipses around the sun). Fundamental laws (e.g., gravitation) explain why observed regularities occur. Spencer's law of evolution describes the course of change throughout all classes of phenomena (inorganic, organic, and superorganic) as an integration of matter and concomitant dissipation of motion; during which the matter passes from a relatively indefinite, incoherent homogeneity to a relatively definite, coherent heterogeneity, and during which the retained motion undergoes a parallel transformation (1862/1911:321). His use of matter and motion to frame this phenomenal law follows logically from his claim that to consolidate the widest generalizations of science, philosophy must use the most general phenomena we can know. This claim also underpins his use of force to frame the fundamental law that explains these experiences of matter and motion. The persistence of force—Spencer's restatement of the law of conservation of energy—occupies a special place in his philosophy of science. As its most general and simple proposition, it cannot be merged into nor derived from any other truth. All other truths are proved by derivation from it. Thus, in the same way that laws of planetary motion can be interpreted as necessary consequences of the law of gravitation, the experiences of matter and motion described by the law of evolution can be interpreted as necessary consequences of the principle that force can neither be created nor destroyed. The greater certainty accorded to this deductive proof does not follow from the process of deductive reasoning *per se* but rather from the confidence that results from the fit between its results and *a posteriori* observations.

The methodology for sociology set out in *The Study of Sociology* and *Principles of Sociology* must be read against the backdrop of this philosophy of science. Because the natural sciences and the social sciences share a common canonical standard, there can be no radical break between them. Sociology has the same logical structure as the natural sciences and extends their concern with control through prediction to the social environment. Its goal, like the goal of all science, is causal explanation.

This emphasis on causal explanation led Spencer to another shared premise of Whewell, Herschel, and Mill: the premise that good scientific systems are hypothetico-deductive systems that use observations to confirm or disprove hypotheses. Where and how scientists obtain these hypotheses does not matter. What matters is that these hypotheses are subjected to observational or experimental tests. Spencer's naturalistic conception of sociology follows logically from this view of how science ought to be done. So does his argument that lawful relations can be discovered only through the systematic study of empirically observable phenomena and his strategy of eliminating competing hypotheses on the basis of lack of agreement with observations.

Spencer's argument for the unity of science did not blind him to three sets of "difficulties" that set sociology apart from other sciences. The first set identifies sources of error in the data of sociology that follow from the fact that sociological phenomena are not directly perceptible and thus cannot be studied with measurement instruments analogous to thermometers or microscopes. Sociologists must rely on the observational-comparative method to study social structures and functions in terms of their origins, development, and transformation. The second set identifies difficulties that arise from the intellectual and emotional faculties of the social scientists who analyze and interpret these comparative data (i.e., faculties that are neither complex enough nor flexible enough and feelings of impatience, sympathy, and antipathy). The final set points to distortions that result from the participation of observers in the social arrangements they study: the bias of education, the bias of patriotism, the class bias, the political bias, and the theological bias. Spencer's rules of sociological method are designed to eliminate these preconceptions and biases or to make allowances for the errors they introduce.

Recognizing the differences between sociology and the other sciences and the importance of the comparative method is necessary but not sufficient for the development of a science of sociology. For Spencer, the Lamarckian, "preliminary studies" are also necessary, not to provide requisite data but to evolve a habit of thought which is appropriate for the scientific study of evolution in its most complex form. To prepare sociologists for studying the complex causal chains that connect social phenomena, the analytical habit of mind, the synthetical habit of mind, and consciousness of causation must all be exercised—preferably by preparation in biology and psychology. Because these are the very traits Spencer believed he had inherited from his father and then developed further by writing his biological and psychological works, he could claim to be uniquely positioned to undertake the successful study of sociology.

SPENCER'S EVOLUTIONARY SOCIAL THEORY

Sociology, for Spencer, is the study of social evolution. Like any theory of social change at the historical scale, Spencer's evolutionary theory must answer three questions: What is changing? What is the course of change? What is the mechanism of change? Spencer did not make the modern distinction between organic evolution (information that is transmitted through genetic mechanisms) and cultural evolution (information that is transmitted through nongenetic mechanisms like learning). He could thus argue that organic evolution and social evolution do not just have the same courses; they also have the same mechanism. Social change is a response to environmentally induced changes in the physical, emotional, and intellectual traits of individuals. In more explicitly Lamarckian terms, environmental changes create new needs; new needs require new habits, which, in turn, require changes in the physical, emotional, and intellectual traits of individuals. These changed individuals then mold societies into corresponding forms. Because the environmental changes that trigger this process can originate in the social relations that make up a society and in the relations among societies (Spencer's superorganic environment), the individual-society relationship is reciprocal, with societies and people modifying each other through successive generations. Spencer's answer to the question "What is changing" is society, where societies are conditions and consequences of the actions and interactions of their members. "Be it rudimentary or be it advanced, every society displays phenomena that are ascribable to the characters of its units and to the conditions under which they exist" (Spencer 1896:8–9).

This argument for the social environment as the major source of adaptational variation in social evolution also grounds Spencer's use of the militant-industrial distinction to classify societies. The distinction was not original to Spencer, but the way in which he used it was. Whether the organization for offense and defense or the sustaining organization is more developed depends on the nature of the interactions that occur between a society and its neighboring societies in the struggle for existence. If these interactions are hostile, then militancy evolves; if peaceful, then industrialism is adaptive. For Spencer, then, the transition from the militant to the industrial type of social organization is not inevitable; it is contingent on favorable environmental conditions. The argument for environmental specificity also holds where societies are classified by degree of composition as simple, compound, doubly compound, or trebly compound. In social organisms, as in biological organisms,

structural change occurs in response to environmental pressures. More heterogeneous structures develop only if the environment demands more complex habits. In other environments, there will be stasis or retrogression.

Spencer's hypotheses about the course and mechanism of social evolution, his theory of micro-macro linkage, and his evolutionary systems for classifying societies are all framed at the societal level. The institutional analysis that makes up the bulk of *Principles of Sociology* uses the data on societies that exist and have existed compiled in the *Descriptive Sociology* to extend this analysis of superorganic complexity and diversity to the institutional level. These levels are linked through the definition of society as a cluster of social institutions that Spencer used to divide the field of sociology into domestic institutions, ceremonial institutions, political institutions, ecclesiastical institutions, professional institutions, and industrial institutions.

Spencer's institutional analysis can be read as an empirical demonstration of the explanatory power of his evolutionary approach to the study of social phenomena. Reading it in this way highlights the methodological suppositions, approach to the micro-macro link, and explanatory form of the evolutionary social theory it builds on and elaborates. Spencer's rules of sociological method are reflected in his strategies for eliminating preconceptions and biases and in his use of the comparative method to establish inductive generalizations and test hypotheses. His theory of micro-macro linkage underpins his relational conception of social institution. The use of Lamarckism as the mechanism that links micro- and macro-levels also explains why the militant-industrial system of classification dominates this comparative institutional analysis.

Spencer's analysis of marital relations provides compelling evidence that domestic institutions depend on variations in the biophysical and social environments. Polyandry is adaptive in environments with small carrying capacities. Here, the low birth rate that results from the marriage of one woman to more than one man helps to prevent overpopulation and to ensure the needs of children. In environments where food supply is not a limiting factor and where intersocietal hostility is chronic, polyandry is maladaptive. The high death rate of men and surplus of women produced by chronic warfare mean that the rapid replacement of members necessary for offense and defense can occur only through the marriage of one man to more than one woman. In this environment polygyny is adaptive.

Domestic institutions guide, direct, and regulate the private conduct of individuals. Their public conduct is the domain of the ceremonial, political, and ecclesiastical institutions that make up the regulating system. Spencer's comparative analysis of ceremonial institutions showed that as expressions of subordination and deference, marks of superordination (e.g., titles) and subordination (e.g., mutilations) are concomitants of militancy. His findings for political institutions provide a particularly clear demonstration of how social institutions depend on the nature of their environments and the physical, emotional, and intellectual traits of their members. This analysis refined the militant-industrial classification to specify two radically different types of political organization. The militant type of society specifies the nature of political organization that accompanies chronic militancy. In this environment, the society as a whole must survive if any individual is to survive. Cooperation is therefore compulsory. Where intersocietal conflict is rare or absent altogether, joint action for offense and defense is unnecessary. Here, voluntary cooperation confers survival advantages in the struggle for existence, and the industrial type of society is adaptive. If individuals and societies reciprocally determine each other, then the physical, intellectual, and emotional traits of members of industrial societies should differ from those of their militant counterparts. This is exactly what Spencer found. In industrial societies, sentiments like loyalty, faith in government, and patriotism are rarely exercised, while humane sentiments like honesty, truthfulness, forgiveness, and kindness evolve because of high levels of use.

Spencer also found that individuals in militant societies deal with fellow members and supernatural beings in the same way. Because coercive, centralized civil rule and coercive, centralized religious rule go hand in hand, Spencer concluded that ecclesiastical institutions evolve in response to pressures from the environment. The industrial institutions that make up the sustaining system of a society are also environment specific. Slavery, serfdom, and guilds are found in societies that exist in environments where militant activities predominate. Forms of industrial regulation that do not demand compulsory cooperation (e.g., free labor, contract) become increasingly important as the superorganic environment becomes more industrial.

These empirically verified statements of the causes and conditions under which different kinds of institutions and the societies they constitute originate, persist, or change are framed at the level of what Spencer called proximate causation. Produced by inductive inference and the testing of hypotheses against facts about societies that exist and have existed, these explanations are distinctly sociological. But like other scientists of his day who accepted the Whewell-Herschel-Mill view of how science ought to be done, Spencer felt compelled to interpret these findings in terms of matter, motion, and force. Only ultimate causal explanations can do this, where ultimate is used in the Herschellian sense of incapable of further analysis. Induction and hypothetico-deduction must be joined with deduction, where this deduction is used in Mill's sense of the verification of special laws by their deduction from simpler and more general laws. Because the principles of sociology are the most general laws of the science of sociology, they can be deductively interpreted only by documenting their affiliation on

the law of evolution. Spencer thus verified these proximate causal explanations by showing that the evolution of domestic institutions, ceremonial institutions, political institutions, ecclesiastical institutions, professional institutions, and industrial institutions conformed to the law of evolution. This strategy is practicable only because the law of evolution and the persistence of force that explains why this is the course of transformation satisfy the Whewell-Herschel-Mill canons of good science.

THE FATE OF SPENCER'S EVOLUTIONARY SOCIAL THEORY

It would be hard to overstate the importance of use inheritance to Spencer's evolutionary theorizing. It is no surprise, then, that Spencer took a leading role in the controversy that surrounded the claim by the "neo-Darwinian" August Weismann that natural selection was the sole cause of organic change. By this time in his life (his 70s) Spencer was no stranger to controversy. But persistent health problems had long before forced him to ignore most attacks on his ideas. What was it about this controversy that led him to abandon this strategy? Simply this: Spencer believed that the inheritance of acquired characters was the primary mechanism of evolution and, therefore, that the outcome of this debate would profoundly affect views of life, mind, morals, and politics. Played out in major general and speciality journals, the controversy ended with Spencer and Weismann agreeing to disagree. The neo-Darwinian threat to Spencer's evolutionary theory and the synthetic philosophy that it unified was thus avoided. At the time of his death, Spencer could be eulogized as a member of the British scientific elite and as one of Britain's greatest philosophers. The former focused attention on his evolutionary theories of organic and social change; the latter on his contribution of his synthetic philosophy.

Spencer's contemporaries believed that his synthetic philosophy offered the most complete synthesis and generalization of knowledge of the time he wrote and that this accomplishment alone would ensure his place in the history of thought. Where they speculated on how he would be received by later thinkers, they offered two prescient observations: First, these thinkers would feel compelled to engage his ideas, whether or not they agreed with him. Second, advances in science would undermine at least some of Spencer's ideas—an outcome that Spencer himself would have accepted just as he accepted successful challenges during his lifetime. What they did not anticipate was the extent to which these advances would influence the rules for engaging Spencer and his ideas.

When the Spencer-Weismann debate ended, the verdict was still not in on use inheritance. But since the development of the modern evolutionary synthesis in the 1940s, biologists have accepted natural selection as the sole mechanism of organic evolution. Once it was established that acquired characters cannot be inherited, Spencer's reliance on this mechanism rendered his theory of organic evolution obsolete. In biology today, Spencer is almost forgotten. Some evolutionary sociologists today also distance themselves from Spencer for this reason. Those who regard Spencer as the leading proponent of Social Darwinism use the unrelenting attack on this application of evolutionary theory to human society. Others take a very different tack. They join forces with critics of evolutionary theorizing in sociology to justify the neglect of Spencer in sociology. They argue that Spencer's evolutionary theory is a form of developmentalism (i.e., immanent causation), that developmentalism cannot account adequately for social change, and therefore, that Spencer is dead. They defend this developmental interpretation of Spencer's theory on the grounds that (1) it confounds evolutionary and developmental models of change, (2) its mechanism is the Lamarckian law of progressive development, or (3) its mechanism is a metaphysical principle, the persistence of force. The first argument acknowledges Spencer's debt to von Baer but misrepresents his law of individual development as a source analogy for Spencer's specification of the mechanism of organic evolution and social evolution. It only specified the course of organic and social change. The second argument assigns Lamarckism its proper role but is marred by the fundamental misunderstanding that, for Spencer, Lamarckism meant an inherent tendency toward progress or perfection. For Spencer, Lamarckism meant use inheritance. The third argument misconstrues the logical status of the persistence of force and its role in Spencer's sociology. The persistence of force is a fundamental law. By tying together facts from biology and sociology, it points to a fundamental unity that underlies their apparent diversity—exactly what the Whewell-Herschel-Mill canons of good science prescribed.

The developmental reconstruction does not adequately represent Spencer's social theory. Its prominence in the scholarship on Spencer has nonetheless proven particularly damaging to his current reputational standing. The developmental reconstruction of Spencer's social theory has also made it almost impossible for sociologists today to grasp why Spencer's contemporaries took him so seriously. How Spencer was a product of his time and how he transcended it by offering ideas and arguments that can be exploited in debates of contemporary theoretical consequence become clear only when he is read as an evolutionary theorist.

— Valerie A. Haines

See also Evolutionary Theory; Social Darwinism

FURTHER READINGS AND REFERENCES

Darwin, Charles. 1859/1964. *On the Origin of Species: A Facsimile of the First Edition.* Cambridge, MA: Harvard University Press.

Duncan, David. 1908. *Life and Letters of Herbert Spencer.* 2 vols. New York: D. Appleton.

Haines, Valerie A. 1997. "Spencer and His Critics." Pp. 81–111 in *Reclaiming the Sociological Classics: The State of the Scholarship,* edited by C. Camic. Oxford, UK: Blackwell.

Offer, John, ed. 2000. *Herbert Spencer: Critical Assessments.* New York: Routledge.

Peel, J. D. Y. 1971. *Herbert Spencer: The Evolution of a Sociologist.* New York: Basic Books.

Perrin, Robert G. 1993. *Herbert Spencer: A Primary and Secondary Bibliography.* New York: Garland.

Richards, Robert J. 1987. *Darwin and the Emergence of Evolutionary Theories of Mind and Behavior.* Chicago: University of Chicago Press.

Spencer, Herbert. [1862] 1911. *First Principles.* London: Williams & Norgate.

———. 1864–1867. *Principles of Biology.* 2 vols. New York: D. Appleton.

———. [1855]1870–1872. *Principles of Psychology.* 2 vols. London: Williams & Norgate.

———. 1876–1896. *Principles of Sociology.* 3 vols. New York: D. Appleton.

———. 1879–1893. *Principles of Ethics.* 2 vols. New York: D. Appleton.

———. [1873] 1961. *The Study of Sociology.* Ann Arbor: University of Michigan Press.

———. 1904. *An Autobiography.* 2 vols. London: Williams & Norgate.

SPORT

Sport—loosely defined as the regulated manifestation of competitively based physical activity—is a complex phenomenon that operates simultaneously within numerous social realms (i.e., physical, commercial, media, and political) and can be experienced in a number of different ways (i.e., as participant, spectator, viewer, owner, investor, and worker). Adding to its complexity, sport is also a fluid category whose precise constitution is bound to the specificities of the context in question. Despite this historical and cultural contingency, sport can still be considered a universal practice. Virtually all societies exhibit some form of sporting activity, which, to varying degrees and in varying ways, provides a vehicle for the embodied expression of local identity and difference. Therefore, in deriving from, and contributing toward, the structural, institutional, processional, and behavioral dimensions of social life, sport represents a potentially illuminating field of sociological inquiry; something fully recognized by those within the sociology of sport. Indeed, the approximately four-decade evolution of the sociology of sport subdiscipline has generated an empirically rich, politically prescient, and both theoretically sophisticated and diverse body of work.

Propelled by a growing band of scholars located in, among other places, Australia, Canada, Finland, France, Holland, Japan, New Zealand, Norway, South Africa, South Korea, the United Kingdom, and the United States, the sociology of sport can be considered a truly global academic community. As well as an expanding array of sport-focused books and book series, the primary vehicle for the dissemination of sociology of sport research has been through the field's major academic journals: *Sport in Society; International Review for the Sociology of Sport; Journal of Sport and Social Issues;* and the *Sociology of Sport Journal.* The accumulated body of work represented within these various publication outlets demonstrates an understandable lack of uniformity with regard to the manner in which sport is addressed as a sociological problem. Sport's multidimensional character means there is no, nor has there ever been, an empirical, methodological, or theoretical orthodoxy within the sociology of sport. With regard to social theory, it is possible to discern exponents of virtually every major strand—from structural functionalism to postmodernism—among sociologically informed sport scholars. To illustrate the breadth of this theoretical diversity, the remainder of this brief overview will concentrate on the five major social theorists whose influence is most evident within contemporary sociology of sport research.

As in other subdisciplines within the social sciences, Karl Marx's impact on the sociology of sport has been extensive yet varied. He may have referred to sport only once in his voluminous writings; nevertheless, there are a number of insightful analyses of the political economy of contemporary sport from a Marxist perspective. Shifting from the economy to culture as the locus of critical engagement, Marx's influence is also apparent within an array of Gramscian-inflected sport studies that, from various different vantage points (be they ethnic, race, gender, sexuality, or nation oriented), approach sport as a cultural terrain on which everyday identities and experiences are immersed in a process of continual contestation.

While perhaps not as prevalent as Marxist-oriented scholarship, Max Weber's theorizing has also been a consistent feature of sociologically based sport studies. His concept of rationalization, and more specifically, the notion of instrumental rationality, has proved particularly useful for those interested in theorizing the increasingly commercialized and bureaucratized nature of sport organizations.

Of all social theories Elias's figurational approach has made the most direct contribution to the sociological understanding of sport. Elias identified the processes responsible for the emergence of modern sport forms as being illustrative of his core theory of the civilizing process. According to Elias, the development of modern societies, and sports, was attributed to the formation of increasingly complex and extensive social figurations (chains of interdependence between individuals) that increased pressures on individuals to control their expressive impulses—hence, the emergence of modern sport forms as regulated and codified expressions of physical culture. In addition to accounting for the modernization of sport in general, and that of specific sports in particular, the figurational approach has also been used to study issues pertaining to sport crowd behavior, sport and globalization, race and sport, gender and sport, and drugs and sport.

As with Elias, although not to the same extent, Bourdieu's work discussed sport's importance as a social phenomenon. In addition, each of these theorists focused on sport's fundamentally expressive relationship with the body—for both, sport being the bodily incorporation and practice of socially constructed conventions. Bourdieu identified the sporting body as a vehicle for materializing the status differences, in terms of particular lifestyle choices, through which class-based hierarchies are enacted. This observation has been engaged within numerous studies focused on various aspects of the relationship between sport, physical activity, and social status, and using sporting practices as diverse as basketball, boxing, extreme sports, football, rugby, and wrestling, as the vehicle of empirical analysis.

Last, but certainly not least in terms of its influence on the sociology of sport, Michel Foucault's theory of modern disciplinary power has generated a substantial body of work focused on the relationship between sport, power, and the body. Like Foucault's project itself, this sport-related research can be broadly characterized into two related strands. First, those studies focusing on sport as a disciplinary institution that contributes to the discursive normalization of the modern subject. Second, those studies concerned with the micropolitics of discursive power and more discrete examinations of technologies of the sporting self.

— David L. Andrews

See also Body; Bourdieu, Pierre; Civilizing Process; Cultural Marxism and British Cultural Studies; Elias, Norbert; Figurational Sociology; Foucault, Michel; Gramsci, Antonio; Marxism

FURTHER READINGS AND REFERENCES

Coakley, Jay and Eric Dunning, eds. 2000. *Handbook of Sport Studies.* London: Sage.

Giulianotti, R. 2004. *Sport: A Critical Sociology.* Cambridge: Polity Press.

Ingham, Alan G. and Peter Donnelly. 1997. "A Sociology of North American Sociology of Sport: Disunity in Unity, 1965 to 1996." *Sociology of Sport Journal* 14(4):362–418.

Jarvie, Grant and Joseph A. Maguire. 1994. *Sport and Leisure in Social Thought.* London: Routledge.

Maguire, Joseph A. and Kevin Young, eds. 2002. *Theory, Sport and Society.* Oxford, UK: JAI.

STANDPOINT THEORY

The idea of a standpoint theory is most widely used in feminist theory and most strongly rooted in a broader sense of multicultural theory. Most generally, a standpoint theory is one that gives light to the specific circumstances and insider knowledge available only to members of a certain collective standpoint. This collective need not be a group in the strictest sense of the word but rather a shared location identified by some heterogeneous commonality. In other words, the idea of a collective standpoint does not imply an essential overarching characteristic but rather a sense of belonging to a group bounded by a shared experience.

The idea of a standpoint theory is a group-based ideology. An individual can be a member of several standpoints (black, woman, Jew, or black female Jew) at once, although the ways in which various forms of oppression intersect will have the strongest impact on the standpoint theory of the individual.

Standpoint theorists rally around the idea of social justice and support protesting, organizing, and testifying to one's unique social location as a means of raising awareness of, and giving validity to, all lived social experiences. There is a goal of empowering those who lack power and to diminish the line between traditional theory and other narratives. Standpoint theories are value laden and seek to disrupt the intellectual and social world but only as a means of opening them up to diversity. There is an edge to standpoint theory that is both self-critical as well as critical of other theories and the social world more broadly. Most important, standpoint theories recognize their own limitations by virtue of their unique historical, social, and cultural locations and seek to open the social stage to all members of society.

— Michael Ryan

See also Collins, Patricia Hill; Hartsock, Nancy; Identity Politics; Smith, Dorothy

FURTHER READING AND REFERENCES

Collins, Patricia Hill. 1998. *Fighting Words: Black Women and the Search for Justice.* Minneapolis: University of Minnesota Press.

Hartsock, Nancy C. M. 1998. *The Feminist Standpoint Revisited & Other Essays.* Boulder, CO: Westview.

STATE

The state is a set of institutions and agencies that has the authority to define and enforce collectively binding decisions on members of a society in the name of their common interest or general will. As noted by Max Weber, the state is distinct from other political entities by its system of legitimate domination based on rational-legal authority. The state possesses distinctive capacities that include, for example, the ability to raise taxes and the right to make decisions and laws that regulate the conduct of individuals and groups in society. The state can also be characterized by its distinctive political logic or governmentality that includes the maintenance of territorial sovereignty and the promotion of social solidarity and a national identity. Hence, the state includes a system of legal rules that bind individuals to the society, civil service bureaucracy, elected representatives, and coercive institutions such as the police and armed forces. Thus, the state is not a unified entity, nor does it have fixed institutional boundaries. It is, rather, an ensemble of multifunctional institutions and organizations. The state has no unitary interest but, rather, contains many competing interests in different parts of the state. These interests develop through negotiation, bargaining, and compromise among different groups in society, among different state actors, and between state actors and societal groups.

It is difficult to specify the relationship between the state with other institutional orders and society. Early political thinkers such as Aristotle, Augustine, and Georg Hegel believed that the state was a political abstraction standing over and above society. Karl Marx believed that the state arises with the development of modern capitalism. For Marx, the appearance of the state coincides with the development of *civil society,* which protects private property, promotes individual pursuit of private interest, and fosters the illusion that competitive market relations can create democratic and egalitarian societies. Later Marxists, including Antonio Gramsci and Louis Althusser, questioned the distinction between the state and civil society. Althusser maintained that civil organizations such as political parties, the church, and schools are part of the *ideological state apparatus.* Some aspects of civil society have a close relationship to the state and play an important role in developing public policy. The state also regulates parts of civil society by providing laws, charters, regulations, and financial support that influence the actions and decisions of organizations. Moreover, the institutional boundaries of the state are not static. They are always changing through devolution (transferring responsibilities from the national government to subnational governments), privatization (transferring responsibilities from the government to the private sector), and deregulating public policy or creating new regulatory agencies. Often, the establishment of quasi public-private organizations blurs the boundaries between the state and civil society. As the articulation of the state and civil society changes, the state becomes both a site and an object of political struggle among different groups.

The role of the state is complex and multidimensional. Five major themes are addressed: conceptualizations of the state and state power, which groups control the state policy, the development of middle-range state theory, the question of *governance,* and relationship between globalization and the state.

CONCEPTUALIZATIONS OF THE STATE AND STATE POWER

No single usage of the concept of the "state" is self-evidently correct, nor does one definition necessarily exclude other definitions in different contexts. While the state is a contested concept, empirical research and generalizations about the state and state power vary according to the theoretical orientation and level of analysis. In the *Manifesto of the Communist Party,* Marx and Engels treated the state as a committee for managing the common affairs of the bourgeois. For Max Weber, the state claims a monopoly on the legitimate use of physical force within a specific territory. Following Weber, Anthony Giddens (1987) defines the state as a "bordered power container." The boundaries of the state are not merely administrative divisions but potentially, at least, lines along which violence may erupt. The mechanisms of state power include the state's capacity for making war, its capacity to extract resources to fund its operations, the expansion of surveillance capabilities and the policing of deviance, and the active construction and maintenance of consensus and legitimacy.

For Marxian scholars, however, the role of the modern state is to reproduce the social conditions necessary for capital accumulation. Early work conceptualized the state in several different ways—for example, as an instrument of class rule, a factor of cohesion, or an institutional ensemble that mediates class conflict. Later accounts highlighted the conflicts the state faces in managing social antagonisms and crisis tendencies within capitalism. On one hand, the state must sustain the process of capital accumulation, since its own survival depends on a continuous flow of revenue; on the other hand, the state must preserve the belief in itself as a neutral arbiter of divergent societal interests to legitimate its power. For James O'Connor and Claus Offe, the state cannot effectively secure the market conditions necessary for capitalist accumulation unless it can conceal its class bias behind the cloak of democratic legitimacy. In so far as the state is increasingly called on to compensate for the failures of market mechanisms without infringing on the primacy of private production, the state will be faced with a fiscal crisis or a crisis of legitimacy. This means that crisis management will assume the form of trial-and-error responses, the content of which is determined by the changing balance of class forces.

Feminist scholars have conceptualized the state and state power in several different ways. Early work focused on the state's role in reproducing patriarchal social relations by institutionalizing male dominance over women in social policy and law. More recently, feminist scholars have focused empirical attention on how different aspects of state power, policy, and action shape, and are shaped by, gender relations. Based on studies covering welfare policy, law, and crime, feminist theorists have developed a conception of the state as a differentiated entity, composed of multiple and conflicting gender arrangements. The result has been a proliferation and diversification of feminist analyses of the state. Much of this new feminist scholarship proceeds analytically, focusing on particular state apparatuses rather than on the state as whole. In her examination of the *politics of need interpretation,* Nancy Fraser (1989) argued that state actions and practices—the *juridical-administrative-therapeutic state apparatus* (JAT)—construct women and women's needs according to certain specific but contestable interpretations, such as *caregiving, homemaker-mothers, deserving* and *undeserving* poor, among others. Other feminist work has looked at the discourse underlying state policy, examining how meanings and interpretations of femininity, masculinity, and other gender stereotypes derive in part from the shape and administration of state programs. Over the last decade, feminist theory has shifted away from discussions of how or why the state oppresses women to analyses that identify the different *gendered regimes* that women and men encounter in different parts of the state apparatus (Haney 2000).

Sociologists of race focus on the racial bases of state power, the racial biases of state actors, and the discriminatory effects of state policy. Most accounts focus on the socially constructed nature of *race* and racism and reject the notion that the state is inherently *racist* or that it is necessary or inevitable that the state policies will always reproduce racial divisions and inequality. Rather, race must be understood as occupying different degrees of importance in different state institutions at different historical moments. Such an approach sensitizes us to the inherent improbability of a unified state and the need to examine the economic, political, and cultural factors that contribute to the racialization of state policy. Thus, some state agencies may challenge racial divisions, others may be neutral, and still others may reinforce racial divisions through policies and institutional practices that are explicitly or implicitly racial (e.g., education programs, family law, and procedures for punishment, treatment, and surveillance of the criminal, deviant, and mentally ill). Examples include the use of racial criteria to assign unequal political rights to different races, different punishments for equivalent crimes according to the race of criminals and victims, the segregation of schoolchildren according to race, and other policies that discriminate on the basis of race. In short, the racial intents and effects of state policy cannot be established a priori, but only through a historical examination of specific state agencies, political processes, and historical contingencies that shape the formulation and implementation of particular policies, and exclude other policy options (Gotham 2000).

THE STATE AND SOCIAL POLICY

A second major topic concerns which groups control the policy formulation process, who supports and opposes policy proposals, and which groups benefit and suffer once the state enacts and implements certain social policies. Pluralists view the state as containing different spheres of power and influence that mediate social conflict. State actions are responses to different group pressures. For some pluralists, power is broadly shared among different political and economic interests with no one group dominating. Decision making in the political arena involves a division of labor among top decision makers. Interest groups all compete more or less equally within the political system to influence political decisions. Important policy decisions are not made by a small number of powerful individuals or groups. While large corporations might influence decisions by contributing to political candidates, for example, labor unions also contribute to their candidates. Over the long run, different interest groups share equally in the decisions made by elected officials. Control of the state by any one interest group over the long term is not possible.

Marxian theories focus on the degree to which state is subject to influence and control by the capitalist class. In his famous book, the *State in Capitalist Society*, Ralph Miliband (1969) argued that the "ruling class of capitalist society" which "owns and controls the means of production" is able "to use the state as its instrument for the domination of society" (p. 32). In a debate with Miliband, Nicos Poulantzas (1976) argued that the direct participation of members of the capitalist class in the state apparatus is not important since there are structural factors that make the state serve capitalist ends regardless of whether capitalists intervene directly, indirectly, or not at all. Whereas Miliband analyzed the state in terms of the individual human subjects who control it, Poulantzas conceptualized the state in relation to its structurally determined role in capitalist society.

The famous Miliband-Poulantzas debate helped launch a three-way debate between *class dominance theory, state-centered theory,* and *Marxian structuralism* during the 1980s and 1990s. Class dominance theorists argue that state policy is intentionally dictated by corporate interests whose representatives have captured or control the state. Some proponents maintain that corporate leaders are *overrepresented* in high decision-making positions and therefore dominate the policy-making process. Others argue that classwide rationality is articulated by representatives of the capitalist class who sit on multiple corporate boards. These representatives influence policy by acting on the basis of what is best for business as a whole. In short, class dominance theorists emphasize the class basis of state power; interactions among corporate elites, especially the largest corporations and financial institutions; and the specific political, economic, and organizational resources that allow corporate leaders to dominate the policy-making process in the face of resistance.

State-centered theory views the formulation and enactment of social policy as contingent on previous policy precedents, the *autonomous* power of state managers, and the capacities of state structures. State institutions and party organizations can be *independent* determinants of political conflicts and outcomes because officials within the state may have interests fundamentally opposed to interests in society. Once instituted, social policies reshape the organization of the state itself and affect the goals and alliances of social groups involved in ongoing political struggle. Business unity, division, and influence are only tangentially related to state economic policy since it is state managers, and not individual capitalists, who implement state policy.

Marxian structuralists focus on the structural foundations of capitalism and the process of capital accumulation as salient factors in the formulation of social policies. Influenced by Poulantzas's (1980) work, structuralists do not deny that business leaders play a central role in the policy formulation process, but they view this role as symptomatic of the structural forces of capitalism, not an ultimate cause. State policy and state structures constitute a relatively autonomous political arena that groups of capitalists use to organize political coalitions that compete for political dominance. Those coalitions that overcome opposition become the dominant power bloc. However, these political coalitions and actors cannot formulate policies at their behest but operate within a capitalist context that defines the major contending interests and sets limits on the range of likely solutions. This perspective suggests that states can be *relatively autonomous* from the capitalist class only because both are part of the mode of production.

THE DEVELOPMENT OF MIDDLE-RANGE STATE THEORY

The 1990s witnessed a third development in state theory—the development of middle-range approaches to show the complementary nature of state theories when examining state policy at different levels of analysis. Proponents of *middle-range state theory* attempt to identify the conditions under which the policy formulation mechanisms specified by the different theories—variants of Marxism, state-centric, class dominance theory, and so on—augment each other. Current research does not assume that the state, the capitalist class, or selected class factions are unified at all times. Capitalist class unity is affected by accumulation opportunities and constraints of particular class factions. Whether the needs and interests of factions of capital are contradictory or whether unity exists within the capitalist class are historically contingent questions. According to Harland Prechel (2001), the key issue to understand when considering capital-state relations is not whether class segments are united or divided, but rather the conditions under which the capitalist class is more or less divided. Similarly, the issue is not whether states are autonomous from the capitalist class or class segments, but rather the conditions under which the state is more or less autonomous. (p. 152)

Middle-range adaptations of state theories do not preclude the possibility for making general statements about the state. They do, however, challenge scholars to clearly identify the social conditions (e.g., war, depression, mass protest, and disorder) that facilitate or constrain policy choices. Gregory Hooks's (1993:40–41) analysis of World War II and postwar investment processes in the United States synthesizes three state theories—that is, class dominance, structural Marxism, and state-centered theory—to demonstrate how the U.S. federal government participated in the post-World War II industrial mobilization. At particular historical moments, state agencies and legislative committees are heavily influenced by business and business elites. Other agencies are insulated from the direct influence of business elites and may promote policies that harm certain capitalist groups. Still other agencies pursue an agenda that suits the state's administrative goals despite the resistance of business elites. Thus, state theories can complement one another: The challenge is to analyze the institutional context in which the state conceives and implements certain policies. In short, middle-range positions compel the analysis to situate historical analyses of state agencies in relation to other processes and actors (e.g., class segments, business elites) to specify the conditions that produce the outcomes asserted by each theory.

THE QUESTION OF GOVERNANCE OF THE ECONOMY

A fourth topic in state research concerns the question of *governance*. A burgeoning literature on the relationships between states and markets focuses on how market creation and regulation takes place through states. States provide an array of governance structures or mechanisms (e.g., property rights, laws, regulations, rules of exchange, etc.) that define relations of competition and enable actors in markets to organize themselves. The development of capitalist economies, including the establishment of stable and reliable conditions under which economic actors organize, compete, cooperate, and exchange is part of the core of state building. One of the central tenets of institutional theory, as it applies to the link between political actors and the state, is that the development of markets is causally related to the emergence and consolidation of specific symbiotic relationships that form between economic actors, state structures, and rules of exchange. The state's enforcement of laws, property rights, and rules of exchange affect what conceptions of control produce stable markets, disrupt some kinds of economic activity, and create new markets. Changes in property rights, rules of exchange, and legal regulations promote changes in market institutions and state-firm relations.

All forms of economic activity are embedded in social relations, and states create the institutional conditions for markets to be stable. As economic crises and new circumstances arise, powerful organized interests and market actors will attempt to influence government organizations, including legislators and the courts, to destabilize old markets and create new rules and legal opportunities to establish and expand markets. As governance structures and institutions develop, they tend to *feed back* onto economic activity. Through such feedback loops, new market networks and relationships develop symbiotically into specific state structures and regulatory frameworks that gradually embed actors' orientations and understandings of existing arrangements. This process is not static but dynamic. It means that economic actors and networks of actors exist in a competitive political climate where they must constantly struggle to influence state officials to create new rules and adapt existing rules to changing circumstances. The basic insight is that the state provides the political and legal framework that permanently shapes the economy.

GLOBALIZATION AND THE STATE

A fifth and final concern is the relationship between globalization and the state. The recent focus on globalization in state theory directs attention to the ways in which global-level forces are transforming social relations and influencing the activities and operations of states. Globalization recasts the state debate in terms of the relationship between the state and transnational processes and struggles. So-called *hyperglobalist* perspectives stress the omnipresence of globalization, maintaining that globalization imposes a financial discipline on governments, leading to a decline in the ability of states to regulate economic and social activities within their borders. In this respect, many scholars believe that the emergence of new institutions of global financial regulation (e.g., the World Bank and the International Monetary Fund) and increasing cross-border capital flows are evidence of a new global economy that prefigures the erosion or disempowering of the state (Jessop 2002). So-called *statist* perspectives emphasize the continuing significance of state institutions and national policy in organizing global economic flows and constituting the global economy. While globalization may have pushed forward a new geographic extension of state authority or a transformation of state capacities, the modern state remains a vehicle of globalization. In this conception, globalization is not a novel socioeconomic condition, nor does it undermine the power of national governments or state sovereignty. Globalization may affect the attributes of states, but it does not change their basic identity or disrupt their capacity to act.

It is not the state that is pressured by globalization or that generates globalization. Some parts of the state are actively involved in promoting some kinds of globalization, other parts of the state may be harmed by these state actions, other parts of the state may see their capacities strengthen or weaken as a result of global pressures, and other parts of the state may actively resist globalization. Even as some parts of the state may disengage from the market economy (e.g., through privatization, deregulation, and trade liberalization), they may intervene in other extra-market sectors and attempt to create the social conditions for marketization, commodification, and valorization. In doing so, they may favor some factions, classes, and social forces over others; they may prompt struggles to reorganize state capacities; they may constrain the actions of firms and alter networks; and they may aggravate economic contradictions and crisis tendencies.

— Kevin Fox Gotham

See also Capitalism; Civil Society; Globalization; Marxism; Power

FURTHER READINGS AND REFERENCES

Fraser, Nancy. 1989. *Unruly Practices: Power Discourse, and Gender in Contemporary Social Theory.* Minneapolis: University of Minnesota Press.

Giddens, Anthony. 1987. *Nation-State and Violence.* Berkeley: University of California Press.

Gotham, Kevin Fox. 2000. "Racialization and the State: The Housing Act of 1934 and the Origins of the Federal Housing Administration (FHA)." *Sociological Perspectives* 43(2): 291–316.

Haney, Lynne. 2000. "Feminist State Theory: Applications to Jurisprudence, Criminology, and the Welfare State." *Annual Review of Sociology* 26:641-66.

Hooks, Gregory. 1993. "The Weakness of Strong Theories: The U.S. State's Dominance of the World War II Investment Process." *American Sociological Review* 58:37–53.

Jessop, Bob. 2002. *The Future of the Capitalist State.* New York: Blackwell.

Miliband, Ralph. 1969. *The State in Capitalist Society.* New York: Basic Books.

Poulantzas, Nicos. 1976. "The Capitalist State: A Reply to Miliband and Laclau." *New Left Review* 95:63–83.

———. 1980. *State, Power, and Socialism.* New York: New Left Books.

Prechel, Harland. 2001. *Big Business and the State: Historical Transformations and Corporate Transformation, 1880s-1990s.* Albany: State University of New York Press.

STATICS AND DYNAMICS

Contemporary usage of the terms *statics* and *dynamics* has its roots in the work of Auguste Comte (1798–1857). Comte developed social physics, or what he eventually referred to as *sociology* (Comte was the first to use this term), during the 1830s in France. He believed that sociology should be strongly modeled after the hard sciences, particularly biology. He saw society as a social organism and was interested in studying how various components, or subsystems, contributed to the social system as a whole. Comte was relatively unconcerned with the domain of the individual (although his thinking was shaped by basic assumptions about individuals) but, rather, was concerned with the social groupings of individuals, collective existence, and macro-level phenomena (especially the family). Furthermore, Comte gave priority to theory over empirical research.

Statics and dynamics are cornerstones of Comtean theory. Comte argued that sociology should be concerned with both existing social structures, or social statics, and social change, or social dynamics. Comte's study of social statics is a forerunner to much contemporary work in sociology in general, and sociological theory in particular, especially structural-functionalism. He was interested in the ways in which the various parts of the society functioned and, more important, with their relationship to the social whole. He saw the parts of society and the whole in a state of harmony (what would later be called equilibrium) and privileged starting from the social whole and proceeding to the parts. Social statics, as the name implies, also meant freezing time to get a look at society as it existed at a particular historical moment.

In contrast to social statics, social dynamics involves looking at the ways in which society changes over time. Time is a necessary element for the study of social dynamics since it is inherent in what Comte saw to be the natural evolution of society toward a final harmonious state. Comte ([1830–42]1855) even refers to social dynamics as the "theory of Natural Progress of Human Society" (p. 515). He believed that society was continually improving and that the same law of progressive development applied universally to all societies. Thus, although the speed of social evolution may vary from one society to another, or from one time period to another within a given society, there is a continual progression toward the goal of a more harmonious society.

Although Comte felt that studying both social statics and social dynamics were important for understanding society, he placed a greater emphasis on social dynamics. This relates to Comte's view that society did not need a revolution in order to make things better (he was largely critical of the French Revolution and its effects on society) because the natural progress of things would eventually deal with the ills that were plaguing the social world. Therefore, he advocated reforms, but only as a means of helping along the natural evolution of society. Since society was constantly evolving, and such evolution brought with it continual improvement, the study of social dynamics was privileged over the study of social statics.

Comte's work on statics and dynamics influenced many future sociologists. Émile Durkheim was particularly influenced by his ideas on macrosociology and the social body as an organism (especially in his thinking on material and nonmaterial social facts), evolution (Durkheim focused on the change from mechanical to organic solidarity), and the promotion of reforms to cure the pathologies of society.

Herbert Spencer was also heavily influenced by Comte and his thinking on social statics and dynamics. Spencer, however, did not want to be seen as a disciple of Comte but rather as one of his antagonists. Thus, although he held Comte in the highest esteem, he believed that his ideas were of a very different nature. Ironically, Spencer's first book was titled *Social Statics* ([1850]1954). He claimed that at the time of its publication he had knowledge of Comte only insofar as that he knew he was a French philosopher and not at all his body of work. Thus, Spencer ([1850] 1954) gives quite different meanings to the terms *statics* and *dynamics* in his work. He takes social statics to mean "the equilibrium of a perfect society" and social dynamics to mean "the forces by which society is advanced toward perfection" (p. 367).

Structural functionalists in general, as well as their leading figure Talcott Parsons, were another group of social thinkers influenced by Comte's (as well as Spencer's) emphasis on social statics in their focus on social structures and social institutions. Furthermore, later in his career, Parsons developed an evolutionary theory that bore at least some resemblance to Comte's.

The entire field of sociology owes a great deal to Comte. His emphasis on social statics and dynamics continues to be of importance to many in sociology today in the often-made distinction between social structure and social change.

— Michael Ryan

See also Comte, August; Dahrendorf, Ralf; Parsons, Talcott; Spencer, Herbert; Time

FURTHER READINGS AND REFERENCES

Comte, Auguste. [1830–1842] 1855. *The Positive Philosophy of Auguste Comte.* New York: Calvin Blanchard.
———. [1854] 1968. *System of Positive Polity.* Vol. 4. New York: Burt Franklin.
Spencer, Herbert. [1850] 1954. *Social Statics.* New York: Robert Schalkenbach Foundation.

STATUS RELATIONS

Status generally refers to an individual's position or rank, along a standard of honor or respect, within a group or social hierarchy. As such, *status relations* are defined as observable rank-ordered pairings of individuals in some social situation. For instance, when male presidential advisors are more influential than females, when senior partners in a legal firm are given access to the beach home but junior partners are excluded, or when attractive children dominate the best playground equipment, relations are affected by status. In each case, a characteristic (i.e., gender, seniority, or beauty) produces advantages wherein some individuals are ranked more highly than others. What follows is a brief examination of historical accounts of status relations, their causes and consequences in group interaction, and prevailing theories of this phenomenon. We conclude by surveying contemporary directions in status research.

BACKGROUND

Interest in status relations is as varied and diverse as sociology itself. The first systematic writings can be traced to Aristotle, who claimed that status, merit, or excellence is one basis for the allocation of social rewards. Max Weber applied the concept of status more broadly, noting that status groups (i.e., white-collar workers vs. blue-collar workers) share common lifestyles as indicated by housing, dress, and leisure time activities. For Weber, status is an important dimension of social stratification. Thorstein Veblen linked status and economic behaviors, noting that people express status through the conspicuous consumption of material wealth. Modern theorists tend to use the term *status* more uniformly, in reference to the honor or prestige one is granted in a social situation.

That status relations have captured the attention of social theorists probably stems from the numerous interesting properties such relations exhibit. Status relations are seemingly universal, quite robust, and often paradoxical. First, status relations are universal in that they emerge among turkeys eating bugs, macaques living in captivity, and humans deliberating on a jury. That humans and animals order themselves along a standard of respect or deference is a phenomenon that spans the phylogenetic scale. Second, status relations are fairly robust in that they emerge quickly and are mostly stable. In human groups, status ordering typically emerges within the first few minutes of interaction and tends to change very little over time. Finally, perhaps the most compelling and bothersome property is that status relations frequently pose a paradox. That is, status ordering frequently exists even when the most competent or capable individuals are not those with the most input or influence in the group. The combination of these three factors may account for the widespread interest in status and status relations. Some of the ways that status affects social relationships are considered next.

EFFECTS OF STATUS

Over five decades of research has been aimed at understanding how status affects behavior, cognition, and emotion. In terms of behavior, early studies found that high status tends to produce social influence. For instance, in a classic military study of three-person decision-making teams, it was found that pilots were more influential than navigators, and navigators were more influential than gunners. In essence, the participants act as if those with more prestigious occupations (i.e., pilots) have better ideas than those with lower occupational prestige (i.e., gunners) even when the task is not related to occupation. Such early studies set the stage for more detailed inquiry and the discovery that status relations tend to produce a complex web of interrelated behaviors, perceptions, and emotions. The most significant program in this regard was initiated by Robert Freed Bales.

Bales studied relatively small groups of individuals (2 to 20) working together on a common task. A graduate student of Bales, Joseph Berger, noticed that within a relatively short period of time, a structure of inequality emerged wherein some individuals dominate the interaction more than others. For instance, some people in the group (1) receive more opportunities to perform, (2) perform more often, (3) are evaluated more positively for their performance, and (4) have more influence over the group decisions. Berger noted that such measures tend to be highly correlated, such that individuals high on one dimension tended to be high on all dimensions. He conceived of these interrelated measures as reflecting a single *observable power and prestige order.* Today, we know that the primary effect of status is that it leads to an observable power and prestige order wherein some individuals are advantaged over others.

Status not only affects overt behavior but also influences perceptions, cognitions, and emotional reactions. For instance, high-status individuals are perceived to be generally more competent at a range of tasks, viewed as better group leaders, and largely regarded as more socially important than lower-status individuals. Martha Foschi and associates have shown that status beliefs often result in a "double standard," wherein the same activity by high- and low-status people (i.e., scoring 82 on a math test) is treated as differentially reflecting math ability. Another line of research tracks how status alters emotions and sentiments. Here, it has been shown that high status is associated with positive emotions while low status tends to produce negative emotions. High-status people tend to experience pride, satisfaction, and happiness from interaction, while low-status

individuals often report feelings of fear, resentment, and anger. Not only does status affect how one feels, it also affects what one can express. Some research shows that high-status members are normatively free to publicly express their emotions more so than low-status members.

CAUSES OF STATUS

In general, status is a result of the traits people possess, the resources they control, and their actions in group situations. The lion's share of research to date has focused on how observable traits, either achieved or ascribed, lead to status. Achieved status occurs when a person earns some level of honor or respect by way of individual merit or achievement. For example, Bill Gates, founder of Microsoft, may be said to have achieved his high status as a result of his entrepreneurial ability and business savvy. Ascribed status, on the other hand, occurs when a person attains status based on inherent characteristics or family lineage. For instance, George W. Bush, the 43rd president of the United States, may be said to have ascribed status based on his membership in a wealthy and politically powerful family. Also notable is that he possesses other significant characteristics, such as race and gender, that tend to carry social advantages. For instance, studies generally find that men are allocated higher status than women when the two interact, and whites are allocated higher status than African Americans.

More broadly, any trait that systematically produces advantages and disadvantages in a given culture is known as a *status characteristic.* The theory of status characteristics and expectation states, developed by Berger and associates, conceptualizes two kinds of status characteristics. *Specific status characteristics* exist when (1) there are two or more states that are differentially evaluated, and (2) each state is associated with specific performance expectations. For example, algebra skill is a specific status characteristic when being good at algebra is preferable to being bad at algebra and when one expects an algebra expert to be competent at a range of other math-related tasks. Specific status characteristics generate status for a relatively narrow range of tasks.

Diffuse status characteristics are broader in their effect. The defining characteristic of a diffuse status characteristic is that, in addition to having two or more states that are differentially valued, and carrying specific performance expectations, such traits also produce a wide range of general performance expectations. For example, gender is a diffuse status characteristic when one state (e.g., male) is more highly valued than the other state (e.g., female), when men are expected to be more competent than women at specific tasks such as sports, and when men are generally expected to be more logical, intelligent, and capable at a wide range of tasks. Studies in the United States show that race, gender, age, physical attractiveness, education, and occupation are diffuse status characteristics that affect social interaction. In each case, individuals who possess the positive state (i.e., white, male, older, attractive, educated) are treated as if they are more competent than those who possess the negative state (i.e., African American, female, younger, unattractive, uneducated).

Although it is easy to understand why status might be granted to a person with a specific skill (i.e., knowledge of algebra) related to a group task (i.e., completing a math assignment), it is more difficult to understand how status comes to be associated with inherent traits such as gender, race, and physical attractiveness. Why would whites/men/ attractive people be viewed as more competent? From where do such beliefs arise in the first place, and how are they perpetuated? Cecilia Ridgeway's *Status Construction Theory* offers one explanation. The theory asserts that traits become status characteristics when they are systematically linked to another valued characteristic. Thus, imagine a group whose members contain different levels of some social reward (i.e., call them rich vs. poor) and some other distinguishing attribute that has no status significance (i.e., dark vs. fair hair). Now, if for some reason people observe that more dark-haired individuals are resource rich, and more fair-haired individuals are resource poor, then those people may come to view dark hair as indicating higher status or worthiness. It is as if people presume that dark-haired individuals are resource rich because they are more deserving. Ridgeway and associates have shown that once such beliefs emerge, people act on the beliefs in social interaction and can even spread them to others. In this manner, a particular status belief may eventually become consensual within a society, and part of the overall cultural framework.

To illustrate, consider a basketball team that has bearded and nonbearded players (i.e., a nominal difference with no status value). Now imagine that the bearded players happen to perform better than the nonbearded players during the very first game. Even if there is no "real" difference in the players' abilities, the members of the team are likely to walk away from the game (mis)attributing greater competence to the bearded players. In addition, they will carry that expectation with them to other games and other social situations. Moreover, since the players, both bearded and nonbearded, expect the bearded players to perform better, chances are they will be given more opportunities to do so (i.e., more opportunities to shoot and more influence over team strategy). This results in a sort of self-fulfilling prophecy that bolsters and reinforces the initial status belief. Over time, we can imagine that the "bearded is better" idea will be spread throughout the league and become normatively accepted.

THEORIES CONNECTING CAUSE AND EFFECT

Perhaps the most influential theory, in terms of spawning a proliferation of other theories, was developed by Joseph Berger and associates in the 1960s. Berger's *expectation states theory* proposes the notion of a performance expectation to explain status in groups. A *performance expectation* is a belief about an actor's future task performance. Performance expectations are not generally conscious; rather, they are hunches, of which one is unaware, about whose suggestions are likely to be better. The theory claims that through social interaction, individuals develop performance expectations for themselves and others regarding task competency. Because performance expectations are formed on the basis of observable acts and shared understandings of the world, these beliefs are generally consensual across members of a group. Those perceived to be more competent are higher in the ordering of expectations; those perceived to be less competent are lower. In turn, performance expectations are postulated to be the key theoretical construct that shapes differentiation along an observable order of power and prestige. Later elaborations of expectation states theory give critical insights into the traits and behaviors that yield expectations and status in groups.

Status characteristics theory is a related branch of the larger expectation states program that emerged in the 1970s to connect culturally specific beliefs and performance expectations. Briefly, status characteristics theory consists of five interrelated assumptions that explain how status characteristics translate into behavioral outcomes. First, status characteristics become salient if they differentiate members of a task group or are directly relevant to the task at hand. Second, salient status characteristics are assumed to be task relevant unless they are explicitly shown to be irrelevant. Third, status information is incorporated and maintained, according to the principles described in the first two assumptions above, as individuals enter or leave the group. Fourth, all salient status information is combined to form an aggregated performance expectation associated with each member. Finally, aggregated performance expectations give rise to observable differences in social interaction. Those with relatively higher performance expectations are predicted to receive more opportunities to perform, perform more often, be evaluated more positively, and have greater social influence over the group's decisions. Tests have generally supported the basic claims of the theory.

Another branch of the expectation states program focuses on the relation between rewards and performance expectations. The principle idea undergirding *reward expectations theory* is that levels of reward can induce performance expectations and, subsequently, status. In one study, Karen Cook (1975) showed that when experimental subjects received high versus low levels of payment, those subjects used their payment level to infer they had greater or lesser task ability. Studies find that individuals receiving higher levels of rewards are presumed to be more competent, or somehow better, than those receiving lower levels of reward. Imagine choosing between two doctors, knowing only that Dr. Jones makes $100,000 while Dr. Smith makes $40,000. It is easy to attribute a causal link between pay and skill, as in "Dr. Jones would not be so highly paid if he were not a great doctor." This illustrates how performance expectations can be inferred from associated rewards.

Finally, other theoretical research shows that overt behaviors can produce status in groups. Actions such as taking the head seat at a table, talking in a confident and firm manner, maintaining an upright posture, making direct eye contact, and various other actions are seen as indicators of competence and can thereby produce status. Berger and colleagues refer to such factors as *task cues,* because they tend to signal who is most comfortable and competent at completing the group task. A more complex kind of behavioral sequence, in which behavioral cycles between two or more actors come to reinforce the status order, is called a *behavior interchange pattern.* For example, a repetitive pattern of one individual asserting, "I think that we should do X" while a second individual agrees, "I think this is a good idea," serves to reinforce the higher status of the first person relative to the second. M. Hamit Fisek and associates have recently developed a theory that explains how behavior interchange patterns interact with status cues to produce participation rates in groups.

CURRENT TRENDS

The majority of research to date has aimed to understand the cause and effect of status in isolation of other social processes—status neat, as it were. With a basic understanding of status now in place, investigators recently have examined how status interacts with other social forces such as legitimacy, power, identity, and organizational structure. For instance, Henry Walker and Morris Zelditch (1993) have sought to understand how status inequalities come to be accepted, or treated as normatively appropriate, in groups. Their studies document a range of conditions under which status inequalities are legitimated and come to persist over time.

Although the two are distinct, status also is linked to social power, defined as a structural ability to extract valued resources from another person. For instance, Shane Thye (2000) has demonstrated that resources controlled by high-status actors are seen as more valuable than resources controlled by lower-status actors. This provides high-status individuals with an advantage when they negotiate with lower-status partners. This phenomenon has also been documented in the field, where studies find that African American women are sharply disadvantaged in car negotiations. Interestingly, although status produces power, the converse is not necessarily true. That is, having high power does not necessarily lead to high status. High-power actors who exercise their power (i.e., a dictator exercising political power) can often stir negative emotions within those whom power is used against. Michael Lovaglia and Jeffrey Houser have shown that high power yields high status only when negative emotions are blocked.

Perhaps the latest trend in status research is to combine status, social identity, and organizational structure. A recent series of tests by William Kalkhoff and Chris Barnum have determined that status and social identity have comparable effects in producing influence. That is, given a disagreement with another person, subjects were about as influenced by higher-status partners as they were by in-group members. In addition, Ridgeway and associates have argued that status-organizing processes are also affected by organizational structure. That is, imagine an all-female group in an otherwise male-dominated organization. It is not difficult to imagine that, in such a context, gender status will become salient for those women in the group and affect their performance. Research in this domain will inevitably shed light on gender-based inequalities found in the modern organization and promises to be an important avenue for investigation as future research unfolds.

— Shane Thye and Christine Witkowski

See also Berger, Joseph; Cook, Karen; Identity; Power; Social Class; Social Interaction; Veblen, Thorstein; Weber, Max

FURTHER READINGS AND REFERENCES

Berger, Joseph, Thomas L. Conner, and M. Hamit Fisek, eds. 1974. *Expectation States Theory: A Theoretical Research Program.* Cambridge, MA: Winthrop.

Berger, Joseph, M. Hamit Fisek, Robert Z. Norman, and David G. Wagner. 1985. "The Formation of Reward Expectations in Status Situations." Pp. 215–61 in *Status, Rewards, and Influence,* edited by Joseph Berger and Morris Zelditch, Jr. San Francisco: Jossey-Bass.

Berger, Joseph, M. Hamit Fisek, Robert Z. Norman, and Morris Zelditch Jr. 1977. *Status Characteristics and Social Interaction.* New York: Elsevier.

Cook, Karen S. 1975. "Expectations, Evaluations, and Equity." *American Sociological Review* 40:372–88.

Ridgeway, Cecilia L. and Henry A. Walker. 1995. "Status Structures." Pp. 281–310 in *Sociological Perspectives on Social Psychology,* edited by Karen S. Cook, Gary Alan Fine, and James S. House. Boston: Allyn & Bacon.

Thye, Shane. 2000. "A Status Value Theory of Power in Exchange Relations." *American Sociological Review* 65:407–32.

Wagner, David G. and Joseph Berger. 1993. "Status Characteristics Theory: The Growth of a Program." Pp. 23–63 in *Theoretical Research Programs: Studies in the Growth of Theory,* edited by Joseph Berger and Morris Zelditch Jr. Stanford, CA: Stanford University Press.

Walker, Henry A. and Morris Zelditch Jr. 1993. "Power, Legitimacy and Stability of Authority: A Theoretical Research Program." Pp. 364–81 in *Theoretical Research Programs:*

Studies in the Growth of Theory, edited by Joseph Berger and Morris Zelditch Jr. Stanford, CA: Stanford University Press.

Webster, Murray. 2003. "Puzzles, Provisional Solutions, and New Provinces." Pp. 281–310 in *Advances in Group Processes: Power and Status,* edited by Shane R. Thye and John Skvoretz. London: Elsevier.

STRATIFICATION

Stratification describes the differential arrangement of persons or positions within a society. The term can also be used to refer to the hierarchical ordering of societies or other macrolevel entities.

Many of the founding fathers of sociology were interested in issues of stratification. Karl Marx was most interested in economic stratification and how it spelled itself out in the capitalist system. He saw two broad layers (although an argument can be made that he actually saw more) in society—capitalists at the top and proletariat at the bottom. His means for determining the social strata were purely economic and based on the ownership of the means of production.

Max Weber took Marx's theory of stratification one step further to also include dimensions of status and power as well as economics. Weber's ideas about economic stratification are found in what he termed *class.* The concept of a class does not refer to a community of actors but rather to any group of actors whose shared class location is, or at least could be, the basis of some form of action. Status, on the other hand, does represent a shared community. While class refers to economic production, class refers largely to consumption. Hence, status is based on one's lifestyle. A third dimension of stratification, the concept of a party, is oriented solely toward the attainment of power. This is the most highly organized of the three and is found in the political realm.

Kingsley Davis and Wilbert Moore (1945) wrote what is perhaps the best-known piece of structural-functional literature on the topic of stratification. They argued that social stratification is both functional and necessary for a society to continue and be healthy. They argued that no society had ever been totally classless because all societies need a system of stratification, and this need brings such a system into existence. This is not to imply that the creation of a stratified system is a conscious undertaking of the society but rather that it is an "unconsciously evolved device." Their theoretical orientation of structural-functionalism also led them to view society not in terms of actors but in terms of positions. Consequently, their main interest was in how certain positions come to be ranked higher or lower in the system, not how certain people come to fill those particular positions.

Davis and Moore believed that one of the major problems in society was how to get the right people into the right positions and after they are there, how to keep them there. This was a problem because some positions are more pleasant to occupy than others, some are more important to the continuity of society, and different positions require different skills. They argued that those positions that are deemed higher up in society (e.g., doctors, lawyers, politicians) were less pleasant to occupy, more important to the overall society, and required the greatest level of ability. Hence, these positions had to be rewarded with the highest levels of prestige, money, and leisure.

The structural-functional approach to stratification has been criticized on many levels. First, it is seen as simply perpetuating the privilege of those who already enjoy it. Second, it assumes that simply because stratification has existed in the past, it must continue in the future. Third, it is difficult to support that there are positions in society that are more or less important than others. Are nurses any less important than the doctor's they assist? Fourth, any shortage of people willing to occupy higher positions in that stratified system is caused primarily by the stratified system itself through differential access to means such as education and training. Finally, it negates the possibility of one's being motivated to accept a higher position solely, or even in part, for its intrinsic rewards.

A more contemporary theory of stratification was put forth by Randall Collins (1975, 1990). Unlike Marx, Weber, or Davis and Moore, Collins focused on the microlevel effects of stratification. He studied stratification because he sees this phenomenon affecting nearly ever aspect of people's daily lives. He was especially interested in showing that "stratification and organization are grounded in the interactions of everyday life" (Collins 1990:72). For this reason, although he drew from Marx and Weber's theories, he drew most heavily from ethnomethodology and phenomenology.

Collins's theory begins with the assumption that people are inherently social but that they are also self-interested and hence conflict prone as they seek to outdo others. Three basic tenets outline his conflict approach: (1) People live in self-constructed subjective worlds, (2) people other than the individual actor may have the power to affect that actor's subjective experience, and (3) these outside people often try to control the actor's experience, which leads to a conflict. These tenets led Collins to his five basic principles of conflict analysis in social stratification: (1) There should be a focus on real-life experiences rather than abstract ideologies, (2) an examination should be made into how each actor is able to manipulate or is restricted by possession of material factors or lack thereof, (3) there is a conscious or unconscious exploitation of those with fewer resources by those with greater access to resources, (4) beliefs and idea systems should be analyzed with consideration to interests, resources, and power, and (5) the study of stratification should be undertaken in a scientific way, using hypothesis testing, empirical research, and whenever possible, causal explanations.

The study of stratification is also undertaken within feminist theory. For example, Janet Chafetz (1984, 1990) uses analytic conflict theory to focus on gender inequality, or what she calls sex stratification. She seeks to understand the structural conditions that lead to sex stratification across time and cultures. She explores the conditions that affect its intensity, including fertility patterns, economic surplus, and patriarchal ideologies among others. These variables are considered important because they are the framework of the home and the economic marketplace and how women are able to move between these two locations. Chafetz asserts that women will experience the least disadvantage when they are able to find an equilibrium between the responsibilities in the home environment and an autonomous role in the economic marketplace. She also outlines what she perceives as important locations in the structure where gender equity might be achieved by improving women's conditions.

— Michael Ryan

See also Chafetz, Janet; Collins, Randall; Conflict Theory; Marx, Karl; Weber, Max

FURTHER READINGS AND REFERENCES

Chafetz, Janet Saltzman. 1984. *Sex and Advantage.* Totowa, NJ: Rowman & Allanheld.

———. 1990. *Gender Equity: An Integrated Theory of Stability and Change.* Newbury Park, CA: Sage.

Collins, Randall. 1975. *Conflict Sociology: Toward an Exploratory Science.* New York: Academic Press.

———. 1990. "Conflict Theory and the Advance of Macro-Historical Sociology." Pp. 68–87 in *Frontiers of Social Theory: The New Synthesis,* edited by G. Ritzer. New York: Columbia University Press.

Davis, Kingsley and Wilbert Moore. 1945. "Some Principles of Stratification." *American Sociological Review* 10:242–49.

Lengermann, Patricia Madoo and Jill Niebrugge-Brantley. 2000. "Contemporary Feminist Theory." Pp. 307–55 in *Modern Sociological Theory,* edited by George Ritzer. Boston: McGraw-Hill.

STRAUSS, ANSELM

Anselm L. Strauss (1916–1996) was an American symbolic interactionist and cofounder of the grounded theory method. Strauss advocated developing middle-range theories from systematic analysis of qualitative data. His noted works span his career from his major coauthored textbook with Alfred Lindesmith, *Social Psychology,* in 1949 to his culminating volume, *Continuous Permutations of Actions* in 1993. Among Strauss's principal contributions are his coauthored works, *Awareness of Dying* (1965) and *The Discovery of Grounded Theory* (1967) as well as numerous theoretical analyses of empirical research that reconceptualized ideas in their respective substantive fields. Strauss received his baccalaureate degree from the University of Virginia, where the writings of Robert Park awakened his sociological consciousness. He received his doctorate from the University of Chicago. While at Chicago, the works of pragmatists George Herbert Mead, John Dewey, and Charles Peirce influenced him, and numerous conversations with Herbert Blumer inspired his quest to integrate theory and research. His involvement in the vibrant intellectual climate at Chicago among faculty and graduate students made Strauss a vital part of the "second Chicago school" (Fine 1995).

Strauss brought the freshness and fluidity of pragmatist thought to his studies and integrated pragmatist concerns with action throughout his lengthy career. Agency and acts—and their meanings to the actors themselves—were fundamental to Strauss's sociological research and theorizing. This stance distinguished his work from midcentury structural-functionalists who discounted firsthand studies of research participants' views, endeavors, and accounts and distrusted theorizing that began with them. Strauss's work provided a major source of continuity and development of Chicago school sociology during the latter half of the twentieth century. He began theorizing by challenging deterministic views with a social psychology that was open-ended, emergent, and thus, somewhat indeterminate. The originality of his thought is evident in his early essay, *Mirrors and Masks: The Search for Identity* (1959) in which he treats identity as a way to organize ideas and to permit new theoretical insights to emerge that take into account social processes and their symbolic underpinnings. Strauss argues that language plays a crucial role in human behavior and in the complex weaving of subjective and social identities. Through naming, individuals locate, evaluate, and understand self and others as well as objects and events and subsequently direct their actions.

Although first known as a social psychologist, Strauss developed the concept of *negotiated order* in his 1978 publication of *Negotiations: Varieties, Processes, Contexts, and Social Order.* This treatise brought symbolic interactionism to the mesolevel of analysis and recast conceptualizations of how organizations work. By looking at the mesolevel, Strauss addressed the collective life of social worlds and organizations that lie between micro-interactions and macrosocietal structure. Rather than assuming order as a given in social life, Strauss showed that people negotiated and renegotiated order as they interacted individually and collectively. However, Strauss's explicit constructionist statement did not deny the existence of social structural constraints. Instead, it fostered seeing how interacting individuals acted toward, contested, or reproduced them through taken-for-granted understandings and routines.

Consistent with Strauss's interest in action and organization, his coauthored study with Barney G. Glaser, *Awareness of Dying* (1965), provided a theoretical explication of the organization of information about the dying patient's status, including who knew the patient was dying, when they knew, and what, if anything, they said or did about it. The temporal features of the patient's dying also intersect with work, careers, and earlier predictions—all of which affect information control. Glaser and Strauss's types of *awareness contexts* had wide applicability in situations in which vital information is withheld from certain central participants.

Glaser and Strauss attempted to delineate their methods of conceptual development in their study of dying in *The Discovery of Grounded Theory* (1967). This book advanced both theory construction and methodological rigor by offering a flexible set of systematic guidelines to develop inductive middle-range theories from empirical data that, in turn, explain those data. The authors combined the Chicago school emphases on symbolic interactionism and qualitative research with codified methods of theory construction. Glaser and Strauss's book challenged the theoretical and methodological hegemony of the day, legitimated conducting qualitative research in its own right, and ultimately advanced theory development in many substantive fields, disciplines, and professions.

Grounded theory involves simultaneous data collection and analytic procedures in which the emerging analysis shapes further data collection. Coding is aimed to identify processes and their categories and to define the properties of categories theoretically. Grounded theory is an inherently comparative method. Grounded theorists compare data with data, data with category, and category to category. They use each level of comparison to illuminate properties and to specify conditions under which their categories are germane. As grounded theorists' categories become more conceptual, they engage in *theoretical sampling*. This type of sampling means seeking data to fill out, refine, and test their theoretical categories. Grounded theorists work across substantive fields to develop generic theoretical categories with broad explanatory power. The resulting grounded theories fit the data they explain, provide useful, dense, and integrated explanations, offer insights to research participants, and are modifiable through further research.

The *Discovery* book laid out the logic and justifications for building middle-range theory from qualitative research. Strauss developed his position and explicated how to construct grounded theories in two important qualitative analysis textbooks, *Qualitative Analysis for Social Scientists* (1987) and *Basics of Qualitative Research* (1998), coauthored with Juliet Corbin. In these books, he moved toward technical advancement of grounded theory methodology and verification, although he maintained the earlier emphasis on comparative methods and theoretical sampling.

Strauss's contributions cut across several substantive areas. He gave a new depth to urban sociology through studying symbolic imagery in *Images of the American City,* published in 1961. The images that people hold of cities influence their actions and moral stance toward them. Strauss brought a processural view to occupations and professions by looking at differentiation and interaction between sectors of professions and how they advanced their positions. His work made conceptual advances in medical sociology that informed the entire discipline when this subfield might have otherwise developed only as an applied area. Strauss's numerous studies in medical sociology move from managing information and illness to larger theoretical questions of body and identity and biographical disruption. In addition, his interest in the organization of medical work sparked generic organizational concepts. Strauss proposed a concept of *social worlds* as a new unit of theoretical analysis in organizational studies. The concept assumes permeable group boundaries, individual and collective commitments, the temporality of social structures, and viewed process and change as routine. This perspective takes how people organize themselves into account—despite structural constraints and actual or potential conflict.

The concerns with which Strauss began his career resound in his final theoretical statement, *Continual Permutations of Action* (1993): the theoretical significance of meaning and action, dynamic—and open-ended—relations between individuals and social structures, the integration of social psychology and social organization, tensions between negotiated orders and habitual routines, and the explication of a pragmatist theory of action. Strauss (1) articulates anew the significance of language, fluidity of complex relations, the emergence of contingencies, and the blurred collective boundaries that he implied decades before in *Mirrors and Masks;* (2) extends his theoretical insights about relations between body, self, time, and symbols that informed his medical sociology; (3) argues against the presumed objective consequences of status variables; and (4) develops his statement of action as interactions between and among group members. In the introduction to the book, Strauss describes himself as someone who has devoted himself to working out the sociological implications of the pragmatist/interactionist traditions. His opus stands as testimony to the significance of this effort.

— Kathy Charmaz

See also Pragmatism; Social Constructionism; Social Worlds; Symbolic Interaction

FURTHER READINGS AND REFERENCES

Fine, Gary A., ed. 1995. *A Second Chicago School? The Development of a Postwar American Sociology.* Chicago, IL: University of Chicago Press.

Glaser, Barney G. and Anselm L. Strauss. 1965. *Awareness of Dying.* Chicago, IL: Aldine.

———. 1967. *The Discovery of Grounded Theory: Strategies for Qualitative Research.* Chicago. IL: Aldine.

Strauss, Anselm. 1993. *Continual Permutations of Action.* Hawthorne, NY: Aldine.

Strauss, Anselm and Juliet Corbin. 1998. *Basics of Qualitative Research: Grounded Theory Procedures and Techniques.* 2d ed. Thousand Oaks, CA: Sage.

STRENGTH OF WEAK TIES

The concept of the "strength of weak ties" was first proposed and developed by Mark Granovetter in a 1973 article of the same title. The argument is that while one might think strong interpersonal ties are more significant than weak for most purposes, this may not be so when what people need is information. Because our close friends tend to move in the same circles that we do, the information they receive overlaps considerably with what we already know. Acquaintances, by contrast, know people that we do not, and thus receive more novel information. This is in part because acquaintances are typically less similar to one another than close friends and in part because they spend less time together. Moving in different circles from ours, they connect us to a wider world. They may therefore be better sources when we need to go beyond what our own group knows, as in finding a new job or obtaining a scarce service. This is so even though close friends may be more interested than acquaintances in helping us; social structure dominates motivation.

This argument also has macrolevel implications. If each person's close friends know one another, they form a close-knit clique. This suggests that individuals are connected to other cliques through their weak ties and not their strong ones. Thus, from an "aerial" view of social networks, cliques are connected to one another, if at all, mainly by weak ties. It is, then, weak ties that determine the extent of information diffusion in large-scale social structures (playing, in this regard, a role similar to that of hydrogen bonds in chemical reactions). One outcome of this is that in scientific fields, new information and ideas are more efficiently diffused through weak ties (see Granovetter 1983). Another application is to community organization. Granovetter (1973) argued that communities lacking in weak ties may be fragmented into discrete cliques that have great difficulty organizing across these to confront a common threat. See,

for example, his comments on the inability of some communities to resist destruction brought by "urban renewal" (pp. 1373–76) and his exchange with Herbert Gans (Granovetter 1974) who had proposed a more cultural argument to explain the same phenomenon.

Though Granovetter was the first to develop the sociological implications of this argument in detail, he drew on earlier research that strongly suggested this effect. For example, Rapoport and Horvath (1961) had shown that if you ask junior high school students to name their eight best friends in order, best, next best, and so on, and you then trace out networks of all those reached from randomly chosen starting points, considerably more people can be reached through seventh and eighth best friends than through first and second best. They attributed this to the greater overlap of networks among closer friends.

Later work has extended these arguments. Granovetter (1983) reviewed a series of studies that used or assessed the validity of the weak ties idea. Marsden and Campbell (1984) made the first serious attempt to assess the validity of different measures of tie strength, concluding that "closeness" or "emotional intensity" was a better indicator than three others Granovetter had mentioned in his original article—amount of time spent together, reciprocal services, and mutual confiding. Burt (1992) extended the weak ties argument by emphasizing the importance of "structural holes" in social networks. His approach emphasizes the importance of whether ties bridge separate parts of social networks and the strategic advantage for those who can operate through those bridging ties and thus control the only route for important information or resources to flow from one segment to another. Beginning in the late 1990s, the idea of weak ties became one part of a new interdisciplinary literature on complex networks, which developed more sophisticated arguments than before on flows, connectivity, and the robustness or fragility of large networks, including metabolic reactions in biochemistry, systems of electric power distribution, and the World Wide Web (see Barabasi 2002; Buchanan 2002; Watts 2003).

— Mark Granovetter

See also Levels of Social Structure; Network Theory; Relational Cohesion; Social Capital; Social Exchange Theory

FURTHER READINGS AND REFERENCES

Barabasi, Albert-Laszlo. 2002. *Linked: The New Science of Networks.* New York: Perseus.

Buchanan, Mark. 2002. *Nexus: Small Worlds and the Groundbreaking Science of Networks.* New York: Norton.

Burt, Ronald. 1992. *Structural Holes: The Social Structure of Competition.* Cambridge, MA: Harvard University Press.

Granovetter, Mark. 1973. "The Strength of Weak Ties." *American Journal of Sociology* 78(6):1360–80.

———. 1974. "Exchange with Herbert Gans." *American Journal of Sociology* 80(2):524–31.

———. 1983. "The Strength of Weak Ties: A Network Theory Revisited." *Sociological Theory* 1:201–33.

Marsden, Peter and Karen Campbell. 1984. "Measuring Tie Strength." *Social Forces* 63(2):482–501.

Rapoport, Anatol and William Horvath. 1961. "A Study of a Large Sociogram." *Behavioral Science* 6:279–91.

Watts, Duncan. 2003. *Six Degrees: The Science of a Connected Age.* New York: Norton.

STRUCTURAL FUNCTIONALISM

Although it was once the dominant sociological theory, structural functionalism is now more of a relic. Recent decades have seen this theoretical orientation slip into the background as more contemporary theories (including neofunctionalism) have taken its place.

Structural functionalism is one type of consensus theory— it posits that society is based on mutual agreements, sees the creation and maintenance of shared values and norms as crucial to society, and views social change as a slow, orderly process. Examples of prominent consensus theorists include Auguste Comte, Émile Durkheim, Talcott Parsons, and Robert Merton. These theories stand in contrast to conflict theories, such as those of Karl Marx, that view the world as based on a system of oppressive hierarchies, social order at the whim of dominant groups, and social change as rapid and disorderly resulting from struggles between groups.

The term *structural functionalism* can be broken down into its constituent parts. An analysis can be made of structures without reference to functions, and conversely, an analysis can be made of functions without reference to structures. Generally, however, these two are used in conjunction with one another. Furthermore, most theorists in this field were particularly interested in societal functionalism, or the specific structures and functions of society as a whole.

Parsons (1937, 1970) was the founder of, and perhaps the most prominent contributor to, structural functionalism. He was concerned with the question of how society was able to maintain order and not fall into utter chaos. He answered this question from the viewpoint of structural functionalism and outlined what he believed are its major tenets: (1) Systems are ordered and their parts are all interdependent; (2) systems tend toward a goal of equilibrium or self-maintenance; (3) systems may be either inert or change in an ordered manner; (4) each part of the system has an effect on the forms the other parts can take; (5) systems create and maintain boundaries separating them from their environments; (6) allocation and integration are necessary for a system to reach a certain state of equilibrium;

and (7) systems will tend toward self-maintenance by maintaining their boundaries, the interdependent relationship among parts, and the relationship between parts and the whole; by controlling variations in the environment; and by controlling tendencies of the system to change from within.

In addition to structures, Parsons was also concerned with functions. Parsons saw functions as those activities that had the goal of fulfilling a need of the system. He believed that there were four necessary functional imperatives of all systems: [A] adaptation (how a system copes with its outside environment by both adapting to it and by adapting the environment to meet the needs of the system), [G] goal attainment (the definition and achievement of the primary goals of the system), [I] integration (how the system regulates the relationship of its various parts as well as the relationship among the other three functional imperatives), and [L] latency, or pattern maintenance (how the system provides, maintains, and rejuvenates the motivation of individuals and the cultural patterns that stimulate and maintain that motivation). These functional imperatives are known as Parsons's AGIL scheme.

Functions become integrated with systems in Parsons's theory as each component of the AGIL scheme is handled by a different system. Most generally, adaptation is handled by the behavioral organism that adjusts to and transforms the outside world. Goal attainment is handled by the personality system that defines the goals of the system and mobilizes the necessary resources to reach outlined goals. Integration is done by the social system that controls the various components of the system. Latency is performed by the cultural system that provides individuals with norms and values to motivate them to action.

Merton (1968), a student of Parsons, continued and enriched the tradition of structural functionalism. He argued that traditional postulates in functionalism, as outlined mainly by anthropologists such as Malinowski, were grounded too heavily in abstract theory and lacked the empirical evidence needed to give them credence. He believed that to conduct proper functional analyses, theory must be coupled with empirical research. Merton helped define his viewpoint by criticizing several postulates of functional analysis. First, he criticized the postulate of functional unity by arguing that in complex societies not all components had to be integrated to a high degree. Second, he criticized the postulate of universal functionalism by contending that not all forms and structures in society have positive consequences or functions. Finally, he criticized the postulate of indispensability and rejected the idea that every aspect of society served a necessary and vital purpose; there are components that the society could function without.

Merton defined functions as those consequences that lead to the adjustment or adaptation of a system. In addition, he argued that not all functions had positive consequences and that some, in fact, were better described as dysfunctions. In addition, nonfunctions are those consequences that have no effect at all on the system.

The development of dysfunctions and nonfunctions to complement the existing theory of functions led Merton to develop the idea of a net balance. A net balance is an understanding of the relative weight of functions and dysfunctions in a given system. It is more of a theoretical orientation then an empirical tool because the magnitude and evaluation of what constitutes functions and dysfunctions are highly subjective.

The issue of how to study a net balance led Merton to the idea of levels of functional analysis. He argued that society did not have to be studied as a whole but that organizations, groups, and other subcomponents of society were also valid as research topics. Merton, in fact, was a proponent of "middle-range" theories. Thus, what is the net balance of those functions, and dysfunctions, at one level may well be different at another level.

Another valuable contribution of Merton to the field of structural functionalism was the idea of manifest and latent functions. Manifest functions are those that are intended, whereas latent functions are those that are unintended yet still functional for the system. Closely related to the idea of latent functions is that of unanticipated consequences, although this term encompasses not only those unintended consequences that are functional for the system but also those that are dysfunctional and nonfunctional as well.

Merton defined culture as a system of norms and values that is present in society and is common to, and governs the behavior of, its members. He defined social structure as the ordered system of social interactions in which the members of a given society are occupied. In addition, Merton was interested in the relationship between culturally defined ends and the structurally possible means of achieving those ends. *Anomie*, or a state of normlessness, occurs when the available means make it difficult, if not impossible, for members of a society to achieve the culturally defined goals. The reaction of individuals to this discrepancy can involve deviant behavior because they are forced to attempt alternate (sometimes illegal) means to achieve their desired (as prescribed by society) ends. Anomie, for Merton, represents the disjuncture between social structures and cultural goals and hence can be dysfunctional for society.

Kingsley Davis and Wilbert Moore (1945) wrote what is perhaps the best-known piece of structural functional literature on the topic of social stratification. They argued that a system of stratification is not only functional but also necessary for societies to persist and remain healthy. This idea led them to argue that a classless society had never existed because the need for a system of stratification had always created such a system. They did not, however, believe that the creation of such a stratified system was always a conscious undertaking on the part of society but, rather, that it could be, and often was, an "unconsciously evolved device."

Following their structural functional orientation, Davis and Moore saw stratification in society not in terms of people but in terms of positions. This meant that they were primarily interested in how certain positions came to be ranked higher or lower than other positions, not in how certain individuals came to fill those ranked positions. They did believe, however, that one of the biggest problems faced by society was how to get the right people to fill the right positions and then, more important, how to keep them there.

Their argument was that some positions in society are more pleasant to occupy, some are more crucial for the health and continuity of the society as a whole, and different types of positions require different types of knowledge and skills. Those positions that are generally attributed with a higher social ranking (e.g., politicians, bankers, lawyers) are not as pleasant to occupy, are more important to the overall health of society, and require the highest level of skill and education. Consequently, it is these positions that must also carry the highest level of social prestige, monetary compensation, and available leisure time.

Davis and Moore's structural functional explanation of stratification has been criticized by many for a number of reasons. First, it assumes that a system of stratification has always existed in every society and that such a system will exist in all societies in the future. Second, it provides a theoretical rationale for perpetuating the privileges of the elite. Third, many find it difficult to accept that any position in society is more or less important than any other position. Garbage collectors, for example, are arguably as important as politicians. Fourth, the stratified system makes it difficult for those in lower rankings to obtain the education and training necessary to achieve a higher ranking. Finally, there is no consideration of individuals being motivated to accept a higher (or lower) position based solely on intrinsic rewards.

Given that it was the dominant theory in sociology for such a long time, structural functionalism has also been critiqued by many in the field. A number of the more noteworthy critiques include (1) that it is ahistorical (it did in fact develop in reaction to the historical evolutionary approach of many anthropologists at that time); (2) it is unable to deal with contemporary processes of social change; (3) it cannot adequately deal with conflict (it is generally viewed as a consensus theory and hence in contradiction to conflict theory); (4) it has a conservative bias that maintains the status quo and the dominating power of the elite class; (5) it is generally too abstract, vague, and ambiguous to bear much relationship to the real world; (6) the theories are too grand and ambitious when more historically and situation relevant theories might be more appropriate; (7) there are inadequate methods to research the questions of interest; and (8) comparative analysis is virtually impossible.

Turner and Maryanski (1979) also saw the problems of teleology and tautology plaguing structural functionalism.

More specifically, they saw illegitimate teleology as a problem. It is legitimate to assume that society has certain goals and that it brings certain structures and functions into creation to achieve these goals. What many structural functionalists do, however, that is illegitimate is to assume that the current structures and functions in society are the only ones that could have been created to achieve these goals. In addition, tautology is a problem because both the whole and its parts are defined in terms of the other. The whole is defined in terms of its parts and the various parts are then defined in terms of the whole. Hence, neither is truly defined at all.

At the barrage of such critiques as those outlined above, structural functionalism eventually fell out of the limelight of sociology. Jeffrey Alexander and Paul Colomy (1985), however, made an attempt to revive interest in the topic by developing neofunctionalism in the mid-1980s. The term itself, *neofunctionalism*, implies both a strong relationship to "functionalism" as well as the implications of a new, "neo," direction. This is exactly what Alexander and Colomy had in mind; they saw neofunctionalism as broader and more integrative than traditional structural functionalism.

Although neofunctionalism is not considered so much a fully developed theory as a "tendency," Alexander (1985) has outlined some of its basic tenets: (1) It sees society as composed of interacting elements (that are not controlled by an overarching force) that form a pattern that allows it to be differentiated from the outside environment; (2) approximately equal attention is given to action and order; (3) integration is seen as a possibility rather than an accomplishment; (4) there is still an emphasis on personality, culture, and social systems, although the tension between these systems is seen as a source of control as well as change; (5) there is a focus on social change found in the differentiation within the personality, culture, and social systems; and (6) it implies a promise to the autonomy of conceptualization and theorizing from additional levels of sociological investigation.

Although it did succeed in its goal of reviving interest in the work of structural functionalists, and particularly Parsons, neofunctionalism seems to have gone the way of its predecessor and fallen out of style. This is even acknowledged by Alexander (1998) who has abandoned this orientation in lieu of pursuing what he believes will be a new wave in the creation of theory that is able to go beyond even the advances made by neofunctionalism.

— Michael Ryan

See also Alexander, Jeffrey; Anomie; Comte, Auguste; Durkheim, Émile; Merton, Robert; Parsons, Talcott

REFERENCES

Alexander, Jeffrey C., ed. 1985. *Neofunctionalism.* Beverly Hills, CA: Sage.

———. 1998. *Neofunctionalism and After.* Malden, MA: Blackwell.

Alexander, Jeffrey C. and Paul Colomy. 1985. "Toward Neo-Functionalism." *Sociological Theory* 3:11–23.

Davis, Kingsley and Wilbert Moore. 1945. "Some Principles of Stratification." *American Sociological Review* 10:242–49.

Merton, Robert K. 1968. *Social Theory and Social Structure.* New York: Free Press.

Parsons, Talcott. 1937. *The Structure of Social Action.* New York: McGraw-Hill.

———. 1970. *Social Structure and Personality.* New York: Free Press.

Turner, Jonathan H. and A. Z. Maryanski. 1979. *Functionalism.* Menlo Park, CA: Benjamin/Cummings.

STRUCTURALISM

It is important to understand structuralism not only in and for itself but also as a precursor to poststructuralism and ultimately to postmodern social theory. Structuralism came to be most highly developed in France (and hence is often called French structuralism). Its greatest flowering involved, at least in part, a backlash against the humanism, and especially the existentialism (Sartre was the major exponent of this perspective), that was so pervasive in post-World War II France. Humanists such as Sartre gave considerable attention to individuals and afforded them a great deal of autonomy and agency. Structuralists turned this perspective on its head by focusing on the structures that they saw as the true base of the social world. Instead of having autonomy and agency, people were seen as being impelled, if not determined, by structures.

The roots of structuralism are not in sociology but, rather, are traceable to various disciplines.

Many structuralists focus on what they believe are the deep underlying structures of society. For example, Karl Marx focuses on the underlying economic structures of society that he sees structuring not only the economy but much of society. For the economy and the larger society to change, these structures need to be uncovered, understood, and transformed. Later structural Marxists (Althusser, Poulantzas) came to see Marx as a structuralist as evidenced by his concern with the largely invisible economic structure of a capitalist society. It is this concern with underlying invisible economic structures and a rejection of empirical analysis that makes structural Marxism a form of structuralism.

Other thinkers focus on the underlying structures of the mind, especially those found in the unconscious. Sigmund Freud was a leading exponent of this idea and thought it was important not only to understand these underlying structures but also to uncover them and their operations in order to allow people to deal better with the impact of these structures on their thoughts and actions. Jacques Lacan was a French psychoanalyst who took the ideas of Freud and combined them with those of Saussure to develop the idea that the unconscious is structured in the same way as language. This position sees language as pivotal in the formation of the individual and also as central to the way in which the unconscious mind is structured.

Still others define structures as the models they build of social reality. One example of this is Pierre Bourdieu. Although generally considered a poststructuralist, Bourdieu exhibited elements of structuralism in his theory on habitus and field by asserting that structures can exist in the social world itself independent of language and culture.

Finally, a fourth group, such as anthropologist Claude Lévi-Strauss (often referred to as "the father of structuralism" [Kurzweil 1980:13]), can be seen as being concerned with the dialectical relationship between structures of the mind and the structures found in society.

Although it arose in a number of different disciplines (Marx [as well as the structural Marxists] in political economy, Freud in psychiatry, and Lévi-Strauss in anthropology, among many others), the greatest interest in and development of structuralism is to be found in linguistics, especially the work of Ferdinand de Saussure (1857–1913). However, the field of linguistics in general, and Saussure in particular, has had a profound impact outside the field of linguistics. They helped give rise to the linguistic turn, or a shift in focal concern from social to linguistic structures, that has altered many of the social sciences.

Saussure was interested in the differences between *langue,* or the universal structure underlying all language, and *parole,* or the way speakers actually use the langue. *Langue,* however, was the more important of the two to Saussure; he believed it was most relevant to look at the formal system of language rather than the ways in which individuals made use of this structure. *Langue* can be seen as a system of signs where each sign depends on the other signs in the system for meaning. This is clearest in the case of binary oppositions. For example, the word *high* does not convey a sense of elevated positioning without at least an implied reference to its binary opposite low. The structure of *langue* is not one that is shaped by individuals but, rather, one that shapes the meanings of words, the mind, and ultimately the social structure. Lévi-Strauss took the work of Saussure on linguistic structuralism and applied it to anthropology. He reconceptualized a number of social phenomena (most notably kinship systems) as communication systems in order to subject them to a structural analysis.

Eventually, the concern for an underlying structure and the system of signs grew into a discipline in its own right. *Semiotics* is the field of study concerned with structure of sign systems. Semiotics is concerned not only with language but with all sign and symbol systems, in other words, with all forms (verbal and nonverbal) of communication.

— Michael Ryan

See also Althusser, Louis; Bourdieu, Pierre; Discourse; Lévi-Strauss, Claude; Poststructuralism; Saussure, Ferdinand de; Semiology; Structuralist Marxism

FURTHER READINGS AND REFERENCES

Althusser, Louis. 1969. *For Marx.* Harmondsworth, UK: Penguin.
Kurzweil, Edith. 1980. *The Age of Structuralism: Levi-Strauss to Foucault.* New York: Columbia University Press.
Lacan, Jacques. 1977. *Ecrits: A Selection.* New York: Norton.
Saussure, Ferdinand de. 1966. *Course in General Linguistics.* New York: McGraw-Hill.

STRUCTURALIST MARXISM

Marxism that came under the influence of structuralism—with its emphasis on meaning as deriving from a system of differences—criticised Marxist humanism, as found, for example, in the work of Jean-Paul Sartre (1905–1980) and Herbert Marcuse (1898–1979). Humanist Marxism placed the epistemological figure of "man" at the heart in its framework of the analysis of society, without always seeing that this was an epistemological stance, preferring instead to believe in the intentions and the will of "actual" human beings.

At its height in the decade 1965 to 1975, structuralist Marxism, was no doubt strongest in France, possibly, in part, because of that nation's rationalist tradition. The specification of such clear chronological markers, however, implies that such a Marxism's day has passed. But as will be noted later, it lives on in aspects of the epistemological stance of sociologists, such as Pierre Bourdieu (1930–2002), influenced by the epistemological school inspired by the work of Gaston Bachelard (1884–1962).

Structuralist Marxism has several strands, including the philosophical, and "scientific" Marxism promoted by Louis Althusser (1918–1990) in France; the genetic Marxism of Lucien Goldman (1913–1970), again in France; and Galvano della Volpe (1895–1968) and Lucio Colletti (1924–2001) in Italy. Structuralist Marxism consisted, first, of a method: The key achievement here was a "return to Marx," which opened up Marx's work to a critical and "symptomatic" reading (in the manner of Freud's interpretation of dreams). This reoriented political Marxism away from a crude, humanist, "battle of ideologies" approach, derived from Marx's early works, toward an understanding of the implicit structure of the relations of production in political economy. Second, Structuralist Marxism, as with the movement of structuralism in general, de-centered the subject, so that history ceased to be seen as the expression of a subjective human essence. Third, history becomes discontinuous because it is not the history of a subject (whether this be man or nature or the state) but, rather, is the autonomous evolution of time in which numerous forces are at work.

Of course, no explanation of structuralism—whether or not of the Marxist variety—can avoid considering the innovation brought to the understanding of language by Ferdinand de Saussure (1857–1913); nor can it avoid noting the importance attributed to language in the social sciences influenced by a structuralist approach. The work of Claude Lévi-Strauss in anthropology is a case in point. The structure of language becomes the methodological point of departure par excellence; the social world itself is like a language, based on relations, not on essential attributes.

For the structuralist view, then, language is a system of relations, not a collection of static elements (words). Value (e.g., meaning) is established through analysing the differential relations pertaining between the elements. Value emerges only in the relation between the elements themselves. As Saussure famously said, "Language is a system without positive terms." At another, more historical, level, structuralist Marxism was also developed by thinkers (Althusser, Balibar, Rancière et al.) for whom epistemology was the point of departure for analysing economic and political phenomena. Influential in this regard is the "father" of epistemology and the history of science in France, Gaston Bachelard. Indeed, if one looks to Bachelard here, structuralist Marxism begins to fall within a program of thinking and research that would clearly include philosophers and sociologists such as Michel Foucault (1926–1984) and Pierre Bourdieu (1930–2002), even though their allegiance to Marxism was always weak.

Three aspects of Bachelard's thought endeared him to a structuralist approach. The first is his emphasis on epistemology, which implied that scientists should not be blinded by positivism but should develop a reflexive sense. In other words, knowledge of the subjective dimension is also important to the scientific project. Scientists need to grasp the real space in which they are working as well as the represented space they are studying. An appreciation of the difference between real and represented space requires recourse to theory. This is not to deny the real. For connected to Bachelard's emphasis on theory is his strongly held position that a rationalist framework (field of interpretation and reason) in science is impotent when detached from experimentation. Thus, although experiment without theory leads to naive empiricism, theory without experimentation is sterile.

Second, Bachelard proposes a nonsequential, noncausal (in the simple sense) explanation of history. Science, for example, evolves in fits and starts; it exemplifies "discontinuity" as much as, or more than, continuities. Newton's work cannot predict Einstein's, for example. In fact, this aspect of Bachelard's work was reinforced by his anti-Cartesian stance. So whereas Descartes had aimed to reduce reality to its simplest element, Bachelard argues that after the revolution brought by quantum physics, even an apparently simple element turns out to be complex. Thus, complexity (or "complex causation" as Althusser expressed it) is at the heart of things not simplicity.

Third, Bachelard made the imagination a fundamental object of analysis, a fact that opened the way to a structural view of subjectivity, even if Bachelard's own credentials as a structuralist were at best ambiguous.

In raising method to pride of place in understanding society and class struggle, structuralist Marxism focused on the relations between elements—whether in politics, or the economy—as Saussure had done in his revision of linguistics. Althusser thus argued that the nature, meaning, and importance of Marx's concepts were not given in advance in a self-evident, obvious way. Rather, they had to be produced through a symptomatic reading—particularly of *Capital*—to arrive at Marx's truly original insights, insights of which Marx himself might not have been entirely aware because the theoretical and philosophical language available to him was quite literally, pre-Marxist. More specifically, this language was anthropological and placed "man" at the center of a secular universe. To confirm this, Dostoyevsky (1821–1881), Nietzsche (1844–1900), and others proclaimed the death of God, without always recognising that if God is dead, so is man. For the anthropology in question is indebted to the same metaphysics as the religious orientation it opposes. Thus is Ludwig Feuerbach's (1804–1872) critique of Christianity reinforced by the same anthropological view of the world when he claims that things can be put to rights by substituting man for God—or rather, by saying that God is man's creation (Feuerbach [1841]1989).

Historically, a key question for Western intellectuals in the post-World War II period in light of dominance of Stalinism, concerned the true nature of Marxism. Was it necessary to accept that Stalin and the gulag were the inevitable outcome of Marx's intellectual and political legacy? For a number of key philosophers and thinkers, such as György Lukács (1885–1971), the discovery of Marx's early writings, which focused on the concept of "man," the answer was "no." Indeed, by way of these early writings, a case could be made, Lukács claimed, for saying that, within the capitalist system, the notion of alienation explained why human life had become so degraded. With the generalised commodification—and thus, objectification—resulting from the dominance of exchange-value under capitalism, this argument said, humanity had lost touch with its natural human essence founded in community. The object had become a force over and against "man," not a force for liberation and enrichment. And it emerged that in France and elsewhere between 1945 and 1960, Marx's theoretical and metaphysical writings giving "man" pride of place in economic and political affairs came to be seen as the secret to all Marx's other works, including *Capital.*

When Jean-Paul Sartre called Marxism the "unsurpassable philosophy of the modern era," he meant by this that Marx had alerted the world to the necessity of an essentially humanist critique of capitalism, a critique that would reveal the importance of human subjectivity—thus, morality—in political matters and that, furthermore, would see history as the reflection of human consciousness caught at a given moment of time. To write history thus meant giving a phenomenological description of human consciousness. Through such a strategy, the determinist approach of economistic Marxism, inherited from the Second International, could be avoided.

Humanist Marxism had another feature, however, one that was more problematic. This is highlighted by Claude Lévi-Strauss's critique of Sartre's theory of history. Briefly, Lévi-Strauss argued that it is a mistake to raise the "I" to the power of "we," as Sartre's Cartesian notion of the subject had led him to do. In other words, it is inadequate to project qualities of the individual onto the collectivity. Sartre's approach entailed deducing the nature of collective entities, such as "the people," "the state," "the party," "the species" (man), from the nature of individual consciousness and inserting the result into a historical narrative hailing the triumph of the collectivity, whatever name one gave to it. By the 1960s, a number of intellectuals realised that Stalinism and totalitarian Marxism could be understood as regimes that precisely forced subservience to such collective entities. In this sense, Stalinism, rather than being the antithesis of Marxist humanism, could be seen as its continuation.

Moreover, if Marxism was a humanism because it focused on the relation between man and nature and between self and other, it would, from an epistemological and metaphysical perspective, be little different from a host of nineteenth-century philosophies of man that inherited the Enlightenment push for the secularisation of society, a principle underlying the French Revolution. It was necessary, then, to discover the truly unique qualities of Marx's thought, and it was this that raised questions of method. Marx cannot be inserted into the Enlightenment secular heritage so easily if the originality of his thought is to be preserved. Moreover, it is the humanist approach to Marxism that made a reconciliation possible between Marxism and certain strands of Catholicism, especially in France.

Consequently, through Althusser, structuralist Marxism argued for an "epistemological break" between Marx and Hegel and between Marx and Feuerbach, and it rejected the idea of a quiet and continuous evolution between the essential qualities of Marx's thought and what had gone before. "Epistemological break" implies that there is not even a continuity between Marx's method and concepts and those invoked by humanists of every stripe. Structuralist Marxism famously became a "theoretical anti-humanism," which opponents claimed was equivalent to its being Stalinist (cf. C. P. Thompson). Certainly, it was abstract rather than concrete or empirical, but whether it was inhuman in a moral sense is another matter. For, in fact, the whole field of moral and ethical action raises key questions that could be addressed only through the idea, developed in the theory of the French psychoanalyst, Jacques Lacan (1901–1980), of the unconscious understood structurally as a specific kind of discourse. For Lacan, the subject is the subject in language, the subject as formed in and through the symbolic order oriented around the relationship between signifier and signified. Here, it is not that ethical action is impossible but, rather, that it is never the spontaneous process that the conscious ego often believes it to be. Here, there is no subject independent of the signifier. There is, in other words, no original human nature (or natural sexuality), giving rise to a subject identical with itself (where the subject is the self-conscious subject, entirely present to itself). The structural unconscious decenters the subject, and this is the view that structuralist Marxism also took before it—in the work of Althusser, in particular.

For its part, genetic structuralism, derived largely from two moments: The first was the debate around the historical relationship between Hegel and Marx, inaugurated by Jean Hyppolite (1969), where the key question centered on the extent to which Marx was, or was not, the inheritor of Hegel's system. The second moment came from psychology, where its chief instigator was Jean Piaget (1896–1980). The chief claim of genetic structuralism and its Marxist variant, as articulated in the work of Goldman, was that it soft-pedalled discontinuity in favour of a historical and evolutionist approach to the study of art and society. In effect, it sought to balance the overemphasis on "synchrony" (the same time: a static moment favoured by those influenced by Saussure) with diachrony (time as movement and evolution).

ECONOMIC DETERMINISM

Marxism of the Second International, which collapsed in 1914, espoused an "official" Marxism that gave primacy to economic activity in the evolutionary transformation of society: The economic laws governing society would inevitably bring about a socialist, and then communist, society. Culture, by contrast, was seen to be "superstructural": the level of ideas and idealism, if not of false consciousness. Here we have an abiding issue in theoretical Marxism: The nature of the separation of the ideological superstructure from the economic—therefore material—infrastructure. For the economistic view, the laws of the formation of the infrastructure determine the superstructure. Such was confirmed by the Comintern founded by Stalin in 1938. In other words, living, real communism promoted a blatant economic determinism.

It was precisely this simple determinism—implying that the economy was a totality that *expressed* underlying forces of production—that structuralist Marxism set out to contest. Instead, it offered a nuanced philosophical view of the relation between the economic and cultural spheres by saying that the economic never appears simply in its own right for all to see but, rather, appears in a displaced form in a wide range of activities, from art production and education to politics and religion. For this approach, it is not a matter of the economic sphere on one side and the superstructural dimension on the other. There is, rather, a fundamental imbrication of the two, to the point that it has to be admitted that a knowledge of material life can be gained only through the prism of ideas emerging in the superstructure. The argument is not unlike Freud's when he talks about the relationship between primary and secondary (or symbolic) psychical processes. The latter constitute the prism through which knowledge of the displaced actions of the primary processes becomes possible.

Or again we could point to a nondeterminist way of understanding technology—technology being fundamental to economic development, even for Marx. Thus, instead of technology determining social relations, it becomes a feature of, and is implicated in, the cultural field itself. Had not Marcel Mauss, the anthropologist most influential for structuralism before Lévi-Strauss, said that techniques of the body (even spitting) imply that, through techniques, technology crosses over into the psychical and social domains instead of being separate from them? It is not essentially, in the words of Marx, a "mode of production," found uniquely in the economy understood as the accumulation of goods. Or we could say that the economy is more than the quantitative version of it. The economic, as exchange—as giving and receiving—and as the search for equilibrium, as the principle of "zero-sum," and, above all, as the principle of differential relations between elements in the productive process, penetrates all the hitherto superstructural domains of society.

More specifically, Althusser and Etienne Balibar argue, in *Reading Capital* (1970), that Marx shows that it is the capitalist system itself that valorises a narrow view of the economy as determining the nature of social and cultural forms. Within the capitalist system, the economy appears only in the version in which consumers adopt a fetishistic attitude to commodities, meaning that goods are desired for their own sake rather than for the deeper insights into society at large that production provides—insights about how, for example, kinship relations might be structured by the mode of production, without being reducible to it.

The uneven development of the various levels of the socioeconomic formation mean that it is impossible to have a homogeneous whole that, mirrorlike, reflects society and the economy. Rather, it is a matter of "the effectivity of a structure on its elements" (Althusser and Balibar 1970:29). That is to say, at any given historical moment, one aspect of the whole can come into dominance. At one time, it might be the economy narrowly understood; at another time, it might be politics; at another, cultural elements. What emerges in dominance is a historical, not a theoretical question. The conditions of possibility of the historical determination, however, depend on the nature of the articulation of the socioeconomic structure, which is itself in time. Although it is not a simple whole, this structure has its laws and its order, and these are accessible only through grasping the nature of the relations between the elements themselves.

"Structuralist Marxism" is thus also a reading of *Capital* in terms of an epistemological position. The latter entails the idea that Marx founded a science, the science of history, and that this science can be found embedded in Marx's writing, if one knows how to look for it—that is, if one has a sophisticated idea of reading based on a scientific theory or if one has a rigorous method enabling a passage beyond the self-evident aspect of the text, a self-evidency that in all probability is governed by ideology.

By contrast, humanist Marxism in France was driven by Sartre's claim that existentialism is a humanism, ultimately subservient to Marxism. For Sartre, the main focus had to be on the moral status of particular acts. With the discovery of Marx's early writings in the 1930s, the members of the Frankfurt School, such as Herbert Marcuse, also claimed a humanist heritage for Marx and added that this humanism led to the conscious determination to escape the alienation implicit in the capitalist system. But where was humanist Marxism going? What would be the result if alienation were finally overcome? Is it equivalent to the end of politics?

For its part, structuralist Marxism (Althusser, Balibar, Badiou, Godelier) saw the gaining of a knowledge of the form and content of the "social formation" as the central issue. Thus, in the work of Althusser and Balibar, the idea of "economic" is broadened to include ideological and political factors that interact with the economy—an interaction that is crucial, even if the economy is still determinate "in the last instance" (which never comes: the origin is never present). Here, there is—again following the lead of Freud—an issue of "overdetermination," meaning that there is a complex and not a simple relation between cause and effect. There are contradictions between different levels of the social formation. And in any case, the economy can, at mininmum, be seen as the scene of exchanges at a structural level: exchange of goods, exchange of women.

GENETIC AND NONGENETIC MARXISM

Along with Goldman and Piaget, structure emerged in a genetic form in the work of the historians of the *Annales* school in France, for whom the "*longue durée*" (long span) is beyond the consciousness of *histoire evenmentielle* (history of discrete, everyday events). The *longue durée* is the slow centuries of time, barely perceptible and yet inexorable. It is history equivalent to the changes in climate patterns and geographic transformations. Indeed, the *longue durée* is a "spatialisation of time" as structure is in the field of nongenetic structural Marxism. The objective of the history with this very broad focus is to escape the narrowness of history as chronicle, where individual events are recounted but where a deep understanding of their logic and complexity is impossible. Events history is inherently simple, for it is always reducible to the individual events themselves.

HISTORICAL MOMENT OF STRUCTURALIST MARXISM

Although structuralist Marxism had its formal beginning with the work of Althusser in the mid-1960s, its roots were in fact more concrete. They were linked, not only to the dissatisfaction with the moral Marxism propounded by Sartre, and with the subjectivist Marxism promoted by the Frankfurt School, but also to opposition to all movements that valorised the agent of action to the exclusion of social conditions. The context of action needed attention. Back in 1947, Heidegger (1889–1976), in his "Letter on Humanism" ([1947]1993), criticised Sartre and his insistence that the human subject was its acts: that existence preceded essence. Such an approach privileged consciousness inordinately as well as the idea of moral responsibility. "Man" became responsible for what he did, despite the situation. However, Heidegger was less concerned to criticise consciousness and moral bearing and more concerned to question the privileging of beings (existence) at the expense of Being.

In keeping with the critique of agency and consciousness inaugurated by structuralist Marxism, Pierre Bourdieu articulated a structuralist sociology aiming to provide a complex theory of the individual in a given society as both constituted by and constituting the social world in which he or she is located. Forms of perception, apperception and appreciation are in large measure articulated through Bourdieu's concept of "habitus," which is also defined by the levels of cultural and economic capital specific to a given agent. Saying this implies that, through the concept of habitus, a structuralist approach "breaks" with a commonsense epistemology based on the obviousness of perception—the level of empiricism for Althusser. The complexity that habitus points to evokes the space where the scientist works and, thus, the influence of Bachelard. For Bourdieu, complexity also arises because, as Marx said,

human beings *produce* their way of life. More specifically, habitus is a kind of grammar that sets the limits to action without determining how a specific individual will act within it, just as the grammar of a natural language sets the limits to possible speech acts without determining the kind of speech that will be enacted in any contingent situation. Overall, Bourdieu's claim is that class struggle is a struggle between the habitus of the dominant and the habitus of the dominated class as much as it is a struggle between social positions based on the differential possession of economic and other forms of capital. In fact, the reproduction of the unequal distribution of economic capital cannot occur, Bourdieu argues, outside the framework of the habitus that enables the unequal distribution of economic wealth to become manifest. Even though he belongs to no Marxist school, Bourdieu, like Marx, refuses to accept the status quo, a status quo in favour, clearly, of the dominant class. Class struggle is therefore the name of the political and social game for both Marx and Bourdieu, and the reality and truth of this game can be revealed through rigorous scientific research—what Bourdieu calls a knowledge of necessity.

Where Bourdieu differs from both Marx and structuralism is in his refusal to see class in solely economic terms—however broadly *economic* is defined—and in his refusal to accept what he calls the "objectivist," or "scholastic" illusion of structuralism, an illusion that gives too little weight to "practice" or to agency. In short, actions, often couched in complex strategies, for Bourdieu, do make a difference.

Like Althusser's, Bourdieu's work is also marked by the approach to epistemological questions in science inaugurated by Gaston Bachelard, where the notion of an epistemological break is crucial. Bourdieu, however, includes in the equation, the social disposition of the researcher. The researcher can thus go through a kind of "mental transformation," or "conversion of thought," which breaks with spontaneous yet preconstructed perspectives that support the existing social system.

With his emphasis on the way privilege is reproduced—especially through education, where the next generation inherits the benefits of its forebears—Bourdieu has an affinity with genetic structuralism. For it is in the passage of inheritance that time enters the picture and the exclusively synchronic (= one time) approach of "pure" structuralism is modified if it is not entirely rejected. On this basis, too, the agent of the system can play a part in the determination of social conditions through the implementation of strategies—strategies that the idea of agents as mere supports for the structure (as in the work of Althusser) leaves out.

PLACE OF IDEOLOGY

For structuralist Marxism, ideology becomes a practice. Writing of the phenomenon of ideology, Althusser cites

Pascal who offers advice to the one without faith, the one who does not know how to pray: kneel down, move your lips and you will believe, entreats Pascal. Believing—ideology—is thus in the everyday practice, not in a prior faith worked out intellectually. Thus for Althusser, ideology is not a competing intellectual system, but a way of being and acting. Ideology interpellates—calls—individuals to come to be what the system wants them to be. Ideology is a way of using identity to create human supports for the system. In addition, according to Althusser, "ideology has no history."

Slovoj Žižek follows up this practical structuralist Marxist approach to ideology by arguing that ideology is what cannot be rationally justified: We might know that consumer behaviour is furthering the interests of capitalism, but we engage in it all the same. For ideology cannot be explained by false consciousness, which would imply that once people become enlightened, they would change their behaviour. It is rather a set of practices through which individuals constitute themselves in the social world. Only an unthought-out voluntarism could argue that it is enlightenment and education that will bring people to their senses. Such an approach cannot meet Marx's point in the theses on Feuerbach that "the educator also needs to be educated."

KINSHIP AND THE MODE OF PRODUCTION

It would be wrong to think that stucturalist Marxism attempted to analyse and explain only modern capitalist societies of the Western sort. There was, in addition, a lively debate about the status (historical, political, philosophical) of precapitalist economic formations. Could the latter be explained by a Marxist science, or would it have to be conceded that Marx still had work to do here and that therefore the notion of mode of production is limited in relation to explaining the dynamics of noncapitalist, or precapitalist societies and cultures? Certainly, it was recognised that a narrow conception of the "economic base" had little to offer in interpreting societies structured around kinship relations.

When discussing the question of the economic base versus kinship as the determining factor in the reproduction of society, a number of writers in the field made the mode of production sui generis, an entity in its own right that either dominated or did not dominate the spheres of power and social relations. This, however, is to take a very narrow view of "economic." For the latter could be defined, in keeping with Marx's early writings, as the way humanity produces its means of subsistence—that is, the economic field is the one in which humans first of all survive and then do, or do not, flourish. On this basis, the opposition to Marx is not so much that he privileges the economy, which, as structural Marxism argued, can be articulated throughout a system in a highly displaced form but that the economic thesis cannot envisage the nonsurvival, or self-destruction,

of a society. To say "economic" (and the reproductive power that accompanies this) is to say no to death—forever, if possible.

CRITICISMS OF STRUCTURALIST MARXISM

However, some societies have a destructive principle at their very heart: Only in such social formations can a noneconomic way of life not based in physical needs be envisaged. This is the sense, then, of Marx's reductionism—a reductionism that is also an essentialism, because it says that the economy is determinate, not historically, but in principle, as has been noted by several major commentators (Baudrillard 1981; Laclau and Mouffe 1985). Ultimately, therefore, as sophisticated as structuralist Marxism was in its theoretical approach, it nevertheless gave into the idea of a founding principle revealed philosophically rather than historically.

Moreover, in wishing to keep a tight reign on the role of the subject and of agency, structuralist Marxism added a further essentialist aspect to its framework. For while it is true that subjectivity and the notion of the subject can also lead to a certain essentialism when the subject is defined in a noncontingent, or analytical, way, it is also true that subjectivity can be seen as the place where action changes things. Subjectivity is action—or, the subject is always "in process" (Kristeva), an "open system," restructuring itself in light of new experiences and, reciprocally, changes a small part of social reality in the process.

Of course, the ultimate criticism of structural Marxism was, and is, that it is intellectualist. In this, it goes beyond Bachelard's call for theory to grasp the place from where the scientist works—a use of theory that accepts the synthetic, open-ended nature of reality—and becomes an end in itself, a law unto itself, unable to identify with what Pierre Bourdieu called the "logic of practice." Instead of opening things up with its theoretical boldness, structuralist Marxism closed things down; it privileged the production of a theoretical practice of analysis articulated in discourse, a discourse having the structure of language as Saussure ([1916]1983) has outlined it, therefore a discourse eminently analysable at every point. In effect, against structuralist Marxism, reality cannot be reduced to discourse. There is a nondiscursive reality. Reality, like the subject, is also difference, otherness, the event, the shock of history, the revelations of time, what cannot be easily, if at all, assimilated into a structure.

To suggest that the structuralist version of Marxism is flawed is not to say—far from it—that the opposing humanist position and its variants is superior in its explanatory power. Even if structuralist Marxism was determinist and intellectualist, there was a historical reason for its emergence, and this was to show an interpretation of Marx that privileged neither consciousness nor an essentialist idea of "man," as was common in the nineteenth century. Moreover, if the strictures about a Marxist science, as proposed by Althusser, ultimately turned out to be dogmatic, they had the effect, at the same time, of forcing intellectuals and others to think again about what science is. And in this regard, a more rigorous approach to the study of society shows that there are aspects of social and cultural life that are simply not available to consciousness, and all the self-conscious work in the world will never give access to the crucially "hidden" structures of social life, in the same way that consciousness cannot have access to the structure of language because it is also a product of language. In Freudian terms, there is an *un*conscious dimension to life and society.

It nevertheless remains true that if the "truth" of politics and society resides in the unconscious social structures, it would seem necessary for intellectuals to take on the responsibility of revealing these to the public at large. There is, then, the easy accusation against structuralism that, for it, society has to be run by elites as the keepers of truth. Such an issue opens up the question Nietzsche raises of the *ressentiment* of those who perceive that they are in the position of slave and not of master. For while a claim to science is problematic in the domain of politics, the claim that scientific knowledge cannot be directly available to all surely goes without saying.

Such questions, which cannot be answered fully here, serve to show that, for all its faults, structuralist Marxism raised serious and fundamental questions about how scientific and intellectual work is carried out in supposedly liberal democracies.

— John Lechte

See also Althusser, Louis; *Annales* School; Bourdieu, Pierre; Discourse; German Idealism; Habitus; Marx, Karl; Marxism; Saussure, Ferdinand de; Žižek, Slavoj

FURTHER READINGS AND REFERENCES

Althusser, Louis and Etienne Balibar. 1970. *Reading Capital.* Translated by Ben Brewster. London: New Left Books.

Baudrillard, Jean. 1981. *For a Political Economy of the Sign.* Translated by Charles Levin. St. Louis, MO: Telos Press.

Benton, Ted. 1984. *The Rise and Fall of Structural Marxism: Althusser and His Influence.* London & Basingstoke, UK: Macmillan.

Feuerbach, Ludwig. [1841] 1989. *The Essence of Christianity.* Translated by George Eliot. Buffalo, NY: Prometheus.

Heidegger, Martin. [1947] 1993. "Letter on Humanism." Translated by Frank A. Capuzzi. Pp. 213–66 in *Martin Heidegger: Basic Writings,* edited by David Farrell Krell. London: Routledge. Hyppolite, Jean. 1969. *Studies on Hegel and Marx.* Translated by John O'Neill. New York: Harper and Row.

Laclau, Ernesto and Chantal Mouffe. 1985. *Hegemony and Socialist Strategy: Towards a Radical Democratic Politics.* London & New York: Verso.

Rademacher, Lee M. 2002. *Structuralism vs. Humanism in the Formation of the Political Self: The Philosophy of Politics of Jean-Paul Sartre and Louis Althusser.* Lewiston, NY: E. Mellen.

Saussure, Ferdinand de. [1916] 1983. *Course in General Linguistics.* Translated by Roy Harris. London: Duckworth.

Schaff, Adam. 1978. *Structuralism and Marxism.* Oxford, UK, & New York: Pergamon.

Sturrock, John. 2003. *Structuralism.* 2d ed. Oxford, UK, & Malden, MA: Blackwell.

STRUCTURATION

Structuration theory is a broad-ranging sociological ontology in which social practices are postulated as the basic constituents of the social world. Sociological ontologies differ from ontologies in the philosophical sense of the term. Whereas philosophical ontologies derive from primordial metaphysical questions such as what is the ultimate nature of being and existence, sociological ontologies begin more modestly by asking questions about the generic (i.e., transcultural and transhistoric) properties of social life subject to sociological inquiry. Prior to structuration theory, two antithetical positions dominated ontological thinking in sociology. On the one hand, individualism maintained that the social world is constituted by actors impelled to behave in certain ways by their own interests or motives or by their interpretations of their situations. On the other hand, collectivism maintained that the social world is constituted through the effects of social groups that shape, channel, and constrain social action. Structuration theory develops a third approach to sociological ontology that is neither individualistic nor collectivist, although it incorporates key insights from each.

Structuration theory maintains that social praxis is the most basic property of all phenomena of sociological interest. Social praxis is simply the generic term for practices of all kinds in the same sense that the individual is a generic term for actors of all kinds. Structuration theory's emphasis on praxis begins from the intuitively appealing insight that whatever types of social events or forms of structured collectivities may arise or change in a given culture or historical era, these types of events or forms of collectivities are generated in the course of social conduct and through the consequences of this conduct. Long-lasting forms of events and enduring collectivities that maintain their structural features for extended periods of time result from the reproduction of broadly similar forms of praxis. Conversely, when new forms of events or features of collectivities arise, we can be sure that these changes are driven by widespread transformations in social praxis. For example, when capitalism supplanted the political economy of feudalism as the prevailing mode of European production and exchange, the transformation pivoted on newly devised practices of labor, trade, investment, and consumption. Similarly, the new form of political culture that developed in the late eighteenth century in the United States was generated by numerous shifts in praxis, including new forms of political gatherings, political language, and even new forms of public interaction that generated what we now term civil society. It is true, of course, that individuals and collectivities also changed during these transformative periods. However, from a structurational standpoint, without the changes in praxis, these other changes would not have come about.

Structuration theory originated in the writings of the British social theorist Anthony Giddens during the period from 1976 to 1991 when Giddens was on the faculty at the University of Cambridge. Giddens had become interested in sociologies of praxis during several trips to North America in the early 1970s. In his first book on structuration theory, Giddens (1976) began to synthesize points of emphasis from American theories of praxis, including ethnomethodology, social phenomenology, and Erving Goffman's accounts of the interaction order. Continuing his synthetic approach, Giddens found that these American theories shared common ground with British and Continental conceptions of praxis, including works inspired by the later philosophy of Ludwig Wittgenstein, the hermeneutic philosophy of Hans-Georg Gadamer, and Jürgen Habermas's early writings on critical theory.

While Giddens was heavily influenced by these theories of praxis, he was dissatisfied with their neglect of the collective dimensions of social life. Conversely, Giddens was also highly critical of collectivist theories for their neglect of social praxis. Among collectivist theorists Giddens paid close attention to Marx, Durkheim, Merton, and Parsons, as well as French structuralists including Levi-Strauss, Althusser, and Derrida. In addition, Giddens imported significant insights into his writings on collectivities from the new field of time geography. In Giddens's most widely cited writings on structuration theory (1979, 1984; see also Cohen 1989), he synthesized key insights from his sources to open theories of praxis to issues regarding social collectivities and, conversely, to open theories of collectivities to issues in the production and reproduction of everyday social life.

The integration of social praxis with the collective dimensions of social life in structuration theory is sometimes referred to as a solution to the problem of structure and agency. However, this catchphrase actually condenses a number of different problems, particularly on the collectivist side. Indeed, the notion of structure is one of three different dimensions of collectivities interwoven in the structurationist ontology. In addition to structure, Giddens also takes into account recurring patterns of social relations such as networks and systems, as well as the nature of domination and relations of power in social life.

A singularly important step in reconciling praxis and collectivities is to methodologically suspend the ever-present possibility of innovations in social praxis. The justification for this move is as follows: While it is true that on any given occasion actors may do something new, or make a mistake, or simply refuse to do what others expect or demand, it is also true that, except in periods of great social transformation such as wars, revolutions, or disasters, most social practices are routinely performed. For example, in modern societies, people coordinate their affairs according to clocks and watches innumerable times each day. They also ride in autos, speak a common language, prepare and eat familiar foods, and use commonly practiced interaction rituals for greetings, departures, and other conventional moves in personal encounters. All sorts of organizations from schools to business firms to armies to hospitals operate according to scheduled routines. Family life and personal life operate according to repetitive everyday routines as well. Overall, not only each day, but each week, each year, and for periods that may span several generations, commonplace social routines maintain the continuity and order in social life. No two instances of any given practice may be precisely the same in every respect, but the similarities are sufficient to generate a world in which participants know their way around. This is a world structured through the reproduction of common practices. Or in Giddens's terms, this is a world that is structured through structuration.

One of Giddens's central concepts, the duality of structure, provides an abstract image of how processes of structuration occur. In structuration theory, the reproduction of routines is a reflexive process. Unlike those who make fine-grained investigations of everyday life that ignore the preconditions of praxis in local settings, Giddens emphasizes that social actors bring a large repertoire of previously acquired competencies with them as they enter a new social scene. The reflexivity at the center of the duality of structure arises because, in appropriate circumstances, actors draw on these competencies to reproduce familiar practices and social contexts in a new social moment. Thus, as I write these words, I reproduce familiar elements of everything from English grammar and syntax to a narrative voice and expository form appropriate for an entry in a reference work. In these practices, I draw on preestablished competencies to reproduce a new instance of a familiar form. I thereby regenerate a small, structured feature of the academic world. Any commonly reproduced practice may be understood the same way.

But it is not practices performed one at a time that gives the duality of structure its expansive significance. Rather, it is the manifold reproduction of the same practice in a multitude of situations. For example, although one simple act of preparing a meal may not structure the dietary practices of an entire culture, the fact that on any given day a multitude of meals are prepared in the same way does indeed provide structure to the diet within that culture. The duality of structure refers to this recurrent process of reproducing familiar practices to structure the present as it was structured in the past. Of course, once we withdraw the methodological brackets, the duality of structure works just as well to account for change as for reproduction. Thus, cooks may systematically alter old culinary practices or combine several old practices in new ways. If these innovations are disseminated and appropriated by a given population, the diet of an entire culture may be restructured as a result. But whether reproduction or social change is at issue, the reflexivity in the duality of structure continues to operate so long as people use competencies for structuration acquired in the past to structure situations in the present.

The duality of structure provides the means to understand how the social world can be a world of constant praxis and yet a world that remains much the same from one day to the next. But the idea of a structured social world on this everyday scale may seem a long way from the structuration of large-scale cultures, societies, or historical eras. And it is after all the structured properties of large collectivities that have been the focus of a great deal of social theory beginning with the foundational writings of Marx and Durkheim. There is nothing in structuration theory that approaches the conceptual specificity of Marx's concept of the mode of production or Durkheim's concept of the *conscience collective*. However, Giddens does provide a set of conceptual tools for structural analysis that permit a similarly expansive view. One advantage of these conceptual tools is that they permit Giddens to sidestep the intractable theoretical debates over the primacy of materialist or idealist factors in the constitution of large collectivities as well as in historical stasis and change. Along with an increasing number of contemporary theorists, Giddens believes that history offers too many different cultures and civilizations with diverse historical trajectories to postulate the primacy of one set of structural factors over all others. Therefore, he simply offers four categories for the analysis of structural properties that are ultimately no more than conceptual tools for structural analysis. The four forms are (1) *performative rules* that analytically refer to the enactment of routines, (2) *normative rules* that refer to the appropriate circumstances and manner in which routines are performed, (3) *authoritative resources* that refer to the nature and use of capacities to control the doings of others, and (4) *allocative resources* that refer to the nature and capacities of control over material resources.

While Giddens's treatment of structuration is widely regarded as the most innovative aspect of his synthesis of collective and agentic dimensions of social life, he also contributes new directions to the sociological understanding of social morphology—that is, enduring patterns of social relations. Giddens begins with familiar images of systems and networks composed of links between nodes. However, whereas mid-twentieth-century social morphologists such as Peter Blau, Mark Granovetter, and Ronald Burt generally conceive collective patterns of relations as emergent entities, Giddens conceives them as patterns of relations reproduced in social practices that "stretch" across time and space. Thus, in structuration theory, the familiar links-between-nodes imagery that represents networks in a virtual social space becomes a series of reproduced relations that Giddens terms *circuits of reproduction*. Within these circuits, some of the links may be reproduced in regularly scheduled face-to-face encounters, while other links may be forged through media of communication and transportation that span diverse settings across time and space. Initially, Giddens devised this imagery of the time-space distanciation of social relations from his readings of time geographers such as Torsten Hägerstrand and Allan Pred. In addition, Giddens incorporated key insights from functional analysis to account for the organization of social systems, although his only original contribution here is to eliminate the illegitimate hypostatization of functional systems by insisting on conceptions of systemic coordination and control that operate through social praxis. Giddens's conception of the time-space distanciation of social systems is not only one of the basic elements of structuration theory, it also serves as the basis for his analyses of late modernity—that is, the social and cultural circumstances of our time. Here, Giddens argues that the late-modern era, or what he terms posttraditional society has been shaped in substantial ways by instantaneous electronic communications media and increasingly rapid and efficient transport media that "stretch" the reach of social systems indefinitely around the globe. As spelled out in Giddens's own writings and those of other theorists of globalization such as David Harvey and David Held, this idea of the full eclipse of time and the partial eclipse of space has transformed philosophical speculation about what is truly new in modern life into empirically researchable sociological propositions.

Structuration theory includes a comprehensive and balanced account of the political dimensions of social life. Like Max Weber, Giddens distinguishes between power as a ubiquitous feature of conduct, and power as a characteristic set of relations of domination between superordinates and subordinates in institutional orders. Like Weber, Giddens views relations of domination as an inescapable feature of all large collectivities. But unlike Weber, Giddens does not rest content to focus exclusively on domination from a "top-down" point of view. Indeed, his most noteworthy contributions to theories of power in collectivities look at relations of power between the dominant and the dominated with an eye toward the balance of power between them.

Whereas most theories of power stress the capacity of powerholders to realize their objectives, Giddens proposes a dialectic of control. In this concept, as in most others, dominant groups hold their power through their control of scarce resources, the nature of which varies depending on historical circumstances. However, powerholders cannot realize their objectives without the active compliance of the dominated. Through their compliance or resistance to the orders they receive, the dominated maintain some degree of leverage over their political circumstances. When this leverage is skillfully employed, as is most easily illustrated in the case of strikes and other tactics used by labor unions, subordinate groups may claim some rights to autonomy from the dictates of those who control the most powerful resources. Beyond labor unions, one may see examples of the dialectic of control on a large scale in the origins of citizenship rights that commoners wrested from nobles and aristocrats in Western polities and, on a small scale, in the control of domestic arrangements by women in conventional bourgeois families where men controlled the dominant cultural and social capital as well as the bulk of the economic resources.

No full-scale social ontology can avoid an account of human consciousness and motivation. Giddens's account (see especially 1991, chap. 2) is both a strength and a weakness of his thought. On one hand, it introduces a way of conceiving consciousness that is well suited to the praxiological orientation of structuration theory. On the other hand, it leaves many human capacities for existential meaning and emotional experience unaddressed (see Craib 1992). To begin, Giddens divides human consciousness into three segments: (1) discursive consciousness, which is the familiar idea of fully focused thought and fully engaged attention; (2) practical consciousness; and (3) the unconscious. Although fully focused thought plays a substantial role in Giddens's theoretical analyses of modernity, Giddens's conceptions of practical consciousness and the unconscious are more central to the development of structuration theory.

Practical consciousness refers to the tacit form of awareness that is all that actors require when they perform familiar routines or when they recognize familiar elements of social situations. Although this tacit form of consciousness takes account only of the unexceptional and commonplace elements of human experience, it acquires great importance in structuration theory on two grounds. First, practical consciousness is maintained in the mundane routines that reproduce social life in the duality of structure. Second, practical consciousness is tied into what Giddens proposes as a basic and generalized human need for ontological security, a need that arises in the human unconscious.

Ontological security is a condition in which humans feel comfortable with their activities, their environment and with their fellow actors with whom they interact. The connection between routine praxis and ontological security is obvious: Routine praxis produces ontological security. However, ontological security is an unconscious state of mind that is generally inaccessible in everyday life. The existence of this need becomes evident during wars and catastrophic disasters. In these circumstances, when most of the practices that structure social life are no longer possible, actors experience the acute psychic effects of anomie. In these circumstances, actors will go to great lengths to establish a new daily round of activities. While some of these activities may be necessary for material survival, the recurrent and predictable familiarity of the routine quickly begins to serve as both a social and psychological anchor for daily life. The powerful urge to devise and maintain basic processes of structuration that is so evident in these situations supports Giddens's insights into ontological security as a basic need. However, Giddens has nothing to say about whether humans also have ontological needs for meaning or emotional attachments. Thus, primordial philosophical questions about human ontology lie beyond the scope of structuration theory.

— Ira J. Cohen

See also Ethnomethodology; Giddens, Anthony; Individualism; Social Action; Social Space; Social Structure; Time

FURTHER READINGS AND REFERENCES

Bryant, C. G. A. and D. Jary, eds. 1996. *Anthony Giddens: Critical Assessments.* 4 Vols. London: Routledge.

Cohen, Ira J. 1989. *Structuration Theory: Anthony Giddens and the Constitution of Social Life.* Basingstoke, UK: Macmillan.

Craib, Ian. 1992. *Anthony Giddens.* London: Routldge.

Giddens, Anthony. 1976. *New Rules of Sociological Method.* London: Hutchinson.

———. 1979. *Central Problems in Social Theory: Action, Structure, and Contradiction in Social Analysis.* Basingstoke, UK: Macmillan.

———. 1984. *The Constitution of Society: Outline of the Theory of Structuration.* Cambridge, UK: Polity.

———. 1991. *Modernity and Self-Identity: Self and Society in the Late Modern Age.* Cambridge, UK: Polity.

Stones, Rob. 1996. *Sociological Reasoning.* Basingstoke, UK: Macmillan.

SUMNER, WILLIAM GRAHAM

William Graham Sumner (1840–1910) is credited with teaching the first sociology course in the United States. He was one of the founders of the American Sociological Society movement and its second president. Sumner was greatly influenced by Herbert Spencer and became an American proponent of social Darwinism and laissez-faire.

Sumner was born in Paterson, New Jersey, and spent his childhood in Hartford, Connecticut. His parents had emigrated from England and raised William in a strict religious environment. After spending four years at Yale (1859–1863), Sumner attended the Universities of Geneva, Goettingen, and Oxford (1863–1866) in preparation for the ministry. While in Europe he changed his religion from the Congregational to the Protestant Episcopal faith, becoming ordained a deacon in 1867. Sumner began doubting mystical theory and shifted his focus to the concrete facts and theories of social science. In 1872, he solidified his decision by accepting a position as professor of political and social science at Yale. He taught Spencer's *Study of Sociology* and almost lost his position in 1881 because of it. Sumner had become a complete advocate for social evolutionism and the expansion of industrial and capitalist society in the United States.

Sumner's most significant contribution to sociological theory rests with his best-known work, *Folkways* (1906), a book that describes the origins of *folkways* found in society and their consequential influence on manners, customs, mores, and morals. Folkways are a societal force produced by frequent repetition of petty acts, often by great numbers acting collectively or, at least, when acting in the same way when faced with the same need. As Sumner explained in *Folkways*,

> Folkways are habits of the individual and customs of the society which arise from efforts to satisfy needs, they are intertwined with goblinism and demonism and primitive notions of luck and so they win traditional authority. . . . they become regulated for future generations and take on the character of a social force. (p. iv)

Folkways are made unconsciously, they are the product of recurrent habits, guided by recurrent needs of the individual and of the group. As Sumner had learned from Spencer, "guidance by custom" is the most common thread among diverse groups of people. *Custom* is the product of concurrent action, over time, by mass actions driven by mass needs and wants. Mass action is stimu-lated by the desire of people to act collectively with one another. Sumner stated that there are four great motives of human action: hunger, sex passion, vanity, and fear (of ghosts and spirits). Associated with each of these motives are interests. Human life revolves around satisfying these interests. Society dictates which courses of action (folkways) are proper in the attempt to satisfy basic needs and desires.

When certain folkways become associated with philosophical and ethical issues of proper behavior, they are elevated to another plane. These coercive and constraining norms are called *mores*. Mores come down to us from the past and take on the authority of facts. Each individual is born into them and are subjected to their "legitimacy." Mores serve as regulators of the political, social, and religious behaviors of individuals, and they are not affected by "scientific facts." Mores often consist of *taboos*, which indicate the things that must not be done. Taboos are linked to past behaviors that have been proven to cause unwelcome results and therefore contain reference to a reason as to why specific acts should not be allowed. Sumner acknowledged that folkways, mores, and taboos vary from society to society and therefore promotes the field of ethology. *Ethology* is the term he used for the study of manners, customs, usages, and mores, including the study of the way in which they are formed; how they grow or decay; and how they affect the interests of those who are affected by them. The sociologist in particular must pay attention to the folkways and mores of a society, for they have a great impact on human behavior.

Sumner applied Spencer's survival-of-the-fittest approach to the social world. Those who work hard—the fittest—will find a way to survive in society. He believed that poverty could be eliminated in a few generations if people simply worked hard; were industrious, prudent, and wise; and raised their children to do likewise. Sumner felt that it was the duty of everyone to be self-reliant, to look to oneself for help and certainly not to look for aid from others. One either survives or perishes. The "survival of the fittest" concept is viewed as a *natural* law and not a social creation. From this approach, society is viewed as constantly improving, or evolving—the strong, or fit, survive, while the weak, or unfit, die off. Consequently, any interference, especially by the government, could cause a negative disruption in the social order. Sumner opposed governmental sponsorship, believing that each member of society must bear his or her own burdens. Sumner embraced the idea of *laissez-faire,* which he described as the unrestrained action of nature without any intelligent interference by man. Sumner stated that *laissez-faire* means, "Do not meddle; wait and observe; be teachable. Do not enter upon any rash experiments; be patient until you see how it will work out" (Keller and Davie 1934b:472). Sumner was against all forms of paternalism—state assistance to the poor and needy—especially when applied through legislative methods. Sumner's worry over of the role of government is reflected in his concern for individual rights and liberties.

The concept of *liberty* is of great appeal to Sumner; he used it over and over to justify his views on many issues. He associated liberty primarily as a justification for the right of competition and *laissez-faire*, even to the extent to justify industrial warfare. Sumner contended that individuals are guaranteed the use of all their powers and means to secure their own welfare. Consistent with the laissez-faire school of thought, Sumner viewed property rights as a primary concern and supported the human rights of traditional democracy that does allow for governmental interference with an individual's pursuit of personal welfare. The American ideal of such things as "natural" rights is due to the fact that such rights originate in the mores of society. Sumner stated, "the notion of 'natural' rights is the notion that rights have independent authority in absolute right, so that they are not relative or contingent, but absolute" (Keller and Davie 1934a:358). Inevitably, interests of individuals come into conflict with the interests of others. Determining rights arise from within the in-group. Sumner believed that rights come with responsibilities. Rights and liberties are to be protected by civil law. Law should not restrict liberty, but it should provide proper discipline and punishment to protect the rights of citizens. In addition, Sumner recognized the right of individuals to protect themselves collectively.

As many sociological thinkers believe, Sumner felt that conflict is a natural response to competition over scarce resources. In the struggle for survival, life conditions often create conflict situations between members of the same society. Ironically, individual members of society also depend on one another for their daily survival needs. Sumner (1906) coined the term *antagonistic cooperation* to draw attention to this paradoxical feature of human life. He pointed out that individuals are brought into association and held there by the compulsion of self-interest. He believed that human cooperation exists simultaneously with suppressed antagonisms. Thus, conflict and cooperation are often intertwined and built-in realities of intra-group behavior.

— Tim Delaney

See also Social Darwinism; Spencer, Herbert

FURTHER READINGS AND REFERENCES

Adams, Bert N. and R. A. Sydie. 2001. *Sociological Theory.* Thousand Oaks, CA: Pine Forge.

Bernard, L. L. 1940. "The Social Science Theories of William Graham Sumner." *Social Forces* 19(2):153–75.

Keller, Albert Galloway and Maurice R. Davie, eds. 1934a. *Essays of William Graham Sumner.* Vol. 1. New Haven, CT: Yale University.

———. 1934b. *Essays of William Graham Sumner.* Vol. 2. New Haven, CT: Yale University Press.

Sumner, William Graham. 1906. *Folkways.* New York: Dover.

Sumner, William Graham and Albert Galloway Keller. 1927. *The Science of Society.* Vol. 1. New Haven, CT: Yale University Press.

SURVEILLANCE AND SOCIETY

TRADITIONAL SURVEILLANCE

An organized crime figure is sentenced to prison based on telephone wiretaps. A member of a protest group is discovered to be a police informer. These are instances of *traditional surveillance*—defined by the dictionary as, "close observation, especially of a suspected person."

Yet surveillance goes far beyond its popular association with crime and national security. To varying degrees, it is a property of any social system—from two friends to a workplace to government. Consider, for example, a supervisor monitoring an employee's productivity, a doctor assessing the health of a patient, a parent observing his child at play in the park, or the driver of a speeding car asked to show her driver's license. Each of these also involves surveillance.

Information boundaries and contests are found in all societies and beyond that in all living systems. Humans are curious and also seek to protect their informational borders. To survive, individuals and groups engage in, and guard against, surveillance. Seeking information about others (whether within or beyond one's group) is characteristic of all societies. However, the form, content, and rules of surveillance vary considerably—from relying on informers to intercepting smoke signals to taking satellite photographs.

In the fifteenth century, religious surveillance was a powerful and dominant form. This involved the search for heretics, devils, and witches, as well as the more routine policing of religious consciousness, rituals, and rules (e.g., adultery and wedlock). Religious organizations also kept basic records of births, marriages, baptisms, and deaths.

In the sixteenth century, with the appearance and growth of the embryonic nation-state, which had both new needs and a developing capacity to gather and use information, political surveillance became increasingly important relative to religious surveillance. Over the next several centuries, there was a gradual move to a "policed" society in which agents of the state and the economy came to exercise control over ever-wider social, geographical, and temporal areas. Forms such as an expanded census, police and other registries, identity documents, and inspections appeared, blurring the line between direct political surveillance and a neutral (even in some ways) more benign, governance or administration. Such forms were used for taxation, conscription, law enforcement, border control (both immigration and emigration), and later, to determine citizenship, eligibility for democratic participation, and in social planning.

In the nineteenth and twentieth centuries, with the growth of the factory system, national and international economies, bureaucracy, and the regulated and welfare states, the content of surveillance expanded yet again to the collection of detailed personal information to enhance productivity and commerce, to protect public health, to determine conformity with an ever-increasing number of laws and regulations, and to determine eligibility for various welfare and intervention programs such as Social Security and the protection of children.

Government uses, in turn, have been supplemented (and on any quantitative scale, likely overtaken) by contemporary private sector uses of surveillance at work, in the marketplace and in medical, banking, and insurance settings. The contemporary commercial state is inconceivable without the massive collection of personal data.

A credentialed state, bureaucratically organized around the certification of identity, experience, and competence depends on the collection of personal information. Reliance on surveillance technologies for authenticating identity has increased as remote non-face-to-face interactions across distances and interactions with strangers have increased. Modern urban society contrasts markedly with the small-town or rural community where face-to-face interaction with those personally known was more common. When individuals and organizations don't know the reputation of, or can't be sure of, the person with whom they are dealing, they may turn to surveillance technology to increase authenticity and accountability.

The microchip and computer are, of course, central to surveillance developments and, in turn, reflect broader social forces set in motion with industrialization. The increased availability of personal information is a tiny strand in the constant expansion of knowledge witnessed in the last two centuries, but it is exemplary of the centrality of information to the workings of contemporary society.

THE NEW SURVEILLANCE

The traditional forms of surveillance noted in the opening paragraph contrast in important ways with what can be called the *new surveillance,* a form that became increasingly prominent toward the end of the twentieth century. The new social surveillance can be defined as, "scrutiny through the use of technical means to extract or create personal or group data, whether from individuals or contexts." Examples include video cameras; computer matching, profiling, and data mining; work, computer, and electronic location monitoring; DNA analysis; drug tests; brain scans for lie detection; various self-administered tests; and thermal and other forms of imaging to reveal what is behind walls and enclosures.

The use of "technical means" to extract and create the information implies the ability to go beyond what is offered to the unaided senses or voluntarily reported. Much new surveillance involves an automated process and extends the senses and cognitive abilities through using material artifacts or software.

Using the broader verb *scrutinize* rather than *observe* in the definition, calls attention to the fact that contemporary forms often go beyond the visual image to involve sound, smell, motion, numbers, and words. The eyes do contain the vast majority of the body's sense receptors, and the visual is a master metaphor for the other senses (e.g., saying "I see" for understanding). Yet the eye as the major means of direct surveillance is increasingly joined or replaced by other means. The use of multiple senses and sources of data is an important characteristic of much of the new surveillance.

Traditionally, surveillance involved close observation by a person, not a machine. But with contemporary practices, surveillance may be carried out from afar, as with satellite images or the remote monitoring of communications and work. Nor need it be close, as in detailed—much initial surveillance involves superficial scans looking for patterns of interest to be pursued later in greater detail. Surveillance has become both farther away and closer than in previous times. It occurs with spongelike absorbency and laserlike specificity.

In a striking innovation, surveillance is also applied to contexts (geographical places and spaces, particular time periods, networks, systems, and categories of person), not just to a particular person whose identity is known beforehand. For example, police may focus on "hot spots" where street crimes most commonly occur or seek to follow a money trail across borders to identify drug smuggling and related criminal networks. The new surveillance technologies are often applied *categorically* (e.g., all employees are drug tested or all travelers are searched, not just those whom there is some reason to suspect).

Traditional surveillance often implied a noncooperative relationship and a clear distinction between the object of surveillance and the person carrying it out. In an age of servants listening behind closed doors, binoculars, and telegraph interceptions, that separation made sense. It was easy to distinguish the watcher from the person watched. Yet for the new surveillance with its expanded forms of self-surveillance and cooperative surveillance, the easy distinction between agent and subject of surveillance can be blurred.

In analyzing the rise of modern forms of social control the French philosopher Michel Foucault (1977) drew on British legal theorist Jeremy Bentham's idea for the *panopticon.* Bentham proposed a highly organized system for managing large populations within physically enclosed structures, such as prisons, factories, or schools, in which authorities could see all but not be seen. From a standpoint of social control, this created uncertainty. Inmates could never be sure when they were being watched, and hence through self-interest and habit, it was hoped they would engage in self-discipline.

Well-publicized contemporary warnings (e.g., that an area is under video surveillance) reflect this pattern in seeking to create self-restraint. A general ethos of self-surveillance is also encouraged by the availability of products that permit individuals to test themselves (e.g., for alcohol level, blood pressure, or pregnancy).

In related forms, subjects may willingly cooperate—submitting to personal surveillance to have consumer benefits (e.g., frequent flyer and shopper discounts) or for convenience (e.g., fast track lanes on toll roads in which fees are paid in advance).

Implanted chips transmitting identity and location, which were initially offered for pets, are now available for their owners (and others) as well. In some work settings, smart badges worn by individuals do the same thing, although not with the same degree of voluntarism.

The new surveillance relative to traditional surveillance has low visibility or is invisible. Manipulation as against direct coercion has become more prominent. Monitoring may be purposefully disguised, as with a video camera hidden in a teddy bear or a clock, or it may simply come to be routinized and taken for granted as data collection is integrated into everyday activities (e.g., use of a credit card for purchases automatically conveys information about consumption, time, and location).

With the trend toward ubiquitous computing, surveillance and sensors in one sense disappear into ordinary activities and objects—cars, cell phones, toilets, buildings, clothes. and even bodies. The relatively labor-intensive bar code on consumer goods that requires manually scanning may soon be replaced with inexpensive embedded RFID (radio frequency identification) computer chips that can be automatically read from short distances.

The remote sensing of preferences and behavior offers many advantages, such as controlling temperature and lighting in a room or reducing shipping and merchandising costs, while also generating records that can be used for surveillance.

There may be only a short interval between the discovery of the information and the automatic taking of action. The individual as a subject of data collection and analysis may also almost simultaneously become the object of an intervention, whether this involves triggering an alarm or granting (or denying) some form of access (e.g., to enter a door, use a computer, or make a purchase).

The new forms are relatively inexpensive per unit of data collected. Relative to traditional forms, it is easy to combine visual, auditory, text, and numerical data. It is relatively easier to organize, store, retrieve, analyze, send, and receive data. Data are available in real time, and data collection can be continuous and offer information on the past, present, and future (ala statistical predictions). Simulated models of behavior are created.

The new surveillance is more comprehensive, intensive, and extensive. The ratio of what individuals know about themselves relative to what the surveilling organization knows is lower than in the past, even if objectively much more is known. One way to think about the topic is to note that many of the kinds of surveillance once found only in high-security military and prison settings are seeping into the society at large. Are we moving toward becoming a *maximum security society* where more and more of our behavior is known and subject to control?

Six features of the maximum security society are (1) a *dossier* society in which computerized records play a major role; (2) an *actuarial* society in which decisions are increasingly made on the basis of predictions about future behavior as a result of membership in, and comparisons to, aggregate categories; (3) a *suspicious* society in which everyone is suspected; (4) an *engineered* society in which choices are increasingly limited and determined by the physical and social environment; (5) a *transparent* society in which the boundaries of time, distance, darkness, and physical barriers that traditionally protected information are weakened; and (6) a *self-monitored* society in which autosurveillance plays a prominent role.

SURVEILLANCE STRUCTURES

Several kinds of social structure define surveillance relationships. There is an important difference between *organizational surveillance* and the *nonorganizational surveillance* carried about by individuals.

Large organizations have become ever more important in affecting the life chances of individuals. Organizations are the driving force in the instrumental collection of personal data. At the organizational level, formal surveillance involves a constituency. *Constituency* is used broadly to refer to those with some rule-defined relationship or potential connection to the organization, whether this involves formal membership or merely forms of interaction with it, such as renting a video or showing a passport at a border. All organizations have varying degrees of internal and external surveillance.

The many kinds of employee or inmate monitoring, such as within the "total institutions" studied by Goffman (1961), are examples of the *internal constituency surveillance* found in organizations. Here individuals "belong" to the organization in a double sense. They belong as members. They also in a sense are "belongings" of the organization, being directly subject to its control in ways that nonmembers are not. There is often a loose analogy to the ownership of property.

External constituency surveillance involves watching those who have some patterned contact with the organization—for example, as customers, patients, malefactors, or citizens subject to laws of the state—but who do not "belong" to the organization the way that an employee or inmate does. Credit card companies and banks, for example, monitor client transactions and also seek potential clients by mining and combining databases. Or consider the control activities of a government agency charged with enforcing health and safety regulations. Such an organization is responsible for seeing that categories of persons subject to its rules are in compliance, even though they are not members of the organization. Nongovernmental organizations that audit and grant ratings, licenses, and certifications have the same compliance function.

Organizations also engage in *external nonconstituency* surveillance in monitoring their broader environment in watching other organizations and social trends. The rapidly growing field of business intelligence seeks information about competitors, social conditions, and trends that may effect an organization. Industrial espionage is one variant. Planning also requires such data, although it is usually treated in the aggregate rather than in personally identifiable form.

With the widespread accessibility (democratization?) of surveillance techniques and the perception that they are needed and justified, whether for protective, strategic, or prurient reasons, *personal surveillance,* in which an individual watches another individual apart from an organizational role, is commonplace.

This may involve *role relationship surveillance* as with family members (parents and children, the suspicious spouse) or friends looking out for each other (e.g., monitoring location through a cell phone). Or it can involve *non-role relationship surveillance,* as with the free-floating activities of the voyeur whose watching is unconnected to a legitimate role.

With respect to the roles played, we can identify the *surveillance agent* (watcher/observer/seeker) who desires personal information about a *surveillance subject.* All persons play both roles, although hardly in the same form or degree, and this shifts depending on the context and over the life cycle, and as noted the roles are sometimes blurred.

Within the surveillance agent category, the surveillance function may be *central* to the role, as with police, private detectives, spies, work supervisors, and investigative reporters. Or it may simply be a *peripheral* part of a broader role whose main goals are elsewhere, as with checkout clerks who are trained to look for shoplifters, or dentists who are encouraged (or required) to report suspected child abuse when seeing bruises on the face.

A distinction rich with empirical and ethical implications is whether the situation involves those who are a party to the generation and collection of data (*direct participants*) or instead involves a *third party.* A third party may legitimately obtain personal information through contracting with the surveillance agent (e.g., to carry out drug tests or to purchase consumer preference lists). Or personal information may be obtained because confidentiality is violated by the agent or because an outsider illegitimately obtains it (wiretaps, hacking). The presence of third parties raises an important "secondary use" issue—that is, can data collected for one purpose be used without an individual's permission for unrelated purposes? In Europe, the answer generally is "no," although that is less the case in the United States where a much freer market in personal information exists.

An important distinction that often involves power differentials is whether the surveillance is *nonreciprocal* or *reciprocal.* The former is one-way, with personal data going from the watched to the watcher (e.g., employers, merchants, police, wardens, teachers, parents). With reciprocal surveillance, it is bidirectional (e.g., many conflicts, contests, and recreational games).

Surveillance that is reciprocal may be *asymmetrical* or *symmetrical* with respect to means and goals. Thus, in a democratic society, citizens and government engage in reciprocal but distinct forms of mutual surveillance. For example, citizens can watch government through freedom-of-information requests, open hearings and meetings, and conflict-of-interest and other disclosures required as a condition for running for office. But citizens cannot legally wiretap, carry out Fourth Amendment searches, or see others' tax returns. In bounded settings, such as a protest demonstration, there may be greater equivalence with respect to particular means (e.g., police and demonstrators videotaping each other).

In organizational settings, power is rarely all on one side, whatever the contours of formal authority. Lower-status members are not without resources to watch their superiors and to neutralize or limit surveillance. Video and audio monitoring tools are widely available. Employees may document harassment and discrimination with a hidden recorder and file complaints that will mobilize others to scrutinize a superior.

Even without equipment, being on the scene permits surveillance through the senses. In spite of the power differences, butlers, servants, and valets are often believed to know much more about their employers than the reverse, although this is not formally defined by the role.

Many settings of organizational conflict show *symmetrical reciprocated surveillance* in which the contending parties are roughly equivalent. Games such as poker involve this, as do some contractual agreements and treaties (e.g., the mutual deterrence of nuclear arms control sought through reciprocal watching).

Symmetrical forms may be present even in the absence of formal agreements. Spies (or more neutrally) intelligence agents, whether working for countries, companies, or athletic teams are often mirror images of each other. They offensively seek to discover their opponent's information and defensively to protect their own.

Agent-initiated surveillance, which is particularly characteristic of compliance checks such as an inspection of a truck or a boat, can be differentiated from *subject-initiated surveillance* such as submitting one's transcript, undergoing osteoporosis screening, or applying for a job requiring an extensive background investigation. In these cases, the individual makes a claim or seeks help and essentially invites, or at least agrees to, scrutiny.

With agent-initiated surveillance, the intention is always to serve the goals of the organization. Yet this need not necessarily conflict with the interests of the subject; consider, for example, the protection offered by school-crossing guards or efficient library service dependent on good circulation records. Public health and medical surveillance have multiple goals, protecting the community as well as the individual. Efficiently run companies provide jobs and services. Providing a limited amount of personal information on a warranty form and having a chip record usage of an appliance such as a lawn mower or a car may serve the interest of both consumers and businesses (e.g., being notified if the manufacturer finds a problem or offering proof of correct usage if the device fails).

Subject-initiated surveillance may reflect goals that serve the interests of the initiator, but these goals often overlap the goals of the surveilling organization. Consider some protection services that have the capability to remotely monitor home and business interiors (video, audio, heat, gas, motion detection) or health systems for remotely monitoring the elderly and ill (e.g., an alarm sent if the refrigerator of a person living alone is not opened after 24 hours). As forms of surveillance more likely to involve informed consent, these are less controversial than surveillance carried out secretly by an agent.

What is good for the organization may also be good for the individual, although that is not always the case and, of course, depends on the context. Social understanding and moral evaluation require attending to the varied contexts and goals of surveillance. The many settings and forms of surveillance preclude any easy explanation for what causes it. A multiplicity of causes at different levels can be identified, and their relative importance varies over time and across areas and on the kind of question asked (e.g., the development of a technology, patterns of diffusion, initial adoption vs. continued use or disappearance).

Two broad opposed views of the new surveillance can be identified. One optimistically places great faith in the power of technology and welcomes ever more powerful surveillance as necessary in today's world where efficiency is so valued and where there are a multiplicity of dangers and risks. More pessimistic is the Frankensteinian/Luddite view that surveillance technology is inhuman, destructive of liberty and untrustworthy. Clearly, surveillance is a sword with multiple edges. The area is fascinating precisely because there are no easy scientific or moral answers.

Value conflicts and ironic conflicting needs and consequences make it difficult to take a broad and consistent position in favor of, or against, expanding or restricting surveillance. For example, we value both the individual and the community. We want both liberty and order. We seek privacy and often anonymity, but we also know that secrecy can hide dastardly deeds and that visibility can bring accountability. But too much visibility may inhibit experimentation, creativity, and risk taking.

In our media-saturated society, we want to be seen and to see, yet we also want to be left alone. We value freedom of expression and a free press, but we do not wish to see individuals defamed or harassed. We desire honesty in communication and also civility and diplomacy. We value the right to know but also the right to control personal information. The broad universalistic treatment citizens expect may conflict with the efficiency-driven specific treatment made possible by fine-honed personal surveillance.

Whatever action is taken, there are likely costs, gains, and trade-offs. At best, we can hope to find a compass rather than a map and a moving equilibrium rather than a fixed point for decision making.

Surveillance practices are shaped by manners, organizational policies, and laws that draw on a number of background value principles. Many of these were first expressed in the Code of Fair Information Practices developed in 1973 for the U.S. Department of Health, Education and Welfare.

The code offered (1) a *principle of informed consent* that says the data collection is not to be done in secret—individuals are to be made aware of how it will be used and, under ideal circumstances, consent to it; (2) a principle of *inspection and correction* that says individuals are entitled to know what kind of information has been collected and to offer corrections and emendations; (3) a *principle of data security* that says the information will be protected and precautions must be taken to prevent misuses of the data; (4) *a principle of validity and reliability* that says organizations have a responsibility to ensure the appropriateness of the means used and the accuracy of the data gathered; and (5) *a principle of unitary usage* that says information gathered for one purpose is not to be used for another without consent.

As new surveillance technologies and problems have appeared, additional principles have emerged. These include (1) a *principle of minimization* such that only information directly relevant to the task at hand is gathered; (2) a *principle of restoration* such that in a communications monopoly context those altering the privacy status quo should bear the cost of restoring it; (3) *a safety net or equity principle* such that a minimum threshold of information should be available to all; (4) a *sanctity of the individual and dignity principle* in which there are limits (even with consent) on the commodification and offering of personal information; (5) a *principle of timeliness* such that data are expected to be current and information that is no longer timely should be destroyed; (6) *principle of joint ownership of transactional data* such that both parties to a data-creating transaction should agree to any subsequent use of the data, including the sharing of benefits if appropriate; (7) a *principle of consistency* such that broad ideals rather than specific characteristics of a technology govern surveillance practices; (8) a *principle of human review* such that an automated decision is always subject to review by a person; and (9) a *principle of redress* such that those subject to inappropriate surveillance have adequate mechanisms for discovering and being compensated for the harm.

— Gary T. Marx

See also Body; Deviance; Disneyization; Fordism and post-Fordism; Foucault, Michel; Male Gaze; Public Sphere; Total Institutions

FURTHER READINGS AND REFERENCES

Allen, A. 2003. *Accountability for Private Life.* Lanham, MD: Rowman & Littlefield.

Bennett, C. and R. Grant, eds. 1999. *Visions of Privacy.* Toronto, Canada: University of Toronto Press.

Brinn, D. 1999. *The Transparent Society.* New York: Perseus.

Ericson, R. and K. Haggerty. 1997. *Policing the Risk Society.* Toronto, Canada: University of Toronto Press.

Foucault, M. 1977. *Discipline and Punish: The Birth of the Prison.* New York: Pantheon.

Goffman, E. 1961. *Asylums Essays in the Social Situation of Mental Patients and Other Inmates.* Garden City, NY: Anchor.

Lyon, D. 2001. *The Electronic Eye: The Rise of Surveillance Society.* Minneapolis: University of Minnesota Press.

Marguilis, S. T., ed. 2003. "Contemporary Perspectives on Privacy: Social, Psychological, Political." *Journal of Social Issues* 59(1).

Marx, G. 2004. *Windows into the Soul: Surveillance and Society in an Age of High Technology.* Chicago, IL: University of Chicago Press.

Regan, P. 1995. *Legislating Privacy: Technology, Social Values, and Public Policy.* Chapel Hill: University of North Carolina Press.

Staples, W. 2000. *Everyday Surveillance: Vigilance and Visibility in Postmodern Life.* Lanham, MD: Rowman & Littlefield.

SYMBOLIC INTERACTION

Symbolic interaction is a perspective in sociology that places meaning, interaction, and human agency at the center of understanding social life. This perspective grew out of the American philosophical tradition of pragmatism, an approach developed in the late nineteenth century by Charles Peirce, William James, and John Dewey. Challenging the assumptions of classical rationalism, these thinkers regarded people as actors rather than reactors, treated "reality" as dynamic and pluralistic, linked meanings to social acts and perspectives, and viewed knowledge as a key resource for problem solving and reorganizing the world.

George Herbert Mead brought pragmatist philosophy to sociology, working its assumptions into a theory and method for the social sciences. Drawing on the ideas of the pragmatist founders, as well as the theories of Charles Horton Cooley, Charles Darwin, and Wilhelm Wundt, Mead developed a distinctly sociological account of human consciousness, selfhood, and action. He presented this perspective in a series of social psychology lectures that became the basis for his best-known book, *Mind, Self, and Society* (1934). Mead's insights impressed many of his students, notably Herbert Blumer, who later became a distinguished sociologist at the University of California at Berkeley and president of the American Sociological Association. Blumer's compilation of writings, *Symbolic Interactionism* (1969), is still widely acknowledged as the major statement of the symbolic interactionist perspective. Mead and Blumer belonged to a group of other early sociologists, including Robert Park, W. I. Thomas, and Everett Hughes, who studied related topics such as roles, selves, social definitions, and socialization. Because most of these scholars were affiliated with the University of Chicago, symbolic interactionism is often referred to as the Chicago School of Sociology, even though another variant of the perspective emerged later at the University of Iowa.

Blumer coined the label "symbolic interactionism" in 1937 while writing an essay on social psychology for a social science textbook. In that essay, Blumer emphasized how Mead's work could provide the basis for a new social psychological approach that would transcend the deterministic theories of the time. Mead is usually credited as the originator of symbolic interactionism, even though Blumer's analysis drew heavily on the ideas of other theorists and, according to some critics, differed in important respects from Mead's writings.

Blumer, along with Everett Hughes, influenced cohorts of graduate students he taught at the University of Chicago in the 1940s and early 1950s. These students, including Howard Becker, Fred Davis, Elliot Friedson, Erving Goffman, Joseph Gusfield, Helena Lopata, Tamotsu Shibutani, Gregory Stone, Anselm Strauss, and Ralph Turner, further developed the symbolic interactionist perspective and shaped a number of its subfields, such as deviance, social problems, self and identity, and collective behavior. They have since become recognized as the Second Chicago School.

GUIDING PRINCIPLES AND ASSUMPTIONS

Blumer (1969) articulated the core premises of symbolic interactionism:

> The first premise is that human beings act toward things on the basis of the meanings those things have for them. . . . The second premise is that the meaning of such things is derived from, or arises out of, the social interaction that one has with one's fellows. The third premise is that these meanings are handled in, and modified through, an interpretive process used by the person in dealing with the things he [or she] encounters. (p. 2)

Other related assumptions inform and guide this perspective:

1. *Human beings are unique in their ability to use symbols.* Because people rely on and use symbols, we do not usually respond to stimuli in a direct or automatic way; instead, we give meanings to stimuli and then act in relation to these meanings. Our behavior is different from that of other animals or organisms, which act through instincts or reflexes. We learn what things mean as we interact with others. In doing so, we rely heavily on language and the processes of role taking and communication it facilitates. We learn to see and respond to symbolically mediated objects—objects that have names such as water, ground, student, professor, book, and library. These objects become part of the reality we create and negotiate through interaction.

2. *People become human through interaction.* Through social interaction, we learn to use symbols, to think and make plans, to take the perspective of others, to develop a sense of self, and to participate in complex forms of communication and social organization. Interactionists do not believe that we are born human. They argue instead that we develop into human beings only through interaction with others. Interactionists acknowledge that we are born with certain kinds of biological "hardware" (e.g., a highly developed nervous system) that gives us the potential to become fully human, but they contend that involvement in society is essential for realizing this potential.

3. *People are conscious, self-reflexive beings who shape their own behavior.* The most important capacities that we develop through our involvement in social interaction are the "mind" and the "self." By developing the capacity to see and respond to ourselves as objects, we learn to interact with ourselves, or think. As we think, we shape the meaning of objects in our world, accepting them, rejecting them, or changing them in accord with how we define and act toward them. Our behavior, then, is an interplay of social stimuli and our responses to those stimuli. In making this assertion, interactionists embrace a voluntaristic image of human behavior. They suggest that we exercise an important element of autonomy in our actions. At the same time, interactionists understand that a variety of social factors, such as language, culture, race, class, and gender, constrain our interpretations and behaviors. Thus, interactionists can be characterized as "soft determinists"; they presume that our actions are influenced but not determined by social constraints.

4. *People are purposive creatures who act in and toward situations.* For interactionists, we don't "release" our behavior, like tension in a spring, in response to biological drives, psychological needs, or social expectations. Rather, we act *toward situations.* Our actions are based on the meaning we attribute to the situation in which we find ourselves. This "definition of the situation" emerges from our interactions with others. We determine the meaning of a situation (and our subsequent actions) by taking account of others' intentions, actions, and expressions. We select lines of behavior that we believe will lead to our desired ends. Our predictions may be wrong; we do not necessarily act wisely or correctly. Nor do we always pursue goals in a clear-cut or single-minded way. Once we begin acting, we may encounter obstacles and contingencies that may block or distract us from our original goals and direct us toward new ones. Our actions and intentions, then, are dynamic and emergent.

5. *Society consists of people engaging in symbolic interaction.* Following Blumer, interactionists conceive of the relationship between society and the individual as both fluid and structured. This relationship is grounded in individuals' abilities to assume each other's perspectives (or "role take"), to adjust and coordinate their unfolding acts, and to interpret and communicate these acts. In emphasizing that society consists of people interacting symbolically, interactionists part company with psychologistic theories that see society as existing primarily "in our heads," either in the form of reward histories or socially shaped cognitions. Interactionists also depart from structuralists who conceive of society as an entity that exists independently of individuals, dictating our actions through imposed rules, roles, statuses, and structures. We are born into a society that frames our actions through patterns of meaning and rewards, but we also shape our identities and behaviors as we make plans, seek goals, and interact with others in specific situations. That which we call "society" and "structure" are human products, rooted in joint action. Thus, "'society' and 'individual' do not denote separable phenomena" (Cooley 1902/1964:36–37). People acquire and realize their individuality (or selfhood) through interaction and, at the same time, maintain or alter society.

6. *Emotions are central to meaning and behavior.* Since the late 1970s, interactionists have attended more to the importance of emotions in understanding social life. Although other sociologists have bracketed emotions, relegating them to the psychological or biological realm, interactionists have recognized that "social factors enter not simply before and after but *interactively* during the experience of emotion" (Hochschild 1983:211). Arlie Hochschild, Candace Clark, Spencer Cahill, Sherryl Kleinman, and other interactionists have studied feeling rules—guidelines for how we are expected to feel in particular situations—and the emotion work we do when our feelings do not measure up to situational norms. Feelings may also put our moral identities into question: Can we believe we are good people if we have feelings that violate our ideals? Groups and organizations have different cultures of emotions; participants expect members to experience

particular emotions and to display them. In their research, interactionists ask not only what objects mean to participants but also how they feel about them and whether those feelings fit with or challenge the norms of the group.

7. *The social act is the fundamental unit of analysis.* Interactionists contend that the social act, or what Blumer referred to as joint action, is the central concern of sociology. A "social act" refers to behavior that in some way takes account of others and is guided by what they do; it is formulated so that it fits together with the behavior of another person, group, or social organization. It also depends on and emerges through communication and interpretation. This covers a diverse array of human action, ranging from a handshake, a kiss, a wink, and a fistfight to a lecture, a beer bash, a funeral, or a religious revival. Whenever we orient ourselves to others and their actions, regardless of whether we are trying to hurt them, help them, convert them, or destroy them, we are engaging in a social act. We align our behaviors with others, whether acting as individuals or as representatives of a group or organization.

In focusing on social acts, interactionists are not limited to examining the behavior of individuals or even small groups. They also consider the social conduct of crowds, industries, political parties, school systems, hospitals, religious cults, therapeutic organizations, occupational groups, social movements, and the mass media. Inspired by Herbert Blumer (1969), they regard the domain of sociology as "constituted precisely by the study of joint action and the collectivities that engage in joint action" (p. 17).

8. *Sociological methods should enable researchers to grasp people's meanings.* Blumer noted that people act on the basis of the meanings we give to things. Interactionists believe it is essential to understand those meanings, seeing them from the point of view of the individuals or groups under study. To develop this insider's view, researchers learn to empathize with—"take the role of"—the individuals or groups they are studying (Blumer 1969). In addition, interactionists observe and interact with these individuals or groups in their "natural" setting. This in-depth approach enables researchers to learn how social actors accept, defy, or reconstruct their everyday worlds.

RECENT TRENDS AND NEW DIRECTIONS IN INTERACTIONIST ANALYSIS

Critics contend that interactionists' emphasis on how people make roles, define situations, and negotiate identities leads them to ignore or downplay how our individual behavior is constrained by social structure. Yet analysis of the link between individual agency and social structure has a long history in interactionist thought, especially in the writings of Mead, Cooley, Blumer, and Goffman. In recent years, it has become the focus of interactionist studies of

social organization and collective action, power and inequality, and the nature and foundations of the self.

Social Organization and Collective Action

Symbolic interactionism addresses issues that extend beyond microsociological concerns. Even in the early years of interactionism, Herbert Blumer wrote about organizations in his studies of collective behavior, industrial relations, and race relations. As a professor at the University of Chicago, Blumer served as a labor negotiator and deeply appreciated the power of unions, corporations, and interest groups. During the past couple of decades, interactionists have addressed macrosociological issues through the concept of *mesostructure,* an intermediate level of analysis between the microstructural concerns of social psychology and the macrostructural concerns of organizational theory (Maines 1977). Mesostructure refers to the level of organization within which interaction occurs.

In examining mesostructure, interactionists analyze how power relations and social constraints play out in organizational actors' behaviors. For example, Harvey Farberman studied how the practices of used car dealers are shaped by the structure of their relationships with car manufacturers. The manufacturers impose a system of sales on the dealers that force them to operate with a small profit margin. Consequently, the dealers have to squeeze every dollar they can from their customers, exploiting them through a variety of money-making "rackets," including "charging for labor time not actually expended, billing for repairs not actually done, replacing parts unnecessarily, and using rebuilt parts but charging for new parts" (Farberman 1975:457).

Since the late 1970s, interactionists have used mesostructural analysis to study a wide array of organizations, including hospitals, churches, restaurants, court systems, the mass media, the arts, welfare agencies, scientific groups, athletic teams, educational institutions, and even civilizations. They have used concepts such as meaning, frame, network, career, metapower, and negotiated order to examine the links between "micro" and "macro" levels of social reality.

They have shown how interactions in local organizations, such as a business, emerge from and are influenced by the structural conditions in which they are embedded. For example, restaurants strive to fit into a market niche. Every owner wants to develop a strong and loyal customer base so that the restaurant will be predictably profitable. To do this, the owner must consider likely customers, their culinary desires, and how much they are willing to spend. These factors influence how much the owner or manager spends on food, how many cooks he or she hires, and how much he or she pays them. Ultimately, the restaurant as an organization depends on its customers and on the owner's need for profit. As a result, many dishwashers or "potmen" are high school students, undocumented immigrants, or individuals with developmental disabilities. In each case, the restaurant management hires those who are willing to work for minimum wage, largely because of their structural position in our society. Thus, although a restaurant is an interactional arena, it is also an organization that operates within the structural parameters of a market economy. The dynamics of this economy shape the structure and interactions that occur within the organization (Fine 1996).

In addition to studying how people reproduce structure within the interactional arena of organizations, interactionists have turned their attention to the dynamics of collective action and social movement organizations. David Snow and his colleagues (1986) have illustrated how social movements are organized through "frames" and frame alignments that shape the outlooks and behavioral choices of participants. Members of social movements search for frameworks of meaning to answer the question, "What is going on here?" Some frames legitimate violent protest (the frame of oppression), whereas other frames (the frame of moral justice) diminish the probability of violence.

Interactionist analyses of social structure and collective action have revealed how organizational relations are shaped and reproduced by means of symbolic negotiation, thus sharing common features with smaller-scale, face-to-face negotiations. Even large-scale organizations—governments, multinational corporations, and international social movements—depend on symbolic meaning and are grounded in and sustained through patterns of interaction.

POWER AND INEQUALITY

Some interactionists analyzed power and politics over 30 years ago, but others were slow in following their lead. During the past decade, interactionists have done more extensive research on political power, conflict, and negotiation, especially when examining the construction of social problems. In exploring how issues get defined as social problems, interactionist scholars have studied the interpretive, claims-making activities of social problems of entrepreneurs. Scholars have pointed out how these activities unfold in a context of competing and conflicting claims—a context in which some actors are privileged over others for various political and structural reasons.

This approach to social problems has led interactionists to analyze broader sociohistorical changes in U.S. society, such as the medicalization of deviance. Interactionists have examined how people use metaphorical images and rhetorical strategies to define certain phenomena as social problems and to build consensus that action needs to be taken to constrain the behaviors of others. Studies of social problems have enabled interactionists to integrate macrosociological questions more fully into their analyses and, in so doing, to develop the foundations for a "critical interactionist" approach to social life.

Perhaps the best example of a critical interactionism is found in the work of Michael Schwalbe, who has blended the insights of Marx and Mead in studying the labor process, identity work, and the reproduction of inequality. Recently, Schwalbe and his colleagues (2001) have identified four generic social processes through which inequalities are created and sustained. These include (1) *oppressive othering* (how powerful groups seek and sustain advantage through defining members of less powerful groups as inferior), (2) *boundary maintenance* (how dominant groups protect their economic and cultural privileges by maintaining boundaries between themselves and subordinate groups), (3) *emotion management* (how groups suppress or manage potentially destabilizing feelings, such as anger, resentment, sympathy, and despair), and (4) *subordinate adaptations* (how members of subordinate groups adapt to their unequal status and, in some cases, reproduce it). These four social processes provide links between local, everyday interactions and larger structural inequalities.

Peter Hall has integrated neo-Marxist and interactionist perspectives in analyzing power, politics, and the organization of the policy process. Hall has examined how politicians, including U.S. presidents, manage impressions and manipulate symbols to "reassure" the public, promote the public's quiescence, and discourage people's participation in the political process. In his investigations of policymaking, Hall has revealed how and why the organizational context of policy shapes and mediates the policy process.

Another variant of critical interactionism is found in analyses that blend feminist and interactionist perspectives. What distinguishes these analyses is their focus on how everyday practices sustain or disrupt gender inequalities. For example, Candace West and Don Zimmerman (1987) used feminist, interactionist, and ethnomethodological insights to explain how people "do gender" through their routine conversations and interactions. West and Zimmerman highlight how people perform and reproduce gender, individually and institutionally. By showing that gender is a performance, West and Zimmerman acknowledge that people can change or undermine the gender order.

Scholars adopting a feminist interactionist approach have also analyzed power relations, studying how men exercise and maintain conversational advantage through interruptions, topic changes, and language style. In addition, they have studied the "sexual politics" that characterize family relationships, organizational life, and a wide range of face-to-face communications.

Feminist interactionism has had a large impact on the sociology of emotions. Research conducted at airlines, law firms, power plants, police departments, alternative health care clinics, and weight loss associations reveal how organizations manufacture sentiments and regulate emotional display while requiring women to engage in unrecognized and devalued work.

The Nature and Foundations of the Self

Interactionists have always emphasized the social nature and roots of the self. As Mead noted, people develop the capacity for reflexive selfhood through interacting with others. It is through interaction that we learn to take the role of others and see ourselves as social objects, much like other social objects. Moreover, it is through interaction that we experience, sustain, and transform our sense of who we are. Our sense of selfhood, then, is inextricably linked to our relationships with others. It is both a social product and a social process.

Interactionists generally agree about how the self emerges and develops, but they differ in the relative weight they accord to the structure of the self, on one hand, and the processes through which the self is created and enacted, on the other. Scholars who place emphasis on the structure of the self are sometimes referred to as "structural interactionists." They focus on the nature and relevance of the "self-concept," or the overarching view that an individual has of himself or herself. In analyzing the self-concept, structural interactionists highlight its contents and organization and consider how it shapes a person's behavior across different situations. They also propose that it is best to study and measure the self-concept through traditional quantitative methods (e.g., survey questionnaires or laboratory experiments).

Interactionists who emphasize the self-as-process focus on how people create and enact selves; they also assert that the self is best studied through ethnographic methods. Some of these "processual interactionists" embrace Erving Goffman's dramaturgical perspective. In this view, there is no "real" self, only a set of masks and situated performances that a person enacts. Instead of carrying a core self from situation to situation, the person fashions a self anew in each social interaction, generating expressive cues and managing the impressions of an audience to realize desired identities and outcomes. Other processual interactionists adopt a less situational perspective on the self. They acknowledge that people bring fairly stable self-concepts to social situations while also recognizing that these self-concepts change over time. Some analysts focus on the broad changes in American culture that have produced differences in the places where people anchor their fundamental images of self. In the 1950s and 1960s, Americans had relatively enduring and consistent conceptions of self that were anchored in the social institutions to which they belonged, such as families, workplaces, churches, or schools. More recently, Americans have developed a "mutable" sense of self, anchored more in impulses than institutions and flexibly adaptive to the demands of a rapidly changing society (Turner 1976).

Although differing in the relative weight they accord to the structural and processual aspects of the self, the vast majority of interactionists acknowledge the influence of social structural factors (e.g., race, class, gender, and culture) on the development and expression of selves. Their disagreements revolve around the degree of agency that people have in addressing and negotiating these structural constraints. Even postmodern interactionists, who are less structural in orientation than many interactionists, link the expression of the self to the dynamics of late capitalist or "postmodern" societies. For example, Gergen argues that the faster pace of life and communications in postmodern societies has overwhelmed people, leaving them with selves "under siege." Consequently, identities have become fragmented and incoherent. Under postmodern conditions, the concept of the self becomes uncertain and "the fully saturated self becomes no self at all" (Gergen 1991:7). People face a daunting challenge in building and sustaining an integrated sense of self because the social structures that surround the self are fleeting and unstable. As James Holstein and Jaber Gubrium (2000) observe, contemporary times are challenging for the self because it is being produced in a rapidly growing, widely varying, and increasingly competitive set of institutions. Self-construction has become a big business, characterized by the proliferation of institutions that make it their stock-in-trade to design and discern identities for us. Gubrium and Holstein call for interactionists to shift the focus of their analyses beyond the situational construction of selves toward the institutional production of selves. By doing so, interactionist scholars can continue to push their perspective beyond traditional social psychological concerns and toward the domains of macrosociology.

FUTURE PROSPECTS

Symbolic interactionism is likely to maintain an influential voice in sociology, especially through its academic journal (*Symbolic Interaction*) and its ongoing contributions to various substantive areas and theoretical debates. Given recent trends, interactionist researchers will place greater emphasis on the development of macrolevel concepts and analyses, attending not only on mesostructural phenomena but also on the construction, dynamics, and interrelations of large-scale social structures. Interactionism will become characterized by even greater theoretical and methodological diversity in the next few decades, making it necessary to abandon the old (and somewhat illusory) distinction drawn between the Chicago and Iowa Schools and to speak of interactionist sociologies rather than interactionist sociology. And symbolic interactionism may become a victim of its recent and continuing theoretical successes, hastening its "sad demise" and eventual disappearance within sociology (Fine 1993). As the concepts of interactionism become the concepts of sociology, its voice will become increasingly integrated with, and indistinguishable from, the other voices that make up the discipline. This has already become evident in the analyses that can be found in many prominent sociological books and journal articles.

Symbolic interactionism's prospects in the twenty-first century will be determined largely by its central mission. If interactionists decide that their key mission is to continue formulating a pragmatic approach to social life—the power of symbol creation and interaction that is at the heart of the sociological imagination—then the future of interactionism will be bright. Guided by this goal, interactionists can expect to build on and extend the inroads they have gained within sociology in recent years. They can also expect their work to have a growing impact on related disciplines, such as gender studies, communication studies, cultural studies, education, and psychology.

— Kent Sandstrom and Sherryl Kleinman

See also Blumer, Herbert; Dramaturgy; Goffman, Erving; Mead, George Herbert; Negotiated Order; Self and Self-Concept; Social Interaction; Strauss, Anselm

FURTHER READINGS AND REFERENCES

Blumer, Herbert. 1969. *Symbolic Interactionism.* Englewood Cliffs, NJ: Prentice-Hall.

Cooley, Charles Horton. [1902] 1964. *Human Nature and the Social Order.* New York: Scribner's.

Gergen, Kenneth. 1991. *The Saturated Self.* New York: Basic Books.

Farberman, Harvey. 1975. "A Criminogenic Market Structure: The Automobile Industry." *Sociological Quarterly* 16:438–57.

Fine, Gary Alan. 1993. "The Sad Demise, Mysterious Disappearance, and Glorious Triumph of Symbolic Interactionism." *Annual Review of Sociology* 19:61–87.

———. 1996. *Kitchens: The Culture of Restaurant Work.* Berkeley: University of California Press.

Hochschild, Arlie. 1983. *The Managed Heart.* Berkeley: University of California Press.

Holstein, James A. and Jaber Gubrium. 2000. *The Self We Live By: Narrative Identity in a Postmodern World.* New York: Oxford University Press.

Maines, David. 1977. "Social Organization and Social Structure in Symbolic Interactionist Thought." *Annual Review of Sociology* 3:235–59.

Schwalbe, Michael, Sandra Godwin, Daphne Holden, Douglas Schrock, Shealy Thompson, and Michele Wolkomir. 2000. "Generic Processes in the Reproduction of Inequality: An Interactionist Analysis." *Social Forces* 79:419–52.

Snow, David A., E. Burke Rochford Jr., Steven K. Worden, and Robert D. Benford. 1986. "Frame Alignment Processes, Micromobilization and Movement Participation." *American Sociological Review* 51:464–81.

Turner, Ralph S. 1976. "Real Self: From Institution to Impulse" *American Journal of Sociology.* 81(5):989–1016.

West, Candace and Don H. Zimmerman. 1987. "Doing Gender." *Gender and Society* 1:125–51.

T

TAYLOR, CHARLES

Charles Taylor (b. 1931), Canadian social theorist and philosopher of modernity, is an advocate of the hermeneutic approach to social scientific research and author of the highly regarded *Sources of the Self: The Making of the Modern Identity* (1989). Educated at McGill and Oxford, Taylor combines Anglo-American and Continental philosophies to address problems across the social and human sciences. Most notably, Taylor has offered a sustained critique of the naturalist and reductionist accounts of human behavior that have predominated in modern philosophy and social science. More recently, this critique has addressed the nihilistic implications of postmodern and poststructuralist philosophies. As an alternative for the social sciences, Taylor proposes a hermeneutic understanding of human behavior that valorizes the integrity and agency of persons. Human beings are self-interpreting animals who struggle to articulate their position within culturally constituted frameworks of meaning and moral worth. In elaborating this perspective, Taylor has written on issues of broad concern to the social sciences, including epistemology, ethics, language, the self, multiculturalism, the liberal-communitarian debate in political philosophy, and religion. Taylor situates his project within the tradition of philosophical anthropology, indicating his interest in tracing the history of the changing conceptions of human nature in Western philosophy and culture. Although this philosophical anthropology is most clearly exemplified in *Sources of the Self,* its influence on Taylor's method of research and style of argument is also apparent in shorter essays such as his often-cited "The Politics of Recognition" (1994). Taylor is also recognized as an interpreter of the German idealist philosopher Georg Hegel and a commentator on Canadian politics, especially on the question of Quebec's sovereignty within Canada.

Taylor's critique of reductionist social science extends as far back as his first book, *The Explanation of Behavior* (1964), in which he criticizes behaviorist psychology for its efforts to explain human behavior through the lawlike statements exemplified in the natural sciences. In the 1970s and the 1980s, he extended this critique to cognitive psychological and neurophysiological explanations of behavior. Similarly, in "Interpretation and the Sciences of Man" (1971), Taylor finds fault in the kind of political science scholarship that reduces the shared meanings contained in political cultures to the interests of atomistic individuals. Common to these social sciences is the expectation that reductive theories provide explanations of human behavior that can be verified against empirical evidence. This hope, Taylor claims, is dangerously misplaced, because it leads to the elaboration of sciences that cannot help us to understand important aspects of human life. In this respect, Taylor shares much in common with postmodern and poststructuralist authors who aim to deconstruct the scientistic, foundationalist, and individualistic bias of Western thought. However, even as he sympathizes with authors such as Michel Foucault and Jacques Derrida, Taylor argues that poststructuralism reproduces the epistemological errors of Western philosophy by ignoring the integrity of lived personal experience. As such, Taylor advocates a hermeneutic epistemology in which the self-possessed interpretive capacities of human beings assume center stage. Human beings are self-interpreting animals who understand and reflect on the meaning of their lives and their relations to other people. This kind of self-interpretive activity is not based on a priori epistemological principles but on practical knowledge and everyday encounters with cultural frameworks. Furthermore, Taylor marks himself as a philosopher of morality by arguing that interpretation necessarily involves evaluations of moral worth. Human beings are not simply self-interpreters, but they are the kind of interpreters for whom things matter. Precisely what matters is worked out as individuals articulate their position within the moral spaces constituted by historical communities.

Taylor's hermeneutic project is supported by a philosophy of language that makes appearances throughout his writings but that is most thoroughly developed in the essays contained in the first volume of his philosophical papers, *Human Agency and Language* (1985a). Here, twentieth-century philosophy is characterized by its concern with language and the relation between language and meaning. Two conceptions of language have vied for superiority in twentieth-century thought. Taylor traces the first of these conceptions to Enlightenment scholarship, and in particular, to the influence of John Locke. On this "designative" view, language serves the utilitarian purpose of accurately picturing or representing a preexistent reality. In contrast, the Romantic counter-Enlightenment, as represented in the work of Johann Gottfried von Herder and Jean-Jacques Rousseau, provides a "constitutive" or "expressive" conception of language. In this view, language does not represent a preexisting reality but gives expression to unarticulated sensibilities and feelings. The act of articulation clarifies the meaning of these feelings and constitutes new forms of human understanding. Insofar as they are constituted in language, these newly articulated understandings are communal possessions that deepen self-awareness. While twentieth-century social science has been committed to the designative view of language, Taylor argues that language is most properly an expressive medium.

These philosophical arguments come together in Taylor's history of the modern self, *Sources of Self: The Making of the Modern Identity*. In this book, Taylor argues that selfhood and morality are inextricably intertwined, and he sets out to describe the history of the relation between the self and the good. Taylor is particularly critical of the strand of modernism that seeks to objectify and naturalize all accounts of human selfhood. He deems these incapable of providing an account of the self that captures the depth of personal experience. Nevertheless, Taylor argues that there are elements of modernity that potentially provide for a rich account of the self. Taylor's task, then, is not to reject the modern project but to recover those elements of the project that revivify the idea of authentic selfhood. These arguments overlap with Taylor's work in political philosophy. Like his project on the self, Taylor views his work in political philosophy as an effort to define the political culture of modernity. In this capacity, Taylor has written on the liberal-communitarian debate, defending the communitarian position against the atomism and methodological individualism of political liberalism. As a Canadian in Quebec, Taylor has written on the topic of French-English relations in Canada and has also been called on by parliamentary commissions to address the viability of a continuing Canadian federalism. In these capacities, Taylor has passionately argued for a renewed federalism in which cultural diversity is deepened and sustained through ongoing efforts at cross-cultural communication and mutual understanding. Here, Taylor has also addressed broader issues of nationalism, multiculturalism, and ethnocentricity. He argues that debates about multiculturalism and ethnocentricity emerge from the modern concern with a demand for recognition. While the liberal perspective employs a procedural mechanism to ensure that all cultures are granted equal opportunity for recognition, Taylor adopts a communitarian stance to argue that cross-cultural encounters should involve conversations about the relative worth of cultures and their valued goods.

— Jeffrey Stepnisky

See also Hermeneutics; Modernity; Nationalism; Philosophical Anthropology; Rousseau, Jean-Jacques; Self and Self-Concept

FURTHER READINGS AND REFERENCES

Taylor, C. 1985a. *Philosophical Papers 1: Human Agency and Language.* New York: Cambridge University Press.
———. 1985b. *Philosophical Papers 2: Philosophy and the Human Sciences.* New York: Cambridge University Press.
———. 1989. *Sources of the Self: The Making of the Modern Identity.* Cambridge, MA: Harvard University Press.
———. 1991. *The Ethics of Authenticity.* Cambridge, MA: Harvard University Press.
———. 1993. *Reconciling the Solitudes: Essays on Canadian Federalism and Nationalism.* Montreal, Canada: McGill-Queen's University Press.
———. 1995. *Philosophical Arguments.* Cambridge, MA: Harvard University Press.
Taylor, C. K., with Anthony Appiah, Jürgen Habermas, Steven C. Rockefeller, Michael Walzer, and Susan Wolf. 1994. *Multiculturalism: Examining the Politics of Recognition.* Edited and with an introduction by Amy Gutmann. 2d ed. Princeton, NJ: Princeton University Press.

TELEVISION AND SOCIAL THEORY

Television has been the object of theoretical reflection beginning with debates on "mass society" that heated up in the years following World War II. Residual concerns over the totalitarian temptation to which the vanquished Axis nations fell prey leading up to the war, the rise of the consumer capitalist economy in the West, and Cold War politics focusing on the Soviet Union and its allies made for serious discussion concerning the role of television within democratic society. In the postwar period, researchers and theorists turned the formerly pejorative phrase "mass society" into a descriptor of popular democracy and "liberal-pluralism triumphant." (Bennett 1982:40)

Television loomed large in this rethinking of postwar liberal democracy.

The relationship between the academic study of social communication and the development of contemporary social theory is surveyed by Hanno Hardt in *Critical Communication Studies: Communication, History & Theory in America* (1992). This comprehensive overview identifies two primary tendencies within the field. As it concerns television in specific, the pragmatic tradition in the United States manifests itself in empirically oriented "effects" research, which concerns the psychology of individual reception and the social psychology of resultant group behavior. The challenge to the tradition of "administrative research" is represented by British Cultural Studies beginning in the 1950s, whose intellectual heritage reaches back to the Frankfurt School of critical theory. More recent developments include critiques that owe to feminism, postmodernist thought, critical race theory, and a return to institutional-historical approaches to television and social theory.

So far as any discussion of the relationship between television and social theory is even addressed, the research questions asked by those interested in the "effects" of television tend to assume that the political and economic order that gave rise to this new postwar mass medium of communication is in itself not problematic. Contrary to this approach, those writing specifically about television in the cultural studies tradition understand that the very basis of the sociocultural, political, and economic system needs to be examined in understanding both the mundane reality and transformative potential of the medium. Moreover, the empiricist thrust of conventional research on television in the United States is "marked by a built-in inconclusiveness that forestalls the linkage with social theory, the proper goal of research in the social sciences" (Hamamoto 1989:10).

Most social science literature on television, despite its pose of objectivity, is informed by liberal pluralist social theory whereby conflicting beliefs and values compete for supremacy within a fictive marketplace of ideas. From this matrix of supposedly free exchange has emerged a political-economic system—capitalism—that has proved its fitness by its sheer ability to deliver the greatest good to the largest number within the polity. *The People Look at Television: A Study of Audience Attitudes* (1963) by Gary A. Steiner is a prime example of social science research that legitimates the for-profit system of the three U.S. national networks of the day. Financed by CBS and conducted under the aegis of the Bureau of Applied Social Research at Columbia University, the report combines an argument laden with populist and democratic rhetoric (*vide* "The People") with a show of social science data marshaled to blunt then-current criticism of network television by the Federal Communications Commission (FCC).

The landmark study by Raymond Williams, *Television: Technology and Cultural Form* (1975) represents a rejection of abstracted empiricist social science research in communications. It also put to rest the "technological determinism" of Marshall McLuhan's *Understanding Media: The Extensions of Man* (1964), which had exerted much influence both within academia and among the educated public. Instead, Williams argues that technologies such as television must be understood as the outcome of historical forces arising from bourgeois class interests within advanced capitalism while appreciating the communitarian and democratic values of television's vast audience.

The preliminary attempt by Williams to delve more deeply into the phenomenology of the television viewing experience characterized by what he calls "flow" was taken systematically to a new level by John Fiske in *Television Culture* (1987). This foundational study draws from a number of seminal methodological strategies, including semiotics, discourse theory, ideological criticism, and feminist insights into issues of gender. Fiske advances the claim that audiences often "resist" the dominant reading of television texts and thereby poses a challenge to its otherwise hegemonic power.

Specific television genres such as the "soap opera" and TV creations such as pop star Madonna have been examined from a variety of critical approaches under the heading of "feminist" theory. Liberal, Marxist, poststructuralist, and postmodern feminist theory have given rise to an array of scholarship that explores the relationship between women and patriarchy within capitalist society. The strict focus on women as the object of analysis in feminist theory more recently has been broadened to address more general questions of gender in society. Bearing the influence of postmodern feminist strains of thought in their study of audience "consumption" of TV, Ien Ang and Joke Hermes (1991) argue that even in the face of "hegemonic gender discourse" a fluid gender identity is ever in the process of being "articulated, disarticulated, and rearticulated" (p. 321).

It seems inevitable that the medium of television as a postwar "technology and cultural form" would become emblematic of the "postmodern condition." According to David Harvey in *The Condition of Postmodernity: An Enquiry into the Origins of Cultural Change* (1989), the emergence of postmodernity can be attributed to the proliferation of television viewing in almost all societies. The intertextual semiotic excess, self-reflexive irony, and multivalent meanings generated by TV programs in all their sheer pervasiveness within the larger consumer capitalist culture seem to embody all that is unique to postmodernity. The internal debate among theorists of the postmodern ranges widely and is rife with dubious claims and counterclaims. Where postmodern theory pertains specifically to television studies, however, John Fiske warns against divorcing critical reflection from the politics of capitalist society. He stresses that postmodern critique must remain rooted in material realities.

Race, racial identity, and racism have long been minor components of empirically inflected social science research in television studies. Qualitative and interpretative approaches in television studies emerging from the humanities similarly relegated race to the category of second-class status. Perhaps in response to the political ineffectuality of high theory as it had become enshrined in academia, a return to "race" as a basic category of sociocultural analysis began in earnest beginning in the 1990s. Inspired by pioneering work by J. Fred MacDonald who recounts both the repressive social climate and institutional barriers to racial equality in *Blacks and White TV: Afro-Americans in Television Since 1948* (1983), Darrell Y. Hamamoto provides a radical analysis of U.S. militarism, empire, and immigration and relates this conflicted history to the portrayal of yellow peoples in *Monitored Peril: Asian American and the Politics of TV Representation* (1994).

With the appearance of *Communication and Race: A Structural Perspective* (1998) by Oscar H. Gandy Jr., social constructivist theories of race and racism have been pushed to the foreground in current discussions of the private, for-profit "media system." In particular, the growing body of contemporary scholarship described as critical race theory has done much to shed explanatory light on the origins of institutionalized racism within the system of corporate oligopoly television.

Douglas Kellner in *Television and the Crisis of Democracy* (1990) views the capitalist foundations and imperatives of the commercial "broadcasting system" as antithetical to democracy itself. Respectful of the critical theory tradition while rejecting the tendency of its more elitist proponents to be dismissive of mass media and popular culture, Kellner sees the interlocking system of government, the FCC, and television networks as depriving the television audience of truly democratic communication due to the lack of corporate accountability, highly restricted access to the airwaves, and the narrowness of political perspective presented.

By the turn of the century, the problems identified by Kellner have only expanded and intensified with the supranational global reach of U.S. television and allied media, such as films, recorded music, and publishing. The "global media system" in its megacorporate manifestations is presented in exacting detail by Robert W. McChesney in *Rich Media, Poor Democracy: Communication Politics in Dubious Times* (1999). He argues that the concentration of power among vertically integrated corporate oligopolies poses a grave threat to the free flow of information and diverse opinion vital to the sustenance of democratic society. McChesney concludes with an agenda for "structural media reform" that will allow television to realize its potential for the spread of democratic values and social practices.

— Darrell Y. Hamamoto

See also Feminist Cultural Studies; Media Critique; Positivism; Postmodernism; Power-Dependence Relations

FURTHER READINGS AND REFERENCES

Ang, Ien and Joke Hermes 1991. Pp. 307–28 in *Mass Media and Society,* edited by James Curran and Michael Gurevitch. New York: Routledge.

Bennett, T. 1982. "Theories of the Media, Theories of Society. Pp. 30–55 in *Culture, Society and the Media,* edited by Michael Gurevitch, Tony Bennett, James Curran, and Janet Woollacott. New York: Routledge.

Gandy, Oscar H. Jr. 1998. *Communication and Race: A Structural Perspective.* London: Arnold.

Hamamoto, Darrell Y. 1989. *Nervous Laughter: Television Situation Comedy and Liberal Democratic Ideology.* New York: Praeger.

Kellner, Douglas. 1990. *Television and the Crisis of Democracy.* Boulder, CO: Westview.

McChesney, Robert W. 1999. *Rich Media, Poor Democracy: Communication Politics in Dubious Times.* New York: New Press.

THEORY CONSTRUCTION

Theory construction is the process of developing theories in accord with criteria for their production and analysis. A number of texts offer methods for constructing sociological theories; however, at the present time, the field of sociology has no widely agreed-upon set of criteria for building and evaluating theories.

This entry presents criteria for theory construction and theory analysis that are consistent with some of the sociological prescriptions and, more important, with criteria that are widely accepted in other sciences. Before doing so, it is first necessary to discuss briefly some broader issues.

THE CONTEXT OF THEORIES

Theories are repositories of general knowledge. Through testing and refinement, scientific theories change over time in ways that lead them to provide increasingly accurate explanations for ever-widening ranges of phenomena. Their accumulated wisdom far exceeds the ability of common sense to explain the complex world around us. However, sociologists hold different conceptions of what a theory actually is and so do not all agree on criteria for building and evaluating them. Some use the term very broadly so that it includes virtually any sociological conjecture. Others apply more stringent criteria that actually rule out much that usually is called "theory" in sociology. The compromise adopted here is to distinguish two different kinds of intellectual products: theories and quasi-theories.

Quasi-theories are known by a variety of labels, including *perspectives, frameworks, orientations, metatheories,* and somewhat confusingly, *theories.* As will be illustrated shortly, there are explicit criteria for defining, constructing, and evaluating theories. In contrast, there is no such thing as a uniform set of criteria for quasi-theories. They are loosely bound areas of theoretical work that may include raw ideas, classic statements, discussions about theories or other quasi-theories, sensitizing concepts, empirical observations, research strategies, provisional generalizations, expressions of values, authoritative proclamations, and so on. Despite their indefinite form, however, quasi-theories have played a key role in sociology's development, mainly because they inspire research and new theorizing.

Quasi-theory is just one of several contextual factors that influence the development of theory. Others include prior theories and research findings. Brand-new theories are relatively uncommon, and most new theoretical developments build on existing theories in response to empirical observations. Sociologists of science and other scholars identify still more factors that influence theories directly and indirectly: norms and mechanisms for funding; review and publication practices; the politics of academic disciplines; and even personal characteristics of the theorists themselves. These affect theory primarily by coloring value judgments regarding which issues warrant attention, but they also may introduce bias into the process whereby theories are accepted or rejected. However, upholding rigorous standards for theory construction (and for the empirical testing of theories) at least reduces the unwanted impact of factors unrelated to the accuracy of the theory's claims.

THE ELEMENTS OF THEORIES

A well-constructed theory should have several identifiable components that work together as a system. Although some theorists develop these components in an explicit and self-conscious way, this is generally not the case. However, inattention to a theory's form can impede its function by making it more difficult to identify weaknesses. The various components of theories and their connections to the empirical world are identified next. Following that, there is a discussion of some of the qualities that distinguish better theories.

Arguments

At the heart of every theory is an *argument.* The author of the theory offers the argument in an attempt to convince readers that one or more *conclusions* must follow from a series of assumptions or *premises.* The reader is under no obligation to believe a theory if the premises do not actually support the conclusion or if the theory is ambiguous because some of its terms are undefined. In other words, the theorist is obliged to communicate the theory so that the meanings of its statements are clear to members of an intended audience and the logic by which its conclusions are reached is accessible to anyone interested in using the theory. When inadequate attention is paid to an argument's logical structure, closer inspection often reveals that the conclusions the author wishes to derive do not actually follow from his or her premises—that the conclusions are *invalid.* When this is the case, empirical tests are irrelevant until the problems are repaired.

Ideally, theoretical statements are organized in accord with some explicit logic that provides rules for manipulating statements and deriving new conclusions from them. The theorist may choose from a variety of logical systems, depending on the kinds of statements he or she wants to express. For instance, *sentential logic* applies to natural language statements, and mathematical systems such as *calculus* or *graph theory* apply to statements expressed using specialized symbolic languages.

Premises

In discussions of the logic of argumentation, a *premise* is a conditional statement that links two simpler statements. For example, consider these three simple statements: (A) A group is stratified. (B) A group has a division of labor. (C) Workers are highly productive. These can serve as building blocks for compound statements that serve as premises of a theory:

Premise 1: If a group is stratified, then it has a division of labor.
Premise 2: If a group has a division of labor, then its workers are highly productive.

These may be written symbolically as

A → B (Premise 1)
B → C (Premise 2)

The first simple statement in each premise is the *antecedent condition,* and the second statement is the *consequent.* A well-formed theory contains two or more premises, although they can appear in other formats (e.g., English, algebraic, graphical) and may be referred to by other labels (e.g., *propositions, assumptions, axioms,* or *postulates*) or even obscured by a mountain of extraneous text. More important than formats or labels, however, is their role within the structure of theories: Premises specify the relationships that the theorist assumes to be true and from which implications may be derived and tested. Furthermore, to play any role in the theoretical argument, each premise must "connect" with one or more other premises—a criterion fulfilled by Statement B in the example.

Conclusions

It is by virtue of their interconnectedness that premises and rules of logic may combine to generate and justify a *conclusion*—another term with special meaning in the world of logic. Conclusions are akin to premises in that they are conditional statements, and they may appear under various labels, including *derivation, theorem,* and *hypothesis*. A conclusion is derived from two or more premises by applying an explicit logical or mathematical principle. For example, a complete argument can be formed using the premises introduced earlier:

$$A \rightarrow B \text{ (Premise 1)}$$
$$B \rightarrow C \text{ (Premise 2)}$$
$$\overline{}$$
$$A \rightarrow C \text{ (Conclusion)}$$

In this case, the conclusion is a new statement that takes the argument beyond what was asserted by the premises. It was derived from the two premises by applying a logical principle known as the "Law of Hypothetical Syllogism." Although the logic is fairly intuitive in this case, with richer sets of premises and logical systems it is often possible to generate unexpected and counterintuitive conclusions. If these hold up under empirical testing, they provide compelling evidence that the theory behind them is sound.

Terms

The burden of communicating the precise meanings of a theory's statements rests on its *terms*—the set of words or symbols chosen by the theorist to express premises. Whereas attending to the logical form of a theory helps ensure that its conclusions follow from its premises, attending to a theory's semantic form increases the likelihood that the authors' intended meanings will follow from the terms used to express them.

All terms fall into three categories: *primitive terms, defined terms,* and *logical connectives.* Logical connectives are components of a theory's logical system. They may include terms such as *if, then,* and *therefore* in sentential logic, or symbols such as =, +, and Σ if a mathematical framework is used. Logical connectives need not be defined within the theory because they are well defined within the logical framework that the theory invokes.

Primitive terms also are not defined within the theory. They must be chosen by the theorist with the intended readership in mind, and they provide the foundation for

the theory's terminological system. If the primitive terms fall short insofar as accurately communicating the theorist's intended ideas, the theory's assertions will be misunderstood by some readers. This will lead to problems in attempting to validate the theory via empirical testing. Whether or not a given test is valid may come down to the interpretation of a single theoretical term. Therefore, the theorist must know what terms will be understood without explicit definition.

Words do not have inherent meanings. To assume so would be committing the "fallacy of essentialism"—that is, assuming that a given term has a "true" or essential meaning. Terms have only the meanings that people give to them. When a theorist cannot be certain that members of the theory's intended audience will share the meaning that he or she intends for a term, then an explicit definition is warranted. Ideally, a definition should specify criteria necessary and sufficient to identify any empirical instance of the term.

Terms used in a definition are part of the theory and so must be chosen with care. The reason for having primitive terms is simple: One cannot define all terms in a theory because of the "infinite regress" problem. Terms in definitions would have to be defined, then all the terms in *those* definitions must be defined, and so on. Instead, primitive terms create a foundation, new terms are defined using those primitive terms, and more specialized terms may be defined using primitive terms and/or previously defined terms. Just as one may diagram the interrelationships of the statements comprising the theoretical argument, one may also diagram the structure of the terminological system to ensure that there are no circularities or gaps.

Scope

For a variety of reasons, a theorist may wish to state provisional limits on the applicability of his or her theory. *Scope conditions* place abstract and general boundaries around the domain in which a theory is intended to apply. Newer theories may be expected to have narrower scope, but with time and the accumulation of research, the scope conditions of the maturing theory are gradually relaxed. From the theorist's standpoint, scope conditions protect the theory from being tested under conditions never intended by the theorist. At the same time, the constraints imposed by scope conditions are abstract and general, and so even a theory with many such conditions still in principle may apply to an infinite number of empirical cases.

Hypotheses

Theoretical statements exist in an abstract world of their own, referring to general classes of phenomena but to nothing in particular. If they are to be convincing, sociological theories must connect to observable phenomena, and they must conform to those phenomena in reliable and accurate ways. Although sometimes the term is used differently, here we treat *hypotheses* as theoretically motivated statements about relationships between empirical phenomena. Ultimately, a theory must be tested through hypotheses consistent with both theoretical statements and empirical observations.

For abstract theoretical statements to produce hypotheses that pertain to phenomena in the "real world," connections must be established between terms of the theory and *indicators* for those terms. To illustrate using the earlier example, the derived conclusion was "A → C" or "If a group is stratified, then workers are highly productive." To test this claim, we would need to use the definitions of the theoretical terms ("group," "stratified," "workers," "highly productive") to guide the selection of empirical instances. This translation process goes by various names, including *operationalization, instantiation,* and *interpretation.* Finally, the same logical connectives that frame the theoretical statement are used to complete the hypothesis. These relationships may be diagrammed as follows:

$$\begin{array}{ll} \text{From the Theory:} & A \to C \\ \text{Operationalizations:} & \vdots \quad \vdots \\ \text{Hypothesis:} & a \to c \end{array}$$

For example, suppose that the definition of *group* used by a particular theory is "A set of actors, each of which identifies himself or herself as belonging to a common entity." Then one possible operationalization could be "Sociology 330, University of South Carolina, Fall semester 2002," if it is indeed the case that all members of this class would identify themselves as such in a questionnaire or interview. If this class also satisfies the theory's definition of *stratified,* then the antecedent condition of the hypothesis is fulfilled. If *c* is observed—that is, if "highly productive workers" are observed as specified by the definitions of those terms—then the hypothesis is confirmed and we would be justified in raising our confidence in the theory.

Hypotheses may fail tests for any of a number of reasons, some pertaining to the theory, some pertaining to measurement procedures. In other words, a failed test does not immediately necessitate revising or discarding the theory. This is especially true if the theory is well corroborated by other tests and if there is some uncertainty about the empirical methods used in the falsifying test. On the other hand, if the failed hypothesis clearly does operationalize an explicit theoretical assertion and there is high confidence in the integrity of the test itself, then the relevant community of scholars would be obliged to lower their confidence in the theory.

BUILDING GOOD THEORIES

Merely describing the elements of theories neither justifies them nor explains the process by which they evolve over time. One way to address both issues is to review some of the desirable qualities that characterize theories built with explicit attention to these elements, and some of the undesirable qualities that theorists should strive to avoid.

Self-Contradiction

A single contradiction can invalidate an entire argument, so it is very much in the theorist's interest to employ a set of tools designed to detect and eliminate such problems. Careful attention to the theory's logical structure greatly reduces the potential for mutually contradictory statements, circular arguments, invalid deductions, and any number of other fallacies that characterize informal discourse.

Ambivalence and Ambiguity

If there are terms in a theory with multiple meanings, or if the meanings of some terms are unclear, it is highly unlikely that the theory can be communicated effectively to its intended audience. The consequences are important. Readers not applying rigorous standards for theory construction will readily infer meanings for undefined terms. They will assume, often incorrectly, that the meanings they infer are accurate reflections of the theorist's intended meanings. A healthy research-driven discipline depends on accurately communicated theories so that members of a *community* of scholars may submit them to analyses and tests. If a misunderstanding leads to an invalid operationalization of theoretical terms, results of empirical tests have no bearing on the theory and valuable time and resources will have been wasted.

Abstractness and Generality

If theories were supposed to be descriptions of phenomena that occur in specific places and times, there would have to be a theory for each phenomenon at each time and place. Instead, a theory uses *abstract* terms that may connect it to potentially limitless numbers of specific cases and that capitalize on underlying connections between what may appear to be unrelated phenomena. This permits the development of *general* theories—that is, theories that accurately explain wide-ranging phenomena under broad-scope conditions.

Tests and Testability

At crucial points in their development, *tests* subject the implications of theories to the harsh light of empirical reality. The more tests a theory survives, the more believable the theory. Furthermore, a theory is more compelling to the extent that its tests are stringent and diverse, and that the tested theory performs better than any alternative theories. If a theory is not *testable,* it is not credible. The testability of a theory is diminished by problems with its language or its logic. For example, a theory may be so ambivalent that it can never be disproved, in the same way that "If *x,* then either *y* or not *y*" cannot be falsified. The most powerful theories tend to be those that make the riskiest claims in the sense that there are clearly stipulated ways for them to fail tests.

Parsimony

All else being equal, small and simple theories—those having fewer and simpler terms, premises and scope conditions—are preferable to big complex theories. This is the criterion of *parsimony.* Simpler theories are easier to evaluate and to communicate efficiently and accurately. The expression "theory *construction*" can be misleading in that theories sometimes are improved by *removing* components such as redundant terms and statements with no logical connection to the theory's central arguments.

Evolutionary Progress

In a progressive discipline, theories are not created to be put on display for future generations to admire. They are works in progress that become more general, precise, parsimonious, and so on, through trial and error over extended periods of time. The trial-and-error process operates on several fronts: Definitions are adjusted and sharpened, new conjectures are formulated and tested, old premises are subsumed and extended by new ones, scope conditions are relaxed. The long-term effect is an evolving, ever-improving theory.

— Barry Markovsky

See also Metatheory; Positivism

FURTHER READINGS AND REFERENCES

Berger, Joseph and Morris Zelditch Jr., eds. 2002. *New Directions in Contemporary Sociological Theory.* Lanham, MD: Rowman & Littlefield.

Cederblom, Jerry and David W. Paulson. 2001. *Critical Reasoning.* 5th ed. Belmont, CA: Wadsworth.

Cohen, Bernard P. 1989. *Developing Sociological Knowledge.* 2d ed. Chicago, IL: Nelson-Hall.

Markovsky, Barry. 1994. "The Structure of Theories." Pp. 3–24 in *Group Processes: Sociological Analyses,* edited by Martha Foschi and Edward J. Lawler. Chicago, IL: Nelson-Hall.

Turner, Jonathan H. 2002. *The Structure of Sociological Theory.* 7th ed. Belmont, CA: Wadsworth.

THOMAS, WILLIAM ISAAC

William Isaac Thomas (1863–1947), American sociologist and social psychologist, directed the field of sociology away from the abstractions of an earlier generation of "system builders" to concrete studies of group life and social behavior. Thomas was widely regarded as one of the University of Chicago's most productive and original scholars, first as a graduate student (1893–1896) and then as one of the sociology faculty (1896–1918). His greatest, most lasting influence was as a framer of sociological concepts and methodologies, establishing the *life history* (a self-reported narration of life) and the personal document (letters, diaries, archival records) as basic sources for social research. Thomas proposed that social problems required an understanding of both "social organization" and the subjective (experiential) aspects of social reality and a commitment to sociology and social psychology, respectively. He was also an early champion of comparative methods in social science, pioneering comparative studies in culture and personality. *The Polish Peasant in Europe and America* (1918–1920), written with Florian Znaniecki, has been regarded as one of the most important works in American social science and was the subject of several scholarly reappraisals in the years after its publication, the first by Herbert Blumer in 1939. The influence of Thomas on U.S. sociology was also felt through his close friendship and association with Robert E. Park. They met at the 1910 International Conference on the Negro held at the Tuskegee Institute, a meeting that eventually led to Park's appointment at Chicago and their lifelong collaboration.

Thomas was born in rural Virginia and entered the University of Tennessee at Knoxville, graduating in 1884, where he remained as a teacher of Greek and modern languages while undertaking graduate studies in English literature and modern languages, receiving a doctorate in 1886. By his own account, he was moved to pursue learning through the examples of two teachers—a professor of Greek language and culture and a natural scientist who taught him evolutionary science, fields of study that remained part of his distinct interdisciplinary focus throughout his life. In his "Life History," Thomas described his youthful "conversion" to the intellectual and scientific life and his plans to travel to Germany to pursue that life through the study of modern and ancient languages. While on a leave from Tennessee from 1888 to 1889, he studied at Göttingen and Berlin, working in languages and in the new fields of ethnology and the folk psychology of Moritz Lazarus and Heymann Steinthal.

On his return to America in 1889, he accepted his first full-time academic post at Oberlin College as a teacher of English and comparative literature. These early years of reading, learning, and teaching he described as "the most satisfactory of my life." At Oberlin, his interest in social science was further stimulated by his reading of Herbert Spencer's *Principles of Sociology* from which he took his evolutionary and anthropological view of human development. In 1893, Thomas went to the newly established University of Chicago to pursue a second doctorate in sociology, working under the direction of Albion W. Small and Charles R. Henderson. Thomas's second doctoral dissertation, "On a Difference of the Metabolism of the Sexes," was later developed and published as *Sex and Society: Studies in the Social Psychology of Sex* (1907) and is numbered among the early sociological studies of the social aspects of sexual behavior and relations. It is also an example of Thomas's interest in the social problems of his day that evoked intense moral discussion, such as prostitution and sexual behavior, issues he addressed as problems of "human behavior," using research methods from anthropology, clinical case studies, and fieldwork.

In a second visit to Europe (1896–1897), the year after receiving his doctorate in sociology and while on faculty leave from Chicago, he began to formulate a method and topic he called a "comparative study of European nationalities" and began to outline a study of European peasants and the problem of *immigration.* In 1914, he began a four-year collaboration with Florian Znaniecki that culminated in *The Polish Peasant in Europe and America,* a five-volume work regarded as monumental both for its insights into groups and group processes and for its range of topics: life historical method, including the life history of Wladek, a Polish peasant; theories of personality, culture, and culture change; an attitude-value schema where "attitudes" are the meanings of individual subjects and "values" are the objective social and situational conditions of social actors. This work incorporated a new definition of "attitude," a concept then in use in sociology and psychology; attitudes are distinguished from psychic states and involve a disposition to act toward an object according to its meaning.

A period of major changes in Thomas's professional life began in 1918 with the sudden termination of his faculty appointment at Chicago following a public scandal closely recounted in the *Chicago Tribune.* The charges, violation of the Mann Act and false hotel registration, were later dismissed, but the publicity led to his swift dismissal by the university president and trustees. At age 55, Thomas was never again to secure another full-time academic position. He moved to New York in 1918 where he worked for a year on the Carnegie Corporation's Americanization Studies and collaborated with Robert Park on *Old World Traits Transplanted* (1921). He relied for many years on the support of philanthropists, private foundations, and research institutes for the continuance of his work and for occasional appointments, including research projects culminating in *The Unadjusted Girl* (1923) and another published as *The Child in America* (1928). The latter, sponsored by the Laura Spellman Rockefeller Memorial, was written in collaboration

with the sociologist and demographer Dorothy Swaine Thomas whom he married in 1934 and who was elected the first woman president of the American Sociological Society in 1952. His first marriage to Harriet Park, with whom he also collaborated on works of social reform and social policy, ended in divorce in 1934. Thomas worked on the staff of the Social Science Research Council from 1932 to 1933 and lectured at Harvard in 1936 and 1937. His last book *Primitive Behavior* (1936) was a study of cultural history from a "sociopsychological standpoint." Thomas died at age 84 in Berkeley, California.

Thomas is often identified with the concept of the "four wishes" (desires for new experience, mastery, recognition, security), an emphasis in his early thought and work on human instincts and desires. His concept of the "definition of the situation" represents Thomas's later "situational" approach to the study of human behavior, which argues that all determinants of behavior require study and should not be assumed by postulating needs, instincts, or wishes. How situations are defined is a problem about the group and its standards, codified in norms and laws. But it is also a matter of how situations are defined by individuals, since different social experiences lead to different and unique perceptions and evaluations of situations. Human action always begins with this process of defining the situation, but the outcomes of these processes in action are always real: "If men define situations as real they are real in their consequences" (1928:572).

The situational theory of human behavior, the topic of his 1927 presidential address at the American Sociological Society ("Situational Analysis: The Behavior Pattern and the Situation"), shows the influence of, among others, the pragmatist philosophers on his thinking, particularly their efforts to depart from the notion of human beings as mechanisms: Human actions occur in group structures and according to cultural norms, but their activities include the idea that human beings assume attitudes toward these situations and act according to their own definitions of what those situations mean.

— E. Doyle McCarthy

See also Park, Robert; Pragmatism; Symbolic Interaction; Znaniecki, Florian Witold

FURTHER READINGS AND REFERENCES

Janowitz, Morris. 1966. "Introduction." Pp. vii–lviii in *W. I. Thomas on Social Organization and Social Personality,* edited and with an introduction by Morris Janowitz. Chicago & London: University of Chicago Press.

Thomas, William I. 1907. *Sex and Society: Studies in the Social Psychology of Sex.* Chicago, IL: University of Chicago Press.

———. 1923. *The Unadjusted Girl: With Cases and Standpoint for Behavior Analysis.* Boston: Little, Brown.

———. 1936. *Primitive Behavior: An Introduction to the Social Sciences.* New York: McGraw-Hill.

Thomas, William I., Robert E. Park, and Herbert A. Miller. 1921. *Old World Traits Transplanted.* New York: Harper & Brothers.

Thomas, William I. and Dorothy Swaine Thomas. 1928. *The Child in America: Behavior Problems and Programs.* New York: Knopf.

Thomas, William I. and Florian Znaniecki. 1918–1919. *The Polish Peasant in Europe and America.* 5 vols. Boston: Badger. Vols. I and II originally published by University of Chicago Press, 1918.

Young, Kimball. 1962–1963. "The Contribution of William Isaac Thomas to Sociology." *Sociology and Social Research* 47(1,2,3,4):3–24; 123–37; 251–72; 381–97.

TILLY, CHARLES

Charles Tilly (b. 1929) is a U.S. social historian who revolutionized the way that social scientists think about revolutions, social movements, and social change. Educated at Harvard, Oxford, and Angers (France), Tilly provides the metatheoretical and historical framework for resource mobilization and political process theories of collective action, social movements, and social change in his analyses of state making, revolution, and enduring inequality. Tilly incorporates elements of utilitarianism (John Stuart Mill), Max Weber, and Karl Marx in a scathing critique of Émile Durkheim's approach to social change and offers a synthetic theory of collective action based on Marxian interests, Millian opportunities, and Weberian organization. Tilly applies this model in historical analyses of state making and capital accumulation as these affect and are affected by changing forms (*repertoires*) of political protest, particularly in England and France, circa 1500 to 1900. Much of this research was focused on the organization of, and opportunities for, political protest, but his recent work includes a return to the topic of interests, their base in exploitation and opportunity hoarding and their reproduction and institutionalization through processes of emulation and accommodation. Thus, Tilly completes the synthesis of Marx and Weber, leaving unresolved the Millian (utilitarian or rational choice) concerns with rationality and game theory and the relationship between individual and organizational processes. Tilly remains an organizational theorist who uses Mill and Weber to specify the organizational processes through which state making and capitalism have transformed and been transformed by political challenges (based on interests, opportunities, and organizations).

Tilly's dissertation (Harvard 1958), expanded and published as *The Vendee* in 1964, offered French historians a sociological perspective on how urbanization affected the interests and organization of various local actors who mobilized in opposition to the Revolution of 1789. By 1978, in *From Mobilization to Revolution,* Tilly had developed both theory and method to guide the work of social historians and students of social movements and social change. He began with Marx's materialist, relational model of interests rooted in exploitation and added Weberian concepts of political organization to construct a mobilization model in which interest, organization, and opportunities predict collective action. Interests predict organization, and both interests and organization predict the mobilization of resources in preparation for collective action. Interests also affect political opportunity (or threat) for gains (or losses) from collective action and the likelihood and extent of repression (or toleration or facilitation) by governments or other polity members (this, in turn affects power, which, together with mobilization, also predicts opportunity or threat).

Based on this model, Tilly predicts collective action based on mobilization, opportunity or threat, and power. Thus, Tilly challenged the prevailing wisdom of the 1970s by arguing that collective action was rational and purposive rather than affective and expressive. Tilly maintained that collective action was rational at the organizational level (but not necessarily at the individual level) and generally sided with Mill and the utilitarians in opposition to Durkheim and the functionalists, but he insisted that interests were rooted in social relations rather than in personal predispositions. This was particularly evident in his tribute to George Homans (his former teacher) and his scathing review of Durkheim, in *As Sociology Meets History* (1981). Thus, Tilly anticipated the concerns of rational choice while offering a base in classical theory for resource mobilization and political process theories, which became the dominant perspective on social movements and social change in the 1980s.

Equally important, Tilly introduced history as both cause and effect of collective action. Collective action in any particular time and place is rooted in the familiar ways in which people protest injustice, but these repertoires of collective action—these arrays of interactive performances—change substantially in form and content over time. Tilly argues, in *The Contentious French* (1986), that between 1650 and 1850 popular protest was parochial and patronized. Between 1850 and 1980, the modern social movement was born, as the repertoire of collective action became increasingly national and autonomous. The general change from local festivals to modern demonstrations was in large part a response to state making and capitalism, which significantly altered interests, organizations, and opportunities for collective action. Tilly documents a similar change in *Popular Contention in Great Britain, 1758–1834* (1995). Here, however, Tilly clarifies two important points. First, repertoire changes differ across countries, just as state making and capitalism differ. Second, repertoire change is not determined by changes in economic and political institutions. In fact, collective action is not simply an effect of institutional change but is also a contributing cause.

Tilly argues, in *Roads from Past to Future* (1997), that political challengers are a necessary if not sufficient cause of the revolutionary situations from which modern states and modern capitalism emerged. Here, he shifts emphasis from the effects of institutions on collective action to the effects of collective action on institutional change. This was, however, a major concern in his initial conceptualization. Tilly consistently distinguished *revolutionary situations,* where control of the state is challenged, from *revolutionary outcomes,* which involve a transfer of governing authority to the challengers. Tilly argues, in *European Revolutions, 1492–1992* (1993), that there was considerable variation in revolutionary struggles over time and place but that these variations were explicable within the general framework of the mobilization model. Specifically, variations in interests and organization associated with demands of state making (particularly taxation) and opportunities (including powerful allies and vulnerable authorities) combined to create very different types of revolutionary situations and outcomes.

By 1998, Tilly had returned to the problem of the foundational basis for identifying interests and explaining enduring inequality. In *Durable Inequality* Tilly argues that categorical distinctions (e.g., male-female) are used by organizations to establish, accommodate, or reproduce inequality in organizational relations (e.g., supervisor-supervised). The foundation or goal in establishing these relations is either exploitation (surplus appropriation, as defined by Marx) or opportunity hoarding (monopolizing life-chances, as defined by Weber). Particular instances of inequality (e.g., race) endure, however, because organizations find it cost-effective (efficient, as Millians might define it) to reproduce (or emulate and thereby generalize) forms of inequality that exist in the larger society. Organizations similarly attempt to accommodate these general forms of inequality by adapting organizational relations and thereby institutionalizing this form of inequality as part of the taken-for-granted external environment within which the organization must operate.

— Richard Hogan

See also Historical and Comparative Theory; Revolution; Social Movement Theory

FURTHER READING AND REFERENCES

Tilly, Charles. 1964. *The Vendee.* Cambridge, MA: Harvard University Press.
———. 1978. *From Mobilization to Revolution.* Reading, MA: Addison-Wesley.
———. 1981. *As Sociology Meets History.* New York: Academic Press.
———. 1986. *The Contentious French.* Cambridge, MA: Harvard University Press.
———. 1993. *European Revolutions, 1492–1992.* Oxford, UK: Blackwell.
———. 1995. *Popular Contention in Great Britain, 1758–1834.* Cambridge, MA: Harvard University Press.
———. 1997. *Roads from Past to Future.* Lanham, MD: Rowman & Littlefield.
———. 1998. *Durable Inequality.* Berkeley: University of California Press.

TIME AND SOCIAL THEORY

Social theorists writing about time generally agree that in the hands of humans this single linear, objective, natural physical dimension is transformed into multiple structured sociocultural dimensions. "Social" time is overlaid with meaning and value, and the linearity of physical time is reshaped by convention into all manner of "unnatural" forms. Beyond the agreement that *social* must be distinguished from *natural* time, however, there is a great deal of diversity in how social theorists see time and temporality and their relevance to understanding the social.

Social theory's questions begin by asking whether there is a "social" time distinct from both natural-cosmological time and personal-subjective time. How are social processes conditioned by their temporality? How is social reality constituted in and across time? Are there multiple social times associated with different social structures?

THREE BRANCHES

Treatments of time in social theory can be somewhat crudely divided into three categories. The first includes the work of thinkers who have made explicit attempts to do a "sociology of time." The second is composed of work that deals with time explicitly in the course of theorizing other social phenomena. In the third category, we find social theories in which time plays an important, if only implicit, role.

"Sociology of time" perspectives include attempts to define social time, catalog forms of temporal regularity, describe multiple temporalities associated with different forms of social organization, and explain cross-cultural or transhistorical differences in the experience and organization of time. Representative authors in this category are Émile Durkheim, Marcel Mauss and Henri Hubert, Pitirim Sorokin and Robert K. Merton, Georges Gurvitch, Wilbert Moore, Julius A. Roth, and Eviatar Zerubavel.

The second strand—corollary theories of time—has to do with theories of social time elaborated as key components of theories of other phenomena. Included here is work by Karl Marx, Max Weber, Karl Mannheim, George Herbert Mead, Alfred Schütz, Norbert Elias, Niklas Luhmann, Michel Foucault, and Anthony Giddens.

The third strand includes theories of diverse social phenomena—social change, development, diffusion, planning, for example—in which, even though not explicitly thematized, time plays a critical role.

DISTINGUISHING PHILOSOPHY OF TIME FROM SOCIAL THEORY OF TIME

Although there are many overlaps and interdependencies, it is useful to distinguish "time and social theory" from "the philosophy of time." To the latter are generally left questions such as what time is, whether time is real, how time is perceived or experienced, and how human existence is conditioned by its temporality.

Philosophical theories variously identify the origins of temporality in the actual experience of change, birth, growth, decay, and death and the experience of memory, planning, and expectation. For Aristotle (Book IV of the *Physics*) the "sense of time" depends on the mind registering change. St. Augustine, in *The Confessions,* argues that time is a creation of God who is outside of time. Isaac Newton, to the contrary, argued that time is independent of both motion and God. For Immanuel Kant, time is real insofar as all experience is in time, but it is also ideal because it is a form of intuition, logically prior to experience, a contribution of the mind. Henri Bergson distinguished between the time of experience and the mind from the objectified time of clocks, mathematics, and physics. Edmund Husserl employed the phenomenological method to analyze the experience of inner time consciousness. William James described the temporality of the stream of consciousness. Martin Heidegger looks at *Dasein's* continual participation in its coming into being and its being toward death.

From these writers and others, philosophy has bequeathed social theory several dualities which, even if rejected by many theorists, continue to serve as theoretical touchstones. These include *chronos* (time/interval/while) versus *kairos* (opportunity, critical/right moment in time), *aeternitas* (spreading out of time) versus *tempus* (differentiation between past and future), *temps* (objective time) versus *durée* (flow of duration), and linear versus cyclical time.

SOCIOLOGY OF TIME: TIME AS THE OBJECT OF SOCIAL THEORIES

Durkheim is often seen as the founder of the sociology of time. His *Elementary Forms of the Religious Life* is ostensibly about the nature of religion, but its overarching goal is to demonstrate, contra Kant, the social origin of the categories of thought—time, space, class, causality. He locates the social epistemologically between the empiricists' "mind as *tabula rasa*" and the a priorists' "mind as hardwired." Durkheim acknowledges the reality of the subjective experience of time, but suggests that this is not the "time" we are talking about when we ask what time is. As a category, time is not for me, but for us. The framework against which things are temporally located is taken from collective social life. "A calendar expresses the rhythm of the collective activities, while at the same time its function is to assure their regularity. . . . what the category of time expresses is a time common to the group, a social time, so to speak. In itself it is a veritable social institution" (Durkheim [1915]1965:23).

Hubert and Mauss extended this idea, showing how social perception allowed groups to assign to mathematically equal times socially unequal meanings as when the year between 20 and 21 brings new legal rights, but that between 30 and 31 is relatively uneventful. This theme is continued and extended by Sorokin and Merton (1937) who argue that social time is not merely different from astronomical time but that it admits of many variants—social time varies qualitatively across social space. Different calendars, systems of time reckoning, and meanings of temporality are to be expected in different societies, locations within societies, and even in association with different activities.

The idea of a multiplicity of social times is taken up by Gurvitch in *The Spectrum of Social Time* (1964). Gurvitch identifies eight kinds of social time, each associated with specific manifestations of sociability (communion, community, and mass) or "levels of we-ness," types of social groupings, and degrees of continuity-discontinuity and contingency-certainty. "Enduring time" is the time of kinship, families, and local demography, the enduring nowadays of everyday life. "Deceptive time" is the time of the daily round with its routines and surprises. "Erratic time" is the time of irregular life and world events, the uncertainties of ongoing history. "Cyclical time" is the time of dependable recurrences in life. "Retarded time" is the time of social symbols and institutions, which, by the time they attain "reality," they are anchored backward in the past. As tradition and convention, they are used in life moving forward, but are marked by permanence that is backward reaching. By contrast, "alternating time" is the time of rules and algorithms and recipes. It is also based on the past and settled, but it is used in moving forward toward change. The time of economy and industry is alternating time—it depends on what has been learned but is not about mere repetition. "Pushing forward time" is the time of aspiration and innovation. In it, we reach out to the future, pulling the present forward. Finally, "explosive time" is the time of collective creation and revolution. It is the time that allows existing structures to be superseded and replaced.

A different tack on the multiplicities of social time was taken by social ecologists and functionalist thinkers. Here, we see explicit concern with developing taxonomies and typologies of temporal patterning associated with different forms of social organization. Sorokin identified synchronicity and order, rhythm and phases, periodicity and tempo; Hawley focused on rhythm, tempo, and timing. Moore discusses synchronization, sequence, and rates as fundamental sociotemporal processes with respect to a variety of institutions (the family, career, organizations, voluntary associations, and the city). He examines the phenomena of temporal concentration and segregation (as when fresh food wholesaling takes place in the wee hours so that produce is in the stores during shopping hours), temporal complementarity and schedule staggering that ease loads on systems (as when flextime reduces rush hour traffic) but that can also result in temporal mismatches between individuals or institutions (as when shift-working spouses never see one another or working mothers cannot chaperone school trips). Roth described "timetable norms" as collective understandings of proper timing of life events (such as when one can expect to be up for promotion or how long a couple can date before they ought to "get serious").

Zerubavel, in several influential works, consolidates much previous work and explicitly aims to establish a sociology of time (e.g., Zerubavel 1981, 1985) by examining phenomena such as schedules, calendars, public or private time, the week, and holidays. In contrast to more ecological approaches above, which focus on the temporal patterning of social life, Zerubavel's objective is to elucidate the *social foundations* of temporal patterning. By analogy to Goffman's public order, he focuses on "sociotemporal order," which he differentiates from biotemporal and physiotemporal orders. His analysis is built around the recognition of four forms of sociotemporal regularity that are neither natural nor individually voluntaristic but are, rather, conventional: (1) sequential structure (collective agreement about the proper temporal order of activities), (2) duration (how long things should last), (3) temporal location (what should be done when—schedules), and (4) rates of recurrence (how often things occur). These forms can be found at scales ranging from cognition and social interaction to organizations and whole societies. They are typically overlaid with normative prescriptions, and temporal ordering is implicated in the general social order.

COROLLARY THEORIES OF TIME

Many writers have developed treatments of time and temporality as corollaries to the investigations of other phenomenon. Time plays a role, for example, in Schütz's theory of social action, Mannheim's sociology of knowledge, and Giddens's theory of structuration. Mead, Elias, and Luhmann are often cited as theorists of time, but here,

too, their analyses of temporality are in service of other issues. Yet another set of theorists who deal with temporality in their analyses of the rationalization of society includes Marx, Weber, and Foucault, among others.

Temporal considerations in Alfred Schütz's work on the meaning of action, routinization, social relationships, and multiple realities are important both in the field of phenomenological sociology and beyond it. Schütz used Husserl's phenomenology to provide a social psychological foundation for Weber's theory of meaningful social action. If meaning is retrospective and requires reflection, how can forward-looking action be meaningful? How can an actor be consciously rational, aware of his or her "in-order-to" motive? Schütz employs Husserl's theory of inner time consciousness to show how a future act can be apprehended in the future perfect tense and hence be a part of the actor's choosing projects of action. Routinization is the process whereby such chosen, meaningful courses of action become typified and taken for granted as "I can do it again." The world of others is temporally structured. Schütz divides it first into those who are temporally inaccessible (predecessors and successors) and those who are temporally accessible. Those with whom we share time are further divided into those who are spatially not accessible (contemporaries) and those who are (consociates). With the latter group, there is the possibility of sociation in its ideal form, the We-relation, in which, Schütz says, our inner times gear into one another and we "grow older together." In addition to everyday waking reality, Schütz has theorized "multiple realities" of fantasy, dreaming, and scientific theory. Each reality, according to Schütz, has its own distinctive "temporal style."

Marx's analysis of ideology introduced the idea that knowledge and ideas are historically contingent. More generally, Mannheim's sociology of knowledge implies a temporal component in the meaning of all social and cultural phenomena. He also introduced the idea of time as identity and social location, and generations as collective identities in his essay "The Problem of Generations" (1952). Contemporary work on cohorts and historical generations, the importance of biographical phases, and the life course as a structure of analysis continues this tradition.

Giddens's theory of structuration is an attempt to transcend structure-agency dualism by holding that structure and agency are recursively related: Structures both constrain and enable actors even as actions constitute and reproduce those structures. From Hägerstrand's time geography Giddens borrows five basic spatial-temporal constraints: (1) the indivisibility of the body; (2) the finitude of life span; (3) duration/sequence/one task at a time; (4) movement in space is always movement in time; and (5) finite packing capacity of time/space. Giddens suggests that the central task in social theory is to explain "time-space distanciation"—the stretching of social systems across space and time—in the face of these fundamental constraints. Time, however, is not a mere environment of action, a dimension against which it takes place. Social life—from the reflexive self to enduring social institutions—is both subject to and constitutive of social temporality. Three "times" are key here: (1) the time of Heidegger's *Dasein,* the basic finite temporality of being which is always a part of human existence; (2) *durée,* the time of the day-to-day flow of intentional action; and (3) *longue durée,* the time of institutional duration. These times and their corresponding structures and practices are not hierarchical building blocks of one another. Rather, they are always co-constituting; everyday routine involves all three.

If Durkheim and his descendants had built a sociology of time around the dualism of natural and social time, others begin with the analysis of the origins of "social" time and move toward subsuming natural time. Mead develops his ideas about time in the context of his general theory about the evolution of consciousness and society. In *The Philosophy of the Present*, Mead (1959) suggests the primacy of sociality as constitutive of mind and self, which, in turn, apprehend time as the emergent contrast of past and future with the present. For Mead, the social and the psychological are an instance of "nature," so this explanation of the psychology and sociology of time is an explanation of time itself.

Luhmann develops a similar perspective on time in his systems theory. Like Mead, he sees time as emerging from the difference between past and future relating to one another in the present, and like Mead, he sees temporality not as uniquely human but as a part of the natural world of which humanity finds itself a part.

Several theorists posit changes in the meaning of time, attitudes toward time, and ways of experiencing time as a component or effect of cultural evolution. Elias suggests, for example, that as societies develop they require more complex forms of coordination and so from generation to generation, humans acquire improved capacity for symbolizing time and using it as a "means of orientation." Weber and others describe the progressive rationalization of time as a component of the rationalization of society beginning with the development of the Rule of St. Benedict. The primary theme here is change from "natural" and preindustrial time to "rationalized" time. The former is continuous and spontaneous, while the latter is subdivided and regimented. More recently, Foucault has written about the microdivision of time as a manifestation of power, echoing and generalizing the observations of critics of F. W. Taylor's scientific management time and motion analyses. Marx, Tönnies, and Simmel all allude to the replacement of natural pace with artificial and standardized pace of life as city time displaces the time of villages. "In the city," Lewis Mumford famously wrote, "time becomes visible" (Mumford 1938:4).

TIME AS AN IMPLICIT COMPONENT OF SOCIAL THEORIES

A discussion of time and social theory would not be complete without mention of how time and temporality are frequently implicit components of social theories, most often as a taken-for-granted dimension along which a process plays out. Despite making little or no attempt to problematize time, these lines of thought offer potentially fertile territory for theoretical exploration in examining their unexamined temporal content.

Time is implicit in theories of social change, social mobility, cultural lag, life course and life cycle, careers, diffusion, planning, narrative, biography, and collective memory.

Nineteenth-century social theory paid a lot of attention to the question of how societies evolve and develop in an attempt to understand where European society had been and where it was going. Condorcet, Comte, Hegel, Marx, and Spencer all offered teleological theories of the stages of societal development in which time is a taken-for-granted dimension. Social mobility theories invoke time as a measure of movement in social space. Cultural lag theories depend on a background temporal dimension. Life course, life cycle, and career theories look at lives in time. Studies of information and innovation diffusion connect social space and time. Time scales are also implicated in planning. Recent work implicating time includes investigations of collective memory, narrative, and network dynamics.

— Dan Ryan

See also Durkheim, Émile; Giddens, Anthony; Schütz, Alfred; Social Space; Structuration

FURTHER READINGS AND REFERENCES

Adam, B. 1990. *Time and Social Theory.* Philadelphia, PA: Temple University Press.

Durkheim, E. [1915]1965. *The Elementary Forms of the Religious Life.* New York: Free Press.

Giddens, A. 1984. *The Constitution of Society: Introduction of the Theory of Structuration.* Berkeley: University of California Press.

Gurvitch, G. 1964. *The Spectrum of Social Time.* Dordrecht, Holland: D. Reidel.

Moore, W. E. 1963. *Man, Time, and Society.* New York: Wiley.

Mumford, L. 1938. *The Culture of Cities.* New York: Harcourt, Brace.

Sorokin, P. A. and R. K. Merton. 1937. "Social Time: A Methodological and Functional Analysis." *American Journal of Sociology* 42:615–29.

Schütz, A. [1932] 1967. *The Phenomenology of the Social World.* Evanston, IL: Northwestern University Press.

Zerubavel, E. 1981. *Hidden Rhythms: Schedules and Calendars in Social Life.* Chicago, IL: University of Chicago Press.

———. 1985. *The Seven Day Circle: The History and Meaning of the Week.* New York: Free Press.

TOCQUEVILLE, ALEXIS DE

Alexis de Tocqueville (1805–1859) was a French statesman, political thinker, and founder of comparative-historical sociology. Tocqueville was born in Paris to an aristocratic family that had suffered the depredations of the French Revolution. He traveled to the United States in 1831–1832—on the pretext of researching the novel penitentiary system of Pennsylvania and New York—and based his masterpiece *Democracy in America* on his observations and inquiries of American society. Shortly after returning to France, Tocqueville got involved in politics and served in the Chamber of Deputies from 1839 to 1851, participated in drafting a new constitution in 1848, and served briefly as Louis Bonaparte's Minister of Foreign Affairs. Tocqueville left public office in 1851 after protesting Bonaparte's coup d'état and immediately set to work researching and writing *The Old Regime and the French Revolution.* Tocqueville's most significant contributions to social theory include his arguments on democratization as a world-historical process of transformation, his views on the role of voluntary associations in democracies, and his analysis of the disintegration of the *ancien régime* and the transformations wrought by the French Revolution.

Tocqueville presented his views on democratization most clearly in *Democracy in America.* Tocqueville asked two central questions about democratic society in the United States in the 1830s. First, how did democratic society, characterized above all by the equality of social conditions and liberty, come to be? Second, he asks, how could Americans safeguard democratic society and democratic political institutions against the tendency to slide into uniformity, mediocrity, and despotism? The equality of social conditions refers not to economic equality or even formal political equality in Tocqueville's work. Rather, the equality of social conditions refers above all to the result of the gradual elimination of hereditary distinctions of titles and honors. Furthermore, Tocqueville's notion of the equality of social conditions entails that occupations and professions are open to all, regardless of birth. It refers to the absence (or the successful abolition) of the power and privilege of an aristocracy (Aron 1968:24; Tocqueville 1969:50–60).

The process of democratization occurred over the course of centuries. In Tocqueville's view, war had battered the nobility of medieval Europe, distributing their lands and encouraging the development of municipal institutions and liberties in the towns. The introduction of gunpowder weaponry leveled social distinctions on the battlefield. The printing press and rudimentary postal systems spread ideas of equality and liberty to villages, towns, and cities across the continent. Furthermore, the Reformation introduced many strains of Protestantism, which preached that all persons stand in a direct relationship to God and therefore broke the Church's monopoly on the means of salvation. The discovery and colonization of America, moreover, provided manifold opportunities for aggrandizement regardless of social rank (Tocqueville 1969:11).

In Tocqueville's view, democratic society in the United States, with its proclivity for liberty and equality, had emerged for three central reasons. First, the geographical location of the United States meant that it had few military risks and an abundance of land (1969:23–30). Second, according to Tocqueville, the laws of the colonies promoted liberty, which in turn influenced the emphasis on federalism and the protection of liberty in the Constitution (1969:31–46). Third, Tocqueville argued that the religious devotion of American colonists promoted customs, beliefs, and manners conducive to freedom: "Religion is considered as the guardian of mores, and mores are regarded as the guarantee of the laws and pledge for the maintenance of freedom itself" (p. 47). For Tocqueville, the customs, beliefs, and manners of the people were paramount in the establishment of American democracy.

According to Tocqueville, the equality of social conditions—and therefore democracy—in the United States had several negative consequences. First, it tended to encourage a tyranny of the majority in both politics and opinion (1969:250–59). Second, the tyranny of the majority promoted mediocrity (p. 257). Third, under certain circumstances—for example, "when free institutions seem to be functioning badly" (Aron 1968:284)—equality comes into conflict with freedom. Finally, the relentless pursuit of equality at the expense of freedom could lead to the centralization of administration, as was the case in France (Aron 1968:285). When this is the case, Tocqueville maintained, people in democratic societies—which he assumed are also commercial and industrial societies—tended to turn toward individualism in their pursuit of material gain and pleasures. This leads not to interdependence (as in, for example, Adam Smith's view) but to isolation, which threatens democratic societies with despotism.

While Tocqueville's description and diagnosis of the United States in the 1830s appears obsolete for many reasons—for example, today we tend to emphasize the lack of equality at the time—his account of the institutions that counter the slide toward despotism is still quite powerful. Tocqueville wrote at length about the separation of powers in the U.S. Constitution and the freedom of the press, but his most trenchant argument in this respect focuses on the role of voluntary associations in maintaining American democracy. The thrust of Tocqueville's argument consists of the claim that the laws and mores of American democracy bind people, or at least encourage them, to participate in politics. Tocqueville (1969) extends this line of argumentation to participation in associations: "There are not only commercial and industrial associations in which all take part, but others of a thousand different types—religious, moral, serious, futile, very general and very limited, immensely large and very minute" (p. 513). Tocqueville remarks that in Europe, one would find states or territorial magnates taking up these roles, while in the United States people form associations. The crucial conclusion to make here is that, for Tocqueville, associations counter the centrifugal force of individualism by teaching people how to act out of self-interest yet in cooperation with one another, thus countering the threat of despotism and centralization in democracy.

Tocqueville's study of *The Old Regime and the French Revolution* attempts a sociological explanation of a profound historical transformation. His sociological explanation of the collapse of the *ancien régime* and the revolution emphasizes the importance of conflict between the orders and estates of the old regime and the emerging social classes of modernity, the spread of ideas of liberty and equality, irreconcilable political and social divisions between the elites, the prerevolutionary centralization of the state administration and political power, and the financial crisis of the late 1780s. Moreover, Tocqueville ties the collapse of the old regime and the consequences of the revolution to the tendency of democracy in France toward despotism. The republican and imperial administrations continued the centralizing, bureaucratic trends that were already occurring under the *ancien régime,* thus further undermining the power of representative institutions.

— James M. Murphy

See also Democracy; Revolution; Social Capital

FURTHER READINGS AND REFERENCES

Aron, Raymond. 1968. *Main Currents in Sociological Thought.* Vol. 1. Translated by R. Howard. New York: Doubleday Anchor.

Tocqueville, Alexis de. 1969. *Democracy in America.* Translated by G. Lawrence. New York: Anchor.

———. 1995. *Recollections: The Revolutions of 1848,* edited by J. P. Mayer and A. P. Kerr. Translated by G. Lawrence. New Brunswick, NJ: Transaction.

———. 1998. *The Old Regime and the French Revolution,* edited by F. Furet and F. Melonio. Translated by A. S. Kahan. Chicago, IL: University of Chicago Press.

Wolin, Sheldon S. 2001. *Tocqueville between Two Worlds.* Princeton, NJ: Princeton University Press.

TÖNNIES, FERDINAND

Ferdinand Tönnies (1855–1936) is considered one of sociology's founding fathers. He studied in Strassburg, Jena, Bonn, Leipzig, and Tübingen where he received his doctorate in classical philology in 1877. His famous *Gemeinschaft und Gesellschaft* served as his *Habilitationsschrift* in 1881. His father's wealth enabled him to follow his private, especially political, interests and to be relatively distant from the academic milieu. Nevertheless, he was appointed to a chair for economics and statistics in 1913 from which he retired only three years later. He resumed teaching sociology as professor emeritus in Kiel in 1921.

Tönnies took an active interest in the socialist and trade union movements and in consumer cooperatives. He joined the Social Democratic Party, protesting against the National Socialist Movement, which led to the discharge from his position as professor by the Hitler government in 1932–1933. Tönnies was president of the German Sociological Society from 1909 to 1933, which he had founded together with Georg Simmel, Max Weber, and Werner Sombart.

Tönnies perceived of all human interactions as creations of thought and will. This distinguishes Tönnies's concept of the social from a behavioristic view, which regards any kind of interaction as social. Social entities in Tönnies's sense are creations of their members' will so that they are felt as a quasi-objective reality with its own obligations and rights. They can be classified roughly as social collectives (*Samtschaften*), social corporations (*soziale Körperschaften*), and social relationships (*soziale Verhältnisse*). Social relationships exist insofar as they are willed by their participants (even though they may well, as in the case of parent and child, rest on a psychological or biological basis). They are prevalent within social corporations and social collectives, as well. Social collectives (which as a concept is found only in Tönnies's later writings) stand for unorganized groups that have grown enough in size to be independent of the participation of particular individuals. The concept of social corporation refers to groups capable of acting collectively through representatives. They constitute the most "artificial" level because the participants' will to maintain a social relationship becomes manifest in their conformity with specific rules and norms.

Tönnies uses the term *will* in a broad sense. Similar to Max Weber's distinction of four ideal types of social action, Tönnies differentiates the will that creates a social entity according to its relation to ends and means. The main distinction here is between *Wesenwille* (derived from Arthur Schopenhauer and Wilhelm Wundt) and *Kürwille* (which stems from Thomas Hobbes and the rationalist tradition of natural law). The latter corresponds to Weber's purposive-rational orientation of social action and is derived from an ancient Germanic word for choosing. The action is consciously motivated toward an end, and the actor chooses among several possible means to achieve that end. In contrast, *Wesenwille* manifests the actor's nature and has several degrees of rationality according to affect, tradition, and value orientation.

In applying these classifications to social entities, Tönnies distinguishes between *Gemeinschaft* and *Gesellschaft*, which was meant as a conceptual framework for the analysis of modern society. Certain entities are willed for their intrinsic value and depend on the members' sympathy, habit, and shared beliefs (e.g., clubs, sects, family, neighborhood). Other entities must be conceived of as means to specific ends such as the business association that constitutes the paradigm of the "*Gesellschaft*" and "*Kürwille*"-type of social entity. Kinship, neighborhood, and spiritual community form prototypes of "community." Contractual relationships and special-purpose associations stand for "society." Like Weber, Tönnies sees these categories as ideal types. In reality, we find neither pure *Gemeinschaft* nor pure *Gesellschaft*. Rather, social entities are *more or less Gesellschaft-* and *Gemeinschaft*-like because human conduct is never exclusively determined by reason or sympathy. Tönnies illustrates this concept by comparing the ideal types to chemical elements that are combined in different proportions. Accordingly, Tönnies identifies empirical mixtures that he combines with the question whether social relationships are conceived of as equal or unequal. A *Genossenschaft* is a *Gemeinschaft*-like relationship of equal peers, whereas *Herrschaft* implies social super- and subordination. The relationship of husband and wife constitutes a mixture of perceived equality and superordination. *Gesellschaft*-like types of social entities create inequality by delegating authority to certain members while at the same time assuming a conceptual peer equality.

Tönnies's conceptual framework of social entities aims at a synthesis of the social theories of rationalism with romantic and historical concepts of society. It tries to overcome the antagonism of organicist and contractual views of society. According to Tönnies, these seemingly irreconcilable concepts lay within the realm of sociology as real historical phenomena. Consequently, he reconciled Aristotle's *zoon politikon* with Hobbes's pessimistic *homo homini lupus* and conceptualized the relation between individual and society in a new way, leading to the division of society into subdivisions of analysis and calling for a basic systematization of divergent social phenomena. Some social entities must be seen as prior to individual will, while other social relationships are the result of contractual agreement. Thus, all social relationships and human conduct can be conceptualized as voluntaristic, existing only insofar as they are created by acting individuals. The object of social theory becomes pluralistic without being fragmented.

Tönnies laid the foundation for a sociology that was further developed by Durkheim, Weber, and Simmel. Tönnies's conceptual framework has become so much taken for granted that it is difficult to specify exactly his influence on social theory. The *Gemeinschaft-Gesellschaft* distinction can be found in Parsons's pattern variables, in Habermas's distinction between communicative and instrumental types of action, between system and lifeworld, and in Coleman's asymmetric society.

— Gerd Nollmann

See also Durkheim, Émile; Simmel, Georg; Sombart, Werner; Weber, Max

FURTHER READINGS AND REFERENCES

Tönnies, Ferdinand. [1887]1957. *Gemeinschaft und Gesellschaft* (Community and Society). East Lansing: Michigan State University Press.

———. [1909] 1961. *Custom: An Essay on Social Codes.* New York: Free Press.

Wirth, Louis. 1926. "The Sociology of Ferdinand Tönnies." *American Journal of Sociology* 32:412–22.

TOTAL INSTITUTIONS

Erving Goffman created the concept of total institution in his essay "On the Characteristics of Total Institutions" published in 1961 in *Asylums*. Total institutions are social hybrids, part residential community and part formal organization intended for the bureaucratic management of large groups of people. Goffman (1961) offers this definition:

A total institution may be defined as a place of residence and work where a large number of like-situated individuals, cut off from the wider society for an appreciable period of time, together lead an enclosed, formally administered round of life. (p. xiii)

Goffman provides this taxonomy of the five groups of total institutions:

Institutions that care for those who are incapable of caring for themselves but are considered harmless—the blind, aged, orphaned, and indigent

Institutions that sequester groups who are incapable of caring for themselves and pose a threat to others—sanitarium, leprosarium, or mental hospital

Institutions designed to protect the community from those perceived as threats where the welfare of the inmates is not a concern—prisons, prisoner of war camps, and concentration camps

Institutions established to pursue a worklike task—army barracks, ships, boarding schools, and work camps

Institutions that form cloistered retreats or monastic orders designed for training and the pursuit of a religious vocation

Supported by the National Institute of Mental Health, Goffman spent a year from 1955 to 1956 conducting field-work in a mental hospital, St. Elizabeth's Hospital in Washington, D.C. He developed this analysis drawing on eclectic evidence from the sociological literature on prisons and organizations and from ethnographies, novels, auto-biographies, and theology. Despite the breadth of this scholarship, the formal concept of total institution focuses primarily on psychiatric institutions, and his intention was to explore the social world of the patient and the subjective, lived experiences of inmates.

Total institutions are distinguished by their varying degrees of closure or separation from the outside world. All activities of the daily round occur in the same place, under a single authority, and in the immediate company of a large batch of others. Total institutions create the rationalization of life through tight scheduling, regimentation, and bureau-cratic rules that foster the disciplinary control of inmates. Thus, the bureaucratic management of inmates and *batch living* promote the rational plan or official purpose of the institution (Burns 1992).

Goffman identifies the radical split between the *inmate world* and the *staff world* as a critical feature of these institu-tions. He offers a detailed discussion of the *moral career of mental patients,* documenting the systematic stripping of their socially constructed conventional identity in the outside home world by the denigrations, mortifications, and humili-ations of the admissions process. Through welcoming cere-monies, staff members take a life history, photograph, weigh, fingerprint, assign numbers, search, list personal possessions for storage, undress, bathe, disinfect, cut hair, and issue insti-tutional clothing. Without access to civilian clothing, towels, soap, shaving kits, and bathing facilities, inmates are stripped of their usual appearance and suffer a personal defacement. Through obedience tests and abusive welcome rituals, inmates come to understand their powerlessness. Inmates may be required to hold their body in a humiliating stance and provide humiliating verbal responses to staff members as part of the enforced deference pattern of total institutions.

Once persons are transformed into patients and enter the inmate world, they experience a civil death that denies them adultlike autonomy and control over their fate. From the most mundane or trivial matters to important life decisions, patients no longer act with agency or self-determination. The structure of the hospital regulations as enforced by staff and staff decisions, and justified by therapeutic ratio-nales, determines the fate of inmates.

Although patients suffer the loss of their socially constructed identity grounded in their home world, they strive to reconstruct their social self and protect themselves from the mortification of self so characteristic of life in total institutions. Patients use secondary adjustments, "practices that do not directly challenge staff but allow inmates to obtain forbidden satisfactions or obtain permit-ted ones by forbidden means." (Goffman 1961:54) Secondary adjustments provide evidence that the patient can act with agency and can claim an inner soul beyond the reach of institutional profanations.

Patients also achieve a degree of personal reorganization and recovery of self through conformity to house rules and the opportunities and rewards available to them through the privilege system. Good behavior and compliance ostensibly demonstrate improving mental health and are rewarded by privileges and the prospect of a timely release. In addition, inmates are resocialized into the inmate social system—a parallel and countercultural complex of values, meanings, and informal structures that oppose bureaucratic regimenta-tion or psychotherapeutic rationales. Instead of the belief that time spent in treatment is beneficial, patients learn that time spent in the institution is wasted time in exile from living. Rather than learning to take responsibility for one's actions, the inmate belief system instructs patients about externalizing responsibility and blaming others. Patients construct *sad tales* to explain how bad luck or forces out-side their control brought them to the institution. Through solidarity and defiance, inmates create cliques and adopt strategies of withdrawal and intransigence. Other inmates become colonizers as they view the institution as their home. Most inmates adopt a combination of secondary adjustments and coping strategies, responding to situations by embracing the stance of *playing it cool* to maximize their chances of getting out of the institution without physical or psychological injury.

The staff world defines these institutions as storage dumps where staff members, motivated by the constraints of institutional efficiency, work on people as a kind of biosocial material. This staff rationale conflicts with the idealized public aims of the institution and the Kantian ethical imperative that people are ends in themselves and are deserving of humane standards of care. The staff artic-ulates a theory of human nature that depersonalizes each patient, equating the inmate with the cluster of symptoms associated with the diagnosis.

The concept of total institution incorporates the key ideas of the dominant sociological theoretical perspective in the 1950s—structural functionalism—and the work of Talcott Parsons (1951) and Amitai Etzioni (1961). A total institution is a structural form, a formal organization and residential community that adopts institutional ceremonies and strategies to integrate staff and inmate worlds into a func-tional social system by elaborating complementary roles between inmates and staff. Goffman's conceptualization of total institutions created a unique descriptive and analytic framework by which to understand the structural determinants of the inmates' subjectively experienced social reality.

Goffman's reliance on a structural analysis of the roles, rules, and relationships between inmates and staff members differed from his earlier work, *The Presentation of Self in Everyday Life* (1959). Here, he developed a *dramaturgical analysis* of social interaction within social institutions by viewing interaction as theater where actors use fronts, scripts, and props, and collude with others to enact impression management before various audiences.

The concept of total institutions has enjoyed a long and influential career. Theorists in interpretive sociology and labeling theory (Howard Becker), ethnomethodology (Harold Garfinkel), the antipsychiatry movement (Thomas Szasz, R. D. Laing), the sociology of organizations, and policymakers concerned with deinstitutionalization and community mental health have been influenced by Goffman's work (Steudler 2001).

As a theoretical construct, total institution has significant limitations. By constructing an ahistorical formal theory in the spirit of Georg Simmel (Weil 2001) and incorporating a structural-functional dynamic, Goffman emphasized the legitimate exercise of bureaucratic authority in total institutions. He largely ignored the question of political ideology, domination, and power in the wider society where the total institution was situated. Power, domination, and social conflict were never problematic for Goffman. For example, Stalinist work camps (gulag), the Soviet abuse of psychiatry to stifle internal political dissent after World War II, and Nazi concentration camps illustrate how totalitarian regimes have employed total institutions as a means to abuse power and to oppress citizens. Concentration camps were total institutions dedicated to racial purification through state-sponsored genocide and crimes against humanity. For Goffman, however, total institutions were a social form that existed in a social vacuum, without blood or social conflict and unrelated to ideology or dogma.

Goffman formulated a taxonomy of the types of total institutions and an analysis of the structural-functional aspects of this social form derived from his fieldwork and an examination of mid-twentieth-century institutions. He did not concern himself with the historical development of total institutions in the West during the transition to modernity from the seventeenth through nineteenth centuries. Goffman never addressed the questions raised by the important work of his contemporary, French theorist Michel Foucault, who examined the formation of the asylum, the birth of the clinic, the establishment of the modern penitentiary, and the elaboration of official *discourse,* the systematized knowledge that situated elites like psychiatrists employ as a key medium of power within the bureaucratic state and total institutions (Foucault 1965).

— Julius H. Rubin

See also Becker, Howard; Discourse; Dramaturgy; Ethnomethodology; Foucault, Michel; Garfinkel, Harold; Goffman, Erving; Labeling Theory; Parsons, Talcott

FURTHER READINGS AND REFERENCES

Burns, T. 1992. *Erving Goffman.* London: Routledge.
Etzioni, A. 1961. *Complex Organizations: A Sociological Reader.* New York: Holt, Rinehart & Winston.
Foucault, M. 1965. *Madness and Civilization: A History of Insanity in the Age of Reason.* New York: Pantheon.
Goffman, E. 1959. *The Presentation of Self in Everyday Life.* Garden City, NY: Doubleday Anchor.
———. 1961. *Asylums: Essays on the Social Situation of Mental Patients and Other Inmates.* Garden City, NY: Anchor Books.
Parsons, T. 1951. *The Social System.* New York: Free Press.
Steudler, F. 2001. "Les institutions totales et la vie d'un concept" [Total Institutions and the Life of a Concept]. Pp. 247–89 in *Erving Goffman et Les Institutions Totales* [Erving Goffman and Total Institutions], edited by C. Amourous and A. Blanc. Paris: L'Harmattan.
Weil, R. 2001. "Les institutions totales dans l'oeuvre de Goffman" [Total Institutions in Goffman's Work]. Pp. 25–43 in *Erving Goffman et Les Institutions Totales* [Erving Goffman and Total Institutions], edited by C. Amourous and A. Blanc. Paris: L'Harmattan.

TOURAINE, ALAIN

Alain Touraine (b. 1925) is a French sociologist and engaged public intellectual in the democratic socialist tradition. He has been involved in a long-term project that seeks to assess the transformative potential of collective social actors, particularly in the advanced industrial nations. In so doing, Touraine has sought to articulate an antifunctionalist and post-Marxist theoretical perspective that he has described as both a *"sociologie actionnaliste"* and the sociology of the "self-production of society." His work reflects a distinctive engagement with the sociological classics, resulting in a unique blend of Marxist and non-Marxist social theory. Unlike contemporary theorists who have sought to unite agency and structure into one comprehensive theoretical framework, Touraine has tended to simply ignore structure because he is convinced that action is antecedent to structure and thus the latter is to be understood within the framework of action. His perspective is thus a version of social constructionism, although unlike most interpretive theories, one that is preoccupied with the collective actor rather than the individual.

Educated at the École Normale Supérieure, he has taught at the University of Paris-Nanterre and worked for both the French National Research Council (CNRS) and as a senior researcher at the École des Hautes Études en Sciences Sociales. He founded the Center for Sociological Analysis and Intervention in 1981 and is currently professor of sociology at the École des Hautes Études en Sciences Sociales. Touraine has published over 20 books, about half of which have been translated into English. While he has had a major impact on French sociology, his reception in the English-speaking world is decidedly more mixed.

In his earliest publications, Touraine engaged in a series of empirical inquiries into the changing character of the class structure of postwar French society, which included studies of workers at Renault and agricultural workers. He sought to challenge the literature of the time that proclaimed the embourgeoisement of the working class and thus the end of the conflicts that have pitted labor against capital throughout the history of industrial capitalism. However, what separated him from those Marxists and neo-Marxists who sought to find in various sectors of the working class new potential locations for revolutionary vanguards, he does not consider the present to be a revolutionary era. Moreover, in the wake of the student movement that shook the foundations of French politics in May 1968, he began to view the university rather than the factory as an increasingly crucial locus of political and cultural conflict.

This perspective is connected to his claim that the advanced industrial nations were rapidly moving into a postindustrial era. In the late 1960s, Touraine was one of the key figures associated with discussions about the advent of postindustrial society, which focused on the shift from manufacturing-based economies to information-based ones. His contribution reveals his penchant for viewing the world in terms of sharp dichotomies. Thus, in an early formulation, he suggested that the transition from industrial to postindustrial society amounted to a developmental leap akin to the transition from agrarian to industrial society. He contended that we were entering societies "of pure change, without structure or nature" (Touraine 1977:6). Reflecting a particular moment in the history of the contemporary welfare state, he argued that the economic realm no longer functioned autonomously, but instead, economic decisions were increasingly made at the political level, and therefore the boundaries between the economic and the political increasingly dissolved, with political decision making being of paramount importance in shaping the economy. Under the influence of Weberian thought, he contended that these changes amount to the bureaucratisation of society as decision making became increasingly centralized in the state apparatus. It is in this sense that he suggests that a synonym for postindustrial society is the programmed society. In such societies, knowledge takes on a new importance, and as a consequence, universities come to play an increasingly pivotal role in training the new cadres of information elites necessary for the functioning of advanced industrial economics.

Whereas Daniel Bell, the other key formulator of the postindustrial concept, contended that the tensions within postindustrial societies came about because the economic, political, and cultural realms operate on different axial principles, Touraine saw the state increasingly subsuming control of the economy, while in the cultural realm, it increasingly seeks to manipulate public opinion. In this scenario, the enormous power of the state can lead to a paralysing of social actors intent on challenging the programmed society, thereby posing a threat to democracy. Within this general perspective, Touraine concluded that the working class could no longer be seen as the main challenger to domination. Although he was not prepared to write them off as potential social actors as was, for example, Andre Gorz, he saw them as representing only one of several potential progressive social movements.

In this view, 1968 was to postindustrial society what 1848 was to industrial society: a preview of the new conflicts characteristic of the emerging new social order. Touraine's perspective on social movements begins with his attempt to fuse two central concepts: historicity and class relations. Historicity refers to the self-production of society based on its capacity to act on the nonsocial world, its methods for determining ways of investing economic surpluses into noneconomic ventures, and the cultural framework that informs social actors about their capacity for social transformation. A legacy of the Marxist heritage, class relations are viewed in dichotomous terms, pitting a dominant or ruling class against a dominated popular class. These are meant as analytical terms that involve congeries of collectivities. The dominant class includes technocrats, managers, political elites, economic entrepreneurs, and the like, while the popular class is best seen reflected in the new social movements that have emerged in recent decades, which in addition to the labor movement includes the environmental, student, antinuclear, and feminist movements.

Cognizant of the manipulative power of the dominant class to marginalize conflict, Touraine sees a novel role for sociology as an interpretative tool. He contends that social movements can use sociology to achieve a heightened level of self-awareness that can help them act, not merely defensively, but as truly contestatory participants in the self-production of society. Like resource mobilization theory, he views social movements as rational responses to institutionally embedded discontents, and he considers their chances of success to be partially determined by their capacity to muster sufficient organizational, financial, and ideological resources and their ability to make appropriate strategic decisions. He differs from resource mobilization theorists insofar as he is always intent on determining the transformative potential of various movements or, in other words, on their ability to change the course of social development that has been advanced by the dominant class.

Touraine believes that sociology has an especially critical role to play in assisting social movements in making these determinations. To this end, his role as an engaged sociologist took the form of developing a method of analysis that he termed "sociological intervention," whereby sociologists work in the interests of segments of the popular class rather than the state apparatus. Thus, the purpose of sociological intervention is to promote societal transformation rather than social integration. More explicitly, the method is intended to assist progressive social movements in acquiring the ability to engage in self-analysis as a prelude to locating their sense of collective identity and their definition of opposition and domination in a way that transcends the limits of movement ideologies and raises consciousness to that of a system of historicity. The sociologist functions for the collective actor as a psychoanalyst does for the individual, by helping to make visible social relations that are "masked by order and domination" (Touraine 1981:139) and distorted by ideology. The techniques used in intervention, developed in collaboration with Michel Wieviorka and other researchers at the Center for Sociological Analysis and Intervention, were detailed in *The Voice and the Eye* (1981). A number of publications appeared as the result of sociological interventions, including books on solidarity in Poland and the antinuclear, workers, and student movements in France.

In his more recent work, Touraine has explored the challenges posed by modernity in the era of globalization and the central dilemmas of citizenship in the wake of multiculturalism as ideology and social policy. He has sought to articulate an appropriate response to the rise of neoliberalism in the Western democracies that accepts the persistence of capitalist markets without abandoning the prospect of challenging the inequities that unbridled markets bring in their wake. In all this work, there is a remarkable continuity with publications dating back to the 1960s insofar as he remains insistent that autonomous collective social actors from the popular class are capable of playing a significant role in shaping the contours of social change.

— Peter Kivisto

See also Bell, Daniel; Industrial Society; Social Movement Theory

FURTHER READINGS AND REFERENCES

Touraine, Alain. 1965. *Sociologie de l'action.* Paris: Editions du Seuil.
———. 1971. *The Post-Industrial Society.* New York: Random House.
———. 1977. *The Self-Production of Society.* Chicago, IL: University of Chicago Press.
———. 1981. *The Voice and the Eye.* Cambridge, UK: Cambridge University Press.
———. 2000. *Can We Live Together?* Cambridge, UK: Polity.
———. 2001. *Beyond Neoliberalism.* Cambridge, UK: Polity.

TRUST

Scholars as well as ordinary citizens agree that trust is an important lubricant for social relations and that trust helps build a prosperous society. Beyond the importance of trust in our social and personal lives, however, there is little consensus concerning the nature and function of trust. Even the broadest definition of trust as an expectation of natural and social order, a definition on which many Westerners agree, meets objections in some non-Western cultures. For example, a Japanese person will never say, "I trust that the sun will rise again tomorrow." Furthermore, trust as expectations of the trustee's *ability* to perform a trusted action is different from trust as expectations of the trustee's *intention* to perform the same action (Barber 1983). The lack of consensus among the social scientists interested in trust reflects the fact that trust is a multifaceted concept. The definitions and theories of trust vary as different facets of the concept are examined.

There are three common usages of the word *trust*. First, the word trust is used to refer to *trustworthiness*. When people talk of the "decline in trust in American society," this meaning is being employed. Second, trust is used to refer to *trustfulness*. Scales used to measure trust by psychologists (e.g., Rotter 1971) are measuring individual differences in the degree to which individuals expect others to be trustworthy. Third and finally, trust is used to refer to the *act of trust*.

The act of trust is easy to define. The most common and the easiest way to understand what we mean by the act of trust is illustrated in the game of trust. The game of trust is played by two players. One of the players, Player A, makes a choice to trust (T) or to not trust (NT) the second player, Player B. When A chooses NT, the game ends there, and the status quo is maintained. When Player A chooses to trust, the game continues and Player B is given a choice between honoring Player A's trust (H, honor trust) and not honoring Player A's trust (NH, not honor trust). The outcome for Player B if he chooses *not to honor* Player A's trust is better than the outcome for Player B if he chooses *to honor* Player A's trust (NH > H for B). The outcome for Player A if Player B chooses not to honor her trust (NH) is less than the status quo (NH < 0 for A), and the outcome for Player A if Player B chooses to honor her trust (H) is greater than the status quo (H > 0 for A). If Player A believes that Player B will honor her trust, T is a better choice for him than NT. If Player A does not believe that Player B will honor her trust, NT is a better choice than T. Thus, A's choice in this game reflects his trust in B, and B's choice reflects her trustworthiness in this relationship. If we assume that both players are rational in the sense that they care only about their own welfare, and expect that others are similarly rational, B will not honor A's trust. Thus, A, expecting that B will not honor her trust, will not choose T. However, most experimental studies using the game of trust between anonymous players find that a substantial proportion of B's choose to honor the trust of A's (H). *And* they find that a sizable proportion of A's choose to trust B's (T). Social scientists are interested in finding out why people behave in both a trustworthy manner and a trustful manner.

The degree to which the game of trust is embedded in a larger social and cultural context provides a key to the question posed above. There are factors in the social context surrounding the game of trust that encourage trustworthy behavior. Examples of such factors are long-term relationships, social mechanisms that effectively spread reputations, and legal systems that detect and punish untrustworthy behavior. When these factors are present, not only trustworthy behavior but also trustful behavior becomes a rational choice for individuals. Many social scientists seek to identify these contextual factors and describe the ways in which they encourage trustworthy behavior. The decision to trust or not to trust in a particular game of trust is often determined by an individual's ability to correctly read the presence or the absence of these contextual factors. Russell Hardin (2002) refers to this understanding of trust as the "encapsulated" interest of the trusted.

While Hardin views trustfulness as a reflection of encapsulated contextual ingredients that encourage the trustee to behave in a trustworthy manner, other researchers understand trustfulness differently. In David Lewis and Andrew Weigert's (1985) words, "Trust begins where simple prediction ends" (p. 976). According to these scholars, the act of trust involves not only the reading of the encapsulated ingredients that make the trusted behave in a trustworthy manner but also a willingness to take *social risks*. Toshio Yamagishi and his colleagues argue that trust as social risk taking is grounded in the adaptive role of trust. Specifically, trust as social risk taking is viewed as adaptive because it reduces the opportunity costs for remaining in a committed social relation in which transaction costs are small. Ironically, institutional arrangements that encourage trustworthy behavior reduce the need to trust others (or take social risks) since trustworthy behavior is then institutionally ensured. In a society in which an individual's behavior is completely monitored and sanctioned (such that cheating is impossible), people no longer need to trust others.

Ultimate explanations of trust, including both trustworthiness and trustfulness, reside in the identification of the sociocontextual factors that encourage trusting and trustworthy behaviors. When the sociocontextual factors lead to short-term personal rewards for trusting (or when the consequences of trust are calculable), trust is explained as a rational behavior. When the personal rewards of trust take a long time to accrue, trust can be conceived as irrational and yet *adaptive*. For example, it is irrational to behave in a trustworthy or a trustful manner in a game of trust that is artificially created in a laboratory. However, acquiring a psychological mechanism (i.e., values, beliefs, heuristics, emotion, or a cognitive module such as a cheater detection module) encouraging people to disregard some of the immediate incentive features and behave in a trustful or trustworthy manner can be adaptive if, for example, such behavior helps establish a good reputation of the actor as a desirable exchange partner. What makes an irrational behavior adaptive or not is whether the long-term benefits of behaving in an irrational manner outweigh the immediate costs. Trust can be rational, irrational and adaptive, or irrational and maladaptive, depending on the nature of the social context.

— Toshio Yamagishi

See also Evolutionary Theory; Rational Choice; Risk Society

FURTHER READINGS AND REFERENCES

Barber, Bernard. 1983. *The Logic and Limit of Trust*. New Brunswick, NJ: Rutgers University Press.

Hardin, Russell. 2002. *Trust and Trustworthiness*. New York: Russell Sage.

Lewis, J. David and Andrew Weigert. 1985. "Trust as a Social Reality." *Social Forces* 63:967–85.

Rotter, Julian B. 1971. "Generalized Expectancies for Interpersonal Trust. *American Psychologist* 26:443–52.

Yamagishi, Toshio and Midori Yamagishi. 1994. "Trust and Commitment in the United States and Japan." *Motivation and Emotion* 18:129–66.

TURNER, BRYAN

Bryan Turner's (b. 1945) work is best understood as an attempt to revive action sociology from the perspective of embodiment. Together with "emplacement" (the relation of humans to the environment), embodiment is understood to be a universal category of human experience. Turner's work is a critique of both social constructionism and cultural relativism. The body is theorized as the material basis for social solidarity with the potential to transcend cultural difference and social variation. In the application of this theory, embodiment and emplacement are explored as the basis for a universal theory of citizenship and human rights. In particular, the need for companionship and the material facts of bodily frailty and vulnerability are articulated as the incentive for the formal recognition of sympathy and practice of empathy at the level of civil society. Aspects of Heidegger's ontology, especially the emphasis on being and choice, are enlisted to develop a sociological approach centered on the phenomenology of the body.

Turner's recent work introduces the concept of *cosmopolitan virtue* to elaborate the argument. As a contribution to the theory of social action, the concept introduces six dimensions: (1) *irony*—the recognition of the contingency and partiality of perspective; (2) *reflexivity*—the location of values and action in the context of biography, history, and structure; (3) *skepticism*—the distrust of grand narratives and totalitarian politics; (4) *care for others*—the recognition of sympathy, mutuality, and reciprocity; (5) *social inclusiveness*—the cohesion of the body politic and civil society around principles of sympathy, mutuality, and reciprocity; (6) *nomadism*—a version of *flanerie,* attributing travel and displacement as sources of sympathy, mutuality, and reciprocity in civil society.

Turner's sociology is firmly located in the classical tradition, especially the writings of Max Weber. It is committed to the investigation of the subjective meaning of social actions. Unlike some other versions of action sociology, notably symbolic interactionism, exchange theory and ethnomethodology, it emphasizes the *situated* character of the social actor in both the historical and comparative dimensions. Although Turner sees the state as both the enabler and abuser of human rights, it highlights processes of globalization and the porosity of national boundaries. Following Foucault, embodiment and emplacement are understood as shaped by a network of *social institutions of normative coercion.* The state is a significant agent, but so are the corporation, the media, education, medicine and the professional-knowledge class. To some extent, Turner's work elaborates Thomas Hobbes in regarding human life as "nasty, brutish and short." Human beings are considered to be ontologically frail and to inhabit natural environments that are precarious. A variety of social consequences follow from this, which are explored historically and comparatively in terms of the means and ends of social action. The theory of citizenship and human rights aims to invest social institutions of normative coercion with a binding system of moral conscience and accountability and to acknowledge a global dimension in civil society.

This concern with the question of social integration reflects Turner's reading of Parsons, in as much as it holds that all human societies face economic dilemmas of resource allocation and political issues of goal definition. This reinforces the emphasis placed on embodiment and emplacement as universal categories in human society that constitute a common basis for government. It also identifies scarcity as fundamental in investigating social cohesion and change. However, unlike Parsons, Turner's approach assigns greater analytic weight to social conflict deriving from inequality and the clash of human values. For example, his discussion of vulnerability and rights holds that the increasing fragmentation and hybridity of culture threaten social solidarity.

Turner's perspective holds that there are identifiable, cumulative research traditions that are independent of contexts of class, gender, race, and culture and repudiates a priori reasoning. It submits that sociological investigation must be *attentiste* rather than relativist and is committed to the production of value-free knowledge, which presupposes a consistently reflexive approach to social enquiry. It is distanced from linguistic or discursive approaches to social investigation because it maintains that societies constitute material systems of cohesion and restraint that are independent of language. In as much as this is the case, his perspective is skeptical about both the cultural and linguistic turns, preferring instead to treat society in Durkheimian terms as a *social fact* that exerts priority, externality, and constraint over the individual. However, it also regards the normative institutions of coercion as enabling and subject to critical revision by actors. Indeed, one function of sociology is to continuously subject these institutions to critical investigation.

These concerns are explored in an impressive range of enquiries into, inter alia, medicine, the body, disability, social stratification, citizenship, generations, equality, human rights, religion, Islamic society, and classical and contemporary social theory, making Turner one of the most prolific postwar sociologists. With hindsight, one might say that he prepared his understanding of cosmopolitan virtue *practically,* by way of a variety of academic appointments in Lancaster, Aberdeen, Essex, the Netherlands, and Australia. He is currently professor of sociology at the University of Cambridge.

— Chris Rojek

See also Body; Citizenship; Cosmopolitan Sociology; Marxism

FURTHER READINGS AND REFERENCES

Abercombie, N., S. Hill, and B. S. Turner. 1980. *The Dominant Ideology Thesis.* London: Allen & Unwin.

———. 1986. *Sovereign Individuals of Capitalism.* London: Unwin Hyman.

Turner, B. S. 1984. *Weber and Islam.* London: Routledge.

———. 1984. *The Body and Society.* Oxford, UK: Blackwell.

———. 1991. *Religion and Social Theory.* 2d ed. London & Thousand Oaks, CA: Sage.

Turner, B. S. and C. Rojek. 2001. *Society and Culture.* London: Sage.

TURNER, JONATHAN

Over the last 35 years, Jonathan H. Turner (b. 1942) has advocated a positivistic view of sociological theory, arguing that the goal of sociology is ultimately the production of abstract laws or principles and analytical models that explain basic social forces operating in all times and places (e.g., Turner 1991). For many years, Turner engaged in metatheoretical analysis, formalizing both early and contemporary theories into propositions and models. The goal of these efforts was to highlight the scientific contribution of the classical theorists to explaining the operative dynamics of the social universe (e.g., Turner 2002b; Turner, Beeghley, and Powers 2002) and to argue that some contemporary theories are better than others as scientific theory. As this advocacy and metatheorizing was being produced, Turner also began to implement his strategy for developing scientific theory. This strategy revolved around formalizing existing theories to see what they had to say about a given topic, extracting the useful elements of these theories, and adding new elements in order to produce a more robust theory. Generally, Turner produced abstract models that displayed in visual space the causal flow of social forces, highlighting the direct, indirect, and reverse causal effects of forces in the social universe. Along side these models, Turner would also produce a list of abstract propositions that stated the fundamental relationships among forces in the social universe. The goal of these theories was to define concepts clearly, to specify precisely the nature of their relationship to each other, and to list the conditions that changed the value of each concept.

Turner's work is thus synthetic, pulling together diverse strands of thought, making necessary corrections and additions, and then presenting a theory in a formal way so that, in principle, it can be tested. Early work revolved around the process of conflict (beginning with Turner 1973), especially in the context of ethnic relations (Turner and Singleton 1978). These works became part of a general theory of societal stratification (1984) that conceptualized stratification along several dimensions (the unequal distribution of power, material wealth, and prestige; the formation of homogeneous subpopulations; the ranking of subpopulations; and mobility across subpopulations). For each of these dimensions, a formal law, stated mathematically, was formulated.

In the late 1980s, Turner produced a theory of social interaction that sought to synthesize existing theories into a series of analytical models on motivational, interactional, and structuring processes (e.g., Turner 1987). Motivational dynamics are those processes that energize actors to behave, interactional processes revolve around the mutual signaling and interpreting of people in face-to-face contact, and structuring processes are those dynamics that stabilize the flow of interaction in space and time. Over a decade later, Turner produced a new theory of interaction, incorporating some of the ideas of this earlier theory but adding an entirely new framework as well as ideas on emotional dynamics that he had developed during the course of the 1990s and into the new century (2000, 2002a). This new theory adopted a conceptual scheme developed in the course of work on more macro-social processes (Turner 1995), and it appears that this simple conceptual edifice is influencing all of Turner's current theorizing. The scheme simply argues that the social universe unfolds at three levels: micro, meso, and macro. These are more than analytical distinctions; in Turner's view, they are reality. For each level of reality, there are forces that drive the formation and operation of structures at that level. At the micro level, the key structure is the encounter; at the meso level, the generic structures are corporate units (with a division of labor organized to achieve goals) and categoric units (the social distinctions that people use to define others); and at the macro level, the units are institutional systems. Each unit is embedded in the other, as well as in human biology. Thus, institutions are composed of corporate and categoric units; the latter are built from encounters, and encounters are possible only because of the biological makeup of humans. But in contrast to much theorizing that seeks to connect the micro and macro, Turner argues that each level of reality is driven by its own distinctive forces, and these forces are to be the subject of theoretical principles (Turner 2002a). That is, the goal of sociological theory is to isolate those forces that drive each level of social reality, and for each force, theorists should be able to state an abstract principle about its dynamic properties and, if desired, to develop an analytical model that lays out the causal connections among those properties of the social world that influence values and valences of each force.

In his most recent work on micro-social processes, Turner (2000a, 2002b) has specified six forces driving encounters: emotions, transactional needs, symbols, roles, status, and demographic/ecological properties. Earlier in the 1990s, Turner (1995) developed a theory of macro-dynamics that sought to explain those forces driving the formation of institutional systems. In this work, Turner postulated that there are seven forces driving the social universe at the macro level: population, production, distribution, power, space, differentiation, and disintegration. Turner has yet to work out a theory of mesodynamics, although his earlier theory of stratification hints at some of the dynamics that drive the formation of categoric units.

While these more general theoretical schemes were in development, Turner also pursued inquiry into human biology and evolution, arguing that sociologists must conceptualize biological processes to fully understand the social universe. Most of this evolutionary theorizing has involved analysis of humans' closest relative, the primates, to see what clues they offer to the hominid ancestors of humans. Turner has produced a number of works, ranging from a reanalysis of human nature (e.g., Maryanski and Turner 1992) to a theory on the evolution of human emotions (Turner 2000). At the same time, Turner has sought to revive and revise stage model theories of evolution by examining with a theory of selection processes and with principles of macrodynamics the development of institutional systems (Turner 2003). In this way, Turner hopes to overcome the obvious flaws of earlier functional theories of societal evolution.

Thus, Jonathan Turner is one of the few "grand theorists" remaining in sociology.

— Charles Powers

See also Conflict Theory; Evolutionary Theory; Metatheory; Positivism

FURTHER READINGS AND REFERENCES

Maryanski, Alexandra and Jonathan H. Turner. 1992. *The Social Cage: Human Nature and the Evolution of Society.* Stanford, CA: Stanford University Press.

Turner, Jonathan H. 1973. "From Utopia to Where? A Strategy for Reformulating the Dahrendorf Conflict Model." *Social Forces* 52:236–44.

————. 1984. *Societal Stratification: A Theoretical Analysis.* New York: Columbia University Press.

————. 1987. "Toward a Sociological Theory of Motivation." *American Sociological Review* 52:15–25.

————. 1991. "Using Metatheory to Develop Cumulative and Practical Knowledge." *Sociological Perspectives* 34:249–68.

————. 1995. *Macrodynamics: Toward a Theory on the Organization of Human Populations.* New Brunswick, NJ: Rutgers University Press for Rose Monograph.

————. 2000. *On the Origins of Human Emotions.* Stanford, CA: Stanford University Press.

————. 2002a. *Face-to-Face: Toward a Sociological Theory of Interpersonal Behavior.* Stanford, CA: Stanford University Press.

————. 2002b. *The Structure of Sociological Theory.* Belmont, CA: Wadsworth.

————. 2003. *Human Institutions: A Theory of Societal Evolution.* Boulder, CO: Rowman & Littlefield.

Turner, Jonathan H., Leonard Beeghley, and Charles H. Powers. 2002. *The Emergence of Sociological Theory.* Belmont, CA: Wadsworth.

Turner, Jonathan H. and Royce R. Singleton. 1978. "A Theory of Ethnic Oppression." *Social Forces* 56:1001–19.

URBANIZATION

THE NATURE OF URBANIZATION

Urbanization is the process whereby large numbers of people congregate and settle in an area, eventually developing social institutions, such as businesses and government, to support themselves. Urban areas, or those pockets of people and institutions thereby created, are generally characterized as relatively dense settlements of people. Furthermore, it is claimed, they sometimes originate from the effort by authorities to consciously concentrate power, capital, or both at a particular site.

The process of urbanization has gone on throughout history. Large congregations of people have existed across the world, from ancient China to ancient Rome and Greece. Although the numbers of residents of such cities pale by comparison with urban areas today, the relatively large and dense congregations of people still helped to foster new institutions and, in general, to make urban life in many ways preferable to that of living in relatively isolated rural areas. Urban residents typically benefit from better forms of education, improved medical care, the availability and distribution of information, and the greater supply of life-sustaining goods, such as food and shelter.

Today, more than half the world's population resides in urban areas. Furthermore, demographers project that between 2000 and 2025 the population growth of urban areas will constitute about 90 percent of all world population growth. Major concentrations of people today can be found on all continents (see Table 1).

Yet urbanization is more than just the process leading to dense settlements. Social theorists across the ages have wrestled to understand it. Indeed, one might say that the process of urbanization is a focal point for many sociological concerns; the urban area serves, in effect, as a major stage on which social change plays itself out. If one takes a dim view of such change, then urbanization tends to be criticized for the evils it unleashes. Yet if one takes a positive view of social change, then urbanization is claimed to produce many benefits. The next section examines the varying theories of urbanization more closely to discover how, and why, social theorists differ in their views of the process.

THEORIES OF URBANIZATION

Even though observers generally agree on the nature of urbanization, there is widespread disagreement both as to its social sources and consequences. Moreover, there is also disagreement over the extent to which human actors can intervene in the process. Here, some of the leading views

Table U.1 Fifteen Largest Metropolitan Areas of the World

Name	Size
Tokyo (Japan)	33,750,000
Mexico City (Mexico)	21,850,000
New York (United States)	21,750,000
Seoul (South Korea)	21,700,000
Sao Paulo (Brazil)	20,200,000
Bombay (India)	18,800,000
Delhi (India)	18,100,000
Los Angeles (United States)	17,450,000
Osaka (Japan)	16,700,000
Jakarta (Indonesia)	16,300,000
Cairo (Egypt)	15,600,000
Moscow (Russia)	15,350,000
Calcutta (India)	14,950,000
Manila (Philippines)	14,000,000
Buenos Aires (Argentina)	13,900,000

Source: Thomas Brinkhoff, City Population http://www.citypopulation.de, as of September 2003.

are considered, noting how, and why, they differ from one another.

The German Perspective

One of the first theorists to acknowledge the deep and important impact of urbanization on social life was the German scholar, Georg Simmel. Simmel developed a sociology that focused on the special ways that forms, such as the numbers of people in groups, influenced social life. His effort to understand the nature of urbanization and, in particular, the metropolis of the late nineteenth and early twentieth centuries, displayed his characteristic method of analysis.

In a famous article, "The Metropolis and Mental Life," Simmel argued that there were certain features of the modern metropolis that rendered it different from all prior forms of social organization. In particular, life in the metropolis requires that people engage in social interactions with large numbers of different people. It also requires that they carry on their social life with a good deal more rapidity than other forms of settlement. The characteristic type of relationship in the metropolis, he suggested, was the relationship between the customer and clerk in a business exchange. Both treat one another not as intimates but, rather, simply as people engaged in business with one another. The impersonal and instrumental qualities of such relationships were, Simmel argued, essential features of the modern metropolis. Moreover, these features extended to life throughout the metropolis. People tend not to know one another as individuals but, rather, as passersby or mere acquaintances. The consequence of all such relationships was to give life in the modern metropolis an air of anonymity. Money, not interpersonal trust, lies at the heart of the metropolis, so Simmel insisted.

Simmel was not the only German theorist to take the difference between the metropolitan form and prior social forms seriously. Ferdinand Tönnies, a fellow German, insisted on a somewhat similar contrast. Unlike Simmel, who cast his argument in terms primarily about the modern form, that of the metropolis, Tönnies developed a theoretical polarity between what he termed *Gemeinschaft,* on one hand, and *Gesellschaft,* on the other. The former represents the close-knit community, whereas the latter refers to society. *Gemeinschaft* suggested intimacy, warmth, and human closeness, whereas *Gesellschaft* clearly suggests impersonal exchanges, based on forms such as business exchanges. Like Simmel, Tönnies's intention was to capture in theoretical analysis a real social change that was unfolding across Europe over the course of the eighteenth and, especially, nineteenth centuries.

The Chicago School

These themes—impersonality, anonymity, and economic exchange in the metropolis—heavily influenced the writings of American sociologists in the early twentieth century as they sought to unravel the nature of the expanding metropolis. The influence was by no means accidental. The leading figure of what came to be known as the Chicago School of Sociology—so-called because all the sociologists were located at the University of Chicago—was Robert Park, a man trained as an American journalist who studied in Germany with Georg Simmel.

The central theoretical argument about the nature of urbanization, the metropolis, in particular, is to be found in the writing of Chicago sociologist, Louis Wirth. In another famous article, "Urbanism as a Way of Life," Wirth (1938) amplified themes that first appear in the writing of Simmel and, to a lesser extent, Tönnies. Wirth insisted that urbanism, or urbanization, produced any of several important social consequences among people: (1) impersonality and anonymity in everyday life, (2) loss of trust among people, and (3) various forms of social disorganization, as in higher rates of crime than in rural areas. Yet unlike Simmel and Tönnies, there was growing empirical evidence on which Wirth could draw. Like other members of the Chicago School, his attention was principally focused on the city of Chicago and the period of the late nineteenth and early twentieth centuries during which it multiplied in size enormously. Chicago, in fact, seemed to fit all the theoretical forecasts of urbanism, showing, among other things, a high crime rate and an abundance of urban gangs. In effect, the theoretical portrait that first emerged in the writings of Simmel and Tönnies, later appearing in that of Wirth, was more than just a social theory: It was a theory that seemed to be well grounded in empirical facts.

While Wirth's work expanded on the broad social consequences of urbanization, other Chicago sociologists expanded on other parts. Ernest Burgess, a longtime collaborator of Robert Park, produced a famous model of the growth of the urban area. The model consisted of a series of concentric zones. Each zone was composed of a different set of businesses and residential characteristics. The interior zone, for example, consisted of major business and financial firms; the immediately adjacent zone consisted of the red-light district as well as certain ethnic settlements, such as Little Sicily. And in the farthest reaches of the metropolis, one found wealthier residents as well as the apartment houses and fancier hotels. The model was based entirely on the city of Chicago, yet it eventually gave rise to many efforts to discover the extent to which it reappeared in many other growing metropolises. Moreover, there were additional efforts to show that the concentric pattern of growth was not the only one; other theories suggested, for example, that cities could develop in the form of a variety of different social and economic nuclei.

Human Ecology. Besides the theory of urbanism and the concentric pattern of metropolitan growth, the Chicago School also gave rise to a general theoretical perspective on the nature of the metropolis, one rooted in a view of the city in terms of its population and broad social environment. Robert Park was the major developer of this view. And because it was inspired by the writings of ecologists—again an influence Park came under in Germany—it became known as the "human ecology" paradigm. The human ecology perspective was especially focused on the ways in which the population of areas expanded or declined. It concentrated its attention on how the change of specific areas of the city occurred, and which economic social actors were winners and losers in the process. Any of several outcomes could happen, Park believed—among them, conflict, accommodation, and in certain cases, assimilation by the newcomers of the cultural patterns of the natives. Indeed, it was Park's conception of human ecology and the city that eventually gave rise to his theory of the race relations cycle, and the nature of assimilation among immigrants, in general.

Park's theory was relatively simple and never extensively developed as a fully integrated theory. Amos Hawley, a sociologist who taught at the University of Michigan and North Carolina, took it upon himself to make the human ecology paradigm far more systematic. He fleshed out the ideas of the environment as well as the processes of adaptation and competition through which social groups adjusted both to one another and to the environment. Moreover, he advanced certain ideas about the nature of dominance and power among actors, among them the claim, later confirmed, that metropolitan areas with higher concentrations of professional and managerial workers would be more effective in getting broad civic actions implemented than those with smaller concentrations.

Theoretical Alternatives to the Chicago School

The Chicago School's theories of urbanization remained dominant among sociologists until the early 1970s. Then they were challenged by other points of view. The result was to create both reforms in the theories as well as to provide other theories grounded in different principles about the working of societies.

The City as Neighborhood and Community. One of the first and most important critiques of the Chicago School view of the city came from the sociologist Claude Fischer. Fischer challenged the Wirth/Simmel interpretation of the city. Fischer argued that the city was not characterized by impersonality and anonymity but, rather, by a variety of social ties and subcultures that connected people to one another. Fischer found the characteristic form of urban life in the neighborhood, not, as Wirth and Simmel had, in business or economic exchanges. Thus, he insisted, cities are not sites of impersonality but, rather, sites of trust and friendship:

Such relationships are to be found in the neighborhood, not in the department store.

The Political Economy Perspective. The dominant critique and most substantial alternative to the view of the Chicago School came, as one might anticipate, in the writings of Marxist scholars who began to build their alternative theory in the early 1970s. There are several variants of this perspective; although each is a rich and compelling portrait by itself, the discussion here must be abbreviated because of space limitations.

The leading Marxist theorist on the city is Henri Lefebvre, a French scholar. Lefebvre argued that the urbanization process is not one driven by population expansion and mobility, per se, but rather by the actions of key social actors. Social agents, he insisted, produce, and reproduce, the spaces in cities; and, to the extent that such agents reflect the dominant forms of social and economic inequalities, those inequalities will be re-created in the nature of metropolitan space. Lefebvre extended his basic insights in several directions, insisting that we must study not simply the different parts of the metropolitan area but also the way that social rhythms are created therein, such as the rhythm to work life and that to the nature of life on the streets.

Lefebvre inspired several important theorists. Among them are the sociologist Manuel Castells. Castells leveled the most major charges at the Chicago School view of the city. He argued specifically that it was not simply population growth that created the various forms of social disorganization, such as higher crime rates in the city, but instead it was the forces of capitalism. Capitalism created the inequalities, between residents as well as between sectors of the city. Moreover, Castells suggested, the Marxist view of the world, when applied carefully to the city and to the process of urbanization, emphasized the forces of collective consumption, not those of production, as Marx himself originally argued. Thus, Castells argued, it is the conditions of public housing and of other forms in which urban laborers are exploited as consumers, to which sociologists, studying urbanization, must turn their attention and seek to correct.

A third Marxist writer on urban areas is the British geographer, David Harvey. Harvey has had the widest influence over modern writings about the city. He maintains that from a Marxist perspective the major economic activity in urbanization is that which deals with the use and value of land. Thus, those social actors, such as real estate developers and bankers, actually exploit the value of urban space through their investment and selling strategies. Whereas capitalist employers secure profit by, for example, paying workers low wages, real estate developers and bankers secure their profits by setting high prices on the land in cities. Furthermore, Harvey argues, the inequalities characteristic of urban areas, such as the wide differential in values between suburban and inner-city areas, are also the product of how capitalism manipulates the value of land. There is nothing natural to the disparate values of suburban and inner-city land; it is simply that bankers and real estate developers constantly seek to divest themselves of property that produces little income, as within the interior of the city, and reinvest their funds in other portions of the city, those especially in the outlying areas, where they can expect both to set higher prices and secure greater profits from the sales of land and housing. In recent years, it might be noted, that process has been reversed to some degree, as bankers and developers now turn their attention back to the central city, creating new housing developments where they can expect to lure both wealthy young professionals and older former suburban residents.

Other writers, taking a similar political economic perspective on urbanization, have developed similar critiques of the Chicago School as well as their own special theoretical portraits. John Logan and Harvey Molotch, in a famous work, argue that the city must be viewed as a "growth machine." Cities expand not because of the dynamics of population but, rather, because there are key social groups that benefit from such expansion. Such groups include, among others, real estate developers, bankers, and even political officials. All of them profit from growth, Logan and Molotch insist: Developers and bankers gain financial profit, while political officials garner the key political support of the business community if they insist on expansion.

MODERN FORMS OF URBAN GROWTH

Urbanization today is different in important respects from its form in the past. Here are a few of the significant twists and turns it has taken.

The Megalopolis

In the early 1960s, the urban scholar Jean Gottesman sought to capture the novelty of the growing interconnectedness of various major metropolitan areas in the world. He claimed that regions such as that from Boston south to Washington, D.C., along the Eastern seaboard of the United States represented new forms of metropolitan expansion in which major cities came to overlap with one another. He insisted that in the future more and more such megalopolises would emerge in the world, providing ever more dense concentrations of people. Such patterns, in fact, are to be found increasingly in the United States, in the West as well as the Southwest. There are many other countries as well, such as Japan, in which similar patterns of urban expansion are also to be found.

Suburbanization

Urbanization that produces new residential communities on the outskirts of major cities has become known as suburbanization. In the United States, suburbanization has become the fundamental form of urban growth since the end of World War II, suburbs taking root outside virtually all major cities. There are different explanations for the process. Unlike the Chicago School, which insisted that suburban growth was a simple part of the inexorable expansion of the city, the historian Kenneth Jackson has argued convincingly that the suburb represents a symbolic place rooted deep in American culture, a setting rooted in the imagination wherein people come to expect they can live a satisfying life, with their own yards and neighbors, intimately embedded in the natural environment. But Jackson has also shown that political actors play a key role in the creation of suburbs. In particular, he shows, the Federal Housing Agency after World War II provided low-interest loans to returning veterans, the effect of which was to make suburban housing far more affordable than it had ever been in the past. To this day, the process of suburbanization continues to engage the writings of social scientists as they seek to better understand the nature of urban growth, especially in the United States.

Edge Cities

Yet an even newer wrinkle to the process of urbanization today is the growth of what the journalist, Joel Garreau, has called "edge cities." Edge cities are those congregations of people, residences, and businesses that have grown up alongside major thoroughfares and, especially, highways around cities. They seem to occur everywhere that the highway system transports people, and they account for much of the most recent urban growth. Places such as Naperville, Illinois, and Georgetown, Texas, serve as examples of such expansion: Indeed, without the highway system, such rapidly growing cities would never have developed.

Global Cities

The growth of megacities such as London, Shanghai, and Mexico City, cities that number in the millions, has given rise to various explanations. Some, of course, would simply see such cities as the inevitable outcome of the urbanization process. But other scholars see in such megacities a new historic phenomenon.

The most popular writer on large cities today is the sociologist Saskia Sassen. Sassen argues that over the course of the last three decades the urbanization process has produced a tendency for people to congregate in enormous numbers on relatively small spaces. Three cities typify the process of urban globalization: Tokyo, New York, and London. All three cities, Sassen finds, are based on new and emerging economic foundations, in particular, the concentration of financial, real estate, and communications industries. Moreover, the growth of these cities has also led to their bifurcation along economic lines. Two major economic groups have emerged: on one hand, a large and expanding class of service employees and, on the other hand, a much smaller but far more wealthy group of professional workers. The effect, she argues, is to increase economic inequalities in the city; moreover, she insists, the growth of the service sector jobs has also prompted the influx of many immigrants who are willing to take on the low-paying positions. Finally, she argues that these global cities have become disconnected from their nation-states; they tend to act as strong political and economic actors on their own, relatively autonomous from nations. Sassen's argument has proven very influential, but it also has its critics, some of whom charge that she underplays the key political role of the nation-state in today's world.

It is notable that among these major novelties to urban growth in the recent past, only the work of Sassen on global cities and globalization is based on important theoretical work. The other new elements, such as edge cities and even suburbanization, are regarded by urban scholars as significant, although they have not yet prompted extensive theoretical work by sociologists.

POVERTY, IMMIGRATION, AND URBANIZATION

New patterns of urban expansion have helped to modify the earlier theoretical views of the city and suggested not only the limitations of such theories but also the importance of human actors in the construction of the metropolis. One of the most important areas of contemporary work on urban expansion and change lies in research on poverty and immigration.

Poverty and Urbanization

The sociologist, William Julius Wilson, has had an important impact on these writings. In his various writings Wilson inspired a line of research on the modern city in which work, and its absence, he believed, played a powerful role in shaping the urban area. His claim is that over the course of two decades, from about 1970 until 1990, the nature of cities in the United States changed dramatically. Parts of the city declined, while other parts expanded. Those parts that declined, almost always located in the inner-city areas inhabited by black residents, did so, he insisted, because major industries abandoned these areas in favor of labor markets elsewhere, especially overseas. The result was to create a huge group of unemployed people, those whom he came to describe as the "underclass." In turn, new jobs tended to show up on the fringe of urban areas, at those sites generally occupied by the white middle class. Moreover, such jobs became part of the suburbanization phenomenon, even in many cases integral to the emergence of "edge cities."

Unlike the Chicago School of sociologists, however, Wilson believed that such decline was not inevitable but, rather, directly traceable to the decisions of industries to leave the city. Hence, he became a strong advocate of efforts to encourage new public policies that would promote a revitalization of the inner city along with efforts to increase the growth of low-income housing in the suburbs, thereby bringing low-income people closer to the location of the new employment opportunities.

This work on poverty has also led to further studies of the nature of social disorganization and decline in the inner-city areas of the modern metropolis. Sociologists such as Robert Sampson have argued that some neighborhoods are much more able to deal with issues of social disorganization, attributing their success to the "collective efficacy," or the capacity of residents to take common and effective local action. Many other social scientists are following up similar leads, with efforts now under way to create more viable and successful communities among the poor and minority residents of the inner city.

Immigration and Urbanization

Immigration in the contemporary period also represents an important new social element to the picture of urban growth. In the past, immigrants tended to settle in the interior of major cities, partly because that is where they first arrived and partly because, in the absence of highways, mobility to the outlying areas was virtually impossible. Today, however, there are new patterns of immigrant growth and communities in urban areas. Part of the difference is to be found in the vast numbers and movement of people across the world. Since 1945, there have been massive shifts of people from one country to another, most of whom settle in or around urban areas. In cities from London to Paris, Berlin to Toronto, one can find new and relatively large immigrant settlements. Some such settlements have arisen because of a government's selective use of guest worker programs, like the *bracero* program in the United States or the *Gastarbeiter* program in Germany; but many others have emerged simply because immigrants come to a new place for the job opportunities it offers. In the United States, today's immigrants are remaking the metropolitan area, not only through the introduction of groups of people from Latin America, Asia, and Africa—nations formerly underrepresented—but also by a host of new settlements across the entire metropolitan region. Thanks to the system of highways and public transportation, today's immigrants can settle not only in the inner core of the metropolis but also on the suburban fringes as well. Because of such new patterns of settlement by immigrants in the metropolis, sociologists have modified their older theories and developed new arguments about the growth of a multicultural metropolis.

THE FUTURE OF URBANIZATION

Urbanization will continue as long as people form communities, move from one place to another, and settle in sites where new friends, old family, and good job opportunities can be found. Whether it will tend to improve the condition of humankind, or detract from it, depends on many things. One thing is now very clear: Human beings and social institutions can play a far more important role in the shaping of urban areas than early twentieth-century theorists ever thought possible. Indeed, one might say that the early theorists tended to view urbanization as a broad structural process, in part simply to make the new enterprise of scientific sociology a legitimate one. Today's urban writers and thinkers tend to see the process of urban expansion both as one more subject to the exercise of human agency as well as one heavily influenced by events and actions rooted in international circumstances.

— Anthony Orum

See Also Ecological Theory; Globalization; Hawley, Amos; Lefebvre, Henri; Park, Robert; Political Economy; Simmel, Georg; Tönnies, Ferdinand

Further Readings and References

Castells, Manuel. [1972] 1977. *The Urban Question*. Translated by Alan Sheridan. Cambridge, MA: MIT. Originally published as *La Question Urbaine* (Paris: Francois Maspero, 1972).

Harvey, David. [1973] 1988. *Social Justice and the City*. Oxford, UK: Basil Blackwell.

Hawley, Amos. 1950. *Human Ecology: A Theory of Community Structure*. New York: Ronald Press.

Jacobs, Jane. 1961. *The Death and Life of Great American Cities*. New York: Random House.

Lefebvre, Henri. 1991. *The Production of Space*. Translated by Donald Nicholson-Smith. Oxford, UK: Blackwell. Originally published as *Production de l'espace* (Paris: Anthropos, 1974).

Logan, John and Harvey Molotch. 1987. *Urban Fortunes: Toward a Political Economy of Place*. Berkeley: University of California Press.

Orum, Anthony M. and Xiangming Chen. 2003. *The World of Cities*. Malden, MA, & Oxford, UK: Blackwell.

Sassen, Saskia. 2001. *The Global City: New York, London, Tokyo*. 2d ed. Princeton, NJ: Princeton University Press.

Wirth, Louis. 1938. "Urbanism as a Way of Life." *American Journal of Sociology* 44(January):1–24.

Zukin, Sharon. 1995. *The Cultures of Cities*. Oxford, UK: Blackwell.

UTOPIA

THE INVENTION OF UTOPIA

The term *utopia* was coined by the English writer Sir Thomas More in his book, *Utopia* (1516). More combined, in a punning way, two Greek words, *eutopia* = the good place, and *outopia* = no place. Utopia is therefore the good place that is nowhere.

This would seem to lend itself to the most fantastic products of the imagination, unchecked by any considerations of reality or rationality. The wider reaches of science fiction, as well as the fantasies of the dream, would seem to belong to its province. If utopia, by definition, is not and never can be somewhere, why restrict ourselves to the merely practicable, let alone the realistically probable? Why not give the freest plays to our fancies, let our imaginations rip in the devising of schemes for the fullest fulfillment of our desires?

There are indeed, it seems, at all times and in all societies, forms of thought and popular culture that express this kind of longing. Nearly all societies have traditions of Paradise or the Golden Age, a time and a place where the pain and privations of everyday life did not exist and all lived freely and blissfully. There are folk images of the Land of Cockaygne and Schlaraffenland, places of exuberantly unrestrained wishes and more or less instant gratification. There are El Dorados and Shangri-las where people live in peace, harmony, and everlasting contentment.

But these are not utopia—not, at least, as that form has been understood and practiced for more than 500 years in the West. From the very beginning, from More's own rational and restrained vision in his Utopia, utopia has displayed a certain sobriety, a certain wish to walk in step with current realities. It is as if it has wanted deliberately to distinguish itself from the wilder fancies of the popular imagination. Typically, it has been a form of the high literary culture of the age. Certainly it has wished to go beyond its own time and place. It has sought to create a picture of a good, even perfect, society. But it has wanted to remain within the realm of the possible. It has wanted to work with the human and social materials at hand; it has accepted the psychological and sociological realities of human society. The realm of utopia is wide, but it is not boundless. Utopia, while it liberates the imagination, also sets limits. This is perhaps the source of its fascination—and its strength.

More's *Utopia* initiated a tradition of social thought that has had a continuous history ever since (More's own book, remarkably, has been in print in one language or another without a break since its original publication). In addition to *Utopia*, certain major utopian works inspired by it—Anton Francesco Doni's *I Mondi* (1553), Johann Valentin Andreae's *Christianopolis* (1619), Tommaso Campanella's *City of the Sun* (1623), and Bacon's *New Atlantis* (1627)—achieved great fame among European men of letters. All utopian writers were aware of these great exemplars even when they sought, as in Bishop Hall's *Mundus Alter et Idem* (1605) or Jonathan Swift's *Gulliver's Travels* (1726), to satirize or rebut them (thus inventing the anti-utopia or dystopia). Right down to the twentieth century, we can trace the continuing influence of the great early modern utopias.

UTOPIA AND SOCIAL THEORY

With his *Utopia,* More coined not just a new word, but he invented a new form. Not that there were not important precursors. More was influenced by works such as Plato's *Republic* (fifth century BCE) and in general the Hellenic literary genre of devising the ideal city. He was probably also influenced by Christian monasticism and the Christian idea of the millennium, from the Book of Revelation in the New Testament. But neither Plato's *Republic* nor the Christian millennium looks like More's *Utopia.* The *Republic* is essentially a treatise on justice, while, apart from the fact that More's Utopians are pagans, the Book of Revelation's sketch of the coming millennial dispensation is shadowy in the extreme. What the Hellenic ideal city contributed to utopia was the element of design, the planning of the perfect city or society. What the Christian millennium contributed was the element of time or history. The expectation of Christ's second coming, which would inaugurate a terrestrial millennium of peace and plenty, gave to utopia a sense of urgency and hope. There would be an "end of days," an end of history, which would lead to the annulment of the old order and the commencement of the new. Utopia was slow to incorporate this dynamic dimension in its imagination—it is not found, for instance, in More's *Utopia.* Not until the eighteenth century, with the decisive temporalization of European thought, did the millennial theme come fully into its own in utopian thought.

So classical and Christian ideas have undoubtedly played their part in the utopian tradition. But in synthesizing them, More went beyond them in inventing a new literary form. Utopia is a form of fiction closely related to the novel—indeed, it probably contributed to the development of the novel form as it emerged in the eighteenth century. It uses all the techniques of the novel—plot, characterization, incident—to paint its picture of the ideal society. This distinguishes it from the form of social and political theory that, following Friedrich Engels, we might call "utopian social theory." Examples of such theory would be the writings of Robert Owen, Henri Saint-Simon, Charles Fourier, and indeed those of Karl Marx. These give an account of future societies in which misery, injustice, oppression, and pain have been eliminated.

To that extent they are utopian. But their accounts are couched in the terms of social-scientific analysis. They claim to be giving scientifically truthful accounts of history and society. Indeed so concerned are they to do so that they are markedly hesitant, especially in the case of Marx, in giving full-blooded accounts of the new society ("I do not," Marx wrote contemptuously, "write recipes for the cookshops of the future"). This may have advantages in certain respects, but in comparison with the utopia proper, it also suffers from a serious weakness.

What makes the literary utopia superior to other ways of promoting the good society? We can compare, say, the

accounts of socialism in the writings of theoreticians such as Marx and Engels and those provided in socialist utopias such as Edward Bellamy's *Looking Backward* (1888) and William Morris's *News from Nowhere* (1890). We have many testimonies to the effect that, while impressed by the theoretical writings of the socialists, it was these socialist utopias that converted many Europeans and Americans to socialism. There can be many reasons for this, including the obvious one of the attractions of a well-told story over abstract analysis. But there is also the point that utopias are more persuasive because they allow us to make a more honest test of theory than abstract formulations, however profound.

The utopian mode of persuasion is to paint pleasing pictures of daily life, such that we are driven to want to make the world they portray. They are concerned as much with what Miguel Abensour calls "the education of desire" as with the particular portrait of the good society. But in painting such pictures, utopian writers are forced to provide the wealth of details of daily life that are entirely lacking in abstract theory. Unlike the theoretician, who asks us to accept as it were on trust that the desirable consequences will follow from the application of the relevant theoretical principles—that happiness will, indeed, follow upon "the expropriation of the expropriators," for example—the utopian writer is under the obligation to present a fully developed and detailed picture of the happy world that is expected to result from the application of the relevant principles. We see people at work and at play, at home and in the public spaces of society, in their personal and in their political lives. We experience, through involvement with characters and events, as well as through the descriptions of the scenes and settings of daily life, a "good day" in the new society. We can therefore judge of both the plausibility and the desirability of the life so presented. When William Morris, in *News from Nowhere,* vividly depicts the revitalized and rebeautified landscape of the Thames valley in a transformed socialist England of the future, we intensely want to be there, to experience such beauty. But we also understand, in a way not possible from a reading of socialist theory, what precisely might be involved in the construction of the new society, and how far we can imagine such things coming about. It is exactly in this way, too, because we can see in detail how it looks and feels, that we can choose between the competing visions of socialism offered by Bellamy and Morris—Bellamy's utilitarian paradise where the machines do all the work and Morris's more arcadian vision where work is restored to everyone as a labor of love.

UTOPIA IN SPACE AND TIME

The utopias of the sixteenth and seventeenth century—those of More, Campanella, Bacon, and others—can be called objects of contemplation. They were philosophical speculations, sometimes religious in inspiration, on the nature of good and evil, and how humans might aspire to lead the good life, so far as it might be humanly possible on earth. Typically, they held up a satiric mirror to their own societies, using the utopian society as a foil to their own disordered societies. There was little suggestion that they were intended as practical schemes of human betterment. Even Bacon's utopia of science, *The New Atlantis,* merely suggested the boundless possibilities opened up by the new scientific and technical discoveries of the age. Although the House of Saloman has often been seen as anticipating the foundation of the Royal Society in 1660, its social and political setting in *The New Atlantis* gives no guide whatsoever as to how to achieve the scientifically advanced society that spawns it.

With the growth of the idea of progress in the eighteenth century, utopia took on a more secular and realistic form. It now came to be inserted in history, in the story of humanity's growth in knowledge and power. Utopia was displaced from space—the space of contemplation—to time, the time of the culmination of human development. Utopia would be found not on some hitherto unknown island nor in a remote mountain valley on the other side of the world, but in the future. Louis Sebastien Mercier's utopia, *L'An 2240* (1770) decisively sounded the new note. The epigraph was taken from Leibniz: "The present is pregnant with the future."

There was however an unexpected side to this development. While Enlightenment utopias made full use of the new temporal resources, the occurrence of the French and Industrial Revolutions prompted the thought that utopia might not be some distant eventuality but a more or less imminent possibility. In the hands of Saint-Simon, Comte, and their sociological successors, in the thinking of the socialists Owen, Fourier, and the early Marx, utopia passed into a species of social science in which it was argued that the good society could be constructed with the tools at hand and that, moreover, it was a society struggling to be born in the thinker's own times. There seemed no need, and no room, for imaginary pictures of the good society. Utopia proper went for a while into abeyance. Its place was taken by schemes for reform and regeneration that, drawing on the new social sciences, offered to show the way to utopia as a strictly rational and scientific enterprise. Most prominent among these were the varieties of socialism.

But although utopia, as a literary form, underwent a temporary suppression, the temporalizing impulse underlying social thought remained powerful in the evolutionary schemes of the social scientists, to mark strongly the utopias that reemerged toward the end of the nineteenth century. Ironically, it was the very failure of socialism to generate the expected support or to realize its aims that seemed to have stimulated the revival of utopia. Socialists came to see the need to show society as it might be, in all its glowing colors. That was the aim of Bellamy's *Looking Backward,* Morris's *News from Nowhere,* H. G. Wells's *A Modern Utopia* (1905), and a host of others that crowded the field at the end

of the nineteenth and the early twentieth centuries. In nearly all these, the temporal dimension was paramount. Society needed time to develop the fullness of its powers and the consciousness of its members. In such a way, and to such an extent, did the millennial underpinnings of utopia—the supplying of the elements of hope and of history—continue to show their power up until recent times.

THE FATE AND FUTURE OF UTOPIA

The twentieth-century world, at least in the first part of the century, was markedly inhospitable to utopia. Two world wars, a global economic depression, fascism and communism, Hiroshima and the subsequent "balance of terror" between the West and the Soviet bloc: All these not unnaturally militated against the hopes that had sustained utopia throughout "the long nineteenth century." All these developments equally naturally provided rich material for utopia's *doppelgänger,* the anti-utopia. Evgeny Zamyatin's *We* (1920), Aldous Huxley's *Brave New World* (1932), and George Orwell's *Nineteen Eighty-Four* (1949), with their chilling portraits of totalitarian societies governed by scientific techniques and power-hungry elites, were the works that stamped themselves on the imaginations of Western societies in the first half of the century and beyond. Equally persuasive were varied works such as Arthur Koestler's novel *Darkness at Noon* (1940) and the philosopher Karl Popper's *The Open Society and Its Enemies* (1945), both of them swingeing attacks on the utopian temperament and the pass to which it had brought the world.

There were some isolated attempts, especially in the Marxist camp, to keep the utopian flame alive, of which Ernst Bloch's voluminous *The Principle of Hope* (1949) was the most exuberant expression. The psychologist B. F. Skinner's *Walden Two* (1948), a utopia of "behavioral engineering," was also a brave attempt to revive utopian hopes in dark times. And indeed in the second half of the twentieth century, despite the ever-present threat of nuclear war between the two superpowers, utopia found new forms and new ideas. Partly this may have been the result of the enormous vitality shown by Western economies in the post-1945 period, allowing many thinkers to argue that "the economic problem" had been solved. Certainly, this seemed the underlying assumption of the upsurge of utopian thought that was found in the student movements and the "counter-culture" of the 1960s (right on cue, the old anti-utopian Aldous Huxley stepped forward to answer his own critique with a sex-and-drugs utopia, *Island* [1962], which fused Western science and Eastern philosophy). In the French "May Events" of 1968, Parisian students for a short time even attempted to put utopia into practice by turning the city into a liberated zone of spontaneity and pleasure.

Out of the movements of the 1960s also came two new kinds of utopias—the ecological utopia or "ecotopia" and the feminist utopia. Neither was entirely new—Morris's *News from Nowhere* was an ecotopia in all but name, and the feminist utopia had precedents in works such as Charlotte Perkins Gilman's *Herland* (1915). But both showed that the utopian imagination was far from exhausted and was capable of being put to effective use in the new concerns of the age. Ernest Callenbach's *Ecotopia* (1975) named the form, although some of its best expressions were to be found in genre science fiction, such as Frank Herbert's portrait of the Fremen in *Dune* (1965). Ecological sympathies were generally also strong in the feminist utopia, such as Marge Piercy's *Woman on the Edge of Time* (1976) and, most notably, Ursula Le Guin's *The Dispossessed* (1974). And in a familiar fashion, these vigorous utopias were matched by equally energetic anti-utopias, such as John Brunner's *Stand on Zanzibar* (1969)—a warning against overpopulation—and Margaret Attwood's *The Handmaid's Tale* (1986), in which women are simple breeding machines and the playthings of men.

The problem for recent utopias has been that, unlike earlier ones, they tend to be addressed to, and read by, the faithful. It is mainly those already possessed by an ecological or feminist consciousness that tend to be attracted to these utopias. Utopia does not, as with Bellamy's *Looking Backward* or Skinner's *Walden Two*, become a hotly disputed vision of present and future society. It has been exiled to the margins of society, becoming a subgenre of science fiction or feminist literature. So far, this too seems to have been the fate of the "virtual utopia," the many private utopias to be found scattered all over the Internet. The anti-utopia seems to have fared better, at least in the popular medium of the cinema, judging by the success of films such as *The Matrix* trilogy (1999, 2003, 2003) and *Minority Report* (2002). And perhaps it is in the new visual technologies that utopia, too,

will find new themes and forms, if it has a future. That at least has been the view of certain theorists of postmodernity, such as Frederick Jameson and David Harvey. But it is hard to see how the typical postmodernist attitude—skeptical, ironic, playful, distrustful of the "grand narratives" of reason and history—can stimulate utopian thinking.

Utopia has had a more or less continuous 500-year history. In our own era of globalization, the information technology revolution, splintered societies, and mass migrations, one would think that never was there more need for unifying and clarifying visions. That has been utopia's function throughout its long history. It is difficult to imagine that it has now ceased. Social and political theory has its invaluable contribution to make, but it is utopia that issues the clarion call.

— Krishan Kumar

See Also Ecological Theory; Gilman, Charlotte Perkins; Internet and Cyberculture; Mannheim, Karl; Situationists; Socialism

Further Readings and References

Claeys, Gregory and Lyman Tower Sargent, eds. 1999. *The Utopia Reader.* New York & London: New York University Press.

Fortunati, Vita and Raymond Trousson, eds. 2000. *Dictionary of Literary Utopias.* Paris: Editions Champion; Geneva, Switzerland: Editions Slatkine.

Kateb, George. 1972. *Utopia and Its Enemies.* New York: Schocken.

Kumar, Krishan. 1987. *Utopia and Anti-Utopia in Modern Times.* Oxford, UK, & New York: Basil Blackwell.

Levitas, Ruth. 1990. *The Concept of Utopia.* Hemel Hempstead, UK: Philip Allan.

Manuel, Frank and Fritzie Manuel. 1979. *Utopian Thought in the Western World.* Cambridge, MA: Harvard University Press.

VEBLEN, THORSTEIN

Thorstein Veblen (1857–1929), along with Max Weber, Vilfredo Pareto, and Werner Sombart, worked at the intersection of economics and sociology. Veblen's memorable concept of "conspicuous consumption" formed a lasting link between economics and sociology by focusing attention on status seeking, which motivates a great deal of economic behavior but must be understood in sociological rather than in purely economic terms. Veblen is also remembered as one of the founding figures of the "institutional economics' tradition in economics, with its focus on legal forms and developments in governance. Finally, Veblen was an insightful social critic who helped shape the thinking of subsequent generations of analysts like C. Wright ("the power elite") Mills.

Thorstein Veblen was an economist who, in the process of trying to understand the economy, underwent a transformation that carried him clearly into sociology. Veblen's departure from conventional economics began with his rejection of the idea that most behavior is guided by rational calculation aimed at maximizing material well-being. A key to understanding Veblen is his awareness of human beings as status seekers. Veblen viewed society as a giant arena in which people struggle to acquire social approval. His enduring contribution unfolds from the recognition that what often appears as materialism is actually status seeking in disguise.

Veblen maintained that the specific steps people take to pursue recognition will be constrained by the character of the property system, the nature of banking, and other institutional forms. Informed economic analysis must consequently pay considerable attention to organizational and legal forms as they have evolved over time in different countries. Although he was indebted to the German "historical" economists in this regard, Veblen is nevertheless remembered for having provided some of the intellectual inspiration and energy for the subdiscipline of "institutional" economics.

Thorstein Veblen's parents were Norwegian immigrants farming in Wisconsin when Thorstein Veblen was born in 1857, the sixth of 12 children. The family moved to a larger farm in Minnesota in 1865, where Veblen grew up speaking Norwegian in a rural, religiously conservative setting. Smart and acerbic, Veblen didn't fit in very well when he was sent to newly established Carleton College to train for the Lutheran ministry. Veblen generally disliked Carleton when he was there (1874–1880), but he did grow close to one faculty member, and this proved to be very important. The faculty member was John Bates Clark (1847–1938), who had just completed his graduate studies in Germany, where he had studied economics with Wilhelm Roscher and Karl Knies of the historical school of economics.

After graduating from Carleton, Veblen taught at a local school for a year. He began graduate studies at Johns Hopkins in 1881 and rather quickly transferred to Yale where he completed a doctorate in philosophy in 1884. Veblen's mentor at Yale was Yale's president, the Reverend Noah Porter, and Veblen was also very close to William Graham Sumner. But Veblen was unable to find a faculty position on completion of his program of study, so he returned to Minnesota where he married former Carleton classmate Ellen Rolfe in 1888. They moved to one of her father's farms in Iowa, where they shared a life of hard work but also studious reflection about the state of America's farm economy. Beginning in the late 1880s, there was a serious drought in the upper plains states, lasting five years. Farm foreclosures reached record proportions in some areas. Within a short time Veblen enrolled in graduate school at Cornell University to study economics (1890–1892). Upon leaving Cornell in 1892, Veblen accepted an entry-level position as a teaching fellow in economics at the University of Chicago. He remained at the University of Chicago until 1906, producing his best-known work, *The Theory of the Leisure Class* (1899), editing the *Journal of Political Economy* for a time, and enjoying lively collegial exchange with some of the best minds of his time but never feeling fully appreciated.

Thorstein Veblen's *The Theory of the Leisure Class* introduces the observation that rich and near rich and merely prosperous, and even rather poor people in America, engage in conspicuous consumption as a way of elevating their status by flaunting things people equate with success or interpret as signs of accomplishment and worth. Conspicuous consumption is easiest to use as a strategy for acquiring social recognition in a country like the United States where there is a lot of geographic movement and people are very busy and are therefore apt to make quick judgments on the basis of visible signs. But status accrued through conspicuous consumption is not necessarily deserved. Veblen saw rich people in general and absentee owners in particular as social parasites who impede rather than foster the advancement of society. His evolutionary view of a society's development focused on technology that makes new things possible (a good thing), class structure that tries to fossilize old inequalities (a bad thing), and institutions that (no longer contemporary, having evolved in the past) can act as a brake inhibiting further progress unless they evolve with the times.

Veblen's *The Theory of the Leisure Class* was an instant success and attracted a cult following for its insightful social criticism. His later books were less successful, however. Veblen's *The Theory of Business Enterprise* (1904) is difficult to read and antagonized a lot of people because of its antibusiness stance. This put Veblen at the center of a firestorm at the University of Chicago. And when the firestorm was not about his critical analysis of the American economy it was about his social life, for Veblen was accused of having too much magnetic appeal for members of the opposite sex.

In 1906, Veblen went to Stanford University, but controversy regarding his social life followed him. His wife left him for good, and he moved to the University of Missouri in 1910. While at Missouri, Veblen produced *The Instinct of Workmanship* (1914), *Imperial Germany and the Industrial Revolution* (1917), and other works, extending ideas introduced in his first books. After America entered World War I in 1917, Veblen held advisory posts in the government, but he provided advice that would have been politically difficult for the administration to embrace. After the war, Veblen moved to New York City to edit *The Dial*, a politically charged, reformist-minded magazine. Veblen's editorship ended after one year. He was then invited to join the faculty of the New School for Social Research. At the New School, Veblen was renowned but somewhat marginal. In 1927, aging and losing energy, he returned to California where he led a rather impoverished existence until his death in 1929.

—Charles Powers

See also Consumer Culture; Industrial Society; Pareto, Vilfredo; Sumner, William Graham; Weber, Max

FURTHER READINGS AND REFERENCES

Coser, Lewis. 1977. *Masters of Sociological Thought.* 2d ed. New York: Harcourt Brace Jovanovich.

Veblen, Thorstein. 1954. *Absentee Ownership and Business Enterprise in Recent Times: The Case of America.* New York: Viking.

———. [1917] 1939. *Imperial Germany and the Industrial Revolution.* New York: Viking.

———. [1914] 1946. *The Instinct of Workmanship.* New York: Viking.

———. 1970. *The Portable Veblen,* edited by Max Lerner. New York: Viking.

———. [1904] 1912. *The Theory of Business Enterprise.* New York: Scribner's.

———. [1899] 1953. *The Theory of the Leisure Class: An Economic Study of Institutions.* New York: Viking.

VERSTEHEN

In contrast to explanation, the listing of the causal rules governing events, scientifically observable processes, or functional relationships, "understanding" addresses itself toward meaningful human behavior and the resultant meaningful objectified forms this behavior takes on within the fields of economy, politics, culture, and the arts. In comparison to the (philosophical) term *knowledge, understanding* is as a term more extensive, yet at the same time subject to greater limitations. It is more extensive in that it connotes a familiarity with the lifeworld, and everything belonging to this context. For this familiarity constitutes a precondition for the acquisition of knowledge through reason. The limitations of the term become apparent in relation to the interpretation of individual constructs of meaning: values, behavioral patterns, and motives. However, these very same constructs of meaning cannot be adequately interpreted either through identifying the laws of causality behind them or by recourse to "nomological" insights attained through pure reason. Only the interpretative reconstruction of the meaning behind the given behavior achieves this end. Although the additional knowledge gained through this interpretative understanding is in comparison to explanation on the basis of observation "bought at the price of the fundamentally more hypothetical and fragmentary character of the results won through interpretation," these gains attained through the process of understanding designate "exactly the specific nature of sociological knowledge" (Weber [1922] 1978:15, § 1).

CONSTRUCTION AND RECONSTRUCTION

Sociology, insofar as we mean it in Max Weber's sense of the term, has disclosed that the human processes of perception, recognition, understanding, and explanation establishes images and constructions of "reality," believe these constructions to be real, define them as reality, and orient themselves according to them. The transcendental-philosophical, Kantian development in the theory of perception carried on by Husserl; the social theories and protosociologies of Schütz, Berger, and Luckmann in this context; the anthropological expansion of the phenomenological point of view by Scheler, Plessner, and even Gehlen: all these have contributed to the systematic description and analysis of this phenomenon. A construct's attainment of meaningful intersubjectivity within a monadic community (Husserl), the subjects of the "social constructions of reality" with an egologic perspective (Berger and Luckmann 1966, 1970) the social constitution of the "structures of the life-world" (Schütz and Luckmann 1979, 1984), and the principally symbol boundedness of human perception and action (Peirce, Wittgenstein, Buehler) all serve here as examples.

Sociology as the science of reality aims to comprehend and explain all social constructions: the products of human activity, the forms of socialization and economy as well as the conceptions of the world, interpretive figures, and world outlooks. It presupposes that the symbol boundedness of human perception and action conceives of all social constructions in "symbolic forms" (Cassirer), that we move, interpreting, through a human preinterpreted and overinterpreted world, that we are trapped in our own symbols and fictions or constructions of reality, and that, in the orientation of our actions, we must grapple with the reality or, respectively, with the validity of these fictions and constructions.

It does not follow that the social sciences and humanities must once again fight the battles against realism, empiricism, and idealism fought by Carneades, Augustinus, Kant, and Husserl just because some natural scientists and cyberneticists—quite belatedly and with astounding coarseness—have uncovered (or discovered) what for them are new insights. The realization that subjects construct "their" reality according to their type-specific and individual abilities and that which is collectively held to be "real" is indeed a social construct, is of great consequence. However, this insight is not new. Thus, it should not lead to the repetition of old debates about our inability to perceive an outside world per se. Rather, the social sciences must address the various social constructions and offer comparative explanations for these sketches of reality as a result of their historical and social structural conditions. Sociology is primarily hindsighted prophecy—the reconstruction of social constructions and the conditions of constructions of reality. Thus, sociological prognoses are made up of the—often dubious—attempt to imagine one's self and others on the basis of scientific interpretations and reconstructions of past realities, possibilities, or probabilities of "new" social sketches of reality.

EVERYDAY AND SCIENTIFIC CONSTRUCTIONS

From a pragmatic perspective, the everyday actor must—however faulty the results may be—prognosticate. Otherwise, setting goals and planning actions would not be possible: Survival requires more of us than reaction. In contrast, before he or she dares to prognosticate, the social scientist must first deal with the description and analysis of the particular construction on which the actions and plans of members of society in everyday, pragmatic perspectives are based. These are the first order constructions—the everyday, sociohistorically anchored types, models, routines, plausibilities, forms of knowledge, resources of knowledge, and (often implicitly) conclusions.

In that the social scientist is occupied with it, the reconstruction does not double the constructs of everyday action. Indeed, in the processes of describing, understanding, and explaining the construction of "the everyday," a network of categorizations, ideal-typical suppositions, ex-post conclusions and causalities, or finalizations is established ("in order to" and "because motives"). In short, one designs second-order constructions. These are (demonstrable theoretically as well as in formal models) controlled, methodically examined and checkable, comprehensive reconstructions of the first-order constructions.

There is more than just a logical difference between first- and second-order constructions. When a reconstruction begins, the action to which it refers is already finished, past, and unrepeatable. Insofar as it is open to interpretation, it must be represented in certain data, and it "presents" itself in the data as a completed action. Since social scientists are interested in testable—that is, intersubjectively, rationally understandable—reconstructions, they can neither understand the action in the same way as the actor, nor can they project themselves into the souls and minds, thoughts and feelings of the actor. Instead, they develop "reconstructive-hermeneutic" models of possibilities for the processes of action as well as for the actor.

The data recording past events are, after all, *not* the "original" situations in which the action took place but their records. To the same small degree, the interpretations are *not* the repeated and "rationally explicit" original action in the reconstruction. Rather, they are models of objectively possible symbolic figures that are based on and refer only to the records of the action (indeed for the purpose of interpretation, all human products share the status of records of action). Thus, interpretations do not "contain" "the actor who truly existed" (or, respectively, the first-order constructions formed by partners in action in specific situations) anymore but, rather, models of the actors. These, in turn, are put in a situation that they did not choose themselves—in no small part due to the way a social scientist has posed the question with which he or she is concerned. "He [or she] has created these figures, these homunculi," in order to understand and explain their doings according to his or her own as well as general conceptions of comprehensible and rational action. In the case of all logical, "existential" differences between everyday perception, interpretation, action, and understanding on one hand and, on the other hand, the scientific reconstruction of the first-order constructions on which they rely and the conditions of their reconstruction, it can be determined that everyday and scientific constructions are based on the same framework (that of the human condition) and on a largely shared repertoire consisting of experiences, sociohistorically conveyable and learnable skills and methods. In other words, our everyday and our scientific actions and interpretations are each part of different "provinces of meaning" (Schütz) and each represents a different attitude, a different method of recognition with regard to ourselves and the world around us, but the scientific capacity to understand is to a great extent structured similarly to everyday life—from which science derives and the methods and criteria of which are borrowed more subconsciously and implicitly than consciously and in a controlled manner.

Despite all attempts to distinguish between the two, the results of scientific (which remain mostly inexplicit) and prescientific comprehensions demonstrate a series of similarities. Both meet in the formulation of explanations, and these explanations rest often enough on nothing other than standards of plausibility that seem to be closely tied to a supposed common sense. These certainties, in turn, are derived from unknown or no longer known routines of typifications and connections of standard experiences, from processes of "interpret however" and collective semantics that are no longer questioned. It is similar to or the same for the prescientific and the scientific explications of experiences that their explanations are typified and classified observations, enumerations, and relations of data that have always been rationally constructed. The social world is constructed understandably, and we move interpreting in a preinterpreted and overly interpreted world, a sociohistorical symbolic a priori.

With regard to their basic structure, scientific comprehension and explanation are probably analogous to everyday thought but have been more formalized and institutionalized. In contrast to past paradigms of interpretation and

comprehension, both methods of explanation—the scientific and everyday—are generally equally unreflective. Of course, social scientists in particular like to deal with the "ideologies" and "myths of the everyday," but seldom do they pursue the question of how much their own myths rely on exactly those of the everyday, how much they are derived from the latter, or—in case this compositional wrong tree has not been barked up—whether and to what degree they differ at all structurally or formally analytically from quasi-mythological thinking.

UNDERSTANDING AND EXPLAINING

A systematic examination of the structural conditions for the constitution of these myths is even more seldom undertaken in practical research: the genres and types of narration, symbolism, and components of construction; historical lines of argumentation and quotation ("discourses"); the process of the construction of perspective, expectation, and consensus. If, however, the subject is meant to be the description, an interpreted understanding and explanation of social orientation as well as social action and its products, then one cannot get around these fundamental analyses—unless, of course, one is content with these individual myths.

The analysis of human subjects, "groups," or societies' historical, "individual," or "collective" conception of self is not possible without the identification, description, and analysis of the "practices," "rules," "patterns." and "communicative types of presentation"—foregoing all the constructions of "contents," opinions, dogmas, and worldviews—that we employ when we orient, reassure, and acquaint ourselves—when we act, produce, and interpret. There can be no rational sociology of the content of knowledge and of action without a sociology of the forms that shape knowledge and action and without which both would be rendered unrecognizable as well as not sustainable. Often enough, "contents," opinions, and convictions are nothing more than decorations—colorful trim on the forms that practically lend action social sense and are content—"forms are the food of faith" (Gehlen 1988)

It may be fascinating to be devoted to ideas, assertions, and convictions; to read and "reread anew" certain authors and books; to introduce, for example, to the Marxist method of reading from yesterday something new from today. As long as a historical-reconstructive analysis of the structures of the text and argumentation and the symbolic networks and discursive references of Marxist texts are partially tackled and, in Bultmann's sense of the word, *de-mythologized*, while at the same time this same method is not applied to the description of the patterns of reception, of the series of quotes and recitations rampant in them, there is nothing to expect of the "new" literature other than a continuation of the never-ending story of old approaches. Something totally different would be a literature on the horizon of sociology, a sociology that has as a necessary component a developed and systematically proceeding sociology of comprehension.

The scientific "comprehension of something" necessarily requires the description and explication of the implicit procedures and perspectives of comprehension—the comprehension of comprehension itself. In the same way, speaking of sociology as a "science of experience" only then makes sense, when it is not simply understood as a collection of and an analytical historicizing renarration of experiences, but as a science of the social constitution, recording, and transmission of experiences as well.

Inasmuch as one understands sociology in a "social scientific hermeneutical," a basic theoretical, "protosociological" (Luckmann) as well as a practical research sense, it will appear—theoretically necessarily—as the sociology of knowledge. This means no more and no less than the science of the reconstruction of the social constitution of experiences and the social construction of reality. Only as a "comprehensive," hermeneutic-reconstructive science of the social can sociology fulfill its role as the science of reality *and* experiences.

Pulling together the thoughts of Max Weber and Alfred Schütz, one can help bring to an end a widespread prejudice, which, simplifying Schleiermacher, states that social scientific comprehension concerns itself inductively and more or less empathically with the specific, while explanations according to preset principles subsume the specific to a general. Beyond this, "comprehension" is more a process of humanities, "explanation" more a natural science-oriented method. One does not encounter this prejudice in just the shrinking, dedicated community of colleagues who work with theoretical models, pure quantification, or both. Rather, this is also seen in various conventicles in the colorful camp of "qualitative social research"—by those who use expressions such as "hermeneutics" and "comprehension" as war cries against explanative = mathematicalizing, overmeasuring, and soulless—in short, Cartesian sociology.

Max Weber's ([1922]1978) famous definition of "interpretive" sociology, in the first sentence of the first section of *Economy and Society,* has either been forgotten or was never taken particularly seriously. "Sociology . . . is a science concerning itself with the interpretive understanding of a social action and thereby with a causal explanation of its course and consequence" (p. 4, § 1). The methodological consequences of this definition can be sketched onto four steps: observe, describe, understand, explain.

Scientific "observation," which assumes a limited inquiry and a preliminary establishment of what the case should be, is to be understood here as controlled investigation and production of data. At the same time, the observer's perception as such cannot at all be controlled, or at best, only to a certain degree. Attention, then, must be directed all the more closely to those processes in which, in connection with—nonlingual—perception, linguistically set data are derived from impressions. The social scientist in this case becomes a scribe. Actions are translated into language, speaking into writing. The written text lends a new and different structure—that of text—to the structure of action, conversation, or both. The structure of text has its own rules of organization and procedure. Its chronological and procedural structures have hardly anything in common with those of nonlingual action and its perception. In this way, the immediate, reciprocal relationship in which interaction partners perceive and react to each other, for example, is turned into a dramatic text broken up into sequences and made up of director's comments and dialogue. The perception of the simultaneous becomes a sequence of text.

Controlling the difference between observation and transcripts of observation is as much a part of controlling the description as it is a reflection on the fabrication and "artificiality" of the data. Limiting what the case should be provides benefits not only for the selection of what the description will entail but also often for the style of presentation. Aside from implicit and explicit contextual judgments, just through its formal arrangement (or its belonging to a specific genre: from an ostensibly neutral explanatory text to the report oriented closely on the field to the narration enhanced by literature), it contains its own explanatory rules for subsequent interpretations. Whatever may be the result of the control, it leads principally to the insight that the scientific interpretation of data is a secondhand interpretation of life.

Scientific understanding (the controlled putting forth of data to which of course all products and documents of human activity count as or can be made into natural data) can only then begin systematically and methodically reflectively if the data are provided discursively. They must be recorded in some way. It must be possible for interpreters to examine them, interpret them, and turn them around again and again. In short, the "fleeting," as it is not fixed, attention of everyday interaction can, by way of the establishment and continuous recallability of the data, be made permanent. Then even "the most unremitting attention," as Dilthey ([1900]1962) knew,

> can become a skillful method, in which a controllable degree of objectivity is reached, only if the expression of life is fixed and we are able to return to it again and again. We call such skillful comprehension of constantly fixed expressions of life exegesis or interpretation." (p. 318)

Beyond this, it becomes apparent that both scientifically "constructed" and "natural" data are actually constructions. Both are given (back) the status of first-order constructions if one inquires beyond their specific contexts, integrates them into a more general horizon of understanding, and thereby indicates their objectively possible, general potential for meaning—that is, if the case-specific significance of action is made evident in contrast to a general horizon of significance. Such an interpretation aims for a reconstruction of a social first-order construction, oriented along the lines of the case structure of the documented action. It is case specifically laid out, elaborating for the case, "interpretive understanding" of social action in Weber's sense of the term.

The path from the interpretive understanding to the "causal" explanation of the procedure and the effects of social action passes through the construction of a *theoretically pure type* of subjective meaning attributed to the hypothetical actor or actors in a given type of action: a second-order construction. Only in the realm of the ideal-typical constructions of rational action can it be decided how an actor "would act in a scenario of ideal rational action" and would have acted. Only with the help of these ideal-typical constructions, which better serve their purpose terminologically, classificationally, and heuristically the more "abstract and unrealistic" they are, can comparisons with the documented actors be made. Only then is it possible "to explain causally" the gap between action in ideal-typical rational action on one hand and documented action on the other so that the elements of the case being examined that were mixed in with the "pure rational action" can be identified.

The specific individual case is thus exclusively causally explained with regard t*o its distance from and difference to the terminologically "pure" ideal type of rational action.* The individual case cannot be understood by the causal explanation of the difference—the opposite is true. By way of the interpretive understanding of social action, the constructions of ideal types can be found, which in turn cast light on the individual case and help it get its just deserve. In that they explain the case's difference to the ideal type, they aid in the understanding of a case in its singularity and concretion.

In this sense, sociology is the progressive interpretive understanding of social action that takes seriously the individual case and thereby people, their orders, and their history. The scientific second-order constructions, the historic-genetic ideal types, aim exactly and equally for this historical understanding of the individual case and the understanding of history.

Social scientific, historic reconstructive hermeneutics is thus much more than a methodology and the repertoire of procedures that spring from it. It is a specific historic self-reflexive style of perception with the background supposition that there is no conclusive, ahistorical, ensurable knowledge, no social theory of a final solution. And this style of perception succeeds in naming good reasons for its background supposition.

— Hans-Georg Soeffner

See also Dilthey, Wilhelm; Historicism; Ideal Type; Phenomenology; Schütz, Alfred; Simmel, Georg; Weber, Max

FURTHER READINGS AND REFERENCES

Berger, P. L. and T. Luckmann. 1966. *The Social Construction of Reality: A Treatise in the Sociology of Knowledge.* Garden City, NY: Doubleday.

Dilthey, Wilhelm. [1900] 1962. "Die Entstehung der Hermeneutik" [The Emergence of Hermeneutics]. In *Gesammelte Schriften* [Collected Writings], edited by W. Dilthey. [Leipzig/Berlin 1914–1936, fortgeführt.] Stuttgart, Germany: Göttingen.

Gehlen, A. 1988. *Man, His Nature and Place in the World.* New York: Columbia University Press.

Giddens, Anthony. 1976. *New Rules of Sociological Method.* Cambridge, UK: Polity.

Outhwaite, William. 1975. *Understanding Social Life: The Method Called Verstehen.* New York: Holmes & Meier.

Schütz, A. and T. Luckmann. 1974. *The Structures of the Life-World.* Vol. 1. London: Heinemann.

———. 1989. *The Structures of the Life-World.* Vol. 2. Evanston, IL: Northwestern University Press.

———. 1975. *Strukturen der Lebenswelt* [Structures of the Life-World]. Bd. 1. Neuwied, Germany: Luchterhand.

———. 1984. *Strukturen der Lebenswelt* [Structures of the Life-World]. Bd. 2. Frankfurt am Main, Germany: Suhrkamp.

Weber, Max. 1976. *Wirtschaft und Gesellschaft: Grundriss der verstehenden Soziologie* [Economy and Society: An Outline of Interpretive Sociology]. 5th ed. Tübingen, Germany: Mohr.

Wright, G. H. 1971. *Explanation and Understanding.* Ithaca, NY: Cornell University Press.

VIDEO AND COMPUTER GAMES

An ever-expanding category, the term, *computer games*, may refer to almost any recreational activity that can be performed using digital technologies and may include games played on self-contained machines within an arcade space, games played on self-contained platforms (Nintendo, Sega, X-Box, Sony PlayStation) attached to the television set, games played on the personal computer, games played online, and games played using portable handheld technologies. An inherently imprecise category, the term collapses distinctions historically drawn between games, sports, toys, play, stories, and role-playing.

The first games were played on computers within the programming community starting in the early 1960s, but they did not reach the commercial marketplace until 1971 with the introduction of the first arcade technologies and in 1972 with the release of the first home computer game consoles. From this modest start, and following some commercial setbacks in the 1980s, computer games have expanded into one of the most profitable sectors of the American entertainment industry and a significant force for technological and aesthetic innovation.

The medium had an enormous impact on the generation of American youth that has come of age since the early 1980s. Some studies have found that as many as 92 percent of Americans between the ages of 2 and 17 have played games, with adolescent males typically the heaviest game players. Some evidence suggests that boys' earlier and more frequent interactions with computer games makes them more self-confident in their relationships with new media technologies and thus contributes to a gender gap in computer access and use. Periodically, the games industry has made efforts to broaden its offerings to attract female consumers with mixed results. The number of girls playing computer games has dramatically increased over the past decade but still lags behind boys in almost every classification; the notable exception would be Web-based games where women slightly outnumber men.

Games technologies emerged at a moment when American youth had diminished access to real-world play space, and the technology seemed to respond to the need to provide entertainment and recreation to a generation of latchkey children who spent much of their out-of-school hours at home. In many ways, the traditional values and activities associated with boys' backyard play culture were mapped onto digital space, with the computer offering more opportunities for exploratory play than these youths would have experienced otherwise. Paralleling traits that E. Anthony Rotundo identified in boys' culture historically, players saw digital space as a realm of autonomy from adult supervision, sought recognition from their peers on the basis of daring and risk-taking, used games as a means of demonstrating self-control and mastery and as a means of social bonding through competition, and relied on digital environments to enact adult roles. With the emergence of multiplayer online games, opportunities for team-based competition expanded, with advocates claiming that participating in "brigades' might offer teens some of the same opportunities for building self-confidence and developing leadership and collaboration skills as traditional team sports. Other games-related activities, such as amateur-level design and game modification might be read as the contemporary equivalent of building crystal radios, constructing balsa wood models, or working with erector sets, hobbies that helped boys develop technical skills and insights.

Game arcades inherited a space in American teen culture previously occupied by pool halls or pinball parlors and also inherited adult concerns that these gathering places encouraged truancy and gang-related activities. As games moved into the home, the concern shifted from the idea that games drew kids together outside of school toward the idea that games were socially isolating and addictive, distracting kids from schoolwork or social interaction. Games also embraced and built on a tradition of blood and thunder imagery that had run through boys' books since the nineteenth century and remained a persistent concern of adult reformers; with each improvement in computer technology, games perfected the ability to represent graphic violence through game play and thus provoked anxieties about whether media violence contributed to real-world aggression.

Over several decades of debate, two strands of thinking about youth access to game technologies has emerged: (a) one seeing games as a normative part of childhood culture and largely continuing traditional forms of boys' play into digital realms and (b) the other seeing games as disruptive technologies with a largely negative impact on child development. A series of school shootings in the late 1990s, including those in Paducah, Kentucky, and Littleton, Colorado, intensified this debate. The marketing of media violence to youths became the focus of a series of congressional hearings and governmental investigations; court cases were filed in several jurisdictions by parents whose children had been killed in school shootings seeking claims against specific game companies whose products had been found in the shooters' possession; state and local ordinances sought to regulate youth access to violent or sexually explicit video games drawing parallels to the regulation of youth access to cigarettes, alcohol, or pornography.

David Grossman (1999), a military psychologist, has emerged as the most visible reformer, echoing many of the same concerns raised by previous generations of media reformers, such as Frederick Wertham's charges that comic books contributed to an alleged increased in juvenile crime in the 1950s: "If we had a clear-cut objective of raising a generation of assassins and killers who are unrestrained by either authority or the nature of the victim, it is difficult to imagine how we could do a better job. The inflicting of pain and suffering has become a source of entertainment and vicarious pleasure rather than revulsion. We are learning to kill, and we are learning to like it." Citing the use of games in military training, Grossman argued that games were murder simulators that would desensitize their users to the consequences of real-world violence and thus psychologically prepare them to pull the trigger. Grossman's criticisms of video game violence have attracted support from other reform groups, most notably The Lion and the Lamb Project and the National Institute on Media and the Family. They are also embraced by a range of political leaders, including Senator Joseph Lieberman (D-CT.) and conservative think tank leader William Bennett.

Others, such as journalist Jon Katz (2001), challenges such arguments, noting that despite the pervasiveness of games in contemporary youth culture, federal crime statistics indicate that youth violence was at a 20-year low. They charged that the moral panic about youth access to video games was inspiring adult authorities to punish young gamers, citing the use of recreational habits as a criteria in many school districts for determining whether teens needed to receive therapy, or the suspension or expulsion of students for ideas expressed in classroom discussions or in assigned papers dealing with the controversy. Some writers, notably Gerard Jones (2002), go further, making an affirmative case that aggressive fantasies play important developmental roles for children, helping them to work through their aggression and antisocial impulses and granting them a space of fantasy empowerment at a time in their lives when they feel limited control over their physical surroundings.

Mirroring larger debates in the social sciences, these disagreements often center on competing research methodologies: The reformers most often rely on quantitative evidence, mostly derived from the media effects tradition, whereas critics of the reform movement rely primarily on qualitative findings, mostly from ethnographic research, with a few researchers also examining broad sociological trends or correlational research. Some powerful organizations, such as American Psychological Association and American Academy of Pediatrics, issued reports claiming conclusive links between media and real-world violence, whereas other equally influential bodies, including the U.S. Surgeon General and the Australian National Censorship Board, concluded that the case had not yet been satisfactorily made. A group of scholars, representing a diverse range of academic disciplines and affiliated with the Free Expression Network, filed a succession of amicus briefs in court cases testing the regulation of violent game content, arguing that the media effects research significantly distorted the cultural phenomenon it sought to document, reducing game play to simple variables that could be tested in a laboratory.

Much of the controversy centered on titles, such as *Quake, Doom,* and *Grand Theft Auto 3,* which the industry itself rates as inappropriate for teens. These titles emerged as the industry sought more mature content to reflect its market demographics, which showed that 66 percent of all PC gamers and 54 percent of all platform gamers were over 18. The generation that grew up with Nintendo in the 1980s was continuing to play games but now demanded new content. Many parents still perceive games as predominantly a children's entertainment and often fail to distinguish adult from youth-oriented content. The Federal Trade Commission charged the games industry with actively marketing the more violent game titles to underage consumers, although the same study found that 85 percent of game purchases for youth consumers were made either by parents or by parents and children together, suggesting that adults were important mediators between the games industry and their younger consumers. Reform groups called for tighter enforcement of ratings at the point of sale, while the industry argued for greater efforts to educate parents about game content.

Adult uncertainty about the place of games in American youth culture reflects a significant generational gap in access and comfort with digital technologies. As with earlier communications technologies, youth are often early adopters and display greater competence with the emerging media than do their parents. One can also position the controversy within the context of a long-standing debate about whether theatricality and role-playing constitutes forms of deception that are apt to lead participants to confusion about the line between fantasy and reality, as well as a much more recent debate about the place of play in adult life, which reflects the expansion of consumer and leisure culture in the twentieth century. Finally, by the early twenty-first century, the number of people under the age of 18 in the United States equaled the number of people in the so-called baby boom generation, placing generational issues front and center on the American political agenda.

In the midst of these controversies, educational technologists began to make the case that games could become a powerful force in American education. For some, such as Marc Prensky (2000), the argument rests on the need to develop new modes of teaching for the so-called "twitch generation," whose learning style was shaped by their early and consistent access to digital technologies. Others, such as MIT's Education Arcade project, make the case that games can enable powerful simulations inside and outside the classroom, enable and support peer-to-peer learning, become important motivators of learning, and encourage exploratory play and intuitive experience of complex content. Mark Lepper's educational psychology research group at Stanford examined games as an extraordinary example of intrinsically motivated play and developed principles of designing engaging instructional materials based on studies of video game players. Other groups, such as the OnRamp project in South Central Los Angeles, worked with teams of kids to plan and develop Web-based games, seeing the design process as itself educationally beneficial.

— Henry Jenkins

See also Consumer Culture; Internet and Cyberculture; Sport

FURTHER READINGS AND REFERENCES

Cassell, Justine and Henry Jenkins, eds. 1998. *From Barbie to Mortal Kombat: Gender and Computer Games.* Cambridge, MA: MIT Press.

Grossman, David. 1999. *Stop Teaching Our Kids to Kill: A Call to Action Against TV, Movie and Video Game Violence.* New York: Random House.

Jones, Gerard. 2002. *Killing Monsters: Why Children Need Fantasy, Superheros, and Make-Believe Violence.* New York: Basic.

Katz, Jon. 2001. *Geeks.* New York: Broadway.

Poole, Steven. 2000. *Trigger Happy: Video Games and the Entertainment Revolution.* New York: Arcade.

Prensky, Marc. 2000. *Digital Game-Based Learning.* New York: McGraw-Hill.

VIRILIO, PAUL

Paul Virilio (b. 1932), the French self-styled "urbanist" and "critic of the art of technology," was, until his retirement in 1998, professor of architecture at the École Spéciale d'Architecture in Paris. Virilio's importance for understanding contemporary culture arises from his constant engagement with many of the most significant theoretical questions within the field of cultural studies. In his writings Virilio has made a vital and wide-ranging contribution to the understanding of the cultural features of modern architecture as well as offering critical studies of urban planning, speed, and war, including several volumes of critique on cinema, technology, political organizations, social hierarchies, and aesthetic practices. Encompassing "military space" and "dromology" (the study of the compulsive logic of speed), Virilio's "war model" is a highly stylized methodological line of attack on postmodern culture that spurns the analysis of such concepts and realities as mere objects for cultural or theoretical reflection. By way of his conception of the "aesthetics of disappearance" (art founded on retinal and materially persistent reality), Virilio has also idiosyncratically reinterpreted the cultural history of modernism, inclusive of the writings of artistic revolutionaries, philosophical leaders, and technoscientific thinkers such as Filippo Tommaso Marinetti, Maurice Merleau-Ponty, and Albert Einstein.

Accordingly, in *Bunker Archeology* (1994), Virilio focused his attention on the military space of the Atlantic Wall—the 15,000 Nazi bunkers constructed during World War II along the French coastline to prevent an Allied landing. Virilio and the French architect Claude Parent's *The Function of the Oblique* (1996), by contrast, argues for the establishment of an urban system founded on the theory of the "oblique function." Introducing sloping planes and corporeal dislocation, the theory nonetheless culminated in the concrete edifice of the bunkerlike Church of Sainte-Bernadette du Banlay at Nevers. Likewise, Virilio's *The Lost Dimension* (1991) is not literally involved with the inner city and structural design. Rather, it is concerned with urbanism and architecture as the military spaces of the "overexposed city" that is permeated by "morphological irruption," "improbable architecture," and critically, those new political "speed-spaces" of information, communications, and vision technologies such as the Internet.

Virilio's conception of speed-space may persuade readers to contemplate merely the overexposed city. But adhering to the terminology created in his *Speed & Politics* (1986), the genuine difficulties of the development of "dromocratic" culture and society emerge from its unending "state of emergency." Dromology has nothing to do with urban peace and, as in the military space of war, everything to do with the increasingly technologically induced death of distance that has become a planned certainty effecting immense sociocultural consequences, while it also ties in with the annihilation of space during wartime. Virilio's "dromological" war model therefore tracks the metropolitan, architectural, and technopolitical vectors of the military machine. Hence, the "logistics of perception," maintains Virilio in his *War and Cinema* (1989), elucidate a future in which the technological functioning of contemporary civilian vision machines (e.g., surveillance cameras) and war machines progress simultaneously. Harmonizing the tasks of the human eye and the technology of weaponry, the military field of perception turns into a machine that produces a telescopic regime that lies far beyond the capacities of human sight. In *Popular Defense & Ecological Struggles* (1990), by comparison, Virilio reflects on "pure power," the enforcement of surrender without engagement, and "revolutionary resistance" to war. In so doing, he refuses to comprehend, for instance, the present-day Palestinian struggle as simply "popular defense," insisting that it is also a "popular assault" against its own geopolitical disappearance.

While modernism rather than postmodernism is the focus of Virilio's *The Aesthetics of Disappearance* (1991), artistic, philosophical, and technoscientific ideas have increasingly assumed greater intricacy in his *The Vision Machine* (1994), *The Art of the Motor* (1995), *Open Sky* (1997), and *Polar Inertia* (1999). Specifically, Virilio's conception of the aesthetics of disappearance permits vision and other technologies to be observed from his stance as a critic of the art of technology. Effectively, Virilio questions the aesthetics of disappearance and particularly the extraordinary bias it retains for contemporary cinematic or televisual and videographic disappearance over ancient appearance-based art such as Greek marble sculptures. It is a further affirmation of the creative cultural power of Virilio's texts that the current crises in contemporary "motorized" and other cybernetic forms of art converge on their "disappearance" into the Internet and the elimination of the difference between here and now.

Critical assessments of Virilio's writings have to entail an acknowledgment that they presently contemplate a space ruled by speed or what he labels *A Landscape of Events* (2000), as against what the American postmodern cultural theorist Fredric Jameson (1991:16) calls the contemporary domination of categories of speed by space. Yet in *The Information Bomb* (2000), Virilio frequently appears ensnared in binary logic. Certainly, Virilio gives the impression of being unacquainted with "deconstructive" debates over the critique of binary oppositions (e.g., "civilianization" over "militarization") that structure his cultural theory. Virilio's work might then profit from an engagement with the French poststructuralist Jacques Derrida's concept of "différance" where the meaning of binary terms is constantly reconstructed. Finally, it is important to appraise Virilio's texts on the Gulf and Kosovo wars in *Desert*

Screen (2002) and *Strategy of Deception* (2000) because it is only lately that other cultural critics have acknowledged his exceptional contribution to the understanding of war at the speed of light. Visualizing the wars of the future, in these works Virilio pinpoints the move from territorial or industrial warfare to extraterritorial or postindustrial information warfare conducted in "real time." Arguing that we currently exist in a duplicitous realm of global terror and surveillance, spatial and temporal disintegration, he depicts an uncaring world in which the strategic deliberations and politics of state- and military-controlled new information and especially mass media technologies prohibit any ethical or diplomatic debates. It is appropriate, then, that Virilio's most recent book, on the attack and repercussions of the terrorist assault on and ruin of the World Trade Center in New York City on September 11 2001, *Ground Zero* (2002), is currently being fervently examined by an increasing number of cultural theorists.

— John Armitage

See also Baudrillard, Jean; Derrida, Jacques; Deleuze, Gilles; Jameson, Frederic; Simulation

FURTHER READINGS AND REFERENCES

Armitage, John. ed. 2000. *Paul Virilio: From Modernism to Hypermodernism and Beyond.* London: Sage.
———. 2001. *Virilio Live: Selected Interviews.* London: Sage.
Der Derian, James, ed. 1998. *The Virilio Reader.* Oxford, UK: Blackwell.
Jameson, Fredric. 1991. *Postmodernism, or, The Cultural Logic of Late Capitalism.* Durham, NC: Duke University Press.
Virilio, Paul. 1986. *Speed & Politics: An Essay on Dromology.* New York: Semiotext(e).
———. 1991. *The Lost Dimension.* New York: Semiotext(e).
———. 2000. *The Information Bomb.* London: Verso.

VOCABULARIES OF MOTIVES

Efforts to explain human behavior simply cannot avoid questions of motives. To ask "why" human beings do what they do necessarily involves inquiry into the forces, social factors, energies, drives, or mechanisms that push along human acts. Social science and lay theorists alike must ascertain the motives that lie behind or channel their own and others' past, present, and likely future behaviors. However, social science theories differ in the way they conceptualize motives and understand them to operate in human affairs. The notion of "vocabularies of motives," most primarily credited to Charles Wright Mills, offers a thoroughly sociological version of the nature and operation of motives by understanding them as arising socially—from a person's

social circles—rather than as forces or drives innately a part of human nature or somehow rooted in biology.

Although Mills's (1940) now famous paper titled "Situated Actions and Vocabularies of Motive" is recognized as the single most powerful articulation of the idea, his thinking on motives is part of a longer intellectual lineage. In particular, the idea that we best conceive motives as visible only when people must explain socially questionable actions appears in the multiple and complex works of Kenneth Burke (1936, 1945, 1950), a theorist and literary critic who sought to understand the linkages among language, power, cultural discourses, and symbolic actions. Building on Burke's observation that motives are the linguistic names given to acts, Mills reads motives as located in the immediate acting situation of an individual rather than within the person (or as part of their psychic structure, as Freudian psychoanalytic theory would have it). In their well-known book *Character and Social Structure,* published after his initial analysis, Mills and Hans Gerth (Gerth and Mills 1953) draw inspiration from Max Weber who defined motive as "a complex of meaning, which appears to the actor himself, or to the observer to be an adequate ground for his actions" (p. 116). Motives, in short, are intrinsically social since they are learned and are tied intimately to the expectations of others in the immediate contexts of our behaviors. Motives are "conceived as acceptable grounds for social action" (p. 117).

Essential to Mills's theorizing is the observation that different contexts are often circumscribed by quite different ideologies, thus requiring different explanations for conduct. Just as symbolic interaction theorists advocate the idea of "multiple realities," there are multiple vocabularies of motives that both channel behaviors and are available to justify one's acts. Vocabularies of motives vary from one social circle to another, vary in different institutions and organizations, and like all symbolic systems, are subject to change. Acceptable explanations for behavior will, for example, differ in military, business, religious, and educational institutions. Moreover, vocabularies of motives are lodged within the larger frame of history. Justifications for behaviors that might make sense in one situation or point in time may well be viewed as illegitimate in other times and settings.

Different historical periods are guided by what Carl Becker (in his 1952 book *Modern History*) has called different "climates of opinion" that shape consciousness and behaviors. The United States, for example, has witnessed the rise, over the last half century, of a therapeutic culture. Americans are now prone to think of deviant, often morally reprehensible behaviors, as propelled by flawed selves that can and ought to be repaired via therapy. A "recovery" vocabulary is reflected in institutions such as television talk shows and self-help programs. There is a linear connection between pervasive cultural discourses, the emergence of particular institutions bounded by these explanatory schemas, and ultimately, the ways individuals account for their everyday acts.

Motive talk is, in fact, a central feature of everyday experience. It provides one of the organizing techniques of social interaction, determining how acts are interpreted, including the moral evaluations attached to them. To explain our motives when actions are seen as deviant or identity damaging, we use linguistic devices called "accounts." In an extension of the vocabulary of motives idea, Stanford Lyman and Marvin Scott (1968) define an account as a verbal statement made to explain "unanticipated or untoward behavior."

Accounts, Lyman and Scott argue, can take the form of excuses or justifications for questionable behaviors in a given situation. Excuses (for example, "We had a flat tire and couldn't get home on time") appeal potential charges of deviance by citing events beyond a person's control. Justifications, alternatively, are used to neutralize possible negative definitions of acts by providing nondeviant interpretations of them (for example, "It's true we harassed them but, after all, they were being unpatriotic"). Motive talk may also take the form of "disclaimers" (Hewitt and Stokes 1975), which are verbal strategies used *in advance* to counter negative evaluations that could result from intended conduct (for example, "This may seem strange to you, but . . ."; "Don't get me wrong, but . . ."). Because different settings are defined by different vocabularies of motives, explanations of conduct acceptable in one setting may not work elsewhere. In this regard, people who routinely offer culturally unacceptable motives for their behaviors may be labeled mentally ill.

The vocabulary of motives idea has been greatly influential because it so clearly links motives to social life rather than to mysterious and invisible forces within persons. While Mills's treatment leaves unresolved questions about a person's "true" motives, it nevertheless seems clear that any view of motives discounting social expectations is incomplete. In this regard, Mills's thinking has been powerfully influential in framing social science understandings of behaviors such as rape or domestic violence that are often seen as instances of psychopathology only. The vocabularies-of-motives notion does not require that we accept, applaud, or agree with others' explanations for their behaviors. It does require, however, that social science theories of behavior move beyond reductionist biological or psychological explanations to consider how available social vocabularies generate, sustain, and justify the extraordinary range of what human beings think, feel, and do.

— David A. Karp

See also Blumer, Herbert; Cooley, Charles Horton; Impression Management; Mills, C. Wright; Social Interaction

FURTHER READINGS AND REFERENCES

Burke, Kenneth. 1936. *Permanence and Change: An Anatomy of Purpose.* Berkeley: University of California Press.

———. 1945. *A Grammar of Motives.* Berkeley: University of California Press.

———. 1950. *A Rhetoric of Motives.* Berkeley: University of California Press.

Gerth, H. and C. Wright Mills. 1953. *Character and Social Structure: The Psychology of Social Institutions.* New York: Harcourt, Brace.

Hewitt, J. and R. Stokes. 1975. "Disclaimers." *American Sociological Review* 40:1–11.

Lyman, S. and M. Scott. 1968. "Accounts." *American Sociological Review* 33:46–62.

Mills, C. W. 1940. "Situated Actions and Vocabularies of Motive." *American Sociological Review* 5:904–13.

WALLERSTEIN, IMMANUEL

Immanuel Wallerstein (b. 1930) is certainly among the most influential social theorists of his generation despite his explicit denials of the possibility of general theory in social science. Wallerstein's conceptual approach to world history, what he has called the "world-systems perspective," has had a wide and deep impact in both the social sciences and the humanities wherever scholars and organic intellectuals have tried to penetrate what Giovanni Arrighi has called "the fog of globalization." He is the cofounder, with Terence Hopkins, of the Fernand Braudel Center at Binghamton University and is now a senior research scholar at Yale. Wallerstein is past president of the International Sociological Association and has published more than 30 books and over 200 articles and book chapters.

With Samir Amin, Andre Gunder Frank, and Giovanni Arrighi, Wallerstein discovered, or rediscovered, the modern system of societies as it arose with European hegemony. Born in 1930, Wallerstein grew up in the pungent broth of the New York Left. The *Monthly Review* scholars were putting together the third worldist rendering of Marxism, and Wallerstein took up the political sociology of African nationalism and pan-Africanism. Dependency theory emerged from the effort of Latin American social scientists and activists to confront sociological modernization theory (Talcott Parsons and his minions) with the realities of 500 years of European colonialism and U.S. neocolonialism. Wallerstein saw the relevance of this approach to the history of Africa, and when he read Fernand Braudel's *The Mediterranean* and Marian Malowist's studies of sixteenth-century Poland, he realized that core-periphery relations have been fundamental to the rise of capitalism in Europe for centuries. Thus, did Wallerstein discover the core-periphery hierarchy as a crucial dimension for understanding the last 500 years of world history.

Wallerstein's metatheoretical stance is signified by his use of the term *historical system*, which is meant to radically collapse the separation in the disciplinary structure of the modern academy between social science and history—the contrast between nomothetic ahistoricism and idiographic historicism. His narrative of the history of the modern world-system tells the story of a hierarchical intersocietal system in which class relations, state formation, nation building, race relations, geopolitics, capitalist competition, and core-periphery domination and resistance have constituted the main outlines of social change.

Wallerstein formulated the modern core-periphery hierarchy as an asymmetrical division of labor between producers of highly profitable core commodities and producers of much less profitable peripheral goods. He also asserted the systemic importance of an intermediate zone, the semiperiphery. This tripartite spatial division of labor, reproduced over the centuries despite some upward and downward mobility, is the most important of the conceptual schemas that Wallerstein's historical-structural analysis of world history has produced.

Wallerstein's big point is that it is impossible to truly understand and explain the development of modern capitalism without attention to the core-periphery hierarchy. The ability of core capitalists and their states to exploit peripheral resources and labor has been a major factor in the competition among core contenders, and the resistance to exploitation and domination mounted by peripheral peoples has also played a powerful role in world history.

There have been two major critiques of Wallerstein's work. Some Marxists have alleged that Wallerstein pays too little attention to class relations as the key to capitalist development. His claim that peripheral class relations—serfdom and slavery—have played a fundamental role in shaping the modern world-system is alleged to water down Marx's insistence on wage labor as the sine qua non of modern capitalism. And Wallerstein has been lumped with other "Smithian

Marxists" (such as Paul Sweezy) because his emphasis on the centrality of core-periphery relations is argued to privilege the importance of exchange relations (trade) over production relations (the appropriation of surplus value by capitalist exploitation of wage labor). These oft-repeated critiques have allowed many Marxists to continue to indulge in an analysis of societal class relations as if national societies were separate and autonomous entities, at least until the allegedly recent emergence of globalization.

The second main critique has come from those who contend that Wallerstein has privileged economic factors over and above politics and states. Some political sociologists have argued that Wallerstein's focus on the core-periphery division of labor glosses over important differences between the institutional structures of particular state apparatuses and struggles over policy changes that have occurred in the realm of politics. Curiously, both the point-of-production Marxists and the "bringing the state back in" political sociologists seem to have missed the specifics of Wallerstein's narrative account of the historical development of the modern world-system. He repeatedly tells how differences in regional or national class structures led to significant outcomes such as Portugal's leading role in fifteenth-century European expansion or the rise of the Dutch and British hegemonies. Wallerstein's insistence on the study of the whole world system and his resonant avowal of the relevance of historical and comparative knowledge scare those scholars whose specialized expertise is spatially or temporally narrow.

Despite all the breathless claims about globalization having changed everything since 1960, Wallerstein contends that globalization is as much a cycle as a trend and that the wave of global integration that has swept the world in the last decades is best understood by studying its similarities and differences with the wave of international trade and foreign investment in the last half of the nineteenth century. Wallerstein insists that U.S. economic hegemony is continuing to decline, and he sees the current U.S. unilateralism as a repetition of the mistakes of earlier declining hegemons who attempted to substitute military superiority for economic comparative advantage. Once the world system cycles and trends, and the game of musical chairs that is capitalist uneven development are taken into account, Wallerstein sees far more continuities than radical transformations. The title of one of his essays is "What Globalization?"

Wallerstein's stellar performance as brilliant historical sociologist and brave public intellectual demonstrates that social theory is not merely a pastime for academics. It still has voice on the stage of world politics.

— Christopher Chase-Dunn

See also *Annales* School; Capitalism; Globalization; Historical and Comparative Theory; Imperialism; Marxism; World-Systems Theory

FURTHER READINGS AND REFERENCES

Goldfrank, Walter L. 2000. "Paradigm Regained? The Rules of Wallerstein's World-System Method." In *Festschrift for Immanuel Wallerstein*, edited by Giovanni Arrighi and Walter L. Goldfrank. *Journal of World-Systems Research* 6(2):150–95. Retrieved March 20, 2004 (http://jwsr.ucr.edu/ archive/vol6/ number2/index.shtml).

Wallerstein, Immanuel. 2000. *The Essential Wallerstein*. New York: New Press.

WEBER, MARIANNE

Marianne Schnitger Weber (1870–1954) is best known for her marriage to sociologist Max Weber and her efforts to ensure his scholarly legacy by editing 10 volumes of his writings and penning his biography, published in 1926. In Germany during the latter part of the nineteenth and early twentieth centuries, Weber was recognized as a feminist intellectual who wrote and spoke widely on women's issues. Her feminist theoretical writings provided a counterpoise to sociological theories by contemporaneous male academicians, which brought to sociological discourse a focus on women's roles in society. Weber rejected the assumption that sociological theory written from a male standpoint is applicable to all social actors.

In 1896, Weber was one of the first generation of women to study at the University of Heidelberg. Here, she joined a feminist organization and began to develop her sociological investigations that begin with women's experiences and situations. Weber completed a dissertation at the University of Freiburg titled, "Fichte's Socialism and Its Relationship to Marxist Doctrine" (1900). In 1904, she traveled to America, meeting a number of women activists, reformers, and educators, including Jane Addams and Florence Kelly of Hull House and Lillian Wald of the Henry Street Settlement. It was M. Carey Thomas, president of Bryn Mawr College, and Ethel Puffer Howes, professor of philosophy and psychology at Wellesley College, however, who most shared Weber's belief that women should be given the opportunity for intellectual development through coeducation. Weber based her arguments concerning women and education not on economic opportunity but on feminist Charlotte Perkins Gilman's thesis that women would experience financial and marital freedom through paid employment. Weber's critique, informed by an awareness of social differentiation as well as current statistics assumed that the majority of women would endure the double burden of low-wage physical labor plus the duties of motherhood and housekeeping. Weber argued that housework and child care be given economic value in her essay "On the Valuation of Housework" (1912). In this essay, Weber posits that the underlying moral and economic operative within marriage should be one of equality rather than based on a patriarchal system of inequality. A new valuation of the partnership calls for a means of economic independence so wives have freedom to shape their personal lives. Weber notes that constant economic dependency relevant to the subjective responses of another is demeaning. The subordinate loses self-respect and is induced to using methods of trickery and deception as found in the master-slave relationship. To alleviate this destructive marital pattern, Weber proposes the enacting of marriage laws so that a fixed amount of the husband's income be apportioned for household and personal use by the wife. She is aware that the redistribution of familial economic power by a patriarchal legislation will not readily occur; her ulterior objective is to raise public consciousness concerning marital economic inequity and transform not only marital law but marital custom.

Weber penned a series of writings titled *Reflections on Women and Women's Issues* (1904–1919). Her writings presage Carol Gilligan's work on difference as well as other feminists who find that using male models and male culture obscures the riches found in female culture. In 1907, she published an in-depth study, *Marriage, Motherhood and the Law*, critiquing the historical and structural development of marital relationships as dictated by patriarchy. Her 1912 composition, "Authority and Autonomy in Marriage," looks critically at how marital relationships based on subordinate and superordinate positions are destructive to both men and women. Her 1913 essay, "Woman and Objective Culture," is a treatise responding to Georg Simmel's supposition that men create objective culture and women, due to an undifferentiated nature, are engaged by subjective culture. In addressing Simmel's dialectical method of defining men and women, Weber disputes his thesis that a dramatic metaphysical difference exists between the genders. She brings a focus to their similarities, framing the sexes as overlapping circles. Each circle maintains its unique areas of distinction; however, areas of commonality are greater than differences. Weber notes that the creation of objective culture requires rationality, objectivity, and goal orientation, human qualities applicable to both men and women. She states that due to social regulation women are excluded from the realms where objective culture is created, and she draws a link between women's work and the transference of objective culture into subjective knowledge. Her thesis is that women's participation in the development of objective culture would expand and enrich cultural arenas.

Weber's writings coupled with her feminist activism led to her being the first woman elected to the legislature in Baden (1919). In 1920, the year Max died unexpectedly of pneumonia, she was chair of the Federation of German Women's Organizations, Germany's largest and most active feminist group. After Max's death, Weber withdrew from public life for several years. In 1924, she was awarded an honorary doctorate from the University of Heidelberg for her compilation of Max's works and her own scholarly writings. In 1936, she published the book *Women and Love*, and in 1948 completed her autobiography *Memoirs of a Life*. These works have not yet been translated into English. The largest impediment to the study of Weber's theoretical writings for those who speak only English is a lack of translated works.

— Nina Lohr-Valdez

See also Gilligan, Carol; Gilman, Charlotte Perkins; Simmel, Georg; Weber, Max

FURTHER READING AND REFERENCES

Lengermann, Patricia M. and Jill Niebrugge-Brantley. 1998. "Marianne Weber: A Woman-Centered Sociology." Pp. 193–228 in *The Women Founders: Sociology and Social Theory, 1830–1630*. New York: McGraw-Hill.

Roth, Guenther. 1990. "Marianne Weber and Her Circle." *Society* 27(2):63–69.

Scaff, Lawrence. 1998. "The 'Cool Objectivity of Sociation': Max Weber and Marianne Weber in America." *History of the Human Sciences* 11(2):61–82.

Weber, Marianne. 1975. *Max Weber: A Biography*. Translated by Harry Zohn. New York: John Wiley.

———. [1912] 2003. "Authority and Autonomy in Marriage." Translation with introduction by Craig R. Bermingham. *Sociological Theory* 21(2):85–102.

WEBER, MAX

Max Weber (1864–1920) was born in Prussia in 1864. His father started his career as a journalist, became a local city official in Erfurt, and then moved to Berlin on his election to the parliament as a National Liberal—the political party that supported the chancellorship of Bismarck and hence the unification of Germany under Prussian rule. His mother was descended from a rich family of international merchants based in Frankfurt. She was brought up somewhat severely in a beautiful villa overlooking the River Neckar and the old town of Heidelberg. She was devoutly religious but in an ethical rather than a superstitious way. In Berlin, she supported the social-evangelical movement whose aim was to improve the welfare of the poor through the work of the church and through reform politics. She was not a Calvinist, as is often (mistakenly) stated.

Weber studied history and law at the universities of Heidelberg, Göttingen, and Berlin. His doctoral dissertation investigated how legal forms of partnership were developed to spread the risk on medieval trading ventures. His habilitation thesis, required for teaching in a German university, examined the changing forms of property ownership in ancient Rome. Both studies required an intensive involvement in primary materials (and so foreign languages and handwritten documents). Weber, in this and also his other intellectual interests, was a beneficiary of the research seminar, which had placed the German universities in the forefront of research in the study of cultures, history, theology, languages, and archaeology. One of Weber's greatest achievements was the comparative study of the economic ethics of the world religions, an achievement made possible in large part by German scholarship and the techniques of interpreting documents.

He rose to national academic prominence with the publication in 1892 of an empirical survey of large landowners in the eastern provinces of Germany. The study was started when he was still completing his research on ancient Rome, and he was only 29 when he presented the findings in Berlin in 1893 to Germany's premier social policy association. The survey investigated the reasons behind the crisis in agricultural profits, the move of farm-labourers off the land, and the use of migrant labourers from Poland and the Ukraine. Prussia's rise to hegemony over all other German states had been based for over two centuries on its well-disciplined armies conscripted from peasants in the eastern provinces. During the decade of the 1890s, Weber pursued the controversial political question of how Prussia's ruling class (the Junkers) were using protectionist measures to support their own, uneconomic, farms while at the same time using cheap immigrant wage labourers and so displacing the settled German farmworkers.

Weber is pivotal to the "conversation" of social theory, and it needs to be made clear how his social theory relates to social science and how social science relates to politics and social policy. The farm study is beyond doubt firmly rooted in empirical social science methods. But what Weber brought to the survey was a demand to include the psychological or subjective factors of why farmworkers were leaving their traditional villages. What part did the desire for freedom and independence (from their Junker landlords) play in their decisions to move to the cities? This was a question additional to and separate from the Marxist thesis of immiserization that regarded the flight from the land solely in material terms. The "psychological magic of freedom" had to be placed alongside "bread and butter questions" as Weber expressed it. In addition, Weber considered what political conclusions should be drawn and debated from the fact that politicians were benefiting directly from state economic policies at the cost of national defence (of the eastern border against Russia).

In short, what Weber presents in the 1890s are the triple and interrelated issues of social science, questions of social and cultural meaning, and the debating of political and policy questions. He formulated his solution to this set of issues in a series of pathbreaking essays on methodology.

But first Weber needs to be placed in context. He has been greatly misconstrued during the twentieth century, not least by social and cultural theorists. Weber, as Karl Löwith (1982) has commented, wanted to make intelligible how we are today, how we have become, and to show to us the history of the present that in universal historical terms is only an excerpt in the destiny of humankind. This acute sense of historicity (that has been so overlaid by the uniformity of modernity) and the anticipation of what can happen in the future, in its turn, is understandable only by returning for a moment to the outlook of around 1900.

WEBER'S VIEW OF THE TWENTIETH CENTURY

Weber viewed the coming twentieth century in ways not dissimilar to how today's conventional wisdom views the twenty-first. He assumed the widespread development of capitalism on a rational, systematic basis in emerging countries like Russia and China and that there would be growing international markets in trade and finance. He thought the socialist alternative to capitalism, while once a threat, to have receded as a possibility. International relations would remain conflictual since the major national states wished to extend their influence beyond their borders, but he did not envisage major and sustained war on a global basis. Religions would decline in proportion as education and science increased. The modern world would experience a degree of disenchantment—that is, a loss of magic, revelation, and the mystery of the unknown—but Weber was also concerned that substitute religions could be a source of irrationality and instability.

The twentieth century, however, became "Weberian" only in its last decades. The outbreak of a world war in 1914 was completely unexpected by Weber, although he had noted an increased tension between the major European states. He died soon after the war, in June 1920, not realizing the full extent and enormity of the conflict or the causes for its outbreak. The maleficent legacy of that war led to European fascism, another world war culminating in the greatest technological violence, and the institutionalization of ideological politics on a global scale. This has meant that all readings of Weber in the twentieth century have been overdetermined by events. In the 1920s, he was ignored as a German intellectual; in the 1930s, he was shunned for political reasons; and after the Second World War, he became a weapon in the ideological struggle against Marxist communisms—the "bourgeois Marx," as it was then said. In Germany, the reception of Weber has been highly ambivalent, with the Frankfurt School regarding him as condoning the formal rationality of capitalism and ignoring its irrationalities (Marcuse [1965]1971) and with liberals condemning his national viewpoints (Mommsen 1984). But to return to 1900, capitalism was a progressive force, and it was for politics to decide on reform agendas, and the idea of nationalism was still connected to nation building and democracy (Scott 2000:33–55).

In the last two decades of the twentieth century, there has been a cultural turn in the social sciences and a less ideologically encumbered appreciation of his work (see Scaff 1989; Whimster and Lash 1987). There has been a return to the issues of science, knowledge, and politics that Weber considered crucial for a mature understanding of the dynamics, both cultural and societal, of modernity. Weber argued that politics was a realm of competing values, that there were no longer any fundamental beliefs from which norms and values could be prioritized, and that the validity of scientific knowledge did not rest on fixed and undisputed foundations. The condition of living in modernity required a maturity to come to terms with these new realities.

Over 1904–1905, Weber published his essay "The Protestant Ethic and the Spirit of Capitalism" and his methodological essay "The 'Objectivity' of Knowledge in Social Science and Social Policy." These two works contain the components of the Weberian programme: (1) social and cultural theory that addresses the meanings that direct and mould people's lives, (2) the methods used to validate such knowledge, and (3) how the implications of investigative findings are to be debated and acted on.

THE PROTESTANT ETHIC STUDY

The Protestant Ethic and the Spirit of Capitalism (*PESC*) ([1904-1905]1930) addressed an association that had been long recognized but hitherto unexplained. Capitalistic enterprises appeared to flourish in Protestant inhabited areas, more so than in Catholic areas. This statistical evidence was of the same nature as Durkheim's observation that suicide rates were lower in Catholic areas and countries, compared with Protestant regions. Given these facts, how can the respective issues be explained? For Durkheim, the explanation resided in the suicidogenic forces that different levels of collective consciousness generated; forces generated at the level of society act as external forces on people's individual lives. For Weber, the emergence of the distinctive form of modern capitalism, as systematically rational, is an effect or repercussion of individually held meanings. The everyday behaviour of Puritans is the outcome of a religiously determined psychology where individuals look inward to their conscience as a regulator of their actions. Puritanism, in its various forms—and Weber provides historical case studies of Calvinism, Pietism, Methodism, and the Baptist sects—is a religion of reform that constantly admonishes the individual to control and monitor his or her conduct. Puritanism abolished the mediation of church and confession, made accessible sacred texts in the vernacular language, and placed an enormous responsibility on each person to remain pure according to the salvation message of the sacred text. The case of Calvinism is psychologically more complex, for here, actions alone do not suffice to secure salvation and avoid damnation. Calvinist beliefs posited the idea of predestination: that an unknown and unseen god has already determined the salvation of each individual prior to his or her birth. The resulting salvation anxiety was allayed by acting as if one had been chosen (predestined) to go to heaven.

Weber's social-cultural theory identifies an irrational belief held with great intensity as a crucial causal factor in the development of modern capitalism. These beliefs—more generally, cultural meanings—result in a systematic style of life. The Puritans avoid pleasure, they work hard, they save their money. Weber refers to this as "inner-worldly" asceticism. A lifestyle as austere and pleasure averse as the Puritans involves training. In Christianity, as well as other religions, asceticism is practised by monks, usually within the closed community of the monastery. Weber terms this "other-worldly" asceticism. Monasteries are cut off from the rest of the world and follow their own regime of disciplined observance. The Puritan lives within the world, carrying out normal social and work activities. Strong religious meanings structure the personality of the Puritan, permitting an ascetic style of life carried on within the world with all its temptations of a more relaxed code of life. The Puritan always is aware of the salvation message. This is his or her "calling" or vocation. Religious beliefs become solidified in ascetic practice, and Weber terms this a style of life (*Lebensstil*) or a conduct of life (*Lebensführung*).

In a further step in his argument, Weber holds that conduct of life is passed on as a social form, irrespective of its religious origins. He provides the example of the American entrepreneur, scientist, and diplomat, Benjamin Franklin, whose father was a Calvinist. Franklin was secular in his outlook but nevertheless retained the discipline of his upbringing. Indeed, he formulated a kind of lifestyle handbook that provided an instruction manual on how to get on in business and life by improving one's ability to work. Once this attitude or mentality becomes generalized through a population (here a Protestant population), the social scientist can then frame the thesis that such a mentality will have significant economic consequences. In causal terms, Weber frames this as codetermination. There already existed in Northwestern Europe fairly advanced forms of capitalist trade, banking, technology, and legal frameworks. Puritanism did not produce capitalism "out of a hat"; Puritan sects that settled in Patagonia did not produce an economic miracle; they remained farmers. But where this systematic, sober, rational approach to life existed in conjunction with an already developing capitalism, then to use Weber's phrase there was an "elective affinity" between the two. There occurred a sort of chemical bonding, to produce the distinctively new compound, modern rational capitalism.

The last pages of *PESC* pursues the argument to a final stage, and it has been highly influential in social and cultural theory; indeed its phrases have entered popular consciousness as a shorthand way of thinking about the rigidities and impersonality of modern capitalism and modern life. Weber speaks of asceticism being released from the monastic cell into everyday life, "building the tremendous cosmos of the modern economic order." It was an order bound to the technical and economic conditions of machine production that controlled the lives of those born into the mechanism and that had become an "iron cage" (Weber 1930:181). Talcott Parsons's translation used "iron cage" in place of the more accurate "a housing as hard as steel," so emphasizing imprisonment over rigidity. But either image is a powerful metaphor of the loss of individual autonomy in the face of an impersonal, rational order. This was a theme that Weber also developed in his analysis of modern bureaucracy that has come to dominate in any large organization, whether voluntary, business, or governmental. Bureaucratic apparatus was the organizational equivalent of mechanical production, allowing precision, speed, certainty, knowledge of the files, continuity, discretion, unity, strict subordination, reduction of friction, and reduction of material and personal costs. Business was conducted according to calculable rules and without regard for the status of the person and, as such, represents a move to dehumanization (Weber 1968:973–75).

Rational conduct on the basis of the idea of calling comes to pervade not only modern capitalism but modern culture as well (*PESC*:180). Any achievement in the modern world is a specialized one and involves what Weber termed "the renunciation of the Faustian universality of man." That latter idea was part of the Renaissance ideal of the "universal man"—the courtier, the artist, the scientist, the poet, the soldier as all the varied accomplishments of a single person. Religious duty undermined such an ideal, regarding it as a creaturely vanity that needed to be replaced by dogged pursuit of a single vocation. Weber's contemporary, the novelist Stefan Zweig, illustrated this phenomenon in his Chess novella (translated as *The Royal Game*). On a trans-Atlantic liner, two chess-masters compete. One is an educated humanist and the better, and faster, player. The other is a chess specialist, ignorant of everything but chess, where he is ploddingly efficient. The humanist makes an unforced error and loses to the specialist, and rational efficiency wins out over amateur brilliance. In sport, business, politics, education, and administration, the specialist type today is of course completely prevalent. In his 1915 essay, "Intermediate Reflection," Weber expanded the idea of specialism into the fragmentation of life orders with their own autonomous values. The decisive life orders in modernity were politics, economics, and science; the other life orders were more personal and consolatory and included aesthetics and the erotic. And in "The Vocation of Politics," Weber went on to argue that the demand of politics follows its own internal logic that is incompatible with Christian ethics.

Goodness and love of one's neighbour transposed to the unforgiving arena of politics will produce outcomes vary much at variance with those virtues (Weber 2003:259–62). The modern individual, then, pursues a life separated into individual spheres with no overarching scheme of values. The individual person, Weber suggests, has to choose in which sphere and by what guiding values he or she will live life—as politician, businessperson, scientist, artist, or lover.

At the end of *PESC,* Weber concludes, of this "last stage of cultural development, it might well be truly said: 'Specialists without spirit, sensualists without heart; this nullity imagines that it has attained a level of civilization never before achieved'" (*PESC:*182). Weber here is expressing Nietzsche's contempt for modern civilization that brings forward the type who Nietzsche refers to as "the Last Man" who makes everything small and who Nietzsche compares to a fly—inexterminable. This is strong language, where irony and contempt are used to scathing effect. Overall, Weber is expressing a mood of cultural pessimism as an old civilization makes the transition to modern, rational industrial-based capitalism. The loss of this older, less knowing, and more personal world Weber refers to as disenchantment. In the Nietzschean formulation, the specialist is vilified as a nonentity and the search for happiness as illusory. The rudiments of modern happiness, for Nietzsche, consisted of material well-being and security without any other aspiration. In the Nietzschean view of the world, the higher ideals could include religious and philosophical insight, artistic perfection, and courage, any of which are likely to exclude material happiness.

Weber is far more realistic about material well-being, for his comparative economic sociology demonstrated the search for wealth as a universal feature of humankind. Likewise, following his visit to America in 1804, he failed to share some of his German colleagues' distaste for American consumerism. But even allowing for Weber's acceptance of consumerism, the above quotes certainly express a disquiet that happiness could, or should, be a goal in itself. This suggests that other values, as goals in themselves, were worth pursuing. This theme has been taken up fairly recently in Weber commentary. David Owen (1994) argues that an alternative idea of happiness underlies Weber's standpoint. Happiness in this conception is the Aristotelian notion of human flourishing. Wilhelm Hennis (2000a, 2000b) has interpreted the Nietzschean theme in Weber in terms of conduct of life. The Puritan had through religious belief and everyday behaviour formed a coherent way of life. Likewise in Weber's comparative sociology, the Confucian mandarin and the Hindu Brahman had a way of life whose values and beliefs remained beyond question that was embedded within an existing social structure. Modernity, to use Karl Polanyi's phrase, disembeds conduct from social structure. Hennis's response to this predicament is a philosophical anthropology that seeks to reconnect the higher-level values, such as integrity, truth, and professionalism, to the social process of upbringing and education.

These debates, while being at the heart of contemporary social and cultural theory and also can be extended to the work of Foucault (Gane 2002; Gordon 1987), cannot be said to be strictly scientific. As Weber admonishes himself, "But this brings us to the world of judgements of value and faith, with which this purely historical discussion need not be burdened" (*PESC:*182). To see how he handles the inter-relation of science to matters of belief and values, his methodological position needs to be understood.

METHODOLOGY AND SOCIAL THEORY

"The 'Objectivity' in Social Science and Social Policy" was published in the *Archiv für Sozialwissenschaft und Sozialpolitik* in the same year (1904) as the Protestant ethic essay was appearing. Immediate points to note are the title of the journal and that "Objectivity" appears in quotation marks. The journal, whose editorship Weber had taken over along with the economic historian Werner Sombart and the banking expert Edgar Jaffé, was committed to the analysis of economic phenomena and their cultural relevance. As the title says, it was a social science journal with a reformist social policy agenda. So its function was to analyse culture and economics, be committed to science, and to comment on policy implications. It was to pursue truth dispassionately without party political bias and, most certainly, without a totalizing worldview like scientific monism, Marxism, or Hegelianism. Yet Weber's concept of objectivity was not to be confused with an objectivist account of reality. By today's standards this programme sounds contradictory, and this is one of the reasons why Weber's legacy has been split into empiricist, interpretivist, and positivist strands (see Eliaeson 2000).

The unity of Weber's scientific method, however, can be grasped only if the deliberate paradoxes of his position are understood. Objectively valid truths belong to the domain of the sciences of cultural life. Truth is arrived at by a valid conceptual ordering of empirical reality. But the domain of science is constituted not by the objective relation between things but by relations between problems in thought (and what is now termed "constructivism") (Weber 2003:365). "The real" for Weber is a constant and chaotic flux that can never, ever be contained and explained by a system of scientific thought. Reality is not only in flux; it is infinite in its extension through time and infinite in its complexity at any one point in time. There is no inherent patterning within this reality, and it is a grand conceit and illusion to believe that the human mind can discern laws that determine the infinite complexity of social and cultural reality. This was an assumption he took from the neo-Kantian philosopher Heinrich Rickert.

However, the scientist does have ways of coming to terms with what would appear to be insuperable difficulties. Scientific thought starts, for Weber, with the invention of the concept. Concepts give humankind a handle on the representation of reality, although not reality itself. Moreover, Weber's notion of truth is not the Platonic one that equated truth with timeless forms. Weber can be identified with an older tradition that can be traced back to Democritus where reality is assumed to possess no timeless structure but consists of the flux of atoms. Concepts, for Weber, are postulates or hypotheses thrown out like a beam of torchlight to interrogate reality—an idea comprehensively (and subsequently) developed by Karl Popper.

Weber's second large assumption is that human beings are cultural beings and as such are endowed with the capacity to lend meaning to an otherwise external and hostile world. This capacity separates a science of culture from a science of nature. In a science like biology, classificatory systems reflect an empirical reality of life forms. In a cultural science, the scientist forms a relationship with reality. The social scientist chooses a topic or a problem that has interest and significance for research, and in turn, this reflects an ongoing problematic like "orientalism" or "the underclass." This isolates a class of phenomena for causal analysis and explanation, and the class itself is defined by selection through cultural interest. This, argues Weber, is the only way to grasp a part of social reality's infinite complexity.

Some features of Weber's position run parallel to Richard Rorty's (1991) on objectivity. For both, science is not a "mirror of nature" where truth can be faithfully represented by a scientific language. The findings of science, for both, do not correspond to a knowable reality "out there." Rorty's cultural being is always in an unending and nongraspable (in sense of closure) conversation with self, others, and the world, where no truth can be underpinned and values cannot be derived from a scientific truth. Science, for Rorty, is a powerful tool for getting what one wants from the world; his pragmatism concerns questions of "how" not objective definitions of "what is." This interaction with the world does not allow the specification of timeless truths.

Weber's programme for social science appears close to Rorty's pragmatism. There is no objective reality that can be represented through scientific language. The researcher is always in an interaction with the world, and a research problematic is generated within the social and cultural world and is not derived from science itself. But Weber turns what for Rorty is a problem for science into a solution. Because we are endowed with the capacity to confer meaning on the world, our interaction becomes a framing device defining a portion of infinite reality. Within this frame, truth can be verified at the level of specific causes and effects. Compared with Platonic truth, this might be a prosaic version of truth, but nonetheless it is empirical and concerns the ascertainment of facts. Social theorists who, like Rorty, enlist Nietzsche in their attack on the impossibility of social science, need to be wary of including Weber as part of their argument. Both Nietzsche and Weber draw on non-Platonic understandings of external reality—a brute and chaotic force. This creates an obligation on the individual both to cognitively master this reality and to endow it with values. Unlike Rorty, Weber specifies a scientific methodology for establishing regularities in social reality.

The ideal type is the specific method employed by the cultural scientist. Social and cultural reality is a non-logical chaos of meanings. It is like a crowded party where the noise in the room is an undifferentiated hubbub until one starts listening to particular conversations. In listening, one creates a relation or "rapport" with a conversation. In history and other cultural sciences that interpret the past, the conversation can be imaginatively re-created. This is often referred to as empathetic understanding, an idea Weber took from Wilhelm Dilthey who had established it as a method in the historical sciences.

Meanings have to be isolated and placed within a specific context. This is a scientific operation. Isolation is achieved through the accentuation of a specific meaning to its logically pure state. Weber gives the example of church and sect. For the historian and theologian, these terms each have multiple and overlapping meanings. In Weber's [(1905)2002] hands, they are construed as oppositional concepts, the church open and the sect closed with different criteria of membership. The motivational logic of a sect will be entirely different to a church. But in empirical reality, these distinctions will be obscured. Actual sects, in the present or in the past, are then compared to the ideal-typical yardstick. Where they approach the pure type, they can be presumed to generate specific communal motivations among its members. Churches, on the other hand, as a pure type generate specific associational forces. Complex social reality, then, is dissected by these two ideal-type instruments and the causal forces at work can be weighted. (Note: A heuristic should not be confused with a hermeneutic. Heuristics are analogous to modelling in natural science. Indeed, Weber invokes the idea of a limiting case, like a perfect vacuum. Only through such a device can the constant force of gravity be isolated and demonstrated. By contrast, a hermeneutic is a totalizing device that attempts to intuit an empirically existing cultural artifact.)

Broadly speaking, Weber refers to two sorts of causality. People either react to impersonal forces—such as climate, population growth, their own biological structure, and market forces—or they have their own reasons for acting, and these reasons are derived from the cultural context of which they are part. Returning to the *PESC*, modern capitalism was in part the outcome of impersonal forces like demography, technology, geography, and markets, but it was also an indirect outcome of a strongly religiously determined context of meaning. The former is the determination of outside forces on the individual and group; the latter, the grounds, reasons, or motives for actions by an individual or group.

Using ideal types, so to speak parting the tangled undergrowth of past reality, the historian can assign empirical validity to specific concrete causes having particular outcomes. Truth can be ascertained at the level of the concrete. For example, neo-Calvinist sects in the seventeenth century Low Countries really did have a formative effect on the capitalist economy. This is Weber's concept of objectivity and, to repeat, it is confined to the level of concrete cause and effect. Objectivity is not able to achieve total certainty; even at the level of the concrete, knowledge remains partial, so truth can never be validated with full certainty—there may be other, unknown factors to be discovered.

This tends to condemn social and cultural science to permanent adolescence, says Weber. New questions and new problematics come along, and the old issues are left aside not fully resolved. Complete truth remains elusive, and general laws are a chimera, but despite this, the determination of factual truth is a scientific obligation.

The framing questions or problematics posed by the scientist are relative to society and its values, but factual truth can be confirmed by the social scientist, and in this sense truth is universal.

Scientific objectivity is compatible with *conviction*. The latter term is a strong word for value judgements. In the area of policy analysis, social scientists can undertake scientific analyses, say, of the causes of the "underclass" phenomenon. They can also undertake predictive studies on policy solutions and their outcomes. Weber recognized that differences will exist among social scientists as well as politicians as to what counts as a desirable outcome. Social science cannot scientifically validate the differing ends desired by people. One policy scientist might wish to promote the maximisation of happiness, another the maintenance of inequality (very roughly the difference approximates to liberal vs. neoliberal values). Weber argued that scientific analysis of causes and policy solutions must proceed impartially to whatever personal values an individual scientist holds. But outside the field of science, the social scientist can plead for his or her values as much as the next citizen. A moment's observation of the contemporary university and think tank will demonstrate that this scientific ideal is comprehensively breached, and with this comes an accompanying loss of scientific reputation of the social "sciences." Gunnar Myrdal was an exemplar in the Weberian mould. He conducted policy analysis in a way that was "objective," realizing that such analyses raised questions of values choice (Eliaeson 2000:118–22.); or as Weber expressed it, his own journal stood for "the training of judgement in respect of practical problems arising from social circumstances," and his "Objectivity" essay explains how this is achieved (Weber 2003:359).

It is important not to "overcook" Weber's writings from a methodological point of view. His insistent message is that human and cultural values have to be analysed and debated. The social and cultural scientist takes a position on values in deciding what to study, and social scientific analysis with the help of the ideal type sifts through the complexity of values. Issues of judgement, choice, and debate follow on after the social scientific investigation. Subsequent to Weber, the "demarcationists" (of the Vienna Circle, Popper's critical rationalism, and other neopositivist schools) have pencilled in thick black lines that stipulate that "valid" science must exclude the analysis of cultural meanings and that value judgements are no part of the scientific enterprise. With Weber these are, rather, dotted lines. His methodology strongly argues against perverse procedures, such as allowing a person's prior values to be legitimated through a scientific procedure, or the incursion of semi-religious worldviews into social science. But social science—and this is his contribution to the canon of scientific humanism—is about values and their analysis.

At the end of *PESC,* Weber issued a warning that the "immense economic cosmos" and the "iron cage" had the potential to eject the *Mensch* and the pathos of human values and install the automaton of the *Fachmensch*. The social pathologies of the twentieth century—the death camps, the soulless bureaucracies, the separation of the administration of people from justice for people—can all be analysed along Weberian lines, as Zygmunt Bauman, unforgettably, has shown (Bauman 1989). Weber himself did not think he was issuing a storm warning. He probably thought that he had achieved enough by showing that social and cultural theory, used correctly and incisively, can reveal fundamental contradictions in the nature of modernity—that modern capitalism in its formative stage was constructed to honour an absent god. The significance of this finding indicated a rationalization process that distanced the modern individual from religious, ethical, and community values and an integrated sense of self. It is probably a lesson relevant for the twenty-first century.

— Sam Whimster

See also Bureaucracy; Capitalism; Enchantment/Disenchantment; Ideal Type; Modernity; Neo-Kantianism; Positivism; Pragmatism; Rationalization; Rorty, Richard; Sombart, Werner; Werturteilsstreit (Value Judgment Dispute)

FURTHER READINGS AND REFERENCES

Bauman, Zygmunt. 1989. *Modernity and the Holocaust.* Cambridge, UK: Polity.

Eliaeson, Sven. 2000. *Max Weber's Methodologies.* Cambridge, UK: Polity.

Gane, Nicholas. 2002. *Max Weber and Postmodern Theory. Rationalization versus Re-enchantment.* London: Palgrave.

Gordon, Colin. 1987. "The Soul of the Citizen: Max Weber and Michel Foucault on Rationality and Government." Pp. 293–316 in *Max Weber, Rationality and Modernity,* edited by S. Whimster and S. Lash. London: Allen & Unwin.

Hennis, Wilhelm. 2000a. *Max Weber's Central Questions.* Translated by Keith Tribe. Newbury, UK: Threshold.

———. 2000b. *Max Weber's Science of Man.* Translated by Keith Tribe. Newbury, UK: Threshold.

Löwith, Karl. 1982. *Max Weber and Karl Marx.* London: Allen & Unwin.

Marcuse, Herbert. [1965] 1971. "Industrialization and Capitalism." Pp. 133–51 in *Max Weber Today,* edited by Otto Stammer. Translated by Kathleen Morris. Oxford, UK: Blackwell.

Mommsen, Wolfgang J. 1984. *Max Weber and German Politics: 1890–1920.* Translated by Michael Steinberg. Chicago, IL: Chicago University Press.

Owen, David. 1994. *Maturity and Modernity: Nietzsche, Weber, Foucault and the Ambivalence of Reason.* London: Routledge.

Rorty, Richard. 1991. *Objectivity, Relativism and Truth.* Cambridge, UK: Cambridge University Press.

Scaff, Lawrence. 1989. *Fleeing the Iron Cage.* Berkeley: University of California Press.

Scott, Alan. 2000. "Capitalism, Weber and Democracy." *Max Weber Studies* 1(1):33–35.

Weber, Max. [1904-1905] 1930. *The Protestant Ethic and the Spirit of Capitalism.* Translated by Talcott Parsons. London: Allen & Unwin.

———. 1968. *Economy and Society,* edited by G. Roth and C. Wittich. New York: Bedminster.

———. [1905] 2002. "'Churches' and 'Sects' in North America." Pp. 203–20 in *The Protestant Ethic and the "Spirit" of Capitalism and Other Writings,* edited and translated by Peter Baehr and Gordon Wells. Harmondsworth, UK: Penguin.

———. 2003. *The Essential Weber,* edited by S. Whimster. London: Routledge.

Whimster, Sam and Scott Lash, eds. 1987. *Max Weber, Rationality and Modernity.* London: Allen & Unwin.

WERTURTEILSSTREIT (VALUE JUDGMENT DISPUTE)

The *Werturteilsstreit* is part of the methodological controversies dominating the historical social and cultural sciences, especially in Germany, in the late nineteenth and early twentieth century. The central issue was the problem of whether those sciences were legitimated and able to derive ultimate and universally binding value judgments (*Werturteile*) from their empirical findings and explanations.

The most important advocate of a value-free social science in this sense was Max Weber. At the same time, however, he stressed that as far as the selection and forming

("*Auswahl und Formung*") of their subjects is concerned, no science could do without a value relevance (*Wertbeziehung*) and that values and judgments are of course an important issue of the cultural sciences.

The most determined criticism of the postulate of value freedom always came from those who wanted to engage and employ the social sciences for their own political (or religious) purposes.

This interest was the stronger the more marked or more radical the particular political and ideological position was. Therefore, it is not surprising that the criticism of the postulate of ethical neutrality was uttered with particular strictness from the right and left pole of the political spectrum. Initially, Max Weber encountered the political abuse of the social sciences in the works of the nationalist historian Heinrich von Treitschke, whereas in the *Verein für Socialpolitik* (Association for Social Politics) he had to argue above all with moderate Leftist colleagues, the so-called Kathedersozialisten (see Nau 1996). Absolutely intolerable and even life threatening was the postulate of an ethically neutral science in both of the totalitarian systems of the twentieth century. And in the socialist or communist parts of the student movement of the 1960s and 1970s, it became the pivotal element of the non-Marxist, bourgeois science in general and the sociology in particular that had to be overcome (Weiss 1998). That's why the controversies of that time, at least in Germany, are frequently referred to as "second *Werturteilsstreit*" (Adorno et al. 1984).

As long as this interest was sufficiently strong, the *Werturteilsstreit* went on for years, with changing front lines and varying intensity. It seems, however, to be finally settled. As far as Weber's actually irrefutable logical and methodological arguments meet a general approval, one can, at least in this regard, almost refer to a generalized Weberianism in the social sciences.

Almost no one still claims that from a theoretical or empirical analysis of societal facts or tendencies a "scientific" moral or political strategy can be deduced. Likewise only rarely the opinion can be found that correct and relevant sociological findings were to be gained only within the framework of a specific moral or political orientation. As far as these fundamental questions are concerned, the *Werturteilsstreit* does not exist anymore. Despite this, very different ideas remain prevalent as to whether or not sociology has to regard itself as an integral part of the societal and political process (as Pierre Bourdieu believed) or if for the sake of its intellectual independence and honesty it must keep itself away from any sort of political engagement (as, for example, Niklas Luhmann demanded and practiced). In logical and empirical respect, the better arguments lie on the side of the second position. Nevertheless, one can argue, if not by formal logical but by pragmatic and maybe also transcendental logical reasons, that sociologists at least should suspend (as the value basis of their research) those

kinds of moral or political options that are incompatible with the requirements and objectives of free scientific research, like the totalitarian ideologies of the twentieth century. In this case, there is a kind of value relevance that derives from the reflection on the meaning and the prerequisites of science itself.

— Johannes Weiss

See also Bourdieu, Pierre; Luhmann, Niklas; Positivismusstreit (Positivist Dispute); Socialism; Weber, Max

FURTHER READINGS AND REFERENCES

Adorno, Theodor W. et al., eds. 1984. *Der Positivismusstreit in der Deutschen Soziologie* [The Positivist Dispute in German Sociology]. 11th ed. Neuwied & Berlin, Germany: Luchterhand.

Albert, Hans and Ernst Topitsch, ed. 1971. *Der Werturteilsstreit* [The Value Judgment Dispute]. Darmstadt, Germany: Wissenschaftliche Buchgesellschaft.

Ciaffra, Jay A. 1998. *Max Weber and the Problems of Value-Free Social Science: A Critical Examination of the Werturteils-Streit.* Lewisburg, NJ: Bucknell University Press.

Ferber, Christian von. 1965. "Der Werturteilsstreit 1909/1959: Versuch einer wissenschaftsgeschichtlichen Interpretation" [The Value Judgement Dispute 1909/1959: An Attempt at an Interpretation in the Context of History of Science]. Pp. 165–80 in *Logik der Sozialwissenschaften* [Logic of the Social Sciences], edited by Ernst Topitsch. Koeln & Berlin, Germany: Kiepenheuer & Witsch.

Nau, Heino Heinrich. ed. 1996. *Der Werturteilsstreit: Die Aeusserungen zur Werturteilsdiskussion im Ausschuss des Vereins für Socialpolitik* [The Value Judgement Dispute: The Statements in the Discussion about Value Judgements in the Committee of the Verein für Socialpolitik Marburg]. Germany: Metropolis.

Weber, Max. 1968. "Der Sinn der 'Wertfreiheit' der soziologischen und oekonomischen Wissenschaften." Pp. 489–540 in *Max Weber: Gesammelte Aufsaetze zur Wissenschaftslehre.* 3d ed. Tüebingen, Germany: J. C. B. Mohr. English ed. 1949. "The Meaning of 'Ethical New Neutrality' in Sociology and Economics." Pp. 1–112, in *Max Weber: The Methodology of the Social Sciences,* edited by E. A. Shils and H. A. Finch. New York: Free Press.

Weiss, Johannes. 1998. *Weber and the Marxist World,* with an introduction by Bryan S. Turner. London & New York: Routledge.

WHITE, HARRISON

Harrison Colyar White (b. 1930), American sociologist, structuralist thinker, network phenomenologist, and mathematical modeler, contributes theory, models, and conceptualization that focus on concrete, interconnected sets of actors beyond the level of the individual person or group but below the level of total cultures or societies. Having earned doctorates in theoretical physics (at MIT) and in sociology (at Princeton), White addresses problems of social structure that cut across the range of the social sciences. Most notably, he has contributed (1) theories of role structures encompassing classificatory kinship systems of native Australian peoples and institutions of the contemporary West; (2) models based on equivalences of actors across networks of multiple types of social relation; (3) theorization of social mobility in systems of organizations; (4) a structural theory of social action that emphasizes control, agency, narrative, and identity; (5) a theory of artistic production; (6) a theory of economic production markets leading to the elaboration of a network ecology for market identities and new ways of accounting for profits, prices, and market shares; and (7) a theory of language use that emphasizes switching between social, cultural, and idiomatic domains within networks of discourse. His most explicit theoretical statement is *Identity and Control: A Structural Theory of Social Action* (1992), although several of the major components of his theory of the mutual shaping of networks, institutions, and agency are also readily apparent in *Careers and Creativity: Social Forces in the Arts* (1993), written for a less-specialized audience.

The relation of White's work to strands of classical European structuralism is evident in his first book, *An Anatomy of Kinship* (1963), which includes in an appendix a translation (by Cynthia A. White) of a portion of Chapter 14 of Claude Lévi-Strauss's *Elementary Structures of Kinship* (1949, English translation 1969). Like André Weil, a mathematician who endeavored to formalize a portion of Lévi-Strauss's kinship theory, White is interested in the algebraic modeling of social relations. In his 1963 book, however, White brought to bear several distinctive themes that he has been developing throughout his later work. One of these is based on the observation of a certain similarity between charts of kinship roles among native Australian peoples and tables of organization for modern businesses. The more general concern is what White termed "structures of cumulated roles." In his first book, this preoccupation with roles led to the formulation of eight axioms relating clan structure to marriage rules for Australian societies (e.g., children whose fathers are in different clans must themselves be in different clans), derivations of ideal-type models of all possible societies that conformed to the axioms, and comparison of these models against extant anthropological accounts.

In subsequent work, White and collaborators loosened up the models (moving from algebraic group theory to the algebra of semigroups) so as to make them applicable to organizations and informal groups in a modern, Western context; now he defined role structures as positions of social actors across multiple networks of social relations (such as friendship, enmity, and the provision of help). In particular, in a seminal 1971 paper, White and François P. Lorrain defined "structural equivalence" with reference to sets of individuals who are placed similarly with respect to all other such sets, to the extent that relations and flows across multiple networks are captured by an aggregation of detailed relations. This equivalence concept allowed the representation of complex networks by reduced-form images that were obtained by aggregating equivalent actors. Further loosening of the underlying mathematics led White and collaborators to many analyses of social networks under the term *blockmodeling* (reviewed in White 1992).

Another concept that bridges several of White's contributions is duality. Anthropologists' notions of dual organization appeared in White's first book to motivate his interest in classificatory kinship systems that are invariant under transformations of matrilineal into patrilineal descent conventions. In the modeling of social mobility presented in *Chains of Opportunity* (1970), White defines duality as invariance in models of social structure and process under the interchange of named individuals and named jobs. A key innovation of this work was to stand conventional mobility modeling on its head, as applied to certain systems of moves of individuals between organizations. Vacancies, not individual persons, are free to move between categories according to fixed-transition probabilities, in White's view; therefore, conventional mobility models such as Markov chains should be applied to a study of the vacancies, not directly to analyze the mobility of persons. The latter can nonetheless be inferred from White's system models for mobility in organizations, as illustrated in his empirical analyses of the mobility of Episcopalian, Methodist, and Presbyterian clergy among congregations. In this work, careers of vacancies are seen not only as dual to, but as causally prior to careers of persons. More recently, in *Markets from Networks* (2002), the duality concept appears in White's characterization of the relation between upstream markets (with their emphasis on buyers "pulling" from their suppliers) and downstream markets (where producers are "pushing" their chosen volumes of product). Upstream and downstream markets are dual in the sense that producers' commitments are not directly governed by the underlying network of firms' concrete relations, which nonetheless constrain them. White therefore characterizes the upstream-downstream relation as a duality of decoupling and embeddedness.

In addition to concepts and principles (such as cumulated role, structural equivalence, duality, and reduced-form, ideal-type images of social networks) that cut across many of White's contributions and provide some considerable degree of unity to them, there has also been, over the course of his work to date, an evolution away from a formal structuralism and attendant concern for abstract patterning of relations and toward an enhanced focus on action, agency, cultural meaning, and concern with institutional practices. Searches and struggles for identity and control are taken as the trigger for all social action in White's 1992 volume rethinking network theory. Here the ties in networks are seen in their narrative aspects, and a social network is conceptualized as a network of meanings. "Switching" is a concept that White and Ann Mische use in their exploration of how conversations transit across multiple domains and sets of expectations, and in *Markets from Networks,* White also uses the concept to indicate shifts between the different market modes, noting that switching implies agency (purposive action) and disruption.

— Ronald L. Breiger

See also Network Theory; Structuralism

FURTHER READINGS AND REFERENCES

Azarian, Reza. 2003. *The General Sociology of Harrison White.* Stockholm, Sweden: Stockholm Studies in Social Mechanisms.

White, Harrison C. 1963. *An Anatomy of Kinship: Mathematical Models for Structures of Cumulated Roles.* Englewood Cliffs, NJ: Prentice-Hall.

————. 1970. *Chains of Opportunity: System Models of Mobility in Organizations.* Cambridge, MA: Harvard University Press.

————. 1992. *Identity and Control: A Structural Theory of Social Action.* Princeton, NJ: Princeton University Press.

————. 1993. *Careers and Creativity: Social Forces in the Arts.* Boulder, CO: Westview.

————. 2002. *Markets from Networks: Socioeconomic Models of Production.* Princeton, NJ: Princeton University Press.

WILLER, DAVID

Willer, David (b. 1937) is a theorist and researcher whose work exemplifies the use of formal methods for theory construction and experimental methods for testing derived predictions. His first book, *Scientific Sociology: Theory and Method* (1967), emphasized building models of social phenomena using systems of mathematical equations, and meticulous investigation aimed at developing and applying scientific laws to society. The work contended that such laws are not found by generalizing from empirical findings, a theme developed further in *Systematic Empiricism: Critique of a PseudoScience* (Willer and Willer 1973). This book developed a historically grounded analysis of empiricism and science. Its fundamental assertion was that sociology is a pseudoscience because of its reliance on empirical generalizations in lieu of abstract, general theories.

Believing that sociology could be scientific only by developing explicit, testable theories, Willer began work on a program of research driven by his new "elementary theory." The theory first appeared in *Networks, Exchange and Coercion* (1981), coedited by Willer and Bo Anderson. The theory builds on a foundation of simple defined concepts, combining them into more sophisticated concepts, and then into a small set of logically connected principles and laws used to predict social phenomena. *Networks, Exchange and Coercion* developed theoretical models for normatively controlled social exchange systems at the micro level and for structures of economic exchange and coercion at the macro level. Applied research reported in the book employed a variety of methods, including experiments, comparative-historical analysis, institutional analysis, and ethnographic case studies.

One of the basic principles in the theory, inspired by the work of Max Weber, is that actors are strategically rational. That is, actors' decisions take into account behaviors expected to be enacted by others. Karl Marx's thinking also has influenced Elementary Theory through the assumption that actors' values reflect the social structures and relations in which they are embedded. This contrasts with egocentric rationality assumptions in economics and allows Elementary Theory to account for a broad array of phenomena affected by social structures and contexts. Willer's next book, *Theory and the Experimental Investigation of Social Structures* (1987), reported a series of laboratory experiments investigating structural conditions for exchange and coercion. Elementary Theory identified commonalities between the structural conditions that produce power differences in social exchange networks and conditions in coercive structures. In other applications, Willer found that strong power differences are produced by mobility in hierarchies and by exclusion processes in exchange structures.

Soon after the 1987 book, Willer's collaborative work on the Network Exchange Theory (NET) branch of the Elementary Theory also came to fruition. The seminal article "Power Relations in Exchange Networks" (Markovsky, Willer, and Patton 1988) was the first to offer the Graph Theoretic Power Index. This mathematical model uses patterns of network connections to predict relative power for all positions in a network based on broader patterns of connections with other positions. It also predicts when and how larger networks will decompose into smaller networks, and when structural changes in one part of a network will or will not affect exchanges in other parts of the network.

Willer supports the idea that competition among different theories promotes rapid advancements in science. Thus, in 1992 he edited a special edition of the journal *Social Networks* that compared predictions from five competing theories of power in social exchange networks. Soon thereafter, published experiments identified NET as the most accurate. Subsequent collaborations have extended NET to more subtle "weak power" structures, and work continues toward the goals of increasing the theory's generality, precision, and parsimony. Progress in NET's development over the course of more than a decade is reviewed and analyzed in Willer's edited volume *Network Exchange Theory* (1999).

The future development of the science of sociology is, according to Willer, bound up with the development of advanced instrumentation for precisely testing theories. Fortuitously, the need for such instrumentation comes at the same time as the growth of the Internet. Willer has taken the lead in developing software for the construction and execution of experiments administered via the Internet. Interested scholars will be able to run experiments under the umbrella of Elementary Theory or modified to suit the testing requirements of other theories.

Although extensively tested in the laboratory, a central concern of Elementary Theory remains institutional and historical explanations and predictions. Theory provides the common ground for all of these empirical endeavors; however, natural settings place special demands on the theories. For instance, it may be difficult or impossible to control all of the factors in natural settings that impinge on the phenomenon of interest or to ensure that empirical tests satisfy all of a theory's scope conditions. To deal with this issue, Elementary Theory now includes a typology of seven structural power conditions, each with a unique set of properties. The implications of all seven have been tested in experiments, both individually and in combination.

In the course of extending Elementary Theory into new domains, Willer has contributed to the process of building integrative bridges to some other long-standing group process theories. For example, by linking his Elementary Theory to the theory of Status Characteristics and Expectation States, we now have a better understanding of the relationships between status, power, and social exchange. Similarly, connections forged to theories of legitimation help to explain interactions between power, network, and legitimacy phenomena. As such integrative projects develop further, increasingly rich and complex social phenomena may be expected to fall within the purview of Willer's program.

— Barry Markovsky

See also Exchange Networks; Network Exchange Theory; Theory Construction

FURTHER READINGS AND REFERENCES

Markovsky, Barry, David Willer, and Travis Patton. 1988. "Power Relations in Exchange Networks." *American Sociological Review* 53:220–36.
Willer, David. 1967. *Scientific Sociology: Theory and Method.* Englewood Cliffs, NJ: Prentice Hall.
———. 1987. *Theory and the Experimental Investigation of Social Structures.* New York: Gordon & Breach.
———, ed. 1999. *Network Exchange Theory.* Westport, CT: Praeger.
Willer, David and Bo Anderson, eds. 1981. *Networks, Exchange and Coercion.* New York: Elsevier.
Willer, David and Judith Willer. 1973. *Systematic Empiricism: Critique of a Pseudoscience.* Englewood Cliffs, NJ: Prentice-Hall.

WORLD-SYSTEMS THEORY

The world-systems perspective is a strategy for explaining social change that focuses on whole intersocietal systems. The main insight is that important interaction networks (trade, alliances, conflict, etc.) weave polities and cultures together since the beginning of human social evolution, so the explaining of change needs to take intersocietal systems (world-systems) as the units that "develop."

The intellectual history of world-systems theory has roots in classical sociology, Marxian revolutionary theory, geopolitical strategizing, and theories of social evolution. But in explicit form, the world-systems perspective emerged only in the 1970s when Samir Amin, Andre Gunder Frank, and Immanuel Wallerstein began to formulate the concepts and narrate the analytic history of the modern world-system.

This entry uses an intentionally inclusive definition of "world-systems/world systems theory" (with and without the hyphen). The hyphen emphasizes the idea of the *whole system,* the point being that all the human interaction networks small and large, from the household to global trade, constitute the world-system. It is not just a matter of "international relations" or global-scale institutions such as the World Bank. Rather at the present time it is all the people of the Earth and all their cultural, economic, and political institutions and the interactions and connections among them. This said, the hyphen has also come to connote a degree of loyalty to Wallerstein's approach. Other versions often drop the hyphen. Hyphen or not, the world(-)systems approach has long been far more internally differentiated than most of its critics have understood.

The world-systems perspective looks at human institutions over long periods of time and employs the spatial scale required for comprehending whole interaction systems. Single societies have always interacted in consequential ways with neighboring societies, so intersocietal interaction must be studied to understand social change. This does not mean that all the important processes causing social change are intersocietal but, rather, that enough of them are so that it is usually disastrous to ignore intersocietal relations.

The world-systems perspective is neither Eurocentric nor core-centric, at least in principle. The main idea is simple: Human interaction networks have been increasing in spatial scale for millennia as new technologies of communications and transportation have been developed. Since the emergence of oceangoing transportation in the fifteenth century, the multicentric Afroeurasian system incorporated the Western Hemisphere. Before the incorporation of the Americas into the Afroeurasian system, there were many local and regional world-systems (intersocietal networks). Most of these became inserted into the expanding European-centered system largely by force, and their populations were mobilized to supply labor for a colonial economy that was repeatedly reorganized by the changing geopolitical and economic forces emanating from the European and (later) North American core societies.

This whole process can be understood structurally as a stratification system composed of economically and politically dominant core societies (themselves in competition with one another) and dependent peripheral and semiperipheral regions, a few of which have been successful in improving their positions in the larger core-periphery hierarchy, while most have simply maintained their relative positions.

This structural perspective on world history allows us to analyze the cyclical features of social change and the long-term trends of development in historical and comparative perspective. We can see the development of the modern world-system as driven primarily by capitalist accumulation and geopolitics in which businesses and states compete with one another for power and wealth. Competition among states and capitals is conditioned by the dynamics of struggle among classes and by the resistance of peripheral and semiperipheral peoples to domination and exploitation from the core. In the modern world-system, the semiperiphery is composed of large and powerful countries in the third world (e.g., Mexico, India, Brazil, China) as well as smaller countries that have intermediate levels of economic development (e.g., the East Asian NICs, or newly industrialized countries). It is not possible to understand the history of social change in the system as a whole without taking into account both the strategies of the winners and the strategies and organizational actions of those who have resisted domination and exploitation.

It is also difficult to understand why and where innovative social change emerges without a conceptualization of the world-system as a whole. New organizational forms that transform institutions and that lead to upward mobility most often emerge from societies in semiperipheral locations. Thus, all the countries that became hegemonic core states in the modern system had formerly been semiperipheral (the Dutch, the British, and the United States). This is a continuation of a long-term pattern of social evolution that Christopher Chase-Dunn and Thomas D. Hall have called "semiperipheral development." Semiperipheral marcher states and semiperipheral capitalist city-states had acted as the main agents of empire formation and commercialization for millennia. This phenomenon arguably also includes organizational innovations in contemporary semiperipheral countries (e.g., Mexico, India, South Korea, Brazil) that may transform the now-global system.

This approach requires that we think structurally. We must be able to abstract from the particularities of the game of musical chairs that constitutes uneven development in the system to see the structural continuities. The core-periphery hierarchy remains, although some countries have moved up or down. The interstate system remains, although the internationalization of capital has further constrained the abilities of states to structure national economies. States have always been subjected to larger geopolitical and economic forces in the world-system, and as is still the case, some have been more successful at exploiting opportunities and protecting themselves from liabilities than others.

In this perspective, many of the phenomena that have been called "globalization" correspond to recently expanded international trade, financial flows, and foreign investment by transnational corporations and banks. The globalization discourse generally assumes that until recently there were separate national societies and economies and that these have now been superseded by an expansion of international integration driven by information and transportation technologies. Rather than a wholly unique and new phenomenon, globalization is primarily international economic integration, and as such it is a feature of the world-system that has been oscillating as well as increasing for centuries. Recent research comparing the nineteenth and twentieth centuries has shown that trade globalization is both a cycle and a trend.

The great chartered companies of the seventeenth century were already playing an important role in shaping the development of world regions. Certainly, the transnational corporations of the present are much more important players, but the point is that "foreign investment" is not an institution that became important only since 1970 (nor since World War II). Giovanni Arrighi has shown that finance capital has been a central component of the commanding heights of the world-system since the fourteenth century. The current floods and ebbs of world money are typical of the late phase of very long "systemic cycles of accumulation."

An inclusive bounding of the circle of world(-)system scholarship should include all those who see the global system of the late twentieth century as having important systemic continuities with the nearly global system of the nineteenth century. While this is a growing and interdisciplinary band, the temporal depth criterion excludes most of the breathless globalization scholars who see such radical recent discontinuities that they need know nothing about what happened before 1960. The information age, the new economy, global cities, the transnational capitalist class, and other hypothetically new and radical departures are seen as digging a huge chasm between recent decades and earlier world history. Those who believe that everything has changed must be left outside the circle.

A second criterion that might be invoked to draw a boundary around world(-)systems scholarship is a concern for analyzing international stratification, what some world-systemists call the core-periphery hierarchy. Certainly, this was a primary focus for Wallerstein, Amin, and the classical Gunder Frank. These progenitors were themselves influenced by the Latin American dependency school and by the third worldism of *Monthly Review* Marxism. Wallerstein was an Africanist when he discovered Fernand Braudel and Marion Malowist and the dependent development of Eastern Europe in the long sixteenth century. The epiphany that Latin America and Africa were like Eastern Europe—that they had all been peripheralized and underdeveloped by core exploitation and domination over a period of centuries—mushroomed into the idea that international stratification is a fundamental part of capitalist development and that core-periphery inequalities are systematically reproduced.

It is possible to have good temporal depth but still ignore the periphery and the dynamics of global inequalities. The important theoretical and empirical work of political scientists George Modelski and William R. Thompson is an example. Modelski and Thompson theorize a "power cycle" in which "system leaders" rise and fall since the Portuguese led European expansion in the fifteenth century. They also study the important phenomenon of "new lead industries" and the way in which the Kondratieff wave, a 40- to 60-year business cycle, is regularly related to the rise and decline of "system leaders." Modelski and Thompson largely ignore core-periphery relations to concentrate on the "great powers." But so does Giovanni Arrighi's masterful 600-year examination of "systemic cycles of accumulation." Andre Gunder Frank's latest reinvention of himself shines the spotlight on the centrality of China in the Afroeurasian world system and the allegedly abrupt rise of European power around 1800, a perspective that also largely ignores core-periphery exploitation.

So too does the "world polity school" led by sociologist John W. Meyer. This institutionalist approach adds a valuable sensitivity to the civilizational assumptions of Western Christendom and their diffusion from the core to the periphery. But rather than a dynamic struggle with authentic resistance from the periphery and the semiperiphery, the world polity school stresses how the discourses of resistance, national self-determination, and individual liberties have mainly been constructed out of the assumptions of the European Enlightenment. This is not wrong, but the focus on the ideology of distributive justice deflects attention from the real expansion of material global inequalities.

Most world-systems scholars contend that leaving out the core-periphery dimension or treating the periphery as inert are grave mistakes, not only for reasons of completeness but also because the ability of core capitalists and their states to exploit peripheral resources and labor has been a major factor in deciding the winners of the competition among core contenders. And the resistance to exploitation and domination mounted by peripheral peoples has played a powerful role in shaping the historical development of world orders. The comparison of the modern world-system with earlier regional systems has also revealed that all hierarchical world-systems have experienced a process of semiperipheral development in which some of the societies "in the middle" innovate and implement new technologies of power that drive the processes of expansion and systemic transformation. Thus, world history cannot be properly understood without attention to the core-periphery hierarchy.

COMPARING WORLD-SYSTEMS

It is often assumed that world-systems must necessarily be of large geographical scale. But systemness means that groups are tightly wound so that an event in one place has important consequences for people in another place. By that criterion, intersocietal systems have become global (Earthwide) only with the emergence of intercontinental seafaring. Earlier world-systems were smaller regional affairs. An important determinant of system size is the kind of transportation and communications technologies available. At the very small extreme, we have intergroup networks of sedentary foragers who primarily used "backpacking" to transport goods. This kind of hauling produces rather local networks. Such small systems still existed until the nineteenth century in some regions of North America and Australia. But they were similar in many respects with small world-systems all over the Earth before the emergence of states. An important theoretical task is to specify how to bound the spatial scale of human interaction networks. Working this out makes it possible to compare small, medium-sized, and large world-systems and to use world-systems concepts to rethink theories of human social evolution on a millennial time scale.

METATHEORETICAL ISSUES

Especially for Wallerstein, the study of the modern world-system was explicitly delineated as a perspective rather than a theory or a set of theories. A terminology was deployed to tell the story. The guiding ideas were explicitly *not* a set of precisely defined concepts being used to formulate theoretical explanations. Universalistic theoretical explanations were rejected and the historicity of all social science was embraced. Indeed, Wallerstein radically collapsed the metatheoretical opposites of nomothetic ahistoricism/ideographic historicism into the contradictory unity of "historical systems." Efforts to formalize a theory or theories out of the resulting analytic narratives are only confounded if they assume that the changing meanings of "concepts" are unintentional. Rather, there has been sensitivity to context and difference that has abjured specifying definitions and formalizing propositions.

Thomas Richard Shannon's (1996) *Introduction to the World-Systems Perspective* remains the most valuable tool for introducing the main ideas to undergraduates. But Shannon displays a misplaced exasperation when he encounters apparently inconsistent terminological usages in Wallerstein's work. This is because Shannon's effort to explicate assumes a single and unvarying set of meanings, while Wallerstein allows his vocabulary to adapt to the historical context that it is being used to analyze.

Some theorists have adopted a more nomothetic and structuralist approach to world-systems theory with the understanding that model building can interact fruitfully with the more historicist approach. All macrosociologists may be arrayed along a continuum from purely nomothetic ahistoricism to completely descriptive idiographic historicism. The possible metatheoretical stances are not two, but many, depending on the extent to which different institutional realms are thought to be lawlike or contingent and conjunctural. Fernand Braudel was more historicist than Wallerstein. Amin, an economist, is more nomothetic. Giovanni Arrighi's monumental work on 600 years of "systemic cycles of accumulation" sees qualitative differences in each hegemony, while Wallerstein, despite his aversion to explicating models, sees rather more continuity in the logic of the system, even extending to the most recent era of globalization. Andre Gunder Frank now claims that there was no transition to capitalism and that the logic of "capital imperialism" has not changed since the emergence of cities and states in Mesopotamia 5,000 years ago. Metatheory comes before theory. It focuses our theoretical spotlight on some questions while leaving others in the shadows.

Because of alleged overemphasis on large-scale social structures like the core-periphery hierarchy, some critics have asserted that the world-systems perspective denies the possibility of agency. On the contrary, the focus is on both how successful power holders concoct new strategies of domination and exploitation, and how dominated and exploited peoples struggle to protect themselves and build new institutions of justice. The structuralist aspects of the world-systems perspective make it possible to understand where agency is more likely to be successful and where not.

THE FUTURE OF THE WORLD SYSTEM

Phillip McMichael has studied the "globalization project"—the abandoning of Keynesian models of national development and a new (or renewed) emphasis on deregulation and opening national commodity and financial markets to foreign trade and investment. This approach focuses on the ideological aspects of the recent wave of international economic integration. The term many prefer for this turn in global discourse is *neoliberalism*, but it has also been called "Reaganism/Thatcherism" and the "Washington Consensus." The worldwide decline of the political Left predated the revolutions of 1989 and the demise of the Soviet Union, but it was certainly also accelerated by these events. The structural basis of the rise of the globalization project is the new level of integration reached by the global capitalist class. The internationalization of capital has long been an important part of the trend toward economic globalization. And there have been many claims to represent the general interests of business before. Indeed, every modern hegemon has made this claim. But the real integration of the interests of capitalists all over the world has very likely reached a level greater than at the peak of the nineteenth-century wave of globalization.

This is the part of the theory of a global stage of capitalism that must be taken most seriously, although it can certainly be overdone. The world-system has now reached a point at which both the old interstate system based on separate national capitalist classes and new institutions representing the global interests of capital exist and are powerful simultaneously. In this light, each country can be seen to have an important ruling class faction that is allied with the transnational capitalist class. The big question is whether or not this new level of transnational integration will be strong enough to prevent competition among states for world hegemony from turning into warfare, as it has always done in the past, during a period in which a hegemon (the United States) is declining.

Neoliberalism began as the Reagan–Thatcher attack on the welfare state and labor unions. It evolved into the structural adjustment policies of the International Monetary Fund (IMF) and the triumphalism of the ideologues of corporate globalization after the demise of the Soviet Union. In U.S. foreign policy, it has found expression in a new emphasis on "democracy promotion" in the periphery and semiperiphery. Rather than propping up military dictatorships in Latin America, the emphasis has shifted toward coordinated action between the CIA and the U.S. National Endowment for Democracy to promote electoral institutions in Latin America and other semiperipheral and peripheral regions. William I. Robinson points out that the kind of "low intensity democracy" promoted is really best understood as "polyarchy," a regime form in which elites orchestrate a process of electoral competition and governance that legitimates state power and undercuts more radical political alternatives that might threaten their ability to maintain their wealth and power by exploiting workers and peasants. Robinson convincingly argues that polyarchy and democracy promotion are the political forms most congruent with a globalized and neoliberal world economy in which capital is given free reign to generate accumulation wherever profits are greatest.

The insight that capitalist globalization has occurred in waves, and that these waves of integration are followed by periods of globalization backlash has important implications for the future. Capitalist globalization increased both intranational and international inequalities in the nineteenth century, and it did the same thing in the late twentieth century. Those countries and groups left out of the "beautiful époque" either mobilize to challenge the hegemony of the powerful or retreat into self-reliance or both. Globalization protests emerged in the noncore with the anti-IMF riots of the 1980s. The several transnational social movements that participated in the 1999 protest in Seattle brought globalization protest to the attention of observers in the core, and this resistance to capitalist globalization has continued and grown despite the setback that occurred in response to the terrorist attacks on New York and Washington in 2001. The 2003 global antiwar demonstrations against the Bush administration's "preventative" war against Iraq involve many of the same movements as well as some new recruits. The several transnational social movements face difficult problems of forming alliances and cooperative action. The idea of semiperipheral development implies that support for more democratic institutions of global governance will come from democratic socialist regimes that come to power in the semiperiphery. This has already happened in Brazil, where the new labor government strongly supports the movement for global social justice.

There is an apparent tension between those who advocate deglobalization and delinking from the global capitalist economy and the building of stronger, more cooperative and self-reliant social relations in the periphery and semiperiphery, on one hand, and those who seek to mobilize support for new or reformed institutions of democratic global governance. But in fact these strategies are complementary, and each can benefit by supporting the other. Self-reliance by itself, although an understandable reaction to exploitation, is not likely to solve the problems of humanity in the long run. The great challenge of the twenty-first century will be the building of a democratic and collectively rational global commonwealth. World-systems theory can be an important contributor to this effort.

— Christopher Chase-Dunn

See also *Annales* School; Capitalism; Globalization; Historical and Comparative Theory; Imperialism; Marxism; Wallerstein, Immanuel

FURTHER READINGS AND REFERENCES

Amin, Samir. 1997. *Capitalism in the Age of Globalization.* London: Zed.

Arrighi, Giovanni. 1994. *The Long Twentieth Century.* London: Verso.

Chase-Dunn, Christopher. 1998. *Global Formation.* Lanham, MD: Rowman & Littlefield.

Chase-Dunn, Christopher and Thomas D. Hall. 1997. *Rise and Demise: Comparing World-Systems.* Boulder, CO: Westview.

Frank, Andre Gunder. 1998. *Reorient.* Berkeley: University of California Press.

McMichael, Philip. 2000. *Development and Social Change: A Global Perspective.* Thousand Oaks, CA: Pine Forge.

Meyer, John W., John Boli, George M. Thomas, and Francisco Ramirez. 1997. "World Society and the Nation-State." *American Journal of Sociology* 103:144–81.

Modelski, George and William R. Thompson. 1996. *Leading Sectors and World Powers.* Columbia: University of South Carolina Press.

Robinson, William I. 1994. *Promoting Polyarchy.* Cambridge, UK: Cambridge University Press.

Shannon, Thomas R. 1996. *An Introduction to the World-Systems Perspective.* Boulder, CO: Westview.

Wallerstein, Immanuel. 2000. *The Essential Wallerstein.* New York: New Press.

WRIGHT, ERIK OLIN

Erik Olin Wright is a radical sociologist working within the Marxist tradition. Raised in a family of academics in Kansas, Wright studied history and social science at Harvard and Oxford University before entering the sociology program at Berkeley in the early 1970s. Upon completing his PhD degree in 1976, he secured a position in the Sociology Department at the University of Wisconsin, where he has been ever since. Wright thus made his appearance on the intellectual scene in the mid-1970s, along with an entire generation of young academics who were radicalized by the Vietnam War and the civil rights movement. What is remarkable about his career is not its initiation in Marxist debates—in this, it is not unlike many other careers of the "generation of '68"; rather, it is Wright's steady commitment to his research agenda for more than a quarter century, long after most of his peers had ended their dalliance with Marxist theory. Even more noteworthy is that, throughout this period, Wright has ceaselessly confronted mainstream sociology while at the same time carefully modifying his views in response to criticism. The result has been as unusual as it is significant: Over a long arc of theoretical innovation and conceptual clarification, Wright has quite successfully developed a nuanced and sophisticated version of Marxian class analysis and has managed to place it at the very core of contemporary social theory.

The Components of a Research Agenda. Wright's research agenda has been exceptionally clear and consistent. Throughout his career, he has been centrally concerned with interrogating the concept of "class" in Marxian theory. The bulk of this work has concentrated on how class operates as a mechanism for social differentiation in contemporary capitalism. In three successive book-length attempts, Wright has offered a careful discussion of the theoretical status of the term in Marxian theory and then proceeded to investigate how it maps on to contemporary society, mainly Europe and the United States. In addition to this component of his work, however, Wright has also expended considerable energy analyzing the importance of class on another axis in Marxian theory: its importance as a marker of qualitatively different social formations and a mechanism for the traversal from one historical epoch to another.

Class as a Mechanism for Social Differentiation. The trajectory of Erik Wright's theoretical innovations has been driven by a puzzle central to Marxism: how to marry the simple, polarized picture of class society to the empirically rich and quite diverse topography of capitalist societies—a puzzle that is most pointedly embodied in the problem of conceptualizing the "middle class." Marxists insist that, in every social formation, agents are slotted into two basic groups: producers, who generate a social surplus, and exploiters, who usurp a portion of this surplus. Every social formation is therefore characterized by two fundamental classes of exploited and exploiters. But it is also the case that this simple polarized picture does not sit easily with the reality of modern society. It is easy to find agents who, while technically belonging to one of the two "classes," also have features that set them apart from members of that same class. This is most famously exemplified in the case of professionals; while they do not directly control material productive assets, it strains our intuitions to slot them in the same category as workers on the production line. Wright's solution, which he briefly abandoned and then resurrected in a more nuanced version, is to conceptualize such members of social classes as simultaneously occupying locations in more than one class: they are in *contradictory class locations,* pulled in different and opposing directions (Wright 1978, 1985, 2000). The reason for this is that they reproduce themselves through mechanisms that include those typical of workers *and* those of capitalists. This allows Wright to move away from thinking of the middle class as a residual category, encompassing everyone who doesn't "fit" neatly into one of the two basic classes, to a category that is robustly defined.

Class and Historical Variation. The concept of class performs two functions in the broader Marxist theory of history. First, it serves as the central axis on which social formations are distinguished. Second, it is supposed to be the means through which these formations are propelled across time—through class struggle. But the notion of class struggle as the motor of history sits uneasily with another part of the Marxist canon, broadly known as technological determinism. On the latter argument, class struggle itself is subservient to a deeper force—namely, the developmental requirements of society's productive forces. Class struggle still plays a role but only to the extent that its outcomes are functional for the needs of the productive forces. The contingency and drama of class struggle is thus pit against a highly deterministic theory of technological development. Wright's solution to this tension has been a synthesis of sorts: He allows that there is a cumulative character to technological development across history. But technology does not drive history; rather, because humans tend to prefer greater productive power over less, technological achievements, when they occur, tend not to be abandoned. Technological growth therefore gives history a trajectory, preventing it from becoming a random walk. Within the broad trajectory imparted by this accumulation of productive power, there is enormous room for variation of social forms. And this variation is generated by the conflicts between classes. Which class wins, and which loses, is at best underdetermined by the needs of the productive forces. Class struggle is thus married to a weak technological determinism (Wright, Levine, and Sober 1993).

Wright has argued that this elevation of class struggle over the functional requirements of the productive forces comes at a cost: Marxists can no longer be confident that capitalism will necessarily give way to socialism, since the theory's determinism is now drastically weakened. Furthermore, after the collapse of the Eastern Bloc, it is no longer clear just what socialism entails. This implies that progressives must expend a great deal of energy on doing just what Marx himself strenuously abjured: drawing up designs—blueprints, as Marx called them—of the institutions necessary for a just social order, since they are no longer guaranteed by history and since the ones presented in the name of socialism failed on so many counts. In his most recent work, Wright has not only developed, but also sponsored through a series of conferences and book volumes, arguments about "Real Utopias"—realistic visions of a future society, inspired by the utopias of the present (see, e.g., Wright and Fong 2003).

Over the course of a quarter century, Wright has, in this fashion, explored the importance of class for the past, the present, and possible futures.

— Vivek Chibber

See also Capitalism; Historical Materialism; Marx, Karl; Social Class; Structuralist Marxism

FURTHER READINGS AND REFERENCES

Wright, Erik Olin. 1978. *Class, Crisis, and the State.* London: Verso.

———. 1985. *Classes.* London: Verso

———. 2000. *Class Counts.* Cambridge, MA: Harvard University Press.

Wright, Erik Olin et al. 1989. *The Debate on Classes.* London: Verso.

Wright, Erik Olin and Archon Fong, eds. 2003. *Deepening Democracy: Institutional Innovation in Empowered Participatory Governance.* London: Verso.

Wright, Erik Olin, Andrew Levine, and Elliott Sober. 1993. *Reconstructing Marxism.* London: Verso.

WUTHNOW, ROBERT

Robert Wuthnow (b. 1946), an American sociologist, is best known as a highly prolific, empirically oriented cultural sociologist and a sociologist of religion who has, along the way, created a novel theory of cultural change to use in his empirical investigations. Wuthnow received his BA from the University of Kansas and his PhD in sociology from University of California, Berkeley, in 1975 with a dissertation supervised by Charles Glock and Robert Bellah. He joined the faculty at Princeton University in 1976 and has been there ever since.

Like Pierre Bourdieu and Robert Merton, Wuthnow is a social theorist whose theories arise from and serve his empirical research into social life. For example, of Wuthnow's 22 published books, 9 edited volumes, and over 160 articles, few are devoted to sociological theory per se but are primarily devoted to topics in the sociology of religion and culture.

However, his theories have been influential because they provide tools for empirical investigations in the recently popular field of cultural sociology. Wuthnow's only purely theoretical book is *Meaning and Moral Order: Explorations in Cultural Analysis* (1987). The 730-page *Communities of Discourse: Ideology and Social Structure in the Reformation, the Enlightenment and European Socialism* (1989), apparently written at approximately the same time, is a detailed empirical study demonstrating his theory of cultural change.

Wuthnow is probably best known for the controversial proposal in these books to, in his words, go "beyond the problem of meaning" in cultural sociology. The dominant form of cultural analysis in the social sciences is what Wuthnow calls the "subjective" approach, where the analyst focuses on the beliefs, attitudes, opinions, or values of the individual. The point in this type of research is to figure out what is inside the person's head, and many readily accessible methods—such as opinion surveys—appear to be available for use. The problem of meaning is central in this tradition: What symbols "mean" to the individual is the central question.

According to Wuthnow, the primary problem with the subjective tradition is that we can never know what is really inside of people's heads—what people *really* think. We have access only to what they say, write, or do, from which we infer these inner states. Why not just use what we can observe and forget about the inner states of consciousness? Wuthnow's proposal is to stop investigating meaning and instead look at the patterns of observable symbolic codes such as words, movements, and texts. With this method, "Data are more readily observable kinds of behavior rather than being locked away in people's private ruminations" (1987:56). This results in a form of cultural structuralism, not unlike an analysis of Michel Foucault. We can, for example, identify the structure of codes in Protestant discourse—perhaps that the symbols "friend" and "Jesus" are more closely related in the more highly individualistic evangelicalism than in mainline Protestantism. While this does not tell us the "meaning" of these terms for any one Protestant, it is observable and can be correlated with observable action.

Where do these symbolic patterns come from? The relationship of culture to social structure is one of the original debates in sociological theory, and this is the other distinctive contribution of Wuthnow to social theory. Where, for example, did the set of symbols called "the discourse of the Protestant reformation" come from? His theory is premised on the insight that all symbols are explicitly produced by actors in particular environments; they do not somehow rise like ether from structural relationships. There are three stages of this cultural production. First, innumerable symbols are produced by innumerable people, a stage Wuthnow calls "cultural production." For example, Martin Luther was not the only person producing ideas during his life, but many others were as well. The next stage, "selection," explains why Luther's ideas become known. Some ideas are selected over others because they are able to obtain resources from the environment to be produced more broadly because they articulate with that environment. The final stage is "institutionalization," where routinized mechanisms are put into place for the continued production of the discourse. Publishing houses are set up, schools founded, denominations created—all devoted to the promotion of certain cultural symbols. Some cultural systems—like science—are so deeply institutionalized, with so many interlocking institutions devoted to their propagation, that we think of them as "reality." A critical part of Wuthnow's analysis is to ask why a particular cultural producer obtained the resources to institutionalize their preferred symbols.

Wuthnow's call to look at observable patterns of symbols, and to closely examine who exactly produced these symbols, along with a commitment to empirical research, has resulted in an unusual methodological stance among cultural sociologists. Bemoaning the fact that cultural sociology "has sometimes become a preserve for those disdainful of the positivism implicit in more dominant quantitative sub-fields" Wuthnow argues for "drawing on the hermeneutic literature" to be aware of interpretive limitations but to do "empirical work with as much attention to rigor and systematization as any unrepentant positivist might give" (1992:5). While he does not think this will produce positive knowledge, it will leave "tracks" of what was done so that the author's biases can be revealed. This call for positivist-like methods has meant that Wuthnow is one of the few advocates in cultural sociology of quantifying cultural symbols. For example, his students have quantified the symbols in flags, national anthems, popular songs, and academic texts.

— John H. Evans

See also Culture and Civilization; Foucault, Michel; Structuralism

FURTHER READINGS AND REFERENCES

Wuthnow, Robert. 1987. *Meaning and Moral Order: Explorations in Cultural Analysis.* Berkeley: University of California Press.

———. 1989. *Communities of Discourse: Ideology and Social Structure in the Reformation, the Enlightenment and European Socialism.* Cambridge, MA: Harvard University Press.

———. 1992. "Introduction: New Directions in the Empirical Study of Cultural Codes." Pp. 1–18 in *Vocabularies of Public Life: Empirical Essays in Symbolic Structure,* edited by Robert Wuthnow. New York: Routledge.

Z

ŽIŽEK, SLAVOJ

Slavoj Žižek (b. 1949) is one of the most outspoken proponents of Lacanian psychoanalysis working in contemporary social theory. Born in 1949 in Ljubljana, Slovenia, Žižek holds a PhD in philosophy from the Department of Philosophy, Faculty of Arts, Ljubljana and a PhD in psychoanalysis from the Université Paris-VIII. Over the last 15 years, the aptly nicknamed "Giant of Ljubljana" has attended over 250 international philosophical and cultural studies conferences, published over 25 books, and is currently the senior researcher in the Department of Philosophy at the University of Ljubljana. Not only is he an internationally recognized social theorist, he has also been known to dabble in politics, campaigning for the Slovenian presidency in 1990. Overall, Žižek is a provocative voice that has challenged many assumptions both inside and outside of academia.

While the scope of Žižek writings is far too vast to cover in this brief entry, there is a clear theoretical argument that runs throughout his work. His overarching theoretical program is perhaps best outlined in the book *The Sublime Object of Ideology* (1989) in which he presents a Lacanian-inspired form of ideological critique. For Žižek, ideology attempts to stitch together the fractured social field, which is traversed by inconsistencies and antagonisms. Social antagonisms, such as class struggle, are for Žižek equivalent to Lacan's notion of the Real as a traumatic kernel that resists symbolization. There are essentially two mechanisms by which ideology reconstructs the social as a unified, harmonious, and coherent totality. To effectively erase internal contradictions, ideology propagates sublime objects such as "the nation" or "the people." These symbolic fictions act as virtual stand-ins, repressing internal social antagonisms, which nonetheless reappear in the form of symptoms (e.g., class conflict, World Trade Organization [WTO] protests, global warming, or the increasing homeless population). Second, to purify its harmonious self-image, ideology not only represses social ambiguities but also externalizes them. In this manner, internal contestations are projected outward onto the proverbial other. Through ideology as a fantasy construct, the social is able to maintain its illusory integrity.

For Žižek, a Lacanian-inspired form of ideological critique is paramount to going through the social fantasy until the subject is able to identify with the symptom. As an example, Žižek references the Nazi construction of the Jew. Within the ideological fantasy of National Socialism, the Jew becomes the stumbling block that prevents the realization of the perfected Aryan race. The internal antagonisms found within the German social field are conveniently projected onto the Jew as the external other. To deconstruct this ideological projection, the subject should "traverse the phantasy" of Nazism, realizing that the traumatic kernel preventing the full realization of the Aryan myth is not external but internal to the Nazi project itself. Through the application of Lacanian concepts to the study of ideology, Žižek thus equips cultural critics with powerful analytical tools that complement and enlarge the leftist vocabulary.

In texts such as *Looking Awry* (1991), *Enjoy Your Symptom!* (1992), and *Everything You Always Wanted to Know About Lacan (But Were Afraid to Ask Hitchcock)* (1992), Žižek brings cultural studies and Lacan into dialog with one another. As a philosophical DJ, Žižek likes to mix it up, often employing a surprising combination of Kant, Marx, Hegel, Schelling, Badiou, and of course, Lacan to explore a wide range of contemporary cultural phenomena that include, but are by no means limited to, the Internet, Hollywood films, television, tea bag mantras, and other banal aspects of the American cultural sphere. While other cultural theorists see popular culture as merely an ideological mystification, Žižek believes that an understanding of the media is paramount to understanding the human psyche as such. According to Lacan, the unconscious is quite literally the symbolic order, or the discourse of the Other. Rather than a deep, dark, secret hidden within our minds, the unconscious resides outside us, embedded within everyday institutions, media culture, and social practices. Taking advantage of the ubiquity and the popularity of the American media, Žižek often employs concrete examples drawn from mainstream culture to clearly elucidate rather opaque Lacanian concepts. In perhaps his most famous example, Žižek uses sitcom laugh tracks to demonstrate the Lacanian maxim "desire is the desire of the other." In a typical Žižekian inversion of commonsense assumptions, he argues that laugh tracks do not tell us when to laugh, instead they literally laugh for us. The symbolic order—that is, the Lacanian Big Other—has relieved the viewer of the burden to laugh, laughing in our place.

Žižek also uses the explanatory power of Lacanian concepts to analyze contemporary politics. In particular, Žižek attacks New Agers, liberals, feminists, postmodernists, and multiculturalists. For Žižek, these movements are forms of micropolitics that do not challenge the hegemonic rule of capitalism or its political counterpart, liberal democracy. In fact, identity politics are endorsed and even encouraged by the new, flexible, transnational capitalist order. In *The Ticklish Subject* (2000), Žižek observes, "The depoliticized economy is the disavowed 'fundamental fantasy' of postmodern politics" (p. 355). Through a Lacanian perspective, Žižek argues that these movements are in fact forms of "interpassivity." In psychoanalysis, the interpassive subject remains fanatically active to prevent something from occurring. Applying this term to the realm of politics, Žižek contends that postmodern social movements constantly produce new pleasures, new identities, and new desires that remain fully within the scope of capitalism, thus preventing radical social transformation. Although identity politics have made important strides that should not be forgotten or abandoned, Žižek nevertheless sees such forms of activism as limited.

Consequentially, Žižek calls for the recentralization or a repoliticization of the economy in leftist politics. In *Repeating Lenin* (2001), Žižek endorses the radical political imagination of V. I. Lenin as an intervention that does not accept the "natural" and "unavoidable" status of the global economy. Instead of simply returning to Lenin's political project, Žižek instead argues for a rehabilitation of the spirit of Lenin's radical break with the hegemonic status quo. As opposed to identity politics, which remain situated within the logic of the capitalist market and the ideologies of liberal democracy, an extreme break with the status quo would be the embodiment of a "Lacanian act," creating new horizons of political, cultural, and economic possibilities. Thus Žižek views Lenin's project as a true historical event—an articulation of the void at the heart of symbolic order that opens up a space for radical social and political alternatives.

In conclusion, Žižek is important for social theory because he has demonstrated the wide-reaching explanatory power of Lacanian psychoanalysis. While receiving praise for his theoretical innovations, Žižek is no stranger to criticism. In the book *Contingency, Hegemony, and Universality* (2000), Žižek, Judith Butler, and Ernesto Laclau enter into an extended debate concerning these three concepts. Butler in particular questions Žižek's ability to account for the historical specificity of trauma. From her perspective, his Lacanian approach reduces all forms of oppression to the ahistorical category of the Real. In response, Žižek has argued that Butler is in fact ahistorical, creating a teleological narrative that posits her own theory of performative identity as a universal "truth" rather than a historically and culturally embedded form of knowledge. Furthermore, the Lacanian real is not really ahistorical but is rather the traumatic, unsymbolized kernel that is unique to each historical period. Thus, Žižek remains a highly controversial figure whose theories are read and debated across disciplines.

— Tyson Lewis

See also Butler, Judith; Lacan, Jacques; Marx, Karl; Marxism; Media Critique; Psychoanalysis and Social Theory; Simulation

FURTHER READINGS AND REFERENCES

Butler, J., E. Laclau, and S. Žižek. 2000. *Contingency, Hegemony, Universality: Contemporary Dialogues on the Left.* London & New York: Verso.

Žižek, S. 1989. *The Sublime Object of Ideology.* New York: London, Verso.

———. 1991. *Looking Awry: An Introduction to Jacques Lacan Through Popular Culture.* Cambridge, MA: MIT Press.

———. 1999. *The Ticklish Subject: The Absent Centre of Political Ontology.* New York: Verso.

———. 2001. *Repeating Lenin.* Zagreb, Croatia: Arkzin d.o.o.

ZNANIECKI, FLORIAN WITOLD

Florian Znaniecki (1882–1958) was a Polish and American sociologist and philosopher of culture, born on January 15, 1882, in Świątniki, Poland. He died on March 23, 1958, in Urbana-Champaign, Illinois. He formulated a theory of cultural systems with a humanistic coefficient that relates to the active experience of meaning and the axiological significance of cultural data. For Znaniecki, cultural data consist of values, and these differ from the mere "things" that are the object of research in the natural sciences. With his writings in Polish and English, Znaniecki developed a systematic sociological theory built on a theory of action that aimed at the understanding and explanation of the social dynamics of culture, change, and creativity. Znaniecki considered sociology the centerpiece of the cultural sciences because all systems of culture in their existence depend on social interactions. Sociology is a special cultural science that takes systems of social actions as its subject matter. They bear on social values—individuals and collectivities—as they appear to others and to themselves. Social values are the most complex and changeable among all cultural values—economic, religious, aesthetic, and others. Znaniecki investigated the ontology and theory of cultural and interactional foundations of more complex social systems, as they emerged from social actions, in sociological studies of knowledge, education, and national cultures. Znaniecki was also a researcher of civilizational processes and of the world society. His remarkable contribution to the methodology of cultural sciences was shaped by the principle of the humanistic coefficient that demands the comparative study of the experience of individuals and collectivities as historical subjects, since every element of a cultural system is what it appears to be in the experience of people who are actively dealing with it. To this end, he relied on case studies and biographical methods and assumed as a general rule of qualitative methodology analytic induction leading to abstraction and generalization.

Znaniecki studied in Geneva and Zurich, as well as at the Sorbonne in Paris, and took a doctoral degree in 1910 at the Jagiellonian University in Cracow where he presented the dissertation *The Problem of Value in Philosophy* (in Polish). In addressing the debates between idealists and realists, Znaniecki formulated an original humanistic stance, which was subsequently developed into the system of the philosophy of culturalism. A synthesis of these theses was presented in *Cultural Reality,* published in Chicago in 1919. The basic principles of his system were actions and values, through which he assumed a constructivist, relativist, and pluralist view of reality as a changeable historical world. In this respect, he held much in common with pragmatists.

Znaniecki came to the United States in 1914 at the invitation of William I. Thomas, whom he met as the director of the Bureau of the Society for the Protection of Emigrants in Warsaw. He was lecturer in Polish history and institutions at the Department of Sociology of the University of Chicago in the years 1917 to 1919. Together with Thomas, Znaniecki wrote the classic work of the Chicago School *The Polish Peasant in Europe and America* (1918–1920), considered a turning point in the development of theory and method in the social sciences. Here, Thomas and Znaniecki made unprecedented use of personal documents, including the letters and memoirs of migrants. Znaniecki took the initiative to write the *Methodological Note,* in which were formulated the conceptions of values and attitudes comprised by people's definition of the situation. This provided a theoretical schema of social becoming through the interaction of subjective and objective factors—that is, the

interplay of personality and culture. Action patterns were analyzed focusing on social psychological factors such as wishes or motives for recognition, the need for security, the exercise of power, and the impact of new experiences. They also drew on sociological factors such as the formation of institutions and organizations.

In 1920, Znaniecki returned to Poland, where he took the chair of sociology and philosophy of culture at Poznań University. Further theoretical assumptions were formulated in *Introduction to Sociology* (1922, in Polish), articulating the conception of social systems. He argued that from elementary social action emerges the constructed reality of more complex, dynamic systems: social relations, social roles, and social groups. Later, Znaniecki incorporated into social systems analytically conceived societies—political, religious, and national, as well as the world society, the development of which he predicted. Connections between systems of social actions and social self elaborated in *The Laws of Social Psychology* (1926) were developed into the pioneering conception of social role in *Sociology of Education* (1928–1930, in Polish). In the years 1931 to 1933, he lectured at Columbia University, as well as directed research on education and social change.

After his return to Poland, *Present-Day People and the Civilization of the Future* (1934, in Polish) was published, based on the result of this project, in which he also continued to explore the issues earlier discussed in *The Fall of Western Civilization* (1921, in Polish). Znaniecki published a systematic synthesis of theoretical conceptions in *The Method of Sociology* (1934), in which rules of qualitative research of social systems based on the conception of the cultural data were formulated as well as of analytic induction and case study logic. The analysis and taxonomy of social actions as the dynamic systems of values culminated in *Social Actions* (1936). In 1939, Znaniecki lectured at Columbia University on complex relations between the creators and users of knowledge. Those investigations were published in the masterpiece *The Social Role of the Man of Knowledge* (1940). World War II and the subsequent installation of communism made Znaniecki's return to Poland impossible. From 1940, he worked at the University of Illinois, where he wrote *Modern Nationalities* (1952) and his magnum opus: *Cultural Sciences* (1952). The development of secular literary cultures and the growth of organizations for their expansion gave origin to modern national culture societies. The sociologist's task is to study axionormative models and patterns of actions and the mediation of social organization in the development and integration of various categories of cultural systems.

Further works on systematic sociology where published posthumously in *Social Relations and Social Roles* (1965). Proof of the recognition of Znaniecki's creative output was his election as president of the American Sociological Society in 1953.

There are many affinities between Znaniecki's theory and symbolic interactionism. The eminence and distinct character of Znaniecki's theory among other interpretative theories stems from assumptions of culturalism that makes it possible to avoid the microsociological bias inherent in many other interpretive theories. Social systems and axionormative cultural orders are intertwined. The constructivism of the conception of reality's creative evolution, and the historical changeability of worldviews through creating meanings and values in interactions, erase the dualistic oppositions of thought and reality, subjectivity and objectivity, and consequently, the neo-Kantian opposition of nature and culture. The epistemological equivalent of the ontological conception of values and actions is the conception of the humanistic coefficient of cultural data, applied to sociological data. A researcher of cultural systems, including the social one, comes into contact with phenomena that are always somebody else's data, given first in the active experience of the participants in culture who create and re-create them. Valuable sources of sociological knowledge are personal experience of the sociologist, observation by the sociologist, and the communicated experiences and observations conducted by other people as group members, including those expressed through literature. Phenomenological and interpretive method is legitimized but in the context of objective systems of actions.

For Znaniecki, the analysis of social systems is rooted in the study of civilizational processes as a social integration of culture and the vision of a more fluid and peaceful future civilization. By discerning the political society or the state from the national culture society, Znaniecki explained the specific, cultural objectivity of the nation's existence, the cultural sources of conflicts between nations as well as the possibility of their cooperation. The opportunity for the emergence of a supranational, worldwide social system on the grounds of relative cultural values has been emphasized.

Znaniecki created a comprehensive theoretical system of humanistic sociology, based on an ontology of cultural values and concentrated on the meaningful and axiological dimension of reality. Meaningful cultural data may have a negative or positive significance depending on different systems, and their axiological significance is relative. The analytical conception of social systems as the subject matter in the cluster of other cultural systems of actions and values also encourages a cross-disciplinary approach. Znaniecki proclaimed the need for efforts in the direction of a new way of thinking about culture and the cultural sciences, which should lead to casting off the dogmas of naturalism and formal rationalisms as well as idealism unable to grasp the creative evolution of meanings and values and also as duration and specific objectivity of culture that prevailed in the twentieth century. He underlined the need for researching the cultural differences in the dynamics of conflicts and social changes in order to understand and control them and also to properly prepare people for creative leadership and peaceful cooperation.

— Elżbieta Hałas

See also Cosmopolitan Sociology; Nationalism; Phenomenology; Pragmatism; Social Constructionism; Symbolic Interaction; Thomas, William Isaac

FURTHER READINGS AND REFERENCES

Bierstedt, Robert. 1968. "Znaniecki Florian." Pp. 599–602 in *International Encyclopedia of the Social Sciences,* edited by D. L. Sills. Vol. 16. New York: Macmillan.

Thomas, William I. and Znaniecki Florian. 1918–1920. *The Polish Peasant in Europe and in America.* 5 vols. Chicago, IL: University of Chicago Press.

Znaniecki, Florian. 1934. *The Method of Sociology.* New York: Farrar & Rinehart.

———. 1952. *Cultural Sciences. Their Origin and Development.* Urbana: University of Illinois Press.

———. 1952. *Modern Nationalities.* Urbana, IL: University of Illinois Press.

———. 1998. *Education and Social Change,* edited by E. Hałas. Frankfurt am Main, Germany: Peter Lang Verlag.

Chronology of Social Theory

Jon A. Lemich

Early Roots

1406   Abdel Rahman Ibn-Khaldun dies, leaving written works on social topics that closely resemble the sociology of today.

Early Enlightenment

1651   Thomas Hobbes's *Leviathan* announces that "Life is nasty, brutish and short."

1690   John Locke publishes *Essay Concerning Human Understanding* and *Second Treatise on Government.*

18th Century

1739   David Hume's *Treatise on Human Nature* insists on studying human nature through observation rather than through pure philosophy.

1748   Hume publishes *An Enquiry Concerning Human Understanding.*

1748   Charles de Secondat, Baron de Montesquieu anonymously publishes *The Spirit of Laws.*

1751   Hume completes his *Enquiry Concerning the Principals of Morals.*

1762   With Jean-Jacques Rousseau's *The Social Contract,* we go from a "stupid and unimaginative animal" to "an intelligent being and a man."

1776   The Age of Revolution begins, and the flames are fanned by Thomas Paine's *Common Sense.*

1776   Adam Smith releases *An Inquiry into the Nature and Causes of the Wealth of Nations.*

1776   A landmark of the American Revolution and statement of political theory, the Declaration of Independence of the United States of America is published.

1781   Immanuel Kant argues against Hume's radical empiricism in *Critique of Pure Reason.*

1788   Kant publishes *Critique of Practical Reason,* emphasizing free will.

1789   Jeremy Bentham develops a theory of social morals based on the greatest happiness principle in *Introduction to the Principles of Morals and Legislation.*

1791   Olympe de Gouges, a butcher's daughter, writes an alternate version of *Declaration of the Rights of Man* titled *Declaration of the Rights of Woman.*

1792   Mary Wollstonecraft publishes *A Vindication of the Rights of Woman,* urging women to "acquire strength."

1792   Parisians storm the Bastille, beginning the French Revolution.

1798   Thomas Malthus theorizes on the social and demographic effects of scarcity with his *Essay on the Principle of Population.*

1800–1850

1807   Georg Hegel publishes the *Phenomenology of Spirit.*

1817   David Ricardo offers a new vision for political economy with *The Principles of Political Economy and Taxation.*

1821   Claude-Henry de Rouvroy, Comte de Saint-Simon publishes *The Industrial System.*

1837   Hegel publishes the *Philosophy of History.*

1838   Harriet Martineau's *How to Observe Morals and Manners* argues that the goal of sociology is to describe the historically situated relationship between manners and morals.

1840   Alexis de Tocqueville, a French intellectual, offered an early insight into *Democracy in America.*

1841   Ludwig Feuerbach's *The Essence of Christianity* articulates a materialist influence contrary to Hegelian idealism, inspiring Karl Marx.

1830–   Auguste Comte describes a positivistic, evolutionary
1842   view of the world in his *Positive Philosophy.*

1843   Feuerbach inspires secular, humanistic, scientific study of human behavior with *The Philosophy of the Future.*

1843   J. S. Mill publishes *System of Logic* in which he refines logic in its applications to social as well as purely natural phenomena.

1844   Friedrich Engels publishes *Outline of a Critique of Political Economy.*

1844   Karl Marx completes what will become known as his *Economic and Philosophic Manuscripts of 1844;* however, the manuscript is not published in entirety until 1932. The manuscript highlights Marx's early humanistic thinking.

1846   Marx publishes *The German Ideology*, proposing a study of historical materialism.

1848   Marx and Engels publish and distribute *The Communist Manifesto*, which serves as a clarion call for revolution based on Marx's theoretical principles.

1848   Workers revolt across Europe.

1848   Mill debates the ideas of socialism in his *Principles of Political Economy*.

1850–1900

1850   Herbert Spencer publishes *Social Statics*, developing his basic ideas of social structure and change, as well as arguing for rights for women and children.

1851   Feuerbach publishes *Lectures on the Essence of Religion*.

1851   The Great Exhibition of the Works of Industry of All Nations is held in London, primarily inside the iron-and-glass Crystal Palace. It is the first of a series of extravagant world fairs that proclaim the arrival of the industrial revolution.

1852   Marx offers an analysis of the French Revolution titled *The Eighteenth Brumaire of Louis Bonaparte*.

1856   Tocqueville publishes *Ancien Regime in Old Europe*.

1858   Marx develops ideas that will later be refined in *Capital* in *Grundrisse: Foundations of the Critique of Political Economy*.

1859   Charles Darwin publishes *The Origin of the Species*. With Darwinian evolutionary theory, biology takes its first real steps into philosophy's traditional terrain.

1859   Mill publishes *On Liberty*, echoing Tocqueville's fears about democracy.

1863   Lincoln's Emancipation Proclamation decrees that all slaves in the United States "shall be then, thenceforward, and forever free."

1865   The 13th Amendment to the United States Constitution abolishes slavery.

1867   Marx publishes Volume 1 of *Capital: A Critique of Political Economy*.

1871   The Paris Commune is formed.

1872   Friedrich Nietzsche publishes *The Birth of Tragedy, Out of the Spirit of Music* declaring that modern Europe is Apollonian in spirit and needs a recovery of the Dionysian.

1873   Spencer publishes *Study of Sociology*, the textbook used in the first course in sociology in the United States.

1882   Nietzsche publishes *The Gay Science* pronouncing that God is dead.

1877–   Spencer publishes the three volumes of *The Principles of*
1882   *Sociology*, which later inspire Sumner's concept of social Darwinism.

1884   Marx (posthumously) publishes Volume 2 of *Capital: A Critique of Political Economy*.

1884   Engels publishes *The Origins of the Family, Private Property and the State*, declaring that women's subordination is the result of society, not biology.

1887   Ferdinand Tönnies publishes *Gemeinschaft und Gesellschaft*, comparing urban and small town society.

1890   William James publishes *Principles of Psychology* before Sigmund Freud's psychoanalytic methods have become widespread.

1890   Gabriel Tarde discusses the difference between the imitative and the inventive in *Laws of Imitation*.

1893   Émile Durkheim publishes *The Division of Labor in Society* explicating the evolution from mechanical to organic solidarity.

1894   Volume 3 of Marx's *Capital* is published.

1894   Durkheim joins Emile Zola and Jean Jaures in defending Captain Alfred Dreyfus, a Jew unfairly accused of spying. The affair highlighted French anti-Semitism, which Durkheim saw as a deep social pathology.

1895   Durkheim develops the notion of a social fact, the basis for positivism in modern sociology, in *Rules of Sociological Method*.

1897   Durkheim publishes *Suicide* an application of the principles of the new method of sociology. He shows that suicide is a social fact, not an individual problem.

1899   Thorstein Veblen coins the now-famous term "conspicuous consumption" in his *Theory of the Leisure Class*.

1900–1910

1900   Sigmund Freud publishes *The Interpretation of Dreams*, an early statement of Freud's psychoanalytic principals.

1900–   In *Logical Investigations*, Edmund Husserl establishes
1901   the basis for the science of phenomenology.

1900   Georg Simmel finishes his *Philosophy of Money*, a wide-ranging analysis that points to, among other things, the tragedy of culture.

1900   The most well-known World's Fair in Paris exhibits the latest industrial marvels.

1902   Charles H. Cooley publishes *Human Nature and Social Order* at the University of Michigan. His work there is closely associated with the Chicago School.

1903   W. E. B. Du Bois writes *The Souls of Black Folk*, introducing the important concepts of double consciousness and the veil.

1903   Durkheim publishes *Moral Education*.

1904   Robert Park publishes *The Crowd and the Public*.

1905   Max Weber relates the idea systems of Calvinism to the emergence of the "iron cage" in *The Protestant Ethic and the Spirit of Capitalism*.

1907   William James publishes *Pragmatism*, which later inspires the development of symbolic interactionism.

1907   William G. Sumner first develops the concept of social Darwinism in his book *Folkways*.

1908   Georg Simmel publishes *Soziologie*, a wide-ranging set of essays on social phenomena reflecting Simmel's distinctive approach.

1910–1920

1911   In *Political Parties*, Roberto Michels devises the Iron Law of Oligarchy to explain how oligarchy develops in bureaucracy.

1912   In *Elementary Forms of the Religious Life*, Émile Durkheim introduces anthropological evidence to argue that religious experience lies at the foundation of the social order.

1913   The term "behaviorism" is first used by J. B. Watson.

1914   World War I begins.

1915   Vifredo Pareto publishes *General Treatise on Sociology* a systemic, equilibrium-based theory of society.

1916   Ferdinand de Saussure's *Course in General Linguistics* forms the basis for structuralism.

1916   Lenin advances Marx's ideas in *Imperialism, The Highest Stage of Capitalism,* identifying the inherent global expansionistic tendencies of capitalist societies.

1917   The Russian Revolution, inspired by Marxist ideals, overthrows the Czars.

1918   With Florian Znaniecki, W. I. Thomas publishes *The Polish Peasant in Europe and America,* a study that draws on multiple investigative methods.

1919   Pitrim Sorokin's *System of Sociology* lays out his theory of cultural organization and helps develop the ontology of integralism.

1920–1930

1920   American women win the right to vote.

1921   Robert E. Park and Ernest W. Burgess write the first major textbook in sociology: *Introduction to the Science of Sociology.*

1922   Weber's *Economy and Society,* his comparative historical social theory, is published in three volumes.

1922   Bronislaw Malinowski discusses indirect exchange in the Kula rings of the Trobriand Islands in *Argonauts of the Western Pacific.*

1922   Sir James G. Fraser's controversial *The Golden Bough* shows that the Christian story of the man-god sacrificed on the tree is borrowed from other ancient myths.

1922   Cooley introduces the concept of the "looking-glass self" in *Human Nature and the Social Order.*

1923   György Lukács publishes *History and Class Consciousness.*

1923   The Institute of Social Research, also known as the Frankfurt School, is founded.

1923   Ernst Cassirer publishes the first part of "The Philosophy of Symbolic Forms," a series that examines various forms of symbolic representation.

1924   John Maynard Keynes offers a brilliant analysis of the effects of inflation and deflation in his most influential work, *A Tract on Monetary Reform.*

1925   Marcel Mauss develops his theory of gift exchange in *The Gift.*

1925   Burgess and Park publish *The City.*

1925   Maurice Halbwachs publishes *The Social Frameworks of Memory,* a pioneering text in social memory studies.

1927   Martin Heidegger publishes *Being and Time.*

1928   Margaret Mead drops the proof for her controversial *Coming of Age in Samoa* off at the publisher before embarking for New Guinea.

1929   Lucien Febvre and Marc Bloch found the *Annales* School, which is famous for its work on social history.

1929   Karl Mannheim develops his sociology of knowledge in *Ideology and Utopia.*

1929   The U.S. stock market crashes, leading to a worldwide depression.

1930–1940

1930   Psychiatrist J. L. Moreno invents sociometry, the keystone concept for network exchange theory.

1932   Alfred Schütz's *The Phenomenology of the Social World* extends the philosophy of phenomenology into social theory.

1933   Nazis open the first concentration camp at Dachau.

1934   George H. Mead's lectures are compiled and published as *Mind, Self and Society,* the basic text for symbolic interactionism.

1935   Mannheim proposes a planned society in *Man and Society in an Age of Reconstruction.*

1936   Keynes publishes *General Theory of Employment, Interest and Money,* the text that immortalizes his economic theory.

1937   Talcott Parsons publishes the *Structure of Social Action,* in which he introduces grand European theory to an American audience.

1938   B. F. Skinner publishes *The Behavior of Organisms.*

1939   The first shots of World War II are fired as German forces invade Poland.

1939   Norbert Elias publishes *The Civilizing Process* in which he links changes in everyday life to changes in broader social structure.

1940–1950

1940   A. R. Radcliffe-Brown writes *Structure and Function in Primitive Society,* which has a great influence on structural functionalism.

1927– 1940   Walter Benjamin compiles his notes on the Paris Arcades, which are published as *Das Passagen-Werk* in 1982.

1941   At Auschwitz, Nazis begin the use of Zyklon-B gas to murder Jews.

1942   Margaret Mead's *Growing Up in New Guinea* draws a parallel between the primitive Manus and Western civilization.

1942   Joseph Schumpeter revises Marx's predictions on the downfall of capitalism in *Capitalism, Socialism and Democracy.*

1943   Jean-Paul Sartre elaborates contemporary existentialism in *Being and Nothingness,* partially written in a German war prison from 1940–1941.

1944   Karl Polanyi analyzes the industrial revolution, free trade, and socialism in *The Great Transformation.*

1945   In the same year, Hitler commits suicide as America unleashes the atom bomb on Japan.

1947   In *The Accursed Share,* Georges Bataille values the concepts of excess, waste, and sacrifice in his social theory.

1948   Alfred Kinsey publishes *The Sexual Behavior of the Human Male* along with Wardell Pomeroy and Clyde Martin.

1949   Talcott Parsons publishes *Essays in Sociological Theory, Pure and Applied.*

1949   Claude Lévi-Strauss publishes *Elementary Structures of Kinship.*

1949   Max Horkheimer and Theodor Adorno seek to explain why the Enlightenment failed to deliver on its promises of progress, reason, and order in *The Dialectic of Enlightenment.*

1949   Robert Merton publishes *Social Theory and Social Structure.*

1949   Simone de Beauvoir publishes *The Second Sex* in which she provides an existential analysis of the concept of woman.

1950–1960

1950   David Reisman's *The Lonely Crowd* develops the concepts of inner- and other-directedness.

1951   C. Wright Mills publishes *White Collar,* a critical analysis of the work lives of Americans.

1951   Parsons publishes *The Social System* and *Toward a General Theory of Action,* which further refine his structural-functional theory and develop action theory.

1952   The American Psychiatric Association publishes the first edition of the *Diagnostic and Statistical Manual of Mental Disorders (DSM-I).*

1954   Abraham Maslow delineates his famous hierarchy of needs in *Motivation and Personality.*

1955   L. J. Moreno gives his book, *Sociometry,* to the American Sociological Association for publication.

1956   Mills publishes *The Power Elite,* anticipating Dwight Eisenhower's ideas on the military-industrial complex.

1956   Ralf Dahrendorf's *Class and Class Conflict in Industrial Society* becomes the basic text in conflict theory.

1956   Lewis Coser publishes *The Functions of Social Conflict* in which he integrates Simmel's ideas on conflict with a structural-functional approach.

1957   Roland Barthes examines myths and cultural objects as a language of signs in society in *Mythologies.*

1958   John K. Galbraith's *The Affluent Society* challenges the American myth of consumer sovereignty.

1959   Karl R. Popper debates the philosophy and rules of science in *The Logic of Scientific Discovery.*

1959   Mills articulates his famous view of sociology in *The Sociological Imagination,* where he also critiques Parsons's structural functionalism.

1959   Erving Goffman develops his dramaturgical theory and famous ideas of front- and backstage in *The Presentation of Self in Everyday Life.*

1960–1970

1961   George C. Homans publishes *Social Behavior: Its Elementary Forms,* the pioneering text in exchange theory.

1962   Richard Emerson's article, "Power-Dependence Relations" is published in the *American Sociological Review.*

1962   Thomas Kuhn develops a revolutionary rather than evolutionary theory of the advance of science in *The Structure of Scientific Revolutions.* This book also popularizes the term *paradigm.*

1963   Goffman publishes *Stigma,* a critical book for labeling theory.

1963   200,000 people march for civil rights in Washington, D.C. Martin Luther King Jr. gives his famous "I Have a Dream" speech at the Lincoln Memorial.

1963   The second wave of feminism is marked by Betty Friedan's *The Feminine Mystique.*

1964   Peter Blau develops a micro-macro theory of exchange in *Exchange and Power in Social Life.*

1964   Marshall McLuhan declares that the medium is the message in *Understanding Media: The Extensions of Man.*

1964   Herbert Marcuse publishes *One Dimensional Man: Studies in the Ideology of Advanced Industrial Society* describing society's destructive impact on people.

1965   Michel Foucault's *Madness and Civilization* is published.

1966   William Masters and Virginia Johnson publish *Human Sexual Response,* introducing large numbers of people to the study of sexuality.

1966   Peter Berger and Thomas Luckmann's *The Social Construction of Reality: A Treatise in the Sociology of Knowledge* extends phenomenology to macrolevel issues.

1967   Jacques Derrida finishes *On Grammatology,* which becomes a central text in the emerging field of poststructuralism.

1967   Guy Debord publishes *The Society of the Spectacle,* a critique of media and consumption in contemporary social life.

1967   Harold Garfinkel's *Studies in Ethnomethodology* creates a new micro-social theory.

1968   Student revolts form an epicenter in Paris and sweep through Europe.

1969   Herbert Blumer publishes *Symbolic Interactionism: Perspectives and Methods,* offering an overview of the symbolic interactionist perspective.

1970–1980

1970   Alvin Gouldner's *The Coming Crisis of Western Sociology* critiques many trends in Western sociology, especially Parsonsian structural functionalism.

1970   Jean Baudrillard releases *Consumer Society: Myths and Structures,* a groundbreaking text in the studies of consumption.

1971   Jürgen Habermas relates material interest to idea systems in *Knowledge and Human Interests.*

1972   The demolition of the modernist Pruitt-Igoe housing project in St. Louis marks the end of the reign of modernity for some postmodernist theorists.

1973   Howard Becker publishes *Outsiders: Studies in the Sociology of Deviance,* a key text in the sociology of deviance.

1973   Baudrillard's *The Mirror of Production* marks his break from his Marxian roots.

1973   Clifford Geertz publishes *The Interpretation of Cultures.*

1974   Herbert Marcuse publishes *Eros and Civilization: A Philosophical Inquiry into Freud* where he translates Freud for critical theory.

1974   The first part of Immanuel Wallerstein's 3-volume *The Modern World System* shifts the focus of Marxian theory to exploitation between nations on a global scale.

1974   First issue of *Theory & Society* published.

1974   Luce Irigaray's *Speculum of the Other Woman* argues that psychoanalysis is phallocentric and thus has no place for the feminine.

1974   Daniel Bell's *The Coming of Post-Industrial Society* predicts the coming of "knowledge society."

1974   Goffman's *Frame Analysis: An Essay on the Organization of Experience* creates a new theoretical methodology.

1974   Glen H. Elder Jr. argues for a life course perspective in social psychology in *Children of the Great Depression.*

1974   Henri LeFebvre publishes *The Production of Space* provoking social analysis of space.

1975   Randall Collins publishes *Conflict Sociology: Toward an Explanatory Science,* in which Collins develops a micro orientation to conflict theory.

1975   E. O. Wilson introduces the term *sociobiology* in *Socio-Biology: The New Synthesis.*

1975   Foucault publishes *Discipline and Punish: The Birth of the Prison* in which he depicts the origins of the carceral society.

1976   Baudrillard argues that the modern world has lost the ability to engage in symbolic exchange in *Symbolic Exchange and Death.*

1977   Pierre Bourdieu publishes *Outline of a Theory of Practice* formulating his constructivist structuralism and his concepts of habitus and field.

1978   Marcuse publishes *The Aesthetic Dimension: Toward a Critique of Marxist Aesthetics.*

1978   In *The Reproduction of Mothering: Psychoanalysis and the Sociology of Gender,* Nancy Chodorow draws on object relations theories to rethink gender and the mother-child relationship.

1978   Edward Said's *Orientalism* opens cultural studies to postcolonial theory.

1979   Arlie Hochschild's article "Emotion Work, Feeling Rules and Social Structure" is published, introducing social theorists to the effects of emotional labor.

1979   Theda Skocpol's *States and Social Revolutions* shows that state structures, international forces, and class relations contribute to revolutionary transformations.

1979   Jean-Francois Lyotard publishes *The Postmodern Condition.*

1979   Bruno Latour and Steve Woolgar publish *Laboratory Life: The Social Construction of Scientific Facts,* a key document for the social studies of science; it also inspires actor network theory.

1979   Richard Rorty's *Philosophy and the Mirror of Nature* rejects foundationalist and essentialist epistemologies and argues for the merits of pragmatic philosophy.

1980–1990

1980   Foucault publishes the first of his three-volume opus, *The History of Sexuality,* major works on poststructuralist and queer theory.

1980   In a famous essay of the same name, Stuart Hall introduces the "Encoding/Decoding" model of television viewing, arguing that audiences interpret the meaning of programs in many ways.

1980   Adrienne Rich writes her essay "Compulsory Heterosexuality and Lesbian Existence," creating the lesbian continuum and coining the term *compulsory heterosexuality.*

1982   First issue of *Theory, Culture and Society* is published.

1982   Niklas Luhmann develops his distinctive version of systems theory in *The Differentiation of Society.*

1982–   Jeffrey Alexander releases *Theoretical Logic in Sociology*
1983   in four volumes, paralleling Parsons's *The Structure of Social Action,* synthesizing and updating functionalism.

1983   Cook, Emerson, Gillmore, and Yamagishi publish "The Distribution of Power in Exchange Networks: Theory and Experimental Results."

1983   Baudrillard's *Simulations* develops the concepts of simulation and simulacra in society.

1983   Nancy Hartsock publishes "The Feminist Standpoint: Developing the Ground for a Specifically Feminist Historical Materialism," an article crucial to the definition of standpoint theory.

1983   Hochschild publishes *The Managed Heart: Commercialization of Human Feeling.*

1983   The first issue of *Sociological Theory* is published.

1983   French philosopher Paul Ricoeur publishes volume 1 of *Time and Narrative,* a series that describes the centrality of narrative to lived experience.

1984   Pierre Bourdieu publishes *Distinction: A Social Critique of the Judgment of Taste* in which he applies his constructivist structuralism to consumption and culture in France.

1984   Anthony Giddens publishes *The Constitution of Society: Outline of the Theory of Structuration*, the most complete statement of his structuration theory.

1984   Habermas publishes *The Theory of Communicative Action*, vol. 1, *Reason and the Rationalization of Society*, reinterpreting and extending Weber's social theory and developing his ideas of communicative rationality.

1985   Gilles Deleuze and Felix Guattari oppose psychoanalysis and offer a political analysis of desire in *Anti-Oedipus: Capitalism and Schizophrenia*.

1985   Robert Bellah et al. publish *Habits of the Heart: Individualism and Commitment in American Life*, a micro-macro look at democratic community and individualism.

1985   Jonathan Turner's essay, "In Defense of Positivism" is published.

1986   Ulrich Beck completes *Risk Society: Towards a New Modernity*, which begins a widespread interest in the concept of risk in late modern life.

1986   Jacques Lacan publishes *Écrits*, in which he revises Freud's psychoanalysis in the context of Saussurian linguistics.

1986   Paul Virilio publishes *Speed and Politics*, introducing the concept of speed to social theory.

1987   Dorothy Smith combines phenomenology and feminism in *The Everyday World as Problematic: A Feminist Sociology*.

1987   Habermas explores the colonization of the lifeworld in *The Theory of Communicative Action*, vol. 2, *Lifeworld and System, a Critique of Functionalist Reason*.

1988   Noam Chomsky and Edward Herman declare, in *Manufacturing Consent: The Political Economy of the Mass Media*, that the mass media is used as a tool of political propaganda.

1989   In *The Sublime Object of Ideology*, Slavoj Žižek draws on Lacanian psychoanalysis to develop his theory of ideology critique and cultural analysis.

1989   Zygmunt Bauman argues that the Holocaust is a consequence of modernity in *Modernity and the Holocaust*.

1989   David Harvey introduces the idea of time-space compression and develops social geography in *The Condition of Postmodernity: An Enquiry into the Origins of Cultural Change*.

1989   In his influential *Sources of the Self*, Charles Taylor explores the cultural and intellectual origins of modern selfhood.

1990–2000

1990   James S. Coleman publishes *Foundations of Social Theory*, laying the foundations for sociologically relevant rational choice theory.

1990   Judith Butler calls for the subversion of the hegemony of gender in *Gender Trouble*.

1990   Giddens publishes *The Consequences of Modernity*, introducing the idea of the juggernaut of modernity.

1990   Donna Haraway's essay "A Manifesto for Cyborgs: Science, Technology, and Socialist Feminism" becomes an important postmodern contribution to feminist theory.

1990   Patricia Hill Collins publishes *Black Feminist Thought: Knowledge, Consciousness and Empowerment*, where, among other things, she develops the concept of intersectionality.

1991   Frederic Jameson writes *Postmodernism, or, the Cultural Logic of Late Capitalism*.

1991   Kenneth Gergen publishes *The Saturated Self: Dilemmas of Identity in Contemporary Life*, an account of the chaos of postmodern selfhood.

1992   Marc Augé publishes *Non-Places: An Introduction to an Anthropology of Supermodernity*.

1992   Roland Robertson's *Globalization: Social Theory and Global Culture*, building on his work in religion, develops a series of ideas, including the concept of glocalization.

1992   Paul Gilroy revisits the origins of Atlantic African cultural diaspora in *The Black Atlantic*.

1993   George Ritzer extends Weber's theory of rationalization to the realm of consumption and culture in *The McDonaldization of Society*.

1994   Cornell West publishes *Race Matters*.

1995   Luhmann's *Social Systems* further develops his version of systems theory.

1996   Manuel Castells conceives of a world dominated by the flow of information in *The Rise of the Network Society*.

1996   Arjun Appadurai develops his concept of global "scapes" in *Modernity at Large: Cultural Dimensions of Globalization*.

1997   Chomsky publishes "Media Control: The Spectacular Achievements of Propaganda."

1998   Patricia Hill Collins's *Fighting Words: Black Women and the Search for Justice* further develops her theory of intersectionality.

1999   David Willer publishes *Network Exchange Theory*.

2000   In *Empire*, Michael Hardt and Antonio Negri propose that the age of imperialism is over, being replaced by an empire without a national base.

Master Bibliography

Abbott, Andrew. 1988. *The System of Professions: Essays on the Expert Division of Labor.* Chicago, IL: University of Chicago Press.

Abelshauser, Werner. 1997. "Erhard oder Bismarck? Die Richtungsentscheidung der deutschen Sozialpolitik am Beispielder Reform der Sozialversicherung in den Fünziger Jahren" [Erhard or Bismarck? Strategical Options of German Social Policy: The Debate on the Social Security System in Germany in the 50s]. *Geschichte und Gesellschaft* 22:376–92.

Abercombie, N., S. Hill, and B. S. Turner. 1980. *The Dominant Ideology Thesis.* London: Allen & Unwin.

Abercrombie, N., S. Hill, and B. S. Turner. 1986. *Sovereign Individuals of Capitalism.* London: Allen & Unwin.

Abernathy, David B. 2000. *The Dynamics of Global Dominance.* New Haven, CT: Yale University Press.

Abramovitz, M. 1988. *Regulating the Lives of Women.* Boston, MA: South End.

Adam, B. 1990. *Time and Social Theory.* Philadelphia, PA: Temple University Press.

Adam, B. 1998. *Timescapes of Modernity.* London: Routledge.

Adam, B., U. Beck, and J. van Loon. 2000. *The Risk Society and Beyond.* London: Sage.

Adams, Bert N. and R. A. Sydie. 2001. *Sociological Theory.* Thousand Oaks, CA: Pine Forge.

Adorno, T. W. 1991. *The Culture Industry.* London: Routledge.

Adorno, T. W. 1994. *The Stars Down to Earth and Other Essays on the Irrational in Culture.* London: Routledge.

Adorno, Theodor and Max Horkheimer. 1972. *Dialectic of Enlightenment.* Translated by J. Cumming. New York: Seabury Press.

Adorno, Theodor W. and Max Horkheimer. 1977. "The Culture Industry: Enlightenment as Mass Deception." Pp. 349–83 in *Mass Communication and Society,* edited by James Curran, Michael Gurevitch, and Janet Woollacott. London: Edward Arnold.

Adorno, Theodor, Hans Albert, Ralf Dahrendorf, Jürgen Habermas, Harald Pilot, and Karl R. Popper. 1976. *The Positivist Dispute in German Sociology.* London: Heinemann.

Aglietta, M. 1979. *A Theory of Capitalist Regulation: The U.S. Experience.* London: Verso.

Aglietta, M. 1997. *Régulation et crises du capitalism* [A Theory of Capitalist Regulation]. New ed. Paris: Odile Jacob.

Ahearne, Jeremy. 1995. *Michel de Certeau: Interpretation and Its Other.* Cambridge, UK: Polity.

Alaimo, Stacy. 2000. *Undomesticated Ground: Recasting Nature as Feminist Space.* Ithaca, NY, & London: Cornell University Press.

Albert, Hans and Ernst Topitsch, eds. 1971. *Der Werturteilsstreit* [The Value Judgment Dispute]. Darmstadt, Germany: Wissenschaftliche Buchgesellschaft.

Albrow, Martin. 1997. *The Global Age: State and Society Beyond Modernity.* Stanford, CA: Stanford University Press.

Aldrich, Howard. 1979. *Organizations and Environments.* Englewood Cliffs, NJ: Prentice-Hall.

Aldrich, Howard. 1999. *Organizations Evolving.* Thousand Oaks, CA: Sage.

Alexander, Jeffrey C. 1982. *Theoretical Logic in Sociology.* vol. 1, *Positivism, Presuppositions, and Current Controversies.* Berkeley: University of California Press.

Alexander, Jeffrey C. 1982–1983. *Theoretical Logic in Sociology.* 4 vols. Berkeley: University of California Press.

Alexander, Jeffrey C., ed. 1985. *Neofunctionalism.* Beverly Hills, CA: Sage.

Alexander, Jeffrey C. 1987. *Twenty Lectures: Sociological Theory Since World War Two.* New York: Columbia University Press.

Alexander, Jeffrey C. 1988. *Action and Its Environments.* New York: Columbia University Press.

Alexander, Jeffrey C. 1988. *Durkheimian Sociology: Cultural Studies.* Cambridge, UK: Cambridge University Press.

Alexander, Jeffrey C. 1995. *Fin-de-Siècle Social Theory: Relativism, Reduction, and the Problem of Reason.* London: Verso.

Alexander, Jeffrey C., ed. 1998. *Neofunctionalism and After.* Malden, MA: Blackwell.

Alexander, Jeffrey C., ed. 1998. *Real Civil Societies: Dilemmas of Institutionalization.* Thousand Oaks, CA: Sage.

Alexander, Jeffrey C. 2001. *Evil and Good: A Cultural Sociology.* Cambridge, UK: Cambridge University Press.

Alexander, Jeffrey C. Forthcoming. *The Possibilities of Justice: Civil Society and Its Contradictions.* Oxford, UK: Oxford University Press.

Alexander, Jeffrey C. and Paul Colomy. 1985. "Toward Neo-Functionalism." *Sociological Theory* 3:11–23.

Alexander, Jeffrey C. and Paul Colomy, eds. 1990. *Differentiation Theory and Social Change: Historical and Comparative Perspectives.* New York: Columbia University Press.

Alexander, Jeffrey C., Gary T. Marx, and Christine Williams. 2004. *Self, Social Structure and Beliefs: Essays in Honor of Neil Smelser.* Berkeley: University of California Press.

Alexander, M. Jacqui and Chandra Talpade Mohanty, eds. 1997. *Feminist Genealogies, Colonial Legacies, Democratic Futures.* New York: Routledge.

Alford, C. Fred. 1991. *The Self in Social Theory: A Psychoanalytic Account of Its Construction in Plato, Hobbes, Locke, Rawls, and Rousseau.* New Haven, CT: Yale University Press.

Allan, S. 2003. *Media, Risk and Science.* Buckingham, UK, & Philadelphia, PA: Open University Press.

Allen, A. 2003. *Accountability for Private Life.* Lanham, MD: Rowman & Littlefield.

Allen, Philip J., ed. 1963. *Pitirim A. Sorokin in Review.* Durham, NC: Duke University.

Alter, Peter. 1989. *Nationalism.* London: Edward Arnold.

Althusser, Louis. 1970. *For Marx.* Translated by Ben Brewster. New York: Vintage.

Althusser, Louis. 1971. "Ideology and Ideological State Apparatuses." In *Lenin and Philosophy and Other Essays.* Translated by Ben Brewster. London: New Left Books.

Althusser, Louis. 1972. "Montesquieu: Politics and History." Pp. 13–109 in *Politics and History, Montesquieu, Rousseau, Hegel and Marx.* Translated by Ben Brewster. London: NLB.

Althusser, Louis. 1972. "Rousseau: The Social Contract (The Discrepancies)." Pp. 111–60 in *Politics and History: Montesquieu, Rousseau, Marx.* Translated by Ben Brewster. London: NLB.

Althusser, Louis and Etienne Balibar. 1970. *Reading Capital.* Translated by Ben Brewster. London: New Left Books.

Amin, Ash, ed. 1994. *Post-Fordism: A Reader.* Oxford, UK: Blackwell.

Amin, Samir. 1997. *Capitalism in the Age of Globalization.* London: Zed.

Amott, Teresa L. and Julie A. Matthaei. 1996. *Race, Gender, and Work: A Multicultural Economic History of Women in the United States.* Boston, MA: South End.

Andersen, Margaret and Patricia Hill Collins. 1995. *Race, Class, and Gender.* 2d ed. Belmont, CA: Wadsworth.

Anderson, Benedict. 1991. *Imagined Communities.* Rev. ed. London: Verso.

Anderson, Benedict. 1996. "Introduction." In *Mapping the Nation,* edited by Gopal Balakrishnan. London: Verso.

Anderson, Perry. 1976. *Considerations on Western Marxism.* London: New Left Books.

André, Serge. 1999. *What Does a Woman Want?* New York: Other Press.

Ang, Ien and Joke Hermes 1991. "Gender and/in Media Consumption." Pp. 307–28 in *Mass Media and Society,* edited by James Curran and Michael Gurevitch. New York: Routledge.

Anzaldua, Gloria. 1987. *Borderlands/La Frontera: The New Mestiza.* San Francisco, CA: Aunt Lute.

Appadurai, Arjun, 1986. *The Social Life of Things: Commodities in Cultural Perspective.* Cambridge, UK: Cambridge University Press.

Appadurai, Arjun. 1990. "Disjuncture and Difference in the Global Cultural Economy." *Theory, Culture and Society* 7: 295–310.

Appadurai, Arjun. 1990. "Disjuncture and Difference in the Global Cultural Economy." Pp. 295–310 in *Global Culture,* edited by M. Featherstone. London: Sage.

Appadurai, Arjun. 1996. *Modernity at Large: Cultural Dimensions of Globalization.* Minneapolis, MN: University of Minnesota Press.

Archer, Margaret. 1982. "Morphogenesis versus Structuration: On Combining Structure and Action." *British Journal of Sociology* 33:455–83.

Archer, Margaret S. 1995. *Realist Social Theory: The Morphogenetic Approach.* New York: Cambridge University Press.

Archibugi, Daniele and David Held, eds. 1995. *Cosmopolitan Democracy: An Agenda for a New World Order.* Cambridge, UK: Polity.

Arditi, George. 1998. *A Genealogy of Manners: Transformations of Social Relations in France and England from the Fourteenth to the Eighteenth Century.* Chicago, IL: Chicago University Press.

Arendt, Hannah. 1950. "Social Science Techniques and the Study of Concentration Camps." *Jewish Social Studies* 12: 49–64.

Arendt, Hannah. 1963. *Eichmann in Jerusalem: A Report on the Banality of Evil.* New York: Viking.

Arendt, Hannah. 1965. *On Revolution.* New York: Viking.

Aristotle. 1991. *On Rhetoric: A Theory of Civic Discourse.* Translated by George A. Kennedy. Oxford, UK: Oxford University Press.

Armitage, John, ed. 2000. *Paul Virilio: From Modernism to Hypermodernism and Beyond.* London: Sage.

Armitage, John, ed. 2001. *Virilio Live: Selected Interviews.* London: Sage.

Arnason, J. P. 1987. "Figurational Sociology as a Counter-Paradigm." *Theory, Culture and Society* 4(2–3):444.

Arnason, J. P. 2001. "Capitalism in Context: Sources, Trajectories and Alternatives." *Thesis Eleven* 66:99–125.

Arnheim, Rudolf. 1969. *Film as Art.* London: Faber & Faber.

Aron, Raymond. 1960. "Macht, Power, Puissance: Prose Democratique ou Poesie Demoniacque?" *Archives Europeenes de Sociologie* 1:27–51.

Aron, Raymond. 1967. *The Industrial Society: Three Essays on Ideology and Development.* London: Weidenfeld & Nicolson.

Aron, Raymond. 1968. *Main Currents in Sociological Thought.* Vol. 1. Translated by R. Howard. New York: Doubleday Anchor.

Arrighi, Giovanni. 1994. *The Long Twentieth Century.* London: Verso.

Augé, Marc. 1995. *Non-Places: Introduction to an Anthropology of Supermodernity.* Translated by John Howe. London: Verso.

Augé, Marc. 1998. *An Anthropology for Contemporaneous Worlds.* Translated by Amy Jacobs. Stanford, CA: Stanford University Press.

Augé, Marc. 1998. *A Sense for the Other: The Timeliness and Relevance of Anthropology.* Translated by Amy Jacobs. Stanford, CA: Stanford University Press.

Augé, Marc. 1999. *The War of Dreams: Studies in Ethno Fiction.* Translated by Liz Heron. London: Pluto.

Augé, Marc. 2002. *In the Metro.* Translated by Tom Conley. Minneapolis: University of Minnesota Press.

Aust, Andreas, Sigrid Leitner, and Stephan Lessenich, eds. 2000. "Sozialmodell Europa: Kontouren eines Phänomens" [The Social Model of Europe: Outline of a Phenomenon]. *Jahrbuch für Europa- und Nordamerikastudien.* No. 4. Opladen, Germany: Leske and Budrich.

Avalle, D'Arco Silvio. [1973] 1986. *L'Ontologia del Segno in Saussure.* 2d ed., revised and expanded edition. Turin, Italy: Editore G. Giappichelli.

Avritzer, Leonardo. 2002. *Democracy and the Public Space in Latin America.* Princeton, NJ: Princeton University Press.

Axelrod, Robert. 1984. *The Evolution of Cooperation.* New York: Basic Books.

Axelrod, Robert. 1997. "Advancing the Art of Simulation in the Social Sciences." Pp. 21–40 in *Simulating Social Phenomena,* edited by R. Conte, R. Hegselmann, and P. Terna. Berlin, Germany: Springer-Verlag.

Axelrod, Robert. 1997. *The Complexity of Cooperation: Agent-based Models of Competition and Collaboration.* Princeton, NJ: Princeton University Press.

Azarian, Reza. 2003. *The General Sociology of Harrison White.* Stockholm, Sweden: Stockholm Studies in Social Mechanisms.

Bailey, Edward. 1998. "'Implicit Religion': What Might That Be?" *Implicit Religion* 1:9–22.

Bailey, Kenneth D. 1990. *Social Entropy Theory.* Albany: State University of New York Press.

Bailey, Kenneth D. 1994. *Sociology and the New Systems Theory.* Albany: State University of New York Press.

Baldry, H. C. 1965. *The Unity of Mankind in Greek Thought.* Cambridge, UK: Cambridge University Press.

Bar On, Bat-Ami. 1993. "Marginality and Epistemic Privilege." Pp. 83–100 in *Feminist Epistemologies,* edited by Linda Alcoff and Elizabeth Potter. New York: Routledge.

Barabasi, Albert-Laszlo. 2002. *Linked: The New Science of Networks.* New York: Perseus.

Baran, P. A. and P. M. Sweezy. 1977. *Monopoly Capital: An Essay on the American Economic and Social Order.* Harmondsworth, UK: Penguin.

Barber, Bernard. 1983. *The Logic and Limit of Trust.* New Brunswick, NJ: Rutgers University Press.

Barrett, Michèle. 2000. "Sociology and the Metaphorical Tiger." In *Without Guarantees: In Honour of Stuart Hall,* edited by Paul Gilroy, Lawrence Grossberg, and Angela McRobbie. London & New York: Verso.

Bartky, Sandra Lee. 1990. *Femininity and Domination: Studies in the Phenomenology of Oppression.* New York: Routledge.

Bartky, Sandra Lee. 1993. "Reply to Commentators on *Femininity and Domination.*" *Hypatia: A Journal of Feminist Philosophy* 8:192–96.

Bartky, Sandra Lee. 1995. "Agency: What's the Problem?" Pp. 178–93 in *Provoking Agents: Gender and Agency in Theory and Practice,* edited by Judith Kegan Gardiner. Urbana & Chicago: University of Illinois Press.

Bartky, Sandra Lee. 1998. "Foucault, Femininity, and the Modernization of Patriarchal Power." Pp. 61–86 in *Feminism & Foucault,* edited by I. Diamond and L. Quinby. Boston, MA: Northeastern University Press.

Bartky, Sandra Lee. 2002. *"Sympathy and Solidarity" and Other Essays.* Lanham, MD: Rowman & Littlefield.

Bataille, Georges. 1970–1988. *Œuvres complètes.* Paris: Gallimard.

Bataille, Georges. 1979. *The Story of the Eye.* London: Penguin.

Bataille, Georges. 1983. *Manet.* London: Macmillan.

Bataille, Georges. [1933] 1985. "The Psychological Structure of Fascism." In *Georges Bataille: Visions of Excess: Selected Writings 1927–1939,* edited by A. Stoekl. Minneapolis: University of Minnesota Press.

Bataille, Georges. 1985. *Visions of Excess.* Allan Stoekl, ed. Minneapolis: University of Minnesota Press.

Bataille, Georges. 1986. "Autobiographical Note." *October* 36(Spring).

Bataille, Georges. 1987. *Eroticism.* London & New York: Calder & Boyars.

Bataille, Georges. 1988. *Guilty.* Venice, CA: Lapis.

Bataille, Georges. 1988. *Inner Experience.* Albany: State University of New York Press.

Bataille, Georges. 1991. *The Accursed Share.* New York: Zone.

Bataille, Georges. 1992. *Theory of Religion.* New York: Zone.

Bataille, Georges. 1999. *L'apprenti sorcier: Georges Bataille, textes, lettres et documents, rassemblés, présentés et annotés par Marina Galletti* [The Apprentice Sorcerer: Georges Bataille, Texts, Letters and Documents, Collected, Presented and Annotated by Marina Galletti]. Paris: Éditions de la Différence.

Baudrillard, Jean. 1981. *For a Critique of the Political Economy of the Sign.* St. Louis, MO: Telos.

Baudrillard, Jean. 1981. *For a Political Economy of the Sign.* Translated by Charles Levin. St. Louis, MO: Telos Press.

Baudrillard, Jean. 1983. *Simulations.* Translated by P. Patton, P. Foss, and P. Beitchman. New York: Semiotext(e).

Baudrillard, Jean. 1989. *America.* London: Verso.

Baudrillard, Jean. [1983] 1990. *Fatal Strategies* [Les stratégies fatales]. Translated by P. Beitchman and W. G. J. Nieslucjowski. New York: Semiotexte(e).

Baudrillard, Jean. [1976] 1993. *Symbolic Exchange and Death* [L'échange symbolique et la mort]. Translated by Iain Hamilton Grant. London: Sage.

Baudrillard, Jean. 1994. *Simulacra and Simulation.* Translated by Sheila Faria Glaser. Ann Arbor: University of Michigan Press.

Baudrillard, Jean. 1996. *The Perfect Crime.* Translated by Chris Turner. London: Verso.

Baudrillard, Jean. [1970] 1998. *Consumer Society* [La société de consommation]. London: Sage.

Bauman, Janina. 1986. *Winter in the Morning.* London: Virago.

Bauman, Zygmunt. 1989. *Modernity and the Holocaust.* Cambridge, UK: Polity.

Bauman, Zygmunt. 1991. *Modernity and Ambivalence.* Oxford, UK. Polity.

Bauman, Zygmunt. 1993. *Postmodern Ethics.* Oxford, UK: Blackwell.

Bauman, Zygmunt. 1998. *Globalization.* Oxford, UK: Polity.

Bauman, Zygmunt. 2000. *Liquid Modernity.* Oxford, UK: Polity.

Baumeister, Roy, ed. 1999. *The Self in Social Psychology.* Ann Arbor, MI: Edwards Brothers.

Beardsworth, Alan and Alan Bryman. 2001. "The Wild Animal in Later Modernity: The Case of the Disneyization of Zoos." *Tourist Studies* 1:83–104.

Beauvoir, Simone de. [1949] 1961. *The Second Sex.* Edited and translated by H. M. Parshley. New York: Bantam.

Beauvoir, Simone de. [1958] 1963. *Memoirs of a Dutiful Daughter.* Translated by James Kirkup. Harmondsworth, UK: Penguin.

Beauvoir, Simone de. [1974] 1994. *The Ethics of Ambiguity.* Translated by Bernard Frechtman. New York: Citadel.

Beck, Ulrich. 1986. *Risikogesellschaft: Auf dem Weg in eine andere Moderne.* Frankfurt, Germany: Suhrkamp. Translated as *Risk Society* (London: Sage, 1992).

Beck, Ulrich. 1988. *Gegengifte: Die organisierte Verantwortlichkeit.* Frankfurt, Germany: Suhrkamp. Translated as *Ecological Enlightenment* (London: Polity, 1995).

Beck, Ulrich. 1992. *Risk Society: Towards a New Modernity.* London: Sage.

Beck, Ulrich. 1993. *Die Erfindung des Politischen: Zu einer Theorie reflexiver Modernisierung.* Frankfurt, Germany: Suhrkamp. Translated as *The Reinvention of Politics* (London: Polity, 1997).

Beck, Ulrich. 1999. *Was ist Globalisierung?* Frankfurt, Germany: Suhrkamp. Tranlsated as *What Is Globalization?* (London: Polity, 1999).

Beck, Ulrich. 1999. *World Risk Society.* Cambridge, UK: Polity.

Beck, Ulrich. 2000. "The Cosmopolitan Perspective: Sociology in the Second Age of Modernity." *British Journal of Sociology* 51(1):79–106.

Beck, Ulrich. 2002. "The Cosmopolitan Society and Its Enemies." *Theory, Culture & Society* 19(1–2):17–44.

Beck, Ulrich. 2002. *Macht und Gegenmacht im globalen Zeitalter. Neue weltpolitische Ökonomie.* Frankfurt, Germany: Suhrkamp. To be published as *Power and Counter Power in the Global Age: New World-Political Economy* (London: Polity).

Beck, Ulrich. With Elizabeth Gernsheim Beck. 1990. *Das Ganz Normale Chaos der Liebe.* Frankfurt, Germany: Suhrkamp. Translated as *The Normal Chaos of Love* (London: Polity, 1995).

Beck, Ulrich. With Anthony Giddens and Scott Lash. 1996. *Reflexive Modernisierung—Eine Debatte.* Frankfurt, Germany: Suhrkamp. Originally published as *Reflexive Modernization* (Stanford, CA: Stanford University Press, 1994).

Becker, Howard S. 1963. *Outsiders: Studies in the Sociology of Deviance.* New York: Free Press.

Becker, Howard S. 1982. *Art Worlds.* Berkeley: University of California Press.

Becker, Howard S. 2000. "The Etiquette of Improvisation." *Mind, Culture, and Activity* 7:171–76.

Becker, Howard S., Blanche Geer, and Everett C. Hughes. 1968. *Making the Grade: The Academic Side of College Life.* New York: Wiley.

Becker, Howard S., Blanche Geer, Everett C. Hughes, and Anselm Strauss. 1961. *Boys in White: Student Culture in Medical School.* Chicago, IL: University of Chicago Press.

Becker, Howard S. and Michal M. McCall. 1990. "Performance Science." *Social Problems* 37:117–32.

Beilharz, Peter. 1987. *Trotsky, Trotskyism and the Transition to Socialism.* London: Croom Helm.

Beilharz, Peter. 1992. *Labour's Utopias: Bolshevism, Fabianism, Social Democracy.* London: Routledge.

Beilharz, Peter. 1994. *Postmodern Socialism.* Melbourne, Australia: Melbourne University Press.

Beilharz, Peter. 2000. *Zygmunt Bauman: Dialectic of Modernity.* London: Sage.

Beilharz, Peter, ed. 2001. *The Bauman Reader.* Oxford, UK: Blackwell.

Beilharz, Peter, ed. 2002. *Zygmunt Bauman,* 4 vols. London: Sage.

Bell, Daniel. 1973. *The Coming of Post-Industrial Society: A Venture in Social Forecasting.* New York: Basic Books.

Bell, Daniel. 1976. *The Cultural Contradictions of Capitalism.* New York: Basic Books.

Bell, David. 1990. *Husserl.* London: Routledge.

Bell, Richard, Henry Walker, and David Willer. 2000. "Power, Influence and Legitimacy in Organizations: Implications of Three Theoretical Research Programs." *Research in the Sociology of Organizations* 17:131–77.

Bellah, Robert N. 1991. *Beyond Belief: Essays on Religion in a Post-Traditional World.* 2d ed. Berkeley: University of California Press.

Bellah, Robert N. 1992. *The Broken Covenant: American Civil Religion in Time of Trial.* 2d ed. Chicago, IL: University of Chicago Press.

Bellah, Robert N., Richard Madsen, William M. Sullivan, Ann Swidler, and Steven M. Tipton. 1985. *Habits of the Heart: Individualism and Commitment in American Life.* Berkeley: University of California Press.

Benford, Robert D. and David A. Snow. 2000. "Framing Processes and Social Movements: An Overview and Assessment." *Annual Review of Sociology* 26:611–39.

Benhabib, Seyla. 1992. "Models of Public Space: Hannah Arendt, the Liberal Tradition, and Jürgen Habermas." Pp. 73–98 in *Habermas and the Public Sphere,* edited by Craig Calhoun. Cambridge, MA: MIT Press.

Benjamin, Jessica. 1988. *The Bonds of Love: Psychoanalysis, Feminism and the Problem of Domination.* New York: Pantheon.

Benjamin, Jessica. 1995. *Like Subjects, Love Objects: Essays on Recognition and Sexual Difference.* New Haven, CT: Yale University Press.

Benjamin, Jessica. 1998. *Shadow of the Other: Intersubjectivity and Gender in Psychoanalysis.* New York: Routledge.

Benjamin, Walter. 1969. "The Work of Art in the Age of Mechanical Reproduction." Pp. 217–51 in *Illuminations,* edited by H. Arendt. Translated by H. Zohn. New York: Schocken.

Benjamin, Walter. [1955] 1973. *Illuminations.* Translated by Harry Zohn. Glasgow, Scotland: Fontana/Collins.

Benjamin, Walter. [1928] 1985. *One-Way Street and Other Writings.* Translated by Edmund Jephcott and Kingsley Shorter. London: Verso.

Benjamin, Walter. [1928] 1985. *The Origin of German Tragic Drama.* Translated by John Osborne. London: Verso.

Benjamin, Walter. 1989. *Charles Baudelaire: A Lyric Poet in the Era of High Capitalism.* London: Verso.

Benjamin, Walter. 1996. "Critique of Violence." Pp. 236–52 in *Walter Benjamin: Selected Writings.* vol. 1, *1913–1926,* edited by Marcus Bullock and Michael Jennings. Cambridge, MA, & London: Harvard University, Belknap Press.

Benjamin, Walter. [1934] 1999. "The Artist as Producer." In *Collected Writings,* Vol. 2. Cambridge, MA: Harvard University Press.

Benjamin, Walter. 2000. *The Arcades Project.* Cambridge, MA: Harvard University Press.

Bennett, C. and R. Grant, eds. 1999. *Visions of Privacy.* Toronto, Canada: University of Toronto Press.

Bennett, T. 1982. "Theories of the Media, Theories of Society. Pp. 30–55 in *Culture, Society and the Media,* edited by Michael Gurevitch, Tony Bennett, James Curran, and Janet Woollacott. New York: Routledge.

Benton, Ted. 1984. *The Rise and Fall of Structural Marxism: Althusser and His Influence.* London & Basingstoke, UK: Macmillan.

Berelson, B. R., P. F. Lazarsfeld, and W. N. McPhee. 1954. *Voting.* Chicago, IL: University of Chicago Press.

Berger, Joseph. 1992. "Expectations, Theory, and Group Processes." *Social Psychology Quarterly* 55:3–11.

Berger, Joseph, Bernard P. Cohen, J. Laurie Snell, and Morris Zelditch Jr. 1962. *Types of Formalization in Small-Group Research.* Boston, MA: Houghton Mifflin.

Berger, Joseph, Bernard P. Cohen, and Morris Zelditch Jr. 1972. "Status Characteristics and Social Interaction." *American Sociological Review* 37:241–55.

Berger, Joseph, Thomas L. Conner, and M. Hamit Fisek, eds. 1974. *Expectation States Theory: A Theoretical Research Program.* Cambridge, MA: Winthrop.

Berger, Joseph, M. Hamit Fisek, Robert Z. Norman, and David G. Wagner. 1985. "The Formation of Reward Expectations in Status Situations." Pp. 215–61 in *Status, Rewards, and Influence,* edited by Joseph Berger and Morris Zelditch, Jr. San Francisco, CA: Jossey-Bass.

Berger, Joseph, M. Hamit Fisek, Robert Z. Norman, and Morris Zelditch Jr. 1977. *Status Characteristics and Social Interaction.* New York: Elsevier.

Berger, Joseph, Cecilia L. Ridgeway, and Morris Zelditch Jr. 2002. "Construction of Status and Referential Structures." *Sociological Theory* 20:157–79.

Berger, Joseph and Morris Zelditch Jr. 1998. *Status, Power and Legitimacy: Strategies and Theories.* New Brunswick, NJ: Transaction.

Berger, Joseph and Morris Zelditch Jr., eds. 2002. *New Directions in Contemporary Sociological Theory.* Lanham, MD: Rowman & Littlefield.

Berger, Peter L. 1963. *Invitation to Sociology.* Garden City, NY: Anchor.

Berger, Peter L. 1969. *The Sacred Canopy: Elements of a Sociological Theory of Religion.* Garden City, NY: Doubleday.

Berger, Peter L., Brigitte Berger, and Hansfried Kellner. 1974. *The Homeless Mind: Modernization and Consciousness.* New York: Vintage.

Berger, Peter L. and Thomas Luckmann. 1966. *The Social Construction of Reality: A Treatise in the Sociology of Knowledge.* Garden City, NY: Doubleday.

Bergrstraesser, A. 1947. "Wilhelm Dilthey and Max Weber: An Empirical Approach to Historical Synthesis." *Ethics* 57(2): 92–110.

Bergson, Henri. 1935. *Two Sources of Morality and Religion.* Translated by R. Ashley Audra and Cloudesley Brereton, with the assistance of W. Horsfall Carter. New York: Henry Holt.

Bernard, L. L. 1940. "The Social Science Theories of William Graham Sumner." *Social Forces* 19(2):153–75.

Bertalanffy, Ludwig von. 1968. *General System Theory: Foundations, Development, Applications.* New York: George Braziller.

Berthelot, Jean Michel. 1992. "The Body as a Discursive Operator: Or the Aporias of a Sociology of the Body." *Body & Society* 1(1):13–23.

Best, Steven and Douglas Kellner. 2001. *The Postmodern Adventure: Science Technology, and Cultural Studies at the Third Millennium.* New York & London: Guilford & Routledge.

Bestor, Theodore C. 2000. "How Sushi Went Global." *Foreign Policy* November-December.

Bhaba, Homi. 1994. *The Location of Culture.* London: Routledge.

Biddle, Bruce J. 1986. "Recent Developments in Role Theory." *Annual Review of Sociology* 12:67–92.

Biddle, Bruce J. 2000. "Role Theory." Pp. 2415–20 in *Encyclopedia of Sociology.* 2d ed. Vol. 4, edited by Edgar F. Borgatta and Rhonda J. V. Montgomery. New York: Macmillan Reference.

Bidney, David. 1966. *"Ernst Cassirers Stellung in der Geschichte der philosophischen Anthropologie."* Pp. 335–403 in *Ernst Cassirer,* edited by Paul A. Schilpp. Stuttgart, Germany: Kohlhammer. Originally published in *The Philosophy of Ernst Cassirer,* edited by P. A. Schilpp (Evanston, IL: Library of Living Philosophers, 1949).

Biemel, Walter. 1959. "Die entscheidenden Phasen der Entfaltung von Husserls Philosophie." *Zeitschrift für philosophische Forschung* 13:187–214.

Bienenstock, Elisa Jayne and Phillip Bonacich. 1993. "Game-Theory Models for Exchange Networks: Experimental Results." *Sociological Perspectives* 36:117–35.

Bierstedt, Robert. 1968. "Znaniecki Florian." Pp. 599–602 in *International Encyclopedia of the Social Sciences,* edited by D. L. Sills. Vol. 16. New York: Macmillan.

Bierstedt, Robert. 1974. *Power and Progress: Essays on Sociological Theory.* New York: McGraw-Hill.

Billig, Michael. 1995. *Banal Nationalism.* London: Sage.

Biskind, Peter. 1998. *Easy Riders, Raging Bulls.* New York: McGraw-Hill.

Blanchot, Maurice. 1988. *The Unavowable Community.* Barrytown, NY: Station Hill.

Blau, Peter M. 1964. *Exchange and Power in Social Life.* New York: Wiley.

Blau, Peter M. 1970. "A Formal Theory of Differentiation in Organizations." *American Sociological Review* 35:201–18.

Blau, Peter M. 1994. *Structural Context of Opportunities.* Chicago, IL: University of Chicago Press.

Blau, Peter M., Terry C. Blum, and Joseph E. Schwartz. 1982. "Heterogeneity and Intermarriage." *American Sociological Review* 47:45–62.

Blau, Peter M. and Otis Dudley Duncan. 1974. *The American Occupational Structure.* New York: Wiley.

Bleicher, Joseph. 1980. *Contemporary Hermeneutics: Hermeneutics as Method, Philosophy, and Critique.* London: Routledge & Kegan Paul.

Bloch, Ernst. 1986. *The Principle of Hope.* Cambridge, MA: MIT Press.

Bloch, Marc. 1961. *Feudal Society,* 2 vols. Translated by L. A. Manyon. Chicago, IL: University of Chicago Press.

Bloch, Marc. 1973. *The Royal Touch.* Translated by J. E. Anderson. London: Routledge.

Blumberg, Rae Lesser. 1978. *Stratification: Socioeconomic and Sexual Inequality.* Dubuque, IA: William C. Brown.

Blumberg, Rae Lesser. 1984. "A General Theory of Gender Stratification." *Sociological Theory* 2:23–101.

Blumer, Herbert. 1931. "Science Without Concepts." *American Journal of Sociology* 36:515–33.

Blumer, Herbert. 1933. *Movies and Conduct.* New York: Macmillan.

Blumer, Herbert. 1937. "Social Psychology." Pp. 144–98 in *Man and Society,* edited by Emerson Schmidt. New York: Prentice-Hall.

Blumer, Herbert. 1948. "Public Opinion and Public Opinion Polling." *American Sociological Review* 13:542–54.

Blumer, Herbert. 1962. "Society as Symbolic Interaction." Pp. 179–92 in *Human Behavior and Social Processes,* edited by Arnold Rose. Boston, MA: Houghton Mifflin.

Blumer, Herbert. 1966. "Sociological Implications of the Thought of George Herbert Mead." *American Journal of Sociology* 71:535–44.

Blumer, Herbert. 1969. *Symbolic Interaction: Perspective and Method.* Englewood Cliffs, NJ: Prentice-Hall.

Blumer, Herbert. 1981. "George Herbert Mead." Pp. 136–69 in *The Future of the Sociological Classics,* edited by B. Rhea. London: Allen & Unwin.

Blumer, Herbert. 1990. *Industrialization as an Agent of Social Change.* Edited with an Introduction by David R. Maines and Thomas J. Morrione. Hawthorne, NY: Aldine de Gruyter.

Bob, Jacqueline. 1995. *Black Women as Cultural Readers.* New York: Columbia University Press.

Bogard, William. 1996. *The Simulation of Surveillance: Hypercontrol in Telematic Societies.* Cambridge, UK: Cambridge University Press.

Boggs, Carl and Tom Pollard. 2003. *A World in Chaos: Social Crisis and the Rise of Postmodern Cinema.* Lanham, MD: Rowman & Littlefield.

Böhm, Franz. 1961. "Demokratie und ökonomische Macht" (Democracy and Economic Power). Pp. 1-23 in *Institut fuer Auslaendisches und Internationales Wirtschaftsrecht* (Institute for Foreign and International Economic Law), edited by Kartelle und Monopole im modernen Recht (Cartels in Modern Law). Karlsruhe, Germany: Mueller.

Bohman, James and Mathias Lutz-Bachmann, eds. 1997. *Perpetual Peace: Essays on Kant's Cosmopolitan Ideal.* Cambridge, MA: MIT Press.

Boltanski, Luc. 2002. "The Left after 1968 and the Longing for Total Revolution." *Thesis Eleven: Critical Theory and Historical Sociology* 69:1–20.

Boltanski, Luc and Eve Chiapello. 1999. *Le nouvel esprit du capitalisme* [The New Spirit of Capitalism]. Paris: Gallimard.

Bonald, Louis de. 1817–1843. *Législation primitif* [Primitive Legislation]. Vol. 1, *Oeuvres,* 16 vols. Paris: Leclerc.

Bonald, Louis de. 1817–1843. *Théorie du pouvoir* [Theory of Power]. Vol. 13, *Oeuvres,* 16 vols. Paris: Leclerc.

Borgatti, Stephen P. and Martin G. Everett. 1989. "The Class of All Regular Equivalences: Algebraic Structure and Computation." *Social Networks* 11:65–88.

Bourdieu, Pierre. 1971. "Intellectual Field and Creative Project." Pp. 161–88 in *Knowledge and Control,* edited by M. F. D. Young. London: Collier-Macmillan.

Bourdieu, Pierre. 1977. *Outline of a Theory of Practice.* Cambridge, UK: Cambridge University Press. Originally published as *Esquisse d'un théorie de la pratique,* 1972.

Bourdieu, Pierre. 1983. "The Forms of Capital." Pp. 241–58 in *Handbook of Theory and Research for the Sociology of Education,* edited by J. G. Richardson. Westport, CT: Greenwood.

Bourdieu, Pierre. 1984. *Distinction: A Social Critique of the Judgement of Taste.* Translated by Richard Nice. Cambridge, MA: Harvard University Press.

Bourdieu, Pierre. 1987. "What Makes a Social Class?" *Berkeley Journal of Sociology* 22:1–18.

Bourdieu, Pierre. [1984] 1988. *Homo Academicus.* Cambridge, UK: Polity.

Bourdieu, Pierre. 1990. *In Other Words: Essays toward a Reflexive Sociology.* Cambridge, UK: Polity.

Bourdieu, Pierre. 1990. *The Logic of Practice.* Cambridge, UK: Polity. Originally published as *La sens pratique,* 1980.

Bourdieu, Pierre. 1999. *The Weight of the World: Social Suffering in Contemporary Society.* Cambridge, UK: Polity. Originally published as *La misère du monde,* 1993.

Bourdieu, Pierre and Jean-Claude Passeron. 1977. *Reproduction in Education, Society and Culture.* Beverly Hills, CA: Sage.

Bourdieu, Pierre and Monique de St. Martin. 1996. *The State Nobility: Elite Schools in the Field of Power.* Cambridge, UK: Polity. Originally published as *La noblesse d'état,* 1989.

Bourdieu, Pierre and Loïc J. D. Wacquant. 1992. *An Invitation to Reflexive Sociology.* Chicago, IL: University of Chicago Press.

Braczyk, Hans-Joachim and Gerd Schienstock, eds. 1996. *Kurswechsel in der Industrie: Lean Production in Baden-Württemberg* [Change of Direction in Industry: Lean Production in Baden-Württemberg/Germany]. Stuttgart, Germany: Kohlhammer.

Bradley, Harriet. 1989. *Men's Work, Women's Work: A Sociological History of the Sexual Division of Labour in Employment.* Minneapolis: University of Minnesota Press.

Bradley, Owen. 1999. *A Modern Maistre.* Lincoln: University of Nebraska Press.

Braidotti, Rosi. 1993. "Embodiment, Sexual Difference, and the Nomadic Subject." *Hypatia: A Journal of Women and Philosophy* 8(Winter):1–13.

Braithwaite, John. 1989. *Crime, Shame and Reintegration.* Cambridge, UK: Cambridge University Press.

Braudel, Fernand. 1972. *The Mediterranean and the Mediterranean World in the Age of Philip II,* 2 vols. Translated by Sian Reynolds. New York: Harper and Row.

Braudel, Fernand. 1980. *On History.* Translated by Sarah Matthews. Chicago, IL: University of Chicago Press.

Braudel, Fernand. 1981–1984. *Civilization and Capitalism, 15th-18th Century,* 3 vols. New York: Harper and Row.

Braudy, Leo. 1986. *The Frenzy of Reknown.* New York: Vintage.

Braun, Christoph. 1992. *Max Weber's "Musiksoziologie."* Laaber, Germany: Laaber-Verlag.

Breuilly, John. 1993. *Nationalism and the State.* Rev. ed. Chicago, IL: University of Chicago Press.

Brewer, Anthony. 1980. *Marxist Theories of Imperialism: A Critical Survey.* London: Routledge & Kegan Paul.

Brewer, Anthony. 1984. *A Guide to Marx's Capital.* Cambridge, UK: Cambridge University Press.

Brinn, D. 1999. *The Transparent Society.* New York: Perseus.

Brint, Steven. 1992. "Hidden Meanings: Cultural Content and Context in Harrison White's Structural Sociology." *Sociological Theory* 10:194–208.

Brint, Steven. 1994. *In an Age of Experts: The Changing Role of Professionals in Politics and Public Life.* Princeton, NJ: Princeton University Press.

Brinton, Crane. 1950. *Ideas and Men: The Story of Western Thought.* New York: Prentice-Hall.

Brinton, Mary C. and Victor Nee, eds. 1998. *The New Institutionalism in Sociology.* New York: Russell Sage.

Brisett, Dennis and Charles Edgley, eds. 1990. *Life as Theater: A Dramaturgical Source Book.* New York: Aldine de Gruyter.

Broad, Robin, ed. 2002. *Global Backlash: Citizen Initiatives for a Just World Economy.* Lanham, MD: Rowman & Littlefield.

Brook, Thomas. 1991. *The New Historicism and Other Old-Fashioned Topics.* Princeton, NJ: Princeton University Press.

Brown, Lyn Mikel and Carol Gilligan. 1992. *Meeting at the Crossroads: Women's Psychology and Girls' Development.* Cambridge, MA: Harvard University Press.

Brown, Richard H. 1977. *A Poetic for Sociology.* Cambridge, UK: Cambridge University Press.

Brown, Richard Harvey. 1987. *Society as Text: Essays on Rhetoric, Reason, and Reality.* Chicago, IL: University of Chicago Press.

Brown, Richard Harvey. 1989. *Social Science as Civic Discourse: Essays on the Invention, Legitimation, and Uses of Social Theory.* Chicago, IL: University of Chicago Press.

Brubaker, Rogers. 1992. *Citizenship and Nationhood in France and Germany.* Cambridge, UK: Cambridge University Press.

Brubaker, Rogers. 1996. *Nationalism Reframed: Nationhood and the National Question in the New Europe.* Cambridge, UK: Cambridge University Press.

Bryant, C. G. A. and D. Jary, eds. 1996. *Anthony Giddens: Critical Assessments.* 4 vols. London: Routledge.

Bryant, Christopher and David Jary. 2001. *The Contemporary Giddens: Social Theory in a Globalizing Age.* London: Palgrave Macmillan.

Bryman, Alan. 1999. "The Disneyization of Society." *Sociological Review* 47:25–47.

Bryman, Alan. 2003. "McDonald's as a Disneyized Institution: Global Implications." *American Behavioral Scientist* 47:2.

Bryman, Alan. 2004. *The Disneyization of Society.* London: Sage.

Buber, Martin. 1972. *Briefwechsel aus sieben Jahrzehnten* [Correspondence from Seven Decades]. Vol. 1, *1897–1918,* edited by Grete Schaeder. Heidelberg, Germany: Verlag Lambert Schneider.

Buchanan, Ian. 1999. "Non-Places: Space in the Age of Supermodernity." Pp. 169–76 in *Imagining Australian Space,* edited by R. Barcan and I. Buchanan. Perth, Australia: University of Western Australia Press.

Buchanan, Ian. 2000. *Michel de Certeau: Cultural Theorist.* London: Sage.

Buchanan, Ian. 2002. *De Certeau in the Plural.* Durham, NC: Duke University Press.

Buchanan, Mark. 2002. *Nexus: Small Worlds and the Groundbreaking Science of Networks.* New York: Norton.

Bucolo, Placido. 1980. *The Other Pareto.* New York: St. Martin's.

Bühl, Walter L. 2002. *Phänomenologische Soziologie.* Konstanz, Germany: Universitätsverlag.

Bürger, Peter. 1984. *Theory of the Avant-Garde.* Minneapolis: University of Minnesota Press.

Burger, Thomas. 1976. *Max Weber's Theory of Concept Formation: History, Laws, and Ideal Types.* Durham, NC: Duke University Press.

Burgess, Robert L. and Don Bushell Jr., eds. 1969. *Behavioral Sociology.* New York: Columbia University Press.

Burke, C., N. Schor, and M. Whitford, eds. 1994. *Engaging with Irigaray.* New York: Columbia University Press.

Burke, Kenneth. 1936. *Permanence and Change: An Anatomy of Purpose.* Berkeley: University of California Press.

Burke, Kenneth. 1945. *A Grammar of Motives.* Berkeley: University of California Press.

Burke, Kenneth. 1950. *A Rhetoric of Motives.* Berkeley: University of California Press.

Burke, Kenneth. 1969. *A Grammar of Motives.* Berkeley: University of California Press.

Burke, Kenneth. 1969. *A Rhetoric of Motives.* Berkeley: University of California Press.

Burke, Kenneth. 1984. *Permanence and Change: An Anatomy of Purpose.* Berkeley: University of California Press.

Burke, Peter. 1990. *The French Historical Revolution: The Annales School, 1929–1989.* Stanford, CA: Stanford University Press.

Burns, T. 1992. *Erving Goffman.* London: Routledge.

Burr, Vivien. 1995. *An Introduction to Social Constructionism.* London: Routledge.

Burt, Ronald S. 1987. "Social Contagion and Innovation: Cohesion versus Structural Equivalence." *American Journal of Sociology* 92:1287–1335.

Burt, Ronald S. 1992. *Structural Holes: The Social Structure of Competition.* Cambridge, MA: Harvard University Press.

Burt, Ronald S. 2002. "The Social Capital of Structural Holes." Pp. 148–90 in *The New Economic Sociology: Developments in an Emerging Field,* edited by M. F. Guillén, R. Collins, P. England, and M. Meyer. New York: Russell Sage.

Butler, Judith. 1988. "Performative Acts & Gender Constitution: An Essay in Phenomenology and Feminist Theory." *Theatre Journal* 40:519–31.

Butler, Judith. 1990. *Gender Trouble: Feminism and the Subversion of Identity.* New York: Routledge.

Butler, Judith. 1992. "Contingent Foundations: Feminism and the Question of 'Postmodernism.'" Pp. 3–21 in *Feminists Theorize the Political,* edited by Judith Butler and Joan W. Scott. New York: Routledge.

Butler, Judith. 1993. *Bodies That Matter: On the Discursive Limits of "Sex"* New York: Routledge.

Butler, Judith. 1997. *Excitable Speech.* New York & London: Routledge.

Butler, Judith. 1997. "Imitation and Gender Insubordination." Pp. 300–16 in *The Second Wave: A Reader in Feminist Theory,* edited by Linda Nicholson. New York: Routledge.

Butler, Judith, Ernesto Laclau, and Slavoj Žižek. 2000. *Contingency, Hegemony, Universality: Contemporary Dialogues on the Left.* London & New York: Verso.

Buttler, Friedrich, ed. 1995. *International Frameworks and Labor Market Performance: Comparative Views on the US and German Economies.* London: Routledge.

Byrne, David. 1998. *Complexity Theory and the Social Sciences.* London: Routledge.

Cahill, Spencer and Lyn Lofland, eds. 1994. *The Community of the Streets: Research in Community Sociology.* Suppl. 1. Greenwich, CT: JAI.

Caillois, Roger. 1975. "The Collège de Sociologie: Paradox of an Active Sociology." *Substance* 11–12.

Calhoun, Craig, ed. 1992. *Habermas and the Public Sphere.* Cambridge, MA: MIT Press.

Calhoun, Craig. 1997. *Nationalism.* Milton Keynes, UK: Open University Press.

Calkins, Mary Whiton. 1919. "The Self in Recent Psychology." *Psychological Bulletin* 16:111–18.

Callon, Michel. 1986. "The Sociology of an Actor-Network: The Case of the Electric Vehicle." In *Mapping the Dynamics of Science and Technology: Sociology of Science in the Real World,* edited by M. Callon, J. Law, and A. Rip. Houndmills, UK: Macmillan.

Callon, Michel. 1986. "Some Elements of a Sociology of Translation: Domestication of the Scallops and the Fishermen of St. Brieuc Bay." In *Power, Action, and Belief: A New Sociology of Knowledge?* edited by J. Law. London: Routledge & Kegan Paul.

Campbell, C. 1989. *The Romantic Ethic and the Spirit of Modern Consumerism.* Oxford, UK: Blackwell.

Campbell, Marie L. and Ann Manicom, eds. 1995. *Knowledge, Experience, and Ruling Relations: Studies in the Social Organization of Knowledge.* Toronto, Canada: University of Toronto Press.

Canclini, N. 2001. *Consumers and Citizens.* Minneapolis: University of Minnesota Press.

Card, Claudia, ed. 2003. *The Cambridge Companion to Simone de Beauvoir.* Cambridge & New York: Cambridge University Press.

Carrithers, David W., Michael A. Mosher, and Paul A. Rahe. 2001. *Montesquieu's Science of Politics: Essays on the Spirit of Laws.* Lanham, MD: Rowman & Littlefield.

Carroll, Glenn R. 1985. "Concentration and Specialization: Dynamics of Niche Width in Populations of Organizations." *American Journal of Sociology* 90:1262–83.

Carroll, Glenn R., ed. 1988. *Ecological Models of Organization.* Cambridge, MA: Ballinger.

Carroll, Glenn R. and Michael T. Hannan. 2000. *The Demography of Corporations and Industries.* Princeton, NJ: Princeton University Press.

Casanova, José. 1994. *Public Religions in the Modern World.* Chicago, IL: University of Chicago Press.

Cassell, Justine and Henry Jenkins, eds. 1998. *From Barbie to Mortal Kombat: Gender and Computer Games.* Cambridge, MA: MIT Press.

Cassirer, Ernst. 1944. *An Essay on Man: An Introduction to a Philosophy of Human Culture.* New Haven, CT: Yale University Press.

Cassirer, Ernst. [1923] 1953. *The Philosophy of Symbolic Forms.* vol. 1, *Language.* Translated by Ralph Manheim. New Haven, CT: Yale University Press.

Cassirer, Ernst. [1925] 1955. *The Philosophy of Symbolic Forms.* vol. 2, *Mythical Thought.* Translated by Ralph Manheim. New Haven, CT: Yale University Press.

Cassirer, Ernst. [1929] 1957. *The Philosophy of Symbolic Forms.* vol. 3, *The Phenomenology of Knowledge.* Translated by Ralph Manheim. New Haven, CT: Yale University Press.

Cassirer, Ernst. [1923–1999] 1997. *Philosophie der symbolischen Formen* [Philosophy of Symbolic Forms]. Vol. 1: *Die Sprache* [Language/Speech]; Vol. 2: *Das mythische Denken* [Mythological Thought]; Vol. 3: *Phänomenologie der Erkenntnis* [Phenomenology of Knowledge]. Darmstadt, Germany: Primus Verlag.

Castells, Manuel. [1972] 1977. *The Urban Question.* Translated by Alan Sheridan. Cambridge, MA: MIT. Originally published as *La Question Urbaine* (Paris: Francois Maspero, 1972).

Castells, Manuel. 1996. *The Rise of the Network Society.* Malden, MA; Oxford, UK: Blackwell.

Castells, *The Power of Identity*. 1997. *The Power of Identity.* vol. 2, *The Information Age: Economy, Society and Culture.* Oxford, UK: Blackwell.

Castoriadis, Cornelius. 1987. *The Imaginary Institution of Society.* Cambridge, MA: MIT Press.

Castoriadis, Cornelius. 1991. *Philosophy, Politics, Autonomy.* New York: Oxford University Press.

Castoriadis, Cornelius. 1997. *Castoriadis Reader.* Oxford, UK: Blackwell.

Castoriadis, Cornelius. 1997. *World in Fragments.* Stanford, CA: Stanford University Press.

Caughey, J. L. 1984. *Imaginary Social Worlds.* Lincoln: University of Nebraska Press.

Cederblom, Jerry and David W. Paulson. 2001. *Critical Reasoning.* 5th ed. Belmont, CA: Wadsworth.

Certeau, Michel de. 1984. *The Practice of Everyday Life.* Translated by Steven Rendall. Berkeley: University of California Press.

Certeau, Michel de. 1986. *Heterologies: Discourse on the Other.* Translated by Brian Massumi. Minneapolis: University of Minnesota Press.

Certeau, Michel de. 1988. *The Writing of History.* 1975. Translated by Tom Conley. New York: Columbia University Press.

Cerulo, Karen A. 1997. "Identity Construction: New Issues, New Directions." *Annual Review of Sociology* 23:385–409.

Cerulo, Karen A. 2002. *Culture in Mind: Toward a Sociology of Culture and Cognition.* New York: Routledge.

Chafetz, Janet Saltzman. 1984. *Sex and Advantage: A Comparative Macro-Structural Theory of Sexual Stratification.* Totowa, NJ: Rowman & Allanheld.

Chafetz, Janet Saltzman. 1988. *Feminist Sociology: An Overview of Contemporary Theories.* Itasca, IL: F. E. Peacock.

Chafetz, Janet Saltzman. 1990. *Gender Equity: An Integrated Theory of Stability and Change.* Newbury Park, CA: Sage.

Chapoulie, Jean-Michel. 1996. "Everett Hughes and the Chicago Tradition." Translated by Howie Becker. *Sociological Theory* 14:3–29.

Chase-Dunn, Christopher. 1998. *Global Formation.* Lanham, MD: Rowman & Littlefield.

Chase-Dunn, Christopher and Thomas D. Hall. 1997. *Rise and Demise: Comparing World-Systems.* Boulder, CO: Westview.

Chatterjee, Partha. 1986. *Nationalist Thought and the Colonial World: A Derivative Discourse?* Atlantic Highlands, NJ: Zed.

Chatterjee, Partha. 1994. *The Nation and Its Fragments: Studies in Colonial and Post-Colonial Histories.* Princeton, NJ: Princeton University Press.

Chaves, Mark A. 1994. "Secularization as Declining Religious Authority." *Social Forces* 72:749–74.

Cheah, Pheng and Bruce Robbins, eds. 1998. *Cosmopolitcs: Thinking and Feeling beyond the Nation.* Minneapolis: University of Minnesota Press.

Chesters, Graeme and Ian Welsh. 2004. *Complexity and Social Movements: Protest at the Edge of Chaos.* London: Routledge.

Chilcote, Ronald H., ed. 1999. *The Political Economy of Imperialism.* Boston, MA: Kluwer.

Chodorow, Nancy. 1989. *Feminism and Psychoanalytic Theory.* Cambridge, UK: Polity; New Haven, CT: Yale University Press.

Chodorow, Nancy. 1994. *Femininities, Masculinities, Sexualities: Freud and Beyond.* Lexington: University Press of Kentucky & London: Free Association Books.

Chodorow, Nancy. 1999. *The Power of Feelings: Personal Meaning in Psychoanalysis, Gender and Culture.* New Haven, CT: Yale University Press.

Chodorow, Nancy. [1978] 1999. *The Reproduction of Mothering: Psychoanalysis and the Sociology of Gender.* Berkeley: University of California Press.

Chriss, James J. 1999. *Alvin W. Gouldner: Sociologist and Outlaw Marxist.* Aldershot, UK: Ashgate.

Ciaffra, Jay A. 1998. *Max Weber and the Problems of Value-Free Social Science: A Critical Examination of the Werturteils-Streit.* Lewisburg, NJ: Bucknell University Press.

Cicourel, Aaron. 1974. *Cognitive Sociology: Language and Meaning in Social Interaction.* New York: Free Press.

Cilliers, Paul. 1998. *Complexity and Postmodernism.* London: Routledge.

Claeys, Gregory and Lyman Tower Sargent, eds. 1999. *The Utopia Reader.* New York & London: New York University Press.

Claparède, Ed. 1916. Review of the *Cours de Linguistique Générale* (C Bally and A Sechehaye, eds, Lausanne & Paris: Payot, 1916). *Archives de Psychologie* 61:93–95.

Clark, J., C. Modgil, and S. Modgil, eds. 1990. *Robert K. Merton: Consensus and Controversy.* London: Falmer.

Clark, Stuart, ed. 1999. *The Annales School,* 4 vols. New York: Routledge.

Clarke, Adele. 1991. "Social Worlds/Arenas Theory as Organizational Theory." Pp. 119–58 in *Social Organization and Social Processes: Essays in Honor of Anselm Strauss,* edited by David R. Maines. New York: Aldine de Gruyter.

Clarke, Adele E. 1998. *Disciplining Reproduction: Modernity, Life Sciences, and "the Problems of Sex."* Berkeley: University of California Press.

Clarke, Adele E. and Joan H. Fujimura, eds. 1992. *The Right Tools for the Job: At Work in Twentieth-Century Life Sciences.* Princeton, NJ: Princeton University Press.

Clifford, James. 1988. *The Predicament of Culture.* Cambridge, MA: Harvard University Press.

Clough, Patricia T. 1998. *The End(s) of Ethnography: From Realism to Social Criticism.* 2d ed. New York: Peter Lang.

Coakley, Jay and Eric Dunning, eds. 2000. *Handbook of Sport Studies.* London: Sage.

Code, Lorraine. 1993. "Taking Subjectivity into Account." Pp. 15–48 in *Feminist Epistemologies,* edited by Linda Alcoff and Elizabeth Potter. New York: Routledge.

Cohen, Bernard P. 1989. *Developing Sociological Knowledge.* 2d ed. Chicago, IL: Nelson-Hall.

Cohen, Gerald A. 1978. *Karl Marx's Theory of History: A Defense.* Princeton, NJ: Princeton University Press.

Cohen, Ira. 1989. *Structuration Theory: Anthony Giddens and the Constitution of Social Life.* London: Macmillan.

Cohen, Jean L. and Andrew Arato. 1992. *Civil Society and Political Theory.* Cambridge, MA: MIT Press.

Cole, G. D. H. 1953–1960. *A History of Socialist Thought.* 5 vols., 7 parts. London: Macmillan.

Coleman, James S. 1961. *The Adolescent Society.* Glencoe, IL: Free Press.

Coleman, James S. 1964. *Introduction to Mathematical Sociology.* Glencoe, IL: Free Press.

Coleman, James S. 1973. *Power and the Structure of Society.* New York: Norton.

Coleman, James S. 1982. *The Asymmetric Society.* Syracuse, NY: Syracuse University Press.

Coleman, James S. 1986. "Microfoundations and Macrosocial Theory." Pp. 345–63 in *Approaches to Social Theory,* edited by S. Lindenberg, J. S. Coleman, and S. Nowak. New York: Russell Sage.

Coleman, James S. 1986. "Social Theory, Social Research, and a Theory of Action." *American Journal of Sociology* 91:1309–35.

Coleman, James S. 1988. "Social Capital in the Creation of Human Capital." *American Journal of Sociology* 94:S95–20.

Coleman, James S. 1990. *Foundation of Social Theory.* Cambridge, MA: Harvard University Press.

Coleman, James S., with E. Q. Campbell, C. J. Hobson, J. McPartland, A. M. Mood, F. D. Weinfeld, and R. L. York. 1966. *Equality of Educational Opportunity.* Washington, DC: Government Printing Office.

Coleman, James S. and Thomas Hoffer. 1987. *Public and Private High Schools: The Impact of Communities.* New York: Basic Books.

Collins, Patricia Hill. 1986. "Learning from the Outsider Within: The Sociological Significance of Black Feminist Thought." *Social Problems* 33(6):14–32.

Collins, Patricia Hill. 1990. *Black Feminist Thought: Knowledge, Consciousness, and the Politics of Empowerment.* London: Unwin Hyman.

Collins, Patricia Hill. 1993. "Toward a New Vision: Race, Class, and Gender as Categories of Analysis and Connection." *Race, Sex, & Class* 1:25–45.

Collins, Patricia Hill. 1994. "Shifting the Center: Race, Class, and Feminist Theorizing about Motherhood." Pp. 47–8 in *Mothering: Ideology, Experience, and Agency,* edited by Evelyn Nakano Glenn, Grace Chang, and Linda Rennie Forcey. New York: Routledge.

Collins, Patricia Hill. 1998. *Fighting Words: Black Women and the Search for Justice.* Minneapolis: University of Minnesota Press.

Collins, Patricia Hill. 2004. *Black Sexual Politics: African Americans, Gender, and the New Racism.* New York: Routledge.

Collins, Randall. 1972. *Conflict Sociology: Toward an Explanatory Science.* New York: Academic Press.

Collins, Randall. 1981. "On the Microfoundations of Macrosociology." *American Journal of Sociology* 86:984–1014.

Collins, Randall. 1981. "Micro-Translation as Theory-Building Strategy." Pp. 81–108 in *Advances in Social Theory and Methodology,* edited by K. Knorr-Cetina and A. Cicourel. New York: Methuen.

Collins, Randall. 1986. *Weberian Sociological Theory.* Cambridge, UK: Cambridge University Press.

Collins, Randall. 1990. "Conflict Theory and the Advance of Macro-Historical Sociology." Pp. 68–87 in *Frontiers of Social Theory: The New Synthesis,* edited by G. Ritzer. New York: Columbia University Press.

Collins, Randall. 1990. "Stratification, Emotional Energy, and the Transient Emotions." Pp. 27–57 in *Research Agendas in the Sociology of Emotions,* edited by Theodore D. Kemper. Albany: State University of New York Press.

Collins, Randall. 1998. *The Sociology of Philosophies: A Global Theory of Intellectual Change.* Cambridge, MA: Harvard University Press.

Collins, Randall. 1999. *Macro-History: Essays in Sociology of the Long Run.* Stanford, CA: Stanford University Press.

Coltrane, Scott. 1998. *Gender and Families.* Thousand Oaks, CA: Pine Forge.

Combahee River Collective. 1997. "A Black Feminist Statement." Pp. 63–70 in *The Second Wave: A Reader in Feminist Theory,* edited by Linda Nicholson. New York: Routledge.

Compaine, Benjamin M. and Douglas Gomery. 2000. *Who Owns the Media? Competition and Concentration in the Mass Media Industry.* 3d ed. Mahwah, NJ: Erlbaum.

Comte, Auguste. [1830–1842] 1855. *The Positive Philosophy of Auguste Comte.* New York: Calvin Blanchard.

Comte, Auguste. [1854] 1968. *System of Positive Polity.* Vol. 4. New York: Burt Franklin.

Comte, Aguste. 1970. *Oeuvres d'August Comte,* 12 vols. Edited by Sylvain Pérignon. Paris: Éditions Anthropos.

Conley, Tom. 2002. "Afterword: Riding the Subway with Marc Augé." Pp. 73–113 in *In the Metro,* by M. Augé. Translated by Tom Conley. Minneapolis: University of Minnesota Press.

Conley, Tom. 2002. "Introduction: Marc Augé, 'A Little History.'" Pp. vii–xxii in *In the Metro,* by M. Augé. Translated by Tom Conley. Minneapolis: University of Minnesota Press.

Connell, R. W. 1987. *Gender and Power.* Cambridge, UK: Polity.

Connor, Walker. 1994. *Ethnonationalism.* Princeton, NJ: Princeton University Press.

Conrad, Peter and Joseph W. Schneider. 1992. *Deviance and Medicalization: From Badness to Sickness.* Philadelphia, PA: Temple University Press.

Constant, B. 1988. *Benjamin Constant: Political Writings.* Cambridge, UK: Cambridge University Press.

Cook, Gary A. 1993. *George Herbert Mead: The Making of a Social Pragmatist.* Urbana: University of Illinois Press.

Cook, Karen S. 1975. "Expectations, Evaluations, and Equity." *American Sociological Review* 40:372–88.

Cook, Karen S. 2000. "Advances in the Microfoundations of Sociology: Recent Developments and New Challenges for Social Psychology." *Contemporary Sociology* 29:685–92.

Cook, Karen S., ed. 2001. *Trust in Society.* New York: Russell Sage.

Cook, Karen S. and Richard M. Emerson. 1978. "Power, Equity and Commitment in Exchange Networks." *American Sociological Review* 43:712–39.

Cook, Karen S. and Richard M. Emerson. 1984. "Exchange Networks and the Analysis of Complex Organizations." *Research in the Sociology of Organizations* 3:1–30.

Cook, Karen S., Richard M. Emerson, Mary R. Gillmore, and Toshio Yamagishi. 1983. "The Distribution of Power in Exchange Networks: Theory and Experimental Results." *American Journal of Sociology* 89:275–305.

Cook, Karen S., Eric R. W. Rice, and Alexandra Gerbasi. 2004. "The Emergence of Trust Networks under Uncertainty: The Case of Transitional Economies—Insights from Social Psychological Research." In *Problems of Post Socialist Transition: Creating Social Trust,* edited by Susan Rose-Ackerman, Bo Rothstein, and Janos Kornai. New York: Palgrave Macmillan.

Cook, Karen S. and Toshio Yamagishi. 1992. "Power in Exchange Networks: A Power-Dependence Formulation." *Social Networks* 14:245–65.

Cooley, Charles Horton. 1918. *Social Process.* New York: Scribner's.

Cooley, Charles Horton. 1923. "Heredity and Instinct in Human Life." *Survey* 49:454–69.

Cooley, Charles Horton. [1909] 1963. *Social Organization: A Study of the Larger Mind.* New York: Schocken.

Cooley, Charles Horton. [1902] 1964. *Human Nature and the Social Order.* New York: Schocken.

Cooley, Charles Horton. [1918] 1966. *Social Process.* Carbondale & Edwardsville, IL: Southern Illinois Press.

Cooley, Charles Horton. [1894] 1969. "The Theory of Transportation." In *Sociological Theory and Social Research: Selected Papers of Charles Horton Cooley,* edited by Robert Cooley Angell. New York: Kelley.

Cooley, Charles Horton. [1928] 1969. "The Development of Sociology at Michigan." Pp. 3–14 in *Sociological Theory and Social Research: Selected Papers of Charles Horton Cooley,* edited by Robert Cooley Angell. New York: Kelley.

Cooley, Charles Horton. 1998. *On Self and Social Organization,* edited by Hans-Joachim Schubert. Chicago, IL: University of Chicago Press.

Copjec, Joan. 1994. *Read My Desire: Lacan against the Historicists.* Cambridge, MA: MIT Press.

Cornell, Stephen and Douglas Hartman. 1998. *Ethnicity and Race: Making Identities in a Changing World.* Thousand Oaks, CA: Pine Forge.

Corra, Mamadi and David Willer. 2002. "The Gatekeeper." *Sociological Theory* 20:180–205.

Coser, Lewis. 1956. *The Functions of Social Conflict.* New York: Free Press.

Coser, Lewis. 1965. *Men of Ideas: A Sociologist's View.* New York: Free Press.

Coser, Lewis. 1967. *Continuities in the Study of Social Conflict.* New York: Free Press.

Coser, Lewis. 1974. *Greedy Institutions: Patterns of Undivided Commitment.* New York: Free Press.

Coser, Lewis. 1977. *Masters of Sociological Thought.* 2d ed. New York: Harcourt Brace Jovanovich.

Coser, Lewis. 1993. "A Sociologist's Atypical Life." *Annual Review for Sociology* 19:1–15.

Craib, Ian. 1992. *Anthony Giddens.* London: Routldge.

Crehan, K. 2002. *Gramsci, Culture and Anthropology.* London: Pluto.

Culler, Jonathan. 1982. *On Deconstruction: Theory and Criticism after Structuralism.* Ithaca, NY: Cornell University Press.

Culture and Cognition Research Network. 2003. *A division of the American Sociological Association's Culture Section.* Available at http://sociology.rutgers.edu/cultcog/.

Cuomo, Chris J. 1998. *Feminism and Ecological Communities: An Ethic of Flourishing.* New York: Routledge.

Cvetkovich, Ann and Douglas Kellner. 1997. *Articulating the Global and the Local. Globalization and Cultural Studies.* Boulder, CO: Westview.

Dahl, Robert A. 1998. *On Democracy.* New Haven, CT: Yale University Press.

Dahms, Hans-Joachim. 1994. *Positivismusstreit: Die Auseinandersetzungen der Frankfurter Schule mit dem logischen Positivismus, dem amerikanischen Pragmatismus und dem kritischen Rationalismus.* Translated as *The Positivist Dispute: The Heated Discussion of the Frankfurt School against Logical Positivism, American Pragmatism and Critical Rationalism* (Frankfurt, Germany: Suhrkamp).

Dahrendorf, Ralf. 1958. "Toward a Theory of Social Conflict." *Journal of Conflict Resolution* 2(June):170–83.

Dahrendorf, Ralf. 1959. *Class and Class Conflict in Industrial Society.* Stanford, CA: Stanford University Press.

Dahrendorf, Ralf. 1964. "Amba und die Amerikaner: Bemerkungen zur These der Universalität von Herrschaft [Amba and the Americans: Some Notes on the Thesis of the Universality of Herrschaft]." *Europäisches Archiv für Soziologie* 5:83–98.

Dahrendorf, Ralf. 1968. *Essays in the Theory of Society.* London: Routledge & Kegan Paul.

Dahrendorf, Ralf. 1977. *Homo Sociologicus. Ein Versuch zur Geschichte, Bedeutung und Kritik der Kategorie der sozialen Rolle* [An Essay on History, Meaning and Criticism of the Term "Social Role"]. 15th ed. Opladen, Germany: Westdeutscher Verlag.

Dahrendorf, Ralf. 1979. *Life Chance: Aproaches to Social and Political Theory.* Chicago, IL: University of Chicago Press.

Dahrendorf, Ralf. 1979. *Society and Democracy in Germany.* New York: Norton.

Dahrendorf, Ralf. 1988. *The Modern Social Conflict: An Essay on the Politics of Liberty.* New York: Weidenfeld & Nicolson.

Darwin, Charles. 1901. *The Descent of Man and Selection in Relation to Sex.* London: Murray.

Darwin, Charles. [1859] 1964. *On the Origin of Species: A Facsimile of the First Edition.* Cambridge, MA: Harvard University Press.

Davidson, A. 1977. *Antonio Gramsci: Towards an Intellectual Biography.* London: Merlin.

Davie, Grace. 2002. *Europe: The Exceptional Case: Parameters of Faith in the Modern World.* London: Darton, Longman, & Todd.

Davis, Angela. 1981. *Women, Race and Class.* New York: Random House.

Davis, Angela. 1985. *Violence against Women and the Ongoing Challenge of Racism.* Tallahassee, FL: Women of Color Press.

Davis, Kingsley and Wilbert Moore. 1945. "Some Principles of Stratification." *American Sociological Review* 10:242–49.

Dawes, Robyn M. 1980. "Social Dilemmas." *Annual Review of Psychology* 31:169–93.

Dawkins, Richard. 1989. *The Selfish Gene.* Harmondsworth, UK: Penguin.

Dawson, Michael. 1994. "A Black Counterpublic? Economic Earthquakes, Racial Agenda(s), and Black Politics." *Public Culture* 7:195–223.

Debord, Guy. 1967. *La société du spectacle.* Paris: Buchet/Chastel. Rev. ed., no translator credit. Published as *The Society of the Spectacle* (Detroit, MI: Black & Red, 1977).

Debord, Guy. 1990. *Comments on the Society of the Spectacle.* Translated by Malcolm Imrie. London: Verso.

Debord, Guy. 1991. *Panegyric.* Translated by James Brook. London: Verso.

Debord, Guy. 1995. *Society of the Spectacle.* New York: Zone.

Debord, Guy. 2001. *Considerations on the Assassination of Gérard Lebovici.* Translated by Robert Greene. Los Angeles, CA: Tam Tam.

Debord, Guy and Gianfranco Sanguinetti. 1985. *The Veritable Split in the International: Public Circular of the Situationist International.* No translator credit. London: Chronos.

Degenne, Alain and Michel Forsé. 1999. *Introducing Social Networks.* Thousand Oaks, CA: Sage.

Delanty, G. 2000. *Citizenship in a Global Age.* Buckingham, UK: Open University Press.

Deleuze, Gilles. 1990. *The Logic of Sense.* London: Athlone.

Deleuze, Gilles. 1992. "Ethology: Spinoza and Us." In *Incorporations,* edited by Jonathan Crary and Sanford Kwinter. New York: Zone Books.

Deleuze, Gilles. 1994. *Difference and Repetition.* London: Athlone.

Deleuze, Gilles and Felix Guattari. 1980. *Milles Plateaux: Capitalisme et Schizophrénie.* Translated as *Thousand Plateaus* (Minneapolis: University of Minnesota Press, 1987).

Deleuze, Gilles and Félix Guattari. 1984. *Anti-Oedipus: Capitalism and Schizophrenia.* London: Athlone.

Deleuze, Gilles and Félix Guattari. 1987. *A Thousand Plateaus: Capitalism and Schizophrenia.* Minneapolis: University of Minnesota Press.

Delphy, Christine. 1984. *Close to Home: A Materialist Analysis of Women's Oppression,* edited and translated by Diana Leonard. Amherst: University of Massachusetts Press.

Delphy, Christine. 1993. "Rethinking Sex and Gender." *Women's Study International Forum* 16:1–9.

Demerath, N. J., Peter Dobkin Hall, Terry Schmitt, and Rhys H. Williams, eds. 1998. *Sacred Companies: Organizational Aspects of Religion and Religious Aspects of Organizations.* New York: Oxford University Press.

Denzin, Norman. 1995. *The Cinematic Society.* London: Sage.

Der Derian, James, ed. 1998. *The Virilio Reader.* Oxford, UK: Blackwell.

Derathé, Robert. 1950. *Jean-Jacques Rousseau et la science politique de son temps* [Jean-Jacques Rousseau and the Political Science of His Time]. Paris: Presses Universitaires de France.

Derrida, Jacques. 1966. "Structure, Sign, and Play in the Discourse of the Human Sciences." Reprinted as chap. 10 in *Writing and Difference* (Chicago, IL: University of Chicago Press, 1978).

Derrida, Jacques. 1973. *Speech and Phenomena: And Other Essays on Husserl's Theory of Signs.* Translated by David B. Allison. Evanston, IL: Northwestern University Press.

Derrida, Jacques. 1974. *Of Grammatology.* Translated by G. Spivak. Baltimore, MD: Johns Hopkins University Press.

Derrida, Jacques. 1978. *Writing and Difference.* Translated by A. Bass. Chicago, IL: Chicago University Press.

Derrida, Jacques. 1981. *Dissemination.* London: Athlone.

Derrida, Jacques. 1981. *Positions.* Chicago, IL: University of Chicago Press.

Derrida, Jacques. 1982. "The Ends of Man." Pp. 111–36 in *Margins of Philosophy.* Translated by Alan Bass. Chicago, IL: University of Chicago Press.

Deutsch, Karl W. 1966. *Nationalism and Social Communication: An Inquiry into the Foundations of Nationality,* 2d ed. Cambridge, MA: MIT Press.

Dewey, John. 1960. *Dewey on Experience, Nature, and Freedom.* Edited by Richard J. Bernstein. Indianapolis, IN: Bobbs-Merrill.

Dickens, D. R. and A. Fontana. 1994. *Postmodernism and Social Inquiry.* New York: Guilford.

Dickens, Peter. 2000. *Social Darwinism.* Buckingham, UK: Open University Press.

Dickens, Peter. 2003. *Society and Nature. Evolution, Industry, Community, Risk.* Oxford, UK: Polity Press.

Diekmann, A. and Lindenberg, S. 2001. "Cooperation: Sociological Aspects." Pp. 2751–56 in *International Encyclopedia of the Social and Behavioral Sciences,* edited by N. J. Smelser and P. B. Baltes. Vol. 4. Oxford, UK: Pergamon-Elsevier.

Dilthey, Wilhelm. 1957–1960. *Gesammelte Schriften* [Collected Writings]. 12 vols. 2d ed. Stuttgart Germany: & Göttingen.

Dilthey, Wilhelm. [1900] 1962. "Die Entstehung der Hermeneutik" [The Emergence of Hermeneutics]. In *Gesammelte Schriften* [Collected Writings], edited by W. Dilthey. [Leipzig/Berlin 1914–1936, fortgeführt.] Stuttgart, Germany: Göttingen.

Dilthey, Wilhelm. 1962. *Pattern and Meaning in History: Thought on History and Society.* Edited and translated by H. P. Rickman. New York: Harper and Row.

Dilthey, Wilhelm. [1883] 1989. *Selected Works.* vol. I, *Introduction to the Human Sciences,* edited and translated by Rudolf Makreel and Firthjof Rodi. Princeton, NJ: Princeton University Press.

Dilthey, Wilhelm. [1900] 1996. "The Rise of Hermeneutics." Pp. 235–58 in *Wilhelm Dilthey: Selected Works.* vol. 4, *Hermeneutics and the Study of History,* edited by Rudolf A. Makkreel and Frithjof Rodi. Princeton, NJ: Princeton University Press.

DiMaggio, Paul. 1997. "Culture and Cognition: An Interdisciplinary Review. *Annual Review of Sociology* 23: 263–87.

DiMaggio, Paul and John Mohr. 1985. "Cultural Capital, Educational Attainment and Marital Selection." *American Journal of Sociology* 90:1231–61.

Dobb, Maurice H. 1973. *Theories of Value and Distribution since Adam Smith.* Cambridge, UK: Cambridge University Press.

Dobbelaere, Karel. 1981. *Secularization: A Multidimensional Concept.* London: Sage.

Domhoff, G. William and Hoyt B. Ballard, eds. 1968. *C. Wright Mills and the Power Elite.* Boston, MA: Beacon.

Dor, Joël. 1997. *Introduction to the Reading of Lacan.* Northvale, NJ: Jason Aronson.

Dorfman, Ariel and Armand Mattelart. 2000. *Para leer al pato Donald: Comunicación de masa y colonialismo.* Mexico City, Mexico: Siglo Veintiuno Editores.

Dosse, François. 1997. *History of Structuralism.* 2 vols. Minneapolis, MN: Minnesota University Press.

Dosse, François. 2002. *Michel de Certeau, chemins d'histoire.* Paris: Éditions Complexe.

Dosse, François. 2002. *Michel de Certeau, le marcheur blessé.* Paris: La Découverte.

Douglas, J., P. A. Adler, P. Adler, A. Fontana, C. R. Freeman, and J. Kotarba. 1980. *Introduction to the Sociologies of Everyday Life.* Boston, MA: Allyn & Bacon.

Douglas, M. and B. Isherwood. 1979. *The World of Goods: Toward an Anthropology of Consumption.* Harmondsworth, UK: Penguin.

Draghici, Simona. 2001. *The Pauper/Georg Simmel.* Washington, DC: Plutarch.

Draper, H. 1977–1986. *Karl Marx's Theory of Revolution.* 4 vols. New York: Monthly Review.

Drew, P. and A. Wootten, eds. 1988. *Erving Goffman: Exploring the Interaction Order.* Cambridge, UK: Polity.

Dreyfus, Hubert and Paul Rabinow. 1983. *Michel Foucault: Beyond Structuralism and Hermeneutics.* Berkeley: University of California Press.

Du Bois, W. E. B. 1896. *The Suppression of the African Slave-Trade to the United States of America, 1638–1870.* New York: Longmans, Green.

Du Bois, W. E. B. 1899. *The Philadelphia Negro: A Social Study.* Boston, MA: Ginn & Company.

Du Bois, W. E. B. 1903. *The Souls of Black Folk.* Chicago, IL: A. C. McClurg.

Du Bois, W. E. B. 1920. *Darkwater: Voices from within the Veil.* New York: Harcourt, Brace, & Howe.

Du Bois, W. E. B. 1935. *Black Reconstruction: An Essay toward a History of the Part Which Black Folk Played in the Attempt to Reconstruct Democracy in America, 1860–1880.* New York: Harcourt, Brace.

Du Bois, W. E. B. 1940. *Dusk of Dawn: An Essay toward an Autobiography of a Race Concept.* New York: Harcourt, Brace.

Du Bois, W. E. B. 1947. *The World and Africa: An Inquiry into the Part Which Africa Has Played in World History.* New York: Viking.

Du Gay, P., S. Hall, L. Janes, H. Mackay, and K. Negus. 1997. *Doing Cultural Studies: The Story of the Sony Walkman.* London: Sage.

Duerr, Hans-Peter. 1988–1997. *Der Mythos vom Zivilisationsprozeße.* 4 vols. Frankfurt/Main, Germany: Suhrkamp.

Duggan, Lisa and Nan D. Hunter. 1995. *Sex Wars: Sexual Dissent and Political Culture.* New York & London: Routledge.

Dumont, L. 1986. *Essays on Individualism, Modern Ideology in Anthropological Perspective.* Chicago, IL: University of Chicago Press.

Duncan, David. 1908. *Life and Letters of Herbert Spencer.* 2 vols. New York: D. Appleton.

Dunlap, R. E., F. H. Buttel, P. Dickens, and A. Gijswijt, eds. 2002. *Sociological Theory and the Environment: Classical Foundations, Contemporary Insights.* Boulder, CO: Rowman & Littlefield.

Durant, Will. 2001. *Heroes of History: A Brief History of Civilization from Ancient Times to the Dawn of the Modern Age.* New York: Simon & Schuster.

Durham, Meenakshi Gigi and Douglas Kellner, eds. 2001. *Media and Cultural Studies: KeyWorks.* Malden, MA, and Oxford, UK: Blackwell.

Durkheim, Émile. [1893] 1933. *The Division of Labor in Society.* New York: Macmillan.

Durkheim, Émile. [1897] 1951. *Suicide: A Sociological Study.* Translated by John Spaulding and George Simpson. New York: Free Press.

Durkheim, Émile. 1957. *Professional Ethics and Civic Morals.* Translated by Cornelia Brookfield. London: Routledge & Kegan Paul.

Durkheim, Émile. [1892] 1960. "Montesquieu's Contribution to the Rise of Social Science." Pp. 1–64 in *Montesquieu and Rousseau: Forerunners of Sociology.* Ann Arbor: University of Michigan Press.

Durkheim, Émile. 1960. "Rousseau's Social Contract." Pp. 65–138 in *Montesquieu and Rousseau: Forerunners of Sociology.* Ann Arbor: University of Michigan Press.

Durkheim, Émile. [1895] 1964. *The Rules of the Sociological Method.* New York: Free Press.

Durkheim, Émile. [1912] 1965. *The Elementary Forms of Religious Life.* New York: Dutton.

Durkheim, Émile. [1898] 1973. "Individualism and the Intellectuals." In *Émile Durkheim on Morality and Society,* edited by Robert N. Bellah. Chicago, IL: University of Chicago Press.

Durkheim, Émile. 1973. *Moral Education: A Study in the Theory and Application of the Sociology of Education.* New York: Free Press.

Durkheim, Émile. [1897b] 1982. "Marxism and Sociology: Review of Antonio Labriola 'Essais sur la conception materialiste de l'histoire.'" In *The Rules of Sociological Method,* edited by Steven Lukes. Translated by W. D. Halls. New York: Free Press.

Durkheim, Émile and Elijah Anderson, 1990. *Street Wise: Race, Class and Change in an Urban Community.* Chicago, IL: University of Chicago Press.

Dworkin, Andrea. 1981. *Pornography: Men Possessing Women.* New York: Perigee.

Dworkin, Andrea. 2002. *Heartbreak: The Political Memoir of a Feminist Militant.* New York: Basic Books.

Dyer, Richard. 1998. *Stars.* New ed. London: British Film Institute.

Eagleton, Terry. 1998. *The Ideology of the Aesthetic.* Oxford, UK: Blackwell.

Eagleton, Terry, Frederic Jameson, and Edward Said. 1990. *Nationalism, Colonialism and Literature.* Minneapolis: University of Minnesota Press.

Eaubonne, Françoise d'. 1974. "Le Feminisme ou la Mort" [Feminism or Death]. Women and the Environment Conference. Berkeley, CA: University of California.

Ebaugh, Helen Rose. 1987. *Becoming an Ex.* Chicago, IL: University of Chicago Press.

Eckberg, Douglas E. and Lester Hill. 1979. "The Paradigm Concept and Sociology: A Critical Review." *American Sociological Review* 44: 925–37.

Eco, Umberto. 1986. *Faith in Fakes: Travels in Hyperreality.* Translated by William Weaver. London: Minerva.

Eder, K. and B. Giesen, eds. 2001. *European Citizenship: National Legacies and Transnational Projects.* Oxford, UK: Oxford University Press.

Eggertson, Thráinn. 1990. *Economic Behaviour and Institutions.* Cambridge, UK: Cambridge University Press.

Eisenstadt, Shmuel N. 1963. *The Political Systems of Empires.* New York: Free Press.

Eisenstadt, Shmuel N. 1973. *Tradition, Change, and Modernity.* New York: Wiley.

Eisenstadt, Shmuel N. 1978. *Revolution and the Transformation of Societies: A Comparative Study of Civilizations.* New York: Free Press.

Eisenstadt, Shmuel N., ed. 1986. *The Origins and Diversity of Axial Civilizations.* Albany: State University of New York Press.

Eisenstadt, Shmuel N. 1987. *Patterns of Modernity.* London: Pinter.

Eisenstadt, Shmuel N. 2002. *Multiple Modernities.* New Brunswick, NJ: Transaction.

Eisenstein, Zillah R. 1981. *The Radical Future of Liberal Feminism.* New York: Longman.

Ekeh, P. P. 1974. *Social Exchange Theory: The Two Traditions.* Cambridge, MA: Harvard University Press.

Eldridge, J. E. T. 1983. *C. Wright Mills.* New York: Tavistock.

Eliaeson, Sven. 2000. *Max Weber's Methodologies.* Cambridge, UK: Polity.

Elias, Norbert. 1978. *What Is Sociology?* Translated by Stephen Mennell and Grace Morrissey. New York: Columbia University Press.

Elias, Norbert. 1982. *The Civilizing Process.* 2 vols. Translated by E. Jephcott. New York: Pantheon.

Elias, Norbert. 1983. *The Court Society.* Translated by Edmund Jephcott. Oxford, UK: Blackwell.

Elias, Norbert. 1986. "Introduction." Pp. 19–62 in *Quest for Excitement: Sport and Leisure in the Civilizing Process,* edited by N. Elias and E. Dunning. Oxford, UK: Blackwell.

Elias, Norbert. 1987. "Norbert Elias and Figurational Sociology" (Special issue). *Theory, Culture & Society* 4(2–3).

Elias, Norbert. 1987. *Involvement and Detachment.* Edited by Michael Schröter. Translated by Edmund Jephcott. Oxford, UK: Blackwell.

Elias, Norbert. 1988. "Violence and Civilization: The State Monopoly of Physical and Its Infringement." Pp. 177–98 in *Civil Society and the State,* edited by John Keane. London: Verso.

Elias, Norbert. 1990. *Über die Zeit: Arbeiten zur Wissenssoziologie II* [On Time: Studies on the Sociology of Knowledge]. Frankfurt, Germany: Suhrkamp.

Elias, Norbert. 1991. *The Society of Individuals.* Edited by Michael Schröter. Translated by Edmund Jephcott. Oxford, UK: Blackwell.

Elias, Norbert. 1996. *The German's Power Struggles and the Development of Habitus in the Nineteenth and Twentieth Centuries.* Edited by Michael Schröter. Translated by Eric Dunning and Stephen Mennell. Cambridge, UK: Polity.

Elias, Norbert and Eric Dunning. 1986. *Quest for Excitement.* Oxford, UK: Blackwell.

Elias, Norbert, with John L. Scotson. 1994. *The Established and Outsiders: A Sociological Study into Community Problems.* 2d ed. London: Sage.

Elliott, Anthony. 1999. *Social Theory and Psychoanalysis in Transition: Self and Society from Freud to Kristeva.* 2d ed. New York: Free Association Books.

Elliott, Anthony. 2001. *Concepts of the Self.* Oxford, UK: Blackwell.

Elliott, Gregory. 1994. *Althusser: A Critical Reader.* Oxford, UK: Blackwell.

Elster, Jon. 1998. "Emotions and Economic Theory." *Journal of Economic Literature* 36:47–74.

Embree, Lester, ed. 1999. *Schutzian Social Science.* Dordrecht, Netherlands: Kluwer.

Embree, Lester et al., eds. 1997. *Encyclopedia of Phenomenology.* Dordrecht, Netherlands: Kluwer.

Emerson, Richard M. 1962. "Power-Dependence Relations." *American Sociological Review* 27:31–41.

Emerson, Richard M. 1964. "Power-Dependence Relations: Two Experiments." *Sociometry* 27:282–98.

Emerson, Richard M. 1972. "Exchange Theory, Part I: A Psychological Basis for Social Exchange" and "Exchange Theory, Part II: Exchange Relations and Network Structures." Pp. 38–87 in *Sociological Theories in Progress,* Vol. 2, edited by J. Berger, M. Zelditch Jr., and B. Anderson. Boston, MA: Houghton Mifflin.

Emge, Richard Martinus. 1987. *Saint-Simon.* Munich, Germany: Oldenbourg.

Emirbayer, Mustafa and Jeff Goodwin. 1994. "Network Analysis, Culture, and the Problem of Agency." *American Journal of Sociology* 99:1411–54.

Engels, F. [1890] 1972. "Letter to J. Bloch, September 21, 1890," in *On Historical Materialism (Marx, Engels, Lenin).* Moscow, Russia: Progress.

Epstein, J. and R. Axtell. 1996. *Growing Artificial Societies: Social Science from the Bottom Up.* Cambridge, MA: MIT Press.

Erickson, Bonnie H. 1988. "The Relational Basis of Attitudes." Pp. 99–121 in *Social Structures: A Network Approach,* edited by Barry Wellman and S. D. Berkowitz. New York: Cambridge University Press.

Erickson, Bonnie H. 1996. "Culture, Class and Connections." *American Journal of Sociology* 102:217–51.

Ericson, R. and K. Haggerty. 1997. *Policing the Risk Society.* Toronto, Canada: University of Toronto Press.

Eriksson, Björn. 1993. "The First Formulation of Sociology: A Discursive Innovation of the 18th Century." *European Journal of Sociology* 34:251–76.

Etzioni, A. 1961. *Complex Organizations: A Sociological Reader.* New York: Holt, Rinehart & Winston.

Falk, Richard. 1999. *Predatory Globalization: A Critique.* Cambridge, UK: Polity.

Fanon, Frantz. 1967. *Black Skins, White Masks.* New York: Grove.

Fararo, Thomas J. 2001. *Social Action Systems.* Westport, CT: Praeger.

Farberman, Harvey. 1975. "A Criminogenic Market Structure: The Automobile Industry." *Sociological Quarterly* 16:438–57.

Farrell, Thomas. 1993. *Norms of Rhetorical Culture.* New Haven, CT: Yale University Press.

Febvre, Lucien. 1973. *A New Kind of History and Other Essays,* edited by Peter Burke. Translated by K. Folca. New York: Harper Torchbooks.

Febvre, Lucien. 1982. *The Problem of Unbelief in the Sixteenth Century: The Religion of Rabelais.* Translated by Beatrice Gottlieb. Cambridge, MA: Harvard University Press.

Fee, D., ed. 2000. *Pathology and the Postmodern: Mental Illness and Discourse as Experience.* Thousand Oaks, CA: Sage.

Feffer, Andrew. 1990. "Sociability and Social Conflict in George Herbert Mead's Interactionism, 1900–1919." *Journal of the History of Ideas* 51:233–54.

Fehr, Ernst and Simon Gächter. 2000. "Fairness and Retaliation: The Economics of Reciprocity." *Journal of Economic Perspective* 14:159–81.

Ferber, Christian von. 1965. "Der Werturteilsstreit 1909/1959: Versuch einer wissenschaftsgeschichtlichen Interpretation." [The Value Judgement Dispute 1909/1959: An Attempt at an Interpretation in the Context of History of Science]. Pp. 165–80 in *Logik der Sozialwissenschaften* [Logic of the Social Sciences], edited by Ernst Topitsch. Koeln & Berlin, Germany: Kiepenheuer & Witsch.

Ferguson, Adam. [1767] 1966. *An Essay on the History of Civil Society.* Edinburgh, Scotland: Edinburgh University Press.

Ferguson, Anne. 1981. "Patriarchy, Sexual Identity, and the Sexual Revolution." *Signs* 7:158–72.

Ferguson, Ann. 1991. *Sexual Democracy: Women, Oppression, and Revolution.* Boulder, CO: Westview.

Ferrante, Joan. 2000. *Sociology: A Global Perspective.* Belmont, CA: Wadsworth.

Feuerbach, Ludwig. 1975. *Werke in sechs Bänden.* Frankfurt, Germany: Suhrkamp.

Feuerbach, Ludwig. [1841] 1989. *The Essence of Christianity.* Translated by George Eliot. Buffalo, NY: Prometheus.

Fichte, J. G. [1794] 1982. *The Science of Knowledge: With the First and Second Introductions.* New York: Cambridge University Press.

Fichte, J. G. [1798] 1995. [1798] 1995. *Das System der Sittenlehre nach den Prinzipien der Wissenschaftslehre* [The System of Moral Philosophy according to the Knowledge of Science]. Hamburg, Germany: Meiner.

Fichte, J. G. 2004. *System of Ethics.* New York: Cambridge University Press.

Filloux, J. C. 1997. *Durkheim et le socialisme.* Geneva, Switzerland: Libraire Droz.

Fine, Gary Alan. 1979. "Small Groups and Culture Creation: The Idioculture of Little League Baseball Teams." *American Sociological Review* 44:733–45.

Fine, Gary Alan. 1983. *Shared Fantasy: Role-Playing Games as Social Worlds.* Chicago, IL: University of Chicago Press.

Fine, Gary Alan. 1984. "Negotiated Orders and Organizational Cultures." *Annual Review of Sociology* 10:239–62.

Fine, Gary Alan. 1993. "The Sad Demise, Mysterious Disappearance, and Glorious Triumph of Symbolic Interactionism." *Annual Review of Sociology* 19:61–87.

Fine, Gary Alan, ed. 1995. *A Second Chicago School? The Development of a Postwar American Sociology.* Chicago, IL: University of Chicago Press.

Fine, Gary Alan. 1996. *Kitchens: The Culture of Restaurant Work.* Berkeley: University of California Press.

Fine, Gary Alan. 2001. *Difficult Reputations: Collective Memories of the Evil, Inept, and Controversial.* Chicago, IL: University of Chicago Press.

Fine, Gary Alan and Philip Manning. 2000. "Erving Goffman: Shifting Impressions and Tight Frames." In *Blackwell Companion to Major Social Theorists,* edited by George Ritzer. Oxford, UK: Blackwell.

Fine, Gary Alan and Daniel D. Martin. 1990. "A Partisan View: Sarcasm, Satire and Irony in Erving Goffman's *Asylums. Journal of Contemporary Ethnography* 19:89–115.

Fink, Bruce. 1995. *The Lacanian Subject.* Princeton, NJ: Princeton University Press.

Finke, Roger and Rodney Stark. 1992. *The Churching of America, 1776–1990: Winners and Losers in Our Religious Economy.* New Brunswick, NJ: Rutgers University Press.

Fiske, John. 1994. "Audiencing. Cultural Practice and Cultural Studies." Pp. 189–98 in *Handbook of Qualitative Research,* edited by Norman Denzin and Yvonna S. Lincoln. Thousand Oaks, CA: Sage.

Fletcher, John and Andrew Benjamin, eds. 1990. *Abjection, Melancholia, and Love: The Work of Julia Kristeva.* London: Routledge.

Flyvbjerg, Bent. 2001. *Making Social Science Matter: Why Social Inquiry Fails and How It Can Succeed Again.* Cambridge, UK: Cambridge University Press.

Fontana, A. Forthcoming. "The Postmodern Turn in Interactionism." *Studies in Symbolic Interaction.*

Fortunati, Vita and Raymond Trousson, eds. 2000. *Dictionary of Literary Utopias.* Paris: Editions Champion; Geneva, Switzerland: Editions Slatkine.

Foucault, M. 1965. *Madness and Civilization: A History of Insanity in the Age of Reason.* Translated (abridged) by Richard Howard. New York: Pantheon. Originally published as *Folie et déraison: Histoire de la folie à l'âge classique* (Paris: Plon, 1961).

Foucault, Michel. 1966. *Les Mots et les choses.* Translated as *The Order of Things: An Archaeology of the Human Sciences* (New York: Random House, 1970).

Foucault, Michel. 1969. *The Archaeology of Knowledge and the Discourse on Language.* New York: HarperColophon.

Foucault, Michel. 1969. *L'archéologie du savoir.* Translated as *Archaeology of Knowledge* (New York: Pantheon, 1972).

Foucault, Michel. 1973. *Birth of the Clinic: An Archaeology of Medical Perception.* Translated by A. M. Sheridan Smith. New York: Pantheon. Originally published as *Naissance de la clinique* (Paris: Presses Universitaires de France, 1963).

Foucault, Michel. 1977. *Discipline and Punish: The Birth of the Prison.* Translated by A. M Sheridan Smith. New York: Pantheon. Originally published as *Surveillir et punir: Naissance de la prison* (Paris: Gallimard, 1975).

Foucault, Michel. 1977. "Preface to Transgression." Pp. 29–52 in *Language, Counter-Memory and Practice.* Ithaca, NY: Cornell University Press.

Foucault, Michel. 1978. *The History of Sexuality.* vol. 1, *An Introduction.* Translated by Robert Hurley. New York: Pantheon. Originally published as *La volonté savoir: Histoire de la sexualité I* (Paris: Gallimard, 1976).

Foucault, Michel. 1985. *History of Sexuality.* vol. 2, *The Use of Pleasure.* Translated by Robert Hurley. New York: Pantheon. Originally published as *L'usage des plaisirs: Histoire de la sexualité II* (Paris: Gallimard, 1984).

Foucault, Michel. 1986. *Le Souci de soi* [The Care of the Self: The History of Sexuality. Vol. 3]. New York: Random House.

Foucault, Michel. 1985. *L'usage des plasir* [The Use of Pleasure: The History of Sexuality. Vol. 2]. New York: Pantheon.

Foucault, Michel. 1986. *History of Sexuality.* vol. 3, *The Care of the Self.* Translated by Robert Hurley. New York: Pantheon. Originally published as *Le souci de soi: Histoire de la sexualité, III* (Paris: Gallimard, 1984).

Fox, W. 1990. *Towards a Transpersonal Ecology.* London: Shambala.

Frank, Andre Gunder. 1998. *Reorient.* Berkeley: University of California Press.

Frank, Arthur, W. 1995. *The Wounded Storyteller: Body, Illness, and Ethics.* Chicago, IL: University of Chicago Press.

Frank, R. 1988. *Passions within Reason: The Strategic Role of the Emotions.* New York: Norton.

Frank, T. 2001. *One Market Under God: Extreme Capitalism, Market Populism and the End of Economic Democracy.* London: Secker & Warburg.

Fraser, Nancy. 1989. *Unruly Practices: Power Discourse, and Gender in Contemporary Social Theory.* Minneapolis: University of Minnesota Press.

Fraser, Nancy. 1992. "Rethinking the Public Sphere: A Contribution to Critique of Actually Existing Democracy." Pp. 109–42 in *Habermas and the Public Sphere,* edited by Craig Calhoun. Cambridge, MA: MIT Press.

Frazer, Elizabeth. 1998. "Feminist Political Theory." Pp. 50–61 in *Contemporary Feminist Theories,* edited by Stevi Jackson and Jackie Jones. New York: New York University Press.

Freire, Paulo. 1972. *Pedagogy of the Oppressed.* New York: Herder & Herder.

Freud, Sigmund. [1900] 1953. *The Interpretation of Dreams.* Standard Edition, 4, 1–338; Standard Edition, 5, 339–627. London: Hogarth.

Freud, Sigmund. [1921] 1955. *Group Psychology and the Analysis of the Ego.* Standard Edition, 18, 65–143. London: Hogarth.

Freud, Sigmund. [1915] 1959. *The Unconscious.* Standard Edition, 14, 159–215. London: Hogarth.

Freud, Sigmund. [1923] 1961. *The Ego and the Id.* Standard Edition, 19, 1–66. London: Hogarth.

Freud, Sigmund. 1962. *Three Essays on the Theory of Sexuality.* New York: Basic Books.

Freud, Sigmund. [1930] 1975. *Civilization and Its Discontents.* Standard edition, 21. London: Hogarth.

Freud, Sigmund. [1913] 1975. *Totem and Taboo.* Standard edition, 12. London: Hogarth.

Friedan, Betty. 1963. *The Feminine Mystique.* New York: Dell.

Friedkin, Noah E. 1992. "An Expected Value Model of Social Power: Predictions for Selected Exchange Networks." *Social Networks* 14:213–29.

Friedlander, Saul, ed. 1992. *Probing the Limits of Representation: Nazism and the Final Solution.* Cambridge, MA: Harvard University Press.

Friedman, Susan W. 1996. *Marc Bloch, Sociology, and Geography.* New York: Cambridge University Press.

Friedson, Elliot. 1994. *Professionalism Reborn: Theory, Prophesy and Policy.* Chicago, IL: University of Chicago Press.

Frings, Manfred. 1965. *Max Scheler: A Concise Introduction into the World of a Great Thinker.* Pittsburgh, PA: Duquesne University Press.

Frisby, David. 1976. *The Positivist Dispute in German Sociology.* London: Heinemann.

Frow, John and Meaghan Morris. 2000. "Cultural Studies." Pp. 315–46 in *Handbook of Qualitative Research,* 2d ed., edited by Norman Denzin and Yvonna S. Lincoln. Thousand Oaks, CA: Sage.

Fujimura, Joan H. 1992. "Crafting Science: Standardized Packages, Boundary Objects, and 'Translation.'" Pp. 168–211 in *Science as Practice and Culture,* edited by Andrew Pickering. Chicago, IL: University of Chicago Press.

Fukuyama, Francis. 2002. *Our Posthuman Future: Consequences of the Biotechnology Revolution.* New York: Farrar, Straus & Giroux.

Fullbrook, Kate and Edward Fullbrook. 1998. *Simone de Beauvoir: A Critical Introduction.* Cambridge, UK: Polity.

Furet, F. 2000. *The Passing of an Illusion.* Cambridge, MA: Harvard University Press.

Furfey, Paul H. 1965. *The Scope and Method of Sociology: A Metasociological Treatise.* New York: Cooper Square.

Fuss, Diana. 1989. *Essentially Speaking.* New York: Routledge.

Fuss, Diana. 1991. *Inside/Outside: Lesbian Theories, Gay Theories.* New York: Routledge.

Gaard, Greta. 1998. *Ecological Politics: Ecofeminists and the Greens.* Philadelphia, PA: Temple University Press.

Gadamer, Hans-Georg. 1975. *Truth and Method.* New York: Seabury.

Galletti, Marina. 1999. "Comunautés Morales, Communautés Politiques." *Les Tempes Modernes* 54(Janvier–Février):153–67.

Galletti, Marina. 2003. "The Secret and the Sacred in Leiris and Bataille." In "The Collège de Sociologie and French Social Thought." Special issue. *Economy and Society* 32(1).

Gamson, Joshua. 1994. *Claims to Fame: Celebrity in Contemporary America.* Berkeley: University of California Press.

Gamson, William A. 1975. *The Strategy of Social Protest.* Homewood, IL: Dorsey.

Gandy, Oscar H. Jr. 1998. *Communication and Race: A Structural Perspective.* London: Arnold.

Gane, Mike. 1991. *Baudrillard's Bestiary: Baudrillard and Culture.* London: Routledge.

Gane, Mike. 1991. *Baudrillard: Critical and Fatal Theory.* London: Routledge.

Gane, Mike, ed. 1992. *The Radical Sociology of Durkheim and Mauss.* London: Routledge.

Gane, Mike. 2000. *Jean Baudrillard: In Radical Uncertainty.* London: Pluto.

Gane, Mike. 2002. *French Social Theory from Comte to Baudrillard.* Thousand Oaks, CA: Sage.

Gane, Nicholas. 2002. *Max Weber and Postmodern Theory. Rationalization versus Re-enchantment.* London: Palgrave.

Ganz, Marshall. 2000. "Resources and Resourcefulness: Strategic Capacity in the Unionization of California Agriculture, 1959–1966." *American Journal of Sociology* 105(4):1003–62.

Gardner, Carol Brooks. 1995. *Passing By: Gender and Public Harassment.* Berkeley: University of California Press.

Garfinkel, Harold. 1939. "Color Trouble." In *Best Short Stories of 1939,* edited by Edward O'Brien. Boston, MA: Houghton Mifflin.

Garfinkel, Harold. 1956. "Conditions for Successful Degradation Ceremonies." *American Journal of Sociology* 61:420–24.

Garfinkel, Harold. 1967. *Studies in Ethnomethodology.* Englewood Cliffs, NJ: Prentice-Hall.

Garfinkel, Harold. 2002. *Ethnomethodology's Program: Working Out Durkheim's Aphorism.* Lanham, MD: Rowman & Littlefield.

Garfinkel, Harold and Harvey Sacks. 1970. "On Formal Structures of Practical Action." In *Theoretical Sociology,* edited by Edward Tiryakian and John McKinney. New York: Appleton Century Crofts.

Garnham, Nicholas. 1987. "Concepts of Culture: Public Policy and the Culture Industries." *Cultural Studies* 1:23–37.

Garofalo, Reebee. 2001. *Rockin Out: Popular Music in the U.S.A.* 2d ed. New York: Prentice Hall.

Gates, Bill. 1995. *The Road Ahead.* New York: Viking.

Gecas, Viktor and Peter Burke. 1995. "Self and Identity." Pp. 41–67 in *Sociological Perspectives on Social Psychology,* edited by K. S. Cook, G. A. Fine, and J. S. House. Boston, MA: Allyn & Bacon.

Geertz, Clifford. 1963. *Old Societies and New States.* New York: Free Press.

Gehlen, Arnold. [1962] 1988. *Man: His Nature and His Place in the World.* 7th ed. New York: Columbia University Press. Originally published as *Der Mensch. Seine Natur und seine Stellung in der Welt.* 7th ed. (Frankfurt, Germany: Klostermann, 1940).

Gellner, Ernest. 1983. *Nations and Nationalism.* Oxford, UK: Blackwell.

Genosko, Gary. 1994. *Baudrillard and Signs.* London: Routledge.

Genosko, Gary. 1999. *McLuhan and Baudrillard: The Masters of Implosion.* London: Routledge.

Gergen, Kenneth. 1991. *The Saturated Self: Dilemmas of Identity in Contemporary Life.* New York: Basic Books.

Gerritsen, Jan-Willem. 2000. *The Control of Fuddle and Flash: A Sociological History of the Regulation of Alcohol and Opiates.* Leiden, Holland: Brill.

Gerth, H. and C. Wright Mills. 1953. *Character and Social Structure: The Psychology of Social Institutions.* New York: Harcourt, Brace.

Gerth, H. and C. W. Mills. 1958. *From Max Weber*. New York: Oxford University Press.

Gibson, William. 1984. *Neuromancer*. New York: Dell.

Gibson-Graham, J. K. 1996. "Reflections on Postmodern Feminist Social Research." In *Bodyspace: Destabilizing Geographies of Gender and Sexuality*, edited by Nancy Duncan. London: Routledge.

Giddens, Anthony. 1971. *Capitalism and Modern Social Theory: An Analysis of the Writings of Marx, Durkheim and Max Weber*. Cambridge, UK: Cambridge University Press.

Giddens, Anthony. 1971. *The Sociology of Suicide*. London: Cass.

Giddens, Anthony, ed. 1974. *Positivism and Sociology*. London: Heinemann.

Giddens, Anthony. 1976. *New Rules of Sociological Method: A Positive Critique of Interpretative Sociologies*. London: Macmillan.

Giddens, Anthony. 1978. "Positivism and Its Critics." In *A History of Sociological Analysis*, edited by Tom Bottomore and Robert Nisbet. New York: Basic Books.

Giddens, Anthony. 1979. *Central Problems in Social Theory: Action, Structure and Contradiction in Social Analysis*. London: Macmillan.

Giddens, Anthony. 1981. *A Contemporary Critique of Historical Materialism*. vol. 1, *Power, Property and the State*. London: Macmillan.

Giddens, Anthony. 1984. *The Constitution of Society: Outline of the Theory of Structuration*. Berkeley: University of California Press.

Giddens, Anthony. 1985. *The Nation-State and Violence*. vol. 2, *A Contemporary Critique of Historical Materialism*. Cambridge, UK: Polity.

Giddens, Anthony. 1987. *Nation-State and Violence*. Berkeley: University of California Press.

Giddens, Anthony. 1989. "A Reply to My Critics." Pp. 249–301 in *Social Theory of Modern Societies: Anthony Giddens and His Critics,* edited by D. Held and J. B. Thompson. Cambridge, UK: Cambridge University Press.

Giddens, Anthony. 1990. *The Consequences of Modernity*. Cambridge, UK: Polity.

Giddens, Anthony 1991. *Modernity and Self-Identity: Self and Society in the Late Modern Age*. Stanford, CA: Stanford University Press.

Giddens, Anthony 1992. *The Transformation of Intimacy: Sexuality, Love and Eroticism in Modern Societies*. Stanford, CA: Stanford University Press.

Giddens, Anthony. 1994. *Beyond Left and Right: The Future of Radical Politics*. Cambridge, UK: Polity.

Giddens, Anthony. 1998. *The Third Way: The Renewal of Social Democracy*. Cambridge, UK: Polity.

Giddens, Anthony. 2000. *The Third Way and Its Critics*. Cambridge, UK: Polity.

Gilbert, Margaret. 1992. *On Social Facts*. Princeton, NJ: Princeton University Press.

Giles, David. 2000. *Illusions of Immortality: A Psychology of Fame and Celebrity*. London: Macmillan.

Gilligan, Carol. 1982. *In a Different Voice: Psychological Theory and Women's Development*. Cambridge, MA: Harvard University Press.

Gilligan, Carol. 1990. "Joining the Resistance: Psychology, Politics, Girls and Women." *Michigan Quarterly Review* 29:501–31.

Gilligan, Carol. 1995. "Hearing the Difference: Theorizing Connection." *Hypatia* 10(2):120–28.

Gilligan, Carol. 2002. *The Birth of Pleasure*. New York: Knopf.

Gilligan, Carol, N. Lyons, and T. Hanmer, eds. 1990. *Making Connections: The Relational Worlds of Adolescent Girls at Emma Willard School*. Cambridge, MA: Harvard University Press.

Gilligan, Carol, A. Rogers, and D. Tolman, eds. 1991. *Women, Girls, and Psychotherapy: Reframing Resistance*. New York: Hayworth.

Gilligan, Carol, R. Spencer, M. K. Weinberg, and T. Bertsch. 2003. "On the Listening Guide: A Voice-Centered Relational Model." In *Qualitative Research in Psychology: Expanding Perspectives in Methodology and Design*, edited by P. M. Camic, J. E. Rhodes, and L. Yardley. Washington, DC: American Psychological Association Press.

Gilligan, Carol, J. Ward, and J. Taylor, with B. Bardige, eds. 1988. *Mapping the Moral Domain: A Contribution of Women's Thinking to Psychological Theory and Education*. Cambridge, MA: Harvard University Press.

Gilman, Charlotte Perkins. 1903. *The Home: Its Work and Influence*. New York: McClure, Phillips.

Gilman, Charlotte Perkins. 1904. *Human Work*. New York: McClure, Phillips.

Gilman, Charlotte Perkins. 1914. *The Man-Made World or, Our Androcentric Culture*. New York: Charlton.

Gilman, Charlotte Perkins. [1923] 1976. *His Religion and Hers: A Study of the Faith of Our Fathers and the Work of Our Mothers*. Westport, CT: Hyperion.

Gilman, Sander. 1985. *Difference and Pathology*. Ithaca, NY: Cornell University Press.

Gintis, Herbert. 2000. *Game Theory Evolving*. Princeton, NJ: Princeton University Press.

Giobbe, Evilina. 1995. "Surviving Commercial Sexual Exploitation." Pp. 314–18 in *Gender, Race and Class in Media: A Text-Reader,* edited by Gail Dines and Jean Humez. Thousand Oaks, CA: Sage.

Giroux, Henry A. 1999. *The Mouse That Roared: Disney and the End of Innocence*. Lanham, MD: Rowman & Littlefield.

Giroux, Henry A. 2001. *Public Spaces, Private Lives. Beyond the Culture of Cynicism*. Lanham, MD: Rowman & Littlefield.

Giroux, Henry A. 2002. *Breaking in to the Movies. Film and the Culture of Politics*. Oxford, UK: Blackwell.

Giroux, Henry A. and Peter McLaren. 1995. "Radical Pedagogy as Cultural Politics: Beyond the Discourse of Critique and Anti-Utopianism." Pp. 29–57 in *Critical Pedagogy and*

Predatory Culture: Oppositional Politics in a Postmodern Era, edited by Peter McLaren. New York & London: Routledge.

Glaser, Barney G. and Anselm L. Strauss. 1965. *Awareness of Dying.* Chicago, IL: Aldine.

Glaser, Barney G. and Anselm L. Strauss. 1967. *The Discovery of Grounded Theory: Strategies for Qualitative Research.* Chicago. IL: Aldine.

Glover, Jonathan. 1988. *I: The Philosophy and Psychology of Personal Identity.* London: Allen Lane, Penguin.

Goffman, Erving. 1959. *The Presentation of Self in Everyday Life.* Garden City, NY: Doubleday Anchor.

Goffman, Erving. 1961. *Asylums: Essays in the Social Situation of Mental Patients and Other Inmates.* Garden City, NY: Anchor.

Goffman, Erving. 1961. *Encounters: Two Studies in the Sociology of Interaction.* Indianapolis, IN: Bobbs-Merrill.

Goffman, Erving. 1963. *Behavior in Public Places: Notes on the Social Organization of Gatherings.* New York: Free Press.

Goffman, Erving. 1963. *Stigma: Notes on the Management of Spoiled Identity.* Englewood Cliffs, NJ: Prentice-Hall.

Goffman, Erving. 1967. *Interaction Ritual.* New York: Random House.

Goffman, Erving. 1969. *Strategic Interaction.* Philadelphia, PA: University of Philadelphia Press.

Goffman, Erving. 1971. *Relations in Public: Microstudies of the Public Order.* New York: Basic Books.

Goffman, Erving. 1974. *Frame Analysis: An Essay on the Organization of Experience.* Cambridge, MA: Harvard Univesity Press.

Goffman, Erving. 1983. "Felicity's Condition." *American Journal of Sociology* 89:1–51.

Goffman, Erving. 1983. "The Interaction Order." *American Sociological Review* 48:1–17.

Goldfrank, Walter L. 2000. "Paradigm Regained? The Rules of Wallerstein's World-System Method." In *Festschrift for Immanuel Wallerstein,* edited by Giovanni Arrighi and Walter L. Goldfrank. *Journal of World-Systems Research* 6(2):150–95. Retrieved March 20, 2004 (http://jwsr.ucr.edu/archive/vol6/number2/index.shtml).

Goldmann, L. 1964. *The Hidden God: A Study of Tragic Vision in the Pensees of Pascal and the Tragedies of Racine.* London: Routledge & Kegan Paul.

Goldstein, Jeffrey. 1999. "Emergence as a Construct: History and Issues." *Emergence* 1:49–72.

Goldstone, Jack A. 1991. *Revolution and Rebellion in the Early Modern World.* Berkeley: University of California Press.

Goldstone, Jack A. 1997. "Methodological Issues in Comparative Macrosociology," *Comparative Social Research* 16:107–20.

Goldstone, Jack A. 2002. "Efflorescences and Economic Growth in World History: Rethinking the 'Rise of the West' and the British Industrial Revolution." *Journal of World History* 13:323–89.

Goldstone, Jack A. 2004. *The Happy Chance: The Rise of the West in Global Context, 1500–1800.* Cambridge, MA: Harvard University Press.

Goldstone, Jack A. and Bert Useem. 1999. "Prison Riots as Micro-Revolutions: An Extension of State-Centered Theories of Revolution." *American Journal of Sociology* 104:985–1029.

Goldthorpe, John H. 1980. *Social Mobility and Class Structure in Modern Britain.* Oxford, UK: Clarendon.

Gomery, Douglas. 2000. "Hollywood as Industry." Pp. 19–28 in *American Cinema and Hollywood: Critical Approaches,* edited by John Hill and Pamela Church Gibson. Oxford, UK: Oxford University Press.

Gordon, Colin. 1987. "The Soul of the Citizen: Max Weber and Michel Foucault on Rationality and Government." Pp. 293–316 in *Max Weber, Rationality and Modernity,* edited by S. Whimster and S. Lash. London: Allen & Unwin.

Gotham, Kevin Fox. 2000. "Racialization and the State: The Housing Act of 1934 and the Origins of the Federal Housing Administration (FHA)." *Sociological Perspectives* 43(2): 291–316.

Gothlin, Eva. 1999. "Simone de Beauvoir's Notions of Appeal, Desire, and Ambiguity and Their Relationship to Jean-Paul Sartre's Notions of Appeal and Desire." *Hypatia: A Journal of Feminist Philosophy* 14(4):83–95.

Goudsblom, Johan and Stephen Mennell. 1997. "Civilizing Processes—Myth or Reality?" Review article on Hans-Peter Duerr, *Der Mythos vom Zivilisationsprozeße* [The Myth of the Civilising Process]. *Comparative Studies in Society and History* 39(4):727–31.

Gouhier, H. 1965. *La vie d'Auguste Comte.* Paris: Vrin.

Gould, C. 1978. *Marx's Social Ontology: Individuality and Community in Marx's Theory of Social Reality.* Cambridge, MA: MIT Press.

Gould, Deborah B. 2002. "Life during Wartime: Emotions and the Development of ACT UP." *Mobilization* 7(2):177–200.

Gould, Roger, ed. 2000. *The Rational Choice Controversy in Historical Sociology.* Chicago, IL: University of Chicago Press.

Gouldner, Alvin W. 1954. *Patterns of Industrial Democracy.* Glencoe, IL: Free Press.

Gouldner, Alvin W. 1960. "The Norm of Reciprocity: A Preliminary Statement." *American Sociological Review* 25:161–178.

Gouldner, Alvin W. 1970. *The Coming Crisis of Western Sociology.* New York: Avon.

Gouldner, Alvin W. 1973. *For Sociology: Renewal and Critique in Sociology Today.* New York: Basic Books.

Gouldner, Alvin W. 1979. *The Future of Intellectuals and the Rise of the New Class.* New York: Seabury.

Gouldner, Alvin W. 1980. *The Two Marxisms: The Ambiguous Legacy.* New York: Seabury.

Grace, Victoria. 2000. *Baudrillard's Challenge: A Feminist Reading.* London: Routledge.

Grace, Victoria H., Worth, and L. Simmons, eds. 2003. *Baudrillard: West of the Dateline.* Palmerston North, New Zealand: Dunmore.

Gramsci, Antonio. 1971. *Selections from the Prison Notebooks of Antonio Gramsci,* edited and translated by Quintin Hoare and Geoffrey Nowell Smith. New York: International.

Gramsci, Antonio. 1975. *Letters from Prison*. London: Cape.

Gramsci, Antonio. 1985. *Selections from Cultural Writings,* edited by David Forgacs and Geoffrey Nowell-Smith. London: Lawrence & Wishart.

Gramsci, Antonio. [1926] 1995. *The Southern Question.* Translated by Pasquale Verdicchio. Lafayette, IN: Bordighera.

Granfield, Robert. 1991. "Making It by Faking It: Working-Class Students in an Elite Academic Environment." *Journal of Contemporary Ethnology* 20:331-51.

Granovetter, Mark S. 1973. "The Strength of Weak Ties." *American Journal of Sociology* 78:1360–80.

Granovetter, Mark S. 1983. "The Strength of Weak Ties: A Network Theory Revisited." *Sociological Theory* 1:201–33.

Granovetter, Mark S. 1974. "Exchange with Herbert Gans." *American Journal of Sociology* 80(2):524–31.

Granovetter, Mark S. 1985. "*Economic Action and Social Structure: The Problem of Embeddedness.*" *American Journal of Sociology* 91(3):481–510.

Grant, Judith. 1993. *Fundamental Feminism: Contesting the Core Concepts of Feminist Theory.* New York: Routledge.

Green, Donald P. and Ian Shapiro. 1994. *Pathologies of Rational Choice Theory: A Critique of Applications in Political Science.* New Haven, CT: Yale University Press.

Greenfeld, Leah. 1992. *Nationalism: Five Paths to Modernity.* Cambridge, MA: Harvard University Press.

Greenwald, Anthony G. and Anthony R. Pratkanis. 1984. "The Self." Pp. 129–78 in *Handbook of Social Cognition,* edited by R. S. Wyer and T. K. Srull. Hillsdale, NJ: Lawrence Erlbaum.

Grimshaw, Jean. 1986. *Philosophy and Feminist Thinking.* Minneapolis: University of Minnesota Press.

Grosrichard, Alain. 1988. *The Sultan's Court: European Fantasies of the East.* New York: Verso.

Grossberg, Lawrence. 1992. *We Gotta Get Out of This Place: Popular Conservatism and Popular Culture.* New York & London: Routledge.

Grossman, David. 1999. *Stop Teaching Our Kids to Kill: A Call to Action Against TV, Movie and Video Game Violence.* New York: Random House.

Grundmann, Reiner and Nico Stehr. 2001. "Introduction." Pp. ix–lxii in *Werner Sombart: Economic Life in the Modern Age,* edited by N. Stehr and R. Grundmann. New Brunswick, NJ, & Oxford, UK: Transaction.

Gubrium, J. and J. Holstein. 1997. *The New Language of Qualitative Methods.* New York: Oxford University Press.

Guillén, Mauro F. 2001. "Is Globalization Civilizing, Destructive or Feeble? A Critique of Five Key Debates in the Social Science Literature." *Annual Review of Sociology* 27:235–60.

Gurvitch, Georges. 1950. *La vocation actuelle de la sociologie.* Paris: Presses Universitaires de France.

Gurvitch, Georges. 1964. *The Spectrum of Social Time.* Dordrecht, Holland: D. Reidel.

Haas, Ernst B. 1958. *The Uniting of Europe.* Stanford, CA: Stanford University Press.

Haas, Ernst B. 1975. *The Obsolescence of Regional Integration Theory.* Berkeley: University of California Press.

Habermas, Jürgen. 1969. "Kritische und konservative Aufgaben der Soziologie" [Critical and Conservative Tasks of Sociology]. Pp. 215–30 in *Theorie und Praxis* [Theory and Practice]. Neuwied, Germany: Luchterhand.

Habermas, Jürgen. 1984. *The Theory of Communicative Action.* 2 vols. Translated by T. McCarthy. Boston, MA: Beacon.

Habermas, Jürgen. 1987. *The Philosophical Discourse of Modernity: Twelve Lectures.* Translated by Fredrick Lawrence. Cambridge, MA: MIT Press.

Habermas, Jürgen. 1987. *The Theory of Communicative Action.* 2 vols. Translated by Thomas McCarthy. Boston, MA: Beacon.

Habermas, Jürgen. 1988. *Postmetaphysical Thinking.* Cambridge, MA: MIT Press.

Habermas, Jürgen. [1962]1989. *The Structural Transformation of the Public Sphere: An Inquiry into a Category of Bourgeois Society.* Translated by T. Burger with F. Lawrence. Cambridge, MA: MIT Press. Originally published as *Strukturwandel der Öffentlichkeit: Untersuchung zu einer Kategorie der bügerlichen Gesellschaft.*

Habermas, Jürgen. 1991. "A Reply." Pp. 215–64 in *Communicative Action: Essays on Jürgen Habermas's "The Theory of Communicative Action,"* edited by A. Honneth and H. Joas. Cambridge, UK: Cambridge University Press.

Habermas, Jürgen. 1992. *Between Facts and Norms: Contributions to a Discourse Theory of Law and Democracy.* Cambridge, MA: MIT Press.

Habermas, Jürgen. 1992. "Further Reflections on the Public Sphere." Pp. 421–61 in *Habermas and the Public Sphere,* edited by Craig Calhoun. Cambridge, MA: MIT Press.

Habermas, Jürgen. 1998. *The Inclusion of the Other: Studies in Political Theory,* edited by Ciaran Cronin and Pablo De Greif. Cambridge, MA: MIT Press.

Habermas, Jürgen and Niklas Luhmann, eds. 1971. *Theorie der Gesellschaft oder Sozialtechnologie* [Theory of Society or Social Technology]. Frankfurt, Germany: Suhrkamp.

Hacking, Ian. 1999. *The Social Construction of What?* Cambridge, MA: Harvard University Press.

Hadden, Jeffrey K. 1987. "Toward Desacralizing Secularization Theory." *Social Forces* 65:587–611.

Hage, Jerald and Charles H. Powers. 1992. *Post-Industrial Lives: Roles and Relationships in the 21st Century.* Newbury Park, CA: Sage.

Hägerstrand, Torsten. 1984. "Presence and Absence: A Look at Conceptual Choices and Bodily Necessities." *Regional Studies* 18:373–80.

Hahn, Kornelia and Günter Burkart, eds. 1998. *Love at the End of the 20th Century: Studies in the Sociology of Intimate Relationships I.* Opladen, Germany: Leske & Budrich.

Haines, Herbert H. 1984. "Black Radicalization and the Funding of Civil Rights: 1957–1970." *Social Problems* 32(1):31–43.

Haines, Valerie A. 1997. "Spencer and His Critics." Pp. 81–111 in *Reclaiming the Sociological Classics: The State of the Scholarship,* edited by C. Camic. Oxford, UK: Blackwell.

Halbwachs, Maurice. [1925] 1992. *On Collective Memory.* Chicago, IL: University of Chicago Press.

Halbwachs, Maurice. [1925] 1992. *Social Frameworks of Memory.* Chicago, IL: University of Chicago Press.

Halfpenny, Peter. 2001. "Positivism in the Twentieth Century." Pp. 371–85 in *Handbook of Social Theory,* edited by G. Ritzer and B. Smart. London: Sage.

Halfpenny, Peter and Peter McMylor, eds. 1994. *Positivist Sociology and Its Critics.* 3 vols. Aldershot, UK: E. Elgar.

Hall, John. 1995. *Civil Society: Theory, History, Comparison.* Cambridge, MA: Harvard University Press.

Hall, John A. and R. Schroeder, eds. 2003. *An Anatomy of Power: The Social Theory of Michael Mann.* Cambridge, MA: Cambridge University Press.

Hall, Peter A., and David Soskice, eds. 2001. *Varieties of Capitalism: The Institutional Foundations of Comparative Advantage.* Oxford, UK: Oxford University Press.

Hall, Stuart. 1973. *Encoding and Decoding in the Television Discourse.* Stencilled Occasional Paper, Birmingham Centre for Contemporary Cultural Studies.

Hall, Stuart. 1980. "Cultural Studies: Two Paradigms." *Media, Culture & Society* 2(1):57–72.

Hall, Stuart. 1980. "Cultural Studies and the Centre: Some Problematics and Problems." Pp. 15–47 in *Culture, Media, Language.* London: Hutchinson.

Hall, Stuart. 1980. "Encoding/Decoding." Pp. 128–38 in *Culture, Media, Language.* London: Hutchinson.

Hall, Stuart. 1986. "The Problem of Ideology: Marxism without Guarantees." *Journal of Communication Inquiry* 10:28–44.

Hall, Stuart. 1988. *The Hard Road to Renewal.* London: Verso.

Hall, Stuart. 1991. "Globalization and Ethnicity" (Lecture on Videotape). University of Minnesota, Minneapolis.

Hall, Stuart. 1992. "Cultural Studies and Its Theoretical Legacies." Pp. 277–94 in *Cultural Studies,* edited by Lawrence Grossberg, Cary Nelson, and Paula Treichler. New York: Routledge.

Hall, Stuart. 1992. "The West and the Rest." Pp. 1–16 in *Formations of Modernity,* edited by S. Hall and B. Gieben. Cambridge, UK: Polity.

Hall, Stuart, C. Critcher, T. Jefferson, J. Clarke, and R. Roberts. 1978. *Policing the Crisis: Mugging, the State, and Law and Order.* London: Macmillan.

Hall, Stuart and M. Jacques, eds. 1990. *New Times.* London: Verso.

Hall, Stuart, M. Langan, and B. Schwarz, eds. 1985. *1880–1930: Crises in the British State.* London: Hutchinson.

Hall, Stuart, B. Lumley, and G. McLennan, eds. 1978. *On Ideology.* London: Hutchinson.

Hall, Stuart and P. Whannel. 1964. *The Popular Arts.* London: Hutchinson.

Halton, Eugene. 1995. *Bereft of Reason: On the Decline of Social Thought and Prospects for Its Renewal.* Chicago, IL: University of Chicago Press.

Hamamoto, Darrell Y. 1989. *Nervous Laughter: Television Situation Comedy and Liberal Democratic Ideology.* New York: Praeger.

Haney, Lynne. 2000. "Feminist State Theory: Applications to Jurisprudence, Criminology, and the Welfare State." *Annual Review of Sociology* 26:641–66.

Hanifan, Lyda Judson. 1916. "The Rural School Community Center." *Annals of the American Academy of Political and Social Science* 67:130–38.

Hanigsberg, Julia E. and Sara Ruddick. 1999. *Mother Troubles: Rethinking Contemporary Maternal Dilemmas.* Boston, MA: Beacon.

Hannan, Michael T. 1984. "Structural Inertia an Organizational Change." *American Sociological Review* 49:149–64.

Hannan, Michael T. 1989. *Organizational Ecology.* Cambridge, MA: Harvard University Press.

Hannan, Michael T. and Glenn R. Carroll. 1992. *Dynamics of Organizational Populations: Density, Legitimation and Competition.* New York: Oxford University Press.

Hannan, Michael T. and John Freeman. 1977. "The Population Ecology of Organizations." *American Journal of Sociology* 82:929–64.

Hannerz, Ulf. 1996. *Transnational Connections: Culture, People, Places.* London: Routledge.

Hansen, Mogens Herman. 1991. *The Athenian Democracy in the Age of Demosthenes: Structure, Principles and Ideology.* Oxford, UK: Blackwell.

Harary, Frank. 1994. *Graph Theory.* Reading, MA: Addison-Wesley.

Haraway, Donna. 1986. "Primatology Is Politics by Other Means." Pp. 77–118 in *Feminist Approaches to Science.* New York: Pergamon.

Haraway, Donna. 1990. "A Manifesto for Cyborgs: Science, Technology, and Socialist Feminism in the 1980s." In *Feminism/ Postmodernism,* edited by Linda J. Nicholson. New York: Routledge.

Haraway, Donna. 1991. *Simians, Cyborgs, and Women: The Reinvention of Nature.* New York & London: Routledge.

Haraway, Donna. 1992. "Ecce Homo, Ain't (Ar'n't) I a Woman, and Inappropriate/d Others: The Human in a Post-Humanist Landscape." Pp. 86–100 in *Feminists Theorize the Political,* edited by Judith Butler and Joan W. Scott. New York: Routledge.

Haraway, Donna. 1993. "Situated Knowledges: The Science Question in Feminism and the Privilege of Partial Perspective." In *Feminism and Science,* edited by Evelyn Fox Keller and Helen E. Longino. Oxford, UK: Oxford University Press.

Haraway, Donna. 1997. *Modest-Witness@Second-Millennium. FemaleMan©-Meets-Oncomouse™: Feminism and Technoscience.* New York: Routledge.

Hardin, Russell. 2002. *Trust and Trustworthiness.* New York: Russell Sage.

Harding, Sandra. 1986. *The Science Question in Feminism.* Ithaca, NY: Cornell University Press.

Harding, Sandra. 1990. "Feminism, Science, and the Anti-Enlightenment Critiques." Pp. 83–106 in *Feminism/Postmodernism,* edited by Linda J. Nicholson. New York: Routledge.

Harding, Sandra. 1991. "Who Knows? Identities and Feminist Epistemology." Pp. 100–15 in *(En)Gendering Knowledge: Feminists in Academe,* edited by Joan E. Hartman and Ellen Messer-Davidow. Knoxville: University of Tennessee Press.

Harding, Sandra. 1991. *Whose Science? Whose Knowledge? Thinking from Women's Lives.* Ithaca, NY: Cornell University Press.

Harding, Sandra. 1993. "Rethinking Standpoint Epistemology: What Is 'Strong Objectivity'?" Pp. 49–82 in *Feminist Epistemologies,* edited by Linda Alcoff and Elizabeth Potter. New York: Routledge.

Harding, Sandra. 1994. "The Instability of the Analytical Categories of Feminist Theory." Pp. 17–24 in *Different Roles, Different Voices: Women and Politics in the United States and Europe,* edited by Marianne Githens, Pippa Norris, and Joni Lovenduski. New York: HarperCollins.

Harding, Sandra and Jean F. O'Barr, eds. 1987. *Sex and Scientific Inquiry.* Chicago, IL: University of Chicago Press.

Hardt, Michael and Antonio Negri. 2000. *Empire.* Cambridge, MA: Harvard University Press.

Harré, Rom. 1979. *Social Being.* Oxford, UK: Blackwell.

Harris, Roy. 2001. *Rethinking Writing.* London & New York: Continuum.

Hartmann, Heidi. 1976. "Capitalism, Patriarchy and Job Segregation by Sex." *Signs* 1:137–68.

Hartmann, Heidi. 1981. "The Unhappy Marriage of Marxism and Feminism: Towards a More Progressive Union." In *Women and Revolution,* edited by Lydia Sargent. Boston, MA: South End.

Hartsock, Nancy. 1983. *Money, Sex and Power: Towards a Feminist Historical Materialism.* New York: Longman.

Hartsock, Nancy C. M. 1998. *The Feminist Standpoint Revisited & Other Essays.* Boulder, CO: Westview.

Harvey, David. [1973] 1988. *Social Justice and the City.* Oxford, UK: Basil Blackwell.

Harvey, David. 1989. *The Condition of Postmodernity.* Cambridge, UK: Blackwell.

Harvey, David. 1990. *The Condition of Postmodernity.* Cambridge, UK: Blackwell.

Harvey, David. 1996. *Justice, Nature and the Geography of Difference.* Cambridge, UK: Blackwell.

Hassan, Uhab. 1985. "The Culture of Postmodernism." *Theory, Culture and Society* 2:119–32.

Hawkesworth, Mary. 1999. "Analyzing Backlash: Feminist Standpoint Theory as Analytical Tool." *Women's Studies International Forum* 22(2):135–55.

Hawkins, Mike. 1997. *Social Darwinism in European and American Thought.* Cambridge, UK: Cambridge University Press.

Hawley, Amos H. 1950. *Human Ecology: A Theory of Community Structure.* New York: Ronald Press.

Hawley, Amos H. 1971. *Urban Society: An Ecological Approach.* New York: Ronald Press.

Hawley, Amos H. 1986. *Human Ecology: A Theoretical Essay.* Chicago, IL: University of Chicago Press.

Hawley, Amos H. 1992. "The Logic of Macrosociology." *Annual Review of Sociology* 18:1–14.

Hayashi, Nohoko and Toshio Yamagishi. 1998. "Selective Play: Choosing Partners in an Uncertain World." *Personality and Social Psychology Review* 2: 276–89.

Hayes, Carlton J. H. 1931. *The Historical Evolution of Modern Nationalism.* New York: R. R. Smith.

Hebdige, Dick. 1979. *Subculture: The Meaning of Style.* London: Methuen.

Hechter, Michael. 2000. *Containing Nationalism.* New York: Oxford University Press.

Hediger, Vinzenz. 2001. *Verführung zum Film: Der amerikanische Kinotrailer, 1912–1998.* Zurich, Switzerland: Schüren.

Hegel, Georg Wilhelm Friedrich. [1821] 1967. *Hegel's Philosophy of Right.* New York: Oxford University Press.

Hegel, Georg Wilhelm Friedrich. [1807] 1988. *Phenomenology of Mind.* New York: Oxford University Press.

Hegel, Georg Wilhelm Friedrich. [1840] 1995. *Lectures on the History of Philosophy.* vol. 3, *Medieval and Modern Philosophy.* Translated by E. S. Haldane and Francis H. Simson. Lincoln: University of Nebraska Press.

Hegtvedt, Karen A. and Barry Markovsky. 1995. "Justice and Injustice." Pp. 257–80 in *Sociological Perspectives on Social Psychology,* edited by Karen Cook, Gary Alan Fine, and James House. Boston, MA: Allyn & Bacon.

Heidegger, Martin. [1931] 1950. *Cartesianische Meditationen und Pariser Vorträge, Husserliana 1.* The Hague, Netherlands: Nijhoff. Translated as *Cartesian Meditations* (The Hague, Netherlands: Nijhoff. 1960).

Heidegger, Martin. ([1936] 1954. *Die Krisis der europäischen Wissenschaften und die transzendentale Phänomenologie, Husserliana 6:* The Hague, Netherlands: Nijhoff. Translated as *The Crisis of European Sciences and the Transcendental Phenomenology* (Evanston, IL: Northwestern University Press, 1970).

Heidegger, Martin. 1962. *Being and Time.* New York: Harper and Row.

Heidegger, Martin. 1963. *Holzwege.* Frankfurt, Germany: V. Klostermann.

Heidegger, Martin. [1911] 1965. *Phänomenologie als strenge Wissesnchaft.* Frankfurt, Germany: M. Klostermann.

Heidegger, Martin. [1928] 1966. *Zur Phänomenologie des inneren Zeitbewußtseins, Husserliana 10.* The Hague, Netherlands: Nijhoff. Translated as *On the Phenomenology of the Consciousness of Internal Time* (Dordrecht, Netherlands: Kluwer, 1991).

Heidegger, Martin. [1913] 1976. *Ideen zu einer reinen Phänomenologie und phänomenologischen Philosophie, Erstes Buch, Huserliana 3/1.* The Hague, Netherlands: Nijhoff. Translated as *Ideas Pertaining to a Pure Phenomenology and to a Phenomenological Philosophy. First Book* (The Hague, Netherlands: Nijhoff, 1982).

Heidegger, Martin. [1927] 1977. *Sein und Zeit.* Frankfurt, Germany: M Kostermann.

Heidegger, Martin. [1947] 1993. "Letter on Humanism." Translated by Frank A. Capuzzi. Pp. 213–66 in *Martin Heidegger: Basic Writings,* edited by David Farrell Krell. London: Routledge.

Heimer, Carol. 2001. "Solving the Problem of Trust." Pp. 40–88 in *Trust in Society,* edited by Karen Cook. New York: Russell Sage.

Heise, David R. 1979. *Understanding Events: Affect and the Construction of Social Action.* New York: Cambridge University Press.

Hekman, Susan. 1997. "Truth and Method: Feminist Standpoint Theory Revisited." *Signs: Journal of Women in Culture and Society* 22(2):341–65.

Held, David. 1995. *Democracy and the Global Order: From the Modern State to Cosmopolitan Governance.* Stanford, CA: Stanford University Press.

Held, David, Anthony McGrew, David Goldblatt, and Jonathan Perraton. 1999. *Global Transformations.* Stanford, CA: Stanford University Press.

Helle, von Horst J. 2001. *Georg Simmel: Introduction to His Theory and Method.* München and Wien, Germany: R. Oldenbourg Verlag.

Heller, Agnes. 1972. "Towards a Marxist Theory of Value." *Kinesis* 5:6–72.

Heller, Agnes, ed. 1983. *Lukács Revalued.* Oxford, UK: Blackwell.

Heller, Agnes. 1984. *A Radical Philosophy.* Oxford, UK: Blackwell.

Heller, Agnes. 1985. *The Power of Shame.* London: Routledge & Kegan Paul.

Heller, Agnes. 1988. *General Ethics.* Oxford, UK: Blackwell.

Heller, Agnes. 1999. *A Theory of Modernity.* Oxford, UK: Blackwell.

Heller, Agnes and Ferenc Fehér. 1988. *The Postmodern Political Condition.* Cambridge, UK: Polity.

Heller, Agnes and Ferenc Fehér. 1991. *The Grandeur and Twilight of Radical Universalism.* New Brunswick, NJ: Transaction.

Helmes-Hayes, Rick. 1943. *French Canada in Transition.* Chicago, IL: University of Chicago Press.

Helmes-Hayes, Rick. 1969. "Social Institutions." Pp. 123–85 in *New Outline of the Principles of Sociology,* 3d ed., edited by A. M. Lee. New York: Barnes & Noble.

Helmes-Hayes, Rick. 1971. *The Sociological Eye: Parts I and II.* Chicago, IL: Aldine.

Helmes-Hayes, Rick. 1998. "Everett Hughes: Theorist of the Second Chicago School." *International Journal of Politics, Culture and Society* 11:621–73.

Hennessy, Rosemary. 1993. "Women's Lives/Feminist Knowledge: Feminist Standpoint as Ideology Critique." *Hypatia: A Journal of Women and Philosophy* (Winter):14–34.

Hennis, Wilhelm. 2000. *Max Weber's Central Questions.* Translated by Keith Tribe. Newbury, UK: Threshold.

Hennis, Wilhelm. 2000. *Max Weber's Science of Man.* Translated by Keith Tribe. Newbury, UK: Threshold.

Heritage, John. 1984. "Conversation Analysis." Pp. 233–92 in *Garfinkel and Ethnomethodology,* by John Heritage. Cambridge, UK: Polity.

Herrnstein, R. J. and P. Drazin 1991. "Meliorization: A Theory of Distributed Choice." *Journal of Economic Perspectives* 5:137–56.

Hertz, Robert. [1907] 1960. *Death and the Right Hand.* Glencoe, IL: Free Press.

Heussi, Karl. 1932. *Die Krisis des Historismus* [The Crisis of Historism]. Tübingen, Germany: Mohr-Siebeck.

Hewitt, J. and R. Stokes. 1975. "Disclaimers." *American Sociological Review* 40:1–11.

Hewitt, John P. 1998. *The Myth of Self-Esteem.* New York: St. Martin's.

Higgins, Winton and Nixon Apple. 1983. "How Limited Is Reformism?" *Theory and Society* 12(5):603–60.

Hilberg, Raul. 1961. *The Destruction of the European Jews.* Chicago, IL: Quadrangle.

Hilger, M. -E. and L. Hölscher. 1982. "Kapital, Kapitalist, Kapitalismus." Pp. 399–454 in *Geschichtliche Grundbegriffe,* Vol. 3, edited by O. Brunner et al. Stuttgart, Germany: Klett-Cotta.

Hirsh, Elizabeth and Gary A. Olson. 1995. "Starting from Marginalized Lives: A Conversation with Sandra Harding." Pp. 3–42 in *Women Writing Culture,* edited by Gary A. Olson and Elizabeth Hirsh. Albany: State University of New York Press.

Hirst, Paul. 1994. *Associational Democracy: New Forms of Economic and Social Governance.* Cambridge, UK: Polity.

Hoagland, Sarah Lucia. 1989. *Lesbian Ethics.* Palo Alto, CA: Institute of Lesbian Studies.

Hobsbawm, Eric. 1969. *Industry and Empire.* Middlesex, UK: Penguin.

Hobsbawm, Eric. 1990. *Nations and Nationalism Since 1780: Programme, Myth, Reality.* Cambridge, UK: Cambridge University Press.

Hobsbawm, Eric and Terence Ranger. 1983. *The Invention of Tradition.* Cambridge, UK: Cambridge University Press.

Hochschild, Arlie. 1979. "Emotion Work, Feeling Rules, and Social Structure." *American Sociological Review* 85(3):551–75.

Hochschild, Arlie. 1983. *The Managed Heart.* Berkeley: University of California Press.

Hochschild, Arlie R. 1997. *The Time Bind: When Work Becomes Home and Home Becomes Work.* New York: Metropolitan Books.

Hodges, H. A. 1952. *The Philosophy of Wilhelm Dilthey.* London: Routledge & Kegan Paul.

Hodges, H. A. 1969. *Wilhelm Dilthey: An Introduction.* New York: H. Fertig.

Hodgson, Geoffrey M. 2001. *How Economics Forgot History: The Problem of Historical Specificity in Social Science.* London: Routledge.

Hofstadter, Richard. 1959. *Social Darwinism in American Thought.* New York: Braziller.

Hoggart, R. 1957. *The Uses of Literacy.* London: Chatto & Windus.

Hollier, Denis. 1988. *The College of Sociology (1937–1939).* Minneapolis: University of Minnesota Press.

Holstein, James A. and Jaber Gubrium. 2000. *The Self We Live By: Narrative Identity in a Postmodern World.* New York: Oxford University Press.

Holstein, James A. and Gale Miller, eds. 1993. *Reconsidering Social Constructionism: Debates in Social Problems Theory.* Hawthorne, NY: de Gruyter.

Holton, R. J. and B. S. Turner. 1989. "Has Class Analysis a Future? Max Weber and the Challenge of Liberalism to *Gemeinschaftlich* Accounts of Class." Pp. 160–96 in *Max Weber on Economics and Society,* edited by R. J. Holton and B. S. Turner. London: Routledge & Kegan Paul.

Homans, George C. 1950. *The Human Group.* New York: Harcourt, Brace.

Homans, George C. 1958. "Social Behavior as Exchange." *American Journal of Sociology* 63:597–606.

Homans, George C. 1961. *Social Behavior: Its Elementary Forms.* New York: Harcourt Brace & Jovanovich.

Homans, George C. 1964. "Bringing Men Back In." *American Sociological Review* 29(6):809–18.

Homans, George C. 1964. "Contemporary Theory in Sociology." In *Handbook of Modern Sociology,* edited by R. E. L. Faris. Chicago, IL: Rand McNally.

Homans, George C. 1967. *The Nature of Social Science.* New York: Harcourt, Brace, & World.

Homans, George C. [1961] 1974. *Social Behavior: Its Elementary Forms.* New York: Harcourt, Brace, & World.

Homans, George C. 1984. *Coming to My Senses: The Autobiography of a Sociologist.* New Brunswick, NJ: Transaction.

Honneth, A. 1996. *The Struggle for Recognition: The Moral Grammar of Social Conflicts.* Cambridge, MA: MIT Press.

hooks, bell. 1989. *Talking Back: Thinking Feminist, Thinking Black.* Boston, MA: South End.

hooks, bell. 1994. *Teaching to Transgress: Education as the Practice of Freedom.* New York: Routledge.

Hooks, Gregory. 1993. "The Weakness of Strong Theories: The U.S. State's Dominance of the World War II Investment Process." *American Sociological Review* 58:37–53.

Horkheimer, Max and T. Adorno. [1944] 1972. *The Dialectic of Enlightenment.* Translated by J. Cumming. New York: Herder & Herder.

Horowitz, Asher. 1987. *Rousseau, Nature and History.* Toronto, Canada: University of Toronto Press.

Horrocks, Christopher. 1999. *Baudrillard and the Millennium.* London: Icon.

Howard, Michael C. and John E. King. 1985. *The Political Economy of Marx.* 2d ed. Harlow, UK: Longman.

Howard, Michael C. and John E. King. 1989. *A History of Marxian Economics.* vol. 1, *1883–1929.* London: Macmillan.

Howard, Michael C. and John E. King. 1992. *A History of Marxian Economics.* vol. 2, *1929–1990.* London: Macmillan.

Howells, Christina, ed. 1991. *The Cambridge Companion to Sartre.* New York: Cambridge University Press.

Hoyningen-Huene, Paul. 1993. *Reconstructing Scientific Revolutions: Thomas S. Kuhn's Philosophy of Science.* Chicago, IL: University of Chicago Press.

Hughes, Everett. 1928. "The Growth of an Institution: The Chicago Real Estate Board." PhD dissertation, Department of Sociology, University of Chicago.

Hume, David. [1739–40] 1964. *A Treatise of Human Nature.* Vols. 1–2. London/New York: Dent/Dutton.

Husserl, Edmund. [1900–1901] 1975–1984. *Logische Untersuchungen.* 2 vols. The Hague, Netherlands: Nijhoff. Translated as *Logical Investigations* (London: Routledge & Kegan Paul, 1970).

Hyppolite, Jean. 1969. *Studies on Hegel and Marx.* Translated by John O'Neill. New York: Harper and Row.

Illich, Ivan. 1982. *Medical Nemesis: The Expropriation of Health.* New York: Pantheon.

Ingham, Alan G. and Peter Donnelly. 1997. "A Sociology of North American Sociology of Sport: Disunity in Unity, 1965 to 1996." *Sociology of Sport Journal* 14(4):362–418.

Irigaray, Luce. 1985. *Speculum of the Other Woman.* Translated by Gillian C. Gill. Ithaca, NY: Cornell University Press.

Irigaray, Luce. 1993. *An Ethics of Sexual Difference.* Translated by Carolyn Burke and Gillian C. Gill. Ithaca, NY: Cornell University Press.

Irigaray, Luce. 1994. *Thinking the Difference: For a Peaceful Revolution.* Translated by Karin Montin. New York: Routledge.

Irigaray, Luce. 1996. *I Love to You: Sketch of a Possible Felicity in History.* Translated by Alison Martin. New York: Routledge.

Isin, E. and B. Turner, eds. 2002. *Handbook of Citizenship Studies.* London: Sage.

Jacobs, Jane. 1961. *The Death and Life of Great American Cities.* New York: Random House.

Jacobs, Ronald N. 1996. "Civil Society and Crisis: Culture, Discourse, and the Rodney King Beating." *American Journal of Sociology* 101(5):1238–72.

Jaggar, Alison 1991. "Feminist Ethics: Projects, Problems, Prospects." Pp. 78–106 in *Feminist Ethics,* edited by C. Card. Lawrence: University of Kansas Press.

James, William. 1890. *Principles of Psychology.* New York: Henry Holt.

James, William. 1977. *The Writings of William James: A Comprehensive Edition.* Edited by John J. McDermott. Chicago, IL: University of Chicago Press.

Jameson, Fredric. 1971. *Marxism and Form.* Princeton, NJ: Princeton University Press.

Jameson, Fredric. 1972. *The Prison-House of Language.* Princeton, NJ: Princeton University Press.

Jameson, Fredric. 1979. *Fables of Aggression.* Berkeley: University of California Press.

Jameson, Fredric. 1981. *The Political Unconscious.* Ithaca, NY: Cornell University Press.

Jameson, Fredric. 1990. *Late Marxism: Adorno, or, the Persistence of the Dialectic.* London: Verso.

Jameson, Fredric. 1990. *Signatures of the Visible.* New York: Routledge.

Jameson, Fredric. 1991. *Postmodernism, or the Cultural Logic of Late Capitalism.* Durham, NC: Duke University Press.

Jameson, Fredric. 2000. *Brecht and Method.* London: Verso.

Jameson, Fredric. 2002. *A Singular Modernity.* London: Verso.

Janoski, T. 1998. *Citizenship and Civil Society.* Cambridge, UK: Cambridge University Press.

Janowitz, Morris. 1966. "Introduction." Pp. vii–lviii in *W. I. Thomas on Social Organization and Social Personality,* edited and with an introduction by Morris Janowitz. Chicago & London: University of Chicago Press.

Jarvie, Grant and Joseph A. Maguire. 1994. *Sport and Leisure in Social Thought.* London: Routledge.

Jasanoff, Sheila, Gerald Markle, James Peterson, and Trevor Pinch, eds. 1994. *Handbook of Science, Technology & Society.* Beverly Hills, CA: Sage.

Jasinski, James. 2001. *Sourcebook on Rhetoric: Key Concepts in Contemporary Rhetorical Studies.* Thousand Oaks, CA: Sage.

Jasso, Guillermina. 1980. "A New Theory of Distributive Justice." *American Sociological Review* 45:3–32.

Jasso, Guillermina. 2001. "Formal Theory." Pp. 37–68 in *Handbook of Sociological Theory,* edited by Jonathan H. Turner. New York: Kluwer Academic/Plenum.

Jay, Martin. 1984. *Marxism and Totality: The Adventures of a Concept from Lukács to Habermas.* Berkeley: University of California Press.

Jefferson, T., ed. 1976. *Resistance through Rituals.* London: Hutchinson.

Jenkins, Richard 2002. *Pierre Bourdieu.* Rev. ed. London: Routledge.

Jepperson, Ronald L. 2002. "The Development and Application of Sociological Neoinstitutionalism." Pp. 229–66 in *New Directions in Contemporary Sociological Theory,* edited by Joseph Berger and Morris Zelditch Jr. New York: Rowman & Littlefield.

Jessop, Bob. 2002. *The Future of the Capitalist State.* New York: Blackwell.

Jessop, Bob, Kevin Bonnet, Simon Bromley, and Tom Ling. 1984. "Authoritarian Populism, Two Nations, and Thatcherism." *New Left Review* 147.

Joas, Hans. 1985. *G. H. Mead: A Contemporary Re-examination of His Thought.* Translated by R. Meyer. Cambridge, MA: MIT Press.

Johnson, Allan G. 1997. *The Gender Knot: Unraveling Our Patriarchal Legacy.* Philadelphia, PA: Temple University Press.

Johnson, Allan, G. 2001. *Privilege, Power, and Difference.* Boston, MA: McGraw-Hill.

Johnson, Harry M. 1985. "Social Structure." Pp. 787–89 in *The Social Sciences Encyclopedia,* edited by A. Kuper and J. Kuper. London: Routledge.

Johnson, Paul. 1991. *The Birth of the Modern: World Society 1815–1830.* New York: HarperCollins.

Johnson, Steven. 2001. *Emergence: The Connected Lives of Ants, Brains, Cities, and Software.* New York: Scribner.

Johnston, Barry V. 1995. *Pitirim A. Sorokin: An Intellectual Biography.* Lawrence: University Press of Kansas.

Jones, Gerard. 2002. *Killing Monsters: Why Children Need Fantasy, Superheros, and Make-Believe Violence.* New York: Basic.

Jones, Robert Alun. 2000. "Émile Durkheim." Pp. 205–50 in *The Blackwell Companion to Major Social Theorists,* edited by George Ritzer. Malden, MA: Blackwell.

Jouvenal, Bertrand de. 1958. "Authority: The Efficient Imperative." Pp. 159–69 in *Authority,* Nomos 1, edited by Carl J. Friedrich. Cambridge, MA: Harvard University Press.

Joy, James. 1998. *The Angela Y. Davis Reader.* Malden, MA: Blackwell.

Julien, Phillippe. 1994. *Jacques Lacan's Return to Freud.* New York: New York University Press.

Kant, Immanuel. [1798] 1964. "Anthropologie in pragmatischer Hinsicht abgefasst." Pp. 399–690 in *Werke* 12. Frankfurt, Germany: Suhrkamp.

Kant, Immanuel. [1795] 1982. *On Perpetual Peace.* Indianapolis, IN: Hackett.

Kant, Immanuel. [1781] 1999. *Critique of Pure Reason.* New York: Cambridge University Press.

Kant, Immanuel. [1790] 2000. *The Critique of Judgment.* Amherst, NY: Prometheus.

Kant, Immanuel. [1788] 2002. *Critique of Practical Reason.* Indianapolis, IN: Hackett.

Kaplan, E. Ann and Michael Sprinker. 1984. *The Althusserian Legacy.* London: Verso.

Kasson, John. 1990. *Rudeness and Civility: Manners in Nineteenth-Century Urban America.* New York: Hill & Wang.

Kateb, George. 1972. *Utopia and Its Enemies.* New York: Schocken.

Katz, Jon. 2001. *Geeks.* New York: Broadway.

Kauffman, Stuart. 1993. *At Home in the Universe: The Search for the Laws of Complexity.* Oxford, UK: Oxford University Press.

Kedourie, Elie. 1993. *Nationalism.* 4th ed. Oxford, UK: Blackwell.

Keller, Albert Galloway and Maurice R. Davie, eds. 1934a. *Essays of William Graham Sumner.* Vol. 1. New Haven, CT: Yale University.

Keller, Albert Galloway and Maurice R. Davie, eds. 1934b. *Essays of William Graham Sumner.* Vol. 2. New Haven, CT: Yale University Press.

Keller, Evelyn Fox and Helen E. Longino. 1996. "Introduction." Pp. 1–14 in *Feminism and Science,* edited by Evelyn Fox Keller and Helen E. Longino. New York and Oxford, UK: Oxford University Press.

Kellner, Douglas. 1989. *Critical Theory, Marxism, and Modernity.* Cambridge, UK, & Baltimore, MD: Polity and Johns Hopkins University Press.

Kellner, Douglas. 1989. *Jean Baudrillard: From Marxism to Postmodernism and Beyond.* Stanford, CA: Stanford University Press.

Kellner, Douglas, ed. 1989. *Postmodernism/Jameson/Critique.* Washington, DC: Maisonneuve.

Kellner, Douglas. 1990. *Television and the Crisis of Democracy.* Boulder, CO: Westview.

Kellner, Douglas. 1995. *Media Culture: Cultural Studies, Identity, and Politics between the Modern and the Postmodern.* New York & London: Routledge.

Kellner, Douglas. 1997. "Critical Theory and Cultural Studies: The Missed Articulation." Pp. 12–41 in *Cultural Methodologies,* edited by J. McGuigan. London: Sage.

Kellner, Douglas. 2000. "Habermas, the Public Sphere, and Democracy: A Critical Intervention." In *Perspectives on Habermas,* edited by Lewis Hahn. Chicago, IL: Open Court Press.

Kellner, Douglas. 2002. "New Media and New Literacies. Reconstructing Education for the New Millennium." Pp. 90–104 in *Handbook of New Media: Social Shaping and Consequences of ICTs,* edited by Leah H. Lievrouw and Sonia Livingstone. Thousand Oaks, CA: Sage.

Kellner, Douglas. 2003. "Cultural Studies, Multiculturalism and Media Culture." Pp. 9–20 in *Gender, Race and Class in Media: A Text-Reader,* 2d ed., edited by Gail Dines and Jean Humez. Thousand Oaks, CA: Sage.

Kellner, Douglas. 2003. *Media Spectacle.* New York & London: Routledge.

Kellner, Douglas., ed. 1994. *Baudrillard: A Critical Reader.* Oxford, UK: Blackwell.

Kerr, Clark, T. Dunlap, F. Harrison, and C. A. Myers. 1960. *Industrialism and Industrial Man.* Cambridge, MA: Harvard University Press.

Kessler-Harris, Alice. 1990. *A Woman's Wage: Historical Meanings and Social Consequences.* Lexington, KY: University Press of Kentucky.

Kierkegaard, Søren. 1967–1978. *Journals and Papers.* 7 vols. Bloomington, IN: Indiana University Press.

Kierkegaard, Søren. 1978. *Two Ages: The Age of Revolution and the Present Age.* Princeton, NJ: Princeton University Press.

Kimmel, M. 1990. *Revolution.* Oxford, UK. Polity.

Kittay, Eva Feder. 1999. *Love's Labor: Essays on Women, Equality, and Dependency.* New York: Routledge.

Kittler, Friedrich A. 1997. *Literature, Media, Information Systems: Essays.* Edited and with an introduction by John Johnston. Amsterdam, Netherlands: G+B Arts International.

Kiyonari, Toko, Shigehito Tanida, and Toshio Yamagishi. 2000. "Social Exchange and Reciprocity: Confusion or a Heuristic." *Evolution and Human Behavior* 21:411–27.

Klandermans, Bert. 1997. *The Social Psychology of Protest.* Oxford, UK: Blackwell.

Klapp, Orrin. 1969. *Collective Search for Identity.* New York: Holt, Rinehart & Winston.

Klein, N. 2000. *No Logo.* London: Flamingo.

Kleingeld, Pauline. 1999. "Six Varieties of Cosmopolitanism in Late Eighteenth-Century Germany." *Journal of the History of Ideas* 60:505–24.

Klima, Rolf. 1995. *Positivismusstreit.* 3d enl. ed. [The Positivist Dispute]. Pp. 505–507 in *Lexikon zur Soziologie* [Dictionary of Sociology], edited by Werner Fuchs-Henritz, Rüdiger Lautmann, Otthein Rammstedt, and Hanns Wienold. Opladen, Germany: Westdeutscher Verlag.

Klink, David. 1996. *The French Counter-Revolutionary Theorist Louis de Bonald (1754–1840).* New York: Peter Lang.

Knabb, Ken, ed., trans. 1981. *Situationist International Anthology.* Rev. ed. Berkeley, CA: Bureau of Public Secrets.

Knorr Cetina, Karin. 1981. *The Manufacture of Knowledge: An Essay on the Constructivist and Contextual Nature of Science.* Oxford, UK: Pergamon.

Knorr Cetina, Karin. 1997. "Sociality with Objects. Social Relations in Postsocial Knowledge Societies." *Theory, Culture and Society* 14:1–30.

Kohn, Hans. 1944. *The Age of Nationalism.* New York: Harper and Row.

Kojève, Alexandre. 1969. *Introduction to the Reading of Hegel.* New York: Basic Books.

Kolakowski, L. 1978. *Main Currents in Marxism.* 3 vols. Oxford, UK: Oxford University Press.

Kollock, Peter. 1994. "The Emergence of Exchange Structures: An Experimental Study of Uncertainty, Commitment and Trust." *American Journal of Sociology* 100:313–45.

Kollock, Peter. 1998. "Social Dilemmas." *Annual Review of Sociology* 24:183–214.

König, René. 1949. *Soziologie heute* [Sociology Today]. Zurich, Switzerland: Regio-Verl.

Kontopoules, Kyriakos. 1993. *The Logics of Social Structure.* Cambridge, UK: Cambridge University Press.

Korsch, K. 1938. *Karl Marx.* New York: Russell & Russell.

Kotarba, J. and J. Johnson, eds. 2002. *Postmodern Existential Sociology.* Walnut Creek, CA: Alta Mira.

Krishna, Anirudh. 2000. "Creating and Harnessing Social Capital." Pp. 71–93 in *Social Capital: A Multifaceted Perspective,* edited by P. Dasgupta and I. Serageldin. Washington, DC: World Bank.

Kristeva, Julia. 1981. "Women's Time." *Signs* 7:13–35.

Kristeva, Julia. 1982. *Powers of Horror: An Essay on Abjection.* New York: Columbia University Press.

Kroker, Arthur and David. Cook. 1986. *The Postmodern Scene.* Montreal, Canada: New World Perspectives.

Kruszewski, Mikolaj Habdank. [1880] Forthcoming. "Novejsie Otkrytija v Oblasti Ario-Evropejskogo Vokalisma" [The Latest Discoveries in the Area of Indo-European Vocalism]. Translated by Gregory M. Eramian. In *Saussure: Critical Assessments,* edited by Paul J. Thibault. London & New York: Routledge. (Originally published in *Russkij Filologièeskij Vestnik* [Russian Philological Herald] 4:33–45.)

Kuhn, Thomas. 1970. *The Structure of Scientific Revolutions.* 2d ed. Chicago, IL: University of Chicago Press.

Kumar, Krishan. 1987. *Utopia and Anti-Utopia in Modern Times.* Oxford, UK, & New York: Basil Blackwell.

Kurz, Heinz D. and Neri Salvadori. 1995. *Theory of Production.* Cambridge, UK: Cambridge University Press.

Kurzweil, Edith. 1980. *The Age of Structuralism: Levi-Strauss to Foucault.* New York: Columbia University Press.

Kymlicka, W. and W. Norman, eds. 2000. *Citizenship in Diverse Societies.* Oxford, UK: Oxford University Press.

Labinger, Jay and Harry M. Collins, eds. 2001. *The One Culture? A Conversation about Science.* Chicago, IL: University of Chicago Press.

Lacan, Jacques. 1966. *Écrits.* Translated as *Écrits: A Selection* (New York: Norton, 1977).

Lacan, Jacques. 1978. *The Four Fundamental Concepts of Psycho-analysis.* Translated by A. Sheridan. New York: Norton.

Laclau, Ernesto and Chantal Mouffe. 1985. *Hegemony and Socialist Strategy: Towards a Radical Democratic Politics.* London & New York: Verso.

LaDuke, Winona. 1997. "Voices from White Earth: Gaawaabaa-biganikaag." Pp. 22–37 in *People, Land, and Community: Collected E. F. Schumacher Society Lectures,* edited by Hildegarde Hannum. New Haven, CT: Yale University Press.

Lakatos, Imre. 1970. "Falsification and the Methodology of Scientific Research Programmes." Pp. 91–6 in *Criticism and the Growth of Knowledge,* edited by I. Lakatos and A. Musgrave. Cambridge, UK: Cambridge University Press.

Landlois, Richard M., ed. 1986. *Economics as a Process: Essays in the New Institutional Economics.* New York: Cambridge University Press.

Langer, Susanne K. 1957. *Philosophy in a New Key: A Study in the Symbolism of Reason, Rite, and Art.* Cambridge, MA: Harvard University Press.

Larsen, M. S. 1977. *The Rise of Professionalism: A Sociological Analysis.* Berkeley: University of California Press.

Lasch, Christopher. 1978. *The Culture of Narcissism: American Life in an Age of Diminishing Expectations.* New York: Norton.

Lasch, Christopher. 1995. "Philip Rieff and the Religion of Culture." Pp. 213–29 in *The Revolt of the Elites and the Betrayal of Democracy.* New York: Norton.

Lash, Scott and John Urry. 1987. *The End of Organized Capitalism.* Cambridge, UK: Polity.

Lash, Scott and John Urry. 1994. *Economies of Signs and Space.* London: Sage.

Lash, Scott. 2003. "Empire and Vitalism." Presented at the annual meeting of the Eastern Sociological Society, February 27–March 2, Philadelphia, PA.

Latour, Bruno. 1987. *Science in Action: How to Follow Scientists and Engineers through Society.* Cambridge, MA: Harvard University Press.

Latour, Bruno. 1986. "Visualization and Cognition: Thinking with Hands and Eyes." Pp. 1–40 in *Knowledge and Society: Studies in the Sociology of Culture Past and Present,* Vol. 6, edited by R. Jones and H. Kuklick. Greenwich, CT: JAI.

Latour, Bruno. 1988. *The Pasteurization of France.* Cambridge, MA: Harvard University Press.

Latour, Bruno. 1993. *We Have Never Been Modern.* Cambridge, MA: Harvard University Press.

Latour, Bruno. 1999. "On Recalling ANT." Pp. 15–25 in *Actor Network Theory and After,* edited by J. Law and J. Hassard. Malden, MA: Blackwell.

Latour, Bruno. 1999. *Pandora's Hope: Essays in the Reality of Science Studies.* Cambridge, MA: Harvard University Press.

Latour, Bruno. 2002. *War of the Worlds: What about Peace?* Chicago, IL: Prickly Paradigm.

Latour, Bruno. 2003. "Is Re-modernization Occurring—And If So, How to Prove It?" *Theory, Culture & Society* 20(2):35–48.

Latour, Bruno and Steve Woolgar. 1979. *Laboratory Life: The Social Construction of Scientific Facts.* Thousand Oaks, CA: Sage.

Law, John. 1992. "Notes on the Theory of Actor-Network: Ordering, Strategy and Heterogeneity." *Systems Practice* 5:379–93.

Law, John. 1999. "After ANT: Complexity, Naming, and Topology." In *Actor Network Theory and After,* edited by J. Law and J. Hassard. Malden, MA: Blackwell.

Lawler, Edward J. 1998. "Network Structure and Emotion in Exchange Relations." *American Sociological Review* 63:871–94.

Lawler, Edward J. 2001. "An Affect Theory of Social Exchange." *American Journal of Sociology* 107:321–52.

Lawler, Edward J. and Shane R. Thye. 1999. "Bringing Emotions into Social Exchange Theory." *Annual Review of Sociology* 25:217–44.

Lawler, Edward J., Shane R. Thye, and Jeongkoo Yoon. 2000. "Emotion and Group Cohesion in Productive Exchange." *American Journal of Sociology* 106(3):616–57.

Lawler, Edward J. and Jeongkoo Yoon. 1996. "Commitment in Exchange Relations: Test of a Theory of Relational Cohesion." *American Sociological Review* 61:89–108.

Lawler, Edward J. and Jeongkoo Yoon. 1998. "Network Structure and Emotion in Exchange Relations." *American Sociological Review* 63: 871–94.

Lazarsfeld, Paul. 1941. "Administrative and Critical Communications Research." *Studies in Philosophy and Social Science* 9(1):2–16.

Le Roy Ladurie, Emmanuel. 1978. *Montaillou: The Promised Land of Error.* Translated by Barbara Bray. New York: George Braziller.

Leach, Edmund. 1989. *Claude Lévi-Strauss.* Rev. ed. Chicago, IL: University of Chicago Press.

Leader, Darian and Judy Groves. 1966. *Introducing Lacan.* New York: Totem.

Leary, Mark and Robin Kowalski. 1990. "Impression Management: A Literature Review and Two-Component Model." *Psychological Bulletin* 107(1):34–47.

Lebrun, Richard. 1988. *Joseph de Maistre: An Intellectual Militant.* Montreal, Canada: McGill-Queens University Press.

Lebrun, Richard, ed. 2001. *Joseph de Maistre's Life, Thought, and Influence: Selected Studies.* Montreal, Canada: McGill-Queens University Press.

Lechner, Frank J. and John Boli, eds. 2003. *The Globalization Reader.* Oxford, UK: Blackwell.

Lee, Martyn. 1993. *Consumer Culture Reborn.* London: Routledge.

Lefebvre, Henri. [1940] 1968. *Dialectical Materialism.* Translated by J. Sturrock. London: Jonathan Cape.

Lefebvre, Henri. 1970. *Beyond Marx.* Paris: PUF.

Lefebvre, Henri. 1971. *Everyday Life in the Modern World.* Translated by S. Rabinovitch. Harmondsworth, UK: Penguin.

Lefebvre, Henri. 1991. *The Production of Space.* Translated by Donald Nicholson-Smith. Oxford, UK: Blackwell. Originally published as *Production de l'espace* (Paris: Anthropos, 1974).

Lefebvre, Henri. [1962] 1995. *Introduction to Modernity.* Translated by J. Moore. London: Verso.

Lehmann, William C. 1930. *Adam Ferguson and the Beginning of Modern Sociology.* New York: Columbia University Press.

Lehmann, William C. 1960. *John Millar of Glasgow, 1735–1801: His Life and Thought and His Contribution to Sociological Analysis.* London: Cambridge University Press.

Leicht, Kevin T. and Mary L. Fennell. 2001. *Professional Work: A Sociological Approach.* Oxford, UK: Blackwell.

Leimar, O. and P. Hammerstein. 2001. "Evolution of Cooperation through Indirect Reciprocity." *Proceedings of the Royal Society of London Series B: Biological Sciences* 268:745–53.

Leledakis, K. 1995. *Society and Psyche.* Oxford, UK: Berg.

Lemert, Charles. 1997. *Postmodernism Is Not What You Think.* Malden, MA: Blackwell.

Lenger, Friedrich. 1994. *Werner Sombart 1963–1941: Eine Biographie.* München, Germany: C. H. Beck.

Lengermann, Patricia M. and Jill Niebrugge-Brantley. 1998. "Marianne Weber: A Woman-Centered Sociology." Pp. 193–228 in *The Women Founders: Sociology and Social Theory, 1830–1630.* New York: McGraw-Hill.

Lengermann, Patricia Madoo, and Jill Niebrugge-Brantley. 1998. *The Women Founders: Sociology and Social Theory, 1830–1930, A Text with Readings.* New York: McGraw-Hill.

Lengermann, Patricia Madoo and Jill Niebrugge-Brantley. 2000. "Contemporary Feminist Theory." Pp. 307–55 in *Modern Sociological Theory,* edited by George Ritzer. Boston, MA: McGraw-Hill.

Lenski, Gerhard. 1964. *Power and Privilege.* New York: McGraw-Hill.

Lerner, Gerda. 1993. "Reconceptualizing Differences among Women." Pp. 237–48 in *Feminist Frameworks,* 3d ed., edited by Alison M. Jaggar and Paula S. Rothenberg. New York: McGraw-Hill.

Leventhal, Gerald S., J. Karuza Jr., and W. R. Fry. 1980. "Beyond Fairness: A Theory of Allocation Preferences." Pp. 167–218 in *Justice and Social Interaction,* edited by Gerold Mikula. New York: Plenum.

Levine, Andrew. 2003. *A Future for Marxism? Althusser, the Analytical Turn and Revival of Socialist Theory.* London; Stirling, VA: Pluto.

Levine, Donald N. 1977. "Simmel at a Distance: On the History and the Systematics of the Sociology of the Stranger." *Sociological Focus* 10:15–29.

Levine, Donald Nathan. 1985. *The Flight from Ambiguity: Essays in Social and Cultural Theory.* Chicago, IL: University of Chicago Press.

Lévi-Strauss, Claude. 1957. "The Principle of Reciprocity." P. 90 in *Sociological Theory,* edited by L. A. Coser and B. Rosenberg. New York: Macmillan.

Lévi-Strauss, Claude. 1958. *Anthropologie structurale.* Translated as *Structural Anthopology* (New York: Basic Books, 1963).

Lévi-Strauss, Claude. 1987. *Anthropology and Myth: Lectures 1951–1982.* Oxford, UK: Blackwell.

Lévi-Strauss, Claude. 1995. *Myth and Meaning: Cracking the Code of Culture.* New York: Knopf.

Lévi-Strauss, Claude and Didier Eribon. 1991. *Conversations with Claude Lévi-Strauss.* Translated by Paula Wissing. Chicago, IL: University of Chicago Press.

Levitas, Ruth. 1990. *The Concept of Utopia.* Hemel Hempstead, UK: Philip Allan.

Levy, Daniel and Natan Sznaider. 2002. "Memory Unbound: The Holocaust and the Formation of Cosmopolitan Memory." *European Journal of Social Theory* 5:87–106.

Lévy, Henri-Bernard. 1995. *Adventures on the Freedom Road: The French Intellectuals in the 20th Century.* London: Harvill.

Lewis, J. David and Andrew Weigert. 1985. "Trust as a Social Reality." *Social Forces* 63:967–85.

Lewis, John, ed. 1998. *The New American Cinema.* Durham, NC: Duke University Press.

Lilla, Mark. 2002. "A Battle for Religion." *New York Review of Books,* December 5, pp. 60–65.

Lilly, J. R., F. T. Cullen, and R. A. Ball. 2001. *Criminological Theory.* 3d ed. Thousand Oaks, CA: Sage.

Lin, Nan. 2001. *Social Capital: A Theory of Social Structure and Action.* Cambridge, UK: Cambridge University Press.

Lind, E. A. and T. R. Tyler. 1988. *The Social Psychology of Procedural Justice.* New York: Plenum.

Lindenberg, Siegwart. 1989. "Social Production Functions, Deficits, and Social Revolutions: Pre-revolutionary France and Russia." *Rationality and Society* 1:51–77.

Lindenberg, Siegwart. 1992. "An Extended Theory of Institutions and Contractual Discipline." *Journal of Institutional and Theoretical Economics* 148:25–54.

Lindenberg, Siegwart. 1992. "The Method of Decreasing Abstraction." Pp. 3–20 in *Rational Choice Theory: Advocacy and Critique,* edited by J. S. Coleman and T. J. Feraro. Newbury Park, CA: Sage.

Lindenberg, Siegwart. 1997. "Grounding Groups in Theory: Functional, Cognitive, and Structural Interdependencies." *Advances in Group Processes* 14:281–331.

Lindenberg, Siegwart. 1998. "Solidarity: Its Microfoundations and Macro-Dependence. A Framing Approach. Pp. 61–112 in *The Problem of Solidarity: Theories and Models,* edited by P. Doreian and T. J. Fararo. Amsterdam, Netherlands: Gordon & Breach.

Lindenberg, Siegwart. 2000. "James Coleman." Pp. 513–44 in *The Blackwell Companion to Major Social Theorists,* edited by G. Ritzer. Oxford, UK: Blackwell.

Lindenberg, Siegwart. 2000. "It Takes Both Trust and Lack of Mistrust: The Workings of Cooperation and Relational Signaling in Contractual Relationships." *Journal of Management and Governance* 4:11–33.

Lindenberg, Siegwart. 2001. "Intrinsic Motivation in a New Light." *Kyklos* 54:317–42.

Lindenberg, Siegwart. 2001. "Social Rationality versus Rational Egoism." Pp. 635–68 in *Handbook of Sociological Theory,* edited by J. Turner. New York: Kluwer Academic/Plenum.

Lindenberg, Siegwart. 2003. "The Cognitive Side of Governance." *Research in the Sociology of Organizations* 20:47–76.

Lindsay, Vachel. 1970. *The Art of the Moving Picture.* New York: Liveright.

Linz, Juan J. and Alfred Stepan. 1996. *Problems of Democratic Transition and Consolidation: Southern Europe, South America, and Post-Communist Europe.* Baltimore, MD: Johns Hopkins University Press.

Lipset, Seymour Martin. 1981. *Political Man: The Social Bases of Politics.* Expanded and updated ed. Baltimore, MD: Johns Hopkins University Press.

Lipset, Seymour Martin and Gary Marks. 1999. *It Didn't Happen Here: Why Socialism Failed in the United States.* New York: Norton.

Lisbon European Council. 2000, March 23–24. "Modernizing the European Social Model by Investing in People and Building an Active Welfare State." Presidential Conclusions. Lisbon, Portugal. (http://www.ces.fas.harvard.edu/working_papers/Manow.pdf)

Liska, Allen. 1990. "The Significance of Aggregate Dependent Variables and Contextual Independent Variables for Linking Macro and Micro Theories." *Social Psychology Quarterly* 53: 292–301.

Loewith, K. 1982. *Max Weber and Karl Marx.* London: Allen & Unwin.

Lofland, Lyn. 1998. *The Public Realm: Exploring the City's Quintessential Social Territory.* New York: Aldine de Gruyter.

Logan, John and Harvey Molotch. 1987. *Urban Fortunes: Toward a Political Economy of Place.* Berkeley: University of California Press.

Lorde, Audre. 1980. *The Cancer Journals.* San Francisco, CA: Aunt Lute Books.

Lorde, Audre. 1982. *Zami: A New Spelling of My Name.* Watertown, MA: Persephone.

Lorde, Audre. 1984. "Age, Race, Class, and Sex: Redefining Difference." In *Sister Outsider: Essays and Speeches* by Audre Lorde. Freedom, CA: Crossing.

Lorde, Audre. 1984. *Sister Outsider: Essays and Speeches.* Trumansburg, NY: Crossing.

Lorde, Audre. 1985. *I Am Your Sister: Black Women Organizing across Sexualities.* Latham, NY: Kitchen Table, Women of Color Press.

Lorde, Audre. 1991. *Burst of Light.* Ithaca, NY: Firebrand.

Lorrain, Francois and Harrison C. White. 1971. "Structural Equivalence of Individuals in Social Networks." *Journal of Mathematical Sociology* 1:49–80.

Lowenthal, David. 1985. *The Past Is a Foreign Country.* New York: Cambridge University Press.

Lowenthal, Leo. 1961. *Literature, Popular Culture and Society.* Englewood Cliffs, NJ: Prentice-Hall.

Löwith, Karl. 1982. *Max Weber and Karl Marx.* London: Allen & Unwin.

Löwy, Michael. 1979. *Georg Lukács: From Romanticism to Bolshevism.* Translated by P. Camiller. London: NLB.

Loyal, Steven. 2003. *The Sociology of Anthony Giddens.* London: Pluto.

Luckmann. Thomas. 1967. *The Invisible Religion: The Problem of Religion in Modern Society.* New York: Macmillan.

Lugones, María and Elizabeth Spelman. 1992. "Have We Got a Theory For You! Feminist Theory, Cultural Imperialism and the Demand for 'The Woman's Voice.'" Pp. 382–83 in *Feminist Philosophies: Problems, Theories, and Applications,* edited by J. A. Kourany, J. P. Sterba, and R. Tong. Englewood Cliffs, NJ: Prentice-Hall.

Luhmann, Niklas. 1970. "Soziologie als Theorie sozialer Systeme" [Sociology as a Theory of Social Systems]. Pp. 113–36 in *Soziologische Aufklärung 1* [Sociological Enlightenment]. Opladen, Germany: Westdeutscher Verlag.

Luhmann, Niklas. 1973. "Die Zurechnung von Beförderungen im öffentlichen Dienst [The Attribution of Promotions among Civil Servants]." *Zeitschrift für Soziologie* 2:326–51.

Luhmann, Niklas. 1982. *The Differentiation of Society.* New York: Columbia University Press.

Luhmann, Niklas. 1990. "Meaning as Sociology´s Basic Concept." Pp. 21–79 in *Essays on Self-Reference,* New York: Columbia University Press.

Luhmann, Niklas. 1995. *Social Systems.* Translated by J. Bednarz. Stanford, CA: Stanford University Press.

Luhmann, Niklas. 1997. *Die Gesellschaft der Gesellschaft* [The Society of the Society]. 2 vols. Frankfurt, Germany: Suhrkamp.

Luhmann, Niklas. 1998. *Love as Passion: The Codification of Intimacy.* Stanford, CA: Stanford University Press.

Lukács, Georg. [1910] 1971. *The Theory of the Novel.* Cambridge, MA: MIT University Press.

Lukács, György. [1923] 1971. *History and Class Consciousness: Studies in Marxist Dialectics.* Translated by R. Livingstone. Cambridge, MA: MIT Press.

Lukács, György. 1978. *The Ontology of Social Being.* vol. 3, *Labour.* Translated by D. Fernbach. London: Merlin.

Lukács, György. [1916] 1978. *The Theory of the Novel.* Translated by A. Bostock. London: Merlin.

Lukacs, John. 2002. "It's the End of the Modern Age." *The Chronicle Review: Chronicle of Higher Education,* April 26, pp. B7-B11. [Excerpted from his book *At the End of an Age,* New Haven, CT: Yale University Press, 2002.]

Lukes, Steven. 1973. *Émile Durkheim: His Life and Work.* Stanford, CA: Stanford University Press.

Lukes, Steven. 1974. *Power: A Radical View.* London: Macmillan.

Lyman, S. and M. Scott. 1968. "Accounts." *American Sociological Review* 33:46–62.

Lyman, Stanford and Arthur Vidich. 1988. *Social Order and the Public Philosophy: An Analysis and Interpretation of the Work of Herbert Blumer.* Fayetteville: University of Arkansas Press.

Lynch, Michael. 1993. *Scientific Practice & Ordinary Action: Ethnomethodology and Social Studies of Science.* New York: Cambridge University Press.

Lyon, David. 1999. *Postmodernity.* 2d ed. Minneapolis: University of Minnesota Press.

Lyon, David. 2001. *The Electronic Eye: The Rise of Surveillance Society.* Minneapolis: University of Minnesota Press.

Lyotard, Jean-Francois. 1984. *The Postmodern Condition: A Report on Knowledge.* Translated by Regis Durand. Minneapolis: University of Minnesota Press.

Lyotard, Jean-Francois. 1988. *The Differend: Phrases in Dispute,* Manchester, UK: Manchester University Press.

MacFarlane, A. 1978. *The Origins of English Individualism.* Oxford, UK: Blackwell.

Macherey, P. 1989. *Comte: La philosophie et la science.* Presses Universitaires de France.

Machiavelli, Niccolo. [1532] 1979. *The Prince.* Middlesex, UK: Penguin.

MacIntyre, Alasdair. 1981. *After Virtue: A Study in Moral Theory.* London: Duckworth.

MacIver, Robert. 1931. *Society: Its Structure and Changes.* New York: Ray Long and Richard R. Smith.

Mackay, Robert W. 1974. "Words, Utterances and Activities." Pp. 197–215 in *Ethnomethodology: Selected Readings,* edited by R. Turner. Harmondsworth, UK: Penguin.

MacKinnon, Catherine. *Feminism Unmodified: Discourses on Life and Law.* Cambridge, MA: Harvard University Press.

MacKinnon, Neil J. 1994. *Symbolic Interaction as Affect Control.* Albany: State University of New York Press.

Macpherson, C. B. 1962. *The Political Theory of Possessive Individualism.* Oxford, UK: Oxford University Press.

Macy, M. and A. Flache. 2002. "Learning Dynamics in Social Dilemmas." *Proceedings of the National Academy of Sciences* 99:7229–36.

Maguire, Joseph A. and Kevin Young, eds. 2002. *Theory, Sport and Society.* Oxford: JAI.

Maines, David. 1977. "Social Organization and Social Structure in Symbolic Interactionist Thought." *Annual Review of Sociology* 3:235–59.

Maines, David R. 1982. "In Search of Mesostructure: Studies in the Negotiated Order." *Urban Life* 11:267–79.

Maines, David R. 2001. *The Faultline of Consciousness: A View of Interactionism in Sociology.* Hawthorne, NY: Aldine de Gruyter.

Maistre, Joseph de. [1797] 1974. *Considerations on France.* Translated by Richard Lebrun. Montreal, Canada: McGill-Queens University Press.

Maistre, Joseph de. [1820] 1975. *The Pope.* Translated by Aeneas Dawson. Reprint of 1850 edition. New York: Howard Fertig.

Maistre, Joseph de. [1821] 1993. *Saint Petersburg Dialogues.* Translated by Richard Lebrun. Montreal, Canada: McGill-Queens University Press.

Makreel, R. 1975. *Dilthey: Philosopher of the Human Sciences.* Princeton, NJ: Princeton University Press.

Mann, Michael. 1973. *Workers on the Move.* Cambridge, MA: Cambridge University Press.

Mann, Michael. 1986. *The Sources of Social Power.* vol. 1, *From the Beginning to 1760 AD.* Cambridge, MA: Cambridge University Press.

Mann, Michael. 1993. *The Sources of Social Power.* vol. 2, *The Rise of Classes and Nation-States, 1760–1914.* Cambridge, MA: Cambridge University Press.

Mannheim, Karl. 1936. *Ideology and Utopia.* New York: Harcourt, Brace, & World.

Mannheim, Karl. 1936. "The Sociology of Knowledge." Pp. 264–311 in K. Mannheim, *Ideology and Utopia.* New York: Harcourt, Brace, & World.

Mannheim, Karl. 1940. *Man and Society in an Age of Reconstruction.* New York: Harcourt, Brace, & World.

Mannheim, Karl. [1944] 1971. "Education, Sociology and the Problem of Social Awareness." Pp. 367–84 in *From Karl Mannheim,* edited by K. H. Wolff. New York: Oxford University Press.

Mannheim, Karl. [1952] 1971. "On the Interpretation of Weltanschauung." Pp. 8–58 in *From Karl Mannheim,* edited by K. H. Wolff. New York: Oxford University Press.

Manning, P. 1992. *Erving Goffman and Modern Sociology.* Stanford, CA: Stanford University Press.

Manow, Philip. 2002. *Modell Deutschland as an Interdenominational Compromise.* Max Planck Institute for the Study of Societies—Program for the Study of Germany and Europe, Working Paper No. 00.3. Cologne, Germany.

Manuel, Frank E. 1963. *The New World of Henri Saint-Simon.* 2d ed. Notre Dame, IN: University of Notre Dame Press.

Manuel, Frank and Fritzie Manuel. 1979. *Utopian Thought in the Western World.* Cambridge, MA: Harvard University Press.

March, James G. and Johan P. Olsen. 1989. *Rediscovering Institutions: The Organizational Basis of Politics.* New York: Free Press.

March, James G. and H. A. Simon. 1958. *Organizations.* New York: Wiley.

Marcuse, Herbert. 1941. "Some Social Implications of Modern Technology." *Studies in Philosophy and Social Science* 9(3):414–39.

Marcuse, Herbert. 1964. *One Dimensional Man.* London: Abacus.

Marcuse, Herbert. 1971. "Industrialization and Capitalism." Pp. 133–51 in *Max Weber Today,* edited by Otto Stammer. Translated by Kathleen Morris. Oxford, UK: Blackwell.

Marguilis, S. T. ed. 2003. "Contemporary Perspectives on Privacy: Social, Psychological, Political." *Journal of Social Issues* 59(1).

Markoff, John. 1996. *Waves of Democracy. Social Movements and Political Change.* Thousand Oaks, CA: Pine Forge.

Markovsky, Barry. 1985. "Toward a Multilevel Distributive Justice Theory." *American Sociological Review* 50:822–39.

Markovsky, Barry. 1988. "Injustice Arousal." *Social Justice Research* 2:223–33.

Markovsky, Barry. 1994. "The Structure of Theories." Pp. 3–24 in *Group Processes: Sociological Analyses,* edited by Martha Foschi and Edward J. Lawler. Chicago, IL: Nelson Hall.

Markovsky, Barry and Edward J. Lawler. 1994. "A New Theory of Group Solidarity." In *Advances in Group Processes,* Vol. 1, edited by B. Markovsky, Jodi O'Brien, and Karen Heimer. Greenwich, CT: JAI.

Markovsky, Barry, John Skvoretz, David Willer, Michael J. Lovaglia, and Jeffrey Erger. 1993. "The Seeds of Weak Power: An Extension of Network Exchange Theory." *American Sociological Review* 58:197–209.

Markovsky, Barry, Le Roy F. Smith, and Joseph Berger. 1984. "Do Status Interventions Persist?" *American Sociological Review* 49:373–82.

Markovsky, Barry, David Willer, and Travis Patton. 1988. "Power Relations in Exchange Networks." *American Sociological Review* 53: 220–36.

Markus, G. 1982. "Alienation and Reification in Marx and Lukács." *Thesis Eleven* 5–6:139–61.

Marsden, Peter and Karen Campbell. 1984. "Measuring Tie Strength." *Social Forces* 63(2):482–501.

Marshall, Barbara L. 1994. *Engendering Modernity: Feminism, Social Theory and Social Change.* Boston, MA: Northeastern University Press.

Marshall, G. 1997. *Repositioning Class: Social Inequality in Industrial Societies.* London: Sage.

Marshall, T. H. [1950] 1992. *Citizenship and Social Class.* London: Pluto.

Martin, Daniel and Gary Alan Fine. 1991. "Satanic Cults, Satanic Play: Is Dungeons & Dragons a Breeding Ground for the Devil?" Pp. 107–26 in *The Satanism Scare,* edited by James T. Richardson, Joel Best, and David Bromley. Chicago IL: Aldine de Gruyter.

Marx, Gary. 2004. *Windows into the Soul: Surveillance and Society in an Age of High Technology.* Chicago, IL: University of Chicago Press.

Marx, Karl. 1848. *The Communist Manifesto.* Any edition.

Marx, Karl. 1959. "Excerpt from *A Contribution to the Critique of Political Economy*." In *Marx and Engels: Basic Writings on Politics and Philosophy,* edited by Lewis S. Feuer. Garden City, NY: Doubleday.

Marx, Karl. [1852] 1963. *The Eighteenth Brumaire of Louis Bonaparte.* New York: International.

Marx, Karl. [1857–1858] 1964. *Pre-Capitalist Economic Foundations.* Edited by Eric J. Horsham. New York: International.

Marx, Karl. 1967. "Except Notes of 1844" and "Economic and Philosophic Manuscripts (1844)." In *Writings of the Young Marx on Philosophy and Society,* edited and translated by Lloyd D. Easton and Kurt H. Guddat. New York: Anchor.

Marx, Karl. [1867] 1967. *Capital: A Critique of Political Economy.* 3 vols. New York: International.

Marx, Karl. 1969. *Zur Kritik der politischen Ökonomie.* MEW, Bd. 13. Berlin, Germany: Dietz.

Marx, Karl. [1859] 1971. *Contribution to the Critique of Political Economy.* London: Lawrence & Wishart.

Marx, Karl. [1953] 1973. *Grundrisse.* New York: Vintage.

Marx, Karl. 1975. *Early Writings.* Harmondsworth, UK: Penguin.

Marx, Karl. [1844] 1975. *Paris Manuscripts.* In *Marx: Early Writings,* edited by L. Colletti. Harmondsworth, UK: Penguin.

Marx, Karl. [1867] 1977. "Chapter 1: The Commodity." Pp. 125–77 in *Capital: A Critique of Political Economy.* Vol. 1. New York: Vintage.

Marx, Karl. [1848] 1983. "Wage Labour and Capital." In *Selected Works in Three Volumes,* Vol. 1, by Karl Marx and Frederick Engels. Moscow, Russia: Progress.

Marx, Karl. 1983. "Wages, Price and Profit." In Karl Marx and Frederick Engels, *Selected Works in Three Volumes.* Vol. 2. Moscow, Russia: Progress.

Marx, Karl and Frederick Engels. [1845–1846] 1965. *The German Ideology.* London: Lawrence & Wishart.

Marx, Karl and Frederick Engels. [1848] 1983. *The Manifesto of the Communist Party.* In *Selected Works in Three Volumes,* Vol. 1, by Karl Marx and Frederick Engels. Moscow, Russia: Progress.

Massumi, B. 1992. *A User's Guide to Capitalism and Schizophrenia: Deviations from Deleuze and Guatarri.* Cambridge, MA: MIT Press.

Matthews, Fred H. 1977. *Quest for an American Sociology: Robert E. Park and the Chicago School.* Montreal & London: McGill-Queen's University Press.

Mauss, Marcel. 1966. *The Gift: Forms and Functions of Exchange in Archaic Societies.* London: Routledge & Kegan Paul.

Mauss, Marcel. [1935] 1973. "The Techniques of the Body." *Economy & Society* 2(1):70–88.

May, Martha. 1982. "The Historical Problem of the Family Wage: The Ford Motor Company and the Five Dollar Day." *Feminist Studies* 8(2):399–424.

Mayberry, Maralee, Banu Subramaniam, and Lisa Weasel, eds. 2001. *Feminist Science Studies: A New Generation.* New York: Routledge.

McAdam, Doug. 1986. "Recruitment to High-Risk Activism: The Case of Freedom Summer." *American Journal of Sociology* 92:64–90.

McAdam, Doug. 1996. "Conceptual Origins, Current Problems, Future Directions." Pp. 23–40 in *Comparative Perspectives on Social Movements,* edited by Doug McAdam, John

D. McCarthy, and Mayer N. Zald. Cambridge, UK, & New York: Cambridge University Press.

McAdam, Doug, Sidney Tarrow, and Charles Tilly. 2001. *Dynamics of Contention.* Cambridge, UK: Cambridge University Press.

McCarthy, Thomas. 1986, "Komplexität und Demokratie— die Versuchungen der Systemtheorie." Pp. 177–215 in *Kommunikatives Handeln. Beiträge zu Jürgen Habermas' "Theorie des kommunikativen Handelns,"* edited by Axel Honneth and Hans Joas. Frankfurt, Germany: Suhrkamp.

McChesney, Robert W. 1999. *Rich Media, Poor Democracy: Communication Politics in Dubious Times.* New York: New Press.

McChesney. Robert W. 2000. "The Political Economy of Communications and the Future of the Field." *Media, Culture and Society* 22:109–16.

McCole, John. 1993. *Walter Benjamin and the Antinomies of Tradition.* Ithaca, NY: Cornell University Press.

McDonough, Tom, ed. 2002. *Guy Debord and the Situationist International: Texts and Documents.* Cambridge, MA: MIT Press.

McGuigan, Jim. 1992. *Cultural Populism.* New York & London: Routledge.

McGuigan, Jim. 1997. "Cultural Populism Revisited." Pp. 138–54 in *Cultural Studies in Question,* edited by M. Ferguson and P. Golding. London: Sage.

McKinney, John C. 1955. "The Contribution of George H. Mead to the Sociology of Knowledge." *Social Forces* 34:144–9.

McKinnon, Catherine. 1993. *Only Words.* Cambridge, MA: Harvard University Press.

McLaren, Margaret. 1993. "Possibilities for a Nondominated Female Subjectivity." *Hypatia: A Journal of Feminist Philosophy* 8:153–58.

McLaren, Peter. 1995. *Critical Pedagogy and Predatory Culture: Oppositional Politics in a Postmodern Era.* New York & London: Routledge.

McLellan, D. 1980. *Marxism after Marx.* London: Macmillan.

McLorg, Penelope A. and Diane E. Taub. 1987. "Anorexia Nervosa and Bulimia: The Development of Deviant Identities." *Deviant Behavior* 8:177–89.

McLuhan, Marshall. 1974. *Understanding Media: The Extensions of Man.* Aylesbury, UK: Abacus.

McMichael, Philip. 2000. *Development and Social Change: A Global Perspective.* Thousand Oaks, CA: Pine Forge.

McNaghten, P. and J. Urry. 1998. *Contested Natures.* London: Sage.

McNall, S. G., R. F. Levine, and R. Fantasia, eds. 1991. *Bringing Class Back In: Contemporary and Historical Perspectives.* Boulder, CO: Westview.

McPherson, J. Miller. 1983. "An Ecology of Affiliation." *American Sociological Review* 48:519–32.

McPherson, J. Miller and James R. Ranger-Moore. 1991. "Evolution on a Dancing Landscape: Organizations and Networks in Dynamic Blau Space." *Social Forces* 70:19–42.

McPherson, J. Miller and Thomas Rotolo. 1996. "Testing a Dynamic Model of Social Composition: Diversity and Change in Voluntary Groups." *American Sociological Review* 61:179–202.

McQuillan, Martin, ed. 2001. *Deconstruction: A Reader.* New York: Routledge.

Mead, George Herbert. 1927. "The Objective Reality of Perspectives." Pp. 100–13 in *Proceedings of the Sixth International Congress of Philosophy*, edited by E. S. Brightman. New York: Longmans, Green.

Mead, George Herbert. 1929–1930. "The Philosophies of Royce, James, and Dewey in Their American Setting." *International Journal of Ethics* 40:211–31.

Mead, George Herbert. 1934. *Mind, Self, and Society: From the Standpoint of a Social Behaviorist,* edited by C. W. Morris. Chicago, IL: University of Chicago Press.

Mead, George Herbert. 1938. *The Philosophy of the Act,* edited by C. W. Morris. Chicago, IL: University of Chicago Press.

Mead, George Herbert. 1956. *George Herbert Mead: On Social Psychology,* edited by A. Strauss. Chicago, IL: University of Chicago Press.

Mead, George Herbert. 1959. *The Philosophy of the Present,* edited by A. E. Murphy. LaSalle, IL: Open Court.

Mead, George Herbert. [1930] 1964. "Cooley's Contribution to American Social Thought." Foreword to *Human Nature and the Social Order,* by Charles Horton Cooley. New York: Schocken.

Mead, George Herbert. [1922] 1981. "A Behavioristic Account of the Significant Symbol." In *Mead: Selected Writings,* edited by A. J. Reck. Chicago, IL: University of Chicago Press.

Meek, Ronald L. 1971. "Smith, Turgot, and the 'Four Stages' Theory." *History of Political Economy* 3:9–27.

Meja, Volker and Nico Stehr, eds. 1987. *Modern German Sociology.* New York: Columbia University Press.

Melucci, A. 1996. *Challenging Codes: Collective Action in the Information Age.* Cambridge, UK: Cambridge University Press.

Mennell, Stephen. 1989. *Norbert Elias: Civilization and the Human Self-Image.* Oxford, UK: Blackwell.

Mennell, Stephen. 1998. *Norbert Elias: An Introduction.* Dublin, Ireland: University College Dublin Press.

Merton, Robert. 1938. "Social Structure and Anomie." *American Sociological Review* 3:672–82.

Merton, Robert K. 1949. *Social Theory and Social Structure.* New York: Free Press.

Merton, Robert K. 1968. "Bureaucratic Structure and Personality." In *Social Theory and Social Structure.* New York: Free Press.

Merton, Robert K. 1973. *The Sociology of Science: Theoretical and Empirical Investigations,* edited by N. W. Storer. Chicago, IL: University of Chicago Press.

Merton, Robert K. 1976. *Sociological Ambivalence and Other Essays.* New York: Free Press.

Merton, Robert K. 1982. "Alvin W. Gouldner: Genesis and Growth of a Friendship." *Theory and Society* 11:915–38.

Merton, Robert K. 1996. *On Social Structure and Science,* edited by P. Sztompka. Chicago, IL: University of Chicago Press.

Mestrovic, I. 1988. *Émile Durkheim and the Reformation of Sociology.* Totowa, NJ: Rowman & Littlefield.

Metz, Christian. 1974. *Film Language: A Semiotics of the Cinema.* Translated by Michael Taylor. New York: Oxford University Press.

Meyer, John W., John Boli, George M. Thomas, and Francisco O. Ramirez. 1997. "World Society and the Nation-State." *American Journal of Sociology* 103:144–81.

Meyer, John W. and W. Richard Scott. 1983. *Organizational Environments: Ritual and Rationality.* Beverly Hills, CA: Sage.

Micklethwait, John and Adrian Wooldridge. 2000. *A Future Perfect: The Challenge and Hidden Promise of Globalization.* New York: Crown.

Mies, M. and V. Shiva. 1993. *Ecofeminism.* London: Routledge.

Milbank, J. 1993. *Theology and Social Theory: Beyond Secular Reason.* Oxford, UK: Blackwell.

Miliband, Ralph. 1969. *The State in Capitalist Society.* New York: Basic Books.

Mill, John Stuart. [1861] 1977. "Considerations on Representative Government." Pp. 371–577 in *Collected Works of John Stuart Mill.* Vol. 19. Toronto and London: University of Toronto Press and Routledge & Kegan Paul.

Millar, John. [1787] 1803. *An Historical View of the English Government: From the Settlement of the Saxons in Britain to the Revolution in 1688; to which are Subjoined Some Dissertations Connected with the History of Government from the Revolution to the Present Time.* Vols. 1–4. London: Mawman.

Millar, John. [1771] 1806. *The Origin of the Distinction of Ranks: Or, an Inquiry into the Circumstances Which Give Rise to Influence and Authority, in the Different Members of Society.* Edinburgh, Scotland: Blackwood.

Miller, Daniel. 1987. *Material Culture and Mass Consumption.* Oxford, UK: Blackwell.

Miller, David L. 1973. *George Herbert Mead: Self, Language, and the World.* Austin, TX: University of Texas Press.

Miller, David, ed. 1985. *Popper: Selections.* Princeton, NJ: Princeton University Press.

Miller, James Grier. 1978. *Living Systems.* New York: McGraw-Hill.

Miller, Toby, ed. 2003. *Television: Critical Concepts in Media and Cultural Studies.* 5 vols. London: Routledge.

Miller, Toby, Nitin Govil, John McMurria, and Richard Maxwell. 2001. *Global Hollywood.* London: British Film Institute.

Millet, Kate. 1981. *Sexual Politics.* New York: Avon.

Mills, C. W. 1940. "Situated Actions and Vocabularies of Motive." *American Sociological Review* 5:904–13.

Mills, C. Wright. 1956. *The Power Elite.* New York: Oxford University Press.

Mills, C. Wright. 1959. *The Sociological Imagination.* New York: Oxford University Press.

Minnich, Elizabeth Kamarck. 1990. *Transforming Knowledge.* Philadelphia, PA: Temple University Press.

Misztal, Barbara A. 2001. "Civil Society: A Signifier of Plurality and Sense of Wholeness." Pp. 73–85 in *Blackwell Companion to Sociology,* edited by Judith Blau. Oxford, UK: Blackwell.

Mitchell, Juliet. 1974. *Psychoanalysis and Feminism.* New York: Vintage.

Mitchell, Juliet and J. Rose, eds. 1985. *Feminine Sexuality: Jacques Lacan and the École Freudienne.* Translated by J. Rose. New York: Norton.

Modelski, George and William R. Thompson. 1996. *Leading Sectors and World Powers.* Columbia: University of South Carolina Press.

Modleski, Tania. 1991. *Feminism without Women: Culture and Criticism in a "Postfeminist" Age.* New York: Routledge.

Mohr, John and Paul DiMaggio. 1995. "The Intergenerational Transmission of Cultural Capital." *Research in Social Stratification and Mobility* 14:167–99.

Moi, Toril. 1985. *Sexual/Texual Politics.* London: Methuen.

Moi, Toril, ed. 1986. *The Kristeva Reader.* New York: Columbia University Press.

Molm, Linda D. 1981. "The Legitimacy of Behavioral Theory as a Sociological Perspective." *American Sociologist* 16:153–66.

Molm, Linda D. 1984. "The Disruption and Recovery of Dyadic Social Interaction." Pp. 183–227 in *Advances in Group Processes: Theory and Research*, Vol. 1, edited by Edward J. Lawler. Greenwich, CT: JAI.

Molm, Linda D. 1997. *Coercive Power in Social Exchange.* Cambridge, UK: Cambridge University Press.

Molm, Linda D. and Karen S. Cook. 1995. "Social Exchange and Exchange Netowkrds." Pp. 209–35 in *Sociological Perspectives on Social Psychology,* edited by Karen S. Cook, Gary A. Fine, and James S. House. Needham Heights, MA: Allyn & Bacon.

Molm, Linda D., Gretchen Peterson, and Nobuyuki Takahashi. 1999. "Power in Negotiated and Reciprocal Exchange." *American Sociological Review* 64:876–90.

Molm, Linda D., Nobuyuki Takahashi, and Gretchen Peterson. 2000. "Risk and Trust in Social Exchange: An Experimental Test of a Classical Proposition." *American Journal of Sociology* 105:1396–427.

Molm, Linda D., Nobuyuki Takahashi, and Gretchen Peterson. 2003. "Perceptions of Fairness and Forms of Exchange." *American Sociological Review* 68:1–160.

Mommsen, Wolfgang J. 1984. *Max Weber and German Politics: 1890–1920.* Translated by Michael Steinberg. Chicago, IL: Chicago University Press.

Moore, Barrington. 1966. *Social Origins of Dictatorship and Democracy: Lord and Peasant in the Making of the Modern World.* Boston, MA: Beacon.

Moore, W. E. 1963. *Man, Time, and Society.* New York: Wiley.

Moraga, Cherrie and Gloria Anzaldua, eds. 1981. *This Bridge Called My Back: Writings by Radical Women of Color.* Watertown, MA: Persephone.

Morgan, Robin. 1982. *The Anatomy of Freedom: Feminism, Physics, and Global Politics.* Garden City, NY: Anchor Press/ Doubleday.

Morrione, Thomas. 1999. "Blumer, Herbert George." Pp. 73–6 in *American National Biography,* 24 vols., edited by John Garraty and Mark Carnes. New York: Oxford University Press.

Morris, Charles W. 1934. "Introduction: George H. Mead as Social Psychologist and Social Philosopher." Pp. ix–xxxv in *Mind, Self, and Society: From the Standpoint of a Social Behaviorist,* edited by C. W. Morris. Chicago, IL: University of Chicago Press.

Mortimer, Jeylan T., Jon Lorence, and Donald S. Kumka. 1986. *Work, Family and Personality: Transition to Adulthood.* Norwood, NJ: Ablex.

Mosca, Gaetano. [1884] 1939. *The Ruling Class.* New York: McGraw-Hill.

Mosse, Werner. 1987. *Jews in the German Economy.* Oxford, UK: Clarendon.

Müller-Armack, Alfred. 1966. *Wirtschaftsordnung und Wirtschaftspolitik* (Economic Order and Economic Policy). Freiburg, Germany: Krombach.

Mulvey, Laura. 1975. "Visual Pleasure and Narrative Cinema." *Screen* 16:6–18.

Mumford, L. 1938. *The Culture of Cities.* New York: Harcourt, Brace.

Münch, Richard. 1988. *Theorie des Handelns.* Frankfurt, Germany: Suhrkamp.

Münch, Richard. 1995. *Dynamik der Kommunikationsgesellschaft.* Frankfurt, Germany: Suhrkamp.

Nancy, Jean-Luc. 1991. *The Inoperative Community.* Minneapolis: University of Minnesota Press

Neuman, Franz. 1944. *Behemoth: The Structure and Practice of National Socialism.* New York: Oxford University Press.

Newcomb, Horace. 1974. *TV: The Most Popular Art.* Garden City, NY: Anchor/Doubleday.

Nicholson, Linda. 1995. "Interpreting Gender." Pp. 39–57 in *Social Postmodernism: Beyond Identity Politics,* edited by Linda Nicholson and Steven Siedman. New York: Cambridge University Press.

Nicholson, Linda. 1997. *The Second Wave: A Reader in Feminist Theory.* New York: Routledge.

Nicholson, Linda and Steven Seidman. 1995. *Interpreting Gender in Social Postmodernism: Beyond Identity Politics.* New York: Cambridge University Press.

Nielsen, Donald A. 1999. *Three Faces of God: Society, Religion and the Categories of Totality in the Philosophy of Émile Durkheim.* Albany: State University of New York Press.

Nietzsche, Fredrick. [1887] 1927. *Genealogy of Morals.* New York: Modern Library.

Nietzsche, Friedrich. 1982. *Daybreak: Thoughts on the Prejudices of Morality.* Cambridge, UK: Cambridge University Press.

Nizan, Paul. 1973. *The Watchdogs.* New York: Monthly Review Press.

Noddings, Nel. 1984. *Caring: A Feminine Approach to Ethics and Moral Education.* Berkeley: University of California Press.

Nora, Pierre. 1996–1998. *Realms of Memory: The Construction of the French Past,* 3 vols. New York: Columbia University Press.

Norris, Christopher. 1992. *Uncritical Theory: Postmodernism, Intellectuals and the Gulf War.* London: Lawrence & Wishart.

North, Douglass C. 1990. *Institutions, Institutional Change, and Economic Performance.* Cambridge, UK: Cambridge University Press.

Norton, Robert Edward. 2002. *Secret Germany: Stefan George and His Circle.* Ithaca, NY, & London: Cornell University Press.

Nowak, M. A. and K. Sigmund. 1998. "Evolution of Indirect Reciprocity by Image Scoring." *Nature* 393:573–7.

Oakes, Guy. 1987. "Weber and the Southwest German School: The Genesis of the Concept of the Historical Individual." Pp. 434–46 in *Max Weber and His Contemporaries,* edited by Wolfgang J. Mommsen and Jürgen Osterhammel. London: Unwin Hyman.

Obeyesekere, G. 1990. *The Work of Culture: Symbolic Transformation in Psychoanalysis and Anthropology.* Chicago, IL: University of Chicago Press.

Ofer, Dalia and Lenore Weitzman, eds. 1998. *Women in the Holocaust.* New Haven, CT: Yale University Press.

Offer, John, ed. 2000. *Herbert Spencer: Critical Assessments.* New York: Routledge.

Olick, Jeffrey. 1999. "Collective Memory: The Two Cultures." *Sociological Theory* 17:333–48.

Olick, Jeffrey and Joyce Robbins. 1998. "Social Memory Studies: From 'Collective Memory' to the Historical Sociology of Mnemonic Practices." *Annual Review of Sociology* 24:105–40.

Oliver, Kelly. 1993. "Julia Kristeva's Feminist Revolutions." *Hypatia: A Journal of Feminist Philosophy* 8:94–114.

Oliver, Kelly, ed. 1997. *The Portable Kristeva.* New York: Columbia University Press.

Ollig, Hans-Ludwig, ed. 1982. *Neukantianismus. Texte der Marburger und Südwestdeutschen Schule, ihrer Vorläufer und Kritiker* [Neo-Kantianism: Texts of the Marburg and South-West German Schools, Their Predecessors and Critics]. Stuttgart, Germany: Reclam.

Ollman, B. 1976. *Alienation: Marx's Conception of Man in Capitalism Society.* 2d ed. New York: Cambridge University Press.

Olson, Mancur. 1965. *The Logic of Collective Action.* Cambridge, MA: Harvard University Press.

Ong, A. 1999. *Flexible Citizenship: The Cultural Logics of Transnationality.* Durham, NC: Duke University Press.

Orbach, Susie. 1978. *Fat Is a Feminist Issue.* New York: Penguin.

Orum, Anthony M. and Xiangming Chen. 2003. *The World of Cities.* Malden, MA, & Oxford, UK: Blackwell.

Outhwaite, William. 1975. *Understanding Social Life: The Method Called Verstehen.* New York: Holmes & Meier.

Owen, David. 1994. *Maturity and Modernity: Nietzsche, Weber, Foucault and the Ambivalence of Reason.* London: Routledge.

Owen, Guillermo. 1995. *Game Theory.* 3d ed. San Diego, CA: Academic Press.

Pace, David. 1983. *Claude Lévi-Strauss, the Bearer of Ashes.* London: Routledge.

Padgett, John F. and Christopher K. Ansell. 1993. "Robust Action and the Rise of the Medici, 1400–1434." *American Journal of Sociology* 98:1259–1319.

Pahl, R. E. 1989. "Is the Emperor Naked? Some Comments on the Adequacy of Sociological Theory in Urban and Regional Reserach." *International Journal of Urban and Regional Research* 13:127–29.

Paige, Jeffrey. 1975. *Agrarian Revolution: Social Movements and Export Agriculture in the Underdeveloped World*. New York: Free Press.

Pakulski, J. and M. Waters. 1996. *The Death of Class*. London: Sage.

Palmer, R. E. 1969. *Hermeneutics*. Evanston, IL: Northwestern University Press.

Pangle, Thomas L. 1973. *Montesquieu's Philosophy of Liberalism: A Commentary on the Spirit of the Laws*. Chicago, IL: University of Chicago Press.

Parekh Report. 2000. *The Future of Multi-Ethnic Britain*. London: Runnymede Trust.

Pareto, Vilfredo. [1901] 1968. *The Rise and Fall of the Elites*. Totowa, NJ: Bedminster.

Pareto, Vilfredo. [1906] 1971. *Manual of Political Economy*. New York: Augustus Kelley.

Pareto, Vilfredo. [1916] 1980. *Trattato di Sociologia Generale* [The Mind and Society]. Edited and abridged by Giulio Farina. Minneapolis: University of Minnesota Press

Park, Robert E. 1914. "Racial Assimilation in Secondary Groups with Particular Reference to the Negro." *American Journal of Sociology* 19:606–23.

Park, Robert E. 1915. "The City: Suggestions for the Investigation of Human Behavior in the City Environment." *American Journal of Sociology* 20:577–612.

Park, Robert E. 1922. *The Immigrant Press and Its Control*. New York: Harper.

Park, Robert E. 1923. "The Natural History of the Newspaper." *American Journal of Sociology* 29:273–89.

Park, Robert E. 1926. "The Urban Community as a Spatial Pattern and a Moral Order." In *The Urban Community*, edited by Ernest W. Burgess. Chicago, IL: University of Chicago Press.

Park, Robert E. 1929. "The City as a Social Laboratory." In *Chicago: An Experiment in Social Science Research*, edited by T. V. Smith and Leonard D. White. Chicago, IL: University of Chicago Press.

Park, Robert E. [1904] 1972. *The Crowd and the Public, and Other Essays*. Translated by Charlotte Elsner. Chicago, IL: University of Chicago Press.

Park, Robert E. and Ernest W. Burgess. 1921. *An Introduction to the Science of Sociology*. Chicago, IL: University of Chicago Press.

Parker, John. 2000. *Structuration*. Buckingham, UK: Open University Press.

Parsons, Talcott. 1937. *The Structure of Social Action*. New York: Free Press.

Parsons, Talcott. 1951. *The Social System*. Glencoe, IL: Free Press.

Parsons, Talcott. 1959. "General Theory in Sociology." Pp. 3–38 in *Sociology Today: Problems and Prospects*, edited by R. K. Merton, L. Bloom, and L. S. Cottrell. New York: Basic Books.

Parsons, Talcott. 1964. *Social Structure and Personality*. New York: Free Press.

Parsons, Talcott. 1964. "The Superego and the Theory of Social Systems." In *Social Structure and Personality*. New York: Free Press.

Parsons, Talcott. 1966. *Societies: Evolutionary and Comparative Perspectives*. Englewood Cliffs, NJ: Prentice-Hall.

Parsons, Talcott. 1967. "Evolutionary Universals in Society." Pp. 490–520 in *Sociological Theory and Modern Society* by T. Parsons. New York: Free Press.

Parsons, Talcott. 1969. "On the Concept of Influence." Pp. 405–38 in *Politics and Social Structure*, by T. Parsons. New York: Free Press.

Parsons, Talcott. 1969. "On the Concept of Political Power." Pp. 352–404 in *Politics and Social Structure*, by T. Parsons. New York: Free Press.

Parsons, Talcott. 1969. "On the Concept of Value Commitments." Pp. 439–72 in *Politics and Social Structure*, by T. Parsons. New York: Free Press.

Parsons, Talcott. 1969. "Voting and the Equilibrium of the American Political System." Pp. 204–40 in *Politics and Social Structure*, by T. Parsons. New York: Free Press.

Parsons, Talcott. 1971. *The System of Modern Societies*. Englewood Cliffs. NJ: Prentice-Hall.

Parsons, Talcott. 1977. "Some Theoretical Considerations on the Nature and Trends of Change of Ethnicity." Pp. 383–404 in *Social Systems and the Evolution of Action Theory*, by T. Parsons. New York: Free Press.

Parsons, Talcott. 1978. *Action Theory and the Human Condition*. New York: Free Press.

Parsons, Talcott, Robert F. Bales, and Edward A. Shils. 1953. *Working Papers in the Theory of Action*. New York: Free Press.

Parsons, Talcott and G. M. Platt. 1973. *The American University*. Cambridge, MA: Harvard University Press.

Parsons, Talcott and E. A. Shils, eds. 1951. *Toward a General Theory of Action*. Cambridge, MA: Harvard University Press.

Parsons, Talcott and Neil J. Smelser. 1956. *Economy and Society: A Study of the Integration of Economic and Social Theory*. New York: Free Press.

Pateman, Carole. 1979. *The Problem of Political Obligation: A Critical Analysis of Liberal Theory*. Chichester, UK: John Wiley.

Paternoster, R. and Bachman, R. 2001. *Explaining Crime and Criminals*. Los Angeles, CA: Roxbury.

Paternoster, R., R. Brame, R. Bachman, and L. W. Sherman. 1997. "Do Fair Procedures Matter? The Effect of Procedural Justice on Spouse Assault. *Law and Society Review* 31:163–204.

Pearce, Frank. 2001. *The Radical Durkheim*. 2d ed. Toronto, Canada: Canadian Scholars Press.

Pearce, Frank, ed. 2003. "The Collège de Sociologie and French Social Thought." Special issue. *Economy and Society* 32(1).

Peel, J. D. Y. 1971. *Herbert Spencer: The Evolution of a Sociologist.* New York: Basic Books.

Peirce, Charles Sanders. 1931–1938. *The Collected Papers of Charles Sanders Peirce,* 6 vols, edited by Charles Hartshorne and Paul Weiss. Cambridge, MA: Harvard University Press.

Peirce, Charles Sanders. [1878] 1992. "How to Make Our Ideas Clear." In *The Essential Peirce: Selected Philosophical Writings,* vol. 1, *1867–1893,* edited by Nathan Houser and Christian Kloesel. Bloomington: Indiana University Press.

Perelman, Chaim and Lucy Olbrechts-Tyteca. 1971. *The New Rhetoric: A Treatise on Argumentation.* Notre Dame, IN: Notre Dame University Press.

Perrin, Robert G. 1993. *Herbert Spencer: A Primary and Secondary Bibliography.* New York: Garland.

Petersen, Trond, Ishak Saporta, and Marc-David Seidel. 2000. "Offering a Job: Meritocracy and Social Networks." *American Journal of Sociology* 106:763–816.

Peterson, Richard A. and Roger M. Kern. 1996. Highbrow Taste: From Snob to Omnivore." *American Sociological Review* 61(5):900–07.

Pfeffer, J. 1994. *Competitive Advantage through People.* Cambridge, MA: Harvard University Press.

Pfohl, Stephen. 1994. *Images of Deviance and Social Control: A Sociological History.* 2d ed. New York: McGraw-Hill.

Phelan, Shane. 1989. *Identity Politics: Lesbian Feminism and the Limits of Community.* Philadelphia, PA: Temple University Press.

Phelan, Shane. 1994. *Getting Specific: Postmodern Lesbian Politics.* Minneapolis: University of Minnesota Press

Pickering, M. 1993. *Auguste Comte, an Intellectual Biography.* Vol. 1. Cambridge, UK: Cambridge University Press.

Piore, Michael and Charles Sabel. 1984. *The Second Industrial Divide.* New York: Basic Books.

Plant, Sadie. 1992. *The Most Radical Gesture: The Situationist International in a Postmodern Age.* London: Routledge.

Plessner, Helmut. [1928] 1965. *Die Stufen des Organischen und der Mensch* [Man and the States of the Organic]. 2d ed. Berlin, Germany: de Gruyter.

Poggi, Gianfranco. 2001. *Forms of Power.* Oxford, UK: Blackwell.

Polan, A. 1984. *Lenin and the End of Politics.* London: Methuen.

Polanyi, K. 1944. *The Great Transformation: The Political and Economic Origin of Our Time.* Boston, MA: Beacon.

Polletta, Francesca and James M. Jasper. 2001. "Collective Identity and Social Movements." *Annual Review of Sociology* 27:283–305.

Poole, Steven. 2000. *Trigger Happy: Video Games and the Entertainment Revolution.* New York: Arcade.

Popielarz, Pamela A. and J. Miller McPherson. 1995. "Niche Position, Niche Overlap, and the Duration of Voluntary Memberships." *American Journal of Sociology* 101:698–720.

Popper, Karl. 1960. *The Poverty of Historicism.* London: Routledge & Kegan Paul.

Porter, Jack Nusan and Steve Hoffman, eds. 1999. *The Sociology of the Holocaust and Genocide: A Teaching and Learning Guide.* Washington, DC: American Sociological Association.

Porter, R. 2002. *Madness: A Brief History.* New York: Oxford University Press.

Portes, A. 1998. "Social Capital: Its Origins and Applications in Modern Sociology." *Annual Review of Sociology* 24:1–24.

Poster, M. 1975. *Existential Marxism in Postwar France.* Princeton, NJ: Princeton University Press.

Poulantzas, Nicos. 1976. "The Capitalist State: A Reply to Miliband and Laclau." *New Left Review* 95:63–83.

Poulantzas, Nicos. 1980. *State, Power, and Socialism.* New York: New Left Books.

Powell, Walter W. and Paul J. DiMaggio, eds. 1991. *The New Institutionalism in Organizational Analysis.* Chicago, IL: University of Chicago Press.

Powell, Walter W. and Daniel L. Jones, eds. 2003. *How Institutions Work.* Chicago, IL: University of Chicago Press.

Prager, J. 1998. *Presenting the Past: Psychoanalysis and the Sociology of Misremembering.* Cambridge, MA: Harvard University Press.

Pratt, Ray. 1990. *Rhythm and Resistance: Political Uses of American Popular Music.* New York: Praeger.

Prawer, S. S. 1978. *Karl Marx and World Literature.* Oxford, UK: Oxford University Press.

Prechel, Harland. 2001. *Big Business and the State: Historical Transformations and Corporate Transformation, 1880s-1990s.* Albany: State University of New York Press.

Prendergast, Christopher and J. David Knottnerus. 1994. "Introduction: Recent Developments in the Theory of Social Structure." *Current Perspectives in Social Theory,* Supplement 1:1–26.

Prensky, Marc. 2000. *Digital Game-Based Learning.* New York: McGraw-Hill.

Price, Janet and Margaret Shildrick. 1999. *Feminist Theory and the Body.* New York: Routledge.

Priddat, Birger, ed. 1996. *Der Werturteilsstreit: Die Aeusserungen zur Werturteilsdiskussion im Ausschuss des Vereins für Socialpolitik* [The Value Judgement Dispute: The Statements in the Discussion about Value Judgements in the Committee of the Verein für Socialpolitik Marburg]. Marburg, Germany: Metropolis.

Probyn, Elspeth. 2000. *Carnal Appetites: Food Sex Identity.* New York & London: Routledge.

Pruitt, Dean G. and Melvin J. Kimmel. 1977. "Twenty Years of Experimental Gaming: Critique, Synthesis, and Suggestions for the Future." *Annual Review of Psychology* 28: 363–92.

Przeworski, Adam, Michael Alvarez, Jose Antonio Cheibub, and Fernando Limongi. 2000. *Democracy and Development: Political Institutions and Material Well-Being in the World, 1950–1990.* Cambridge, UK: Cambridge University Press.

Psathas, George, ed. 1973. *Phenomenological Sociology, Issues and Applications.* New York: John Wiley.

Putnam, Robert D. 1994. *Making Democracy Work: Civic Institutions in Modern Italy.* Princeton, NJ: Princeton University Press.

Putnam, Robert D. 2000. *Bowling Alone: The Collapse and Revival of American Community.* New York: Simon & Schuster.

Putnam, Robert D, with Roberto Leonardi and Raffaella Y. Nanetti. 1993. *Making Democracy Work: Civic Traditions in Modern Italy.* Princeton, NJ: Princeton University Press.

Rabinbach, Anson. 1996. "Social Knowledge, Social Risk, and the Politics of Industrial Accidents in Germany and France." Pp. 48–89 in *States, Social Knowledge, and the Origins of Modern Social Policies*, edited by D. Rueschemeyer and T. Skocpol. Princeton, NJ: Princeton University Press.

Rademacher, Lee M. 2002. *Structuralism vs. Humanism in the Formation of the Political Self: The Philosophy of Politics of Jean-Paul Sartre and Louis Althusser,* Lewiston, NY: E. Mellen.

Ragin, Charles and David Zaret. 1983. "Theory and Method in Comparative Research: Two Strategies." *Social Forces* 61:731–54.

Randall Jr., John Herman. [1926] 1976. *The Making of the Modern Mind: Survey of the Intellectual Background to the Present.* 50th anniversary ed. New York: Columbia University Press.

Ransom, John Crowe. 1984. *Selected Essays of John Crowe Ransom.* Edited by T. Young and J. Hindle. Baton Rouge: Louisiana State University Press.

Rapoport, Anatol. 1953. "Spread of Information through a Population with Socio-structural Bias: III. Suggested Experimental Procedures." *Bulletin of Mathematical Biophysics* 16:75–81.

Rapoport, Anatol and William Horvath. 1961. "A Study of a Large Sociogram." *Behavioral Science* 6:279–91.

Raushenbush, Winifred. 1979. *Robert E. Park: Biography of a Sociologist.* Durham, NC: Duke University Press.

Rawls, Anne W. 1996. "Durkheim's Epistemology: The Neglected Argument." *American Journal of Sociology* 102:430–82.

Regan, P. 1995. *Legislating Privacy: Technology, Social Values, and Public Policy.* Chapel Hill: University of North Carolina Press.

Reismann, D., N. Glazer, and R. Denney. 1950. *The Lonely Crowd: A Study of the Changing American Character.* New Haven, CT: Yale University Press.

Renan, Ernst. [1871] 1990. "What Is a Nation?" Pp. 8–22 in *Nation and Narration,* edited by Homi Bhabha. London: Routledge.

Rex, John. 1961. *Key Problems of Sociological Theory.* London: Routledge & Kegan Paul.

Reynolds, Charles and Ralph V. Norman, eds. 1988. *Community in America. The Challenge of Habits of the Heart.* Berkeley: University of California Press.

Rheinberger, Hans-Jörg. 1992. "Experiment, Difference, and Writing: I. Tracing Protein Synthesis." *Studies in History and Philosophy of Science* 23:305–31.

Rich, Adrienne. 1980. "Compulsory Heterosexual and Lesbian Experience." Pp. 62–91 in *Women, Sex, and Sexuality,* edited by C. R. Stimson and E. S. Person. Chicago, IL: University of Chicago Press.

Rich, Adrienne. 1986. "Compulsory Heterosexuality and Lesbian Existence (1980)." Pp. 23–75 in *Blood, Bread, and Poetry: Selected Prose, 1979–1985.* New York: Norton.

Richards, Robert J. 1987. *Darwin and the Emergence of Evolutionary Theories of Mind and Behavior.* Chicago, IL: University of Chicago Press.

Richardson, Laurel. 1997. *Fields of Play: Constructing an Academic Life.* New Brunswick, NJ: Rutgers University Press.

Richman, Michèle. 2002. *Sacred Revolutions: Durkheim and the Collège de Sociologie.* Minneapolis: University of Minnesota Press.

Rickert, Heinrich. [1926] 1986. *Kulturwissenschaft und Naturwissenschaft* [Cultural Science and Natural Science]. Stuttgart, Germany: Reclam.

Rickert, Heinrich. 1986. *The Limits of Concept Formation in Natural Sciences: A Logical Introduction to the Historical Sciences,* edited by Guy Oakes. London: Cambridge University Press.

Ricoeur, Paul. *History and Truth.* Evanston IL: Northwestern University Press.

Ridgeway, Cecilia L. and Henry A. Walker. 1995. "Status Structures." Pp. 281–310 in *Sociological Perspectives on Social Psychology,* edited by Karen S. Cook, Gary Alan Fine, and James S. House. Boston, MA: Allyn & Bacon.

Rieff, Philip. [1959, 1961] 1979. *Freud: The Mind of the Moralist.* Chicago, IL: University of Chicago Press.

Rieff, Philip. [1970] 1982-83. "The Impossible Culture: Wilde as a Modern Prophet." *Salmagundi* 58–59:406–26. Expanded version of introduction to *The Soul of Man Under Socialism and Other Essays* (New York: Harper and Row, 1970).

Rieff, Philip. [1972, 1973] 1985. *Fellow Teachers: Of Culture and Its Second Death.* Chicago, IL: University of Chicago Press.

Rieff, Philip. [1966] 1987. *The Triumph of the Therapeutic: Uses of Faith after Freud.* Chicago, IL: University of Chicago Press.

Rieff, Philip. 1990. *The Feeling Intellect: Selected Writings.* Edited and with an introduction by Jonathan B. Imber. Chicago, IL: University of Chicago Press.

Riesman, David. 1950. *The Lonely Crowd.* New York: Doubleday.

Ritzer, George. 1979. "Toward an Integrated Sociological Paradigm." Pp. 25–46 in *Contemporary Issues in Theory and Research*, edited by W. Snizek, E. Fuhrman, and M. Miller. Westport, CT: Greenwood.

Ritzer, G. 1981. *Toward an Integrated Sociological Paradigm: The Search for an Exemplar and an Image of the Subject Matter.* Boston, MA: Allyn & Bacon.

Ritzer, George. 1980. *Sociology: A Multiple Paradigm Science.* Boston, MA: Allyn & Bacon.

Ritzer, George. 1988. "Sociological Metatheory: A Defense of a Subfield by a Delineation of its Parameters." *Sociological Theory* 6:187–200.

Ritzer, George. 1991. *Metatheorizing in Sociology.* Lexington, MA: Lexington Books.

Ritzer, George. 1992. *Sociological Theory.* 3d ed. New York: McGraw-Hill.

Ritzer, George. 1993. *The McDonaldization of Society.* Thousand Oaks, CA: Pine Forge.

Ritzer, George. 1995. *Expressing America: A Critique of the Global Credit Card Society.* Thousand Oaks, CA: Pine Forge.

Ritzer, George. 1998. *The McDonaldization Thesis: Explorations and Extensions.* London & Thousand Oaks, CA: Sage.

Ritzer, George. 1999. *Enchanting a Disenchanted World: Revolutionizing the Means of Consumption.* Thousand Oaks, CA: Pine Forge.

Ritzer, George. 2000. *The McDonaldization of Society: New Century Edition.* Thousand Oaks, CA: Pine Forge.

Ritzer, George. 2000. *Sociological Theory.* New York: McGraw-Hill.

Ritzer, George. 2001. "From Exclusion to Inclusion to Chaos (?) in Sociological Theory." Pp. 145–53 in *Explorations in Social Theory: From Metatheorizing to Rationalization,* by George Ritzer. London: Sage.

Ritzer, George. 2002. *McDonaldization: The Reader.* Thousand Oaks, CA: Pine Forge.

Ritzer, George. 2004. *The Globalization of Nothing.* Thousand Oaks, CA: Pine Forge.

Ritzer, George and Douglas J. Goodman. 2004. *Modern Sociological Theory.* 6th ed. New York: McGraw-Hill.

Robbins, Derek, 1999. *Bourdieu and Culture.* London: Sage.

Robertson, Roland. 1992. *Globalization: Social Theory and Global Culture.* London: Sage.

Robertson, Roland. 1995. "Glocalization: Time-Space and Homogeneity-Heterogeneity." Pp. 25–44 in *Global Modernities,* edited by Roland Robertson et al. London: Sage.

Robertson, Roland and Kathleen White, eds. 2003. *Globalization.* 6 vols. London: Routledge.

Robins, Kevin and Frank Webster. 1999. *Times of the Technoculture.* New York: Routledge.

Robinson, Dawn T. and Lynn Smith-Lovin. 1992. "Selective Interaction as a Strategy for Identity Maintenance: An Affect Control Model." *Social Psychology Quarterly* 55:12–28.

Robinson, Joan. 1973. "What Has Become of the Keynesian Revolution?" Pp.1–11 in *After Keynes,* edited by Joan Robinson. Oxford, UK: Basil Blackwell.

Robinson, Matthew B. 2003. "The Mouse Who Ruled the World! How American Criminal Justice Reflects the Themes of Disneyization." *Journal of Criminal Justice and Popular Culture,* 10(1):69–86.

Robinson, William I. 1994. *Promoting Polyarchy.* Cambridge, UK: Cambridge University Press.

Roche, M. 1992. *Rethinking Citizenship: Welfare, Ideology and Change in Modern Society.* Cambridge, UK: Polity.

Rocher, Guy. 1975. *Talcott Parsons and American Sociology.* New York: Barnes & Noble.

Rochon, Thomas R. 1998. *Culture Moves: Ideas, Activism, and Changing Values.* Princeton, NJ: Princeton University Press.

Rogers, Annie G. 1993. "Voice, Play, and a Practice of Ordinary Courage in Girls' and Women's Lives." *Harvard Educational Review* 63(3):265–92.

Rogers, Mary F. 1998. "The Economy, Work, and Money." Pp. 243–57 in *Contemporary Feminist Theory: A Text Reader,* edited by Mary F. Rogers. New York: McGraw-Hill.

Rogers, Mary F. 2001. "Feminist Theory." Pp. 285–96 in *The Handbook of Social Theory,* edited by George Ritzer & Barry Smart. London: Sage.

Rojek, Chris. 2001. *Celebrity.* London: Reaktion Books.

Rojek, Chris. 2003. *Stuart Hall.* Cambridge, MA: Polity.

Rosa, Gabriele de. 1962. *Carteggi Paretiani, 1892–1923* [Pareto's Letters]. Rome, Italy: Roma.

Rorty, Richard. 1989. *Contingency, Irony, and Solidarity.* New York: Cambridge University Press.

Rorty, Richard. 1991. *Objectivity, Relativism, and Truth: Philosophical Papers.* Vol. 1. Cambridge, UK: Cambridge University Press.

Rorty, Richard. 1991. *Essays on Heidegger and Others: Philosophical Papers.* Vol. 2. Cambridge, UK: Cambridge University Press.

Rorty, Richard. 1998. *Achieving Our Country: Leftist Thought in Twentieth-Century America.* Cambridge, MA: Harvard University Press.

Rorty, Richard. 1998. *Truth and Progress: Philosophical Papers.* Vol. 3. Cambridge, UK: Cambridge University Press.

Rose, Hilary. 1986. "Beyond Masculinist Realities: A Feminist Epistemology for the Sciences." Pp. 59–76 in *Feminist Approaches to Science,* edited by Ruth Bleier. New York: Pergamon.

Rosen, Stanley. 1980. *The Limits of Analysis.* New Haven, CT: Yale University Press.

Rosenberg, Justin. 1994. *The Empire of Civil Society.* London: Verso.

Rosenberg, Morris and Howard B., Kaplan, eds. 1982. *Social Psychology of the Self-Concept.* Arlington Heights, IL: Harlan Davidson.

Rossi, Ino, ed. 1974. *The Unconscious in Culture: The Structuralism of Claude Lévi-Strauss in Perspective.* New York: Dutton.

Rossi, Ino, ed. 1982. *Structural Sociology.* New York: Columbia University Press.

Rossi, Ino. 1983. *From the Sociology of Symbols to the Sociology of Signs: Toward a Dialectic Sociology.* Translated in Japanese. New York: Columbia University Press.

Rossi, Ino. 1993. *Community Reconstruction after an Earthquake: Dialectic Sociology in Action.* Westport, CT: Praeger.

Roth, Guenther, 1963. *The Social Democrats in Imperial Germany: A Study in Working-Class Isolation and National Integration.* Totowa, NJ: Bedminster:

Roth, Guenther. 1990. "Marianne Weber and Her Circle." *Society* 27(2):63–69.

Rotolo, Thomas and J. Miller McPherson. 2001. "The System of Occupations: Modeling Occupations in Sociodemographic Space." *Social Forces* 79:1095–1130.

Rotter, Julian B. 1971. "Generalized Expectancies for Interpersonal Trust. *American Psychologist* 26:443–52.

Roudinesco, Elisabeth. 1997. *Jacques Lacan.* New York: Columbia University Press.

Rubin, Gayle. 1975. "The Traffic in Women: Notes on the 'Political Economy' of Sex." Pp. 157–210 in *Toward an Anthropology of Women,* edited by Rayna R. Reiter. New York: Monthly Review.

Rubin, Gayle. 1981. "The Leather Menace: Comments on Politics and S/M." Pp. 194–229 in *Coming to Power: Writings and Graphics on Lesbian S/M,* edited by Samois. 3d ed. Rev. and updated. Boston, MA: Alyson.

Rubin, Gayle. 1984. "Thinking Sex: Notes for a Radical Theory of the Politics of Sexuality." Pp. 267–319 in *Pleasure and Danger: Exploring Female Sexuality,* edited by Carole S. Vance. Boston, MA: Routledge. Reprinted in *The Lesbian and Gay Studies Reader,* edited by Henry Abelove, Michele Aina Barale, and David M. Halperin (New York: Routledge, 1993).

Rubin, Gayle. 1992. "Of Catamites and Kings: Reflections on Butch, Gender, and Boundaries." Pp. 466–42 in *The Persistent Desire: A Femme-Butch Reader,* edited by Joan Nestle. Boston, MA: Alyson.

Rubin, Gayle with Judith Butler. 1997. "Sexual Traffic, Interview." Pp. 80–84 in *Feminism Meets Queer Theory,* edited by Elizabeth Weed and Naomi Schor. Bloomington: Indiana University Press.

Ruddick, Sara. 1980. "Maternal Thinking." *Feminist Studies* 6:342–67.

Ruddick, Sara. 1995. *Maternal Thinking: Toward a Politics of Peace.* Boston, MA: Beacon.

Ruddick, Sara. 1997. "Rethinking 'Maternal' Politics." Pp. 369–81 in *The Politics of Motherhood: Activist Voices from Left to Right,* edited by A. Jetter, A. Orleck, and D. Taylor. Hanover, NH: University Press of New England.

Ruddick, Sara. 1998. "Care as Labor and Relationship." Pp. 3–25 in *Norms and Values: Essays on the Work of Virginia Held,* edited by J. G. Haber and M. S. Halfon. Lanham, MD: Rowman & Littlefield.

Ruddick, Sara. 1998. "'Woman of Peace': A Feminist Construction." Pp. 213–26 in *The Women and War Reader,* edited by L. A. Lorentzen and J. Turpin. New York: New York University Press.

Ruddick, Sara. 2003. "The Moral Horror of the September Attacks." *Hypatia* 11:212–22.

Ruggie, John Gerard. 1993. "Territoriality and Beyond: Problematizing Modernity in International Relations. *International Organization* 47:139–74.

Rundell, John and Stephen Mennell, eds. 1998. *Classical Readings in Culture and Civilization.* London: Routledge.

Russell, Bertrand. 1938. *Power: A New Social Analysis.* London: George Allen & Unwin.

Russell, Diana. 1998. *Dangerous Relationships: Pornography, Misogyny, and Rape.* Thousand Oaks, CA: Sage.

Ryan, Alan. 2003. "The Power of Positive Thinking." *New York Review of Books,* January 16, pp. 43–6.

Ryan, Michael and Douglas Kellner. 1988. *Camera Politica.* Bloomington: University of Indiana Press.

Sacks, Harvey. 1992. *Lectures on Conversation,* edited by Gail Jefferson. New York: Cambridge University Press.

Sacks, Harvey, Emmanuel Schegloff, and Gail Jefferson. 1977. "The Simplest Systematics for Turntaking in Conversation." *Language* 50:696–735.

Said, Edward W. 1994. *Culture and Imperialism.* New York: Vintage.

Saint-Simon, Claude Henri de. 1966. *Œuvres* [Collected Works]. Paris: Anthropos.

Sanders, Joseph and V. Lee Hamilton, eds. 2001. *Handbook of Justice Research in Law.* New York: Kluwer Academic/Plenum.

Sartre, Jean-Paul. 1947. "Un Nouveau Mystique." Pp. 143–88 in *Situations I.* Paris: Gallimard.

Sartre, Jean-Paul. 1957. *Transcendence and the Ego.* New York: Noonday.

Sartre, Jean-Paul. 1977. *Existentialism and Humanism.* Brooklyn, NY: Haskell House.

Sartre, Jean-Paul. 1989. *No Exit and Three Other Plays.* New York: Vintage.

Sartre, Jean-Paul. 1993. *Being and Nothingness.* New York: Washington Square Press.

Sartre, Jean-Paul. 2001. *Critique of Dialectical Reason.* vol. 1, *Theory of Practical Ensembles.* New York: Verso.

Sarup, Madan. 1993. *An Introductory Guide to Post-Structuralism and Postmodernism.* Athens: University of Georgia Press.

Sassen, Saskia. 1991. *The Global City: New York, London, Tokyo.* Princeton, NJ: Princeton University Press.

Saussure, Ferdinand de. 1879. *Mémoire sur le Système Primitif des Voyelles dans les Langues Indoeuropéennes* [Memory on the Primitive System of the Vowels in the Indo-European Languages]. Leipzig, Germany: Teubner.

Saussure, Ferdinand de. 1881. "De l'Emploi du Génitif Absolu en Sanscrite" [On the Use of the Absolute Genitive in Sanskrit]. Doctoral thesis, Faculty of Philosophy, University of Leipzig. (Reprinted in Saussure 1922.)

Saussure, Ferdinand de. 1922. *Recueil des Publications Scientifiques de Ferdinand de Saussure* [Collected Scientific Publications of Ferdinand de Saussure], edited by Charles Bally and M. Léopold Gautier. Geneva, Switzerland: Éditions Sonor.

Saussure, Ferdinand de. 1966. *Course in General Linguistics.* New York: McGraw-Hill.

Saussure, Ferdinand de. 1978. "Essai pour Reduire les Mots du Grec, du Latin & de l'Allemand à un Petit Nombre de Racines" [Essay for Reducing the Words of Greek, Latin, & German to a Small Number of Roots], edited by B. Davis. *Cahiers Ferdinand de Saussure* 32:73–101.

Saussure, Ferdinand de. 1986. *Le Leggende Germaniche: Scritti Scelti e Annotati* [The Germanic Legends: Selected and

Annotated Writings], edited by Anna Marinetti and Marcello Meli. Padua, Italy: Libreria Editrice Zielo–Este.

Saussure, Ferdinand de. 1995. *Phonétique: Il Manoscritto di Harvard* [Phonetics: The Harvard Manuscript], edited by Maria Pia Marchese. *Houghton Library bMS Fr 266 (8)*.Quaderni del Dipartimento di Linguistica, Università degli Studi di Firenze–Studi 3. Florence, Italy: Unipress.

Sawyer, R. Keith. 2001. "Emergence in Sociology: Contemporary Philosophy of Mind and Some Implications for Sociological Theory." *American Journal of Sociology* 107:551–85.

Sawyer, R. Keith. 2003. "Artificial Societies: Multi-Agent Systems and the Micro-Macro Link in Sociological Theory." *Sociological Methods and Research* 31:37–75.

Sayer, D. 1991. *Capitalism and Modernity. An Excursus on Marx and Weber.* New York & London: Routledge.

Scaff, Lawrence A. 1989. *Fleeing the Iron Cage: Culture, Politics, and Modernity in the Thought of Max Weber.* Berkeley: University of California Press.

Scaff, Lawrence. 1998. "The 'Cool Objectivity of Sociation': Max Weber and Marianne Weber in America." *History of the Human Sciences* 11(2):61–82.

Schaff, Adam. 1978. *Structuralism and Marxism.* Oxford, UK, & New York: Pergamon.

Scharff, R. 1995. *Comte after Positivism.* Cambridge, UK: Cambridge University Press.

Schatz, Thomas. 1988. *The Genius of the System.* New York: Henry Holt.

Scheff, Thomas. 1966. *Being Mentally Ill: A Sociological Theory.* Chicago, IL: Aldine.

Scheler, Max. 1961. *Man's Place in Nature.* New York: Noonday Press. Originally published as *Die Stellung des Menschen im Kosmos* (Muenchen, Germany: Nymphenburger Verlagsbuchhandlung, 1928).

Scheler, Max. 1973. *Formalism in Ethics and Non-Formal Ethics of Values: A New Attempt Toward a Foundation of an Ethical Personalism.* Translated by Manfred S. Frings and Roger L. Funk. Evanston, IL: Northwestern University Press.

Scheler, Max. 1980. *Problems of a Sociology of Knowledge.* Translated by Manfred Frings. Edited and introduction by Kenneth W. Stikkers. London: Routledge & Kegan Paul.

Schelling, F. W. 1978. *System of Transcendental Idealism.* Charlottesville, VA: University of Virginia Press.

Schelling, F. W. [1797] 1988. *Ideas for a Philosophy of Nature.* New York: Cambridge University Press. Originally published as *Ausgewählte Werke. Schriften von 1799–1801. Einleitung zu dem Entwurf eines Systems der Naturphilosophie* (Darmstadt, Germany: Wissenschaftliche Buchgesellschaft [1966] 1997).

Schelling, T. C. 1969. *Models of Segregation.* Memorandum RM-6014-RC. Santa Monica, CA: RAND.

Schelsky, Helmut, 1959. *Ortsbestimmung der deutschen Soziologie.* Düsseldorf, Germany: Diederichs.

Scheper-Hughes, Nancy. 1996. "Maternal Thinking and the Politics of War." *Peace Review* 8:353–8.

Schiller, Herbert I. 1969. *Mass Communications and American Empire.* Boston, MA: Beacon.

Schlipp, Paul A., ed. 1994. *The Philosophy of Ernst Cassirer.* Chicago, IL: Open Court.

Schluchter, Wolfgang 1972. *Aspekte bürokratischer Herrschaft* [Aspects of Bureaucratic Herrschaft]. Munich, Germany: List.

Schluchter, Wolfgang. 1989. *Rationalism, Religion, and Domination: A Weberian Perspective.* Translated by N. Solomon. Berkeley: University of California Press.

Schmidt, Gert, with Karen Williams. 2002. "German Management Facing Globalization: The 'German Model' on Trial." Pp. 281–93 in *Challenges for European Management in a Global Context: Experiences from Britain and Germany,* edited by Mike Geppert, Dirk Matten, and Karen Williams. Houndsmills, UK: Palgrave Macmillan.

Schneider, Louis, ed. 1967. *The Scottish Moralists: On Human Nature and Society.* Chicago, IL: University of Chicago Press.

Schneider, Wolfgang-Ludwig. 1991. *Objektives Verstehen: Rekonstruktion eines Paradigmas: Gadamer, Popper, Toulmin, Luhmann* [Objective Understanding: Reconstruction of a Paradigm]. Opladen, Germany: Westdeutscher Verlag.

Scholte, Jan Aart. 2000. *Globalization: A Critical Introduction.* Houndmills, UK: Palgrave.

Schubert, Hans-Joachim. 1995. *Demokratische Identität: Der soziologische Pragmatismus von Charles Horton Cooley.* Frankfurt am Main, Germany: Suhrkamp.

Schuman, Howard and Jacqueline Scott. 1989. "Generations and Collective Memory." *American Sociological Review* 54:359–81.

Schumpeter, J. A. [1911] 1934. *The Theory of Economic Development.* Cambridge, MA: Harvard University Press.

Schütz, Alfred. 1932. *The Phenomenology of the Social World.* London: Heinemann.

Schütz, Alfred. 1973. *Collected Papers.* vol. 1, *The Problem of Social Reality.* The Hague, Netherlands: Martinus Nijhoff.

Schütz, Alfred and Thomas Luckmann. 1974. *The Structures of the Life-World.* Vol. 1. London: Heinemann.

Schütz, Alfred and Thomas Luckmann. 1989. *The Structures of the Life-World.* Vol. 2. Evanston, IL: Northwestern University Press.

Schütz, Alfred and Talcott Parsons. 1977. *Zur Theorie Sozialen Handelns. Ein Briefwechsel* [The Theory of Social Action: An Exchange of Letters]. Frankfurt, Germany: Suhrkamp.

Schwalbe, Michael, Sandra Godwin, Daphne Holden, Douglas Schrock, Shealy Thompson, and Michele Wolkomir. 2000. "Generic Processes in the Reproduction of Inequality: An Interactionist Analysis." *Social Forces* 79:419–52.

Schwartz, Barry. 2000. *Abraham Lincoln and the Forge of National Memory.* Chicago, IL: University of Chicago Press.

Schweickart, Patrocinio P. 1993. "In Defense of Femininity: Commentary on Sandra Bartky's *Femininity and Domination.*" *Hypatia: A Journal of Feminist Philosophy* 8:178–91.

Scott, Alan. 2000. "Capitalism, Weber and Democracy." *Max Weber Studies* 1(1):33–35.

Scott, Joan W. 1991. "Experience." *Critical Inquiry* 17 (Summer):773–97.

Scott, Joan W. 1992. "Experience." Pp. 22–40 in *Feminists Theorize the Political,* edited by Judith Butler and Joan W. Scott. New York: Routledge.

Scott, Joan W. 1996. "Introduction." Pp. 1–13 in *Feminism and History,* edited by Joan Wallach Scott. New York: Oxford University Press.

Scott, W. Richard. 1982. "Managing Professional Work: Three Models of Control of Healthcare Organizations." *Health Services Research* 17:213–40.

Scott, W. Richard. 2001. *Institutions and Organizations.* 2d ed. Thousand Oaks, CA: Sage.

Scull, A. 1989. *Social Order/Mental Disorder: Anglo-American Psychiatry in Historical Perspective.* Berkeley: University of California Press.

Secord, Paul F. and Carl W. Backman. 1964. *Social Psychology.* New York: McGraw-Hill.

Sedgwick, Eve Kosofsky. 1990. *Epistemology of the Closet.* Berkeley: University of California Press.

Seidman, Steven. 1994. "Symposium: Queer Theory/Sociology: A Dialogue." *Sociological Theory* 12:166–77.

Seidman, Steven. 1996. *Queer Theory/Sociology.* Cambridge, MA: Blackwell.

Seidman, Steven. 2002. *Beyond the Closet: The Transformation of Gay and Lesbian Life.* New York: Routledge.

Sen, A. 1985. *Commodities and Capabilities.* Amsterdam, Netherlands: Elsevier.

Shafai, Fariborz. 1996. *The Ontology of Georg Lukács: Studies in Materialist Dialectic.* Aldershot, UK: Avebury.

Shalin, Dmitri, ed. 1992. "Habermas, Pragmatism, and Critical Theory." Special issue of *Symbolic Interaction* 15(3).

Shannon, Thomas R. 1996. *An Introduction to the World-Systems Perspective.* Boulder, CO: Westview.

Sheringham, Michael. 1995. "Marc Augé and the Ethno-Analysis of Contemporary Life." *Paragraph* 18(2):210–22.

Shiach, Morag. 1999. *Feminism and Cultural Studies.* Oxford, UK: Oxford University Press.

Shibutani, Tamotsu 1955. "Reference Groups as Perspectives." *American Journal of Sociology* 60:562–69.

Shiner, Larry. 1967. "The Concept of Secularization in Empirical Research." *Journal for the Scientific Study of Religion* 6:207–20.

Showstack Sassoon, A. 1980. *Gramsci's Politics.* London: Croom.

Shubik, Martin. 1989. *Game Theory in the Social Sciences: Concepts and Solutions.* Cambridge, MA: MIT Press.

Sica, Alan. 1988. *Weber, Irrationality, and Social Order.* Berkeley: University of California Press.

Silberman, Marc. 2000. *Bertolt Brecht on Film and Radio.* London: Metheun.

Silver, David. 2000. "Looking Backwards, Looking Forward: Cyberculture Studies 1990–2000." Pp. 19–30 in *Web.studies: Rewiring Media Studies for the Digital Age,* edited by David Gauntlett. Oxford, UK: Oxford University Press.

Silverman, Kaja. 1992. *Male Subjectivity at the Margins.* New York: Routledge.

Sim, S. 2000. *Post-Marxism: An Intellectual History.* London: Routledge.

Sim, S., ed. 1998. *Post-Marxism: A Reader.* Edinburgh, Scotland: Edinburgh University Press.

Simmel, Georg. 1882. "Psychologische und Ethnologische Studien über Musik" [Studies in psychology and cultural anthropology on music]. *Zeitschrift für Völkerpsychologie und Srachwissenschaft* 13:261–305.

Simmel, Georg. 1907. *Philosophie des Geldes* [Philosophy of Money]. 2d ed. Leipzig, Germany: Duncker & Humblot.

Simmel, Georg. 1908. *Soziologie: Untersuchungen über die Formen der Vergesellschaftung* [Sociology: Inquiries into the Forms of Socialization]. Leipzig, Germany: Duncker & Humblot.

Simmel, Georg. 1910. *Hauptprobleme der Philosophie* [Main problems of Philosophy]. Leipzig, Germany: G. J. Göschen.

Simmel, Georg. 1918. *Lebensanschauung: Vier metaphysische Kapitel* [Life-anschauung: Four metaphysical chapters]. München & Leipzig, Germany: Duncker & Humblot.

Simmel, Georg. 1950. "The Isolated Individual and the Dyad." Pp. 118–44 in *The Sociology of Georg Simmel,* edited by Kurt Wolff. New York: Free Press.

Simmel, Georg. 1950. "The Metropolis and Mental Life." In *The Sociology of Georg Simmel,* edited by K. Wolff. London: Collier-Macmillan.

Simmel, Georg. 1955. *The Web of Group Affiliation.* New York: Free Press.

Simmel, Georg. 1971. *On Individuality and Social Forms,* edited by Donald Levine. Chicago, IL: University of Chicago Press.

Simmel, Georg. 1977. *The Problems of the Phosophy of History: An Epistemological Essay.* Translated and edited, with an introduction by Guy Oakes. New York: Free Press.

Simmel, Georg. 1997. *Essays on Religion.* New Haven, CT & London: Yale University Press.

Simons, Margaret A. 1999. *Beauvoir and the Second Sex: Feminism, Race, and the Origins of Existentialism.* New York: Rowman & Littlefield.

Skinner, B. F. 1953. *Science and Human Behavior.* New York: Free Press.

Skinner, B. F. 1971. *Beyond Freedom and Dignity.* New York: Knopf.

Skinner, B. F. 1974. *About Behaviorism.* New York: Knopf.

Sklair, Leslie. 2001. *The Transnational Capitalist Class.* Malden, MA: Blackwell.

Skocpol, Theda. 1979. *States and Social Revolutions: A Comparative Analysis of France, Russia and China.* New York: Cambridge University Press.

Skocpol, Theda, ed. 1985. *Vision and Method in Historical Sociology.* Cambridge, UK: Cambridge University Press.

Skvoretz, John and David Willer. 1993. "Exclusion and Power: A Test of Four Theories of Power in Exchange Networks." *American Sociological Review* 58:801–18.

Skyrms, Brian. 1996. *Evolution of the Social Contract*. New York: Cambridge University Press.

Slater, D. R. 1997. *Consumer Culture and Modernity*. Cambridge, UK: Polity.

Slater, P. 1963. "On Social Regression." *American Sociological Review* 28:339–64.

Smart, Barry. 1990. "Modernity, Postmodernity, and the Present." Pp. 14–30 in *Theories of Modernity and Postmodernity*, edited by Bryan Turner. London: Sage.

Smart, Barry. 1999. *Resisting McDonaldization*. London: Sage.

Smelser, Neil. 1968. *Essays in Sociological Explanation*. Englewood Cliffs, NJ: Prentice-Hall.

Smelser, Neil. 1974. "Growth, Structural Change, and Conflict in California Public Higher Education, 1950–1970." Pp. 9–142 in *Public Higher Education in California*, edited by Neil Smelser and Gabriel Almond. Berkeley & Los Angeles: University of California Press.

Smelser, Neil. 1991. *Social Paralysis and Social Change: British Working Class Education in the Nineteenth Century*. Berkeley & Los Angeles: University of California Press.

Smelser, Neil. 1997. *Problematics of Sociology: The George Simmel Lectures, 1995*. Berkeley & Los Angeles: University of California Press.

Smelser, Neil. 1998. *The Social Edges of Psychoanalysis*. Berkeley & Los Angeles: University of California Press.

Smelser, Neil. 1998. "Vicissitudes of Work and Love in Anglo-American Society." Pp. 93–107 in *The Social Edges of Psychoanalysis*. Berkeley & Los Angeles: University of California Press.

Smelser, Neil. 2004. "Psychological Trauma and Cultural Trauma." Pp. 31–59 in *Cultural Trauma and Collective Identity*, edited by Jeffrey C. Alexander, Ron Eyerman, Bernhard Giesen, Neil J. Smelser, and Piotr Sztompka. Berkeley & Los Angeles: University of California Press.

Smelser, Neil J. and Dean Gerstein, eds. 1986. *Behavioral and Social Science: Fifty Years of Discovery*. Washington DC: National Academy Press.

Smelser, Neil J. and Robert S. Wallerstein. 1998. "Psychoanalysis and Sociology: Articulations and Applications." Pp. 3–35 in *The Social Edges of Psychoanalysis*, by Neil J. Smelser. Berkeley & Los Angeles: University of California Press.

Smiles, Samuel. 1861. *Self Help*. London: Penguin.

Smith, Adam. [1776] 1976. *An Inquiry into the Nature and Causes of the Wealth of Nations*. Vols. 1–2. Oxford, UK: Clarendon.

Smith, Adam. [1759] 1982. *The Theory of Moral Sentiments*. Indianapolis, IN: Liberty Fund.

Smith, Anthony. 1986. *The Ethnic Origins of Nations*. Oxford, UK: Blackwell.

Smith, Dorothy E. 1971. "The Ideological Practice of Sociology." *Catalyst* 8:39–54.

Smith, Dorothy E. 1987. *The Everyday World as Problematic: A Feminist Sociology*. Boston, MA: Northeastern University Press.

Smith, Dorothy E. 1990. "Femininity as Discourse." Pp. 159–208 in *Texts, Facts, and Femininity: Exploring the Relations of Ruling*, edited by Dorothy E. Smith. New York: Routledge.

Smith, Dorothy E. 1990. *Texts, Facts, and Femininity: Exploring the Relations of Ruling*. New York: Routledge.

Smith, Dorothy E. 1990. *Conceptual Practices of Power: A Feminist Sociology of Knowledge*. Boston, MA: Northeastern University Press.

Smith, Dorothy E. 1993. "High Noon in Textland: A Critique of Clough." *Sociological Quarterley* 34(1):183–92.

Smith, Dorothy E. 1997. "Comment on Hekman's 'Truth and Method': Feminist Standpoint Theory Revisited." *Signs: Journal of Women in Culture and Society* 22(2):392–97.

Smith, Dorothy E. 1999. *Writing the Social: Critique, Theory, and Investigations*. Toronto, Canada: University of Toronto Press.

Smith, Gary, ed. 1989. *Benjamin: Philosophy, Aesthetics, History*. Chicago, IL, & London: Chicago University Press.

Smith, Greg, ed. 1999. *Goffman and Social Organization: Studies in a Sociological Legacy*. London: Routledge.

Smith-Lovin, Lynn. 1990. "Emotion as the Confirmation and Disconfirmation of Identity: An Affect Control Model." Pp. 238–70 in *Research Agendas in the Sociology of Emotions*, edited by Theodore D. Kemper. Albany: State University of New York Press.

Smith-Lovin, Lynn and David R. Heise. 1988. *Affect Control Theory: Research Advances*. New York: Gordon & Breach.

Snow, David A. 2002. "Social Movements as Challenges to Authority: Resistance to an Emerging Cultural Hegemony." Paper presented at the conference on "Authority in Contention" sponsored by the Collective Behavior and Social Movements section of the American Sociological Association, August 14–15, University of Notre Dame, South Bend, Indiana.

Snow, David A. and Leon Anderson. 1987. "Identity Work among the Homeless: The Verbal Construction and Avowal of Personal Identities." *American Journal of Sociology* 92:1336–71.

Snow, David A. and Robert D. Benford. 1992. "Master Frames and Cycles of Protest." Pp. 133–55 in *Frontiers in Social Movement Theory*, edited by Aldon D. Morris and Carol M. Mueller. New Haven, CT: Yale University Press.

Snow, David A., E. Burke Rochford Jr., Steven K. Worden, and Robert D. Benford. 1986. "Frame Alignment Processes, Micromobilization, and Movement Participation." *American Sociological Review* 51(4):464–81.

Snow, David A. and Pamela E. Oliver. 1995. "Social Movements and Collective Behavior: Social Psychological Dimensions and Considerations." Pp. 571–99 in *Sociological Perspectives on Social Psychology*, edited by Karen S. Cook, Gary Alan Fine, and James S. House. Boston, MA: Allyn & Bacon.

Soja, Edward W. 1989. *Postmodern Geographies: The Reassertion of Space in Critical Social Theory*. London: Verso.

Sokal, Alan D. 1996. "Transgressing the Boundaries: Toward a Transformative Hermeneutics of Quantum Gravity." *Social Text* 46/47:217–52.

Sombart, Werner. 1902. *Der Moderne Kapitalismus.* Leipzig, Germany: Duncker & Humblot.

Sombart, Werner. 1937. *A New Social Philosophy.* Translated and edited by Karl F. Geisser. [Translation of *Deutscher Sozialismus*]. Oxford, UK: Oxford University Press.

Sombart, Werner. 1976. *Why Is There No Socialism in the United States?* London: Macmillan.

Sombart, Werner. [1916–1927] 1987. *Der moderne Kapitalismus* [Modern Capitalism] Bd. I-III. München, Germany: DTV.

Sombart, Werner. [1913] 2001. "The Origins of the Capitalist Spirit," Pp. 33–54 in *Werner Sombart: Economic Life in the Modern Age,* edited by N. Stehr and R. Grundmann. New Brunswick, NJ, & Oxford, UK: Transaction.

Sorokin, Pitirim A. 1941. *The Crisis of Our Age.* New York: E. P. Dutton.

Sorokin, Pitirim A. 1947. *Culture, Society, and Personality.* New York: Harper & Brothers.

Sorokin, Pitirim A. 1954. *The Ways and Power of Love.* Boston, MA: Beacon.

Sorokin, Pitirim A. 1957. *Social and Cultural Dynamics.* 1 vol. ed. Boston, MA: Beacon.

Sorokin, Pitirim A. 1959. *Social and Cultural Mobility.* Glencoe, IL: Free Press.

Sorokin, Pitirim A. 1966. *Sociological Theories of Today.* New York: Harper and Row.

Sorokin, Pitirim A. and Merton, R. K. 1937. "Social Time: A Methodological and Functional Analysis." *American Journal of Sociology* 42:615–29.

Soysal, Y. 1994. *The Limits of Citzenship.* Chicago, IL: Chicago University Press.

Spector, Malcolm and John I. Kitsuse. [1977] 2001. *Constructing Social Problems.* New Brunswick, NJ: Transaction.

Speier, Matthew. 1970. "The Everyday World of the Child." Pp. 188–217 in *Understanding Everyday Life,* edited by J. Douglas. Chicago, IL: Aldine.

Spencer, Herbert. 1864–1867. *Principles of Biology.* 2 vols. New York: D. Appleton.

Spencer, Herbert. [1855] 1870–1872. *Principles of Psychology.* 2 vols. London: Williams & Norgate.

Spencer, Herbert. 1876–1896. *Principles of Sociology.* 3 vols. New York: D. Appleton.

Spencer, Herbert. 1879–1893. *Principles of Ethics.* 2 vols. New York: D. Appleton.

Spencer, Herbert. [1864] 1892. *First Principles.* New York: Appleton.

Spencer, Herbert. 1904. *An Autobiography.* 2 vols. London: Williams & Norgate.

Spencer, Herbert. [1862] 1911. *First Principles.* London: Williams & Norgate.

Spencer, Herbert. [1850] 1954. *Social Statics.* New York: Robert Schalkenbach Foundation.

Spencer, Herbert. [1873]1961. *The Study of Sociology.* Ann Arbor: University of Michigan Press.

Spiegelberg, Herbert. 1965. *The Phenomenological Movement.* The Hague, Netherlands: Nijhoff.

Stack, Carol B. 1994. "Different Voices, Different Visions: Gender, Culture, and Moral Reasoning." Pp. 291–302 in *Women of Color in U.S. Society,* edited by M. B. Zinn and B. T. Dill. Philadelphia, PA: Temple University Press.

Staiger, Janet. 1990. "Announcing Wares, Winning Patrons, Voicing Ideals: Thinking about the History and Theory of Film Advertising." *Cinema Journal* 29(3):3–31.

Stam, Robert and Toby Miller, eds. 2000. *Film and Theory: An Anthology.* Oxford, UK: Blackwell.

Staples, Brent. 1992. "Black Men and Public Space." Pp. 29–32 in *Life Studies,* edited by David Cavitch. Boston, MA: Bedford Books.

Staples, W. 2000. *Everyday Surveillance: Vigilance and Visibility in Postmodern Life.* Lanham, MD: Rowman & Littlefield.

Star, Susan Leigh and James R. Griesemer. 1989. "Institutional Ecology, 'Translations' and Boundary Objects: Amateurs and Professionals in Berkeley's Museum of Vertebrate Zoology, 1907–39." *Social Studies of Science* 19:387–420.

Stark, Rodney and William Sims Bainbridge. 1985. *The Future of Religion: Secularization, Revival, and Cult Formation.* Berkeley: University of California Press.

Stark, Rodney and Roger Finke. 2000. *Acts of Faith: Explaining the Human Side of Religion.* Berkeley: University of California Press.

Starobinski, Jean. 1988. *Jean-Jacques Rousseau: Transparency and Obstruction.* Translated by Arthur Goldhammer. Chicago, IL: University of Chicago Press.

Stedman-Jones, Susan. 2001. *Durkheim Reconsidered.* Cambridge, UK: Polity.

Steenbergen, B., ed. 1994. *The Condition of Citizenship.* London: Sage.

Stein, Arlene and Ken Plummer. 1996. "'I Can't Even Think Straight': 'Queer' Theory and the Missing Sexual Revolution in Sociology." Pp. 129–44 in *Queer Theory/Sociology,* edited by Steven Seidman. Cambridge, MA: Blackwell.

Steinmo, Sven, Kathleen Thelen, and Frank Longstreth, eds. 1992. *Structuring Politics: Historical Institutionalism in Comparative Analysis.* Cambridge, UK: Cambridge University Press.

Stern, Daniel. 1985. *The Interpersonal World of the Infant.* New York: Basic Books.

Stetson, Charlotte Perkins. 1898. *Women and Economics: A Study of the Economic Relation between Men and Women as a Factor in Social Evolution.* Boston, MA: Small, Maynard.

Steudler, F. 2001. "Les institutions totales et la vie d'un concept" [Total Institutions and the Life of a Concept]. Pp. 247–89 in *Erving Goffman et Les Institutions Totales* [Erving Goffman and Total Institutions], edited by C. Amourous and A. Blanc. Paris: L'Harmattan.

Stevenson, Nick, ed. 2000. *Culture and Citizenship.* London: Sage.

Stewart, Dugald. 1854. *The Collected Works of Dugald Stewart.* Vol. 10. Edinburgh, Scotland: Constable.

Stinchcombe, A. 1986. "Reason and Rationality." *Sociological Theory* 4(2):151–66.

Stoekl, Alan, ed. 1985. *Georges Bataille: Visions of Excess.* Minneapolis: University of Minnesota Press

Stoianovich, Traian. With a foreword by Fernand Braudel. 1976. *French Historical Method: The Annales Paradigm.* Ithaca, NY: Cornell University Press.

Stones, Rob. 1996. *Sociological Reasoning.* Basingstoke, UK: Macmillan.

Stones, Rob. 2004. *Structuration Theory.* London: Palgrave Macmillan.

Strauss, Anselm. 1959. *Mirrors and Masks: The Search for Identity.* Glencoe, IL: Free Press.

Strauss, Anselm. 1978. *Negotiations: Varieties, Contexts, Processes, and Social Order.* San Francisco, CA: Jossey-Bass.

Strauss, Anselm. 1993. *Continual Permutations of Action.* New York: Aldine de Gruyter.

Strauss, Anselm and Juliet Corbin. 1998. *Basics of Qualitative Research: Grounded Theory Procedures and Techniques.* 2d ed. Thousand Oaks, CA: Sage.

Strauss, Anselm, Leonard Schatzman, Danuta Ehrlich, Rue Bucher, and Melvin Sabshin. 1963. "The Hospital and Its Negotiated Order." Pp. 147–69 in *The Hospital in Modern Society,* edited by Eliot Freidson. New York: Free Press.

Strenski, Ivan. 1997. *Durkheim and the Jews of France.* Chicago, IL: University of Chicago Press.

Strobel, Margaret. 1995. "Consciousness and Action: Historical Agency in the Chicago Women's Liberation Union." Pp. 52–68 in *Provoking Agents: Gender and Agency in Theory and Practice,* edited by Judith Kegan Gardiner. Urbana & Chicago: University of Illinois Press.

Strossen, Nadine. 1995. *Defending Pornography: Free Speech, Sex, and the Fight for Women's Rights.* New York: Scribner.

Strydom, Piet. 2000. *Discourse and Knowledge: The Making of Enlightenment Sociology.* Liverpool, UK: Liverpool University Press.

Stryker, Sheldon. 1980. *Symbolic Interactionism: A Social Structural Version.* Menlo Park, CA: Benjamin-Cummings.

Sturgeon, Noel. 1997. *Ecofeminist Natures: Race, Gender, Feminist Theory and Political Action.* New York: Routledge.

Sturrock, John. 2003. *Structuralism.* 2d ed. Oxford, UK, & Malden, MA: Blackwell.

Sumner, Colin. 1994. *The Sociology of Deviance: An Obituary.* Buckingham, UK: Open University Press.

Sumner, William Graham. 1906. *Folkways.* New York: Dover.

Sumner, William Graham and Albert Galloway Keller. 1927. *The Science of Society.* Vol. 1. New Haven, CT: Yale University Press.

Surya, Georges. 2002. *Georges Bataille: An Intellectual Biography.* London: Verso.

Sussman, Elizabeth, ed. 1989. *On the Passage of a Few People Through a Rather Brief Moment in Time: The Situationist International, 1957–1972.* Cambridge, MA: MIT Press.

Swartz, David. 1997. *Culture and Power: The Sociology of Pierre Bourdieu.* Chicago, IL: University of Chicago Press.

Swatos, William H. Jr. and Daniel V. A. Olson. 2000. *The Secularization Debate.* Lanham, MD: Rowman & Littlefield.

Swedberg, Richard. 1998. *Max Weber and the Idea of Economic Sociology.* Princeton, NJ: Princeton University Press.

Swenson, James. 2000. *On Jean-Jacques Rousseau: Considered as One of the First Authors of the Revolution.* Stanford, CA: Stanford University Press.

Swingewood, Alan. 1991. *A Short History of Sociological Thought.* Houndsmills, UK: Macmillan.

Sztompka, P. 1986. *Robert K. Merton: An Intellectual Profile.* London & New York: Macmillan & St. Martin's.

Takagi, E. 1996. "The Generalized Exchange Perspective on the Evolution of Altruism." Pp. 311–36 in *Frontiers in Social Dilemmas Research,* edited by W. B. G. Liebrand and D. M. Messick. Berlin, Germany: Springer-Verlag.

Takahashi, N. 2000. "The Emergence of Generalized Exchange." *American Journal of Sociology* 105:1105–34.

Tarnas, Richard. 1991. *The Passion of the Western Mind.* New York: Harmony.

Tarrow, Sidney. 1998. *Power in Movement: Social Movements and Contentious Politics.* 2d ed. New York: Cambridge University Press.

Taylor, C. 1985. *Philosophical Papers 1: Human Agency and Language.* New York: Cambridge University Press.

Taylor, C. 1985. *Philosophical Papers 2: Philosophy and the Human Sciences.* New York: Cambridge University Press.

Taylor, C. 1989. *Sources of the Self: The Making of the Modern Identity.* Cambridge, MA: Harvard University Press.

Taylor, C. 1991. *The Ethics of Authenticity.* Cambridge, MA: Harvard University Press.

Taylor, C. 1993. *Reconciling the Solitudes: Essays on Canadian Federalism and Nationalism.* Montreal, Canada: McGill-Queen's University Press.

Taylor, C. 1995. *Philosophical Arguments.* Cambridge, MA: Harvard University Press.

Taylor, C. K., with Anthony Appiah, Jürgen Habermas, Steven C. Rockefeller, Michael Walzer, and Susan Wolf. 1994. *Multiculturalism: Examining the Politics of Recognition.* Edited and with an introduction by Amy Gutmann. 2d ed. Princeton, NJ: Princeton University Press.

Taylor, K., ed. 1975. *Henri Saint-Simon (1760–1825): Selected Writings.* New York: Holmes & Meier.

Taylor, Mark C. 2001. *The Moment of Complexity: Emerging Network Culture.* Chicago, IL: University of Chicago Press.

Taylor, Verta and Nancy E. Whitter. 1992. "Collective Identity in Social Movement Communities: Lesbian Feminist Mobilization." Pp. 104–29 in *Frontiers in Social Movement Theory,* edited by Aldon D. Morris and Carol M. Mueller. New Haven, CT: Yale University Press.

Terry, Jennifer. 1995. "Anxious Slippages Between 'Us' and 'Them.'" Pp. 129–67 in *Deviant Bodies,* edited by Jennifer Terry and Jacqueline Urla. Bloomington: Indiana University Press.

Tesser, Abraham and Richard Felson, eds. 2000. *Psychological Perspectives on Self and Identity.* Washington DC: American Psychological Association.

Tester, K. 1994. *Media, Culture, and Morality.* New York: Routledge.

Tester, K. 1997. *Moral Culture,* London: Sage.

Therborn, Goran. 2003. "Entangled Modernities." *European Journal of Social Theory* 6(3):293–305.

Thibault, Paul J. 1996. "Speech and Writing: Two Distinct Systems of Signs." Lecture 1 in the course Saussure and Beyond. University of Toronto, Cyber Semiotics Institute. Retrieved February 27, 2004 (http://www.chass.utoronto.ca/epc/srb/cyber/thi1.html).

Thibault, Paul J. 1996. "The Problematic of *Écriture.*" Lecture 2 in the course Saussure and Beyond. University of Toronto, Cyber Semiotics Institute. Retrieved February 27, 2004 (http://www.chass.utoronto.ca/epc/srb/cyber/thi2.html).

Thibault, Paul J. 1997. *Re-reading Saussure: The Dynamics of Signs in Social Life.* London & New York: Routledge.

Thibaut, J. and L. Walker. 1975. *Procedural Justice.* Hillsdale, NJ: Lawrence Erlbaum.

Thiele, L. P. 1990. *Friedrich Nietzsche and the Politics of the Soul: A Study of Heroic Individualism.* Princeton, NJ: Princeton University Press.

Thomas, Edwin J. and Bruce J. Biddle. 1966. "The Nature and History of Role Theory." Pp. 3–19 in *Role Theory: Concepts and Research,* edited by Edwin Thomas and Bruce Biddle. New York: John Wiley.

Thomas, William I. 1907. *Sex and Society: Studies in the Social Psychology of Sex.* Chicago, IL: University of Chicago Press.

Thomas, William I. 1923. *The Unadjusted Girl: With Cases and Standpoint for Behavior Analysis.* Boston, MA: Little, Brown.

Thomas, William I. 1936. *Primitive Behavior: An Introduction to the Social Sciences.* New York: McGraw-Hill.

Thomas, William I., Robert E. Park, and Herbert A. Miller. 1921. *Old World Traits Transplanted.* New York: Harper & Brothers.

Thomas, William I. and Dorothy Swaine Thomas. 1928. *The Child in America: Behavior Problems and Programs.* New York: Knopf.

Thomas, William I. and Florian Znaniecki. 1918–1919. *The Polish Peasant in Europe and America.* 5 vols. Boston, MA: Badger. Vols. 1 and 2 originally published by University of Chicago Press, 1918.

Thorndike, E. L. 1898. *Animal Intelligence: An Experimental Study of the Associative Processes in Animals: Psychological Review.* Monograph Supplements, 8. New York: Macmillan.

Thornham, Sue. 2000. *Feminist Theory and Cultural Studies: Stories of Unsettled Relations.* London: Arnold.

Thye, Shane. 2000. "A Status Value Theory of Power in Exchange Relations." *American Sociological Review* 65:407–32.

Tibbetts, Paul. 1975. "Peirce and Mead on Perceptual Immediacy and Human Action." *Philosophy and Phenomenological Research* 36:222–32.

Tickle, A. and I. Welsh, eds. 1998. *Environment and Society in Eastern Europe.* Harlow, UK: Longman.

Tilly, Charles. 1964. *The Vendee.* Cambridge, MA: Harvard University Press.

Tilly, Charles. 1978. *From Mobilization to Revolution.* Reading, MA: Addison-Wesley.

Tilly, Charles. 1981. *As Sociology Meets History.* New York: Academic Press.

Tilly, Charles. 1986. *The Contentious French.* Cambridge, MA: Harvard University Press.

Tilly, Charles. 1989. *Big Structures, Large Processes, Huge Comparisons.* New York: Russell Sage.

Tilly, Charles. 1990. *Coercion, Capital and European States, AD 990–1990.* Cambridge, UK: Blackwell.

Tilly, Charles. 1993. *European Revolutions, 1492–1992.* Oxford, UK: Blackwell.

Tilly, Charles. 1995. *Popular Contention in Great Britain, 1758–1834.* Cambridge, MA: Harvard University Press.

Tilly, Charles. 1997. *Roads from Past to Future.* Lanham, MD: Rowman & Littlefield.

Tilly, Charles. 1998. *Durable Inequality.* Berkeley: University of California Press.

Tilly, Charles. Forthcoming. *Contention and Democracy in Europe, 1650–2000.* New York: Cambridge University Press.

Tocqueville, Alexis de. 1969. *Democracy in America.* Translated by G. Lawrence. New York: Anchor.

Tocqueville, Alexis de. 1995. *Recollections: The Revolutions of 1848,* edited by J. P. Mayer and A. P. Kerr. Translated by G. Lawrence. New Brunswick, NJ: Transaction.

Tocqueville, Alexis de. 1998. *The Old Regime and the French Revolution,* edited by F. Furet and F. Melonio. Translated by A. S. Kahan. Chicago, IL: University of Chicago Press.

Tong, Rosemarie Putnam. 1998. *Feminist Thought: A More Comprehensive Introduction.* 2d ed. Boulder, CO: Westview.

Tönnies, Ferdinand [1887] 1957. *Community and Society* [Gemeinschaft und Gesellschaft]. East Lansing: Michigan State University Press.

Tönnies, Ferdinand. [1909] 1961. *Custom: An Essay on Social Codes.* New York: Free Press.

Tönnies, Ferdinand. [1887] 2001. *Community and Civil Society.* Translated by J. Harris and M. Hollis. Cambridge, UK: Cambridge University Press.

Touraine, Alain. 1965. *Sociologie de l'action.* Paris: Editions du Seuil.

Touraine, Alain. 1971. *The Post-Industrial Society.* New York: Random House.

Touraine, Alain. 1977. *The Self-Production of Society.* Chicago, IL: University of Chicago Press.

Touraine, Alain. 1981. *The Voice and the Eye.* Cambridge, UK: Cambridge University Press.

Touraine, Alain. 2000. *Can We Live Together?* Cambridge, UK: Polity.

Touraine, Alain. 2001. *Beyond Neoliberalism.* Cambridge, UK: Polity.

Treviño, A. Javier. 2001. "Introduction: The Theory and Legacy of Talcott Parsons." Pp. xv–lviii in *Talcott Parsons Today: His Theory and Legacy in Contemporary Sociology,* edited by A. Javier Treviño. Lanham, MD: Rowman & Littlefield.

Trevor-Roper, Hugh. 1983. "The Invention of Tradition: The Highland Tradition of Scotland." Pp. 15–42 in *The Invention of Tradition,* edited by E. Hobsbawm and T. Ranger. Cambridge, UK: Cambridge University Press.

Tschannen, Olivier. 1991. "The Secularization Paradigm: A Systematization." *Journal for the Scientific Study of Religion* 30:395–415.

Tseelon, Efrat. 1992. "Is the Presented Self Sincere? Goffman, Impression Management and the Postmodern Self." *Theory, Culture and Society* 9:115–28.

Tuchman, Gaye, Arlene Kaplan Daniels, and James Benet, eds. 1978. *Hearth and Home: Images of Women in the Mass Media.* New York: Oxford University Press.

Tudor, H. 1988. *Marxism and Social Democracy.* New York: Cambridge University Press.

Turkle, Sherry. 1995. *Life on the Screen: Identity in the Age of the Internet.* New York: Simon & Schuster.

Turner, B. S. 1984. *The Body and Society.* Oxford, UK: Blackwell.

Turner, B. S. 1984. *Weber and Islam.* London: Routledge.

Turner, B. S. 1991. *Religion and Social Theory.* 2d ed. London & Thousand Oaks, CA: Sage.

Turner, B. S., ed. 1993. *Citizenship and Social Theory.* London: Sage.

Turner, B. S., Alexandra Maryanski, and Jonathan H. Turner. 1992. *The Social Cage: Human Nature and the Evolution of Society.* Stanford, CA: Stanford University Press.

Turner, B. S. and C. Rojek. 2001. *Society and Culture.* London: Sage.

Turner, G. 2003. *British Cultural Studies: An Introduction.* 3d ed. London: Routledge.

Turner, Jonathan H. 1973. "From Utopia to Where? A Strategy for Reformulating the Dahrendorf Conflict Model." *Social Forces* 52:236–44.

Turner, Jonathan H. 1975. "A Strategy for Reformulating the Dialectical and Functional Theories of Conflict." *Social Forces* 53:433–44.

Turner, Jonathan H. 1984. *Societal Stratification: A Theoretical Analysis.* New York: Columbia University Press.

Turner, Jonathan H. 1987. "Toward a Sociological Theory of Motivation." *American Sociological Review* 52:15–25.

Turner, Jonathan H. 1991. "Using Metatheory to Develop Cumulative and Practical Knowledge." *Sociological Perspectives* 34:249–68.

Turner, Jonathan. 1994. "The Ecology of Macrostructure." Pp. 113–37 in *Advances in Human Ecology.* Vol 3. Greenwich, CT. JAI.

Turner, Jonathan H. 1995. *Macrodynamics: Toward a Theory on the Organization of Human Populations.* New Brunswick, NJ: Rutgers University Press for Rose Monograph.

Turner, Jonathan H. 2000. *On the Origins of Human Emotions.* Stanford, CA: Stanford University Press.

Turner, Jonathan H. 2002. *Face-to-Face: Toward a Sociological Theory of Interpersonal Behavior.* Stanford, CA: Stanford University Press.

Turner, Jonathan H. 2002. *The Structure of Sociological Theory.* 7th ed. Belmont, CA: Wadsworth.

Turner, Jonathan H. 2003. "Behavioristic Exchange Theory: George C. Homans." Ch. 17 in *The Structure of Sociological Theory.* 7th ed. Belmont, CA: Wadsworth.

Turner, Jonathan H. 2003. *Human Institutions: A Theory of Societal Evolution.* Lanham, MD: Rowman & Littlefield.

Turner, Jonathan H., Leonard Beeghley, and Charles H. Powers. 2002. *The Emergence of Sociological Theory.* Belmont, CA: Wadsworth.

Turner, Jonathan and Alexandra Maryanski. 1979. *Functionalism.* Menlo Park, CA: Benjamin/Cummings.

Turner, Jonathan H. and Royce R. Singleton. 1978. "A Theory of Ethnic Oppression." *Social Forces* 56:1001–19.

Turner, Ralph H. 1962. "Role Taking: Process versus Conformity." Pp. 20–40 in *Human Behavior and Social Processes,* edited by Arnold M. Rose. Boston, MA: Houghton Mifflin.

Turner, Ralph S. 1976. "Real Self: From Institution to Impulse." *American Journal of Sociology* 81(5):989–1016.

Turner, Stephen, ed. 2000. *The Cambridge Companion to Weber.* Cambridge, UK: Cambridge University Press.

Tyler, T. R. 1990. *Why People Obey the Law.* New Haven, CT: Yale University Press.

Tyler, T. R. 2000. "Social Justice: Outcome and Procedure." *International Journal of Psychology* 35:117–25.

Tyler, T. R. and S. Blader. 2000. *Cooperation in Groups.* Philadelphia, PA: Psychology Press.

Tyler, Tom R., Robert J. Boeckmann, Heather J. Smith, and Yuen J. Huo. 1997. *Social Justice in a Diverse Society.* Boulder, CO: Westview.

Tyler, Tom R. and Yuen J. Huo. 2002. *Trust in the Law.* New York: Russell Sage.

Tyler, Tom R. and Heather J. Smith. 1997. "Social Justice and Social Movements." Pp. 595–629 in *Handbook of Social Psychology,* 4th ed., Vol. 2, edited by D. Gilbert, S. Fiske, and G. Lindzey. New York: Addison-Wesley.

Unruh, D. R. 1980. "The Nature of Social Worlds." *Pacific Sociological Review* 23:271–96.

Urry, John. 2000. *Sociology beyond Societies: Mobilities for the Twenty-First Century.* London: Routledge.

Urry, John 2003. *Global Complexity.* Cambridge, UK: Polity.

Ussher, J. 1992. *Women's Madness: Misogyny or Mental Illness.* Amherst, MA: University of Massachusetts Press.

van Vree, Wilbert. 1999. *Meetings, Manners and Civilization: The Development of Modern Meeting Behavior.* London: Leicester University Press.

Vaneigem, Raoul. [1979] 1983. *The Book of Pleasures.* Translated by John Fullerton. London: Pending Press.

Veblen, Thorstein. [1904] 1912. *The Theory of Business Enterprise.* New York: Scribner's.

Veblen, Thorstein. [1917] 1939. *Imperial Germany and the Industrial Revolution.* New York: Viking.

Veblen, Thorstein. [1914] 1946. *The Instinct of Workmanship.* New York: Viking.

Veblen, Thorstein. [1899] 1953. *The Theory of the Leisure Class: An Economic Study of Institutions.* New York: Viking.

Veblen, Thorstein. 1954. *Absentee Ownership and Business Enterprise in Recent Times: The Case of America.* New York: Viking.

Veblen, Thorstein. 1970. *The Portable Veblen,* edited by Max Lerner. New York: Viking.

Verhoeven, J. 1993. "An Interview with Erving Goffman, 1980." *Research on Language and Social Interaction* 26:317–48.

Vertovec, Steven and Robin Cohen, eds. 2002. *Conceiving Cosmopolitanism: Theory, Context, and Practice.* Oxford, UK: Oxford University Press.

Vincenzi, Giuseppe Carlo. 1976. "'Sistema' e 'fonema' nel primo Saussure" [System and Phoneme in the early Saussure]. *Studi Italiani di Linguistica Teorica ed Applicata* [Italian Studies of Theoretical and Applied Linguistics] 1–2:229–51.

Vintges, Karen. 1999. "Simone de Beauvoir: A Feminist Thinker for Our Times." *Hypatia: A Journal of Feminist Philosophy* 14(4):133–44.

Virilio, Paul. 1986. *Speed & Politics: An Essay on Dromology.* New York: Semiotext(e).

Virilio, Paul. 1991. *The Lost Dimension.* New York: Semiotext(e).

Virilio, Paul. 2000. *The Information Bomb.* London: Verso.

Virilio, Paul and Sylvère Lotringer. 2002. *Crepuscular Dawn.* Translated by Mike Taormina. New York: Semiotext(e).

Wagner, David G. and Joseph Berger. 1993. "Status Characteristics Theory: The Growth of a Program." Pp. 23–63 in *Theoretical Research Programs: Studies in the Growth of Theory,* edited by Joseph Berger and Morris Zelditch Jr. Stanford, CA: Stanford University Press.

Wagner, David G. and Joseph Berger. 2002. "Expectation States Theory: An Evolving Research Program." Pp. 41–76 in *New Directions in Contemporary Sociological Theory,* edited by Joseph Berger and Morris Zelditch Jr. New York: Rowman & Littlefield.

Wagner, Helmut R. 1983. *Alfred Schutz: An Intellectual Biography.* Chicago, IL: University of Chicago Press.

Wagner, P. 1999. "The Resistance That Modernity Constantly Provokes: Europe, America and Social Theory." *Thesis Eleven: Critical Theory and Historical Sociology* 58:35–58.

Waldron, J., ed. 1987. *Nonsense on Stilts: Bentham, Burke and Marx on the Rights of Man.* London: Methuen.

Walker, Henry A. and Morris Zelditch Jr. 1993. "Power, Legitimacy and Stability of Authority: A Theoretical Research Program." Pp. 364–81 in *Theoretical Research Programs: Studies in the Growth of Theory,* edited by Joseph Berger and Morris Zelditch Jr. Stanford, CA: Stanford University Press.

Wall, D. 1994. *Earth First! UK.* London: Routledge.

Wallace, David. 1967. "Reflections on the Education of George Herbert Mead." *American Journal of Sociology* 72:396–408.

Wallace, Ruth and Alison Wolf. *Contemporary Sociological Theory.* 5th ed. Upper Saddle River, NJ: Prentice-Hall.

Wallerstein, Immanuel. 1974. *The Modern World System,* 3 vols. New York: Academic Press.

Wallerstein, Immanuel. 1995. *After Liberalism.* New York: New Press.

Wallerstein, Immanuel. 2000. *The Essential Wallerstein.* New York: New Press.

Wallerstein, Immanuel. 2001. *Unthinking Social Science: The Limits of Nineteenth-Century Paradigms.* 2d ed. Philadelphia, PA: Temple University Press.

Walster, Elaine, George Walster, and Ellen Berscheid. 1978. *Equity: Theory and Research.* Boston, MA: Allyn & Bacon.

Wanderer, Jules J. 1995. "Adventure in a Theme Park." Pp. 171–88 in *Georg Simmel Between Modernity and Postmodernity,* edited by Dörr-Backes and L. Nieder. Würzburg, Germany: Königshausen & Neumann.

Warner, R. Stephen. 1993. "Work in Progress Toward a New Paradigm for the Sociological Study of Religion in the United States." *American Journal of Sociology* 98:1044–93.

Warner, W. Lloyd. 1959. *The Living and the Dead: A Study of the Symbolic Life of Americans.* New Haven, CT: Yale University Press.

Warner, W. Lloyd. [1949] 1960. *Social Class in America.* New York: Harper and Row.

Wasserman, Stanley and Katherine Faust. 1994. *Social Network Analysis: Methods and Applications.* New York: Cambridge University Press.

Waters, Malcolm. 1996. *Daniel Bell.* New York & London: Routledge.

Watts, Duncan. 2003. *Six Degrees: The Science of a Connected Age.* New York: Norton.

Weber, Marianne. 1975. *Max Weber: A Biography.* Translated by Harry Zohn. New York: John Wiley.

Weber, Marianne. [1912] 2003. "Authority and Autonomy in Marriage." Translation with introduction by Craig R. Bermingham. *Sociological Theory* 21(2):85–102.

Weber, Max. [1904–1905] 1930. *The Protestant Ethic and the Spirit of Capitalism.* Translated by Talcott Parsons. London: Allen & Unwin.

Weber, Max. 1946. *From Max Weber,* edited by C. Wright Mills and H. H. Gerth. New York: Oxford University Press.

Weber, Max. 1946. "Religious Rejections of the World and Their Directions." Pp. 323–58 in *From Max Weber: Essays in Sociology.* Translated and edited by H. Gerth and C. W. Mills. New York: Oxford University Press.

Weber, Max. 1949. *The Methodology of the Social Sciences.* Translated and edited by Edward A. Shils and Henry A. Finch. New York: Free Press.

Weber, Max. 1958. *The Rational and Social Foundations of Music.* Translated and edited by D. Martindale et al. Carbondale: Southern Illinois University Press.

Weber, Max. 1968. "Der Sinn der 'Wertfreiheit' der soziologischen und oekonomischen Wissenschaften." Pp. 489–540 in *Max Weber: Gesammelte Aufsaetze zur Wissenschaftslehre.* 3d ed. Tüebingen, Germany: J. C. B. Mohr. English ed. 1949. "The Meaning of 'Ethical New Neutrality' in Sociology and Economics." Pp. 1–112, in *Max Weber: The Methodology of the Social Sciences,* edited by E. A. Shils and H. A. Finch. New York: Free Press.

Weber, Max. [1921] 1968. *Economy and Society,* edited by Guenther Roth and Claus Wittich. New York: Bedminster.

Weber, Max. [1904–1906] 1998. *The Protestant Ethic and the Spirit of Capitalism.* Reprint. Los Angeles: Roxbury.

Weber, Max. [1905] 2002. "'Churches' and 'Sects' in North America." Pp. 203–20 in *The Protestant Ethic and the "Spirit" of Capitalism and Other Writings,* edited and translated by Peter Baehr and Gordon Wells. Harmondsworth, UK: Penguin.

Weber, Max. 2003. *The Essential Weber,* edited by S. Whimster. London: Routledge.

Webster, Murray. 2003. "Puzzles, Provisional Solutions, and New Provinces." Pp. 281–310 in *Advances in Group Processes: Power and Status,* edited by Shane R. Thye and John Skvoretz. London: Elsevier.

Weeks, Jeffrey. 1986. *Sexuality.* London: Tavistock.

Weil, R. 2001. "Les institutions totales dans l'oeuvre de Goffman" [Total Institutions in Goffman's Work]. Pp. 25–43 in *Erving Goffman et Les Institutions Totales* [Erving Goffman and Total Institutions], edited by C. Amourous and A. Blanc. Paris: L'Harmattan.

Weingart, Peter. 1969. "Beyond Parsons? A Critique of Ralf Dahrendorf's Conflict Theory." *Social Forces* 48:151–65.

Weiss, Johannes. 1998. *Weber and the Marxist World.* With an introduction by Bryan S. Turner. London & New York: Routledge.

Weiss, Linda. 2003. "Introduction: Bringing Domestic Institutions Back In." Pp. 1–33 in *States in the Global Economy: Bringing Domestic Institutions Back In,* edited by Linda Weiss. Cambridge, UK: Cambridge University Press.

Welsh, I. 2000. *Mobilising Modernity: The Nuclear Moment.* London: Routledge.

Wernick, Andrew. 2000. *Auguste Comte and the Religion of Humanity: The Post-Theistic Programme of French Social Theory.* Cambridge, UK: Cambridge University Press.

West, Candace and Don H. Zimmerman. 1987. "Doing Gender." *Gender & Society* 1:125–51.

Wharton, Martha. 1995. "A Report on Black Women in the Academy: Defending Our Name, 1894–1994." *Sage: A Scholarly Journal on Black Women* 9:90–91.

Whimster, Sam and Scott Lash, eds. 1987. *Max Weber, Rationality and Modernity.* London: Allen & Unwin.

White, Harrison C. 1963. *An Anatomy of Kinship: Mathematical Models for Structures of Cumulated Roles.* Englewood Cliffs, NJ: Prentice Hall.

White, Harrison C. 1970. *Chains of Opportunity: System Models of Mobility in Organizations.* Cambridge, MA: Harvard University Press.

White. Harrison. 1992. *Identity and Control: A Structural Theory of Social Action.* Princeton, NJ: Princeton University Press.

White, Harrison C. 1993. *Careers and Creativity: Social Forces in the Arts.* Boulder, CO: Westview.

White, Harrison C. 2002. *Markets from Networks: Socioeconomic Models of Production.* Princeton, NJ: Princeton University Press.

Whitebook, J. 1997. "Intersubjectivity and the Monadic Core of the Psyche: Habermas and Castoriadis on the Unconscious." In *Habermas and the Unfinished Project of Modernity,* edited by M. Passerin D'entreves and S. Benhabib. Cambridge, MA: MIT Press.

Whitford, Margaret, ed. 1991. *The Irigaray Reader.* Cambridge, UK: Blackwell.

Wiggershaus, Rolf. 1994. *The Frankfurt School.* Cambridge, UK: Polity.

Wilde, Oscar. 1891. "The Decay of Lying," *Intentions.* London: Methuen.

Wilensky, H. L. 1964. "The Professionalization of Everyone?" *American Journal of Sociology* 70:137–58.

Wiley, Norbert. 1994. *The Semiotic Self.* Chicago, IL: University of Chicago Press.

Wilke, Henk A. M., Dave M. Messick, and Christel G. Rutte, eds. 1986. *Experimental Social Dilemmas.* Frankfurt, Germany: Verlage Peter Lang.

Willer, David. 1967. *Scientific Sociology: Theory and Method.* Englewood Cliffs, NJ: Prentice-Hall.

Willer, David. 1987. *Theory and the Experimental Investigation of Social Structures.* New York: Gordon & Breach.

Willer, David. 1992. "Predicting Power in Exchange Networks: A Brief History and Introduction to the Issues." *Social Networks* 14:187–211.

Willer, David, ed. 1992. *Social Networks* (special issue on locating power in exchange networks) 14(3–4):187–344.

Willer, David, ed. 1999. *Network Exchange Theory.* Westport, CT: Praeger.

Willer, David and Bo Anderson, eds. 1981. *Networks, Exchange, and Coercion.* New York: Elsevier.

Willer, David and Judith Willer. 1973. *Systematic Empiricism: Critique of a Pseudoscience.* Englewood Cliffs, NJ: Prentice-Hall.

Williams, Patrick and Laura Chrisman, eds. 1994. *Colonial Discourse and Post-Colonial Theory: A Reader.* New York: Columbia University Press.

Williams, Raymond. 1961. *The Long Revolution.* London: Chatto & Windus.

Williams, Raymond. 1966. *Communications.* Harmondsworth, UK: Penguin.

Williams, Rhys H. and Robert D. Benford. 2000. "Two Faces of Collective Action Frames: A Theoretical Consideration." *Current Perspectives in Social Theory* 20:127–51. Greenwich, CT: JAI.

Williamson, Oliver E. 1985. *The Economic Institutions of Capitalism.* New York: Free Press.

Willis, P. 1990. *Common Culture: Symbolic Work at Play in the Everyday Cultures of the Young.* Milton Keynes, UK: Open University Press.

Winkin, Y. 1988. *Erving Goffman: Les Moments et Leurs Hommes.* Paris: Minuit.

Winship, Christopher. 1988. "Thoughts About Roles and Relations: An Old Document Revisited." *Social Networks* 10:209–31.

Winter, Rainer. 2001. *Die Kunst des Eigensinns: Cultural Studies als Kritik der Macht.* Weilerswist, Germany: Velbrück Wissenschaft.

Wirth, Louis. 1926. "The Sociology of Ferdinand Tönnies." *American Journal of Sociology* 32:412–22.

Wirth, Louis. 1938. "Urbanism as a Way of Life." *American Journal of Sociology* 44(January):1–24.

Wittrock, Björn and Peter Wagner. 1996. "Social Science and the Building of the Early Welfare State: Toward a Comparison of Statist and Non-Statist Western Societies." Pp. 90–116 in *States, Social Knowledge, and the Origins of Modern Social Policies,* edited by D. Rueschemeyer and T. Skocpol. Princeton, NJ: Princeton University Press.

Wolfe, Alan. 1997. "Public and Private in Theory and Practice." Pp. 182–203 in *Public and Private in Thought and Practice,* edited by J. Weintraub and K. Kuman. Chicago, IL: Chicago University Press.

Wolin, Sheldon S. 2001. *Tocqueville between Two Worlds.* Princeton, NJ: Princeton University Press.

Wollstoncraft, Mary. [1792] 1988. *A Vindication of the Rights of Women.* New York: Norton.

Women's Studies Group, Centre for Contemporary Cultural Studies. 1978. *Women Take Issue: Aspects of Women's Subordination.* London: Hutchinson.

Woolf, Virginia. [1924] 1984. "Mr. Bennett and Mrs. Brown." In *The Virginia Woolf Reader,* edited by Mitchell Leaska. New York: Harcourt Brace Jovanovich.

Wouters, Cas. 1986. "Formalization and Informalization: Changing Tension Balances in Civilizing Processes." *Theory, Culture and Society* 3(2):1–18.

Wright, A. 1986. *Socialisms.* New York: Oxford University Press.

Wright, Erik Olin. 1978. *Class, Crisis, and the State.* London: Verso.

Wright, Eric Olin. 1979. *Class Structure and Income Determination.* New York: Academic Press.

Wright, Eric Olin. 1985. *Classes.* London: Verso.

Wright, Eric Olin. 1997. *Class Counts: Comparative Studies in Class Analysis.* Cambridge, UK: Cambridge University press.

Wright, Eric Olin. 2002. "The Shadow of Exploitation in Weber's Class Analysis." *American Sociological Review* 67:832–53.

Wright, Erik Olin and Archon Fong, eds. 2003. *Deepening Democracy: Institutional Innovation in Empowered Participatory Governance.* London: Verso.

Wright, Erik Olin, Andrew Levine, and Elliott Sober. 1993. *Reconstructing Marxism.* London: Verso.

Wright, Erik Olin, Peter F. Meiksins, and Philippe Van Parijs. 1989. *The Debate on Classes.* London: Verso.

Wright, G. H. 1971. *Explanation and Understanding.* Ithaca, NY: Cornell University Press.

Wright, Hayden. 1975. "Historicism, History, and the Figurative Imagination." *History and Theory* 14:48–67.

Wright, S. 2002. *Storming Heaven: Class Composition and Struggle in Italian Autonomist Marxism.* London: Pluto.

Wrong, Dennis H. 1995. *Power: Its Forms, Bases, and Uses.* New Brunswick, NJ: Transaction.

Wuthnow, Robert. 1987. *Meaning and Moral Order: Explorations in Cultural Analysis.* Berkeley: University of California Press.

Wuthnow, Robert. 1989. *Communities of Discourse: Ideology and Social Structure in the Reformation, the Enlightenment and European Socialism.* Cambridge, MA: Harvard University Press.

Wuthnow, Robert. 1992. "Introduction: New Directions in the Empirical Study of Cultural Codes." Pp. 1–18 in *Vocabularies of Public Life: Empirical Essays in Symbolic Structure,* edited by Robert Wuthnow. New York: Routledge.

Wyatt, Justin. 1998. *High Concept. Movies and Marketing in Hollywood.* Austin: University of Texas Press.

Wyer, Mary, Donna Giesman, Mary Barbercheck, Hatice Ozturk, and Marta Wayne, eds. 2000. *Women, Science and Technology: A Reader in Feminist Science Studies.* New York: Routledge.

Yamagishi, Toshio and Karen S. Cook. 1993. "Generalized Exchange and Social Dilemmas." *Social Psychology Quarterly* 56:235–48.

Yamagishi, Toshio, Karen S. Cook, and M. Watabe. 1998. "Uncertainty, Trust and Commitment Formation in the United States and Japan." *American Journal of Sociology* 104:165–94.

Yamagishi, Toshio and Midori Yamagishi. 1994. "Trust and Commitment in the United States and Japan." *Motivation and Emotion* 18:129–66.

Young, James. 1993. *The Texture of Memory: Holocaust Memorials and Meaning.* New Haven, CT: Yale University Press.

Young, Kimball. 1962–1963. "The Contribution of William Isaac Thomas to Sociology." *Sociology and Social Research* 47(1,2,3,4):3–24; 123–37; 251–72; 381–97.

Young, Robert J. C. 2001. *Postcolonialism: An Historical Introduction.* Oxford, UK: Blackwell.

Zald, Mayer N. 2000. "Ideologically Structured Action: An Enlarged Agenda for Social Movement Research." *Mobilization* 5(1): 1–16.

Zaret, David. 2000. *Origins of Democratic Culture.* Princeton, NJ: Princeton University Press.

Zeitlin, Irving. 1994. *Ideology and the Development of Sociological Theory.* 5th ed. Englewood Cliffs, NJ: Prentice-Hall.

Zerubavel, E. 1981. *Hidden Rhythms: Schedules and Calendars in Social Life.* Chicago, IL: University of Chicago Press.

Zerubavel, E. 1985. *The Seven Day Circle: The History and Meaning of the Week.* New York: Free Press.

Zerubavel, Eviatar. 1997. *Social Mindscapes: An Invitation to Cognitive Sociology.* Cambridge, MA: Harvard University Press.

Zhao, Shanyang. 1991. "Metatheory, Metamethod, Meta-Data-Analysis: What, Why, and How?" *Sociological Perspectives* 34:377–90.

Zimmer, Lyn. 1987. "How Women Shape the Prison Guard Role." *Gender & Society* 1:415–31.

Žižek, Slavoj. 1989. *The Sublime Object of Ideology.* London: Verso.

Žižek, Slavoj. 1991. *Looking Awry: An Introduction to Jacques Lacan Through Popular Culture.* Cambridge, MA: MIT Press.

Žižek, Slavoj. 1999. *The Ticklish Subject: The Absent Centre of Political Ontology.* New York: Verso.

Žižek, Slavoj. 2001. *Repeating Lenin.* Zagreb, Croatia: Arkzin d.o.o.

Žižek, Slavoj. 2002. *Revolution at the Gates.* London: Verso.

Znaniecki, Florian. 1934. *Method of Sociology.* New York: Farrar & Rinehart.

Znaniecki, Florian. 1952. *Cultural Sciences. Their Origin and Development.* Urbana: University of Illinois Press.

Znaniecki, Florian. 1952. *Modern Nationalities.* Urbana: University of Illinois Press.

Znaniecki, Florian. 1998. *Education and Social Change,* edited by E. Hałas. Frankfurt am Main, Germany: Peter Lang Verlag.

Zukin, Sharon. 1995. *The Cultures of Cities.* Oxford, UK: Blackwell.

Zuriff, G. E. 1985. *Behaviorism: A Conceptual Reconstruction.* New York: Columbia University Press.

Index

Entry titles are in boldface type.